Collins

— POCKET —

French
Dictionary

HarperCollins Publishers
Westerhill Road
Bishopbriggs
Glasgow
G64 2QT

Seventh Edition 2013

10 9 8 7 6 5 4

© HarperCollins Publishers 2013,
2010, 2007, 2002, 2001, 1998,

ISBN 978-0-00-748547-5
US ISBN 978-0-06-200743-8

Collins® is a registered trademark of
HarperCollins Publishers Limited

www.collins.co.uk

A catalogue record for this book is
available from the British Library

Typeset by Aptara in India and
Davidsons Publishing Solutions,
Glasgow

Printed and bound by Grafica Veneta

Acknowledgements
We would like to thank those authors
and publishers who kindly gave
permission for copyright material
to be used in the Collins Corpus.
We would also like to thank Times
Newspapers Ltd for providing
valuable data.

TABLE DES MATIÈRES   CONTENTS

PROJECT MANAGEMENT
Carol McCann

CONTRIBUTORS
Teresa Álvarez García
Gaëlle Amiot-Cadey
Sabine Citron
Cordelia Lilly
Val McNulty
Complexli
Jean-François Allan

COMPUTING
Thomas Callan

FOR THE PUBLISHER
Lucy Cooper
Kerry Ferguson
Ruth O'Donovan
Elaine Higgleton

SERIES EDITOR
Rob Scriven

Based on the first edition of
the Collins Gem French
Dictionary under the
direction of Pierre-Henri
Cousin.

INTRODUCTION

Nous sommes très heureux que vous ayez choisi ce dictionnaire et espérons que vous aimerez l'utiliser et que vous en tirerez profit au lycée, à la maison, en vacances ou au travail.

Cette introduction a pour but de vous donner quelques conseils sur la façon d'utiliser au mieux votre dictionnaire, en vous référant non seulement à son importante nomenclature mais aussi aux informations contenues dans chaque entrée. Ceci vous aidera à lire et à comprendre, mais aussi à communiquer et à vous exprimer en anglais contemporain.

Au début du dictionnaire, vous trouverez la liste des abréviations utilisées dans le texte et celle de la transcription des sons par des symboles phonétiques. Vous y trouverez également la liste des verbes irréguliers en anglais, suivis d'une section finale sur les nombres et sur les expressions de temps.

COMMENT UTILISER VOTRE DICTIONNAIRE
Ce dictionnaire offre une richesse d'informations et utilise diverses formes et tailles de caractères, symboles, abréviations, parenthèses et crochets. Les conventions et symboles utilisés sont expliqués dans les sections qui suivent.

ENTRÉES
Les mots que vous cherchez dans le dictionnaire – les entrées – sont classés par ordre alphabétique. Ils sont imprimés en couleur pour pouvoir être repérés rapidement. Les entrées figurant en haut de page indiquent le premier (sur la page de gauche) et le dernier mot (sur la page de droite) des deux pages en question.

Des informations sur l'usage ou sur la forme de certaines entrées sont données entre parenthèses, après la transcription phonétique. Ces indications apparaissent sous forme abrégée et en italiques (par ex. (*fam*), (*Comm*)).

Pour plus de facilité, les mots de la même famille sont regroupés sous la même entrée (**ronger, rongeur; accept, acceptance**) et apparaissent également en couleur.

Les expressions courantes dans lesquelles apparaît l'entrée sont indiquées par des caractères romains gras différents (par exemple **retard** : [...] **avoir du ~**).

TRANSCRIPTION PHONÉTIQUE
La transcription phonétique de chaque entrée (indiquant sa prononciation) est indiquée entre crochets immédiatement après l'entrée (par ex. **fumer** [fyme]; **knee** [niː]). La liste des symboles phonétiques figure page xiii.

TRADUCTIONS
Les traductions des entrées apparaissent en caractères ordinaires ; lorsque plusieurs sens ou usages coexistent, ces traductions sont séparées par un point-virgule. Vous trouverez des synonymes de l'entrée en italiques entre parenthèses avant les traductions (par ex. **poser** (*installer* : *moquette, carrelage*)) ou des mots qui fournissent le contexte dans lequel l'entrée est susceptible d'être utilisée (par ex. **poser** (*question*)).

MOTS-CLÉS
Une importance particulière est accordée à certains mots français et anglais qui sont considérés comme des « mots-clés » dans chacune des langues. Cela peut être dû à leur utilisation très fréquente ou au fait qu'ils ont divers types d'usage (par ex. **vouloir**, **plus**; **get**; **that**). L'utilisation de triangles et de chiffres aide à distinguer différentes catégories grammaticales et différents sens. D'autres renseignements utiles apparaissent en italiques et entre parenthèses dans la langue de l'utilisateur.

DONNÉES GRAMMATICALES

Les catégories grammaticales sont données sous forme abrégée et en italiques après la transcription phonétique (par ex. *vt, adv, conj*). Les genres des noms français sont indiqués de la manière suivante : *nm* pour un nom masculin et *nf* pour un nom féminin. Le féminin et le pluriel irréguliers de certains noms sont également indiqués (par ex. **directeur, -trice** ; **cheval, -aux**).

Le masculin et le féminin des adjectifs sont indiqués lorsque ces deux formes sont différentes (par ex. **noir, e**). Lorsque l'adjectif a un féminin ou un pluriel irrégulier, ces formes sont clairement indiquées (par ex. **net, nette**). Les pluriels irréguliers des noms, et les formes irrégulières des verbes anglais sont indiqués entre parenthèses, avant la catégorie grammaticale (par ex. **man** [...] (*pl* **men**) *n* ; **give** (*pt* **gave**; *pp* **~n**) *vt*).

INTRODUCTION

We are delighted that you have decided to buy this dictionary and hope you will enjoy and benefit from using it at school, at home, on holiday or at work.

This introduction gives you a few tips on how to get the most out of your dictionary – not simply from its comprehensive wordlist but also from the information provided in each entry. This will help you to read and understand modern French, as well as communicate and express yourself in the language. This dictionary begins by listing the abbreviations used in the text and illustrating the sounds shown by the phonetic symbols. You will also find French verb tables, followed by a final section on numbers and time expressions.

USING YOUR DICTIONARY

A wealth of information is presented in the dictionary, using various typefaces, sizes of type, symbols, abbreviations and brackets. The various conventions and symbols used are explained in the following sections.

HEADWORDS

The words you look up in a dictionary – 'headwords' – are listed alphabetically. They are printed in **colour** for rapid identification. The headwords appearing at the top of each page indicate the first (if it appears on a left-hand page) and last word (if it appears on a right-hand page) dealt with on the page in question.

Information about the usage or form of certain headwords is given in brackets after the phonetic spelling. This usually appears in abbreviated form and in italics (e.g. (*fam*), (*Comm*)).

Where appropriate, words related to headwords are grouped in the same entry (**ronger, rongeur; accept, acceptance**) and are also in colour. Common expressions in which the headword appears are shown in a bold roman type (e.g. **retard:** [...] **avoir du ~**).

PHONETIC SPELLINGS

The phonetic spelling of each headword (indicating its pronunciation) is given in square brackets immediately after the headword (e.g. **fumer**[fyme]; **knee**[niː]). A list of these symbols is given on page xiii.

TRANSLATIONS

Headword translations are given in ordinary type and, where more than one meaning or usage exists, these are separated by a semi-colon. You will often find other words in italics in brackets before the translations. These offer suggested contexts in which the headword might appear (e.g. **rough** (*voice*), [...] (*weather*)) or provide synonyms (e.g. **rough** (*violent*)). The gender of the translation also appears in italics immediately following the key element of the translation.

KEY WORDS

Special status is given to certain French and English words which are considered as 'key' words in each language. They may, for example, occur very frequently or have several types of usage (e.g. **vouloir, plus; get, that**). A combination of triangles and numbers helps you to distinguish different parts of speech and different meanings. Further helpful information is provided in brackets and italics.

GRAMMATICAL INFORMATION

Parts of speech are given in abbreviated form in italics after the phonetic spellings of headwords (e.g. *vt, adv, conj*). Genders of French nouns are indicated as follows: *nm* for a masculine and *nf* for a feminine noun. Feminine and irregular plural forms of nouns are also shown (**directeur, -trice; cheval, -aux**).

Adjectives are given in both masculine and feminine forms where these forms are different (e.g. **noir, e**). Clear information is provided where adjectives have an irregular feminine or plural form (e.g. **net, nette**).

ABRÉVIATIONS

ABBREVIATIONS

abréviation	*ab(b)r*	abbreviation
adjectif, locution adjectivale	*adj*	adjective, adjectival phrase
administration	*Admin*	administration
adverbe, locution adverbiale	*adv*	adverb, adverbial phrase
agriculture	*Agr*	agriculture
anatomie	*Anat*	anatomy
architecture	*Archit*	architecture
article défini	*art déf*	definite article
article indéfini	*art indéf*	*indefinite* article
automobile	*Aut(o)*	the motor car and motoring
aviation, voyages aériens	*Aviat*	flying, air travel
biologie	*Bio(l)*	biology
botanique	*Bot*	botany
anglais britannique	*BRIT*	British English
chimie	*Chem*	chemistry
commerce, finance, banque	*Comm*	commerce, finance, banking
informatique	*Comput*	computing
conjonction	*conj*	conjunction
construction	*Constr*	building
nom utilisé comme adjectif	*cpd*	compound element
cuisine	*Culin*	cookery
article défini	*def art*	definite article
déterminant: article; adjectif démonstratif ou indéfini *etc*	*dét*	determiner: article, demonstrative *etc*
économie	*Écon, Econ*	economics
électricité, électronique	*Élec, Elec*	electricity, electronics
en particulier	*esp*	especially
exclamation, interjection	*excl*	exclamation, interjection
féminin	*f*	feminine
langue familière (! emploi vulgaire)	*fam(!)*	colloquial usage (! particularly offensive)
emploi figuré	*fig*	figurative use
(verbe anglais) dont la particule est inséparable	*fus*	(phrasal verb) where the particle is inseparable
généralement	*gén, gen*	generally
géographie, géologie	*Géo, Geo*	geography, geology
géométrie	*Géom, Geom*	geometry
langue familière (! emploi vulgaire)	*inf(!)*	colloquial usage (! particularly offensive)
infinitif	*infin*	infinitive
informatique	*Inform*	computing
invariable	*inv*	invariable
irrégulier	*irreg*	irregular
domaine juridique	*Jur*	law

ABRÉVIATIONS

ABBREVIATIONS

grammaire, linguistique	*Ling*	grammar, linguistics
masculin	*m*	masculine
mathématiques, algèbre	*Math*	mathematics, calculus
médecine	*Méd, Med*	medical term, medicine
masculin ou féminin	*m/f*	masculine or feminine
domaine militaire, armée	*Mil*	military matters
musique	*Mus*	music
nom	*n*	noun
navigation, nautisme	*Navig, Naut*	sailing, navigation
nom ou adjectif numéral	*num*	numeral noun or adjective
	o.s.	oneself
péjoratif	*péj, pej*	derogatory, pejorative
photographie	*Phot(o)*	photography
physiologie	*Physiol*	physiology
pluriel	*pl*	plural
politique	*Pol*	politics
participe passé	*pp*	past participle
préposition	*prép, prep*	preposition
pronom	*pron*	pronoun
psychologie, psychiatrie	*Psych*	psychology, psychiatry
temps du passé	*pt*	past tense
quelque chose	*qch*	
quelqu'un	*qn*	
religion, domaine ecclésiastique	*Rel*	religion
	sb	somebody
enseignement, système scolaire et universitaire	*Scol*	schooling, schools and universities
singulier	*sg*	singular
	sth	something
subjonctif	*sub*	subjunctive
sujet (grammatical)	*su(b)j*	(grammatical) subject
superlatif	*superl*	superlative
techniques, technologie	*Tech*	technical term, technology
télécommunications	*Tél, Tel*	telecommunications
télévision	*TV*	television
typographie	*Typ(o)*	typography, printing
anglais des USA	*US*	American English
verbe (auxiliaire)	*vb (aux)*	(auxiliary) verb
verbe intransitif	*vi*	intransitive verb
verbe transitif	*vt*	transitive verb
zoologie	*Zool*	zoology
marque déposée	®	registered trademark
indique une équivalence culturelle	≈	introduces a cultural equivalent

TRANSCRIPTION PHONÉTIQUE

CONSONNES

CONSONANTS

NB. **p**, **b**, **t**, **d**, **k**, **g** sont suivis d'une aspiration en anglais.

NB. **p**, **b**, **t**, **d**, **k**, **g** are not aspirated in French.

pou**p**ée	p	**p**u**pp**y
bom**b**e	b	**b**a**b**y
ten**t**e **th**ermal	t	**t**en**t**
din**d**e	d	**d**a**dd**y
co**q** **q**ui **k**épi	k	**c**ork **k**iss **ch**ord
ga**g**e ba**gu**e	g	**g**a**g** **gu**ess
sale **c**e na**ti**on	s	**s**o ri**c**e ki**ss**
zéro ro**s**e	z	cou**s**in bu**zz**
ta**ch**e **ch**at	ʃ	**sh**eep **s**ugar
gilet **j**uge	ʒ	plea**s**ure bei**ge**
	tʃ	**ch**ur**ch**
	dʒ	**j**u**dge** **g**eneral
fer **ph**are	f	**f**arm ra**ff**le
ver**v**eine	v	**v**ery re**v**el
	θ	**th**in ma**th**s
	ð	**th**at o**th**er
lent sa**ll**e	l	**l**itt**l**e ba**ll**
rare **r**ent**r**er	ʀ	
	r	**r**at **r**are
ma**m**an fe**mm**e	m	**m**u**mm**y co**mb**
non bo**nn**e	n	**n**o ra**n**
a**gn**eau vi**gn**e	ɲ	
	ŋ	si**ng**ing ba**n**k
	h	**h**at re**h**earse
yeux pa**ill**e p**i**ed	j	**y**et
no**u**er o**ui**	w	**w**all **w**ail
h**ui**le l**u**i	ɥ	
	x	lo**ch**

DIVERS

MISCELLANEOUS

pour l'anglais: le r final se prononce en liaison devant une voyelle — r — in English transcription: final r can be pronounced before a vowel

pour l'anglais: précède la syllabe accentuée — ' — in French wordlist: no liaison before aspirate h

En règle générale, la prononciation est donnée entre crochets après chaque entrée. Toutefois, du côté anglais-français et dans le cas des expressions composées de deux ou plusieurs mots non réunis par un trait d'union et faisant l'objet d'une entrée séparée, la prononciation doit être cherchée sous chacun des mots constitutifs de l'expression en question.

PHONETIC TRANSCRIPTION

VOYELLES		VOWELS
NB. La mise en équivalence de certains sons n'indique qu'une ressemblance approximative.		NB. The pairing of some vowel sounds only indicates approximate equivalence.
ici vie lyrique	i i:	heel bead
	ɪ	hit pity
jouer été	e	
lait jouet merci	ɛ	set tent
plat amour	a æ	bat apple
bas pâte	ɑ ɑ:	after car calm
	ʌ	fun cousin
le premier	ə	over above
beurre peur	œ	
peu deux	ø ə:	urgent fern work
or homme	ɔ	wash pot
mot eau gauche	o ɔ:	born cork
genou roue	u	full hook
	u:	boom shoe
rue urne	y	

DIPHTONGUES		DIPHTHONGS
	ɪə	beer tier
	ɛə	tear fair there
	eɪ	date plaice day
	aɪ	life buy cry
	au	owl foul now
	əu	low no
	ɔɪ	boil boy oily
	uə	poor tour

NASALES		NASAL VOWELS
matin plein	ɛ̃	
brun	œ̃	
sang an dans	ɑ̃	
non pont	ɔ̃	

In general, we give the pronunciation of each entry in square brackets after the word in question. However, on the English-French side, where the entry is composed of two or more unhyphenated words, each of which is given elsewhere in this dictionary, you will find the pronunciation of each word in its alphabetical position.

FRENCH VERB TABLES

a Present participle **b** Past participle **c** Present **d** Imperfect **e** Future
f Conditional **g** Present subjunctive

1 ARRIVER **a** arrivant **b** arrivé
  c arrive, arrives, arrive, arrivons,
  arrivez, arrivent **d** arrivais
  e arriverai **f** arriverais **g** arrive

2 FINIR **a** finissant **b** fini **c** finis, finis,
  finit, finissons, finissez, finissent
  d finissais **e** finirai **f** finirais
  g finisse

3 PLACER **a** plaçant **b** placé **c** place,
  places, place, plaçons, placez,
  placent **d** plaçais, plaçais, plaçait,
  placions, placiez, plaçaient
  e placerai, placeras, placera,
  placerons, placerez, placeront
  f placerais, placerais, placerait,
  placerions, placeriez, placeraient
  g place

3 BOUGER **a** bougeant **b** bougé
  c bouge, bougeons **d** bougeais,
  bougions **e** bougerai **f** bougerais
  g bouge

4 appeler **a** appelant **b** appelé
  c appelle, appelons **d** appelais
  e appellerai **f** appellerais **g** appelle

4 jeter **a** jetant **b** jeté **c** jette, jetons
  d jetais **e** jetterai **f** jetterais **g** jette

5 geler **a** gelant **b** gelé **c** gèle, gelons
  d gelais **e** gèlerai **f** gèlerais **g** gèle

6 CÉDER **a** cédant **b** cédé **c** cède,
  cèdes, cède, cédons, cédez, cèdent
  d cédais, cédais, cédait, cédions,
  cédaient **e** céderai, céderas,
  cédera, céderons, céderez, céderont
  f céderais, céderais, céderait,
  céderions, céderiez, céderaient
  g cède

7 épier **a** épiant **b** épié **c** épie, épions
  d épiais **e** épierai **f** épierais **g** épie

8 noyer **a** noyant **b** noyé **c** noie,
  noyons **d** noyais **e** noierai
  f noierais **g** noie

9 ALLER **a** allant **b** allé **c** vais, vas, va,
  allons, allez, vont **d** allais **e** irai
  f irais **g** aille

10 HAÏR **a** haïssant **b** haï **c** hais, hais,
  hait, haïssons, haïssez, haïssent
  d haïssais, haïssais, haïssait,
  haïssions, haïssiez, haïssaient
  e haïrai, haïras, haïra, haïrons,
  haïrez, haïront **f** haïrais, haïrais,
  haïrait, haïrions, haïriez,
  haïraient **g** haïsse

11 courir **a** courant **b** couru **c** cours,
  courons **d** courais **e** courrai
  g coure

12 cueillir **a** cueillant **b** cueilli
  c cueille, cueillons **d** cueillais
  e cueillerai **g** cueille

13 assaillir – **a** assaillant **b** assailli
  c assaille, assaillons **d** assaillais
  e assaillirai **g** assaille

14 servir **a** servant **b** servi **c** sers,
  servons **d** servais **g** serve

15 bouillir **a** bouillant **b** bouilli
  c bous, bouillons **d** bouillais
  g bouille

16 partir **a** partant **b** parti **c** pars,
  partons **d** partais **g** parte

17 fuir **a** fuyant **b** fui **c** fuis, fuyons,
  fuient **d** fuyais **g** fuie

18 couvrir **a** couvrant **b** couvert
  c couvre, couvrons **d** couvrais
  g couvre

19 mourir **a** mourant **b** mort
  c meurs, mourons, meurent
  d mourais **e** mourrai **g** meure

20 vêtir **a** vêtant **b** vêtu **c** vêts,
  vêtons **d** vêtais **e** vêtirai **g** vête

21 acquérir **a** acquérant **b** acquis
  c acquiers, acquérons,
  acquièrent **d** acquérais
  e acquerrai **g** acquière

22 **venir** **a** venant **b** venu **c** viens, venons, viennent **d** venais **e** viendrai **g** vienne

23 **pleuvoir** **a** pleuvant **b** plu **c** pleut, pleuvent **d** pleuvait **e** pleuvra **g** pleuve

24 **prévoir** *like* voir **e** prévoirai

25 **pourvoir** **a** pourvoyant **b** pourvu **c** pourvois, pourvoyons, pourvoient **d** pourvoyais **g** pourvoie

26 **asseoir** **a** asseyant **b** assis **c** assieds, asseyons, asseyez, asseyent **d** asseyais **e** assiérai **g** asseye

28 **RECEVOIR** **a** recevant **b** reçu **c** reçois, reçois, reçoit, recevons, recevez, reçoivent **d** recevais **e** recevrai **f** recevrais **g** reçoive

29 **valoir** **a** valant **b** valu **c** vaux, vaut, valons **d** valais **e** vaudrai **g** vaille

30 **voir** **a** voyant **b** vu **c** vois, voyons, voient **d** voyais **e** verrai **g** voie

31 **vouloir** **a** voulant **b** voulu **c** veux, veut, voulons, veulent **d** voulais **e** voudrai **g** veuille; *impératif* veuillez!

32 **savoir** **a** sachant **b** su **c** sais, savons, savent **d** savais **e** saurai **g** sache *impératif* sache! sachons! sachez!

33 **pouvoir** **a** pouvant **b** pu **c** peux, peut, pouvons, peuvent **d** pouvais **e** pourrai **g** puisse

34 **AVOIR** **a** ayant **b** eu **c** ai, as, a, avons, avez, ont **d** avais **e** aurai **f** aurais **g** aie, aies, ait, ayons, ayez, aient

35 **conclure** **a** concluant **b** conclu **c** conclus, concluons **d** concluais **g** conclue

36 **rire** **a** riant **b** ri **c** ris, rions **d** riais **g** rie

37 **dire** **a** disant **b** dit **c** dis, disons, dites, disent **d** disais **g** dise

38 **nuire** **a** nuisant **b** nui **c** nuis, nuisons **d** nuisais **e** nuirai **f** nuirais **g** nuise

39 **écrire** **a** écrivant **b** écrit **c** écris, écrivons **d** écrivais **g** écrive

40 **suivre** **a** suivant **b** suivi **c** suis, suivons **d** suivais **g** suive

41 **RENDRE** **a** rendant **b** rendu **c** rends, rends, rend, rendons, rendez, rendent **d** rendais **e** rendrai **f** rendrais **g** rende

42 **vaincre** **a** vainquant **b** vaincu **c** vaincs, vainc, vainquons **d** vainquais **g** vainque

43 **lire** **a** lisant **b** lu **c** lis, lisons **d** lisais **g** lise

44 **croire** **a** croyant **b** cru **c** crois, croyons, croient **d** croyais **g** croie

45 **CLORE** **a** closant **b** clos **c** clos, clos, clôt, closent **e** clorai, cloras, clora, clorons, clorez, cloront **f** clorais, clorais, clorait, clorions, cloriez, cloraient

46 **vivre** **a** vivant **b** vécu **c** vis, vivons **d** vivais **g** vive

47 **MOUDRE** **a** moulant **b** moulu **c** mouds, mouds, moud, moulons, moulez, moulent **d** moulais, moulais, moulait, moulions, mouliez, moulaient **e** moudrai, moudras, moudra, moudrons, moudrez, moudront **f** moudrais, moudrais, moudrait, moudrions, moudriez, moudriaent **g** moule

48 **coudre** **a** cousant **b** cousu **c** couds, cousons, cousez, cousent **d** cousais **g** couse

49 **joindre** **a** joignant **b** joint **c** joins, joignons **d** joignais **g** joigne

50 **TRAIRE** **a** trayant **b** trait **c** trais, trais, trait, trayons, trayez, traient **d** trayais, trayais, trayait, trayions, trayiez, trayaient **e** trairai, trairas, traira, trairons, trairez, trairont **f** trairais, trairais, trairait, trairions, trairiez, trairiaent **g** traie

51 **ABSOUDRE** **a** absolvant **b** absous **c** absous, absous, absout, absolvons, absolvez, absolvent

d absolvais, absolvais, absolvait, absolvions, absolviez, absolvaient **e** absoudrai, absoudras, absoudra, absoudrons, absoudrez, absoudront **f** absoudrais, absoudrais, absoudrait, absoudrions, absoudriez, absoudraient **g** absolve

52 **craindre a** craignant **b** craint **c** crains, craignons **d** craignais **g** craigne

53 **boire a** buvant **b** bu **c** bois, buvons, boivent **d** buvais **g** boive

54 **plaire a** plaisant **b** plu **c** plais, plaît, plaisons **d** plaisais **g** plaise

55 **croître a** croissant **b** crû, crue, crus, crues **c** croîs, croissons **d** croissais **g** croisse

56 **mettre a** mettant **b** mis **c** mets, mettons **d** mettais **g** mette

57 **connaître a** connaissant **b** connu **c** connais, connaît, connaissons **d** connaissais **g** connaisse

58 **prendre a** prenant **b** pris **c** prends, prenons, prennent **d** prenais **g** prenne

59 **naître a** naissant **b** né **c** nais, naît, naissons **d** naissais **g** naisse

60 **FAIRE a** faisant **b** fait **c** fais, fais, fait, faisons, faites, font **d** faisais **e** ferai **f** ferais **g** fasse

61 **ÊTRE a** étant **b** été **c** suis, es, est, sommes, êtes, sont **d** étais **e** serai **f** serais **g** sois, sois, soit, soyons, soyez, soient

VERBES IRRÉGULIERS ANGLAIS

PRÉSENT	PASSÉ	PARTICIPE	PRÉSENT	PASSÉ	PARTICIPE
arise	arose	arisen	**fall**	fell	fallen
awake	awoke	awoken	**feed**	fed	fed
be	was, were	been	**feel**	felt	felt
(am, is,			**fight**	fought	fought
are; being)			**find**	found	found
bear	bore	born(e)	**flee**	fled	fled
beat	beat	beaten	**fling**	flung	flung
become	became	become	**fly**	flew	flown
begin	began	begun	**forbid**	forbad(e)	forbidden
bend	bent	bent	**forecast**	forecast	forecast
bet	bet,	bet,	**forget**	forgot	forgotten
	betted	betted	**forgive**	forgave	forgiven
bid (*at auction,*	bid	bid	**forsake**	forsook	forsaken
cards*)			**freeze**	froze	frozen
bid (*say*)	bade	bidden	**get**	got	got,
bind	bound	bound			(*US*) gotten
bite	bit	bitten	**give**	gave	given
bleed	bled	bled	**go** (goes)	went	gone
blow	blew	blown	**grind**	ground	ground
break	broke	broken	**grow**	grew	grown
breed	bred	bred	**hang**	hung	hung
bring	brought	brought	**hang** (*execute*)	hanged	hanged
build	built	built	**have**	had	had
burn	burnt,	burnt,	**hear**	heard	heard
	burned	burned	**hide**	hid	hidden
burst	burst	burst	**hit**	hit	hit
buy	bought	bought	**hold**	held	held
can	could	(*been able*)	**hurt**	hurt	hurt
cast	cast	cast	**keep**	kept	kept
catch	caught	caught	**kneel**	knelt,	knelt,
choose	chose	chosen		kneeled	kneeled
cling	clung	clung	**know**	knew	known
come	came	come	**lay**	laid	laid
cost	cost	cost	**lead**	led	led
cost (*work	costed	costed	**lean**	leant,	leant,
out price of*)				leaned	leaned
creep	crept	crept	**leap**	leapt,	leapt,
cut	cut	cut		leaped	leaped
deal	dealt	dealt	**learn**	learnt,	learnt,
dig	dug	dug		learned	learned
do (does)	did	done	**leave**	left	left
draw	drew	drawn	**lend**	lent	lent
dream	dreamed,	dreamed,	**let**	let	let
	dreamt	dreamt	**lie** (lying)	lay	lain
drink	drank	drunk	**light**	lit,	lit,
drive	drove	driven		lighted	lighted
dwell	dwelt	dwelt	**lose**	lost	lost
eat	ate	eaten	**make**	made	made

PRÉSENT	PASSÉ	PARTICIPE	PRÉSENT	PASSÉ	PARTICIPE
may	might	–	speed	sped,	sped,
mean	meant	meant		speeded	speeded
meet	met	met	spell	spelt,	spelt,
mistake	mistook	mistaken		spelled	spelled
mow	mowed	mown,	spend	spent	spent
		mowed	spill	spilt,	spilt,
must	(had to)	(had to)		spilled	spilled
pay	paid	paid	spin	spun	spun
put	put	put	spit	spat	spat
quit	quit,	quit,	spoil	spoiled,	spoiled,
	quitted	quitted		spoilt	spoilt
read	read	read	spread	spread	spread
rid	rid	rid	spring	sprang	sprung
ride	rode	ridden	stand	stood	stood
ring	rang	rung	steal	stole	stolen
rise	rose	risen	stick	stuck	stuck
run	ran	run	sting	stung	stung
saw	sawed	sawed,	stink	stank	stunk
		sawn	stride	strode	stridden
say	said	said	strike	struck	struck
see	saw	seen	strive	strove	striven
seek	sought	sought	swear	swore	sworn
sell	sold	sold	sweep	swept	swept
send	sent	sent	swell	swelled	swollen,
set	set	set			swelled
sew	sewed	sewn	swim	swam	swum
shake	shook	shaken	swing	swung	swung
shear	sheared	shorn,	take	took	taken
		sheared	teach	taught	taught
shed	shed	shed	tear	tore	torn
shine	shone	shone	tell	told	told
shoot	shot	shot	think	thought	thought
show	showed	shown	throw	threw	thrown
shrink	shrank	shrunk	thrust	thrust	thrust
shut	shut	shut	tread	trod	trodden
sing	sang	sung	wake	woke,	woken,
sink	sank	sunk		waked	waked
sit	sat	sat	wear	wore	worn
slay	slew	slain	weave	wove	woven
sleep	slept	slept	weave(*wind*)	weaved	weaved
slide	slid	slid	wed	wedded,	wedded,
sling	slung	slung		wed	wed
slit	slit	slit	weep	wept	wept
smell	smelt,	smelt,	win	won	won
	smelled	smelled	wind	wound	wound
sow	sowed	sown,	wring	wrung	wrung
		sowed	write	wrote	written
speak	spoke	spoken			

LES NOMBRES

un (une)	1
deux	2
trois	3
quatre	4
cinq	5
six	6
sept	7
huit	8
neuf	9
dix	10
onze	11
douze	12
treize	13
quatorze	14
quinze	15
seize	16
dix-sept	17
dix-huit	18
dix-neuf	19
vingt	20
vingt et un (une)	21
vingt-deux	22
trente	30
quarante	40
cinquante	50
soixante	60
soixante-dix	70
soixante-et-onze	71
soixante-douze	72
quatre-vingts	80
quatre-vingt-un (-une)	81
quatre-vingt-dix	90
cent	100
cent un (une)	101
deux cents	200
deux cent un (une)	201
quatre cents	400
mille	1000
cinq mille	5000
un million	1000000

NUMBERS

one	
two	
three	
four	
five	
six	
seven	
eight	
nine	
ten	
eleven	
twelve	
thirteen	
fourteen	
fifteen	
sixteen	
seventeen	
eighteen	
nineteen	
twenty	
twenty-one	
twenty-two	
thirty	
forty	
fifty	
sixty	
seventy	
seventy-one	
seventy-two	
eighty	
eighty-one	
ninety	
a hundred, one hundred	
a hundred and one	
two hundred	
two hundred and one	
four hundred	
a thousand	
five thousand	
a million	

LES NOMBRES

premier (première), 1er (1ère)
deuxième, 2e or 2ème
troisième, 3e or 3ème
quatrième, 4e or 4ème
cinquième, 5e or 5ème
sixième, 6e or 6ème
septième
huitième
neuvième
dixième
onzième
douzième
treizième
quartorzième
quinzième
seizième
dix-septième
dix-huitième
dix-neuvième
vingtième
vingt-et-unième
vingt-deuxième
trentième
centième
cent-unième
millième

LES FRACTIONS ETC

un demi
un tiers
un quart
un cinquième
zéro virgule cinq, 0,5
trois virgule quatre, 3,4
dix pour cent
cent pour cent

EXEMPLES

elle habite au septième (étage)
il habite au sept
au chapitre/à la page sept
il est arrivé (le) septième

NUMBERS

first, 1st
second, 2nd
third, 3rd
fourth, 4th
fifth, 5th
sixth, 6th
seventh
eighth
ninth
tenth
eleventh
twelfth
thirteenth
fourteenth
fifteenth
sixteenth
seventeenth
eighteenth
nineteenth
twentieth
twenty-first
twenty-second
thirtieth
hundredth
hundred-and-first
thousandth

FRACTIONS ETC

a half
a third
a quarter
a fifth
(nought) point five, 0.5
three point four, 3.4
ten per cent
a hundred per cent

EXAMPLES

she lives on the 7th floor
he lives at number 7
chapter/page 7
he came in 7th

L'HEURE

quelle heure est-il?

il est ...

minuit
une heure (du matin)

une heure cinq
une heure dix
une heure et quart

une heure vingt-cinq

une heure et demie, une heure trente
deux heures moins vingt-cinq, une
 heure trente-cinq
deux heures moins vingt, une heure
 quarante
deux heures moins le quart, une heure
 quarante-cinq
deux heures moins dix, une heure
 cinquante
midi

deux heures (de l'après-midi),
 quatorze heures
sept heures (du soir), dix-sept heures

à quelle heure?

à minuit
à sept heures

dans vingt minutes
il y a un quart d'heure

THE TIME

what time is it?

it's ou it is ...

midnight, twelve p.m.
one o'clock (in the
 morning), one (a.m.)
five past one
ten past one
a quarter past one,
 one fifteen
twenty-five past one,
 one twenty-five
half-past one, one thirty
twenty-five to two,
 one thirty-five
twenty to two, one forty

a quarter to two,
 one forty-five
ten to two, one fifty

twelve o'clock, midday,
 noon
two o'clock (in the
 afternoon), two (p.m.)
seven o'clock (in the
 evening), seven (p.m.)

(at) what time?

at midnight
at seven o'clock

in twenty minutes
fifteen minutes ago

a [a] vb voir **avoir**

MOT-CLÉ

à [a] (à + le = **au**, à + les = **aux**) prép **1**
(endroit, situation) at, in; **être à Paris/
au Portugal** to be in Paris/Portugal;
être à la maison/à l'école to be at
home/at school; **à la campagne**
in the country; **c'est à 10 m/km/à
20 minutes (d'ici)** it's 10 m/km/20
minutes away
2 (direction) to; **aller à Paris/au
Portugal** to go to Paris/Portugal;
aller à la maison/à l'école to go
home/to school; **à la campagne** to
the country
3 (temps): **à 3 heures/minuit** at 3
o'clock/midnight; **au printemps** in
the spring; **au mois de juin** in June;
à Noël/Pâques at Christmas/Easter;
à demain/la semaine prochaine!
see you tomorrow/next week!

4 (attribution, appartenance) to; **le
livre est à Paul/à lui/à nous** this
book is Paul's/his/ours; **donner qch
à qn** to give sth to sb; **un ami à moi**
a friend of mine
5 (moyen) with; **se chauffer au gaz**
to have gas heating; **à bicyclette** on
a ou by bicycle; **à pied** on foot; **à la
main/machine** by hand/machine
6 (provenance) from; **boire à la
bouteille** to drink from the bottle
7 (caractérisation, manière): **l'homme
aux yeux bleus** the man with the
blue eyes; **à la russe** the Russian way
8 (but, destination): **tasse à café**
coffee cup; **maison à vendre** house
for sale; **je n'ai rien à lire** I don't have
anything to read; **à bien réfléchir ...**
thinking about it ..., on reflection ...
9 (rapport, évaluation, distribution):
100 km/unités à l'heure 100 km/
units per ou an hour; **payé à l'heure**
paid by the hour; **cinq à six** five to six
10 (conséquence, résultat): **à ce qu'il
prétend** according to him; **à leur
grande surprise** much to their
surprise; **à nous trois nous n'avons
pas su le faire** we couldn't do it even
between the three of us; **ils sont
arrivés à quatre** four of them arrived
(together)

abaisser [abese] /1/ vt to lower,
bring down; (manette) to pull down;
s'abaisser vi to go down; (fig) to
demean o.s.
abandon [abɑ̃dɔ̃] nm abandoning;
giving up; withdrawal; **être à l'~** to
be in a state of neglect; **laisser à l'~**
to abandon
abandonner [abɑ̃dɔne] /1/ vt
(personne) to leave, abandon, desert;
(projet, activité) to abandon, give up;
(Sport) to retire ou withdraw from;
(céder) to surrender; **s'~ à** (paresse,
plaisirs) to give o.s. up to
abat-jour [abaʒuʀ] nm inv
lampshade

abats [aba] *nmpl* (*de bœuf, porc*) offal *sg*; (*de volaille*) giblets

abattement [abatmã] *nm*: **~ fiscal** ≈ tax allowance

abattoir [abatwaʀ] *nm* slaughterhouse

abattre [abatʀ] /41/ *vt* (*arbre*) to cut down, fell; (*mur, maison*) to pull down; (*avion, personne*) to shoot down; (*animal*) to shoot, kill; (*fig*) to wear out, tire out; to demoralize; **s'abattre** *vi* to crash down; **ne pas se laisser ~** to keep one's spirits up, not to let things get one down; **s'~ sur** to beat down on; (*coups, injures*) to rain down on; **~ du travail** *ou* **de la besogne** to get through a lot of work

abbaye [abei] *nf* abbey

abbé [abe] *nm* priest; (*d'une abbaye*) abbot

abcès [apsɛ] *nm* abscess

abdiquer [abdike] /1/ *vi* to abdicate

abdominal, e, -aux [abdɔminal, -o] *adj* abdominal; **abdominaux** *nmpl*: **faire des abdominaux** to do sit-ups

abeille [abɛj] *nf* bee

aberrant, e [abeʀɑ̃, -ɑ̃t] *adj* absurd

aberration [abeʀasjɔ̃] *nf* aberration

abîme [abim] *nm* abyss, gulf

abîmer [abime] /1/ *vt* to spoil, damage; **s'abîmer** *vi* to get spoilt *ou* damaged

aboiement [abwamɑ̃] *nm* bark, barking *no pl*

abolir [abɔliʀ] /2/ *vt* to abolish

abominable [abɔminabl] *adj* abominable

abondance [abɔ̃dɑ̃s] *nf* abundance

abondant, e [abɔ̃dɑ̃, -ɑ̃t] *adj* plentiful, abundant, copious; **abonder** /1/ *vi* to abound, be plentiful; **abonder dans le sens de qn** to concur with sb

abonné, e [abɔne] *nm/f* subscriber; season ticket holder

abonnement [abɔnmɑ̃] *nm* subscription; (*pour transports en commun, concerts*) season ticket

abonner [abɔne] /1/ *vt*: **s'abonner à** to subscribe to, take out a subscription to

abord [abɔʀ] *nm*: **abords** *nmpl* (*environs*) surroundings; **d'~** first; **au premier ~** at first sight, initially

abordable [abɔʀdabl] *adj* (*personne*) approachable; (*prix*) reasonable

aborder [abɔʀde] /1/ *vi* to land ▷ *vt* (*sujet, difficulté*) to tackle; (*personne*) to approach; (*rivage etc*) to reach

aboutir [abutiʀ] /2/ *vi* (*négociations etc*) to succeed; **~ à/dans/sur** to end up at/in/on; **n'~ à rien** to come to nothing

aboyer [abwaje] /8/ *vi* to bark

abréger [abʀeʒe] /3, 6/ *vt* to shorten

abreuver [abʀœve] /1/: **s'abreuver** *vi* to drink; **abreuvoir** *nm* watering place

abréviation [abʀevjasjɔ̃] *nf* abbreviation

abri [abʀi] *nm* shelter; **être à l'~** to be under cover; **se mettre à l'~** to shelter; **à l'~ de** sheltered from; (*danger*) safe from

abricot [abʀiko] *nm* apricot

abriter [abʀite] /1/ *vt* to shelter; **s'abriter** *vi* to shelter, take cover

abrupt, e [abʀypt] *adj* sheer, steep; (*ton*) abrupt

abruti, e [abʀyti] *adj* stunned, dazed ▷ *nm/f* (*fam*) idiot; **~ de travail** overworked

absence [apsɑ̃s] *nf* absence; (*Méd*) blackout; **en l'~ de** in the absence of; **avoir des ~s** to have mental blanks

absent, e [apsɑ̃, -ɑ̃t] *adj* absent ▷ *nm/f* absentee; **absenter** /1/: **s'absenter** *vi* to take time off work; (*sortir*) to leave, go out

absolu, e [apsɔly] *adj* absolute; **absolument** *adv* absolutely

absorbant, e [apsɔʀbɑ̃, -ɑ̃t] *adj* absorbent

absorber [apsɔrbe] /1/ vt to absorb; (gén, Méd: manger, boire) to take

abstenir [apstənir] /22/: **s'abstenir** vi: **s'~ de qch/de faire** to refrain from sth/from doing

abstrait, e [apstrɛ, -ɛt] adj abstract

absurde [apsyrd] adj absurd

abus [aby] nm abuse; **~ de confiance** breach of trust; **il y a de l'~!** (fam) that's a bit much!; **abuser** /1/ vi to go too far, overstep the mark; **s'abuser** vi (se méprendre) to be mistaken; **abuser de** (violer, duper) to take advantage of; **abusif, -ive** adj exorbitant; (punition) excessive

académie [akademi] nf academy; (Scol: circonscription) ≈ regional education authority; see note **"Académie française"**

⊕ **ACADÉMIE FRANÇAISE**
⊕
⊕ The Académie française was founded
⊕ by Cardinal Richelieu in 1635,
⊕ during the reign of Louis XIII. It is
⊕ made up of forty elected scholars
⊕ and writers who are known as 'les
⊕ Quarante' or 'les Immortels'. One
⊕ of the Académie's functions is to
⊕ keep an eye on the development
⊕ of the French language, and its
⊕ recommendations are frequently
⊕ the subject of lively public debate.
⊕ It has produced several editions
⊕ of its famous dictionary and also
⊕ awards various literary prizes.

acajou [akaʒu] nm mahogany

acariâtre [akarjɑtr] adj cantankerous

accablant, e [akablɑ̃, -ɑ̃t] adj (chaleur) oppressive; (témoignage, preuve) overwhelming

accabler [akable] /1/ vt to overwhelm, overcome; **~ qn d'injures** to heap ou shower abuse on sb; **~ qn de travail** to overwork sb

accalmie [akalmi] nf lull

accaparer [akapare] /1/ vt to monopolize; (travail etc) to take up (all) the time ou attention of

accéder [aksede] /6/: **~ à** vt (lieu) to reach; (accorder: requête) to grant, accede to

accélérateur [akseleratœr] nm accelerator

accélérer [akselere] /6/ vt to speed up ▷ vi to accelerate

accent [aksɑ̃] nm accent; (Phonétique, fig) stress; **mettre l'~ sur** (fig) to stress; **~ aigu/grave/circonflexe** acute/grave/circumflex accent; **accentuer** /1/ vt (Ling) to accent; (fig) to accentuate, emphasize; **s'accentuer** vi to become more marked ou pronounced

acceptation [aksɛptasjɔ̃] nf acceptance

accepter [aksɛpte] /1/ vt to accept; **~ de faire** to agree to do

accès [aksɛ] nm (à un lieu) access; (Méd: de toux) fit; (: de fièvre) bout; **d'~ facile/malaisé** easily/not easily accessible; **facile d'~** easy to get to; **~ de colère** fit of anger; **accessible** adj accessible; (livre, sujet): **accessible à qn** within the reach of sb

accessoire [akseswar] adj secondary; (frais) incidental ▷ nm accessory; (Théât) prop

accident [aksidɑ̃] nm accident; **par ~** by chance; **~ de la route** road accident; **accidenté, e** adj damaged ou injured (in an accident); (relief, terrain) uneven; hilly; **accidentel, le** adj accidental

acclamer [aklame] /1/ vt to cheer, acclaim

acclimater [aklimate] /1/: **s'acclimater** vi to become acclimatized

accolade [akɔlad] nf (amicale) embrace; (signe) brace

accommoder [akɔmɔde] /1/ vt (Culin) to prepare; **s'accommoder**

de to put up with; (*se contenter de*) to make do with

accompagnateur, -trice [akɔ̃paɲatœʀ, -tʀis] *nm/f* (*Mus*) accompanist; (*de voyage*) guide; (*de voyage organisé*) courier

accompagner [akɔ̃paɲe] /1/ *vt* to accompany, be *ou* go *ou* come with; (*Mus*) to accompany

accompli, e [akɔ̃pli] *adj* accomplished

accomplir [akɔ̃pliʀ] /2/ *vt* (*tâche, projet*) to carry out; (*souhait*) to fulfil; **s'accomplir** *vi* to be fulfilled

accord [akɔʀ] *nm* agreement; (*entre des styles, tons etc*) harmony; (*Mus*) chord; **se mettre d'~** to come to an agreement (with each other); **être d'~** to agree; **d'~!** OK!

accordéon [akɔʀdeɔ̃] *nm* (*Mus*) accordion

accorder [akɔʀde] /1/ *vt* (*faveur, délai*) to grant; **~ de l'importance/de la valeur à qch** to attach importance/value to sth; (*harmoniser*) to match; (*Mus*) to tune

accoster [akɔste] /1/ *vt* (*Navig*) to draw alongside ▷ *vi* to berth

accouchement [akuʃmɑ̃] *nm* delivery, (child)birth; labour

accoucher [akuʃe] /1/ *vi* to give birth, have a baby; **~ d'un garçon** to give birth to a boy

accouder [akude] /1/: **s'accouder** *vi*: **s'~ à/contre/sur** to rest one's elbows on/against/on; **accoudoir** *nm* armrest

accoupler [akuple] /1/ *vt* to couple; (*pour la reproduction*) to mate; **s'accoupler** *vi* to mate

accourir [akuʀiʀ] /11/ *vi* to rush *ou* run up

accoutumance [akutymɑ̃s] *nf* (*gén*) adaptation; (*Méd*) addiction

accoutumé, e [akutyme] *adj* (*habituel*) customary, usual

accoutumer [akutyme] /1/ *vt*: **s'accoutumer à** to get accustomed *ou* used to

accroc [akʀo] *nm* (*déchirure*) tear; (*fig*) hitch, snag

accrochage [akʀoʃaʒ] *nm* (*Auto*) (minor) collision; (*dispute*) clash, brush

accrocher [akʀoʃe] /1/ *vt* (*suspendre*) to hang; (*fig*) to catch, attract; **s'accrocher** (*se disputer*) to have a clash *ou* brush; **~ qch à** (*suspendre*) to hang sth (up) on; (*attacher: remorque*) to hitch sth (up) to; (*déchirer*) to catch sth (on); **il a accroché ma voiture** he bumped into my car; **s'~ à** (*rester pris à*) to catch on; (*agripper, fig*) to hang on *ou* cling to

accroissement [akʀwasmɑ̃] *nm* increase

accroître [akʀwatʀ] /55/ *vt*: **s'accroître** *vi* to increase

accroupir [akʀupiʀ] /2/: **s'accroupir** *vi* to squat, crouch (down)

accru, e [akʀy] *pp de* **accroître**

accueil [akœj] *nm* welcome; **comité/centre d'~** reception committee/centre; **accueillir** /12/ *vt* to welcome; (*aller chercher*) to meet, collect

accumuler [akymyle] /1/ *vt* to accumulate, amass; **s'accumuler** *vi* to accumulate; to pile up

accusation [akyzasjɔ̃] *nf* (*gén*) accusation; (*Jur*) charge; (*partie*): **l'~** the prosecution

accusé, e [akyze] *nm/f* accused; (*prévenu(e)*) defendant ▷ *nm*: **~ de réception** acknowledgement of receipt

accuser [akyze] /1/ *vt* to accuse; (*fig*) to emphasize, bring out; (: *montrer*) to show; **~ qn de** to accuse sb of; (*Jur*) to charge sb with; **~ réception de** to acknowledge receipt of

acéré, e [aseʀe] *adj* sharp

acharné, e [aʃaʀne] *adj* (*lutte, adversaire*) fierce, bitter; (*travail*) relentless

acharner [aʃaʀne] /1/: **s'acharner** *vi*: **s'~ sur** to go at fiercely; **s'~ contre**

to set o.s. against; (*malchance*) to hound; **s'~ à faire** to try doggedly to do; to persist in doing

achat [aʃa] *nm* purchase; **faire l'~ de** to buy; **faire des ~s** to do some shopping

acheter [aʃte] /5/ *vt* to buy, purchase; (*soudoyer*) to buy; **~ qch à** (*marchand*) to buy ou purchase sth from; (*ami etc*: *offrir*) to buy sth for; **acheteur, -euse** *nm/f* buyer; shopper; (*Comm*) buyer

achever [aʃ(ə)ve] /5/ *vt* to complete, finish; (*blessé*) to finish off; **s'achever** *vi* to end

acide [asid] *adj* sour, sharp; (*Chimie*) acid(ic) ▷ *nm* acid; **acidulé, e** *adj* slightly acid; **bonbons acidulés** acid drops

acier [asje] *nm* steel; **aciérie** *nf* steelworks *sg*

acné [akne] *nf* acne

acompte [akɔ̃t] *nm* deposit

à-côté [akote] *nm* side-issue; (*argent*) extra

à-coup [aku] *nm*: **par ~s** by fits and starts

acoustique [akustik] *nf* (*d'une salle*) acoustics *pl*

acquéreur [akerœr] *nm* buyer, purchaser

acquérir [akerir] /21/ *vt* to acquire

acquis, e [aki, -iz] *pp de* **acquérir** ▷ *nm* (accumulated) experience; **son aide nous est ~e** we can count on ou be sure of his help

acquitter [akite] /1/ *vt* (*Jur*) to acquit; (*facture*) to pay, settle; **s'~ de** to discharge; (*promesse, tâche*) to fulfil

âcre [akʀ] *adj* acrid, pungent

acrobate [akʀɔbat] *nm/f* acrobat; **acrobatie** *nf* acrobatics *sg*

acte [akt] *nm* act, action; (*Théât*) act; **prendre ~ de** to note, take note of; **faire ~ de présence** to put in an appearance; **faire ~ de candidature** to submit an application; **~ de**

mariage/naissance marriage/birth certificate

acteur [aktœr] *nm* actor

actif, -ive [aktif, -iv] *adj* active ▷ *nm* (*Comm*) assets *pl*; (*fig*): **avoir à son ~** to have to one's credit; **population active** working population

action [aksjɔ̃] *nf* (*gén*) action; (*Comm*) share; **une bonne/mauvaise ~** a good/an unkind deed; **actionnaire** *nm/f* shareholder; **actionner** /1/ *vt* (*mécanisme*) to activate; (*machine*) to operate

activer [aktive] /1/ *vt* to speed up; **s'activer** *vi* to bustle about; (*se hâter*) to hurry up

activité [aktivite] *nf* activity; **en ~** (*volcan*) active; (*fonctionnaire*) in active life

actrice [aktʀis] *nf* actress

actualité [aktɥalite] *nf* (*d'un problème*) topicality; (*événements*): **l'~** current events; **les ~s** (*Ciné, TV*) the news; **d'~** topical

actuel, le [aktɥɛl] *adj* (*présent*) present; (*d'actualité*) topical; **à l'heure ~le** at this moment in time; **actuellement** [aktɥɛlmɑ̃] *adv* at present, at the present time

■ Attention à ne pas traduire *actuellement* par *actually*.

acuponcture [akypɔ̃ktyʀ] *nf* acupuncture

adaptateur, -trice [adaptatœr, -tʀis] *nm/f* adapter

adapter [adapte] /1/ *vt* to adapt; **s'~ (à)** (*personne*) to adapt (to); **~ qch à** (*approprier*) to adapt sth to (fit); **~ qch sur/dans/à** (*fixer*) to fit sth on/into/to

addition [adisjɔ̃] *nf* addition; (*au café*) bill; **additionner** /1/ *vt* to add (up)

adepte [adɛpt] *nm/f* follower

adéquat, e [adekwa(t), -at] *adj* appropriate, suitable

adhérent, e [aderɑ̃, -ɑ̃t] *nm/f* member

adhérer [adere] /6/: **~ à** (coller) to adhere ou stick to; (se rallier à: parti, club) to join; **adhésif, -ive** adj adhesive, sticky; **ruban adhésif** sticky ou adhesive tape

adieu, x [adjø] excl goodbye ▷ nm farewell

adjectif [adʒɛktif] nm adjective

adjoint, e [adʒwɛ̃, -wɛ̃t] nm/f assistant; **~ au maire** deputy mayor; **directeur ~** assistant manager

admettre [admɛtʀ] /56/ vt (visiteur, nouveau-venu) to admit; (candidat: Scol) to pass; (tolérer) to allow, accept; (reconnaître) to admit, acknowledge

administrateur, -trice [administʀatœʀ, -tʀis] nm/f (Comm) director; (Admin) administrator

administration [administʀasjɔ̃] nf administration; **l'A~** ≈ the Civil Service

administrer [administʀe] /1/ vt (firme) to manage, run; (biens, remède, sacrement etc) to administer

admirable [admiʀabl] adj admirable, wonderful

admirateur, -trice [admiʀatœʀ, -tʀis] nm/f admirer

admiration [admiʀasjɔ̃] nf admiration

admirer [admiʀe] /1/ vt to admire

admis, e [admi, -iz] pp de **admettre**

admissible [admisibl] adj (candidat) eligible; (comportement) admissible, acceptable

ADN sigle m (= acide désoxyribonucléique) DNA

adolescence [adolesɑ̃s] nf adolescence

adolescent, e [adolesɑ̃, -ɑ̃t] nm/f adolescent, teenager

adopter [adopte] /1/ vt to adopt; **adoptif, -ive** adj (parents) adoptive; (fils, patrie) adopted

adorable [adoʀabl] adj adorable

adorer [adoʀe] /1/ vt to adore; (Rel) to worship

adosser [adose] /1/ vt: **~ qch à** ou **contre** to stand sth against; **s'~ à** ou **contre** to lean with one's back against

adoucir [adusiʀ] /2/ vt (goût, température) to make milder; (avec du sucre) to sweeten; (peau, voix, eau) to soften; **s'adoucir** vi (caractère) to mellow

adresse [adʀɛs] nf (voir adroit) skill, dexterity; (domicile) address; **~ électronique** email address

adresser [adʀese] /1/ vt (lettre: expédier) to send; (: écrire l'adresse sur) to address; (injure, compliments) to address; **s'adresser à** (parler à) to speak to, address; (s'informer auprès de) to go and see (: bureau) to enquire at; (livre, conseil) to be aimed at; **~ la parole à qn** to speak to ou address sb

adroit, e [adʀwa, -wat] adj skilled

ADSL sigle m (= asymmetrical digital subscriber line) ADSL, broadband

adulte [adylt] nm/f adult, grown-up ▷ adj (personne, attitude) adult, grown-up; (chien, arbre) fully-grown, mature

adverbe [advɛʀb] nm adverb

adversaire [advɛʀsɛʀ] nm/f (Sport, gén) opponent, adversary

aération [aeʀasjɔ̃] nf airing; (circulation de l'air) ventilation

aérer [aeʀe] /6/ vt to air; (fig) to lighten

aérien, ne [aeʀjɛ̃, -ɛn] adj (Aviat) air cpd, aerial; (câble, métro) overhead; (fig) light; **compagnie ~ne** airline (company)

aéro: aérobic nf aerobics sg; **aérogare** nf airport (buildings); (en ville) air terminal; **aéroglisseur** nm hovercraft; **aérophagie** nf (Méd) wind, aerophagia (Méd); **aéroport** nm airport; **aérosol** nm aerosol

affaiblir [afebliʀ] /2/: **s'affaiblir** vi to weaken

affaire [afɛʀ] nf (problème, question) matter; (criminelle, judiciaire) case; (scandaleuse etc) affair; (entreprise)

business; (*marché, transaction*)
(business) deal, (piece of) business
no pl; (*occasion intéressante*) good
deal; **affaires** *nfpl* affairs; (*activité
commerciale*) business *sg*; (*effets
personnels*) things, belongings; **~s de
sport** sports gear; **tirer qn/se tirer
d'~** to get sb/o.s. out of trouble; **ceci
fera l'~** this will do (nicely); **avoir ~
à** (*en contact*) to be dealing with; **ce
sont mes ~s** (*cela me concerne*) that's
my business; **occupe-toi de tes
~s!** mind your own business!; **les
~s étrangères** (*Pol*) foreign affairs;
affairer /1/: **s'affairer** *vi* to busy o.s.,
bustle about

affamé, e [afame] *adj* starving

affecter [afɛkte] /1/ *vt* to affect;
~ qch à to allocate *ou* allot sth to;
~ qn à to appoint sb to; (*diplomate*)
to post sb to

affectif, -ive [afɛktif, -iv] *adj*
emotional

affection [afɛksjɔ̃] *nf* affection;
(*mal*) ailment; **affectionner** /1/ *vt*
to be fond of; **affectueux, -euse** *adj*
affectionate

affichage [afiʃaʒ] *nm* billposting;
(*électronique*) display; **"~ interdit"**
"stick no bills"; **~ à cristaux liquides**
liquid crystal display, LCD

affiche [afiʃ] *nf* poster; (*officielle*)
(public) notice; (*Théât*) bill; **être à
l'~** to be on

afficher [afiʃe] /1/ *vt* (*affiche*) to
put up; (*réunion*) to put up a notice
about; (*électroniquement*) to display;
(*fig*) to exhibit, display; **s'afficher** *vi*
(*péj*) to flaunt o.s.; (*électroniquement*)
to be displayed; **"défense d'~"** "no
bill posters"

affilée [afile]: **d'~** *adv* at a stretch

affirmatif, -ive [afiʀmatif, -iv] *adj*
affirmative

affirmer [afiʀme] /1/ *vt* to assert

affligé, e [afliʒe] *adj* distressed,
grieved; **~ de** (*maladie, tare*) afflicted
with

affliger [afliʒe] /3/ *vt* (*peiner*) to
distress, grieve

affluence [aflyɑ̃s] *nf* crowds *pl*;
heures d'~ rush hour *sg*; **jours d'~**
busiest days

affluent [aflyɑ̃] *nm* tributary

affolement [afɔlmɑ̃] *nm* panic

affoler [afɔle] /1/ *vt* to throw into a
panic; **s'affoler** *vi* to panic

affranchir [afʀɑ̃ʃiʀ] /2/ *vt* to put a
stamp *ou* stamps on; (*à la machine*)
to frank (*BRIT*), meter (*US*); (*fig*) to
free, liberate; **affranchissement**
nm postage

affreux, -euse [afʀø, -øz] *adj*
dreadful, awful

affront [afʀɔ̃] *nm* affront;
affrontement *nm* clash,
confrontation

affronter [afʀɔ̃te] /1/ *vt* to confront,
face

affût [afy] *nm*: **à l'~ (de)** (*gibier*)
lying in wait (for); (*fig*) on the look-
out (for)

Afghanistan [afganistɑ̃] *nm*: **l'~**
Afghanistan

afin [afɛ̃]: **~ que** *conj* so that, in order
that; **~ de faire** in order to do, so
as to do

africain, e [afʀikɛ̃, -ɛn] *adj* African
▷ *nm/f*: **A~, e** African

Afrique [afʀik] *nf*: **l'~** Africa;
l'~ australe/du Nord/du Sud
southern/North/South Africa

agacer [agase] /3/ *vt* to irritate

âge [ɑʒ] *nm* age; **quel ~ as-tu?** how
old are you?; **prendre de l'~** to be
getting on (in years); **le troisième
~** (*personnes âgées*) senior citizens;
(*période*) retirement; **âgé, e** *adj* old,
elderly; **âgé de 10 ans** 10 years old

agence [aʒɑ̃s] *nf* agency, office;
(*succursale*) branch; **~ immobilière**
estate agent's (office) (*BRIT*), real
estate office (*US*); **~ de voyages**
travel agency

agenda [aʒɛ̃da] *nm* diary;
~ électronique PDA

Attention à ne pas traduire *agenda* par le mot anglais *agenda*.

agenouiller [aʒ(ə)nuje] /1/: **s'agenouiller** *vi* to kneel (down)

agent, e [aʒɑ̃, -ɑ̃t] *nm/f* (*aussi*: **~(e) de police**) policeman (policewoman); (*Admin*) official, officer; **~ immobilier** estate agent (*BRIT*), realtor (*US*)

agglomération [aglɔmeʀasjɔ̃] *nf* town; (*Auto*) built-up area; **l'~ parisienne** the urban area of Paris

aggraver [agʀave] /1/: **s'aggraver** *vi* to worsen

agile [aʒil] *adj* agile, nimble

agir [aʒiʀ] /2/ *vi* to act; **il s'agit de** it's a matter *ou* question of; (*ça traite de*) it is about; **il s'agit de faire** we (*ou* you *etc*) must do; **de quoi s'agit-il?** what is it about?

agitation [aʒitasjɔ̃] *nf* (hustle and) bustle; (*trouble*) agitation, excitement; (*politique*) unrest, agitation

agité, e [aʒite] *adj* fidgety, restless; (*troublé*) agitated, perturbed; (*mer*) rough

agiter [aʒite] /1/ *vt* (*bouteille, chiffon*) to shake; (*bras, mains*) to wave; (*préoccuper, exciter*) to trouble

agneau, x [aɲo] *nm* lamb

agonie [agɔni] *nf* mortal agony, death pangs *pl*; (*fig*) death throes *pl*

agrafe [agʀaf] *nf* (*de vêtement*) hook, fastener; (*de bureau*) staple; **agrafer** /1/ *vt* to fasten; to staple; **agrafeuse** [agʀaføz] *nf* stapler

agrandir [agʀɑ̃diʀ] /2/ *vt* to extend; **s'agrandir** *vi* (*ville, famille*) to grow, expand; (*trou, écart*) to get bigger; **agrandissement** *nm* (*photographie*) enlargement

agréable [agʀeabl] *adj* pleasant, nice

agréé, e [agʀee] *adj*: **concessionnaire ~** registered dealer

agréer [agʀee] /1/ *vt* (*requête*) to accept; **~ à** to please, suit; **veuillez ~, Monsieur/Madame,**

mes salutations distinguées (*personne nommée*) yours sincerely; (*personne non nommée*) yours faithfully

agrégation [agʀegasjɔ̃] *nf* highest teaching diploma in France; **agrégé, e** *nm/f* holder of the *agrégation*

agrément [agʀemɑ̃] *nm* (*accord*) consent, approval; (*attraits*) charm, attractiveness; (*plaisir*) pleasure

agresser [agʀese] /1/ *vt* to attack; **agresseur** *nm* aggressor, attacker; (*Pol, Mil*) aggressor; **agressif, -ive** *adj* aggressive

agricole [agʀikɔl] *adj* agricultural; **agriculteur, -trice** *nm/f* farmer; **agriculture** *nf* agriculture; farming

agripper [agʀipe] /1/ *vt* to grab, clutch; **s'~ à** to cling (on) to, clutch, grip

agroalimentaire [agʀɔalimɑ̃tɛʀ] *nm* farm-produce industry

agrumes [agʀym] *nmpl* citrus fruit(s)

aguets [agɛ]: **aux ~** *adv*; **être aux ~** to be on the look-out

ai [ɛ] *vb voir* **avoir**

aide [ɛd] *nm/f* assistant ▷ *nf* assistance, help; (*secours financier*) aid; **à l'~ de** with the help *ou* aid of; **appeler (qn) à l'~** to call for help (from sb); **à l'~!** help!; **~ judiciaire** legal aid; **~ ménagère** *nf* ≈ home help (*BRIT*) *ou* helper (*US*); **aide-mémoire** *nm inv* memoranda pages *pl*; (key facts) handbook

aider [ede] /1/ *vt* to help; **~ à qch** to help (towards) sth; **~ qn à faire qch** to help sb to do sth; **s'~ de** (*se servir de*) to use, make use of

aide-soignant, e [ɛdswaɲɑ̃, -ɑ̃t] *nm/f* auxiliary nurse

aie *etc* [ɛ] *vb voir* **avoir**

aïe [aj] *excl* ouch!

aigle [ɛgl] *nm* eagle

aigre [ɛgʀ] *adj* sour, sharp; (*fig*) sharp, cutting; **aigre-doux, -douce** *adj* (*sauce*) sweet and sour; **aigreur** *nf* sourness; sharpness

aigu, ë [egy] *adj* (*objet, arête*) sharp; (*son, voix*) high-pitched, shrill; (*note*) high(-pitched)

aiguille [egɥij] *nf* needle; (*de montre*) hand; **~ à tricoter** knitting needle

aiguiser [egize] /1/ *vt* to sharpen; (*fig*) to stimulate (: *sens*) to excite

ail [aj] *nm* garlic

aile [ɛl] *nf* wing; **aileron** *nm* (*de requin*) fin; **ailier** *nm* winger

aille *etc* [aj] *vb voir* **aller**

ailleurs [ajœʀ] *adv* elsewhere, somewhere else; **partout/nulle part ~** everywhere/nowhere else; **d'~** (*autre reste*) moreover, besides; **par ~** (*d'autre part*) moreover, furthermore

aimable [ɛmabl] *adj* kind, nice

aimant [ɛmɑ̃] *nm* magnet

aimer [eme] /1/ *vt* to love; (*d'amitié, affection, par goût*) to like; **j'aimerais …** (*souhait*) I would like …; **j'aime faire du ski** I like skiing; **je t'aime** I love you; **bien ~ qn/qch** to like sb/sth; **j'aime mieux Paul (que Pierre)** I prefer Paul (to Pierre); **j'aimerais autant** *ou* **mieux y aller maintenant** I'd sooner *ou* rather go now

aine [ɛn] *nf* groin

aîné, e [ene] *adj* elder, older; (*le plus âgé*) eldest, oldest ▷ *nm/f* oldest child *ou* one, oldest boy *ou* son/girl *ou* daughter

ainsi [ɛ̃si] *adv* (*de cette façon*) like this, in this way, thus; (*ce faisant*) thus ▷ *conj* thus, so; **~ que** (*comme*) (just) as; (*et aussi*) as well as; **pour ~ dire** so to speak; **et ~ de suite** and so on (and so forth)

air [ɛʀ] *nm* air; (*mélodie*) tune; (*expression*) look, air; **paroles/ menaces en l'~** empty words/ threats; **prendre l'~** to get some (fresh) air; **avoir l'~** (*sembler*) to look, appear; **avoir l'~ triste** to look *ou* seem sad; **avoir l'~ de qch** to look like sth; **avoir l'~ de faire** to look as though one is doing

airbag [ɛʀbag] *nm* airbag

aisance [ɛzɑ̃s] *nf* ease; (*richesse*) affluence

aise [ɛz] *nf* comfort; **être à l'~** *ou* **à son ~** to be comfortable; (*pas embarrassé*) to be at ease; (*financièrement*) to be comfortably off; **se mettre à l'~** to make o.s. comfortable; **être mal à l'~** *ou* **à son ~** to be uncomfortable; (*gêné*) to be ill at ease; **en faire à son ~** to do as one likes; **aisé, e** *adj* easy; (*assez riche*) well-to-do, well-off

aisselle [ɛsɛl] *nf* armpit

ait [ɛ] *vb voir* **avoir**

ajonc [aʒɔ̃] *nm* gorse *no pl*

ajourner [aʒuʀne] /1/ *vt* (*réunion*) to adjourn; (*décision*) to defer, postpone

ajouter [aʒute] /1/ *vt* to add

alarme [alaʀm] *nf* alarm; **donner l'~** to give *ou* raise the alarm; **alarmer** /1/ *vt* to alarm; **s'alarmer** *vi* to become alarmed

Albanie [albani] *nf*: **l'~** Albania

album [albɔm] *nm* album

alcool [alkɔl] *nm*: **l'~** alcohol; **un ~** a spirit, a brandy; **bière sans ~** non-alcoholic *ou* alcohol-free beer; **~ à brûler** methylated spirits (BRIT), wood alcohol (US); **~ à 90°** surgical spirit; **alcoolique** *adj, nm/f* alcoholic; **alcoolisé, e** *adj* alcoholic; **une boisson non alcoolisée** a soft drink; **alcoolisme** *nm* alcoholism; **alco(o)test**® *nm* Breathalyser® ; (*test*) breath-test

aléatoire [aleatwaʀ] *adj* uncertain; (*Inform, Statistique*) random

alentour [alɑ̃tuʀ] *adv* around (about); **alentours** *nmpl* surroundings; **aux ~s de** in the vicinity *ou* neighbourhood of, around about; (*temps*) around about

alerte [alɛʀt] *adj* agile, nimble; (*style*) brisk, lively ▷ *nf* alert; warning; **~ à la bombe** bomb scare; **alerter** /1/ *vt* to alert

algèbre [alʒɛbʀ] *nf* algebra

Alger [alʒe] n Algiers

Algérie [alʒeʀi] nf: **l'~** Algeria; **algérien, ne** adj Algerian ▷ nm/f: **Algérien, ne** Algerian

algue [alg] nf seaweed no pl; (Bot) alga

alibi [alibi] nm alibi

aligner [aliɲe] /1/ vt to align, line up; (idées, chiffres) to string together; (adapter): **~ qch sur** to bring sth into alignment with; **s'aligner** (soldats etc) to line up; **s'~ sur** (Pol) to align o.s. with

aliment [alimɑ̃] nm food; **alimentation** nf (en eau etc, de moteur) supplying; (commerce) food trade; (régime) diet; (Inform) feed; **alimentation (générale)** (general) grocer's; **alimenter** /1/ vt to feed; (Tech): **alimenter (en)** to supply (with), feed (with); (fig) to sustain, keep going

allaiter [alete] /1/ vt to (breast-)feed, nurse; (animal) to suckle

allécher [aleʃe] /6/ vt: **~ qn** to make sb's mouth water; to tempt sb, entice sb

allée [ale] nf (de jardin) path; (en ville) avenue, drive; **~s et venues** comings and goings

allégé, e [aleʒe] adj (yaourt etc) low-fat

alléger [aleʒe] /6, 3/ vt (voiture) to make lighter; (chargement) to lighten; (souffrance) to alleviate, soothe

Allemagne [almaɲ] nf: **l'~** Germany; **allemand, e** adj German ▷ nm (Ling) German ▷ nm/f: **Allemand, e** German

aller [ale] /9/ nm (trajet) outward journey; (billet) single (BRIT) ou one-way ticket (US) ▷ vi (gén) to go; **~ simple** (billet) single (BRIT) ou one-way ticket; **~ (et) retour (AR)** return trip ou journey (BRIT), round trip (US); (billet) return (BRIT) ou round-trip (US) ticket; **~ à** (convenir) to suit; (forme, pointure etc) to fit; **~ avec** (couleurs, style etc) to go (well) with; **je vais le faire/me fâcher** I'm going to do it/to get angry; **~ voir/ chercher qn** to go and see/look for sb; **comment allez-vous?** how are you?; **comment ça va?** how are you?; (affaires etc) how are things?; **il va bien/mal** he's well/not well, he's fine/ill; **ça va bien/mal** (affaires etc) it's going well/not going well; **~ mieux** to be better; **allez!** come on!; **allons!** come now!

allergie [alɛʀʒi] nf allergy

allergique [alɛʀʒik] adj: **~ à** allergic to

alliance [aljɑ̃s] nf (Mil, Pol) alliance; (bague) wedding ring

allier [alje] /7/ vt (Pol, gén) to ally; (fig) to combine; **s'allier** to become allies; (éléments, caractéristiques) to combine

allô [alo] excl hullo, hallo

allocation [alɔkasjɔ̃] nf allowance; **~ (de) chômage** unemployment benefit; **~s familiales** ≈ child benefit

allonger [alɔ̃ʒe] /3/ vt to lengthen, make longer; (étendre: bras, jambe) to stretch (out); **s'allonger** to get longer; (se coucher) to lie down, stretch out; **~ le pas** to hasten one's step(s)

allumage [alymaʒ] nm (Auto) ignition

allume-cigare [alymsigaʀ] nm inv cigar lighter

allumer [alyme] /1/ vt (lampe, phare, radio) to put ou switch on; (pièce) to put ou switch the light(s) on in; (feu, bougie, cigare, pipe, gaz) to light; **s'allumer** vi (lumière, lampe) to come ou go on

allumette [alymɛt] nf match

allure [alyʀ] nf (vitesse) speed; (: à pied) pace; (démarche) walk; (aspect, air) look; **avoir de l'~** to have style; **à toute ~** at full speed

allusion [a(l)lyzjɔ̃] nf allusion; (sous-entendu) hint; **faire ~ à** to allude ou refer to; to hint at

MOT-CLÉ

alors [alɔʀ] *adv* **1** (*à ce moment-là*) then, at that time; **il habitait alors à Paris** he lived in Paris at that time **2** (*par conséquent*) then; **tu as fini? alors je m'en vais** have you finished? I'm going then **3**: **et alors?** so (what)?
▸*conj*: **alors que** (*au moment où*) when, as; **il est arrivé alors que je partais** he arrived as I was leaving; (*tandis que*) whereas, while; **alors que son frère travaillait dur, lui se reposait** while his brother was working hard, HE would rest; (*bien que*) even though; **il a été puni alors qu'il n'a rien fait** he was punished, even though he had done nothing

alourdir [aluʀdiʀ] /2/ *vt* to weigh down, make heavy
Alpes [alp] *nfpl*: **les ~** the Alps
alphabet [alfabɛ] *nm* alphabet; (*livre*) ABC (book)
alpinisme [alpinism] *nm* mountaineering, climbing
Alsace [alzas] *nf* Alsace; **alsacien, ne** *adj* Alsatian ▷ *nm/f*: **Alsacien, ne** Alsatian
altermondialisme [altɛʀmɔ̃djalism] *nm* anti-globalism; **altermondialiste** *adj*, *nm/f* anti-globalist
alternatif, -ive [altɛʀnatif, -iv] *adj* alternating ▷ *nf* alternative; **alternative** *nf* (*choix*) alternative; **alterner** /1/ *vt* to alternate
altitude [altityd] *nf* altitude, height
alto [alto] *nm* (*instrument*) viola
aluminium [alyminjɔm] *nm* aluminium (BRIT), aluminum (US)
amabilité [amabilite] *nf* kindness
amaigrissant, e [amegʀisɑ̃, -ɑ̃t] *adj*: **régime ~** slimming (BRIT) *ou* weight-reduction (US) diet
amande [amɑ̃d] *nf* (*de l'amandier*) almond; **amandier** *nm* almond (tree)

amant [amɑ̃] *nm* lover
amas [amɑ] *nm* heap, pile; **amasser** /1/ *vt* to amass
amateur [amatœʀ] *nm* amateur; **en ~** (*péj*) amateurishly; **~ de musique/ sport** *etc* music/sport *etc* lover
ambassade [ɑ̃basad] *nf* embassy; **l'~ de France** the French Embassy; **ambassadeur, -drice** *nm/f* ambassador/ambassadress
ambiance [ɑ̃bjɑ̃s] *nf* atmosphere; **il y a de l'~** everyone's having a good time
ambigu, ë [ɑ̃bigy] *adj* ambiguous
ambitieux, -euse [ɑ̃bisjø, -jøz] *adj* ambitious
ambition [ɑ̃bisjɔ̃] *nf* ambition
ambulance [ɑ̃bylɑ̃s] *nf* ambulance; **ambulancier, -ière** *nm/f* ambulanceman/woman (BRIT), paramedic (US)
âme [ɑm] *nf* soul; **~ sœur** kindred spirit
amélioration [ameljɔʀasjɔ̃] *nf* improvement
améliorer [ameljɔʀe] /1/ *vt* to improve; **s'améliorer** *vi* to improve, get better
aménager [amenaʒe] /3/ *vt* (*agencer*) to fit out; (: *terrain*) to lay out; (: *quartier, territoire*) to develop; (*installer*) to fix up, put in; **ferme aménagée** converted farmhouse
amende [amɑ̃d] *nf* fine; **faire ~ honorable** to make amends
amener [am(ə)ne] /5/ *vt* to bring; (*causer*) to bring about; **s'amener** *vi* (*fam*) to show up, turn up; **~ qn à qch/à faire** to lead sb to sth/to do
amer, amère [amɛʀ] *adj* bitter
américain, e [ameʀikɛ̃, -ɛn] *adj* American ▷ *nm/f*: **A~, e** American
Amérique [ameʀik] *nf* America; **l'~ centrale** Central America; **l'~ latine** Latin America; **l'~ du Nord** North America; **l'~ du Sud** South America
amertume [amɛʀtym] *nf* bitterness

ameublement [amœbləmɑ̃] *nm*
furnishing; (*meubles*) furniture
ami, e [ami] *nm/f* friend; (*amant/
maîtresse*) boyfriend/girlfriend ▷ *adj*:
pays/groupe ~ friendly country/
group; **petit ~/petite ~e** boyfriend/
girlfriend
amiable [amjabl] **à l'~** *adv* (*Jur*) out
of court; (*gén*) amicably
amiante [amjɑ̃t] *nm* asbestos
amical, e, -aux [amikal, -o] *adj*
friendly; **amicalement** *adv* in a
friendly way; (*formule épistolaire*)
regards
amincir [amɛ̃siʀ] /2/ *vt*: **~ qn**
to make sb thinner *ou* slimmer;
(*vêtement*) to make sb look slimmer
amincissant, e [amɛ̃sisɑ̃, -ɑ̃t] *adj*
slimming; **régime ~** diet; **crème ~e**
slimming cream
amiral, -aux [amiʀal, -o] *nm*
admiral
amitié [amitje] *nf* friendship;
prendre en ~ to take a liking to;
faire *ou* **présenter ses ~s à qn** to
send sb one's best wishes; **~s** (*formule
épistolaire*) (with) best wishes
amonceler [amɔ̃s(ə)le] /4/ *vt* to pile
ou heap up; **s'amonceler** to pile *ou*
heap up; (*fig*) to accumulate
amont [amɔ̃] **en ~** *adv* upstream
amorce [amɔʀs] *nf* (*sur un hameçon*)
bait; (*explosif*) cap; (*tube*) primer;
(: *contenu*) priming; (*fig: début*)
beginning(s), start
amortir [amɔʀtiʀ] /2/ *vt* (*atténuer:
choc*) to absorb, cushion; (: *bruit,
douleur*) to deaden; (*Comm: dette*)
to pay off; **~ un abonnement** to
make a season ticket pay (for itself);
amortisseur *nm* shock absorber
amour [amuʀ] *nm* love; **faire l'~** to
make love; **amoureux, -euse** *adj*
(*regard, tempérament*) amorous; (*vie,
problèmes*) love *cpd*; (*personne*): **être
amoureux (de qn)** to be in love
(with sb) ▷ *nmpl* courting couple(s);
amour-propre *nm* self-esteem, pride

ampère [ɑ̃pɛʀ] *nm* amp(ere)
amphithéâtre [ɑ̃fiteatʀ] *nm*
amphitheatre; (*d'université*) lecture
hall *ou* theatre
ample [ɑ̃pl] *adj* (*vêtement*) roomy,
ample; (*gestes, mouvement*) broad;
(*ressources*) ample; **amplement**
adv: **amplement suffisant** more
than enough; **ampleur** *nf* (*de dégâts,
problème*) extent
amplificateur [ɑ̃plifikatœʀ] *nm*
amplifier
amplifier [ɑ̃plifje] /7/ *vt* (*fig*) to
expand, increase
ampoule [ɑ̃pul] *nf* (*électrique*) bulb;
(*de médicament*) phial; (*aux mains,
pieds*) blister
amusant, e [amyzɑ̃, -ɑ̃t] *adj*
(*divertissant, spirituel*) entertaining,
amusing; (*comique*) funny, amusing
amuse-gueule [amyzgœl] *nm inv*
appetizer, snack
amusement [amyzmɑ̃] *nm* (*voir
amusé*) amusement; (*jeu etc*) pastime,
diversion
amuser [amyze] /1/ *vt* (*divertir*) to
entertain, amuse; (*égayer, faire rire*) to
amuse; **s'amuser** *vi* (*jouer*) to amuse
o.s.; (*se divertir*) to enjoy o.s., have
fun; (*fig*) to mess around
amygdale [amidal] *nf* tonsil
an [ɑ̃] *nm* year; **être âgé de** *ou* **avoir
3 ans** to be 3 (years old); **le jour de
l'an, le premier de l'an, le nouvel
an** New Year's Day
analphabète [analfabɛt] *nm/f*
illiterate
analyse [analiz] *nf* analysis; (*Méd*)
test; **analyser** /1/ *vt* to analyse;
(*Méd*) to test
ananas [anana(s)] *nm* pineapple
anatomie [anatɔmi] *nf* anatomy
ancêtre [ɑ̃sɛtʀ] *nm/f* ancestor
anchois [ɑ̃ʃwa] *nm* anchovy
ancien, ne [ɑ̃sjɛ̃, -jɛn] *adj* old; (*de
jadis, de l'antiquité*) ancient; (*précédent,
ex-*) former, old; (*par l'expérience*)
senior ▷ *nm/f* (*dans une tribu etc*) elder;

ancienneté *nf* (*Admin*) (length of) service; (*privilèges obtenus*) seniority

ancre [ɑ̃kʀ] *nf* anchor; **jeter/lever l'~** to cast/weigh anchor; **ancrer** /1/ *vt* (*Constr*: *câble etc*) to anchor; (*fig*) to fix firmly

Andorre [ɑ̃dɔʀ] *nf* Andorra

andouille [ɑ̃duj] *nf* (*Culin*) sausage *made of chitterlings*; (*fam*) clot, nit

âne [ɑn] *nm* donkey, ass; (*péj*) dunce

anéantir [aneɑ̃tiʀ] /2/ *vt* to annihilate, wipe out; (*fig*) to obliterate, destroy

anémie [anemi] *nf* anaemia; **anémique** *adj* anaemic

anesthésie [anɛstezi] *nf* anaesthesia; **~ générale/locale** general/local anaesthetic; **faire une ~ locale à qn** to give sb a local anaesthetic

ange [ɑ̃ʒ] *nm* angel; **être aux ~s** to be over the moon

angine [ɑ̃ʒin] *nf* throat infection; **~ de poitrine** angina (pectoris)

anglais, e [ɑ̃glɛ, -ɛz] *adj* English ▷ *nm* (*Ling*) English ▷ *nm/f*: **A~, e** Englishman/woman; **les A~** the English; **filer à l'~e** to take French leave

angle [ɑ̃gl] *nm* angle; (*coin*) corner

Angleterre [ɑ̃glətɛʀ] *nf*: **l'~** England

anglo... [ɑ̃glɔ] *préfixe* Anglo-, anglo(-); **anglophone** *adj* English-speaking

angoisse [ɑ̃gwas] *nf*: **l'~** anguish *no pl*; **angoissé, e** *adj* (*personne*) distressed

anguille [ɑ̃gij] *nf* eel

animal, e, -aux [animal, -o] *adj*, *nm* animal

animateur, -trice [animatœʀ, -tʀis] *nm/f* (*de télévision*) host; (*de groupe*) leader, organizer

animation [animasjɔ̃] *nf* (*voir animé*) busyness; liveliness; (*Ciné*: *technique*) animation

animé, e [anime] *adj* (*rue, lieu*) busy, lively; (*conversation, réunion*) lively, animated

animer [anime] /1/ *vt* (*ville, soirée*) to liven up; (*mettre en mouvement*) to drive

anis [ani(s)] *nm* (*Culin*) aniseed; (*Bot*) anise

ankyloser [ɑ̃kiloze] /1/: **s'ankyloser** *vi* to get stiff

anneau, x [ano] *nm* (*de rideau, bague*) ring; (*de chaîne*) link

année [ane] *nf* year

annexe [anɛks] *adj* (*problème*) related; (*document*) appended; (*salle*) adjoining ▷ *nf* (*bâtiment*) annex(e); (*jointe à une lettre, un dossier*) enclosure

anniversaire [anivɛʀsɛʀ] *nm* birthday; (*d'un événement, bâtiment*) anniversary

annonce [anɔ̃s] *nf* announcement; (*signe, indice*) sign; (*aussi*: **~ publicitaire**) advertisement; **les petites ~s** the small *ou* classified ads

annoncer [anɔ̃se] /3/ *vt* to announce; (*être le signe de*) to herald; **s'annoncer bien/difficile** to look promising/difficult

annuaire [anɥɛʀ] *nm* yearbook, annual; **~ téléphonique** (telephone) directory, phone book

annuel, le [anɥɛl] *adj* annual, yearly

annulation [anylasjɔ̃] *nf* cancellation

annuler [anyle] /1/ *vt* (*rendez-vous, voyage*) to cancel, call off; (*jugement*) to quash (BRIT), repeal (US); (*Math, Physique*) to cancel out

anonymat [anɔnima] *nm* anonymity; **garder l'~** to remain anonymous

anonyme [anɔnim] *adj* anonymous; (*fig*) impersonal

anorak [anɔʀak] *nm* anorak

anorexie [anɔʀɛksi] *nf* anorexia

anormal, e, -aux [anɔʀmal, -o] *adj* abnormal

ANPE *sigle f* (= *Agence nationale pour l'emploi*) national employment agency (*functions include job creation*)

antarctique [ɑ̃taʀktik] *adj* Antarctic
▷ *nm*: **l'A~** the Antarctic

antenne [ɑ̃tɛn] *nf* (*de radio, télévision*)
aerial; (*d'insecte*) antenna, feeler;
(*poste avancé*) outpost; (*petite
succursale*) sub-branch; **passer
à/avoir l'~** to go/be on the air;
~ parabolique satellite dish

antérieur, e [ɑ̃teʀjœʀ] *adj* (*d'avant*)
previous, earlier; (*de devant*) front

anti... [ɑ̃ti] *préfixe* anti...;
antialcoolique *adj* anti-alcohol;
antibiotique *nm* antibiotic;
antibrouillard *adj*: **phare
antibrouillard** fog lamp

anticipation [ɑ̃tisipasjɔ̃] *nf*: **livre/
film d'~** science fiction book/film

anticipé, e [ɑ̃tisipe] *adj*: **avec mes
remerciements ~s** thanking you in
advance *ou* anticipation

anticiper [ɑ̃tisipe] /1/ *vt* (*événement,
coup*) to anticipate, foresee

anti: anticorps *nm* antibody;
antidote *nm* antidote; **antigel** *nm*
antifreeze; **antihistaminique** *nm*
antihistamine

antillais, e [ɑ̃tijɛ, -ɛz] *adj* West
Indian, Caribbean ▷ *nm/f*: **A~, e** West
Indian, Caribbean

Antilles [ɑ̃tij] *nfpl*: **les ~** the West
Indies; **les Grandes/Petites ~** the
Greater/Lesser Antilles

antilope [ɑ̃tilɔp] *nf* antelope

anti: antimite(s) *adj, nm*: **(produit)
antimite(s)** mothproofer, moth
repellent; **antimondialisation** *nf*
anti-globalization; **antipathique**
adj unpleasant, disagreeable;
antipelliculaire *adj* anti-dandruff

antiquaire [ɑ̃tikɛʀ] *nm/f* antique
dealer

antique [ɑ̃tik] *adj* antique; (*très
vieux*) ancient, antiquated; **antiquité**
nf (*objet*) antique; **l'Antiquité**
Antiquity; **magasin/marchand
d'antiquités** antique shop/dealer

anti: antirabique *adj* rabies *cpd*;
antirouille *adj inv* anti-rust *cpd*;

antisémite *adj* anti-Semitic;
antiseptique *adj, nm* antiseptic;
antivirus *nm* (*Inform*) antivirus
(program); **antivol** *adj, nm*:
(dispositif) antivol antitheft device

anxieux, -euse [ɑ̃ksjø, -jøz] *adj*
anxious, worried

AOC *sigle f* (= *Appellation d'origine
contrôlée*) *guarantee of quality of wine*

août [u(t)] *nm* August

apaiser [apeze] /1/ *vt* (*colère*) to calm;
(*douleur*) to soothe; (*personne*) to calm
(down), pacify; **s'apaiser** *vi* (*tempête,
bruit*) to die down, subside; (*personne*)
to calm down

apercevoir [apɛʀsəvwaʀ] /28/ *vt* to
see; **s'apercevoir de** *vt* to notice; **s'~
que** to notice that

aperçu [apɛʀsy] *nm* (*vue d'ensemble*)
general survey

apéritif, -ive [apeʀitif, -iv] *adj*
which stimulates the appetite ▷ *nm*
(*boisson*) aperitif; (*réunion*) (pre-lunch
ou -dinner) drinks *pl*

à-peu-près [apøpʀɛ] *nm inv* (*péj*)
vague approximation

apeuré, e [apœʀe] *adj* frightened,
scared

aphte [aft] *nm* mouth ulcer

apitoyer [apitwaje] /8/ *vt* to move
to pity; **s'~ (sur qn/qch)** to feel pity
ou compassion (for sb/over sth)

aplatir [aplatiʀ] /2/ *vt* to flatten;
s'aplatir *vi* to become flatter; (*écrasé*)
to be flattened

aplomb [aplɔ̃] *nm* (*équilibre*) balance,
equilibrium; (*fig*) self-assurance
nerve; **d'~** steady

apostrophe [apɔstʀɔf] *nf* (*signe*)
apostrophe

apparaître [apaʀɛtʀ] /57/ *vi* to
appear

appareil [apaʀɛj] *nm* (*outil, machine*)
piece of apparatus, device; (*électrique
etc*) appliance; (*avion*) (aero)plane,
aircraft *inv*; (*téléphonique*) telephone;
(*dentier*) brace (BRIT), braces (US); **qui
est à l'~?** who's speaking?; **dans le**

plus simple ~ in one's birthday suit; **~ (photo)** camera; **~ numérique** digital camera; **appareiller** /1/ vi (*Navig*) to cast off, get under way ▷ vt (*assortir*) to match up

apparemment [aparamɑ̃] adv apparently

apparence [aparɑ̃s] nf appearance; **en ~** apparently

apparent, e [aparɑ̃, -ɑ̃t] adj visible; (*évident*) obvious; (*superficiel*) apparent

apparenté, e [aparɑ̃te] adj: **~ à** related to; (*fig*) similar to

apparition [aparisjɔ̃] nf appearance; (*surnaturelle*) apparition

appartement [apartəmɑ̃] nm flat (*BRIT*), apartment (*US*)

appartenir [apartənir] /22/: **~ à** vt to belong to; **il lui appartient de** it is up to him to

apparu, e [apary] pp de **apparaître**

appât [apɑ] nm (*Pêche*) bait; (*fig*) lure, bait

appel [apɛl] nm call; (*nominal*) roll call (: *Scol*) register; (*Mil: recrutement*) call-up; **faire ~ à** (*invoquer*) to appeal to; (*avoir recours à*) to call on; (*nécessiter*) to call for, require; **faire ou interjeter ~** (*Jur*) to appeal; **faire l'~** to call the roll; (*Scol*) to call the register; **~ (fig)** final, irrevocable; **~ d'offres** (*Comm*) invitation to tender; **faire un ~ de phares** to flash one's headlights; **~ (téléphonique)** (*tele*)phone call

appelé [ap(ə)le] nm (*Mil*) conscript

appeler [ap(ə)le] /4/ vt to call; (*faire venir: médecin etc*) to call, send for; **s'appeler** vi: **elle s'appelle Gabrielle** her name is Gabrielle, she's called Gabrielle; **comment vous appelez-vous?** what's your name?; **comment ça s'appelle?** what is it *ou* that called?

appendicite [apɑ̃disit] nf appendicitis

appesantir [apəzɑ̃tir] /2/: **s'appesantir** vi to grow heavier; **s'~ sur** (*fig*) to dwell at length on

appétissant, e [apetisɑ̃, -ɑ̃t] adj appetizing, mouth-watering

appétit [apeti] nm appetite; **bon ~!** enjoy your meal!

applaudir [aplodir] /2/ vt to applaud ▷ vi to applaud, clap; **applaudissements** nmpl applause sg, clapping sg

appli [apli] nf app

application [aplikasjɔ̃] nf application

appliquer [aplike] /1/ vt to apply; (*loi*) to enforce; **s'appliquer** vi (*élève etc*) to apply o.s.; **s'~ à** to apply to

appoint [apwɛ̃] nm (*extra*) contribution *ou* help; **avoir/faire l'~** to have/give the right change *ou* money; **chauffage d'~** extra heating

apporter [aporte] /1/ vt to bring

appréciable [apresjabl] adj appreciable

apprécier [apresje] /7/ vt to appreciate; (*évaluer*) to estimate, assess

appréhender [apreɑ̃de] /1/ vt (*craindre*) to dread; (*arrêter*) to apprehend

apprendre [aprɑ̃dr] /58/ vt to learn; (*événement, résultats*) to learn of, hear of; **~ qch à qn** (*informer*) to tell sb (of) sth; (*enseigner*) to teach sb sth; **~ à faire qch** to learn to do sth; **~ à qn à faire qch** to teach sb to do sth; **apprenti, e** nm/f apprentice; **apprentissage** nm learning; (*Comm, Scol: période*) apprenticeship

apprêter [aprete] /1/: **s'apprêter** vi: **s'~ à qch/à faire qch** to prepare for sth/for doing sth

appris, e [apri, -iz] pp de **apprendre**

apprivoiser [aprivwaze] /1/ vt to tame

approbation [aprobasjɔ̃] nf approval

approcher [aprɔʃe] /1/ vi to approach, come near ▷ vt to approach; (*rapprocher*): **~ qch (de qch)** to bring *ou* put *ou* move sth near (to sth); **s'approcher de** to approach, go *ou* come *ou* move near to; **~ de** (*lieu, but*) to draw near to; (*quantité, moment*) to approach

approfondir [apʀɔfɔ̃diʀ] /2/ *vt* to deepen; (*question*) to go further into

approprié, e [apʀɔpʀije] *adj*: **~ (à)** appropriate (to), suited (to)

approprier [apʀɔpʀije] /7/: **s'approprier** *vt* to appropriate, take over; **s'~ en** to stock up with

approuver [apʀuve] /1/ *vt* to agree with; (*trouver louable*) to approve of

approvisionner [apʀɔvizjɔne] /1/ *vt* to supply; (*compte bancaire*) to pay funds into; **s'~ en** to stock up with

approximatif, -ive [apʀɔksimatif, -iv] *adj* approximate, rough; (*imprécis*) vague

appt *abr* = **appartement**

appui [apɥi] *nm* support; **prendre ~ sur** to lean on; (*objet*) to rest on; **l'~ de la fenêtre** the windowsill, the window ledge

appuyer [apɥije] /8/ *vt* (*poser, soutenir: personne, demande*) to support, back (up) ▷ *vi*: **~ sur** (*bouton*) to press, push; (*mot, détail*) to stress, emphasize; **s'appuyer sur** *vt* to lean on; (*compter sur*) to rely on; **~ qch sur/contre/à** to lean *ou* rest sth on/ against/on; **~ sur le frein** to brake, to apply the brakes

après [apʀɛ] *prép* after ▷ *adv* afterwards; **deux heures ~** two hours later; **~ qu'il est parti/avoir fait** after he left/having done; **courir ~ qn** to run after sb; **crier ~ qn** to shout at sb; **être toujours ~ qn** (*critiquer etc*) to be always at sb; **~ quoi** after which; **d'~** (*selon*) according to; **~ coup** after the event, afterwards; **~ tout** (*au fond*) after all; **et (puis) ~?** so what?; **après-demain** *adv* the day after tomorrow; **après-midi** [apʀɛmidi] *nm ou f inv* afternoon; **après-rasage** *nm inv* after-shave; **après-shampooing**
nm inv conditioner; **après-ski** *nm inv* snow boot

après-soleil [apʀɛsɔlɛj] *adj inv* after-sun *cpd* ▷ *nm* after-sun cream *ou* lotion

apte [apt] *adj*: **~ à qch/faire qch** capable of sth/doing sth; **~ (au service)** (*Mil*) fit (for service)

aquarelle [akwaʀɛl] *nf* watercolour

aquarium [akwaʀjɔm] *nm* aquarium

arabe [aʀab] *adj* Arabic; (*désert, cheval*) Arabian; (*nation, peuple*) Arab ▷ *nm* (*Ling*) Arabic ▷ *nm/f*: **A~** Arab

Arabie [aʀabi] *nf*: **l'~ Saoudite** *ou* **Séoudite** Saudi Arabia

arachide [aʀaʃid] *nf* groundnut (plant); (*graine*) peanut, groundnut

araignée [aʀeɲe] *nf* spider

arbitraire [aʀbitʀɛʀ] *adj* arbitrary

arbitre [aʀbitʀ] *nm* (*Sport*) referee (: *Tennis, Cricket*) umpire; (*fig*) arbiter, judge; (*Jur*) arbitrator; **arbitrer** /1/ *vt* to referee; to umpire; to arbitrate

arbre [aʀbʀ] *nm* tree; (*Tech*) shaft

arbuste [aʀbyst] *nm* small shrub

arc [aʀk] *nm* (*arme*) bow; (*Géom*) arc; (*Archit*) arch; **en ~ de cercle** semi-circular

arcade [aʀkad] *nf* arch(way); **~s** arcade *sg*, arches

arc-en-ciel [aʀkɑ̃sjɛl] *nm* rainbow

arche [aʀʃ] *nf* arch; **~ de Noé** Noah's Ark

archéologie [aʀkeɔlɔʒi] *nf* arch(a)eology; **archéologue** *nm/f* arch(a)eologist

archet [aʀʃɛ] *nm* bow

archipel [aʀʃipɛl] *nm* archipelago

architecte [aʀʃitɛkt] *nm* architect

architecture [aʀʃitɛktyʀ] *nf* architecture

archives [aʀʃiv] *nfpl* (*collection*) archives

arctique [aʀktik] *adj* Arctic ▷ *nm*: **l'A~** the Arctic

ardent, e [aʀdɑ̃, -ɑ̃t] *adj* (*soleil*) blazing; (*amour*) ardent, passionate; (*prière*) fervent

ardoise [aʀdwaz] nf slate

ardu, e [aʀdy] adj (travail) arduous; (problème) difficult

arène [aʀɛn] nf arena; **arènes** nfpl bull-ring sg

arête [aʀɛt] nf (de poisson) bone; (d'une montagne) ridge

argent [aʀʒɑ̃] nm (métal) silver; (monnaie) money; **~ de poche** pocket money; **~ liquide** ready money, (ready) cash; **argenterie** nf silverware

argentin, e [aʀʒɑ̃tɛ̃, -in] adj Argentinian ▷ nm/f: **A~, e** Argentinian

Argentine [aʀʒɑ̃tin] nf: **l'~** Argentina

argentique [aʀʒɑ̃tik] adj (appareil photo) film cpd

argile [aʀʒil] nf clay

argot [aʀɡo] nm slang; **argotique** adj slang cpd; (très familier) slangy

argument [aʀɡymɑ̃] nm argument

argumenter [aʀɡymɑ̃te] /1/ vi to argue

aride [aʀid] adj arid

aristocratie [aʀistɔkʀasi] nf aristocracy; **aristocratique** adj aristocratic

arithmétique [aʀitmetik] adj arithmetic(al) ▷ nf arithmetic

arme [aʀm] nf weapon; **armes** nfpl weapons, arms; (blason) (coat of) arms; **~ à feu** firearm; **~s de destruction massive** weapons of mass destruction

armée [aʀme] nf army; **~ de l'air** Air Force; **~ de terre** Army

armer [aʀme] /1/ vt to arm; (arme à feu) to cock; (appareil photo) to wind on; **s'armer** vi: **s'~ de** to arm o.s. with; **~ qch de** to reinforce sth with

armistice [aʀmistis] nm armistice; **l'A~** ≈ Remembrance (BRIT) ou Veterans (US) Day

armoire [aʀmwaʀ] nf (tall) cupboard; (penderie) wardrobe (BRIT), closet (US)

armure [aʀmyʀ] nf armour no pl, suit of armour; **armurier** nm gunsmith

arnaque [aʀnak] (fam) nf swindling; **c'est de l'~** it's daylight robbery; **arnaquer** /1/ (fam) vt to do (fam)

arobase [aʀɔbaz] nf (Inform) 'at' symbol; **"paul ~ société point fr"** "paul at société dot fr"

aromates [aʀɔmat] nmpl seasoning sg, herbs (and spices)

aromathérapie [aʀɔmateʀapi] nf aromatherapy

aromatisé, e [aʀɔmatize] adj flavoured

arôme [aʀom] nm aroma

arracher [aʀaʃe] /1/ vt to pull out; (page etc) to tear off, tear out; (légume, herbe, souche) to pull up; (bras etc) to tear off; **s'arracher** vt (article très recherché) to fight over; **~ qch à qn** to snatch sth from sb; (fig) to wring sth out of sb

arrangement [aʀɑ̃ʒmɑ̃] nm arrangement

arranger [aʀɑ̃ʒe] /3/ vt to arrange; (réparer) to fix, put right; (régler) to settle, sort out; (convenir à) to suit, be convenient for; **cela m'arrange** that suits me (fine); **s'arranger** vi (se mettre d'accord) to come to an agreement ou arrangement; **je vais m'~** I'll manage; **ça va s'~** it'll sort itself out

arrestation [aʀɛstasjɔ̃] nf arrest

arrêt [aʀɛ] nm stopping; (de bus etc) stop; (Jur) judgment, decision; **être à l'~** to be stopped; **rester** ou **tomber en ~ devant** to stop short in front of; **sans ~** non-stop; (fréquemment) continually; **~ de travail** stoppage (of work)

arrêter [aʀete] /1/ vt to stop; (chauffage etc) to turn off, switch off; (fixer: date etc) to appoint, decide on; (criminel, suspect) to arrest; **s'arrêter** vi to stop; **~ de faire** to stop doing

arrhes [aʀ] nfpl deposit sg

arrière [aʀjeʀ] nm back; (Sport) fullback ▷ adj inv: **siège/roue**

~ back *ou* rear seat/wheel; **à l'~** behind, at the back; **en ~** behind; (*regarder*) back, behind; (*tomber, aller*) backwards; **arrière-goût** *nm* aftertaste; **arrière-grand-mère** *nf* great-grandmother; **arrière-grand-père** *nm* great-grandfather; **arrière-pays** *nm inv* hinterland; **arrière-pensée** *nf* ulterior motive; (*doute*) mental reservation; **arrière-plan** *nm* background; **à l'arrière-plan** in the background; **arrière-saison** *nf* late autumn

arrimer [aʀime] /1/ *vt* (*cargaison*) to stow; (*fixer*) to secure

arrivage [aʀivaʒ] *nm* consignment

arrivée [aʀive] *nf* arrival; (*ligne d'arrivée*) finish

arriver [aʀive] /1/ *vi* to arrive; (*survenir*) to happen, occur; **il arrive à Paris à 8 h** he gets to *ou* arrives in Paris at 8; **~ à** (*atteindre*) to reach; **~ à (faire) qch** to manage (to do) sth; **en ~ à faire ...** to end up doing ...; **il arrive que ...** it happens that ...; **il lui arrive de faire ...** he sometimes does ...

arrobase [aʀɔbaz] *nf* (*Inform*) 'at' symbol

arrogance [aʀɔgɑ̃s] *nf* arrogance

arrogant, e [aʀɔgɑ̃, -ɑ̃t] *adj* arrogant

arrondissement [aʀɔ̃dismɑ̃] *nm* (*Admin*) ≈ district

arroser [aʀoze] /1/ *vt* to water; (*victoire etc*) to celebrate (over a drink); (*Culin*) to baste; **arrosoir** *nm* watering can

arsenal, -aux [aʀsənal, -o] *nm* (*Navig*) naval dockyard; (*Mil*) arsenal; (*fig*) gear, paraphernalia

art [aʀ] *nm* art

artère [aʀtɛʀ] *nf* (*Anat*) artery; (*rue*) main road

arthrite [aʀtʀit] *nf* arthritis

artichaut [aʀtiʃo] *nm* artichoke

article [aʀtikl] *nm* article; (*Comm*) item, article; **à l'~ de la mort** at the point of death

articulation [aʀtikylasjɔ̃] *nf* articulation; (*Anat*) joint

articuler [aʀtikyle] /1/ *vt* to articulate

artificiel, le [aʀtifisjɛl] *adj* artificial

artisan [aʀtizɑ̃] *nm* artisan, (self-employed) craftsman; **artisanal, e, -aux** [aʀtizanal, -o] *adj* of *ou* made by craftsmen; (*péj*) cottage industry *cpd*; **de fabrication artisanale** home-made; **artisanat** [aʀtizana] *nm* arts and crafts *pl*

artiste [aʀtist] *nm/f* artist; (*Théât, Mus*) performer; (*de variétés*) entertainer; **artistique** *adj* artistic

as *vb* [a]; *voir* **avoir** ▷ *nm* [ɑs] ace

ascenseur [asɑ̃sœʀ] *nm* lift (*BRIT*), elevator (*US*)

ascension [asɑ̃sjɔ̃] *nf* ascent; (*de montagne*) climb; **l'A~** (*Rel*) the Ascension

⊕ **L'ASCENSION**

⊕ The *fête de l'Ascension* is a public
⊕ holiday in France. It always falls on
⊕ a Thursday, usually in May. Many
⊕ French people take the following
⊕ Friday off work too and enjoy a long
⊕ weekend.

asiatique [azjatik] *adj* Asian, Asiatic ▷ *nm/f*: **A~** Asian

Asie [azi] *nf*: **l'~** Asia

asile [azil] *nm* (*refuge*) refuge, sanctuary; **droit d'~** (*Pol*) (political) asylum

aspect [aspɛ] *nm* appearance, look; (*fig*) aspect, side; **à l'~ de** at the sight of

asperge [aspɛʀʒ] *nf* asparagus *no pl*

asperger [aspɛʀʒe] /3/ *vt* to spray, sprinkle

asphalte [asfalt] *nm* asphalt

asphyxier [asfiksje] /7/ *vt* to suffocate, asphyxiate; (*fig*) to stifle

aspirateur [aspiʀatœʀ] *nm* vacuum cleaner; **passer l'~** to vacuum

aspirer [aspiʀe] /1/ vt (air) to inhale; (liquide) to suck (up); (appareil) to suck ou draw up; **~ à** to aspire to

aspirine [aspiʀin] nf aspirin

assagir [asaʒiʀ] /2/ vt, **s'assagir** vi to quieten down, settle down

assaillir [asajiʀ] /13/ vt to assail, attack

assaisonnement [asɛzɔnmɑ̃] nm seasoning

assaisonner [asɛzɔne] /1/ vt to season

assassin [asasɛ̃] nm murderer; assassin; **assassiner** /1/ vt to murder; (Pol) to assassinate

assaut [aso] nm assault, attack; **prendre d'~** to (take by) storm, assault; **donner l'~ (à)** to attack

assécher [aseʃe] /6/ vt to drain

assemblage [asɑ̃blaʒ] nm (action) assembling; **un ~ de** (fig) a collection of

assemblée [asɑ̃ble] nf (réunion) meeting; (public, assistance) gathering; (Pol) assembly; **l'A~ nationale (AN)** the (French) National Assembly

assembler [asɑ̃ble] /1/ vt (joindre, monter) to assemble, put together; (amasser) to gather (together), collect (together); **s'assembler** vi to gather

asseoir [aswaʀ] /26/ vt (malade, bébé) to sit up; (personne debout) to sit down; (autorité, réputation) to establish; **s'asseoir** vi to sit (o.s.) down

assez [ase] adv (suffisamment) enough, sufficiently; (passablement) rather, quite, fairly; **~ de pain/ livres** enough ou sufficient bread/ books; **vous en avez ~?** have you got enough?; **j'en ai ~!** I've had enough!

assidu, e [asidy] adj assiduous, painstaking; (régulier) regular

assied etc [asje] vb voir **asseoir**

assiérai etc [asjeʀe] vb voir **asseoir**

assiette [asjɛt] nf plate; (contenu) plate(ful); **il n'est pas dans son ~** he's not feeling quite himself; **~ à dessert** dessert ou side plate; **~ anglaise** assorted cold meats; **~ creuse** (soup) dish, soup plate; **~ plate** (dinner) plate

assimiler [asimile] /1/ vt to assimilate, absorb; (comparer): **~ qch/qn à** to liken ou compare sth/ sb to; **s'assimiler** vi (s'intégrer) to be assimilated ou absorbed

assis, e [asi, -iz] pp de **asseoir** ▷ adj sitting (down), seated

assistance [asistɑ̃s] nf (public) audience; (aide) assistance; **enfant de l'A~ (publique)** child in care

assistant, e [asistɑ̃, -ɑ̃t] nm/f assistant; (d'université) probationary lecturer; **~e sociale** social worker

assisté, e [asiste] adj (Auto) power-assisted; **~ par ordinateur** computer-assisted; **direction ~e** power steering

assister [asiste] /1/ vt to assist; **~ à** (scène, événement) to witness; (conférence) to attend, be (present) at; (spectacle, match) to be at, see

association [asɔsjasjɔ̃] nf association

associé, e [asɔsje] nm/f associate; (Comm) partner

associer [asɔsje] /7/ vt to associate; **~ qn à** (profits) to give sb a share of; (affaire) to make sb a partner in; (joie, triomphe) to include sb in; **~ qch à** (joindre, allier) to combine sth with; **s'associer** vi to join together; **s'~ à** (couleurs, qualités) to be combined with; (opinions, joie de qn) to share in; **s'~ à** ou **avec qn pour faire** to join (forces) ou join together with sb to do

assoiffé, e [aswafe] adj thirsty

assommer [asɔme] /1/ vt (étourdir, abrutir) to knock out, stun

Assomption [asɔ̃psjɔ̃] nf: **l'~** the Assumption

● **L'ASSOMPTION**
●
● The *fête de l'Assomption*, more
● commonly known as "le 15 août"
● is a national holiday in France.
● Traditionally, large numbers of
● holidaymakers leave home on
● 15 August, frequently causing
● chaos on the roads.

assorti, e [asɔʀti] *adj* matched,
matching; **fromages/légumes**
~s assorted cheeses/vegetables;
~ à matching; **assortiment** *nm*
assortment, selection

assortir [asɔʀtiʀ] /2/ *vt* to match;
~ qch à to match sth with; **~ qch de**
to accompany sth with

assouplir [asupliʀ] /2/ *vt* to make
supple; (*fig*) to relax; **assouplissant**
nm (fabric) softener

assumer [asyme] /1/ *vt* (*fonction,*
emploi) to assume, take on

assurance [asyʀɑ̃s] *nf* (*certitude*)
assurance; (*confiance en soi*) (self-)
confidence; (*contrat*) insurance
(policy); (*secteur commercial*) insurance;
~ au tiers third party insurance;
~ maladie (AM) health insurance;
~ tous risques (*Auto*) comprehensive
insurance; **~s sociales (AS)** ≈
National Insurance (BRIT), ≈ Social
Security (US); **assurance-vie** *nf* life
assurance *ou* insurance

assuré, e [asyʀe] *adj* (*réussite, échec,*
victoire etc) certain, sure; (*démarche,*
voix) assured; (*pas*) steady ▷ *nm/f*
insured (person); **assurément** *adv*
assuredly, most certainly

assurer [asyʀe] /1/ *vt* (*Comm*)
to insure; (*victoire etc*) to ensure;
(*frontières, pouvoir*) to make secure;
(*service, garde*) to provide, operate;
s'assurer (contre) (*Comm*) to insure
o.s. (against); **~ à qn que** to assure sb
that; **~ qn de** to assure sb of; **s'~ de/**
que (*vérifier*) to make sure of/that;
s'~ (de) (*aide de qn*) to secure

asthmatique [asmatik] *adj, nm/f*
asthmatic

asthme [asm] *nm* asthma

asticot [astiko] *nm* maggot

astre [astʀ] *nm* star

astrologie [astʀɔlɔʒi] *nf* astrology

astronaute [astʀonot] *nm/f*
astronaut

astronomie [astʀɔnɔmi] *nf*
astronomy

astuce [astys] *nf* shrewdness,
astuteness; (*truc*) trick, clever way;
astucieux, -euse *adj* clever

atelier [atəlje] *nm* workshop; (*de*
peintre) studio

athée [ate] *adj* atheistic ▷ *nm/f*
atheist

Athènes [atɛn] *n* Athens

athlète [atlɛt] *nm/f* (*Sport*) athlete;
athlétisme *nm* athletics *sg*

atlantique [atlɑ̃tik] *adj* Atlantic
▷ *nm*: **l'(océan) A~** the Atlantic
(Ocean)

atlas [atlɑs] *nm* atlas

atmosphère [atmɔsfɛʀ] *nf*
atmosphere

atome [atom] *nm* atom; **atomique**
adj atomic; nuclear

atomiseur [atɔmizœʀ] *nm* atomizer

atout [atu] *nm* trump; (*fig*) asset

atroce [atʀɔs] *adj* atrocious

attachant, e [ataʃɑ̃, -ɑ̃t] *adj*
engaging, likeable

attache [ataʃ] *nf* clip, fastener; (*fig*) tie

attacher [ataʃe] /1/ *vt* to tie up;
(*étiquette*) to attach, tie on; (*ceinture*)
to fasten; (*souliers*) to do up ▷ *vi* (*poêle,*
riz) to stick; **s'~ à** (*par affection*) to
become attached to; **~ qch à** to tie *ou*
fasten *ou* attach sth to

attaque [atak] *nf* attack; (*cérébrale*)
stroke; (*d'épilepsie*) fit

attaquer [atake] /1/ *vt* to attack;
(*en justice*) to sue ▷ *vi* to attack;
s'attaquer à *vt* (*personne*) to attack;
(*épidémie, misère*) to tackle

attarder [ataʀde] /1/: **s'attarder**
vi to linger

atteindre [atɛ̃dʀ] /49/ vt to reach; (blesser) to hit; (émouvoir) to affect; **atteint, e** adj (Méd): **être atteint de** to be suffering from ▷ nf attack; **hors d'atteinte** out of reach; **porter atteinte à** to strike a blow at

attendant [atɑ̃dɑ̃]: **en ~** adv meanwhile, in the meantime

attendre [atɑ̃dʀ] /41/ vt to wait for; (être destiné ou réservé à) to await, be in store for ▷ vi to wait; **s'~ à (ce que)** to expect (that); **attendez-moi, s'il vous plaît** wait for me, please; **~ un enfant** to be expecting a baby; **~ de faire/d'être** to wait until one does/is; **attendez qu'il vienne** wait until he comes; **~ qch de** to expect sth of;

▌ Attention à ne pas traduire attendre par to attend.

attendrir [atɑ̃dʀiʀ] /2/ vt to move (to pity); (viande) to tenderize

attendu, e [atɑ̃dy] adj (événement) long-awaited; (prévu) expected; **~ que** considering that, since

attentat [atɑ̃ta] nm assassination attempt; **~ à la pudeur** indecent assault no pl; **~ suicide** suicide bombing

attente [atɑ̃t] nf wait; (espérance) expectation

attenter [atɑ̃te] /1/: **~ à** vt (liberté) to violate; **~ à la vie de qn** to make an attempt on sb's life

attentif, -ive [atɑ̃tif, -iv] adj (auditeur) attentive; (travail) careful; **~ à** paying attention to

attention [atɑ̃sjɔ̃] nf attention; (prévenance) attention, thoughtfulness no pl; **à l'~ de** for the attention of; **faire ~ (à)** to be careful (of); **faire ~ (à ce) que** to be ou make sure that; **~!** careful!, watch out!; **~ à la voiture!** watch out for that car!; **attentionné, e** [atɑ̃sjɔne] adj thoughtful, considerate

atténuer [atenɥe] /1/ vt (douleur) to alleviate, ease; (couleurs) to soften;

s'atténuer vi to ease; (violence etc) to abate

atterrir [ateʀiʀ] /2/ vi to land; **atterrissage** nm landing

attestation nf certificate

attirant, e [atiʀɑ̃, -ɑ̃t] adj attractive, appealing

attirer [atiʀe] /1/ vt to attract; (appâter) to lure, entice; **~ qn dans un coin/vers soi** to draw sb into a corner/towards one; **~ l'attention de qn** to attract sb's attention; **~ l'attention de qn sur qch** to draw sb's attention to sth; **s'~ des ennuis** to bring trouble upon o.s., get into trouble

attitude [atityd] nf attitude; (position du corps) bearing

attraction [atʀaksjɔ̃] nf attraction; (de cabaret, cirque) number

attrait [atʀɛ] nm appeal, attraction

attraper [atʀape] /1/ vt to catch; (habitude, amende) to get, pick up; (fam: duper) to con; **se faire ~** (fam) to be told off

attrayant, e [atʀɛjɑ̃, -ɑ̃t] adj attractive

attribuer [atʀibɥe] /1/ vt (prix) to award; (rôle, tâche) to allocate, assign; (imputer): **~ qch à** to attribute sth to; **s'attribuer** vt (s'approprier) to claim for o.s.

attrister [atʀiste] /1/ vt to sadden

attroupement [atʀupmɑ̃] nm crowd

attrouper [atʀupe] /1/: **s'attrouper** vi to gather

au [o] prép voir **à**

aubaine [obɛn] nf godsend

aube [ob] nf dawn, daybreak; **à l'~** at dawn ou daybreak

aubépine [obepin] nf hawthorn

auberge [obɛʀʒ] nf inn; **~ de jeunesse** youth hostel

aubergine [obɛʀʒin] nf aubergine

aucun, e [okœ̃, -yn] adj, pron no; (positif) any ▷ pron none; (positif) any(one); **sans ~ doute** without any doubt; **plus qu'~ autre** more than any other; **il le fera mieux qu'~ de nous** he'll do it better than any of us; **~ des deux** neither of the two; **~ d'entre eux** none of them

audace [odas] *nf* daring, boldness; (*péj*) audacity; **audacieux, -euse** *adj* daring, bold

au-delà [od(ə)la] *adv* beyond ▷ *nm*: **l'~** the hereafter; **~ de** beyond

au-dessous [odsu] *adv* underneath; below; **~ de** under(neath), below; (*limite, somme etc*) below, under; (*dignité, condition*) below

au-dessus [odsy] *adv* above; **~ de** above

au-devant [od(ə)vã]: **~ de** *prép*: **aller ~ de** (*personne, danger*) to go (out) and meet; (*souhaits de qn*) to anticipate

audience [odjãs] *nf* audience; (*Jur: séance*) hearing

audio-visuel, le [odjovizɥɛl] *adj* audio-visual

audition [odisjɔ̃] *nf* (*ouïe, écoute*) hearing; (*Jur: de témoins*) examination; (*Mus, Théât: épreuve*) audition

auditoire [oditwaʀ] *nm* audience

augmentation [ogmɑ̃tasjɔ̃] *nf* increase; **~ (de salaire)** rise (in salary) (*BRIT*), (pay) raise (*US*)

augmenter [ogmɑ̃te] /1/ *vt* to increase; (*salaire, prix*) to increase, raise, put up; (*employé*) to increase the salary of ▷ *vi* to increase

augure [ogyʀ] *nm*: **de bon/mauvais ~** of good/ill omen

aujourd'hui [oʒuʀdɥi] *adv* today

aumône [omon] *nf* alms *sg* (*pl inv*); **aumônier** *nm* chaplain

auparavant [oparavã] *adv* before(hand)

auprès [opʀɛ]: **~ de** *prép* next to, close to; (*recourir, s'adresser*) to; (*en comparaison de*) compared with

auquel [okɛl] *pron voir* **lequel**

aurai *etc* [ɔʀe] *vb voir* **avoir**

aurons *etc* [ɔʀɔ̃] *vb voir* **avoir**

aurore [ɔʀɔʀ] *nf* dawn, daybreak

ausculter [ɔskylte] /1/ *vt* to sound

aussi [osi] *adv* (*également*) also, too; (*de comparaison*) as ▷ *conj* therefore, consequently; **~ fort que** as strong as; **moi ~** me too

aussitôt [osito] *adv* straight away, immediately; **~ que** as soon as

austère [ɔstɛʀ] *adj* austere

austral, e [ɔstʀal] *adj* southern

Australie [ɔstʀali] *nf*: **l'~** Australia; **australien, ne** *adj* Australian ▷ *nm/f*: **Australien, ne** Australian

autant [otɑ̃] *adv* so much; **je ne savais pas que tu la détestais ~** I didn't know you hated her so much; (*comparatif*): **~ (que)** as much (as); (*nombre*) as many (as); **~ (de)** so much (*ou* many); as much (*ou* many); **~ partir** we (*ou* you *etc*) may as well leave; **~ dire que ...** one might as well say that ...; **pour ~** for all that; **d'~ plus/mieux (que)** all the more/the better (since)

autel [otɛl] *nm* altar

auteur [otœʀ] *nm* author

authentique [otɑ̃tik] *adj* authentic, genuine

auto [oto] *nf* car; **autobiographie** *nf* autobiography; **autobronzant** *nm* self-tanning cream (*or* lotion *etc*); **autobus** *nm* bus; **autocar** *nm* coach

autochtone [ɔtɔktɔn] *nm/f* native

auto: **autocollant, e** *adj* self-adhesive; (*enveloppe*) self-seal ▷ *nm* sticker; **autocuiseur** *nm* pressure cooker; **autodéfense** *nf* self-defence; **autodidacte** *nm/f* self-taught person; **auto-école** *nf* driving school; **autographe** *nm* autograph

automate [ɔtɔmat] *nm* (*machine*) (automatic) machine

automatique [ɔtɔmatik] *adj* automatic ▷ *nm*: **l'~** ≈ direct dialling

automne [ɔtɔn] *nm* autumn (*BRIT*), fall (*US*)

automobile [ɔtɔmɔbil] *adj* motor *cpd* ▷ *nf* (motor) car; **automobiliste** *nm/f* motorist

autonome [ɔtɔnɔm] *adj* autonomous; **autonomie** *nf* autonomy; (*Pol*) self-government, autonomy

autopsie [ɔtɔpsi] *nf* post-mortem (examination), autopsy

autoradio [otoʀadjo] *nf* car radio

autorisation [ɔtɔʀizasjɔ̃] *nf* permission, authorization; (*papiers*) permit

autorisé, e [ɔtɔʀize] *adj* (*opinion, sources*) authoritative

autoriser [ɔtɔʀize] /1/ *vt* to give permission for, authorize; (*fig*) to allow (of)

autoritaire [ɔtɔʀitɛʀ] *adj* authoritarian

autorité [ɔtɔʀite] *nf* authority; **faire ~** to be authoritative

autoroute [otoʀut] *nf* motorway (BRIT), expressway (US); **~ de l'information** (*Inform*) information superhighway

auto-stop [otostɔp] *nm*: **faire de l'~** to hitch-hike; **prendre qn en ~** to give sb a lift; **auto-stoppeur, -euse** *nm/f* hitch-hiker

autour [otuʀ] *adv* around; **~ de** around; **tout ~** all around

MOT-CLÉ

autre [otʀ] *adj* **1** (*différent*) other, different; **je préférerais un autre verre** I'd prefer another *ou* a different glass

2 (*supplémentaire*) other; **je voudrais un autre verre d'eau** I'd like another glass of water

3: **autre chose** something else; **autre part** somewhere else; **d'autre part** on the other hand

▶ *pron*: **un autre** another (one); **nous/vous autres** us/you; **d'autres** others; **l'autre** the other (one); **les autres** the others; (*autrui*) others; **l'un et l'autre** both of them; **se détester l'un l'autre/les uns les autres** to hate each other *ou* one another; **d'une semaine/minute à l'autre** from one week/minute *ou* moment to the next; (*incessamment*) any week/minute *ou* moment now; **entre autres** (*personnes*) among others; (*choses*) among other things

autrefois [otʀəfwa] *adv* in the past

autrement [otʀəmɑ̃] *adv* differently; (*d'une manière différente*) in another way; (*sinon*) otherwise; **~ dit** in other words

Autriche [otʀiʃ] *nf*: **l'~** Austria; **autrichien, ne** *adj* Austrian ▷ *nm/f*: **Autrichien, ne** Austrian

autruche [otʀyʃ] *nf* ostrich

aux [o] *prép voir* **à**

auxiliaire [ɔksiljɛʀ] *adj, nm/f* auxiliary

auxquels, auxquelles [okɛl] *pron voir* **lequel**

avalanche [avalɑ̃ʃ] *nf* avalanche

avaler [avale] /1/ *vt* to swallow

avance [avɑ̃s] *nf* (*de troupes etc*) advance; (*progrès*) progress; (*d'argent*) advance; (*opposé à retard*) lead; **avances** *nfpl* (*amoureuses*) advances; **(être) en ~** (to be) early; (*sur un programme*) (to be) ahead of schedule; **d'~, à l'~** in advance

avancé, e [avɑ̃se] *adj* advanced; (*travail etc*) well on, well under way

avancement [avɑ̃smɑ̃] *nm* (*professionnel*) promotion

avancer [avɑ̃se] /3/ *vi* to move forward, advance; (*projet, travail*) to make progress; (*montre, réveil*) to be fast to gain ▷ *vt* to move forward, advance; (*argent*) to advance; (*montre, pendule*) to put forward; **s'avancer** *vi* to move forward, advance; (*fig*) to commit o.s.

avant [avɑ̃] *prép* before ▷ *adj inv*: **siège/roue ~** front seat/wheel ▷ *nm* (*d'un véhicule, bâtiment*) front; (*Sport: joueur*) forward; **~ qu'il parte/de partir** before he leaves/ leaving; **~ tout** (*surtout*) above all; **à l'~** (*dans un véhicule*) in (the) front; **en ~** (*se pencher, tomber*) forward(s); **partir en ~** to go on ahead; **en ~ de** in front of

avantage [avɑ̃taʒ] *nm* advantage; **~s sociaux** fringe benefits; **avantager** /3/ *vt* (*favoriser*) to favour; (*embellir*) to flatter; **avantageux, -euse** *adj* (*prix*) attractive

avant: **avant-bras** *nm inv* forearm; **avant-coureur** *adj inv*: **signe avant-coureur** advance indication *ou* sign; **avant-dernier, -ière** *adj, nm/f* next to last, last but one; **avant-goût** *nm* foretaste; **avant-hier** *adv* the day before yesterday; **avant-première** *nf* (*de film*) preview; **avant-veille** *nf*: **l'avant-veille** two days before

avare [avaʀ] *adj* miserly, avaricious ▷ *nm/f* miser; **~ de compliments** stingy *ou* sparing with one's compliments

avec [avɛk] *prép* with; (*à l'égard de*) to(wards), with; **et ~ ça** (*dans un magasin*) anything *ou* something else?

avenir [avniʀ] *nm*: **l'~** the future; **à l'~** in future; **carrière/politicien d'~** career/politician with prospects *ou* a future

aventure [avɑ̃tyʀ] *nf*: **l'~** adventure; **une ~** (*amoureuse*) an affair;

aventureux, -euse *adj* adventurous, venturesome; (*projet*) risky, chancy

avenue [avny] *nf* avenue

avérer [aveʀe] /6/: **s'avérer** *vr*: **s'~ faux/coûteux** to prove (to be) wrong/expensive

averse [avɛʀs] *nf* shower

averti, e [avɛʀti] *adj* (well-) informed

avertir [avɛʀtiʀ] /2/ *vt*: **~ qn (de qch/que)** to warn sb (of sth/that); (*renseigner*) to inform sb (of sth/ that); **avertissement** *nm* warning; **avertisseur** *nm* horn, siren

aveu, x [avø] *nm* confession

aveugle [avœgl] *adj* blind ▷ *nm/f* blind person

aviation [avjasjɔ̃] *nf* aviation; (*sport, métier de pilote*) flying; (*Mil*) air force

avide [avid] *adj* eager; (*péj*) greedy, grasping

avion [avjɔ̃] *nm* (aero)plane (BRIT), (air)plane (US); **aller (quelque part) en ~** to go (somewhere) by plane, fly (somewhere); **par ~** by airmail; **~ à réaction** jet (plane)

aviron [aviʀɔ̃] *nm* oar; (*sport*): **l'~** rowing

avis [avi] *nm* opinion; (*notification*) notice; **à mon ~** in my opinion; **changer d'~** to change one's mind; **jusqu'à nouvel ~** until further notice

aviser [avize] /1/ *vt* (*informer*): **~ qn de/que** to advise *ou* inform *ou* notify sb of/that ▷ *vi* to think about things, assess the situation; **nous aviserons sur place** we'll work something out once we're there; **s'~ de qch/que** to become suddenly aware of sth/ that; **s'~ de faire** to take it into one's head to do

avocat, e [avɔka, -at] *nm/f* (*Jur*) ≈ barrister (BRIT), lawyer ▷ *nm* (*Culin*) avocado (pear); **l'~ de la défense/partie civile** the counsel for the defence/plaintiff; **~ général** assistant public prosecutor

avoine [avwan] *nf* oats *pl*

MOT-CLÉ

avoir [avwaʀ] /34/ vt **1** (*posséder*)
to have; **elle a deux enfants/une
belle maison** she has (got) two
children/a lovely house; **il a les yeux
bleus** he has (got) blue eyes; **vous
avez du sel?** do you have any salt?;
avoir du courage/de la patience to
be brave/patient

2 (*éprouver*): **avoir de la peine** to be
ou feel sad; *voir aussi* **faim, peur**

3 (*âge, dimensions*) to be; **il a 3 ans** he
is 3 (years old); **le mur a 3 mètres de
haut** the wall is 3 metres high

4 (*fam: duper*) to do, have; **on vous a
eu!** you've been done ou had!; (*fait une
plaisanterie*) we ou they had you there

5: **en avoir contre qn** to have a
grudge against sb; **en avoir assez**
to be fed up; **j'en ai pour une demi-
heure** it'll take me half an hour

6 (*obtenir, attraper*) to get; **j'ai réussi
à avoir mon train** I managed to
get ou catch my train; **j'ai réussi à
avoir le renseignement qu'il me
fallait** I managed to get (hold of) the
information I needed

▶vb aux **1** to have; **avoir mangé/
dormi** to have eaten/slept

2 (*avoir +à +infinitif*): **avoir à faire
qch** to have to do sth; **vous n'avez
qu'à lui demander** you only have
to ask him

▶vb impers **1**: **il y a** (+ *singulier*)
there is; (+ *pluriel*) there are; **il y
avait du café/des gâteaux** there
was coffee/there were cakes; **qu'y
a-t-il?, qu'est-ce qu'il y a?** what's
the matter?, what is it?; **il doit y
avoir une explication** there must
be an explanation; **il n'y a qu'à ...**
we (*ou* you *etc*) will just have to ...; **il
ne peut y en avoir qu'un** there can
only be one

2: **il y a** (*temporel*): **il y a 10 ans**
10 years ago; **il y a 10 ans/
longtemps que je le connais** I've
known him for 10 years/a long time;
il y a 10 ans qu'il est arrivé it's 10
years since he arrived

▶nm assets pl, resources pl;(*Comm*)
credit

avortement [avɔʀtəmã] *nm*
abortion

avouer [avwe] /1/ vt (*crime, défaut*)
to confess (to); **~ avoir fait/que** to
admit ou confess to having done/that

avril [avʀil] *nm* April

axe [aks] *nm* axis (*pl* axes); (*de roue etc*)
axle; (*fig*) main line; **~ routier** trunk
road (BRIT), main road, highway (US)

ayons *etc* [ɛjɔ̃] *vb voir* **avoir**

bâbord [babɔʀ] *nm*: **à** *ou* **par ~** to port, on the port side

baby-foot [babifut] *nm inv* table football

baby-sitting [babisitiŋ] *nm* baby-sitting; **faire du ~** to baby-sit

bac [bak] *nm* (*récipient*) tub

baccalauréat [bakalɔʀea] *nm* ≈ high school diploma

bâcler [bakle] /1/ *vt* to botch (up)

baffe [baf] *nf* (*fam*) slap, clout

bafouiller [bafuje] /1/ *vi, vt* to stammer

bagage [bagaʒ] *nm*: **~s** luggage *sg*; (*connaissances*) background, knowledge; **~s à main** hand-luggage

bagarre [bagaʀ] *nf* fight, brawl; **bagarrer** /1/: **se bagarrer** *vi* to (have a) fight

bagnole [baɲɔl] *nf* (*fam*) car

bague [bag] *nf* ring; **~ de fiançailles** engagement ring

baguette [bagɛt] *nf* stick; (*cuisine chinoise*) chopstick; (*de chef d'orchestre*) baton; (*pain*) stick of (French) bread; **~ magique** magic wand

baie [bɛ] *nf* (*Géo*) bay; (*fruit*) berry; **~ (vitrée)** picture window

baignade [bɛɲad] *nf* bathing; **"~ interdite"** "no bathing"

baigner [bɛɲe] /1/ *vt* (*bébé*) to bath; **se baigner** *vi* to go swimming *ou* bathing; **baignoire** *nf* bath(tub)

bail (*pl* **baux**) [baj, bo] *nm* lease

bâiller [baje] /1/ *vi* to yawn; (*être ouvert*) to gape

bain [bɛ̃] *nm* bath; **prendre un ~** to have a bath; **se mettre dans le ~** (*fig*) to get into (the way of) it *ou* things; **~ de bouche** mouthwash; **~ moussant** bubble bath; **~ de soleil; prendre un ~ de soleil** to sunbathe; **bain-marie** *nm*: **faire chauffer au bain-marie** (*boîte etc*) to immerse in boiling water

baiser [beze] /1/ *nm* kiss ▷ *vt* (*main, front*) to kiss; (*fam!*) to screw (!)

baisse [bɛs] *nf* fall, drop; **en ~** falling

baisser [bese] /1/ *vt* to lower; (*radio, chauffage*) to turn down ▷ *vi* to fall, drop, go down; (*vue, santé*) to fail, dwindle; **se baisser** *vi* to bend down

bal [bal] *nm* dance; (*grande soirée*) ball; **~ costumé/masqué** fancy-dress/masked ball

balade [balad] (*fam*) *nf* (*à pied*) walk, stroll; (*en voiture*) drive; **balader** /1/ (*fam*): **se balader** *vi* to go for a walk *ou* stroll; to go for a drive; **baladeur** [baladœʀ] *nm* personal stereo, Walkman®

balai [balɛ] *nm* broom, brush

balance [balɑ̃s] *nf* scales *pl*; (*signe*): **la B~** Libra; **~ commerciale** balance of trade

balancer [balɑ̃se] /3/ *vt* to swing; (*lancer*) to fling, chuck; (*renvoyer, jeter*) to chuck out; **se balancer** *vi* to swing; to rock; **se ~ de qch** (*fam*) not to give a toss about sth; **balançoire** nf swing; (sur pivot) seesaw

balayer [baleje] /8/ vt (feuilles etc) to sweep up, brush up; (pièce, cour) to sweep; (chasser) to sweep away ou aside; (radar) to scan; **balayeur, -euse** [balejœR, -øz] nm/f road sweeper ▷ nf (engin) road sweeper

balbutier [balbysje] /7/ vi, vt to stammer

balcon [balkɔ̃] nm balcony; (Théât) dress circle

Bâle [bal] n Basle ou Basel

Baléares [baleaR] nfpl: **les ~** the Balearic Islands, the Balearics

baleine [balɛn] nf whale

balise [baliz] nf (Navig) beacon, (marker) buoy; (Aviat) runway light, beacon; (Auto, Ski) sign, marker; **baliser** /1/ vt to mark out (with beacons ou lights etc)

balle [bal] nf (de fusil) bullet; (de sport) ball; (fam: franc) franc

ballerine [bal(ə)Rin] nf (danseuse) ballet dancer; (chaussure) pump, ballet shoe

ballet [balɛ] nm ballet

ballon [balɔ̃] nm (de sport) ball; (jouet, Aviat) balloon; **~ de football** football; **~ d'oxygène** oxygen bottle

balnéaire [balneɛR] adj seaside cpd; **station ~** seaside resort

balustrade [balystRad] nf railings pl, handrail

bambin [bɑ̃bɛ̃] nm little child

bambou [bɑ̃bu] nm bamboo

banal, e [banal] adj banal, commonplace; (péj) trite; **banalité** nf banality

banane [banan] nf banana; (sac) waist-bag, bum-bag

banc [bɑ̃] nm seat, bench; (de poissons) shoal; **~ d'essai** (fig) testing ground

bancaire [bɑ̃kɛR] adj banking; (chèque, carte) bank cpd

bancal, e [bɑ̃kal] adj wobbly

bandage [bɑ̃daʒ] nf bandage

bande [bɑ̃d] nf (de tissu etc) strip; (Méd) bandage; (motif, dessin) stripe; (groupe) band; (péj): **une ~ de** a bunch ou crowd of; **faire ~ à part** to keep to o.s.; **~ dessinée (BD)** comic strip; **~ magnétique** magnetic tape; **~ sonore** sound track

bande-annonce [bɑ̃danɔ̃s] nf trailer

bandeau, x [bɑ̃do] nm headband; (sur les yeux) blindfold

bander [bɑ̃de] /1/ vt (blessure) to bandage; **~ les yeux à qn** to blindfold sb

bandit [bɑ̃di] nm bandit

bandoulière [bɑ̃duljɛR] nf: **en ~** (slung ou worn) across the shoulder

Bangladesh [bɑ̃gladɛʃ] nm: **le ~** Bangladesh

banlieue [bɑ̃ljø] nf suburbs pl; **quartiers de ~** suburban areas; **trains de ~** commuter trains

bannir [baniR] /2/ vt to banish

banque [bɑ̃k] nf bank; (activités) banking; **~ de données** data bank

banquet [bɑ̃kɛ] nm dinner; (d'apparat) banquet

banquette [bɑ̃kɛt] nf seat

banquier [bɑ̃kje] nm banker

banquise [bɑ̃kiz] nf ice field

baptême [batɛm] nm christening; baptism; **~ de l'air** first flight

baptiser [batize] /1/ vt to christen; to baptize

bar [baR] nm bar

baraque [baRak] nf shed; (fam) house; **~ foraine** fairground stand; **baraqué, e** (fam) adj well-built, hefty

barbant, e [baRbɑ̃, -ɑ̃t] adj (fam) deadly (boring)

barbare [baRbaR] adj barbaric

barbe [baRb] nf beard; **(au nez et) à la ~ de qn** (fig) under sb's very nose; **la ~!** (fam) damn it!; **quelle ~!** (fam) what a drag ou bore!; **~ à papa** candy-floss (BRIT), cotton candy (US)

barbelé [baRbəle] adj, nm: **(fil de fer) ~** barbed wire no pl

barbiturique [baʀbityʀik] *nm* barbiturate

barbouiller [baʀbuje] /1/ *vt* to daub; **avoir l'estomac barbouillé** to feel queasy *ou* sick

barbu, e [baʀby] *adj* bearded

barder [baʀde] /1/ *vi* (*fam*): **ça va ~** sparks will fly

barème [baʀɛm] *nm* (*Scol*) scale; (*liste*) table

baril [baʀi(l)] *nm* barrel; (*de poudre*) keg

bariolé, e [baʀjɔle] *adj* many-coloured, rainbow-coloured

baromètre [baʀɔmɛtʀ] *nm* barometer

baron [baʀɔ̃] *nm* baron

baronne [baʀɔn] *nf* baroness

baroque [baʀɔk] *adj* (*Art*) baroque; (*fig*) weird

barque [baʀk] *nf* small boat

barquette [baʀkɛt] *nf* small boat-shaped tart; (*récipient: en aluminium*) tub; (*: en bois*) basket; (*pour repas*) tray; (*pour fruits*) punnet

barrage [baʀaʒ] *nm* dam; (*sur route*) roadblock, barricade

barre [baʀ] *nf* (*de fer etc*) rod; (*Navig*) helm; (*écrite*) line, stroke

barreau, x [baʀo] *nm* bar; (*Jur*): **le ~** the Bar

barrer [baʀe] /1/ *vt* (*route etc*) to block; (*mot*) to cross out; (*chèque*) to cross (*BRIT*); (*Navig*) to steer; **se barrer** *vi* (*fam*) to clear off

barrette [baʀɛt] *nf* (*pour cheveux*) (hair) slide (*BRIT*) *ou* clip (*US*)

barricader [baʀikade] /1/: **se barricader** *vi*: **se ~ chez soi** to lock o.s. in

barrière [baʀjɛʀ] *nf* fence; (*obstacle*) barrier; (*porte*) gate

barrique [baʀik] *nf* barrel, cask

bar-tabac [baʀtaba] *nm* bar (*which sells tobacco and stamps*)

bas, basse [bɑ, bɑs] *adj* low ▷ *nm* (*vêtement*) stocking; (*partie inférieure*): **le ~ de** the lower part *ou* foot *ou* bottom of ▷ *adv* low; (*parler*) softly;

au ~ mot at the lowest estimate; **enfant en ~ âge** young child; **en ~** down below; (*d'une liste, d'un mur etc*) at (*ou* to) the bottom; (*dans une maison*) downstairs; **en ~ de** at the bottom of; **à ~ la dictature!** down with dictatorship!

bas-côté [bakote] *nm* (*de route*) verge (*BRIT*), shoulder (*US*)

basculer [baskyle] /1/ *vi* to fall over, topple (over); (*benne*) to tip up ▷ *vt* (*contenu*) to tip out; (*benne*) tip up

base [bɑz] *nf* base; (*fondement, principe*) basis (*pl* bases); **la ~** (*Pol*) the rank and file; **de ~** basic; **à ~ de café** etc coffee etc -based; **~ de données** database; **baser** /1/ *vt*: **baser qch sur** to base sth on; **se baser sur** (*données, preuves*) to base one's argument on

bas-fond [bafɔ̃] *nm* (*Navig*) shallow; **bas-fonds** *nmpl* (*fig*) dregs

basilic [bazilik] *nm* (*Culin*) basil

basket [baskɛt] *nm* basketball

baskets [baskɛt] *nfpl* trainers (*BRIT*), sneakers (*US*)

basque [bask] *adj* Basque ▷ *nm/f*: **B~** Basque; **le Pays ~** the Basque country

basse [bɑs] *adj voir* **bas** ▷ *nf* (*Mus*) bass; **basse-cour** *nf* farmyard

bassin [basɛ̃] *nm* (*pièce d'eau*) pond, pool; (*de fontaine, Géo*) basin; (*Anat*) pelvis; (*portuaire*) dock

bassine [basin] *nf* basin; (*contenu*) bowl, bowlful

basson [basɔ̃] *nm* bassoon

bat [ba] *vb voir* **battre**

bataille [bataj] *nf* battle; (*rixe*) fight; **elle avait les cheveux en ~** her hair was a mess

bateau, x [bato] *nm* boat; ship; **bateau-mouche** *nm* (*passenger*) pleasure boat (*on the Seine*)

bâti, e [bati] *adj* (*terrain*) developed; **bien ~** well-built

bâtiment [batimɑ̃] *nm* building; (*Navig*) ship, vessel; (*industrie*): **le ~** the building trade

bâtir [batiʀ] /2/ vt to build
bâtisse [batis] nf building
bâton [batɔ̃] nm stick; **parler à ~s rompus** to chat about this and that
bats [ba] vb voir **battre**
battement [batmɑ̃] nm (de cœur) beat; (intervalle) interval (between classes, trains etc); **10 minutes de ~** 10 minutes to spare
batterie [batʀi] nf (Mil, Élec) battery; (Mus) drums pl, drum kit; **~ de cuisine** kitchen utensils pl; (casseroles etc) pots and pans pl
batteur [batœʀ] nm (Mus) drummer; (appareil) whisk
battre [batʀ] /41/ vt to beat; (blé) to thresh; (cartes) to shuffle; (passer au peigne fin) to scour ▷ vi (cœur) to beat; (volets etc) to bang, rattle; **se battre** vi to fight; **~ la mesure** to beat time; **~ son plein** to be at its height, be going full swing; **~ des mains** to clap one's hands
baume [bom] nm balm
bavard, e [bavaʀ, -aʀd] adj (very) talkative; gossipy; **bavarder** /1/ vi to chatter; (indiscrètement) to gossip; (révéler un secret) to blab
baver [bave] /1/ vi to dribble; (chien) to slobber, slaver; **en ~** (fam) to have a hard time (of it)
bavoir [bavwaʀ] nm bib
bavure [bavyʀ] nf smudge; (fig) hitch; (policière etc) blunder
bazar [bazaʀ] nm general store; (fam) jumble; **bazarder** /1/ vt (fam) to chuck out
BCBG sigle adj (= bon chic bon genre) smart and trendy, ≈ preppy
BD sigle f = **bande dessinée**
bd abr = **boulevard**
béant, e [beɑ̃, -ɑ̃t] adj gaping
beau (bel), belle, beaux [bo, bɛl] adj beautiful, lovely; (homme) handsome ▷ adv: **il fait ~** the weather's fine ▷ nm: **un ~ jour** one (fine) day; **de plus belle** more than ever, even more; **bel et bien** well

and truly; **le plus ~ c'est que ...** the best of it is that ...; **on a ~ essayer** however hard ou no matter how hard we try; **faire le ~** (chien) to sit up and beg

MOT-CLÉ

beaucoup [buku] adv 1 a lot; **il boit beaucoup** he drinks a lot; **il ne boit pas beaucoup** he doesn't drink much ou a lot
2 (suivi de plus, trop etc) much, a lot; **il est beaucoup plus grand** he is much ou a lot ou far taller; **c'est beaucoup plus cher** it's a lot ou much more expensive; **il a beaucoup plus de temps que moi** he has much ou a lot more time than me; **il y a beaucoup plus de touristes ici** there are a lot ou many more tourists here; **beaucoup trop vite** much too fast; **il fume beaucoup trop** he smokes far too much
3: **beaucoup de** (nombre) many, a lot of; (quantité) a lot of; **beaucoup d'étudiants/de touristes** a lot of ou many students/tourists; **beaucoup de courage** a lot of courage; **il n'a pas beaucoup d'argent** he hasn't got much ou a lot of money
4: **de beaucoup** by far

beau: beau-fils nm son-in-law; (remariage) stepson; **beau-frère** nm brother-in-law; **beau-père** nm father-in-law; (remariage) stepfather
beauté [bote] nf beauty; **de toute ~** beautiful; **finir qch en ~** to complete sth brilliantly
beaux-arts [bozaʀ] nmpl fine arts
beaux-parents [bopaʀɑ̃] nmpl wife's/husband's family, in-laws
bébé [bebe] nm baby
bec [bɛk] nm beak, bill; (de cafetière etc) spout; (de casserole etc) lip; (fam) mouth; **~ de gaz** (street) gaslamp

bêche [bɛʃ] nf spade; **bêcher** /1/ vt to dig

bedaine [bədɛn] nf paunch

bedonnant, e [bədɔnã, -ãt] adj potbellied

bée [be] adj: **bouche ~** gaping

bégayer [begeje] /8/ vt, vi to stammer

beige [bɛʒ] adj beige

beignet [bɛɲɛ] nm fritter

bel [bɛl] adj m voir **beau**

bêler [bele] /1/ vi to bleat

belette [bəlɛt] nf weasel

belge [bɛlʒ] adj Belgian ▷ nm/f: **B~** Belgian

Belgique [bɛlʒik] nf: **la ~** Belgium

bélier [belje] nm ram; (signe): **le B~** Aries

belle [bɛl] adj voir **beau** ▷ nf (Sport): **la ~** the decider; **belle-fille** nf daughter-in-law; (remariage) stepdaughter; **belle-mère** nf mother-in-law; (remariage) stepmother; **belle-sœur** nf sister-in-law

belvédère [bɛlvedɛr] nm panoramic viewpoint (or small building there)

bémol [bemɔl] nm (Mus) flat

bénédiction [benediksjɔ̃] nf blessing

bénéfice [benefis] nm (Comm) profit; (avantage) benefit; **bénéficier** /7/ vi: **bénéficier de** to enjoy; (profiter) to benefit by ou from; **bénéfique** adj beneficial

Benelux [benelyks] nm: **le ~** Benelux, the Benelux countries

bénévole [benevɔl] adj voluntary, unpaid

bénin, -igne [benɛ̃, -iɲ] adj minor, mild; (tumeur) benign

bénir [benir] /2/ vt to bless; **bénit, e** adj consecrated; **eau bénite** holy water

benne [bɛn] nf skip; (de téléphérique) (cable) car; **~ à ordures** (amovible) skip

béquille [bekij] nf crutch; (de bicyclette) stand

berceau, x [bɛrso] nm cradle, crib

bercer [bɛrse] /3/ vt to rock, cradle; (musique etc) to lull; **~ qn de** (promesses etc) to delude sb with; **berceuse** nf lullaby

béret [berɛ] nm (aussi: **~ basque**) beret

berge [bɛrʒ] nf bank

berger, -ère [bɛrʒe, -ɛr] nm/f shepherd/shepherdess; **~ allemand** alsatian (dog) (BRIT), German shepherd (dog) (US)

Berlin [bɛrlɛ̃] n Berlin

Bermudes [bɛrmyd] nfpl: **les (îles) ~** Bermuda

Berne [bɛrn] n Bern

berner [bɛrne] /1/ vt to fool

besogne [bəzɔɲ] nf work no pl, job

besoin [bəzwɛ̃] nm need; (pauvreté): **le ~** need, want; **faire ses ~s** to relieve o.s.; **avoir ~ de qch/faire qch** to need sth/to do sth; **au ~** if need be; **être dans le ~** to be in need ou want

bestiole [bɛstjɔl] nf (tiny) creature

bétail [betaj] nm livestock, cattle pl

bête [bɛt] nf animal; (bestiole) insect, creature ▷ adj stupid, silly; **chercher la petite ~** to nit-pick; **~ noire** pet hate; **~ sauvage** wild beast

bêtise [betiz] nf stupidity; (action, remarque) stupid thing (to say ou do)

béton [betɔ̃] nm concrete; **(en) ~** (fig: alibi, argument) cast iron; **~ armé** reinforced concrete

betterave [bɛtrav] nf beetroot (BRIT), beet (US); **~ sucrière** sugar beet

Beur [bœr] nm/f see note **"Beur"**

● **BEUR**

● Beur is a term used to refer to a
● person born in France of North
● African immigrant parents. It is
● not racist and is often used by the
● media, anti-racist groups and
● second-generation North Africans
● themselves. The word itself comes
● from back slang or 'verlan'.

beurre [bœʀ] nm butter; **beurrer**/1/ vt to butter; **beurrier** nm butter dish

biais [bjɛ] nm (moyen) device, expedient; (aspect) angle; **en ~, de ~** (obliquement) at an angle; **par le ~ de** by means of

bibelot [biblo] nm trinket, curio

biberon [bibʀɔ̃] nm (feeding) bottle; **nourrir au ~** to bottle-feed

bible [bibl] nf bible

bibliobus [biblijobys] nm mobile library van

bibliothécaire nm/f librarian

bibliothèque nf library; (meuble) bookcase

bic® [bik] nm Biro®

bicarbonate [bikaʀbɔnat] nm: **~ (de soude)** bicarbonate of soda

biceps [bisɛps] nm biceps

biche [biʃ] nf doe

bicolore [bikɔlɔʀ] adj two-coloured

bicoque [bikɔk] nf (péj) shack

bicyclette [bisiklɛt] nf bicycle

bidet [bidɛ] nm bidet

bidon [bidɔ̃] nm can ▷ adj inv (fam) phoney

bidonville [bidɔ̃vil] nm shanty town

bidule [bidyl] nm (fam) thingamajig

MOT-CLÉ

bien [bjɛ̃] nm **1** (avantage, profit): **faire du bien à qn** to do sb good; **dire du bien de** to speak well of; **c'est pour son bien** it's for his own good

2 (possession, patrimoine) possession, property; **son bien le plus précieux** his most treasured possession; **avoir du bien** to have property; **biens (de consommation** etc) (consumer etc) goods

3 (moral): **le bien** good; **distinguer le bien du mal** to tell good from evil

▶ adv **1** (de façon satisfaisante) well; **elle travaille/mange bien** she works/eats well; **croyant bien faire, je/il …** thinking I/he was doing the right thing, I/he …; **tiens-toi bien!** (assieds-toi correctement)

sit up straight!; (debout) stand up straight!; (sois sage) behave yourself!; (prépare-toi) wait for it!

2 (valeur intensive) quite; **bien jeune** quite young; **bien assez** quite enough; **bien mieux** (very) much better; **bien du temps/des gens** quite a time/a number of people; **j'espère bien y aller** I do hope to go; **je veux bien le faire** (concession) I'm quite willing to do it; **il faut bien le faire** it has to be done; **cela fait bien deux ans que je ne l'ai pas vu** I haven't seen him for at least ou a good two years; **Paul est bien venu, n'est-ce pas?** Paul HAS come, hasn't he?; **où peut-il bien être passé?** where on earth can he have got to?

▶ excl right!, OK!, fine!; **(c'est) bien fait!** it serves you (ou him etc) right!; **bien sûr!** certainly!

▶ adj inv **1** (en bonne forme, à l'aise): **je me sens bien** I feel fine; **je ne me sens pas bien** I don't feel well; **on est bien dans ce fauteuil** this chair is very comfortable

2 (joli, beau) good-looking; **tu es bien dans cette robe** you look good in that dress

3 (satisfaisant) good; **elle est bien, cette maison/secrétaire** it's a good house/she's a good secretary; **c'est très bien (comme ça)** it's fine (like that); **c'est bien?** is that all right?

4 (moralement) right; (: personne) good, nice; (respectable) respectable; **ce n'est pas bien de …** it's not right to …; **elle est bien, cette femme** she's a nice woman, she's a good sort; **des gens bien** respectable people

5 (en bons termes): **être bien avec qn** to be on good terms with sb; **bien-aimé, e** adj, nm/f beloved; **bien-être** nm well-being; **bienfaisance** nf charity; **bienfait** nm act of generosity, benefaction; (de la science etc) benefit; **bienfaiteur, -trice**

nm/f benefactor/benefactress;
bien-fondé *nm* soundness; **bien que**
conj although

bientôt [bjɛ̃to] *adv* soon; **à ~** see
you soon
bienveillant, e [bjɛ̃vɛjɑ̃, -ɑ̃t] *adj*
kindly
bienvenu, e [bjɛ̃vny] *adj* welcome
▷ *nf*: **souhaiter la ~e à** to welcome;
~e à welcome to
bière [bjɛʀ] *nf* (*boisson*) beer; (*cercueil*)
bier; **~ blonde** lager; **~ brune** brown
ale (*BRIT*), dark beer (*US*); **~ (à la)
pression** draught beer
bifteck [biftɛk] *nm* steak
bigorneau, x [bigɔʀno] *nm* winkle
bigoudi [bigudi] *nm* curler
bijou, x [biʒu] *nm* jewel; **bijouterie**
nf jeweller's (shop); **bijoutier, -ière**
nm/f jeweller
bikini [bikini] *nm* bikini
bilan [bilɑ̃] *nm* (*Comm*) balance
sheet(s); (*fig*) (*net*) outcome (: *de
victimes*) toll; **faire le ~ de** to assess;
to review; **déposer son ~** to file a
bankruptcy statement; **~ de santé**
check-up
bile [bil] *nf* bile; **se faire de la ~** (*fam*)
to worry o.s. sick
bilieux, -euse [biljø, -øz] *adj* bilious;
(*fig: colérique*) testy
bilingue [bilɛ̃g] *adj* bilingual
billard [bijaʀ] *nm* billiards *sg*; (*table*)
billiard table
bille [bij] *nf* ball; (*du jeu de billes*)
marble
billet [bijɛ] *nm* (*aussi*: **~ de banque**)
(bank)note; (*de cinéma, de bus
etc*) ticket; (*courte lettre*) note;
~ électronique e-ticket; **billetterie**
nf ticket office; (*distributeur*) ticket
dispenser; (*Banque*) cash dispenser
billion [biljɔ̃] *nm* billion (*BRIT*),
trillion (*US*)
bimensuel, le [bimɑ̃sɥɛl] *adj*
bimonthly
bio [bjo] *adj* organic

bio... [bjo] *préfixe* bio...;
biocarburant [bjokaʀbyʀɑ̃] *nm*
biofuel; **biochimie** *nf* biochemistry;
biographie *nf* biography; **biologie**
nf biology; **biologique** *adj*
biological; **biométrie** *nf* biometrics;
biotechnologie *nf* biotechnology;
bioterrorisme *nm* bioterrorism
Birmanie [biʀmani] *nf* Burma
bis¹, e [bi, biz] *adj* (*couleur*) greyish
brown ▷ *nf* (*baiser*) kiss; (*vent*) North
wind; **faire une** *ou* **la ~e à qn** to kiss
sb; **grosses ~es (de)** (*sur lettre*) love
and kisses (from)
bis² [bis] *adv*: **12 ~** 12a *ou* A ▷ *excl*,
nm encore
biscotte [biskɔt] *nf* toasted bread
(*sold in packets*)
biscuit [biskɥi] *nm* biscuit (*BRIT*),
cookie (*US*)
bise [biz] *nf voir* **bis²**
bisexuel, le [bisɛksɥɛl] *adj*
bisexual
bisou [bizu] *nm* (*fam*) kiss
bissextile [bisɛkstil] *adj*: **année ~**
leap year
bistro(t) [bistʀo] *nm* bistro, café
bitume [bitym] *nm* asphalt
bizarre [bizaʀ] *adj* strange, odd
blague [blag] *nf* (*propos*) joke; (*farce*)
trick; **sans ~!** no kidding!; **blaguer**
/1/ *vi* to joke
blaireau, x [blɛʀo] *nm* (*Zool*) badger;
(*brosse*) shaving brush
blâme [blɑm] *nm* blame; (*sanction*)
reprimand; **blâmer** /1/ *vt* to blame
blanc, blanche [blɑ̃, blɑ̃ʃ] *adj* white;
(*non imprimé*) blank ▷ *nm/f* white,
white man/woman ▷ *nm* (*couleur*)
white; (*espace non écrit*) blank; (*aussi*:
~ d'œuf) (egg-)white; (*aussi*: **~ de
poulet**) breast, white meat; (*aussi*:
vin ~) white wine ▷ *nf* (*Mus*) minim
(*BRIT*), half-note (*US*); **chèque
en ~** blank cheque; **à ~** (*chauffer*)
white-hot; (*tirer, charger*) with blanks;
~ cassé off-white; **blancheur** *nf*
whiteness

blanchir [blɑ̃ʃiʀ] /2/ vt (gén) to whiten; (linge) to launder; (Culin) to blanch; (fig: disculper) to clear ▷ vi (cheveux) to go white; **blanchisserie** nf laundry

blason [blazɔ̃] nm coat of arms

blasphème [blasfɛm] nm blasphemy

blazer [blazɛʀ] nm blazer

blé [ble] nm wheat; **~ noir** buckwheat

bled [blɛd] nm (péj) hole

blême [blɛm] adj pale

blessé, e [blese] adj injured ▷ nm/f injured person, casualty

blesser [blese] /1/ vt to injure; (délibérément) to wound; (offenser) to hurt; **se blesser** to injure o.s.; **se ~ au pied** etc to injure one's foot etc; **blessure** nf (accidentelle) injury; (intentionnelle) wound

bleu, e [blø] adj blue; (bifteck) very rare ▷ nm (couleur) blue; (contusion) bruise; (vêtement: aussi: **~s**) overalls pl; **fromage ~** blue cheese; **~ marine/ nuit/roi** navy/midnight/royal blue; **bleuet** nm cornflower

bloc [blɔk] nm (de pierre etc) block; (de papier à lettres) pad; (ensemble) group, block; **serré à ~** tightened right down; **en ~** as a whole; **~ opératoire** operating ou theatre block; **blocage** nm (des prix) freezing; (Psych) hang-up; **bloc-notes** nm note pad

blog, blogue [blɔg] nm blog; **bloguer** /1/ vi to blog

blond, e [blɔ̃, -ɔ̃d] adj fair; blond; (sable, blés) golden

bloquer [blɔke] /1/ vt (passage) to block; (pièce mobile) to jam; (crédits, compte) to freeze

blottir [blɔtiʀ] /2/: **se blottir** vi to huddle up

blouse [bluz] nf overall

blouson [bluzɔ̃] nm blouson (jacket); **~ noir** (fig) ≈ rocker

bluff [blœf] nm bluff

bobine [bɔbin] nf reel; (Élec) coil

bobo [bobo] sigle m/f (= bourgeois bohème) boho

bocal, -aux [bɔkal, -o] nm jar

bock [bɔk] nm glass of beer

bœuf (pl **bœufs**) [bœf, bø] nm ox; (Culin) beef

bof [bɔf] excl (fam: indifférence) don't care!; (pas terrible) nothing special

bohémien, ne [bɔemjɛ̃, -ɛn] nm/f gipsy

boire [bwaʀ] /53/ vt to drink; (s'imprégner de) to soak up; **~ un coup** to have a drink

bois [bwa] nm wood; **de ~, en ~** wooden; **boisé, e** adj woody, wooded

boisson [bwasɔ̃] nf drink

boîte [bwat] nf box; (fam: entreprise) firm; **aliments en ~** canned ou tinned (BRIT) foods; **~ à gants** glove compartment; **~ à ordures** dustbin (BRIT), trash can (US); **~ aux lettres** letter box; **~ d'allumettes** box of matches; (vide) matchbox; **~ de conserves** can ou tin (BRIT) (of food); **~ de nuit** night club; **~ de vitesses** gear box; **~ postale (BP)** PO box; **~ vocale** voice mail

boiter [bwate] /1/ vi to limp; (fig: raisonnement) to be shaky

boîtier [bwatje] nm case

boive etc [bwav] vb voir **boire**

bol [bɔl] nm bowl; **un ~ d'air** a breath of fresh air; **en avoir ras le ~** (fam) to have had a bellyful; **avoir du ~** (fam) to be lucky

bombarder [bɔ̃baʀde] /1/ vt to bomb; **~ qn de** (cailloux, lettres) to bombard sb with

bombe [bɔ̃b] nf bomb; (atomiseur) (aerosol) spray

 MOT-CLÉ

bon, bonne [bɔ̃, bɔn] adj **1** (agréable, satisfaisant) good; **un bon repas/ restaurant** a good meal/restaurant; **être bon en maths** to be good at maths

2 (*charitable*): **être bon (envers)** to be good (to)

3 (*correct*) right; **le bon numéro/moment** the right number/moment

4 (*souhaits*): **bon anniversaire!** happy birthday!; **bon courage!** good luck!; **bon séjour!** enjoy your stay!; **bon voyage!** have a good trip!; **bonne année!** happy New Year!; **bonne chance!** good luck!; **bonne fête!** happy holiday!; **bonne nuit!** good night!

5 (*approprié*): **bon à/pour** fit to/for; **à quoi bon (…)?** what's the point ou use (of …)?

6: **bon enfant** *adj inv* accommodating, easy-going; **bonne femme** (*péj*) woman; **de bonne heure** early; **bon marché** cheap; **bon mot** witticism; **bon sens** common sense; **bon vivant** jovial chap; **bonnes œuvres** charitable works, charities
▶*nm* **1** (*billet*) voucher; (*aussi:* **bon cadeau**) gift voucher; **bon d'essence** petrol coupon; **bon du Trésor** Treasury bond
2: **avoir du bon** to have its good points; **pour de bon** for good
▶*adv*: **il fait bon** it's ou the weather is fine; **sentir bon** to smell good; **tenir bon** to stand firm
▶*excl* good!; **ah bon?** really?; **bon, je reste** right, I'll stay; *voir aussi* **bonne**

bonbon [bɔ̃bɔ̃] *nm* (boiled) sweet
bond [bɔ̃] *nm* leap; **faire un ~** to leap in the air
bondé, e [bɔ̃de] *adj* packed (full)
bondir [bɔ̃dir] /2/ *vi* to leap
bonheur [bɔnœr] *nm* happiness; **porter ~ (à qn)** to bring (sb) luck; **au petit ~** haphazardly; **par ~** fortunately
bonhomme [bɔnɔm] (*pl* **bonshommes**) *nm* fellow; **~ de neige** snowman

bonjour [bɔ̃ʒur] *excl, nm* hello; (*selon l'heure*) good morning (ou afternoon); **c'est simple comme ~!** it's easy as pie!
bonne [bɔn] *adj f voir* **bon** ▷ *nf* (*domestique*) maid
bonnet [bɔnɛ] *nm* hat; (*de soutien-gorge*) cup; **~ de bain** bathing cap
bonsoir [bɔ̃swar] *excl* good evening
bonté [bɔ̃te] *nf* kindness *no pl*
bonus [bɔnys] *nm* (*Assurances*) no-claims bonus; (*de DVD*) extras *pl*
bord [bɔr] *nm* (*de table, verre, falaise*) edge; (*de rivière, lac*) bank; (*de route*) side; **(monter) à ~** (to go) on board; **jeter par-dessus ~** to throw overboard; **le commandant de ~/les hommes du ~** the ship's master/crew; **au ~ de la mer/route** at the seaside/roadside; **être au ~ des larmes** to be on the verge of tears
bordeaux [bɔrdo] *nm* Bordeaux ▷ *adj inv* maroon
bordel [bɔrdɛl] *nm* brothel; (*fam!*) bloody (BRIT) ou goddamn (US) mess (!)
border [bɔrde] /1/ *vt* (*être le long de*) to line, border; (*qn dans son lit*) to tuck up; **~ qch de** (*garnir*) to trim sth with
bordure [bɔrdyr] *nf* border; **en ~ de** on the edge of
borne [bɔrn] *nf* boundary stone; (*aussi:* **~ kilométrique**) kilometre-marker, ≈ milestone; **bornes** *nfpl* (*fig*) limits; **dépasser les ~s** to go too far
borné, e [bɔrne] *adj* (*personne*) narrow-minded
borner [bɔrne] /1/ *vt*: **se ~ à faire** (*se contenter de*) to content o.s. with doing; (*se limiter à*) to limit o.s. to doing
bosniaque [bɔznjak] *adj* Bosnian ▷ *nm/f*: **B~** Bosnian
Bosnie-Herzégovine [bɔsniɛrzegovin] *nf* Bosnia-Herzegovina
bosquet [bɔskɛ] *nm* grove

bosse [bɔs] nf (de terrain etc) bump; (enflure) lump; (du bossu, du chameau) hump; **avoir la ~ des maths** etc (fam) to have a gift for maths etc; **il a roulé sa ~** (fam) he's been around

bosser [bɔse] /1/ vi (fam) to work; (: dur) to slave (away)

bossu, e [bɔsy] nm/f hunchback

botanique [bɔtanik] nf botany ▷ adj botanic(al)

botte [bɔt] nf (soulier) (high) boot; (gerbe): **~ de paille** bundle of straw; **~ de radis/d'asperges** bunch of radishes/asparagus; **~s de caoutchouc** wellington boots

bottine [bɔtin] nf ankle boot

bouc [buk] nm goat; (barbe) goatee; **~ émissaire** scapegoat

boucan [bukɑ̃] nm din, racket

bouche [buʃ] nf mouth; **faire du ~ à ~ à qn** to give sb the kiss of life (BRIT), give sb mouth-to-mouth resuscitation; **rester ~ bée** to stand open-mouthed; **~ d'égout** manhole; **~ d'incendie** fire hydrant; **~ de métro** métro entrance

bouché, e [buʃe] adj (flacon etc) stoppered; (temps, ciel) overcast; (péj: personne) thick; **avoir le nez ~** to have a blocked(-up) nose; **c'est un secteur ~** there's no future in that area; **l'évier est ~** the sink's blocked

bouchée [buʃe] nf mouthful; **~s à la reine** chicken vol-au-vents

boucher [buʃe] /1/ nm butcher ▷ vt (pour colmater) to stop up; (trou) to fill up; (obstruer) to block (up); **se boucher** vi (tuyau etc) to block up, get blocked up; **j'ai le nez bouché** my nose is blocked; **se ~ le nez** to hold one's nose

bouchère [buʃɛʀ] nf butcher

boucherie nf butcher's (shop); (fig) slaughter

bouchon [buʃɔ̃] nm (en liège) cork; (autre matière) stopper; (de tube) top; (fig: embouteillage) holdup; (Pêche) float

boucle [bukl] nf (forme, figure) loop; (objet) buckle; **~ (de cheveux)** curl; **~ d'oreille** earring

bouclé, e [bukle] adj (cheveux) curly

boucler [bukle] /1/ vt (fermer: ceinture etc) to fasten; (terminer) to finish off; (enfermer) to shut away; (quartier) to seal off ▷ vi to curl

bouder [bude] /1/ vi to sulk ▷ vt (personne) to refuse to have anything to do with

boudin [budɛ̃] nm: **~ (noir)** black pudding; **~ blanc** white pudding

boue [bu] nf mud

bouée [bwe] nf buoy; **~ (de sauvetage)** lifebuoy

boueux, -euse [bwø, -øz] adj muddy

bouffe [buf] nf (fam) grub, food

bouffée [bufe] nf (de cigarette) puff; **une ~ d'air pur** a breath of fresh air; **~ de chaleur** hot flush (BRIT) ou flash (US)

bouffer [bufe] /1/ vi (fam) to eat

bouffi, e [bufi] adj swollen

bouger [buʒe] /3/ vi to move; (dent etc) to be loose; (s'activer) to get moving ▷ vt to move; **les prix/les couleurs n'ont pas bougé** prices/ colours haven't changed

bougie [buʒi] nf candle; (Auto) spark(ing) plug

bouillabaisse [bujabɛs] nf type of fish soup

bouillant, e [bujɑ̃, -ɑ̃t] adj (qui bout) boiling; (très chaud) boiling (hot)

bouillie [buji] nf (de bébé) cereal; **en ~** (fig) crushed

bouillir [bujiʀ] /15/ vi to boil ▷ vt to boil; **~ de colère** etc to seethe with anger etc

bouilloire [bujwaʀ] nf kettle

bouillon [bujɔ̃] nm (Culin) stock no pl; **bouillonner** /1/ vi to bubble; (fig: idées) to bubble up

bouillotte [bujɔt] nf hot-water bottle

boulanger, -ère [bulɑ̃ʒe, -ɛʀ] nm/f baker; **boulangerie** nf bakery

boule [bul] *nf* (*gén*) ball; (*de pétanque*) bowl; **~ de neige** snowball

boulette [bulɛt] *nf* (*de viande*) meatball

boulevard [bulvaʀ] *nm* boulevard

bouleversement [bulvɛʀsəmɑ̃] *nm* upheaval

bouleverser [bulvɛʀse] /1/ *vt* (*émouvoir*) to overwhelm; (*causer du chagrin à*) to distress; (*pays, vie*) to disrupt; (*papiers, objets*) to turn upside down

boulimie [bulimi] *nf* bulimia

boulimique [bulimik] *adj* bulimic

boulon [bulɔ̃] *nm* bolt

boulot¹ [bulo] *nm* (*fam: travail*) work

boulot², te [bulo, -ɔt] *adj* plump, tubby

boum [bum] *nm* bang ▷ *nf* (*fam*) party

bouquet [bukɛ] *nm* (*de fleurs*) bunch (of flowers), bouquet; (*de persil etc*) bunch; **c'est le ~!** that's the last straw!

bouquin [bukɛ̃] *nm* (*fam*) book; **bouquiner** /1/ *vi* (*fam*) to read

bourdon [buʀdɔ̃] *nm* bumblebee

bourg [buʀ] *nm* small market town (*ou* village)

bourgeois, e [buʀʒwa, -waz] *adj* ≈ (upper) middle class; **bourgeoisie** *nf* ≈ upper middle classes *pl*

bourgeon [buʀʒɔ̃] *nm* bud

Bourgogne [buʀgɔɲ] *nf*: **la ~** Burgundy ▷ *nm*: **b~** Burgundy (wine)

bourguignon, ne [buʀɡiɲɔ̃, -ɔn] *adj* of *ou* from Burgundy, Burgundian

bourrasque [buʀask] *nf* squall

bourratif, -ive [buʀatif, -iv] (*fam*) *adj* filling, stodgy

bourré, e [buʀe] *adj* (*rempli*): **~ de** crammed full of; (*fam: ivre*) pickled, plastered

bourrer [buʀe] /1/ *vt* (*pipe*) to fill; (*poêle*) to pack; (*valise*) to cram (full)

bourru, e [buʀy] *adj* surly, gruff

bourse [buʀs] *nf* (*subvention*) grant; (*porte-monnaie*) purse; **la B~** the Stock Exchange

bous [bu] *vb voir* **bouillir**

bousculade [buskylad] *nf* (*hâte*) rush; (*poussée*) crush; **bousculer** /1/ *vt* (*heurter*) to knock into; (*fig*) to push, rush

boussole [busɔl] *nf* compass

bout [bu] *vb voir* **bouillir** ▷ *nm* bit; (*d'un bâton etc*) tip; (*d'une ficelle, table, rue, période*) end; **au ~ de** at the end of, after; **pousser qn à ~** to push sb to the limit (of his patience); **venir à ~ de** to manage to finish (off) *ou* overcome; **à ~ portant** at point-blank range

bouteille [butɛj] *nf* bottle; (*de gaz butane*) cylinder

boutique [butik] *nf* shop

bouton [butɔ̃] *nm* button; (*Bot*) bud; (*sur la peau*) spot; **boutonner** /1/ *vt* to button up; **boutonnière** *nf* buttonhole; **bouton-pression** *nm* press stud

bovin, e [bɔvɛ̃, -in] *adj* bovine ▷ *nm*: **~s** cattle *pl*

bowling [boliŋ] *nm* (tenpin) bowling; (*salle*) bowling alley

boxe [bɔks] *nf* boxing

BP *sigle f* = **boîte postale**

bracelet [bʀaslɛ] *nm* bracelet

braconnier [bʀakɔnje] *nm* poacher

brader [bʀade] /1/ *vt* to sell off; **braderie** *nf* cut-price (BRIT) *ou* cut-rate (US) stall

braguette [bʀagɛt] *nf* fly, flies *pl* (BRIT), zipper (US)

braise [bʀɛz] *nf* embers *pl*

brancard [bʀɑ̃kaʀ] *nm* (*civière*) stretcher; **brancardier** *nm* stretcher-bearer

branche [bʀɑ̃ʃ] *nf* branch

branché, e [bʀɑ̃ʃe] *adj* (*fam*) trendy

brancher [bʀɑ̃ʃe] /1/ *vt* to connect (up); (*en mettant la prise*) to plug in

brandir [bʀɑ̃diʀ] /2/ *vt* to brandish

braquer [bʀake] /1/ *vi* (*Auto*) to turn (the wheel) ▷ *vt* (*revolver etc*): **~ qch sur** to aim sth at, point sth at; (*mettre en colère*): **~ qn** to antagonize sb

bras [bʀɑ] *nm* arm; **~ dessus ~ dessous** arm in arm; **se retrouver avec qch sur les ~** (*fam*) to be landed with sth; **~ droit** (*fig*) right hand man

brassard [bʀasaʀ] *nm* armband

brasse [bʀas] *nf* (*nage*) breast-stroke; **~ papillon** butterfly(-stroke)

brassée [bʀase] *nf* armful

brasser [bʀase] /1/ *vt* to mix; **~ l'argent/les affaires** to handle a lot of money/ business

brasserie [bʀasʀi] *nf* (*restaurant*) bar (*selling food*); (*usine*) brewery

brave [bʀav] *adj* (*courageux*) brave; (*bon, gentil*) good, kind

braver [bʀave] /1/ *vt* to defy

bravo [bʀavo] *excl* bravo! ▷ *nm* cheer

bravoure [bʀavuʀ] *nf* bravery

break [bʀɛk] *nm* (*Auto*) estate car

brebis [bʀəbi] *nf* ewe; **~ galeuse** black sheep

bredouiller [bʀəduje] /1/ *vi, vt* to mumble, stammer

bref, brève [bʀɛf, bʀɛv] *adj* short, brief ▷ *adv* in short; **d'un ton ~** sharply, curtly; **en ~** in short, in brief

Brésil [bʀezil] *nm*: **le ~** Brazil

Bretagne [bʀətaɲ] *nf*: **la ~** Brittany

bretelle [bʀətɛl] *nf* (*de vêtement*) strap; (*d'autoroute*) slip road (BRIT), entrance *ou* exit ramp (US); **bretelles** *nfpl* (*pour pantalon*) braces (BRIT), suspenders (US)

breton, ne [bʀətɔ̃, -ɔn] *adj* Breton ▷ *nm/f*: **B~, ne** Breton

brève [bʀɛv] *adj f voir* **bref**

brevet [bʀəvɛ] *nm* diploma, certificate; **~ (des collèges)** *school certificate, taken at approx. 16 years*; **~ (d'invention)** patent; **breveté, e** *adj* patented

bricolage [bʀikɔlaʒ] *nm*: **le ~** do-it-yourself (jobs)

bricoler [bʀikɔle] /1/ *vi* (*en amateur*) to do DIY jobs; (*passe-temps*) to potter about ▷ *vt* (*réparer*) to fix up; **bricoleur, -euse** *nm/f* handyman/woman, DIY enthusiast

bridge [bʀidʒ] *nm* (*Cartes*) bridge

brièvement [bʀijɛvmɑ̃] *adv* briefly

brigade [bʀigad] *nf* (*Police*) squad; (*Mil*) brigade; **brigadier** *nm* ≈ sergeant

brillamment [bʀijamɑ̃] *adv* brilliantly

brillant, e [bʀijɑ̃, -ɑ̃t] *adj* (*remarquable*) bright; (*luisant*) shiny, shining

briller [bʀije] /1/ *vi* to shine

brin [bʀɛ̃] *nm* (*de laine, ficelle etc*) strand; (*fig*): **un ~ de** a bit of

brindille [bʀɛ̃dij] *nf* twig

brioche [bʀijɔʃ] *nf* brioche (bun); (*fam: ventre*) paunch

brique [bʀik] *nf* brick; (*de lait*) carton

briquet [bʀikɛ] *nm* (cigarette) lighter

brise [bʀiz] *nf* breeze

briser [bʀize] /1/ *vt* to break; **se briser** *vi* to break

britannique [bʀitanik] *adj* British ▷ *nm/f*: **B~** Briton, British person; **les B~s** the British

brocante [bʀɔkɑ̃t] *nf* (*objets*) secondhand goods *pl*, junk; **brocanteur, -euse** *nm/f* junk shop owner; junk dealer

broche [bʀɔʃ] *nf* brooch; (*Culin*) spit; (*Méd*) pin; **à la ~** spit-roasted

broché, e [bʀɔʃe] *adj* (*livre*) paper-backed

brochet [bʀɔʃɛ] *nm* pike *inv*

brochette [bʀɔʃɛt] *nf* (*ustensile*) skewer; (*plat*) kebab

brochure [bʀɔʃyʀ] *nf* pamphlet, brochure, booklet

broder [bʀɔde] /1/ *vt* to embroider ▷ *vi*: **~ (sur des faits** *ou* **une histoire)** to embroider the facts; **broderie** *nf* embroidery

bronches [bʀɔ̃ʃ] *nfpl* bronchial tubes; **bronchite** *nf* bronchitis

bronze [bʀɔ̃z] *nm* bronze

bronzer [bʀɔ̃ze] /1/ *vi* to get a tan; **se bronzer** to sunbathe

brosse [bʀɔs] *nf* brush; **coiffé en ~** with a crewcut; **~ à cheveux**

hairbrush; **~ à dents** toothbrush; **~ à habits** clothesbrush; **brosser** /1/ *vt* (*nettoyer*) to brush; (*fig: tableau etc*) to paint; **se brosser les dents** to brush one's teeth

brouette [bʀuɛt] *nf* wheelbarrow

brouillard [bʀujaʀ] *nm* fog

brouiller [bʀuje] /1/ *vt* (*œufs, message*) to scramble; (*idées*) to mix up; (*rendre trouble*) to cloud; (*désunir: amis*) to set at odds; **se brouiller** *vi* (*ciel, vue*) to cloud over; **se ~ (avec)** to fall out (with)

brouillon, ne [bʀujɔ̃, -ɔn] *adj* (*sans soin*) untidy; (*qui manque d'organisation*) disorganized ▷ *nm* (first) draft; **(papier) ~** rough paper

broussailles [bʀusaj] *nfpl* undergrowth *sg*; **broussailleux, -euse** *adj* bushy

brousse [bʀus] *nf*: **la ~** the bush

brouter [bʀute] /1/ *vi* to graze

brugnon [bʀyɲɔ̃] *nm* nectarine

bruiner [bʀɥine] /1/ *vb impers*: **il bruine** it's drizzling, there's a drizzle

bruit [bʀɥi] *nm*: **un ~** a noise, a sound; (*fig: rumeur*) a rumour; **le ~** noise; **sans ~** without a sound, noiselessly; **~ de fond** background noise

brûlant, e [bʀylɑ̃, -ɑ̃t] *adj* burning (hot); (*liquide*) boiling (hot)

brûlé, e [bʀyle] *adj* (*fig: démasqué*) blown ▷ *nm*: **odeur de ~** smell of burning

brûler [bʀyle] /1/ *vt* to burn; (*eau bouillante*) to scald; (*consommer: électricité, essence*) to use; (: *feu rouge, signal*) to go through (without stopping) ▷ *vi* to burn; **se brûler** to burn o.s.; (*s'ébouillanter*) to scald o.s.; **tu brûles** (*jeu*) you're getting warm ou hot

brûlure [bʀylyʀ] *nf* (*lésion*) burn; **~s d'estomac** heartburn *sg*

brume [bʀym] *nf* mist

brumeux, -euse [bʀymø, -øz] *adj* misty

brun, e [bʀœ̃, -yn] *adj* (*gén, bière*) brown; (*cheveux, personne, tabac*) dark; **elle est ~e** she's got dark hair

brunch [bʀœntʃ] *nm* brunch

brushing [bʀœʃiŋ] *nm* blow-dry

brusque [bʀysk] *adj* abrupt

brut, e [bʀyt] *adj* (*diamant*) uncut; (*soie, minéral*) raw; (*Comm*) gross; **(pétrole) ~** crude (oil)

brutal, e, -aux [bʀytal, -o] *adj* brutal

Bruxelles [bʀysɛl] *n* Brussels

bruyamment [bʀɥijamɑ̃] *adv* noisily

bruyant, e [bʀɥijɑ̃, -ɑ̃t] *adj* noisy

bruyère [bʀɥijɛʀ] *nf* heather

BTS *sigle m* (= *Brevet de technicien supérieur*) *vocational training certificate taken at end of two-year higher education course*

bu, e [by] *pp de* **boire**

buccal, e, -aux [bykal, -o] *adj*: **par voie ~e** orally

bûche [byʃ] *nf* log; **prendre une ~** (*fig*) to come a cropper (*BRIT*), fall flat on one's face; **~ de Noël** Yule log

bûcher [byʃe] /1/ *nm* (*funéraire*) pyre; (*supplice*) stake ▷ *vi* (*fam*) to swot, slave (away) ▷ *vt* to swot up, slave away at

budget [bydʒɛ] *nm* budget

buée [bɥe] *nf* (*sur une vitre*) mist

buffet [byfɛ] *nm* (*meuble*) sideboard; (*de réception*) buffet; **~ (de gare)** (station) buffet, snack bar

buis [bɥi] *nm* box tree; (*bois*) box(wood)

buisson [bɥisɔ̃] *nm* bush

bulbe [bylb] *nm* (*Bot, Anat*) bulb

Bulgarie [bylgaʀi] *nf*: **la ~** Bulgaria

bulle [byl] *nf* bubble

bulletin [byltɛ̃] *nm* (*communiqué, journal*) bulletin; (*Scol*) report; **~ d'informations** news bulletin; **~ (de vote)** ballot paper; **~ météorologique** weather report

bureau, x [byʀo] *nm* (*meuble*) desk; (*pièce, service*) office; **~ de change** (foreign) exchange office *ou* bureau;

~ **de poste** post office; ~ **de tabac** tobacconist's (shop); **bureaucratie** [byʀokʀasi] *nf* bureaucracy

bus¹ *vb* [by] *voir* **boire**

bus² *nm* [bys] (*véhicule*) bus

buste [byst] *nm* (*Anat*) chest (: *de femme*) bust

but [by] *vb voir* **boire** ▷ *nm* (*cible*) target; (*fig*) goal, aim; (*Football etc*) goal; **de ~ en blanc** point-blank; **avoir pour ~ de faire** to aim to do; **dans le ~ de** with the intention of

butane [bytan] *nm* butane; (*domestique*) calor gas® (BRIT), butane

butiner [bytine] /1/ *vi* (*abeilles*) to gather nectar

buvais *etc* [byvε] *vb voir* **boire**

buvard [byvaʀ] *nm* blotter

buvette [byvεt] *nf* bar

c' [s] *pron voir* **ce**

ça [sa] *pron* (*pour désigner*) this (: *plus loin*) that; (*comme sujet indéfini*) it; **ça m'étonne que** it surprises me that; **ça va?** how are you?; how are things?; (*d'accord?*) OK?, all right?; **où ça?** where's that?; **pourquoi ça?** why's that?; **qui ça?** who's that?; **ça alors!** (*désapprobation*) well!, really!; **c'est ça** that's right; **ça y est** that's it

cabane [kaban] *nf* hut, cabin

cabaret [kabaʀε] *nm* night club

cabillaud [kabijo] *nm* cod *inv*

cabine [kabin] *nf* (*de bateau*) cabin; (*de piscine etc*) cubicle; (*de camion, train*) cab; (*d'avion*) cockpit; ~ **d'essayage** fitting room; ~ **(téléphonique)** call *ou* (tele) phone box

cabinet [kabinε] *nm* (*petite pièce*) closet; (*de médecin*) surgery (BRIT), office (US); (*de notaire etc*) office (: *clientèle*) practice; (*Pol*) cabinet;

cabinets *nmpl* (*w.-c.*) toilet *sg*; **~ de toilette** toilet

câble [kɑbl] *nm* cable; **le ~** (*TV*) cable television, cablevision (*us*)

cacahuète [kakaɥɛt] *nf* peanut

cacao [kakao] *nm* cocoa

cache [kaʃ] *nm* mask, card (*for masking*)

cache-cache [kaʃkaʃ] *nm*: **jouer à ~** to play hide-and-seek

cachemire [kaʃmir] *nm* cashmere

cacher [kaʃe] /1/ *vt* to hide, conceal; **~ qch à qn** to hide *ou* conceal sth from sb; **se cacher** *vi* (*volontairement*) to hide; (*être caché*) to be hidden *ou* concealed

cachet [kaʃɛ] *nm* (*comprimé*) tablet; (*de la poste*) postmark; (*rétribution*) fee; (*fig*) style, character

cachette [kaʃɛt] *nf* hiding place; **en ~** on the sly, secretly

cactus [kaktys] *nm* cactus

cadavre [kadɑvr] *nm* corpse, (dead) body

Caddie® [kadi] *nm* (supermarket) trolley (*brit*), (grocery) cart (*us*)

cadeau, x [kado] *nm* present, gift; **faire un ~ à qn** to give sb a present *ou* gift; **faire ~ de qch à qn** to make a present of sth to sb, give sb sth as a present

cadenas [kadnɑ] *nm* padlock

cadet, te [kadɛ, -ɛt] *adj* younger; (*le plus jeune*) youngest ▷ *nm/f* youngest child *ou* one

cadran [kadrɑ̃] *nm* dial; **~ solaire** sundial

cadre [kadr] *nm* frame; (*environnement*) surroundings *pl* ▷ *nm/f* (*Admin*) managerial employee, executive; **dans le ~ de** (*fig*) within the framework *ou* context of

cafard [kafar] *nm* cockroach; **avoir le ~** to be down in the dumps

café [kafe] *nm* coffee; (*bistro*) café ▷ *adj inv* coffee *cpd*; **~ au lait** white coffee; **~ noir** black coffee; **café-tabac** *nm* tobacconist's or newsagent's

also serving coffee and spirits; **cafétéria** [kafeterja] *nf* cafeteria; **cafetière** *nf* (*pot*) coffee-pot

cage [kaʒ] *nf* cage; **~ d'escalier** (stair) well; **~ thoracique** rib cage

cageot [kaʒo] *nm* crate

cagoule [kagul] *nf* (*passe-montagne*) balaclava

cahier [kaje] *nm* notebook; **~ de brouillons** rough book, jotter; **~ d'exercices** exercise book

caille [kaj] *nf* quail

caillou, x [kaju] *nm* (little) stone; **caillouteux, -euse** *adj* stony

Caire [kɛr] *nm*: **le ~** Cairo

caisse [kɛs] *nf* box; (*où l'on met la recette*) till; (*où l'on paye*) cash desk (*brit*), checkout counter; (: *au supermarché*) checkout; (*de banque*) cashier's desk; **~ enregistreuse** cash register; **~ d'épargne (CE)** savings bank; **~ de retraite** pension fund; **caissier, -ière** *nm/f* cashier

cake [kɛk] *nm* fruit cake

calandre [kalɑ̃dr] *nf* radiator grill

calcaire [kalkɛr] *nm* limestone ▷ *adj* (*eau*) hard; (*Géo*) limestone *cpd*

calcul [kalkyl] *nm* calculation; **le ~** (*Scol*) arithmetic; **~ (biliaire)** (*gall*) stone; **calculateur** *nm*, **calculatrice** *nf* calculator; **calculer** /1/ *vt* to calculate, work out; **calculette** *nf* (pocket) calculator

cale [kal] *nf* (*de bateau*) hold; (*en bois*) wedge

calé, e [kale] *adj* (*fam*) clever, bright

caleçon [kalsɔ̃] *nm* (*d'homme*) boxer shorts; (*de femme*) leggings

calendrier [kalɑ̃drije] *nm* calendar; (*fig*) timetable

calepin [kalpɛ̃] *nm* notebook

caler [kale] /1/ *vt* to wedge ▷ *vi* (*moteur, véhicule*) to stall

calibre [kalibr] *nm* calibre

câlin, e [kɑlɛ̃, -in] *adj* cuddly, cuddlesome; (*regard, voix*) tender

calmant [kalmɑ̃] *nm* tranquillizer, sedative; (*contre la douleur*) painkiller

calme [kalm] *adj* calm, quiet ▷ *nm* calm(ness), quietness; **sans perdre son ~** without losing one's cool *ou* calmness; **calmer** /1/ *vt* to calm (down); (*douleur, inquiétude*) to ease, soothe; **se calmer** *vi* to calm down

calorie [kalɔʀi] *nf* calorie

camarade [kamaʀad] *nm/f* friend, pal; (*Pol*) comrade

Cambodge [kɑ̃bɔdʒ] *nm*: **le ~** Cambodia

cambriolage [kɑ̃bʀijɔlaʒ] *nm* burglary; **cambrioler** /1/ *vt* to burgle (*BRIT*), burglarize (*US*); **cambrioleur, -euse** *nm/f* burglar

camelote [kamlɔt] (*fam*) *nf* rubbish, trash, junk

caméra [kameʀa] *nf* (*Ciné, TV*) camera; (*d'amateur*) cine-camera

Cameroun [kamʀun] *nm*: **le ~** Cameroon

caméscope® [kameskɔp] *nm* camcorder

camion [kamjɔ̃] *nm* lorry (*BRIT*), truck; **~ de dépannage** breakdown (*BRIT*) *ou* tow (*US*) truck; **camionnette** *nf* (small) van; **camionneur** *nm* (*entrepreneur*) haulage contractor (*BRIT*), trucker (*US*); (*chauffeur*) lorry (*BRIT*) *ou* truck driver

camomille [kamɔmij] *nf* camomile; (*boisson*) camomile tea

camp [kɑ̃] *nm* camp; (*fig*) side

campagnard, e [kɑ̃paɲaʀ, -aʀd] *adj* country *cpd*

campagne [kɑ̃paɲ] *nf* country, countryside; (*Mil, Pol, Comm*) campaign; **à la ~** in/to the country

camper [kɑ̃pe] /1/ *vi* to camp ▷ *vt* to sketch; **se ~ devant** to plant o.s. in front of; **campeur, -euse** *nm/f* camper

camping [kɑ̃piŋ] *nm* camping; **(terrain de) ~** campsite, camping site; **faire du ~** to go camping; **camping-car** *nm* camper, motorhome (*US*); **camping-gaz®** *nm inv* camp(ing) stove

Canada [kanada] *nm*: **le ~** Canada; **canadien, ne** *adj* Canadian ▷ *nm/f*: **Canadien, ne** Canadian ▷ *nf* (*veste*) fur-lined jacket

canal, -aux [kanal, -o] *nm* canal; (*naturel, TV*) channel; **canalisation** *nf* (*tuyau*) pipe

canapé [kanape] *nm* settee, sofa

canard [kanaʀ] *nm* duck; (*fam: journal*) rag

cancer [kɑ̃sɛʀ] *nm* cancer; (*signe*): **le C~** Cancer

cancre [kɑ̃kʀ] *nm* dunce

candidat, e [kɑ̃dida, -at] *nm/f* candidate; (*à un poste*) applicant, candidate; **candidature** *nf* (*Pol*) candidature; (*à poste*) application; **poser sa candidature à un poste** to apply for a job

cane [kan] *nf* (female) duck

canette [kanɛt] *nf* (*de bière*) (flip-top) bottle

canevas [kanva] *nm* (*Couture*) canvas (for tapestry work)

caniche [kaniʃ] *nm* poodle

canicule [kanikyl] *nf* scorching heat

canif [kanif] *nm* penknife, pocket knife

canne [kan] *nf* (walking) stick; **~ à pêche** fishing rod; **~ à sucre** sugar cane

cannelle [kanɛl] *nf* cinnamon

canoë [kanɔe] *nm* canoe; (*sport*) canoeing; **~ (kayak)** kayak

canot [kano] *nm* ding(h)y; **~ pneumatique** rubber *ou* inflatable ding(h)y; **~ de sauvetage** lifeboat

cantatrice [kɑ̃tatʀis] *nf* (opera) singer

cantine [kɑ̃tin] *nf* canteen

canton [kɑ̃tɔ̃] *nm* district (consisting of several communes); (*en Suisse*) canton

caoutchouc [kautʃu] *nm* rubber; **~ mousse** foam rubber; **en ~** rubber *cpd*

CAP *sigle m* (= *Certificat d'aptitude professionnelle*) vocational training certificate taken at secondary school

cap [kap] nm (Géo) cape; (promontoire) headland; (fig: tournant) watershed; (Navig): **changer de ~** to change course; **mettre le ~ sur** to head ou steer for

capable [kapabl] adj able, capable; **~ de qch/faire** capable of sth/doing

capacité [kapasite] nf (compétence) ability; (Jur, Inform, d'un récipient) capacity

cape [kap] nf cape, cloak; **rire sous ~** to laugh up one's sleeve

CAPES [kapɛs] sigle m (= Certificat d'aptitude au professorat de l'enseignement du second degré) secondary teaching diploma

capitaine [kapitɛn] nm captain

capital, e, -aux [kapital, -o] adj (œuvre) major; (question, rôle) fundamental ▷ nm capital; (fig) stock ▷ nf (ville) capital; (lettre) capital (letter); **d'une importance ~e** of capital importance; **capitaux** nmpl (fonds) capital sg; **~ (social)** authorized capital; **~ d'exploitation** working capital; **capitalisme** nm capitalism; **capitaliste** adj, nm/f capitalist

caporal, -aux [kapɔral, -o] nm lance corporal

capot [kapo] nm (Auto) bonnet (BRIT), hood (US)

câpre [kɑpr] nf caper

caprice [kapris] nm whim, caprice; **faire des ~s** to be temperamental; **capricieux, -euse** adj (fantasque) capricious; whimsical; (enfant) temperamental

Capricorne [kaprikɔrn] nm: **le ~** Capricorn

capsule [kapsyl] nf (de bouteille) cap; cap; (Bot etc, spatiale) capsule

capter [kapte] /1/ vt (ondes radio) to pick up; (fig) to win, capture

captivant, e [kaptivɑ̃, -ɑ̃t] adj captivating

capturer [kaptyre] /1/ vt to capture

capuche [kapyʃ] nf hood

capuchon [kapyʃɔ̃] nm hood; (de stylo) cap, top

car [kar] nm coach (BRIT), bus ▷ conj because, for

carabine [karabin] nf rifle

caractère [karaktɛr] nm (gén) character; **en ~s gras** in bold type; **en petits ~s** in small print; **en ~s d'imprimerie** in block capitals; **avoir bon/mauvais ~** to be good-/ ill-natured ou tempered

caractériser [karakterize] /1/ vt to characterize; **se ~ par** to be characterized ou distinguished by

caractéristique [karakteristik] adj, nf characteristic

carafe [karaf] nf decanter; (pour eau, vin ordinaire) carafe

caraïbe [karaib] adj Caribbean; **les Caraïbes** nfpl the Caribbean (Islands)

carambolage [karɑ̃bɔlaʒ] nm multiple crash, pileup

caramel [karamɛl] nm (bonbon) caramel, toffee; (substance) caramel

caravane [karavan] nf caravan; **caravaning** nm caravanning

carbone [karbɔn] nm carbon; (double) carbon (copy)

carbonique [karbɔnik] adj: **gaz ~** carbon dioxide; **neige ~** dry ice

carbonisé, e [karbɔnize] adj charred

carburant [karbyrɑ̃] nm (motor) fuel

carburateur [karbyratœr] nm carburettor

cardiaque [kardjak] adj cardiac, heart cpd ▷ nm/f heart patient; **être ~** to have a heart condition

cardigan [kardigɑ̃] nm cardigan

cardiologue [kardjɔlɔg] nm/f cardiologist, heart specialist

Carême [karɛm] nm: **le ~** Lent

carence [karɑ̃s] nf (manque) deficiency

caresse [karɛs] nf caress

caresser [karese] /1/ vt to caress; (animal) to stroke

cargaison [kaʁgɛzɔ̃] *nf* cargo, freight
cargo [kaʁgo] *nm* cargo boat, freighter
caricature [kaʁikatyʁ] *nf* caricature
carie [kaʁi] *nf*: **la ~ (dentaire)** tooth decay; **une ~** a bad tooth
carnaval [kaʁnaval] *nm* carnival
carnet [kaʁnɛ] *nm* (*calepin*) notebook; (*de tickets, timbres etc*) book; **~ de chèques** cheque book
carotte [kaʁɔt] *nf* carrot
carré, e [kaʁe] *adj* square; (*fig: franc*) straightforward ▷ *nm* (*Math*) square; **mètre/kilomètre ~** square metre/kilometre
carreau, x [kaʁo] *nm* (*en faïence etc*) (floor) tile; (*au mur*) (wall) tile; (*de fenêtre*) (window) pane; (*motif*) check, square; (*Cartes: couleur*) diamonds *pl*; **tissu à ~x** checked fabric
carrefour [kaʁfuʁ] *nm* crossroads *sg*
carrelage [kaʁlaʒ] *nm* (*sol*) (tiled) floor
carrelet [kaʁlɛ] *nm* (*poisson*) plaice
carrément [kaʁemɑ̃] *adv* (*franchement*) straight out, bluntly; (*sans détours, sans hésiter*) straight; (*intensif*) completely; **c'est ~ impossible** it's completely impossible
carrière [kaʁjɛʁ] *nf* (*de roches*) quarry; (*métier*) career; **militaire de ~** professional soldier
carrosserie [kaʁɔsʁi] *nf* body, bodywork *no pl* (BRIT)
carrure [kaʁyʁ] *nf* build; (*fig*) stature, calibre
cartable [kaʁtabl] *nm* satchel, (school)bag
carte [kaʁt] *nf* (*de géographie*) map; (*marine, du ciel*) chart; (*de fichier, d'abonnement etc, à jouer*) card; (*au restaurant*) menu; (*aussi:* **~ postale**) (post)card; (*aussi:* **~ de visite**) (visiting) card; **avoir/donner ~ blanche** to have/give carte blanche *ou* a free hand; **à la ~** (*au restaurant*) à la carte; **~ à puce**

smartcard; **~ bancaire** cash card; **C~ Bleue®** debit card; **~ de crédit** credit card; **~ de fidélité** loyalty card; **~ d'identité** identity card; **la ~ grise** (*Auto*) ≈ the (car) registration document; **~ mémoire** (*d'appareil photo numérique*) memory card; **~ routière** road map; **~ de séjour** residence permit; **~ SIM** SIM card; **~ téléphonique** phonecard
carter [kaʁtɛʁ] *nm* sump
carton [kaʁtɔ̃] *nm* (*matériau*) cardboard; (*boîte*) (cardboard) box; **faire un ~** to score a hit; **~ (à dessin)** portfolio
cartouche [kaʁtuʃ] *nf* cartridge; (*de cigarettes*) carton
cas [kɑ] *nm* case; **ne faire aucun ~ de** to take no notice of; **en aucun ~** on no account; **au ~ où** in case; **en ~ de** in case of, in the event of; **en ~ de besoin** if need be; **en tout ~** in any case, at any rate
cascade [kaskad] *nf* waterfall, cascade
case [kɑz] *nf* (*hutte*) hut; (*compartiment*) compartment; (*sur un formulaire, de mots croisés*) box
caser [kɑze] /1/ (*fam*) *vt* (*mettre*) to put; (*loger*) to put up; **se caser** *vi* (*se marier*) to settle down; (*trouver un emploi*) to find a (steady) job
caserne [kɑzɛʁn] *nf* barracks
casier [kɑzje] *nm* (*case*) compartment; (*pour courrier*) pigeonhole (: *à clef*) locker; **~ judiciaire** police record
casino [kazino] *nm* casino
casque [kask] *nm* helmet; (*chez le coiffeur*) (hair-)dryer; (*pour audition*) (head-)phones *pl*, headset
casquette [kaskɛt] *nf* cap
casse-croûte [kaskʁut] *nm inv* snack
casse-noisettes, casse-noix [kasnwazɛt, kasnwa] *nm inv* nutcrackers *pl*
casse-pieds [kaspje] *nm/f inv* (*fam*): **il est ~, c'est un ~** he's a pain (in the neck)
casser [kɑse] /1/ *vt* to break; (*Jur*) to quash; **se casser** *vi, vt* to break; **~ les**

pieds à qn (*fam: irriter*) to get on sb's nerves; **se ~ la tête** (*fam*) to go to a lot of trouble

casserole [kasʀɔl] *nf* saucepan

casse-tête [kastɛt] *nm inv* (*difficultés*) headache (*fig*)

cassette [kasɛt] *nf* (*bande magnétique*) cassette; (*coffret*) casket

cassis [kasis] *nm* blackcurrant

cassoulet [kasulɛ] *nm* sausage and bean hotpot

catalogue [katalɔg] *nm* catalogue

catalytique [katalitik] *adj*: **pot ~** catalytic converter

catastrophe [katastʀɔf] *nf* catastrophe, disaster

catéchisme [kateʃism] *nm* catechism

catégorie [kategɔʀi] *nf* category; **catégorique** *adj* categorical

cathédrale [katedʀal] *nf* cathedral

catholique [katɔlik] *adj, nm/f* (Roman) Catholic; **pas très ~** a bit shady *ou* fishy

cauchemar [koʃmaʀ] *nm* nightmare

cause [koz] *nf* cause; (*Jur*) lawsuit, case; **à ~ de** because of, owing to; **pour ~ de** on account of; **(et) pour ~** and for (a very) good reason; **être en ~** (*intérêts*) to be at stake; **remettre en ~** to challenge; **causer** /1/ *vt* to cause ▷ *vi* to chat, talk

caution [kosjɔ̃] *nf* guarantee, security; (*Jur*) bail (bond); (*fig*) backing, support; **libéré sous ~** released on bail

cavalier, -ière [kavalje, -jɛʀ] *adj* (*désinvolte*) offhand ▷ *nm/f* rider; (*au bal*) partner ▷ *nm* (*Échecs*) knight

cave [kav] *nf* cellar

caverne [kavɛʀn] *nf* cave

CD *sigle m* (= *compact disc*) CD

CD-ROM [sedeʀɔm] *nm inv* CD-Rom

 MOT-CLÉ

ce, cette [sə, sɛt] (*devant nm* **cet** + *voyelle ou h aspiré; pl* **ces**) *adj dém*

(*proximité*) this; these *pl*; (*non-proximité*) that; those *pl*; **cette maison(-ci/là)** this/that house; **cette nuit** (*qui vient*) tonight; (*passée*) last night

▶ *pron* 1 : **c'est** it's, it is; **c'est un peintre** he's *ou* he is a painter; **ce sont des peintres** they're *ou* they are painters; **c'est le facteur** *etc* (*à la porte*) it's the postman *etc*; **qui est-ce?** who is it?; (*en désignant*) who is he/she?; **qu'est-ce?** what is it?; **c'est toi qui lui as parlé** it was you who spoke to him

2 : **c'est ça** (*correct*) that's right

3 : **ce qui, ce que** what; **ce qui me plaît, c'est sa franchise** what I like about him *ou* her is his *ou* her frankness; **il est bête, ce qui me chagrine** he's stupid, which saddens me; **tout ce qui bouge** everything that *ou* which moves; **tout ce que je sais** all I know; **ce dont j'ai parlé** what I talked about; **ce que c'est grand!** it's so big!; *voir aussi* **c'est-à-dire; -ci; est-ce que; n'est-ce pas**

ceci [səsi] *pron* this

céder [sede] /6/ *vt* to give up ▷ *vi* (*pont, barrage*) to give way; (*personne*) to give in; **~ à** to yield to, give in to

cédérom [sedeʀɔm] *nm* CD-ROM

CEDEX [sedɛks] *sigle m* (= *courrier d'entreprise à distribution exceptionnelle*) accelerated postal service for bulk users

cédille [sedij] *nf* cedilla

ceinture [sɛ̃tyʀ] *nf* belt; (*taille*) waist; **~ de sécurité** safety *ou* seat belt

cela [s(ə)la] *pron* (*comme sujet indéfini*) it; **~ m'étonne que** it surprises me that; **quand/où ~?** when/where (was that)?

célèbre [selɛbʀ] *adj* famous; **célébrer** /6/ *vt* to celebrate

céleri [sɛlʀi] *nm*: **~(-rave)** celeriac; **~ (en branche)** celery

célibataire [selibatɛʀ] *adj* single, unmarried ▷ *nm/f* bachelor/

unmarried *ou* single woman; **mère ~** single *ou* unmarried mother

celle, celles [sɛl] *pron voir* **celui**

cellule [selyl] *nf* (*gén*) cell; **~ souche** stem cell

cellulite [selylit] *nf* cellulite

MOT-CLÉ

celui, celle (*mpl* **ceux**, *fpl* **celles**) [səlɥi, sɛl] *pron* **1** : **celui-ci/là, celle-ci/là** this one/that one; **ceux-ci, celles-ci** these (ones); **ceux-là, celles-là** those (ones); **celui de mon frère** my brother's; **celui du salon/du dessous** the one in (*ou* from) the lounge/below

2 (+ *relatif*): **celui qui bouge** the one which *ou* that moves; (*personne*) the one who moves; **celui que je vois** the one (which *ou* that) I see; (*personne*) the one (whom) I see; **celui dont je parle** the one I'm talking about

3 (*valeur indéfinie*): **celui qui veut** whoever wants

cendre [sɑ̃dʀ] *nf* ash; **~s** (*d'un défunt*) ashes; **sous la ~** (*Culin*) in (the) embers; **cendrier** *nm* ashtray

censé, e [sɑ̃se] *adj*: **être ~ faire** to be supposed to do

censeur [sɑ̃sœʀ] *nm* (*Scol*) deputy head (BRIT), vice-principal (US)

censure [sɑ̃syʀ] *nf* censorship; **censurer** /1/ *vt* (*Ciné, Presse*) to censor; (*Pol*) to censure

cent [sɑ̃] *num* a hundred, one hundred ▷ *nm* (US, Canada, partie de l'euro etc) cent; **centaine** *nf*: **une centaine (de)** about a hundred, a hundred or so; **des centaines (de)** hundreds (of); **centenaire** *adj* hundred-year-old ▷ *nm* (*anniversaire*) centenary; (*monnaie*) cent; **centième** *num* hundredth; **centigrade** *nm* centigrade; **centilitre** *nm* centilitre ; **centime** *nm* centime; **centime**

d'euro euro cent; **centimètre** *nm* centimetre; (*ruban*) tape measure, measuring tape

central, e, -aux [sɑ̃tʀal, -o] *adj* central ▷ *nm*: **~ (téléphonique)** (telephone) exchange ▷ *nf* power station; **~e électrique/nucléaire** electric/nuclear power station

centre [sɑ̃tʀ] *nm* centre ; **~ commercial/sportif/culturel** shopping/sports/arts centre; **~ d'appels** call centre; **centre-ville** *nm* town centre (BRIT) *ou* center (US)

cèpe [sɛp] *nm* (*edible*) boletus

cependant [s(ə)pɑ̃dɑ̃] *adv* however, nevertheless

céramique [seʀamik] *nf* ceramics *sg*

cercle [sɛʀkl] *nm* circle; **~ vicieux** vicious circle

cercueil [sɛʀkœj] *nm* coffin

céréale [seʀeal] *nf* cereal

cérémonie [seʀemɔni] *nf* ceremony; **sans ~** (*inviter, manger*) informally

cerf [sɛʀ] *nm* stag

cerf-volant [sɛʀvɔlɑ̃] *nm* kite

cerise [səʀiz] *nf* cherry; **cerisier** *nm* cherry (tree)

cerner [sɛʀne] /1/ *vt* (*Mil etc*) to surround; (*fig: problème*) to delimit, define

certain, e [sɛʀtɛ̃, -ɛn] *adj* certain; **~ (de/que)** certain *ou* sure (of/that); **d'un ~ âge** past one's prime, not so young; **un ~ temps** (quite) some time; **sûr et ~** absolutely certain; **un ~ Georges** someone called Georges; **~s** *pron* some; **certainement** *adv* (*probablement*) most probably *ou* likely; (*bien sûr*) certainly, of course

certes [sɛʀt] *adv* (*sans doute*) admittedly; (*bien sûr*) of course; indeed (yes)

certificat [sɛʀtifika] *nm* certificate

certifier [sɛʀtifje] /7/ *vt*: **~ qch à qn** to guarantee sth to sb

certitude [sɛʀtityd] *nf* certainty

cerveau, x [sɛʀvo] *nm* brain

cervelas [sɛʀvəla] *nm* saveloy

cervelle [sɛrvɛl] *nf* (*Anat*) brain; (*Culin*) brain(s)

CES *sigle m* (= *Collège d'enseignement secondaire*) ≈ (junior) secondary school

ces [se] *adj dém voir* **ce**

cesse [sɛs]: **sans ~** *adv* (*tout le temps*) continually, constantly; (*sans interruption*) continuously; **il n'avait de ~ que** he would not rest until; **cesser** /1/ *vt* to stop ▷ *vi* to stop, cease; **cesser de faire** to stop doing; **cessez-le-feu** *nm inv* ceasefire

c'est-à-dire [sɛtadir] *adv* that is (to say)

cet [sɛt] *adj dém voir* **ce**

ceux [sø] *pron voir* **celui**

chacun, e [ʃakœ̃, -yn] *pron* each; (*indéfini*) everyone, everybody

chagrin, e [ʃagrɛ̃, -in] *adj* morose ▷ *nm* grief, sorrow; **avoir du ~** to be grieved *ou* sorrowful

chahut [ʃay] *nm* uproar; **chahuter** /1/ *vt* to rag, bait ▷ *vi* to make an uproar

chaîne [ʃɛn] *nf* chain; (*Radio, TV: stations*) channel; **travail à la ~** production line work; **réactions en ~** chain reactions; **~ (haute-fidélité** *ou* **hi-fi)** hi-fi system; **~ (de montagnes)** (mountain) range

chair [ʃɛr] *nf* flesh; **avoir la ~ de poule** to have goose pimples *ou* goose flesh; **bien en ~** plump, well-padded; **en ~ et en os** in the flesh; **~ à saucisse** sausage meat

chaise [ʃɛz] *nf* chair; **~ longue** deckchair

châle [ʃal] *nm* shawl

chaleur [ʃalœr] *nf* heat; (*fig: d'accueil*) warmth; **chaleureux, -euse** *adj* warm

chamailler [ʃamaje] /1/: **se chamailler** *vi* to squabble, bicker

chambre [ʃɑ̃br] *nf* bedroom; (*Pol*) chamber; (*Comm*) chamber; **faire ~ à part** to sleep in separate rooms; **~ à un lit/deux lits** single/twin-bedded room; **~ à air** (*de pneu*) (inner) tube; **~ d'amis** spare *ou* guest room; **~ à**

coucher bedroom; **~ d'hôte** ≈ bed and breakfast (*in private home*); **~ meublée** bedsit(ter) (BRIT), furnished room; **~ noire** (*Photo*) dark room

chameau, x [ʃamo] *nm* camel

chamois [ʃamwa] *nm* chamois

champ [ʃɑ̃] *nm* field; **~ de bataille** battlefield; **~ de courses** racecourse

champagne [ʃɑ̃paɲ] *nm* champagne

champignon [ʃɑ̃piɲɔ̃] *nm* mushroom; (*terme générique*) fungus; **~ de couche** *ou* **de Paris** button mushroom

champion, ne [ʃɑ̃pjɔ̃, -ɔn] *adj, nm/f* champion; **championnat** *nm* championship

chance [ʃɑ̃s] *nf*: **la ~** luck; **chances** *nfpl* (*probabilités*) chances; **avoir de la ~** to be lucky; **il a des ~s de gagner** he has a chance of winning; **bonne ~!** good luck!

change [ʃɑ̃ʒ] *nm* (*Comm*) exchange

changement [ʃɑ̃ʒmɑ̃] *nm* change; **~ climatique** climate change; **~ de vitesse** gears *pl*; (*action*) gear change

changer [ʃɑ̃ʒe] /3/ *vt* (*modifier*) to change, alter; (*remplacer, Comm*) to change ▷ *vi* to change, alter; **se changer** *vi* to change (o.s.); **~ de** (*remplacer: adresse, nom, voiture etc*) to change one's; **~ de train** to change trains; **~ d'avis, ~ d'idée** to change one's mind; **~ de vitesse** to change gear; **~ qn/qch de place** to move sb/sth to another place

chanson [ʃɑ̃sɔ̃] *nf* song

chant [ʃɑ̃] *nm* song; (*art vocal*) singing; (*d'église*) hymn

chantage [ʃɑ̃taʒ] *nm* blackmail; **faire du ~** to use blackmail

chanter [ʃɑ̃te] /1/ *vt, vi* to sing; **si cela lui chante** (*fam*) if he feels like it *ou* fancies it; **chanteur, -euse** *nm/f* singer

chantier [ʃɑ̃tje] *nm* (*building*) site; (*sur une route*) roadworks *pl*; **mettre en ~** to start work on; **~ naval** shipyard

chantilly [ʃɑ̃tiji] *nf voir* **crème**

chantonner [ʃɑ̃tɔne] /1/ *vi*, *vt* to sing to oneself, hum

chapeau, x [ʃapo] *nm* hat; **~!** well done!

chapelle [ʃapɛl] *nf* chapel

chapitre [ʃapitʁ] *nm* chapter

chaque [ʃak] *adj* each, every; (*indéfini*) every

char [ʃaʁ] *nm*: **~ (d'assaut)** tank; **~ à voile** sand yacht

charbon [ʃaʁbɔ̃] *nm* coal; **~ de bois** charcoal

charcuterie [ʃaʁkytʁi] *nf (magasin)* pork butcher's shop and delicatessen; (*produits*) cooked pork meats *pl*; **charcutier, -ière** *nm/f* pork butcher

chardon [ʃaʁdɔ̃] *nm* thistle

charge [ʃaʁʒ] *nf (fardeau)* load; (*Élec, Mil, Jur*) charge; (*rôle, mission*) responsibility; **charges** *nfpl (du loyer)* service charges; **à la ~ de** (*dépendant de*) dependent upon; (*aux frais de*) chargeable to; **prendre en ~** to take charge of; (*véhicule*) to take on; (*dépenses*) to take care of; **~s sociales** social security contributions

chargement [ʃaʁʒəmɑ̃] *nm (objets)* load

charger [ʃaʁʒe] /3/ *vt (voiture, fusil, caméra)* to load; (*batterie*) to charge ▷ *vi (Mil etc)* to charge; **se ~ de** to see to, take care of

chargeur [ʃaʁʒœʁ] *nm (de batterie)* charger

chariot [ʃaʁjo] *nm* trolley; (*charrette*) waggon

charité [ʃaʁite] *nf* charity; **faire la ~ à** to give (something) to

charmant, e [ʃaʁmɑ̃, -ɑ̃t] *adj* charming

charme [ʃaʁm] *nm* charm; **charmer** /1/ *vt* to charm

charpente [ʃaʁpɑ̃t] *nf* frame(work); **charpentier** *nm* carpenter

charrette [ʃaʁɛt] *nf* cart

charter [tʃaʁtœʁ] *nm (vol)* charter flight

chasse [ʃas] *nf* hunting; (*au fusil*) shooting; (*poursuite*) chase; (*aussi*: **~ d'eau**) flush; **prendre en ~** to give chase to; **tirer la ~ (d'eau)** to flush the toilet, pull the chain; **~ à courre** hunting; **chasse-neige** *nm inv* snowplough (BRIT), snowplow (US); **chasser** /1/ *vt* to hunt; (*expulser*) to chase away *ou* out, drive away *ou* out; **chasseur, -euse** *nm/f* hunter ▷ *nm (avion)* fighter

chat¹ [ʃa] *nm* cat

chat² [tʃat] *nm (Internet: salon)* chat room; (: *conversation*) chat

châtaigne [ʃatɛɲ] *nf* chestnut

châtain [ʃatɛ̃] *adj inv* chestnut (brown); (*personne*) chestnut-haired

château, x [ʃato] *nm (forteresse)* castle; (*résidence royale*) palace; (*manoir*) mansion; **~ d'eau** water tower; **~ fort** stronghold, fortified castle

châtiment [ʃatimɑ̃] *nm* punishment

chaton [ʃatɔ̃] *nm (Zool)* kitten

chatouiller [ʃatuje] /1/ *vt* to tickle; **chatouilleux, -euse** [ʃatujø, -øz] *adj* ticklish; (*fig*) touchy, over-sensitive

chatte [ʃat] *nf* (she-)cat

chatter [tʃate] /1/ *vi (Internet)* to chat

chaud, e [ʃo, -od] *adj (gén)* warm; (*très chaud*) hot ▷ *nm*: **il fait ~** it's warm; it's hot; **avoir ~** to be warm; to be hot; **ça me tient ~** it keeps me warm; **rester au ~** to stay in the warm

chaudière [ʃodjɛʁ] *nf* boiler

chauffage [ʃofaʒ] *nm* heating; **~ central** central heating

chauffe-eau [ʃofo] *nm inv* water heater

chauffer [ʃofe] /1/ *vt* to heat ▷ *vi* to heat up, warm up; (*trop chauffer: moteur*) to overheat; **se chauffer** *vi* (*au soleil*) to warm o.s.

chauffeur [ʃofœʁ] *nm* driver; (*privé*) chauffeur

chaumière [ʃomjɛʁ] *nf* (thatched) cottage

chaussée [ʃose] *nf* road(way)

chausser [ʃose] /1/ vt (bottes, skis) to put on; (enfant) to put shoes on; **~ du 38/42** to take size 38/42

chaussette [ʃosɛt] nf sock

chausson [ʃosɔ̃] nm slipper; (de bébé) bootee; **~ (aux pommes)** (apple) turnover

chaussure [ʃosyʀ] nf shoe; **~s basses** flat shoes; **~s montantes** ankle boots; **~s de ski** ski boots

chauve [ʃov] adj bald; **chauve-souris** nf bat

chauvin, e [ʃovɛ̃, -in] adj chauvinistic

chaux [ʃo] nf lime; **blanchi à la ~** whitewashed

chef [ʃɛf] nm head, leader; (de cuisine) chef; **général/commandant en ~** general-/commander-in-chief; **~ d'accusation** charge; **~ d'entreprise** company head; **~ d'état** head of state; **~ de famille** head of the family; **~ de file** (de parti etc) leader; **~ de gare** station master; **~ d'orchestre** conductor; **chef-d'œuvre** nm masterpiece; **chef-lieu** nm county town

chemin [ʃəmɛ̃] nm path; (itinéraire, direction, trajet) way; **en ~** on the way; **~ de fer** railway (BRIT), railroad (US)

cheminée [ʃəmine] nf chimney; (à l'intérieur) chimney piece, fireplace; (de bateau) funnel

chemise [ʃəmiz] nf shirt; (dossier) folder; **~ de nuit** nightdress

chemisier [ʃəmizje] nm blouse

chêne [ʃɛn] nm oak (tree); (bois) oak

chenil [ʃənil] nm kennels pl

chenille [ʃənij] nf (Zool) caterpillar

chèque [ʃɛk] nm cheque (BRIT), check (US); **faire/toucher un ~** to write/cash a cheque; **par ~** by cheque; **~ barré/sans provision** crossed (BRIT)/bad cheque; **~ de voyage** traveller's cheque; **chéquier** [ʃekje] nm cheque book

cher, -ère [ʃɛʀ] adj (aimé) dear; (coûteux) expensive, dear ▷ adv: **cela coûte ~** it's expensive

chercher [ʃɛʀʃe] /1/ vt to look for; (gloire etc) to seek; **aller ~** to go for, go and fetch; **~ à faire** to try to do; **chercheur, -euse** nm/f researcher, research worker

chéri, e [ʃeʀi] adj beloved, dear; **(mon) ~** darling

cheval, -aux [ʃəval, -o] nm horse; (Auto): **~ (vapeur)** horsepower no pl; **faire du ~** to ride; **à ~** on horseback; **à ~ sur** astride; (fig) overlapping; **~ de course** race horse

chevalier [ʃəvalje] nm knight

chevalière [ʃəvaljɛʀ] nf signet ring

chevaux [ʃəvo] nmpl voir **cheval**

chevet [ʃəvɛ] nm: **au ~ de qn** at sb's bedside; **lampe de ~** bedside lamp

cheveu, x [ʃəvø] nm hair ▷ nmpl (chevelure) hair sg; (: avoir les **~x courts/en brosse** to have short hair/a crew cut

cheville [ʃəvij] nf (Anat) ankle; (de bois) peg; (pour enfoncer une vis) plug

chèvre [ʃɛvʀ] nf (she-)goat

chèvrefeuille [ʃɛvʀəfœj] nm honeysuckle

chevreuil [ʃəvʀœj] nm roe deer inv; (Culin) venison

 MOT-CLÉ

chez [ʃe] prép **1** (à la demeure de) at; (: direction) to; **chez qn** at/to sb's house ou place; **je suis chez moi** I'm at home; **je rentre chez moi** I'm going home; **allons chez Nathalie** let's go to Nathalie's

2 (+profession) at; (: direction) to; **chez le boulanger/dentiste** at ou to the baker's/dentist's

3 (dans le caractère, l'œuvre de) in; **chez ce poète** in this poet's work; **c'est ce que je préfère chez lui** that's what I like best about him

chic [ʃik] adj inv chic, smart; (généreux) nice, decent ▷ nm stylishness; **avoir**

le ~ de ou **pour** to have the knack of ou for; **~!** great!
chicorée [ʃikɔʀe] nf (café) chicory; (salade) endive
chien [ʃjɛ̃] nm dog; (de pistolet) hammer; **~ d'aveugle** guide dog; **~ de garde** guard dog
chienne [ʃjɛn] nf (she-)dog, bitch
chiffon [ʃifɔ̃] nm (piece of) rag; **chiffonner** /1/ vt to crumple; (tracasser) to concern
chiffre [ʃifʀ] nm (représentant un nombre) figure; numeral; (montant, total) total, sum; **en ~s ronds** in round figures; **~ d'affaires (CA)** turnover; **chiffrer** /1/ vt (dépense) to put a figure to, assess; (message) to (en)code, cipher ▷ vi: **chiffrer à, se chiffrer à** to add up to
chignon [ʃiɲɔ̃] nm chignon, bun
Chili [ʃili] nm: **le ~** Chile; **chilien, ne** adj Chilean ▷ nm/f: **Chilien, ne** Chilean
chimie [ʃimi] nf chemistry; **chimiothérapie** [ʃimjɔteʀapi] nf chemotherapy; **chimique** adj chemical; **produits chimiques** chemicals
chimpanzé [ʃɛ̃pɑ̃ze] nm chimpanzee
Chine [ʃin] nf: **la ~** China; **chinois, e** adj Chinese ▷ nm (Ling) Chinese ▷ nm/f: **Chinois, e** Chinese
chiot [ʃjo] nm pup(py)
chips [ʃips] nfpl crisps (BRIT), (potato) chips (US)
chirurgie [ʃiʀyʀʒi] nf surgery; **~ esthétique** cosmetic ou plastic surgery; **chirurgien, ne** nm/f surgeon
chlore [klɔʀ] nm chlorine
choc [ʃɔk] nm (heurt) impact; shock; (collision) crash; (moral) shock; (affrontement) clash
chocolat [ʃɔkɔla] nm chocolate; **~ au lait** milk chocolate
chœur [kœʀ] nm (chorale) choir; (Opéra, Théât) chorus; **en ~** in chorus
choisir [ʃwaziʀ] /2/ vt to choose, select

choix [ʃwa] nm choice; selection; **avoir le ~** to have the choice; **de premier ~** (Comm) class ou grade one; **de ~** choice cpd, selected; **au ~** as you wish ou prefer
chômage [ʃomaʒ] nm unemployment; **mettre au ~** to make redundant, put out of work; **être au ~** to be unemployed ou out of work; **chômeur, -euse** nm/f unemployed person
chope [ʃɔp] nf tankard
choquer [ʃɔke] /1/ vt (offenser) to shock; (commotionner) to shake (up)
chorale [kɔʀal] nf choir
chose [ʃoz] nf thing; **c'est peu de ~** it's nothing much
chou, x [ʃu] nm cabbage; **mon petit ~** (my) sweetheart; **~ à la crème** cream bun (made of choux pastry); **~ de Bruxelles** Brussels sprout; **choucroute** nf sauerkraut
chouette [ʃwɛt] nf owl ▷ adj (fam) great, smashing
chou-fleur [ʃuflœʀ] nm cauliflower
chrétien, ne [kʀetjɛ̃, -ɛn] adj, nm/f Christian
Christ [kʀist] nm: **le ~** Christ; **christianisme** nm Christianity
chronique [kʀɔnik] adj chronic ▷ nf (de journal) column, page; (historique) chronicle; (Radio, TV): **la ~ sportive/théâtrale** the sports/theatre review
chronologique [kʀɔnɔlɔʒik] adj chronological
chronomètre [kʀɔnɔmɛtʀ] nm stopwatch; **chronométrer** /6/ vt to time
chrysanthème [kʀizɑ̃tɛm] nm chrysanthemum

- **CHRYSANTHÈME**
-
- Chrysanthemums are strongly
- associated with funerals in France,
- and therefore should not be given
- as gifts.

chuchotement [ʃyʃɔtmɑ̃] nm whisper

chuchoter [ʃyʃɔte] /1/ vt, vi to whisper

chut excl [ʃyt] sh!

chute [ʃyt] nf fall; (déchet) scrap; **faire une ~ (de 10 m)** to fall (10 m); **~s de pluie/neige** rain/snowfalls; **~ (d'eau)** waterfall; **~ libre** free fall

Chypre [ʃipʀ] nf Cyprus

-ci [si] adv voir **par** ▷ adj dém: **ce garçon~/-là** this/that boy; **ces femmes~/-là** these/those women

cible [sibl] nf target

ciboulette [sibulɛt] nf (small) chive

cicatrice [sikatʀis] nf scar; **cicatriser** /1/ vt to heal

ci-contre [sikɔ̃tʀ] adv opposite

ci-dessous [sidəsu] adv below

ci-dessus [sidəsy] adv above

cidre [sidʀ] nm cider

Cie abr (= compagnie) Co

ciel [sjɛl] nm sky; (Rel) heaven

cieux [sjø] nmpl voir **ciel**

cigale [sigal] nf cicada

cigare [sigaʀ] nm cigar

cigarette [sigaʀɛt] nf cigarette

ci-inclus, e [siɛ̃kly, -yz] adj, adv enclosed

ci-joint, e [siʒwɛ̃, -ɛ̃t] adj, adv enclosed

cil [sil] nm (eye)lash

cime [sim] nf top; (montagne) peak

ciment [simɑ̃] nm cement

cimetière [simtjɛʀ] nm cemetery; (d'église) churchyard

cinéaste [sineast] nm/f film-maker

cinéma [sinema] nm cinema

cinq [sɛ̃k] num five; **cinquantaine** nf: **une cinquantaine (de)** about fifty; **avoir la cinquantaine** (âge) to be around fifty; **cinquante** num fifty; **cinquantenaire** adj, nm/f fifty-year-old; **cinquième** num fifth ▷ nf (Scol) year 8 (BRIT), seventh grade (US)

cintre [sɛ̃tʀ] nm coat-hanger

cintré, e [sɛ̃tʀe] adj (chemise) fitted

cirage [siʀaʒ] nm (shoe) polish

circonflexe [siʀkɔ̃flɛks] adj: **accent ~** circumflex accent

circonstance [siʀkɔ̃stɑ̃s] nf circumstance; (occasion) occasion; **~s atténuantes** mitigating circumstances

circuit [siʀkɥi] nm (trajet) tour, (round) trip; (Élec, Tech) circuit

circulaire [siʀkylɛʀ] adj, nf circular

circulation [siʀkylasjɔ̃] nf circulation; (Auto): **la ~** (the) traffic

circuler [siʀkyle] /1/ vi (véhicules) to drive (along); (passants) to walk along; (train etc) to run; (sang, devises) to circulate; **faire ~** (nouvelle) to spread (about), circulate; (badauds) to move on

cire [siʀ] nf wax; **ciré** nm oilskin; **cirer** [siʀe] /1/ vt to wax, polish

cirque [siʀk] nm circus; (fig) chaos, bedlam; **quel ~!** what a carry-on!

ciseau, x [sizo] nm: **~ (à bois)** chisel ▷ nmpl (paire de ciseaux) (pair of) scissors

citadin, e [sitadɛ̃, -in] nm/f city dweller

citation [sitasjɔ̃] nf (d'auteur) quotation; (Jur) summons sg

cité [site] nf town; (plus grande) city; **~ universitaire** students' residences pl

citer [site] /1/ vt (un auteur) to quote (from); (nommer) to name; (Jur) to summon

citoyen, ne [sitwajɛ̃, -ɛn] nm/f citizen

citron [sitʀɔ̃] nm lemon; **~ pressé** (fresh) lemon juice; **~ vert** lime; **citronnade** nf still lemonade

citrouille [sitʀuj] nf pumpkin

civet [sivɛ] nm: **~ de lapin** rabbit stew

civière [sivjɛʀ] nf stretcher

civil, e [sivil] adj (Jur, Admin, poli) civil; (non militaire) civilian; **en ~** in civilian clothes; **dans le ~** in civilian life

civilisation [sivilizasjɔ̃] nf civilization

clair, e [klɛʀ] adj light; (chambre) light, bright; (eau, son, fig) clear ▷ adv:

voir ~ to see clearly ▷ *nm*: **mettre au ~** (*notes etc*) to tidy up; **tirer qch au ~** to clear sth up, clarify sth; **~ de lune** moonlight; **clairement** *adv* clearly

clairière [klɛʀjɛʀ] *nf* clearing

clandestin, e [klɑ̃dɛstɛ̃, -in] *adj* clandestine, covert; (*Pol*) underground, clandestine; (*travailleur, immigration*) illegal; **passager ~** stowaway

claque [klak] *nf* (*gifle*) slap; **claquer** /1/ *vi* (*porte*) to bang, slam; (*fam: mourir*) to snuff it ▷ *vt* (*porte*) to slam, bang; (*doigts*) to snap; (*fam: dépenser*) to blow; **elle claquait des dents** her teeth were chattering; **être claqué** (*fam*) to be dead tired; **se claquer un muscle** to pull ou strain a muscle; **claquettes** *nfpl* tap-dancing *sg*; (*chaussures*) flip-flops

clarinette [klaʀinɛt] *nf* clarinet

classe [klɑs] *nf* class; (*Scol: local*) class(room); (*: leçon*) class; (*: élèves*) class; **aller en ~** to go to school; **classement** *nm* (*rang: Scol*) place; (*: Sport*) placing; (*liste: Scol*) class list (in order of merit); (*: Sport*) placings *pl*

classer [klɑse] /1/ *vt* (*idées, livres*) to classify; (*papiers*) to file; (*candidat, concurrent*) to grade; (*Jur: affaire*) to close; **se ~ premier/dernier** to come first/last; (*Sport*) to finish first/last; **classeur** *nm* (*cahier*) file

classique [klasik] *adj* (*sobre, coupe etc*) classic(al), classical; (*habituel*) standard, classic

clavecin [klav(ə)sɛ̃] *nm* harpsichord

clavicule [klavikyl] *nf* collarbone

clavier [klavje] *nm* keyboard

clé [kle] *nf* key; (*Mus*) clef; (*de mécanicien*) spanner (*BRIT*), wrench (*US*); **prix ~s en main** (*d'une voiture*) on-the-road price; ; **~ de contact** ignition key; **~ USB** USB key

clergé [klɛʀʒe] *nm* clergy

cliché [kliʃe] *nm* (*fig*) cliché; (*Photo*) negative; print; (*Typo*) (printing) plate; (*Ling*) cliché

client, e [klijɑ̃, -ɑ̃t] *nm/f* (*acheteur*) customer, client; (*d'hôtel*) guest, patron; (*du docteur*) patient; (*de l'avocat*) client; **clientèle** *nf* (*du magasin*) customers *pl*, clientèle; (*du docteur, de l'avocat*) practice

cligner [kliɲe] /1/ *vi*: **~ des yeux** to blink (one's eyes); **~ de l'œil** to wink; **clignotant** *nm* (*Auto*) indicator; **clignoter** /1/ *vi* (*étoiles etc*) to twinkle; (*lumière*) to flicker

climat [klima] *nm* climate

climatisation [klimatizasjɔ̃] *nf* air conditioning; **climatisé, e** *adj* air-conditioned

clin d'œil [klɛ̃dœj] *nm* wink; **en un ~** in a flash

clinique [klinik] *nf* (*private*) clinic

clip [klip] *nm* (*pince*) clip; (*boucle d'oreille*) clip-on; **(vidéo) ~** pop (*ou* promotional) video

cliquer [klike] /1/ *vi* (*Inform*) to click; **~ deux fois** to double-click ▷ *vt* to click; **~ sur** to click on

clochard, e [klɔʃaʀ, -aʀd] *nm/f* tramp

cloche [klɔʃ] *nf* (*d'église*) bell; (*fam*) clot; **clocher** /1/ *nm* church tower; (*en pointe*) steeple ▷ *vi* (*fam*) to be ou go wrong; **de clocher** (*péj*) parochial

cloison [klwazɔ̃] *nf* partition (wall)

clonage [klɔnaʒ] *nm* cloning

cloner [klɔne] /1/ *vt* to clone

cloque [klɔk] *nf* blister

clore [klɔʀ] /45/ *vt* to close

clôture [klotyʀ] *nf* closure; (*barrière*) enclosure

clou [klu] *nm* nail; **clous** *nmpl* = **passage clouté**; **pneus à ~s** studded tyres; **le ~ du spectacle** the highlight of the show; **~ de girofle** clove

clown [klun] *nm* clown

club [klœb] *nm* club

CNRS *sigle m* (= *Centre national de la recherche scientifique*) ≈ SERC (*BRIT*), ≈ NSF (*US*)

coaguler [kɔagyle] /1/ vi, vt, **se coaguler** vi (sang) to coagulate

cobaye [kɔbaj] nm guinea-pig

coca® [kɔka] nm Coke®

cocaïne [kɔkain] nf cocaine

coccinelle [kɔksinɛl] nf ladybird (BRIT), ladybug (US)

cocher [kɔʃe] /1/ vt to tick off

cochon, ne [kɔʃɔ̃, -ɔn] nm pig ▷ adj (fam) dirty, smutty; **~ d'Inde** guinea-pig; **cochonnerie** nf (fam: saleté) filth; (marchandises) rubbish, trash

cocktail [kɔktɛl] nm cocktail; (réception) cocktail party

cocorico [kɔkɔriko] excl, nm cock-a-doodle-do

cocotte [kɔkɔt] nf (en fonte) casserole; **ma ~** (fam) sweetie (pie); **~ (minute)**® pressure cooker

code [kɔd] nm code ▷ adj: **phares ~s** dipped lights; **se mettre en ~(s)** to dip (BRIT) ou dim (US) one's (head) lights; **~ à barres** bar code; **~ civil** Common Law; **~ pénal** penal code; **~ postal** (numéro) postcode (BRIT), zip code (US); **~ de la route** highway code; **~ secret** cipher

cœur [kœr] nm heart; (Cartes: couleur) hearts pl; (: carte) heart; **avoir bon ~** to be kind-hearted; **avoir mal au ~** to feel sick; **par ~** by heart; **de bon ~** willingly; **cela lui tient à ~** that's (very) close to his heart

coffre [kɔfr] nm (meuble) chest; (d'auto) boot (BRIT), trunk (US); **coffre-fort** nm safe; **coffret** nm casket

cognac [kɔɲak] nm brandy, cognac

cogner [kɔɲe] /1/ vi to knock; **se ~ contre** to knock ou bump into; **se ~ la tête** to bang one's head

cohérent, e [kɔerɑ̃, -ɑ̃t] adj coherent, consistent

coiffé, e [kwafe] adj: **bien/mal ~** with tidy/untidy hair; **~ d'un béret** wearing a beret

coiffer [kwafe] /1/ vt (fig: surmonter) to cover, top; **~ qn** to do sb's hair; **se**

coiffer vi to do one's hair; **coiffeur, -euse** nm/f hairdresser ▷ nf (table) dressing table; **coiffure** nf (cheveux) hairstyle, hairdo; (art): **la coiffure** hairdressing

coin [kwɛ̃] nm corner; (pour coincer) wedge; **l'épicerie du ~** the local grocer; **dans le ~** (aux alentours) in the area, around about; (habiter) locally; **je ne suis pas du ~** I'm not from here; **au ~ du feu** by the fireside; **regard en ~** side(ways) glance

coincé, e [kwɛ̃se] adj stuck, jammed; (fig: inhibé) inhibited, with hang-ups

coïncidence [kɔɛ̃sidɑ̃s] nf coincidence

coing [kwɛ̃] nm quince

col [kɔl] nm (de chemise) collar; (encolure, cou) neck; (de montagne) pass; **~ roulé** polo-neck; **~ de l'utérus** cervix

colère [kɔlɛr] nf anger; **une ~** a fit of anger; **être en ~ (contre qn)** to be angry (with sb); **mettre qn en ~** to make sb angry; **se mettre en ~ contre qn** to get angry with sb; **se mettre en ~** to get angry; **coléreux, -euse, colérique** adj quick-tempered, irascible

colin [kɔlɛ̃] nm hake

colique [kɔlik] nf diarrhoea

colis [kɔli] nm parcel

collaborer [kɔ(l)labɔre] /1/ vi to collaborate; **~ à** to collaborate on; (revue) to contribute to

collant, e [kɔlɑ̃, -ɑ̃t] adj sticky; (robe etc) clinging, skintight; (péj) clinging ▷ nm (bas) tights pl; (de danseur) leotard

colle [kɔl] nf glue; (à papiers peints) (wallpaper) paste; (devinette) teaser, riddle; (Scol: fam) detention

collecte [kɔlɛkt] nf collection; **collectif, -ive** adj collective; (visite, billet etc) group cpd

collection [kɔlɛksjɔ̃] nf collection; (Édition) series; **collectionner** /1/ vt (tableaux, timbres) to

collect; **collectionneur, -euse**
[kɔlɛksjɔnœʀ, -øz] nm/f collector
collectivité [kɔlɛktivite] nf group;
les ~s locales local authorities
collège [kɔlɛʒ] nm (école) (secondary)
school; (assemblée) body; **collégien,
ne** nm/f secondary school pupil
(BRIT), high school student (US)
collègue [kɔ(l)lɛg] nm/f colleague
coller [kɔle] /1/ vt (papier, timbre)
to stick (on); (affiche) to stick up;
(enveloppe) to stick down; (morceaux)
to stick ou glue together; (Inform) to
paste; (fam: mettre, fourrer) to stick,
shove; (Scol: fam) to keep in ▷ vi
(être collant) to be sticky; (adhérer) to
stick; **~ à** to stick to; **être collé à un
examen** (fam) to fail an exam
collier [kɔlje] nm (bijou) necklace; (de
chien, Tech) collar
colline [kɔlin] nf hill
collision [kɔlizjɔ̃] nf collision, crash;
entrer en ~ (avec) to collide (with)
collyre [kɔliʀ] nm eye lotion
colombe [kɔlɔ̃b] nf dove
Colombie [kɔlɔ̃bi] nf: **la ~** Colombia
colonie [kɔlɔni] nf colony; **~ (de
vacances)** holiday camp (for children)
colonne [kɔlɔn] nf column; **se
mettre en ~ par deux/quatre** to
get into twos/fours; **~ (vertébrale)**
spine, spinal column
colorant [kɔlɔʀɑ̃] nm colouring
colorer [kɔlɔʀe] /1/ vt to colour
colorier [kɔlɔʀje] /7/ vt to colour (in)
coloris [kɔlɔʀi] nm colour, shade
colza [kɔlza] nm rape(seed)
coma [kɔma] nm coma; **être dans le
~** to be in a coma
combat [kɔ̃ba] nm fight; fighting
no pl; **~ de boxe** boxing match;
combattant nm: **ancien
combattant** war veteran;
combattre /41/ vt to fight; (épidémie,
ignorance) to combat, fight against
combien [kɔ̃bjɛ̃] adv (quantité) how
much; (nombre) how many; **~ de**
how much; (nombre) how many;

~ de temps how long; **~ coûte/
pèse ceci?** how much does this cost/
weigh?; **on est le ~ aujourd'hui?**
(fam) what's the date today?
combinaison [kɔ̃binɛzɔ̃] nf
combination; (astuce) scheme; (de
femme) slip; (de plongée) wetsuit; (bleu
de travail) boilersuit (BRIT), coveralls
pl (US)
combiné [kɔ̃bine] nm (aussi:
~ téléphonique) receiver
comble [kɔ̃bl] adj (salle) packed
(full) ▷ nm (du bonheur, plaisir) height;
combles nmpl (Constr) attic sg, loft sg;
c'est le ~! that beats everything!
combler [kɔ̃ble] /1/ vt (trou) to fill in;
(besoin, lacune) to fill; (déficit) to make
good; (satisfaire) fulfil
comédie [kɔmedi] nf comedy; (fig)
playacting no pl; **faire une ~** (fig) to
make a fuss; **~ musicale** musical;
comédien, ne nm/f actor/actress
comestible [kɔmɛstibl] adj edible
comique [kɔmik] adj (drôle) comical;
(Théât) comic ▷ nm (artiste) comic,
comedian
commandant [kɔmɑ̃dɑ̃] nm (gén)
commander, commandant; (Navig)
captain
commande [kɔmɑ̃d] nf (Comm)
order; **commandes** nfpl (Aviat etc)
controls; **sur ~** to order; **commander**
/1/ vt (Comm) to order; (diriger,
ordonner) to command; **commander
à qn de faire** to command ou order
sb to do

 MOT-CLÉ

comme [kɔm] prép 1 (comparaison)
like; **tout comme son père** just like
his father; **fort comme un bœuf** as
strong as an ox; **joli comme tout**
ever so pretty
2 (manière) like; **faites-le comme ça**
do it like this, do it this way; **comme
ci, comme ça** so-so, middling
3 (en tant que) as a; **donner comme**

prix to give as a prize; **travailler comme secrétaire** to work as a secretary
4: **comme il faut** adv properly
▶ conj 1 (ainsi que) as; **elle écrit comme elle parle** she writes as she talks; **comme si** as if
2 (au moment où, alors que) as; **il est parti comme j'arrivais** he left as I arrived
3 (parce que, puisque) as; **comme il était en retard, il …** as he was late, he …
▶ adv: **comme il est fort/c'est bon!** he's so strong/it's so good!

commencement [kɔmɑ̃smɑ̃] nm beginning, start
commencer [kɔmɑ̃se] /3/ vt, vi to begin, start; **~ à** ou **de faire** to begin ou start doing
comment [kɔmɑ̃] adv how; **~?** (que dites-vous?) (I beg your) pardon?; **et ~!** and how!
commentaire [kɔmɑ̃tɛʀ] nm comment; remark; **~ (de texte)** commentary
commerçant, e [kɔmɛʀsɑ̃, -ɑ̃t] nm/f shopkeeper, trader
commerce [kɔmɛʀs] nm (activité) trade, commerce; (boutique) business; **~ électronique** e-commerce; **~ équitable** fair trade; **commercial, e, -aux** adj commercial, trading; (péj) commercial; **commercialiser** /1/ vt to market
commettre [kɔmɛtʀ] /56/ vt to commit
commissaire [kɔmisɛʀ] nm (de police) ≈ (police) superintendent; **~ aux comptes** (Admin) auditor; **commissariat** nm police station
commission [kɔmisjɔ̃] nf (comité, pourcentage) commission; (message) message; (course) errand; **commissions** nfpl (achats) shopping sg

commode [kɔmɔd] adj (pratique) convenient, handy; (facile) easy; (personne): **pas ~** awkward (to deal with) ▷ nf chest of drawers
commun, e [kɔmœ̃, -yn] adj common; (pièce) communal, shared; (réunion, effort) joint ▷ nf (Admin) commune, ≈ district (: urbaine) ≈ borough; **communs** nmpl (bâtiments) outbuildings; **cela sort du ~** it's out of the ordinary; **le ~ des mortels** the common run of people; **en ~ (faire)** jointly; **mettre en ~** to pool, share; **d'un ~ accord** of one accord
communauté [kɔmynote] nf community
commune [kɔmyn] adj f, nf voir **commun**
communication [kɔmynikasjɔ̃] nf communication
communier [kɔmynje] /7/ vi (Rel) to receive communion
communion [kɔmynjɔ̃] nf communion
communiquer [kɔmynike] /1/ vt (nouvelle, dossier) to pass on, convey; (peur etc) to communicate ▷ vi to communicate; **se ~ à** (se propager) to spread to
communisme [kɔmynism] nm communism; **communiste** adj, nm/f communist
commutateur [kɔmytatœʀ] nm (Élec) (change-over) switch, commutator
compact, e [kɔ̃pakt] adj (dense) dense; (appareil) compact
compagne [kɔ̃paɲ] nf companion
compagnie [kɔ̃paɲi] nf (firme, Mil) company; **tenir ~ à qn** to keep sb company; **fausser ~ à qn** to give sb the slip, slip ou sneak away from sb; **~ aérienne** airline (company)
compagnon [kɔ̃paɲɔ̃] nm companion
comparable [kɔ̃paʀabl] adj: **~ (à)** comparable (to)

comparaison [kɔ̃paʀɛzɔ̃] nf
comparison

comparer [kɔ̃paʀe] /1/ vt to
compare; **~ qch/qn à** ou **et** (*pour
choisir*) to compare sth/sb with ou
and; (*pour établir une similitude*) to
compare sth/sb to ou and

compartiment [kɔ̃paʀtimɑ̃] nm
compartment

compas [kɔ̃pa] nm (*Géom*) (pair of)
compasses *pl*; (*Navig*) compass

compatible [kɔ̃patibl] adj
compatible

compatriote [kɔ̃patʀijɔt] nm/f
compatriot

compensation [kɔ̃pɑ̃sasjɔ̃] nf
compensation

compenser [kɔ̃pɑ̃se] /1/ vt to
compensate for, make up for

compétence [kɔ̃petɑ̃s] nf
competence

compétent, e [kɔ̃petɑ̃, -ɑ̃t] adj (*apte*)
competent, capable

compétition [kɔ̃petisjɔ̃] nf (*gén*)
competition; (*Sport: épreuve*) event; **la
~ automobile** motor racing

complément [kɔ̃plemɑ̃] nm
complement; (*reste*) remainder;
~ d'information (*Admin*)
supplementary ou further
information; **complémentaire**
adj complementary; (*additionnel*)
supplementary

complet, -ète [kɔ̃plɛ, -ɛt] adj
complete; (*plein: hôtel etc*) full ▷ nm
(*aussi:* **~-veston**) suit; **pain ~**
wholemeal bread; **complètement**
adv completely; **compléter** /6/
vt (*porter à la quantité voulue*) to
complete; (*augmenter: connaissances,
études*) to complement, supplement;
(: *garde-robe*) to add to

complexe [kɔ̃plɛks] adj complex
▷ nm: **~ hospitalier/industriel**
hospital/industrial complex;
complexé, e adj mixed-up, hung-up

complication [kɔ̃plikasjɔ̃] nf
complexity, intricacy; (*difficulté, ennui*)
complication; **complications** nfpl
(*Méd*) complications

complice [kɔ̃plis] nm accomplice

compliment [kɔ̃plimɑ̃]
nm (*louange*) compliment;
compliments nmpl (*félicitations*)
congratulations

compliqué, e [kɔ̃plike] adj
complicated, complex; (*personne*)
complicated

comportement [kɔ̃pɔʀtəmɑ̃] nm
behaviour

comporter [kɔ̃pɔʀte] /1/ vt (*consister
en*) to consist of, comprise; (*être
équipé de*) to have; **se comporter** vi
to behave

composer [kɔ̃poze] /1/ vt (*musique,
texte*) to compose; (*mélange, équipe*) to
make up; (*faire partie de*) to make up,
form ▷ vi (*transiger*) to come to terms;
se ~ de to be composed of, be made
up of; **~ un numéro** (*au téléphone*) to
dial a number; **compositeur, -trice**
nm/f (*Mus*) composer; **composition**
nf composition; (*Scol*) test

composter [kɔ̃pɔste] /1/ vt (*billet*)
to punch

● **COMPOSTER**
●
● In France you have to punch your
● ticket on the platform to validate it
● before getting onto the train.

compote [kɔ̃pɔt] nf stewed fruit *no
pl*; **~ de pommes** stewed apples

compréhensible [kɔ̃pʀeɑ̃sibl]
adj comprehensible; (*attitude*)
understandable

compréhensif, -ive [kɔ̃pʀeɑ̃sif, -iv]
adj understanding
Attention à ne pas traduire
compréhensif par *comprehensive*.

comprendre [kɔ̃pʀɑ̃dʀ] /58/ vt
to understand; (*se composer de*) to
comprise, consist of

compresse [kɔ̃pʀɛs] nf compress

comprimé [kɔ̃pʀime] nm tablet

compris, e [kɔ̃pʀi, -iz] *pp de*
comprendre ▷ *adj* (*inclus*) included;
~ entre (*situé*) contained between;
**la maison ~e/non ~e, y/non ~ la
maison** including/excluding the
house; **100 euros tout ~** 100 euros
all inclusive *ou* all in

comptabilité [kɔ̃tabilite] *nf*
(*activité, technique*) accounting,
accountancy; accounts *pl*, books
pl; (*service*) accounts office *ou*
department

comptable [kɔ̃tabl] *nm/f*
accountant

comptant [kɔ̃tɑ̃] *adv*: **payer ~** to pay
cash; **acheter ~** to buy for cash

compte [kɔ̃t] *nm* count; (*total,
montant*) count, (right) number;
(*bancaire, facture*) account; **comptes**
nmpl accounts, books; (*fig*)
explanation *sg*; **en fin de ~** all things
considered; **s'en tirer à bon ~** to get
off lightly; **pour le ~ de** on behalf
of; **pour son propre ~** for one's own
benefit; **travailler à son ~** to work
for oneself; **régler un ~** (*s'acquitter de
qch*) to settle an account; (*se venger*)
to get one's own back; **rendre des ~s à
qn** (*fig*) to be answerable to sb; **tenir
~ de qch** to take sth into account;
~ courant (CC) current account;
~ à rebours countdown; **~ rendu**
account, report; (*de film, livre*) review;
voir aussi **rendre**; **compte-gouttes**
nm inv dropper

compter [kɔ̃te] /1/ *vt* to count;
(*facturer*) to charge for; (*avoir à son
actif, comporter*) to have; (*prévoir*)
to allow, reckon; (*penser, espérer*):
~ réussir/revenir to expect to
succeed/return ▷ *vi* to count; (*être
économe*) to economize; (*figurer*):
~ parmi to be *ou* rank among; **~ sur**
to count (up)on; **~ avec qch/qn** to
reckon with *ou* take account of sth/
sb; **sans ~ que** besides which

compteur [kɔ̃tœʀ] *nm* meter; **~ de
vitesse** speedometer

comptine [kɔ̃tin] *nf* nursery rhyme

comptoir [kɔ̃twaʀ] *nm* (*de magasin*)
counter; (*de café*) counter, bar

con, ne [kɔ̃, kɔn] *adj* (*fam!*) bloody
(BRIT !) *ou* damned stupid

concentrer [kɔ̃sɑ̃tʀe] /1/ *vt* to
concentrate; **se concentrer** *vi* to
concentrate

concerner [kɔ̃sɛʀne] /1/ *vt* to
concern; **en ce qui me concerne** as
far as I am concerned

concert [kɔ̃sɛʀ] *nm* concert; **de ~**
(*décider*) unanimously

concessionnaire [kɔ̃sesjɔnɛʀ]
nm/f agent, dealer

concevoir [kɔ̃s(ə)vwaʀ] /28/ *vt* (*idée,
projet*) to conceive (of); (*comprendre*)
to understand; (*enfant*) to conceive;
maison bien/mal conçue well-/
badly-designed *ou* -planned house

concierge [kɔ̃sjɛʀʒ] *nm/f* caretaker

concis, e [kɔ̃si, -iz] *adj* concise

conclure [kɔ̃klyʀ] /35/ *vt* to
conclude; **conclusion** *nf* conclusion

conçois [kɔ̃swa] *vb voir* **concevoir**

concombre [kɔ̃kɔ̃bʀ] *nm* cucumber

concours [kɔ̃kuʀ] *nm* competition;
(*Scol*) competitive examination;
(*assistance*) aid, help; **~ de
circonstances** combination of
circumstances; **~ hippique** horse
show; *voir* **'hors-concours**

concret, -ète [kɔ̃kʀɛ, -ɛt] *adj*
concrete

conçu, e [kɔ̃sy] *pp de* **concevoir**

concubinage [kɔ̃kybinaʒ] *nm* (*Jur*)
cohabitation

concurrence [kɔ̃kyʀɑ̃s] *nf*
competition; **jusqu'à ~ de** up to;
faire ~ à to be in competition with

concurrent, e [kɔ̃kyʀɑ̃, -ɑ̃t] *nm/f*
(*Sport, Écon etc*) competitor; (*Scol*)
candidate

condamner [kɔ̃dane] /1/ *vt* (*blâmer*)
to condemn; (*Jur*) to sentence; (*porte,
ouverture*) to fill in, block up; **~ qn à
deux ans de prison** to sentence sb to
two years' imprisonment

condensation [kɔ̃dɑ̃sasjɔ̃] nf
condensation

condition [kɔ̃disjɔ̃] nf condition;
conditions nfpl (tarif, prix) terms;
(circonstances) conditions; **sans**
~ unconditionally; **à ~ de** ou **que**
provided that; **conditionnel, le** nm
conditional (tense)

conditionnement [kɔ̃disjɔnmɑ̃]
nm (emballage) packaging

condoléances [kɔ̃dɔleɑ̃s] nfpl
condolences

conducteur, -trice [kɔ̃dyktœʀ,
-tʀis] nm/f driver ▷ nm (Élec etc)
conductor

conduire [kɔ̃dɥiʀ] /38/ vt to drive;
(délégation, troupeau) to lead; **se**
conduire vi to behave; **~ vers/à** to
lead towards/to; **~ qn quelque part**
to take somebody somewhere; to drive somebody
somewhere

conduite [kɔ̃dɥit] nf (comportement)
behaviour; (d'eau, de gaz) pipe; **sous**
la ~ de led by

confection [kɔ̃fɛksjɔ̃] nf (fabrication)
making; (Couture): **la ~** the clothing
industry

conférence [kɔ̃feʀɑ̃s] nf (exposé)
lecture; (pourparlers) conference; **~ de**
presse press conference

confesser [kɔ̃fese] /1/ vt to confess;
confession nf confession; (culte:
catholique etc) denomination

confetti [kɔ̃feti] nm confetti no pl

confiance [kɔ̃fjɑ̃s] nf (en l'honnêteté de
qn) confidence, trust; (en la valeur de qch)
faith; **avoir ~ en** to have confidence
ou faith in, trust; **faire ~ à** to trust;
mettre qn en ~ to win somebody's trust; **~ en**
soi self-confidence; voir **question**

confiant, e [kɔ̃fjɑ̃, -ɑ̃t] adj confident;
trusting

confidence [kɔ̃fidɑ̃s] nf confidence;
confidentiel, le adj confidential

confier [kɔ̃fje] /7/ vt: **~ à qn** (objet
en dépôt, travail etc) to entrust to somebody;
(secret, pensée) to confide to somebody; **se ~ à**
qn to confide in somebody

confirmation [kɔ̃fiʀmasjɔ̃] nf
confirmation

confirmer [kɔ̃fiʀme] /1/ vt to
confirm

confiserie [kɔ̃fizʀi] nf (magasin)
confectioner's ou sweet shop;
confiseries nfpl (bonbons)
confectionery sg

confisquer [kɔ̃fiske] /1/ vt to
confiscate

confit, e [kɔ̃fi, -it] adj: **fruits ~s**
crystallized fruits ▷ nm: **~ d'oie**
potted goose

confiture [kɔ̃fityʀ] nf jam

conflit [kɔ̃fli] nm conflict

confondre [kɔ̃fɔ̃dʀ] /41/ vt (jumeaux,
faits) to confuse, mix up; (témoin,
menteur) to confound; **se confondre**
vi to merge; **se ~ en excuses** to offer
profuse apologies

conforme [kɔ̃fɔʀm] adj: **~ à** (en
accord avec: loi, règle) in accordance
with; **conformément** adv:
conformément à in accordance
with; **conformer** /1/ vt: **se**
conformer à to conform to

confort [kɔ̃fɔʀ] nm comfort; **tout ~**
(Comm) with all mod cons (BRIT) ou
modern conveniences; **confortable**
adj comfortable

confronter [kɔ̃fʀɔ̃te] /1/ vt to
confront

confus, e [kɔ̃fy, -yz] adj (vague)
confused; (embarrassé) embarrassed;
confusion nf (voir confus) confusion;
embarrassment; (voir confondre)
confusion; mixing up

congé [kɔ̃ʒe] nm (vacances) holiday;
en ~ on holiday; **semaine/jour de**
~ week/day off; **prendre ~ de qn** to
take one's leave of somebody; **donner son**
~ à to hand ou give in one's notice
to; **~ de maladie** sick leave; **~ de**
maternité maternity leave; **~s**
payés paid holiday ou leave

congédier [kɔ̃ʒedje] /7/ vt to dismiss

congélateur [kɔ̃ʒelatœʀ] nm
freezer

congeler [kɔ̃ʒ(ə)le] /5/ vt to freeze;
les produits congelés frozen foods;
se congeler vi to freeze
congestion [kɔ̃ʒɛstjɔ̃] nf congestion
Congo [kɔ̃go] nm: **le ~** the Congo
congrès [kɔ̃gʀɛ] nm congress
conifère [kɔnifɛʀ] nm conifer
conjoint, e [kɔ̃ʒwɛ̃, -wɛ̃t] adj joint
▷ nm/f spouse
conjonctivite [kɔ̃ʒɔ̃ktivit] nf
conjunctivitis
conjoncture [kɔ̃ʒɔ̃ktyʀ]
nf circumstances pl; **la ~
(économique)** the economic
climate ou situation
conjugaison [kɔ̃ʒygɛzɔ̃] nf (Ling)
conjugation
connaissance [kɔnɛsɑ̃s] nf (savoir)
knowledge no pl; (personne connue)
acquaintance; **être sans ~** to be
unconscious; **perdre/reprendre
~** to lose/regain consciousness; **à
ma/sa ~** to (the best of) my/his
knowledge; **faire ~ avec qn** ou **la ~
de qn** to meet sb
connaisseur, -euse [kɔnɛsœʀ, -øz]
nm/f connoisseur
connaître [kɔnɛtʀ] /57/ vt to know;
(éprouver) to experience; (avoir: succès)
to have; to enjoy; **~ de nom/vue** to
know by name/sight; **ils se sont
connus à Genève** they (first) met
in Geneva; **s'y ~ en qch** to know
about sth
connecter [kɔnɛkte] /1/ vt to
connect; **se ~ à Internet** to log onto
the Internet
connerie [kɔnʀi] nf (fam) (bloody)
stupid (BRIT) ou damn-fool (US) thing
to do ou say
connexion [kɔnɛksjɔ̃] nf connection
connu, e [kɔny] adj (célèbre) well-
known
conquérir [kɔ̃keʀiʀ] /21/ vt to
conquer; **conquête** nf conquest
consacrer [kɔ̃sakʀe] /1/ vt (Rel) to
consecrate; **~ qch à** (employer) to
devote ou dedicate sth to; **se ~ à**

qch/faire to dedicate ou devote o.s.
to sth/to doing
conscience [kɔ̃sjɑ̃s] nf conscience;
avoir/prendre ~ de to be/become
aware of; **perdre/reprendre ~** to
lose/regain consciousness; **avoir
bonne/mauvaise ~** to have a clear/
guilty conscience; **consciencieux,
-euse** adj conscientious; **conscient, e**
adj conscious
consécutif, -ive [kɔ̃sekytif, -iv] adj
consecutive; **~ à** following upon
conseil [kɔ̃sɛj] nm (avis) piece of
advice; (assemblée) council; **donner
un ~** ou **des ~s à qn** to give sb (a
piece of) advice; **prendre ~ (auprès
de qn)** to take advice (from sb);
~ d'administration (CA) board
(of directors); **~ général** regional
council; **le ~ des ministres** ≈ the
Cabinet; **~ municipal (CM)** town
council
conseiller¹ [kɔ̃seje] vt (personne)
to advise; (méthode, action) to
recommend, advise; **~ à qn de faire
qch** to advise sb to do sth
conseiller², -ière [kɔ̃seje, -ɛʀ]
nm/f adviser; **~ d'orientation** (Scol)
careers adviser (BRIT), (school)
counselor (US)
consentement [kɔ̃sɑ̃tmɑ̃] nm
consent
consentir [kɔ̃sɑ̃tiʀ] /16/ vt: **~ (à
qch/faire)** to agree ou consent (to
sth/to doing)
conséquence [kɔ̃sekɑ̃s] nf
consequence; **en ~ (donc)**
consequently; (de façon appropriée)
accordingly; **conséquent, e** adj
logical, rational; (fam: important)
substantial; **par conséquent**
consequently
conservateur, -trice [kɔ̃sɛʀvatœʀ,
-tʀis] nm/f (Pol) conservative; (de
musée) curator ▷ nm (pour aliments)
preservative
conservatoire [kɔ̃sɛʀvatwaʀ] nm
academy

conserve [kɔ̃sɛʀv] nf (gén pl) canned ou tinned (BRIT) food; **en ~** canned, tinned (BRIT)

conserver [kɔ̃sɛʀve] /1/ vt (faculté) to retain, keep; (amis, livres) to keep; (préserver, Culin) to preserve

considérable [kɔ̃siderabl] adj considerable, significant, extensive

considération [kɔ̃siderasjɔ̃] nf consideration; (estime) esteem

considérer [kɔ̃sidere] /6/ vt to consider; **~ qch comme** to regard sth as

consigne [kɔ̃siɲ] nf (de gare) left luggage (office) (BRIT), checkroom (US); (ordre, instruction) instructions pl; **~ automatique** left-luggage locker

consister [kɔ̃siste] /1/ vi: **~ en/ dans/à faire** to consist of/in/ in doing

consoler [kɔ̃sɔle] /1/ vt to console

consommateur, -trice [kɔ̃sɔmatœʀ, -tʀis] nm/f (Écon) consumer; (dans un café) customer

consommation [kɔ̃sɔmasjɔ̃] nf (Écon) consumption; (boisson) drink; **de ~** (biens, société) consumer cpd

consommer [kɔ̃sɔme] /1/ vt (personne) to eat ou drink, consume; (voiture, usine, poêle) to use, consume; (Jur: mariage) to consummate ▷ vi (dans un café) to (have a) drink

consonne [kɔ̃sɔn] nf consonant

constamment [kɔ̃stamã] adv constantly

constant, e [kɔ̃stã, -ãt] adj constant; (personne) steadfast

constat [kɔ̃sta] nm (de police) report; **~ (à l'amiable)** (jointly agreed) statement for insurance purposes; **~ d'échec** acknowledgement of failure

constatation [kɔ̃statasjɔ̃] nf (remarque) observation

constater [kɔ̃state] /1/ vt (remarquer) to note; (Admin, Jur: attester) to certify

consterner [kɔ̃stɛʀne] /1/ vt to dismay

constipé, e [kɔ̃stipe] adj constipated

constitué, e [kɔ̃stitɥe] adj: **~ de** made up ou composed of

constituer [kɔ̃stitɥe] /1/ vt (comité, équipe) to set up; (dossier, collection) to put together; (éléments, parties: composer) to make up, constitute; (: représenter, être) to constitute; **se ~ prisonnier** to give o.s. up

constructeur [kɔ̃stʀyktœʀ] nm/f manufacturer, builder

constructif, -ive [kɔ̃stʀyktif, -iv] adj constructive

construction [kɔ̃stʀyksjɔ̃] nf construction, building

construire [kɔ̃stʀɥiʀ] /38/ vt to build, construct

consul [kɔ̃syl] nm consul; **consulat** nm consulate

consultant, e adj, nm consultant

consultation [kɔ̃syltasjɔ̃] nf consultation; **heures de ~** (Méd) surgery (BRIT) ou office (US) hours

consulter [kɔ̃sylte] /1/ vt to consult ▷ vi (médecin) to hold surgery (BRIT), be in (the office) (US)

contact [kɔ̃takt] nm contact; **au ~ de** (air, peau) on contact with; (gens) through contact with; **mettre/ couper le ~** (Auto) to switch on/off the ignition; **entrer en ~** to come into contact; **prendre ~ avec** to get in touch ou contact with; **contacter** /1/ vt to contact, get in touch with

contagieux, -euse [kɔ̃taʒjø, -øz] adj infectious; (par le contact) contagious

contaminer [kɔ̃tamine] /1/ vt to contaminate

conte [kɔ̃t] nm tale; **~ de fées** fairy tale

contempler [kɔ̃tãple] /1/ vt to contemplate, gaze at

contemporain, e [kɔ̃tãpɔʀɛ̃, -ɛn] adj, nm/f contemporary

contenir [kɔ̃t(ə)niʀ] /22/ vt to contain; (avoir une capacité de) to hold

content, e [kɔ̃tɑ̃, -ɑ̃t] *adj* pleased, glad; **~ de** pleased with; **contenter** /1/ *vt* to satisfy, please; **se contenter de** to content o.s. with

contenu, e [kɔ̃t(ə)ny] *nm* (*d'un bol*) contents *pl*; (*d'un texte*) content

conter [kɔ̃te] /1/ *vt* to recount, relate

conteste [kɔ̃tɛst]: **sans ~** *adv* unquestionably, indisputably; **contester** /1/ *vt* to question ▷ *vi* (*Pol, gén*) to rebel (against established authority)

contexte [kɔ̃tɛkst] *nm* context

continent [kɔ̃tinɑ̃] *nm* continent

continu, e [kɔ̃tiny] *adj* continuous; **faire la journée ~e** to work without taking a full lunch break; **(courant) ~** direct current, DC

continuel, le [kɔ̃tinɥɛl] *adj* (*qui se répète*) constant, continual; (*continu*) continuous

continuer [kɔ̃tinɥe] /1/ *vt* (*travail, voyage etc*) to continue (with), carry on (with), go on with; (*prolonger: alignement, rue*) to continue ▷ *vi* (*pluie, vie, bruit*) to continue, go on; **~ à ou de faire** to go on *ou* continue doing

contourner [kɔ̃turne] /1/ *vt* to bypass, walk *ou* drive round; (*difficulté*) to get round

contraceptif, -ive [kɔ̃trasɛptif, -iv] *adj, nm* contraceptive; **contraception** *nf* contraception

contracté, e [kɔ̃trakte] *adj* tense

contracter [kɔ̃trakte] /1/ *vt* (*muscle etc*) to tense, contract; (*maladie, dette, obligation*) to contract; (*assurance*) to take out; **se contracter** *vi* (*métal, muscles*) to contract

contractuel, le [kɔ̃traktɥɛl] *nm/f* (*agent*) traffic warden

contradiction [kɔ̃tradiksjɔ̃] *nf* contradiction; **contradictoire** *adj* contradictory, conflicting

contraignant, e [kɔ̃trɛɲɑ̃, -ɑ̃t] *adj* restricting

contraindre [kɔ̃trɛ̃dr] /52/ *vt*: **~ qn à faire** to force *ou* compel sb to do

contraint, e *pp de* **contraindre** ▷ *nf* constraint

contraire [kɔ̃trɛr] *adj, nm* opposite; **~ à** contrary to; **au ~** on the contrary

contrarier [kɔ̃trarje] /7/ *vt* (*personne*) to annoy; (*projets*) to thwart, frustrate; **contrariété** [kɔ̃trarjete] *nf* annoyance

contraste [kɔ̃trast] *nm* contrast

contrat [kɔ̃tra] *nm* contract

contravention [kɔ̃travɑ̃sjɔ̃] *nf* parking ticket

contre [kɔ̃tr] *prép* against; (*en échange*) (in exchange) for; **par ~** on the other hand

contrebande [kɔ̃trəbɑ̃d] *nf* (*trafic*) contraband, smuggling; (*marchandise*) contraband, smuggled goods *pl*; **faire la ~ de** to smuggle

contrebas [kɔ̃trəba]: **en ~** *adv* (down) below

contrebasse [kɔ̃trəbas] *nf* (double) bass

contre: contrecoup *nm* repercussions *pl*; **contredire** /37/ *vt* (*personne*) to contradict; (*témoignage, assertion, faits*) to refute

contrefaçon [kɔ̃trəfasɔ̃] *nf* forgery

contre: contre-indication (*pl* **contre-indications**) *nf* (*Méd*) contra-indication; **"contre-indication en cas d'eczéma"** "should not be used by people with eczema"; **contre-indiqué, e** *adj* (*Méd*) contraindicated; (*déconseillé*) unadvisable, ill-advised

contremaître [kɔ̃trəmɛtr] *nm* foreman

contre-plaqué [kɔ̃trəplake] *nm* plywood

contresens [kɔ̃trəsɑ̃s] *nm* (*erreur*) misinterpretation; (*mauvaise traduction*) mistranslation; **à ~** the wrong way

contretemps [kɔ̃trətɑ̃] *nm* hitch; **à ~** (*fig*) at an inopportune moment

contribuer [kɔ̃tribɥe] /1/: **~ à** *vt* to contribute towards; **contribution** *nf* contribution;

mettre à contribution to call upon; **contributions directes/indirectes** direct/indirect taxation

contrôle [kɔ̃trol] *nm* checking *no pl*, check; monitoring; (*test*) test, examination; **perdre le ~ de son véhicule** to lose control of one's vehicle; **~ continu** (*Scol*) continuous assessment; **~ d'identité** identity check

contrôler [kɔ̃trole] /1/ *vt* (*vérifier*) to check; (*surveiller: opérations*) to supervise; (: *prix*) to monitor, control; (*maîtriser, Comm: firme*) to control; **contrôleur, -euse** *nm/f* (*de train*) (ticket) inspector; (*de bus*) (bus) conductor/tress

controversé, e [kɔ̃troverse] *adj* (*personnage, question*) controversial

contusion [kɔ̃tyzjɔ̃] *nf* bruise, contusion

convaincre [kɔ̃vɛ̃kr] /42/ *vt*: **~ qn (de qch)** to convince sb (of sth); **~ qn (de faire)** to persuade sb (to do)

convalescence [kɔ̃valesɑ̃s] *nf* convalescence

convenable [kɔ̃vnabl] *adj* suitable; (*assez bon*) decent

convenir [kɔ̃vnir] /22/ *vi* to be suitable; **~ à** to suit; **~ de** (*bien-fondé de qch*) to admit (to), acknowledge; (*date, somme etc*) to agree upon; **~ que** (*admettre*) to admit that; **~ de faire qch** to agree to do sth

convention [kɔ̃vɑ̃sjɔ̃] *nf* convention; **conventions** *nfpl* (*convenances*) convention *sg*; **~ collective** (*Écon*) collective agreement; **conventionné, e** *adj* (*Admin*) applying charges laid down by the state

convenu, e [kɔ̃vny] *pp de* **convenir** ▷ *adj* agreed

conversation [kɔ̃versasjɔ̃] *nf* conversation

convertir [kɔ̃vertir] /2/ *vt*: **~ qn (à)** to convert sb (to); **~ qch en** to convert sth into; **se ~ (à)** to be converted (to)

conviction [kɔ̃viksjɔ̃] *nf* conviction

convienne *etc* [kɔ̃vjɛn] *vb voir* **convenir**

convivial, e [kɔ̃vivjal] *adj* (*Inform*) user-friendly

convocation [kɔ̃vɔkasjɔ̃] *nf* (*document*) notification to attend; (*Jur*) summons *sg*

convoquer [kɔ̃vɔke] /1/ *vt* (*assemblée*) to convene; (*subordonné, témoin*) to summon; (*candidat*) to ask to attend

coopération [kɔɔperasjɔ̃] *nf* co-operation; (*Admin*): **la C~** ≈ Voluntary Service Overseas (BRIT) *ou* the Peace Corps (US: *done as alternative to military service*)

coopérer [kɔɔpere] /6/ *vi*: **~ (à)** to co-operate (in)

coordonné, e [kɔɔrdone] *adj* coordinated; **coordonnées** *nfpl* (*détails personnels*) address, phone number, schedule *etc*

coordonner [kɔɔrdone] /1/ *vt* to coordinate

copain, copine *nm/f* pal; (*petit ami*) boyfriend; (*petite amie*) girlfriend

copie [kɔpi] *nf* copy; (*Scol*) script, paper; **copier** /7/ *vt, vi* to copy; **copier coller** (*Inform*) copy and paste; **copier sur** to copy from; **copieur** *nm* (photo)copier

copieux, -euse [kɔpjø, -øz] *adj* copious

copine [kɔpin] *nf voir* **copain**

coq [kɔk] *nm* cockerel

coque [kɔk] *nf* (*de noix, mollusque*) shell; (*de bateau*) hull; **à la ~** (*Culin*) (soft-)boiled

coquelicot [kɔkliko] *nm* poppy

coqueluche [kɔklyʃ] *nf* whooping-cough

coquet, te [kɔkɛ, -ɛt] *adj* appearance-conscious; (*logement*) smart, charming

coquetier [kɔk(ə)tje] *nm* egg-cup

coquillage [kɔkijaʒ] *nm* (*mollusque*) shellfish *inv*; (*coquille*) shell

coquille [kɔkij] nf shell; (Typo) misprint; **~ St Jacques** scallop

coquin, e [kɔkɛ̃, -in] adj mischievous, roguish; (polisson) naughty

cor [kɔʀ] nm (Mus) horn; (Méd): **~ (au pied)** corn

corail, -aux [kɔʀaj, -o] nm coral no pl

Coran [kɔʀɑ̃] nm: **le ~** the Koran

corbeau, x [kɔʀbo] nm crow

corbeille [kɔʀbɛj] nf basket; (Inform) recycle bin; **~ à papier** waste paper basket ou bin

corde [kɔʀd] nf rope; (de violon, raquette, d'arc) string; **usé jusqu'à la ~** threadbare; **~ à linge** washing ou clothes line; **~ à sauter** skipping rope; **~s vocales** vocal cords

cordée [kɔʀde] nf (d'alpinistes) rope, roped party

cordialement [kɔʀdjalmɑ̃] adv (formule épistolaire) (kind) regards

cordon [kɔʀdɔ̃] nm cord, string; **~ sanitaire/de police** sanitary/police cordon; **~ ombilical** umbilical cord

cordonnerie [kɔʀdɔnʀi] nf shoe repairer's ou mender's (shop); **cordonnier** nm shoe repairer ou mender

Corée [kɔʀe] nf: **la ~ du Sud/du Nord** South/North Korea

coriace [kɔʀjas] adj tough

corne [kɔʀn] nf horn; (de cerf) antler

cornée [kɔʀne] nf cornea

corneille [kɔʀnɛj] nf crow

cornemuse [kɔʀnəmyz] nf bagpipes pl

cornet [kɔʀnɛ] nm (paper) cone; (de glace) cornet, cone

corniche [kɔʀniʃ] nf (route) coast road

cornichon [kɔʀniʃɔ̃] nm gherkin

Cornouailles [kɔʀnwaj] fpl Cornwall

corporel, le [kɔʀpɔʀɛl] adj bodily; (punition) corporal

corps [kɔʀ] nm body; **à ~ perdu** headlong; **prendre ~** to take shape; **le ~ électoral** the electorate; **le ~ enseignant** the teaching profession

correct, e [kɔʀɛkt] adj correct; **correcteur, -trice** nm/f (Scol) examiner; **correction** nf (voir corriger) correction; (voir correct) correctness; (coups) thrashing

correspondance [kɔʀɛspɔ̃dɑ̃s] nf correspondence; (de train, d'avion) connection; **cours par ~** correspondence course; **vente par ~** mail-order business

correspondant, e [kɔʀɛspɔ̃dɑ̃, -ɑ̃t] nm/f correspondent; (Tél) person phoning (ou being phoned)

correspondre [kɔʀɛspɔ̃dʀ] /41/ vi to correspond, tally; **~ à** to correspond to; **~ avec qn** to correspond with sb

corrida [kɔʀida] nf bullfight

corridor [kɔʀidɔʀ] nm corridor

corrigé [kɔʀiʒe] nm (Scol: d'exercice) correct version

corriger [kɔʀiʒe] /3/ vt (devoir) to correct; (punir) to thrash; **~ qn de** (défaut) to cure sb of

corrompre [kɔʀɔ̃pʀ] /41/ vt to corrupt; (acheter: témoin etc) to bribe

corruption [kɔʀypsjɔ̃] nf corruption; (de témoins) bribery

corse [kɔʀs] adj Corsican ▷ nm/f: **C~** Corsican ▷ nf: **la C~** Corsica

corsé, e [kɔʀse] adj (café etc) full-flavoured (BRIT) ou -flavored (US); (sauce) spicy; (problème) tough

cortège [kɔʀtɛʒ] nm procession

cortisone [kɔʀtizɔn] nf cortisone

corvée [kɔʀve] nf chore, drudgery no pl

cosmétique [kɔsmetik] nm beauty care product

cosmopolite [kɔsmɔpɔlit] adj cosmopolitan

costaud, e [kɔsto, -od] adj strong, sturdy

costume [kɔstym] nm (d'homme) suit; (de théâtre) costume; **costumé, e** adj dressed up

cote [kɔt] nf (en Bourse etc) quotation; **~ d'alerte** danger ou flood level; **~ de popularité** popularity rating

côte [kot] *nf* (*rivage*) coast(line); (*pente*) hill; (*Anat*) rib; (*d'un tricot, tissu*) rib, ribbing *no pl*; **~ à ~** side by side; **la C~ (d'Azur)** the (French) Riviera

côté [kote] *nm* (*gén*) side; (*direction*) way, direction; **de chaque ~ (de)** on each side of; **de tous les ~s** from all directions; **de quel ~ est-il parti?** which way *ou* in which direction did he go?; **de ce/de l'autre ~** this/the other way; **du ~ de** (*provenance*) from; (*direction*) towards; **du ~ de Lyon** (*proximité*) near Lyons; **de ~** (*regarder*) sideways; **mettre de ~** to put aside, put on one side; **mettre de l'argent de ~** to save some money; **à ~** (*right*) nearby; (*voisins*) next door; **à ~ de** beside; next to; (*fig*) in comparison to; **être aux ~s de** to be by the side of

Côte d'Ivoire [kotdivwaʀ] *nf*: **la ~** Côte d'Ivoire, the Ivory Coast

côtelette [kotlɛt] *nf* chop

côtier, -ière [kotje, -jɛʀ] *adj* coastal

cotisation [kɔtizasjɔ̃] *nf* subscription, dues *pl*; (*pour une pension*) contributions *pl*

cotiser [kɔtize] /1/ *vi*: **~ (à)** to pay contributions (to); **se cotiser** *vi* to club together

coton [kɔtɔ̃] *nm* cotton; **~ hydrophile** cotton wool (*BRIT*), absorbent cotton (*US*)

Coton-Tige® *nm* cotton bud

cou [ku] *nm* neck

couchant [kuʃɑ̃] *adj*: **soleil ~** setting sun

couche [kuʃ] *nf* layer; (*de peinture, vernis*) coat; (*de bébé*) nappy (*BRIT*), diaper (*US*); **~s sociales** social levels *ou* strata

couché, e [kuʃe] *adj* lying down; (*au lit*) in bed

coucher [kuʃe] /1/ *vt* (*personne*) to put to bed (: *loger*) to put up; (*objet*) to lay on its side ▷ *vi* to sleep; **~ avec qn** to sleep with sb; **se coucher** *vi* (*pour dormir*) to go to bed; (*pour se reposer*) to lie down; (*soleil*) to set; **~ de soleil** sunset

couchette [kuʃɛt] *nf* couchette; (*pour voyageur, sur bateau*) berth

coucou [kuku] *nm* cuckoo

coude [kud] *nm* (*Anat*) elbow; (*de tuyau, de la route*) bend; **~ à ~** shoulder to shoulder, side by side

coudre [kudʀ] /48/ *vt* (*bouton*) to sew on ▷ *vi* to sew

couette [kwɛt] *nf* duvet; **couettes** *nfpl* (*cheveux*) bunches

couffin [kufɛ̃] *nm* Moses basket

couler [kule] /1/ *vi* to flow, run; (*fuir: stylo, récipient*) to leak; (: *nez*) to run; (*sombrer: bateau*) to sink ▷ *vt* (*cloche, sculpture*) to cast; (*bateau*) to sink; (*faire échouer: personne*) to bring down, ruin

couleur [kulœʀ] *nf* colour (*BRIT*), color (*US*); (*Cartes*) suit; **en ~s** (*film*) in colo(u)r; **télévision en ~s** colo(u)r television; **de ~** (*homme, femme: vieilli*) colo(u)red

couleuvre [kulœvʀ] *nf* grass snake

coulisse [kulis] *nf* (*Tech*) runner; **coulisses** *nfpl* (*Théât*) wings; (*fig*): **dans les ~s** behind the scenes

couloir [kulwaʀ] *nm* corridor, passage; (*d'avion*) aisle; (*de bus*) gangway; **~ aérien** air corridor *ou* lane; **~ de navigation** shipping lane

coup [ku] *nm* (*heurt, choc*) knock; (*affectif*) blow, shock; (*agressif*) blow; (*avec arme à feu*) shot; (*de l'horloge*) stroke; (*Sport: golf*) stroke; (: *tennis*) shot; (*fam: fois*) time; **~ de coude/genou** nudge (with the elbow)/with the knee; **donner un ~ de balai** to give the floor a sweep; **être dans le/hors du ~** to be/not to be in on it; (*à la page*) to be hip *ou* trendy; **du ~** as a result; **d'un seul ~** (*subitement*) suddenly; (*à la fois*) at one go; **du premier ~** first time *ou* go; **du même ~** at the same time; **à ~ sûr** definitely, without fail; **après ~** afterwards; **~ sur ~** in quick succession; **sur le ~**

outright; **sous le ~ de** (*surprise etc*) under the influence of; **à tous les ~s** every time; **tenir le ~** to hold out; **~ de chance** stroke of luck; **~ de couteau** stab (of a knife); **~ d'envoi** kick-off; **~ d'essai** first attempt; **~ d'état** coup d'état; **~ de feu** shot; **~ de filet** (*Police*) haul; **~ de foudre** (*fig*) love at first sight; **~ franc** free kick; **~ de frein** (sharp) braking *no pl*; **~ de grâce** coup de grâce; **~ de main: donner un ~ de main à qn** to give sb a (helping) hand; **~ d'œil** glance; **~ de pied** kick; **~ de poing** punch; **~ de soleil** sunburn *no pl*; **~ de sonnette** ring of the bell; **~ de téléphone** phone call; **~ de tête** (*fig*) (sudden) impulse; **~ de théâtre** (*fig*) dramatic turn of events; **~ de tonnerre** clap of thunder; **~ de vent** gust of wind; **en ~ de vent** (*rapidement*) in a tearing hurry

coupable [kupabl] *adj* guilty ▷ *nm/f* (*gén*) culprit; (*Jur*) guilty party

coupe [kup] *nf* (*verre*) goblet; (*à fruits*) dish; (*Sport*) cup; (*de cheveux, de vêtement*) cut; (*graphique, plan*) (cross) section

couper [kupe] /1/ *vt* to cut; (*retrancher*) to cut (out); (*route, courant*) to cut off; (*appétit*) to take away; (*vin, cidre: à table*) to dilute (with water) ▷ *vi* to cut; (*prendre un raccourci*) to take a short-cut; **se couper** *vi* (*se blesser*) to cut o.s.; **~ la parole à qn** to cut sb short; **nous avons été coupés** we've been cut off

couple [kupl] *nm* couple

couplet [kuplɛ] *nm* verse

coupole [kupɔl] *nf* dome

coupon [kupɔ̃] *nm* (*ticket*) coupon; (*de tissu*) remnant

coupure [kupyʀ] *nf* cut; (*billet de banque*) note; (*de journal*) cutting; **~ de courant** power cut

cour [kuʀ] *nf* (*de ferme, jardin*) (court) yard; (*d'immeuble*) back yard; (*Jur,*

royale) court; **faire la ~ à qn** to court sb; **~ d'assises** court of assizes; **~ de récréation** playground

courage [kuʀaʒ] *nm* courage, bravery; **courageux, -euse** *adj* brave, courageous

couramment [kuʀamɑ̃] *adv* commonly; (*parler*) fluently

courant, e [kuʀɑ̃, -ɑ̃t] *adj* (*fréquent*) common; (*Comm, gén: normal*) standard; (*en cours*) current ▷ *nm* current; (*fig*) movement; (: *d'opinion*) trend; **être au ~ (de)** (*fait, nouvelle*) to know (about); **mettre qn au ~ (de)** to tell sb (about); (*nouveau travail etc*) to teach sb the basics (of); **se tenir au ~ (de)** (*techniques etc*) to keep o.s. up-to-date (on); **dans le ~ de** (*pendant*) in the course of; **le 10 ~** (*Comm*) the 10th inst.; **~ d'air** draught; **~ électrique** (electric) current, power

courbature [kuʀbatyʀ] *nf* ache

courbe [kuʀb] *adj* curved ▷ *nf* curve

coureur, -euse [kuʀœʀ, -øz] *nm/f* (*Sport*) runner (*ou* driver); (*péj*) womanizer/manhunter

courge [kuʀʒ] *nf* (*Culin*) marrow; **courgette** *nf* courgette (*BRIT*), zucchini (*US*)

courir [kuʀiʀ] /11/ *vi* to run ▷ *vt* (*Sport: épreuve*) to compete in; (: *risque*) to run; (: *danger*) to face; **~ les cafés/bals** to do the rounds of the cafés/ dances; **le bruit court que** the rumour is going round that

couronne [kuʀɔn] *nf* crown; (*de fleurs*) wreath, circlet

courons [kuʀɔ̃] *vb voir* **courir**

courriel [kuʀjɛl] *nm* email

courrier [kuʀje] *nm* mail, post; (*lettres à écrire*) letters *pl*; **est-ce que j'ai du ~?** are there any letters for me?; **~ électronique** email

▮ Attention à ne pas traduire *courrier* par le mot anglais *courier*.

courroie [kuʀwa] *nf* strap; (*Tech*) belt

courrons *etc* [kuʀɔ̃] *vb voir* **courir**

cours [kur] *nm* (*leçon*) class
(*: particulier*) lesson; (*série de leçons*)
course; (*écoulement*) flow; (*Comm:
de devises*) rate; (*: de denrées*) price;
donner libre ~ à to give free
expression to; **avoir ~** (*Scol*) to have a
class *ou* lecture; **en ~** (*année*) current;
(*travaux*) in progress; **en ~ de route**
on the way; **au ~ de** in the course of,
during; **le ~ du change** the exchange
rate; **~ d'eau** waterway; **~ du soir**
night school

course [kurs] *nf* running; (*Sport:
épreuve*) race; (*d'un taxi, autocar*)
journey, trip; (*petite mission*) errand;
courses *nfpl* (*achats*) shopping *sg*;
faire les *ou* **ses ~s** to go shopping

court, e [kur, kurt] *adj* short ⊳ *adv*
short; **~ (de tennis)** (tennis)
court; **à ~ de** short of; **prendre qn
de ~** to catch sb unawares; **court-
circuit** *nm* short-circuit

courtoisie [kurtwazi] *nf* courtesy

couru, e [kury] *pp de* **courir**

cousais *etc* [kuze] *vb voir* **coudre**

couscous [kuskus] *nm* couscous

cousin, e [kuzɛ̃, -in] *nm/f* cousin

coussin [kusɛ̃] *nm* cushion

cousu, e [kuzy] *pp de* **coudre**

coût [ku] *nm* cost; **le ~ de la vie** the
cost of living

couteau, x [kuto] *nm* knife

coûter [kute] /1/ *vt* to cost ⊳ *vi*
to cost; **~ cher** to be expensive;
combien ça coûte? how much is it?,
what does it cost?; **coûte que coûte**
at all costs; **coûteux, -euse** *adj*
costly, expensive

coutume [kutym] *nf* custom

couture [kutyr] *nf* sewing;
(*profession*) dress-making; (*points*)
seam; **couturier** *nm* fashion
designer; **couturière** *nf* dressmaker

couvent [kuvɑ̃] *nm* (*de sœurs*)
convent; (*de frères*) monastery

couver [kuve] /1/ *vt* to hatch;
(*maladie*) to be sickening for ⊳ *vi* (*feu*)
to smoulder ; (*révolte*) to be brewing

couvercle [kuvɛrkl] *nm* lid; (*de
bombe aérosol etc, qui se visse*) cap, top

couvert, e [kuvɛr, -ɛrt] *pp de*
couvrir ⊳ *adj* (*ciel*) overcast ⊳ *nm*
place setting; (*place à table*) place;
couverts *nmpl* (*ustensiles*) cutlery *sg*;
~ de covered with *ou* in; **mettre le ~**
to lay the table

couverture [kuvɛrtyr] *nf* blanket;
(*de livre, fig, Assurances*) cover; (*Presse*)
coverage

couvre-lit [kuvrəli] *nm* bedspread

couvrir [kuvrir] /18/ *vt* to cover;
se couvrir *vi* (*ciel*) to cloud over;
(*s'habiller*) to cover up; (*se coiffer*) to
put on one's hat

cow-boy [kɔbɔj] *nm* cowboy

crabe [krab] *nm* crab

cracher [kraʃe] /1/ *vi* to spit ⊳ *vt*
to spit out

crachin [kraʃɛ̃] *nm* drizzle

craie [krɛ] *nf* chalk

craindre [krɛ̃dr] /52/ *vt* to fear, be
afraid of; (*être sensible à: chaleur, froid*)
to be easily damaged by

crainte [krɛ̃t] *nf* fear; **de ~ de/
que** for fear of/that; **craintif, -ive**
adj timid

crampe [krɑ̃p] *nf* cramp; **j'ai une ~ à
la jambe** I've got cramp in my leg

cramponner [krɑ̃pɔne] /1/: **se
cramponner** *vi*: **se ~ (à)** to hang *ou*
cling on (to)

cran [krɑ̃] *nm* (*entaille*) notch; (*de
courroie*) hole; (*courage*) guts *pl*

crâne [krɑn] *nm* skull

crapaud [krapo] *nm* toad

craquement [krakmɑ̃] *nm* crack,
snap; (*du plancher*) creak, creaking
no pl

craquer [krake] /1/ *vi* (*bois, plancher*)
to creak; (*fil, branche*) to snap;
(*couture*) to come apart; (*fig: accusé*)
to break down, fall apart ⊳ *vt*: **~ une
allumette** to strike a match; **j'ai
craqué** (*fam*) I couldn't resist it

crasse [kras] *nf* grime, filth;
crasseux, -euse *adj* filthy

cravache [kʀavaʃ] nf (riding) crop
cravate [kʀavat] nf tie
crawl [kʀol] nm crawl; **dos ~é**
backstroke
crayon [kʀɛjɔ̃] nm pencil; **~ à bille**
ball-point pen; **~ de couleur** crayon;
crayon-feutre (pl **crayons-feutres**)
nm felt(-tip) pen
création [kʀeasjɔ̃] nf creation
crèche [kʀɛʃ] nf (de Noël) crib;
(garderie) crèche, day nursery
crédit [kʀedi] nm (gén) credit; **crédits**
nmpl funds; **acheter à ~** to buy on
credit ou on easy terms; **faire ~ à**
qn to give sb credit; **créditer** /1/ vt:
créditer un compte (de) to credit an
account (with)
créer [kʀee] /1/ vt to create
crémaillère [kʀemajɛʀ] nf: **pendre**
la ~ to have a house-warming party
crème [kʀɛm] nf cream; (entremets)
cream dessert ▷ adj inv cream; **un**
(café) ~ ≈ a white coffee; **~ anglaise**
(egg) custard; **~ chantilly** whipped
cream; **~ à raser** shaving cream;
~ solaire sun cream
créneau, x [kʀeno] nm (de
fortification) crenel(le); (fig, aussi
Comm) gap, slot; (Auto): **faire un ~** to
reverse into a parking space (between
cars alongside the kerb)
crêpe [kʀɛp] nf (galette) pancake
▷ nm (tissu) crêpe; **crêperie** nf
pancake shop ou restaurant
crépuscule [kʀepyskyl] nm twilight,
dusk
cresson [kʀesɔ̃] nm watercress
creuser [kʀøze] /1/ vt (trou, tunnel)
to dig; (sol) to dig a hole in; (fig) to go
(deeply) into; **ça creuse** that gives
you a real appetite; **se ~ (la cervelle)**
to rack one's brains
creux, -euse [kʀø, -øz] adj hollow
▷ nm hollow; **heures creuses**
slack periods; (électricité, téléphone)
off-peak periods; **avoir un ~** (fam)
to be hungry
crevaison [kʀəvɛzɔ̃] nf puncture

crevé, e [kʀəve] adj (fam: fatigué)
shattered (BRIT), exhausted
crever [kʀəve] /5/ vt (tambour,
ballon) to burst ▷ vi (pneu) to burst;
(automobiliste) to have a puncture
(BRIT) ou a flat (tire) (US); (fam) to die
crevette [kʀəvɛt] nf: **~ (rose)**
prawn; **~ grise** shrimp
cri [kʀi] nm cry, shout; (d'animal:
spécifique) cry, call; **c'est le dernier ~**
(fig) it's the latest fashion
criard, e [kʀijaʀ, -aʀd] adj (couleur)
garish, loud; (voix) yelling
cric [kʀik] nm (Auto) jack
crier [kʀije] /7/ vi (pour appeler) to
shout, cry (out); (de peur, de douleur
etc) to scream, yell ▷ vt (ordre, injure)
to shout (out), yell (out)
crime [kʀim] nm crime; (meurtre)
murder; **criminel, le** nm/f criminal;
murderer
crin [kʀɛ̃] nm (de cheval) hair no pl
crinière [kʀinjɛʀ] nf mane
crique [kʀik] nf creek, inlet
criquet [kʀike] nm grasshopper
crise [kʀiz] nf crisis (pl crises); (Méd)
attack (: d'épilepsie) fit; **~ cardiaque**
heart attack; **avoir une ~ de foie** to
have really bad indigestion; **piquer**
une ~ de nerfs to go hysterical
cristal, -aux [kʀistal, -o] nm crystal
critère [kʀitɛʀ] nm criterion (pl criteria)
critiquable [kʀitikabl] adj open
to criticism
critique [kʀitik] adj critical ▷ nm/f
(de théâtre, musique) critic ▷ nf
criticism; (Théât etc article) review
critiquer [kʀitike] /1/ vt (dénigrer)
to criticize; (évaluer, juger) to assess,
examine (critically)
croate [kʀɔat] adj Croatian ▷ nm
(Ling) Croat, Croatian ▷ nm/f: **C~**
Croat, Croatian
Croatie [kʀɔasi] nf: **la ~** Croatia
crochet [kʀɔʃɛ] nm hook; (détour)
detour; (Tricot: aiguille) crochet hook;
(: technique) crochet; **vivre aux ~s de**
qn to live ou sponge off sb

crocodile [kʀɔkɔdil] nm crocodile

croire [kʀwaʀ] /44/ vt to believe; **se ~ fort** to think one is strong; **~ que** to believe ou think that; **~ à, ~ en** to believe in

croisade [kʀwazad] nf crusade

croisement [kʀwazmã] nm (carrefour) crossroads sg; (Bio) crossing (: résultat) crossbreed

croiser [kʀwaze] /1/ vt (personne, voiture) to pass; (route) to cross, cut across; (Bio) to cross; **se croiser** vi (personnes, véhicules) to pass each other; (routes) to cross; (regards) to meet; **se ~ les bras** (fig) to fold one's arms, to twiddle one's thumbs

croisière [kʀwazjɛʀ] nf cruise

croissance [kʀwasãs] nf growth

croissant, e [kʀwasã, -ãt] adj growing ▷ nm (à manger) croissant; (motif) crescent

croître [kʀwatʀ] /55/ vi to grow

croix [kʀwa] nf cross; **la C~ Rouge** the Red Cross

croque-madame [kʀɔkmadam] nm inv toasted cheese sandwich with a fried egg on top

croque-monsieur [kʀɔkməsjø] nm inv toasted ham and cheese sandwich

croquer [kʀɔke] /1/ vt (manger) to crunch (: fruit) to munch; (dessiner) to sketch; **chocolat à ~** plain dessert chocolate

croquis [kʀɔki] nm sketch

crotte [kʀɔt] nf droppings pl; **crottin** [kʀɔtɛ̃] nm dung, manure; (fromage) (small round) cheese (made of goat's milk)

croustillant, e [kʀustijã, -ãt] adj crisp

croûte [kʀut] nf crust; (du fromage) rind; (Méd) scab; **en ~** (Culin) in pastry

croûton [kʀutɔ̃] nm (Culin) crouton; (bout du pain) crust, heel

croyant, e [kʀwajã, -ãt] nm/f believer

CRS sigle fpl (= Compagnies républicaines de sécurité) state security police force ▷ sigle m member of the CRS

cru, e [kʀy] pp de **croire** ▷ adj (non cuit) raw; (lumière, couleur) harsh; (paroles, langage) crude ▷ nm (vignoble) vineyard; (vin) wine; **un grand ~** a great vintage; **jambon ~** Parma ham

crû [kʀy] pp de **croître**

cruauté [kʀyote] nf cruelty

cruche [kʀyʃ] nf pitcher, (earthenware) jug

crucifix [kʀysifi] nm crucifix

crudité [kʀydite] nf crudeness no pl; **crudités** nfpl (Culin) selection of raw vegetables

crue [kʀy] nf (inondation) flood; voir aussi **cru**

cruel, le [kʀyɛl] adj cruel

crus, crûs etc [kʀy] vb voir **croire**; **croître**

crustacés [kʀystase] nmpl shellfish

Cuba [kyba] nm Cuba; **cubain, e** adj Cuban ▷ nm/f: **Cubain, e** Cuban

cube [kyb] nm cube; (jouet) brick; **mètre ~** cubic metre; **2 au ~ = 8** 2 cubed is 8

cueillette [kœjɛt] nf picking; (quantité) crop, harvest

cueillir [kœjiʀ] /12/ vt (fruits, fleurs) to pick, gather; (fig) to catch

cuiller, cuillère [kɥijɛʀ] nf spoon; **~ à café** coffee spoon; (Culin) ≈ teaspoonful; **~ à soupe** soup spoon; (Culin) ≈ tablespoonful; **cuillerée** nf spoonful

cuir [kɥiʀ] nm leather; (avant tannage) hide; **~ chevelu** scalp

cuire [kɥiʀ] /38/ vt: (aliments) to cook; (au four) to bake ▷ vi to cook; **bien cuit** (viande) well done; **trop cuit** overdone

cuisine [kɥizin] nf (pièce) kitchen; (art culinaire) cookery, cooking; (nourriture) cooking, food; **faire la ~** to cook; **cuisiné, e** adj: **plat cuisiné** ready-made meal ou dish; **cuisiner** /1/ vt to cook; (fam) to grill ▷ vi to cook; **cuisinier, -ière** nm/f cook ▷ nf (poêle) cooker

cuisse [kɥis] nf thigh; (Culin) leg

cuisson [kɥisɔ̃] *nf* cooking
cuit, e [kɥi, -it] *pp de* **cuire**
cuivre [kɥivʀ] *nm* copper; **les ~s**
(*Mus*) the brass
cul [ky] *nm* (*fam!*) arse (!)
culminant, e [kylminɑ̃, -ɑ̃t] *adj*:
point ~ highest point
culot [kylo] (*fam*) *nm* (*effronterie*) cheek
culotte [kylɔt] *nf* (*de femme*) panties
pl, knickers *pl* (BRIT)
culte [kylt] *nm* (*religion*) religion;
(*hommage, vénération*) worship;
(*protestant*) service
cultivateur, -trice [kyltivatœʀ,
-tʀis] *nm/f* farmer
cultivé, e [kyltive] *adj* (*personne*)
cultured, cultivated
cultiver [kyltive] /1/ *vt* to cultivate;
(*légumes*) to grow, cultivate
culture [kyltyʀ] *nf* cultivation;
(*connaissances etc*) culture; **les ~s
intensives** intensive farming;
~ physique physical training;
culturel, le *adj* cultural
cumin [kymɛ̃] *nm* cumin
cure [kyʀ] *nf* (*Méd*) course of
treatment; **~ d'amaigrissement**
slimming course; **~ de repos** rest
cure
curé [kyʀe] *nm* parish priest
cure-dent [kyʀdɑ̃] *nm* toothpick
curieux, -euse [kyʀjø, -øz] *adj*
(*étrange*) strange, curious; (*indiscret*)
curious, inquisitive ▷ *nmpl* (*badauds*)
onlookers; **curiosité** *nf* curiosity;
(*site*) unusual feature *ou* sight
curriculum vitae [kyʀikylɔmvite]
nm inv curriculum vitae
curseur [kyʀsœʀ] *nm* (*Inform*) cursor;
(*de règle*) slide; (*de fermeture-éclair*)
slider
cutané, e [kytane] *adj* skin *cpd*
cuve [kyv] *nf* vat; (*à mazout etc*) tank
cuvée [kyve] *nf* vintage
cuvette [kyvɛt] *nf* (*récipient*) bowl,
basin; (*Géo*) basin
CV *sigle m* (*Auto*); = **cheval (vapeur)**;
(*Admin*) = **curriculum vitae**

cybercafé [sibɛʀkafe] *nm* Internet
café
cyberespace [sibɛʀɛspas] *nm*
cyberspace
cybernaute [sibɛʀnot] *nm/f*
Internet user
cyclable [siklabl] *adj*: **piste ~**
cycle track
cycle [sikl] *nm* cycle; **cyclisme**
[siklism] *nm* cycling; **cycliste**
[siklist] *nm/f* cyclist ▷ *adj* cycle *cpd*;
coureur cycliste racing cyclist
cyclomoteur [siklomɔtœʀ] *nm*
moped
cyclone [siklon] *nm* hurricane
cygne [siɲ] *nm* swan
cylindre [silɛ̃dʀ] *nm* cylinder;
cylindrée *nf* (*Auto*) (cubic) capacity;
une (voiture de) grosse cylindrée a
big-engined car
cymbale [sɛ̃bal] *nf* cymbal
cynique [sinik] *adj* cynical
cystite [sistit] *nf* cystitis

MOT-CLÉ

dans [dɑ̃] *prép* **1** (*position*) in; (: *à l'intérieur de*) inside; **c'est dans le tiroir/le salon** it's in the drawer/ lounge; **dans la boîte** in *ou* inside the box; **marcher dans la ville/la rue** to walk about the town/along the street; **je l'ai lu dans le journal** I read it in the newspaper
2 (*direction*) into; **elle a couru dans le salon** she ran into the lounge; **monter dans une voiture/le bus** to get into a car/on to the bus
3 (*provenance*) out of, from; **je l'ai pris dans le tiroir/salon** I took it out of *ou* from the drawer/lounge; **boire dans un verre** to drink out of *ou* from a glass
4 (*temps*) in; **dans deux mois** in two months, in two months' time
5 (*approximation*) about; **dans les 20 euros** about 20 euros

d' *prép, art voir* **de**
dactylo [daktilo] *nf* (*aussi:* **~graphe**) typist; (*aussi:* **~graphie**) typing
dada [dada] *nm* hobby-horse
daim [dɛ̃] *nm* (fallow) deer *inv*; (*cuir suédé*) suede
daltonien, ne [daltɔnjɛ̃, -ɛn] *adj* colour-blind
dame [dam] *nf* lady; (*Cartes, Échecs*) queen; **dames** *nfpl* (*jeu*) draughts *sg* (BRIT), checkers *sg* (US)
Danemark [danmark] *nm*: **le ~** Denmark
danger [dɑ̃ʒe] *nm* danger; **mettre en ~** (*personne*) to put in danger; (*projet, carrière*) to jeopardize; **être en ~** (*personne*) to be in danger; **être en ~ de mort** to be in peril of one's life; **être hors de ~** to be out of danger; **dangereux, -euse** *adj* dangerous
danois, e [danwa, -waz] *adj* Danish ▷ *nm* (*Ling*) Danish ▷ *nm/f*: **D~, e** Dane

danse [dɑ̃s] *nf*: **la ~** dancing; (*classique*) (ballet) dancing; **une ~** a dance; **danser** /1/ *vi, vt* to dance; **danseur, -euse** *nm/f* ballet dancer; (*au bal etc*) dancer (: *cavalier*) partner
date [dat] *nf* date; **de longue ~** longstanding; **~ de naissance** date of birth; **~ limite** deadline; **dater** /1/ *vt, vi* to date; **dater de** to date from; **à dater de** (as) from
datte [dat] *nf* date
dauphin [dofɛ̃] *nm* (*Zool*) dolphin
davantage [davɑ̃taʒ] *adv* more; (*plus longtemps*) longer; **~ de** more

MOT-CLÉ

de, d' [də, d] (*de + le = **du**, de + les = **des***) *prép* **1** (*appartenance*) of; **le toit de la maison** the roof of the house; **la voiture d'Elisabeth/de mes parents** Elizabeth's/my parents' car
2 (*provenance*) from; **il vient de Londres** he comes from London; **elle**

est sortie du cinéma she came out
of the cinema
3 (*moyen*) with; **je l'ai fait de mes
propres mains** I did it with my own
two hands
4 (*caractérisation, mesure*): **un mur
de brique/bureau d'acajou** a brick
wall/mahogany desk; **un billet de 10
euros** a 10 euro note; **une pièce de
2 m de large** *ou* **large de 2 m** a room
2 m wide, a 2m-wide room; **un bébé
de 10 mois** a 10-month-old baby; **12
mois de crédit/travail** 12 months'
credit/work; **elle est payée 20
euros de l'heure** she's paid 20 euros
an hour *ou* per hour; **augmenter de
10 euros** to increase by 10 euros
5 (*rapport*) from; **de quatre à six**
from four to six
6 (*cause*): **mourir de faim** to die of
hunger; **rouge de colère** red with fury
7 (*vb +de +infin*) to; **il m'a dit de
rester** he told me to stay
▶*art* **1** (*phrases affirmatives*) some
(*souvent omis*); **du vin, de l'eau,
des pommes** (some) wine, (some)
water, (some) apples; **des enfants
sont venus** some children came;
pendant des mois for months
2 (*phrases interrogatives et négatives*)
any; **a-t-il du vin?** has he got any
wine?; **il n'a pas de pommes/
d'enfants** he hasn't (got) any apples/
children, he has no apples/children

dé [de] *nm* (*à jouer*) die *ou* dice; (*aussi:*
dé à coudre) thimble
déballer [debale] /1/ *vt* to unpack
débarcadère [debarkadɛr] *nm* wharf
débardeur [debardœr] *nm* (*pour
femme*) vest top; (*pour homme*)
sleeveless top
débarquer [debarke] /1/ *vt* to
unload, land ▷ *vi* to disembark; (*fig*)
to turn up
débarras [debara] *nm* (*pièce*) lumber
room; (*placard*) junk cupboard; **bon
~!** good riddance!; **débarrasser**/1/ *vt*

to clear ▷ *vi* (*enlever le couvert*) to clear
away; **se débarrasser de** *vt* to get rid
of; **débarrasser qn de** (*vêtements,
paquets*) to relieve sb of
débat [deba] *nm* discussion, debate;
débattre /41/ *vt* to discuss, debate;
se débattre *vi* to struggle
débit [debi] *nm* (*d'un liquide, fleuve*)
(rate of) flow; (*d'un magasin*) turnover
(of goods); (*élocution*) delivery;
(*bancaire*) debit; **~ de boissons**
drinking establishment; **~ de tabac**
tobacconist's (shop)
déblayer [debleje] /8/ *vt* to clear
débloquer [debloke] /1/ *vt* (*frein,
fonds*) to release; (*prix, crédits*) to free
▷ *vi* (*fam*) to talk rubbish
déboîter [debwate] /1/ *vt* (*Auto*)
to pull out; **se ~ le genou** *etc* to
dislocate one's knee *etc*
débordé, e [deborde] *adj*: **être ~
de** (*travail, demandes*) to be snowed
under with
déborder [deborde] /1/ *vi* to
overflow; (*lait etc*) to boil over; **~ (de)
qch** (*dépasser*) to extend beyond sth;
~ de (*joie, zèle*) to be brimming over
with *ou* bursting with
débouché [debuʃe] *nm* (*pour vendre*)
outlet; (*perspective d'emploi*) opening
déboucher [debuʃe] /1/ *vt* (*évier,
tuyau etc*) to unblock; (*bouteille*) to
uncork ▷ *vi*: **~ de** to emerge from;
~ sur (*études*) to lead on to
debout [dəbu] *adv*: **être ~** (*personne*)
to be standing, stand; (*levé, éveillé*) to
be up (and about); **se mettre ~** to get
up (on one's feet); **se tenir ~** to stand;
~! stand up!; (*du lit*) get up!; **cette
histoire ne tient pas ~** this story
doesn't hold water
déboutonner [debutone] /1/ *vt* to
undo, unbutton
débraillé, e [debraje] *adj* slovenly,
untidy
débrancher [debrãʃe] /1/ *vt* (*appareil
électrique*) to unplug; (*téléphone,
courant électrique*) to disconnect

débrayage [debʀɛjaʒ] *nm* (*Auto*) clutch; **débrayer**/8/ *vi* (*Auto*) to declutch; (*cesser le travail*) to stop work

débris [debʀi] *nm* fragment ▷ *nmpl*: **des ~ de verre** bits of glass

débrouillard, e [debʀujaʀ, -aʀd] *adj* smart, resourceful

débrouiller [debʀuje] /1/ *vt* to disentangle, untangle; **se débrouiller** *vi* to manage; **débrouillez-vous** you'll have to sort things out yourself

début [deby] *nm* beginning, start; **débuts** *nmpl* (*de carrière*) début *sg*; **~ juin** in early June; **débutant, e** *nm/f* beginner, novice; **débuter**/1/ *vi* to begin, start; (*faire ses débuts*) to start out

décaféiné, e [dekafeine] *adj* decaffeinated

décalage [dekalaʒ] *nm* gap; **~ horaire** time difference (between time zones), time-lag

décaler [dekale] /1/ *vt* to shift forward *ou* back

décapotable [dekapɔtabl] *adj* convertible

décapsuleur [dekapsylœʀ] *nm* bottle-opener

décédé, e [desede] *adj* deceased

décéder [desede] /6/ *vi* to die

décembre [desɑ̃bʀ] *nm* December

décennie [deseni] *nf* decade

décent, e [desɑ̃, -ɑ̃t] *adj* decent

déception [desɛpsjɔ̃] *nf* disappointment

décès [desɛ] *nm* death

décevoir [des(ə)vwaʀ] /28/ *vt* to disappoint

décharge [deʃaʀʒ] *nf* (*dépôt d'ordures*) rubbish tip *ou* dump; (*électrique*) electrical discharge; **décharger**/3/ *vt* (*marchandise, véhicule*) to unload; (*faire feu*) to discharge, fire; **décharger qn de** (*responsabilité*) to relieve sb of, release sb from

déchausser [deʃose] /1/ *vt* (*skis*) to take off; **se déchausser** *vi* to take

off one's shoes; (*dent*) to come *ou* work loose

déchet [deʃɛ] *nm* (*de bois, tissu etc*) scrap; **déchets** *nmpl* (*ordures*) refuse *sg*, rubbish *sg*; **~s nucléaires** nuclear waste

déchiffrer [deʃifʀe] /1/ *vt* to decipher

déchirant, e [deʃiʀɑ̃, -ɑ̃t] *adj* heart-rending

déchirement [deʃiʀmɑ̃] *nm* (*chagrin*) wrench, heartbreak; (*gén pl*: *conflit*) rift, split

déchirer [deʃiʀe] /1/ *vt* to tear; (*mettre en morceaux*) to tear up; (*arracher*) to tear out; (*fig*) to tear apart; **se déchirer** *vi* to tear, rip; **se ~ un muscle/tendon** to tear a muscle/tendon

déchirure [deʃiʀyʀ] *nf* (*accroc*) tear, rip; **~ musculaire** torn muscle

décidé, e [deside] *adj* (*personne, air*) determined; **c'est ~** it's decided; **décidément** *adv* really

décider [deside] /1/ *vt*: **~ qch** to decide on sth; **~ de faire/que** to decide to do/that; **~ qn (à faire qch)** to persuade sb to do (to do sth); **se ~ à faire** to decide *ou* make up one's mind to do; **se ~ pour qch** to decide on *ou* in favour of sth

décimal, e, -aux [desimal, -o] *adj* decimal

décimètre [desimɛtʀ] *nm* decimetre

décisif, -ive [desizif, -iv] *adj* decisive

décision [desizjɔ̃] *nf* decision

déclaration [deklaʀasjɔ̃] *nf* declaration; (*discours: Pol etc*) statement; **~ (d'impôts)** ≈ tax return; **~ de revenus** statement of income; **faire une ~ de vol** to report a theft

déclarer [deklaʀe] /1/ *vt* to declare; (*décès, naissance*) to register; **se déclarer** *vi* (*feu, maladie*) to break out

déclencher [deklɑ̃ʃe] /1/ *vt* (*mécanisme etc*) to release; (*sonnerie*) to set off; (*attaque, grève*) to launch; (*provoquer*) to trigger off; **se déclencher** *vi* (*sonnerie*) to go off

décliner [dekline] /1/ *vi* to decline
▷ *vt* (*invitation*) to decline; (*nom,
adresse*) to state

décoiffer [dekwafe] /1/ *vt*: **~ qn**
to mess up sb's hair; **je suis toute
décoiffée** my hair is in a real mess

déçois *etc* [deswa] *vb voir* **décevoir**

décollage [dekɔlaʒ] *nm* (*Aviat, Écon*)
takeoff

décoller [dekɔle] /1/ *vt* to unstick ▷ *vi*
(*avion*) to take off; **se décoller** *vi* to
come unstuck

décolleté, e [dekɔlte] *adj* low-cut
▷ *nm* low neck(line); (*plongeant*)
cleavage

décolorer [dekɔlɔʀe] /1/: **se
décolorer** *vi* to fade; **se faire ~ les
cheveux** to have one's hair bleached

décommander [dekɔmɑ̃de] /1/
vt to cancel; **se décommander** *vi*
to cancel

déconcerter [dekɔ̃sɛʀte] /1/ *vt* to
disconcert, confound

décongeler [dekɔ̃ʒ(ə)le] /5/ *vt* to
thaw (out)

déconner [dekɔne] /1/ *vi* (*fam!*)
to talk (a load of) rubbish (BRIT) *ou*
garbage (US)

déconseiller [dekɔ̃seje] /1/ *vt*: **~ qch
(à qn)** to advise (sb) against sth;
c'est déconseillé it's not advised *ou*
advisable

décontracté, e [dekɔ̃tʀakte] *adj*
relaxed, laid-back (*fam*)

décontracter [dekɔ̃tʀakte] /1/: **se
décontracter** *vi* to relax

décor [dekɔʀ] *nm* décor; (*paysage*)
scenery; **décorateur, -trice** *nm/f*
(interior) decorator; **décoration**
nf decoration; **décorer** /1/ *vt* to
decorate

décortiquer [dekɔʀtike] /1/ *vt* to
shell; (*fig: texte*) to dissect

découdre /48/: **se découdre** *vi* to
come unstitched

découper [dekupe] /1/ *vt* (*papier,
tissu etc*) to cut up; (*volaille, viande*) to
carve; (*manche, article*) to cut out

décourager [dekuʀaʒe] /3/ *vt* to
discourage; **se décourager** *vi* to lose
heart, become discouraged

décousu, e [dekuzy] *adj* unstitched;
(*fig*) disjointed, disconnected

découvert, e [dekuvɛʀ, -ɛʀt] *adj*
(*tête*) bare, uncovered; (*lieu*) open,
exposed ▷ *nm* (*bancaire*) overdraft
▷ *nf* discovery; **faire la ~e de** to
discover

découvrir [dekuvʀiʀ] /18/ *vt* to
discover; (*enlever ce qui couvre ou
protège*) to uncover; (*montrer, dévoiler*)
to reveal; **se découvrir** *vi* (*chapeau*)
to take off one's hat; (*se déshabiller*) to
take something off; (*ciel*) to clear

décrire [dekʀiʀ] /39/ *vt* to describe

décrocher [dekʀɔʃe] /1/ *vt* (*dépendre*)
to take down; (*téléphone*) to take
off the hook; (: *pour répondre*): **~ (le
téléphone)** to pick up *ou* lift the
receiver; (*fig: contrat etc*) to get, land
▷ *vi* (*fam: abandonner*) to drop out;
(: *cesser d'écouter*) to switch off

déçu, e [desy] *pp de* **décevoir**

dédaigner [dedeɲe] /1/ *vt* to
despise, scorn; (*négliger*) to disregard,
spurn; **dédaigneux, -euse** *adj*
scornful, disdainful; **dédain** *nm*
scorn, disdain

dedans [dədɑ̃] *adv* inside; (*pas en
plein air*) indoors, inside ▷ *nm* inside;
au ~ inside

dédicacer [dedikase] /3/ *vt*: **~ (à qn)**
to sign (for sb), autograph (for sb)

dédier [dedje] /7/ *vt*: **~ à** to dedicate
to

dédommagement [dedɔmaʒmɑ̃]
nm compensation

dédommager [dedɔmaʒe] /3/ *vt*:
~ qn (de) to compensate sb (for)

dédouaner [dedwane] /1/ *vt* to clear
through customs

déduire [dedɥiʀ] /38/ *vt*: **~ qch (de)**
(*ôter*) to deduct sth (from); (*conclure*)
to deduce *ou* infer sth (from)

défaillance [defajɑ̃s] *nf* (*syncope*)
blackout; (*fatigue*) (sudden) weakness

no pl; (*technique*) fault, failure;
~ cardiaque heart failure

défaire [defɛʀ] /60/ *vt* (*installation, échafaudage*) to take down, dismantle; (*paquet etc, nœud, vêtement*) to undo; **se défaire** *vi* to come undone; **se ~ de** to get rid of

défait, e [defɛ, -ɛt] *adj* (*visage*) haggard, ravaged ▷ *nf* defeat

défaut [defo] *nm* (*moral*) fault, failing, defect; (*d'étoffe, métal*) fault, flaw; (*manque, carence*) **~** shortage of; **prendre qn en ~** to catch sb out; **faire ~** (*manquer*) to be lacking; **à ~ de** for lack ou want of

défavorable [defavɔʀabl] *adj* unfavourable (BRIT), unfavorable (US)

défavoriser [defavɔʀize] /1/ *vt* to put at a disadvantage

défectueux, -euse [defɛktɥø, -øz] *adj* faulty, defective

défendre [defɑ̃dʀ] /41/ *vt* to defend; (*interdire*) to forbid; **se défendre** *vi* to defend o.s.; **~ à qn qch/de faire** to forbid sb sth/to do; **il se défend** (*fig*) he can hold his own; **se ~ de/ contre** (*se protéger*) to protect o.s. from/against; **se ~ de** (*se garder de*) to refrain from

défense [defɑ̃s] *nf* defence; (*d'éléphant etc*) tusk; **ministre de la ~** Minister of Defence (BRIT), Defence Secretary; **"~ de fumer/cracher"** "no smoking/spitting"

défi [defi] *nm* challenge; **lancer un ~ à qn** to challenge sb; **sur un ton de ~** defiantly

déficit [defisit] *nm* (*Comm*) deficit

défier [defje] /7/ *vt* (*provoquer*) to challenge; (*fig*) to defy; **~ qn de faire** to challenge ou defy sb to do

défigurer [defigyʀe] /1/ *vt* to disfigure

défilé [defile] *nm* (*Géo*) (narrow) gorge ou pass; (*soldats*) parade; (*manifestants*) procession, march

défiler [defile] /1/ *vi* (*troupes*) to march past; (*sportifs*) to parade;

(*manifestants*) to march; (*visiteurs*) to pour, stream; **faire ~ un document** (*Inform*) to scroll a document; **se défiler** *vi*: **il s'est défilé** (*fam*) he wriggled out of it

définir [definiʀ] /2/ *vt* to define

définitif, -ive [definitif, -iv] *adj* (*final*) final, definitive; (*pour longtemps*) permanent, definitive; (*sans appel*) definite ▷ *nf*: **en définitive** eventually; (*somme toute*) when all is said and done; **définitivement** *adv* permanently

déformer [defɔʀme] /1/ *vt* to put out of shape; (*pensée, fait*) to distort; **se déformer** *vi* to lose its shape

défouler [defule] /1/: **se défouler** *vi* to unwind, let off steam

défunt, e [defœ̃, -œ̃t] *adj*: **son ~ père** his late father ▷ *nm/f* deceased

dégagé, e [degaʒe] *adj* (*route, ciel*) clear; **sur un ton ~** casually

dégager [degaʒe] /3/ *vt* (*exhaler*) to give off; (*délivrer*) to free, extricate; (*désencombrer*) to clear; (*isoler, mettre en valeur*) to bring out; **se dégager** *vi* (*passage, ciel*) to clear; **~ qn de** (*engagement, parole etc*) to release ou free sb from

dégâts [dega] *nmpl* damage *sg*; **faire des ~** to do damage

dégel [deʒɛl] *nm* thaw; **dégeler** /5/ *vt* to thaw (out)

dégivrer [deʒivʀe] /1/ *vt* (*frigo*) to defrost; (*vitres*) to de-ice

dégonflé, e [degɔ̃fle] *adj* (*pneu*) flat

dégonfler [degɔ̃fle] /1/ *vt* (*pneu, ballon*) to let down, deflate; **se dégonfler** *vi* (*fam*) to chicken out

dégouliner [deguline] /1/ *vi* to trickle, drip

dégourdi, e [deguʀdi] *adj* smart, resourceful

dégourdir [deguʀdiʀ] /2/ *vt*: **se ~ (les jambes)** to stretch one's legs

dégoût [degu] *nm* disgust, distaste; **dégoûtant, e** *adj* disgusting; **dégoûté, e** *adj* disgusted; **dégoûté**

de sick of; **dégoûter** /1/ vt to disgust; **dégoûter qn de qch** to put sb off sth

dégrader [degrade] /1/ vt (*Mil: officier*) to degrade; (*abîmer*) to damage, deface; **se dégrader** vi (*relations, situation*) to deteriorate

degré [dagre] nm degree

dégressif, -ive [degresif, -iv] adj on a decreasing scale

dégringoler [degrēgɔle] /1/ vi to tumble (down)

déguisement [degizmã] nm (*pour s'amuser*) fancy dress

déguiser [degize] /1/: **se déguiser (en)** vi (*se costumer*) to dress up (as); (*pour tromper*) to disguise o.s. (as)

dégustation [degystasjɔ̃] nf (*de fromages etc*) sampling; **~ de vin(s)** wine-tasting

déguster [degyste] /1/ vt (*vins*) to taste; (*fromages etc*) to sample; (*savourer*) to enjoy

dehors [dəɔʀ] adv outside; (*en plein air*) outdoors ▷ nm outside ▷ nmpl (*apparences*) appearances; **mettre** ou **jeter ~** to throw out; **au ~** outside; **au ~ de** outside; **en ~ de** apart from

déjà [deʒa] adv already; (*auparavant*) before, already

déjeuner [deʒœne] /1/ vi to (have) lunch; (*le matin*) to have breakfast ▷ nm lunch

delà [dəla] adv: **en ~ (de), au ~ (de)** beyond

délacer [delase] /3/ vt (*chaussures*) to undo, unlace

délai [delɛ] nm (*attente*) waiting period; (*sursis*) extension (of time); (*temps accordé*) time limit; **sans ~** without delay; **dans les ~s** within the time limit

délaisser [delese] /1/ vt to abandon, desert

délasser [delase] /1/ vt to relax; **se délasser** vi to relax

délavé, e [delave] adj faded

délayer [deleje] /8/ vt (*Culin*) to mix (with water etc); (*peinture*) to thin down

delco® [dɛlko] nm (*Auto*) distributor

délégué, e [delege] nm/f representative

déléguer [delege] /6/ vt to delegate

délibéré, e [delibere] adj (*conscient*) deliberate

délicat, e [delika, -at] adj delicate; (*plein de tact*) tactful; (*attentionné*) thoughtful; **délicatement** adv delicately; (*avec douceur*) gently

délice [delis] nm delight

délicieux, -euse [delisjø, -øz] adj (*au goût*) delicious; (*sensation, impression*) delightful

délimiter [delimite] /1/ vt (*terrain*) to delimit, demarcate

délinquant, e [delɛ̃kɑ̃, -ɑ̃t] adj, nm/f delinquent

délirer [delire] /1/ vi to be delirious; **tu délires!** (*fam*) you're crazy!

délit [deli] nm (*criminal*) offence

délivrer [delivre] /1/ vt (*prisonnier*) to (set) free, release; (*passeport, certificat*) to issue

deltaplane® [dɛltaplan] nm hang-glider

déluge [delyʒ] nm (*biblique*) Flood; (*grosse pluie*) downpour

demain [d(ə)mɛ̃] adv tomorrow; **~ matin/soir** tomorrow morning/evening

demande [d(ə)mɑ̃d] nf (*requête*) request; (*revendication*) demand; (*formulaire*) application; (*Écon*): **la ~** demand; **"~s d'emploi"** "situations wanted"

demandé, e [d(ə)mɑ̃de] adj (*article etc*): **très ~** (very) much in demand

demander [d(ə)mɑ̃de] /1/ vt to ask for; (*date, heure, chemin*) to ask; (*requérir, nécessiter*) to require, demand; **~ qch à qn** to ask sb for sth; **~ à qn de faire** to ask sb to do; **se ~ si/pourquoi** etc to wonder if/why etc; **je ne demande pas mieux** I'm asking nothing more; **demandeur, -euse** nm/f: **demandeur d'asile**

asylum-seeker; **demandeur d'emploi** job-seeker

démangeaison [demãʒɛzɔ̃] nf itching; **avoir des ~s** to be itching

démanger [demãʒe] /3/ vi to itch

démaquillant [demakijã] nm make-up remover

démaquiller [demakije] /1/ vt: **se démaquiller** to remove one's make-up

démarche [demaʀʃ] nf (allure) gait, walk; (intervention) step; (fig: intellectuelle) thought processes pl; **faire les ~s nécessaires (pour obtenir qch)** to take the necessary steps (to obtain sth)

démarrage [demaʀaʒ] nm start

démarrer [demaʀe] /1/ vi (conducteur) to start (up); (véhicule) to move off; (travaux, affaire) to get moving; **démarreur** nm (Auto) starter

démêlant, e [demelã, -ãt] adj: **crème ~e** (hair) conditioner ▷ nm conditioner

démêler [demele] /1/ vt to untangle; **démêlés** nmpl problems

déménagement [demenaʒmã] nm move; **entreprise/camion de ~** removal (BRIT) ou moving (US) firm/van

déménager [demenaʒe] /3/ vt (meubles) to (re)move ▷ vi to move (house); **déménageur** nm removal man

démerder [demɛʀde] /1/: **se démerder** vi (fam!) to bloody well manage for o.s.

démettre [demɛtʀ] /56/ vt: **~ qn de** (fonction, poste) to dismiss sb from; **se ~ l'épaule** etc to dislocate one's shoulder etc

demeurer [d(ə)mœʀe] /1/ vi (habiter) to live; (rester) to remain

demi, e [dəmi] adj half; **et ~: trois heures/bouteilles et ~es** three and a half hours/bottles ▷ nm (bière: = 0.25 litre) ≈ half-pint; **il est 2 heures et ~e** it's half past 2; **il est midi et ~** it's

half past 12; **à ~** half-; **à la ~e** (heure) on the half-hour; **demi-douzaine** nf half-dozen, half a dozen; **demi-finale** nf semifinal; **demi-frère** nm half-brother; **demi-heure** nf: **une demi-heure** a half-hour, half an hour; **demi-journée** nf half-day, half a day; **demi-litre** nm half-litre (BRIT), half-liter (US), half a litre ou liter; **demi-livre** nf half-pound, half a pound; **demi-pension** nf half-board; **demi-pensionnaire** nm/f: **être demi-pensionnaire** to take school lunches

démis, e adj (épaule etc) dislocated

demi-sœur [dəmisœʀ] nf half-sister

démission [demisjɔ̃] nf resignation; **donner sa ~** to give ou hand in one's notice; **démissionner** /1/ vi to resign

demi-tarif [dəmitaʀif] nm half-price; (Transports) half-fare; **voyager à ~** to travel half-fare

demi-tour [dəmituʀ] nm about-turn; **faire ~** to turn (and go) back

démocratie [demɔkʀasi] nf democracy; **démocratique** adj democratic

démodé, e [demɔde] adj old-fashioned

demoiselle [d(ə)mwazɛl] nf (jeune fille) young lady; (célibataire) single lady, maiden lady; **~ d'honneur** bridesmaid

démolir [demɔliʀ] /2/ vt to demolish

démon [demɔ̃] nm (enfant turbulent) devil, demon; **le D~** the Devil

démonstration [demɔ̃stʀasjɔ̃] nf demonstration

démonter [demɔ̃te] /1/ vt (machine etc) to take down, dismantle; **se démonter** vi (meuble) to be dismantled, be taken to pieces; (personne) to lose countenance

démontrer [demɔ̃tʀe] /1/ vt to demonstrate

démouler [demule] /1/ vt to turn out

démuni, e [demyni] adj (sans argent) impoverished; **~ de** without

dénicher [denife] /1/ vt (fam: objet) to unearth; (: restaurant etc) to discover

dénier [denje] /7/ vt to deny

dénivellation [denivelasjɔ̃] nf (pente) ramp

dénombrer [denɔ̃bʀe] /1/ vt to count

dénomination [denɔminasjɔ̃] nf designation, appellation

dénoncer [denɔ̃se] /3/ vt to denounce; **se dénoncer** to give o.s. up, come forward

dénouement [denumɑ̃] nm outcome

dénouer [denwe] /1/ vt to unknot, undo

denrée [dɑ̃ʀe] nf (aussi: ~ **alimentaire**) food(stuff)

dense [dɑ̃s] adj dense; **densité** nf density

dent [dɑ̃] nf tooth; ~ **de lait/sagesse** milk/wisdom tooth; **dentaire** adj dental; **cabinet dentaire** dental surgery

dentelle [dɑ̃tɛl] nf lace no pl

dentier [dɑ̃tje] nm denture

dentifrice [dɑ̃tifʀis] nm: **(pâte) ~** toothpaste

dentiste nm/f dentist

dentition [dɑ̃tisjɔ̃] nf teeth pl

dénué, e [denɥe] adj: ~ **de** devoid of

déodorant [deɔdɔʀɑ̃] nm deodorant

déontologie [deɔ̃tɔlɔʒi] nf (professional) code of practice

dépannage [depanaʒ] nm: **service/ camion de ~** (Auto) breakdown service/truck

dépanner [depane] /1/ vt (voiture, télévision) to fix, repair; (fig) to bail out, help out; **dépanneuse** nf breakdown lorry (BRIT), tow truck (US)

dépareillé, e [depaʀeje] adj (collection, service) incomplete; (gant, volume, objet) odd

départ [depaʀ] nm departure; (Sport) start; **au ~** at the start; **la veille de son ~** the day before he leaves/left

département [depaʀtəmɑ̃] nm department

dépassé, e [depase] adj superseded, outmoded; (fig) out of one's depth

dépasser [depase] /1/ vt (véhicule, concurrent) to overtake; (endroit) to pass, go past; (somme, limite) to exceed; (fig: en beauté etc) to surpass, outshine ▷ vi (jupon) to show; **se dépasser** to excel o.s.

dépaysé, e [depeize] adj disoriented

dépaysement [depeizmɑ̃] nm change of scenery

dépêcher [depefe] /1/: **se dépêcher** vi to hurry

dépendance [depɑ̃dɑ̃s] nf dependence no pl; (bâtiment) outbuilding

dépendre [depɑ̃dʀ] /41/ vt: ~ **de** vt to depend on, to be dependent on; **ça dépend** it depends

dépens [depɑ̃] nmpl: **aux ~ de** at the expense of

dépense [depɑ̃s] nf spending no pl, expense, expenditure no pl; **dépenser** /1/ vt to spend; (fig) to expend, use up; **se dépenser** vi to exert o.s.

dépeupler [depœple] /1/: **se dépeupler** vi to become depopulated

dépilatoire [depilatwaʀ] adj: **crème ~** hair-removing ou depilatory cream

dépister [depiste] /1/ vt to detect; (voleur) to track down

dépit [depi] *nm* vexation, frustration; **en ~ de** in spite of; **en ~ du bon sens** contrary to all good sense; **dépité, e** *adj* vexed, frustrated

déplacé, e [deplase] *adj* (*propos*) out of place, uncalled-for

déplacement [deplasmã] *nm* (*voyage*) trip, travelling *no pl*; **en ~** away (on a trip)

déplacer [deplase] /3/ *vt* (*table, voiture*) to move, shift; **se ~ déplacer** *vi* to move; (*voyager*) to travel; **se ~ une vertèbre** to slip a disc

déplaire [deplɛʀ] /54/ *vi*: **ceci me déplaît** I don't like this, I dislike this; **se ~ quelque part** to dislike it *ou* be unhappy somewhere; **déplaisant, e** *adj* disagreeable

dépliant [deplijã] *nm* leaflet

déplier [deplije] /7/ *vt* to unfold

déposer [depoze] /1/ *vt* (*gén: mettre, poser*) to lay down, put down; (*à la banque, à la consigne*) to deposit; (*passager*) to drop (off), set down; (*roi*) to depose; (*marque*) to register; (*plainte*) to lodge; **se déposer** *vi* to settle; **dépositaire** *nm/f* (*Comm*) agent; **déposition** *nf* statement

dépôt [depo] *nm* (*à la banque, sédiment*) deposit; (*entrepôt, réserve*) warehouse, store

dépourvu, e [depuʀvy] *adj*: **~ de** lacking in, without; **prendre qn au ~** to catch sb unawares

dépression *nf* depression; **~ (nerveuse)** (nervous) breakdown

déprimant, e [depʀimã, -ãt] *adj* depressing

déprimer [depʀime] /1/ *vt* to depress

MOT-CLÉ

depuis [dəpɥi] *prép* **1** (*point de départ dans le temps*) since; **il habite Paris depuis 1983/l'an dernier** he has been living in Paris since 1983/last year; **depuis quand?** since when?;

depuis quand le connaissez-vous? how long have you known him? **2** (*temps écoulé*) for; **il habite Paris depuis cinq ans** he has been living in Paris for five years; **je le connais depuis trois ans** I've known him for three years

3 (*lieu*): **il a plu depuis Metz** it's been raining since Metz; **elle a téléphoné depuis Valence** she rang from Valence

4 (*quantité, rang*) from; **depuis les plus petits jusqu'aux plus grands** from the youngest to the oldest

▶ *adv* (*temps*) since (then); **je ne lui ai pas parlé depuis** I haven't spoken to him since (then); **depuis que** *conj* (ever) since; **depuis qu'il m'a dit ça** (ever) since he said that to me

député, e [depyte] *nm/f* (*Pol*) ≈ Member of Parliament (BRIT), ≈ Congressman/woman (US)

dérangement [deʀãʒmã] *nm* (*gêne, déplacement*) trouble; (*gastrique etc*) disorder; **en ~** (*téléphone*) out of order

déranger [deʀãʒe] /3/ *vt* (*personne*) to trouble, bother; (*projets*) to disrupt, upset; (*objets, vêtements*) to disarrange; **se déranger**; *vi*: **surtout ne vous dérangez pas pour moi** please don't put yourself out on my account; **est-ce que cela vous dérange si …?** do you mind if …?

déraper [deʀape] /1/ *vi* (*voiture*) to skid; (*personne, semelles, couteau*) to slip

dérégler [deʀegle] /6/ *vt* (*mécanisme*) to put out of order; (*estomac*) to upset

dérisoire [deʀizwaʀ] *adj* derisory

dérive [deʀiv] *nf*: **aller à la ~** (*Navig, fig*) to drift

dérivé, e [deʀive] *nm* (*Tech*) by-product

dermatologue [dɛʀmatɔlɔg] *nm/f* dermatologist

dernier, -ière [dɛʀnje, -jɛʀ] *adj* last; (*le plus récent: gén avant n*) latest, last; **lundi/le mois ~** last Monday/ month; **le ~ cri** the last word (in fashion); **en ~** last; **ce ~, cette dernière** the latter; **dernièrement** adv recently

dérogation [deʀɔgasjɔ̃] nf (special) dispensation

dérouiller [deʀuje] /1/ vt: **se ~ les jambes** to stretch one's legs (fig)

déroulement [deʀulmɑ̃] nm (d'une opération etc) progress

dérouler [deʀule] /1/ vt (ficelle) to unwind; **se dérouler** vi (avoir lieu) to take place; (se passer) to go; **tout s'est déroulé comme prévu** everything went as planned

dérouter [deʀute] /1/ vt (avion, train) to reroute, divert; (étonner) to disconcert, throw (out)

derrière [deʀjɛʀ] adv, prép behind ▷ nm (d'une maison) back; (postérieur) behind, bottom; **les pattes de ~** the back legs, the hind legs; **par ~** from behind; (fig) behind one's back

des [de] art voir **de**

dès [dɛ] prép from; **~ que** as soon as; **~ son retour** as soon as he was (ou is) back

désaccord [dezakɔʀ] nm disagreement

désagréable [dezagʀeabl] adj unpleasant

désagrément [dezagʀemɑ̃] nm annoyance, trouble no pl

désaltérer [dezalteʀe] /6/ vt: **se désaltérer** to quench: one's thirst

désapprobateur, -trice [dezapʀɔbatœʀ, -tʀis] adj disapproving

désapprouver [dezapʀuve] /1/ vt to disapprove of

désarmant, e [dezaʀmɑ̃, -ɑ̃t] adj disarming

désastre [dezastʀ] nm disaster; **désastreux, -euse** adj disastrous

désavantage [dezavɑ̃taʒ] nm disadvantage; **désavantager** /3/ vt to put at a disadvantage

descendre [desɑ̃dʀ] /41/ vt (escalier, montagne) to go (ou come) down; (valise, paquet) to take ou get down; (étagère etc) to lower; (fam: abattre) to shoot down ▷ vi to go (ou come) down; (passager: s'arrêter) to get out, alight; **~ à pied/en voiture** to walk/drive down; **~ de** (famille) to be descended from; **~ du train** to get out of ou off the train; **~ d'un arbre** to climb down from a tree; **~ de cheval** to dismount; **~ à l'hôtel** to stay at a hotel

descente [desɑ̃t] nf descent, going down; (chemin) way down; (Ski) downhill (race); **au milieu de la ~** halfway down; **~ de lit** bedside rug; **~ (de police)** (police) raid

description [dɛskʀipsjɔ̃] nf description

déséquilibre [dezekilibʀ] nm (position): **être en ~** to be unsteady; (fig: des forces, du budget) imbalance

désert, e [dezɛʀ, -ɛʀt] adj deserted ▷ nm desert; **désertique** adj desert cpd

désespéré, e [dezɛspeʀe] adj desperate

désespérer [dezɛspeʀe] /6/ vi: **~ de** to despair of; **désespoir** nm despair; **en désespoir de cause** in desperation

déshabiller [dezabije] /1/ vt to undress; **se déshabiller** vi to undress (o.s.)

déshydraté, e [dezidʀate] adj dehydrated

désigner [deziɲe] /1/ vt (montrer) to point out, indicate; (dénommer) to denote; (candidat etc) to name

désinfectant, e [dezɛ̃fɛktɑ̃, -ɑ̃t] adj, nm disinfectant

désinfecter [dezɛ̃fɛkte] /1/ vt to disinfect

désintéressé, e [dezɛ̃teʀese] adj disinterested, unselfish

désintéresser [dezɛ̃teʀese] /1/ vt: **se désintéresser (de)** to lose interest (in)

désintoxication [dezɛ̃tɔksikasjɔ̃]
nf: **faire une cure de ~** to have *ou*
undergo treatment for alcoholism (*ou*
drug addiction)

désinvolte [dezɛ̃vɔlt] *adj* casual,
off-hand

désir [deziʀ] *nm* wish; (*fort, sensuel*)
desire; **désirer** /1/ *vt* to want, wish
for; (*sexuellement*) to desire; **je désire
…** (*formule de politesse*) I would like …

désister [deziste] /1/: **se désister** *vi*
to stand down, withdraw

désobéir [dezɔbeiʀ] /2/ *vi:*
~ (à qn/qch) to disobey (sb/sth);
désobéissant, e *adj* disobedient

désodorisant [dezɔdɔʀizɑ̃] *nm* air
freshener, deodorizer

désolé, e [dezɔle] *adj* (*paysage*)
desolate; **je suis ~** I'm sorry

désordonné, e [dezɔʀdɔne] *adj*
untidy

désordre [dezɔʀdʀ] *nm*
disorder(liness), untidiness; (*anarchie*)
disorder; **en ~** in a mess, untidy

désormais [dezɔʀmɛ] *adv* from
now on

desquels, desquelles [dekɛl]
voir **lequel**

dessécher [deseʃe] /6/: **se
dessécher** *vi* to dry out

desserrer [deseʀe] /1/ *vt* to loosen;
(*frein*) to release

dessert [desɛʀ] *nm* dessert, pudding

desservir [desɛʀviʀ] /14/ *vt* (*ville,
quartier*) to serve; (*débarrasser*): **~ (la
table)** to clear the table

dessin [desɛ̃] *nm* (*œuvre, art*) drawing;
(*motif*) pattern, design; **~ animé**
cartoon (film); **~ humoristique**
cartoon; **dessinateur, -trice**
nm/f drawer; (*de bandes dessinées*)
cartoonist; (*industriel*) draughtsman
(BRIT), draftsman (US); **dessiner** /1/
vt to draw; (*concevoir*) to design; **se
dessiner** *vi* (*forme*) to be outlined; (*fig:
solution*) to emerge

dessous [d(ə)su] *adv* underneath,
beneath ▷ *nm* underside; **les voisins**

du ~ the downstairs neighbours
▷ *nmpl* (*sous-vêtements*) underwear
sg; **en ~** underneath; below; **par ~**
underneath; below; **avoir le ~** to get
the worst of it; **dessous-de-plat** *nm
inv* tablemat

dessus [d(ə)sy] *adv* on top;
(*collé, écrit*) on it ▷ *nm* top; **les
voisins/l'appartement du ~** the
upstairs neighbours/flat; **en ~** above;
par ~ *adv* over it; **prép** over; **au-~**
above; **avoir/prendre le ~** to have/
get the upper hand; **sens ~ dessous**
upside down; **dessus-de-lit** *nm inv*
bedspread

destin [dɛstɛ̃] *nm* fate; (*avenir*) destiny

destinataire [dɛstinatɛʀ] *nm/f*
(*Postes*) addressee; (*d'un colis*)
consignee

destination [dɛstinasjɔ̃] *nf* (*lieu*)
destination; (*usage*) purpose; **à ~ de**
bound for; travelling to

destiner [dɛstine] /1/ *vt:* **~ qch à qn**
(*envisager de donner*) to intend sb to
have sth; (*adresser*) to intend sth for
sb; **se ~ à l'enseignement** to intend
to become a teacher; **être destiné à**
(*usage*) to be intended *ou* meant for

détachant [detaʃɑ̃] *nm* stain remover

détacher [detaʃe] /1/ *vt* (*enlever*)
to detach, remove; (*délier*) to untie;
(*Admin*): **~ qn (auprès de** *ou* **à)**
to post sb (to); **se détacher** *vi*
(*se séparer*) to come off; (*page*) to
come out; (*se défaire*) to come
undone; **se ~ sur** to stand out
against; **se ~ de** (*se désintéresser*) to
grow away from

détail [detaj] *nm* detail; (*Comm*): **le
~** retail; **au ~** (*Comm*) retail; **en ~** in
detail; **détaillant, e** *nm/f* retailer;
détaillé, e *adj* (*récit, plan, explications*)
detailed; (*facture*) itemized; **détailler**
/1/ *vt* (*expliquer*) to explain in detail

détecter [detɛkte] /1/ *vt* to detect

détective [detɛktiv] *nm* detective;
~ (privé) private detective *ou*
investigator

déteindre [detɛ̃dʀ] /52/ vi to fade; (au lavage) to run; **~ sur** (vêtement) to run into; (fig) to rub off on

détendre [detɑ̃dʀ] /41/ vt (personne, atmosphère, corps, esprit) to relax; **se détendre** vi (ressort) to lose its tension; (personne) to relax

détenir [det(ə)niʀ] /22/ vt (fortune, objet, secret) to be in possession of; (prisonnier) to detain; (record) to hold; **~ le pouvoir** to be in power

détente [detɑ̃t] nf relaxation

détention [detɑ̃sjɔ̃] nf (de fortune, objet, secret) possession; (captivité) detention; **~ préventive** (pre-trial) custody

détenu, e [det(ə)ny] pp de **détenir** ▷ nm/f prisoner

détergent [detɛʀʒɑ̃] nm detergent

détériorer [deterjɔre] /1/ vt to damage; **se détériorer** vi to deteriorate

déterminé, e [detɛrmine] adj (résolu) determined; (précis) specific, definite

déterminer [detɛrmine] /1/ vt (fixer) to determine; **~ qn à faire** to decide sb to do; **se ~ à faire** to make up one's mind to do

détester [detɛste] /1/ vt to hate, detest

détour [detuʀ] nm detour; (tournant) bend, curve; **ça vaut le ~** it's worth the trip; **sans ~** (fig) plainly

détourné, e [deturne] adj (sentier, chemin, moyen) roundabout

détourner [deturne] /1/ vt to divert; (par la force) to hijack; (yeux, tête) to turn away; (de l'argent) to embezzle; **se détourner** vi to turn away

détraquer [detrake] /1/ vt to put out of order; (estomac) to upset; **se détraquer** vi to go wrong

détriment [detrimɑ̃] nm: **au ~ de** to the detriment of

détroit [detrwa] nm strait

détruire [detrɥir] /38/ vt to destroy

dette [dɛt] nf debt

DEUG [dœg] sigle m = **Diplôme d'études universitaires générales**

deuil [dœj] nm (perte) bereavement; (période) mourning; **prendre le/être en ~** to go into/be in mourning

deux [dø] num two; **les ~** both; **ses ~ mains** both his hands, his two hands; **~ fois** twice; **deuxième** num second; **deuxièmement** adv secondly; **deux-pièces** nm inv (tailleur) two-piece (suit); (de bain) two-piece (swimsuit); (appartement) two-roomed flat (BRIT) ou apartment (US); **deux-points** nm inv colon sg; **deux-roues** nm inv two-wheeled vehicle

devais etc [dəvɛ] vb voir **devoir**

dévaluation [devalɥasjɔ̃] nf devaluation

devancer [d(ə)vɑ̃se] /3/ vt to get ahead of; (arriver avant) to arrive before; (prévenir) to anticipate

devant [d(ə)vɑ̃] adv in front; (à distance: en avant) ahead ▷ prép in front of; (en avant) ahead of; (avec mouvement: passer) past; (fig) before, in front of (: vu) in view of ▷ nm front; **prendre les ~s** to make the first move; **les pattes de ~** the front legs, the forelegs; **par ~** (boutonner) at the front; (entrer) the front way; **aller au-~ de qn** to go out to meet sb; **aller au-~ de** (désirs de qn) to anticipate

devanture [d(ə)vɑ̃tyr] nf (étalage) display; (vitrine) (shop) window

développement [dev(ə)lɔpmɑ̃]
nm development; **pays en voie de
~** developing countries; **~ durable**
sustainable development

développer [dev(ə)lɔpe] /1/ vt to
develop; **se développer** vi to develop

devenir [dəv(ə)niʀ] /22/ vi to
become; **que sont-ils devenus?**
what has become of them?

devez [dəve] vb voir **devoir**

déviation [devjasjɔ̃] nf (Auto)
diversion (BRIT), detour (US)

devienne etc [dəvjɛn] vb voir **devenir**

deviner [d(ə)vine] /1/ vt to guess;
(apercevoir) to distinguish; **devinette**
nf riddle

devis [d(ə)vi] nm estimate, quotation

devise [dəviz] nf (formule) motto,
watchword; **devises** nfpl (argent)
currency sg

dévisser [devise] /1/ vt to unscrew,
undo; **se dévisser** vi to come
unscrewed

devoir [d(ə)vwaʀ] /28/ nm duty;
(Scol) homework no pl (: en classe)
exercise ▷ vt (argent, respect): **~ qch
(à qn)** to owe (sb) sth; **combien
est-ce que je vous dois?** how
much do I owe you?; **il doit le faire**
(obligation) he has to do it, he must
do it; **cela devait arriver un jour**
it was bound to happen; **il doit
partir demain** (intention) he is due
to leave tomorrow; **il doit être tard**
(probabilité) it must be late

dévorer [devɔʀe] /1/ vt to devour;
(feu, soucis) to consume; **~ qn/qch
des yeux** ou **du regard** (convoitise) to
eye sb/sth greedily

dévoué, e [devwe] adj devoted

dévouer [devwe] /1/: **se dévouer** vi
(se sacrifier): **se ~ (pour)** to sacrifice
o.s. (for); (se consacrer): **se ~ à** to
devote ou dedicate o.s. to

devrai etc [dəvʀe] vb voir **devoir**

dézipper [dezipe] /1/ vt to unzip

diabète [djabɛt] nm diabetes sg;
diabétique nm/f diabetic

diable [djabl] nm devil

diabolo [djabɔlo] nm (boisson)
lemonade and fruit cordial

diagnostic [djagnɔstik] nm
diagnosis sg; **diagnostiquer** /1/ vt
to diagnose

diagonal, e, -aux [djagɔnal, -o] adj,
nf diagonal; **en ~e** diagonally

diagramme [djagʀam] nm chart,
graph

dialecte [djalɛkt] nm dialect

dialogue [djalɔg] nm dialogue

diamant [djamɑ̃] nm diamond

diamètre [djamɛtʀ] nm diameter

diapo [djapo], **diapositive**
[djapozitiv] nf transparency, slide

diarrhée [djaʀe] nf diarrhoea

dictateur [diktatœʀ] nm dictator;
dictature [diktatyʀ] nf dictatorship

dictée [dikte] nf dictation

dicter [dikte] /1/ vt to dictate

dictionnaire [diksjɔnɛʀ] nm
dictionary

dièse [djɛz] nm sharp

diesel [djezɛl] nm, adj inv diesel

diète [djɛt] nf (jeûne) starvation
diet; (régime) diet; **diététique** adj:
magasin diététique health food
shop (BRIT) ou store (US)

dieu, x [djø] nm god; **D~** God; **mon
D~!** good heavens!

différemment [difeʀamɑ̃] adv
differently

différence [difeʀɑ̃s] nf difference; **à
la ~ de** unlike; **différencier** /7/ vt to
differentiate

différent, e [difeʀɑ̃, -ɑ̃t] adj
(dissemblable) different; **~ de** different
from; **~s objets** different ou various
objects

différer [difeʀe] /6/ vt to postpone,
put off ▷ vi: **~ (de)** to differ (from)

difficile [difisil] adj difficult;
(exigeant) hard to please;
difficilement adv with difficulty

difficulté [difikylte] nf difficulty;
en ~ (bateau, alpiniste) in trouble ou
difficulties

diffuser [difyze] /1/ vt (chaleur, bruit, lumière) to diffuse; (émission, musique) to broadcast; (nouvelle, idée) to circulate; (Comm) to distribute

digérer [diʒeʁe] /6/ vt to digest; (fig: accepter) to stomach, put up with; **digestif, -ive** nm (after-dinner) liqueur; **digestion** nf digestion

digne [diɲ] adj dignified; **~ de** worthy of; **~ de foi** trustworthy; **dignité** nf dignity

digue [dig] nf dike, dyke

dilemme [dilɛm] nm dilemma

diligence [diliʒɑ̃s] nf stagecoach

diluer [dilɥe] /1/ vt to dilute

dimanche [dimɑ̃ʃ] nm Sunday

dimension [dimɑ̃sjɔ̃] nf (grandeur) size; (dimensions) dimensions

diminuer [diminɥe] /1/ vt to reduce, decrease; (ardeur etc) to lessen; (dénigrer) to belittle ▷ vi to decrease, diminish; **diminutif** nm (surnom) pet name

dinde [dɛ̃d] nf turkey

dindon [dɛ̃dɔ̃] nm turkey

dîner [dine] /1/ nm dinner ▷ vi to have dinner

dingue [dɛ̃g] adj (fam) crazy

dinosaure [dinɔzɔʁ] nm dinosaur

diplomate [diplɔmat] adj diplomatic ▷ nm diplomat; (fig) diplomatist; **diplomatie** nf diplomacy

diplôme [diplom] nm diploma certificate; **avoir des ~s** to have qualifications; **diplômé, e** adj qualified

dire [diʁ] /37/ vt to say; (secret, mensonge) to tell; **se dire** (à soi-même) to say to oneself ▷ nm: **au ~ de** according to; **~ qch à qn** to tell sb sth; **~ à qn qu'il fasse** ou **de faire** to tell sb to do; **on dit que** they say that; **on dirait que** it looks (ou sounds etc) as though; **que dites-vous de** (penser) what do you think of; **si cela lui dit** if he fancies it; **dis donc!, dites donc!** (pour attirer l'attention)

hey!; (au fait) by the way; **ceci** ou **cela dit** that being said; **ça ne se dit pas** (impoli) you shouldn't say that; (pas en usage) you don't say that

direct, e [diʁɛkt] adj direct ▷ nm: **en ~** (émission) live; **directement** adv directly

directeur, -trice [diʁɛktœʁ, -tʁis] nm/f (d'entreprise) director; (de service) manager/eress; (d'école) head(teacher) (BRIT), principal (US)

direction [diʁɛksjɔ̃] nf (d'entreprise) management; (Auto) steering; (sens) direction; **"toutes ~s"** "all routes"

dirent [diʁ] vb voir **dire**

dirigeant, e [diʁiʒɑ̃, -ɑ̃t] adj (classes) ruling ▷ nm/f (d'un parti etc) leader

diriger [diʁiʒe] /3/ vt (entreprise) to manage, run; (véhicule) to steer; (orchestre) to conduct; (recherches, travaux) to supervise; (arme): **~ sur** to point ou level ou aim at; **se diriger** vi (s'orienter) to find one's way; **~ son regard sur** to look in the direction of; **se ~ vers** ou **sur** to make ou head for

dis [di] vb voir **dire**

discerner [disɛʁne] /1/ vt to discern, make out

discipline [disiplin] nf discipline; **discipliner** /1/ vt to discipline

discontinu, e [diskɔ̃tiny] adj intermittent

discontinuer [diskɔ̃tinɥe] /1/ vi: **sans ~** without stopping, without a break

discothèque [diskɔtɛk] nf (boîte de nuit) disco(thèque)

discours [diskuʁ] nm speech

discret, -ète [diskʁɛ, -ɛt] adj discreet; (fig: musique, style, maquillage) unobtrusive; **discrétion** nf discretion; **à discrétion** as much as one wants

discrimination nf discrimination; **sans ~** indiscriminately

discussion [diskysjɔ̃] nf discussion

discutable [diskytabl] adj debatable

discuter [diskyte] /1/ vt (*contester*) to question, dispute; (*débattre: prix*) to discuss ▷ vi to talk; (*protester*) to argue; **~ de** to discuss

dise etc [diz] vb voir **dire**

disjoncteur [disʒɔ̃ktœʀ] nm (*Élec*) circuit breaker

disloquer [dislɔke] /1/: **se disloquer** vi (*parti, empire*) to break up; (*meuble*) to come apart; **se ~ l'épaule** to dislocate one's shoulder

disons etc [dizɔ̃] vb voir **dire**

disparaître [disparɛtʀ] /57/ vi to disappear; (*se perdre: traditions etc*) to die out; (*personne: mourir*) to die; **faire ~** (*objet, tache, trace*) to remove; (*personne, douleur*) to get rid of

disparition [disparisjɔ̃] nf disappearance; **espèce en voie de ~** endangered species

disparu, e [dispaʀy] nm/f missing person; **être porté ~** to be reported missing

dispensaire [dispɑ̃sɛʀ] nm community clinic

dispenser [dispɑ̃se] /1/ vt: **~ qn de** to exempt sb from

disperser [dispɛʀse] /1/ vt to scatter; **se disperser** vi to scatter

disponible [dispɔnibl] adj available

disposé, e [dispoze] adj: **bien/mal ~** (*humeur*) in a good/bad mood; **~ à** (*prêt à*) willing ou prepared to

disposer [dispoze] /1/ vt to arrange ▷ vi: **vous pouvez ~** you may leave; **~ de** to have (at one's disposal); **se ~ à faire** to prepare to do, be about to do

dispositif [dispozitif] nm device; (*fig*) system, plan of action

disposition [dispozisjɔ̃] nf (*arrangement*) arrangement, layout; (*humeur*) mood; **prendre ses ~s** to make arrangements; **avoir des ~s pour la musique** etc to have a special aptitude for music etc; **à la ~ de qn** at sb's disposal; **je suis à votre ~** I am at your service

disproportionné, e [dispʀopɔʀsjɔne] adj disproportionate, out of all proportion

dispute [dispyt] nf quarrel, argument; **disputer** /1/ vt (*match*) to play; (*combat*) to fight; **se disputer** vi to quarrel

disqualifier [diskalifje] /7/ vt to disqualify

disque [disk] nm (*Mus*) record; (*forme, pièce*) disc; (*Sport*) discus; **~ compact** compact disc; **~ dur** hard disk; **disquette** nf floppy (disk), diskette

dissertation [disɛʀtasjɔ̃] nf (*Scol*) essay

dissimuler [disimyle] /1/ vt to conceal

dissipé, e [disipe] adj (*indiscipliné*) unruly

dissolvant [disɔlvɑ̃] nm nail polish remover

dissuader [disɥade] /1/ vt: **~ qn de faire/de qch** to dissuade sb from doing/from sth

distance [distɑ̃s] nf distance; (*fig: écart*) gap; **à ~** at ou from a distance; **distancer** /3/ vt to outdistance

distant, e [distɑ̃, -ɑ̃t] adj (*réservé*) distant; **~ de** (*lieu*) far away ou a long way from

distillerie [distilʀi] nf distillery

distinct, e [distɛ̃(kt), distɛ̃kt] adj distinct; **distinctement** [distɛ̃ktəmɑ̃] adv distinctly; **distinctif, -ive** adj distinctive

distingué, e [distɛ̃ge] adj distinguished

distinguer [distɛ̃ge] /1/ vt to distinguish; **se distinguer** vi: **se ~ (de)** to distinguish o.s. ou be distinguished (from)

distraction [distʀaksjɔ̃] nf (*manque d'attention*) absent-mindedness; (*passe-temps*) distraction, entertainment

distraire [distʀɛʀ] /50/ vt (*déranger*) to distract; (*divertir*) to entertain, divert; **se distraire** vi to amuse ou enjoy o.s.; **distrait, e** [distrɛ, -ɛt] *pp de* **distraire** ▷ *adj* absent-minded

distrayant, e [distrɛjɑ̃, -ɑ̃t] *adj* entertaining

distribuer [distribɥe] /1/ *vt* to distribute; to hand out; *(Cartes)* to deal (out); *(courrier)* to deliver; **distributeur** *nm (Auto, Comm)* distributor; *(automatique)* (vending) machine; **distributeur de billets** cash dispenser

dit, e [di, dit] *pp de* **dire** ▷ *adj (fixé):* **le jour ~** the arranged day; *(surnommé):* **X, ~ Pierrot** X, known as *ou* called Pierrot

dites [dit] *vb voir* **dire**

divan [divɑ̃] *nm* divan

divers, e [divɛʀ, -ɛʀs] *adj (varié)* diverse, varied; *(différent)* different, various; **~es personnes** various *ou* several people

diversité [divɛʀsite] *nf* diversity, variety

divertir [divɛʀtiʀ] /2/: **se divertir** *vi* to amuse *ou* enjoy o.s.; **divertissement** *nm* entertainment

diviser [divize] /1/ *vt* to divide; **division** *nf* division

divorce [divɔʀs] *nm* divorce; **divorcé, e** *nm/f* divorcee; **divorcer** /3/ *vi* to get a divorce, get divorced; **divorcer de** *ou* **d'avec qn** to divorce sb

divulguer [divylge] /1/ *vt* to disclose

dix [di, dis, diz] *num* ten; **dix-huit** *num* eighteen; **dix-huitième** *num* eighteenth; **dixième** *num* tenth; **dix-neuf** *num* nineteen; **dix-neuvième** *num* nineteenth; **dix-sept** *num* seventeen; **dix-septième** *num* seventeenth

dizaine [dizɛn] *nf:* **une ~ (de)** about ten, ten or so

do [do] *nm (note)* C; *(en chantant la gamme)* do(h)

docile [dɔsil] *adj* docile

dock [dɔk] *nm* dock; **docker** *nm* docker

docteur, e [dɔktœʀ] *nm/f* doctor; **doctorat** *nm:* **doctorat (d'Université)** ≈ doctorate

doctrine [dɔktʀin] *nf* doctrine

document [dɔkymɑ̃] *nm* document; **documentaire** *adj, nm* documentary; **documentation** *nf* documentation, literature; **documenter** /1/ *vt:* **se documenter (sur)** to gather information *ou* material (on *ou* about)

dodo [dodo] *nm:* **aller faire ~** to go to beddy-byes

dogue [dɔg] *nm* mastiff

doigt [dwa] *nm* finger; **à deux ~s de** within an ace *(BRIT) ou* an inch of; **un ~ de lait/whisky** a drop of milk/ whisky; **~ de pied** toe

doit *etc* [dwa] *vb voir* **devoir**

dollar [dɔlaʀ] *nm* dollar

domaine [dɔmɛn] *nm* estate, property; *(fig)* domain, field

domestique [dɔmɛstik] *adj* domestic ▷ *nm/f* servant, domestic

domicile [dɔmisil] *nm* home, place of residence; **à ~** at home; **livrer à ~** to deliver; **domicilié, e** *adj:* **être domicilié à** to have one's home in *ou* at

dominant, e [dɔminɑ̃, -ɑ̃t] *adj (opinion)* predominant

dominer [dɔmine] /1/ *vt* to dominate; *(sujet)* to master; *(surpasser)* to outclass, surpass; *(surplomber)* to tower above, dominate ▷ *vi* to be in the dominant position; **se dominer** *vi* to control o.s.

domino [dɔmino] *nm* domino; **dominos** *nmpl (jeu)* dominoes *sg*

dommage [dɔmaʒ] *nm:* **~s** *(dégâts, pertes)* damage *no pl;* **c'est ~ de faire/que** it's a shame to do/ that; **quel ~!, c'est ~!** what a pity *ou* shame!

dompter [dɔ̃(p)te] /1/ *vt* to tame; **dompteur, -euse** *nm/f* trainer

DOM-ROM [dɔmʀɔm] *sigle m(pl)* (= *Département(s) et Régions/*

Territoire(s) d'outre-mer) French overseas departments and regions

don [dɔ̃] *nm* gift; *(charité)* donation; **avoir des ~s pour** to have a gift *ou* talent for; **elle a le ~ de m'énerver** she's got a knack of getting on my nerves

donc [dɔ̃k] *conj* therefore, so; *(après une digression)* so, then

dongle [dɔ̃gl] *nm* dongle

donné, e [dɔne] *adj (convenu: lieu, heure)* given; *(pas cher)* very cheap; **données** *nfpl* data; **c'est ~** it's a gift; **étant ~ que ...** given that ...

donner [dɔne] /1/ *vt* to give; *(vieux habits etc)* to give away; *(spectacle)* to put on; **~ qch à qn** to give sb sth, give sth to sb; **~ sur** *(fenêtre, chambre)* to look (out) onto; **ça donne soif/faim** it makes you (feel) thirsty/hungry; **se ~ à fond (à son travail)** to give one's all (to one's work); **se ~ du mal** *ou* **de la peine (pour faire qch)** to go to a lot of trouble (to do sth); **s'en ~ à cœur joie** *(fam)* to have a great time (of it)

MOT-CLÉ

dont [dɔ̃] *pron relatif* **1** *(appartenance: objets)* whose, of which; *(: êtres animés)* whose; **la maison dont le toit est rouge** the house the roof of which is red, the house whose roof is red; **l'homme dont je connais la sœur** the man whose sister I know **2** *(parmi lesquel(le)s)*: **deux livres, dont l'un est ...** two books, one of which is ...; **il y avait plusieurs personnes, dont Gabrielle** there were several people, among them Gabrielle; **10 blessés, dont 2 grièvement** 10 injured, 2 of them seriously

3 *(complément d'adjectif, de verbe)*: **le fils dont il est si fier** the son he's so proud of; **le pays dont il est originaire** the country he's from; **ce**

dont je parle what I'm talking about; **la façon dont il l'a fait** the way (in which) he did it

dopage [dɔpaʒ] *nm (Sport)* drug use; *(de cheval)* doping

doré, e [dɔre] *adj* golden; *(avec dorure)* gilt, gilded

dorénavant [dɔrenavɑ̃] *adv* henceforth

dorer [dɔre] /1/ *vt* to gild; **(faire) ~** *(Culin)* to brown

dorloter [dɔrlɔte] /1/ *vt* to pamper

dormir [dɔrmir] /16/ *vi* to sleep; *(être endormi)* to be asleep

dortoir [dɔrtwar] *nm* dormitory

dos [do] *nm* back; *(de livre)* spine; **"voir au ~"** "see over"; **de ~** from the back

dosage [dozaʒ] *nm* mixture

dose [doz] *nf* dose; **doser** /1/ *vt* to measure out; **il faut savoir doser ses efforts** you have to be able to pace yourself

dossier [dɔsje] *nm (renseignements, fichier)* file; *(de chaise)* back; *(Presse)* feature; *(Inform)* folder; **un ~ scolaire** a school report

douane [dwan] *nf* customs *pl*; **douanier, -ière** *adj* customs *cpd* ▷ *nm* customs officer

double [dubl] *adj, adv* double ▷ *nm (autre exemplaire)* duplicate, copy; *(sosie)* double; *(Tennis)* doubles *sg*; *(2 fois plus)*: **le ~ (de)** twice as much *(ou* many) (as); **en ~ (exemplaire)** in duplicate; **faire ~ emploi** to be redundant; **double-cliquer** /1/ *vi (Inform)* to double-click

doubler [duble] /1/ *vt (multiplier par 2)* to double; *(vêtement)* to line; *(dépasser)* to overtake, pass; *(film)* to dub; *(acteur)* to stand in for ▷ *vi* to double

doublure [dublyr] *nf* lining; *(Ciné)* stand-in

douce [dus] *adj f voir* **doux**; **douceâtre** *adj* sickly sweet;

doucement adv gently; (lentement) slowly; **douceur** nf softness; (de climat) mildness; (de quelqu'un) gentleness

douche [duʃ] nf shower; **prendre une ~** to have ou take a shower; **doucher** /1/: **se doucher** vi to have ou take a shower

doué, e [dwe] adj gifted, talented; **être ~ pour** to have a gift for

douille [duj] nf (Élec) socket

douillet, te [dujɛ, -ɛt] adj cosy; (péj: à la douleur) soft

douleur [dulœʀ] nf pain; (chagrin) grief, distress; **douloureux, -euse** adj painful

doute [dut] nm doubt; **sans ~** no doubt; (probablement) probably; **sans nul** ou **aucun ~** without (a) doubt; **douter** /1/ vt to doubt; **douter de** (allié, sincérité de qn) to have (one's) doubts about, doubt; (résultat, réussite) to be doubtful of; **douter que** to doubt whether ou if; **se douter de qch/que** to suspect sth/that; **je m'en doutais** I suspected as much; **douteux, -euse** adj (incertain) doubtful; (péj) dubious-looking

Douvres [duvʀ] n Dover

doux, douce [du, dus] adj soft; (sucré, agréable) sweet; (peu fort: moutarde etc, clément: climat) mild; (pas brusque) gentle

douzaine [duzɛn] nf (12) dozen; (environ 12): **une ~ (de)** a dozen or so

douze [duz] num twelve; **douzième** num twelfth

dragée [dʀaʒe] nf sugared almond

draguer [dʀage] /1/ vt (rivière) to dredge; (fam) to try and pick up

dramatique [dʀamatik] adj dramatic; (tragique) tragic ▷ nf (TV) (television) drama

drame [dʀam] nm drama

drap [dʀa] nm (de lit) sheet; (tissu) woollen fabric

drapeau, x [dʀapo] nm flag

drap-housse [dʀaus] nm fitted sheet

dresser [dʀese] /1/ vt (mettre vertical, monter) to put up, erect; (liste, bilan, contrat) to draw up; (animal) to train; **se dresser** vi (falaise, obstacle) to stand; (personne) to draw o.s. up; **~ l'oreille** to prick up one's ears; **~ qn contre qn d'autre** to set sb against sb else

drogue [dʀɔg] nf drug; **la ~** drugs pl; **drogué, e** nm/f drug addict; **droguer** /1/ vt (victime) to drug; **se droguer** vi (aux stupéfiants) to take drugs; (de médicaments) to dose o.s. up; **droguerie** nf ≈ hardware shop (BRIT) ou store (US); **droguiste** nm ≈ keeper (ou owner) of a hardware shop ou store

droit, e [dʀwa, dʀwat] adj (non courbe) straight; (vertical) upright, straight; (fig: loyal, franc) upright, straight(forward); (opposé à gauche) right, right-hand ▷ adv straight ▷ nm (prérogative) right; (taxe) duty, tax; (: d'inscription) fee; (lois, branche): **le ~** law ▷ nf (Pol) right (wing); **avoir le ~ de** to be allowed to; **avoir ~ à** to be entitled to; **être dans son ~** to be within one's rights; **à ~e** on the right; (direction) (to the) right; **~s d'auteur** royalties; **~s d'inscription** enrolment ou registration fees; **droitier, -ière** adj right-handed

drôle [dʀol] adj (amusant) funny, amusing; (bizarre) funny, peculiar; **un ~ de ...** (bizarre) a strange ou funny ...; (intensif) an incredible ..., a terrific ...

dromadaire [dʀɔmadɛʀ] nm dromedary

du [dy] art voir **de**

dû, due [dy] pp de **devoir** ▷ adj (somme) owing, owed; (causé par): **dû à** due to ▷ nm due

dune [dyn] nf dune

duplex [dyplɛks] nm (appartement) split-level apartment, duplex

duquel [dykɛl] voir **lequel**

dur, e [dyʀ] *adj* (*pierre, siège, travail, problème*) hard; (*lumière, voix, climat*) harsh; (*sévère*) hard, harsh; (*cruel*) hard(-hearted); (*porte, col*) stiff; (*viande*) tough ▷ *adv* hard ▷ *nm* (*fam: meneur*) tough nut; **~ d'oreille** hard of hearing

durant [dyʀɑ̃] *prép* (*au cours de*) during; (*pendant*) for; **des mois ~** for months

durcir [dyʀsiʀ] /2/ *vt, vi* to harden; **se durcir** *vi* to harden

durée [dyʀe] *nf* length; (*d'une pile etc*) life; **de courte ~** (*séjour, répit*) brief

durement [dyʀmɑ̃] *adv* harshly

durer [dyʀe] /1/ *vi* to last

dureté [dyʀte] *nf* hardness; harshness; stiffness; toughness

durit® [dyʀit] *nf* (*car radiator*) hose

duvet [dyvɛ] *nm* down

DVD *sigle m* (= *digital versatile disc*) DVD

dynamique [dinamik] *adj* dynamic; **dynamisme** *nm* dynamism

dynamo [dinamo] *nf* dynamo

dyslexie [dislɛksi] *nf* dyslexia, word blindness

eau, x [o] *nf* water ▷ *nfpl* (*Méd*) waters; **prendre l'~** to leak, let in water; **tomber à l'~** (*fig*) to fall through; **~ de Cologne** eau de Cologne; **~ courante** running water; **~ douce** fresh water; **~ gazeuse** sparkling (mineral) water; **~ de Javel** bleach; **~ minérale** mineral water; **~ plate** still water; **~ salée** salt water; **~ de toilette** toilet water; **eau-de-vie** *nf* brandy

ébène [ebɛn] *nf* ebony; **ébéniste** [ebenist] *nm* cabinetmaker

éblouir [ebluiʀ] /2/ *vt* to dazzle

éboueur [ebwœʀ] *nm* dustman (BRIT), garbage man (US)

ébouillanter [ebujɑ̃te] /1/ *vt* to scald; (*Culin*) to blanch

éboulement [ebulmɑ̃] *nm* rock fall

ébranler [ebʀɑ̃le] /1/ *vt* to shake; (*rendre instable*) to weaken; **s'ébranler** *vi* (*partir*) to move off

ébullition [ebylisjɔ̃] *nf* boiling point; **en ~** boiling

écaille [ekɑj] nf (de poisson) scale; (matière) tortoiseshell; **écailler** /1/ vt (poisson) to scale; **s'écailler** vi to flake ou peel (off)

écart [ekaʀ] nm gap; **à l'~** out of the way; **à l'~ de** away from; **faire un ~** (voiture) to swerve

écarté, e [ekaʀte] adj (lieu) out-of-the-way, remote; (ouvert): **les jambes ~es** legs apart; **les bras ~s** arms outstretched

écarter [ekaʀte] /1/ vt (séparer) to move apart, separate; (éloigner) to push back, move away; (ouvrir: bras, jambes) to spread, open; (: rideau) to draw (back); (éliminer: candidat, possibilité) to dismiss; **s'écarter** vi to part; (personne) to move away; **s'~ de** to wander from

échafaudage [eʃafodaʒ] nm scaffolding

échalote [eʃalɔt] nf shallot

échange [eʃɑ̃ʒ] nm exchange; **en ~ de** in exchange ou return for; **échanger** /3/ vt: **échanger qch (contre)** to exchange sth (for)

échantillon [eʃɑ̃tijɔ̃] nm sample

échapper [eʃape] /1/: **~ à** vt (gardien) to escape (from); (punition, péril) to escape; **~ à qn** (détail, sens) to escape sb; (objet qu'on tient) to slip out of sb's hands; **laisser ~** (cri etc) to let out; **l'~ belle** to have a narrow escape

écharde [eʃaʀd] nf splinter (of wood)

écharpe [eʃaʀp] nf scarf; **avoir le bras en ~** to have one's arm in a sling

échauffer [eʃofe] /1/ vt (métal, moteur) to overheat; **s'échauffer** vi (Sport) to warm up; (discussion) to become heated

échéance [eʃeɑ̃s] nf (d'un paiement: date) settlement date; (fig) deadline; **à brève/longue ~** in the short/long term

échéant [eʃeɑ̃]: **le cas ~** adv if the case arises

échec [eʃɛk] nm failure; (Échecs): **~ et mat/au roi** checkmate/check;

échecs nmpl (jeu) chess sg; **tenir en ~** to hold in check

échelle [eʃɛl] nf ladder; (fig, d'une carte) scale

échelon [eʃ(ə)lɔ̃] nm (d'échelle) rung; (Admin) grade; **échelonner** /1/ vt to space out, spread out

échiquier [eʃikje] nm chessboard

écho [eko] nm echo; **échographie** nf: **passer une échographie** to have a scan

échouer [eʃwe] /1/ vi to fail; **s'échouer** vi to run aground

éclabousser [eklabuse] /1/ vt to splash

éclair [eklɛʀ] nm (d'orage) flash of lightning, lightning no pl; (gâteau) éclair

éclairage [eklɛʀaʒ] nm lighting

éclaircie [eklɛʀsi] nf bright ou sunny interval

éclaircir [eklɛʀsiʀ] /2/ vt to lighten; (fig: mystère) to clear up; (point) to clarify; **s'éclaircir** vi (ciel) to brighten up; **s'~ la voix** to clear one's throat; **éclaircissement** nm clarification

éclairer [eklere] /1/ vt (lieu) to light (up); (personne: avec une lampe de poche etc) to light the way for; (fig: rendre compréhensible) to shed light on ▷ vi: **~ mal/bien** to give a poor/good light; **s'~ à la bougie/l'électricité** to use candlelight/have electric lighting

éclat [ekla] nm (de bombe, de verre) fragment; (du soleil, d'une couleur etc) brightness, brilliance; (d'une cérémonie) splendour; (scandale): **faire un ~** to cause a commotion; **~ de rire** burst ou roar of laughter; **~ de voix** shout

éclatant, e [eklatɑ̃, -ɑ̃t] adj brilliant

éclater [eklate] /1/ vi (pneu) to burst; (bombe) to explode; (guerre, épidémie) to break out; (groupe, parti) to break up; **~ de rire/en sanglots** to burst out laughing/sobbing

écluse [eklyz] nf lock

écœurant, e [ekœʀɑ̃, -ɑ̃t] adj sickening; (gâteau etc) sickly

écœurer [ekœʀe] *vt*: ~ **qn** (*nourriture*) to make sb feel sick; (*fig: conduite, personne*) to disgust sb

école [ekɔl] *nf* school; **aller à l'~** to go to school; ~ **maternelle** nursery school; ~ **primaire** primary (BRIT) *ou* grade (US) school; ~ **secondaire** secondary (BRIT) *ou* high (US) school; **écolier, -ière** *nm/f* schoolboy/girl

écologie [ekɔlɔʒi] *nf* ecology; **écologique** *adj* environment-friendly; **écologiste** *nm/f* ecologist

économe [ekɔnɔm] *adj* thrifty ▷ *nm/f* (*de lycée etc*) bursar (BRIT), treasurer (US)

économie [ekɔnɔmi] *nf* economy; (*gain: d'argent, de temps etc*) saving; (*science*) economics *sg*; **économies** *nfpl* (*Comm*) savings; **économique** *adj* (*avantageux*) economical; (*Écon*) economic; **économiser** /1/ *vt, vi* to save

écorce [ekɔʀs] *nf* bark; (*de fruit*) peel

écorcher [ekɔʀʃe] /1/ *vt*: **s'~ le genou** *etc* to scrape *ou* graze one's knee *etc*; **écorchure** *nf* graze

écossais, e [ekɔsɛ, -ɛz] *adj* Scottish ▷ *nm/f*: **É~, e** Scot

Écosse [ekɔs] *nf*: **l'~** Scotland

écouter [ekute] /1/ *vt* to listen to; **s'écouter** (*malade*) to be a bit of a hypochondriac; **si je m'écoutais** if I followed my instincts; **écouteur** *nm* (*Tél*) receiver; **écouteurs** *nmpl* (*casque*) headphones, headset *sg*

écran [ekʀɑ̃] *nm* screen; **le petit ~** television; ~ **tactile** touchscreen; ~ **total** sunblock

écrasant, e [ekʀɑzɑ̃, -ɑ̃t] *adj* overwhelming

écraser [ekʀɑze] /1/ *vt* to crush; (*piéton*) to run over; **s'~ (au sol)** *vi* to crash; **s'~ contre** to crash into

écrémé, e [ekʀeme] *adj* (*lait*) skimmed

écrevisse [ekʀəvis] *nf* crayfish *inv*

écrire [ekʀiʀ] /39/ *vt, vi* to write; **s'écrire** *vi* to write to one another; **ça s'écrit comment?** how is it spelt?;

écrit *nm* (*examen*) written paper; **par écrit** in writing

écriteau, x [ekʀito] *nm* notice, sign

écriture [ekʀityʀ] *nf* writing; **écritures** *nfpl* (*Comm*) accounts, books; **l'É~ (sainte), les É~s** the Scriptures

écrivain [ekʀivɛ̃] *nm* writer

écrou [ekʀu] *nm* nut

écrouler [ekʀule] /1/: **s'écrouler** *vi* to collapse

écru, e [ekʀy] *adj* (*couleur*) off-white, écru

écume [ekym] *nf* foam

écureuil [ekyʀœj] *nm* squirrel

écurie [ekyʀi] *nf* stable

eczéma [ɛgzema] *nm* eczema

EDF *sigle f* (= *Électricité de France*) national electricity company

Édimbourg [edɛ̃buʀ] *n* Edinburgh

éditer [edite] /1/ *vt* (*publier*) to publish; (*annoter*) to edit; **éditeur, -trice** *nm/f* publisher; **édition** *nf* edition; **l'édition** publishing

édredon [edʀədɔ̃] *nm* eiderdown

éducateur, -trice [edykatœʀ, -tʀis] *nm/f* teacher; (*en école spécialisée*) instructor

éducatif, -ive [edykatif, -iv] *adj* educational

éducation [edykasjɔ̃] *nf* education; (*familiale*) upbringing; (*manières*) (good) manners *pl*; ~ **physique** physical education

éduquer [edyke] /1/ *vt* to educate; (*élever*) to bring up

effacer [efase] /3/ *vt* to erase, rub out; **s'effacer** *vi* (*inscription etc*) to wear off; (*pour laisser passer*) to step aside

effarant, e [efaʀɑ̃, -ɑ̃t] *adj* alarming

effectif, -ive [efɛktif, -iv] *adj* real ▷ *nm* (*Scol*) total number of pupils; (*Comm*) manpower *sg*; **effectivement** *adv* (*réellement*) actually, really; (*en effet*) indeed

effectuer [efɛktɥe] /1/ *vt* (*opération, mission*) to carry out; (*déplacement, trajet*) to make

effervescent, e [efɛʀvesɑ̃, -ɑ̃t] *adj* effervescent

effet [efɛ] *nm* effect; (*impression*) impression; **effets** *nmpl* (*vêtements etc*) things; **faire ~** (*médicament*) to take effect; **faire de l'~** (*impressionner*) to make an impression; **faire bon/ mauvais ~ sur qn** to make a good/ bad impression on sb; **en ~** indeed; **~ de serre** greenhouse effect

efficace [efikas] *adj* (*personne*) efficient; (*action, médicament*) effective; **efficacité** *nf* efficiency; effectiveness

effondrer [efɔ̃dʀe] /1/: **s'effondrer** *vi* to collapse

efforcer [efɔʀse] /3/: **s'efforcer de** *vt*: **s'~ de faire** to try hard to do

effort [efɔʀ] *nm* effort

effrayant, e [efʀɛjɑ̃, -ɑ̃t] *adj* frightening

effrayer [efʀeje] /8/ *vt* to frighten, scare; **s'effrayer (de)** to be frightened *ou* scared (by)

effréné, e [efʀene] *adj* wild

effronté, e [efʀɔ̃te] *adj* insolent

effroyable [efʀwajabl] *adj* horrifying, appalling

égal, e, -aux [egal, -o] *adj* equal; (*constant: vitesse*) steady ▷ *nm/f* equal; **être ~ à** (*prix, nombre*) to be equal to; **ça m'est ~** it's all the same to me, I don't mind; **sans ~** matchless, unequalled; **d'~ à ~** as equals; **également** *adv* equally; (*aussi*) too, as well; **égaler** /1/ *vt* to equal; **égaliser** /1/ *vt* (*sol, salaires*) to level (out); (*chances*) to equalize ▷ *vi* (*Sport*) to equalize; **égalité** *nf* equality; **être à égalité (de points)** to be level

égard [egaʀ] *nm*: **égards** *nmpl* consideration *sg*; **à cet ~** in this respect; **par ~ pour** out of consideration for; **à l'~ de** towards

égarer [egaʀe] /1/ *vt* to mislay; **s'égarer** *vi* to get lost, lose one's way; (*objet*) to go astray

églefin [egləfɛ̃] *nm* haddock

église [egliz] *nf* church; **aller à l'~** to go to church

égoïsme [egɔism] *nm* selfishness; **égoïste** *adj* selfish

égout [egu] *nm* sewer

égoutter [egute] /1/ *vi* to drip; **s'égoutter** *vi* to drip; **égouttoir** *nm* draining board; (*mobile*) draining rack

égratignure [egʀatiɲyʀ] *nf* scratch

Égypte [eʒipt] *nf*: **l'~** Egypt; **égyptien, ne** *adj* Egyptian ▷ *nm/f*: **Égyptien, ne** Egyptian

eh [e] *excl* hey!; **eh bien** well

élaborer [elabɔʀe] /1/ *vt* to elaborate; (*projet, stratégie*) to work out; (*rapport*) to draft

élan [elɑ̃] *nm* (*Zool*) elk, moose; (*Sport*) run up; (*fig: de tendresse etc*) surge; **prendre son ~/de l'~** to take a run up/gather speed

élancer [elɑ̃se] /3/: **s'élancer** *vi* to dash, hurl o.s.

élargir [elaʀʒiʀ] /2/ *vt* to widen; **s'élargir** *vi* to widen; (*vêtement*) to stretch

élastique [elastik] *adj* elastic ▷ *nm* (*de bureau*) rubber band; (*pour la couture*) elastic *no pl*

élection [elɛksjɔ̃] *nf* election

électricien, ne [elɛktʀisjɛ̃, -ɛn] *nm/f* electrician

électricité [elɛktʀisite] *nf* electricity; **allumer/éteindre l'~** to put on/off the light

électrique [elɛktʀik] *adj* electric(al)

électrocuter [elɛktʀɔkyte] /1/ *vt* to electrocute

électroménager [elɛktʀɔmenaʒe] *adj*: **appareils ~s** domestic (electrical) appliances ▷ *nm*: **l'~** household appliances

électronique [elɛktʀɔnik] *adj* electronic ▷ *nf* electronics *sg*

élégance [elegɑ̃s] *nf* elegance

élégant, e [elegɑ̃, -ɑ̃t] *adj* elegant

élément [elemɑ̃] *nm* element; (*pièce*) component, part; **élémentaire** *adj* elementary

éléphant [elefɑ̃] *nm* elephant

élevage [el(ə)vaʒ] *nm* breeding; (*de bovins*) cattle breeding *ou* rearing; **truite d'~** farmed trout

élevé, e [el(ə)ve] *adj* high; **bien/mal ~** well-/ill-mannered

élève [elɛv] *nm/f* pupil

élever [el(ə)ve] /5/ *vt* (*enfant*) to bring up, raise; (*bétail, volaille*) to breed; (*hausser: taux, niveau*) to raise; (*édifier: monument*) to put up, erect; **s'élever** *vi* (*avion, alpiniste*) to go up; (*niveau, température, aussi*) to rise; **s'~ à** (*frais, dégâts*) to amount to, add up to; **s'~ contre** to rise up against; **~ la voix** to raise one's voice; **éleveur, -euse** *nm/f* stock breeder

éliminatoire [eliminatwaʀ] *nf* (*Sport*) heat

éliminer [elimine] /1/ *vt* to eliminate

élire [eliʀ] /43/ *vt* to elect

elle [ɛl] *pron* (*sujet*) she; (: *chose*) it; (*complément*) her; it; **~s** (*sujet*) they; (*complément*) them; **~-même** herself; itself; **~s-mêmes** themselves; *voir* **il**

éloigné, e [elwaɲe] *adj* distant, far-off; (*parent*) distant

éloigner [elwaɲe] /1/ *vt* (*échéance*) to put off, postpone; (*soupçons, danger*) to ward off; **~ qch (de)** to move sth far away (from); **s'éloigner (de)** (*personne*) to go away (from); (*véhicule*) to move away (from); (*affectivement*) to become estranged (from); **~ qn (de)** to take sb away *ou* remove sb (from)

élu, e [ely] *pp de* **élire** ▷ *nm/f* (*Pol*) elected representative

Élysée [elize] *nm*: **(le palais de) l'~** the Élysée palace

émail, -aux [emaj, -o] *nm* enamel

e-mail [imɛl] *nm* email; **envoyer qch par ~** to email sth

émanciper [emɑ̃sipe] /1/: **s'émanciper** *vi* (*fig*) to become emancipated *ou* liberated

emballage [ɑ̃balaʒ] *nm* (*papier*) wrapping; (*carton*) packaging

emballer [ɑ̃bale] /1/ *vt* to wrap (up); (*dans un carton*) to pack (up); (*fig: fam*) to thrill (to bits); **s'emballer** *vi* (*moteur*) to race; (*cheval*) to bolt; (*fig: personne*) to get carried away

embarcadère [ɑ̃baʀkadɛʀ] *nm* landing stage (BRIT), pier

embarquement [ɑ̃baʀkəmɑ̃] *nm* embarkation; (*de marchandises*) loading; (*de passagers*) boarding

embarquer [ɑ̃baʀke] /1/ *vt* (*personne*) to embark; (*marchandise*) to load; (*fam*) to cart off ▷ *vi* (*passager*) to board; **s'embarquer** *vi* to board; **s'~ dans** (*affaire, aventure*) to embark upon

embarras [ɑ̃baʀa] *nm* (*confusion*) embarrassment; **être dans l'~** to be in a predicament *ou* an awkward position; **vous n'avez que l'~ du choix** the only problem is choosing

embarrassant, e [ɑ̃baʀasɑ̃, -ɑ̃t] *adj* embarrassing

embarrasser [ɑ̃baʀase] /1/ *vt* (*encombrer*) to clutter (up); (*gêner*) to hinder, hamper; to put in an awkward position; **s'embarrasser de** to burden o.s. with

embaucher [ɑ̃boʃe] /1/ *vt* to take on, hire

embêtant, e [ɑ̃bɛtɑ̃, -ɑ̃t] *adj* annoying

embêter [ɑ̃bete] /1/ *vt* to bother; **s'embêter** *vi* (*s'ennuyer*) to be bored

emblée [ɑ̃ble]: **d'~** *adv* straightaway

embouchure [ɑ̃buʃyʀ] *nf* (*Géo*) mouth

embourber [ɑ̃buʀbe] /1/: **s'embourber** *vi* to get stuck in the mud

embouteillage [ɑ̃buteijaʒ] *nm* traffic jam, (traffic) holdup (BRIT)

embranchement [ãbrãʃmã] nm (routier) junction

embrasser [ãbrase] /1/ vt to kiss; (sujet, période) to embrace, encompass

embrayage [ãbrɛjaʒ] nm clutch

embrouiller [ãbruje] /1/ vt (fils) to tangle (up); (fiches, idées, personne) to muddle up; **s'embrouiller** vi to get in a muddle

embruns [ãbrœ̃] nmpl sea spray sg

embué, e [ãbɥe] adj misted up

émeraude [em(ə)rod] nf emerald

émerger [emɛrʒe] /3/ vi to emerge; (faire saillie, aussi fig) to stand out

émeri [em(ə)ri] nm: **toile** ou **papier ~** emery paper

émerveiller [emɛrveje] /1/ vt to fill with wonder; **s'émerveiller de** to marvel at

émettre [emɛtr] /56/ vt (son, lumière) to give out, emit; (message etc: Radio) to transmit; (billet, timbre, emprunt, chèque) to issue; (hypothèse, avis) to voice, put forward ▷ vi to broadcast

émeus etc [emø] vb voir **émouvoir**

émeute [emøt] nf riot

émigrer [emigre] /1/ vi to emigrate

émincer [emɛ̃se] /3/ vt to slice thinly

émission [emisjɔ̃] nf (voir émettre) emission; (d'un message) transmission; (de billet, timbre, emprunt, chèque) issue; (Radio, TV) programme, broadcast

emmêler [ãmele] /1/ vt to tangle (up); (fig) to muddle up; **s'emmêler** vi to get into a tangle

emménager [ãmenaʒe] /3/ vi to move in; **~ dans** to move into

emmener [ãm(ə)ne] /5/ vt to take (with one); (comme otage, capture) to take away; **~ qn au cinéma** to take sb to the cinema

emmerder [ãmɛrde] /1/ (!) vt to bug, bother; **s'emmerder** vi to be bored stiff

émoticone [emoticon] nm smiley

émotif, -ive [emotif, -iv] adj emotional

émotion [emosjɔ̃] nf emotion

émouvoir [emuvwar] /27/ vt to move; **s'émouvoir** vi to be moved; to be roused

empaqueter [ãpakte] /4/ vt to pack up

emparer [ãpare] /1/: **s'emparer de** vt (objet) to seize, grab; (comme otage, Mil) to seize; (peur etc) to take hold of

empêchement [ãpɛʃmã] nm (unexpected) obstacle, hitch

empêcher [ãpeʃe] /1/ vt to prevent; **~ qn de faire** to prevent ou stop sb (from) doing; **il n'empêche que** nevertheless; **il n'a pas pu s'~ de rire** he couldn't help laughing

empereur [ãprœr] nm emperor

empiffrer [ãpifre] /1/: **s'empiffrer** vi (péj) to stuff o.s.

empiler [ãpile] /1/ vt to pile (up)

empire [ãpir] nm empire; (fig) influence

empirer [ãpire] /1/ vi to worsen, deteriorate

emplacement [ãplasmã] nm site

emploi [ãplwa] nm use; (poste) job, situation; (Comm, Écon) employment; **mode d'~** directions for use; **~ du temps** timetable, schedule

employé, e [ãplwaje] nm/f employee; **~ de bureau/banque** office/bank employee ou clerk

employer [ãplwaje] /8/ vt to use; (ouvrier, main-d'œuvre) to employ; **s'~ à qch/à faire** to apply ou devote o.s. to sth/to doing; **employeur, -euse** nm/f employer

empoigner [ãpwaɲe] /1/ vt to grab

empoisonner [ãpwazɔne] /1/ vt to poison; (empester: air, pièce) to stink out; (fam): **~ qn** to drive sb mad

emporter [ãpɔrte] /1/ vt to take (with one); (en dérobant ou enlevant, emmener: blessés, voyageurs) to take away; (entraîner) to carry away ou along; (rivière, vent) to carry away; **s'emporter** vi (de colère) to fly into a rage; **l'~ (sur)** to get the upper hand (of); **plats à ~** take-away meals

empreint, e [ɑ̃pʀɛ̃, -ɛ̃t] *adj*: **~ de** marked with ▷ *nf* (*de pied, main*) print; **~e (digitale)** fingerprint; **~e écologique** carbon footprint

empressé, e [ɑ̃pʀese] *adj* attentive

empresser [ɑ̃pʀese] /1/: **s'empresser** *vi*: **s'~ auprès de qn** to surround sb with attentions; **s'~ de faire** to hasten to do

emprisonner [ɑ̃pʀizɔne] /1/ *vt* to imprison

emprunt [ɑ̃pʀœ̃] *nm* loan (*from debtor's point of view*)

emprunter [ɑ̃pʀœ̃te] /1/ *vt* to borrow; (*itinéraire*) to take, follow

ému, e [emy] *pp de* **émouvoir** ▷ *adj* (*gratitude*) touched; (*compassion*) moved

○ **MOT-CLÉ**

en [ɑ̃] *prép* **1** (*endroit, pays*) in; (: *direction*) to; **habiter en France/ ville** to live in France/town; **aller en France/ville** to go to France/town
2 (*moment, temps*) in; **en été/juin** in summer/June; **en 3 jours/20 ans** in 3 days/20 years
3 (*moyen*) by; **en avion/taxi** by plane/taxi
4 (*composition*) made of; **c'est en verre/coton/laine** it's (made of) glass/cotton/wool; **un collier en argent** a silver necklace
5 (*description, état*): **une femme (habillée) en rouge** a woman (dressed) in red; **peindre qch en rouge** to paint sth red; **en T/étoile** T-/star-shaped; **en chemise/chaussettes** in one's shirt sleeves/socks; **en soldat** as a soldier; **cassé en plusieurs morceaux** broken into several pieces; **en réparation** being repaired, under repair; **en vacances** on holiday; **en deuil** in mourning; **le même en plus grand** the same but *ou* only bigger
6 (*avec gérondif*) while; on; **en dormant** while sleeping, as one

sleeps; **en sortant** on going out, as he *etc* went out; **sortir en courant** to run out
7: **en tant que** as; **je te parle en ami** I'm talking to you as a friend
▷ *pron* **1** (*indéfini*): **j'en ai/veux** I have/want some; **en as-tu?** have you got any?; **je n'en veux pas** I don't want any; **j'en ai deux** I've got two; **combien y en a-t-il?** how many (of them) are there?; **j'en ai assez** I've got enough (of it *ou* them); (*j'en ai marre*) I've had enough
2 (*provenance*) from there; **j'en viens** I've come from there
3 (*cause*): **il en est malade/perd le sommeil** he is ill/can't sleep because of it
4 (*complément de nom, d'adjectif, de verbe*): **j'en connais les dangers** I know its *ou* the dangers; **j'en suis fier/ai besoin** I am proud of it/need it

encadrer [ɑ̃kadʀe] /1/ *vt* (*tableau, image*) to frame; (*fig: entourer*) to surround; (*personnel, soldats etc*) to train

encaisser [ɑ̃kese] /1/ *vt* (*chèque*) to cash; (*argent*) to collect; (*fig: coup, défaite*) to take

en-cas [ɑ̃ka] *nm inv* snack

enceinte [ɑ̃sɛ̃t] *adj f*: **~ (de six mois)** (six months) pregnant ▷ *nf* (*mur*) wall; (*espace*) enclosure; **~ (acoustique)** speaker

encens [ɑ̃sɑ̃] *nm* incense

encercler [ɑ̃sɛʀkle] /1/ *vt* to surround

enchaîner [ɑ̃ʃene] /1/ *vt* to chain up; (*mouvements, séquences*) to link (together) ▷ *vi* to carry on

enchanté, e [ɑ̃ʃɑ̃te] *adj* (*ravi*) delighted; (*ensorcelé*) enchanted; **~ (de faire votre connaissance)** pleased to meet you

enchère [ɑ̃ʃɛʀ] *nf* bid; **mettre/ vendre aux ~s** to put up for (sale by)/ sell by auction

enclencher [ãklãʃe] /1/ vt
(*mécanisme*) to engage; **s'enclencher**
vi to engage

encombrant, e [ãkɔ̃bʀã, -ãt] adj
cumbersome, bulky

encombrement [ãkɔ̃bʀəmã] nm:
être pris dans un ~ to be stuck in a
traffic jam

encombrer [ãkɔ̃bʀe] /1/ vt to clutter
(up); (*gêner*) to hamper; **s'encombrer
de** (*bagages etc*) to load ou burden
o.s. with

 MOT-CLÉ

encore [ãkɔʀ] adv **1** (*continuation*)
still; **il y travaille encore** he's still
working on it; **pas encore** not yet
2 (*de nouveau*) again; **j'irai encore
demain** I'll go again tomorrow;
encore une fois (once) again
3 (*en plus*) more; **encore un peu de
viande?** a little more meat?; **encore
deux jours** two more days
4 (*intensif*) even, still; **encore plus
fort/mieux** even louder/better,
louder/better still; **quoi encore?**
what now?
5 (*restriction*) even so ou then, only;
encore pourrais-je le faire si ...
even so, I might be able to do it if ...; **si
encore** if only

encourager [ãkuʀaʒe] /3/ vt to
encourage; **~ qn à faire qch** to
encourage sb to do sth

encourir [ãkuʀiʀ] /11/ vt to incur

encre [ãkʀ] nf ink; **~ de Chine**
Indian ink

encyclopédie [ãsiklɔpedi] nf
encyclopaedia

endetter [ãdete] /1/: **s'endetter** vi to
get into debt

endive [ãdiv] nf chicory no pl

endormi, e [ãdɔʀmi] adj asleep

endormir [ãdɔʀmiʀ] /16/ vt to put
to sleep; (*chaleur etc*) to send to sleep;
(*Méd: dent, nerf*) to anaesthetize; (*fig:*

soupçons) to allay; **s'endormir** vi to
fall asleep, go to sleep

endroit [ãdʀwa] nm place; (*opposé à
l'envers*) right side; **à l'~** (*vêtement*) the
right way out; (*objet posé*) the right
way round

endurance [ãdyʀãs] nf endurance

endurant, e [ãdyʀã, -ãt] adj tough,
hardy

endurcir [ãdyʀsiʀ] /2/: **s'endurcir**
vi (*physiquement*) to become tougher;
(*moralement*) to become hardened

endurer [ãdyʀe] /1/ vt to endure,
bear

énergétique [enɛʀʒetik] adj
(*aliment*) energizing

énergie [enɛʀʒi] nf (*Physique*) energy;
(*Tech*) power; (*morale*) vigour, spirit;
énergique adj energetic, vigorous;
(*mesures*) drastic, stringent

énervant, e [enɛʀvã, -ãt] adj
irritating, annoying

énerver [enɛʀve] /1/ vt to irritate,
annoy; **s'énerver** vi to get excited,
get worked up

enfance [ãfãs] nf childhood

enfant [ãfã] nm/f child; **enfantin, e**
adj childlike; (*langage*) children's cpd

enfer [ãfɛʀ] nm hell

enfermer [ãfɛʀme] /1/ vt to shut up;
(*à clef, interner*) to lock up; **s'enfermer**
to shut o.s. away

enfiler [ãfile] /1/ vt (*vêtement*) to
slip on; (*perles*) to string; (*aiguille*) to
thread; **~ un tee-shirt** to slip into
a T-shirt

enfin [ãfɛ̃] adv at last; (*en énumérant*)
lastly; (*de restriction, résignation*) still;
(*pour conclure*) in a word; (*somme
toute*) after all

enflammer [ãflame] /1/:
s'enflammer vi to catch fire; (*Méd*) to
become inflamed

enflé, e [ãfle] adj swollen

enfler [ãfle] /1/ vi to swell (up)

enfoncer [ãfɔ̃se] /3/ vt (*clou*) to drive
in; (*faire pénétrer*): **~ qch dans** to push
(*ou drive*) sth into; (*forcer: porte*) to

break open; **s'enfoncer** vi to sink; **s'~ dans** to sink into; (forêt, ville) to disappear into

enfouir [ãfwiʀ] /2/ vt (dans le sol) to bury; (dans un tiroir etc) to tuck away

enfuir [ãfɥiʀ] /17/: **s'enfuir** vi to run away ou off

engagement [ãgaʒmã] nm commitment; **sans ~** without obligation

engager [ãgaʒe] /3/ vt (embaucher) to take on; (: artiste) to engage; (commencer) to start; (lier) to bind, commit; (impliquer, entraîner) to involve; (investir) to invest, lay out; (introduire, clé) to insert; (inciter) **~ qn à faire** to urge sb to do; **s'engager** vi (Mil) to enlist; (promettre) to commit o.s.; (débuter: conversation etc) to start (up); **s'~ à faire** to undertake to do; **s'~ dans** (rue, passage) to turn into; (fig: affaire, discussion) to enter into, embark on

engelures [ãʒlyʀ] nfpl chilblains

engin [ãʒɛ̃] nm machine; (outil) instrument; (Auto) vehicle; (Aviat) aircraft inv

   Attention à ne pas traduire engin par le mot anglais engine.

engloutir [ãglutiʀ] /2/ vt to swallow up

engouement [ãgumã] nm (sudden) passion

engouffrer [ãgufʀe] /1/ vt to swallow up, devour; **s'engouffrer dans** to rush into

engourdir [ãguʀdiʀ] /2/ vt to numb; (fig) to dull, blunt; **s'engourdir** vi to go numb

engrais [ãgʀɛ] nm manure; **~ (chimique)** (chemical) fertilizer

engraisser [ãgʀese] /1/ vt to fatten (up)

engrenage [ãgʀənaʒ] nm gears pl, gearing; (fig) chain

engueuler [ãgœle] /1/ vt (fam) to bawl at ou out

enhardir [ãaʀdiʀ] /2/: **s'enhardir** vi to grow bolder

énigme [enigm] nf riddle

enivrer [ãnivʀe] /1/ vt: **s'enivrer** to get drunk

enjamber [ãʒãbe] /1/ vt to stride over

enjeu, x [ãʒø] nm stakes pl

enjoué, e [ãʒwe] adj playful

enlaidir [ãlediʀ] /2/ vt to make ugly ▷ vi to become ugly

enlèvement [ãlɛvmã] nm (rapt) abduction, kidnapping

enlever [ãl(ə)ve] /5/ vt (ôter: gén) to remove; (: vêtement, lunettes) to take off; (emporter: ordures etc) to collect; (kidnapper) to abduct, kidnap; (obtenir: prix, contrat) to win; (prendre) **~ qch à qn** to take sth (away) from sb

enliser [ãlize] /1/: **s'enliser** vi to sink, get stuck

enneigé, e [ãneʒe] adj snowy

ennemi, e [ɛnmi] adj hostile; (Mil) enemy cpd ▷ nm/f enemy

ennui [ãnɥi] nm (lassitude) boredom; (difficulté) trouble no pl; **avoir des ~s** to have problems; **ennuyer** /8/ vt to bother; (lasser) to bore; **s'ennuyer** vi to be bored; **si cela ne vous ennuie pas** if it's no trouble to you; **ennuyeux, -euse** adj boring, tedious; (agaçant) annoying

énorme [enɔʀm] adj enormous, huge; **énormément** adv enormously; **énormément de neige/gens** an enormous amount of snow/number of people

enquête [ãkɛt] nf (de journaliste, de police) investigation; (judiciaire, administrative) inquiry; (sondage d'opinion) survey; **enquêter** /1/ vi to investigate; **enquêter (sur)** to do a survey (on)

enragé, e [ãʀaʒe] adj (Méd) rabid, with rabies; (fig) fanatical

enrageant, e [ãʀaʒã, -ãt] adj infuriating

enrager [ãʀaʒe] /3/ vi to be furious

enregistrement [ãʀ(ə)ʒistʀəmã] nm recording; **~ des bagages** baggage check-in

enregistrer [ɑ̃R(ə)ʒistRe] /1/ vt (Mus) to record; (fig: mémoriser) to make a mental note of; (bagages: à l'aéroport) to check in

enrhumer [ɑ̃Ryme] /1/: **s'enrhumer** vi to catch a cold

enrichir [ɑ̃RiʃiR] /2/ vt to make rich(er); (fig) to enrich; **s'enrichir** vi to get rich(er)

enrouer [ɑ̃Rwe] /1/: **s'enrouer** vi to go hoarse

enrouler [ɑ̃Rule] /1/ vt (fil, corde) to wind (up); **s'enrouler** to coil up; **~ qch autour de** to wind sth (a)round

enseignant, e [ɑ̃sɛɲɑ̃, -ɑ̃t] nm/f teacher

enseignement [ɑ̃sɛɲ(ə)mɑ̃] nm teaching; (Admin) education

enseigner [ɑ̃seɲe] /1/ vt, vi to teach; **~ qch à qn/à qn que** to teach sb sth/sb that

ensemble [ɑ̃sɑ̃bl] adv together ▷ nm (assemblage) set; (vêtements) outfit; (unité, harmonie) unity; **l'~ du/de la** (totalité) the whole ou entire; **impression/idée d'~** overall ou general impression/idea; **dans l'~** (en gros) on the whole

ensoleillé, e [ɑ̃sɔleje] adj sunny

ensuite [ɑ̃sɥit] adv then, next; (plus tard) afterwards, later

entamer [ɑ̃tame] /1/ vt (pain, bouteille) to start; (hostilités, pourparlers) to open

entasser [ɑ̃tɑse] /1/ vt (empiler) to pile up, heap up; **s'entasser** vi (s'amonceler) to pile up; **s'~ dans** to cram into

entendre [ɑ̃tɑ̃dR] /41/ vt to hear; (comprendre) to understand; (vouloir dire) to mean; **s'entendre** vi (sympathiser) to get on; (se mettre d'accord) to agree; **j'ai entendu dire que** I've heard (it said) that; **~ parler de** to hear of

entendu, e [ɑ̃tɑ̃dy] adj (réglé) agreed; (au courant: air) knowing; **(c'est) ~** all right, agreed; **bien ~** of course

entente [ɑ̃tɑ̃t] nf understanding; (accord, traité) agreement; **à double ~** (sens) with a double meaning

enterrement [ɑ̃tɛRmɑ̃] nm (cérémonie) funeral, burial

enterrer [ɑ̃teRe] /1/ vt to bury

entêtant, e [ɑ̃tɛtɑ̃, -ɑ̃t] adj heady

en-tête [ɑ̃tɛt] nm heading; **papier à ~** headed notepaper

entêté, e [ɑ̃tete] adj stubborn

entêter [ɑ̃tete] /1/: **s'entêter** vi: **s'~ (à faire)** to persist (in doing)

enthousiasme [ɑ̃tuzjasm] nm enthusiasm; **enthousiasmer** /1/ vt to fill with enthusiasm; **s'enthousiasmer (pour qch)** to get enthusiastic (about sth); **enthousiaste** adj enthusiastic

entier, -ière [ɑ̃tje, -jɛR] adj whole; (total, complet: satisfaction etc) complete; (fig: caractère) unbending ▷ nm (Math) whole; **en ~** totally; **lait ~** full-cream milk; **entièrement** adv entirely, wholly

entonnoir [ɑ̃tɔnwaR] nm funnel

entorse [ɑ̃tɔRs] nf (Méd) sprain; (fig): **~ à la loi/au règlement** infringement of the law/rule

entourage [ɑ̃tuRaʒ] nm circle; (famille) family (circle); (ce qui enclôt) surround

entourer [ɑ̃tuRe] /1/ vt to surround; (apporter son soutien à) to rally round; **~ de** to surround with; **s'entourer de** to surround o.s. with

entracte [ɑ̃tRakt] nm interval

entraide [ɑ̃tRɛd] nf mutual aid ou assistance

entrain [ɑ̃tRɛ̃] nm spirit; **avec ~** energetically; **faire qch sans ~** to do sth half-heartedly ou without enthusiasm

entraînement [ɑ̃tRɛnmɑ̃] nm training

entraîner [ɑ̃tRene] /1/ vt (charrier) to carry ou drag along; (Tech) to drive; (emmener: personne) to take (off); (mener à l'assaut, influencer) to lead;

(*Sport*) to train; (*impliquer*) to entail; **~ qn à faire** (*inciter*) to lead sb to do; **s'entraîner** *vi* (*Sport*) to train; **s'~ à qch/à faire** to train o.s. for sth/to do; **entraîneur** *nm/f* (*Sport*) coach, trainer ▷ *nm* (*Hippisme*) trainer

entre [ɑ̃tʀ] *prép* between; (*parmi*) among(st); **l'un d'~ eux/nous** one of them/us; **~ autres (choses)** among other things; **ils se battent ~ eux** they are fighting among(st) themselves; **entrecôte** *nf* entrecôte ou rib steak

entrée [ɑ̃tʀe] *nf* entrance; (*accès: au cinéma etc*) admission; (*billet*) (admission) ticket; (*Culin*) first course

entre: entrefilet *nm* (*article*) paragraph, short report; **entremets** *nm* (cream) dessert

entrepôt [ɑ̃tʀəpo] *nm* warehouse

entreprendre [ɑ̃tʀəpʀɑ̃dʀ] /58/ *vt* (*se lancer dans*) to undertake; (*commencer*) to begin ou start (upon)

entrepreneur, -euse [ɑ̃tʀəpʀənœʀ, -øz] *nm/f:* **~ (en bâtiment)** (building) contractor

entrepris, e [ɑ̃tʀəpʀi, -iz] *pp de* **entreprendre** ▷ *nf* (*société*) firm, business; (*action*) undertaking, venture

entrer [ɑ̃tʀe] /1/ *vi* to go (ou come) in, enter ▷ *vt* (*Inform*) to input, enter; **~ dans** (*gén*) to enter; (*pièce*) to go (*ou* come) into, enter; (*club*) to join; (*heurter*) to run into; **(faire) ~ qch dans** to get sth into; **~ à l'hôpital** to go into hospital; **faire ~** (*visiteur*) to show in

entre-temps [ɑ̃tʀətɑ̃] *adv* meanwhile

entretenir [ɑ̃tʀət(ə)niʀ] /22/ *vt* to maintain; (*famille, maîtresse*) to support, keep; **~ qn (de)** to speak to sb (about)

entretien [ɑ̃tʀətjɛ̃] *nm* maintenance; (*discussion*) discussion, talk; (*pour un emploi*) interview

entrevoir [ɑ̃tʀəvwaʀ] /30/ *vt* (*à peine*) to make out; (*brièvement*) to catch a glimpse of

entrevu, e [ɑ̃tʀəvy] *pp de* **entrevoir** ▷ *nf* (*audience*) interview

entrouvert, e [ɑ̃tʀuvɛʀ, -ɛʀt] *adj* half-open

énumérer [enymeʀe] /6/ *vt* to list

envahir [ɑ̃vaiʀ] /2/ *vt* to invade; (*inquiétude, peur*) to come over; **envahissant, e** *adj* (*péj: personne*) intrusive

enveloppe [ɑ̃v(ə)lɔp] *nf* (*de lettre*) envelope; (*crédits*) budget; **envelopper** /1/ *vt* to wrap; (*fig*) to envelop, shroud

enverrai *etc* [ɑ̃veʀe] *vb voir* **envoyer**

envers [ɑ̃vɛʀ] *prép* towards, to ▷ *nm* other side; (*d'une étoffe*) wrong side; **à l'~** (*verticalement*) upside down; (*pull*) back to front; (*vêtement*) inside out

envie [ɑ̃vi] *nf* (*sentiment*) envy; (*souhait*) desire, wish; **avoir ~ de** to feel like; (*désir plus fort*) to want; **avoir ~ de faire** to feel like doing; to want to do; **avoir ~ que** to wish that; **cette glace me fait ~** I fancy some of that ice cream; **envier** /7/ *vt* to envy; **envieux, -euse** *adj* envious

environ [ɑ̃viʀɔ̃] *adv:* **~ 3 h/2 km** (around) about 3 o'clock/2 km; *voir aussi* **environs**

environnant, e [ɑ̃viʀɔnɑ̃, -ɑ̃t] *adj* surrounding

environnement [ɑ̃viʀɔnmɑ̃] *nm* environment

environs [ɑ̃viʀɔ̃] *nmpl* surroundings; **aux ~ de** around

envisager [ɑ̃vizaʒe] /3/ *vt* to contemplate; (*avoir en vue*) to envisage; **~ de faire** to consider doing

envoler [ɑ̃vɔle] /1/: **s'envoler** *vi* (*oiseau*) to fly away ou off; (*avion*) to take off; (*papier, feuille*) to blow away; (*fig*) to vanish (into thin air)

envoyé, e [ɑ̃vwaje] *nm/f* (*Pol*) envoy; (*Presse*) correspondent; **~ spécial** special correspondent

envoyer [ɑ̃vwaje] /8/ *vt* to send; (*lancer*) to hurl, throw; **~ chercher**

to send for; **~ promener qn** (*fam*) to send sb packing

éolien, ne [eɔljɛ̃, -ɛn] *adj* wind ▷ *nf* wind turbine

épagneul, e [epaɲœl] *nm/f* spaniel

épais, se [epɛ, -ɛs] *adj* thick; **épaisseur** *nf* thickness

épanouir [epanwiʀ] /2/: **s'épanouir** *vi* (*fleur*) to bloom, open out; (*visage*) to light up; (*se développer*) to blossom (out)

épargne [epaʀɲ] *nf* saving

épargner [epaʀɲe] /1/ *vt* to save; (*ne pas tuer ou endommager*) to spare ▷ *vi* to save; **~ qch à qn** to spare sb sth

éparpiller [epaʀpije] /1/ *vt* to scatter; **s'éparpiller** *vi* to scatter; (*fig*) to dissipate one's efforts

épatant, e [epatɑ̃, -ɑ̃t] *adj* (*fam*) super

épater [epate] /1/ *vt* (*fam*) to amaze; (: *impressionner*) to impress

épaule [epol] *nf* shoulder

épave [epav] *nf* wreck

épée [epe] *nf* sword

épeler [ep(ə)le] /4/ *vt* to spell

éperon [epʀɔ̃] *nm* spur

épervier [epɛʀvje] *nm* sparrowhawk

épi [epi] *nm* (*de blé, d'orge*) ear; (*de maïs*) cob

épice [epis] *nf* spice

épicé, e [epise] *adj* spicy

épicer [epise] /3/ *vt* to spice

épicerie [episʀi] *nf* grocer's shop; (*denrées*) groceries *pl*; **~ fine** delicatessen (shop); **épicier, -ière** *nm/f* grocer

épidémie [epidemi] *nf* epidemic

épiderme [epidɛʀm] *nm* skin

épier [epje] /7/ *vt* to spy on, watch closely

épilepsie [epilɛpsi] *nf* epilepsy

épiler [epile] /1/ *vt* (*jambes*) to remove the hair from; (*sourcils*) to pluck

épinards [epinaʀ] *nmpl* spinach *sg*

épine [epin] *nf* thorn, prickle; (*d'oursin etc*) spine

épingle [epɛ̃gl] *nf* pin; **~ de nourrice** *ou* **de sûreté** *ou* **double** safety pin

épisode [epizɔd] *nm* episode; **film/ roman à ~s** serial; **épisodique** *adj* occasional

épluche-légumes [eplyʃlegym] *nm inv* potato peeler

éplucher [eplyʃe] /1/ *vt* (*fruit, légumes*) to peel; (*comptes, dossier*) to go over with a fine-tooth comb; **épluchures** *nfpl* peelings

éponge [epɔ̃ʒ] *nf* sponge; **éponger** /3/ *vt* (*liquide*) to mop ou sponge up; (*surface*) to sponge; (*fig: déficit*) to soak up

époque [epɔk] *nf* (*de l'histoire*) age, era; (*de l'année, la vie*) time; **d'~** (*meuble*) period *cpd*

épouse [epuz] *nf* wife; **épouser** /1/ *vt* to marry

épousseter [epuste] /4/ *vt* to dust

épouvantable [epuvɑ̃tabl] *adj* appalling, dreadful

épouvantail [epuvɑ̃taj] *nm* scarecrow

épouvante [epuvɑ̃t] *nf* terror; **film d'~** horror film; **épouvanter** /1/ *vt* to terrify

époux [epu] *nm* husband ▷ *nmpl*: **les ~** the (married) couple

épreuve [epʀœv] *nf* (*d'examen*) test; (*malheur, difficulté*) trial, ordeal; (*Photo*) print; (*Typo*) proof; (*Sport*) event; **à toute ~** unfailing; **mettre à l'~** to put to the test

éprouver [epʀuve] /1/ *vt* (*tester*) to test; to afflict, distress; (*ressentir*) to experience

EPS *sigle f* (= *Éducation physique et sportive*) ≈ PE

épuisé, e [epɥize] *adj* exhausted; (*livre*) out of print; **épuisement** *nm* exhaustion

épuiser [epɥize] /1/ *vt* (*fatiguer*) to exhaust, wear ou tire out; (*stock, sujet*) to exhaust; **s'épuiser** *vi* to wear ou tire o.s. out, exhaust o.s.

épuisette [epɥizɛt] *nf* shrimping net

équateur [ekwatœʀ] *nm* equator; **(la république de) l'É~** Ecuador

équation [ekwasjɔ̃] nf equation

équerre [ekɛʀ] nf (à dessin) (set) square

équilibre [ekilibʀ] nm balance;
garder/perdre l'~ to keep/lose one's balance; **être en ~** to be balanced;
équilibré, e adj well-balanced;
équilibrer /1/ vt to balance;
s'équilibrer vi to balance

équipage [ekipaʒ] nm crew

équipe [ekip] nf team; **travailler en ~** to work as a team

équipé, e [ekipe] adj: **bien/mal ~** well-/poorly-equipped

équipement [ekipmɑ̃] nm equipment

équiper [ekipe] /1/ vt to equip; **~ qn/qch de** to equip sb/sth with

équipier, -ière [ekipje, -jɛʀ] nm/f team member

équitation [ekitasjɔ̃] nf (horse-)riding; **faire de l'~** to go (horse-)riding

équivalent, e [ekivalɑ̃, -ɑ̃t] adj, nm equivalent

équivaloir [ekivalwaʀ] /29/: **~ à** vt to be equivalent to

érable [eʀabl] nm maple

érafler [eʀafle] /1/ vt to scratch;
éraflure nf scratch

ère [ɛʀ] nf era; **en l'an 1050 de notre ~** in the year 1050 A.D.

érection [eʀɛksjɔ̃] nf erection

éroder [eʀɔde] /1/ vt to erode

érotique [eʀɔtik] adj erotic

errer [eʀe] /1/ vi to wander

erreur [eʀœʀ] nf mistake, error; **par ~** by mistake; **faire ~** to be mistaken

éruption [eʀypsjɔ̃] nf eruption;
(boutons) rash

es [ɛ] vb voir **être**

ès [ɛs] prép: **licencié ès lettres/sciences** ≈ Bachelor of Arts/Science

ESB sigle f (= encéphalopathie spongiforme bovine) BSE

escabeau, x [ɛskabo] nm (tabouret) stool; (échelle) stepladder

escalade [ɛskalad] nf climbing no pl; (Pol etc) escalation; **escalader** /1/ vt to climb

escale [ɛskal] nf (Navig: durée) call;
(: port) port of call; (Aviat) stop(over);
faire ~ à (Navig) to put in at; (Aviat) to stop over at; **vol sans ~** nonstop flight

escalier [ɛskalje] nm stairs pl;
dans l'~ ou **les ~s** on the stairs;
~ mécanique ou **roulant** escalator

escapade [ɛskapad] nf: **faire une ~** to go on a jaunt; (s'enfuir) to run away ou off

escargot [ɛskaʀgo] nm snail

escarpé, e [ɛskaʀpe] adj steep

esclavage [ɛsklavaʒ] nm slavery

esclave [ɛsklav] nm/f slave

escompte [ɛskɔ̃t] nm discount

escrime [ɛskʀim] nf fencing

escroc [ɛskʀo] nm swindler, con-man; **escroquer** /1/ vt: **escroquer qn (de qch)/qch à qn** to swindle sb (out of sth)/sth out of sb;
escroquerie [ɛskʀɔkʀi] nf swindle

espace [ɛspas] nm space; **espacer** /3/ vt to space out; **s'espacer** vi (visites etc) to become less frequent

espadon [ɛspadɔ̃] nm swordfish inv

espadrille [ɛspadʀij] nf rope-soled sandal

Espagne [ɛspaɲ] nf: **l'~** Spain;
espagnol, e adj Spanish ▷ nm (Ling) Spanish ▷ nm/f: **Espagnol, e** Spaniard

espèce [ɛspɛs] nf (Bio, Bot, Zool) species inv; (gén: sorte) sort, kind, type; (péj): **~ de maladroit/de brute!** you clumsy oaf/you brute!;
espèces nfpl (Comm) cash sg; **payer en ~s** to pay (in) cash

espérance [esperɑ̃s] nf hope; **~ de vie** life expectancy

espérer [espeʀe] /6/ vt to hope for;
j'espère (bien) I hope so; **~ que/faire** to hope that/to do

espiègle [ɛspjɛgl] adj mischievous

espion, ne [ɛspjɔ̃, -ɔn] nm/f spy;
espionnage nm espionage, spying;
espionner /1/ vt to spy (up)on

espoir [ɛspwaʀ] *nm* hope; **dans l'~ de/que** in the hope of/that; **reprendre ~** not to lose hope

esprit [ɛspʀi] *nm* (*pensée, intellect*) mind; (*humour, ironie*) wit; (*mentalité, d'une loi etc, fantôme etc*) spirit; **faire de l'~** to try to be witty; **reprendre ses ~s** to come to; **perdre l'~** to lose one's mind

esquimau, de, x [ɛskimo, -od] *adj* Eskimo ▷ *nm*: **E~®** ice lolly (BRIT), popsicle (US) ▷ *nm/f*: **E~, de** Eskimo

essai [esɛ] *nm* (*tentative*) attempt, try; (*de produit*) testing; (*Rugby*) try; (*Littérature*) essay; **à l'~** on a trial basis; **mettre à l'~** to put to the test

essaim [esɛ̃] *nm* swarm

essayer [eseje] /8/ *vt* to try; (*vêtement, chaussures*) to try (on); (*restaurant, méthode, voiture*) to try (out) ▷ *vi* to try; **~ de faire** to try *ou* attempt to do

essence [esɑ̃s] *nf* (*de voiture*) petrol (BRIT), gas(oline) (US); (*extrait de plante*) essence; (*espèce: d'arbre*) species *inv*

essentiel, le [esɑ̃sjɛl] *adj* essential; **c'est l'~** (*ce qui importe*) that's the main thing; **l'~ de** the main part of

essieu, x [esjø] *nm* axle

essor [esɔʀ] *nm* (*de l'économie etc*) rapid expansion

essorer [esɔʀe] /1/ *vt* (*en tordant*) to wring (out); (*par la force centrifuge*) to spin-dry; **essoreuse** *nf* spin-dryer

essouffler [esufle] /1/: **s'essouffler** *vi* to get out of breath

essuie-glace [esɥiglas] *nm* windscreen (BRIT) *ou* windshield (US) wiper

essuyer [esɥije] /8/ *vt* to wipe; (*fig: subir*) to suffer; **s'essuyer** (*après le bain*) to dry o.s.; **~ la vaisselle** to dry up

est *vb* [ɛ] *voir* **être** ▷ *nm* [ɛst]: **l'~** the east ▷ *adj inv* [ɛst] east; (*région*) east(ern); **à l'~** in the east; (*direction*) to the east, east(wards); **à l'~ de** (to the) east of

est-ce que [ɛskə] *adv*: **~ c'est cher/c'était bon?** is it expensive/was it good?; **quand est-ce qu'il part?** when does he leave?, when is he leaving?; *voir aussi* **que**

esthéticienne [ɛstetisjɛn] *nf* beautician

esthétique [ɛstetik] *adj* attractive

estimation [ɛstimasjɔ̃] *nf* valuation; (*chiffre*) estimate

estime [ɛstim] *nf* esteem, regard; **estimer** /1/ *vt* (*respecter*) to esteem; (*expertiser: bijou*) to value; (*évaluer: coût etc*) to assess, estimate; (*penser*) **estimer que/être** to consider that/o.s. to be

estival, e, -aux [ɛstival, -o] *adj* summer *cpd*

estivant, e [ɛstivɑ̃, -ɑ̃t] *nm/f* (summer) holiday-maker

estomac [ɛstɔma] *nm* stomach

estragon [ɛstʀagɔ̃] *nm* tarragon

estuaire [ɛstɥɛʀ] *nm* estuary

et [e] *conj* and; **et lui?** what about him?; **et alors?** so what?

étable [etabl] *nf* cowshed

établi, e [etabli] *nm* (work)bench

établir [etabliʀ] /2/ *vt* (*papiers d'identité, facture*) to make out; (*liste, programme*) to draw up; (*gouvernement, artisan etc*) to set up; (*réputation, usage, fait, culpabilité, relations*) to establish; **s'établir** *vi* to be established; **s'~ (à son compte)** to set up in business; **s'~ à/près de** to settle in/near

établissement [etablismɑ̃] *nm* (*entreprise, institution*) establishment; **~ scolaire** school, educational establishment

étage [etaʒ] *nm* (*d'immeuble*) storey, floor; **au 2ème ~** on the 2nd (BRIT) *ou* 3rd (US) floor; **à l'~** upstairs; **c'est à quel ~?** what floor is it on?

étagère [etaʒɛʀ] *nf* (*rayon*) shelf; (*meuble*) shelves *pl*

étai [etɛ] *nm* stay, prop

étain [etɛ̃] *nm* pewter *no pl*

étais etc [etɛ] vb voir **être**

étaler [etale] /1/ vt (carte, nappe) to spread (out); (peinture, liquide) to spread; (échelonner: paiements, dates, vacances) to spread, stagger; (marchandises) to display; (richesses, connaissances) to parade; **s'étaler** vi (liquide) to spread out; (fam) to fall flat on one's face; **s'~ sur** (paiements etc) to be spread over

étalon [etalɔ̃] nm (cheval) stallion

étanche [etɑ̃ʃ] adj (récipient) watertight; (montre, vêtement) waterproof

étang [etɑ̃] nm pond

étant [etɑ̃] vb voir **être**; **donné**

étape [etap] nf stage; (lieu d'arrivée) stopping place; (: Cyclisme) staging point

état [eta] nm (Pol, condition) state; **en bon/mauvais ~** in good/poor condition; **en ~ (de marche)** in (working) order; **remettre en ~** to repair; **hors d'~** out of order; **être en ~/hors d'~ de faire** to be in a state/in no fit state to do; **être dans tous ses ~s** to be in a state; **faire ~ de** (alléguer) to put forward; **l'É~** the State; **~ civil** civil status; **~ des lieux** inventory of fixtures; **États-Unis** nmpl: **les États-Unis (d'Amérique)** the United States (of America)

et cætera, et cetera, etc. [ɛtsetera] adv etc

été [ete] pp de **être** ▷ nm summer

éteindre [etɛ̃dʀ] /52/ vt (lampe, lumière, radio, chauffage) to turn ou switch off; (cigarette, incendie, bougie) to put out, extinguish; **s'éteindre** vi (feu, lumière) to go out; (mourir) to pass away; **éteint, e** adj (fig) lacklustre, dull; (volcan) extinct

étendre [etɑ̃dʀ] /41/ vt (pâte, liquide) to spread; (carte etc) to spread out; (lessive, linge) to hang up ou out; (bras, jambes) to stretch out; (fig: agrandir) to extend; **s'étendre** vi (augmenter, se propager) to spread; (terrain, forêt

etc): **s'~ jusqu'à/de … à** to stretch as far as/from … to; **s'~ sur** (se coucher) to lie down (on); (fig: expliquer) to elaborate ou enlarge (upon)

étendu, e [etɑ̃dy] adj extensive

éternel, le [etɛʀnɛl] adj eternal

éternité [etɛʀnite] nf eternity; **ça a duré une ~** it lasted for ages

éternuement [etɛʀnymɑ̃] nm sneeze

éternuer [etɛʀnɥe] /1/ vi to sneeze

êtes [ɛt(z)] vb voir **être**

Éthiopie [etjɔpi] nf: **l'~** Ethiopia

étiez [etje] vb voir **être**

étinceler [etɛ̃s(ə)le] /4/ vi to sparkle

étincelle [etɛ̃sɛl] nf spark

étiquette [etikɛt] nf label; (protocole): **l'~** etiquette

étirer [etiʀe] /1/ vt to stretch out; **s'étirer** vi (personne) to stretch; (convoi, route): **s'~ sur** to stretch out over

étoile [etwal] nf star; **à la belle ~** (out) in the open; **~ filante** shooting star; **~ de mer** starfish; **étoilé, e** adj starry

étonnant, e [etɔnɑ̃, -ɑ̃t] adj surprising

étonnement [etɔnmɑ̃] nm surprise, amazing

étonner [etɔne] /1/ vt to surprise, amaze; **s'étonner que/de** to be surprised that/at; **cela m'~ait (que)** (j'en doute) I'd be (very) surprised (if)

étouffer [etufe] /1/ vt to suffocate; (bruit) to muffle; (scandale) to hush up ▷ vi to suffocate; **s'étouffer** vi (en mangeant etc) to choke; **on étouffe** it's stifling

étourderie [eturdəri] nf (caractère) absent-mindedness no pl; (faute) thoughtless blunder

étourdi, e [eturdi] adj (distrait) scatterbrained, heedless

étourdir [eturdir] /2/ vt (assommer) to stun, daze; (griser) to make dizzy ou giddy; **étourdissement** nm dizzy spell

étrange [etʀɑ̃ʒ] *adj* strange
étranger, -ère [etʀɑ̃ʒe, -ɛʀ] *adj*
foreign; (*pas de la famille, non familier*)
strange ▷ *nm/f* foreigner; stranger
▷ *nm*: **à l'~** abroad
étrangler [etʀɑ̃gle] /1/ *vt* to
strangle; **s'étrangler** *vi* (*en mangeant
etc*) to choke

MOT-CLÉ

être [ɛtʀ] /61/ *nm* being; **être
humain** human being
▶*vb copule* **1** (*état, description*) to
be; **il est instituteur** he is *ou* he's
a teacher; **vous êtes grand/
intelligent/fatigué** you are *ou* you're
tall/clever/tired
2 (+*à: appartenir*) to be; **le livre est
à Paul** the book is Paul's *ou* belongs
to Paul; **c'est à moi/eux** it is *ou* it's
mine/theirs
3 (+*de: provenance*): **il est de Paris** he
is from Paris; (: *appartenance*): **il est
des nôtres** he is one of us
4 (*date*): **nous sommes le 10 janvier**
it's the 10th of January (today)
▶*vi* to be; **je ne serai pas ici demain**
I won't be here tomorrow
▶*vb aux* **1** to have; to be; **être arrivé/
allé** to have arrived/gone; **il est
parti** he has left, he has gone
2 (*forme passive*) to be; **être fait par**
to be made by; **il a été promu** he has
been promoted
3 (+*à* +*inf, obligation, but*): **c'est à
réparer** it needs repairing; **c'est
à essayer** it should be tried; **il est
à espérer que …** it is *ou* it's to be
hoped that …
▶*vb impers* **1**: **il est** (+ *adj*) it is; **il est
impossible de le faire** it's impossible
to do it
2: **il est** (*heure, date*): **il est 10 heures**
it is *ou* it's 10 o'clock
3 (*emphatique*): **c'est moi** it's me;
c'est à lui de le faire it's up to him
to do it

étrennes [etʀɛn] *nfpl* ≈ Christmas
box *sg*
étrier [etʀije] *nm* stirrup
étroit, e [etʀwa, -wat] *adj*
narrow; (*vêtement*) tight; (*fig: liens,
collaboration*) close; **à l'~** cramped;
~ d'esprit narrow-minded
étude [etyd] *nf* studying; (*ouvrage,
rapport*) study; (*Scol: salle de travail*)
study room; **études** *nfpl* (*Scol*)
studies; **être à l'~** (*projet etc*) to be
under consideration; **faire des ~s
(de droit/médecine)** to study (law/
medicine)
étudiant, e [etydjɑ̃, -ɑ̃t] *nm/f* student
étudier [etydje] /7/ *vt, vi* to study
étui [etɥi] *nm* case
eu, eue [y] *pp de* **avoir**
euh [ø] *excl* er
euro [øʀo] *nm* euro
Europe [øʀɔp] *nf*: **l'~** Europe;
européen, ne *adj* European ▷ *nm/f*:
Européen, ne European
eus *etc* [y] *vb voir* **avoir**
eux [ø] *pron* (*sujet*) they; (*objet*) them
évacuer [evakɥe] /1/ *vt* to evacuate
évader [evade] /1/: **s'évader** *vi* to
escape
évaluer [evalɥe] /1/ *vt* (*expertiser*)
to assess, evaluate; (*juger
approximativement*) to estimate
évangile [evɑ̃ʒil] *nm* gospel; **É~**
Gospel
évanouir [evanwiʀ] /2/: **s'évanouir**
vi to faint; (*disparaître*) to vanish,
disappear; **évanouissement** *nm*
(*syncope*) fainting fit
évaporer [evapɔʀe] /1/: **s'évaporer**
vi to evaporate
évasion [evazjɔ̃] *nf* escape
éveillé, e [eveje] *adj* awake; (*vif*)
alert, sharp; **éveiller** /1/ *vt* to (a)
waken; (*soupçons etc*) to arouse;
s'éveiller *vi* to (a)waken; (*fig*) to be
aroused
événement [evɛnmɑ̃] *nm* event
éventail [evɑ̃taj] *nm* fan; (*choix*)
range

éventualité [evãtɥalite] *nf* eventuality; possibility; **dans l'~ de** in the event of

éventuel, le [evãtɥɛl] *adj* possible

Attention à ne pas traduire *éventuel* par *eventual*.

éventuellement [evãtɥɛlmã] *adv* possibly

Attention à ne pas traduire *éventuellement* par *eventually*.

évêque [evɛk] *nm* bishop

évidemment [evidamã] *adv* (*bien sûr*) of course; (*certainement*) obviously

évidence [evidãs] *nf* obviousness; (*fait*) obvious fact; **de toute ~** quite obviously *ou* evidently; **être en ~** to be clearly visible; **mettre en ~** (*fait*) to highlight; **évident, e** *adj* obvious, evident; **ce n'est pas évident** it's not as simple as all that

évier [evje] *nm* (kitchen) sink

éviter [evite] /1/ *vt* to avoid; **~ de faire/que qch ne se passe** to avoid doing/sth happening; **~ qch à qn** to spare sb sth

évoluer [evɔlɥe] /1/ *vi* (*enfant, maladie*) to develop; (*situation, moralement*) to evolve, develop; (*aller et venir*) to move about; **évolution** *nf* development; evolution

évoquer [evɔke] /1/ *vt* to call to mind, evoke; (*mentionner*) to mention

ex- [ɛks] *préfixe* ex-; **son ~mari** her ex-husband; **son ~femme** his ex-wife

exact, e [ɛgza(kt), ɛgzakt] *adj* exact; (*correct*) correct; (*ponctuel*) punctual; **l'heure ~e** the right *ou* exact time; **exactement** *adv* exactly

ex aequo [ɛgzeko] *adj* equally placed; **arriver ~** to finish neck and neck

exagéré, e [ɛgzaʒere] *adj* (*prix etc*) excessive

exagérer [ɛgzaʒere] /6/ *vt* to exaggerate ⊳ *vi* (*abuser*) to go too far; (*déformer les faits*) to exaggerate

examen [ɛgzamɛ̃] *nm* examination; (*Scol*) exam, examination; **à l'~** under consideration; **~ médical** (medical) examination; (*analyse*) test

examinateur, -trice [ɛgzaminatœr, -tris] *nm/f* examiner

examiner [ɛgzamine] /1/ *vt* to examine

exaspérant, e [ɛgzasperã, -ãt] *adj* exasperating

exaspérer [ɛgzaspere] /6/ *vt* to exasperate

exaucer [ɛgzose] /3/ *vt* (*vœu*) to grant

excéder [ɛksede] /6/ *vt* (*dépasser*) to exceed; (*agacer*) to exasperate

excellent, e [ɛkselã, -ãt] *adj* excellent

excentrique [ɛksãtrik] *adj* eccentric

excepté, e [ɛksɛpte] *adj, prép*: **les élèves ~s, ~ les élèves** except for *ou* apart from the pupils

exception [ɛksɛpsjõ] *nf* exception; **à l'~ de** except for, with the exception of; **d'~** (*mesure, loi*) special, exceptional; **exceptionnel, le** *adj* exceptional; **exceptionnellement** *adv* exceptionally

excès [ɛksɛ] *nm* surplus ⊳ *nmpl* excesses; **faire des ~** to overindulge; **~ de vitesse** speeding *no pl*; **excessif, -ive** *adj* excessive

excitant, e [ɛksitã, -ãt] *adj* exciting ⊳ *nm* stimulant; **excitation** *nf* (*état*) excitement

exciter [ɛksite] /1/ *vt* to excite; (*café etc*) to stimulate; **s'exciter** *vi* to get excited

exclamer [ɛksklame] /1/: **s'exclamer** *vi* to exclaim

exclu, e [ɛkskly] *adj*: **il est/n'est pas ~ que ...** it's out of the question/not impossible that ...

exclure [ɛksklyr] /35/ *vt* (*faire sortir*) to expel; (*ne pas compter*) to exclude, leave out; (*rendre impossible*) to exclude, rule out; **exclusif, -ive** *adj* exclusive; **exclusion** *nf* expulsion; **à l'exclusion de** with the exclusion *ou* exception of; **exclusivité** *nf* (*Comm*)

exclusive rights pl; **film passant en exclusivité à** film showing only at
excursion [εkskyʀsjɔ̃] nf (en autocar) excursion, trip; (à pied) walk, hike
excuse [εkskyz] nf excuse; **excuses** nfpl (regret) apology sg, apologies; **excuser** /1/ vt to excuse; **s'excuser (de)** to apologize (for); **"excusez-moi"** "I'm sorry"; (pour attirer l'attention) "excuse me"
exécuter [εgzekyte] /1/ vt (prisonnier) to execute; (tâche etc) to execute, carry out; (Mus: jouer) to perform, execute; **s'exécuter** vi to comply
exemplaire [εgzɑ̃plεʀ] nm copy
exemple [εgzɑ̃pl] nm example; **par ~** for instance, for example; **donner l'~** to set an example
exercer [εgzεʀse] /3/ vt (pratiquer) to exercise, practise; (influence, contrôle, pression) to exert; (former) to exercise, train; **s'exercer** vi (médecin) to be in practice; (sportif, musicien) to practise
exercice [εgzεʀsis] nm exercise
exhiber [εgzibe] /1/ vt (montrer: papiers, certificat) to present, produce; (péj) to display, flaunt; **s'exhiber** vi to parade; (exhibitionniste) to expose o.s.; **exhibitionniste** nm/f exhibitionist
exigeant, e [εgziʒɑ̃, -ɑ̃t] adj demanding; (péj) hard to please
exiger [εgziʒe] /3/ vt to demand, require
exil [εgzil] nm exile; **exiler** /1/ vt to exile; **s'exiler** vi to go into exile
existence [εgzistɑ̃s] nf existence
exister [εgziste] /1/ vi to exist; **il existe un/des** there is a/are (some)
exorbitant, e [εgzɔʀbitɑ̃, -ɑ̃t] adj exorbitant
exotique [εgzɔtik] adj exotic; **yaourt aux fruits ~s** tropical fruit yoghurt
expédier [εkspedje] /7/ vt (lettre, paquet) to send; (troupes, renfort) to dispatch; (péj: travail etc) to dispose of, dispatch; **expéditeur, -trice**

nm/f sender; **expédition** nf sending; (scientifique, sportive, Mil) expedition
expérience [εkspeʀjɑ̃s] nf (de la vie, des choses) experience; (scientifique) experiment
expérimenté, e [εkspeʀimɑ̃te] adj experienced
expérimenter [εkspeʀimɑ̃te] /1/ vt to test out, experiment with
expert, e [εkspεʀ, -εʀt] adj ▷ nm expert; **~ en assurances** insurance valuer; **expert-comptable** nm ≈ chartered (BRIT) ou certified public (US) accountant
expirer [εkspiʀe] /1/ vi (prendre fin, lit: mourir) to expire; (respirer) to breathe out
explication [εksplikasjɔ̃] nf explanation; (discussion) discussion; (dispute) argument
explicite [εksplisit] adj explicit
expliquer [εksplike] /1/ vt to explain; **s'expliquer** to explain o.s.; **s'~ avec qn** (discuter) to explain o.s. to sb
exploit [εksplwa] nm exploit, feat; **exploitant** nm/f: **exploitant (agricole)** farmer; **exploitation** nf exploitation; (d'une entreprise) running; **exploitation agricole** farming concern; **exploiter** /1/ vt (personne, don) to exploit; (entreprise, ferme) to run, operate; (mine) to exploit, work
explorer [εksplɔʀe] /1/ vt to explore
exploser [εksploze] /1/ vi to explode, blow up; (engin explosif) to go off; (personne: de colère) to explode; **explosif, -ive** adj, nm explosive; **explosion** nf explosion; **explosion de joie/colère** outburst of joy/rage
exportateur, -trice [εkspɔʀtatœʀ, -tʀis] adj export cpd, exporting ▷ nm exporter
exportation [εkspɔʀtasjɔ̃] nf (action) exportation; (produit) export
exporter [εkspɔʀte] /1/ vt to export
exposant [εkspozɑ̃] nm exhibitor

exposé, e [ɛkspoze] nm talk ▷ adj:
~ au sud facing south

exposer [ɛkspoze] /1/ vt
(marchandise) to display; (peinture) to
exhibit, show; (parler de) to explain,
set out; (mettre en danger, orienter,
Photo) to expose; **s'exposer à** (soleil,
danger) to expose o.s. to; **exposition**
nf (manifestation) exhibition; (Photo)
exposure

exprès¹ [ɛksprɛ] adv (délibérément)
on purpose; (spécialement) specially;
faire ~ de faire qch to do sth on
purpose

exprès², -esse [ɛksprɛs] adj inv
(Postes: lettre, colis) express

express [ɛksprɛs] adj, nm: **(café) ~**
espresso; **(train) ~** fast train

expressif, -ive [ɛksprɛsif, -iv] adj
expressive

expression [ɛksprɛsjɔ̃] nf
expression

exprimer [ɛksprime] /1/ vt
(sentiment, idée) to express; (jus,
liquide) to press out; **s'exprimer** vi
(personne) to express o.s.

expulser [ɛkspylse] /1/ vt to expel;
(locataire) to evict; (Football) to
send off

exquis, e [ɛkski, -iz] adj exquisite

extasier [ɛkstɑzje] /7/: **s'extasier** vi:
s'~ sur to go into raptures over

exténuer [ɛkstenɥe] /1/ vt to
exhaust

extérieur, e [ɛksterjœr] adj (porte,
mur etc) outer, outside; (commerce,
politique) foreign; (influences, pressions)
external; (apparent: calme, gaieté etc)
outer ▷ nm (d'une maison, d'un récipient
etc) outside, exterior; (apparence)
exterior; **à l'~** outside; (à l'étranger)
abroad

externat [ɛksterna] nm day school

externe [ɛkstern] adj external, outer
▷ nm/f (Méd) non-resident medical
student, extern (us); (Scol) day pupil

extincteur [ɛkstɛ̃ktœr] nm (fire)
extinguisher

extinction [ɛkstɛ̃ksjɔ̃] nf: **~ de voix**
loss of voice

extra [ɛkstra] adj inv first-rate; (fam)
fantastic ▷ nm inv extra help

extraire [ɛkstrɛr] /50/ vt to extract;
~ qch de to extract sth from; **extrait**
nm extract; **extrait de naissance**
birth certificate

extraordinaire [ɛkstraɔrdinɛr]
adj extraordinary; (Pol, Admin: mesures
etc) special

extravagant, e [ɛkstravagɑ̃, -ɑ̃t]
adj extravagant

extraverti, e [ɛkstraverti] adj
extrovert

extrême [ɛkstrɛm] adj, nm extreme;
d'un ~ à l'autre from one extreme
to another; **extrêmement** adv
extremely; **Extrême-Orient** nm:
l'Extrême-Orient the Far East

extrémité [ɛkstremite] nf
end; (situation) straits pl, plight;
(geste désespéré) extreme action;
extrémités nfpl (pieds et mains)
extremities

exubérant, e [ɛgzyberɑ̃, -ɑ̃t] adj
exuberant

f

F *abr* (= franc) fr.; (*appartement*): **un F2/F3** a 2-/3-roomed flat (BRIT) ou apartment (US)

fa [fa] *nm inv* (*Mus*) F; (*en chantant la gamme*) fa

fabricant, e [fabʀikā, -āt] *nm/f* manufacturer

fabrication [fabʀikasjɔ̄] *nf* manufacture

fabrique [fabʀik] *nf* factory; **fabriquer** /1/ *vt* to make; (*industriellement*) to manufacture; (*fam*): **qu'est-ce qu'il fabrique?** what is he up to?

fac [fak] *nf* (*fam: Scol*) (= *faculté*) Uni (BRIT *fam*), ≈ college (US)

façade [fasad] *nf* front, façade

face [fas] *nf* face; (*fig: aspect*) side ▷ *adj*: **le côté ~** heads; **en ~ de** opposite; (*fig*) in front of; **de ~** face on; **~ à** facing; (*fig*) faced with, in the face of; **faire ~ à** to face; **~ à ~** *adv* facing each other; **face-à-face** *nm inv* encounter

fâché, e [fɑʃe] *adj* angry; (*désolé*) sorry

fâcher [fɑʃe] /1/ *vt* to anger; **se fâcher** *vi* to get angry; **se ~ avec** (*se brouiller*) to fall out with

facile [fasil] *adj* easy; (*caractère*) easy-going; **facilement** *adv* easily; **facilité** *nf* easiness; (*disposition, don*) aptitude; **facilités** *nfpl* (*possibilités*) facilities; (*Comm*) terms; **faciliter** /1/ *vt* to make easier

façon [fasɔ̄] *nf* (*manière*) way; (*d'une robe etc*) making-up; cut; **façons** *nfpl* (*péj*) fuss *sg*; **sans ~** *adv* without fuss; **non merci, sans ~** no thanks, honestly; **de ~ à** so as to; **de ~ à ce que** so that; **de toute ~** anyway, in any case

facteur, -trice [faktœʀ, -tʀis] *nm/f* postman/woman (BRIT), mailman/woman (US) ▷ *nm* (*Math, gén: élément*) factor

facture [faktyʀ] *nf* (*à payer: gén*) bill; (: *Comm*) invoice

facultatif, -ive [fakyltatif, -iv] *adj* optional

faculté [fakylte] *nf* (*intellectuelle, d'université*) faculty; (*pouvoir, possibilité*) power

fade [fad] *adj* insipid

faible [fɛbl] *adj* weak; (*voix, lumière, vent*) faint; (*rendement, intensité, revenu etc*) low ▷ *nm* (*pour quelqu'un*) weakness, soft spot; **faiblesse** *nf* weakness; **faiblir** [fɛbliʀ] /2/ *vi* to weaken; (*lumière*) to dim; (*vent*) to drop

faïence [fajɑ̄s] *nf* earthenware *no pl*

faillir [fajiʀ] /2/ *vi*: **j'ai failli tomber/lui dire** I almost ou nearly fell/told him

faillite [fajit] *nf* bankruptcy; **faire ~** to go bankrupt

faim [fɛ̄] *nf* hunger; **avoir ~** to be hungry; **rester sur sa ~** (*aussi fig*) to be left wanting more

fainéant, e [fɛneā, -āt] *nm/f* idler, loafer

MOT-CLÉ

faire [fɛʀ] /60/ vt **1** (*fabriquer, être l'auteur de*) to make; **faire du vin/ une offre/un film** to make wine/ an offer/a film; **faire du bruit** to make a noise

2 (*effectuer: travail, opération*) to do; **que faites-vous?** (*quel métier etc*) what do you do?; (*quelle activité: au moment de la question*) what are you doing?; **faire la lessive/le ménage** to do the washing/the housework

3 (*études*) to do; (*sport, musique*) to play; **faire du droit/du français** to do law/French; **faire du rugby/ piano** to play rugby/the piano

4 (*visiter*): **faire les magasins** to go shopping; **faire l'Europe** to tour ou do Europe

5 (*distance*): **faire du 50 (à l'heure)** to do 50 (km an hour); **nous avons fait 1000 km en 2 jours** we did ou covered 1000 km in 2 days

6 (*simuler*): **faire le malade/ l'ignorant** to act the invalid/the fool

7 (*transformer, avoir un effet sur*): **faire de qn un frustré/avocat** to make sb frustrated/a lawyer; **ça ne me fait rien** (*m'est égal*) I don't care ou mind; (*me laisse froid*) it has no effect on me; **ça ne fait rien** it doesn't matter; **faire que** (*impliquer*) to mean that

8 (*calculs, prix, mesures*): **deux et deux font quatre** two and two are ou make four; **ça fait 10 m/15 euros** it's 10 m/15 euros; **je vous le fais 10 euros** I'll let you have it for 10 euros; **je fais du 40** I take a size 40

9: **qu'a-t-il fait de sa valise/de sa sœur?** what has he done with his case/his sister?

10: **ne faire que**: **il ne fait que critiquer** (*sans cesse*) all he (ever) does is criticize; (*seulement*) he's only criticizing

11 (*dire*) to say; **vraiment? fit-il** really? he said

12 (*maladie*) to have; **faire du diabète/de la tension** to have diabetes *sg*/high blood pressure

▶*vi* **1** (*agir, s'y prendre*) to act, do; **il faut faire vite** we (*ou* you *etc*) must act quickly; **comment a-t-il fait pour?** how did he manage to?; **faites comme chez vous** make yourself at home

2 (*paraître*) to look; **faire vieux/ démodé** to look old/old-fashioned; **ça fait bien** it looks good

3 (*remplaçant un autre verbe*) to do; **ne le casse pas comme je l'ai fait** don't break it as I did; **je peux le voir? — faites!** can I see it? — please do!

▶*vb impers* **1**: **il fait beau** *etc* the weather is fine *etc*; *voir aussi* **froid; jour** *etc*

2 (*temps écoulé, durée*): **ça fait deux ans qu'il est parti** it's two years since he left; **ça fait deux ans qu'il y est** he's been there for two years

▶*vb aux* **1**: **faire** (+*infinitif: action directe*) to make; **faire tomber/ bouger qch** to make sth fall/ move; **faire démarrer un moteur/ chauffer de l'eau** to start up an engine/heat some water; **cela fait dormir** it makes you sleep; **faire travailler les enfants** to make the children work ou get the children to work; **il m'a fait traverser la rue** he helped me to cross the road

2: **faire** (+*infinitif: indirectement, par un intermédiaire*): **faire réparer qch** to get ou have sth repaired; **faire punir les enfants** to have the children punished

se faire *vr* **1** (*vin, fromage*) to mature

2 (*être convenable*): **cela se fait beaucoup/ne se fait pas** it's done a lot/not done

3 (+*nom ou pron*): **se faire une jupe** to make o.s. a skirt; **se faire des amis** to make friends; **se faire du souci** to worry; **il ne s'en fait pas** he doesn't worry

4 (+*adj*: *devenir*): **se faire vieux** to be getting old; (: *délibérément*): **se faire beau** to do o.s. up
5: **se faire à** (*s'habituer*) to get used to; **je n'arrive pas à me faire à la nourriture/au climat** I can't get used to the food/climate
6 (: +*infinitif*): **se faire examiner la vue/opérer** to have one's eyes tested/have an operation; **se faire couper les cheveux** to get one's hair cut; **il va se faire tuer/punir** he's going to get himself killed/get (himself) punished; **il s'est fait aider** he got somebody to help him; **il s'est fait aider par Simon** he got Simon to help him; **se faire faire un vêtement** to get a garment made for o.s.
7 (*impersonnel*): **comment se fait-il/faisait-il que?** how is it/was it that?

faire-part [fɛRpaR] *nm inv* announcement (*of birth, marriage etc*)
faisan, e [fəzɑ̃, -an] *nm/f* pheasant
faisons [fəzɔ̃] *vb voir* **faire**
fait[1] [fɛ] *nm* (*événement*) event, occurrence; (*réalité, donnée*) fact; **être au ~ (de)** to be informed (of); **au ~** (*à propos*) by the way; **en venir au ~** to get to the point; **du ~ de ceci/qu'il a menti** because of *ou* on account of this/his having lied; **de ce ~** for this reason; **en ~** in fact; **prendre qn sur le ~** to catch sb in the act; **~ divers** (short) news item
fait[2], **e** [fɛ, fɛt] *adj* (*mûr: fromage, melon*) ripe; **c'est bien ~ (pour lui** *ou* **eux** *etc*) it serves him (*ou* them *etc*) right
faites [fɛt] *vb voir* **faire**
falaise [falɛz] *nf* cliff
falloir [falwaR] /29/ *vb impers*: **il faut faire les lits** we (*ou* you *etc*) have to *ou* must make the beds; **il faut que je fasse les lits** I have to *ou* must make the beds; **il a fallu qu'il parte** he had to leave; **il faudrait qu'elle rentre** she should come *ou* go back, she ought to come *ou* go back; **il faut faire attention** you have to be careful; **il me faudrait 100 euros** I would need 100 euros; **il vous faut tourner à gauche après l'église** you have to turn left past the church; **nous avons ce qu'il (nous) faut** we have what we need; **il ne fallait pas** you shouldn't have (done); **s'en falloir** *vi*: **il s'en est fallu de 10 euros/5 minutes** we (*ou* they *etc*) were 10 euros short/5 minutes late (*ou* early); **il s'en faut de beaucoup qu'il soit ...** he is far from being ...; **il s'en est fallu de peu que cela n'arrive** it very nearly happened; **comme il faut** *adj* proper; *adv* properly
famé, e [fame] *adj*: **mal ~** disreputable, of ill repute
fameux, -euse [famø, -øz] *adj* (*illustre*) famous; (*bon: repas, plat etc*) first-rate, first-class; (*intensif*): **un ~ problème** *etc* a real problem *etc*
familial, e, -aux [familjal, -o] *adj* family *cpd*
familiarité [familjaRite] *nf* familiarity
familier, -ière [familje, -jɛR] *adj* (*connu, impertinent*) familiar; (*atmosphère*) informal, friendly; (*Ling*) informal, colloquial ⊳ *nm* regular (visitor)
famille [famij] *nf* family; **il a de la ~ à Paris** he has relatives in Paris
famine [famin] *nf* famine
fana [fana] *adj, nm/f* (*fam*) = **fanatique**
fanatique [fanatik] *adj*: **~ (de)** fanatical (about) ⊳ *nm/f* fanatic
faner [fane] /1/: **se faner** *vi* to fade
fanfare [fɑ̃faR] *nf* (*orchestre*) brass band; (*musique*) fanfare
fantaisie [fɑ̃tezi] *nf* (*spontanéité*) fancy, imagination; (*caprice*) whim ⊳ *adj*: **bijou (de) ~** (piece of) costume jewellery (BRIT) *ou* jewelry (US)

fantasme [fãtasm] *nm* fantasy

fantastique [fãtastik] *adj* fantastic

fantôme [fãtom] *nm* ghost, phantom

faon [fã] *nm* fawn (deer)

FAQ *sigle f* (= foire aux questions) FAQ *pl*

farce [faʀs] *nf* (viande) stuffing; (blague) (practical) joke; (Théât) farce; **farcir** /2/ *vt* (viande) to stuff

farder [faʀde] /1/: **se farder** *vi* to make o.s. up

farine [faʀin] *nf* flour

farouche [faʀuʃ] *adj* shy, timid

fart [faʀt] *nm* (ski) wax

fascination [fasinasjɔ̃] *nf* fascination

fasciner [fasine] /1/ *vt* to fascinate

fascisme [faʃism] *nm* fascism

fasse *etc* [fas] *vb voir* **faire**

fastidieux, -euse [fastidjø, -øz] *adj* tedious, tiresome

fatal, e [fatal] *adj* fatal; (inévitable) inevitable; **fatalité** *nf* (destin) fate; (coïncidence) fateful coincidence

fatidique [fatidik] *adj* fateful

fatigant, e [fatigã, -ãt] *adj* tiring; (agaçant) tiresome

fatigue [fatig] *nf* tiredness, fatigue; **fatigué, e** *adj* tired; **fatiguer** /1/ *vt* to tire, make tired; (fig: agacer) to annoy ▷ *vi* (moteur) to labour, strain; **se fatiguer** to get tired

fauché, e [foʃe] *adj* (fam) broke

faucher [foʃe] /1/ *vt* (herbe) to cut; (champs, blés) to reap; (véhicule) to mow down; (fam: voler) to pinch

faucon [fokɔ̃] *nm* falcon, hawk

faudra *etc* [fodʀa] *vb voir* **falloir**

faufiler [fofile] /1/: **se faufiler** *vi*: **~ dans** to edge one's way into; **se ~ parmi/entre** to thread one's way among/between

faune [fon] *nf* (Zool) wildlife, fauna

fausse [fos] *adj f voir* **faux²**; **faussement** *adv* (accuser) wrongly, wrongfully; (croire) falsely

fausser [fose] /1/ *vt* (objet) to bend, buckle; (fig) to distort; **~ compagnie à qn** to give sb the slip

faut [fo] *vb voir* **falloir**

faute [fot] *nf* (erreur) mistake, error; (péché, manquement) misdemeanour; (Football etc) offence; (Tennis) fault; **c'est de sa/ma ~** it's his/my fault; **être en ~** to be in the wrong; **~ de** (temps, argent) for ou through lack of; **sans ~** without fail; **~ de frappe** typing error; **~ professionnelle** professional misconduct *no pl*

fauteuil [fotœj] *nm* armchair; **~ d'orchestre** seat in the front stalls (BRIT) *ou* the orchestra (US); **~ roulant** wheelchair

fautif, -ive [fotif, -iv] *adj* (incorrect) incorrect, inaccurate; (responsable) at fault, in the wrong; **il se sentait ~** he felt guilty

fauve [fov] *nm* wildcat ▷ *adj* (couleur) fawn

faux¹ [fo] *nf* scythe

faux², fausse [fo, fos] *adj* (inexact) wrong; (piano, voix) out of tune; (billet) fake, forged; (sournois, postiche) false ▷ *adv* (Mus) out of tune ▷ *nm* (copie) fake, forgery; **faire ~ bond à qn** to let sb down; **~ frais** *nm pl* extras, incidental expenses; **~ mouvement** awkward movement; **faire un ~ pas** to trip; (fig) to make a faux pas; **~ témoignage** (délit) perjury; **fausse alerte** false alarm; **fausse couche** miscarriage; **fausse note** wrong note; **faux-filet** *nm* sirloin

faveur [favœʀ] *nf* favour; **traitement de ~** preferential treatment; **en ~ de** in favo(u)r of

favorable [favɔʀabl] *adj* favo(u)rable

favori, te [favɔʀi, -it] *adj, nm/f* favo(u)rite

favoriser [favɔʀize] /1/ *vt* to favour

fax [faks] *nm* fax

fécond, e [fekɔ̃, -ɔ̃d] *adj* fertile; **féconder** /1/ *vt* to fertilize

féculent [fekylã] *nm* starchy food

fédéral, e, -aux [fedeʀal, -o] *adj* federal

fée [fe] *nf* fairy

feignant, e [fɛɲɑ̃, -ɑ̃t] *nm/f*
= **fainéant**

feindre [fɛ̃dʀ] /52/ *vt* to feign; **~ de
faire** to pretend to do

fêler [fele] /1/ *vt* to crack

félicitations [felisitasjɔ̃] *nfpl*
congratulations

féliciter [felisite] /1/ *vt*: **~ qn (de)** to
congratulate sb (on)

félin, e [felɛ̃, -in] *nm* (big) cat

femelle [fəmɛl] *adj, nf* female

féminin, e [feminɛ̃, -in] *adj*
feminine; (*sexe*) female; (*équipe,
vêtements etc*) women's ▷ *nm* (*Ling*)
feminine; **féministe** *adj* feminist

femme [fam] *nf* woman; (*épouse*)
wife; **~ de chambre** chambermaid;
~ au foyer housewife; **~ de ménage**
cleaning lady

fémur [femyʀ] *nm* femur, thighbone

fendre [fɑ̃dʀ] /41/ *vt* (*couper en deux*)
to split; (*fissurer*) to crack; (*traverser*)
to cut through; **se fendre** *vi* to crack

fenêtre [f(ə)nɛtʀ] *nf* window

fenouil [fənuj] *nm* fennel

fente [fɑ̃t] *nf* (*fissure*) crack; (*de boîte à
lettres etc*) slit

fer [fɛʀ] *nm* iron; **~ à cheval** horseshoe;
~ forgé wrought iron; **~ à friser**
curling tongs; **~ (à repasser)** iron

ferai *etc* [fəʀe] *vb voir* **faire**

fer-blanc [fɛʀblɑ̃] *nm* tin(plate)

férié, e [feʀje] *adj*: **jour ~** public
holiday

ferions *etc* [fəʀjɔ̃] *vb voir* **faire**

ferme [fɛʀm] *adj* firm ▷ *adv* (*travailler
etc*) hard ▷ *nf* (*exploitation*) farm;
(*maison*) farmhouse

fermé, e [fɛʀme] *adj* closed, shut;
(*gaz, eau etc*) off; (*fig: milieu*) exclusive

fermenter [fɛʀmɑ̃te] /1/ *vi* to ferment

fermer [fɛʀme] /1/ *vt* to close, shut;
(*cesser l'exploitation de*) to close down,
shut down; (*eau, lumière, électricité,
robinet*) to turn off; (*aéroport, route*)
to close ▷ *vi* to close, shut; (*magasin:
définitivement*) to close down, shut

down; **se fermer** *vi* to close, shut; **~
à clef** to lock

fermeté [fɛʀməte] *nf* firmness

fermeture [fɛʀmətyʀ] *nf* closing;
(*dispositif*) catch; **heure de ~** closing
time; **~ éclair®** *ou* **à glissière** zip
(fastener) (*BRIT*), zipper (*US*)

fermier, -ière [fɛʀmje, -jɛʀ] *nm/f*
farmer

féroce [feʀɔs] *adj* ferocious, fierce

ferons *etc* [fəʀɔ̃] *vb voir* **faire**

ferrer [feʀe] /1/ *vt* (*cheval*) to shoe

ferroviaire [feʀɔvjɛʀ] *adj* rail *cpd*,
railway (*BRIT*), railroad *cpd* (*US*)

ferry(-boat) [feʀe(bɔt)] *nm* ferry

fertile [fɛʀtil] *adj* fertile; **~ en
incidents** eventful, packed with
incidents

fervent, e [fɛʀvɑ̃, -ɑ̃t] *adj* fervent

fesse [fɛs] *nf* buttock; **fessée** *nf*
spanking

festin [fɛstɛ̃] *nm* feast

festival [fɛstival] *nm* festival

festivités [fɛstivite] *nfpl* festivities

fêtard, e [fɛtaʀ, -aʀd] (*fam*) *nm/f* (*péj*)
high liver, merrymaker

fête [fɛt] *nf* (*religieuse*) feast; (*publique*)
holiday; (*réception*) party; (*kermesse*)
fête, fair; (*du nom*) feast day, name
day; **faire la ~** to live it up; **faire ~
à qn** to give sb a warm welcome;
les ~s (de fin d'année) the festive
season; **la salle/le comité des ~s**
the village hall/festival committee;
la ~ des Mères/Pères Mother's/
Father's Day; **~ foraine** (fun)fair; **la
~ de la musique**; *see note* **"fête de la
musique"; fêter** /1/ *vt* to celebrate;
(*personne*) to have a celebration for

* **FÊTE DE LA MUSIQUE**

* The *Fête de la Musique* is a music
* festival which has taken place
* every year since 1981. On 21 June
* throughout France local musicians
* perform free of charge in parks,
* streets and squares.

feu, x [fø] nm (gén) fire; (signal lumineux) light; (de cuisinière) ring; **feux** nmpl (Auto) (traffic) lights; **au ~!** (incendie) fire!; **à ~ doux/vif** over a slow/brisk heat; **à petit ~** (Culin) over a gentle heat; (fig) slowly; **faire ~** to fire; **ne pas faire long ~** not to last long; **prendre ~** to catch fire; **mettre le ~ à** to set fire to; **faire du ~** to make a fire; **avez-vous du ~?** (pour cigarette) have you (got) a light?; **~ rouge/ vert/orange** red/green/amber (BRIT) ou yellow (US) light; **~ arrière** rear light; **~ d'artifice** firework; (spectacle) fireworks pl; **~ de joie** bonfire; **~x de brouillard** fog lights ou lamps; **~x de croisement** dipped (BRIT) ou dimmed (US) headlights; **~x de position** sidelights; **~x de route** (Auto) headlights (on full (BRIT) ou high (US) beam)

feuillage [fœjaʒ] nm foliage, leaves pl

feuille [fœj] nf (d'arbre) leaf; **~ (de papier)** sheet (of paper); **~ de calcul** spreadsheet; **~ d'impôts** tax form; **~ de maladie** medical expenses claim form; **~ de paye** pay slip

feuillet [fœje] nm leaf

feuilleté, e [fœjte] adj: **pâte ~** flaky pastry

feuilleter [fœjte] /4/ vt (livre) to leaf through

feuilleton [fœjtɔ̃] nm serial

feutre [føtʀ] nm felt; (chapeau) felt hat; (stylo) felt-tip(ped pen); **feutré, e** adj (pas, voix, atmosphère) muffled

fève [fɛv] nf broad bean

février [fevʀije] nm February

fiable [fjabl] adj reliable

fiançailles [fjɑ̃saj] nfpl engagement sg

fiancé, e [fjɑ̃se] nm/f fiancé (fiancée) ▷ adj: **être ~ (à)** to be engaged (to)

fibre [fibʀ] nf fibre; **~ de verre** fibreglass

ficeler [fis(ə)le] /4/ vt to tie up

ficelle [fisɛl] nf string no pl; (morceau) piece ou length of string

fiche [fiʃ] nf (carte) (index) card; (formulaire) form; (Élec) plug; **~ de paye** pay slip

ficher [fiʃe] /1/ vt (dans un fichier) to file; (: Police) to put on file; (fam: faire) to do; (: donner) to give; (: mettre) to stick ou shove; **fiche(-moi) le camp** (fam) clear off; **fiche-moi la paix** (fam) leave me alone; **se ~ de** (fam: rire de) to make fun of; (: être indifférent à) not to care about

fichier [fiʃje] nm file; **~ joint** (Inform) attachment

fichu, e [fiʃy] pp de **ficher** ▷ adj (fam: fini, inutilisable) bust, done for; (: intensif) wretched, darned ▷ nm (foulard) (head)scarf; **mal ~** feeling lousy

fictif, -ive [fiktif, -iv] adj fictitious

fiction [fiksjɔ̃] nf fiction; (fait imaginé) invention

fidèle [fidɛl] adj: **~ (à)** faithful (to) ▷ nm/f (Rel): **les ~s** (à l'église) the congregation; **fidélité** nf (d'un conjoint) fidelity, faithfulness; (d'un ami, client) loyalty

fier¹ [fje]: **se ~ à** vt to trust

fier², fière [fjɛʀ] adj proud; **~ de** proud of; **fierté** nf pride

fièvre [fjɛvʀ] nf fever; **avoir de la ~/39 de ~** to have a high temperature/a temperature of 39° C; **fiévreux, -euse** adj feverish

figer [fiʒe] /3/: **se figer** vi to congeal; (personne) to freeze

fignoler [fiɲɔle] /1/ vt to put the finishing touches to

figue [fig] nf fig; **figuier** nm fig tree

figurant, e [figyʀɑ̃, -ɑ̃t] nm/f (Théât) walk-on; (Ciné) extra

figure [figyʀ] nf (visage) face; (image, tracé, forme, personnage) figure; (illustration) picture, diagram

figuré, e [figyʀe] adj (sens) figurative

figurer [figyʀe] /1/ vi to appear ▷ vt to represent; **se ~ que** to imagine that

fil [fil] nm (brin, fig: d'une histoire) thread; (d'un couteau) edge; **au ~ des**

années with the passing of the years; **au ~ de l'eau** with the stream *ou* current; **coup de ~** (*fam*) phone call; **donner/recevoir un coup de ~** to make/get a phone call; **~ électrique** electric wire; **~ de fer** wire; **~ de fer barbelé** barbed wire

file [fil] *nf* line; (*Auto*) lane; **~ (d'attente)** queue (*BRIT*), line (*US*); **à la ~** (*d'affilée*) in succession; **à la** *ou* **en ~ indienne** in single file

filer [file] /1/ *vt* (*tissu, toile, verre*) to spin; (*prendre en filature*) to shadow, tail; (*fam: donner*): **~ qch à qn** to slip sb sth ⊳ *vi* (*bas, maille, liquide, pâte*) to run; (*aller vite*) to fly past *ou* by; (*fam: partir*) to make off; **~ doux** to behave o.s.

filet [file] *nm* net; (*Culin*) fillet; (*d'eau, de sang*) trickle; **~ (à provisions)** string bag

filial, e, -aux [filjal, -o] *adj* filial ⊳ *nf* (*Comm*) subsidiary

filière [filjɛʀ] *nf* (*carrière*) path; **suivre la ~** to work one's way up (through the hierarchy)

fille [fij] *nf* girl; (*opposé à fils*) daughter; **vieille ~** old maid; **fillette** *nf* (little) girl

filleul, e [fijœl] *nm/f* godchild, godson (goddaughter)

film [film] *nm* (*pour photo*) (roll of) film; (*œuvre*) film, picture, movie

fils [fis] *nm* son; **~ à papa** (*péj*) daddy's boy

filtre [filtʀ] *nm* filter; **filtrer** /1/ *vt* to filter; (*fig: candidats, visiteurs*) to screen

fin¹ [fɛ̃] *nf* end; **fins** *nfpl* (*but*) ends; **~ mai** at the end of May; **prendre ~** to come to an end; **mettre ~ à** to put an end to; **à la ~** in the end, eventually; **en ~ de compte** in the end; **sans ~** endless

fin², e [fɛ̃, fin] *adj* (*papier, couche, fil*) thin; (*cheveux, poudre, pointe, visage*) fine; (*taille*) neat, slim; (*esprit, remarque*) subtle ⊳ *adv* (*moudre,*

couper) finely; **~ prêt/soûl** quite ready/drunk; **avoir la vue/l'ouïe ~e** to have keen eyesight/hearing; **or/linge/vin ~** fine gold/linen/wine; **~es herbes** mixed herbs

final, e [final] *adj, nf* final ⊳ *nm* (*Mus*) finale; **quarts de ~e** quarter finals; **finalement** *adv* finally, in the end; (*après tout*) after all

finance [finãs] *nf* finance; **finances** *nfpl* (*situation financière*) finances; (*activités financières*) finance *sg*; **moyennant ~** for a fee *ou* consideration; **financer** /3/ *vt* to finance; **financier, -ière** *adj* financial

finesse [finɛs] *nf* thinness; (*raffinement*) fineness; (*subtilité*) subtlety

fini, e [fini] *adj* finished; (*Math*) finite ⊳ *nm* (*d'un objet manufacturé*) finish

finir [finiʀ] /2/ *vt* to finish ⊳ *vi* to finish, end; **~ de faire** to finish doing; (*cesser*) to stop doing; **~ par faire** to end *ou* finish up doing; **il finit par m'agacer** he's beginning to get on my nerves; **en ~ avec** to be *ou* have done with; **il va mal ~** he will come to a bad end

finition [finisjɔ̃] *nf* (*résultat*) finish

finlandais, e [fɛ̃lɑ̃dɛ, -ɛz] *adj* Finnish ⊳ *nm/f*: **F~, e** Finn

Finlande [fɛ̃lɑ̃d] *nf*: **la ~** Finland

finnois, e [finwa, -waz] *adj* Finnish ⊳ *nm* (*Ling*) Finnish

fioul [fjul] *nm* fuel oil

firme [fiʀm] *nf* firm

fis [fi] *vb voir* **faire**

fisc [fisk] *nm* tax authorities *pl*; **fiscal, e, -aux** *adj* tax *cpd*, fiscal; **fiscalité** *nf* tax system

fissure [fisyʀ] *nf* crack; **fissurer** /1/ *vt* to crack; **se fissurer** *vi* to crack

fit [fi] *vb voir* **faire**

fixation [fiksasjɔ̃] *nf* (*attache*) fastening; (*Psych*) fixation

fixe [fiks] *adj* fixed; (*emploi*) steady, regular ⊳ *nm* (*salaire*) basic salary; (*téléphone*) landline; **à heure ~** at a set time; **menu à prix ~** set menu

fixé, e [fikse] *adj*: **être ~ (sur)** (*savoir à quoi s'en tenir*) to have made up one's mind (about)

fixer [fikse] /1/ *vt* (*attacher*): **~ qch (à/sur)** to fix *ou* fasten sth (to/onto); (*déterminer*) to fix, set; (*poser son regard sur*) to stare at; **se fixer** (*s'établir*) to settle down; **se ~ sur** (*attention*) to focus on

flacon [flakɔ̃] *nm* bottle

flageolet [flaʒɔlɛ] *nm* (Culin) dwarf kidney bean

flagrant, e [flagrɑ̃, -ɑ̃t] *adj* flagrant, blatant; **en ~ délit** in the act

flair [flɛʀ] *nm* sense of smell; (*fig*) intuition; **flairer** /1/ *vt* (*humer*) to sniff (at); (*détecter*) to scent

flamand, e [flamɑ̃, -ɑ̃d] *adj* Flemish ▷ *nm* (Ling) Flemish ▷ *nm/f*: **F~, e** Fleming

flamant [flamɑ̃] *nm* flamingo

flambant [flɑ̃bɑ̃] *adv*: **~ neuf** brand new

flambé, e [flɑ̃be] *adj* (Culin) flambé

flambée [flɑ̃be] *nf* blaze; **~ des prix** (sudden) shooting up of prices

flamber [flɑ̃be] /1/ *vi* to blaze (up)

flamboyer [flɑ̃bwaje] /8/ *vi* to blaze (up)

flamme [flam] *nf* flame; (*fig*) fire, fervour; **en ~s** on fire, ablaze

flan [flɑ̃] *nm* (Culin) custard tart *ou* pie

flanc [flɑ̃] *nm* side; (Mil) flank

flancher [flɑ̃ʃe] /1/ *vi* to fail, pack up

flanelle [flanɛl] *nf* flannel

flâner [flɑne] /1/ *vi* to stroll

flanquer [flɑ̃ke] /1/ *vt* to flank; (*fam: mettre*) to chuck, shove; **~ par terre/à la porte** (*jeter*) to fling to the ground/chuck out

flaque [flak] *nf* (*d'eau*) puddle; (*d'huile, de sang etc*) pool

flash [flaʃ] (*pl* **flashes**) *nm* (Photo) flash; **~ (d'information)** newsflash

flatter [flate] /1/ *vt* to flatter; **se ~ de qch** to pride o.s. on sth; **flatteur, -euse** *adj* flattering

flèche [flɛʃ] *nf* arrow; (*de clocher*) spire; **monter en ~** (*fig*) to soar, rocket; **partir en ~** to be off like a shot; **fléchette** *nf* dart

flétrir [fletʀiʀ] /2/: **se flétrir** *vi* to wither

fleur [flœʀ] *nf* flower; (*d'un arbre*) blossom; **être en ~** (*arbre*) to be in blossom; **tissu à ~s** flowered *ou* flowery fabric

fleuri, e [flœʀi] *adj* (*jardin*) in flower *ou* bloom; (*style, tissu, papier*) flowery; (*teint*) glowing

fleurir [flœʀiʀ] /2/ *vi* (*rose*) to flower; (*arbre*) to blossom; (*fig*) to flourish ▷ *vt* (*tombe*) to put flowers on; (*chambre*) to decorate with flowers

fleuriste [flœʀist] *nm/f* florist

fleuve [flœv] *nm* river

flexible [flɛksibl] *adj* flexible

flic [flik] *nm* (*fam: péj*) cop

flipper [flipœʀ] *nm* pinball (machine)

flirter [flœʀte] /1/ *vi* to flirt

flocon [flɔkɔ̃] *nm* flake

flore [flɔʀ] *nf* flora

florissant, e [flɔʀisɑ̃, -ɑ̃t] *adj* (*économie*) flourishing

flot [flo] *nm* flood, stream; **flots** *nmpl* (*de la mer*) waves; **être à ~** (Navig) to be afloat; **entrer à ~s** to stream *ou* pour in

flottant, e [flɔtɑ̃, -ɑ̃t] *adj* (*vêtement*) loose(-fitting)

flotte [flɔt] *nf* (Navig) fleet; (*fam: eau*) water; (: *pluie*) rain

flotter [flɔte] /1/ *vi* to float; (*nuage, odeur*) to drift; (*drapeau*) to fly; (*vêtements*) to hang loose ▷ *vb impers* (*fam: pleuvoir*): **il flotte** it's raining; **faire ~** to float; **flotteur** *nm* float

flou, e [flu] *adj* fuzzy, blurred; (*fig*) woolly (BRIT), vague

fluide [flɥid] *adj* fluid; (*circulation etc*) flowing freely ▷ *nm* fluid

fluor [flyɔʀ] *nm*: **dentifrice au ~** fluoride toothpaste

fluorescent, e [flyɔʀesɑ̃, -ɑ̃t] *adj* fluorescent

flûte [flyt] nf (aussi: **~ traversière**) flute; (verre) flute glass; (pain) (thin) baguette; **~!** drat it!; **~ (à bec)** recorder

flux [fly] nm incoming tide; (écoulement) flow; **le ~ et le re~** the ebb and flow

foc [fɔk] nm jib

foi [fwa] nf faith; **digne de ~** reliable; **être de bonne/mauvaise ~** to be in good faith/not to be in good faith

foie [fwa] nm liver; **crise de ~** stomach upset

foin [fwɛ̃] nm hay; **faire du ~** (fam) to kick up a row

foire [fwaʀ] nf fair; (fête foraine) (fun)fair; **~ aux questions** (Internet) frequently asked questions; **faire la ~** to whoop it up; **~ (exposition)** trade fair

fois [fwa] nf time; **une/deux ~** once/ twice; **deux ~ deux** twice two; **une ~** (passé) once; (futur) sometime; **une (bonne) ~ pour toutes** once and for all; **une ~ que c'est fait** once it's done; **des ~** (parfois) sometimes; **à la ~** (ensemble) (all) at once

fol [fɔl] adj m voir **fou**

folie [fɔli] nf (d'une décision, d'un acte) madness, folly; (état) madness, insanity; **la ~ des grandeurs** delusions of grandeur; **faire des ~s** (en dépenses) to be extravagant

folklorique [fɔlklɔʀik] adj folk cpd; (fam) weird

folle [fɔl] adj f, nf voir **fou**; **follement** adv (très) madly, wildly

foncé, e [fɔ̃se] adj dark

foncer [fɔ̃se] /3/ vi to go darker; (fam: aller vite) to tear ou belt along; **~ sur** to charge at

fonction [fɔ̃ksjɔ̃] nf function; (emploi, poste) post, position; **fonctions** nfpl (professionnelles) duties; **voiture de ~** company car; **en ~ de** (par rapport à) according to; **faire ~ de** to serve as; **la ~ publique** the state ou civil (BRIT) service; **fonctionnaire** nm/f

state employee ou official; (dans l'administration) ≈ civil servant; **fonctionner** /1/ vi to work, function

fond [fɔ̃] nm voir aussi **fonds**; (d'un récipient, trou) bottom; (d'une salle, scène) back; (d'un tableau, décor) background; (opposé à la forme) content; (Sport): **le ~** long distance (running); **au ~ de** at the bottom of; at the back of; **à ~** (connaître, soutenir) thoroughly; (appuyer, visser) right down ou home; **à ~ (de train)** (fam) full tilt; **dans le ~, au ~** (en somme) basically, really; **de ~ en comble** from top to bottom; **~ de teint** foundation

fondamental, e, -aux [fɔ̃damɑ̃tal, -o] adj fundamental

fondant, e [fɔ̃dɑ̃, -ɑ̃t] adj (neige) melting; (poire) that melts in the mouth

fondation [fɔ̃dasjɔ̃] nf founding; (établissement) foundation; **fondations** nfpl (d'une maison) foundations

fondé, e [fɔ̃de] adj (accusation etc) well-founded; **être ~ à croire** to have grounds for believing ou good reason to believe

fondement [fɔ̃dmɑ̃] nm: **sans ~** (rumeur etc) groundless, unfounded

fonder [fɔ̃de] /1/ vt to found; (fig): **~ qch sur** to base sth on; **se ~ sur** (personne) to base o.s. on

fonderie [fɔ̃dʀi] nf smelting works sg

fondre [fɔ̃dʀ] /41/ vt (aussi: **faire ~**) to melt; (dans l'eau) to dissolve; (fig: mélanger) to merge, blend ▷ vi (à la chaleur) to melt; to dissolve; (fig) to melt away; (se précipiter): **~ sur** to swoop down on; **~ en larmes** to dissolve into tears

fonds [fɔ̃] nm (Comm): **~ (de commerce)** business ▷ nmpl (argent) funds

fondu, e [fɔ̃dy] adj (beurre, neige) melted; (métal) molten ▷ nf (Culin) fondue

font [fõ] vb voir **faire**

fontaine [fõtɛn] nf fountain; (source) spring

fonte [fõt] nf melting; (métal) cast iron; **la ~ des neiges** the (spring) thaw

foot [fut], **football** [futbol] nm football, soccer; **footballeur, -euse** nm/f footballer (BRIT), football ou soccer player

footing [futiŋ] nm jogging; **faire du ~** to go jogging

forain, e [fɔʀɛ̃, -ɛn] adj fairground cpd ▷ nm (marchand) stallholder; (acteur etc) fairground entertainer

forçat [fɔʀsa] nm convict

force [fɔʀs] nf strength; (Physique, Mécanique) force; **forces** nfpl (physiques) strength sg; (Mil) forces; **à ~ de faire** by dint of doing; **de ~** forcibly, by force; **dans la ~ de l'âge** in the prime of life; **les ~s de l'ordre** the police

forcé, e [fɔʀse] adj forced; **c'est ~!** it's inevitable!; **forcément** adv inevitably; **pas forcément** not necessarily

forcer [fɔʀse] /3/ vt to force; (moteur, voix) to strain ▷ vi (Sport) to overtax o.s.; **se ~ à faire qch** to force o.s. to do sth; **~ la dose/l'allure** to overdo it/increase the pace

forestier, -ière [fɔʀɛstje, -jɛʀ] adj forest cpd

forêt [fɔʀɛ] nf forest

forfait [fɔʀfɛ] nm (Comm) all-in deal ou price; **déclarer ~** to withdraw; **forfaitaire** adj inclusive

forge [fɔʀʒ] nf forge, smithy; **forgeron** nm (black)smith

formaliser [fɔʀmalize] /1/: **se formaliser** vi: **se ~ (de)** to take offence (at)

formalité [fɔʀmalite] nf formality; **simple ~** mere formality

format [fɔʀma] nm size; **formater** /1/ vt (disque) to format

formation [fɔʀmasjõ] nf forming; training; **la ~ permanente** ou

continue continuing education; **la ~ professionnelle** vocational training

forme [fɔʀm] nf (gén) form; (d'un objet) shape, form; **formes** nfpl (bonnes manières) proprieties; (d'une femme) figure sg; **en ~ de poire** pear-shaped, in the shape of a pear; **être en (bonne** ou **pleine) ~** (Sport etc) to be on form; **en bonne et due ~** in due form

formel, le [fɔʀmɛl] adj (preuve, décision) definite, positive; **formellement** adv (interdit) strictly; (absolument) positively

former [fɔʀme] /1/ vt to form; (éduquer) to train; **se former** vi to form

formidable [fɔʀmidabl] adj tremendous

formulaire [fɔʀmylɛʀ] nm form

formule [fɔʀmyl] nf (gén) formula; (expression) phrase; **~ de politesse** polite phrase; (en fin de lettre) letter ending

fort, e [fɔʀ, fɔʀt] adj strong; (intensité, rendement) high, great; (corpulent) large; (doué): **être ~ (en)** to be good (at) ▷ adv (serrer, frapper) hard; (sonner) loud(ly); (beaucoup) greatly, very much; (très) very ▷ nm (édifice) fort; (point fort) strong point, forte; **~e tête** rebel; **forteresse** nf fortress

fortifiant [fɔʀtifjã] nm tonic

fortune [fɔʀtyn] nf fortune; **faire ~** to make one's fortune; **de ~** makeshift; **fortuné, e** adj wealthy

forum [fɔʀɔm] nm forum; **~ de discussion** (Internet) message board

fosse [fos] nf (grand trou) pit; (tombe) grave

fossé [fose] nm ditch; (fig) gulf, gap

fossette [fosɛt] nf dimple

fossile [fosil] nm fossil ▷ adj fossilized, fossil cpd

fou (fol), folle [fu, fɔl] adj mad; (déréglé etc) wild, erratic; (fam: extrême, très grand) terrific, tremendous ▷ nm/f madman/woman ▷ nm (du *roi*) jester; **être ~ de** to be mad *ou* crazy about; **avoir le ~ rire** to have the giggles

foudre [fudʀ] *nf:* **la ~** lightning

foudroyant, e [fudʀwajɑ̃, -ɑ̃t] *adj* (*progrès*) lightning *cpd*; (*succès*) stunning; (*maladie, poison*) violent

fouet [fwɛ] *nm* whip; (*Culin*) whisk; **de plein ~** *adv* (*se heurter*) head on; **fouetter** /1/ *vt* to whip; (*crème*) to whisk

fougère [fuʒɛʀ] *nf* fern

fougue [fug] *nf* ardour, spirit; **fougueux, -euse** *adj* fiery

fouille [fuj] *nf* search; **fouilles** *nfpl* (*archéologiques*) excavations; **fouiller** /1/ *vt* to search; (*creuser*) to dig ▷ *vi*: **fouiller dans/parmi** to rummage in/ among; **fouillis** *nm* jumble, muddle

foulard [fulaʀ] *nm* scarf

foule [ful] *nf* crowd; **la ~** crowds *pl*; **une ~ de** masses of

foulée [fule] *nf* stride

fouler [fule] /1/ *vt* to press; (*sol*) to tread upon; **se ~ la cheville** to sprain one's ankle; **ne pas se ~** not to overexert o.s.; **il ne se foule pas** he doesn't put himself out; **foulure** *nf* sprain

four [fuʀ] *nm* oven; (*de potier*) kiln; (*Théât: échec*) flop

fourche [fuʀʃ] *nf* pitchfork

fourchette [fuʀʃɛt] *nf* fork; (*Statistique*) bracket, margin

fourgon [fuʀgɔ̃] *nm* van; (*Rail*) wag(g)on; **fourgonnette** *nf* (delivery) van

fourmi [fuʀmi] *nf* ant; **avoir des ~s dans les jambes/mains** to have pins and needles in one's legs/hands; **fourmilière** *nf* ant-hill; **fourmiller** /1/ *vi* to swarm

fourneau, x [fuʀno] *nm* stove

fourni, e [fuʀni] *adj* (*barbe, cheveux*) thick; (*magasin*): **bien ~ (en)** well stocked (with)

fournir [fuʀniʀ] /2/ *vt* to supply; (*preuve, exemple*) to provide, supply;

(*effort*) to put in; **~ qch à qn** to supply sth to sb, supply *ou* provide sb with sth; **fournisseur, -euse** *nm/f* supplier; **fournisseur d'accès à Internet** (Internet) service provider, ISP; **fourniture** *nf* supply(ing); **fournitures scolaires** school stationery

fourrage [fuʀaʒ] *nm* fodder

fourré, e [fuʀe] *adj* (*bonbon, chocolat*) filled; (*manteau, botte*) fur-lined ▷ *nm* thicket

fourrer [fuʀe] /1/ *vt* (*fam*) to stick, shove; **se ~ dans/sous** to get into/ under

fourrière [fuʀjɛʀ] *nf* pound

fourrure [fuʀyʀ] *nf* fur; (*sur l'animal*) coat

foutre [futʀ] *vt* (*fam!*) = **ficher**; **foutu, e** *adj* (*fam!*) = **fichu**

foyer [fwaje] *nm* (*de cheminée*) hearth; (*famille*) family; (*domicile*) home; (*local de réunion*) (social) club; (*résidence*) hostel; (*salon*) foyer; **lunettes à double ~** bi-focal glasses

fracassant, e [fʀakasɑ̃, -ɑ̃t] *adj* (*succès*) staggering

fraction [fʀaksjɔ̃] *nf* fraction

fracture [fʀaktyʀ] *nf* fracture; **~ du crâne** fractured skull; **fracturer** /1/ *vt* (*coffre, serrure*) to break open; (*os, membre*) to fracture; **se fracturer le crâne** to fracture one's skull

fragile [fʀaʒil] *adj* fragile, delicate; (*fig*) frail; **fragilité** *nf* fragility

fragment [fʀagmɑ̃] *nm* (*d'un objet*) fragment, piece

fraîche [fʀɛʃ] *adj f voir* **frais**; **fraîcheur** *nf* coolness; (*d'un aliment*) freshness; *voir* **frais**; **fraîchir** /2/ *vi* to get cooler; (*vent*) to freshen

frais, fraîche [fʀɛ, fʀɛʃ] *adj* (*air, eau, accueil*) cool; (*petit pois, œufs, nouvelles, couleur, troupes*) fresh ▷ *adv* (*récemment*) newly, fresh(ly) ▷ *nm:* **mettre au ~** to put in a cool place; **prendre le ~** to take a breath of cool air ▷ *nmpl* (*débours*) expenses; (*Comm*) costs; **il fait ~** it's cool; **servir ~** serve chilled; **faire des ~** to go to a lot of expense; **~ généraux** overheads; **~ de scolarité** school fees (BRIT), tuition (US)

fraise [fʀɛz] nf strawberry; **~ des bois** wild strawberry

framboise [fʀɑ̃bwaz] nf raspberry

franc, franche [fʀɑ̃, fʀɑ̃ʃ] adj (personne) frank, straightforward; (visage) open; (net: refus, couleur) clear; (: coupure) clean; (intensif) downright ▷ nm franc

français, e [fʀɑ̃sɛ, -ɛz] adj French ▷ nm (Ling) French ▷ nm/f: **F~, e** Frenchman/woman

France [fʀɑ̃s] nf: **la ~** France; **~ 2, ~ 3** public-sector television channels

---

○ **FRANCE TÉLÉVISION**
○
○ France 2 and France 3 are public-
○ sector television channels. France
○ 2 is a national general interest and
○ entertainment channel; France
○ 3 provides regional news and
○ information as well as programmes
○ for the national network.

---

franche [fʀɑ̃ʃ] adj f voir **franc**; **franchement** adv frankly; clearly; (nettement) definitely; (tout à fait) downright

franchir [fʀɑ̃ʃiʀ] /2/ vt (obstacle) to clear, get over; (seuil, ligne, rivière) to cross; (distance) to cover

franchise [fʀɑ̃ʃiz] nf frankness; (douanière) exemption; (Assurances) excess

franc-maçon [fʀɑ̃masɔ̃] nm Freemason

franco [fʀɑ̃ko] adv (Comm): **~ (de port)** postage paid

francophone [fʀɑ̃kɔfɔn] adj French-speaking

franc-parler [fʀɑ̃paʀle] nm inv outspokenness; **avoir son ~** to speak one's mind

frange [fʀɑ̃ʒ] nf fringe

frangipane [fʀɑ̃ʒipan] nf almond paste

frappant, e [fʀapɑ̃, -ɑ̃t] adj striking

frappé, e [fʀape] adj iced

frapper [fʀape] /1/ vt to hit, strike; (étonner) to strike; **~ dans ses mains** to clap one's hands; **frappé de stupeur** dumbfounded

fraternel, le [fʀatɛʀnɛl] adj brotherly, fraternal; **fraternité** nf brotherhood

fraude [fʀod] nf fraud; (Scol) cheating; **passer qch en ~** to smuggle sth in (ou out); **~ fiscale** tax evasion

frayeur [fʀejœʀ] nf fright

fredonner [fʀədɔne] /1/ vt to hum

freezer [fʀizœʀ] nm freezing compartment

frein [fʀɛ̃] nm brake; **mettre un ~ à** (fig) to put a brake on, check; **~ à main** handbrake; **freiner** /1/ vi to brake ▷ vt (progrès etc) to check

frêle [fʀɛl] adj frail, fragile

frelon [fʀəlɔ̃] nm hornet

frémir [fʀemiʀ] /2/ vi (de froid, de peur) to shudder; (de colère) to shake; (de joie, feuillage) to quiver

frêne [fʀɛn] nm ash (tree)

fréquemment [fʀekamɑ̃] adv frequently

fréquent, e [fʀekɑ̃, -ɑ̃t] adj frequent

fréquentation [fʀekɑ̃tasjɔ̃] nf frequenting; **fréquentations** nfpl (relations) company sg; **avoir de mauvaises ~s** to be in with the wrong crowd, keep bad company

fréquenté, e [fʀekɑ̃te] adj: **très ~** (very) busy; **mal ~** patronized by disreputable elements

fréquenter [fʀekɑ̃te] /1/ vt (lieu) to frequent; (personne) to see; **se fréquenter** to see a lot of each other

frère [fʀɛʀ] nm brother

fresque [fʀɛsk] nf (Art) fresco

fret [fʀɛ(t)] nm freight

friand, e [fʀijã, -ãd] *adj*: **~ de**
very fond of ▷ *nm*: **~ au fromage**
cheese puff

friandise [fʀijãdiz] *nf* sweet

fric [fʀik] *nm (fam)* cash, bread

friche [fʀiʃ]: **en ~** *adj, adv* (lying)
fallow

friction [fʀiksjɔ̃] *nf (massage)* rub,
rub-down; *(Tech, fig)* friction

frigidaire® [fʀiʒidɛʀ] *nm*
refrigerator

frigo [fʀigo] *nm* fridge

frigorifique [fʀigɔʀifik] *adj*
refrigerating

frileux, -euse [fʀilø, -øz] *adj*
sensitive to (the) cold

frimer [fʀime] /1/ *vi (fam)* to show off

fringale [fʀɛ̃gal] *nf (fam)*: **avoir la ~**
to be ravenous

fringues [fʀɛ̃g] *nfpl (fam)* clothes

fripé, e [fʀipe] *adj* crumpled

frire [fʀiʀ] *vt* to fry ▷ *vi* to fry

frisé, e [fʀize] *adj (cheveux)* curly;
(personne) curly-haired

frisson [fʀisɔ̃] *nm (de froid)* shiver;
(de peur) shudder; **frissonner** /1/ *vi*
(de fièvre, froid) to shiver; *(d'horreur)*
to shudder

frit, e [fʀi, fʀit] *pp de* **frire** ▷ *nf*:
(pommes) ~es chips (BRIT), French
fries; **friteuse** *nf* deep fryer, chip
pan (BRIT); **friture** *nf (huile)* (deep)
fat; *(plat)*: **friture (de poissons)**
fried fish

froid, e [fʀwa, fʀwad] *adj* ▷ *nm* cold;
il fait ~ it's cold; **avoir ~** to be cold;
prendre ~ to catch a chill *ou* cold;
être en ~ avec to be on bad terms
with; **froidement** *adv (accueillir)*
coldly; *(décider)* coolly

froisser [fʀwase] /1/ *vt* to crumple
(up), crease; *(fig)* to hurt, offend;
se froisser *vi* to crumple, crease;
(personne) to take offence (BRIT) *ou*
offense (US); **se ~ un muscle** to
strain a muscle

frôler [fʀole] /1/ *vt* to brush against;
(projectile) to skim past; *(fig)* to come

very close to, come within a hair's
breadth of

fromage [fʀɔmaʒ] *nm* cheese;
~ blanc soft white cheese

froment [fʀɔmã] *nm* wheat

froncer [fʀɔ̃se] /3/ *vt* to gather; **~ les
sourcils** to frown

front [fʀɔ̃] *nm* forehead, brow; *(Mil,
Météorologie, Pol)* front; **de ~** *(se
heurter)* head-on; *(rouler)* together (2
or 3 abreast); *(simultanément)* at once;
faire ~ à to face up to

frontalier, -ière [fʀɔ̃talje,
-jɛʀ] *adj* border *cpd*, frontier *cpd*
▷ **(travailleurs) ~s** commuters from
across the border

frontière [fʀɔ̃tjɛʀ] *nf* frontier, border

frotter [fʀɔte] /1/ *vi* to rub, scrape
▷ *vt* to rub; *(pommes de terre, plancher)*
to scrub; **~ une allumette** to strike
a match

fruit [fʀɥi] *nm* fruit *no pl*; **~s de mer**
seafood(s); **~s secs** dried fruit *sg*;
fruité, e [fʀɥite] *adj* fruity; **fruitier,
-ière** *adj*: **arbre fruitier** fruit tree

frustrer [fʀystʀe] /1/ *vt* to frustrate

fuel(-oil) [fjul(ɔjl)] *nm* fuel oil; *(pour
chauffer)* heating oil

fugace [fygas] *adj* fleeting

fugitif, -ive [fyʒitif, -iv] *adj (lueur,
amour)* fleeting ▷ *nm/f* fugitive

fugue [fyg] *nf*: **faire une ~** to run
away, abscond

fuir [fɥiʀ] /17/ *vt* to flee from; *(éviter)*
to shun ▷ *vi* to run away; *(gaz, robinet)*
to leak

fuite [fɥit] *nf* flight; *(divulgation)* leak;
être en ~ to be on the run; **mettre en
~** to put to flight

fulgurant, e [fylgyʀã, -ãt] *adj*
lightning *cpd*, dazzling

fumé, e [fyme] *adj (Culin)* smoked;
(verre) tinted ▷ *nf* smoke

fumer [fyme] /1/ *vi* to smoke; *(liquide)*
to steam ▷ *vt* to smoke

fûmes [fym] *vb voir* **être**

fumeur, -euse [fymœʀ, -øz] *nm/f*
smoker

fumier [fymje] *nm* manure

funérailles [fyneʀɑj] *nfpl* funeral *sg*

fur [fyʀ]: **au ~ et à mesure** *adv* as one goes along; **au ~ et à mesure que** as

furet [fyʀɛ] *nm* ferret

fureter [fyʀ(ə)te] /5/ *vi* (*péj*) to nose about

fureur [fyʀœʀ] *nf* fury; **être en ~** to be infuriated; **faire ~** to be all the rage

furie [fyʀi] *nf* fury; (*femme*) shrew, vixen; **en ~** (*mer*) raging; **furieux, -euse** *adj* furious

furoncle [fyʀɔ̃kl] *nm* boil

furtif, -ive [fyʀtif, -iv] *adj* furtive

fus [fy] *vb voir* **être**

fusain [fyzɛ̃] *nm* (*Art*) charcoal

fuseau, x [fyzo] *nm* (*pantalon*) (ski-)pants *pl*; (*pour filer*) spindle; **~ horaire** time zone

fusée [fyze] *nf* rocket

fusible [fyzibl] *nm* (*Élec: fil*) fuse wire; (: *fiche*) fuse

fusil [fyzi] *nm* (*de guerre, à canon rayé*) rifle, gun; (*de chasse, à canon lisse*) shotgun, gun; **fusillade** *nf* gunfire *no pl*, shooting *no pl*; **fusiller** /1/ *vt* to shoot; **fusiller qn du regard** to look daggers at sb

fusionner [fyzjɔne] /1/ *vi* to merge

fût [fy] *vb voir* **être** ▷ *nm* (*tonneau*) barrel, cask

futé, e [fyte] *adj* crafty; **Bison ~®** TV and radio traffic monitoring service

futile [fytil] *adj* futile; (*frivole*) frivolous

futur, e [fytyʀ] *adj, nm* future

fuyard, e [fɥijaʀ, -aʀd] *nm/f* runaway

g

Gabon [gabɔ̃] *nm*: **le ~** Gabon

gâcher [gɑʃe] /1/ *vt* (*gâter*) to spoil; (*gaspiller*) to waste; **gâchis** *nm* waste *no pl*

gaffe [gaf] *nf* blunder; **faire ~** (*fam*) to watch out

gage [gaʒ] *nm* (*dans un jeu*) forfeit; (*fig: de fidélité*) token; **gages** *nmpl* (*salaire*) wages; **mettre en ~** to pawn

gagnant, e [gaɲɑ̃, -ɑ̃t] *adj*: **billet/ numéro ~** winning ticket/number ▷ *nm/f* winner

gagne-pain [gaɲpɛ̃] *nm inv* job

gagner [gaɲe] /1/ *vt* to win; (*somme d'argent, revenu*) to earn; (*aller vers, atteindre*) to reach; (*s'emparer de*) to overcome; (*envahir*) to spread to ▷ *vi* to win; (*fig*) to gain; **~ du temps/ de la place** to gain time/save space; **~ sa vie** to earn one's living

gai, e [ge] *adj* cheerful; (*un peu ivre*) merry; **gaiement** *adv* cheerfully;

gaieté nf cheerfulness; **de gaieté de cœur** with a light heart

gain [gɛ̃] nm (revenu) earnings pl; (bénéfice: gén pl) profits pl

gala [gala] nm official reception; **soirée de ~** gala evening

galant, e [galɑ̃, -ɑ̃t] adj (courtois) courteous, gentlemanly; (entreprenant) flirtatious, gallant; (scène, rendez-vous) romantic

galerie [galʁi] nf gallery; (Théât) circle; (de voiture) roof rack; (fig: spectateurs) audience; **~ marchande** shopping mall; **~ de peinture** (private) art gallery

galet [galɛ] nm pebble

galette [galɛt] nf flat pastry cake; **la ~ des Rois** cake traditionally eaten on Twelfth Night

🞉 GALETTE DES ROIS

🞉 A galette des Rois is a cake eaten
🞉 on Twelfth Night containing a
🞉 figurine. The person who finds it
🞉 is the king (or queen) and gets a
🞉 paper crown. They then choose
🞉 someone else to be their queen
🞉 (or king).

galipette [galipɛt] nf somersault

Galles [gal] nfpl: **le pays de ~** Wales; **gallois, e** adj Welsh ▷ nm (Ling) Welsh ▷ nm/f: **Gallois, e** Welshman(-woman)

galon [galɔ̃] nm (Mil) stripe; (décoratif) piece of braid

galop [galo] nm gallop; **galoper** /1/ vi to gallop

gambader [gɑ̃bade] /1/ vi (animal, enfant) to leap about

gamin, e [gamɛ̃, -in] nm/f kid ▷ adj mischievous

gamme [gam] nf (Mus) scale; (fig) range

gang [gɑ̃g] nm (de criminels) gang

gant [gɑ̃] nm glove; **~ de toilette** (face) flannel (BRIT), face cloth

garage [gaʁaʒ] nm garage; **garagiste** nm/f garage owner; (mécanicien) garage mechanic

garantie [gaʁɑ̃ti] nf guarantee; **(bon de) ~** guarantee ou warranty slip

garantir [gaʁɑ̃tiʁ] /2/ vt to guarantee; **je vous garantis que** I can assure you that

garçon [gaʁsɔ̃] nm boy; (aussi: **~ de café**) waiter; **vieux ~** (célibataire) bachelor; **~ de courses** messenger

garde [gaʁd] nm (de prisonnier) guard; (de domaine etc) warden; (soldat, sentinelle) guardsman ▷ nf (soldats) guard; **de ~** on duty; **monter la ~** to stand guard; **mettre en ~** to warn; **prendre ~ (à)** to be careful (of); **~ champêtre** nm rural policeman; **~ du corps** nm bodyguard; **à vue** nf (Jur) ≈ police custody; **garde-boue** nm inv mudguard; **garde-chasse** nm gamekeeper

garder [gaʁde] /1/ vt (conserver) to keep; (surveiller: enfants) to look after; (: immeuble, lieu, prisonnier) to guard; **se garder** vi (aliment: se conserver) to keep; **se ~ de faire** to be careful not to do; **~ le lit/la chambre** to stay in bed/indoors; **pêche/chasse gardée** private fishing/hunting (ground)

garderie [gaʁdəʁi] nf day nursery, crèche

garde-robe [gaʁdəʁɔb] nf wardrobe

gardien, ne [gaʁdjɛ̃, -ɛn] nm/f (garde) guard; (de prison) warder; (de domaine, réserve) warden; (de musée etc) attendant; (de phare, cimetière) keeper; (d'immeuble) caretaker; (fig) guardian; **~ de but** goalkeeper; **~ de nuit** night watchman; **~ de la paix** policeman

gare [gaʁ] nf (railway) station ▷ excl: **~ à ... mind ...!; ~ à toi!** watch out!; **~ routière** bus station

garer [gaʁe] /1/ vt to park; **se garer** vi to park

garni, e [gaʁni] adj (plat) served with vegetables (and chips, pasta or rice)

garniture [ɡaʀnityʀ] nf (Culin) vegetables pl; **~ de frein** brake lining

gars [ɡɑ] nm guy

Gascogne [ɡaskɔɲ] nf: **la ~** Gascony; **le golfe de ~** the Bay of Biscay

gas-oil [ɡazɔjl] nm diesel oil

gaspiller [ɡaspije] /1/ vt to waste

gastronome [ɡastʀɔnɔm] nm/f gourmet; **gastronomique** adj gastronomic

gâteau, x [ɡɑto] nm cake; **~ sec** biscuit

gâter [ɡɑte] /1/ vt to spoil; **se gâter** vi (dent, fruit) to go bad; (temps, situation) to change for the worse

gâteux, -euse [ɡɑtø, -øz] adj senile

gauche [ɡoʃ] adj left, left-hand; (maladroit) awkward, clumsy ▷ nf (Pol) left (wing); **le bras ~** the left arm; **le côté ~** the left-hand side; **à ~** on the left; (direction) (to the) left; **gaucher, -ère** adj left-handed; **gauchiste** nm/f leftist

gaufre [ɡofʀ] nf waffle

gaufrette [ɡofʀɛt] nf wafer

gaulois, e [ɡolwa, -waz] adj Gallic ▷ nm/f: **G~, e** Gaul

gaz [ɡaz] nm inv gas; **ça sent le ~** I can smell gas, there's a smell of gas

gaze [ɡaz] nf gauze

gazette [ɡazɛt] nf news sheet

gazeux, -euse [ɡazø, -øz] adj (eau) sparkling; (boisson) fizzy

gazoduc [ɡazodyk] nm gas pipeline

gazon [ɡazɔ̃] nm (herbe) grass; (pelouse) lawn

geai [ʒɛ] nm jay

géant, e [ʒeɑ̃, -ɑ̃t] adj gigantic; (Comm) giant-size ▷ nm/f giant

geindre [ʒɛ̃dʀ] /52/ vi to groan, moan

gel [ʒɛl] nm frost; **~ douche** shower gel

gélatine [ʒelatin] nf gelatine

gelé, e [ʒəle] adj frozen ▷ nf jelly; (gel) frost

geler [ʒəle] /5/ vt, vi to freeze; **il gèle** it's freezing

gélule [ʒelyl] nf (Méd) capsule

Gémeaux [ʒemo] nmpl: **les ~** Gemini

gémir [ʒemiʀ] /2/ vi to groan, moan

gênant, e [ʒenɑ̃, -ɑ̃t] adj (objet) in the way; (histoire, personne) embarrassing

gencive [ʒɑ̃siv] nf gum

gendarme [ʒɑ̃daʀm] nm gendarme; **gendarmerie** nf military police force in countryside and small towns; their police station or barracks

gendre [ʒɑ̃dʀ] nm son-in-law

gêné, e [ʒene] adj embarrassed

gêner [ʒene] /1/ vt (incommoder) to bother; (encombrer) to be in the way of; (embarrasser): **~ qn** to make sb feel ill-at-ease; **se gêner** to put o.s. out; **ne vous gênez pas!** don't mind me!

général, e, -aux [ʒeneʀal, -o] adj, nm general; **en ~** usually, in general; **généralement** adv generally; **généraliser** /1/ vt, vi to generalize; **se généraliser** vi to become widespread; **généraliste** nm/f general practitioner, GP

génération [ʒeneʀasjɔ̃] nf generation

généreux, -euse [ʒeneʀø, -øz] adj generous

générique [ʒeneʀik] nm (Ciné, TV) credits pl

générosité [ʒeneʀozite] nf generosity

genêt [ʒ(ə)nɛ] nm (Bot) broom no pl

génétique [ʒenetik] adj genetic

Genève [ʒ(ə)nɛv] n Geneva

génial, e, -aux [ʒenjal, -o] adj of genius; (fam: formidable) fantastic, brilliant

génie [ʒeni] nm genius; (Mil): **le ~** ≈ the Engineers pl; **~ civil** civil engineering

genièvre [ʒənjɛvʀ] nm juniper (tree)

génisse [ʒenis] nf heifer

génital, e, -aux [ʒenital, -o] adj genital; **les parties ~es** the genitals

génois, e [ʒenwa, -waz] adj Genoese ▷ nf (gâteau) ≈ sponge cake

genou, x [ʒ(ə)nu] nm knee; **à ~x** on one's knees; **se mettre à ~x** to kneel down

genre [ʒɑ̃R] *nm* kind, type, sort; (*Ling*) gender; **avoir bon ~** to look a nice sort; **avoir mauvais ~** to be coarse-looking; **ce n'est pas son ~** it's not like him

gens [ʒɑ̃] *nmpl* (*f in some phrases*) people *pl*

gentil, le [ʒɑ̃ti, -ij] *adj* kind; (*enfant: sage*) good; (*sympathique: endroit etc*) nice; **gentillesse** *nf* kindness; **gentiment** *adv* kindly

géographie [ʒeɔgRafi] *nf* geography

géologie [ʒeɔlɔʒi] *nf* geology

géomètre [ʒeɔmɛtR] *nm*: **(arpenteur-)** (land) surveyor

géométrie [ʒeɔmetRi] *nf* geometry; **géométrique** *adj* geometric

géranium [ʒeRanjɔm] *nm* geranium

gérant, e [ʒeRɑ̃, -ɑ̃t] *nm/f* manager/ manageress; **~ d'immeuble** managing agent

gerbe [ʒɛRb] *nf* (*de fleurs, d'eau*) spray; (*de blé*) sheaf

gercé, e [ʒɛRse] *adj* chapped

gerçure [ʒɛRsyR] *nf* crack

gérer [ʒeRe] /6/ *vt* to manage

germain, e [ʒɛRmɛ̃, -ɛn] *adj*: **cousin ~** first cousin

germe [ʒɛRm] *nm* germ; **germer** /1/ *vi* to sprout; (*semence*) to germinate

geste [ʒɛst] *nm* gesture

gestion [ʒɛstjɔ̃] *nf* management

Ghana [gana] *nm*: **le ~** Ghana

gibier [ʒibje] *nm* (*animaux*) game

gicler [ʒikle] /1/ *vi* to spurt, squirt

gifle [ʒifl] *nf* slap (in the face); **gifler** /1/ *vt* to slap (in the face)

gigantesque [ʒigɑ̃tɛsk] *adj* gigantic

gigot [ʒigo] *nm* leg (of mutton *ou* lamb)

gigoter [ʒigɔte] /1/ *vi* to wriggle (about)

gilet [ʒilɛ] *nm* waistcoat; (*pull*) cardigan; **~ de sauvetage** life jacket

gin [dʒin] *nm* gin; **~-tonic** gin and tonic

gingembre [ʒɛ̃ʒɑ̃bR] *nm* ginger

girafe [ʒiRaf] *nf* giraffe

giratoire [ʒiRatwaR] *adj*: **sens ~** roundabout

girofle [ʒiRɔfl] *nm*: **clou de ~** clove

girouette [ʒiRwɛt] *nf* weather vane *ou* cock

gitan, e [ʒitɑ̃, -an] *nm/f* gipsy

gîte [ʒit] *nm* (*maison*) home; (*abri*) shelter; **~ (rural)** (*country*) holiday cottage *ou* apartment, gîte (*self-catering accommodation in the country*)

givre [ʒivR] *nm* (hoar) frost; **givré, e** *adj* covered in frost; (*fam: fou*) nuts; **citron givré/orange givrée** lemon/ orange sorbet (*served in fruit skin*)

glace [glas] *nf* ice; (*crème glacée*) ice cream; (*miroir*) mirror; (*de voiture*) window

glacé, e [glase] *adj* (*mains, vent, pluie*) freezing; (*lac*) frozen; (*boisson*) iced

glacer [glase] /3/ *vt* to freeze; (*gâteau*) to ice ; **~ qn** (*intimider*) to chill sb; (*fig*) to make sb's blood run cold

glacial, e [glasjal] *adj* icy

glacier [glasje] *nm* (*Géo*) glacier; (*marchand*) ice-cream maker

glacière [glasjɛR] *nf* icebox

glaçon [glasɔ̃] *nm* icicle; (*pour boisson*) ice cube

glaïeul [glajœl] *nm* gladiola

glaise [glɛz] *nf* clay

gland [glɑ̃] *nm* acorn; (*décoration*) tassel

glande [glɑ̃d] *nf* gland

glissade [glisad] *nf* (*par jeu*) slide; (*chute*) slip; **faire des ~s** to slide

glissant, e [glisɑ̃, -ɑ̃t] *adj* slippery

glissement [glismɑ̃] *nm*: **~ de terrain** landslide

glisser [glise] /1/ *vi* (*avancer*) to glide *ou* slide along; (*coulisser, tomber*) to slide; (*déraper*) to slip; (*être glissant*) to be slippery ▷ *vt* to slip; **se ~ dans/ entre** to slip into/between

global, e, -aux [glɔbal, -o] *adj* overall

globe [glɔb] *nm* globe

globule [glɔbyl] *nm* (*du sang*): **~ blanc/rouge** white/red corpuscle

gloire [glwaʀ] *nf* glory

glousser [gluse] /1/ *vi* to cluck; (*rire*) to chuckle

glouton, ne [glutɔ̃, -ɔn] *adj* gluttonous

gluant, e [glyɑ̃, -ɑ̃t] *adj* sticky, gummy

glucose [glykoz] *nm* glucose

glycine [glisin] *nf* wisteria

GO *sigle fpl* (= *grandes ondes*) LW

goal [gol] *nm* goalkeeper

gobelet [gɔblɛ] *nm* (*en métal*) tumbler; (*en plastique*) beaker; (*à dés*) cup

goéland [gɔelɑ̃] *nm* (sea)gull

goélette [gɔelɛt] *nf* schooner

goinfre [gwɛ̃fʀ] *nm* glutton

golf [gɔlf] *nm* golf; (*terrain*) golf course; **~ miniature** crazy *ou* miniature golf

golfe [gɔlf] *nm* gulf; (*petit*) bay

gomme [gɔm] *nf* (*à effacer*) rubber (BRIT), eraser; **gommer** /1/ *vt* to rub out (BRIT), erase

gonflé, e [gɔ̃fle] *adj* swollen; **il est ~** (*fam: courageux*) he's got some nerve; (: *impertinent*) he's got a nerve

gonfler [gɔ̃fle] /1/ *vt* (*pneu, ballon*) to inflate, blow up; (*nombre, importance*) to inflate ▷ *vi* to swell (up); (*Culin: pâte*) to rise

gonzesse [gɔ̃zɛs] *nf* (*fam*) chick, bird (BRIT)

googler [gugle] /1/ *vt* to google

gorge [gɔʀʒ] *nf* (*Anat*) throat; (*Géo*) gorge

gorgé, e [gɔʀʒe] *adj*: **~ de** filled with ▷ *nf* (*petite*) sip; (*grande*) gulp

gorille [gɔʀij] *nm* gorilla; (*fam*) bodyguard

gosse [gɔs] *nm/f* kid

goudron [gudʀɔ̃] *nm* tar; **goudronner** /1/ *vt* to tar(mac) (BRIT), asphalt (US)

gouffre [gufʀ] *nm* abyss, gulf

goulot [gulo] *nm* neck; **boire au ~** to drink from the bottle

goulu, e [guly] *adj* greedy

gourde [guʀd] *nf* (*récipient*) flask; (*fam*) (clumsy) clot *ou* oaf ▷ *adj* oafish

gourdin [guʀdɛ̃] *nm* club, bludgeon

gourmand, e [guʀmɑ̃, -ɑ̃d] *adj* greedy; **gourmandise** *nf* greed; (*bonbon*) sweet

gousse [gus] *nf*: **~ d'ail** clove of garlic

goût [gu] *nm* taste; **de bon ~** tasteful; **de mauvais ~** tasteless; **avoir bon/ mauvais ~** to taste nice/nasty; **prendre ~ à** to develop a taste *ou* a liking for

goûter [gute] /1/ *vt* (*essayer*) to taste; (*apprécier*) to enjoy ▷ *vi* to have (afternoon) tea ▷ *nm* (afternoon) tea; **je peux ~?** can I have a taste?

goutte [gut] *nf* drop; (*Méd*) gout; (*alcool*) nip (BRIT), drop (US); **tomber ~ à** to drip; **goutte-à-goutte** *nm inv* (*Méd*) drip

gouttière [gutjɛʀ] *nf* gutter

gouvernail [guvɛʀnaj] *nm* rudder; (*barre*) helm, tiller

gouvernement [guvɛʀnəmɑ̃] *nm* government

gouverner [guvɛʀne] /1/ *vt* to govern

grâce [gʀɑs] *nf* (*charme, Rel*) grace; (*faveur*) favour; (*Jur*) pardon; **faire ~ à qn de qch** to spare sb sth; **demander ~** to beg for mercy; **~ à** thanks to; **gracieux, -euse** *adj* graceful

grade [gʀad] *nm* rank; **monter en ~** to be promoted

gradin [gʀadɛ̃] *nm* tier; (*de stade*) step; **gradins** *nmpl* (*de stade*) terracing *no pl*

gradué, e [gʀadɥe] *adj*: **verre ~** measuring jug

graduel, le [gʀadɥɛl] *adj* gradual

graduer [gʀadɥe] /1/ *vt* (*effort etc*) to increase gradually; (*règle, verre*) to graduate

graffiti [gʀafiti] *nmpl* graffiti

grain [gʀɛ̃] *nm* (*gén*) grain; (*Navig*) squall; **~ de beauté** beauty spot; **~ de café** coffee bean; **~ de poivre** peppercorn

graine [gʀɛn] nf seed
graissage [gʀɛsaʒ] nm lubrication, greasing
graisse [gʀɛs] nf fat; (*lubrifiant*) grease; **graisser** /1/ vt to lubricate, grease; (*tacher*) to make greasy; **graisseux, -euse** adj greasy
grammaire [gʀamɛʀ] nf grammar
gramme [gʀam] nm gramme
grand, e [gʀɑ̃, gʀɑ̃d] adj (*haut*) tall; (*gros, vaste, large*) large, big; (*long*) long; (*plus âgé*) big; (*adulte*) grown-up; (*important, brillant*) great ▷ adv: **~ ouvert** wide open; **au ~ air** in the open (air); **les ~s blessés/brûlés** the severely injured/burned; **~ ensemble** housing scheme; **~ magasin** department store; **~e personne** grown-up; **~e surface** hypermarket; **~es écoles** prestige university-level colleges with competitive entrance examinations; **~es lignes** (*Rail*) main lines; **~es vacances** summer holidays (*BRIT*) ou vacation (*US*); **grand-chose** nm/f inv: **pas grand-chose** not much; **Grande-Bretagne** nf: **la Grande-Bretagne** (Great) Britain; **grandeur** nf (*dimension*) size; **grandeur nature** life-size; **grandiose** adj imposing; **grandir** /2/ vi to grow; grow ▷ vt: **grandir qn** (*vêtement, chaussure*) to make sb look taller; **grand-mère** nf grandmother; **grand-peine**: **à grand-peine** adv with (great) difficulty; **grand-père** nm grandfather; **grands-parents** nmpl grandparents
grange [gʀɑ̃ʒ] nf barn
granit [gʀanit] nm granite
graphique [gʀafik] adj graphic ▷ nm graph
grappe [gʀap] nf cluster; **~ de raisin** bunch of grapes
gras, se [gʀɑ, gʀɑs] adj (*viande, soupe*) fatty; (*personne*) fat; (*surface, main, cheveux*) greasy; (*plaisanterie*) coarse; (*Typo*) bold ▷ nm (*Culin*) fat; **faire la ~se matinée** to have a lie-in

(*BRIT*), sleep late; **grassement** adv: **grassement payé** handsomely paid
gratifiant, e [gʀatifjɑ̃, -ɑ̃t] adj gratifying, rewarding
gratin [gʀatɛ̃] nm (*Culin*) cheese-(*ou* crumb-)topped dish (: *croûte*) topping; **tout le ~ parisien** all the best people of Paris; **gratiné** adj (*Culin*) au gratin
gratis [gʀatis] adv free
gratitude [gʀatityd] nf gratitude
gratte-ciel [gʀatsjɛl] nm inv skyscraper
gratter [gʀate] /1/ vt (*frotter*) to scrape; (*avec un ongle*) to scratch; (*enlever: avec un outil*) to scrape off; (: *avec un ongle*) to scratch off ▷ vi (*irriter*) to be scratchy; (*démanger*) to itch; **se gratter** to scratch o.s.
gratuit, e [gʀatɥi, -ɥit] adj (*entrée*) free; (*fig*) gratuitous
grave [gʀav] adj (*maladie, accident*) serious, bad; (*sujet, problème*) serious, grave; (*personne, air*) grave, solemn; (*voix, son*) deep, low-pitched; **gravement** adv seriously; (*parler, regarder*) gravely
graver [gʀave] /1/ vt (*plaque, nom*) to engrave; (*CD, DVD*) to burn
graveur [gʀavœʀ] nm engraver; **~ de CD/DVD** CD/DVD burner or writer
gravier [gʀavje] nm (loose) gravel no pl; **gravillons** nmpl gravel sg
gravir [gʀaviʀ] /2/ vt to climb (up)
gravité [gʀavite] nf (*de maladie, d'accident*) seriousness; (*de sujet, problème*) gravity
graviter [gʀavite] /1/ vi to revolve
gravure [gʀavyʀ] nf engraving; (*reproduction*) print
gré [gʀe] nm: **à son ~** to his liking; **contre le ~ de qn** against sb's will; **de son (plein) ~** of one's own free will; **de ~ ou de force** whether one likes it or not; **de bon ~** willingly; **bon ~ mal ~** like it or not; **savoir (bien) ~ à qn de qch** to be (most) grateful to sb for sth

grec, grecque [gʀɛk] adj Greek; (classique: vase etc) Grecian ▷ nm (Ling) Greek ▷ nm/f: **Grec, Grecque** Greek

Grèce [gʀɛs] nf: **la ~** Greece

greffe [gʀɛf] nf (Bot, Méd: de tissu) graft; (Méd: d'organe) transplant; **greffer** /1/ vt (Bot, Méd: tissu) to graft; (Méd: organe) to transplant

grêle [gʀɛl] adj (very) thin ▷ nf hail; **grêler** /1/ vb impers: **il grêle** it's hailing; **grêlon** nm hailstone

grelot [gʀəlo] nm little bell

grelotter [gʀəlɔte] /1/ vi to shiver

grenade [gʀənad] nf (explosive) grenade; (Bot) pomegranate; **grenadine** nf grenadine

grenier [gʀənje] nm attic; (de ferme) loft

grenouille [gʀənuj] nf frog

grès [gʀɛ] nm sandstone; (poterie) stoneware

grève [gʀɛv] nf (d'ouvriers) strike; (plage) shore; **se mettre en/faire ~** to go on/be on strike; **~ de la faim** hunger strike; **~ sauvage** wildcat strike

gréviste [gʀevist] nm/f striker

grièvement [gʀijɛvmɑ̃] adv seriously

griffe [gʀif] nf claw; (d'un couturier, parfumeur) label; **griffer** /1/ vt to scratch

grignoter [gʀiɲɔte] /1/ vt (personne) to nibble at; (souris) to gnaw at ▷ vi to nibble

gril [gʀil] nm steak ou grill pan; **grillade** nf grill

grillage [gʀijaʒ] nm (treillis) wire netting; (clôture) wire fencing

grille [gʀij] nf (portail) (metal) gate; (clôture) railings pl; (d'égout) (metal) grate; grid

grille-pain [gʀijpɛ̃] nm inv toaster

griller [gʀije] /1/ vt (aussi: **faire ~**) (pain) to toast; (viande) to grill; (châtaignes) to roast; (fig: ampoule etc) to burn out; **~ un feu rouge** to jump the lights

grillon [gʀijɔ̃] nm cricket

grimace [gʀimas] nf grimace; (pour faire rire): **faire des ~s** to pull ou make faces

grimper [gʀɛ̃pe] /1/ vi, vt to climb

grincer [gʀɛ̃se] /3/ vi (porte, roue) to grate; (plancher) to creak; **~ des dents** to grind one's teeth

grincheux, -euse [gʀɛ̃ʃø, -øz] adj grumpy

grippe [gʀip] nf flu, influenza; **~ A** swine flu; **~ aviaire** bird flu; **grippé, e** adj: **être grippé** to have (the) flu

gris, e [gʀi, gʀiz] adj grey; (ivre) tipsy

grisaille [gʀizaj] nf greyness, dullness

griser [gʀize] /1/ vt to intoxicate

grive [gʀiv] nf thrush

Groenland [gʀɔɛnlɑ̃d] nm: **le ~** Greenland

grogner [gʀɔɲe] /1/ vi to growl; (fig) to grumble; **grognon, ne** adj grumpy

grommeler [gʀɔmle] /4/ vi to mutter to o.s.

gronder [gʀɔ̃de] /1/ vi to rumble; (fig: révolte) to be brewing ▷ vt to scold; **se faire ~** to get a telling-off

gros, se [gʀo, gʀos] adj big, large; (obèse) fat; (travaux, dégâts) extensive; (large) thick; (rhume, averse) heavy ▷ adv: **risquer/gagner ~** to risk/win a lot ▷ nm/f fat man/woman ▷ nm (Comm): **le ~** the wholesale business; **prix de ~** wholesale price; **par ~ temps/~se mer** in rough weather/ heavy seas; **le ~ de** the bulk of; **en ~** roughly; (Comm) wholesale; **~ lot** jackpot; **~ mot** swearword; **~ plan** (Photo) close-up; **~ sel** cooking salt; **~ titre** headline; **~se caisse** big drum

groseille [gʀozɛj] nf: **~ (rouge)/ (blanche)** red/white currant; **~ à maquereau** gooseberry

grosse [gʀos] adj f voir **gros**; **grossesse** nf pregnancy; **grosseur** nf size; (tumeur) lump

grossier, -ière [gʀosje, -jɛʀ] adj coarse; (insolent) rude; (dessin) rough; (*travail*) roughly done; (*imitation, instrument*) crude; (*évident: erreur*) gross; **grossièrement** *adv* (*vulgairement*) coarsely; (*sommairement*) roughly; crudely; (*en gros*) roughly; **grossièreté** *nf* rudeness; (*mot*): **dire des grossièretés** to use coarse language

grossir [gʀosiʀ] /2/ *vi* (*personne*) to put on weight ▷ *vt* (*exagérer*) to exaggerate; (*au microscope*) to magnify; (*vêtement*): **~ qn** to make sb look fatter

grossiste [gʀosist] *nm/f* wholesaler

grotesque [gʀɔtɛsk] *adj* (*extravagant*) grotesque; (*ridicule*) ludicrous

grotte [gʀɔt] *nf* cave

groupe [gʀup] *nm* group; **~ de parole** support group; **~ sanguin** blood group; **~ scolaire** school complex; **grouper** /1/ *vt* to group; **se grouper** *vi* to get together

grue [gʀy] *nf* crane

GSM [ʒeɛsɛm] *nm, adj* GSM

guenon [gənɔ̃] *nf* female monkey

guépard [gepaʀ] *nm* cheetah

guêpe [gɛp] *nf* wasp

guère [gɛʀ] *adv* (*avec adjectif, adverbe*): **ne ... ~** hardly; (*avec verbe: pas beaucoup*): **ne ... ~** (*tournure négative*) much; (*pas souvent*) hardly ever; (*tournure négative*) (very) long; **il n'y a ~ que/de** there's hardly anybody (*ou* anything) but/hardly any; **ce n'est ~ difficile** it's hardly difficult; **nous n'avons ~ de temps** we have hardly any time

guérilla [geʀija] *nf* guerrilla warfare

guérillero [geʀijeʀo] *nm* guerrilla

guérir [geʀiʀ] /2/ *vt* (*personne, maladie*) to cure; (*membre, maladie*) to heal ▷ *vi* (*personne, malade*) to recover, be cured; (*maladie*) to be cured; (*plaie, chagrin, blessure*) to heal; **guérison** *nf* (*de maladie*) curing; (*de membre, plaie*) healing; (*de malade*) recovery; **guérisseur, -euse** *nm/f* healer

guerre [gɛʀ] *nf* war; **en ~** at war; **faire la ~ à** to wage war against; **~ civile/mondiale** civil/world war; **guerrier, -ière** *adj* warlike ▷ *nm/f* warrior

guet [gɛ] *nm*: **faire le ~** to be on the watch *ou* look-out; **guet-apens** [gɛtapɑ̃] *nm* ambush; **guetter** /1/ *vt* (*épier*) to watch (intently); (*attendre*) to watch (out) for; (: *pour surprendre*) to be lying in wait for

gueule [gœl] *nf* (*d'animal*) mouth; (*fam: visage*) mug; (: *bouche*) gob (!), mouth; **ta ~!** (*fam*) shut up!; **avoir la ~ de bois** (*fam*) to have a hangover, be hung over; **gueuler** /1/ *vi* to bawl

gui [gi] *nm* mistletoe

guichet [giʃɛ] *nm* (*de bureau, banque*) counter; **les ~s** (*à la gare, au théâtre*) the ticket office

guide [gid] *nm* (*personne*) guide; (*livre*) guide(book) ▷ *nf* (*fille scout*) (girl) guide; **guider** /1/ *vt* to guide

guidon [gidɔ̃] *nm* handlebars *pl*

guignol [giɲɔl] *nm* ≈ Punch and Judy show; (*fig*) clown

guillemets [gijmɛ] *nmpl*: **entre ~** in inverted commas *ou* quotation marks

guindé, e [gɛ̃de] *adj* (*personne, air*) stiff, starchy; (*style*) stilted

Guinée [gine] *nf*: **la (République de) ~** (the Republic of) Guinea

guirlande [giʀlɑ̃d] *nf* (*fleurs*) garland; **~ de Noël** tinsel *no pl*

guise [giz] *nf*: **à votre ~** as you wish *ou* please; **en ~ de** by way of

guitare [gitaʀ] *nf* guitar

Guyane [gɥijan] *nf*: **la ~ (française)** (French) Guiana

gym [ʒim] *nf* (*exercices*) gym; **gymnase** *nm* gym(nasium); **gymnaste** *nm/f* gymnast; **gymnastique** *nf* gymnastics *sg*; (*au réveil etc*) keep-fit exercises *pl*

gynécologie [ʒinekɔlɔʒi] *nf* gynaecology; **gynécologique** *adj* gynaecological; **gynécologue** *nm/f* gynaecologist

h

habile [abil] *adj* skilful; (*malin*) clever; **habileté** [abilte] *nf* skill, skilfulness; cleverness

habillé, e [abije] *adj* dressed; (*chic*) dressy

habiller [abije] /1/ *vt* to dress; (*fournir en vêtements*) to clothe; (*couvrir*) to cover; **s'habiller** *vi* to dress (o.s.); (*se déguiser, mettre des vêtements chic*) to dress up

habit [abi] *nm* outfit; **habits** *nmpl* (*vêtements*) clothes; **~ (de soirée)** evening dress; (*pour homme*) tails *pl*

habitant, e [abitā, -āt] *nm/f* inhabitant; (*d'une maison*) occupant; **loger chez l'~** to stay with the locals

habitation [abitasjɔ̃] *nf* house; **~s à loyer modéré (HLM)** ≈ council flats

habiter [abite] /1/ *vt* to live in ▷ *vi*: **~ à/dans** to live in *ou* at/in

habitude [abityd] *nf* habit; **avoir l'~ de faire** to be in the habit of doing; (*expérience*) to be used to doing;

avoir l'**~ des enfants** to be used to children; **d'~** usually; **comme d'~** as usual

habitué, e [abitɥe] *nm/f* (*de maison*) regular visitor; (*client*) regular (customer)

habituel, le [abitɥɛl] *adj* usual

habituer [abitɥe] /1/ *vt*: **~ qn à** to get sb used to; **s'habituer à** to get used to

'hache ['aʃ] *nf* axe

'hacher ['aʃe] /1/ *vt* (*viande*) to mince ; (*persil*) to chop; **'hachis** *nm* mince *no pl*; **hachis Parmentier** ≈ shepherd's pie

'haie ['ɛ] *nf* hedge; (*Sport*) hurdle

'haillons ['ajɔ̃] *nmpl* rags

'haine ['ɛn] *nf* hatred

'haïr ['aiʀ] /10/ *vt* to detest, hate

'hâlé, e ['ɑle] *adj* (sun)tanned, sunburnt

haleine [alɛn] *nf* breath; **hors d'~** out of breath; **tenir en ~** (*attention*) to hold spellbound; (*en attente*) to keep in suspense; **de longue ~** long-term

'haleter ['alte] /5/ *vi* to pant

'hall ['ol] *nm* hall

'halle ['al] *nf* (covered) market; **'halles** *nfpl* (*d'une grande ville*) central food market *sg*

hallucination [alysinasjɔ̃] *nf* hallucination

'halte ['alt] *nf* stop, break; (*escale*) stopping place ▷ *excl* stop!; **faire ~** to stop

haltère [altɛʀ] *nm* dumbbell, barbell; **(poids et) ~s** (*activité*) weightlifting *sg*; **haltérophilie** *nf* weightlifting

'hamac ['amak] *nm* hammock

'hamburger ['ɑ̃buʀɡœʀ] *nm* hamburger

'hameau, x ['amo] *nm* hamlet

hameçon [amsɔ̃] *nm* (fish) hook

'hamster ['amstɛʀ] *nm* hamster

'hanche ['ɑ̃ʃ] *nf* hip

'hand-ball ['ɑ̃dbal] *nm* handball

h

'handicapé, e ['ãdikape] *adj* disabled, handicapped ▷ *nm/f* handicapped person; **~ mental/physique** mentally/physically handicapped person; **~ moteur** person with a movement disorder

'hangar ['ãgaʀ] *nm* shed; (*Aviat*) hangar

'hanneton ['antɔ̃] *nm* cockchafer

'hanter ['ãte] /1/ *vt* to haunt

'hantise ['ãtiz] *nf* obsessive fear

'harceler ['aʀsəle] /5/ *vt* to harass; **~ qn de questions** to plague sb with questions

'hardi, e ['aʀdi] *adj* bold, daring

'hareng ['aʀã] *nm* herring; **~ saur** kipper, smoked herring

'hargne ['aʀɲ] *nf* aggressivity, aggressiveness; **'hargneux, -euse** *adj* aggressive

'haricot ['aʀiko] *nm* bean; **~ blanc/rouge** haricot/kidney bean; **~ vert** French (*BRIT*) *ou* green bean

harmonica [aʀmɔnika] *nm* mouth organ

harmonie [aʀmɔni] *nf* harmony; **harmonieux, -euse** *adj* harmonious; (*couleurs, couple*) well-matched

'harpe ['aʀp] *nf* harp

'hasard ['azaʀ] *nm*: **le ~** chance, fate; **un ~** a coincidence; **au ~** (*sans but*) aimlessly; (*à l'aveuglette*) at random; **par ~** by chance; **à tout ~** (*en espérant trouver ce qu'on cherche*) on the off chance; (*en cas de besoin*) just in case

'hâte ['at] *nf* haste; **à la ~** hurriedly, hastily; **en ~** posthaste, with all possible speed; **avoir ~ de** to be eager *ou* anxious to; **'hâter** /1/ *vt* to hasten; **se 'hâter** to hurry; **'hâtif, -ive** *adj* (*travail*) hurried; (*décision*) hasty

'hausse ['os] *nf* rise, increase; **être en ~** to be going up; **'hausser** /1/ *vt* to raise; **hausser les épaules** to shrug (one's shoulders)

'haut, e ['o, 'ot] *adj* high; (*grand*) tall ▷ *adv* high ▷ *nm* top (part); **de 3 m de**

~ 3 m high, 3 m in height; **en ~ lieu** in high places; **à ~e voix, (tout) ~** aloud, out loud; **des ~s et des bas** ups and downs; **du ~ de** from the top of; **de ~ en bas** from top to bottom; **plus ~** higher up, further up; (*dans un texte*) above; (*parler*) louder; **en ~** (*être/aller*) at (*ou* to) the top; (*dans une maison*) upstairs; **en ~ de** at the top of; **~ débit** broadband

'hautain, e ['otɛ̃, -ɛn] *adj* haughty

'hautbois ['obwa] *nm* oboe

'hauteur ['otœʀ] *nf* height; **à la ~ de** (*sur la même ligne*) level with; (*fig: tâche, situation*) equal to; **à la ~** (*fig*) up to it

'haut-parleur ['opaʀlœʀ] *nm* (loud) speaker

Hawaï [awai] *n* Hawaii; **les îles ~** the Hawaiian Islands

'Haye ['ɛ] *n*: **la '~** the Hague

hebdomadaire [ɛbdɔmadɛʀ] *adj, nm* weekly

hébergement [ebɛʀʒəmã] *nm* accommodation

héberger [ebɛʀʒe] /3/ *vt* (*touristes*) to accommodate, lodge; (*amis*) to put up; (*réfugiés*) to take in

hébergeur [ebɛʀʒœʀ] *nm* (*Internet*) host

hébreu, x [ebʀø] *adj m, nm* Hebrew

Hébrides [ebʀid] *nf*: **les ~** the Hebrides

hectare [ɛktaʀ] *nm* hectare

'hein ['ɛ̃] *excl* eh?

'hélas ['elas] *excl* alas! ▷ *adv* unfortunately

'héler ['ele] /6/ *vt* to hail

hélice [elis] *nf* propeller

hélicoptère [elikɔptɛʀ] *nm* helicopter

helvétique [ɛlvetik] *adj* Swiss

hématome [ematom] *nm* haematoma

hémisphère [emisfɛʀ] *nm*: **~ nord/sud** northern/southern hemisphere

hémorragie [emɔʀaʒi] *nf* bleeding *no pl*, haemorrhage

hémorroïdes [emɔʀɔid] *nfpl* piles, haemorrhoids

hennir [eniʀ] /2/ *vi* to neigh, whinny

hépatite [epatit] *nf* hepatitis

herbe [ɛʀb] *nf* grass; (*Culin, Méd*) herb; **~s de Provence** mixed herbs; **en ~** unripe; (*fig*) budding; **herbicide** *nm* weed-killer; **herboriste** *nm/f* herbalist

héréditaire [eʀeditɛʀ] *adj* hereditary

hérisson [eʀisɔ̃] *nm* hedgehog

héritage [eʀitaʒ] *nm* inheritance; (*coutumes, système*) heritage; legacy

hériter [eʀite] /1/ *vi*: **~ de qch (de qn)** to inherit sth (from sb); **héritier, -ière** *nm/f* heir/heiress

hermétique [ɛʀmetik] *adj* airtight; (*à l'eau*) watertight; (*fig: écrivain, style*) abstruse; (*: visage*) impenetrable

hermine [ɛʀmin] *nf* ermine

hernie ['ɛʀni] *nf* hernia

héroïne [eʀɔin] *nf* heroine; (*drogue*) heroin

héroïque [eʀɔik] *adj* heroic

héron ['eʀɔ̃] *nm* heron

héros ['eʀo] *nm* hero

hésitant, e [ezitɑ̃, -ɑ̃t] *adj* hesitant

hésitation [ezitasjɔ̃] *nf* hesitation

hésiter [ezite] /1/ *vi*: **~ (à faire)** to hesitate (to do)

hétérosexuel, le [eteʀɔsɛksɥɛl] *adj* heterosexual

hêtre ['ɛtʀ] *nm* beech

heure [œʀ] *nf* hour; (*Scol*) period; (*moment, moment fixé*) time; **c'est l'~** it's time; **quelle ~ est-il?** what time is it?; **2 ~s (du matin)** 2 o'clock (in the morning); **être à l'~** to be on time; (*montre*) to be right; **mettre à l'~** to set right; **à toute ~** at any time; **24 ~s sur 24** round the clock, 24 hours a day; **à l'~ qu'il est** at this time (of day); (*fig*) now; **à l'~ actuelle** at the present time; **sur l'~** at once; **à une ~ avancée (de la nuit)** at a late hour (of the night); **de bonne ~** early; **~ de pointe** rush hour; (*téléphone*) peak period; **~s de bureau** office hours; **~s supplémentaires** overtime *sg*

heureusement [œʀøzmɑ̃] *adv* (*par bonheur*) fortunately, luckily

heureux, -euse [œʀø, -øz] *adj* happy; (*chanceux*) lucky, fortunate

heurt ['œʀ] *nm* (*choc*) collision

heurter ['œʀte] /1/ *vt* (*mur*) to strike, hit; (*personne*) to collide with

hexagone [ɛgzagɔn] *nm* hexagon; **l'H~** (*la France*) France (*because of its roughly hexagonal shape*)

hiberner [ibɛʀne] /1/ *vi* to hibernate

hibou, x ['ibu] *nm* owl

hideux, -euse ['idø, -øz] *adj* hideous

hier [jɛʀ] *adv* yesterday; **~ matin/ soir/midi** yesterday morning/ evening/lunchtime; **toute la journée d'~** all day yesterday; **toute la matinée d'~** all yesterday morning

hiérarchie ['jeʀaʀʃi] *nf* hierarchy

hindou, e [ɛ̃du] *adj* Hindu ⊳ *nm/f*: **H~, e** Hindu; (*Indien*) Indian

hippique [ipik] *adj* equestrian, horse *cpd*; **un club ~** a riding centre; **un concours ~** a horse show; **hippisme** [ipism] *nm* (horse-)riding

hippodrome [ipɔdʀom] *nm* racecourse

hippopotame [ipɔpɔtam] *nm* hippopotamus

hirondelle [iʀɔ̃dɛl] *nf* swallow

hisser ['ise] /1/ *vt* to hoist, haul up

histoire [istwaʀ] *nf* (*science, événements*) history; (*anecdote, récit, mensonge*) story; (*affaire*) business *no pl*; (*chichis: gén pl*) fuss *no pl*; **histoires** *nfpl* (*ennuis*) trouble *sg*; **~ géo** humanities *pl*; **historique** *adj* historical; (*important*) historic ⊳ *nm*: **faire l'historique de** to give the background to

hit-parade ['itpaʀad] *nm*: **le ~** the charts

hiver [ivɛʀ] *nm* winter; **hivernal, e, -aux** *adj* winter *cpd*; (*comme en hiver*) wintry; **hiverner** /1/ *vi* to winter

HLM sigle m ou f (= habitations à loyer modéré) low-rent, state-owned housing; **un(e) ~** ≈ a council flat (ou house)

'**hobby** ['ɔbi] nm hobby

'**hocher** ['ɔʃe] /1/ vt: **~ la tête** to nod; (signe négatif ou dubitatif) to shake one's head

'**hockey** ['ɔkɛ] nm: **~ (sur glace/ gazon)** (ice/field) hockey

'**hold-up** ['ɔldœp] nm inv hold-up

'**hollandais, e** ['ɔlɑ̃dɛ, -ɛz] adj Dutch ▷ nm (Ling) Dutch ▷ nm/f: **~, e** Dutchman/woman

'**Hollande** ['ɔlɑ̃d] nf: **la '~** Holland

'**homard** ['ɔmaʀ] nm lobster

homéopathique [ɔmeɔpatik] adj homoeopathic

homicide [ɔmisid] nm murder; **~ involontaire** manslaughter

hommage [ɔmaʒ] nm tribute; **rendre ~ à** to pay tribute ou homage to

homme [ɔm] nm man; **~ d'affaires** businessman; **~ d'État** statesman; **~ de main** hired man; **~ de paille** stooge; **~ politique** politician; **l'~ de la rue** the man in the street

homogène adj homogeneous

homologue nm/f counterpart

homologué, e adj (Sport) ratified; (tarif) authorized

homonyme nm (Ling) homonym; (d'une personne) namesake

homosexuel, le adj homosexual

'**Hong-Kong** ['ɔ̃gkɔ̃g] n Hong Kong

'**Hongrie** ['ɔ̃gʀi] nf: **la ~** Hungary; '**hongrois, e** adj Hungarian ▷ nm (Ling) Hungarian ▷ nm/f: **Hongrois, e** Hungarian

honnête [ɔnɛt] adj (intègre) honest; (juste, satisfaisant) fair; **honnêtement** adv honestly; **honnêteté** nf honesty

honneur [ɔnœʀ] nm honour; (mérite): **l'~ lui revient** the credit is his; **en l'~ de** (personne) in honour of; (événement) on the occasion of; **faire**

~ à (engagements) to honour; (famille, professeur) to be a credit to; (fig: repas etc) to do justice to

honorable [ɔnɔʀabl] adj worthy, honourable; (suffisant) decent

honoraire [ɔnɔʀɛʀ] adj honorary; **honoraires** nmpl fees; **professeur ~** professor emeritus

honorer [ɔnɔʀe] /1/ vt to honour; (estimer) to hold in high regard; (faire honneur à) to do credit to

'**honte** ['ɔ̃t] nf shame; **avoir honte de** to be ashamed of; **faire honte à qn** to make sb (feel) ashamed; '**honteux, -euse** adj ashamed; (conduite, acte) shameful, disgraceful

hôpital, -aux [ɔpital, -o] nm hospital; **où est l'~ le plus proche?** where is the nearest hospital?

'**hoquet** ['ɔkɛ] nm: **avoir le ~** to have (the) hiccups

horaire [ɔʀɛʀ] adj hourly ▷ nm timetable, schedule; **horaires** nmpl (heures de travail) hours; **~ flexible** ou **mobile** ou **à la carte** ou **souple** flex(i)time

horizon [ɔʀizɔ̃] nm horizon

horizontal, e, -aux adj horizontal

horloge [ɔʀlɔʒ] nf clock; **l'~ parlante** the speaking clock; **horloger, -ère** nm/f watchmaker; clockmaker

'**hormis** ['ɔʀmi] prép save

horoscope [ɔʀɔskɔp] nm horoscope

horreur [ɔʀœʀ] nf horror; **quelle ~!** how awful!; **avoir ~ de** to loathe ou detest; **horrible** adj horrible; **horrifier** /7/ vt to horrify

'**hors** ['ɔʀ] prép: **~ de** out of; **~ pair** outstanding; **~ de propos** inopportune; **~ service (HS)**, **~ d'usage** out of service; **être ~ de soi** to be beside o.s.; '**hors-bord** nm inv speedboat (with outboard motor); '**hors-d'œuvre** nm inv hors d'œuvre; '**hors-la-loi** nm inv outlaw; '**hors- taxe** adj (boutique, marchandises) duty-free

hortensia [ɔʀtɑ̃sja] nm hydrangea

hospice [ɔspis] nm (de vieillards) home

hospitalier, -ière [ɔspitalje, -jɛʀ] adj (accueillant) hospitable; (Méd: service, centre) hospital cpd

hospitaliser [ɔspitalize] /1/ vt to take (ou send) to hospital, hospitalize

hospitalité [ɔspitalite] nf hospitality

hostie [ɔsti] nf host

hostile [ɔstil] adj hostile; **hostilité** nf hostility

hôte [ot] nm (maître de maison) host ▷ nm/f (invité) guest

hôtel [otɛl] nm hotel; **aller à l'~** to stay in a hotel; **~ (particulier)** (private) mansion; **~ de ville** town hall; see note **"hôtels"**; **hôtellerie** [otɛlʀi] nf hotel business

⊛ **HÔTELS**
⊛
⊛ There are six categories of hotel
⊛ in France, from zero ('non classé')
⊛ to four stars and luxury four
⊛ stars ('quatre étoiles luxe'). Prices
⊛ include VAT but not breakfast. In
⊛ some towns, guests pay a small
⊛ additional tourist tax, the 'taxe
⊛ de séjour'.

hôtesse [otɛs] nf hostess; **~ de l'air** flight attendant

'**houblon** ['ublɔ̃] nm (Bot) hop; (pour la bière) hops pl

'**houille** ['uj] nf coal; **~ blanche** hydroelectric power

'**houle** ['ul] nf swell; '**houleux, -euse** adj stormy

'**hourra** ['uʀa] excl hurrah!

'**housse** ['us] nf cover

'**houx** ['u] nm holly

'**hovercraft** [ovœʀkʀaft] nm hovercraft

'**hublot** ['yblo] nm porthole

'**huche** ['yʃ] nf: **huche à pain** bread bin

'**huer** ['ɥe] /1/ vt to boo

huile [ɥil] nf oil

huissier [ɥisje] nm usher; (Jur) ≈ bailiff

'**huit** ['ɥi(t)] num eight; **samedi en ~** a week on Saturday; **dans ~ jours** in a week('s time); '**huitaine** ['ɥitɛn] nf: **une huitaine de jours** a week or so; '**huitième** num eighth

huître [ɥitʀ] nf oyster

humain, e [ymɛ̃, -ɛn] adj human; (compatissant) humane ▷ nm human (being); **humanitaire** adj humanitarian; **humanité** nf humanity

humble [œ̃bl] adj humble

'**humer** ['yme] /1/ vt (parfum) to inhale; (pour sentir) to smell

humeur [ymœʀ] nf mood; **de bonne/mauvaise ~** in a good/ bad mood

humide [ymid] adj damp; (main, yeux) moist; (climat, chaleur) humid; (saison, route) wet

humilier [ymilje] /7/ vt to humiliate

humilité [ymilite] nf humility, humbleness

humoristique [ymɔʀistik] adj humorous

humour [ymuʀ] nm humour; **avoir de l'~** to have a sense of humour; **~ noir** sick humour

'**huppé, e** ['ype] adj (fam) posh

'**hurlement** ['yʀləmɑ̃] nm howling no pl, howl; yelling no pl, yell

'**hurler** ['yʀle] /1/ vi to howl, yell

'**hutte** ['yt] nf hut

hydratant, e [idʀatɑ̃, -ɑ̃t] adj (crème) moisturizing

hydraulique [idʀolik] adj hydraulic

hydravion [idʀavjɔ̃] nm seaplane

hydrogène [idʀɔʒɛn] nm hydrogen

hydroglisseur [idʀɔglisœʀ] nm hydroplane

hyène [jɛn] nf hyena

hygiène [iʒjɛn] nf hygiene

hygiénique [iʒenik] adj hygienic

hymne [imn] nm hymn

hyperlien [ipɛʀljɛ̃] nm hyperlink

hypermarché [ipɛrmarʃe] *nm*
hypermarket
hypermétrope [ipermetrɔp] *adj*
long-sighted
hypertension [ipɛrtɑ̃sjɔ̃] *nf* high
blood pressure
hypnose [ipnoz] *nf* hypnosis;
hypnotiser /1/ *vt* to hypnotize
hypocrisie [ipɔkrizi] *nf* hypocrisy;
hypocrite *adj* hypocritical
hypothèque [ipɔtɛk] *nf* mortgage
hypothèse [ipɔtɛz] *nf* hypothesis
hystérique [isterik] *adj* hysterical

iceberg [isbɛrg] *nm* iceberg
ici [isi] *adv* here; **jusqu'~** as far as this;
(*temporel*) until now; **d'~ là** by then;
d'~ demain by tomorrow; in the
meantime; **d'~ peu** before long
icône [ikon] *nf* icon
idéal, e, -aux [ideal, -o] *adj* ideal
▷ *nm* ideal; **idéaliste** *adj* idealistic
▷ *nm/f* idealist
idée [ide] *nf* idea; **se faire des ~s** to
imagine things, get ideas into one's
head; **avoir dans l'~ que** to have an
idea that; **~s noires** black *ou* dark
thoughts; **~s reçues** accepted ideas
ou wisdom
identifier [idɑ̃tifje] /7/ *vt* to identify;
s'identifier *vi*: **s'~ avec** *ou* **à qn/qch**
(*héros etc*) to identify with sb/sth
identique [idɑ̃tik] *adj*: **~ (à)**
identical (to)
identité [idɑ̃tite] *nf* identity
idiot, e [idjo, idjɔt] *adj* idiotic
▷ *nm/f* idiot

idole [idɔl] *nf* idol

if [if] *nm* yew

ignoble [iɲɔbl] *adj* vile

ignorant, e [iɲɔrɑ̃, -ɑ̃t] *adj* ignorant; **~ de** ignorant of, not aware of

ignorer [iɲɔre] /1/ *vt* not to know; (*personne*) to ignore

il [il] *pron* he; (*animal, chose, en tournure impersonnelle*) it; **il neige** it's snowing; **Pierre est-il arrivé?** has Pierre arrived?; **il a gagné** he won; *voir aussi* **avoir**

île [il] *nf* island; **l'~ Maurice** Mauritius; **les ~s anglo-normandes** the Channel Islands; **les ~s Britanniques** the British Isles

illégal, e, -aux [ilegal, -o] *adj* illegal

illimité, e [ilimite] *adj* unlimited

illisible [ilizibl] *adj* illegible; (*roman*) unreadable

illogique [ilɔʒik] *adj* illogical

illuminer [ilymine] /1/ *vt* to light up; (*monument, rue: pour une fête*) to illuminate; (: *au moyen de projecteurs*) floodlight

illusion [ilyzjɔ̃] *nf* illusion; **se faire des ~s** to delude o.s.; **faire ~** to delude *ou* fool people

illustration [ilystrasjɔ̃] *nf* illustration

illustré, e [ilystre] *adj* illustrated ▷ *nm* comic

illustrer [ilystre] /1/ *vt* to illustrate; **s'illustrer** to become famous, win fame

ils [il] *pron* they

image [imaʒ] *nf* (*gén*) picture; (*comparaison, ressemblance*) image; **~ de marque** brand image; (*d'une personne*) (public) image; **imagé, e** *adj* (*texte*) full of imagery; (*langage*) colourful

imaginaire [imaʒinɛr] *adj* imaginary

imagination [imaʒinasjɔ̃] *nf* imagination; **avoir de l'~** to be imaginative

imaginer [imaʒine] /1/ *vt* to imagine; (*inventer: expédient, mesure*) to devise, think up; **s'imaginer** *vt* (*se figurer: scène etc*) to imagine, picture; **s'~ que** to imagine that

imam [imam] *nm* imam

imbécile [ɛ̃besil] *adj* idiotic ▷ *nm/f* idiot

imbu, e [ɛ̃by] *adj*: **~ de** full of

imitateur, -trice [imitatœr, -tris] *nm/f* (*gén*) imitator; (*Music-Hall*) impersonator

imitation [imitasjɔ̃] *nf* imitation; (*de personalité*) impersonation

imiter [imite] /1/ *vt* to imitate; (*contrefaire*) to forge; (*ressembler à*) to look like

immangeable [ɛ̃mɑ̃ʒabl] *adj* inedible

immatriculation [imatrikylasjɔ̃] *nf* registration

● **IMMATRICULATION**
●
● The last two numbers on vehicle
● licence plates used to show which
● 'département' of France the vehicle
● was registered in. For example,
● a car registered in Paris had the
● number 75 on its licence plates. In
● 2009, a new alphanumeric system
● was introduced, in which the
● 'département' number no longer
● features. Displaying this number
● to the right of the plate is now
● optional.

immatriculer [imatrikyle] /1/ *vt* to register; **faire/se faire ~** to register

immédiat, e [imedja, -at] *adj* immediate ▷ *nm*: **dans l'~** for the time being; **immédiatement** *adv* immediately

immense [imɑ̃s] *adj* immense

immerger [imɛrʒe] /3/ *vt* to immerse, submerge

immeuble [imœbl] *nm* building; **~ locatif** block of rented flats

immigration [imigrasjɔ̃] *nf* immigration

immigré, e [imigʀe] *nm/f*
immigrant

imminent, e [iminɑ̃, -ɑ̃t] *adj*
imminent

immobile [imɔbil] *adj* still,
motionless

immobilier, -ière [imɔbilje,
-jɛʀ] *adj* property *cpd* ▷ *nm*: **l'~** the
property *ou* the real estate business

immobiliser [imɔbilize] /1/ *vt* (*gén*)
to immobilize; (*circulation, véhicule,
affaires*) to bring to a standstill;
s'immobiliser (*personne*) to stand
still; (*machine, véhicule*) to come to a
halt *ou* a standstill

immoral, e, -aux [imɔʀal, -o] *adj*
immoral

immortel, le [imɔʀtɛl] *adj* immortal

immunisé e [im(m)ynize] *adj*: **~
contre** immune to

immunité [imynite] *nf* immunity

impact [ɛ̃pakt] *nm* impact

impair, e [ɛ̃pɛʀ] *adj* odd ▷ *nm* faux
pas, blunder

impardonnable [ɛ̃paʀdɔnabl] *adj*
unpardonable, unforgivable

imparfait, e [ɛ̃paʀfɛ, -ɛt] *adj*
imperfect

impartial, e, -aux [ɛ̃paʀsjal, -o] *adj*
impartial, unbiased

impasse [ɛ̃pɑs] *nf* dead-end, cul-de-
sac; (*fig*) deadlock

impassible [ɛ̃pasibl] *adj* impassive

impatience [ɛ̃pasjɑ̃s] *nf* impatience

impatient, e [ɛ̃pasjɑ̃, -ɑ̃t] *adj*
impatient; **impatienter** /1/:
s'impatienter *vi* to get impatient

impeccable [ɛ̃pekabl] *adj* faultless;
(*propre*) spotlessly clean; (*fam*)
smashing

impensable [ɛ̃pɑ̃sabl] *adj* (*événement
hypothétique*) unthinkable; (*événement
qui a eu lieu*) unbelievable

impératif, -ive [ɛ̃peʀatif, -iv] *adj*
imperative ▷ *nm* (*Ling*) imperative;
impératifs *nmpl* (*exigences: d'une
fonction, d'une charge*) requirements;
(: *de la mode*) demands

impératrice [ɛ̃peʀatʀis] *nf* empress

imperceptible [ɛ̃pɛʀsɛptibl] *adj*
imperceptible

impérial, e, -aux [ɛ̃peʀjal, -o] *adj*
imperial

impérieux, -euse [ɛ̃peʀjø, -øz] *adj*
(*caractère, ton*) imperious; (*obligation,
besoin*) pressing, urgent

impérissable [ɛ̃peʀisabl] *adj*
undying

imperméable [ɛ̃pɛʀmeabl] *adj*
waterproof; (*fig*): **~ à** impervious to
▷ *nm* raincoat

impertinent, e [ɛ̃pɛʀtinɑ̃, -ɑ̃t] *adj*
impertinent

impitoyable [ɛ̃pitwajabl] *adj*
pitiless, merciless

implanter [ɛ̃plɑ̃te] /1/: **s'implanter
dans** *vi* to be established in

impliquer [ɛ̃plike] /1/ *vt* to imply;
~ qn (dans) to implicate sb (in)

impoli, e [ɛ̃pɔli] *adj* impolite, rude

impopulaire [ɛ̃pɔpylɛʀ] *adj*
unpopular

importance [ɛ̃pɔʀtɑ̃s] *nf*
importance; (*de somme*) size; **sans ~**
unimportant

important, e [ɛ̃pɔʀtɑ̃, -ɑ̃t] *adj*
important; (*en quantité: somme,
retard*) considerable, sizeable;
(: *gamme, dégâts*) extensive; (*péj: airs,
ton*) self-important ▷ *nm*: **l'~** the
important thing

importateur, -trice [ɛ̃pɔʀtatœʀ,
-tʀis] *nm/f* importer

importation [ɛ̃pɔʀtasjɔ̃] *nf* (*produit*)
import

importer [ɛ̃pɔʀte] /1/ *vt* (*Comm*)
to import; (*maladies, plantes*) to
introduce ▷ *vi* (*être important*) to
matter; **il importe qu'il fasse** it is
important that he should do; **peu
m'importe** (*je n'ai pas de préférence*)
I don't mind; (*je m'en moque*) I don't
care; **peu importe (que)** it doesn't
matter (if); *voir aussi* **n'importe**

importun, e [ɛ̃pɔʀtœ̃, -yn] *adj*
irksome, importunate; (*arrivée, visite*)

inopportune, ill-timed ▷ *nm* intruder;
importuner /1/ *vt* to bother
imposant, e [ɛ̃pozɑ̃, -ɑ̃t] *adj*
imposing
imposer [ɛ̃poze] /1/ *vt* (*taxer*) to
tax; **~ qch à qn** to impose sth on
sb; **s'imposer** (*être nécessaire*) to be
imperative; **en ~ à** to impress; **s'~
comme** to emerge as; **s'~ par** to win
recognition through
impossible [ɛ̃posibl] *adj* impossible;
il m'est ~ de le faire it is impossible
for me to do it, I can't possibly do
it; **faire l'~ (pour que)** to do one's
utmost (so that)
imposteur [ɛ̃pɔstœʀ] *nm* impostor
impôt [ɛ̃po] *nm* tax; **~ sur le chiffre
d'affaires** corporation *ou*
corporate (*us*) tax; **~ foncier** land
tax; **~ sur le revenu** income tax;
~s locaux rates, local taxes (*us*), ≈
council tax (*BRIT*)
impotent, e [ɛ̃pɔtɑ̃, -ɑ̃t] *adj*
disabled
impraticable [ɛ̃pʀatikabl] *adj*
(*projet*) impracticable, unworkable;
(*piste*) impassable
imprécis, e [ɛ̃pʀesi, -iz] *adj*
imprecise
imprégner [ɛ̃pʀeɲe] /6/ *vt*: **~ (de)**
(*tissu, tampon*) to soak *ou* impregnate
(with); (*lieu, air*) to fill (with);
s'imprégner de (*fig*) to absorb
imprenable [ɛ̃pʀənabl] *adj*
(*forteresse*) impregnable; **vue ~**
unimpeded outlook
impression [ɛ̃pʀesjɔ̃] *nf*
impression; (*d'un ouvrage, tissu*)
printing; **faire bonne/mauvaise
~** to make a good/bad impression;
impressionnant, e *adj* (*imposant*)
impressive; (*bouleversant*) upsetting;
impressionner /1/ *vt* (*frapper*) to
impress; (*troubler*) to upset
imprévisible [ɛ̃pʀevizibl] *adj*
unforeseeable
imprévu, e [ɛ̃pʀevy] *adj* unforeseen,
unexpected ▷ *nm* (*incident*)

unexpected incident; **des vacances
pleines d'~** holidays full of surprises;
en cas d'~ if anything unexpected
happens; **sauf ~** unless anything
unexpected crops up
imprimante [ɛ̃pʀimɑ̃t] *nf* printer;
~ à laser laser printer
imprimé [ɛ̃pʀime] *nm* (*formulaire*)
printed form; (*Postes*) printed matter
no pl; (*tissu*) printed fabric; **un ~ à
fleurs/pois** (*tissu*) a floral/polka-
dot print
imprimer [ɛ̃pʀime] /1/ *vt* to print;
(*publier*) to publish; **imprimerie** *nf*
printing; (*établissement*) printing
works *sg*; **imprimeur** *nm* printer
impropre [ɛ̃pʀɔpʀ] *adj*
inappropriate; **~ à** unsuitable for
improviser [ɛ̃pʀɔvize] /1/ *vt, vi* to
improvize
improviste [ɛ̃pʀɔvist]: **à l'~** *adv*
unexpectedly, without warning
imprudence [ɛ̃pʀydɑ̃s] *nf* (*d'une
personne, d'une action*) carelessness *no
pl*; (*d'une remarque*) imprudence *no pl*;
commettre une ~ to do something
foolish
imprudent, e [ɛ̃pʀydɑ̃, -ɑ̃t] *adj*
(*conducteur, geste, action*) careless;
(*remarque*) unwise, imprudent;
(*projet*) foolhardy
impuissant, e [ɛ̃pɥisɑ̃, -ɑ̃t] *adj*
helpless; (*sans effet*) ineffectual;
(*sexuellement*) impotent
impulsif, -ive [ɛ̃pylsif, -iv] *adj*
impulsive
impulsion [ɛ̃pylsjɔ̃] *nf* (*Élec, instinct*)
impulse; (*élan, influence*) impetus
inabordable [inabɔʀdabl] *adj* (*cher*)
prohibitive
inacceptable [inakseptabl] *adj*
unacceptable
inaccessible [inaksesibl] *adj*
inaccessible; **~ à** impervious to
inachevé, e [inaʃve] *adj* unfinished
inactif, -ive [inaktif, -iv] *adj*
inactive; (*remède*) ineffective; (*Bourse:
marché*) slack

inadapté, e [inadapte] *adj* (*Psych*) maladjusted; **~ à** not adapted to, unsuited to

inadéquat, e [inadekwa, -wat] *adj* inadequate

inadmissible [inadmisibl] *adj* inadmissible

inadvertance [inadvɛʀtɑ̃s]: **par ~** *adv* inadvertently

inanimé, e [inanime] *adj* (*matière*) inanimate; (*évanoui*) unconscious; (*sans vie*) lifeless

inanition [inanisjɔ̃] *nf*: **tomber d'~** to faint with hunger (and exhaustion)

inaperçu, e [inapɛʀsy] *adj*: **passer ~** to go unnoticed

inapte [inapt] *adj*: **~ à** incapable of; (*Mil*) unfit for

inattendu, e [inatɑ̃dy] *adj* unexpected

inattentif, -ive [inatɑ̃tif, -iv] *adj* inattentive; **~ à** (*dangers, détails*) heedless of; **inattention** *nf* inattention; **faute d'inattention** careless mistake

inaugurer [inɔgyʀe] /1/ *vt* (*monument*) to unveil; (*exposition, usine*) to open; (*fig*) to inaugurate

inavouable [inavwabl] *adj* (*bénéfices*) undisclosable; (*honteux*) shameful

incalculable [ɛ̃kalkylabl] *adj* incalculable

incapable [ɛ̃kapabl] *adj* incapable; **~ de faire** incapable of doing; (*empêché*) unable to do

incapacité [ɛ̃kapasite] *nf* (*incompétence*) incapability; (*impossibilité*) incapacity; **être dans l'~ de faire** to be unable to do

incarcérer [ɛ̃kaʀseʀe] /6/ *vt* to incarcerate, imprison

incassable [ɛ̃kasabl] *adj* unbreakable

incendie [ɛ̃sɑ̃di] *nm* fire; **~ criminel** arson *no pl*; **~ de forêt** forest fire; **incendier** /7/ *vt* (*mettre le feu à*) to set fire to, set alight; (*brûler complètement*) to burn down

incertain, e [ɛ̃sɛʀtɛ̃, -ɛn] *adj* uncertain; (*temps*) unsettled; (*imprécis: contours*) indistinct, blurred; **incertitude** *nf* uncertainty

incessamment [ɛ̃sesamɑ̃] *adv* very shortly

incident [ɛ̃sidɑ̃] *nm* incident; **~ de parcours** minor hitch *ou* setback; **~ technique** technical difficulties *pl*

incinérer [ɛ̃sineʀe] /6/ *vt* (*ordures*) to incinerate; (*mort*) to cremate

incisif, -ive [ɛ̃sizif, -iv] *adj* incisive ▷ *nf* incisor

inciter [ɛ̃site] /1/ *vt*: **~ qn à (faire) qch** to prompt *ou* encourage sb to do sth; (*à la révolte etc*) to incite sb to do sth

incivilité [ɛ̃sivilite] *nf* (*grossièreté*) incivility; **incivilités** *nfpl* antisocial behaviour *sg*

inclinable [ɛ̃klinabl] *adj*: **siège à dossier ~** reclining seat

inclination [ɛ̃klinasjɔ̃] *nf* (*penchant*) inclination

incliner [ɛ̃kline] /1/ *vt* (*bouteille*) to tilt ▷ *vi*: **~ à qch/à faire** to incline towards sth/doing; **s'incliner** *vi* (*route*) to slope; **s'~ (devant)** to bow (before)

inclure [ɛ̃klyʀ] /35/ *vt* to include; (*joindre à un envoi*) to enclose

inclus, e [ɛ̃kly, -yz] *pp de* **inclure** ▷ *adj* included; (*joint à un envoi*) enclosed; (*compris: frais, dépense*) included; **jusqu'au 10 mars ~** until 10th March inclusive

incognito [ɛ̃kɔɲito] *adv* incognito ▷ *nm*: **garder l'~** to remain incognito

incohérent, e [ɛ̃kɔeʀɑ̃, -ɑ̃t] *adj* (*comportement*) inconsistent; (*geste, langage, texte*) incoherent

incollable [ɛ̃kɔlabl] *adj* (*riz*) that does not stick; (*fam*): **il est ~** he's got all the answers

incolore [ɛ̃kɔlɔʀ] *adj* colourless

incommoder [ɛ̃kɔmɔde] /1/ *vt*: **~ qn** (*chaleur, odeur*) to bother *ou* inconvenience sb

incomparable [ɛ̃kɔ̃paʀabl] *adj*
incomparable

incompatible [ɛ̃kɔ̃patibl] *adj*
incompatible

incompétent, e [ɛ̃kɔ̃petɑ̃, -ɑ̃t] *adj*
incompetent

incomplet, -ète [ɛ̃kɔ̃plɛ, -ɛt] *adj*
incomplete

incompréhensible [ɛ̃kɔ̃pʀeɑ̃sibl]
adj incomprehensible

incompris, e [ɛ̃kɔ̃pʀi, -iz] *adj*
misunderstood

inconcevable [ɛ̃kɔ̃svabl] *adj*
inconceivable

inconfortable [ɛ̃kɔ̃fɔʀtabl] *adj*
uncomfortable

incongru, e [ɛ̃kɔ̃gʀy] *adj* unseemly

inconnu, e [ɛ̃kɔny] *adj* unknown
▷ *nm/f* stranger ▷ *nm*: **l'~** the
unknown ▷ *nf* unknown factor

inconsciemment [ɛ̃kɔ̃sjamɑ̃] *adv*
unconsciously

inconscient, e [ɛ̃kɔ̃sjɑ̃, -ɑ̃t] *adj*
unconscious; (*irréfléchi*) thoughtless,
reckless; (*sentiment*) subconscious
▷ *nm* (*Psych*): **l'~** the unconscious;
~ de unaware of

inconsidéré, e [ɛ̃kɔ̃sideʀe] *adj*
ill-considered

inconsistant, e [ɛ̃kɔ̃sistɑ̃, -ɑ̃t] *adj*
flimsy, weak

inconsolable [ɛ̃kɔ̃sɔlabl] *adj*
inconsolable

incontestable [ɛ̃kɔ̃tɛstabl] *adj*
indisputable

incontinent, e [ɛ̃kɔ̃tinɑ̃, -ɑ̃t] *adj*
incontinent

incontournable [ɛ̃kɔ̃tuʀnabl] *adj*
unavoidable

incontrôlable [ɛ̃kɔ̃tʀolabl]
adj unverifiable; (*irrépressible*)
uncontrollable

inconvénient [ɛ̃kɔ̃venjɑ̃] *nm*
disadvantage, drawback; **si vous
n'y voyez pas d'~** if you have no
objections

incorporer [ɛ̃kɔʀpɔʀe] /1/ *vt*: **~ (à)**
to mix in (with); **~ (dans)** (*paragraphe*
etc) to incorporate (in); (*Mil: appeler*)
to recruit (into); **il a très bien su s'~
à notre groupe** he was very easily
incorporated into our group

incorrect, e [ɛ̃kɔʀɛkt] *adj* (*impropre,
inconvenant*) improper; (*défectueux*)
faulty; (*inexact*) incorrect; (*impoli*)
impolite; (*déloyal*) underhand

incorrigible [ɛ̃kɔʀiʒibl] *adj*
incorrigible

incrédule [ɛ̃kʀedyl] *adj* incredulous;
(*Rel*) unbelieving

incroyable [ɛ̃kʀwajabl] *adj* incredible

incruster [ɛ̃kʀyste] /1/ *vt*;
s'incruster *vi* (*invité*) to take root;
~ qch dans/qch de (*Art*) to inlay sth
into/sth with

inculpé, e [ɛ̃kylpe] *nm/f* accused

inculper [ɛ̃kylpe] /1/ *vt*: **~ (de)** to
charge (with)

inculquer [ɛ̃kylke] /1/ *vt*: **~ qch à** to
inculcate sth in, instil sth into

Inde [ɛ̃d] *nf*: **l'~** India

indécent, e [ɛ̃desɑ̃, -ɑ̃t] *adj* indecent

indécis, e [ɛ̃desi, -iz] *adj* (*par nature*)
indecisive; (*perplexe*) undecided

indéfendable [ɛ̃defɑ̃dabl] *adj*
indefensible

indéfini, e [ɛ̃defini] *adj* (*imprécis,
incertain*) undefined; (*illimité, Ling*)
indefinite; **indéfiniment** *adv*
indefinitely; **indéfinissable** *adj*
indefinable

indélébile [ɛ̃delebil] *adj* indelible

indélicat, e [ɛ̃delika, -at] *adj* tactless

indemne [ɛ̃dɛmn] *adj* unharmed;
indemniser /1/ *vt*: **indemniser qn
(de)** to compensate sb (for)

indemnité [ɛ̃dɛmnite] *nf*
(*dédommagement*) compensation
no pl; (*allocation*) allowance; **~ de
licenciement** redundancy payment

indépendamment [ɛ̃depɑ̃damɑ̃]
adv independently; **~ de** (*abstraction
faite de*) irrespective of; (*en plus de*)
over and above

indépendance [ɛ̃depɑ̃dɑ̃s] *nf*
independence

indépendant, e [ɛ̃depɑ̃dɑ̃, -ɑ̃t] adj independent; **~ de** independent of; **travailleur ~** self-employed worker

indescriptible [ɛ̃dɛskʀiptibl] adj indescribable

indésirable [ɛ̃deziʀabl] adj undesirable

indestructible [ɛ̃dɛstʀyktibl] adj indestructible

indéterminé, e [ɛ̃detɛʀmine] adj (date, cause, nature) unspecified; (forme, longueur, quantité) indeterminate

index [ɛ̃dɛks] nm (doigt) index finger; (d'un livre etc) index; **mettre à l'~** to blacklist

indicateur [ɛ̃dikatœʀ] nm (Police) informer; (Tech) gauge; indicator ▷ adj: **poteau ~** signpost; **~ des chemins de fer** railway timetable; **~ de rues** street directory

indicatif, -ive [ɛ̃dikatif, -iv] adj: **à titre ~** for (your) information ▷ nm (Ling) indicative; (d'une émission) theme ou signature tune; (Tél) dialling code (BRIT), area code (US); **quel est l'~ de ...** what's the code for ...?

indication [ɛ̃dikasjɔ̃] nf indication; (renseignement) information no pl; **indications** nfpl (directives) instructions

indice [ɛ̃dis] nm (marque, signe) indication, sign; (Police: lors d'une enquête) clue; (Jur: présomption) piece of evidence; (Science, Écon, Tech) index; **~ de protection** (sun protection) factor

indicible [ɛ̃disibl] adj inexpressible

indien, ne [ɛ̃djɛ̃, -ɛn] adj Indian ▷ nm/f: **I~, ne** Indian

indifféremment [ɛ̃difeʀamɑ̃] adv (sans distinction) equally

indifférence [ɛ̃difeʀɑ̃s] nf indifference

indifférent, e [ɛ̃difeʀɑ̃, -ɑ̃t] adj (peu intéressé) indifferent; **ça m'est ~ (que ...)** it doesn't matter to me (whether ...); **elle m'est ~e** I am indifferent to her

indigène [ɛ̃diʒɛn] adj native, indigenous; (de la région) local ▷ nm/f native

indigeste [ɛ̃diʒɛst] adj indigestible

indigestion [ɛ̃diʒɛstjɔ̃] nf indigestion no pl; **avoir une ~** to have indigestion

indigne [ɛ̃diɲ] adj: **~ (de)** unworthy (of)

indigner [ɛ̃diɲe] /1/ vt; **s'indigner (de/contre)** to be (ou become) indignant (at)

indiqué, e [ɛ̃dike] adj (date, lieu) given; (adéquat) appropriate; (conseillé) advisable

indiquer [ɛ̃dike] /1/ vt: **~ qch/qn à qn** to point sth/sb out to sb; (faire connaître: médecin, lieu, restaurant) to tell sb of sth/sb; (pendule, aiguille) to show; (étiquette, plan) to show, indicate; (renseigner sur) to point out, tell; (déterminer: date, lieu) to give, state; (dénoter) to indicate, point to; **pourriez-vous m'~ les toilettes/l'heure?** could you direct me to the toilets/tell me the time?

indiscipliné, e [ɛ̃disipline] adj undisciplined

indiscret, -ète [ɛ̃diskʀɛ, -ɛt] adj indiscreet

indiscutable [ɛ̃diskytabl] adj indisputable

indispensable [ɛ̃dispɑ̃sabl] adj indispensable, essential

indisposé, e [ɛ̃dispoze] adj indisposed

indistinct, e [ɛ̃distɛ̃, -ɛkt] adj indistinct; **indistinctement** adv (voir, prononcer) indistinctly; (sans distinction) indiscriminately

individu [ɛ̃dividy] nm individual; **individuel, le** adj (gén) individual; (opinion, livret, contrôle, avantages) personal; **chambre individuelle** single room; **maison individuelle** detached house; **propriété individuelle** personal ou private property

indolore [ɛ̃dɔlɔʀ] *adj* painless
Indonésie [ɛ̃dɔnezi] *nf:* **l'~** Indonesia
indu, e [ɛ̃dy] *adj:* **à une heure ~e** at some ungodly hour
indulgent, e [ɛ̃dylʒɑ̃, -ɑ̃t] *adj* (*parent, regard*) indulgent; (*juge, examinateur*) lenient
industrialisé, e [ɛ̃dystʀijalize] *adj* industrialized
industrie [ɛ̃dystʀi] *nf* industry; **industriel, le** *adj* industrial ▷ *nm* industrialist
inébranlable [inebʀɑ̃labl] *adj* (*masse, colonne*) solid; (*personne, certitude, foi*) unwavering
inédit, e [inedi, -it] *adj* (*correspondance etc*) (hitherto) unpublished; (*spectacle, moyen*) novel, original; (*film*) unreleased
inefficace [inefikas] *adj* (*remède, moyen*) ineffective; (*machine, employé*) inefficient
inégal, e, -aux [inegal, -o] *adj* unequal; (*irrégulier*) uneven; **inégalable** *adj* matchless; **inégalé, e** *adj* (*record*) unequalled; (*beauté*) unrivalled; **inégalité** *nf* inequality
inépuisable [inepɥizabl] *adj* inexhaustible
inerte [inɛʀt] *adj* (*immobile*) lifeless; (*apathique*) passive
inespéré, e [inɛspeʀe] *adj* unhoped-for, unexpected
inestimable [inɛstimabl] *adj* priceless; (*fig: bienfait*) invaluable
inévitable [inevitabl] *adj* unavoidable; (*fatal, habituel*) inevitable
inexact, e [inɛgzakt] *adj* inaccurate
inexcusable [inɛkskyzabl] *adj* unforgivable
inexplicable [inɛksplikabl] *adj* inexplicable
in extremis [inɛkstʀemis] *adv* at the last minute ▷ *adj* last-minute
infaillible [ɛ̃fajibl] *adj* infallible
infarctus [ɛ̃faʀktys] *nm:* **~ (du myocarde)** coronary (thrombosis)

infatigable [ɛ̃fatigabl] *adj* tireless
infect, e [ɛ̃fɛkt] *adj* revolting; (*repas, vin*) revolting, foul; (*personne*) obnoxious; (*temps*) foul
infecter [ɛ̃fɛkte] /1/ *vt* (*atmosphère, eau*) to contaminate; (*Méd*) to infect; **s'infecter** to become infected *ou* septic; **infection** *nf* infection; (*puanteur*) stench
inférieur, e [ɛ̃feʀjœʀ] *adj* lower; (*en qualité, intelligence*) inferior ▷ *nm/f* inferior; **~ à** (*somme, quantité*) less *ou* smaller than; (*moins bon que*) inferior to
infernal, e, -aux [ɛ̃fɛʀnal, -o] *adj* (*insupportable: chaleur, rythme*) infernal; (*: enfant*) horrid; (*méchanceté, complot*) diabolical
infidèle [ɛ̃fidɛl] *adj* unfaithful
infiltrer [ɛ̃filtʀe] /1/: **s'infiltrer** *vi:* **s'~ dans** to penetrate into; (*liquide*) to seep into; (*fig: noyauter*) to infiltrate
infime [ɛ̃fim] *adj* minute, tiny
infini, e [ɛ̃fini] *adj* infinite ▷ *nm* infinity; **à l'~** endlessly; **infiniment** *adv* infinitely; **infinité** *nf:* **une infinité de** an infinite number of
infinitif, -ive [ɛ̃finitif, -iv] *nm* infinitive
infirme [ɛ̃fiʀm] *adj* disabled ▷ *nm/f* disabled person
infirmerie [ɛ̃fiʀməʀi] *nf* sick bay
infirmier, -ière [ɛ̃fiʀmje, -jɛʀ] *nm/f* nurse; **infirmière chef** sister
infirmité [ɛ̃fiʀmite] *nf* disability
inflammable [ɛ̃flamabl] *adj* (in)flammable
inflation [ɛ̃flasjɔ̃] *nf* inflation
influençable [ɛ̃flɥɑ̃sabl] *adj* easily influenced
influence [ɛ̃flɥɑ̃s] *nf* influence; **influencer** /3/ *vt* to influence; **influent, e** *adj* influential
informaticien, ne [ɛ̃fɔʀmatisjɛ̃, -ɛn] *nm/f* computer scientist
information [ɛ̃fɔʀmasjɔ̃] *nf* (*renseignement*) piece of information; (*Presse, TV: nouvelle*) item of

news; (*diffusion de renseignements*, *Inform*) information; (*Jur*) inquiry, investigation; **informations** *nfpl* (*TV*) news *sg*

informatique [ɛ̃fɔʀmatik] *nf* (*technique*) data processing; (*science*) computer science ▷ *adj* computer *cpd*; **informatiser** /1/ *vt* to computerize

informer [ɛ̃fɔʀme] /1/ *vt*: ~ **qn (de)** to inform sb (of); **s'informer (sur)** to inform o.s. (about); **s'~ (de qch/ si)** to inquire *ou* find out (about sth/ whether *ou* if)

infos [ɛ̃fo] *nfpl* (= *informations*) news

infraction [ɛ̃fʀaksjɔ̃] *nf* offence; ~ **à** violation *ou* breach of; **être en ~** to be in breach of the law

infranchissable [ɛ̃fʀɑ̃ʃisabl] *adj* impassable; (*fig*) insuperable

infrarouge [ɛ̃fʀaʀuʒ] *adj* infrared

infrastructure [ɛ̃fʀastʀyktyʀ] *nf* (*Aviat, Mil*) ground installations *pl*; (*Écon: touristique etc*) facilities *pl*

infuser [ɛ̃fyze] /1/ *vt* (*thé*) to brew; (*tisane*) to infuse ▷ *vi* to brew; to infuse; **infusion** *nf* (*tisane*) herb tea

ingénier [ɛ̃ʒenje] /7/: **s'ingénier** *vi*: **s'~ à faire** to strive to do

ingénierie [ɛ̃ʒeniʀi] *nf* engineering

ingénieur [ɛ̃ʒenjœʀ] *nm* engineer; ~ **du son** sound engineer

ingénieux, -euse [ɛ̃ʒenjø, -øz] *adj* ingenious, clever

ingrat, e [ɛ̃gʀa, -at] *adj* (*personne*) ungrateful; (*travail, sujet*) thankless; (*visage*) unprepossessing

ingrédient [ɛ̃gʀedjɑ̃] *nm* ingredient

inhabité, e [inabite] *adj* uninhabited

inhabituel, le [inabitɥɛl] *adj* unusual

inhibition [inibisjɔ̃] *nf* inhibition

inhumain, e [inymɛ̃, -ɛn] *adj* inhuman

inimaginable [inimaʒinabl] *adj* unimaginable

ininterrompu, e [inɛ̃teʀɔ̃py] *adj* (*file, série*) unbroken; (*flot, vacarme*)

uninterrupted, non-stop; (*effort*) unremitting, continuous; (*suite, ligne*) unbroken

initial, e, -aux [inisjal, -o] *adj* initial; **initiales** *nfpl* initials

initiation [inisjasjɔ̃] *nf*: ~ **à** introduction to

initiative [inisjativ] *nf* initiative

initier [inisje] /7/ *vt*: ~ **qn à** to initiate sb into; (*faire découvrir: art, jeu*) to introduce sb to

injecter [ɛ̃ʒɛkte] /1/ *vt* to inject; **injection** *nf* injection; **à injection** (*Auto*) fuel injection *cpd*

injure [ɛ̃ʒyʀ] *nf* insult, abuse *no pl*; **injurier** /7/ *vt* to insult, abuse; **injurieux, -euse** *adj* abusive, insulting

injuste [ɛ̃ʒyst] *adj* unjust, unfair; **injustice** [ɛ̃ʒystis] *nf* injustice

inlassable [ɛ̃lɑsabl] *adj* tireless

inné, e [ine] *adj* innate, inborn

innocent, e [inɔsɑ̃, -ɑ̃t] *adj* innocent; **innocenter** /1/ *vt* to clear, prove innocent

innombrable [inɔ̃bʀabl] *adj* innumerable

innover [inɔve] /1/ *vi*: ~ **en matière d'art** to break new ground in the field of art

inoccupé, e [inɔkype] *adj* unoccupied

inodore [inɔdɔʀ] *adj* (*gaz*) odourless; (*fleur*) scentless

inoffensif, -ive [inɔfɑ̃sif, -iv] *adj* harmless, innocuous

inondation [inɔ̃dasjɔ̃] *nf* flood

inonder [inɔ̃de] /1/ *vt* to flood; ~ **de** to flood *ou* swamp with

inopportun, e [inɔpɔʀtœ̃, -yn] *adj* ill-timed, untimely

inoubliable [inublijabl] *adj* unforgettable

inouï, e [inwi] *adj* unheard-of, extraordinary

inox [inɔks] *nm* stainless (steel)

inquiet, -ète [ɛ̃kjɛ, -ɛt] *adj* anxious; **inquiétant, e** *adj* worrying, disturbing; **inquiéter** /6/ vt to worry; **s'inquiéter** to worry; **s'inquiéter de** to worry about; (s'enquérir de) to inquire about; **inquiétude** nf anxiety

insaisissable [ɛ̃sezizabl] adj (fugitif, ennemi) elusive; (différence, nuance) imperceptible

insalubre [ɛ̃salybʀ] adj insalubrious

insatisfait, e [ɛ̃satisfɛ, -ɛt] adj (non comblé) unsatisfied; (mécontent) dissatisfied

inscription [ɛ̃skʀipsjɔ̃] nf inscription; (à une institution) enrolment

inscrire [ɛ̃skʀiʀ] /39/ vt (marquer: sur son calepin etc) to note ou write down; (: sur un mur, une affiche etc) to write; (: dans la pierre, le métal) to inscribe; (mettre: sur une liste, un budget etc) to put down; **~ qn à** (club, école etc) to enrol sb at; **s'inscrire** (pour une excursion etc) to put one's name down; **s'~ (à)** (club, parti) to join; (université) to register ou enrol (at); (examen, concours) to register ou enter (for)

insecte [ɛ̃sɛkt] nm insect; **insecticide** nm insecticide

insensé, e [ɛ̃sɑ̃se] adj mad

insensible [ɛ̃sɑ̃sibl] adj (nerf, membre) numb; (dur, indifférent) insensitive

inséparable [ɛ̃sepaʀabl] adj: **~ (de)** inseparable (from) ▷ nmpl: **~s** (oiseaux) lovebirds

insigne [ɛ̃siɲ] nm (d'un parti, club) badge ▷ adj distinguished; **insignes** nmpl (d'une fonction) insignia pl

insignifiant, e [ɛ̃siɲifjɑ̃, -ɑ̃t] adj insignificant; trivial

insinuer [ɛ̃sinɥe] /1/ vt to insinuate; **s'insinuer dans** (fig) to worm one's way into

insipide [ɛ̃sipid] adj insipid

insister [ɛ̃siste] /1/ vi to insist; (s'obstiner) to keep on; **~ sur** (détail, note) to stress

insolation [ɛ̃sɔlasjɔ̃] nf (Méd) sunstroke no pl

insolent, e [ɛ̃sɔlɑ̃, -ɑ̃t] adj insolent

insolite [ɛ̃sɔlit] adj strange, unusual

insomnie [ɛ̃sɔmni] nf insomnia no pl; **avoir des ~s** to sleep badly

insouciant, e [ɛ̃susjɑ̃, -ɑ̃t] adj carefree; **~ du danger** heedless of (the) danger

insoupçonnable [ɛ̃supsɔnabl] adj unsuspected; (personne) above suspicion

insoupçonné, e [ɛ̃supsɔne] adj unsuspected

insoutenable [ɛ̃sutnabl] adj (argument) untenable; (chaleur) unbearable

inspecter [ɛ̃spɛkte] /1/ vt to inspect; **inspecteur, -trice** nm/f inspector; **inspecteur d'Académie** (regional) director of education; **inspecteur des finances** ≈ tax inspector (BRIT), ≈ Internal Revenue Service agent (US); **inspecteur (de police)** (police) inspector; **inspection** nf inspection

inspirer [ɛ̃spiʀe] /1/ vt (gén) to inspire ▷ vi (aspirer) to breathe in; **s'inspirer de** to be inspired by

instable [ɛ̃stabl] adj (meuble, équilibre) unsteady; (population, temps) unsettled; (paix, régime, caractère) unstable

installation [ɛ̃stalasjɔ̃] nf (mise en place) installation; **installations** nfpl installations; (industrielles) plant sg; (de sport, dans un camping) facilities; **l'~ électrique** wiring

installer [ɛ̃stale] /1/ vt to put; (meuble) to put in; (rideau, étagère, tente) to put up; (appartement) to fit out; **s'installer** (s'établir: artisan, dentiste etc) to set o.s. up; (emménager) to settle in; (sur un siège, à un emplacement) to settle (down); (fig: maladie, grève) to take a firm hold ou grip; **s'~ à l'hôtel/chez qn** to move into a hotel/in with sb

instance [ɛ̃stɑ̃s] nf (Admin: autorité) authority; **affaire en ~** matter pending; **être en ~ de divorce** to be awaiting a divorce

instant [ɛ̃stɑ̃] nm moment, instant;
dans un ~ in a moment; **à l'~** this
instant; **je l'ai vu à l'~** I've just
this minute seen him, I saw him
a moment ago; **pour l'~** for the
moment, for the time being

instantané, e [ɛ̃stɑ̃tane] adj
(lait, café) instant; (explosion, mort)
instantaneous ▷ nm snapshot

instar [ɛ̃staʀ]: **à l'~ de** prép following
the example of, like

instaurer [ɛ̃stɔʀe] /1/ vt to institute;
(couvre-feu) to impose; **s'instaurer**
vi (collaboration, paix etc) to be
established; (doute) to set in

instinct [ɛ̃stɛ̃] nm instinct;
instinctivement adv instinctively

instituer [ɛ̃stitɥe] /1/ vt to establish

institut [ɛ̃stity] nm institute;
~ de beauté beauty salon; **I~
universitaire de technologie (IUT)**
≈ Institute of technology

instituteur, -trice [ɛ̃stitytœʀ,
-tʀis] nm/f (primary (BRIT) ou grade
(US) school) teacher

institution [ɛ̃stitysjɔ̃] nf institution;
(collège) private school; **institutions**
nfpl (structures politiques et sociales)
institutions

instructif, -ive [ɛ̃stʀyktif, -iv] adj
instructive

instruction [ɛ̃stʀyksjɔ̃] nf
(enseignement, savoir) education;
(Jur) (preliminary) investigation and
hearing; **instructions** nfpl (mode
d'emploi) instructions; **~ civique**
civics sg

instruire [ɛ̃stʀɥiʀ] /38/ vt (élèves)
to teach; (recrues) to train; (Jur:
affaire) to conduct the investigation
for; **s'instruire** to educate o.s.;
instruit, e adj educated

instrument [ɛ̃stʀymɑ̃] nm
instrument; **~ à cordes/vent**
stringed/wind instrument; **~ de
mesure** measuring instrument; **~ de
musique** musical instrument; **~ de
travail** (working) tool

insu [ɛ̃sy] nm: **à l'~ de qn** without
sb knowing

insuffisant, e [ɛ̃syfizɑ̃, -ɑ̃t] adj (en
quantité) insufficient; (en qualité)
inadequate; (sur une copie) poor

insulaire [ɛ̃sylɛʀ] adj island cpd;
(attitude) insular

insuline [ɛ̃sylin] nf insulin

insulte [ɛ̃sylt] nf insult; **insulter** /1/
vt to insult

insupportable [ɛ̃sypɔʀtabl] adj
unbearable

insurmontable [ɛ̃syʀmɔ̃tabl] adj
(difficulté) insuperable; (aversion)
unconquerable

intact, e [ɛ̃takt] adj intact

intarissable [ɛ̃taʀisabl] adj
inexhaustible

intégral, e, -aux [ɛ̃tegʀal, -o] adj
complete; **texte ~** unabridged
version; **bronzage ~** all-over suntan;
intégralement adv in full; **intégralité**
nf whole (ou full) amount; **dans son
intégralité** in its entirety; **intégrant,
e** adj: **faire partie intégrante de** to
be an integral part of

intègre [ɛ̃tegʀ] adj upright

intégrer [ɛ̃tegʀe] /6/: **s'intégrer** vr:
s'~ à ou **dans** to become integrated
into; **bien s'~** to fit in

intégrisme [ɛ̃tegʀism] nm
fundamentalism

intellectuel, le [ɛ̃telɛktɥɛl] adj,
nm/f intellectual; (péj) highbrow

intelligence [ɛ̃teliʒɑ̃s] nf
intelligence; (compréhension): **l'~ de**
the understanding of; (complicité):
regard d'~ glance of complicity;
(accord): **vivre en bonne ~ avec qn**
to be on good terms with sb

intelligent, e [ɛ̃teliʒɑ̃, -ɑ̃t] adj
intelligent

intelligible [ɛ̃teliʒibl] adj intelligible

intempéries [ɛ̃tɑ̃peʀi] nfpl bad
weather sg

intenable [ɛ̃tnabl] adj unbearable

intendant, e [ɛ̃tɑ̃dɑ̃, -ɑ̃t] nm/f (Mil)
quartermaster; (Scol) bursar

intense [ɛ̃tɑ̃s] *adj* intense; **intensif, -ive** *adj* intensive; **cours intensif** crash course

intenter [ɛ̃tɑ̃te] /1/ *vt*: **~ un procès contre** *ou* **à qn** to start proceedings against sb

intention [ɛ̃tɑ̃sjɔ̃] *nf* intention; (*Jur*) intent; **avoir l'~ de faire** to intend to do; **à l'~ de** for; (*renseignement*) for the benefit of; (*film, ouvrage*) aimed at; **à cette ~** with this aim in view; **intentionné, e** *adj*: **bien intentionné** well-meaning *ou* -intentioned; **mal intentionné** ill-intentioned

interactif, -ive [ɛ̃teraktif, -iv] *adj* (*aussi Inform*) interactive

intercepter [ɛ̃tersɛpte] /1/ *vt* to intercept; (*lumière, chaleur*) to cut off

interchangeable [ɛ̃terʃɑ̃ʒabl] *adj* interchangeable

interdiction [ɛ̃terdiksjɔ̃] *nf* ban; **~ de fumer** no smoking

interdire [ɛ̃terdir] /37/ *vt* to forbid; (*Admin*) to ban, prohibit; (*: journal, livre*) to ban; **~ à qn de faire** to forbid sb to do; (*empêchement*) to prevent *ou* preclude sb from doing

interdit, e [ɛ̃terdi, -it] *pp de* **interdire** ▷ *adj* (*stupéfait*) taken aback; **film ~ aux moins de 18/12 ans** ≈ 18-/12A-rated film; **stationnement ~** no parking

intéressant, e [ɛ̃teresɑ̃, -ɑ̃t] *adj* interesting; (*avantageux*) attractive

intéressé, e [ɛ̃terese] *adj* (*parties*) involved, concerned; (*amitié, motifs*) self-interested

intéresser [ɛ̃terese] /1/ *vt* (*captiver*) to interest; (*toucher*) to be of interest *ou* concern to; (*Admin: concerner*) to affect, concern; **s'intéresser à** *vi* to take an interest in

intérêt [ɛ̃terɛ] *nm* interest; (*égoïsme*) self-interest; **tu as ~ à accepter** it's in your interest to accept; **tu as ~ à te dépêcher** you'd better hurry

intérieur, e [ɛ̃terjœr] *adj* (*mur, escalier, poche*) inside; (*commerce, politique*) domestic; (*cour, calme, vie*) inner; (*navigation*) inland ▷ *nm* (*d'une maison, d'un récipient etc*) inside; (*d'un pays, aussi décor, mobilier*) interior; **l'I~** (the Department of) the Interior, ≈ the Home Office (*BRIT*); **à l'~ (de)** inside; **intérieurement** *adv* inwardly

intérim [ɛ̃terim] *nm* interim period; **assurer l'~ (de)** to deputize (for); **président par ~** interim president; **faire de l'~** to temp

intérimaire [ɛ̃terimer] *adj* (*directeur, ministre*) acting; (*secrétaire, personnel*) temporary ▷ *nm/f* (*secrétaire etc*) temporary, temp (*BRIT*)

interlocuteur, -trice [ɛ̃terlɔkytœr, -tris] *nm/f* speaker; **son ~** the person he *ou* she was speaking to

intermédiaire [ɛ̃termedjer] *adj* intermediate; (*solution*) temporary ▷ *nm/f* intermediary; (*Comm*) middleman; **sans ~** directly; **par l'~ de** through

interminable [ɛ̃terminabl] *adj* never-ending

intermittence [ɛ̃termitɑ̃s] *nf*: **par ~** intermittently, sporadically

internat [ɛ̃terna] *nm* boarding school

international, e, -aux [ɛ̃ternasjɔnal, -o] *adj, nm/f* international

internaute [ɛ̃ternot] *nm/f* Internet user

interne [ɛ̃tern] *adj* internal ▷ *nm/f* (*Scol*) boarder; (*Méd*) houseman

Internet [ɛ̃ternet] *nm*: **l'~** the Internet

interpeller [ɛ̃terpele] /1/ *vt* (*appeler*) to call out to; (*apostropher*) to shout at; (*Police*) to take in for questioning; (*Pol*) to question; (*concerner*) to concern

interphone [ɛ̃terfɔn] *nm* intercom; (*d'immeuble*) entry phone

interposer [ɛ̃tɛʀpoze] /1/ vt; **s'interposer** to intervene; **par personnes interposées** through a third party

interprète [ɛ̃tɛʀpʀɛt] nm/f interpreter; (porte-parole) spokesman

interpréter [ɛ̃tɛʀpʀete] /6/ vt to interpret; (jouer) to play; (chanter) to sing

interrogatif, -ive [ɛ̃teʀɔgatif, -iv] adj (Ling) interrogative

interrogation [ɛ̃teʀɔgasjɔ̃] nf question; (Scol) (written ou oral) test

interrogatoire [ɛ̃teʀɔgatwaʀ] nm (Police) questioning no pl; (Jur, aussi fig) cross-examination

interroger [ɛ̃teʀɔʒe] /3/ vt to question; (Inform) to search; (Scol) to test

interrompre [ɛ̃teʀɔ̃pʀ] /41/ vt (gén) to interrupt; (négociations) to break off; (match) to stop; **s'interrompre** to break off; **interrupteur** nm switch; **interruption** nf interruption; (pause) break; **sans interruption** without a break; **interruption volontaire de grossesse** abortion

intersection [ɛ̃tɛʀsɛksjɔ̃] nf intersection

intervalle [ɛ̃tɛʀval] nm (espace) space; (de temps) interval; **dans l'~** in the meantime; **à deux jours d'~** two days apart

intervenir [ɛ̃tɛʀvəniʀ] /22/ vi (gén) to intervene; **~ auprès de/en faveur de qn** to intervene with/on behalf of sb; **intervention** nf intervention; (discours) speech; **intervention (chirurgicale)** operation

interview [ɛ̃tɛʀvju] nf interview

intestin, e [ɛ̃tɛstɛ̃, -in] adj internal ▷ nm intestine

intime [ɛ̃tim] adj intimate; (vie, journal) private; (convictions) inmost; (dîner, cérémonie) quiet ▷ nm/f close friend; **un journal ~** a diary

intimider [ɛ̃timide] /1/ vt to intimidate

intimité [ɛ̃timite] nf: **dans l'~** in private; (sans formalités) with only a few friends, quietly

intolérable [ɛ̃tɔleʀabl] adj intolerable

intox [ɛ̃tɔks] (fam) nf brainwashing

intoxication [ɛ̃tɔksikasjɔ̃] nf: **~ alimentaire** food poisoning

intoxiquer [ɛ̃tɔksike] /1/ vt to poison; (fig) to brainwash

intraitable [ɛ̃tʀɛtabl] adj inflexible, uncompromising

intransigeant, e [ɛ̃tʀɑ̃ziʒɑ̃, -ɑ̃t] adj intransigent

intrépide [ɛ̃tʀepid] adj dauntless

intrigue [ɛ̃tʀig] nf (scénario) plot; **intriguer** /1/ vt to puzzle, intrigue

introduction [ɛ̃tʀɔdyksjɔ̃] nf introduction

introduire [ɛ̃tʀɔdɥiʀ] /38/ vt to introduce; (visiteur) to show in; (aiguille, clef): **~ qch dans** to insert ou introduce sth into; **s'introduire** vi (techniques, usages) to be introduced; **s'~ dans** to gain entry into; (dans un groupe) to get o.s. accepted into

introuvable [ɛ̃tʀuvabl] adj which cannot be found; (Comm) unobtainable

intrus, e [ɛ̃tʀy, -yz] nm/f intruder

intuition [ɛ̃tɥisjɔ̃] nf intuition

inusable [inyzabl] adj hard-wearing

inutile [inytil] adj useless; (superflu) unnecessary; **inutilement** adv needlessly; **inutilisable** adj unusable

invalide [ɛ̃valid] adj disabled ▷ nm/f: **~ de guerre** disabled ex-serviceman

invariable [ɛ̃vaʀjabl] adj invariable

invasion [ɛ̃vazjɔ̃] nf invasion

inventaire [ɛ̃vɑ̃tɛʀ] nm inventory; (Comm: liste) stocklist; (: opération) stocktaking no pl

inventer [ɛ̃vɑ̃te] /1/ vt to invent; (subterfuge) to devise, invent; (histoire, excuse) to make up, invent; **inventeur, -trice** nm/f inventor; **inventif, -ive** adj inventive; **invention** nf invention

inverse [ɛ̃vɛʀs] *adj* opposite ▷ *nm* inverse; **l'~** the opposite; **dans l'ordre ~** in the reverse order; **dans le sens ~ des aiguilles d'une montre** anti-clockwise; **en sens ~** in (*ou* from) the opposite direction; **inversement** *adv* conversely; **inverser** /1/ *vt* to reverse, invert; (*Élec*) to reverse

investir [ɛ̃vɛstiʀ] /2/ *vt* to invest; **~ qn de** (*d'une fonction, d'un pouvoir*) to vest *ou* invest sb with; **s'investir** *vi* (*Psych*) to involve o.s.; **s'~ dans** to put a lot into; **investissement** *nm* investment

invisible [ɛ̃vizibl] *adj* invisible

invitation [ɛ̃vitasjɔ̃] *nf* invitation

invité, e [ɛ̃vite] *nm/f* guest

inviter [ɛ̃vite] /1/ *vt* to invite; **~ qn à faire qch** to invite sb to do sth

invivable [ɛ̃vivabl] *adj* unbearable

involontaire [ɛ̃vɔlɔ̃tɛʀ] *adj* (*mouvement*) involuntary; (*insulte*) unintentional; (*complice*) unwitting

invoquer [ɛ̃vɔke] /1/ *vt* (*Dieu, muse*) to call upon, invoke; (*prétexte*) to put forward (as an excuse); (*loi, texte*) to refer to

invraisemblable [ɛ̃vʀɛsɑ̃blabl] *adj* (*fait, nouvelle*) unlikely, improbable; (*bizarre*) incredible

iode [jɔd] *nm* iodine

irai *etc* [iʀe] *vb voir* **aller**

Irak [iʀak] *nm*: **l'~** Iraq *ou* Irak; **irakien, ne** *adj* Iraqi ▷ *nm/f*: **Irakien, ne** Iraqi

Iran [iʀɑ̃] *nm*: **l'~** Iran; **iranien, ne** *adj* Iranian ▷ *nm/f*: **Iranien, ne** Iranian

irions *etc* [iʀjɔ̃] *vb voir* **aller**

iris [iʀis] *nm* iris

irlandais, e [iʀlɑ̃dɛ, -ɛz] *adj* Irish ▷ *nm/f*: **I~, e** Irishman/woman

Irlande [iʀlɑ̃d] *nf*: **l'~** Ireland; **la République d'~** the Irish Republic; **~ du Nord** Northern Ireland; **la mer d'~** the Irish Sea

ironie [iʀɔni] *nf* irony; **ironique** *adj* ironical; **ironiser** /1/ *vi* to be ironical

irons *etc* [iʀɔ̃] *vb voir* **aller**

irradier [iʀadje] /7/ *vt* to irradiate

irraisonné, e [iʀɛzɔne] *adj* irrational

irrationnel, le [iʀasjɔnɛl] *adj* irrational

irréalisable [iʀealizabl] *adj* unrealizable; (*projet*) impracticable

irrécupérable [iʀekypeʀabl] *adj* beyond repair; (*personne*) beyond redemption *ou* recall

irréel, le [iʀeel] *adj* unreal

irréfléchi, e [iʀefleʃi] *adj* thoughtless

irrégularité [iʀegylaʀite] *nf* irregularity; (*de travail, d'effort, de qualité*) unevenness *no pl*

irrégulier, -ière [iʀegylje, -jɛʀ] *adj* irregular; (*travail, effort, qualité*) uneven; (*élève, athlète*) erratic

irrémédiable [iʀemedjabl] *adj* irreparable

irremplaçable [iʀɑ̃plasabl] *adj* irreplaceable

irréparable [iʀepaʀabl] *adj* beyond repair; (*fig*) irreparable

irréprochable [iʀepʀɔʃabl] *adj* irreproachable, beyond reproach; (*tenue, toilette*) impeccable

irrésistible [iʀezistibl] *adj* irresistible; (*preuve, logique*) compelling; (*amusant*) hilarious

irrésolu, e [iʀezɔly] *adj* irresolute

irrespectueux, -euse [iʀɛspɛktɥø, -øz] *adj* disrespectful

irresponsable [iʀɛspɔ̃sabl] *adj* irresponsible

irriguer [iʀige] /1/ *vt* to irrigate

irritable [iʀitabl] *adj* irritable

irriter [iʀite] /1/ *vt* to irritate

irruption [iʀypsjɔ̃] *nf*: **faire ~ chez qn** to burst in on sb

Islam [islam] *nm*: **l'~** Islam; **islamique** *adj* Islamic; **islamophobie** *nf* Islamophobia

Islande [islɑ̃d] *nf*: **l'~** Iceland

isolant, e [izɔlɑ̃, -ɑ̃t] *adj* insulating; (*insonorisant*) soundproofing

isolation [izɔlasjɔ̃] *nf* insulation; **~ acoustique** soundproofing

isolé, e [izɔle] *adj* isolated; *(contre le froid)* insulated

isoler [izɔle] /1/ *vt* to isolate; *(prisonnier)* to put in solitary confinement; *(ville)* to cut off, isolate; *(contre le froid)* to insulate; **s'isoler** *vi* to isolate o.s.

Israël [israɛl] *nm*: **l'~** Israel; **israélien, ne** *adj* Israeli ▷ *nm/f*: **Israélien, ne** Israeli; **israélite** *adj* Jewish ▷ *nm/f*: **Israélite** Jew/Jewess

issu, e [isy] *adj*: **~ de** *(né de)* descended from; *(résultant de)* stemming from ▷ *nf (ouverture, sortie)* exit; *(solution)* way out, solution; *(dénouement)* outcome; **à l'~e de** at the conclusion *ou* close of; **voie sans ~e** dead end; **~e de secours** emergency exit

Italie [itali] *nf*: **l'~** Italy; **italien, ne** *adj* Italian ▷ *nm (Ling)* Italian ▷ *nm/f*: **Italien, ne** Italian

italique [italik] *nm*: **en ~(s)** in italics

itinéraire [itineʀɛʀ] *nm* itinerary, route; **~ bis** alternative route

IUT *sigle m* = **Institut universitaire de technologie**

IVG *sigle f (= interruption volontaire de grossesse)* abortion

ivoire [ivwaʀ] *nm* ivory

ivre [ivʀ] *adj* drunk; **~ de** *(colère)* wild with; **ivrogne** *nm/f* drunkard

j' [ʒ] *pron voir* **je**

jacinthe [ʒasɛ̃t] *nf* hyacinth

jadis [ʒadis] *adv* formerly

jaillir [ʒajiʀ] /2/ *vi (liquide)* to spurt out; *(cris, réponses)* to burst out

jais [ʒɛ] *nm* jet; **(d'un noir) de ~** jet-black

jalousie [ʒaluzi] *nf* jealousy; *(store)* (venetian) blind

jaloux, -ouse [ʒalu, -uz] *adj* jealous; **être ~ de qn/qch** to be jealous of sb/sth

jamaïquain, e [ʒamaikɛ̃, -ɛn] *adj* Jamaican ▷ *nm/f*: **J~, e** Jamaican

Jamaïque [ʒamaik] *nf*: **la ~** Jamaica

jamais [ʒamɛ] *adv* never; *(sans négation)* ever; **ne ... ~** never; **si ~ ...** if ever ...; **je ne suis ~ allé en Espagne** I've never been to Spain

jambe [ʒɑ̃b] *nf* leg

jambon [ʒɑ̃bɔ̃] *nm* ham

jante [ʒɑ̃t] *nf (wheel)* rim

janvier [ʒɑ̃vje] *nm* January

Japon [ʒapɔ̃] nm: **le ~** Japan; **japonais, e** adj Japanese ▷ nm (Ling) Japanese ▷ nm/f: **Japonais, e** Japanese

jardin [ʒaʀdɛ̃] nm garden; **~ d'enfants** nursery school; **jardinage** nm gardening /1/ vi to garden; **jardinier, -ière** nm/f gardener ▷ nf (de fenêtre) window box; **jardinière (de légumes)** (Culin) mixed vegetables

jargon [ʒaʀgɔ̃] nm (charabia) gibberish; (publicitaire, scientifique etc) jargon

jarret [ʒaʀɛ] nm back of knee; (Culin) knuckle, shin

jauge [ʒoʒ] nf (instrument) gauge; **~ (de niveau) d'huile** (Auto) dipstick

jaune [ʒon] adj, nm yellow ▷ adv (fam): **rire ~** to laugh on the other side of one's face; **~ d'œuf** (egg) yolk; **jaunir** /2/ vi, vt to turn yellow; **jaunisse** nf jaundice

Javel [ʒavɛl] nf voir **eau**

javelot [ʒavlo] nm javelin

J.-C. sigle m = **Jésus-Christ**

je, j' [ʒə, ʒ] pron I

jean [dʒin] nm jeans pl

Jésus-Christ [ʒezykʀi(st)] n Jesus Christ; **600 avant/après ~** 600 B.C./A.D.

jet [ʒɛ] nm (lancer: action) throwing no pl; (: résultat) throw; (jaillissement: d'eaux) jet; (: de sang) spurt; **~ d'eau** spray

jetable [ʒətabl] adj disposable

jetée [ʒəte] nf jetty; (grande) pier

jeter [ʒəte] /4/ vt (gén) to throw; (se défaire de) to throw away ou out; **~ qch à qn** to throw sth to sb; (de façon agressive) to throw sth at sb; **~ un coup d'œil (à)** to take a look (at); **~ un sort à qn** to cast a spell on sb; **se ~ sur** to throw o.s. onto; **se ~ dans** (fleuve) to flow into

jeton [ʒətɔ̃] nm (au jeu) counter

jette etc [ʒɛt] vb voir **jeter**

jeu, x [ʒø] nm (divertissement, Tech: d'une pièce) play; (Tennis: partie, Football etc: façon de jouer) game; (Théât etc) acting; (série d'objets, jouet) set; (Cartes) hand; (au casino): **le ~** gambling; **en ~** at stake; **remettre en ~** to throw in; **entrer/mettre en ~** to come/bring into play; **~ de cartes** pack of cards; **~ d'échecs** chess set; **~ de hasard** game of chance; **~ de mots** pun; **~ de société** board game; **~ télévisé** television quiz; **~ vidéo** video game

jeudi [ʒødi] nm Thursday

jeun [ʒœ̃]: **à ~** adv on an empty stomach; **être à ~** to have eaten nothing; **rester à ~** not to eat anything

jeune [ʒœn] adj young; **les ~s** young people; **~ fille** girl; **~ homme** young man; **~s gens** young people

jeûne [ʒøn] nm fast

jeunesse [ʒœnɛs] nf youth; (aspect) youthfulness

joaillier, -ière [ʒoaje, -jɛʀ] nm/f jeweller

jogging [dʒogiŋ] nm jogging; (survêtement) tracksuit; **faire du ~** to go jogging

joie [ʒwa] nf joy

joindre [ʒwɛ̃dʀ] /49/ vt to join; (contacter) to contact, get in touch with; **~ qch à** (à une lettre) to enclose sth with; **~ un fichier à un mail** (Inform) to attach a file to an email; **se ~ à qn** to join sb; **se ~ à qch** to join in sth

joint, e [ʒwɛ̃, -ɛ̃t] adj: **~ (à)** (lettre, paquet) attached (to), enclosed (with) ▷ nm joint; (ligne) join; **pièce ~e** (de lettre) enclosure; (de mail) attachment; **~ de culasse** cylinder head gasket

joli, e [ʒoli] adj pretty, attractive; **une ~e somme/situation** a nice little sum/situation; **c'est du ~!** (ironique) that's very nice!; **tout ça, c'est bien ~ mais ...** that's all very well but ...

jonc [ʒɔ̃] nm (bul) rush

jonction [ʒɔ̃ksjɔ̃] nf junction

jongleur, -euse [ʒɔ̃glœʀ, -øz] *nm/f* juggler

jonquille [ʒɔ̃kij] *nf* daffodil

Jordanie [ʒɔʀdani] *nf*: **la ~** Jordan

joue [ʒu] *nf* cheek

jouer [ʒwe] /1/ *vt* to play; (*somme d'argent, réputation*) to stake, wager; (*simuler: sentiment*) to affect, feign ▷ *vi* to play; (*Théât, Ciné*) to act; (*au casino*) to gamble; (*bois, porte: se voiler*) to warp; (*clef, pièce: avoir du jeu*) to be loose; **~ sur** (*miser*) to gamble on; **~ de** (*Mus*) to play; **~ à** (*jeu, sport, roulette*) to play; **~ un tour à qn** to play a trick on sb; **~ la comédie** to put on an act; **~ serré** to play a close game; **à toi/nous de ~** it's your/our go *ou* turn; **bien joué!** well done!; **on joue Hamlet au théâtre X** Hamlet is on at the X theatre

jouet [ʒwɛ] *nm* toy; **être le ~ de** (*illusion etc*) to be the victim of

joueur, -euse [ʒwœʀ, -øz] *nm/f* player; **être beau/mauvais ~** to be a good/bad loser

jouir [ʒwiʀ] /2/ *vi* (*sexe: fam*) to come ▷ *vt*: **~ de** to enjoy

jour [ʒuʀ] *nm* day; (*opposé à la nuit*) day, daytime; (*clarté*) daylight; (*fig: aspect, ouverture*) opening; **sous un ~ favorable/nouveau** in a favourable/ new light; **de ~** (*crème, service*) day *cpd*; **travailler de ~** to work during the day; **voyager de ~** to travel by day; **au ~ le ~** from day to day; **de nos ~s** these days; **du ~ au lendemain** overnight; **il fait ~** it's daylight; **au grand ~** (*fig*) in the open; **mettre au ~** to disclose; **mettre à ~** to bring up to date; **donner le ~ à** to give birth to; **voir le ~** to be born; **~ férié** public holiday; **le ~ J** D-day; **~ ouvrable** working day

journal, -aux [ʒuʀnal, -o] *nm* (news)paper; (*personnel*) journal; (*intime*) diary; **~ de bord** log; **~ parlé/ télévisé** radio/television news *sg*

journalier, -ière [ʒuʀnalje, -jɛʀ] *adj* daily; (*banal*) everyday

journalisme [ʒuʀnalism] *nm* journalism; **journaliste** *nm/f* journalist

journée [ʒuʀne] *nf* day; **la ~ continue** the 9 to 5 working day (*with short lunch break*)

joyau, x [ʒwajo] *nm* gem, jewel

joyeux, -euse [ʒwajø, -øz] *adj* joyful, merry; **~ Noël!** Merry *ou* Happy Christmas!; **~ anniversaire!** many happy returns!

jubiler [ʒybile] /1/ *vi* to be jubilant, exult

judas [ʒyda] *nm* (*trou*) spy-hole

judiciaire [ʒydisjɛʀ] *adj* judicial

judicieux, -euse [ʒydisjø, -øz] *adj* judicious

judo [ʒydo] *nm* judo

juge [ʒyʒ] *nm* judge; **~ d'instruction** examining (BRIT) *ou* committing (US) magistrate; **~ de paix** justice of the peace

jugé [ʒyʒe]: **au ~** *adv* by guesswork

jugement [ʒyʒmɑ̃] *nm* judgment; (*Jur: au pénal*) sentence; (: *au civil*) decision

juger [ʒyʒe] /3/ *vt* to judge; (*estimer*) to consider; **~ qn/qch satisfaisant** to consider sb/sth (to be) satisfactory; **~ bon de faire** to consider it a good idea to do

juif, -ive [ʒɥif, -iv] *adj* Jewish ▷ *nm/f*: **J~, -ive** Jew/Jewess *ou* Jewish woman

juillet [ʒɥijɛ] *nm* July

LE 14 JUILLET

Le 14 juillet is a national holiday in France and commemorates the storming of the Bastille during the French Revolution. Throughout the country there are celebrations, which feature parades, music, dancing and firework displays. In Paris a military parade along the Champs-Élysées is attended by the President.

juin [ʒɥɛ̃] nm June

jumeau, -elle, x [ʒymo, -ɛl] adj, nm/f twin

jumeler [ʒymle] /4/ vt to twin

jumelle [ʒymɛl] adj f, nf voir **jumeau**

jument [ʒymɑ̃] nf mare

jungle [ʒɔ̃gl] nf jungle

jupe [ʒyp] nf skirt

jupon [ʒypɔ̃] nm waist slip ou petticoat

juré, e [ʒyʀe] nm/f juror ▷ adj: **ennemi ~** sworn ou avowed enemy

jurer [ʒyʀe] /1/ vt (obéissance etc) to swear, vow ▷ vi (dire des jurons) to swear, curse; (dissoner): **~ (avec)** to clash (with); **~ de faire/que** to swear ou vow to do/that; **~ de qch** (s'en porter garant) to swear to sth

juridique [ʒyʀidik] adj legal

juron [ʒyʀɔ̃] nm curse, swearword

jury [ʒyʀi] nm jury; (Art, Sport) panel of judges; (Scol) board (of examiners), jury

jus [ʒy] nm juice; (de viande) gravy, (meat) juice; **~ de fruits** fruit juice

jusque [ʒysk]: **jusqu'à** prép (endroit) as far as, (up) to; (moment) until, till; (limite) up to; **~ sur/dans** up to; (y compris) even on/in; **jusqu'à ce que** until; **jusqu'à présent** ou **maintenant** so far; **jusqu'où?** how far?

justaucorps [ʒystokɔʀ] nm inv leotard

juste [ʒyst] adj (équitable) just, fair; (légitime) just; (exact, vrai) right; (pertinent) apt; (étroit) tight; (insuffisant) on the short side ▷ adv right; (chanter) in tune; (seulement) just; **~ assez/au-dessus** just enough/above; **pouvoir tout ~ faire** to be only just able to do; **au ~** exactly; **le ~ milieu** the happy medium; **c'était ~** it was a close thing; **justement** adv justly; (précisément) just, precisely; **justesse** nf (précision) accuracy; (d'une remarque) aptness; (d'une opinion) soundness; **de justesse** only just

justice [ʒystis] nf (équité) fairness, justice; (Admin) justice; **rendre ~ à qn** to do sb justice

justificatif, -ive [ʒystifikatif, -iv] adj (document etc) supporting; **pièce justificative** written proof

justifier [ʒystifje] /7/ vt to justify; **~ de** to prove

juteux, -euse [ʒytø, -øz] adj juicy

juvénile [ʒyvenil] adj youthful

j

kit [kit] *nm* kit; **~ piéton** *ou* **mains libres** hands-free kit; **en ~** in kit form
kiwi [kiwi] *nm* kiwi
klaxon [klaksɔn] *nm* horn; **klaxonner**/1/ *vi*, *vt* to hoot (BRIT), honk (one's horn) (US)
km *abr* (= kilomètre) km
km/h *abr* (= kilomètres/heure) km/h, kph
K.-O. *adj inv* shattered, knackered
Kosovo [kɔsɔvo] *nm*: **le ~** Kosovo
Koweit, Kuweit [kɔwɛt] *nm*: **le ~** Kuwait
k-way® [kawɛ] *nm* (lightweight nylon) cagoule
kyste [kist] *nm* cyst

K [ka] *nm inv* K
kaki [kaki] *adj inv* khaki
kangourou [kãguʀu] *nm* kangaroo
karaté [kaʀate] *nm* karate
kascher [kaʃɛʀ] *adj inv* kosher
kayak [kajak] *nm* kayak; **faire du ~** to go kayaking
képi [kepi] *nm* kepi
kermesse [kɛʀmɛs] *nf* bazaar, (charity) fête; village fair
kidnapper [kidnape] /1/ *vt* to kidnap
kilo [kilo] *nm* kilo; **kilogramme** *nm* kilogramme ; **kilométrage** *nm* number of kilometres travelled, ≈ mileage; **kilomètre** *nm* kilometre; **kilométrique** *adj* (*distance*) in kilometres
kinésithérapeute [kineziteʀapøt] *nm/f* physiotherapist
kiosque [kjɔsk] *nm* kiosk, stall
kir [kiʀ] *nm* kir (*white wine with blackcurrant liqueur*)

lâcher [lɑʃe] /1/ vt to let go of; (ce qui tombe, abandonner) to drop; (oiseau, animal: libérer) to release, set free; (fig: mot, remarque) to let slip, come out with ▷ vi (freins) to fail; **~ les amarres** (Navig) to cast off (the moorings); **~ prise** to let go

lacrymogène [lakʀimɔʒɛn] adj: **grenade/gaz ~** tear gas grenade/ tear gas

lacune [lakyn] nf gap

là-dedans [ladədɑ̃] adv inside (there), in it; (fig) in that

là-dessous [ladsu] adv underneath, under there; (fig) behind that

là-dessus [ladsy] adv on there; (fig: sur ces mots) at that point; (: à ce sujet) about that

ladite [ladit] adj f voir **ledit**

lagune [lagyn] nf lagoon

là-haut [lao] adv up there

laid, e [lɛ, lɛd] adj ugly; **laideur** nf ugliness no pl

lainage [lɛnaʒ] nm (vêtement) woollen garment; (étoffe) woollen material

laine [lɛn] nf wool

laïque [laik] adj lay, civil; (Scol) state cpd (as opposed to private and Roman Catholic); ▷ nm/f layman(-woman)

laisse [lɛs] nf (de chien) lead, leash; **tenir en ~** to keep on a lead ou leash

laisser [lese] /1/ vt to leave ▷ vb aux: **~ qn faire** to let sb do; **se ~ aller** to let o.s. go; **laisse-toi faire** let me (ou him) do it; **laisser-aller** nm carelessness, slovenliness; **laissez-passer** nm inv pass

lait [lɛ] nm milk; **frère/sœur de ~** foster brother/sister; **~ écrémé/ entier/concentré/condensé** skimmed/full-fat/concentrated/ evaporated milk; **laitage** nm dairy product; **laiterie** nf dairy; **laitier, -ière** adj dairy cpd ▷ nm/f milkman (dairywoman)

laiton [lɛtɔ̃] nm brass

laitue [lety] nf lettuce

l' [l] art déf voir **le**

la [la] art déf voir **le** ▷ nm (Mus) A; (en chantant la gamme) la

là [la] adv there; (ici) here; (dans le temps) then; **elle n'est pas là** she isn't here; **c'est là que** this is where; **là où** where; **de là** (fig) hence; **par là** (fig) by that; voir aussi **-ci**; **celui**; **là-bas** adv there

labo [labo] nm (= laboratoire) lab

laboratoire [labɔʀatwaʀ] nm laboratory; **~ de langues/ d'analyses** language/(medical) analysis laboratory

laborieux, -euse [labɔʀjø, -øz] adj (tâche) laborious

labourer /1/ vt to plough

labyrinthe [labiʀɛ̃t] nm labyrinth, maze

lac [lak] nm lake

lacet [lasɛ] nm (de chaussure) lace; (de route) sharp bend; (piège) snare

lâche [lɑʃ] adj (poltron) cowardly; (desserré) loose, slack ▷ nm/f coward

lambeau, x [lãbo] *nm* scrap; **en ~x** in tatters, tattered

lame [lam] *nf* blade; (*vague*) wave; (*lamelle*) strip; **~ de fond** ground swell *no pl*; **~ de rasoir** razor blade; **lamelle** *nf* small blade

lamentable [lamãtabl] *adj* appalling

lamenter [lamãte] /1/: **se lamenter** *vi*: **se ~ (sur)** to moan (over)

lampadaire [lãpadɛʀ] *nm* (*de salon*) standard lamp; (*dans la rue*) street lamp

lampe [lãp] *nf* lamp; (*Tech*) valve; **~ à pétrole** oil lamp; **~ à bronzer** sunlamp; **~ de poche** torch (*BRIT*), flashlight (*US*); **~ halogène** halogen lamp

lance [lãs] *nf* spear; **~ d'incendie** fire hose

lancée [lãse] *nf*: **être/continuer sur sa ~** to be under way/keep going

lancement [lãsmã] *nm* launching *no pl*

lance-pierres [lãspjɛʀ] *nm inv* catapult

lancer [lãse] /3/ *nm* (*Sport*) throwing *no pl*, throw ▷ *vt* to throw; (*émettre, projeter*) to throw out, send out; (*produit, fusée, bateau, artiste*) to launch; (*injure*) to hurl, fling; **se lancer** *vi* (*prendre de l'élan*) to build up speed; (*se précipiter*): **se ~ sur** *ou* **contre** to rush at; **~ du poids** putting the shot; **~ qch à qn** to throw sth to sb; (*de façon agressive*) to throw sth at sb; **~ un cri** *ou* **un appel** to shout *ou* call out; **se ~ dans** (*discussion*) to launch into; (*aventure*) to embark on

landau [lãdo] *nm* pram (*BRIT*), baby carriage (*US*)

lande [lãd] *nf* moor

langage [lãgaʒ] *nm* language

langouste [lãgust] *nf* crayfish *inv*; **langoustine** *nf* Dublin Bay prawn

langue [lãg] *nf* (*Anat, Culin*) tongue; (*Ling*) language; **tirer la ~ (à)** to stick out one's tongue (at); **de ~ française** French-speaking; **~ maternelle** native language, mother tongue; **~s vivantes** modern languages

langueur [lãgœʀ] *nf* languidness

languir [lãgiʀ] /2/ *vi* to languish; (*conversation*) to flag; **faire ~ qn** to keep sb waiting

lanière [lanjɛʀ] *nf* (*de fouet*) lash; (*de valise, bretelle*) strap

lanterne [lãtɛʀn] *nf* (*portable*) lantern; (*électrique*) light, lamp; (*de voiture*) (side)light

laper [lape] /1/ *vt* to lap up

lapidaire [lapidɛʀ] *adj* (*fig*) terse

lapin [lapɛ̃] *nm* rabbit; (*peau*) rabbitskin; (*fourrure*) cony; **poser un ~ à qn** to stand sb up

Laponie [laponi] *nf*: **la ~** Lapland

laps [laps] *nm*: **~ de temps** space of time, time *no pl*

laque [lak] *nf* (*vernis*) lacquer; (*pour cheveux*) hair spray

laquelle [lakɛl] *pron voir* **lequel**

larcin [larsɛ̃] *nm* theft

lard [laʀ] *nm* (*graisse*) fat; (*bacon*) (streaky) bacon

lardon [laʀdɔ̃] *nm* piece of chopped bacon

large [laʀʒ] *adj* wide; broad; (*fig*) generous ▷ *adv*: **calculer/voir ~** to allow extra/think big ▷ *nm* (*largeur*): **5 m de ~** 5 m wide *ou* in width; (*mer*): **le ~** the open sea; **au ~ de** off; **~ d'esprit** broad-minded; **largement** *adv* widely; (*de loin*) greatly; (*amplement, au minimum*) easily; (*donner etc*) generously; **c'est largement suffisant** that's ample; **largesse** *nf* generosity; **largesses** *nfpl* (*dons*) liberalities; **largeur** *nf* (*qu'on mesure*) width; (*impression visuelle*) wideness, width; (*d'esprit*) broadness

larguer [laʀge] /1/ *vt* to drop; **~ les amarres** to cast off (the moorings)

larme [laʀm] *nf* tear; (*fig*): **une ~ de** a drop of; **en ~s** in tears; **larmoyer** /8/ *vi* (*yeux*) to water; (*se plaindre*) to whimper

larvé, e [laʀve] *adj* (*fig*) latent
laryngite [laʀɛ̃ʒit] *nf* laryngitis
las, lasse [lɑ, lɑs] *adj* weary
laser [lazɛʀ] *nm*: **(rayon) ~** laser
(beam); **chaîne** *ou* **platine ~**
compact disc (player); **disque ~**
compact disc
lasse [lɑs] *adj f voir* **las**
lasser [lɑse] /1/ *vt* to weary, tire
latéral, e, -aux [lateʀal, -o] *adj* side
cpd, lateral
latin, e [latɛ̃, -in] *adj* Latin ▷ *nm* (*Ling*)
Latin ▷ *nm/f*: **L~, e** Latin
latitude [latityd] *nf* latitude
lauréat, e [lɔʀea, -at] *nm/f* winner
laurier [lɔʀje] *nm* (*Bot*) laurel; (*Culin*)
bay leaves *pl*
lavable [lavabl] *adj* washable
lavabo [lavabo] *nm* washbasin;
lavabos *nmpl* toilet *sg*
lavage [lavaʒ] *nm* washing *no pl*,
wash; **~ de cerveau** brainwashing
no pl
lavande [lavɑ̃d] *nf* lavender
lave [lav] *nf* lava *no pl*
lave-linge [lavlɛ̃ʒ] *nm inv* washing
machine
laver [lave] /1/ *vt* to wash; (*tache*) to
wash off; **se laver** *vi* to have a wash,
wash; **se ~ les mains/dents** to
wash one's hands/clean one's teeth;
~ la vaisselle/le linge to wash the
dishes/clothes; **~ qn de** (*accusation*)
to clear sb of; **laverie** *nf*: **laverie
(automatique)** Launderette®
(BRIT), Laundromat® (US); **lavette** *nf*
dish cloth; (*fam*) drip; **laveur, -euse**
nm/f cleaner; **lave-vaisselle** *nm inv*
dishwasher; **lavoir** *nm* wash house;
(*évier*) sink
laxatif, -ive [laksatif, -iv] *adj, nm*
laxative
layette [lɛjɛt] *nf* layette

MOT-CLÉ

le, la, l' [lə, la, l] (*pl* **les**) *art déf* **1**
the; **le livre/la pomme/l'arbre**

the book/the apple/the tree; **les
étudiants** the students
2 (*noms abstraits*): **le courage/
l'amour/la jeunesse** courage/
love/youth
3 (*indiquant la possession*): **se casser
la jambe** *etc* to break one's leg *etc*;
levez la main put your hand up;
avoir les yeux gris/le nez rouge to
have grey eyes/a red nose
4 (*temps*): **le matin/soir** in the
morning/evening; mornings/
evenings; **le jeudi** *etc* (*d'habitude*) on
Thursdays *etc*; (*ce jeudi-là etc*) on (the)
Thursday
5 (*distribution, évaluation*) a, an; **trois
euros le mètre/kilo** three euros a *ou*
per metre/kilo; **le tiers/quart de** a
third/quarter of
▶ *pron* **1** (*personne: mâle*) him;
(: *femelle*) her; (: *pluriel*) them; **je le/
la/les vois** I can see him/her/them
2 (*animal, chose: singulier*) it; (: *pluriel*)
them; **je le** (*ou* **la**) **vois** I can see it; **je
les vois** I can see them
3 (*remplaçant une phrase*): **je ne le
savais pas** I didn't know (about it);
il était riche et ne l'est plus he was
once rich but no longer is

lécher [leʃe] /6/ *vt* to lick; (*laper:
lait, eau*) to lick *ou* lap up; **se ~ les
doigts/lèvres** to lick one's fingers/
lips; **lèche-vitrines** *nm inv*: **faire
du lèche-vitrines** to go window-
shopping
leçon [ləsɔ̃] *nf* lesson; **faire la ~ à** (*fig*)
to give a lecture to; **~s de conduite**
driving lessons; **~s particulières**
private lessons *ou* tuition *sg* (BRIT)
lecteur, -trice [lɛktœʀ, -tʀis]
nm/f reader; (*d'université*) (foreign
language) assistant ▷ *nm* (*Tech*):
~ de cassettes cassette player;
~ de disquette(s) disk drive; **~ de
CD/DVD** CD/DVD player; **~ MP3**
MP3 player
lecture [lɛktyʀ] *nf* reading

Attention à ne pas traduire *lecture* par le mot anglais *lecture*.

ledit, ladite [lədit, ladit] (*mpl* **lesdits**, *fpl* **lesdites**) *adj* the aforesaid

légal, e, -aux [legal, -o] *adj* legal; **légaliser** /1/ *vt* to legalize; **légalité** *nf* legality

légendaire [leʒãdɛʀ] *adj* legendary

légende [leʒãd] *nf* (*mythe*) legend; (*de carte, plan*) key; (*de dessin*) caption

léger, -ère [leʒe, -ɛʀ] *adj* light; (*bruit, retard*) slight; (*superficiel*) thoughtless; (*volage*) free and easy; **à la légère** (*parler, agir*) rashly, thoughtlessly; **légèrement** *adv* (*s'habiller, bouger*) lightly; **légèrement plus grand** slightly bigger; **manger légèrement** to eat a light meal; **légèreté** *nf* lightness; (*d'une remarque*) flippancy

législatif, -ive [leʒislatif, -iv] *adj* legislative; **législatives** *nfpl* general election *sg*

légitime [leʒitim] *adj* (*Jur*) lawful, legitimate; (*fig*) rightful, legitimate; **en état de ~ défense** in self-defence

legs [lɛg] *nm* legacy

léguer [lege] /6/ *vt*: **~ qch à qn** (*Jur*) to bequeath sth to sb

légume [legym] *nm* vegetable; **~s verts** green vegetables; **~s secs** pulses

lendemain [lãdmɛ̃] *nm*: **le ~** the next *ou* following day; **le ~ matin/ soir** the next *ou* following morning/ evening; **le ~ de** the day after

lent, e [lã, lãt] *adj* slow; **lentement** *adv* slowly; **lenteur** *nf* slowness *no pl*

lentille [lãtij] *nf* (*Optique*) lens *sg*; (*Bot*) lentil; **~s de contact** contact lenses

léopard [leɔpaʀ] *nm* leopard

lèpre [lɛpʀ] *nf* leprosy

MOT-CLÉ

lequel, laquelle [ləkɛl, lakɛl] (*mpl* **lesquels**, *fpl* **lesquelles**) (*à + lequel* = **auquel**, *de + lequel* = **duquel** *etc*)

pron **1** (*interrogatif*) which, which one; **lequel des deux?** which one?
2 (*relatif: personne: sujet*) who; (: *objet, après préposition*) whom; (: *chose*) which
▶ *adj*: **auquel cas** in which case

les [le] *art déf, pron voir* **le**

lesbienne [lɛsbjɛn] *nf* lesbian

lesdits, lesdites [ledi, ledit] *adj pl voir* **ledit**

léser [leze] /6/ *vt* to wrong

lésiner [lezine] /1/ *vi*: **ne pas ~ sur les moyens** (*pour mariage etc*) to push the boat out

lésion [lezjɔ̃] *nf* lesion, damage *no pl*

lessive [lesiv] *nf* (*poudre*) washing powder; (*linge*) washing *no pl*, wash; **lessiver** /1/ *vt* to wash; (*fam: fatiguer*) to tire out, exhaust

lest [lɛst] *nm* ballast

leste [lɛst] *adj* sprightly, nimble

lettre [lɛtʀ] *nf* letter; **lettres** *nfpl* (*étude, culture*) literature *sg*; (*Scol*) arts (subjects); **à la ~** literally; **en toutes ~s** in full; **~ piégée** letter bomb

leucémie [løsemi] *nf* leukaemia

MOT-CLÉ

leur [lœʀ] *adj poss* their; **leur maison** their house; **leurs amis** their friends
▶ *pron* **1** (*objet indirect*) (to) them; **je leur ai dit la vérité** I told them the truth; **je le leur ai donné** I gave it to them, I gave it them
2 (*possessif*): **le (la) leur, les leurs** theirs

levain [ləvɛ̃] *nm* leaven

levé, e [ləve] *adj*: **être ~** to be up; **levée** *nf* (*Postes*) collection

lever [ləve] /5/ *vt* (*vitre, bras etc*) to raise; (*soulever de terre, supprimer: interdiction, siège*) to lift; (*impôts, armée*) to levy ▷ *vi* to rise ▷ *nm*: **au ~** on getting up; **se lever** *vi* to get up; (*soleil*) to rise; (*jour*) to break;

(*brouillard*) to lift; **ça va se ~** (*temps*) it's going to clear up; **~ du jour** daybreak; **~ de soleil** sunrise

levier [ləvje] *nm* lever

lèvre [lɛvʀ] *nf* lip

lévrier [levʀije] *nm* greyhound

levure [ləvyʀ] *nf* yeast; **~ chimique** baking powder

lexique [lɛksik] *nm* vocabulary, lexicon; (*glossaire*) vocabulary

lézard [lezaʀ] *nm* lizard

lézarde [lezaʀd] *nf* crack

liaison [ljɛzɔ̃] *nf* (*rapport*) connection; (*Rail, Aviat etc*) link; (*amoureuse*) affair; (*Culin, Phonétique*) liaison; **entrer/être en ~ avec** to get/be in contact with

liane [ljan] *nf* creeper

liasse [ljas] *nf* wad, bundle

Liban [libɑ̃] *nm*: **le ~** (the) Lebanon

libeller [libele] /1/ *vt* (*chèque, mandat*): **~ (au nom de)** to make out (to); (*lettre*) to word

libellule [libelyl] *nf* dragonfly

libéral, e, -aux [liberal, -o] *adj, nm/f* liberal; **les professions ~es** liberal professions

libérer [libere] /6/ *vt* (*délivrer*) to free, liberate (*Psych*) to liberate; (*relâcher: prisonnier*) to discharge, release; (*gaz, cran d'arrêt*) to release; **se libérer** *vi* (*de rendez-vous*) to get out of previous engagements

liberté [libɛʀte] *nf* freedom; (*loisir*) free time; **libertés** *nfpl* (*privautés*) liberties; **mettre/être en ~** to set/ be free; **en ~ provisoire/surveillée/ conditionnelle** on bail/probation/ parole

libraire [libʀɛʀ] *nm/f* bookseller

librairie [libʀeʀi] *nf* bookshop
Attention à ne pas traduire *librairie* par library.

libre [libʀ] *adj* free; (*route*) clear; (*place etc*) free; (*ligne*) not engaged; (*Scol*) non-state; **~ de qch/de faire** free from sth/to do; **~ arbitre** free will; **libre-échange** *nm* free trade; **libre-service** *nm inv* self-service store

Libye [libi] *nf*: **la ~** Libya

licence [lisɑ̃s] *nf* (*permis*) permit; (*diplôme*) (first) degree; (*liberté*) liberty; **licencié, e** *nm/f* (*Scol*): **licencié ès lettres/en droit** ≈ Bachelor of Arts/Law

licenciement [lisɑ̃simɑ̃] *nm* redundancy

licencier [lisɑ̃sje] /7/ *vt* (*renvoyer*) to dismiss; (*débaucher*) to make redundant

licite [lisit] *adj* lawful

lie [li] *nf* dregs *pl*, sediment

lié, e [lje] *adj*: **très ~ avec** very friendly with *ou* close to

Liechtenstein [liʃtɛnʃtajn] *nm*: **le ~** Liechtenstein

liège [ljɛʒ] *nm* cork

lien [ljɛ̃] *nm* (*corde, fig: affectif, culturel*) bond; (*rapport*) link, connection; **~ de parenté** family tie; **~ hypertexte** hyperlink

lier [lje] /7/ *vt* (*attacher*) to tie up; (*joindre*) to link up; (*fig: unir, engager*) to bind; **~ conversation (avec)** to strike up a conversation (with); **~ connaissance avec** to get to know

lierre [ljɛʀ] *nm* ivy

lieu, x [ljø] *nm* place; **lieux** *nmpl* (*locaux*) premises; (*endroit: d'un accident etc*) scene *sg*; **arriver/être sur les ~x** to arrive/be on the scene; **en premier ~** in the first place; **en dernier ~** lastly; **avoir ~** to take place; **tenir ~ de** to serve as; **donner ~ à** to give rise to; **au ~ de** instead of; **~ commun** commonplace; **lieu-dit** (*pl* **lieux-dits**) *nm* locality

lieutenant [ljøtnɑ̃] *nm* lieutenant

lièvre [ljɛvʀ] *nm* hare

ligament [ligamɑ̃] *nm* ligament

ligne [liɲ] *nf* (*gén*) line; (*Transports: liaison*) service; (: *trajet*) route; (*silhouette*) figure; **garder la ~** to keep one's figure; **en ~** (*Inform*) online; **entrer en ~ de compte** to be taken into account; **~ fixe** (*Tél*) landline

ligné, e [liɲe] *adj*: **papier ~** ruled paper ▷ *nm* line, lineage

ligoter [ligɔte] /1/ *vt* to tie up

ligue [lig] *nf* league

lilas [lila] *nm* lilac

limace [limas] *nf* slug

limande [limɑ̃d] *nf* dab

lime [lim] *nf* file; **~ à ongles** nail file; **limer** /1/ *vt* to file

limitation [limitasjɔ̃] *nf*: **~ de vitesse** speed limit

limite [limit] *nf* (*de terrain*) boundary; (*partie ou point extrême*) limit; **à la ~** (*au pire*) if the worst comes (*ou* came) to the worst; **vitesse/charge ~** maximum speed/load; **cas ~** borderline case; **date ~** deadline; **date ~ de vente/consommation** sell-by/best-before date; **limiter** /1/ *vt* (*restreindre*) to limit, restrict; (*délimiter*) to border; **limitrophe** *adj* border *cpd*

limoger [limɔʒe] /3/ *vt* to dismiss

limon [limɔ̃] *nm* silt

limonade [limɔnad] *nf* lemonade

lin [lɛ̃] *nm* (*tissu, toile*) linen

linceul [lɛ̃sœl] *nm* shroud

linge [lɛ̃ʒ] *nm* (*serviettes etc*) linen; (*aussi*: **~ de corps**) underwear; (*lessive*) washing; **lingerie** *nf* lingerie, underwear

lingot [lɛ̃go] *nm* ingot

linguistique [lɛ̃gɥistik] *adj* linguistic ▷ *nf* linguistics *sg*

lion, ne [ljɔ̃, ljɔn] *nm/f* lion (lioness); (*signe*): **le L~** Leo; **lionceau, x** *nm* lion cub

liqueur [likœʀ] *nf* liqueur

liquidation [likidasjɔ̃] *nf* (*vente*) sale, liquidation; (*Comm*) clearance (sale)

liquide [likid] *adj* liquid ▷ *nm* liquid; (*Comm*): **en ~** in ready money *ou* cash; **je n'ai pas de ~** I haven't got any cash; **liquider** /1/ *vt* to liquidate; (*Comm: articles*) to clear, sell off

lire [liʀ] /43/ *nf* (*monnaie*) lira ▷ *vt*, *vi* to read

lis *vb* [li] *voir* **lire** ▷ *nm* [lis] = **lys**

Lisbonne [lizbɔn] *n* Lisbon

lisible [lizibl] *adj* legible

lisière [lizjɛʀ] *nf* (*de forêt*) edge

lisons [lizɔ̃] *vb voir* **lire**

lisse [lis] *adj* smooth

lisseur [li:sœʀ] *nm* straighteners

liste [list] *nf* list; **faire la ~ de** to list; **~ électorale** electoral roll; **~ de mariage** wedding (present) list; **listing** *nm* (*Inform*) printout

lit [li] *nm* bed; **petit ~, ~ à une place** single bed; **grand ~, ~ à deux places** double bed; **faire son ~** to make one's bed; **aller/se mettre au ~** to go to/get into bed; **~ de camp** camp bed; **~ d'enfant** cot (*BRIT*), crib (*US*)

literie [litʀi] *nf* bedding, bedclothes *pl*

litige [litiʒ] *nm* dispute

litre [litʀ] *nm* litre

littéraire [liteʀɛʀ] *adj* literary ▷ *nm/f* arts student; **elle est très ~** she's very literary

littéral, e, -aux [literal, -o] *adj* literal

littérature [literatyʀ] *nf* literature

littoral, e, -aux [litɔral, -o] *nm* coast

livide [livid] *adj* livid, pallid

livraison [livʀɛzɔ̃] *nf* delivery

livre [livʀ] *nm* book ▷ *nf* (*poids, monnaie*) pound; **~ numérique** e-book; **~ de poche** paperback

livré, e [livʀe] *adj*: **~ à soi-même** left to oneself *ou* one's own devices

livrer [livʀe] /1/ *vt* (*Comm*) to deliver; (*otage, coupable*) to hand over; (*secret, information*) to give away; **se ~ à** (*se rendre*) to give o.s. up to; (*faire: pratiques, actes*) to indulge in; (*enquête*) to carry out

livret [livʀɛ] *nm* booklet; (*d'opéra*) libretto; **~ de caisse d'épargne** (savings) bank-book; **~ de famille** (official) family record book; **~ scolaire** (school) report book

livreur, -euse [livʀœʀ, -øz] *nm/f*
delivery boy *ou* man/girl *ou* woman

local, e, -aux [lɔkal, -o] *adj* local
▷ *nm* (*salle*) premises *pl* ▷ *nmpl*
premises; **localité** *nf* locality

locataire [lɔkatɛʀ] *nm/f* tenant; (*de chambre*) lodger

location [lɔkasjɔ̃] *nf* (*par le locataire*)
renting; (*par le propriétaire*) renting
out, letting; (*bureau*) booking office;
"~ de voitures" "car hire (BRIT) *ou*
rental (US)"; **habiter en ~** to live in
rented accommodation; **prendre
une ~ (pour les vacances)** to rent a
house *etc* (for the holidays)
Attention à ne pas traduire
location par le mot anglais *location*.

locomotive [lɔkɔmɔtiv] *nf*
locomotive, engine

locution [lɔkysjɔ̃] *nf* phrase

loge [lɔʒ] *nf* (*Théât: d'artiste*) dressing
room; (: *de spectateurs*) box; (*de
concierge, franc-maçon*) lodge

logement [lɔʒmɑ̃] *nm* flat (BRIT),
apartment (US); accommodation *no
pl* (BRIT), accommodations *pl* (US);
(*Pol, Admin*): **le ~** housing

loger [lɔʒe] /3/ *vt* to accommodate
▷ *vi* to live; **se loger** *vr*: **trouver à
se ~** to find accommodation; **se ~
dans** (*balle, flèche*) to lodge itself in;
être logé, nourri to have board and
lodging; **logeur, -euse** *nm/f*
landlord (landlady)

logiciel [lɔʒisjɛl] *nm* piece of
software

logique [lɔʒik] *adj* logical ▷ *nf* logic

logo [lɔgo] *nm* logo

loi [lwa] *nf* law; **faire la ~** to lay down
the law

loin [lwɛ̃] *adv* far; (*dans le temps: futur*)
a long way off; (: *passé*) a long time
ago; **plus ~** further; **~ de** far from;
~ d'ici a long way from here; **au ~**
far off; **de ~** from a distance; (*fig: de
beaucoup*) by far

lointain, e [lwɛ̃tɛ̃, -ɛn] *adj* faraway,
distant; (*dans le futur, passé*) distant;

(*cause, parent*) remote, distant ▷ *nm*:
dans le ~ in the distance

loir [lwaʀ] *nm* dormouse

Loire [lwaʀ] *nf*: **la ~** the Loire

loisir [lwaziʀ] *nm*: **heures de ~**
spare time; **loisirs** *nmpl* (*temps libre*)
leisure *sg*; (*activités*) leisure activities;
avoir le ~ de faire to have the time
ou opportunity to do; **(tout) à ~**
at leisure

londonien, ne [lɔ̃dɔnjɛ̃, -ɛn] *adj*
London *cpd*, of London ▷ *nm/f*: **L~,
ne** Londoner

Londres [lɔ̃dʀ] *n* London

long, longue [lɔ̃, lɔ̃g] *adj* long ▷ *adv*:
en savoir ~ to know a great deal
▷ *nm*: **de 3 m de ~** 3 m long, 3 m in
length; **ne pas faire ~ feu** not to last
long; **(tout) le ~ de** (all) along; **tout
au ~ de** (*année, vie*) throughout; **de
~ en large** (*marcher*) to and fro, up
and down

longer [lɔ̃ʒe] /3/ *vt* to go (*ou* walk
ou drive) along(side); (*mur, route*)
to border

longiligne [lɔ̃ʒiliɲ] *adj* long-limbed

longitude [lɔ̃ʒityd] *nf* longitude

longtemps [lɔ̃tɑ̃] *adv* (for) a long
time, (for) long; **avant ~** before
long; **pour/pendant ~** for a long
time; **mettre ~ à faire** to take a long
time to do; **il en a pour ~** he'll be a
long time

longue [lɔ̃g] *adj f voir* **long** ▷ *nf*: **à
la ~** in the end; **longuement** *adv*
(*longtemps*) for a long time; (*en détail*)
at length

longueur [lɔ̃gœʀ] *nf* length;
longueurs *nfpl* (*fig: d'un film etc*)
tedious parts; **en ~** lengthwise; **tirer
en ~** to drag on; **à ~ de journée** all
day long

loquet [lɔkɛ] *nm* latch

lorgner [lɔʀɲe] /1/ *vt* to eye; (*fig*) to
have one's eye on

lors [lɔʀ]: **~ de** *prép* (*au moment de*)
at the time of; (*pendant*) during;
~ même que even though

lorsque [lɔʀsk] *conj* when, as
losange [lɔzɑ̃ʒ] *nm* diamond
lot [lo] *nm (part)* share; *(de loterie)* prize; *(fig: destin)* fate, lot; *(Comm, Inform)* batch; **le gros ~** the jackpot
loterie [lɔtʀi] *nf* lottery
lotion [losjɔ̃] *nf* lotion; **~ après rasage** after-shave (lotion)
lotissement [lɔtismɑ̃] *nm* housing development; *(parcelle)* (building) plot, lot
loto [lɔto] *nm* lotto
lotte [lɔt] *nf* monkfish
louange [lwɑ̃ʒ] *nf*: **à la ~ de** in praise of; **louanges** *nfpl* praise *sg*
loubar(d) [lubaʀ] *nm (fam)* lout
louche [luʃ] *adj* shady, fishy, dubious ▷ *nf* ladle; **loucher** /1/ *vi* to squint
louer [lwe] /1/ *vt (maison: propriétaire)* to let, rent (out); *(: locataire)* to rent; *(voiture etc: entreprise)* to hire out *(BRIT)*, rent (out); *(: locataire)* to hire *(BRIT)*, rent; *(réserver)* to book; *(faire l'éloge de)* to praise; **"à ~"** "to let" *(BRIT)*, "for rent" *(US)*
loup [lu] *nm* wolf; **jeune ~** young go-getter
loupe [lup] *nf* magnifying glass; **à la ~** in minute detail
louper [lupe] /1/ *vt (fam: manquer)* to miss; *(examen)* to flunk
lourd, e [luʀ, luʀd] *adj* heavy; *(chaleur, temps)* sultry; **~ de** *(menaces)* charged with; *(conséquences)* fraught with; **lourdaud, e** *adj* clumsy; **lourdement** *adv* heavily
loutre [lutʀ] *nf* otter
louveteau, x [luvto] *nm* wolf-cub; *(scout)* cub (scout)
louvoyer [luvwaje] /8/ *vi (fig)* to hedge, evade the issue
loyal, e, -aux [lwajal, -o] *adj (fidèle)* loyal, faithful; *(fair-play)* fair; **loyauté** *nf* loyalty, faithfulness; fairness
loyer [lwaje] *nm* rent
lu, e [ly] *pp de* **lire**
lubie [lybi] *nf* whim, craze
lubrifiant [lybʀifjɑ̃] *nm* lubricant

lubrifier [lybʀifje] /7/ *vt* to lubricate
lubrique [lybʀik] *adj* lecherous
lucarne [lykaʀn] *nf* skylight
lucide [lysid] *adj* lucid; *(accidenté)* conscious
lucratif, -ive [lykʀatif, -iv] *adj* lucrative; profitable; **à but non ~** non profit-making
lueur [lɥœʀ] *nf (chatoyante)* glimmer *no pl; (pâle)* (faint) light; *(fig)* glimmer, gleam
luge [lyʒ] *nf* sledge *(BRIT)*, sled *(US)*
lugubre [lygybʀ] *adj* gloomy; dismal

 MOT-CLÉ

lui [lɥi] *pron* **1** *(objet indirect: mâle)* (to) him; *(: femelle)* (to) her; *(: chose, animal)* (to) it; **je lui ai parlé** I have spoken to him (*ou* to her); **il lui a offert un cadeau** he gave him (*ou* her) a present
2 *(après préposition, comparatif: personne)* him; *(: chose, animal)* it; **elle est contente de lui** she is pleased with him; **je la connais mieux que lui** I know her better than he does; I know her better than him; **cette voiture est à lui** this car belongs to him, this is HIS car; **c'est à lui de jouer** it's his turn *ou* go
3 *(sujet, forme emphatique)* he; **lui, il est à Paris** HE is in Paris; **c'est lui qui l'a fait** HE did it
4 *(objet, forme emphatique)* him; **c'est lui que j'attends** I'm waiting for HIM
5: **lui-même** himself; itself

luire [lɥiʀ] /38/ *vi* to shine; *(reflets chauds, cuivrés)* to glow
lumière [lymjɛʀ] *nf* light; **mettre en ~** *(fig)* to highlight; **~ du jour/soleil** day/sunlight
luminaire [lyminɛʀ] *nm* lamp, light
lumineux, -euse [lyminø, -øz] *adj* luminous; *(éclairé)* illuminated; *(ciel, journée, couleur)* bright; *(rayon etc)* of light, light *cpd*; *(fig: regard)* radiant

lunatique [lynatik] *adj* whimsical, temperamental

lundi [lœdi] *nm* Monday; **on est ~** it's Monday; **le(s) ~(s)** on Mondays; **à ~!** see you (on) Monday!; **~ de Pâques** Easter Monday

lune [lyn] *nf* moon; **~ de miel** honeymoon

lunette [lynɛt] *nf*: **~s** glasses, spectacles; (*protectrices*) goggles; **~ arrière** (*Auto*) rear window; **~s noires** dark glasses; **~s de soleil** sunglasses

lustre [lystʀ] *nm* (*de plafond*) chandelier; (*fig: éclat*) lustre; **lustrer** /1/ *vt*: **lustrer qch** to make sth shine

luth [lyt] *nm* lute

lutin [lytɛ̃] *nm* imp, goblin

lutte [lyt] *nf* (*conflit*) struggle; (*Sport*): **la ~** wrestling; **lutter** /1/ *vi* to fight, struggle

luxe [lyks] *nm* luxury; **de ~** luxury *cpd*

Luxembourg [lyksɑ̃buʀ] *nm*: **le ~** Luxembourg

luxer [lykse] /1/ *vt*: **se ~ l'épaule** to dislocate one's shoulder

luxueux, -euse [lyksɥø, -øz] *adj* luxurious

lycée [lise] *nm* (state) secondary (*BRIT*) *ou* high (*US*) school; **lycéen, ne** *nm/f* secondary school pupil

Lyon [ljɔ̃] *n* Lyons

lyophilisé, e [ljɔfilize] *adj* (*café*) freeze-dried

lyrique [liʀik] *adj* lyrical; (*Opéra*) lyric; **artiste ~** opera singer

lys [lis] *nm* lily

M *abr* = **Monsieur**

m' [m] *pron voir* **me**

ma [ma] *adj poss voir* **mon**

macaron [makaʀɔ̃] *nm* (*gâteau*) macaroon; (*insigne*) (round) badge

macaroni(s) [makaʀɔni] *nm* (*pl*) macaroni *sg*; **~ au gratin** macaroni cheese (*BRIT*), macaroni and cheese (*US*)

Macédoine [masedwan] *nf* Macedonia

macédoine [masedwan] *nf*: **~ de fruits** fruit salad; **~ de légumes** mixed vegetables *pl*

macérer [maseʀe] /6/ *vi, vt* to macerate; (*dans du vinaigre*) to pickle

mâcher [mɑʃe] /1/ *vt* to chew; **ne pas ~ ses mots** not to mince one's words

machin [maʃɛ̃] *nm* (*fam*) thingamajig; (*personne*): **M~(e)** what's-his(*ou* her)-name

machinal, e, -aux [maʃinal, -o] *adj*
mechanical, automatic

machination [maʃinasjɔ̃] *nf*
frame-up

machine [maʃin] *nf* machine;
(*locomotive*) engine; **~ à laver/
coudre/tricoter** washing/sewing/
knitting machine; **~ à sous** fruit
machine

mâchoire [maʃwaʀ] *nf* jaw

mâchonner [maʃɔne] /1/ *vt* to
chew (at)

maçon [masɔ̃] *nm* bricklayer;
(*constructeur*) builder; **maçonnerie**
nf (*murs*) brickwork; (: *de pierre*)
masonry, stonework

Madagascar [madagaskaʀ] *nf*
Madagascar

Madame [madam] (*pl* **Mesdames**)
nf: **~ X** Mrs X; **occupez-vous de
~/Monsieur/Mademoiselle**
please serve this lady/gentleman/
(young) lady; **bonjour ~/
Monsieur/Mademoiselle** good
morning; (*ton déférent*) good
morning Madam/Sir/Madam; (*le
nom est connu*) good morning Mrs
X/Mr X/Miss X; **~/Monsieur/
Mademoiselle!** (*pour appeler*)
excuse me!; **~/Monsieur/
Mademoiselle** (*sur lettre*) Dear
Madam/Sir/Madam; **chère ~/cher
Monsieur/chère Mademoiselle**
Dear Mrs X/Mr X/Miss X;
Mesdames Ladies; **mesdames,
mesdemoiselles, messieurs** ladies
and gentlemen

madeleine [madlɛn] *nf* madeleine,
≈ sponge finger cake

Mademoiselle [madmwazɛl] (*pl*
Mesdemoiselles) *nf* Miss; *voir aussi*
Madame

Madère [madɛʀ] *nf* Madeira ▷ *nm*:
madère Madeira (wine)

Madrid [madʀid] *n* Madrid

magasin [magazɛ̃] *nm* (*boutique*)
shop; (*entrepôt*) warehouse; **en ~**
(*Comm*) in stock

MAGASINS

French shops are usually open from
9am to noon and from 2pm to 7pm.
Most shops are closed on Sunday
and some do not open on Monday.
In bigger towns and shopping
centres, most shops are open
throughout the day.

magazine [magazin] *nm* magazine

Maghreb [magʀɛb] *nm*: **le ~**
North(-West) Africa; **maghrébin,
e** *adj* North African ▷ *nm/f*:
Maghrébin, e North African

magicien, ne [maʒisjɛ̃, -ɛn] *nm/f*
magician

magie [maʒi] *nf* magic; **magique** *adj*
magic; (*fig*) magical

magistral, e, -aux [maʒistʀal, -o]
adj (*œuvre, adresse*) masterly; (*ton*)
authoritative; **cours ~** lecture

magistrat [maʒistʀa] *nm*
magistrate

magnétique [maɲetik] *adj*
magnetic

magnétophone [maɲetɔfɔn] *nm*
tape recorder; **~ à cassettes** cassette
recorder

magnétoscope [maɲetɔskɔp] *nm*:
~ (à cassette) video (recorder)

magnifique [maɲifik] *adj*
magnificent

magret [magʀɛ] *nm*: **~ de canard**
duck breast

mai [mɛ] *nm* May; *voir aussi* **juillet**

LE PREMIER MAI

Le premier mai is a public holiday in
France and commemorates the
trades union demonstrations in
the United States in 1886 when
workers demanded the right
to an eight-hour working day.
Sprigs of lily of the valley are
traditionally exchanged. *Le 8
mai* is also a public holiday and

commemorates the surrender of the German army to Eisenhower on 7 May, 1945. It is marked by parades of ex-servicemen and ex-servicewomen in most towns. The social upheavals of May and June 1968, with their student demonstrations, workers' strikes and general rioting, are usually referred to as 'les événements de mai 68'. De Gaulle's Government survived, but reforms in education and a move towards decentralization ensued.

maigre [mɛgʀ] *adj* (very) thin, skinny; (*viande*) lean; (*fromage*) low-fat; (*végétation*) thin, sparse; (*fig*) poor, meagre, skimpy; **jours ~s** days of abstinence, fish days; **maigreur** *nf* thinness; **maigrir** /2/ *vi* to get thinner, lose weight; **maigrir de 2 kilos** to lose 2 kilos

mail [mɛl] *nm* email

maille [maj] *nf* stitch; **~ à l'endroit/à l'envers** plain/purl stitch

maillet [majɛ] *nm* mallet

maillon [majɔ̃] *nm* link

maillot [majo] *nm* (*aussi*: **~ de corps**) vest; (*de sportif*) jersey; **~ de bain** swimming *ou* bathing (BRIT) costume, swimsuit; (*d'homme*) (swimming *ou* bathing (BRIT)) trunks *pl*

main [mɛ̃] *nf* hand; **à la ~** (*tenir, avoir*) in one's hand; (*faire, tricoter etc*) by hand; **se donner la ~** to hold hands; **donner** *ou* **tendre la ~ à qn** to hold out one's hand to sb; **se serrer la ~** to shake hands; **serrer la ~ à qn** to shake hands with sb; **sous la ~** to *ou* at hand; **haut les ~s!** hands up!; **attaque à ~ armée** armed attack; **à remettre en ~s propres** to be delivered personally; **mettre la dernière ~ à** to put the finishing touches to; **se faire/perdre la ~** to get one's hand in/lose one's touch;

avoir qch bien en ~ to have got the hang of sth; **main-d'œuvre** *nf* manpower, labour; **mainmise** *nf* (*fig*): **avoir la mainmise sur** to have a grip *ou* stranglehold on

mains-libres [mɛ̃libʀ] *adj inv* (*téléphone, kit*) hands-free

maint, e [mɛ̃, mɛ̃t] *adj* many a; **~s** many; **à ~es reprises** time and (time) again

maintenant [mɛ̃tnɑ̃] *adv* now; (*actuellement*) nowadays

maintenir [mɛ̃tniʀ] /22/ *vt* (*retenir, soutenir*) to support; (*contenir: foule etc*) to keep in check; (*conserver*) to maintain; **se maintenir** *vi* (*prix*) to keep steady; (*préjugé*) to persist

maintien [mɛ̃tjɛ̃] *nm* maintaining; (*attitude*) bearing

maire [mɛʀ] *nm* mayor; **mairie** *nf* (*bâtiment*) town hall; (*administration*) town council

mais [mɛ] *conj* but; **~ non!** of course not!; **~ enfin** but after all; (*indignation*) look here!

maïs [mais] *nm* maize (BRIT), corn (US)

maison [mɛzɔ̃] *nf* house; (*chez-soi*) home; (*Comm*) firm ▷ *adj inv* (Culin) home-made; (*Comm*) in-house, own; **à la ~** at home; (*direction*) home; **~ close** brothel; **~ des jeunes** ≈ youth club; **~ mère** parent company; **~ de passe** = **maison close**; **~ de repos** convalescent home; **~ de retraite** old people's home; **~ de santé** mental home

maître, -esse [mɛtʀ, mɛtʀɛs] *nm/f* master (mistress); (*Scol*) teacher, schoolmaster/-mistress ▷ *nm* (*peintre etc*) master; (*titre*): **M~ (Mᵉ)** Maître (term of address for lawyers etc) ▷ *adj* (*principal, essentiel*) main; **être ~ de** (*soi-même, situation*) to be in control of; **une maîtresse femme** a forceful woman; **~ chanteur** blackmailer; **~/maîtresse d'école** schoolmaster/-mistress; **~ d'hôtel**

(*domestique*) butler; (*d'hôtel*) head waiter; **~ nageur** lifeguard; **maîtresse de maison** hostess; (*ménagère*) housewife

maîtrise [metʀiz] nf (*aussi*: **~ de soi**) self-control, self-possession; (*habileté*) skill, mastery; (*suprématie*) mastery, command; (*diplôme*) ≈ master's degree; **maîtriser** /1/ vt (*cheval, incendie*) to (bring under) control; (*sujet*) to master; (*émotion*) to control, master; **se maîtriser** to control o.s.

majestueux, -euse [maʒɛstɥø, -øz] adj majestic

majeur, e [maʒœʀ] adj (*important*) major; (*Jur*) of age ▷ nm (*doigt*) middle finger; **en ~e partie** for the most part; **la ~e partie de** most of

majorer [maʒɔʀe] /1/ vt to increase

majoritaire [maʒɔʀitɛʀ] adj majority cpd

majorité [maʒɔʀite] nf (*gén*) majority; (*parti*) party in power; **en ~** (*composé etc*) mainly; **avoir la ~** to have the majority

majuscule [maʒyskyl] adj, nf: **(lettre) ~** capital (letter)

mal (*pl* **maux**) [mal, mo] nm (*opposé au bien*) evil; (*tort, dommage*) harm; (*douleur physique*) pain, ache; (*maladie*) illness, sickness no pl ▷ adv badly ▷ adj: **être ~ (à l'aise)** to be uncomfortable; **être ~ avec qn** to be on bad terms with sb; **il a ~ compris** he misunderstood; **se sentir** ou **se trouver ~** to feel ill ou unwell; **dire/ penser du ~ de** to speak/think ill of; **avoir du ~ à faire qch** to have trouble doing sth; **se donner du ~ pour faire qch** to go to a lot of trouble to do sth; **ne voir aucun ~ à** to see no harm in, see nothing wrong in; **faire du ~ à qn** to hurt sb; **se faire ~** to hurt o.s.; **ça fait ~** it hurts; **j'ai ~ au dos** my back aches; **avoir ~ à la tête/à la gorge** to have a headache/a sore throat; **avoir ~ aux**

dents/à l'oreille to have toothache/ earache; **avoir le ~ du pays** to be homesick; **~ de mer** seasickness; **~ en point** in a bad state; *voir aussi* **cœur**

malade [malad] adj ill, sick; (*poitrine, jambe*) bad; (*plante*) diseased ▷ nm/f invalid, sick person; (*à l'hôpital etc*) patient; **tomber ~** to fall ill; **être ~ du cœur** to have heart trouble ou a bad heart; **~ mental** mentally sick ou ill person; **maladie** nf (*spécifique*) disease, illness; (*mauvaise santé*) illness, sickness; **maladif, -ive** adj sickly; (*curiosité, besoin*) pathological

maladresse [maladʀɛs] nf clumsiness no pl; (*gaffe*) blunder

maladroit, e [maladʀwa, -wat] adj clumsy

malaise [malɛz] nm (*Méd*) feeling of faintness; (*fig*) uneasiness, malaise; **avoir un ~** to feel faint ou dizzy

Malaisie [malɛzi] nf: **la ~** Malaysia

malaria [malaʀja] nf malaria

malaxer [malakse] /1/ vt (*pétrir*) to knead; (*mêler*) to mix

malbouffe [malbuf] nf (*fam*): **la ~** junk food

malchance [malʃɑ̃s] nf misfortune, ill luck no pl; **par ~** unfortunately; **malchanceux, -euse** adj unlucky

mâle [mal] adj (*Élec, Tech*) male; (*viril: voix, traits*) manly ▷ nm male

malédiction [malediksjɔ̃] nf curse

mal: malentendant, e nm/f: **les malentendants** the hard of hearing; **malentendu** nm misunderstanding; **il y a eu un malentendu** there's been a misunderstanding; **malfaçon** nf fault; **malfaisant, e** adj evil, harmful; **malfaiteur** nm lawbreaker, criminal; (*voleur*) burglar, thief; **malfamé, e** adj disreputable

malgache [malgaʃ] adj Malagasy, Madagascan ▷ nm (*Ling*) Malagasy ▷ nm/f: **M~** Malagasy, Madagascan

malgré [malgʀe] prép in spite of, despite; **~ tout** in spite of everything

malheur [malœʀ] nm (situation) adversity, misfortune; (événement) misfortune (: plus fort) disaster, tragedy; **faire un ~** to be a smash hit; **malheureusement** adv unfortunately; **malheureux, -euse** adj (triste) unhappy, miserable; (infortuné, regrettable) unfortunate; (malchanceux) unlucky; (insignifiant) wretched ▷ nm/f poor soul

malhonnête [malɔnɛt] adj dishonest; **malhonnêteté** nf dishonesty

malice [malis] nf mischievousness; (méchanceté): **par ~** out of malice ou spite; **sans ~** guileless; **malicieux, -euse** adj mischievous

  Attention à ne pas traduire malicieux par malicious.

malin, -igne [malɛ̃, -iɲ] adj (futé) (f gén **maline**) smart, shrewd; (Méd) malignant

malingre [malɛ̃gʀ] adj puny

malle [mal] nf trunk; **mallette** nf (small) suitcase; (pour documents) attaché case

malmener [malməne] /5/ vt to manhandle; (fig) to give a rough ride to

malodorant, e [malɔdɔʀɑ̃, -ɑ̃t] adj foul-smelling

malpoli, e [malpɔli] adj impolite

malsain, e [malsɛ̃, -ɛn] adj unhealthy

malt [malt] nm malt

Malte [malt] nf Malta

maltraiter [maltʀete] /1/ vt to manhandle, ill-treat

malveillance [malvɛjɑ̃s] nf (animosité) ill will; (intention de nuire) malevolence

malversation [malvɛʀsasjɔ̃] nf embezzlement

maman [mamɑ̃] nf mum(my)

mamelle [mamɛl] nf teat

mamelon [mamlɔ̃] nm (Anat) nipple

mamie [mami] nf (fam) granny

mammifère [mamifɛʀ] nm mammal

mammouth [mamut] nm mammoth

manche [mɑ̃ʃ] nf (de vêtement) sleeve; (d'un jeu, tournoi) round; (Géo): **la M~** the (English) Channel ▷ nm (d'outil, casserole) handle; (de pelle, pioche etc) shaft; **à ~s courtes/ longues** short-/long-sleeved; **~ à balai** broomstick; (Aviat, Inform) joystick nm inv

manchette [mɑ̃ʃɛt] nf (de chemise) cuff; (coup) forearm blow; (titre) headline

manchot [mɑ̃ʃo] nm one-armed man; armless man; (Zool) penguin

mandarine [mɑ̃daʀin] nf mandarin (orange), tangerine

mandat [mɑ̃da] nm (postal) postal ou money order; (d'un député etc) mandate; (procuration) power of attorney, proxy; (Police) warrant; **~ d'arrêt** warrant for arrest; **~ de perquisition** search warrant; **mandataire** nm/f (représentant, délégué) representative; (Jur) proxy

manège [manɛʒ] nm riding school; (à la foire) roundabout (BRIT), merry-go-round; (fig) game, ploy

manette [manɛt] nf lever, tap; **~ de jeu** joystick

mangeable [mɑ̃ʒabl] adj edible, eatable

mangeoire [mɑ̃ʒwaʀ] nf trough, manger

manger [mɑ̃ʒe] /3/ vt to eat; (ronger: rouille etc) to eat into ou away ▷ vi to eat; **donner à ~ à** (enfant) to feed

mangue [mɑ̃g] nf mango

maniable [manjabl] adj (outil) handy; (voiture, voilier) easy to handle

maniaque [manjak] adj finicky, fussy ▷ nm/f (méticuleux) fusspot; (fou) maniac

manie [mani] nf mania; (tic) odd habit; **avoir la ~ de** to be obsessive about

manier [manje] /7/ vt to handle

maniéré, e [manjeʀe] adj affected

manière [manjɛʀ] nf (façon) way,
manner; **manières** nfpl (attitude)
manners; (chichis) fuss sg; **de ~ à**
so as to; **de cette ~** in this way ou
manner; **d'une ~ générale** generally
speaking, as a general rule; **de toute
~** in any case; **d'une certaine ~** in a
(certain) way

manifestant, e [manifɛstɑ̃, -ɑ̃t]
nm/f demonstrator

manifestation [manifɛstasjɔ̃] nf
(de joie, mécontentement) expression,
demonstration; (symptôme)
outward sign; (fête etc) event; (Pol)
demonstration

manifeste [manifɛst] adj obvious,
evident ▷ nm manifesto; **manifester**
/1/ vt (volonté, intentions) to show,
indicate; (joie, peur) to express, show
▷ vi to demonstrate; **se manifester**
vi (émotion) to show ou express itself;
(difficultés) to arise; (symptômes) to
appear

manigancer [manigɑ̃se] /3/ vt
to plot

manipulation [manipylasjɔ̃] nf
handling; (Pol, génétique) manipulation

manipuler [manipyle] /1/ vt to
handle; (fig) to manipulate

manivelle [manivɛl] nf crank

mannequin [mankɛ̃] nm (Couture)
dummy; (Mode) model

manœuvre [manœvʀ] nf (gén)
manoeuvre (BRIT), maneuver (US)
▷ nm labourer; **manœuvrer** /1/ vt to
manoeuvre (BRIT), maneuver (US);
(levier, machine) to operate ▷ vi to
manoeuvre ou maneuver

manoir [manwaʀ] nm manor ou
country house

manque [mɑ̃k] nm (insuffisance, vide)
emptiness, gap; (Méd) withdrawal;
~ de lack of; **être en état de ~** to
suffer withdrawal symptoms

manqué [mɑ̃ke] adj failed; **garçon
~** tomboy

manquer [mɑ̃ke] /1/ vi (faire défaut)
to be lacking; (être absent) to be

missing; (échouer) to fail ▷ vt to
miss ▷ vb impers: **il (nous) manque
encore 10 euros** we are still 10 euros
short; **il manque des pages (au
livre)** there are some pages missing
ou some pages are missing (from the
book); **~ à qn** (absent etc): **il/cela me
manque** I miss him/that; **~ à** (règles
etc) to be in breach of, fail to observe;
~ de to lack; **ne pas ~ de faire: je ne
manquerai pas de le lui dire** I'll be
sure to tell him; **il a manqué (de) se
tuer** he very nearly got killed

mansarde [mɑ̃saʀd] nf attic;
mansardé, e adj: **chambre
mansardée** attic room

manteau, x [mɑ̃to] nm coat

manucure [manykyʀ] nf manicurist

manuel, le [manɥɛl] adj manual
▷ nm (ouvrage) manual, handbook

manufacture [manyfaktyʀ]
nf factory; **manufacturé, e** adj
manufactured

manuscrit, e [manyskʀi, -it] adj
handwritten ▷ nm manuscript

manutention [manytɑ̃sjɔ̃] nf
(Comm) handling

mappemonde [mapmɔ̃d] nf (plane)
map of the world; (sphère) globe

maquereau, x [makʀo] nm (Zool)
mackerel inv; (fam) pimp

maquette [makɛt] nf (d'un décor,
bâtiment, véhicule) (scale) model

maquillage [makijaʒ] nm making
up; (produits) make-up

maquiller [makije] /1/ vt (personne,
visage) to make up; (truquer: passeport,
statistique) to fake; (: voiture volée) to
do over (respray etc); **se maquiller** vi
to make o.s. up

maquis [maki] nm (Géo) scrub; (Mil)
maquis, underground fighting no pl

maraîcher, -ère [maʀeʃe, maʀeʃɛʀ]
adj: **cultures maraîchères** market
gardening sg ▷ nm/f market gardener

marais [maʀɛ] nm marsh, swamp

marasme [maʀasm] nm stagnation,
sluggishness

marathon [maratɔ̃] nm marathon
marbre [maʀbʀ] nm marble
marc [maʀ] nm (de raisin, pommes) marc
marchand, e [maʀʃɑ̃, -ɑ̃d] nm/f shopkeeper, tradesman/-woman; (au marché) stallholder; **~ de charbon/vins** coal/wine merchant ▷ adj: **prix/valeur ~(e)** market price/value; **~/e de fruits** fruiterer (BRIT), fruit seller (US); **~/e de journaux** newsagent; **~/e de légumes** greengrocer (BRIT), produce dealer (US); **~/e de poisson** fishmonger (BRIT), fish seller (US); **marchander** /1/ vi to bargain, haggle; **marchandise** nf goods pl, merchandise no pl
marche [maʀʃ] nf (d'escalier) step; (activité) walking; (promenade, trajet, allure) walk; (démarche) walk, gait; (Mil, Mus) march; (fonctionnement) running; (des événements) course; **dans le sens de la ~** (Rail) facing the engine; **en ~** (monter etc) while the vehicle is moving ou in motion; **mettre en ~** to start; **se mettre en ~** (personne) to get moving; (machine) to start; **être en état de ~** to be in working order; **~ arrière** reverse (gear); **faire ~ arrière** to reverse; (fig) to backtrack, back-pedal; **~ à suivre** (correct) procedure
marché [maʀʃe] nm market; (transaction) bargain, deal; **faire du ~ noir** to buy and sell on the black market; **~ aux puces** flea market
marcher [maʀʃe] /1/ vi to walk; (Mil) to march; (aller: voiture, train, affaires) to go; (prospérer) to go well; (fonctionner) to work, run; (fam: consentir) to go along, agree; (: croire naïvement) to be taken in; **faire ~ qn** (pour rire) to pull sb's leg; (pour tromper) to lead sb up the garden path; **marcheur, -euse** nm/f walker
mardi [maʀdi] nm Tuesday; **M~ gras** Shrove Tuesday

mare [maʀ] nf pond; (flaque) pool
marécage [maʀekaʒ] nm marsh, swamp; **marécageux, -euse** adj marshy
maréchal, -aux [maʀeʃal, -o] nm marshal
marée [maʀe] nf tide; (poissons) fresh (sea) fish; **~ haute/basse** high/low tide; **~ noire** oil slick
marelle [maʀɛl] nf: **(jouer à) la ~** (to play) hopscotch
margarine [maʀgaʀin] nf margarine
marge [maʀʒ] nf margin; **en ~ de** (fig) on the fringe of; **~ bénéficiaire** profit margin
marginal, e, -aux [maʀʒinal, -o] nm/f (original) eccentric; (déshérité) dropout
marguerite [maʀgəʀit] nf marguerite, (oxeye) daisy; (d'imprimante) daisy-wheel
mari [maʀi] nm husband
mariage [maʀjaʒ] nm marriage; (noce) wedding; **~ civil/religieux** registry office (BRIT) ou civil/church wedding
marié, e [maʀje] adj married ▷ nm/f (bride)groom/bride; **les ~s** the bride and groom; **les (jeunes) ~s** the newly-weds
marier [maʀje] /7/ vt to marry; (fig) to blend; **se ~ (avec)** to marry, get married (to)
marin, e [maʀɛ̃, -in] adj sea cpd, marine ▷ nm sailor ▷ nf navy; **~e marchande** merchant navy
marine [maʀin] adj f voir **marin** ▷ adj inv navy (blue) ▷ nm (Mil) marine
mariner [maʀine] /1/ vt to marinate
marionnette [maʀjɔnɛt] nf puppet
maritalement [maʀitalmɑ̃] adv: **vivre ~** to live together (as husband and wife)
maritime [maʀitim] adj sea cpd, maritime
mark [maʀk] nm mark

marmelade [maʀməlad] *nf* stewed fruit, compote; **~ d'oranges** (orange) marmalade

marmite [maʀmit] *nf* (cooking-) pot

marmonner [maʀmɔne] /1/ *vt, vi* to mumble, mutter

marmotter [maʀmɔte] /1/ *vt* to mumble

Maroc [maʀɔk] *nm*: **le ~** Morocco; **marocain, e** [maʀɔkɛ̃, -ɛn] *adj* Moroccan ▷ *nm/f*: **Marocain, e** Moroccan

maroquinerie [maʀɔkinʀi] *nf* (*commerce*) leather shop; (*articles*) fine leather goods *pl*

marquant, e [maʀkɑ̃, -ɑ̃t] *adj* outstanding

marque [maʀk] *nf* mark; (*Comm*: *de nourriture*) brand; (: *de voiture, produits manufacturés*) make; (: *de disques*) label; **de ~** high-class; (*personnage, hôte*) distinguished; **~ déposée** registered trademark; **~ de fabrique** trademark; **une grande ~ de vin** a well-known brand of wine

marquer [maʀke] /1/ *vt* to mark; (*inscrire*) to write down; (*bétail*) to brand; (*Sport*: *but etc*) to score; (: *joueur*) to mark; (*accentuer*: *taille etc*) to emphasize; (*manifester*: *refus, intérêt*) to show ▷ *vi* (*événement, personnalité*) to stand out, be outstanding; (*Sport*) to score; **~ les points** to keep the score

marqueterie [maʀkɛtʀi] *nf* inlaid work, marquetry

marquis, e [maʀki, -iz] *nm/f* marquis *ou* marquess (marchioness)

marraine [maʀɛn] *nf* godmother

marrant, e [maʀɑ̃, -ɑ̃t] *adj* (*fam*) funny

marre [maʀ] *adv* (*fam*): **en avoir ~ de** to be fed up with

marrer [maʀe] /1/: **se marrer** *vi* (*fam*) to have a (good) laugh

marron, ne [maʀɔ̃, -ɔn] *nm* (*fruit*) chestnut ▷ *adj inv* brown ▷ *adj* (*péj*)

crooked; **~s glacés** marrons glacés; **marronnier** *nm* chestnut (tree)

mars [maʀs] *nm* March

Marseille [maʀsɛj] *n* Marseilles

marteau, x [maʀto] *nm* hammer; **être ~** (*fam*) to be nuts; **marteau-piqueur** *nm* pneumatic drill

marteler [maʀtəle] /5/ *vt* to hammer

martien, ne [maʀsjɛ̃, -ɛn] *adj* Martian, *of ou* from Mars

martyr, e [maʀtiʀ] *nm/f* martyr ▷ *adj* martyred; **enfants ~s** battered children; **martyre** *nm* martyrdom; (*fig*: *sens affaibli*) agony, torture; **martyriser** /1/ *vt* (*Rel*) to martyr; (*fig*) to bully (: *enfant*) to batter

marxiste [maʀksist] *adj, nm/f* Marxist

mascara [maskaʀa] *nm* mascara

masculin, e [maskylɛ̃, -in] *adj* masculine; (*sexe, population*) male; (*équipe, vêtements*) men's; (*viril*) manly ▷ *nm* masculine

masochiste [mazɔʃist] *adj* masochistic

masque [mask] *nm* mask; **~ de beauté** face pack; **~ de plongée** diving mask; **masquer** /1/ *vt* (*cacher*: *porte, goût*) to hide, conceal; (*dissimuler*: *vérité, projet*) to mask, obscure

massacre [masakʀ] *nm* massacre, slaughter; **massacrer** /1/ *vt* to massacre, slaughter; (*texte etc*) to murder

massage [masaʒ] *nm* massage

masse [mas] *nf* mass; (*Élec*) earth; (*maillet*) sledgehammer; **une ~ de** (*fam*) masses ou loads of; **la ~** (*péj*) the masses *pl*; **en ~** (*adv*: *en bloc*) in bulk; (*en foule*) en masse; *adj*: *exécutions, production*) mass *cpd*

masser [mase] /1/ *vt* (*assembler*: *gens*) to gather; (*pétrir*) to massage; **se masser** *vi* (*foule*) to gather; **masseur, -euse** *nm/f* masseur(-euse)

massif, -ive [masif, -iv] *adj* (*porte*) solid, massive; (*visage*) heavy, large;

(*bois, or*) solid; (*dose*) massive; (*déportations etc*) mass *cpd* ▷ *nm* (*montagneux*) massif; (*de fleurs*) clump, bank; **le M~ Central** the Massif Central
massue [masy] *nf* club, bludgeon
mastic [mastik] *nm* (*pour vitres*) putty; (*pour fentes*) filler
mastiquer [mastike] /1/ *vt* (*aliment*) to chew, masticate
mat, e [mat] *adj* (*couleur, métal*) mat(t); (*bruit, son*) dull ▷ *adj inv* (*Échecs*): **être ~** to be checkmate
mât [mɑ] *nm* (*Navig*) mast; (*poteau*) pole, post
match [matʃ] *nm* match; **faire ~ nul** to draw; **~ aller** first leg; **~ retour** second leg, return match
matelas [matla] *nm* mattress; **~ pneumatique** air bed *ou* mattress
matelot [matlo] *nm* sailor, seaman
mater [mate] /1/ *vt* (*personne*) to bring to heel, subdue; (*révolte*) to put down
matérialiser [materjalize] /1/: **se matérialiser** *vi* to materialize
matérialiste [materjalist] *adj* materialistic
matériau, x [materjo] *nm* material; **matériaux** *nmpl* material(s)
matériel, le [materjɛl] *adj* material ▷ *nm* equipment *no pl*; (*de camping etc*) gear *no pl*; (*Inform*) hardware
maternel, le [matɛrnɛl] *adj* (*amour, geste*) motherly, maternal; (*grand-père, oncle*) maternal ▷ *nf* (*aussi*: **école maternelle**) (state) nursery school
maternité [matɛrnite] *nf* (*établissement*) maternity hospital; (*état de mère*) motherhood, maternity; (*grossesse*) pregnancy; **congé de ~** maternity leave
mathématique [matematik] *adj* mathematical; **mathématiques** *nfpl* mathematics *sg*
maths [mat] *nfpl* maths
matière [matjɛr] *nf* matter; (*Comm, Tech*) material; matter *no pl*; (*fig: d'un*

livre etc) subject matter, material; (*Scol*) subject; **en ~ de** as regards; **~s grasses** fat (content) *sg*; **~s premières** raw materials
Matignon [matiɲɔ̃] *nm*: **(l'hôtel) ~** the French Prime Minister's residence
matin [matɛ̃] *nm, adv* morning; **le ~** (*pendant le matin*) in the morning; **demain/hier/dimanche ~** tomorrow/yesterday/Sunday morning; **tous les ~s** every morning; **du ~ au soir** from morning till night; **une heure du ~** one o'clock in the morning; **de grand** *ou* **bon ~** early in the morning; **matinal, e, -aux** [matinal, -o] *adj* (*toilette, gymnastique*) morning *cpd*; **être matinal** (*personne*) to be up early; (*habituellement*) to be an early riser; **matinée** *nf* morning; (*spectacle*) matinée
matou [matu] *nm* tom(cat)
matraque [matrak] *nf* (*de policier*) truncheon (BRIT), billy (US)
matricule [matrikyl] *nm* (*Mil*) regimental number; (*Admin*) reference number
matrimonial, e, -aux [matrimɔnjal, -o] *adj* marital, marriage *cpd*
maudit, e [modi, -it] *adj* (*fam: satané*) blasted, confounded
maugréer [mogree] /1/ *vi* to grumble
maussade [mosad] *adj* sullen; (*ciel, temps*) gloomy
mauvais, e [mɔvɛ, -ɛz] *adj* bad; (*méchant, malveillant*) malicious, spiteful; (*faux*): **le ~ numéro** the wrong number ▷ *adv*: **il fait ~** the weather is bad; **sentir ~** to have a nasty smell, smell bad *ou* nasty; **la mer est ~e** the sea is rough; **~e plaisanterie** nasty trick; **~ joueur** bad loser; **~e herbe** weed; **~e langue** gossip, scandalmonger (BRIT)
mauve [mov] *adj* mauve
maux [mo] *nmpl voir* **mal**

maximum [maksimɔm] *adj, nm*
maximum; **au ~** (*le plus possible*) as
much as one can; (*tout au plus*) at the
(very) most *ou* maximum; **faire le ~**
to do one's level best

mayonnaise [majɔnɛz] *nf*
mayonnaise

mazout [mazut] *nm* (fuel) oil

me, m' [mə, m] *pron* (*direct: téléphoner,
attendre etc*) me; (*indirect: parler, donner
etc*) (to) me; (*réfléchi*) myself

mec [mɛk] *nm* (*fam*) guy, bloke (BRIT)

mécanicien, ne [mekanisjɛ̃,
-ɛn] *nm/f* mechanic; (*Rail*) (train *ou*
engine) driver

mécanique [mekanik] *adj*
mechanical ▷ *nf* (*science*) mechanics
sg; (*mécanisme*) mechanism; **ennui ~**
engine trouble *no pl*

mécanisme [mekanism] *nm*
mechanism

méchamment [meʃamɑ̃] *adv*
nastily, maliciously; spitefully

méchanceté [meʃɑ̃ste] *nf* nastiness,
maliciousness; **dire des ~s à qn** to
say spiteful things to sb

méchant, e [meʃɑ̃, -ɑ̃t] *adj* nasty,
malicious, spiteful; (*enfant: pas sage*)
naughty; (*animal*) vicious

mèche [mɛʃ] *nf* (*de lampe, bougie*)
wick; (*d'un explosif*) fuse; (*de cheveux*)
lock; **se faire faire des ~s** to have
highlights put in one's hair; **de ~ avec**
in league with

méchoui [meʃwi] *nm whole sheep
barbecue*

méconnaissable [mekɔnɛsabl] *adj*
unrecognizable

méconnaître [mekɔnɛtr] /57/
vt (*ignorer*) to be unaware of;
(*mésestimer*) to misjudge

mécontent, e [mekɔ̃tɑ̃, -ɑ̃t]
adj: **~ (de)** discontented *ou*
dissatisfied *ou* displeased
(with); (*contrarié*) annoyed
(at); **mécontentement** *nm*
dissatisfaction, discontent,
displeasure; (*irritation*) annoyance

Mecque [mɛk] *nf*: **la ~** Mecca

médaille [medaj] *nf* medal

médaillon [medajɔ̃] *nm* (*bijou*) locket

médecin [medsɛ̃] *nm* doctor

médecine [medsin] *nf* medicine

média [medja] *nmpl*: **les ~** the
media; **médiatique** *adj* media *cpd*

médical, e, -aux [medikal, -o] *adj*
medical; **passer une visite ~e** to
have a medical

médicament [medikamɑ̃] *nm*
medicine, drug

médiéval, e, -aux [medjeval, -o]
adj medieval

médiocre [medjɔkr] *adj* mediocre,
poor

méditer [medite] /1/ *vi* to meditate

Méditerranée [mediterane]
nf: **la (mer) ~** the Mediterranean
(Sea); **méditerranéen, ne**
adj Mediterranean ▷ *nm/f*:
Méditerranéen, ne Mediterranean

méduse [medyz] *nf* jellyfish

méfait [mefɛ] *nm* (*faute*)
misdemeanour, wrongdoing;
méfaits *nmpl* (*ravages*) ravages,
damage *sg*

méfiance [mefjɑ̃s] *nf* mistrust,
distrust

méfiant, e [mefjɑ̃, -ɑ̃t] *adj*
mistrustful, distrustful

méfier [mefje] /7/: **se méfier** *vi* to be
wary; (*faire attention*) to be careful; **se
~ de** to mistrust, distrust, be wary of

méga-octet [megaɔktɛ] *nm*
megabyte

mégarde [megard] *nf*: **par ~**
(*accidentellement*) accidentally; (*par
erreur*) by mistake

mégère [meʒɛr] *nf* shrew

mégot [mego] *nm* cigarette end
ou butt

meilleur, e [mɛjœr] *adj, adv* better
▷ *nm*: **le ~** the best; **le ~ des deux** the
better of the two; **il fait ~ qu'hier**
it's better weather than yesterday;
~ marché cheaper

mél [mɛl] *nm* email

mélancolie [melɑ̃kɔli] *nf* melancholy, gloom; **mélancolique** *adj* melancholy

mélange [melɑ̃ʒ] *nm* mixture; **mélanger** /3/ *vt* to mix; (*vins, couleurs*) to blend; (*mettre en désordre, confondre*) to mix up, muddle (up)

mêlée [mele] *nf* mêlée, scramble; (*Rugby*) scrum(mage)

mêler [mele] /1/ *vt* (*substances, odeurs, races*) to mix; (*embrouiller*) to muddle (up), mix up; **se mêler** *vi* to mix; **se ~ à** (*personne*) to join; (*s'associer à*) to mix with; **se ~ de** (*personne*) to meddle with, interfere in; **mêle-toi de tes affaires!** mind your own business!

mélodie [melɔdi] *nf* melody; **mélodieux, -euse** *adj* melodious

melon [məlɔ̃] *nm* (*Bot*) (honeydew) melon; (*aussi*: **chapeau ~**) bowler (hat)

membre [mɑ̃bʀ] *nm* (*Anat*) limb; (*personne, pays, élément*) member ▷ *adj* member *cpd*

mémé [meme] *nf* (*fam*) granny

MOT-CLÉ

même [mɛm] *adj* **1** (*avant le nom*) same; **en même temps** at the same time; **ils ont les mêmes goûts** they have the same *ou* similar tastes
2 (*après le nom, renforcement*): **il est la loyauté même** he is loyalty itself; **ce sont ses paroles/celles-là même** they are his very words/the very ones
▷ *pron*: **le (la) même** the same one
▷ *adv* **1** (*renforcement*): **il n'a même pas pleuré** he didn't even cry; **même lui l'a dit** even HE said it; **ici même** at this very place; **même si** even if
2: **à même**: **à même la bouteille** straight from the bottle; **à même la peau** next to the skin; **être à même de faire** to be in a position to do, be able to do
3: **de même** likewise; **faire de même** to do likewise *ou* the same; **lui de même** so does (*ou* did *ou* is) he; **de même que** just as; **il en va de même pour** the same goes for

mémoire [memwaʀ] *nf* memory ▷ *nm* (*Scol*) dissertation, paper; **à la ~ de** to the *ou* in memory of; **de ~** from memory; **~ morte** read-only memory, ROM; **~ vive** random access memory, RAM

mémoires [memwaʀ] *nmpl* memoirs

mémorable [memɔʀabl] *adj* memorable

menace [mənas] *nf* threat; **menacer** /3/ *vt* to threaten

ménage [menaʒ] *nm* (*travail*) housework; (*couple*) (married) couple; (*famille, Admin*) household; **faire le ~** to do the housework; **ménagement** *nm* care and attention

ménager[1] [menaʒe] *vt* (*traiter avec mesure*) to handle with tact; (*utiliser*) to use sparingly; (*prendre soin de*) to take (great) care of, look after; (*organiser*) to arrange

ménager[2], **-ère** *adj* household *cpd*, domestic ▷ *nf* housewife

mendiant, e [mɑ̃djɑ̃, -ɑ̃t] *nm/f* beggar

mendier [mɑ̃dje] /7/ *vi* to beg ▷ *vt* to beg (for)

mener [məne] /5/ *vt* to lead; (*enquête*) to conduct; (*affaires*) to manage ▷ *vi*: **~ à/dans** (*emmener*) to take to/into; **~ qch à bonne fin** *ou* **à terme** *ou* **à bien** to see sth through (to a successful conclusion), complete sth successfully

meneur, -euse [mənœʀ, -øz] *nm/f* leader; (*péj*) ringleader

méningite [menɛ̃ʒit] *nf* meningitis *no pl*

ménopause [menopoz] *nf* menopause

menotte [mənɔt] *nf* (*langage enfantin*) handie; **menottes** *nfpl* handcuffs

mensonge [mɑ̃sɔ̃ʒ] nm: **le ~** lying no pl; **un ~** a lie; **mensonger, -ère** adj false

mensualité [mɑ̃sɥalite] nf (somme payée) monthly payment

mensuel, le [mɑ̃sɥɛl] adj monthly

mensurations [mɑ̃syrasjɔ̃] nfpl measurements

mental, e, -aux [mɑ̃tal, -o] adj mental; **mentalité** nf mentality

menteur, -euse [mɑ̃tœr, -øz] nm/f liar

menthe [mɑ̃t] nf mint

mention [mɑ̃sjɔ̃] nf (note) note, comment; (Scol): **~ (très) bien/passable** (very) good/satisfactory pass; **"rayer la ~ inutile"** "delete as appropriate"; **mentionner** /1/ vt to mention

mentir [mɑ̃tir] /16/ vi to lie

menton [mɑ̃tɔ̃] nm chin

menu, e [məny] adj (mince) slim, slight; (frais, difficulté) minor ▷ adv (couper, hacher) very fine ▷ nm menu; **~ touristique** popular ou tourist menu

menuiserie [mənɥizri] nf (travail) joinery, carpentry; (d'amateur) woodwork; **menuisier** nm joiner, carpenter

méprendre [meprɑ̃dr] /58/: **se méprendre** vi: **se ~ sur** to be mistaken about

mépris, e [mepri, -iz] pp de **méprendre** ▷ nm (dédain) contempt, scorn; **au ~ de** regardless of, in defiance of; **méprisable** adj contemptible, despicable; **méprisant, e** adj scornful; **méprise** nf mistake, error; **mépriser** /1/ vt to scorn, despise; (gloire, danger) to scorn, spurn

mer [mɛr] nf sea; (marée) tide; **en ~** at sea; **en haute** ou **pleine ~** off shore, on the open sea; **la ~ Morte** the Dead Sea; **la ~ Noire** the Black Sea; **la ~ du Nord** the North Sea; **la ~ Rouge** the Red Sea

mercenaire [mɛrsənɛr] nm mercenary, hired soldier

mercerie [mɛrsəri] nf (boutique) haberdasher's (shop) (BRIT), notions store (US)

merci [mɛrsi] excl thank you ▷ nf: **à la ~ de qn/qch** at sb's mercy/the mercy of sth; **~ beaucoup** thank you very much; **~ de** ou **pour** thank you for; **sans ~** merciless; mercilessly

mercredi [mɛrkrədi] nm Wednesday; **~ des Cendres** Ash Wednesday; voir aussi **lundi**

mercure [mɛrkyr] nm mercury

merde [mɛrd] (!) nf shit (!) ▷ excl (bloody) hell (!)

mère [mɛr] nf mother ▷ adj inv mother cpd; **~ célibataire** single parent, unmarried mother; **~ de famille** housewife, mother

merguez [mɛrgɛz] nf spicy North African sausage

méridional, e, -aux [meridjɔnal, -o] adj southern ▷ nm/f Southerner

meringue [mərɛ̃g] nf meringue

mérite [merit] nm merit; **avoir du ~ (à faire qch)** to deserve credit (for doing sth); **mériter** /1/ vt to deserve

merle [mɛrl] nm blackbird

merveille [mɛrvɛj] nf marvel, wonder; **faire ~** ou **des ~s** to work wonders; **à ~** perfectly, wonderfully; **merveilleux, -euse** adj marvellous, wonderful

mes [me] adj poss voir **mon**

mésange [mezɑ̃ʒ] nf tit (mouse)

mésaventure [mezavɑ̃tyr] nf misadventure, misfortune

Mesdames [medam] nfpl voir **Madame**

Mesdemoiselles [medmwazɛl] nfpl voir **Mademoiselle**

mesquin, e [mɛskɛ̃, -in] adj mean, petty; **mesquinerie** nf meanness no pl; (procédé) mean trick

message [mesaʒ] nm message; **~ SMS** text message; **messager, -ère** nm/f messenger; **messagerie** nf

(*Internet*): **messagerie électronique** email; **messagerie instantanée** instant messenger; **messagerie vocale** voice mail

messe [mɛs] *nf* mass; **aller à la ~** to go to mass

Messieurs [mesjø] *nmpl voir* **Monsieur**

mesure [məzyʀ] *nf* (*évaluation, dimension*) measurement; (*étalon, récipient, contenu*) measure; (*Mus: cadence*) time, tempo; (: *division*) bar; (*retenue*) moderation; (*disposition*) measure, step; **sur ~** (*costume*) made-to-measure; **dans la ~ où** insofar as, inasmuch as; **dans une certaine ~** to some *ou* a certain extent; **à ~ que** as; **être en ~ de** to be in a position to

mesurer [məzyʀe] /1/ *vt* to measure; (*juger*) to weigh up, assess; (*modérer: ses paroles etc*) to moderate

métal, -aux [metal, -o] *nm* metal; **métallique** *adj* metallic

météo [meteo] *nf* (*bulletin*) (weather) forecast

météorologie [meteɔʀɔlɔʒi] *nf* meteorology

méthode [metɔd] *nf* method; (*livre, ouvrage*) manual, tutor

méticuleux, -euse [metikylø, -øz] *adj* meticulous

métier [metje] *nm* (*profession: gén*) job; (: *manuel*) trade; (: *artisanal*) craft; (*technique, expérience*) (acquired) skill *ou* technique; (*aussi: ~ à tisser*) (weaving) loom

métrage [metʀaʒ] *nm*: **long/ moyen/court ~** feature *ou* full-length/medium-length/short film

mètre [mɛtʀ] *nm* metre; (*règle*) metre rule; (*ruban*) tape measure; **métrique** *adj* metric

métro [metʀo] *nm* underground (BRIT), subway (US)

métropole [metʀɔpɔl] *nf* (*capitale*) metropolis; (*pays*) home country

mets [mɛ] *nm* dish

metteur [mɛtœʀ] *nm*: **~ en scène** (*Théât*) producer; (*Ciné*) director

 MOT-CLÉ

mettre [mɛtʀ] /56/ *vt* **1** (*placer*) to put; **mettre en bouteille/en sac** to bottle/put in bags *ou* sacks

2 (*vêtements: revêtir*) to put on; (: *porter*) to wear; **mets ton gilet** put your cardigan on; **je ne mets plus mon manteau** I no longer wear my coat

3 (*faire fonctionner: chauffage, électricité*) to put on; (: *réveil, minuteur*) to set; (*installer: gaz, eau*) to put in, lay on; **mettre en marche** to start up

4 (*consacrer*): **mettre du temps/ deux heures à faire qch** to take time/two hours to do sth; **y mettre du sien** to pull one's weight

5 (*noter, écrire*) to say, put (down); **qu'est-ce qu'il a mis sur la carte?** what did he say *ou* write on the card?; **mettez au pluriel ...** put ... into the plural

6 (*supposer*): **mettons que ...** let's suppose *ou* say that ...

se mettre *vr* **1** (*se placer*): **vous pouvez vous mettre là** you can sit (*ou* stand) there; **où ça se met?** where does it go?; **se mettre au lit** to get into bed; **se mettre au piano** to sit down at the piano; **se mettre de l'encre sur les doigts** to get ink on one's fingers

2 (*s'habiller*): **se mettre en maillot de bain** to get into *ou* put on a swimsuit; **n'avoir rien à se mettre** to have nothing to wear

3: **se mettre à** to begin, start; **se mettre à faire** to begin *ou* start doing *ou* to do; **se mettre au piano** to start learning the piano; **se mettre au régime** to go on a diet; **se mettre au travail/à l'étude** to get down to work/one's studies

m

meuble [mœbl] *nm* piece of furniture; (*ameublement*) furniture *no pl*; **meublé** *nm* furnished flat (*BRIT*) *ou* apartment (*US*); **meubler** /1/ *vt* to furnish; **se meubler** to furnish one's house

meuf [mœf] *nf* (*fam*) woman

meugler [møgle] /1/ *vi* to low, moo

meule [møl] *nf* (*à broyer*) millstone; (*de foin, blé*) stack; (*de fromage*) round

meunier, -ière [mønje, -jɛʀ] *nm* miller ▷ *nf* miller's wife

meurs *etc* [mœʀ] *vb voir* **mourir**

meurtre [mœʀtʀ] *nm* murder; **meurtrier, -ière** *adj* (*arme, épidémie, combat*) deadly; (*fureur, instincts*) murderous ▷ *nm/f* murderer(-ess)

meurtrir [mœʀtʀiʀ] /2/ *vt* to bruise; (*fig*) to wound

meus *etc* [mœ] *vb voir* **mouvoir**

meute [møt] *nf* pack

mexicain, e [mɛksikɛ̃, -ɛn] *adj* Mexican ▷ *nm/f*: **M~, e** Mexican

Mexico [mɛksiko] *n* Mexico City

Mexique [mɛksik] *nm*: **le ~** Mexico

mi [mi] *nm* (*Mus*) E; (*en chantant la gamme*) mi

mi... [mi] *préfixe* half(-), mid-; **à la mi-janvier** in mid-January; **à mi-jambes/-corps** (up *ou* down) to the knees/waist; **à mi-hauteur/-pente** halfway up (*ou* down)/up (*ou* down) the hill

miauler [mjole] /1/ *vi* to miaow

miche [miʃ] *nf* round *ou* cob loaf

mi-chemin [miʃmɛ̃]: **à ~** *adv* halfway, midway

mi-clos, e [miklo, -kloz] *adj* half-closed

micro [mikʀo] *nm* mike, microphone; (*Inform*) micro

microbe [mikʀɔb] *nm* germ, microbe

micro: micro-onde *nf*: **four à micro-ondes** microwave oven; **micro-ordinateur** *nm* microcomputer; **microscope** *nm* microscope; **microscopique** *adj* microscopic

midi [midi] *nm* midday, noon; (*moment du déjeuner*) lunchtime; (*sud*) south; **le M~** the South (of France), the Midi; **à ~** at 12 (o'clock) *ou* midday *ou* noon

mie [mi] *nf* inside (of the loaf)

miel [mjɛl] *nm* honey; **mielleux, -euse** *adj* (*personne*) sugary, syrupy

mien, ne [mjɛ̃, mjɛn] *pron*: **le (la) ~(ne), les ~s** mine; **les ~s** my family

miette [mjɛt] *nf* (*de pain, gâteau*) crumb; (*fig: de la conversation etc*) scrap; **en ~s** in pieces *ou* bits

MOT-CLÉ

mieux [mjø] *adv* **1** (*d'une meilleure façon*): **mieux (que)** better (than); **elle travaille/mange mieux** she works/eats better; **aimer mieux** to prefer; **elle va mieux** she is better; **de mieux en mieux** better and better **2** (*de la meilleure façon*) best; **ce que je sais le mieux** what I know best; **les livres les mieux faits** the best made books

▶ *adj inv* **1** (*plus à l'aise, en meilleure forme*) better; **se sentir mieux** to feel better

2 (*plus satisfaisant*) better; **c'est mieux ainsi** it's better like this; **c'est le mieux des deux** it's the better of the two; **le/la mieux, les mieux** the best; **demandez-lui, c'est le mieux** ask him, it's the best thing

3 (*plus joli*) better-looking; **il est mieux que son frère** (*plus beau*) he's better-looking than his brother; (*plus gentil*) he's nicer than his brother; **il est mieux sans moustache** he looks better without a moustache

4: **au mieux** at best; **au mieux avec** on the best of terms with; **pour le mieux** for the best

▶ *nm* **1** (*progrès*) improvement

2: **de mon/ton mieux** as best I/you can (*ou* could); **faire de son mieux** to do one's best

mignon, ne [miɲɔ̃, -ɔn] *adj* sweet, cute

migraine [migʀɛn] *nf* headache; (*Méd*) migraine

mijoter [miʒɔte] /1/ *vt* to simmer; (*préparer avec soin*) to cook lovingly; (*affaire, projet*) to plot, cook up ▷ *vi* to simmer

milieu, x [miljø] *nm* (*centre*) middle; (*aussi*: **juste ~**) happy medium; (*Bio, Géo*) environment; (*entourage social*) milieu; (*familial*) background; (*pègre*): **le ~** the underworld; **au ~ de** in the middle of; **au beau** *ou* **en plein ~ (de)** right in the middle (of)

militaire [militɛʀ] *adj* military, army *cpd* ▷ *nm* serviceman

militant, e [militɑ̃, -ɑ̃t] *adj, nm/f* militant

militer [milite] /1/ *vi* to be a militant

mille [mil] *num* a *ou* one thousand ▷ *nm* (*mesure*): **~ (marin)** nautical mile; **mettre dans le ~** (*fig*) to be bang on (target); **millefeuille** *nm* cream *ou* vanilla slice; **millénaire** *nm* millennium ▷ *adj* thousand-year-old; (*fig*) ancient; **mille-pattes** *nm inv* centipede

millet [mijɛ] *nm* millet

milliard [miljaʀ] *nm* milliard, thousand million (*BRIT*), billion (*US*); **milliardaire** *nm/f* multimillionaire (*BRIT*), billionaire (*US*)

millier [milje] *nm* thousand; **un ~ (de)** a thousand or so, about a thousand; **par ~s** in (their) thousands, by the thousand

milligramme [miligʀam] *nm* milligramme

millimètre [milimɛtʀ] *nm* millimetre

million [miljɔ̃] *nm* million; **deux ~s de** two million; **millionnaire** *nm/f* millionaire

mime [mim] *nm/f* (*acteur*) mime(r) ▷ *nm* (*art*) mime, miming; **mimer** /1/ *vt* to mime; (*singer*) to mimic, take off

minable [minabl] *adj* (*personne*) shabby(-looking); (*travail*) pathetic

mince [mɛ̃s] *adj* thin; (*personne, taille*) slim, slender; (*fig: profit, connaissances*) slight, small; (: *prétexte*) weak ▷ *excl*: **~ (alors)!** darn it!; **minceur** *nf* thinness; (*d'une personne*) slimness, slenderness; **mincir** /2/ *vi* to get slimmer *ou* thinner

mine [min] *nf* (*physionomie*) expression, look; (*extérieur*) exterior, appearance; (*de crayon*) lead; (*gisement, exploitation, explosif*) mine; **avoir bonne ~** (*personne*) to look well; (*ironique*) to look an utter idiot; **avoir mauvaise ~** to look unwell; **faire ~ de faire** to make a pretence of doing; **~ de rien** although you wouldn't think so

miner [mine] /1/ *vt* (*saper*) to undermine, erode; (*Mil*) to mine

minerai [minʀɛ] *nm* ore

minéral, e, -aux [mineʀal, -o] *adj* mineral

minéralogique [mineʀalɔʒik] *adj*: **plaque ~** number (*BRIT*) *ou* license (*US*) plate; **numéro ~** registration (*BRIT*) *ou* license (*US*) number

minet, te [minɛ, -ɛt] *nm/f* (*chat*) pussy-cat; (*péj*) young trendy

mineur, e [minœʀ] *adj* minor ▷ *nm/f* (*Jur*) minor ▷ *nm* (*travailleur*) miner

miniature [minjatyʀ] *adj, nf* miniature

minibus [minibys] *nm* minibus

minier, -ière [minje, -jɛʀ] *adj* mining

mini-jupe [miniʒyp] *nf* mini-skirt

minime [minim] *adj* minor, minimal

minimiser [minimize] /1/ *vt* to minimize; (*fig*) to play down

minimum [minimɔm] *adj, nm* minimum; **au ~** at the very least

ministère [ministɛʀ] *nm* (*cabinet*) government; (*département*) ministry; (*Rel*) ministry

ministre [ministʀ] *nm* minister (*BRIT*), secretary; (*Rel*) minister; **~ d'État** senior minister *ou* secretary

m

Minitel® [minitɛl] *nm* videotext terminal and service

minoritaire [minɔʀitɛʀ] *adj* minority *cpd*

minorité [minɔʀite] *nf* minority; **être en ~** to be in the *ou* a minority

minuit [minɥi] *nm* midnight

minuscule [minyskyl] *adj* minute, tiny ▷ *nf*: **(lettre) ~** small letter

minute [minyt] *nf* minute; **à la ~** (just) this instant; (*passé*) there and then; **minuter** /1/ *vt* to time; **minuterie** *nf* time switch

minutieux, -euse [minysjø, -øz] *adj* (*personne*) meticulous; (*travail*) requiring painstaking attention to detail

mirabelle [miʀabɛl] *nf* (cherry) plum

miracle [miʀakl] *nm* miracle

mirage [miʀaʒ] *nm* mirage

mire [miʀ] *nf*: **point de ~** (*fig*) focal point

miroir [miʀwaʀ] *nm* mirror

miroiter [miʀwate] /1/ *vi* to sparkle, shimmer; **faire ~ qch à qn** to paint sth in glowing colours for sb, dangle sth in front of sb's eyes

mis, e [mi, miz] *pp de* **mettre** ▷ *adj*: **bien ~** well dressed ▷ *nf* (*argent: au jeu*) stake; (*tenue*) clothing; attire; **être de ~e** to be acceptable *ou* in season; **~e de fonds** capital outlay; **~e à jour** update; **~e en plis** set; **~e au point** (*fig*) clarification; **~e en scène** production

miser [mize] /1/ *vt* (*enjeu*) to stake, bet; **~ sur** (*cheval, numéro*) to bet on; (*fig*) to bank *ou* count on

misérable [mizeʀabl] *adj* (*lamentable, malheureux*) pitiful, wretched; (*pauvre*) poverty-stricken; (*insignifiant, mesquin*) miserable ▷ *nm/f* wretch

misère [mizɛʀ] *nf* (extreme) poverty, destitution; **misères** *nfpl* (*malheurs*) woes, miseries; (*ennuis*) little troubles; **salaire de ~** starvation wage

missile [misil] *nm* missile

mission [misjɔ̃] *nf* mission; **partir en ~** (*Admin, Pol*) to go on an assignment; **missionnaire** *nm/f* missionary

mité, e [mite] *adj* moth-eaten

mi-temps [mitɑ̃] *nf inv* (*Sport: période*) half; (: *pause*) half-time; **à ~** part-time

miteux, -euse [mitø, -øz] *adj* seedy

mitigé, e [mitiʒe] *adj* (*sentiments*) mixed

mitoyen, ne [mitwajɛ̃, -ɛn] *adj* (*mur*) common, party *cpd*; **maisons ~nes** semi-detached houses; (*plus de deux*) terraced (BRIT) *ou* row (US) houses

mitrailler [mitʀaje] /1/ *vt* to machine-gun; (*fig: photographier*) to snap away at; **~ qn de** to pelt *ou* bombard sb with; **mitraillette** *nf* submachine gun; **mitrailleuse** *nf* machine gun

mi-voix [mivwa]: **à ~** *adv* in a low *ou* hushed voice

mixage [miksaʒ] *nm* (*Ciné*) (sound) mixing

mixer [miksœʀ] *nm* (food) mixer

mixte [mikst] *adj* (*gén*) mixed; (*Scol*) mixed, coeducational; **cuisinière ~** combined gas and electric cooker

mixture [mikstyʀ] *nf* mixture; (*fig*) concoction

Mlle (*pl* **Mlles**) *abr* = **Mademoiselle**

MM *abr* = **Messieurs**

Mme (*pl* **Mmes**) *abr* = **Madame**

mobile [mɔbil] *adj* mobile; (*pièce de machine*) moving ▷ *nm* (*motif*) motive; (*œuvre d'art*) mobile; **(téléphone)** mobile (phone)

mobilier, -ière [mɔbilje, -jɛʀ] *nm* furniture

mobiliser [mɔbilize] /1/ *vt* to mobilize

mobylette® [mɔbilɛt] *nf* moped

mocassin [mɔkasɛ̃] *nm* moccasin

moche [mɔʃ] *adj* (*fam: laid*) ugly; (*mauvais, méprisable*) rotten

modalité [mɔdalite] *nf* form, mode

mode [mɔd] *nf* fashion ▷ *nm* (*manière*) form, mode; (*Ling*) mood; (*Inform*,

Mus) mode; **à la ~** fashionable, in fashion; **~ d'emploi** directions *pl* (for use); **~ de paiement** method of payment; **~ de vie** way of life
modèle [mɔdɛl] *adj* ▷ *nm* model; (*qui pose: de peintre*) sitter; **~ déposé** registered design; **~ réduit** small-scale model; **modeler** /5/ *vt* to model
modem [mɔdɛm] *nm* modem
modéré, e [mɔdeRe] *adj, nm/f* moderate
modérer [mɔdeRe] /6/ *vt* to moderate; **se modérer** *vi* to restrain o.s
moderne [mɔdɛRn] *adj* modern ▷ *nm* (*Art*) modern style; (*ameublement*) modern furniture; **moderniser** /1/ *vt* to modernize
modeste [mɔdɛst] *adj* modest; **modestie** *nf* modesty
modifier [mɔdifje] /7/ *vt* to modify, alter; **se modifier** *vi* to alter
modique [mɔdik] *adj* modest
module [mɔdyl] *nm* module
moelle [mwal] *nf* marrow
moelleux, -euse [mwalø, -øz] *adj* soft; (*gâteau*) light and moist
mœurs [mœR] *nfpl* (*conduite*) morals; (*manières*) manners; (*pratiques sociales*) habits
moi [mwa] *pron* me; (*emphatique*): **~, je ...** for my part, I ..., I myself ...; **c'est ~ qui l'ai fait** I did it, it was me who did it; **apporte-le-~** bring it to me; **à ~** mine; (*dans un jeu*) my turn; **moi-même** *pron* myself; (*emphatique*) I myself
moindre [mwɛ̃dR] *adj* lesser; lower; **le (la) ~, les ~s** the least; the slightest; **c'est la ~ des choses** it's nothing at all
moine [mwan] *nm* monk, friar
moineau, x [mwano] *nm* sparrow

MOT-CLÉ

moins [mwɛ̃] *adv* **1** (*comparatif*): **moins (que)** less (than); **moins**

grand que less tall than, not as tall as; **il a trois ans de moins que moi** he's three years younger than me; **moins je travaille, mieux je me porte** the less I work, the better I feel

2 (*superlatif*): **le moins** (the) least; **c'est ce que j'aime le moins** it's what I like (the) least; **le (la) moins doué(e)** the least gifted; **au moins, du moins** at least; **pour le moins** at the very least

3: **moins de** (*quantité*) less (than); (*nombre*) fewer (than); **moins de sable/d'eau** less sand/water; **moins de livres/gens** fewer books/people; **moins de deux ans** less than two years; **moins de midi** not yet midday

4: **de moins, en moins**: **100 euros/3 jours de moins** 100 euros/3 days less; **trois livres en moins** three books fewer; three books too few; **de l'argent en moins** less money; **le soleil en moins** but for the sun, minus the sun; **de moins en moins** less and less

5: **à moins de, à moins que** unless; **à moins de faire** unless we do (*ou* he does *etc*); **à moins que tu ne fasses** unless you do; **à moins d'un accident** barring any accident
▷ *prép*: **quatre moins deux** four minus two; **dix heures moins cinq** five to ten; **il fait moins cinq** it's five (degrees) below (freezing), it's minus five; **il est moins cinq** it's five to

mois [mwa] *nm* month
moisi [mwazi] *nm* mould, mildew; **odeur de ~** musty smell; **moisir** /2/ *vi* to go mouldy; **moisissure** *nf* mould *no pl*
moisson [mwasɔ̃] *nf* harvest; **moissonner** /1/ *vt* to harvest, reap; **moissonneuse** *nf* (*machine*) harvester
moite [mwat] *adj* sweaty, sticky

m

moitié [mwatje] *nf* half; **la ~** half; **la ~ de** half (of); **la ~ du temps/des gens** half the time/the people; **à la ~ de** halfway through; **à ~** half (*avant le verbe*), half- (*avant l'adjectif*); **à ~ prix** (at) half price

molaire [mɔlɛʀ] *nf* molar

molester [mɔlɛste] /1/ *vt* to manhandle, maul (about)

molle [mɔl] *adj f voir* **mou**; **mollement** *adv* (*péj: travailler*) sluggishly; (*protester*) feebly

mollet [mɔlɛ] *nm* calf ▷ *adj m:* **œuf ~** soft-boiled egg

molletonné, e [mɔltɔne] *adj* fleece-lined

mollir [mɔliʀ] /2/ *vi* (*personne*) to relent; (*substance*) to go soft

mollusque [mɔlysk] *nm* mollusc

môme [mom] *nm/f* (*fam: enfant*) brat

moment [mɔmɑ̃] *nm* moment; **ce n'est pas le ~** this is not the right time; **au même ~** at the same time; (*instant*) at the same moment; **pour un bon ~** for a good while; **pour le ~** for the moment, for the time being; **au ~ de** at the time of; **au ~ où** as; **à tout ~** at any time *ou* moment; (*continuellement*) constantly, continually; **en ce ~** at the moment; (*aujourd'hui*) at present; **sur le ~** at the time; **par ~s** now and then, at times; **d'un ~ à l'autre** any time (now); **du ~ où** *ou* **que** seeing that, since; **momentané, e** *adj* temporary, momentary; **momentanément** *adv* for a while

momie [mɔmi] *nf* mummy

mon, ma (*pl* **mes**) [mɔ̃, ma, me] *adj poss* my

Monaco [mɔnako] *nm:* **le ~** Monaco

monarchie [mɔnaʀʃi] *nf* monarchy

monastère [mɔnastɛʀ] *nm* monastery

mondain, e [mɔ̃dɛ̃, -ɛn] *adj* (*soirée, vie*) society *cpd*

monde [mɔ̃d] *nm* world; **le ~** (*personnes mondaines*) (high) society; **il**

y a du ~ (*beaucoup de gens*) there are a lot of people; (*quelques personnes*) there are some people; **beaucoup/peu de ~** many/few people; **mettre au ~** to bring into the world; **pas le moins du ~** not in the least; **mondial, e, -aux** *adj* (*population*) world *cpd*; (*influence*) world-wide; **mondialement** *adv* throughout the world; **mondialisation** *nf* globalization

monégasque [mɔnegask] *adj* Monegasque, of *ou* from Monaco ▷ *nm/f:* **M~** Monegasque

monétaire [mɔnetɛʀ] *adj* monetary

moniteur, -trice [mɔnitœʀ, -tʀis] *nm/f* (*Sport*) instructor (instructress); (*de colonie de vacances*) supervisor ▷ *nm* (*écran*) monitor

monnaie [mɔnɛ] *nf* (*Écon: moyen d'échange*) currency; (*petites pièces*): **avoir de la ~** to have (some) change; **faire de la ~** to get (some) change; **avoir/faire la ~ de 20 euros** to have change of/get change for 20 euros; **rendre à qn la ~ (sur 20 euros)** to give sb the change (from *ou* out of 20 euros)

monologue [mɔnɔlɔg] *nm* monologue, soliloquy; **monologuer** /1/ *vi* to soliloquize

monopole [mɔnɔpɔl] *nm* monopoly

monotone [mɔnɔtɔn] *adj* monotonous

Monsieur (*pl* **Messieurs**) [məsjø, mesjø] *nm* (*titre*) Mr; **un/le monsieur** (*homme quelconque*) a/the gentleman; **~, ...** (*en tête de lettre*) Dear Sir, ...; *voir aussi* **Madame**

monstre [mɔ̃stʀ] *nm* monster ▷ *adj* (*fam: effet, publicité*) massive; **un travail ~** a fantastic amount of work; **monstrueux, -euse** *adj* monstrous

mont [mɔ̃] *nm:* **par ~s et par vaux** up hill and down dale; **le M~ Blanc** Mont Blanc

montage [mɔ̃taʒ] *nm* (*d'une machine etc*) assembly; (*Photo*) photomontage; (*Ciné*) editing

montagnard, e [mɔ̃taɲaʀ, -aʀd]
adj mountain *cpd* ▷ *nm/f* mountain-
dweller
montagne [mɔ̃taɲ] *nf* (*cime*)
mountain; (*région*): **la ~** the
mountains *pl*; **~s russes** big dipper
sg, switchback *sg*; **montagneux,
-euse** *adj* mountainous; (*basse
montagne*) hilly
montant, e [mɔ̃tɑ̃, -ɑ̃t] *adj* rising;
(*robe, corsage*) high-necked ▷ *nm*
(*somme, total*) (sum) total, (total)
amount; (*de fenêtre*) upright; (*de
lit*) post
monte-charge [mɔ̃tʃaʀʒ] *nm inv*
goods lift, hoist
montée [mɔ̃te] *nf* rise; (*escalade*)
climb; (*côte*) hill; **au milieu de la ~**
halfway up
monter [mɔ̃te] /1/ *vt* (*escalier, côte*)
to go (*ou* come) up; (*valise, paquet*)
to take (*ou* bring) up; (*étagère*)
to raise; (*tente, échafaudage*) to put up;
(*machine*) to assemble; (*Ciné*) to edit;
(*Théât*) to put on, stage; (*société, coup
etc*) to set up ▷ *vi* to go (*ou* come) up;
(*chemin, niveau, température, voix, prix*)
to go up, rise; (*passager*) to get on;
~ à cheval (*faire du cheval*) to ride (a
horse); **~ sur** to climb up onto; **~ sur**
ou **à un arbre/une échelle** to climb
(up) a tree/ladder; **se ~ à** (*frais etc*) to
add up to, come to
montgolfière [mɔ̃gɔlfjɛʀ] *nf* hot-air
balloon
montre [mɔ̃tʀ] *nf* watch; **contre la ~**
(*Sport*) against the clock
Montréal [mɔ̃ʀeal] *n* Montreal
montrer [mɔ̃tʀe] /1/ *vt* to show;
~ qch à qn to show sb sth
monture [mɔ̃tyʀ] *nf* (*bête*) mount;
(*d'une bague*) setting; (*de lunettes*)
frame
monument [mɔnymɑ̃] *nm*
monument; **~ aux morts** war
memorial
moquer [mɔke] /1/: **se ~ de** *vt*
to make fun of, laugh at; (*fam: se*

désintéresser de) not to care about;
(*tromper*): **se ~ de qn** to take sb
for a ride
moquette [mɔkɛt] *nf* fitted carpet
moqueur, -euse [mɔkœʀ, -øz] *adj*
mocking
moral, e, -aux [mɔʀal, -o] *adj* moral
▷ *nm* morale ▷ *nf* (*conduite*) morals
pl (*règles*); (*valeurs*) moral standards
pl, morality; (*d'une fable etc*) moral;
faire la ~e à to lecture, preach at;
moralité *nf* morality; (*conclusion,
enseignement*) moral
morceau, x [mɔʀso] *nm* piece, bit;
(*d'une œuvre*) passage, extract; (*Mus*)
piece; (*Culin: de viande*) cut; (: *de sucre*)
lump; **mettre en ~x** to pull to pieces
ou bits; **manger un ~** to have a bite
(to eat)
morceler [mɔʀsəle] /4/ *vt* to break
up, divide up
mordant, e [mɔʀdɑ̃, -ɑ̃t] *adj* (*ton,
remarque*) scathing, cutting; (*froid*)
biting ▷ *nm* (*fougue*) bite, punch
mordiller [mɔʀdije] /1/ *vt* to nibble
at, chew at
mordre [mɔʀdʀ] /41/ *vt* to bite ▷ *vi*
(*poisson*) to bite; **~ sur** (*fig*) to go over
into, overlap into; **~ à l'hameçon** to
bite, rise to the bait
mordu, e [mɔʀdy] *nm/f* enthusiast;
un ~ du jazz/de la voile a jazz/
sailing fanatic *ou* buff
morfondre [mɔʀfɔ̃dʀ] /41/: **se
morfondre** *vi* to mope
morgue [mɔʀg] *nf* (*arrogance*)
haughtiness; (*lieu: de la police*)
morgue; (: *à l'hôpital*) mortuary
morne [mɔʀn] *adj* dismal, dreary
morose [mɔʀoz] *adj* sullen, morose
mors [mɔʀ] *nm* bit
morse [mɔʀs] *nm* (*Zool*) walrus; (*Tél*)
Morse (code)
morsure [mɔʀsyʀ] *nf* bite
mort¹ [mɔʀ] *nf* death
mort², e [mɔʀ, mɔʀt] *pp de* **mourir**
▷ *adj* dead ▷ *nm/f* (*défunt*) dead
man/woman; (*victime*): **il y a eu**

m

plusieurs ~s several people were killed, there were several killed; **~ de peur/fatigue** frightened to death/dead tired

mortalité [mɔʀtalite] *nf* mortality, death rate

mortel, le [mɔʀtɛl] *adj* (*poison etc*) deadly, lethal; (*accident, blessure*) fatal; (*silence, ennemi*) deadly; (*danger, frayeur, péché*) mortal; (*ennui, soirée*) deadly (*boring*)

mort-né, e [mɔʀne] *adj* (*enfant*) stillborn

mortuaire [mɔʀtɥɛʀ] *adj*: **avis ~s** death announcements

morue [mɔʀy] *nf* (*Zool*) cod *inv*

mosaïque [mɔzaik] *nf* mosaic

Moscou [mɔsku] *n* Moscow

mosquée [mɔske] *nf* mosque

mot [mo] *nm* word; (*message*) line, note; **~ à ~** word for word; **~ de passe** password; **~s croisés** crossword (puzzle) *sg*

motard [mɔtaʀ] *nm* biker; (*policier*) motorcycle cop

motel [mɔtɛl] *nm* motel

moteur, -trice [mɔtœʀ, -tʀis] *adj* (*Anat, Physiol*) motor; (*Tech*) driving; (*Auto*): **à 4 roues motrices** 4-wheel drive ▷ *nm* engine, motor; **à ~** power-driven, motor *cpd*; **~ de recherche** search engine

motif [mɔtif] *nm* (*cause*) motive; (*décoratif*) design, pattern, motif; **sans ~** groundless

motivation [mɔtivasjɔ̃] *nf* motivation

motiver [mɔtive] /1/ *vt* (*justifier*) to justify, account for; (*Admin, Jur, Psych*) to motivate

moto [mɔto] *nf* (*motor*)bike; **motocycliste** *nm/f* motorcyclist

motorisé, e [mɔtɔʀize] *adj* (*personne*) having one's own transport

motrice [mɔtʀis] *adj f voir* **moteur**

motte [mɔt] *nf*: **~ de terre** lump of earth, clod (of earth); **~ de beurre** lump of butter

mou (mol), molle [mu, mɔl] *adj* soft; (*personne*) sluggish; (*résistance, protestations*) feeble ▷ *nm*: **avoir du ~** to be slack

mouche [muʃ] *nf* fly

moucher [muʃe] /1/: **se moucher** *vi* to blow one's nose

moucheron [muʃʀɔ̃] *nm* midge

mouchoir [muʃwaʀ] *nm* handkerchief, hanky; **~ en papier** tissue, paper hanky

moudre [mudʀ] /47/ *vt* to grind

moue [mu] *nf* pout; **faire la ~** to pout; (*fig*) to pull a face

mouette [mwɛt] *nf* (*sea*)gull

moufle [mufl] *nf* (*gant*) mitt(en)

mouillé, e [muje] *adj* wet

mouiller [muje] /1/ *vt* (*humecter*) to wet, moisten; (*tremper*): **~ qn/qch** to make sb/sth wet ▷ *vi* (*Navig*) to lie *ou* be at anchor; **se mouiller** to get wet; (*fam: prendre des risques*) to commit o.s

moulant, e [mulɑ̃, -ɑ̃t] *adj* figure-hugging

moule [mul] *nf* mussel ▷ *nm* (*Culin*) mould; **à gâteau** *nm* cake tin (BRIT) *ou* pan (US)

mouler [mule] /1/ *vt* (*vêtement*) to hug, fit closely round

moulin [mulɛ̃] *nm* mill; **~ à café** coffee mill; **~ à eau** watermill; **~ à légumes** (vegetable) shredder; **~ à paroles** (*fig*) chatterbox; **~ à poivre** pepper mill; **~ à vent** windmill

moulinet [mulinɛ] *nm* (*de canne à pêche*) reel; (*mouvement*): **faire des ~s avec qch** to whirl sth around

moulinette® [mulinɛt] *nf* (vegetable) shredder

moulu, e [muly] *pp de* **moudre**

mourant, e [muʀɑ̃, -ɑ̃t] *adj* dying

mourir [muʀiʀ] /1/ *vi* to die; (*civilisation*) to die out; **~ de froid/faim/vieillesse** to die of exposure/hunger/old age; **~ de faim/d'ennui** (*fig*) to be starving/be bored to death; **~ d'envie de faire** to be dying to do

mousse [mus] nf (Bot) moss; (de savon) lather; (écume: sur eau, bière) froth, foam; (Culin) mousse ▷ nm (Navig) ship's boy; **~ à raser** shaving foam

mousseline [muslin] nf muslin; **pommes ~** creamed potatoes

mousser [muse] /1/ vi (bière, détergent) to foam; (savon) to lather; **mousseux, -euse** adj frothy ▷ nm: **(vin) mousseux** sparkling wine

mousson [musɔ̃] nf monsoon

moustache [mustaʃ] nf moustache; **moustaches** nfpl (d'animal) whiskers pl; **moustachu, e** adj with a moustache

moustiquaire [mustikɛʀ] nf mosquito net

moustique [mustik] nm mosquito

moutarde [mutaʀd] nf mustard

mouton [mutɔ̃] nm sheep inv; (peau) sheepskin; (Culin) mutton

mouvement [muvmɑ̃] nm movement; (geste) gesture; **avoir un bon ~** to make a nice gesture; **en ~** in motion; on the move; **mouvementé, e** adj (vie, poursuite) eventful; (réunion) turbulent

mouvoir [muvwaʀ] /27/: **se mouvoir** vi to move

moyen, ne [mwajɛ̃, -ɛn] adj average; (tailles, prix) medium; (de grandeur moyenne) medium-sized ▷ nm (façon) means sg, way ▷ nf average; (Statistique) mean; (Scol: à l'examen) pass mark; **moyens** nmpl (capacités) means; **très ~** (résultats) pretty poor; **je n'en ai pas les ~** I can't afford it; **au ~ de** by means of; **par tous les ~s** by every possible means, every possible way; **par ses propres ~s** all by oneself; **~ âge** Middle Ages; **~ de transport** means of transport; **~ne d'âge** average age; **~ne entreprise** (Comm) medium-sized firm

moyennant [mwajɛnɑ̃] prép (somme) for; (service, conditions) in return for; (travail, effort) with

Moyen-Orient [mwajɛnɔʀjɑ̃] nm: **le ~** the Middle East

moyeu, x [mwajø] nm hub

MST sigle f (= maladie sexuellement transmissible) STD

mû, mue [my] pp de **mouvoir**

muer [mɥe] /1/ vi (oiseau, mammifère) to moult; (serpent) to slough (its skin); (jeune garçon): **il mue** his voice is breaking

muet, te [mɥɛ, -ɛt] adj dumb; (fig): **~ d'admiration** etc speechless with admiration etc; (Ciné) silent ▷ nm/f mute

mufle [myfl] nm muzzle; (goujat) boor

mugir [myʒiʀ] /2/ vi (bœuf) to bellow; (vache) to low; (fig) to howl

muguet [mygɛ] nm lily of the valley

mule [myl] nf (Zool) (she-)mule

mulet [mylɛ] nm (Zool) (he-)mule; (poisson) mullet

multinational, e, -aux [myltinasjɔnal, -o] adj, nf multinational

multiple [myltipl] adj multiple, numerous; (varié) many, manifold; **multiplication** nf multiplication; **multiplier** /7/ vt to multiply; **se multiplier** vi to multiply

municipal, e, -aux [mynisipal, -o] adj (élections, stade) municipal; (conseil) town cpd; **piscine/ bibliothèque ~e** public swimming pool/library; **municipalité** nf (corps municipal) town council; (commune) municipality

munir [myniʀ] /2/ vt: **~ qn/qch de** to equip sb/sth with; **se ~ de** to provide o.s. with

munitions [mynisjɔ̃] nfpl ammunition sg

mur [myʀ] nm wall; **~ du son** sound barrier

mûr, e [myʀ] adj ripe; (personne) mature

muraille [myʀaj] nf (high) wall

mural, e, -aux [myʀal, -o] adj wall cpd ▷ nm (Art) mural

m

mûre [myʀ] *nf* blackberry
muret [myʀɛ] *nm* low wall
mûrir [myʀiʀ] /2/ *vi* (*fruit, blé*) to ripen; (*abcès, furoncle*) to come to a head; (*fig: idée, personne*) to mature ▷ *vt* (*personne*) to (make) mature; (*pensée, projet*) to nurture
murmure [myʀmyʀ] *nm* murmur; **murmurer** /1/ *vi* to murmur
muscade [myskad] *nf* (*aussi:* **noix (de) ~**) nutmeg
muscat [myska] *nm* (*raisin*) muscat grape; (*vin*) muscatel (wine)
muscle [myskl] *nm* muscle; **musclé, e** *adj* muscular; (*fig*) strong-arm *cpd*
museau, x [myzo] *nm* muzzle; (*Culin*) brawn
musée [myze] *nm* museum; (*de peinture*) art gallery
museler [myzle] /4/ *vt* to muzzle; **muselière** *nf* muzzle
musette [myzɛt] *nf* (*sac*) lunch bag
musical, e, -aux [myzikal, -o] *adj* musical
music-hall [myzikol] *nm* (*salle*) variety theatre; (*genre*) variety
musicien, ne [myzisjɛ̃, -ɛn] *adj* musical ▷ *nm/f* musician
musique [myzik] *nf* music
musulman, e [myzylmɑ̃, -an] *adj, nm/f* Moslem, Muslim
mutation [mytasjɔ̃] *nf* (*Admin*) transfer
muter [myte] /1/ *vt* to transfer, move
mutilé, e [mytile] *nm/f* disabled person (*through loss of limbs*)
mutiler [mytile] /1/ *vt* to mutilate, maim
mutin, e [mytɛ̃, -in] *adj* (*enfant, air, ton*) mischievous, impish ▷ *nm/f* (*Mil, Navig*) mutineer; **mutinerie** *nf* mutiny
mutisme [mytism] *nm* silence
mutuel, le [mytɥɛl] *adj* mutual ▷ *nf* mutual benefit society
myope [mjɔp] *adj* short-sighted
myosotis [mjɔzɔtis] *nm* forget-me-not

myrtille [miʀtij] *nf* blueberry
mystère [mistɛʀ] *nm* mystery; **mystérieux, -euse** *adj* mysterious
mystifier [mistifje] /7/ *vt* to fool
mythe [mit] *nm* myth
mythologie [mitɔlɔʒi] *nf* mythology

n' [n] *adv voir* **ne**

nacre [nakʀ] *nf* mother-of-pearl

nage [naʒ] *nf* swimming; (*manière*) style of swimming, stroke; **traverser/s'éloigner à la ~** to swim across/away; **en ~** bathed in sweat; **nageoire** *nf* fin; **nager** /3/ *vi* to swim; **nageur, -euse** *nm/f* swimmer

naïf, -ïve [naif, naiv] *adj* naïve

nain, e [nɛ̃, nɛn] *nm/f* (*péj* (!)) dwarf (!)

naissance [nɛsɑ̃s] *nf* birth; **donner ~ à** to give birth to; (*fig*) to give rise to; **lieu de ~** place of birth

naître [nɛtʀ] /59/ *vi* to be born; (*conflit, complications*): **~ de** to arise from, be born out of; **je suis né en 1960** I was born in 1960; **faire ~** (*fig*) to give rise to, arouse

naïveté [naivte] *nf* naivety

nana [nana] *nf* (*fam: fille*) bird (BRIT), chick

nappe [nap] *nf* tablecloth; (*de pétrole, gaz*) layer; **napperon** *nm* table-mat

narguer [naʀge] /1/ *vt* to taunt

narine [naʀin] *nf* nostril

natal, e [natal] *adj* native; **natalité** *nf* birth rate

natation [natasjɔ̃] *nf* swimming

natif, -ive [natif, -iv] *adj* native

nation [nasjɔ̃] *nf* nation; **national, e, -aux** *adj* national ▷ *nf*: **(route) nationale** ≈ A road (BRIT), ≈ state highway (US); **nationaliser** /1/ *vt* to nationalize; **nationalisme** *nm* nationalism; **nationalité** *nf* nationality

natte [nat] *nf* (*tapis*) mat; (*cheveux*) plait

naturaliser [natyʀalize] /1/ *vt* to naturalize

nature [natyʀ] *nf* nature ▷ *adj, adv* (*Culin*) plain, without seasoning or sweetening; (*café, thé*) black; without sugar; (*yaourt*) natural; **payer en ~** to pay in kind; **~ morte** still-life; **naturel, le** *adj* natural ▷ *nm* naturalness; (*caractère*) disposition, nature; **naturellement** *adv* naturally; (*bien sûr*) of course

naufrage [nofʀaʒ] *nm* (ship)wreck; **faire ~** to be shipwrecked

nausée [noze] *nf* nausea; **avoir la ~** to feel sick

nautique [notik] *adj* nautical, water *cpd*; **sports ~s** water sports

naval, e [naval] *adj* naval; (*industrie*) shipbuilding

navet [navɛ] *nm* turnip; (*péj: film*) third-rate film

navette [navɛt] *nf* shuttle; **faire la ~ (entre)** to go to and fro (between)

navigateur [navigatœʀ] *nm* (*Navig*) seafarer; (*Inform*) browser

navigation [navigasjɔ̃] *nf* navigation, sailing

naviguer [navige] /1/ *vi* to navigate, sail; **~ sur Internet** to browse the Internet

navire [naviʀ] *nm* ship

navrer [navʀe] /1/ *vt* to upset, distress; **je suis navré (de/de faire/ que)** I'm so sorry (for/for doing/that)

ne, n' [nə, n] *adv voir* **pas¹**; **plus²**; **jamais** *etc*; (*sans valeur négative, non traduit*): **c'est plus loin que je ne le croyais** it's further than I thought

né, e [ne] *pp de* **naître**; **né en 1960** born in 1960; **née Scott** née Scott

néanmoins [neɑ̃mwɛ̃] *adv* nevertheless

néant [neɑ̃] *nm* nothingness; **réduire à ~** to bring to nought; (*espoir*) to dash

nécessaire [neseseʀ] *adj* necessary ▷ *nm* necessary; (*sac*) kit; **faire le ~** to do the necessary; **~ de couture** sewing kit; **~ de toilette** toilet bag; **nécessité** *nf* necessity; **nécessiter** /1/ *vt* to require

nectar [nɛktaʀ] *nm* nectar

néerlandais, e [neɛʀlɑ̃dɛ, -ɛz] *adj* Dutch

nef [nɛf] *nf* (*d'église*) nave

néfaste [nefast] *adj* (*nuisible*) harmful; (*funeste*) ill-fated

négatif, -ive [negatif, -iv] *adj* negative ▷ *nm* (*Photo*) negative

négligé, e [negliʒe] *adj* (*en désordre*) slovenly ▷ *nm* (*tenue*) negligee

négligeable [negliʒabl] *adj* negligible

négligent, e [negliʒɑ̃, -ɑ̃t] *adj* careless; negligent

négliger [negliʒe] /3/ *vt* (*épouse, jardin*) to neglect; (*tenue*) to be careless about; (*avis, précautions*) to disregard; **~ de faire** to fail to do, not bother to do

négociant, e [negɔsjɑ̃, -jɑ̃t] *nm/f* merchant

négociation [negɔsjasjɔ̃] *nf* negotiation

négocier [negɔsje] /7/ *vi, vt* to negotiate

nègre [nɛgʀ] *nm* (*péj*) Negro (!); (*écrivain*) ghost writer

neige [nɛʒ] *nf* snow; **neiger** /3/ *vi* to snow

nénuphar [nenyfaʀ] *nm* water-lily

néon [neɔ̃] *nm* neon

néo-zélandais, e [neozelɑ̃dɛ, -ɛz] *adj* New Zealand *cpd* ▷ *nm/f*: **N~, e** New Zealander

Népal [nepal] *nm*: **le ~** Nepal

nerf [nɛʀ] *nm* nerve; **être** *ou* **vivre sur les ~s** to live on one's nerves; **nerveux, -euse** *adj* nervous; (*irritable*) touchy, nervy; (*voiture*) nippy, responsive; **nervosité** *nf* excitability, tenseness

n'est-ce pas [nɛspɑ] *adv* isn't it?, won't you? *etc* (*selon le verbe qui précède*)

net, nette [nɛt] *adj* (*sans équivoque, distinct*) clear; (*amélioration, différence*) marked, distinct; (*propre*) neat, clean; (*Comm: prix, salaire, poids*) net ▷ *adv* (*refuser*) flatly ▷ *nm*: **mettre au ~** to copy out; **s'arrêter ~** to stop dead; **nettement** *adv* clearly; (*incontestablement*) decidedly; **netteté** *nf* clearness

nettoyage [netwajaʒ] *nm* cleaning; **~ à sec** dry cleaning

nettoyer [netwaje] /8/ *vt* to clean

neuf¹ [nœf] *num* nine

neuf², neuve [nœf, nœv] *adj* new; **remettre à ~** to do up (as good as new), refurbish; **quoi de ~?** what's new?

neutre [nøtʀ] *adj* (*Ling*) neuter

neuve [nœv] *adj f voir* **neuf²**

neuvième [nœvjɛm] *num* ninth

neveu, x [nəvø] *nm* nephew

New York [njujɔʀk] *n* New York

nez [ne] *nm* nose; **avoir du ~** to have flair; **~ à ~ avec** face to face with

ni [ni] *conj*: **ni ... ni** neither ... nor; **je n'aime ni les lentilles ni les épinards** I like neither lentils nor spinach; **il n'a dit ni oui ni non** he didn't say either yes or no; **elles ne sont venues ni l'une ni l'autre** neither of them came; **il n'a rien vu ni entendu** he didn't see or hear anything

niche [niʃ] *nf* (*du chien*) kennel; (*de mur*) recess, niche; **nicher** /1/ *vi* to nest

nid [ni] *nm* nest; **~ de poule** pothole

nièce [njɛs] *nf* niece

nier [nje] /7/ *vt* to deny

Nil [nil] *nm*: **le ~** the Nile

n'importe [nɛ̃pɔʀt] *adv*: **~ qui/ quoi/où** anybody/anything/ anywhere; **~ quand** any time; **~ quel/quelle** any; **~ lequel/laquelle** any (one); **~ comment** (*sans soin*) carelessly

niveau, x [nivo] *nm* level; (*des élèves, études*) standard; **~ de vie** standard of living

niveler [nivle] /4/ *vt* to level

noble [nɔbl] *adj* noble; **noblesse** *nf* nobility; (*d'une action etc*) nobleness

noce [nɔs] *nf* wedding; (*gens*) wedding party (*ou* guests *pl*); **faire la ~** (*fam*) to go on a binge; **~s d'or/d'argent/de diamant** golden/ silver/diamond wedding

nocif, -ive [nɔsif, -iv] *adj* harmful

nocturne [nɔktyʀn] *adj* nocturnal ▷ *nf* late opening

Noël [nɔɛl] *nm* Christmas

nœud [nø] *nm* knot; (*ruban*) bow; **~ papillon** bow tie

noir, e [nwaʀ] *adj* black; (*obscur, sombre*) dark ▷ *nm/f* black man/ woman ▷ *nm*: **dans le ~** in the dark ▷ *nf* (*Mus*) crotchet (BRIT), quarter note (US); **travailler au ~** to work on the side; **noircir** /2/ *vt*, *vi* to blacken

noisette [nwazɛt] *nf* hazelnut

noix [nwa] *nf* walnut; (*Culin*): **une ~ de beurre** a knob of butter; **à la ~** (*fam*) worthless; **~ de cajou** cashew nut; **~ de coco** coconut; **~ muscade** nutmeg

nom [nɔ̃] *nm* name; (*Ling*) noun; **~ de famille** surname; **~ de jeune fille** maiden name; **~ d'utilisateur** username

nomade [nɔmad] *nm/f* nomad

nombre [nɔ̃bʀ] *nm* number; **venir en ~** to come in large numbers; **depuis ~ d'années** for many years; **au ~ de mes amis** among my friends; **nombreux, -euse** *adj* many, numerous; (*avec nom sg: foule etc*) large; **peu nombreux** few; **de nombreux cas** many cases

nombril [nɔ̃bʀi(l)] *nm* navel

nommer [nɔme] /1/ *vt* to name; (*élire*) to appoint, nominate; **se nommer** *vr*: **il se nomme Pascal** his name's Pascal, he's called Pascal

non [nɔ̃] *adv* (*réponse*) no; (*suivi d'un adjectif, adverbe*) not; **Paul est venu, ~?** Paul came, didn't he?; **~ pas que** not that; **moi ~ plus** neither do I, I don't either; **je pense que ~** I don't think so; **~ alcoolisé** non-alcoholic

nonchalant, e [nɔ̃ʃalɑ̃, -ɑ̃t] *adj* nonchalant

non-fumeur, -euse [nɔ̃fymœʀ, -øz] *nm/f* non-smoker

non-sens [nɔ̃sɑ̃s] *nm* absurdity

nord [nɔʀ] *nm* North ▷ *adj* northern; north; **au ~** (*situation*) in the north; (*direction*) to the north; **au ~ de** to the north of; **nord-africain, e** *adj* North-African ▷ *nm/f*: **Nord-Africain, e** North African; **nord-est** *nm* North-East; **nord-ouest** *nm* North-West

normal, e, -aux [nɔʀmal, -o] *adj* normal ▷ *nf*: **la ~e** the norm, the average; **c'est tout à fait ~** it's perfectly natural; **vous trouvez ça ~?** does it seem right to you?; **normalement** *adv* (*en général*) normally

normand, e [nɔʀmɑ̃, -ɑ̃d] *adj* Norman ▷ *nm/f*: **N~, e** (*de Normandie*) Norman

Normandie [nɔʀmɑ̃di] *nf*: **la ~** Normandy

norme [nɔʀm] *nf* norm; (*Tech*) standard

Norvège [nɔʀvɛʒ] *nf*: **la ~** Norway; **norvégien, ne** *adj* Norwegian ▷ *nm* (*Ling*) Norwegian ▷ *nm/f*: **Norvégien, ne** Norwegian

nos [no] *adj poss voir* **notre**

nostalgie [nɔstalʒi] *nf* nostalgia; **nostalgique** *adj* nostalgic

notable [nɔtabl] *adj* notable, noteworthy; *(marqué)* noticeable, marked ▷ *nm* prominent citizen

notaire [nɔtɛʀ] *nm* solicitor

notamment [nɔtamɑ̃] *adv* in particular, among others

note [nɔt] *nf (écrite, Mus)* note; *(Scol)* mark *(BRIT)*, grade; *(facture)* bill; **~ de service** memorandum

noter [nɔte] */1/ vt (écrire)* to write down; *(remarquer)* to note, notice; *(devoir)* to mark, give a grade to

notice [nɔtis] *nf* summary, short article; *(brochure):* **~ explicative** explanatory leaflet, instruction booklet

notifier [nɔtifje] */7/ vt:* **~ qch à qn** to notify sb of sth, notify sth to sb

notion [nosjɔ̃] *nf* notion, idea

notoire [nɔtwaʀ] *adj* widely known; *(en mal)* notorious

notre *(pl* **nos)** [nɔtʀ(ə), no] *adj poss* our

nôtre [notʀ] *adj* ours ▷ *pron:* **le/la ~** ours; **les ~s** ours; *(alliés etc)* our own people; **soyez des ~s** join us

nouer [nwe] */1/ vt* to tie, knot; *(fig: alliance etc)* to strike up

noueux, -euse [nwø, -øz] *adj* gnarled

nourrice [nuʀis] *nf* ≈ child-minder

nourrir [nuʀiʀ] */2/ vt* to feed; *(fig: espoir)* to harbour, nurse; **nourrissant, e** *adj* nourishing, nutritious; **nourrisson** *nm* (unweaned) infant; **nourriture** *nf* food

nous [nu] *pron (sujet)* we; *(objet)* us; **nous-mêmes** *pron* ourselves

nouveau (nouvel), -elle, x [nuvo, -ɛl] *adj* new ▷ *nm/f* new pupil *(ou* employee) ▷ *nm:* **il y a du ~** there's something new ▷ *nf (piece of)* news *sg; (Littérature)* short story; **nouvelles** *nfpl (Presse, TV)* news; **de ~, à ~** again; **je suis sans nouvelles de lui** I haven't heard from him; **Nouvel An** New Year; **~ venu, nouvelle venue** newcomer; **~x mariés** newly-weds;

nouveau-né, e *nm/f* newborn (baby); **nouveauté** *nf* novelty; *(chose nouvelle)* something new

nouvelle: Nouvelle-Calédonie [nuvɛlkaledɔni] *nf:* **la Nouvelle-Calédonie** New Caledonia; **Nouvelle-Zélande** [nuvɛlzelɑ̃d] *nf:* **la Nouvelle-Zélande** New Zealand

novembre [nɔvɑ̃bʀ] *nm* November; *voir aussi* **juillet**

● **LE 11 NOVEMBRE**
●
● *Le 11 novembre* is a public holiday
● in France and commemorates
● the signing of the armistice, near
● Compiègne, at the end of the First
● World War.

noyade [nwajad] *nf* drowning *no pl*

noyau, x [nwajo] *nm (de fruit)* stone; *(Bio, Physique)* nucleus; *(fig: centre)* core

noyer [nwaje] */8/ nm* walnut (tree); *(bois)* walnut ▷ *vt* to drown; *(moteur)* to flood; **se noyer** to be drowned, drown; *(suicide)* to drown o.s.

nu, e [ny] *adj* naked; *(membres)* naked, bare; *(chambre, fil, plaine)* bare ▷ *nm (Art)* nude; **tout nu** stark naked; **se mettre nu** to strip

nuage [nɥaʒ] *nm* cloud; **nuageux, -euse** *adj* cloudy

nuance [nɥɑ̃s] *nf (de couleur, sens)* shade; **il y a une ~ (entre)** there's a slight difference (between); **nuancer** */3/ vt (pensée, opinion)* to qualify

nucléaire [nykleɛʀ] *adj* nuclear ▷ *nm:* **le ~** nuclear power

nudiste [nydist] *nm/f* nudist

nuée [nɥe] *nf:* **une ~ de** a cloud *ou* host *ou* swarm of

nuire [nɥiʀ] */38/ vi* to be harmful; **~ à** to harm, do damage to; **nuisible** [nɥizibl] *adj* harmful; **(animal) nuisible** pest

nuit [nɥi] *nf* night; **il fait ~** it's dark; **cette ~** *(hier)* last night; *(aujourd'hui)*

tonight; **de ~** (vol, service) night cpd;
~ blanche sleepless night

nul, nulle [nyl] adj (aucun) no;
(minime) nil, non-existent; (non
valable) null; (péj) useless, hopeless
▷ pron none, no one; **résultat ~,
match ~** draw; **nulle part** nowhere;
nullement adv by no means

numérique [nymeʀik] adj
numerical; (affichage, son, télévision)
digital

numéro [nymeʀo] nm number;
(spectacle) act, turn; (Presse) issue,
number; **~ de téléphone** (tele)phone
number; **~ vert** ≈ Freefone® number
(BRIT), ≈ toll-free number (US);
numéroter /1/ vt to number

nuque [nyk] nf nape of the neck

nu-tête [nytɛt] adj inv bareheaded

nutritif, -ive [nytʀitif, -iv] adj
(besoins, valeur) nutritional; (aliment)
nutritious, nourishing

nylon [nilɔ̃] nm nylon

oasis [ɔazis] nm ou f oasis

obéir [ɔbeiʀ] /2/ vi to obey; **~ à** to
obey; **obéissance** nf obedience;
obéissant, e adj obedient

obèse [ɔbɛz] adj obese; **obésité** nf
obesity

objecter [ɔbʒɛkte] /1/ vt: **~ (à qn)
que** to object (to sb) that; **objecteur**
nm: **objecteur de conscience**
conscientious objector

objectif, -ive [ɔbʒɛktif, -iv] adj
objective ▷ nm (Optique, Photo) lens
sg; (Mil, fig) objective

objection [ɔbʒɛksjɔ̃] nf objection

objectivité [ɔbʒɛktivite] nf
objectivity

objet [ɔbʒɛ] nm object; (d'une
discussion, recherche) subject; **être
ou faire l'~ de** (discussion) to be the
subject of; (soins) to be given ou
shown; **sans ~** purposeless; (sans
fondement) groundless; **~ d'art** objet
d'art; **~s personnels** personal items;

~s trouvés lost property *sg* (*BRIT*), lost-and-found *sg* (*US*); **~s de valeur** valuables

obligation [ɔbligasjɔ̃] *nf* obligation; (*Comm*) bond, debenture; **obligatoire** *adj* compulsory, obligatory; **obligatoirement** *adv* necessarily; (*fam: sans aucun doute*) inevitably

obliger [ɔbliʒe] /3/ *vt* (*contraindre*): **~ qn à faire** *ou* oblige sb to do; **je suis bien obligé (de le faire)** I have to (do it)

oblique [ɔblik] *adj* oblique; **en ~** diagonally

oblitérer [ɔblitere] /6/ *vt* (*timbre-poste*) to cancel

obnubiler [ɔbnybile] /1/ *vt* to obsess

obscène [ɔpsɛn] *adj* obscene

obscur, e [ɔpskyR] *adj* dark; (*raisons*) obscure; **obscurcir** /2/ *vt* to darken; (*fig*) to obscure; **s'obscurcir** *vi* to grow dark; **obscurité** *nf* darkness; **dans l'obscurité** in the dark, in darkness

obsédé, e [ɔpsede] *nm/f* fanatic; **~(e) sexuel(le)** sex maniac

obséder [ɔpsede] /6/ *vt* to obsess, haunt

obsèques [ɔpsɛk] *nfpl* funeral *sg*

observateur, -trice [ɔpsɛRvatœR, -tRis] *adj* observant, perceptive ▷ *nm/f* observer

observation [ɔpsɛRvasjɔ̃] *nf* observation; (*d'un règlement etc*) observance; (*reproche*) reproof; **en ~** (*Méd*) under observation

observatoire [ɔpsɛRvatwaR] *nm* observatory

observer [ɔpsɛRve] /1/ *vt* (*regarder*) to observe, watch; (*scientifiquement, aussi: règlement, jeûne etc*) to observe; (*surveiller*) to watch; (*remarquer*) to observe, notice; **faire ~ qch à qn** (*dire*) to point out sth to sb

obsession [ɔpsesjɔ̃] *nf* obsession

obstacle [ɔpstakl] *nm* obstacle; (*Équitation*) jump, hurdle; **faire ~ à**

(*projet*) to hinder, put obstacles in the path of

obstiné, e [ɔpstine] *adj* obstinate

obstiner [ɔpstine] /1/: **s'obstiner** *vi* to insist, dig one's heels in; **s'~ à faire** to persist (obstinately) in doing

obstruer [ɔpstRye] /1/ *vt* to block, obstruct

obtenir [ɔptəniR] /22/ *vt* to obtain, get; (*résultat*) to achieve, obtain; **~ de pouvoir faire** to obtain permission to do

obturateur [ɔptyRatœR] *nm* (*Photo*) shutter

obus [ɔby] *nm* shell

occasion [ɔkazjɔ̃] *nf* (*aubaine, possibilité*) opportunity; (*circonstance*) occasion; (*Comm: article non neuf*) secondhand buy; (: *acquisition avantageuse*) bargain; **à plusieurs ~s** on several occasions; **à l'~** sometimes, on occasions; **d'~** secondhand; **occasionnel, le** *adj* occasional

occasionner [ɔkazjɔne] /1/ *vt* to cause

occident [ɔksidɑ̃] *nm*: **l'O~** the West; **occidental, e, -aux** *adj* western; (*Pol*) Western ▷ *nm/f* Westerner

occupation [ɔkypasjɔ̃] *nf* occupation

occupé, e [ɔkype] *adj* (*Mil, Pol*) occupied; (*personne*) busy; (*place, sièges*) taken; (*toilettes*) engaged; **la ligne est ~e** the line's engaged (*BRIT*) *ou* busy (*US*)

occuper [ɔkype] /1/ *vt* to occupy; (*poste, fonction*) to hold; **s'~ (à qch)** to occupy o.s *ou* keep o.s. busy (with sth); **s'~ de** (*être responsable de*) to be in charge of; (*se charger de: affaire*) to take charge of, deal with; (: *clients etc*) to attend to

occurrence [ɔkyRɑ̃s] *nf*: **en l'~** in this case

océan [ɔseɑ̃] *nm* ocean

octet [ɔktɛ] *nm* byte

octobre [ɔktɔbR] *nm* October

oculiste [ɔkylist] *nm/f* eye specialist
odeur [ɔdœR] *nf* smell
odieux, -euse [ɔdjø, -øz] *adj* hateful
odorant, e [ɔdɔRɑ̃, -ɑ̃t] *adj* sweet-smelling, fragrant
odorat [ɔdɔRa] *nm* (sense of) smell
œil [œj] (*pl* **yeux**) *nm* eye; **avoir un ~ poché** *ou* **au beurre noir** to have a black eye; **à l'~** (*fam*) for free; **à l'~ nu** with the naked eye; **fermer les yeux (sur)** (*fig*) to turn a blind eye (to); **les yeux fermés** (*aussi fig*) with one's eyes shut; **ouvrir l'~** (*fig*) to keep one's eyes open *ou* an eye out
œillères [œjɛR] *nfpl* blinkers (BRIT), blinders (US)
œillet [œjɛ] *nm* (*Bot*) carnation
œuf [œf] *nm* egg; **~ à la coque/dur/mollet** boiled/hard-boiled/soft-boiled egg; **~ au plat/poché** fried/poached egg; **~s brouillés** scrambled eggs; **~ de Pâques** Easter egg
œuvre [œvR] *nf* (*tâche*) task, undertaking; (*ouvrage achevé, livre, tableau etc*) work; (*ensemble de la production artistique*) works *pl* ▷ *nm* (*Constr*): **le gros ~** the shell; **mettre en ~** (*moyens*) to make use of; **~ d'art** work of art; **~s de bienfaisance** charitable works
offense [ɔfɑ̃s] *nf* insult; **offenser** /1/ *vt* to offend, hurt; **s'offenser de** *vi* to take offence (BRIT) *ou* offense (US) at
offert, e [ɔfɛR, -ɛRt] *pp de* **offrir**
office [ɔfis] *nm* (*agence*) bureau, agency; (*Rel*) service ▷ *nm ou f* (*pièce*) pantry; **faire ~ de** to act as; **d'~** automatically; **~ du tourisme** tourist office
officiel, le [ɔfisjɛl] *adj, nm/f* official
officier [ɔfisje] /7/ *nm* officer
officieux, -euse [ɔfisjø, -øz] *adj* unofficial
offrande [ɔfRɑ̃d] *nf* offering
offre [ɔfR] *nf* offer; (*aux enchères*) bid; (*Admin: soumission*) tender; (*Écon*): **l'~ et la demande** supply and demand; **~ d'emploi** job advertised;

"**~s d'emploi**" "situations vacant"; **~ publique d'achat (OPA)** takeover bid
offrir [ɔfRiR] /18/ *vt*: **~ (à qn)** to offer (to sb); (*faire cadeau*) to give to (sb); **s'offrir**, *vt* (*vacances, voiture*) to treat o.s. to; **~ (à qn) de faire qch** to offer to do sth (for sb); **~ à boire à qn** (*chez soi*) to offer sb a drink; **je vous offre un verre** I'll buy you a drink
OGM *sigle m* (= *organisme génétiquement modifié*) GMO
oie [wa] *nf* (*Zool*) goose
oignon [ɔɲɔ̃] *nm* onion; (*de tulipe etc*) bulb
oiseau, x [wazo] *nm* bird; **~ de proie** bird of prey
oisif, -ive [wazif, -iv] *adj* idle
oléoduc [ɔleɔdyk] *nm* (oil) pipeline
olive [ɔliv] *nf* (*Bot*) olive; **olivier** *nm* olive (tree)
OLP *sigle f* (= *Organisation de libération de la Palestine*) PLO
olympique [ɔlɛ̃pik] *adj* Olympic
ombragé, e [ɔ̃bRaʒe] *adj* shaded, shady
ombre [ɔ̃bR] *nf* (*espace non ensoleillé*) shade; (*ombre portée, tache*) shadow; **à l'~** in the shade; **dans l'~** (*fig*) in the dark; **~ à paupières** eye shadow
omelette [ɔmlɛt] *nf* omelette; **~ norvégienne** baked Alaska
omettre [ɔmɛtR] /56/ *vt* to omit, leave out
omoplate [ɔmɔplat] *nf* shoulder blade

MOT-CLÉ

on [ɔ̃] *pron* **1** (*indéterminé*) you, one; **on peut le faire ainsi** you *ou* one can do it like this, it can be done like this **2** (*quelqu'un*): **on les a attaqués** they were attacked; **on vous demande au téléphone** there's a phone call for you, you're wanted on the phone **3** (*nous*) we; **on va y aller demain** we're going tomorrow

4 (les gens) they; **autrefois, on croyait ...** they used to believe ..
5: **on ne peut plus** adv: **on ne peut plus stupide** as stupid as can be

oncle [ɔ̃kl] nm uncle

onctueux, -euse [ɔ̃ktɥø, -øz] adj creamy; smooth

onde [ɔ̃d] nf wave; **~s courtes (OC)** short wave sg; **~s moyennes (OM)** medium wave sg; **grandes ~s (GO), ~s longues (OL)** long wave sg

ondée [ɔ̃de] nf shower

on-dit [ɔ̃di] nm inv rumour

onduler [ɔ̃dyle] /1/ vi to undulate; (cheveux) to wave

onéreux, -euse [ɔnerø, -øz] adj costly

ongle [ɔ̃gl] nm nail

ont [ɔ̃] vb voir **avoir**

ONU sigle f (= Organisation des Nations unies) UN(O)

onze [ɔ̃z] num eleven; **onzième** num eleventh

OPA sigle f = **offre publique d'achat**

opaque [ɔpak] adj opaque

opéra [ɔpeʀa] nm opera; (édifice) opera house

opérateur, -trice [ɔpeʀatœʀ, -tʀis] nm/f operator; **~ (de prise de vues)** cameraman

opération [ɔpeʀasjɔ̃] nf operation; (Comm) dealing

opératoire [ɔpeʀatwaʀ] adj (choc etc) post-operative

opérer [ɔpeʀe] /6/ vt (Méd) to operate on; (faire, exécuter) to carry out, make ▷ vi (remède: faire effet) to act, work; (Méd) to operate; **s'opérer** vi (avoir lieu) to occur, take place; **se faire ~** to have an operation

opérette [ɔpeʀɛt] nf operetta, light opera

opinion [ɔpinjɔ̃] nf opinion; **l'~ (publique)** public opinion

opportun, e [ɔpɔʀtœ̃, -yn] adj timely, opportune; **opportuniste** [ɔpɔʀtynist] nm/f opportunist

opposant, e [ɔpozɑ̃, -ɑ̃t] nm/f opponent

opposé, e [ɔpoze] adj (direction, rive) opposite; (faction) opposing; (opinions, intérêts) conflicting; (contre): **~ à** opposed to, against ▷ nm: **l'~** the other ou opposite side (ou direction); (contraire) the opposite; **à l'~** (fig) on the other hand; **à l'~ de** (fig) contrary to, unlike

opposer [ɔpoze] /1/ vt (personnes, armées, équipes) to oppose; (couleurs, termes, tons) to contrast; **~ qch à** (comme obstacle, défense) to set sth against; (comme objection) to put sth forward against; **s'opposer** vi (équipes) to confront each other; (opinions) to conflict; (couleurs, styles) to contrast; **s'~ à** (interdire, empêcher) to oppose

opposition [ɔpozisjɔ̃] nf opposition; **par ~ à** as opposed to; **entrer en ~ avec** to come into conflict with; **faire ~ à un chèque** to stop a cheque

oppressant, e [ɔpʀesɑ̃, -ɑ̃t] adj oppressive

oppresser [ɔpʀese] /1/ vt to oppress; **oppression** nf oppression

opprimer [ɔpʀime] /1/ vt to oppress

opter [ɔpte] /1/ vi: **~ pour** to opt for; **~ entre** to choose between

opticien, ne [ɔptisjɛ̃, -ɛn] nm/f optician

optimisme [ɔptimism] nm optimism; **optimiste** [ɔptimist] adj optimistic ▷ nm/f optimist

option [ɔpsjɔ̃] nf option; **matière à ~** (Scol) optional subject

optique [ɔptik] adj (nerf) optic; (verres) optical ▷ nf (fig: manière de voir) perspective

or [ɔʀ] nm gold ▷ conj now, but; **en or** gold cpd; **une affaire en or** a real bargain; **il croyait gagner or il a perdu** he was sure he would win and yet he lost

orage [ɔʀaʒ] nm (thunder)storm; **orageux, -euse** adj stormy

oral, e, -aux [ɔʀal, -o] *adj* oral; (*Méd*): **par voie ~e** orally ▷ *nm* oral

orange [ɔʀɑ̃ʒ] *adj inv*, *nf* orange; **orangé, e** *adj* orangey, orange-coloured; **orangeade** *nf* orangeade; **oranger** *nm* orange tree

orateur [ɔʀatœʀ] *nm* speaker

orbite [ɔʀbit] *nf* (*Anat*) (eye-)socket; (*Physique*) orbit

Orcades [ɔʀkad] *nfpl*: **les ~** the Orkneys, the Orkney Islands

orchestre [ɔʀkɛstʀ] *nm* orchestra; (*de jazz, danse*) band; (*places*) stalls *pl* (*BRIT*), orchestra (*US*)

orchidée [ɔʀkide] *nf* orchid

ordinaire [ɔʀdinɛʀ] *adj* ordinary; (*modèle, qualité*) standard; (*péj: commun*) common ▷ *nm* ordinary; (*menus*) everyday fare ▷ *nf* (*essence*) ≈ two-star (petrol) (*BRIT*), ≈ regular (gas) (*US*); **d'~** usually, normally; **comme à l'~** as usual

ordinateur [ɔʀdinatœʀ] *nm* computer; **~ individuel** *ou* **personnel** personal computer; **~ portable** laptop (computer)

ordonnance [ɔʀdɔnɑ̃s] *nf* (*Méd*) prescription; (*Mil*) orderly, batman (*BRIT*)

ordonné, e [ɔʀdɔne] *adj* tidy, orderly

ordonner [ɔʀdɔne] /1/ *vt* (*agencer*) to organize, arrange; (*donner un ordre*): **~ à qn de faire** to order sb to do; (*Rel*) to ordain; (*Méd*) to prescribe

ordre [ɔʀdʀ] *nm* order; (*propreté et soin*) orderliness, tidiness; **à l'~ de** payable to; (*nature*): **d'~ pratique** of a practical nature; **ordres** *nmpl* (*Rel*) holy orders; **mettre en ~** to tidy (up), put in order; **par ~ alphabétique/ d'importance** in alphabetical order/ in order of importance; **être aux ~s de qn/sous les ~s de qn** to be at sb's disposal/under sb's command; **jusqu'à nouvel ~** until further notice; **de premier ~** first-rate; **~ du jour** (*d'une réunion*) agenda; **à l'~ du jour** (*fig*) topical; **~ public** law and order

ordure [ɔʀdyʀ] *nf* filth *no pl*; **ordures** *nfpl* (*balayures, déchets*) rubbish *sg*, refuse *sg*; **~s ménagères** household refuse

oreille [ɔʀɛj] *nf* ear; **avoir de l'~** to have a good ear (for music)

oreiller [ɔʀeje] *nm* pillow

oreillons [ɔʀɛjɔ̃] *nmpl* mumps *sg*

ores [ɔʀ]: **d'~ et déjà** *adv* already

orfèvrerie [ɔʀfɛvʀəʀi] *nf* goldsmith's (*ou* silversmith's) trade; (*ouvrage*) (silver *ou* gold) plate

organe [ɔʀgan] *nm* organ; (*porte-parole*) representative, mouthpiece

organigramme [ɔʀganigʀam] *nm* (*hiérarchique, structure*) organization chart; (*des opérations*) flow chart

organique [ɔʀganik] *adj* organic

organisateur, -trice [ɔʀganizatœʀ, -tʀis] *nm/f* organizer

organisation [ɔʀganizasjɔ̃] *nf* organization; **O~ des Nations unies (ONU)** United Nations (Organization) (UN(O))

organiser [ɔʀganize] /1/ *vt* to organize; (*mettre sur pied: service etc*) to set up; **s'organiser** to get organized

organisme [ɔʀganism] *nm* (*Bio*) organism; (*corps humain*) body; (*Admin, Pol etc*) body

organiste [ɔʀganist] *nm/f* organist

orgasme [ɔʀgasm] *nm* orgasm, climax

orge [ɔʀʒ] *nf* barley

orgue [ɔʀg] *nm* organ

orgueil [ɔʀgœj] *nm* pride; **orgueilleux, -euse** *adj* proud

oriental, e, -aux [ɔʀjɑ̃tal, -o] *adj* (*langue, produit*) oriental; (*frontière*) eastern

orientation [ɔʀjɑ̃tasjɔ̃] *nf* (*de recherches*) orientation; (*d'une maison etc*) aspect; (*d'un journal*) leanings *pl*; **avoir le sens de l'~** to have a (good) sense of direction; **~ professionnelle** careers advisory service

orienté, e [ɔʀjɑ̃te] *adj* (*fig: article, journal*) slanted; **bien/mal ~**

(*appartement*) well/badly positioned; **~ au sud** facing south, with a southern aspect

orienter [ɔʀjɑ̃te] /1/ vt (*tourner: antenne*) to direct, turn; (: *voyageur, touriste, recherches*) to direct; (*fig: élève*) to orientate; **s'orienter** (*se repérer*) to find one's bearings; **s'~ vers** (*fig*) to turn towards

origan [ɔʀigɑ̃] nm oregano

originaire [ɔʀiʒinɛʀ] adj: **être ~ de** to be a native of

original, e, -aux [ɔʀiʒinal, -o] adj original; (*bizarre*) eccentric ▷ nm/f eccentric ▷ nm (*document etc, Art*) original

origine [ɔʀiʒin] nf origin; **origines** nfpl (*d'une personne*) origins; **d'~** (*pays*) of origin; (*pneus etc*) original; **d'~ française** of French origin; **à l'~** originally; **originel, le** adj original

orme [ɔʀm] nm elm

ornement [ɔʀnəmɑ̃] nm ornament

orner [ɔʀne] /1/ vt to decorate, adorn

ornière [ɔʀnjɛʀ] nf rut

orphelin, e [ɔʀfəlɛ̃, -in] adj orphan(ed) ▷ nm/f orphan; **~ de père/mère** fatherless/motherless; **orphelinat** nm orphanage

orteil [ɔʀtɛj] nm toe; **gros ~** big toe

orthographe [ɔʀtɔgʀaf] nf spelling

ortie [ɔʀti] nf (stinging) nettle

os [ɔs] nm bone; **os à moelle** marrowbone

osciller [ɔsile] /1/ vi (*au vent etc*) to rock; (*fig*): **~ entre** to waver ou fluctuate between

osé, e [oze] adj daring, bold

oseille [ozɛj] nf sorrel

oser [oze] /1/ vi, vt to dare; **~ faire** to dare (to) do

osier [ozje] nm willow; **d'~, en ~** wicker(work) cpd

osseux, -euse [ɔsø, -øz] adj bony; (*tissu, maladie, greffe*) bone cpd

otage [ɔtaʒ] nm hostage; **prendre qn comme ~** to take sb hostage

OTAN sigle f (= Organisation du traité de l'Atlantique Nord) NATO

otarie [ɔtaʀi] nf sea-lion

ôter [ote] /1/ vt to remove; (*soustraire*) to take away; **~ qch à qn** to take sth (away) from sb; **~ qch de** to remove sth from

otite [ɔtit] nf ear infection

ou [u] conj or; **ou … ou** either … or; **ou bien** or (else)

 MOT-CLÉ

où [u] pron relatif **1** (*position, situation*) where, that (*souvent omis*); **la chambre où il était** the room (that) he was in, the room where he was; **la ville où je l'ai rencontré** the town where I met him; **la pièce d'où il est sorti** the room he came out of; **le village d'où je viens** the village I come from; **les villes par où il est passé** the towns he went through **2** (*temps, état*) that (*souvent omis*); **le jour où il est parti** the day (that) he left; **au prix où c'est** at the price it is

▷ adv **1** (*interrogation*) where; **où est-il/va-t-il?** where is he/is he going?; **par où?** which way?; **d'où vient que …?** how come …?

2 (*position*) where; **je sais où il est** I know where he is; **où que l'on aille** wherever you go

ouate [wat] nf cotton wool (BRIT), cotton (US)

oubli [ubli] nm (*acte*): **l'~ de** forgetting; (*trou de mémoire*) lapse of memory; (*négligence*) omission, oversight; **tomber dans l'~** to sink into oblivion

oublier [ublije] /7/ vt to forget; (*ne pas voir: erreurs etc*) to miss; (*laisser quelque part: chapeau etc*) to leave behind

ouest [wɛst] nm west ▷ adj inv west; (*région*) western; **à l'~** in the west; (*direction*) (to the) west, westwards; **à l'~ de** (to the) west of

ouf [uf] *excl* phew!

oui [wi] *adv* yes

ouï-dire ['widiʀ]: **par ~** *adv* by hearsay

ouïe [wi] *nf* hearing; **ouïes** *nfpl* (*de poisson*) gills

ouragan [uʀagã] *nm* hurricane

ourlet [uʀlɛ] *nm* hem

ours [uʀs] *nm* bear; **~ brun/blanc** brown/polar bear; **~ (en peluche)** teddy (bear)

oursin [uʀsɛ̃] *nm* sea urchin

ourson [uʀsɔ̃] *nm* (bear-)cub

ouste [ust] *excl* hop it!

outil [uti] *nm* tool; **outiller** /1/ *vt* to equip

outrage [utʀaʒ] *nm* insult; **~ à la pudeur** indecent behaviour *no pl*

outrance [utʀãs]: **à ~** *adv* excessively, to excess

outre [utʀ] *prép* besides ▷ *adv*: **passer ~ à** to disregard, take no notice of; **en ~** besides, moreover; **~ mesure** to excess; (*manger, boire*) immoderately; **outre-Atlantique** *adv* across the Atlantic; **outre-mer** *adv* overseas

ouvert, e [uvɛʀ, -ɛʀt] *pp de* **ouvrir** ▷ *adj* open; (*robinet, gaz etc*) on; **ouvertement** *adv* openly; **ouverture** *nf* opening; (*Mus*) overture; **ouverture d'esprit** open-mindedness; **heures d'ouverture** (*Comm*) opening hours

ouvrable [uvʀabl] *adj*: **jour ~** working day, weekday

ouvrage [uvʀaʒ] *nm* (*tâche, de tricot etc*) work *no pl*; (*texte, livre*) work

ouvre-boîte(s) [uvʀəbwat] *nm inv* tin (BRIT) ou can opener

ouvre-bouteille(s) [uvʀəbutɛj] *nm inv* bottle-opener

ouvreuse [uvʀøz] *nf* usherette

ouvrier, -ière [uvʀije, -jɛʀ] *nm/f* worker ▷ *adj* working-class; (*problèmes, conflit*) industrial; (*mouvement*) labour *cpd*; **classe ouvrière** working class

ouvrir [uvʀiʀ] /18/ *vt* (*gén*) to open; (*brèche, passage*) to open up; (*commencer l'exploitation de, créer*) to open (up); (*eau, électricité, chauffage, robinet*) to turn on; (*Méd: abcès*) to open up, cut open ▷ *vi* to open; to open up; **s'ouvrir** *vi* to open; **s'~ à qn** to open one's heart to sb (about sth); **~ l'appétit à qn** to whet sb's appetite

ovaire [ovɛʀ] *nm* ovary

ovale [oval] *adj* oval

OVNI [ovni] *sigle m* (= *objet volant non identifié*) UFO

oxyder [ɔkside] /1/: **s'oxyder** *vi* to become oxidized

oxygéné, e [ɔksiʒene] *adj*: **eau ~e** hydrogen peroxide

oxygène [ɔksiʒɛn] *nm* oxygen

ozone [ozon] *nm* ozone; **trou dans la couche d'~** hole in the ozone layer

P

pacifique [pasifik] *adj* peaceful ▷ *nm*: **le P~, l'océan P~** the Pacific (Ocean)
pack [pak] *nm* pack
pacotille [pakɔtij] *nf* cheap junk *pl*
PACS *sigle m* (= *pacte civil de solidarité*) ≈ civil partnership; **pacser** /1/: **se pacser** *vi* ≈ to form a civil partnership
pacte [pakt] *nm* pact, treaty
pagaille [pagaj] *nf* mess, shambles *sg*
page [paʒ] *nf* page ▷ *nm* page (boy); **à la ~** (*fig*) up-to-date; **~ d'accueil** (*Inform*) home page; **~ Web** (*Inform*) web page
païen, ne [pajɛ̃, -ɛn] *adj, nm/f* pagan, heathen
paillasson [pajasɔ̃] *nm* doormat
paille [paj] *nf* straw
pain [pɛ̃] *nm* (*substance*) bread; (*unité*) loaf (of bread); (*morceau*): **~ de cire** *etc* bar of wax *etc*; **~ bis/complet** brown/wholemeal (*BRIT*) *ou* wholewheat (*US*) bread; **~ d'épice** ≈ gingerbread; **~ grillé** toast; **~ de mie** sandwich loaf; **~ au chocolat** pain au chocolat; **~ aux raisins** currant pastry
pair, e [pɛʀ] *adj* (*nombre*) even ▷ *nm* peer; **aller de ~ (avec)** to go hand in hand *ou* together (with); **jeune fille au ~** au pair; **paire** *nf* pair
paisible [pezibl] *adj* peaceful, quiet
paix [pɛ] *nf* peace; **faire la ~ avec** to make peace with; **fiche-lui la ~!** (*fam*) leave him alone!
Pakistan [pakistã] *nm*: **le ~** Pakistan
palais [palɛ] *nm* palace; (*Anat*) palate
pâle [pɑl] *adj* pale; **bleu ~** pale blue
Palestine [palɛstin] *nf*: **la ~** Palestine
palette [palɛt] *nf* (*de peintre*) palette; (*de produits*) range
pâleur [pɑlœʀ] *nf* paleness
palier [palje] *nm* (*d'escalier*) landing; (*fig*) level, plateau; **par ~s** in stages
pâlir [pɑliʀ] /2/ *vi* to turn *ou* go pale; (*couleur*) to fade
pallier [palje] /7/ *vt*: **~ à** to offset, make up for
palme [palm] *nf* (*de plongeur*) flipper; **palmé, e** [palme] *adj* (*pattes*) webbed
palmier [palmje] *nm* palm tree; (*gâteau*) heart-shaped biscuit made of flaky pastry
pâlot, te [pɑlo, -ɔt] *adj* pale, peaky
palourde [paluʀd] *nf* clam
palper [palpe] /1/ *vt* to feel, finger
palpitant, e [palpitã, -ãt] *adj* thrilling
palpiter [palpite] /1/ *vi* (*cœur, pouls*) to beat (: *plus fort*) to pound, throb
paludisme [palydism] *nm* malaria
pamphlet [pɑ̃flɛ] *nm* lampoon, satirical tract
pamplemousse [pɑ̃pləmus] *nm* grapefruit
pan [pɑ̃] *nm* section, piece ▷ *excl* bang!
panache [panaʃ] *nm* plume; (*fig*) spirit, panache
panaché, e [panaʃe] *nm* (*bière*) shandy; **glace ~e** mixed ice cream

pancarte [pɑ̃kaʀt] nf sign, notice
pancréas [pɑ̃kʀeɑs] nm pancreas
pandémie [pɑ̃demi] nf pandemic
pané, e [pane] adj fried in breadcrumbs
panier [panje] nm basket; **mettre au ~** to chuck away; **~ à provisions** shopping basket; **panier-repas** nm packed lunch
panique [panik] adj panicky ▷ nf panic; **paniquer** /1/ vi to panic
panne [pan] nf breakdown; **être/ tomber en ~** to have broken down/ break down; **être en ~ d'essence** ou **en ~ sèche** to have run out of petrol (BRIT) ou gas (US); **~ d'électricité** ou **de courant** power ou electrical failure
panneau, x [pano] nm (écriteau) sign, notice; **~ d'affichage** notice (BRIT) ou bulletin (US) board; **~ indicateur** signpost; **~ de signalisation** roadsign
panoplie [panɔpli] nf (jouet) outfit; (d'armes) display; (fig) array
panorama [panɔʀama] nm panorama
panse [pɑ̃s] nf paunch
pansement [pɑ̃smɑ̃] nm dressing, bandage; **~ adhésif** sticking plaster
pantacourt [pɑ̃takuʀ] nm cropped trousers pl
pantalon [pɑ̃talɔ̃] nm trousers pl (BRIT), pants pl (US), pair of trousers ou pants; **~ de ski** ski pants pl
panthère [pɑ̃tɛʀ] nf panther
pantin [pɑ̃tɛ̃] nm puppet
pantoufle [pɑ̃tufl] nf slipper
paon [pɑ̃] nm peacock
papa [papa] nm dad(dy)
pape [pap] nm pope
paperasse [papʀas] nf (péj) bumf no pl, papers pl; **paperasserie** nf (péj) red tape no pl; paperwork no pl
papeterie [papɛtʀi] nf (magasin) stationer's (shop) (BRIT)
papi [papi] nm (fam) granddad
papier [papje] nm paper; (article) article; **papiers** nmpl (aussi: **~s**

d'identité) (identity) papers; **~ (d') aluminium** aluminium (BRIT) ou aluminum (US) foil, tinfoil; **~ calque** tracing paper; **~ hygiénique** ou **(de) toilette** toilet paper; **~ journal** newspaper; **~ à lettres** writing paper, notepaper; **~ peint** wallpaper; **~ de verre** sandpaper
papillon [papijɔ̃] nm butterfly; (fam: contravention) (parking) ticket; **~ de nuit** moth
papillote [papijɔt] nf: **en ~** cooked in tinfoil
papoter [papɔte] /1/ vi to chatter
paquebot [pakbo] nm liner
pâquerette [pɑkʀɛt] nf daisy
Pâques [pɑk] nm, nfpl Easter

paquet [pakɛ] nm packet; (colis) parcel; (fig: tas): **~ de** pile ou heap of; **paquet-cadeau** nm gift-wrapped parcel
par [paʀ] prép by; **finir** etc **~** to end etc with; **~ amour** out of love; **passer ~ Lyon/la côte** to go via ou through Lyons/along by the coast; **~ la fenêtre** (jeter, regarder) out of the window; **trois ~ jour/personne** three a ou per day/head; **deux ~ deux** in twos; **~ ici** this way; (dans le coin) round here; **~-ci, ~-là** here and there; **~ temps de pluie** in wet weather
parabolique [paʀabɔlik] adj: **antenne ~** satellite dish
parachute [paʀaʃyt] nm parachute; **parachutiste** [paʀaʃytist] nm/f parachutist; (Mil) paratrooper
parade [paʀad] nf (spectacle, défilé) parade; (Escrime, Boxe) parry

P

paradis [paʀadi] *nm* heaven, paradise
paradoxe [paʀadɔks] *nm* paradox
paraffine [paʀafin] *nf* paraffin
parages [paʀaʒ] *nmpl*: **dans les ~ (de)** in the area *ou* vicinity (of)
paragraphe [paʀagʀaf] *nm* paragraph
paraître [paʀɛtʀ] /57/ *vb copule* to seem, look, appear ▷ *vi* to appear; (*être visible*) to show; (*Presse, Édition*) to be published, come out, appear ▷ *vb impers*: **il paraît que** it seems *ou* appears that
parallèle [paʀalɛl] *adj* parallel; (*police, marché*) unofficial ▷ *nm* (*comparaison*): **faire un ~ entre** to draw a parallel between ▷ *nf* parallel (line)
paralyser [paʀalize] /1/ *vt* to paralyze
paramédical, e, -aux [paʀamedikal, -o] *adj*: **personnel ~** paramedics *pl*, paramedical workers *pl*
paraphrase [paʀafʀaz] *nf* paraphrase
parapluie [paʀaplɥi] *nm* umbrella
parasite [paʀazit] *nm* parasite; **parasites** *nmpl* (*Tél*) interference *sg*
parasol [paʀasɔl] *nm* parasol, sunshade
paratonnerre [paʀatɔnɛʀ] *nm* lightning conductor
parc [paʀk] *nm* (*public*) park, gardens *pl*; (*de château etc*) grounds *pl*; (*d'enfant*) playpen; **~ d'attractions** amusement park; **~ éolien** wind farm; **~ de stationnement** car park; **~ à thème** theme park
parcelle [paʀsɛl] *nf* fragment, scrap; (*de terrain*) plot, parcel
parce que [paʀsk] *conj* because
parchemin [paʀʃəmɛ̃] *nm* parchment
parc(o)mètre [paʀk(ɔ)mɛtʀ] *nm* parking meter
parcourir [paʀkuʀiʀ] /11/ *vt* (*trajet, distance*) to cover; (*article, livre*) to skim *ou* glance through; (*lieu*) to go all over, travel up and down; (*frisson, vibration*) to run through
parcours [paʀkuʀ] *nm* (*trajet*) journey; (*itinéraire*) route
par-dessous [paʀdəsu] *prép, adv* under(neath)
pardessus [paʀdəsy] *nm* overcoat
par-dessus [paʀdəsy] *prép* over (the top of) ▷ *adv* over (the top); **~ le marché** on top of it all; **~ tout** above all; **en avoir ~ la tête** to have had enough
par-devant [paʀdəvɑ̃] *adv* (*passer*) round the front
pardon [paʀdɔ̃] *nm* forgiveness *no pl* ▷ *excl* (I'm) sorry; (*pour interpeller etc*) excuse me; **demander ~ à qn (de)** to apologize to sb (for); **je vous demande ~** I'm sorry; (*pour interpeller*) excuse me; **pardonner** /1/ *vt* to forgive; **pardonner qch à qn** to forgive sb for sth
pare: pare-brise *nm inv* windscreen (BRIT), windshield (US); **pare-chocs** *nm inv* bumper; **pare-feu** *nm inv* (*de foyer*) fireguard; (*Inform*) firewall ▷ *adj inv*
pareil, le [paʀɛj] *adj* (*identique*) the same, alike; (*similaire*) similar; (*tel*): **un courage/livre ~** such courage/a book, courage/a book like this; **de ~s livres** such books; **faire ~** to do the same (thing); **~ à** the same as; similar to; **sans ~** unparalleled, unequalled
parent, e [paʀɑ̃, -ɑ̃t] *nm/f*: **un/une ~/e** a relative *ou* relation; **parents** *nmpl* (*père et mère*) parents; **parenté** *nf* (*lien*) relationship
parenthèse [paʀɑ̃tɛz] *nf* (*ponctuation*) bracket, parenthesis; (*digression*) parenthesis, digression; **entre ~s** in brackets; (*fig*) incidentally
paresse [paʀɛs] *nf* laziness; **paresseux, -euse** *adj* lazy
parfait, e [paʀfɛ, -ɛt] *adj* perfect ▷ *nm* (*Ling*) perfect (tense); **parfaitement** *adv* perfectly ▷ *excl* (most) certainly

parfois [paʀfwa] adv sometimes
parfum [paʀfœ̃] nm (produit)
perfume, scent; (odeur: de fleur) scent,
fragrance; (goût) flavour ; **parfumé,**
e adj (fleur, fruit) fragrant; (femme)
perfumed; **parfumé au café** coffee-
flavoured (BRIT) ou -flavored (US);
parfumer /1/ vt (odeur, bouquet) to
perfume; (crème, gâteau) to flavour ;
parfumerie nf (produits) perfumes;
(boutique) perfume shop (BRIT) ou
store (US)
pari [paʀi] nm bet; **parier** /7/ vt to bet
Paris [paʀi] n Paris; **parisien, ne**
adj Parisian; (Géo, Admin) Paris cpd
▷ nm/f: **Parisien, ne** Parisian
parité [paʀite] nf: **~ hommes-**
femmes (Pol) balanced
representation of men and women
parjure [paʀʒyʀ] nm perjury
parking [paʀkiŋ] nm (lieu) car park
(BRIT), parking lot (US)

> Attention à ne pas traduire
> parking par le mot anglais parking.

parlant, e [paʀlɑ̃, -ɑ̃t] adj
(comparaison, preuve) eloquent; (Ciné)
talking
parlement [paʀləmɑ̃] nm
parliament; **parlementaire** adj
parliamentary ▷ nm/f ≈ Member of
Parliament (BRIT) ou Congress (US)
parler [paʀle] /1/ vi to speak, talk;
(avouer) to talk; **~ (à qn) de** to
talk ou speak (to sb) about; **~ le/**
en français to speak French/in
French; **~ affaires** to talk business;
sans ~ de (fig) not to mention, to
say nothing of; **tu parles!** (bien sûr)
you bet!
parloir [paʀlwaʀ] nm (d'une prison,
d'un hôpital) visiting room
parmi [paʀmi] prép among(st)
paroi [paʀwa] nf wall; (cloison)
partition
paroisse [paʀwas] nf parish
parole [paʀɔl] nf (mot, promesse)
word; (faculté): **la ~** speech; **paroles**
nfpl (Mus) words, lyrics; **tenir ~** to

keep one's word; **prendre la ~** to
speak; **demander la ~** to ask for
permission to speak; **je le crois sur ~**
I'll take his word for it
parquet [paʀkɛ] nm (parquet) floor;
(Jur) public prosecutor's office; **le ~**
(général) ≈ the Bench
parrain [paʀɛ̃] nm godfather;
parrainer /1/ vt (nouvel adhérent)
to sponsor
pars [paʀ] vb voir **partir**
parsemer [paʀsəme] /5/ vt (feuilles,
papiers) to be scattered over; **~ qch**
de to scatter sth with
part [paʀ] nf (qui revient à qn) share;
(fraction, partie) part; **prendre ~ à**
(débat etc) to take part in; (soucis,
douleur de qn) to share in; **faire ~**
de qch à qn to announce sth to sb,
inform sb of sth; **pour ma ~** as for me,
as far as I'm concerned; **à ~ entière**
full; **de la ~ de** (au nom de) on behalf
of; (donné par) from; **de toute(s) ~(s)**
from all sides ou quarters; **de ~ et**
d'autre on both sides, on either side;
d'une ... d'autre ~ on the one hand
... on the other hand; **d'autre ~** (de
plus) moreover; **à ~** adv separately;
(de côté) aside; prép apart from, except
for; **faire la ~ des choses** to make
allowances
partage [paʀtaʒ] nm sharing (out) no
pl, share-out; dividing up
partager [paʀtaʒe] /3/ vt to share;
(distribuer, répartir) to share (out);
(morceler, diviser) to divide (up); **se**
partager vt (héritage etc) to share
between themselves (ou ourselves
etc)
partenaire [paʀtənɛʀ] nm/f partner
parterre [paʀtɛʀ] nm (de fleurs)
(flower) bed; (Théât) stalls pl
parti [paʀti] nm (Pol) party; (décision)
course of action; (personne à marier)
match; **tirer ~ de** to take advantage
of, turn to good account; **prendre**
~ (pour/contre) to take sides ou a
stand (for/against); **~ pris** bias

partial, e, -aux [paʀsjal, -o] *adj*
biased, partial

participant, e [paʀtisipɑ̃, -ɑ̃t] *nm/f*
participant, e; (*à un concours*) entrant

participation [paʀtisipasjɔ̃]
nf participation; (*financière*)
contribution

participer [paʀtisipe] /1/: **~ à** *vt*
(*course, réunion*) to take part in; (*frais etc*) to contribute to; (*chagrin, succès de qn*) to share (in)

particularité [paʀtikylaʀite] *nf*
(*distinctive*) characteristic

particulier, -ière [paʀtikylje, -jɛʀ]
adj (*personnel, privé*) private; (*étrange*) peculiar, odd; (*spécial*) special, particular; (*spécifique*) particular ▷ *nm* (*individu: Admin*) private individual;
~ à peculiar to; **en ~** (*surtout*) in particular, particularly; (*en privé*) in private; **particulièrement** *adv* particularly

partie [paʀti] *nf* (*gén*) part; (*Jur etc: protagonistes*) party; (*de cartes, tennis etc*) game; **une ~ de campagne/de pêche** an outing in the country/a fishing party *ou* trip; **en ~** partly, in part; **faire ~ de** (*chose*) to be part of; **prendre qn à ~** to take sb to task; **en grande ~** largely, in the main;
~ civile (*Jur*) party claiming damages in a criminal case

partiel, le [paʀsjɛl] *adj* partial ▷ *nm* (*Scol*) class exam

partir [paʀtiʀ] /16/ *vi* (*gén*) to go; (*quitter*) to go, leave; (*tache*) to go, come out; **~ de** (*lieu*) (*quitter*) to leave; (*commencer à*) to start from; **~ pour/à** (*lieu, pays etc*) to leave for/go off to; **à ~ de** from

partisan, e [paʀtizɑ̃, -an] *nm/f*
partisan; **être ~ de qch/faire** to be in favour (BRIT) *ou* favor (US) of sth/doing

partition [paʀtisjɔ̃] *nf* (*Mus*) score

partout [paʀtu] *adv* everywhere;
~ où il allait everywhere *ou* wherever he went

paru [paʀy] *pp de* **paraître**

parution [paʀysjɔ̃] *nf* publication

parvenir [paʀvəniʀ] /22/: **~ à** *vt*
(*atteindre*) to reach; (*réussir*): **~ à faire** to manage to do, succeed in doing;
faire ~ qch à qn to have sth sent to sb

 MOT-CLÉ

pas¹ [pɑ] *adv* **1** (*en corrélation avec ne, non etc*) not; **il ne pleure pas** (*habituellement*) he does not *ou* doesn't cry; (*maintenant*) he's not *ou* isn't crying; **il n'a pas pleuré/ne pleurera pas** he did not *ou* didn't/ will not *ou* won't cry; **ils n'ont pas de voiture/d'enfants** they haven't got a car/any children; **il m'a dit de ne pas le faire** he told me not to do it; **non pas que ...** not that ..
2 (*employé sans ne etc*): **pas moi** not me, I don't (*ou* can't *etc*); **elle travaille, (mais) lui pas** *ou* **pas lui** she works but he doesn't *ou* does not; **une pomme pas mûre** an apple which isn't ripe; **pas du tout** not at all; **pas de sucre, merci** no sugar, thanks; **ceci est à vous ou pas?** is this yours or not?, is this yours or isn't it?
3: **pas mal** (*joli: personne, maison*) not bad; **pas mal fait** not badly done *ou* made; **comment ça va? — pas mal** how are things? — not bad; **pas mal de** quite a lot of

pas² [pɑ] *nm* (*enjambée, Danse*) step; (*bruit*) (*foot*)step; (*trace*) footprint; (*allure, mesure*) pace; **~ à ~** step by step; **au ~** at a walking pace; **marcher à grands ~** to stride along; **à ~ de loup** stealthily; **faire les cent ~** to pace up and down; **faire les premiers ~** to make the first move; **sur le ~ de la porte** on the doorstep

passage [pasaʒ] *nm* (*fait de passer*); *voir* **passer**; (*lieu, prix de la traversée, extrait de livre etc*) passage; (*chemin*) way; **de ~** (touristes) passing through; **~ clouté** pedestrian crossing; **"~ interdit"** "no entry"; **~ à niveau** level (BRIT) ou grade (US) crossing; **~ souterrain** subway (BRIT), underpass

passager, -ère [pasaʒe, -ɛʀ] adj passing ▷ nm/f passenger

passant, e [pasɑ̃, -ɑ̃t] adj (rue, endroit) busy ▷ nm/f passer-by; **remarquer qch en ~** to notice sth in passing

passe [pas] nf (Sport) pass; (Navig) channel; **être en ~ de faire** to be on the way to doing; **être dans une mauvaise ~** to be going through a bad patch

passé, e [pase] adj (événement, temps) past; (dernier: semaine etc) last; (couleur, tapisserie) faded ▷ prép after ▷ nm past; (Ling) past (tense); **~ de mode** out of fashion; **~ composé** perfect (tense); **~ simple** past historic

passe-partout [paspaʀtu] nm inv master ou skeleton key ▷ adj inv all-purpose

passeport [paspɔʀ] nm passport

passer [pase] /1/ vi (se rendre, aller) to go; (voiture, piétons: défiler) to pass (by), go by; (facteur, laitier etc) to come, call; (pour rendre visite) to call ou drop in; (film, émission) to be on; (temps, jours) to pass, go by; (couleur, papier) to fade; (mode) to die out; (douleur) to pass, go away; (Scol): **~ dans la classe supérieure** to go up (to the next class) ▷ vt (frontière, rivière etc) to cross; (douane) to go through; (examen) to sit, take; (visite médicale etc) to have; (journée, temps) to spend; **~ qch à qn** (sel etc) to pass sth to sb; (prêter) to lend sb sth; (lettre, message) to pass sth on to sb; (tolérer) to let sb get away with sth; (enfiler: vêtement) to slip on; (film, pièce) to show, put on; (disque) to play, put on; (commande) to place; (marché, accord) to agree on; **se passer** vi (avoir lieu: scène, action) to take place; (se dérouler: entretien etc) to go; (arriver): **que s'est-il passé?** what happened?; (s'écouler: semaine etc) to pass, go by; **se ~ de** to go ou do without; **~ par** to go through; **~ avant qch/qn** (fig) to come before sth/sb; **~ un coup de fil à qn** (fam) to give sb a ring; **laisser ~** (air, lumière, personne) to let through; (occasion) to let slip, miss; (erreur) to overlook; **~ à la radio/télévision** to be on the radio/on television; **~ à table** to sit down to eat; **~ au salon** to go through to ou into the sitting room; **~ son tour** to miss one's turn; **~ la seconde** (Auto) to change into second; **~ le balai/l'aspirateur** to sweep up/hoover; **je vous passe M. Dupont** (je vous mets en communication avec lui) I'm putting you through to Mr Dupont; (je lui passe l'appareil) here is Mr Dupont, I'll hand you over to Mr Dupont

passerelle [pasʀɛl] nf footbridge; (de navire, avion) gangway

passe-temps [pastɑ̃] nm inv pastime

passif, -ive [pasif, -iv] adj passive

passion [pasjɔ̃] nf passion; **passionnant, e** adj fascinating; **passionné, e** adj (personne, tempérament) passionate; (description, récit) impassioned; **être passionné de** ou **pour qch** to have a passion for sth; **passionner** /1/ vt (personne) to fascinate, grip

passoire [paswaʀ] nf sieve; (à légumes) colander; (à thé) strainer

pastèque [pastɛk] nf watermelon

pasteur [pastœʀ] nm (protestant) minister, pastor

pastille [pastij] nf (à sucer) lozenge, pastille

patate [patat] nf spud; **~ douce** sweet potato

patauger [patoʒe] /3/ vi to splash about

P

pâte [pɑt] *nf* (*à tarte*) pastry; (*à pain*) dough; (*à frire*) batter; **pâtes** *nfpl* (*macaroni etc*) pasta *sg*; **~ d'amandes** almond paste, marzipan; **~ brisée** shortcrust (BRIT) *ou* pie crust (US) pastry; **~ à choux/feuilletée** choux/ puff *ou* flaky (BRIT) pastry; **~ de fruits** crystallized fruit *no pl*; **~ à modeler** modelling clay, Plasticine® (BRIT)

pâté [pɑte] *nm* (*charcuterie*) pâté; (*tache*) ink blot; (*de sable*) sandpie; **~ (en croûte)** ≈ meat pie; **~ de maisons** block (of houses)

pâtée [pɑte] *nf* mash, feed

patente [patɑ̃t] *nf* (Comm) trading licence (BRIT) *ou* license (US)

paternel, le [patɛʀnɛl] *adj* (*amour, soins*) fatherly; (*ligne, autorité*) paternal

pâteux, -euse [pɑtø, -øz] *adj* pasty; **avoir la bouche** *ou* **langue pâteuse** to have a furred (BRIT) *ou* coated tongue

pathétique [patetik] *adj* moving

patience [pasjɑ̃s] *nf* patience

patient, e [pasjɑ̃, -ɑ̃t] *adj, nm/f* patient; **patienter** /1/ *vi* to wait

patin [patɛ̃] *nm* skate; (*sport*) skating; **~s (à glace)** (ice) skates; **~s à roulettes** roller skates

patinage [patinaʒ] *nm* skating

patiner [patine] /1/ *vi* to skate; (*roue, voiture*) to spin; **se patiner** *vi* (*meuble, cuir*) to acquire a sheen; **patineur, -euse** *nm/f* skater; **patinoire** *nf* skating rink, (ice) rink

pâtir [pɑtiʀ] /2/: **~ de** *vt* to suffer because of

pâtisserie [pɑtisʀi] *nf* (*boutique*) cake shop; (*à la maison*) pastry- *ou* cake-making, baking; **pâtisseries** *nfpl* (*gâteaux*) pastries, cakes; **pâtissier, -ière** *nm/f* pastrycook

patois [patwa] *nm* dialect, patois

patrie [patʀi] *nf* homeland

patrimoine [patʀimwan] *nm* (*culture*) heritage

patriotique [patʀijɔtik] *adj* patriotic

patron, ne [patʀɔ̃, -ɔn] *nm/f* boss; (Rel) patron saint ▷ *nm* (Couture) pattern; **patronat** *nm* employers *pl*; **patronner** /1/ *vt* to sponsor, support

patrouille [patʀuj] *nf* patrol

patte [pat] *nf* (*jambe*) leg; (*pied: de chien, chat*) paw; (: *d'oiseau*) foot

pâturage [pɑtyʀaʒ] *nm* pasture

paume [pom] *nf* palm

paumé, e [pome] *nm/f* (*fam*) drop-out

paupière [popjɛʀ] *nf* eyelid

pause [poz] *nf* (*arrêt*) break; (*en parlant, Mus*) pause; **~ de midi** lunch break

pauvre [povʀ] *adj* poor; **les ~s** the poor; **pauvreté** *nf* (*état*) poverty

pavé, e [pave] *adj* (*cour*) paved; (*rue*) cobbled ▷ *nm* (*bloc*) paving stone; cobblestone

pavillon [pavijɔ̃] *nm* (*de banlieue*) small (detached) house; pavilion; (Navig) flag

payant, e [pɛjɑ̃, -ɑ̃t] *adj* (*spectateurs etc*) paying; (*fig: entreprise*) profitable; (*effort*) which pays off; **c'est ~** you have to pay, there is a charge

paye [pɛj] *nf* pay, wages *pl*

payer [peje] /8/ *vt* (*créancier, employé, loyer*) to pay; (*achat, réparations, faute*) to pay for ▷ *vi* to pay; (*métier*) to be well-paid; (*effort, tactique etc*) to pay off; **il me l'a fait ~ 10 euros** he charged me 10 euros for it; **~ qch à qn** to buy sth for sb, buy sb sth; **se ~ la tête de qn** to take the mickey out of sb (BRIT)

pays [pei] *nm* country; (*région*) region; **du ~** local

paysage [peizaʒ] *nm* landscape

paysan, ne [peizã, -an] *nm/f* farmer; (*péj*) peasant ▷ *adj* (*rural*) country *cpd*; (*agricole*) farming

Pays-Bas [peiba] *nmpl*: **les ~** the Netherlands

PC *sigle m* (*Inform*: = personal computer) PC; = **permis de construire**; (= *prêt conventionné*) type of loan for house purchase

PDA *sigle m* (= personal digital assistant) PDA

PDG *sigle m* = **président directeur général**

péage [peaʒ] *nm* toll; (*endroit*) tollgate

peau, x [po] *nf* skin; **gants de ~** leather gloves; **être bien/mal dans sa ~** to be at ease/ill-at-ease; **~ de chamois** (*chiffon*) chamois leather, shammy

péché [peʃe] *nm* sin

pêche [pɛʃ] *nf* (*sport, activité*) fishing; (*poissons pêchés*) catch; (*fruit*) peach; **~ à la ligne** (*en rivière*) angling

pécher [peʃe] /6/ *vi* (*Rel*) to sin

pêcher [peʃe] /1/ *vi* to go fishing ▷ *vt* (*attraper*) to catch; (*chercher*) to fish for ▷ *nm* peach tree

pécheur, -eresse [peʃœʀ, peʃʀɛs] *nm/f* sinner

pêcheur [peʃœʀ] *nm voir* **pêcher** fisherman; (*à la ligne*) angler

pédagogie [pedagɔʒi] *nf* educational methods *pl*, pedagogy; **pédagogique** *adj* educational

pédale [pedal] *nf* pedal

pédalo [pedalo] *nm* pedal-boat

pédant, e [pedã, -ãt] *adj* (*péj*) pedantic ▷ *nm/f* pedant

pédestre [pedɛstʀ] *adj*: **randonnée ~** ramble; **sentier ~** pedestrian footpath

pédiatre [pedjatʀ] *nm/f* paediatrician, child specialist

pédicure [pedikyʀ] *nm/f* chiropodist

pègre [pɛgʀ] *nf* underworld

peigne [pɛɲ] *nm* comb; **peigner** /1/ *vt* to comb (the hair of); **se peigner** *vi* to comb one's hair; **peignoir** *nm* dressing gown; **peignoir de bain** bathrobe

peindre [pɛ̃dʀ] /52/ *vt* to paint; (*fig*) to portray, depict

peine [pɛn] *nf* (*affliction*) sorrow, sadness *no pl*; (*mal, effort*) trouble *no pl*, effort; (*difficulté*) difficulty; (*Jur*) sentence; **faire de la ~ à qn** to distress *ou* upset sb; **prendre la ~ de faire** to go to the trouble of doing; **se donner de la ~** to make an effort; **ce n'est pas la ~ de faire** there's no point in doing, it's not worth doing; **avoir de la ~** to be sad; **à ~** scarcely, barely; **à ... que** hardly ... than, no sooner ... than; **~ capitale** capital punishment; **~ de mort** death sentence *ou* penalty; **peiner** [pene] /1/ *vi* to work hard; to struggle; (*moteur, voiture*) to labour (BRIT), labor (US) ▷ *vt* to grieve, sadden

peintre [pɛ̃tʀ] *nm* painter; **~ en bâtiment** painter and decorator

peinture [pɛ̃tyʀ] *nf* painting; (*couche de couleur, couleur*) paint; (*surfaces peintes: aussi*: **~s**) paintwork; **"~ fraîche"** "wet paint"

péjoratif, -ive [peʒɔʀatif, -iv] *adj* pejorative, derogatory

Pékin [pekɛ̃] *n* Beijing

pêle-mêle [pɛlmɛl] *adv* higgledy-piggledy

peler [pəle] /5/ *vt, vi* to peel

pèlerin [pɛlʀɛ̃] *nm* pilgrim

pèlerinage [pɛlʀinaʒ] *nm* pilgrimage

pelle [pɛl] *nf* shovel; (*d'enfant, de terrassier*) spade

pellicule [pelikyl] *nf* film; **pellicules** *nfpl* (*Méd*) dandruff *sg*

pelote [pəlɔt] *nf* (*de fil, laine*) ball; **~ basque** pelota

peloton [pəlɔtɔ̃] *nm* group; squad; (*Sport*) pack

pelotonner [pəlɔtɔne] /1/: **se pelotonner** *vi* to curl (o.s.) up

pelouse [pəluz] nf lawn

peluche [pəlyʃ] nf: **animal en ~** soft toy, fluffy animal; **chien/lapin en ~** fluffy dog/rabbit

pelure [pəlyʀ] nf peeling, peel no pl

pénal, e, -aux [penal, -o] adj penal; **pénalité** nf penalty

penchant [pãʃã] nm: **un ~ à faire/à qch** a tendency to do/to sth; **un ~ pour qch** a liking ou fondness for sth

pencher [pãʃe] /1/ vi to tilt, lean over ▷ vt to tilt; **se pencher** vi to lean over; (se baisser) to bend down; **se ~ sur** (fig: problème) to look into; **~ pour** to be inclined to favour (BRIT) ou favor (US)

pendant, e [pãdã, -ãt] adj hanging (out) ▷ prép (au cours de) during; (indiquant la durée) for; **~ que** while

pendentif [pãdãtif] nm pendant

penderie [pãdʀi] nf wardrobe

pendre [pãdʀ] /41/ vt, vi to hang; **se ~ (à)** (se suicider) to hang o.s. (on); **~ qch à** (mur) to hang sth (up) on; (plafond) to hang sth (up) from

pendule [pãdyl] nf clock ▷ nm pendulum

pénétrer [penetre] /6/ vi to come ou get in ▷ vt to penetrate; **~ dans** to enter

pénible [penibl] adj (astreignant) hard; (affligeant) painful; (personne, caractère) tiresome; **péniblement** adv with difficulty

péniche [peniʃ] nf barge

pénicilline [penisilin] nf penicillin

péninsule [penɛ̃syl] nf peninsula

pénis [penis] nm penis

pénitence [penitãs] nf (repentir) penitence; (peine) penance; **pénitencier** nm penitentiary (US)

pénombre [penɔ̃bʀ] nf (faible clarté) half-light; (obscurité) darkness

pensée [pãse] nf thought; (démarche, doctrine) thinking no pl; (Bot) pansy; **en ~** in one's mind

penser [pãse] /1/ vi to think ▷ vt to think; **~ à** (prévoir) to think of; (ami, vacances) to think of ou about; **~ faire qch** to be thinking of doing sth, intend to do sth; **faire ~ à** to remind one of; **pensif, -ive** adj pensive, thoughtful

pension [pãsjɔ̃] nf (allocation) pension; (prix du logement) board and lodging, bed and board; (école) boarding school; **~ alimentaire** (de divorcée) maintenance allowance; alimony; **~ complète** full board; **~ de famille** boarding house, guesthouse; **pensionnaire** nm/f (Scol) boarder; **pensionnat** nm boarding school

pente [pãt] nf slope; **en ~** sloping

Pentecôte [pãtkot] nf: **la ~** Whitsun (BRIT), Pentecost

pénurie [penyʀi] nf shortage

pépé [pepe] nm (fam) grandad

pépin [pepɛ̃] nm (Bot: graine) pip; (fam: ennui) snag, hitch

pépinière [pepinjɛʀ] nf nursery

perçant, e [pɛʀsã, -ãt] adj (vue, regard, yeux) sharp; (cri, voix) piercing, shrill

perce-neige [pɛʀsənɛʒ] nm ou f inv snowdrop

percepteur, -trice [pɛʀsɛptœʀ, -tʀis] nm/f tax collector

perception [pɛʀsɛpsjɔ̃] nf perception; (bureau) tax (collector's) office

percer [pɛʀse] /3/ vt to pierce; (ouverture etc) to make; (mystère, énigme) to penetrate ▷ vi to break through; **perceuse** nf drill

percevoir [pɛʀsəvwaʀ] /28/ vt (distinguer) to perceive, detect; (taxe, impôt) to collect; (revenu, indemnité) to receive

perche [pɛʀʃ] nf (bâton) pole

percher [pɛʀʃe] /1/ vt to perch; **se percher** vi to perch; **perchoir** nm perch

perçois etc [pɛʀswa] vb voir **percevoir**

perçu, e [pɛʀsy] pp de **percevoir**

percussion [pɛʀkysjɔ̃] nf percussion

percuter [pɛʀkyte] /1/ vt to strike; (véhicule) to crash into

perdant, e [pɛʀdɑ̃, -ɑ̃t] nm/f loser

perdre [pɛʀdʀ] /41/ vt to lose; (gaspiller: temps, argent) to waste; (personne: moralement etc) to ruin ▷ vi to lose; (sur une vente etc) to lose out; **se perdre** vi (s'égarer) to get lost, lose one's way; (se gâter) to go to waste; **je me suis perdu** (et je le suis encore) I'm lost; (et je ne le suis plus) I got lost

perdrix [pɛʀdʀi] nf partridge

perdu, e [pɛʀdy] pp de **perdre** ▷ adj (isolé) out-of-the-way; (Comm: emballage) non-returnable; (malade): **il est ~** there's no hope left for him; **à vos moments ~s** in your spare time

père [pɛʀ] nm father; **~ de famille** father; **le ~ Noël** Father Christmas

perfection [pɛʀfɛksjɔ̃] nf perfection; **à la ~** to perfection; **perfectionné, e** adj sophisticated; **perfectionner** /1/ vt to improve, perfect; **se perfectionner en anglais** to improve one's English

perforer [pɛʀfɔʀe] /1/ vt (ticket, bande, carte) to punch

performant, e [pɛʀfɔʀmɑ̃, -ɑ̃t] adj: **très ~** high-performance cpd

perfusion [pɛʀfyzjɔ̃] nf: **faire une ~ à qn** to put sb on a drip

péril [peʀil] nm peril

périmé, e [peʀime] adj (Admin) out-of-date, expired

périmètre [peʀimɛtʀ] nm perimeter

période [peʀjɔd] nf period; **périodique** adj periodic ▷ nm periodical; **garniture** ou **serviette périodique** sanitary towel (BRIT) ou napkin (US)

périphérique [peʀifeʀik] adj (quartiers) outlying ▷ nm (Auto): **(boulevard) ~** ring road (BRIT), beltway (US)

périr [peʀiʀ] /2/ vi to die, perish

périssable [peʀisabl] adj perishable

perle [pɛʀl] nf pearl; (de plastique, métal, sueur) bead

permanence [pɛʀmanɑ̃s] nf permanence; (local) (duty) office; **assurer une ~** (service public, bureaux) to operate ou maintain a basic service; **être de ~** to be on call ou duty; **en ~** continuously

permanent, e [pɛʀmanɑ̃, -ɑ̃t] adj permanent; (spectacle) continuous ▷ nf perm

perméable [pɛʀmeabl] adj (terrain) permeable; **~ à** (fig) receptive ou open to

permettre [pɛʀmɛtʀ] /56/ vt to allow, permit; **~ à qn de faire/qch** to allow sb to do/sth; **se ~ de faire qch** to take the liberty of doing sth

permis [pɛʀmi] nm permit, licence; **~ (de conduire)** (driving) licence (BRIT), (driver's) license (US); **~ de construire** planning permission (BRIT), building permit (US); **~ de séjour** residence permit; **~ de travail** work permit

permission [pɛʀmisjɔ̃] nf permission; (Mil) leave; **en ~** on leave; **avoir la ~ de faire** to have permission to do

Pérou [peʀu] nm: **le ~** Peru

perpétuel, le [pɛʀpetɥɛl] adj perpetual; **perpétuité** nf: **à perpétuité** for life; **être condamné à perpétuité** to be sentenced to life imprisonment

perplexe [pɛʀplɛks] adj perplexed, puzzled

perquisitionner [pɛʀkizisjɔne] /1/ vi to carry out a search

perron [pɛʀɔ̃] nm steps pl (in front of mansion etc)

perroquet [pɛʀɔkɛ] nm parrot

perruche [peʀyʃ] nf budgerigar (BRIT), budgie (BRIT), parakeet (US)

perruque [peʀyk] nf wig

persécuter [pɛʀsekyte] /1/ vt to persecute

persévérer [pɛʀseveʀe] /6/ vi to persevere

persil [pɛʀsi] nm parsley

Persique [pɛʀsik] *adj*: **le golfe ~** the (Persian) Gulf

persistant, e [pɛʀsistã, -ãt] *adj* persistent

persister [pɛʀsiste] /1/ *vi* to persist; **~ à faire qch** to persist in doing sth

personnage [pɛʀsɔnaʒ] *nm* (*notable*) personality; (*individu*) character, individual; (*de roman, film*) character; (*Peinture*) figure

personnalité [pɛʀsɔnalite] *nf* personality; (*personnage*) prominent figure

personne [pɛʀsɔn] *nf* person ▷ *pron* nobody, no one; (*avec négation en anglais*) anybody, anyone; **~ âgée** elderly person; **personnel, le** *adj* personal; (*égoïste*) selfish ▷ *nm* personnel; **personnellement** *adv* personally

perspective [pɛʀspɛktiv] *nf* (*Art*) perspective; (*vue, coup d'œil*) view; (*point de vue*) viewpoint, angle; (*chose escomptée, envisagée*) prospect; **en ~** in prospect

perspicace [pɛʀspikas] *adj* clear-sighted, gifted with (*ou* showing) insight; **perspicacité** *nf* insight

persuader [pɛʀsɥade] /1/ *vt*: **~ qn (de/de faire)** to persuade sb (of/to do); **persuasif, -ive** *adj* persuasive

perte [pɛʀt] *nf* loss; (*de temps*) waste; (*fig: morale*) ruin; **à ~ de vue** as far as the eye can (*ou* could) see; **~s blanches** (vaginal) discharge *sg*

pertinent, e [pɛʀtinã, -ãt] *adj* apt, relevant

perturbation [pɛʀtyʀbasjɔ̃] *nf*: **~ (atmosphérique)** atmospheric disturbance

perturber [pɛʀtyʀbe] /1/ *vt* to disrupt; (*Psych*) to perturb, disturb

pervers, e [pɛʀvɛʀ, -ɛʀs] *adj* perverted

pervertir [pɛʀvɛʀtiʀ] /2/ *vt* to pervert

pesant, e [pəzã, -ãt] *adj* heavy; (*fig: présence*) burdensome

pèse-personne [pɛzpɛʀsɔn] *nm* (bathroom) scales *pl*

peser [pəze] /5/ *vt* to weigh ▷ *vi* to be heavy; (*fig: avoir de l'importance*) to carry weight

pessimiste [pesimist] *adj* pessimistic ▷ *nm/f* pessimist

peste [pɛst] *nf* plague

pétale [petal] *nm* petal

pétanque [petãk] *nf* type of bowls

⬥ **PÉTANQUE**
⬥
⬥
⬥ *Pétanque* is a version of the game
⬥ of 'boules', played on a variety of
⬥ hard surfaces. Standing with their
⬥ feet together, players throw steel
⬥ bowls at a wooden jack. *Pétanque*
⬥ originated in the South of France
⬥ and is still very much associated
⬥ with that area.

pétard [petaʀ] *nm* banger (BRIT), firecracker

péter [pete] /6/ *vi* (*fam: casser, sauter*) to bust; (*fam!*) to fart (!)

pétillant, e [petijã, -ãt] *adj* (*eau*) sparkling

pétiller [petije] /1/ *vi* (*flamme, bois*) to crackle; (*mousse, champagne*) to bubble; (*yeux*) to sparkle

petit, e [pəti, -it] *adj* small; (*avec nuance affective*) little; (*voyage*) short, little; (*bruit etc*) faint, slight ▷ *nm/f* (*petit enfant*) little one, child; **petits** *nmpl* (*d'un animal*) young *pl*; **faire des ~s** to have kittens (*ou* puppies *etc*); **la classe des ~s** the infant class; **les tout-~s** toddlers; **~ à ~** bit by bit, gradually; **~(e) ami(e)** boyfriend/girlfriend; **les ~es annonces** the small ads; **~ déjeuner** breakfast; **~ four** petit four; **~ pain** (bread) roll; **~s pois** garden peas; **petite-fille** *nf* granddaughter; **petit-fils** *nm* grandson

pétition [petisjɔ̃] *nf* petition

petits-enfants [pətizãfã] *nmpl* grandchildren

pétrin [petʀɛ̃] nm (fig): **dans le ~** in a jam ou fix

pétrir [petʀiʀ] /2/ vt to knead

pétrole [petʀɔl] nm oil; (pour lampe, réchaud etc) paraffin; **pétrolier, -ière** nm oil tanker

⬛ Attention à ne pas traduire pétrole par le mot anglais petrol.

⬤ MOT-CLÉ

peu [pø] adv 1 (modifiant verbe, adjectif, adverbe): **il boit peu** he doesn't drink (very) much; **il est peu bavard** he's not very talkative; **peu avant/après** shortly before/afterwards
2 (modifiant nom): **peu de: peu de gens/d'arbres** few ou not (very) many people/trees; **il a peu d'espoir** he hasn't (got) much hope, he has little hope; **pour peu de temps** for (only) a short while
3: **peu à peu** little by little; **à peu près** just about, more or less; **à peu près 10 kg/10 euros** approximately 10 kg/10 euros
▶nm 1: **le peu de gens qui** the few people who; **le peu de sable qui** what little sand, the little sand which
2: **un peu** a little; **un petit peu** a little bit; **un peu d'espoir** a little hope; **elle est un peu bavarde** she's rather talkative; **un peu plus de** slightly more than; **un peu moins de** slightly less than; (avec pluriel) slightly fewer than
▶pron: **peu le savent** few know (it); **de peu** (only) just

peuple [pœpl] nm people; **peupler** /1/ vt (pays, région) to populate; (étang) to stock; (hommes, poissons) to inhabit

peuplier [pøplije] nm poplar (tree)

peur [pœʀ] nf fear; **avoir ~ (de/ de faire/que)** to be frightened ou afraid (of/of doing/that); **faire ~ à** to frighten; **de ~ de/que** for fear of/

that; **peureux, -euse** adj fearful, timorous

peut [pø] vb voir **pouvoir**

peut-être [pøtɛtʀ] adv perhaps, maybe; **~ que** perhaps, maybe; **~ bien qu'il fera/est** he may well do/be

phare [faʀ] nm (en mer) lighthouse; (de véhicule) headlight

pharmacie [faʀmasi] nf (magasin) chemist's (BRIT), pharmacy; (armoire) medicine chest ou cupboard; **pharmacien, ne** nm/f pharmacist, chemist (BRIT)

phénomène [fenɔmɛn] nm phenomenon

philosophe [filɔzɔf] nm/f philosopher ▷ adj philosophical

philosophie [filɔzɔfi] nf philosophy

phobie [fɔbi] nf phobia

phoque [fɔk] nm seal

phosphorescent, e [fɔsfɔʀesɑ̃, -ɑ̃t] adj luminous

photo [foto] nf photo; **prendre en ~** to take a photo of; **aimer la/ faire de la ~** to like taking/take photos; **~ d'identité** passport photo; **photocopie** nf photocopy; **photocopier** /7/ vt to photocopy

photocopieur [fɔtɔkɔpjœʀ] nm, **photocopieuse** [fɔtɔkɔpjøz] nf (photo)copier

photo: photographe nm/f photographer; **photographie** nf (procédé, technique) photography; (cliché) photograph; **photographier** /7/ vt to photograph

phrase [fʀɑz] nf sentence

physicien, ne [fizisjɛ̃, -ɛn] nm/f physicist

physique [fizik] adj physical ▷ nm physique ▷ nf physics sg; **au ~** physically; **physiquement** adv physically

pianiste [pjanist] nm/f pianist

piano [pjano] nm piano; **pianoter** /1/ vi to tinkle away (at the piano)

pic [pik] nm (instrument) pick(axe); (montagne) peak; (Zool) woodpecker;

à ~ vertically; (*fig: tomber, arriver*) just at the right time

pichet [piʃɛ] *nm* jug

picorer [pikɔʀe] /1/ *vt* to peck

pie [pi] *nf* magpie

pièce [pjɛs] *nf* (*d'un logement*) room; (*Théât*) play; (*de mécanisme, machine*) part; (*de monnaie*) coin; (*document*) document; (*de drap, fragment, d'une collection*) piece; **deux euros ~** two euros each; **vendre à la ~** to sell separately *ou* individually; **travailler/payer à la ~** to do piecework/pay piece rate; **un maillot une ~** a one-piece swimsuit; **un deux-~s cuisine** a two-room(ed) flat (BRIT) *ou* apartment (US) with kitchen; **~ à conviction** exhibit; **~ d'eau** ornamental lake *ou* pond; **~ d'identité: avez-vous une ~ d'identité?** have you got any (means of) identification?; **~ jointe** (*Inform*) attachment; **~ montée** tiered cake; **~ de rechange** spare (part); **~s détachées** spares, (spare) parts; **~s justificatives** supporting documents

pied [pje] *nm* foot; (*de table*) leg; (*de lampe*) base; **~s nus** barefoot; **à ~** on foot; **au ~ de la lettre** literally; **avoir ~** to be able to touch the bottom, not to be out of one's depth; **avoir le ~ marin** to be a good sailor; **sur ~** (*debout, rétabli*) up and about; **mettre sur ~** (*entreprise*) to set up; **c'est le ~!** (*fam*) it's brilliant!; **mettre les ~s dans le plat** (*fam*) to put one's foot in it; **il se débrouille comme un ~** (*fam*) he's completely useless; **pied-noir** *nm* Algerian-born Frenchman

piège [pjɛʒ] *nm* trap; **prendre au ~** to trap; **piéger** /3, 6/ *vt* (*avec une bombe*) to booby-trap; **lettre/voiture piégée** letter-/car-bomb

piercing [pjɛʀsiŋ] *nm* piercing

pierre [pjɛʀ] *nf* stone; **~ tombale** tombstone; **pierreries** *nfpl* gems, precious stones

piétiner [pjetine] /1/ *vi* (*trépigner*) to stamp (one's foot); (*fig*) to be at a standstill ▷ *vt* to trample on

piéton, ne [pjetɔ̃, -ɔn] *nm/f* pedestrian; **piétonnier, -ière** *adj* pedestrian *cpd*

pieu, x [pjø] *nm* post; (*pointu*) stake

pieuvre [pjœvʀ] *nf* octopus

pieux, -euse [pjø, -øz] *adj* pious

pigeon [piʒɔ̃] *nm* pigeon

piger [piʒe] /3/ *vi* (*fam*) to get it ▷ *vt* (*fam*) to get

pigiste [piʒist] *nm/f* freelance journalist (*paid by the line*)

pignon [piɲɔ̃] *nm* (*de mur*) gable

pile [pil] *nf* (*tas, pilier*) pile; (*Élec*) battery ▷ *adv* (*net, brusquement*) dead; **à deux heures ~** at two on the dot; **jouer à ~ ou face** to toss up (for it); **~ ou face?** heads or tails?

piler [pile] /1/ *vt* to crush, pound

pilier [pilje] *nm* pillar

piller [pije] /1/ *vt* to pillage, plunder, loot

pilote [pilɔt] *nm* pilot; (*de char, voiture*) driver ▷ *adj* pilot *cpd*; **~ de chasse/d'essai/de ligne** fighter/ test/airline pilot; **~ de course** racing driver; **piloter** /1/ *vt* (*navire*) to pilot; (*avion*) to fly; (*automobile*) to drive

pilule [pilyl] *nf* pill; **prendre la ~** to be on the pill

piment [pimɑ̃] *nm* (*Bot*) pepper, capsicum; (*fig*) spice, piquancy; **~ rouge** (*Culin*) chilli; **pimenté, e** *adj* (*plat*) hot and spicy

pin [pɛ̃] *nm* pine (tree)

pinard [pinaʀ] *nm* (*fam*) (cheap) wine, plonk (BRIT)

pince [pɛ̃s] *nf* (*outil*) pliers *pl*; (*de homard, crabe*) pincer, claw; (*Couture: pli*) dart; **~ à épiler** tweezers *pl*; **~ à linge** clothes peg (BRIT) *ou* pin (US)

pincé, e [pɛ̃se] *adj* (*air*) stiff

pinceau, x [pɛ̃so] *nm* (paint)brush

pincer [pɛ̃se] /3/ *vt* to pinch; (*fam*) to nab

pinède [pinɛd] nf pinewood, pine forest

pingouin [pɛ̃gwɛ̃] nm penguin

ping-pong [piŋpɔ̃g] nm table tennis

pinson [pɛ̃sɔ̃] nm chaffinch

pintade [pɛ̃tad] nf guinea-fowl

pion, ne [pjɔ̃, pjɔn] nm/f (Scol: péj) student paid to supervise schoolchildren ▷ nm (Échecs) pawn; (Dames) piece

pionnier [pjɔnje] nm pioneer

pipe [pip] nf pipe; **fumer la** ou **une ~** to smoke a pipe

piquant, e [pikɑ̃, -ɑ̃t] adj (barbe, rosier etc) prickly; (saveur, sauce) hot, pungent; (fig: détail) titillating; (: mordant, caustique) biting ▷ nm (épine) thorn, prickle; (fig) spiciness, spice

pique [pik] nf pike; (fig): **envoyer** ou **lancer des ~s à qn** to make cutting remarks to sb ▷ nm (Cartes) spades pl

pique-nique [piknik] nm picnic; **pique-niquer** /1/ vi to (have a) picnic

piquer [pike] /1/ vt (percer) to prick; (Méd) to give an injection to; (: animal blessé etc) to put to sleep; (insecte, fumée, ortie) to sting; (moustique) to bite; (froid) to bite; (intérêt etc) to arouse; (fam: voler) to pinch ▷ vi (oiseau, avion) to go into a dive

piquet [pikɛ] nm (pieu) post, stake; (de tente) peg

piqûre [pikyʀ] nf (d'épingle) prick; (d'ortie) sting; (de moustique) bite; (Méd) injection, shot (us); **faire une ~ à qn** to give sb an injection

pirate [piʀat] adj ▷ nm pirate; **~ de l'air** hijacker

pire [piʀ] adj worse; (superlatif): **le (la) ~ ...** the worst ... ▷ nm: **le ~ (de)** the worst (of); **au ~** at (the very) worst

pis [pi] nm (de vache) udder ▷ adj, adv worse; **de mal en ~** from bad to worse

piscine [pisin] nf (swimming) pool; **~ couverte** indoor (swimming) pool

pissenlit [pisɑ̃li] nm dandelion

pistache [pistaʃ] nf pistachio (nut)

piste [pist] nf (d'un animal, sentier) track, trail; (indice) lead; (de stade, de magnétophone) track; (de cirque) ring; (de danse) floor; (de patinage) rink; (de ski) run; (Aviat) runway; **~ cyclable** cycle track

pistolet [pistɔlɛ] nm (arme) pistol, gun; (à peinture) spray gun; **pistolet-mitrailleur** nm submachine gun

piston [pistɔ̃] nm (Tech) piston; **avoir du ~** (fam) to have friends in the right places; **pistonner** /1/ vt (candidat) to pull strings for

piteux, -euse [pitø, -øz] adj pitiful, sorry (avant le nom); **en ~ état** in a sorry state

pitié [pitje] nf pity; **il me fait ~** I feel sorry for him; **avoir ~ de** (compassion) to pity, feel sorry for; (merci) to have pity ou mercy on

pitoyable [pitwajabl] adj pitiful

pittoresque [pitɔʀɛsk] adj picturesque

pizza [pidza] nf pizza

PJ sigle f (= police judiciaire) ≈ CID (BRIT), ≈ FBI (US)

placard [plakaʀ] nm (armoire) cupboard; (affiche) poster, notice

place [plas] nf (emplacement, situation, classement) place; (de ville, village) square; (espace libre) room, space; (de parking) space; (siège: de train, cinéma, voiture) seat; (emploi) job; **en ~** (mettre) in its place; **sur ~** on the spot; **faire ~ à** to give way to; **ça prend de la ~** it takes up a lot of room ou space; **à la ~ de** in place of, instead of; **à votre ~ ...** if I were you ...; **se mettre à la ~ de qn** to put o.s. in sb's place ou in sb's shoes

placé, e [plase] adj: **haut ~** (fig) high-ranking; **être bien/mal ~** to be well/badly placed; (spectateur) to have a good/bad seat; **il est bien ~ pour le savoir** he is in a position to know

placement [plasmɑ̃] nm (Finance) investment; **agence** ou **bureau de ~** employment agency

P

placer [plase] /3/ vt to place; (convive, spectateur) to seat; (capital, argent) to place, invest; **se ~ au premier rang** to go and stand (ou sit) in the first row

plafond [plafɔ̃] nm ceiling

plage [plaʒ] nf beach; **~ arrière** (Auto) parcel ou back shelf

plaider [plede] /1/ vi (avocat) to plead ▷ vt to plead; **~ pour** (fig) to speak for; **plaidoyer** nm (Jur) speech for the defence (BRIT) ou defense (US); (fig) plea

plaie [plɛ] nf wound

plaignant, e [plɛɲɑ̃, -ɑ̃t] nm/f plaintiff

plaindre [plɛ̃dR] /52/ vt to pity, feel sorry for; **se plaindre** vi (gémir) to moan; (protester, rouspéter): **se ~ (à qn) (de)** to complain (to sb) (about); **se ~ de** (souffrir) to complain of

plaine [plɛn] nf plain

plain-pied [plɛ̃pje] adv: **de ~ (avec)** on the same level (as)

plaint, e [plɛ̃, -ɛ̃t] pp de **plaindre** ▷ nf (gémissement) moan, groan; (doléance) complaint; **porter ~e** to lodge a complaint

plaire [plɛR] /54/ vi to be a success, be successful; **cela me plaît** I like it; **ça plaît beaucoup aux jeunes** it's very popular with young people; **se ~ quelque part** to like being somewhere; **s'il vous plaît, s'il te plaît** please

plaisance [plɛzɑ̃s] nf (aussi: **navigation de ~**) (pleasure) sailing, yachting

plaisant, e [plɛzɑ̃, -ɑ̃t] adj pleasant; (histoire, anecdote) amusing

plaisanter [plɛzɑ̃te] /1/ vi to joke; **plaisanterie** nf joke

plaisir [plɛziR] nm pleasure; **faire ~ à qn** (délibérément) to be nice to sb, please sb; **ça me fait ~** I'm delighted ou very pleased with this; **j'espère que ça te fera ~** I hope you'll like it; **pour le** ou **pour son** ou **par ~** for pleasure

plaît [plɛ] vb voir **plaire**

plan, e [plɑ̃, -an] adj flat ▷ nm plan; (fig) level, plane; (Ciné) shot; **au premier/second ~** in the foreground/ middle distance; **à l'arrière ~** in the background; **~ d'eau** lake

planche [plɑ̃ʃ] nf (pièce de bois) plank, (wooden) board; (illustration) plate; **~ à repasser** ironing board; **~ (à roulettes)** skateboard; **~ à voile** (sport) windsurfing

plancher [plɑ̃ʃe] /1/ nm floor; (planches) floorboards pl ▷ vi to work hard

planer [plane] /1/ vi to glide; (fam: rêveur) to have one's head in the clouds; **~ sur** (danger) to hang over

planète [planɛt] nf planet

planeur [planœR] nm glider

planifier [planifje] /7/ vt to plan

planning [planiŋ] nm programme , schedule; **~ familial** family planning

plant [plɑ̃] nm seedling, young plant

plante [plɑ̃t] nf plant; **~ d'appartement** house ou pot plant; **~ du pied** sole (of the foot); **~ verte** house plant

planter [plɑ̃te] /1/ vt (plante) to plant; (enfoncer) to hammer ou drive in; (tente) to put up, pitch; (fam: mettre) to dump; **se planter** vi (fam: se tromper) to get it wrong; (: ordinateur) to crash

plaque [plak] nf plate; (de verglas, d'eczéma) patch; (avec inscription) plaque; **~ chauffante** hotplate; **~ de chocolat** bar of chocolate; **~ tournante** (fig) centre

plaqué, e [plake] adj: **~ or/argent** gold-/silver-plated

plaquer [plake] /1/ vt (Rugby) to bring down; (fam: laisser tomber) to drop

plaquette [plakɛt] nf (de chocolat) bar; (de beurre) packet; **~ de frein** brake pad

plastique [plastik] adj ▷ nm plastic ▷ nf plastic arts pl; (d'une statue) modelling; **plastiquer** /1/ vt to blow up

plat, e [pla, -at] adj flat; (style) flat, dull ▷ nm (récipient, Culin) dish; (d'un repas) course; **à ~ ventre** face down; **à ~** (pneu, batterie) flat; (fam: fatigué) dead beat; **~ cuisiné** pre-cooked meal (ou dish); **~ du jour** dish of the day; **~ principal** ou **de résistance** main course

platane [platan] nm plane tree

plateau, x [plato] nm (support) tray; (Géo) plateau; (Ciné) set; **~ à fromages** cheeseboard

plate-bande [platbɑ̃d] nf flower bed

plate-forme [platfɔrm] nf platform; **~ de forage/pétrolière** drilling/oil rig

platine [platin] nm platinum ▷ nf (d'un tourne-disque) turntable; **~ laser** ou **compact-disc** compact disc (player)

plâtre [platr] nm (matériau) plaster; (statue) plaster statue; (Méd) (plaster) cast; **avoir un bras dans le ~** to have an arm in plaster

plein, e [plɛ̃, -ɛn] adj full ▷ nm: **faire le ~ (d'essence)** to fill up (with petrol (BRIT) ou gas (US)); **à ~es mains** (ramasser) in handfuls; **à ~ temps** full-time; **en ~ air** in the open air; **en ~ soleil** in direct sunlight; **en ~e nuit/ rue** in the middle of the night/street; **en ~ jour** in broad daylight

pleurer [plœre] /1/ vi to cry; (yeux) to water ▷ vt to mourn (for); **~ sur** to lament (over), bemoan

pleurnicher [plœrniʃe] /1/ vi to snivel, whine

pleurs [plœr] nmpl: **en ~** in tears

pleut [plø] vb voir **pleuvoir**

pleuvoir [pløvwar] /23/ vb impers to rain ▷ vi (coups) to rain down; (critiques, invitations) to shower down; **il pleut** it's raining; **il pleut des cordes** ou **à verse** ou **à torrents** it's pouring (down), it's raining cats and dogs

pli [pli] nm fold; (de jupe) pleat; (de pantalon) crease

pliant, e [plijɑ̃, -ɑ̃t] adj folding

plier [plije] /7/ vt to fold; (pour ranger) to fold up; (genou, bras) to bend ▷ vi to bend; (fig) to yield; **se ~ à** to submit to

plisser [plise] /1/ vt (yeux) to screw up; (front) to furrow; (jupe) to put pleats in

plomb [plɔ̃] nm (métal) lead; (d'une cartouche) (lead) shot; (Pêche) sinker; (Élec) fuse; **sans ~** (essence) unleaded

plomberie [plɔ̃bri] nf plumbing

plombier [plɔ̃bje] nm plumber

plonge [plɔ̃ʒ] nf: **faire la ~** to be a washer-up (BRIT) ou dishwasher (person)

plongeant, e [plɔ̃ʒɑ̃, -ɑ̃t] adj (vue) from above; (tir, décolleté) plunging

plongée [plɔ̃ʒe] nf (Sport) diving no pl; (: sans scaphandre) skin diving; **~ sous-marine** diving

plongeoir [plɔ̃ʒwar] nm diving board

plongeon [plɔ̃ʒɔ̃] nm dive

plonger [plɔ̃ʒe] /3/ vi to dive ▷ vt: **~ qch dans** to plunge sth into; **se ~ dans** (études, lecture) to bury ou immerse o.s. in; **plongeur, -euse** [plɔ̃ʒœr, -øz] nm/f diver

plu [ply] pp de **plaire**; **pleuvoir**

pluie [plɥi] nf rain

plume [plym] nf feather; (pour écrire) (pen) nib; (fig) pen

plupart [plypar]: **la ~** pron the majority, most (of them); **la ~ des** most, the majority of; **la ~ du temps/d'entre nous** most of the time/of us; **pour la ~** for the most part, mostly

pluriel [plyrjɛl] nm plural

plus¹ [ply] vb voir **plaire**

MOT-CLÉ

plus² [ply] adv **1** (forme négative): **ne ... plus** no more, no longer; **je n'ai plus d'argent** I've got no more money ou

no money left; **il ne travaille plus**
he's no longer working, he doesn't
work any more
2 [ply, plyz + *voyelle*] (*comparatif*)
more, ...+er; (*superlatif*): **le plus**
the most, the ...+est; **plus grand/
intelligent (que)** bigger/more
intelligent (than); **le plus grand/
intelligent** the biggest/most
intelligent; **tout au plus** at the
very most
3 [plys, plyz + *voyelle*] (*davantage*)
more; **il travaille plus (que)** he
works more (than); **plus il travaille,
plus il est heureux** the more he
works, the happier he is; **plus de 10
personnes/trois heures/quatre
kilos** more than *ou* over 10 people/
three hours/four kilos; **trois heures
de plus que** three hours more than;
de plus what's more, moreover; **il
a trois ans de plus que moi** he's
three years older than me; **trois
kilos en plus** three kilos more; **en
plus de** in addition to; **de plus en
plus** more and more; **plus ou moins**
more or less; **ni plus ni moins** no
more, no less
▶ *prép* [plys]: **quatre plus deux** four
plus two

plusieurs [plyzjœʀ] *adj, pron* several;
ils sont ~ there are several of them
plus-value [plyvaly] *nf* (*bénéfice*)
capital gain
plutôt [plyto] *adv* rather; **je ferais
~ ceci** I'd rather *ou* sooner do this;
~ que (de) faire rather than *ou*
instead of doing
pluvieux, -euse [plyvjø, -øz] *adj*
rainy, wet
PME *sigle fpl* (= *petites et moyennes
entreprises*) small businesses
PMU *sigle m* (= *pari mutuel urbain*) (*dans
un café*) betting agency
PNB *sigle m* (= *produit national brut*)
GNP
pneu [pnø] *nm* tyre (BRIT), tire (US)

pneumonie [pnømɔni] *nf*
pneumonia
poche [pɔʃ] *nf* pocket; (*sous les yeux*)
bag, pouch; **argent de ~** pocket
money
pochette [pɔʃɛt] *nf* (*d'aiguilles etc*)
case; (*de femme*) clutch bag; (*mouchoir*)
breast pocket handkerchief; **~ de
disque** record sleeve
podcast [pɔdkast] *nm* podcast;
podcaster /1/ *vi* to podcast
poêle [pwal] *nm* stove ▷ *nf*: **~ (à
frire)** frying pan
poème [pɔɛm] *nm* poem
poésie [pɔezi] *nf* (*poème*) poem; (*art*):
la ~ poetry
poète [pɔɛt] *nm* poet
poids [pwa] *nm* weight; (*Sport*)
shot; **vendre au ~** to sell by weight;
perdre/prendre du ~ to lose/put on
weight; **~ lourd** (*camion*) (big) lorry
(BRIT), truck (US)
poignant, e [pwaɲɑ̃, -ɑ̃t] *adj*
poignant
poignard [pwaɲaʀ] *nm* dagger;
poignarder /1/ *vt* to stab, knife
poigne [pwaɲ] *nf* grip; **avoir de la ~**
(*fig*) to rule with a firm hand
poignée [pwaɲe] *nf* (*de sel etc, fig*)
handful; (*de couvercle, porte*) handle;
~ de main handshake
poignet [pwaɲɛ] *nm* (*Anat*) wrist; (*de
chemise*) cuff
poil [pwal] *nm* (*Anat*) hair; (*de pinceau,
brosse*) bristle; (*de tapis, tissu*) strand;
(*pelage*) coat; **à ~** (*fam*) starkers; **au ~**
(*fam*) hunky-dory; **poilu, e** *adj* hairy
poinçonner [pwɛ̃sɔne] /1/ *vt*
(*bijou etc*) to hallmark; (*billet, ticket*)
to punch
poing [pwɛ̃] *nm* fist; **coup de ~** punch
point [pwɛ̃] *nm* dot; (*de ponctuation*)
full stop, period (US); (*Couture, Tricot*)
stitch ▷ *adv* = **pas¹**; **faire le ~** (*fig*) to
take stock (of the situation); **sur le
~ de faire** (just) about to do; **à tel
~ que** so much so that; **mettre au
~** (*mécanisme, procédé*) to develop;

(*affaire*) to settle; **à ~** (*Culin: viande*) medium; **à ~ (nommé)** just at the right time; **deux ~s** colon; **~ (de côté)** stitch (*pain*); **~ d'exclamation** exclamation mark; **~ faible** weak spot; **~ final** full stop, period (*US*); **~ d'interrogation** question mark; **~ mort** full stop, period (*US*); **~ mort; au ~ mort** (*Auto*) in neutral; **~ de repère** landmark; (*dans le temps*) point of reference; **~ de vente** retail outlet; **~ de vue** viewpoint; (*fig: opinion*) point of view; **~s cardinaux** cardinal points; **~s de suspension** suspension points

pointe [pwɛ̃t] *nf* point; (*clou*) tack; **une ~ d'ail/d'accent** a touch *ou* hint of garlic/of an accent; **être à la ~ de** (*fig*) to be in the forefront of; **sur la ~ des pieds** on tiptoe; **en ~** *adj* pointed, tapered; **de ~** (*technique etc*) leading; **heures/jours de ~** peak hours/days

pointer [pwɛ̃te] /1/ *vt* (*diriger: canon, longue-vue, doigt*): **~ vers qch, ~ sur qch** to point at sth ▷ *vi* (*employé*) to clock in *ou* on

pointeur, -euse [pwɛ̃tœʀ, -øz] *nf* timeclock ▷ *nm* (*Inform*) cursor

pointillé [pwɛ̃tije] *nm* (*trait*) dotted line

pointilleux, -euse [pwɛ̃tijø, -øz] *adj* particular, pernickety

pointu, e [pwɛ̃ty] *adj* pointed; (*voix*) shrill; (*analyse*) precise

pointure [pwɛ̃tyʀ] *nf* size

point-virgule [pwɛ̃viʀɡyl] *nm* semi-colon

poire [pwaʀ] *nf* pear; (*fam, péj*) mug

poireau, x [pwaʀo] *nm* leek

poirier [pwaʀje] *nm* pear tree

pois [pwa] *nm* (*Bot*) pea; (*sur une étoffe*) dot, spot; **à ~** (*cravate etc*) spotted, polka-dot *cpd*; **~ chiche** chickpea

poison [pwazɔ̃] *nm* poison

poisseux, -euse [pwasø, -øz] *adj* sticky

poisson [pwasɔ̃] *nm* fish *gén inv*; **les P~s** (*Astrologie: signe*) Pisces; **~ d'avril** April fool; (*blague*) April fool's day trick; *see note* **"poisson d'avril"**; **~ rouge** goldfish; **poissonnerie** *nf* fishmonger's; **poissonnier, -ière** *nm/f* fishmonger (*BRIT*), fish merchant (*US*)

● **POISSON D'AVRIL**
●
● The traditional April Fools'
● Day prank in France involves
● attaching a cut-out paper fish,
● known as a 'poisson d'avril', to the
● back of one's victim, without being
● caught.

poitrine [pwatʀin] *nf* chest; (*seins*) bust, bosom; (*Culin*) breast

poivre [pwavʀ] *nm* pepper

poivron [pwavʀɔ̃] *nm* pepper, capsicum

polaire [pɔlɛʀ] *adj* polar

pôle [pol] *nm* (*Géo, Élec*) pole; **le ~ Nord/Sud** the North/South Pole

poli, e [pɔli] *adj* polite; (*lisse*) smooth

police [pɔlis] *nf* police; **~ judiciaire (PJ)** ≈ Criminal Investigation Department (CID) (*BRIT*), ≈ Federal Bureau of Investigation (FBI) (*US*); **~ secours** ≈ emergency services *pl* (*BRIT*), ≈ paramedics *pl* (*US*); **policier, -ière** *adj* police *cpd* ▷ *nm* policeman; (*aussi:* **roman policier**) detective novel

polir [pɔliʀ] /2/ *vt* to polish

politesse [pɔlitɛs] *nf* politeness

politicien, ne [pɔlitisjɛ̃, -ɛn] *nm/f* (*péj*) politician

politique [pɔlitik] *adj* political ▷ *nf* politics *sg*; (*principes, tactique*) policies *pl*

politiquement [pɔlitikmɑ̃] *adv* politically; **~ correct** politically correct

pollen [pɔlɛn] *nm* pollen

polluant, e [pɔlɥɑ̃, -ɑ̃t] *adj* polluting ▷ *nm* pollutant; **non ~** non-polluting

polluer [pɔlɥe] /1/ vt to pollute;
pollution nf pollution
polo [pɔlo] nm (tricot) polo shirt
Pologne [pɔlɔɲ] nf: **la ~** Poland;
polonais, e adj Polish ▷ nm (Ling)
Polish ▷ nm/f: **Polonais, e** Pole
poltron, ne [pɔltrɔ̃, -ɔn] adj
cowardly
polycopier [pɔlikɔpje] /7/ vt to
duplicate
Polynésie [pɔlinezi] nf: **la ~** Polynesia;
la ~ française French Polynesia
polyvalent, e [pɔlivalɑ̃, -ɑ̃t] adj
(rôle) varied; (salle) multi-purpose
pommade [pɔmad] nf ointment,
cream
pomme [pɔm] nf apple; **tomber
dans les ~s** (fam) to pass out;
~ d'Adam Adam's apple; **~ de pin**
pine ou fir cone; **~ de terre** potato; **~s
vapeur** boiled potatoes
pommette [pɔmɛt] nf cheekbone
pommier [pɔmje] nm apple tree
pompe [pɔ̃p] nf pump; (faste)
pomp (and ceremony); **~ à eau/
essence** water/petrol pump; **~s
funèbres** undertaker's sg, funeral
parlour sg; **pomper** /1/ vt to pump;
(aspirer) to pump up; (absorber) to
soak up
pompeux, -euse [pɔ̃pø, -øz] adj
pompous
pompier [pɔ̃pje] nm fireman
pompiste [pɔ̃pist] nm/f petrol (BRIT)
ou gas (US) pump attendant
poncer [pɔ̃se] /3/ vt to sand (down)
ponctuation [pɔ̃ktɥasjɔ̃] nf
punctuation
ponctuel, le [pɔ̃ktɥɛl] adj punctual
pondéré, e [pɔ̃dere] adj level-
headed, composed
pondre [pɔ̃dʀ] /41/ vt to lay
poney [pɔnɛ] nm pony
pont [pɔ̃] nm bridge; (Navig) deck;
faire le ~ to take the extra day off;
see note **"faire le pont"**; **~ suspendu**
suspension bridge; **pont-levis** nm
drawbridge

● **FAIRE LE PONT**
●
● The expression 'faire le pont' refers
● to the practice of taking a Monday
● or Friday off to make a long
● weekend if a public holiday falls on
● a Tuesday or Thursday. The French
● commonly take an extra day off
● work to give four consecutive days'
● holiday at 'l'Ascension', 'le 14 juillet'
● and le '15 août'.

pop [pɔp] adj inv pop
populaire [pɔpylɛʀ] adj popular;
(manifestation) mass cpd; (milieux,
clientèle) working-class; (mot etc) used
by the lower classes (of society)
popularité [pɔpylarite] nf
popularity
population [pɔpylasjɔ̃] nf population
populeux, -euse [pɔpylø, -øz] adj
densely populated
porc [pɔʀ] nm pig; (Culin) pork
porcelaine [pɔʀsəlɛn] nf porcelain,
china; (objet) piece of china(ware)
porc-épic [pɔʀkepik] nm porcupine
porche [pɔʀʃ] nm porch
porcherie [pɔʀʃəʀi] nf pigsty
pore [pɔʀ] nm pore
porno [pɔʀno] adj porno ▷ nm porn
port [pɔʀ] nm harbour, port; (ville)
port; (de l'uniforme etc) wearing;
(pour lettre) postage; (pour colis,
aussi: posture) carriage; **~ d'arme**
(Jur) carrying of a firearm; **~ payé**
postage paid
portable [pɔʀtabl] adj (portatif)
portable; (téléphone) mobile
▷ nm (Inform) laptop (computer);
(téléphone) mobile (phone)
portail [pɔʀtaj] nm gate
portant, e [pɔʀtɑ̃, -ɑ̃t] adj: **bien/
mal ~** in good/poor health
portatif, -ive [pɔʀtatif, -iv] adj
portable
porte [pɔʀt] nf door; (de ville,
forteresse) gate; **mettre à la ~** to
throw out; **~ d'entrée** front door

porté, e [pɔrte] *adj*: **être ~ à faire qch** to be apt to do sth; **être ~ sur qch** to be partial to sth
porte: **porte-avions** *nm inv* aircraft carrier; **porte-bagages** *nm inv* luggage rack (*ou* basket *etc*); **porte-bonheur** *nm inv* lucky charm; **porte-clefs** *nm inv* key ring; **porte-documents** *nm inv* attaché *ou* document case
portée [pɔrte] *nf* (*d'une arme*) range; (*fig: importance*) impact, import; (: *capacités*) scope, capability; (*de chatte etc*) litter; (*Mus*) stave, staff; **à/hors de ~ (de)** within/out of reach (of); **à ~ de (la) main** within (arm's) reach; **à la ~ de qn** (*fig*) at sb's level, within sb's capabilities
porte: **portefeuille** *nm* wallet; **portemanteau, x** *nm* coat rack; (*cintre*) coat hanger; **porte-monnaie** *nm inv* purse; **porte-parole** *nm inv* spokesperson
porter [pɔrte] /1/ *vt* to carry; (*sur soi: vêtement, barbe, bague*) to wear; (*fig: responsabilité etc*) to bear, carry; (*inscription, marque, titre, patronyme, fruits, fleurs*) to bear; (*coup*) to deal; (*attention*) to turn; (*apporter*): **~ qch quelque part/à qn** to take sth somewhere/to sb ▷ *vi* to carry; (*coup, argument*) to hit home; **se porter** *vi* (*se sentir*): **se ~ bien/mal** to be well/unwell; **~ sur** (*conférence etc*) to concern; **se faire ~ malade** to report sick
porteur, -euse [pɔrtœr, -øz] *nm/f* ▷ *nm* (*de bagages*) porter; (*de chèque*) bearer
porte-voix [pɔrtəvwa] *nm inv* megaphone
portier [pɔrtje] *nm* doorman
portière [pɔrtjɛr] *nf* door
portion [pɔrsjɔ̃] *nf* (*part*) portion, share; (*partie*) portion, section
porto [pɔrto] *nm* port (wine)
portrait [pɔrtrɛ] *nm* portrait; (*photographie*) photograph; **portrait-**

robot *nm* Identikit® *ou* Photo-fit® (*BRIT*) picture
portuaire [pɔrtɥɛr] *adj* port *cpd*, harbour *cpd*
portugais, e [pɔrtygɛ, -ɛz] *adj* Portuguese ▷ *nm* (*Ling*) Portuguese ▷ *nm/f*: **P~, e** Portuguese
Portugal [pɔrtygal] *nm*: **le ~** Portugal
pose [poz] *nf* (*de moquette*) laying; (*attitude, d'un modèle*) pose; (*Photo*) exposure
posé, e [poze] *adj* calm
poser [poze] /1/ *vt* (*place*) to put down, to put; (*déposer, installer: moquette, carrelage*) to lay; (*rideaux, papier peint*) to hang; (*question*) to ask; (*principe, conditions*) to lay *ou* set down; (*problème*) to formulate; (*difficulté*) to pose ▷ *vi* (*modèle*) to pose; **se poser** *vi* (*oiseau, avion*) to land; (*question*) to arise; **~ qch (sur)** to put sth down (on); **~ qn à** to drop sb at; **~ qch sur qch/quelque part** to put sth on sth/somewhere; **~ sa candidature à un poste** to apply for a post
positif, -ive [pozitif, -iv] *adj* positive
position [pozisjɔ̃] *nf* position; **prendre ~** (*fig*) to take a stand
posologie [pozɔlɔʒi] *nf* dosage
posséder [pɔsede] /6/ *vt* to own, possess; (*qualité, talent*) to have, possess; (*sexuellement*) to possess; **possession** *nf* ownership *no pl*; possession; **être en possession de qch** to be in possession of sth; **prendre possession de qch** to take possession of sth
possibilité [pɔsibilite] *nf* possibility; **possibilités** *nfpl* potential *sg*
possible [pɔsibl] *adj* possible; (*projet, entreprise*) feasible ▷ *nm*: **faire son ~** to do all one can, do one's utmost; **le plus/moins de livres ~** as many/few books as possible; **le plus vite ~** as quickly as possible; **dès que ~** as soon as possible

P

postal, e, -aux [pɔstal, -o] *adj* postal

poste¹ [pɔst] *nf* (*service*) post, postal service; (*administration, bureau*) post office; **mettre à la ~** to post; **~ restante (PR)** poste restante (*BRIT*), general delivery (*US*)

poste² [pɔst] *nm* (*fonction, Mil*) post; (*Tél*) extension; (*de radio etc*) set; **~ d'essence** filling station; **~ d'incendie** fire point; **~ de pilotage** cockpit, flight deck; **~ (de police)** police station; **~ de secours** first-aid post

poster /1/ *vt* [pɔste] to post ▷ *nm* [pɔstɛʀ] poster

postérieur, e [pɔsteʀjœʀ] *adj* (*date*) later; (*partie*) back ▷ *nm* (*fam*) behind

postuler [pɔstyle] /1/ *vi*: **~ à** *ou* **pour un emploi** to apply for a job

pot [po] *nm* (*en verre*) jar; (*en terre*) pot; (*en plastique, carton*) carton; (*en métal*) tin; (*fam: chance*) luck; **avoir du ~** to be lucky; **boire** *ou* **prendre un ~** (*fam*) to have a drink; **petit ~ (pour bébé)** (jar of) baby food; **~ catalytique** catalytic converter; **~ d'échappement** exhaust pipe

potable [pɔtabl] *adj*: **eau (non) ~** (not) drinking water

potage [pɔtaʒ] *nm* soup; **potager, -ère** *adj*: (**jardin**) **potager** kitchen *ou* vegetable garden

pot-au-feu [pɔtofø] *nm inv* (beef) stew

pot-de-vin [podvɛ̃] *nm* bribe

pote [pɔt] *nm* (*fam*) pal

poteau, x [pɔto] *nm* post; **~ indicateur** signpost

potelé, e [pɔtle] *adj* plump, chubby

potentiel, le [pɔtɑ̃sjɛl] *adj, nm* potential

poterie [pɔtʀi] *nf* pottery; (*objet*) piece of pottery

potier, -ière [pɔtje, -jɛʀ] *nm/f* potter

potiron [pɔtiʀɔ̃] *nm* pumpkin

pou, x [pu] *nm* louse

poubelle [pubɛl] *nf* (dust)bin

pouce [pus] *nm* thumb

poudre [pudʀ] *nf* powder; (*fard*) (face) powder; (*explosif*) gunpowder; **en ~: café en ~** instant coffee; **lait en ~** dried *ou* powdered milk

poudreux, -euse [pudʀø, -øz] *adj* dusty; (*neige*) powder *cpd*

poudrier [pudʀije] *nm* (powder) compact

pouffer [pufe] /1/ *vi*: **~ (de rire)** to burst out laughing

poulailler [pulaje] *nm* henhouse

poulain [pulɛ̃] *nm* foal; (*fig*) protégé

poule [pul] *nf* hen; (*Culin*) (boiling) fowl; **~ mouillée** coward

poulet [pulɛ] *nm* chicken; (*fam*) cop

poulie [puli] *nf* pulley

pouls [pu] *nm* pulse; **prendre le ~ de qn** to take sb's pulse

poumon [pumɔ̃] *nm* lung

poupée [pupe] *nf* doll

pour [puʀ] *prép* for ▷ *nm*: **le ~ et le contre** the pros and cons; **~ faire** (so as) to do, in order to do; **~ avoir fait** for having done; **~ que** so that, in order that; **fermé ~ (cause de) travaux** closed for refurbishment *ou* alterations; **c'est ~ ça que ...** that's why ...; **~ quoi faire?** what for?; **~ 20 euros d'essence** 20 euros' worth of petrol; **~ cent** per cent; **~ ce qui est de** as for

pourboire [puʀbwaʀ] *nm* tip

pourcentage [puʀsɑ̃taʒ] *nm* percentage

pourchasser [puʀʃase] /1/ *vt* to pursue

pourparlers [puʀpaʀle] *nmpl* talks, negotiations

pourpre [puʀpʀ] *adj* crimson

pourquoi [puʀkwa] *adv, conj* why ▷ *nm inv*: **le ~ (de)** the reason (for)

pourrai *etc* [puʀe] *vb voir* **pouvoir**

pourri, e [puʀi] *adj* rotten

pourrir [puʀiʀ] /2/ *vi* to rot; (*fruit*) to go rotten *ou* bad ▷ *vt* to rot; (*fig*) to spoil thoroughly; **pourriture** *nf* rot

poursuite [puʀsɥit] *nf* pursuit, chase;
poursuites *nfpl* (*Jur*) legal proceedings
poursuivre [puʀsɥivʀ] /40/ *vt* to
pursue, chase (after); (*obséder*) to
haunt; (*Jur*) to bring proceedings
against, prosecute (: *au civil*) to sue;
(*but*) to strive towards; (*voyage,
études*) to carry on with, continue; **se
poursuivre** *vi* to go on, continue
pourtant [puʀtɑ̃] *adv* yet; **c'est ~
facile** (and) yet it's easy
pourtour [puʀtuʀ] *nm* perimeter
pourvoir [puʀvwaʀ] /25/ *vt*: **~ qch/
qn de** to equip sth/sb with ▷ *vi*: **~ à** to
provide for; **pourvu, e** *adj*: **pourvu
de** equipped with; **pourvu que** (*si*)
provided that, so long as; (*espérons
que*) let's hope (that)
pousse [pus] *nf* growth; (*bourgeon*)
shoot
poussée [puse] *nf* thrust; (*d'acné*)
eruption; (*fig: prix*) upsurge
pousser [puse] /1/ *vt* to push;
(*émettre: cri etc*) to give; (*stimuler:
élève*) to urge on; (*poursuivre: études,
discussion*) to carry on ▷ *vi* to push;
(*croître*) to grow; **se pousser** *vi* to
move over; **~ qn à faire qch** (*inciter*)
to urge ou press sb to do sth; **faire ~**
(*plante*) to grow
poussette [puset] *nf* pushchair
(BRIT), stroller (US)
poussière [pusjɛʀ] *nf* dust;
poussiéreux, -euse *adj* dusty
poussin [pusɛ̃] *nm* chick
poutre [putʀ] *nf* beam

MOT-CLÉ

pouvoir [puvwaʀ] /33/ *nm* power;
(*dirigeants*): **le pouvoir** those in
power; **les pouvoirs publics** the
authorities; **pouvoir d'achat**
purchasing power
▷ *vb aux* **1** (*être en état de*) can, be able
to; **je ne peux pas le réparer** I can't
ou I am not able to repair it; **déçu de
ne pas pouvoir le faire** disappointed

not to be able to do it
2 (*avoir la permission*) can, may, be
allowed to; **vous pouvez aller au
cinéma** you can ou may go to the
pictures
3 (*probabilité, hypothèse*) may, might,
could; **il a pu avoir un accident**
he may ou might ou could have had
an accident; **il aurait pu le dire!** he
might ou could have said (so)!
▷ *vb impers* may, might, could; **il peut
arriver que** it may ou might ou could
happen that; **il pourrait pleuvoir**
it might rain
▷ *vt* can, be able to; **j'ai fait tout ce
que j'ai pu** I did all I could; **je n'en
peux plus** (*épuisé*) I'm exhausted; (*à
bout*) I can't take any more
se pouvoir *vi*: **il se peut que** it may
ou might be that; **cela se pourrait**
that's quite possible

prairie [pʀeʀi] *nf* meadow
praline [pʀalin] *nf* sugared almond
praticable [pʀatikabl] *adj* passable;
practicable
pratiquant, e [pʀatikɑ̃, -ɑ̃t] *nm/f*
(regular) churchgoer
pratique [pʀatik] *nf* practice ▷ *adj*
practical; **pratiquement** *adv* (*pour
ainsi dire*) practically, virtually;
pratiquer /1/ *vt* to practise;
(*l'équitation, la pêche*) to go in for; (*le
golf, football*) to play; (*intervention,
opération*) to carry out
pré [pʀe] *nm* meadow
préalable [pʀealabl] *adj* preliminary;
au ~ beforehand
préambule [pʀeɑ̃byl] *nm* preamble;
(*fig*) prelude; **sans ~** straight away
préau, x [pʀeo] *nm* (*d'une cour d'école*)
covered playground
préavis [pʀeavi] *nm* notice
précaution [pʀekosjɔ̃] *nf*
precaution; **avec ~** cautiously; **par ~**
as a precaution
précédemment [pʀesedamɑ̃] *adv*
before, previously

précédent, e [pʀesedɑ̃, -ɑ̃t] adj
previous ▷ nm precedent; **sans ~**
unprecedented; **le jour ~** the day
before, the previous day
précéder [pʀesede] /6/ vt to precede
prêcher [pʀeʃe] /1/ vt to preach
précieux, -euse [pʀesjø, -øz] adj
precious; (collaborateur, conseils)
invaluable
précipice [pʀesipis] nm drop, chasm
précipitamment [pʀesipitamɑ̃]
adv hurriedly, hastily
précipitation [pʀesipitasjɔ̃] nf
(hâte) haste
précipité, e [pʀesipite] adj hurried;
hasty
précipiter [pʀesipite] /1/ vt (hâter:
départ) to hasten; **se précipiter** vi
to speed up; **~ qn/qch du haut de**
(faire tomber) to throw ou hurl sb/sth
off ou from; **se ~ sur/vers** to rush
at/towards
précis, e [pʀesi, -iz] adj precise;
(tir, mesures) accurate, precise; **à
4 heures ~es** at 4 o'clock sharp;
précisément adv precisely; **préciser**
/1/ vt (expliquer) to be more specific
about, clarify; (spécifier) to state,
specify; **se préciser** vi to become
clear(er); **précision** nf precision;
(détail) point ou detail (made clear or
to be clarified)
précoce [pʀekɔs] adj early; (enfant)
precocious
préconçu, e [pʀekɔ̃sy] adj
preconceived
préconiser [pʀekɔnize] /1/ vt to
advocate
prédécesseur [pʀedesesœʀ] nm
predecessor
prédilection [pʀedileksjɔ̃] nf: **avoir
une ~ pour** to be partial to
prédire [pʀediʀ] /37/ vt to predict
prédominer [pʀedɔmine] /1/ vi to
predominate
préface [pʀefas] nf preface
préfecture [pʀefɛktyʀ] nf prefecture;
~ de police police headquarters

préférable [pʀefeʀabl] adj
preferable
préféré, e [pʀefeʀe] adj, nm/f
favourite
préférence [pʀefeʀɑ̃s] nf
preference; **de ~** preferably
préférer [pʀefeʀe] /6/ vt: **~ qn/qch
(à)** to prefer sb/sth (to), like sb/sth
better (than); **~ faire** to prefer to do;
je préférerais du thé I would rather
have tea, I'd prefer tea
préfet [pʀefɛ] nm prefect
préhistorique [pʀeistɔʀik] adj
prehistoric
préjudice [pʀeʒydis] nm (matériel)
loss; (moral) harm no pl; **porter ~ à**
to harm, be detrimental to; **au ~ de** at
the expense of
préjugé [pʀeʒyʒe] nm prejudice;
avoir un ~ contre to be prejudiced
against
prélasser [pʀelɑse] /1/: **se prélasser**
vi to lounge
prélèvement [pʀelɛvmɑ̃] nm
(montant) deduction; **faire un ~ de
sang** to take a blood sample
prélever [pʀelve] /5/ vt (échantillon)
to take; **~ (sur)** (argent) to deduct
(from); (sur son compte) to withdraw
(from)
prématuré, e [pʀematyʀe] adj
premature ▷ nm premature baby
premier, -ière [pʀəmje, -jɛʀ] adj
first; (rang) front; (fig: fondamental)
basic ▷ nf (Rail, Aviat etc) first
class; (Scol) year 12 (BRIT), eleventh
grade (US); **de ~ ordre** first-rate;
le ~ venu the first person to come
along; **P~ Ministre** Prime Minister;
premièrement adv firstly
prémonition [pʀemɔnisjɔ̃] nf
premonition
prenant, e [pʀənɑ̃, -ɑ̃t] adj
absorbing, engrossing
prénatal, e [pʀenatal] adj (Méd)
antenatal
prendre [pʀɑ̃dʀ] /58/ vt to take;
(repas) to have; (aller chercher) to

get; (*malfaiteur, poisson*) to catch;
(*passager*) to pick up; (*personnel*) to
take on; (*traiter: enfant, problème*) to
handle; (*voix, ton*) to put on; (*ôter*):
~ qch à to take sth from; (*coincer*): **se
~ les doigts dans** to get one's fingers
caught in ▷ *vi* (*liquide, ciment*) to set;
(*greffe, vaccin*) to take; (*feu: foyer*) to
go; (*se diriger*): **~ à gauche** to turn
(to the) left; **~ froid** to catch cold;
se ~ pour to think one is; **s'en ~ à** to
attack; **se ~ d'amitié/d'affection
pour** to befriend/become fond of;
s'y ~ (*procéder*) to set about it

preneur [pʀənœʀ] *nm*: **être ~** to
be willing to buy; **trouver ~** to find
a buyer

prénom [pʀenɔ̃] *nm* first name

préoccupation [pʀeɔkypasjɔ̃]
nf (*souci*) concern; (*idée fixe*)
preoccupation

préoccuper [pʀeɔkype] /1/ *vt*
(*tourmenter, tracasser*) to concern;
(*absorber, obséder*) to preoccupy; **se ~
de qch** to be concerned about sth

préparatifs [pʀepaʀatif] *nmpl*
preparations

préparation [pʀepaʀasjɔ̃] *nf*
preparation

préparer [pʀepaʀe] /1/ *vt* to prepare;
(*café, repas*) to make; (*examen*) to
prepare for; (*voyage, entreprise*) to
plan; **se préparer** *vi* (*orage, tragédie*)
to brew, be in the air; **se ~ (à qch/à
faire)** to prepare (for sth/to do); get
ready (for sth/to do); **~ qch à qn** (*surprise
etc*) to have sth in store for sb

prépondérant, e [pʀepɔ̃deʀɑ̃, -ɑ̃t]
adj major, dominating

préposé, e [pʀepoze] *nm/f*
employee; (*facteur*) postman/woman

préposition [pʀepozisjɔ̃] *nf*
preposition

près [pʀɛ] *adv* near, close; **~ de** near
(to), close to; (*environ*) nearly, almost;
de ~ closely; **à cinq kg ~** to within
about five kg; **il n'est pas à 10
minutes ~** he can spare 10 minutes

présage [pʀezaʒ] *nm* omen

presbyte [pʀɛsbit] *adj* long-sighted

presbytère [pʀɛsbitɛʀ] *nm* presbytery

prescription [pʀɛskʀipsjɔ̃] *nf*
prescription

prescrire [pʀɛskʀiʀ] /39/ *vt* to
prescribe

présence [pʀezɑ̃s] *nf* presence; (*au
bureau etc*) attendance

présent, e [pʀezɑ̃, -ɑ̃t] *adj, nm*
present; **à ~ que** now that

présentation [pʀezɑ̃tasjɔ̃] *nf*
presentation; (*de nouveau venu*)
introduction; (*allure*) appearance;
faire les ~s to do the introductions

présenter [pʀezɑ̃te] /1/ *vt* to
present; (*invité, candidat*) to
introduce; (*félicitations, condoléances*)
to offer; **~ qn à** to introduce sb
to ▷ *vi*: **~ mal/bien** to have an
unattractive/a pleasing appearance;
se présenter *vi* (*à une élection*) to
stand; (*occasion*) to arise; **se ~ à un
examen** to sit an exam; **je vous
présente Nadine** this is Nadine

préservatif [pʀezɛʀvatif] *nm*
condom, sheath

préserver [pʀezɛʀve] /1/ *vt*: **~ de**
(*protéger*) to protect from

président [pʀezidɑ̃] *nm* (*Pol*)
president; (*d'une assemblée, Comm*)
chairman; **~ directeur général**
chairman and managing director

présidentiel, le [pʀezidɑ̃sjɛl] *adj*
presidential; **présidentielles** *nfpl*
presidential election(s)

présider [pʀezide] /1/ *vt* to preside
over; (*dîner*) to be the guest of honour
(*BRIT*) *ou* honor (*US*) at

presque [pʀɛsk] *adv* almost, nearly;
~ rien hardly anything; **~ pas**
hardly (at all); **~ pas de** hardly any;
personne, ou ~ next to nobody,
hardly anyone

presqu'île [pʀɛskil] *nf* peninsula

pressant, e [pʀɛsɑ̃, -ɑ̃t] *adj* urgent

presse [pʀɛs] *nf* press; (*affluence*):
heures de ~ busy times

pressé, e [pʀese] *adj* in a hurry; (*besogne*) urgent; **orange ~e** freshly squeezed orange juice

pressentiment [pʀesɑ̃timɑ̃] *nm* foreboding, premonition

pressentir [pʀesɑ̃tiʀ] /16/ *vt* to sense

presse-papiers [pʀɛspapje] *nm inv* paperweight

presser [pʀese] /1/ *vt* (*fruit, éponge*) to squeeze; (*interrupteur, bouton*) to press; (*allure, affaire*) to speed up; (*inciter*): **~ qn de faire** to urge *ou* press sb to do ▷ *vi* to be urgent; **se presser** *vi* (*se hâter*) to hurry (up); **rien ne presse** there's no hurry; **se ~ contre qn** to squeeze up against sb; **le temps presse** there's not much time

pressing [pʀesiŋ] *nm* (*magasin*) dry-cleaner's

pression [pʀesjɔ̃] *nf* pressure; (*bouton*) press stud (BRIT), snap fastener (US); (*bière*: *bière*) draught beer; **faire ~ sur** to put pressure on; **sous ~** pressurized, under pressure; (*fig*) keyed up; **~ artérielle** blood pressure

prestataire [pʀɛstatɛʀ] *nm/f* person receiving benefits; **~ de services** provider of services

prestation [pʀɛstasjɔ̃] *nf* (*allocation*) benefit; (*d'une entreprise*) service provided; (*d'un joueur, artiste*) performance

prestidigitateur, -trice [pʀɛstidiʒitatœʀ, -tʀis] *nm/f* conjurer

prestige [pʀɛstiʒ] *nm* prestige; **prestigieux, -euse** *adj* prestigious

présumer [pʀezyme] /1/ *vt*: **~ que** to presume *ou* assume that

prêt, e [pʀɛ, pʀɛt] *adj* ready ▷ *nm* (*somme prêtée*) loan; **prêt-à-porter** *nm* ready-to-wear *ou* off-the-peg (BRIT) clothes *pl*

prétendre [pʀetɑ̃dʀ] /41/ *vt* (*affirmer*): **~ que** to claim that; **~ faire qch** (*avoir l'intention de*) to mean *ou* intend to do sth; **prétendu, e** *adj* (*supposé*) so-called

> Attention à ne pas traduire *prétendre* par *to pretend*.

prétentieux, -euse [pʀetɑ̃sjø, -øz] *adj* pretentious

prétention [pʀetɑ̃sjɔ̃] *nf* pretentiousness; (*exigence, ambition*) claim

prêter [pʀete] /1/ *vt*: **~ qch à qn** (*livres, argent*) to lend sth to sb; (*caractère, propos*) to attribute sth to sb

prétexte [pʀetɛkst] *nm* pretext, excuse; **sous aucun ~** on no account; **prétexter** [pʀetɛkste] /1/ *vt* to give as a pretext *ou* an excuse

prêtre [pʀɛtʀ] *nm* priest

preuve [pʀœv] *nf* proof; (*indice*) proof, evidence *no pl*; **faire ~ de** to show; **faire ses ~s** to prove o.s. (*ou* itself)

prévaloir [pʀevalwaʀ] /29/ *vi* to prevail

prévenant, e [pʀevnɑ̃, -ɑ̃t] *adj* thoughtful, kind

prévenir [pʀevniʀ] /22/ *vt* (*éviter: catastrophe etc*) to avoid, prevent; (*anticiper: désirs, besoins*) to anticipate; **~ qn (de)** (*avertir*) to warn sb (about); (*informer*) to tell *ou* inform sb (about)

préventif, -ive [pʀevɑ̃tif, -iv] *adj* preventive

prévention [pʀevɑ̃sjɔ̃] *nf* prevention; **~ routière** road safety

prévenu, e [pʀevny] *nm/f* (*Jur*) defendant, accused

prévision [pʀevizjɔ̃] *nf*: **~s** predictions; (*météorologiques, économiques*) forecast *sg*; **en ~ de** in anticipation of; **~s météorologiques** *ou* **du temps** weather forecast *sg*

prévoir [pʀevwaʀ] /24/ *vt* (*deviner*) to foresee; (*s'attendre à*) to expect, reckon on; (*organiser: voyage etc*) to plan; (*préparer, réserver*) to

allow; **comme prévu** as planned;
prévoyant, e adj gifted with (ou
showing) foresight; **prévu, e** pp de
prévoir

prier [pʀije] /7/ vi to pray ▷ vt
(Dieu) to pray to; (implorer) to beg;
(demander): **~ qn de faire** to ask sb
to do; **se faire ~** to need coaxing ou
persuading; **je vous en prie** (allez-y)
please do; (de rien) don't mention it;
prière nf prayer; **"prière de faire ..."**
"please do ..."

primaire [pʀimɛʀ] adj primary ▷ nm
(Scol) primary education

prime [pʀim] nf (bonification) bonus;
(subside) allowance; (Comm: cadeau)
free gift; (Assurances, Bourse) premium
▷ adj: **de ~ abord** at first glance;
primer /1/ vt (récompenser) to award a
prize to ▷ vi to dominate

primevère [pʀimvɛʀ] nf primrose

primitif, -ive [pʀimitif, -iv] adj
primitive; (originel) original

prince [pʀɛ̃s] nm prince; **princesse**
nf princess

principal, e, -aux [pʀɛ̃sipal, -o]
adj principal, main ▷ nm (Scol) head
(teacher) (BRIT), principal (US);
(essentiel) main thing

principe [pʀɛ̃sip] nm principle; **par ~**
on principle; **en ~** (habituellement) as a
rule; (théoriquement) in principle

printemps [pʀɛ̃tɑ̃] nm spring

priorité [pʀijɔʀite] nf priority;
(Auto)**~ à droite** right of way to
vehicles coming from the right

pris, e [pʀi, pʀiz] pp de **prendre**
▷ adj (place) taken; (journée, mains)
full; (personne) busy; **avoir le nez/
la gorge ~(e)** to have a stuffy nose/a
bad throat; **être ~ de peur/de
fatigue/de panique** to be stricken
with fear/overcome with fatigue/
panic-stricken

prise [pʀiz] nf (d'une ville) capture;
(Pêche, Chasse) catch; (point d'appui ou
pour empoigner) hold; (Élec: fiche) plug;
(: femelle) socket; **être aux ~s avec**
to be grappling with; **~ de courant**
power point; **~ multiple** adaptor;
~ de sang blood test

priser [pʀize] /1/ vt (estimer) to
prize, value

prison [pʀizɔ̃] nf prison; **aller/être
en ~** to go to/be in prison ou jail;
prisonnier, -ière nm/f prisoner ▷ adj
captive

privé, e [pʀive] adj private; (en
punition): **tu es ~ de télé!** no TV for
you! ▷ nm (Comm) private sector; **en
~** in private

priver [pʀive] /1/ vt: **~ qn de** to deprive
sb of; **se ~ de** to go ou do without

privilège [pʀivilɛʒ] nm privilege

prix [pʀi] nm price; (récompense, Scol)
prize; **hors de ~** exorbitantly priced;
à aucun ~ not at any price; **à tout ~**
at all costs

probable [pʀɔbabl] adj likely,
probable; **probablement** adv
probably

problème [pʀɔblɛm] nm problem

procédé [pʀɔsede] nm (méthode)
process; (comportement) behaviour
no pl

procéder [pʀɔsede] /6/ vi to
proceed; (moralement) to behave; **~ à**
to carry out

procès [pʀɔsɛ] nm trial (poursuites)
proceedings pl; **être en ~ avec** to be
involved in a lawsuit with

processus [pʀɔsesys] nm process

procès-verbal, -aux [pʀɔsɛvɛʀbal,
-o] nm (de réunion) minutes pl; (aussi:
PV): **avoir un ~** to get a parking
ticket

prochain, e [pʀɔʃɛ̃, -ɛn] adj next;
(proche: départ, arrivée) impending
▷ nm fellow man; **la ~e fois/semaine
~** next time/week; **prochainement**
adv soon, shortly

proche [pʀɔʃ] adj nearby; (dans
le temps) imminent; (parent, ami)
close; **proches** nmpl (parents) close
relatives; **être ~ (de)** to be near, be
close (to)

p

proclamer [pʀɔklame] /1/ vt to proclaim

procuration [pʀɔkyʀasjɔ̃] nf proxy

procurer [pʀɔkyʀe] /1/ vt (fournir): **~ qch à qn** (obtenir) to get ou obtain sth for sb; (plaisir etc) to bring ou give sb sth; **se procurer** vt to get; **procureur** nm public prosecutor

prodige [pʀɔdiʒ] nm marvel, wonder; (personne) prodigy; **prodiguer** /1/ vt (soins, attentions): **prodiguer qch à qn** to lavish sth on sb

producteur, -trice [pʀɔdyktœʀ, -tʀis] nm/f producer

productif, -ive [pʀɔdyktif, -iv] adj productive

production [pʀɔdyksjɔ̃] nf production; (rendement) output

productivité [pʀɔdyktivite] nf productivity

produire [pʀɔdɥiʀ] /38/ vt to produce; **se produire** vi (acteur) to perform, appear; (événement) to happen, occur

produit, e [pʀɔdɥi, -it] nm product; **~ chimique** chemical; **~ d'entretien** cleaning product; **~s agricoles** farm produce sg; **~s de beauté** beauty products, cosmetics

prof [pʀɔf] nm (fam) teacher

proférer [pʀɔfeʀe] /6/ vt to utter

professeur, e [pʀɔfesœʀ] nm/f teacher; (titulaire d'une chaire) professor; **~ (de faculté)** (university) lecturer

profession [pʀɔfesjɔ̃] nf (libérale) profession; (gén) occupation; **"sans ~"** "unemployed"; **professionnel, le** adj, nm/f professional

profil [pʀɔfil] nm profile; **de ~** in profile

profit [pʀɔfi] nm (avantage) benefit, advantage; (Comm, Finance) profit; **au ~ de** in aid of; **tirer** ou **retirer ~ de** to profit from; **profitable** adj (utile) beneficial; (lucratif) profitable; **profiter** /1/ vi: **profiter de** (situation, occasion) to take advantage of; (vacances, jeunesse etc) to make the most of

profond, e [pʀɔfɔ̃, -ɔ̃d] adj deep; (méditation, mépris) profound; **profondément** adv deeply; **il dort profondément** he is sound asleep; **profondeur** nf depth; **l'eau a quelle profondeur?** how deep is the water?

programme [pʀɔgʀam] nm programme; (Scol) syllabus, curriculum; (Inform) program; **programmer** /1/ vt (organiser, prévoir: émission) to schedule; (Inform) to program; **programmeur, -euse** nm/f (computer) programmer

progrès [pʀɔgʀɛ] nm progress no pl; **faire des/être en ~** to make/ be making progress; **progresser** /1/ vi to progress; **progressif, -ive** adj progressive

proie [pʀwa] nf prey no pl

projecteur [pʀɔʒɛktœʀ] nm projector; (de théâtre, cirque) spotlight

projectile [pʀɔʒɛktil] nm missile

projection [pʀɔʒɛksjɔ̃] nf projection; (séance) showing

projet [pʀɔʒɛ] nm plan; (ébauche) draft; **~ de loi** bill; **projeter** /4/ vt (envisager) to plan; (film, photos) to project; (ombre, lueur) to throw, cast; (jeter) to throw up (ou off ou out)

prolétaire [pʀɔletɛʀ] adj, nm/f proletarian

prolongement [pʀɔlɔ̃ʒmɑ̃] nm extension; **dans le ~ de** running on from

prolonger [pʀɔlɔ̃ʒe] /3/ vt (débat, séjour) to prolong; (délai, billet, rue) to extend; **se prolonger** vi to go on

promenade [pʀɔmnad] nf walk (ou drive ou ride); **faire une ~** to go for a walk; **une ~ (à pied)/en voiture/à vélo** a walk/drive/(bicycle) ride

promener [pʀɔmne] /5/ vt (personne, chien) to take out for a walk; (doigts, regard): **~ qch sur** to run sth over; **se promener** vi to go for (ou be out for) a walk

promesse [pʀɔmɛs] nf promise

promettre [pʀɔmɛtʀ] /56/ vt to promise ⊳ vi to look promising; **~ à qn de faire** to promise sb that one will do

promiscuité [pʀɔmiskɥite] nf lack of privacy

promontoire [pʀɔmɔ̃twaʀ] nm headland

promoteur, -trice [pʀɔmɔtœʀ, -tʀis] nm/f: **~ (immobilier)** property developer (BRIT), real estate promoter (US)

promotion [pʀɔmosjɔ̃] nf promotion; **en ~** on (special) offer

promouvoir [pʀɔmuvwaʀ] /27/ vt to promote

prompt, e [pʀɔ̃, pʀɔ̃t] adj swift, rapid

prôner [pʀone] /1/ vt (préconiser) to advocate

pronom [pʀɔnɔ̃] nm pronoun

prononcer [pʀɔnɔ̃se] /3/ vt to pronounce; (dire) to utter; (discours) to deliver; **se prononcer** vi to be pronounced; **se ~ (sur)** (se décider) to reach a decision (on ou about), give a verdict (on); **ça se prononce comment?** how do you pronounce this?; **prononciation** nf pronunciation

pronostic [pʀɔnɔstik] nm (Méd) prognosis; (fig: aussi: **~s**) forecast

propagande [pʀɔpagɑ̃d] nf propaganda

propager [pʀɔpaʒe] /3/ vt to spread; **se propager** vi to spread

prophète, prophétesse [pʀɔfɛt, pʀɔfetɛs] nm/f prophet(ess)

prophétie [pʀɔfesi] nf prophecy

propice [pʀɔpis] adj favourable

proportion [pʀɔpɔʀsjɔ̃] nf proportion; **toute(s) ~(s) gardée(s)** making due allowance(s)

propos [pʀɔpo] nm (paroles) talk no pl, remark; (intention, but) intention, aim; (sujet): **à quel ~?** what about?; **à ~ de** about, regarding; **à tout ~** for no reason at all; **à ~** by the way; (opportunément) (just) at the right moment

proposer [pʀɔpoze] /1/ vt to propose; **~ qch (à qn)/de faire** (suggérer) to suggest sth (to sb)/ doing, propose sth (to sb)/(to) do; (offrir) to offer (sb) sth/to do; **se ~ (pour faire)** to offer one's services (to do); **proposition** nf suggestion; proposal; (Ling) clause

propre [pʀɔpʀ] adj clean; (net) neat, tidy; (possessif) own; (sens) literal; (particulier): **~ à** peculiar to; (approprié): **~ à** suitable ou appropriate for ⊳ nm: **recopier au ~** to make a fair copy of; **proprement** adv (avec propreté) cleanly; **à proprement parler** strictly speaking; **le village proprement dit** the village itself; **propreté** nf cleanliness

propriétaire [pʀɔpʀijetɛʀ] nm/f owner; (pour le locataire) landlord(-lady)

propriété [pʀɔpʀijete] nf (droit) ownership; (objet, immeuble etc) property

propulser [pʀɔpylse] /1/ vt to propel

prose [pʀoz] nf prose (style)

prospecter [pʀɔspɛkte] /1/ vt to prospect; (Comm) to canvass

prospectus [pʀɔspɛktys] nm leaflet

prospère [pʀɔspɛʀ] adj prosperous; **prospérer** /6/ vi to thrive

prosterner [pʀɔstɛʀne] /1/: **se prosterner** vi to bow low, prostrate o.s.

prostituée [pʀɔstitɥe] nf prostitute

prostitution [pʀɔstitysjɔ̃] nf prostitution

protecteur, -trice [pʀɔtɛktœʀ, -tʀis] adj protective; (air, ton: péj) patronizing ⊳ nm/f protector

protection [pʀɔtɛksjɔ̃] nf protection; (d'un personnage influent: aide) patronage

protéger [pʀɔteʒe] /6, 3/ vt to protect; **se ~ de/contre** to protect o.s. from

protège-slip [pʀɔtɛʒslip] nm panty liner

P

protéine [prɔtein] nf protein
protestant, e [prɔtɛstɑ̃, -ɑ̃t] adj,
nm/f Protestant
protestation [prɔtɛstasjɔ̃] nf
(plainte) protest
protester [prɔtɛste] /1/ vi: ~ **(contre)**
to protest (against ou about); ~ **de** (son
innocence, sa loyauté) to protest
prothèse [prɔtɛz] nf: ~ **dentaire**
denture
protocole [prɔtɔkɔl] nm (fig)
etiquette
proue [pru] nf bow(s pl), prow
prouesse [prues] nf feat
prouver [pruve] /1/ vt to prove
provenance [prɔvnɑ̃s] nf origin;
avion en ~ de plane (arriving) from
provenir [prɔvnir] /22/: ~ **de** vt to
come from
proverbe [prɔvɛrb] nm proverb
province [prɔvɛ̃s] nf province
proviseur [prɔvizœr] nm ≈ head
(teacher) (BRIT), ≈ principal (US)
provision [prɔvizjɔ̃] nf (réserve)
stock, supply; **provisions** nfpl (vivres)
provisions, food no pl
provisoire [prɔvizwar] adj
temporary; **provisoirement** adv
temporarily
provocant, e [prɔvɔkɑ̃, -ɑ̃t] adj
provocative
provoquer [prɔvɔke] /1/ vt (défier)
to provoke; (causer) to cause, bring
about; (inciter): ~ **qn à** to incite sb to
proxénète [prɔksenɛt] nm procurer
proximité [prɔksimite] nf nearness,
closeness; (dans le temps) imminence,
closeness; **à ~** near ou close by; **à ~ de**
near (to), close to
prudemment [prydamɑ̃] adv
carefully; wisely, sensibly
prudence [prydɑ̃s] nf carefulness;
avec ~ carefully; **par (mesure de) ~**
as a precaution
prudent, e [prydɑ̃, -ɑ̃t] adj (pas
téméraire) careful (: en général) safety-
conscious; (sage, conseillé) wise,
sensible; **c'est plus ~** it's wiser

prune [pryn] nf plum
pruneau, x [pryno] nm prune
prunier [prynje] nm plum tree
PS sigle m = **parti socialiste**; (= post-
scriptum) PS
pseudonyme [psødɔnim] nm
(gén) fictitious name; (d'écrivain)
pseudonym, pen name
psychanalyse [psikanaliz] nf
psychoanalysis
psychiatre [psikjatr] nm/f
psychiatrist; **psychiatrique** adj
psychiatric
psychique [psiʃik] adj
psychological
psychologie [psikɔlɔʒi] nf
psychology; **psychologique** adj
psychological; **psychologue** nm/f
psychologist
pu [py] pp de **pouvoir**
puanteur [pɥɑ̃tœr] nf stink, stench
pub [pyb] nf (fam) = **publicité**; **la ~**
advertising
public, -ique [pyblik] adj public;
(école, instruction) state cpd ▷ nm
public; (assistance) audience; **en ~**
in public
publicitaire [pyblisitɛr] adj
advertising cpd; (film, voiture)
publicity cpd
publicité [pyblisite] nf (méthode,
profession) advertising; (annonce)
advertisement; (révélations) publicity
publier [pyblije] /7/ vt to publish
publipostage [pyblipɔstaʒ] nm
(mass) mailing
publique [pyblik] adj f voir **public**
puce [pys] nf flea; (Inform) chip; **carte
à ~** smart card; **(marché aux) ~s** flea
market sg
pudeur [pydœr] nf modesty;
pudique adj (chaste) modest; (discret)
discreet
puer [pɥe] /1/ (péj) vi to stink
puéricultrice [pɥerikyltris] nf ≈
paediatric nurse
puéril, e [pɥeril] adj childish
puis [pɥi] vb voir **pouvoir** ▷ adv then

puiser [pɥize] /1/ vt: **~ (dans)** to draw (from)

puisque [pɥisk] conj since

puissance [pɥisɑ̃s] nf power; **en ~** adj potential

puissant, e [pɥisɑ̃, -ɑ̃t] adj powerful

puits [pɥi] nm well

pull(-over) [pyl(ɔvœʀ)] nm sweater

pulluler [pylyle] /1/ vi to swarm

pulpe [pylp] nf pulp

pulvériser [pylveʀize] /1/ vt to pulverize; (liquide) to spray

punaise [pynɛz] nf (Zool) bug; (clou) drawing pin (BRIT), thumb tack (US)

punch [pɔ̃ʃ] nm (boisson) punch

punir [pyniʀ] /2/ vt to punish; **punition** nf punishment

pupille [pypij] nf (Anat) pupil ▷ nm/f (enfant) ward

pupitre [pypitʀ] nm (Scol) desk

pur, e [pyʀ] adj pure; (vin) undiluted; (whisky) neat; **en ~e perte** to no avail; **c'est de la folie ~e** it's sheer madness

purée [pyʀe] nf: **~ (de pommes de terre)** ≈ mashed potatoes pl; **~ de marrons** chestnut purée

purement [pyʀmɑ̃] adv purely

purgatoire [pyʀɡatwaʀ] nm purgatory

purger [pyʀʒe] /3/ vt (Méd, Pol) to purge; (Jur: peine) to serve

pur-sang [pyʀsɑ̃] nm inv thoroughbred

pus [py] nm pus

putain [pytɛ̃] nf (!) whore (!)

puzzle [pœzl] nm jigsaw (puzzle)

PV sigle m = **procès-verbal**

pyjama [piʒama] nm pyjamas pl (BRIT), pajamas pl (US)

pyramide [piʀamid] nf pyramid

Pyrénées [piʀene] nfpl: **les ~** the Pyrenees

q

QI sigle m (= quotient intellectuel) IQ

quadragénaire [kadʀaʒenɛʀ] nm/f man/woman in his/her forties

quadruple [k(w)adʀypl] nm: **le ~ de** four times as much as

quai [ke] nm (de port) quay; (de gare) platform; **être à ~** (navire) to be alongside

qualification [kalifikasjɔ̃] nf qualification

qualifier [kalifje] /7/ vt to qualify; **~ qch/qn de** to describe sth/sb as; **se qualifier** vi to qualify

qualité [kalite] nf quality

quand [kɑ̃] conj, adv when; **~ je serai riche** when I'm rich; **~ même** all the same; **~ même, il exagère!** really, he overdoes it!; **~ bien même** even though

quant [kɑ̃]: **~ à** prép (pour ce qui est de) as for, as to; (au sujet de) regarding

quantité [kɑ̃tite] nf quantity, amount; **une** ou **des ~(s) de** (grand nombre) a great deal of

quarantaine [kaʀɑ̃tɛn] nf
(isolement) quarantine; **une ~ (de)**
forty or so, about forty; **avoir la ~**
(âge) to be around forty
quarante [kaʀɑ̃t] num forty
quart [kaʀ] nm (fraction) quarter;
(surveillance) watch; **un ~ de vin** a
quarter litre of wine; **le ~ de** a quarter
of; **~ d'heure** quarter of an hour; **~s
de finale** quarter finals
quartier [kaʀtje] nm (de ville) district,
area; (de bœuf, de la lune) quarter;
(de fruit, fromage) piece; **cinéma/
salle de ~** local cinema/hall; **avoir
~ libre** to be free; **~ général (QG)**
headquarters (HQ)
quartz [kwaʀts] nm quartz
quasi [kazi] adv almost, nearly;
quasiment adv almost, (very) nearly;
quasiment jamais hardly ever
quatorze [katɔʀz] num fourteen
quatorzième [katɔʀzjɛm] num
fourteenth
quatre [katʀ] num four; **à ~ pattes**
on all fours; **se mettre en ~ pour
qn** to go out of one's way for sb;
~ à ~ (monter, descendre) four at
a time; **quatre-vingt-dix** num
ninety; **quatre-vingts** num eighty;
quatrième num fourth ▷ nf (Scol)
year 9 (BRIT), eighth grade (US)
quatuor [kwatɥɔʀ] nm quartet(te)

○ **MOT-CLÉ**

que [kə] conj **1** (introduisant complétive)
that; **il sait que tu es là** he knows
(that) you're here; **je veux que tu
acceptes** I want you to accept; **il
a dit que oui** he said he would (ou
it was etc)
2 (reprise d'autres conjonctions): **quand
il rentrera et qu'il aura mangé**
when he gets back and (when) he has
eaten; **si vous y allez ou que vous
...** if you go there or if you ...
3 (en tête de phrase, hypothèse, souhait
etc): **qu'il le veuille ou non** whether

he likes it or not; **qu'il fasse ce qu'il
voudra!** let him do as he pleases!
4 (but): **tenez-le qu'il ne tombe pas**
hold it so (that) it doesn't fall
5 (après comparatif) than, as; voir aussi
plus², **aussi**, **autant** etc
6 (seulement): **ne ... que** only; **il ne
boit que de l'eau** he only drinks
water
7 (temps): **il y a quatre ans qu'il est
parti** it is four years since he left, he
left four years ago
▶ adv (exclamation): **qu'il** ou **qu'est-ce
qu'il est bête/court vite!** he's so
silly!/he runs so fast!; **que de livres!**
what a lot of books!
▶ pron **1** (relatif: personne) whom;
(: chose) that, which; **l'homme que
je vois** the man (whom) I see; **le livre
que tu vois** the book (that ou which)
you see; **un jour que j'étais ...** a day
when I was ...
2 (interrogatif) what; **que fais-tu?**,
qu'est-ce que tu fais? what are you
doing?; **qu'est-ce que c'est?** what
is it?, what's that?; **que faire?** what
can one do?

Québec [kebɛk] nm: **le ~** Quebec
(Province)
québécois, e adj Quebec cpd ▷ nm
(Ling) Quebec French ▷ nm/f: **Q~, e**
Quebecois, Quebec(k)er

○ **MOT-CLÉ**

quel, quelle [kɛl] adj **1** (interrogatif:
personne) who; (: chose) what; **quel
est cet homme?** who is this man?;
quel est ce livre? what is this
book?; **quel livre/homme?** what
book/man?; (parmi un certain choix)
which book/man?; **quels acteurs
préférez-vous?** which actors do you
prefer?; **dans quels pays êtes-vous
allé?** which ou what countries did
you go to?
2 (exclamatif): **quelle surprise/**

coïncidence! what a surprise/coincidence!

3: **quel que soit le coupable** whoever is guilty; **quel que soit votre avis** whatever your opinion (may be)

quelconque [kɛlkɔ̃k] *adj* (*médiocre*: *repas*) indifferent, poor; (*sans attrait*) ordinary, plain; (*indéfini*): **un ami/prétexte ~** some friend/pretext or other

 MOT-CLÉ

quelque [kɛlk] *adj* **1** (*au singulier*) some; (*au pluriel*) a few, some; (*tournure interrogative*) any; **quelque espoir** some hope; **il a quelques amis** he has a few *ou* some friends; **a-t-il quelques amis?** does he have any friends?; **les quelques livres qui** the few books which; **20 kg et quelque(s)** a bit over 20 kg **2**: **quelque ... que**: **quelque livre qu'il choisisse** whatever (*ou* whichever) book he chooses **3**: **quelque chose** something; (*tournure interrogative*) anything; **quelque chose d'autre** something else; anything else; **quelque part** somewhere; anywhere; **en quelque sorte** as it were

▶ *adv* **1** (*environ*): **quelque 100 mètres** some 100 metres **2**: **quelque peu** rather, somewhat

quelquefois [kɛlkəfwa] *adv* sometimes

quelques-uns, -unes [kɛlkəzœ̃, -yn] *pron* some, a few

quelqu'un [kɛlkœ̃] *pron* someone, somebody; (+ *tournure interrogative ou négative*) anyone, anybody; **~ d'autre** someone *ou* somebody else; anybody else

qu'en dira-t-on [kɑ̃diratɔ̃] *nm inv*: **le ~** gossip, what people say

querelle [kərɛl] *nf* quarrel; **quereller** /1/: **se quereller** *vi* to quarrel

qu'est-ce que [kɛskə] *voir* **que**

qu'est-ce qui [kɛski] *voir* **qui**

question [kɛstjɔ̃] *nf* question; (*fig*) matter; issue; **il a été ~ de** we (*ou* they) spoke about; **de quoi est-il ~?** what is it about?; **il n'en est pas ~** there's no question of it; **en ~** in question; **hors de ~** out of the question; **(re)mettre en ~** to question; **questionnaire** *nm* questionnaire; **questionner** /1/ *vt* to question

quête [kɛt] *nf* collection; (*recherche*) quest, search; **faire la ~** (*à l'église*) to take the collection; (*artiste*) to pass the hat round

quetsche [kwɛtʃ] *nf* damson

queue [kø] *nf* tail; (*fig*: *du classement*) bottom; (: *de poêle*) handle; (: *de fruit, feuille*) stalk; (: *de train, colonne, file*) rear; **faire la ~** to queue (up) (*BRIT*), line up (*US*); **~ de cheval** ponytail; **~ de poisson: faire une ~ de poisson à qn** (*Auto*) to cut in front of sb

 MOT-CLÉ

qui [ki] *pron* **1** (*interrogatif*: *personne*) who; (: *chose*): **qu'est-ce qui est sur la table?** what is on the table?; **qui est-ce qui?** who?; **qui est-ce que?** who?; **à qui est ce sac?** whose bag is this?; **à qui parlais-tu?** who were you talking to?, to whom were you talking?; **chez qui allez-vous?** whose house are you going to? **2** (*relatif*: *personne*) who; (+*prép*) whom; **l'ami de qui je vous ai parlé** the friend I told you about; **la dame chez qui je suis allé** the lady whose house I went to **3** (*sans antécédent*): **amenez qui vous voulez** bring who you like; **qui que ce soit** whoever it may be

quiche [kiʃ] *nf* quiche

q

quiconque [kikɔ̃k] *pron (celui qui)*
whoever, anyone who; *(n'importe qui,*
personne) anyone, anybody

quille [kij] *nf:* **(jeu de) ~s** skittles *sg*
(BRIT), bowling (US)

quincaillerie [kɛ̃kajri] *nf (ustensiles)*
hardware; *(magasin)* hardware shop
ou store (US)

quinquagénaire [kɛ̃kaʒenɛr] *nm/f*
man/woman in his/her fifties

quinquennat [kɛ̃kena] *nm five year*
term of office (of French President)

quinte [kɛ̃t] *nf:* **~ (de toux)**
coughing fit

quintuple [kɛ̃typl] *nm:* **le ~ de** five
times as much as

quinzaine [kɛ̃zɛn] *nf:* **une ~ (de)**
about fifteen, fifteen or so; **une ~ (de**
jours) a fortnight (BRIT), two weeks

quinze [kɛ̃z] *num* fifteen; **dans ~**
jours in a fortnight('s time) (BRIT), in
two weeks(' time)

quinzième [kɛ̃zjɛm] *num* fifteenth

quittance [kitɑ̃s] *nf (reçu)* receipt

quitte [kit] *adj:* **être ~ envers qn**
to be no longer in sb's debt; *(fig)* to
be quits with sb; **~ à faire** even if it
means doing

quitter [kite] /1/ *vt* to leave;
(vêtement) to take off; **se quitter**
vi (couples, interlocuteurs) to part;
ne quittez pas *(au téléphone)* hold
the line

qui-vive [kiviv] *nm inv:* **être sur le ~**
to be on the alert

 MOT-CLÉ

quoi [kwa] *pron interrog* **1** what; **~ de**
neuf? what's new?; **~?** *(qu'est-ce que*
tu dis?) what?

2 *(avec prép):* **à ~ tu penses?** what
are you thinking about?; **de ~ parlez-**
vous? what are you talking about?;
à ~ bon? what's the use?

▶ *pron relatif:* **as-tu de ~ écrire?** do
you have anything to write with?; **il**
n'y a pas de ~ *(please)* don't mention

it; **il n'y a pas de ~ rire** there's
nothing to laugh about

▶ *pron (locutions):* **~ qu'il arrive**
whatever happens; **~ qu'il en soit**
be that as it may; **~ que ce soit**
anything at all

▶ *excl* what!

quoique [kwak] *conj* (al)though

quotidien, ne [kɔtidjɛ̃, -ɛn] *adj*
daily; *(banal)* everyday ▷ *nm (journal)*
daily (paper); **quotidiennement** *adv*
daily, every day

R, r *abr* = **route; rue**

rab [Rab] *nm (fam: nourriture)* extra; **est-ce qu'il y a du ~?** are there any seconds?

rabâcher [Rabɑʃe] /1/ *vt* to keep on repeating

rabais [Rabɛ] *nm* reduction, discount; **rabaisser** /1/ *vt (rabattre: prix)* to reduce; *(dénigrer)* to belittle

Rabat [Raba(t)] *n* Rabat

rabattre [RabatR] /41/ *vt (couvercle, siège)* to pull down; *(déduire)* to reduce; **se rabattre** *vi (bords, couvercle)* to fall shut; *(véhicule, coureur)* to cut in; **se ~ sur** to fall back on

rabbin [Rabɛ̃] *nm* rabbi

rabougri, e [RabugRi] *adj* stunted

raccommoder [Rakɔmɔde] /1/ *vt* to mend, repair

raccompagner [Rakɔ̃paɲe] /1/ *vt* to take *ou* see back

raccord [RakɔR] *nm* link; *(retouche)* touch-up; **raccorder** /1/ *vt* to join (up), link up; *(pont etc)* to connect, link

raccourci [RakuRsi] *nm* short cut

raccourcir [RakuRsiR] /2/ *vt* to shorten ▷ *vi (jours)* to grow shorter, draw in

raccrocher [RakRɔʃe] /1/ *vt (tableau, vêtement)* to hang back up; *(récepteur)* to put down ▷ *vi (Tél)* to hang up, ring off

race [Ras] *nf* race; *(d'animaux, fig)* breed; **de ~** purebred, pedigree

rachat [Raʃa] *nm* buying; *(du même objet)* buying back

racheter [Raʃte] /5/ *vt (article perdu)* to buy another; *(davantage)* to buy more; *(après avoir vendu)* to buy back; *(d'occasion)* to buy; *(Comm: part, firme)* to buy up; **se racheter** *(gén)* to make amends; **~ du lait/trois œufs** to buy more milk/another three eggs *ou* three more eggs

racial, e, -aux [Rasjal, -o] *adj* racial

racine [Rasin] *nf* root; **~ carrée/ cubique** square/cube root

racisme [Rasism] *nm* racism

raciste [Rasist] *adj, nm/f* racist

racket [Rakɛt] *nm* racketeering *no pl*

raclée [Rɑkle] *nf (fam)* hiding, thrashing

racler [Rɑkle] /1/ *vt (os, plat)* to scrape; **se ~ la gorge** to clear one's throat

racontars [Rakɔ̃taR] *nmpl* stories, gossip *sg*

raconter [Rakɔ̃te] /1/ *vt*: **~ (à qn)** *(décrire)* to relate (to sb), tell (sb) about; *(dire)* to tell (sb); **~ une histoire** to tell a story

radar [RadaR] *nm* radar

rade [Rad] *nf (natural)* harbour; **rester en ~** *(fig)* to be left stranded

radeau, x [Rado] *nm* raft

radiateur [RadjatœR] *nm* radiator, heater; *(Auto)* radiator; **~ électrique/à gaz** electric/gas heater *ou* fire

radiation [Radjasjɔ̃] *nf (Physique)* radiation

radical, e, -aux [Radikal, -o] *adj* radical

radieux, -euse [ʁadjø, -øz] *adj* radiant

radin, e [ʁadɛ̃, -in] *adj (fam)* stingy

radio [ʁadjo] *nf* radio; *(Méd)* X-ray ▷ *nm* radio operator; **à la ~** on the radio; **radioactif, -ive** *adj* radioactive; **radiocassette** *nf* cassette radio; **radiographie** *nf* radiography; *(photo)* X-ray photograph; **radiophonique** *adj* radio *cpd*; **radio-réveil** (*pl* **radios-réveils**) *nm* radio alarm (clock)

radis [ʁadi] *nm* radish

radoter [ʁadɔte] /1/ *vi* to ramble on

radoucir [ʁadusiʁ] /2/: **se radoucir** *vi (se réchauffer)* to become milder; *(se calmer)* to calm down

rafale [ʁafal] *nf (vent)* gust (of wind); *(de balles, d'applaudissements)* burst

raffermir [ʁafɛʁmiʁ] /2/ *vt*, **se raffermir** *vi* to firm up

raffiner [ʁafine] /1/ *vt* to refine; **raffinerie** *nf* refinery

raffoler [ʁafɔle] /1/: **~ de** *vt* to be very keen on

rafle [ʁɑfl] *nf (de police)* raid; **rafler** /1/ *vt (fam)* to swipe, nick

rafraîchir [ʁafʁeʃiʁ] /2/ *vt (atmosphère, température)* to cool (down); *(boisson)* to chill; *(fig: rénover)* to brighten up; **se rafraîchir** *vi* to grow cooler; *(en se lavant)* to freshen up; *(en buvant etc)* to refresh o.s.; **rafraîchissant, e** *adj* refreshing; **rafraîchissement** *nm (boisson)* cool drink; **rafraîchissements** *nmpl (boissons, fruits etc)* refreshments

rage [ʁaʒ] *nf (Méd)*: **la ~** rabies; *(fureur)* rage, fury; **faire ~** to rage; **~ de dents** (raging) toothache

ragot [ʁago] *nm (fam)* malicious gossip *no pl*

ragoût [ʁagu] *nm* stew

raide [ʁɛd] *adj (tendu)* taut, tight; *(escarpé)* steep; *(droit: cheveux)* straight; *(ankylosé, dur, guindé)* stiff; *(fam: sans argent)* flat broke; *(osé, licencieux)* daring ▷ *adv (en pente)*

steeply; **~ mort** stone dead; **raideur** *nf (rigidité)* stiffness; **avec raideur** *(répondre)* stiffly, abruptly; **raidir** /2/ *vt (muscles)* to stiffen; **se raidir** *vi* to stiffen; *(personne)* to tense up; *(: se préparer moralement)* to brace o.s.; *(fig: devenir intransigeant)* to harden

raie [ʁɛ] *nf (Zool)* skate, ray; *(rayure)* stripe; *(des cheveux)* parting

raifort [ʁɛfɔʁ] *nm* horseradish

rail [ʁaj] *nm* rail; *(chemins de fer)* railways *pl*; **par ~** by rail

railler [ʁaje] /1/ *vt* to scoff at, jeer at

rainure [ʁenyʁ] *nf* groove

raisin [ʁɛzɛ̃] *nm (aussi: ~s)* grapes *pl*; **~s secs** raisins

raison [ʁɛzɔ̃] *nf* reason; **avoir ~** to be right; **donner ~ à qn** to agree with sb; *(fait)* to prove sb right; **se faire une ~** to learn to live with it; **perdre la ~** to become insane; **~ de plus** all the more reason; **à plus forte ~** all the more so; **sans ~** for no reason; **en ~ de** because of; **à ~ de** at the rate of; **~ sociale** corporate name; **raisonnable** *adj* reasonable, sensible

raisonnement [ʁɛzɔnmɑ̃] *nm* reasoning; argument

raisonner [ʁɛzɔne] /1/ *vi (penser)* to reason; *(argumenter, discuter)* to argue ▷ *vt (personne)* to reason with

rajeunir [ʁaʒœniʁ] /2/ *vt (en recrutant)* to inject new blood into ▷ *vi* to become (*ou* look) younger; **~ qn** *(coiffure, robe)* to make sb look younger

rajouter [ʁaʒute] /1/ *vt* to add

rajuster [ʁaʒyste] /1/ *vt (vêtement)* to straighten, tidy; *(salaires)* to adjust

ralenti [ʁalɑ̃ti] *nm*: **au ~** *(fig)* at a slower pace; **tourner au ~** *(Auto)* to tick over, idle

ralentir [ʁalɑ̃tiʁ] /2/ *vt, vi*, **se ralentir** *vi* to slow down

râler [ʁɑle] /1/ *vi* to groan; *(fam)* to grouse, moan (and groan)

rallier [ʁalje] /1/ *vt (rejoindre)* to rejoin; *(gagner à sa cause)* to win over

rallonge [Ralɔ̃ʒ] nf (de table) (extra) leaf

rallonger [Ralɔ̃ʒe] /3/ vt to lengthen

rallye [Rali] nm rally; (Pol) march

ramassage [Ramasaʒ] nm: **~ scolaire** school bus service

ramasser [Ramase] /1/ vt (objet tombé ou par terre) to pick up; (recueillir: copies, ordures) to collect; (récolter) to gather; **ramassis** nm (péj: de voyous) bunch; (de choses) jumble

rambarde [Rãbard] nf guardrail

rame [Ram] nf (aviron) oar; (de métro) train; (de papier) ream

rameau, x [Ramo] nm (small) branch; **les R~x** (Rel) Palm Sunday sg

ramener [Ramne] /5/ vt to bring back; (reconduire) to take back; **~ qch à** (réduire à) to reduce sth to

ramer [Rame] /1/ vi to row

ramollir [Ramɔlir] /2/ vt to soften; **se ramollir** vi to get (ou go) soft

rampe [Rãp] nf (d'escalier) banister(s pl); (dans un garage, d'un terrain) ramp; **la ~** (Théât) the footlights pl; **~ de lancement** launching pad

ramper [Rãpe] /1/ vi to crawl

rancard [Rãkar] nm (fam) date

rancart [Rãkar] nm: **mettre au ~** to scrap

rance [Rãs] adj rancid

rancœur [Rãkœr] nf rancour

rançon [Rãsɔ̃] nf ransom

rancune [Rãkyn] nf grudge, rancour; **garder ~ à qn (de qch)** to bear sb a grudge (for sth); **sans ~!** no hard feelings!; **rancunier, -ière** adj vindictive, spiteful

randonnée [Rãdɔne] nf ride; (à pied) walk, ramble; (en montagne) hike, hiking no pl; **la ~** (activité) hiking, walking; **une ~ à cheval** a pony trek

rang [Rã] nm (rangée) row; (grade, condition sociale, classement) rank; **rangs** nmpl (Mil) ranks; **se mettre en ~s/sur un ~** to get into ou form rows/a line; **au premier ~** in the first row; (fig) ranking first

rangé, e [Rãʒe] adj (vie) well-ordered; (sérieux: personne) steady

rangée [Rãʒe] nf row

ranger [Rãʒe] /3/ vt (classer, grouper) to order, arrange; (mettre à sa place) to put away; (mettre de l'ordre dans) to tidy up; (fig: classer): **~ qn/qch parmi** to rank sb/sth among; **se ranger** vi (véhicule, conducteur) to pull over or in; (piéton) to step aside; (s'assagir) to settle down; **se ~ à** (avis) to come round to

ranimer [Ranime] /1/ vt (personne évanouie) to bring round; (douleur, souvenir) to revive; (feu) to rekindle

rapace [Rapas] nm bird of prey

râpe [Rɑp] nf (Culin) grater; **râper** /1/ vt (Culin) to grate

rapide [Rapid] adj fast; (prompt: intelligence, coup d'œil, mouvement) quick ▷ nm express (train); (de cours d'eau) rapid; **rapidement** adv fast; quickly

rapiécer [Rapjese] /3, 6/ vt to patch

rappel [Rapel] nm (Théât) curtain call; (Méd: vaccination) booster; (d'une aventure, d'un nom) reminder; **rappeler** /4/ vt to call back; (ambassadeur, Mil) to recall; (faire se souvenir): **rappeler qch à qn** to remind sb of sth; **se rappeler** vt (se souvenir de) to remember, recall

rapport [Rapɔr] nm (compte rendu) report; (profit) yield, return; (lien, analogie) relationship; (corrélation) connection; **rapports** nmpl (entre personnes, pays) relations; **avoir ~ à** to have something to do with; **être/ se mettre en ~ avec qn** to be/get in touch with sb; **par ~ à** in relation to; **~s (sexuels)** (sexual) intercourse sg; **~ qualité-prix** value (for money)

rapporter [Rapɔrte] /1/ vt (rendre, ramener) to bring back; (investissement) to yield; (relater) to report ▷ vi (investissement) to give a good return ou yield; (activité) to be very profitable; **se ~ à** to relate to

rapprochement [ʀapʀɔʃmɑ̃] nm (de nations, familles) reconciliation; (analogie, rapport) parallel

rapprocher [ʀapʀɔʃe] /1/ vt (deux objets) to bring closer together; (ennemis, partis etc) to bring together; (comparer) to establish a parallel between; (chaise d'une table): **~ qch (de)** to bring sth closer (to); **se rapprocher** vi to draw closer ou nearer; **se ~ de** to come closer to; (présenter une analogie avec) to be close to

raquette [ʀakɛt] nf (de tennis) racket; (de ping-pong) bat

rare [ʀɑʀ] adj rare; **se faire ~** to become scarce; **rarement** adv rarely, seldom

ras, e [ʀɑ, ʀɑz] adj (tête, cheveux) close-cropped; (poil, herbe) short ▷ adv short; **en ~e campagne** in open country; **à ~ bords** to the brim; **en avoir ~ le bol** (fam) to be fed up

raser [ʀɑze] /1/ vt (barbe, cheveux) to shave off; (menton, personne) to shave; (fam: ennuyer) to bore; (démolir) to raze (to the ground); (frôler) to graze, skim; **se raser** vi to shave; (fam) to be bored (to tears); **rasoir** nm razor

rassasier [ʀasazje] /7/ vt: **être rassasié** to be sated

rassemblement [ʀasɑ̃bləmɑ̃] nm (groupe) gathering; (Pol) union

rassembler [ʀasɑ̃ble] /1/ vt (réunir) to assemble, gather; (documents, notes) to gather together, collect; **se rassembler** vi to gather

rassurer [ʀasyʀe] /1/ vt to reassure; **se rassurer** vi to be reassured; **rassure-toi** don't worry

rat [ʀa] nm rat

rate [ʀat] nf spleen

raté, e [ʀate] adj (tentative) unsuccessful, failed ▷ nm/f (fam: personne) failure

râteau, x [ʀɑto] nm rake

rater [ʀate] /1/ vi (affaire, projet etc) to go wrong, fail ▷ vt (cible, train, occasion) to miss; (démonstration, plat) to spoil; (examen) to fail

ration [ʀasjɔ̃] nf ration

RATP sigle f (= Régie autonome des transports parisiens) Paris transport authority

rattacher [ʀataʃe] /1/ vt (animal, cheveux) to tie up again; **~ qch à** (relier) to link sth with

rattraper [ʀatʀape] /1/ vt (fugitif) to recapture; (retenir, empêcher de tomber) to catch (hold of); (atteindre, rejoindre) to catch up with; (réparer: erreur) to make up for; **se rattraper** vi to make up for it; **se ~ (à)** (se raccrocher) to stop o.s. falling (by catching hold of)

rature [ʀatyʀ] nf deletion, erasure

rauque [ʀok] adj (voix) hoarse

ravages [ʀavaʒ] nmpl: **faire des ~** to wreak havoc

ravi, e [ʀavi] adj: **être ~ de/que** to be delighted with/that

ravin [ʀavɛ̃] nm gully, ravine

ravir [ʀaviʀ] /2/ vt (enchanter) to delight; **à ~** adv beautifully

raviser [ʀavize] /1/: **se raviser** vi to change one's mind

ravissant, e [ʀavisɑ̃, -ɑ̃t] adj delightful

ravisseur, -euse [ʀavisœʀ, -øz] nm/f abductor, kidnapper

ravitailler [ʀavitaje] /1/ vt (en vivres, munitions) to provide with fresh supplies; (véhicule) to refuel; **se ravitailler** vi to get fresh supplies

raviver [ʀavive] /1/ vt (feu) to rekindle; (douleur) to revive; (couleurs) to brighten up

rayé, e [ʀeje] adj (à rayures) striped

rayer [ʀeje] /8/ vt (érafler) to scratch; (barrer) to cross ou score out; (d'une liste) to cross ou strike off

rayon [ʀejɔ̃] nm (de soleil etc) ray; (Géom) radius; (de roue) spoke; (étagère) shelf; (de grand magasin) department; **dans un ~ de** within a radius of; **~ de soleil** sunbeam; **~s X** X-rays

rayonnement [ʀɛjɔnmɑ̃] nm (d'une culture) influence

rayonner [ʀɛjɔne] /1/ vi (fig) to shine forth; (: visage, personne) to be radiant; (touriste) to go touring (from one base)

rayure [ʀɛjyʀ] nf (motif) stripe; (éraflure) scratch; **à ~s** striped

raz-de-marée [ʀɑdmaʀe] nm inv tidal wave

ré [ʀe] nm (Mus) D; (en chantant la gamme) re

réaction [ʀeaksjɔ̃] nf reaction

réadapter [ʀeadapte] /1/: **se ~ (à)** vi to readjust (to)

réagir [ʀeaʒiʀ] /2/ vi to react

réalisateur, -trice [ʀealizatœʀ, -tʀis] nm/f (TV, Ciné) director

réalisation [ʀealizasjɔ̃] nf realization; (Ciné) production; **en cours de ~** under way

réaliser [ʀealize] /1/ vt (projet, opération) to carry out, realize; (rêve, souhait) to realize, fulfil; (exploit) to achieve; (film) to produce; (se rendre compte de) to realize; **se réaliser** vi to be realized

réaliste [ʀealist] adj realistic

réalité [ʀealite] nf reality; **en ~** in (actual) fact; **dans la ~** in reality

réanimation [ʀeanimasjɔ̃] nf resuscitation; **service de ~** intensive care unit

rébarbatif, -ive [ʀebaʀbatif, -iv] adj forbidding

rebattu, e [ʀəbaty] adj hackneyed

rebelle [ʀəbɛl] nm/f rebel ▷ adj (troupes) rebel; (enfant) rebellious; (mèche etc) unruly

rebeller [ʀəbele] /1/: **se rebeller** vi to rebel

rebondir [ʀəbɔ̃diʀ] /2/ vi (ballon: au sol) to bounce; (: contre un mur) to rebound; (fig) to get moving again

rebord [ʀəbɔʀ] nm edge; **le ~ de la fenêtre** the windowsill

rebours [ʀəbuʀ]: **à ~** adv the wrong way

rebrousser [ʀəbʀuse] /1/ vt: **~ chemin** to turn back

rebuter [ʀəbyte] /1/ vt to put off

récalcitrant, e [ʀekalsitʀɑ̃, -ɑ̃t] adj refractory

récapituler [ʀekapityle] /1/ vt to recapitulate; to sum up

receler [ʀəsəle] /5/ vt (produit d'un vol) to receive; (fig) to conceal; **receleur, -euse** nm/f receiver

récemment [ʀesamɑ̃] adv recently

recensement [ʀəsɑ̃smɑ̃] nm census

recenser [ʀəsɑ̃se] /1/ vt (population) to take a census of; (dénombrer) to list

récent, e [ʀesɑ̃, -ɑ̃t] adj recent

récépissé [ʀesepise] nm receipt

récepteur, -trice [ʀesɛptœʀ, -tʀis] adj receiving ▷ nm receiver

réception [ʀesɛpsjɔ̃] nf receiving no pl; (accueil) reception, welcome; (bureau) reception (desk); (réunion mondaine) reception, party; **réceptionniste** nm/f receptionist

recette [ʀəsɛt] nf recipe; (Comm) takings pl; **recettes** nfpl (Comm: rentrées) receipts; **faire ~** (spectacle, exposition) to be a winner

recevoir [ʀəsvwaʀ] /28/ vt to receive; (client, patient, représentant) to see; **être reçu** (à un examen) to pass

rechange [ʀəʃɑ̃ʒ]: **de ~** adj (pièces, roue) spare; (fig: solution) alternative; **des vêtements de ~** a change of clothes

recharge [ʀəʃaʀʒ] nf refill; **rechargeable** adj (stylo etc) refillable; **recharger** /3/ vt (briquet, stylo) to refill; (batterie) to recharge

réchaud [ʀeʃo] nm (portable) stove

réchauffement [ʀeʃofmɑ̃] nm warming (up); **le ~ de la planète** global warming

réchauffer [ʀeʃofe] /1/ vt (plat) to reheat; (mains, personne) to warm; **se réchauffer** vi (température) to get warmer; (personne) to warm o.s. (up)

rêche [ʀɛʃ] adj rough

recherche [ʀəʃɛʀʃ] nf (action): **la ~ de** the search for; (raffinement) studied elegance; (*scientifique etc*): **la ~** research; **recherches** *nfpl* (*de la police*) investigations; (*scientifiques*) research *sg*; **être/se mettre à la ~ de** to be/ go in search of

recherché, e [ʀəʃɛʀʃe] *adj* (*rare, demandé*) much sought-after; (*raffiné*) affected; (*tenue*) elegant

rechercher [ʀəʃɛʀʃe] /1/ *vt* (*objet égaré, personne*) to look for; (*causes d'un phénomène, nouveau procédé*) to try to find; (*bonheur etc, l'amitié de qn*) to seek

rechute [ʀəʃyt] *nf* (*Méd*) relapse

récidiver [ʀesidive] /1/ *vi* to commit a second (*ou* subsequent) offence; (*fig*) to do it again

récif [ʀesif] *nm* reef

récipient [ʀesipjã] *nm* container

réciproque [ʀesipʀɔk] *adj* reciprocal

récit [ʀesi] *nm* story; **récital** *nm* recital; **réciter** /1/ *vt* to recite

réclamation [ʀeklamasjɔ̃] *nf* complaint; **réclamations** *nfpl* complaints department *sg*

réclame [ʀeklam] *nf*: **une ~** an ad(vertisement), an advert (BRIT); **article en ~** special offer; **réclamer** /1/ *vt* to ask for; (*revendiquer*) to claim, demand ▷ *vi* to complain

réclusion [ʀeklyzjɔ̃] *nf* imprisonment

recoin [ʀəkwɛ̃] *nm* nook, corner

reçois *etc* [ʀəswa] *vb voir* **recevoir**

récolte [ʀekɔlt] *nf* harvesting, gathering; (*produits*) harvest, crop; **récolter** /1/ *vt* to harvest, gather (in); (*fig*) to get

recommandé [ʀəkɔmɑ̃de] *nm* (*Postes*): **en ~** by registered mail

recommander [ʀəkɔmɑ̃de] /1/ *vt* to recommend; (*Postes*) to register

recommencer [ʀəkɔmɑ̃se] /3/ *vt* (*reprendre: lutte, séance*) to resume, start again; (*refaire: travail, explications*) to start afresh, start (over) again ▷ *vi* to start again; (*récidiver*) to do it again

récompense [ʀekɔ̃pɑ̃s] *nf* reward; (*prix*) award; **récompenser** /1/ *vt*: **récompenser qn (de *ou* pour)** to reward sb (for)

réconcilier [ʀekɔ̃silje] /7/ *vt* to reconcile; **se réconcilier (avec)** to be reconciled (with)

reconduire [ʀəkɔ̃dɥiʀ] /38/ *vt* (*raccompagner*) to take *ou* see back; (*renouveler*) to renew

réconfort [ʀekɔ̃fɔʀ] *nm* comfort; **réconforter** /1/ *vt* (*consoler*) to comfort

reconnaissance [ʀəkɔnɛsɑ̃s] *nf* (*action de reconnaître*) recognition; (*gratitude*) gratitude, gratefulness; (*Mil*) reconnaissance, recce; **reconnaissant, e** *adj* grateful; **je vous serais reconnaissant de bien vouloir** I should be most grateful if you would (kindly)

reconnaître [ʀəkɔnɛtʀ] /57/ *vt* to recognize; (*Mil: lieu*) to reconnoitre; (*Jur: enfant, dette, droit*) to acknowledge; **~ que** to admit *ou* acknowledge that; **~ qn/qch à** (*l'identifier grâce à*) to recognize sb/sth by; **reconnu, e** *adj* (*indiscuté, connu*) recognized

reconstituer [ʀəkɔ̃stitɥe] /1/ *vt* (*fresque, vase brisé*) to piece together, reconstitute; (*événement, accident*) to reconstruct

reconstruire [ʀəkɔ̃stʀɥiʀ] /38/ *vt* to rebuild

reconvertir [ʀəkɔ̃vɛʀtiʀ] /2/ *vt* to reconvert; **se ~ dans** (*un métier, une branche*) to move into

record [ʀəkɔʀ] *nm, adj* record

recoupement [ʀəkupmɑ̃] *nm*: **par ~** by cross-checking

recouper [ʀəkupe] /1/: **se recouper** *vi* (*témoignages*) to tie *ou* match up

recourber [ʀəkuʀbe] /1/: **se recourber** *vi* to curve (up), bend (up)

recourir [ʀəkuʀiʀ] /11/: **~ à** *vt* (*ami, agence*) to turn *ou* appeal to; (*force, ruse, emprunt*) to resort to

recours [ʀəkuʀ] *nm*: **avoir ~ à = recourir à**; **en dernier ~** as a last resort

recouvrer [ʀəkuvʀe] /1/ *vt* (*vue, santé etc*) to recover, regain

recouvrir [ʀəkuvʀiʀ] /18/ *vt* (*couvrir à nouveau*) to re-cover; (*couvrir entièrement, aussi fig*) to cover

récréation [ʀekʀeasjɔ̃] *nf* (*Scol*) break

recroqueviller [ʀəkʀɔkvije] /1/: **se recroqueviller** *vi* (*personne*) to huddle up

recrudescence [ʀəkʀydesɑ̃s] *nf* fresh outbreak

recruter [ʀəkʀyte] /1/ *vt* to recruit

rectangle [ʀɛktɑ̃gl] *nm* rectangle; **rectangulaire** *adj* rectangular

rectificatif, -ive [ʀɛktifikatif, -iv] *adj* corrected ▷ *nm* correction

rectifier [ʀɛktifje] /7/ *vt* (*calcul, adresse*) to correct; (*erreur, faute*) to rectify

rectiligne [ʀɛktiliɲ] *adj* straight

recto [ʀɛkto] *nm* front (*of a sheet of paper*); **~ verso** on both sides (of the page)

reçu, e [ʀəsy] *pp de* **recevoir** ▷ *adj* (*candidat*) successful; (*admis, consacré*) accepted ▷ *nm* (*Comm*) receipt

recueil [ʀəkœj] *nm* collection; **recueillir** /12/ *vt* to collect; (*voix, suffrages*) to win; (*accueillir: réfugiés, chat*) to take in; **se recueillir** *vi* to gather one's thoughts; to meditate

recul [ʀəkyl] *nm* (*déclin*) decline; (*éloignement*) distance; **avoir un mouvement de ~** to recoil; **prendre du ~** to stand back; **être en ~** to be on the decline; **avec le ~** in retrospect; **reculé, e** *adj* remote; **reculer** /1/ *vi* to move back, back away; (*Auto*) to reverse, back (up); (*fig*) to (be on the) decline ▷ *vt* to move back; (*véhicule*) to reverse, back (up); (*date, décision*) to postpone; **reculer devant** (*danger, difficulté*) to shrink from; **reculons**: **à reculons** *adv* backwards

récupérer [ʀekypeʀe] /6/ *vt* to recover, get back; (*déchets etc*) to salvage (for reprocessing); (*journée, heures de travail*) to make up ▷ *vi* to recover

récurer [ʀekyʀe] /1/ *vt* to scour; **poudre à ~** scouring powder

reçus *etc* [ʀəsy] *vb voir* **recevoir**

recycler [ʀəsikle] /1/ *vt* (*matériau*) to recycle; **se recycler** *vi* to retrain

rédacteur, -trice [ʀedaktœʀ, -tʀis] *nm/f* (*journaliste*) writer; subeditor; (*d'ouvrage de référence*) editor, compiler

rédaction [ʀedaksjɔ̃] *nf* writing; (*rédacteurs*) editorial staff; (*Scol: devoir*) essay, composition

redescendre [ʀədesɑ̃dʀ] /41/ *vi* to go back down ▷ *vt* (*pente etc*) to go down

rédiger [ʀediʒe] /3/ *vt* to write; (*contrat*) to draw up

redire [ʀədiʀ] /37/ *vt* to repeat; **trouver à ~ à** to find fault with

redoubler [ʀəduble] /1/ *vi* (*tempête, violence*) to intensify; (*Scol*) to repeat a year; **~ de patience/prudence** to be doubly patient/careful

redoutable [ʀədutabl] *adj* formidable, fearsome

redouter [ʀədute] /1/ *vt* to dread

redressement [ʀədʀɛsmɑ̃] *nm* (*économique*) recovery

redresser [ʀədʀese] /1/ *vt* (*arbre, mât*) to set upright; (*pièce tordue*) to straighten out; (*situation, économie*) to put right; **se redresser** *vi* (*personne*) to sit (*ou* stand) up; (*pays, situation*) to recover

réduction [ʀedyksjɔ̃] *nf* reduction

réduire [ʀedɥiʀ] /38/ *vt* to reduce; (*prix, dépenses*) to cut; reduce; **réduit** *nm* tiny room

rééducation [ʀeedykasjɔ̃] *nf* (*d'un membre*) re-education; (*de délinquants, d'un blessé*) rehabilitation

réel, le [ʀeɛl] *adj* real; **réellement** *adv* really

réexpédier [ʀeɛkspedje] /7/ vt (à l'envoyeur) to return, send back; (au destinataire) to send on, forward

refaire [ʀəfɛʀ] /60/ vt to do again; (sport) to take up again; (réparer, restaurer) to do up

réfectoire [ʀefɛktwaʀ] nm refectory

référence [ʀefeʀɑ̃s] nf reference; **références** nfpl (recommandations) reference sg

référer [ʀefeʀe] /6/: **se ~ à** vt to refer to

refermer [ʀəfɛʀme] /1/ vt to close again, shut again; **se refermer** vi (porte) to close ou shut (again)

refiler [ʀəfile] /1/ vt (fam): **~ qch à qn** to palm (BRIT) ou fob sth off on sb

réfléchi, e [ʀefleʃi] adj (caractère) thoughtful; (action) well-thought-out; (Ling) reflexive; **c'est tout ~** my mind's made up

réfléchir [ʀefleʃiʀ] /2/ vt to reflect ▷ vi to think; **~ à ou sur** to think about

reflet [ʀəflɛ] nm reflection; (sur l'eau etc) sheen no pl, glint; **refléter** /6/ vt to reflect; **se refléter** vi to be reflected

réflexe [ʀeflɛks] adj, nm reflex

réflexion [ʀeflɛksjɔ̃] nf (de la lumière etc) reflection; (fait de penser) thought; (remarque) remark; **~ faite, à la ~** on reflection; **délai de ~** cooling-off period; **groupe de ~** think tank

réflexologie [ʀeflɛksɔlɔʒi] nf reflexology

réforme [ʀefɔʀm] nf reform; (Rel): **la R~** the Reformation; **réformer** /1/ vt to reform; (Mil) to declare unfit for service

refouler [ʀəfule] /1/ vt (envahisseurs) to drive back; (liquide, larmes) to force back; (désir, colère) to repress

refrain [ʀəfʀɛ̃] nm refrain, chorus

refréner /6/, **réfréner** [ʀəfʀene, ʀefʀene] vt to curb, check

réfrigérateur [ʀefʀiʒeʀatœʀ] nm refrigerator

refroidir [ʀəfʀwadiʀ] /2/ vt to cool; (personne) to put off ▷ vi to cool (down); **se refroidir** vi (temps) to get cooler ou colder; (fig: ardeur) to cool (off); **refroidissement** nm (grippe etc) chill

refuge [ʀəfyʒ] nm refuge; **réfugié, e** adj, nm/f refugee; **réfugier** /7/: **se réfugier** vi to take refuge

refus [ʀəfy] nm refusal; **ce n'est pas de ~** I won't say no, it's very welcome; **refuser** /1/ vt to refuse; (Scol: candidat) to fail; **refuser qch à qn/de faire** to refuse sb sth/to do; **refuser du monde** to have to turn people away; **se refuser à qch** ou **à faire qch** to refuse to do sth

regagner [ʀəɡaɲe] /1/ vt (argent, faveur) to win back; (lieu) to get back to

régal [ʀeɡal] nm treat; **régaler** /1/ vt: **régaler qn de** to treat sb to; **se régaler** vi to have a delicious meal; (fig) to enjoy o.s.

regard [ʀəɡaʀ] nm (coup d'œil) look, glance; (expression) look (in one's eye); **au ~ de** (loi, morale) from the point of view of; **en ~ de** in comparison with

regardant, e [ʀəɡaʀdɑ̃, -ɑ̃t] adj: **très/peu ~ (sur)** quite fussy/very free (about); (économe) very tight-fisted/quite generous (with)

regarder [ʀəɡaʀde] /1/ vt to look at; (film, télévision, match) to watch; (concerner) to concern ▷ vi to look; **ne pas ~ à la dépense** to spare no expense; **~ qn/qch comme** to regard sb/sth as

régie [ʀeʒi] nf (Comm, Industrie) state-owned company; (Théât, Ciné) production; (Radio, TV) control room

régime [ʀeʒim] nm (Pol) régime; (Admin: carcéral, fiscal etc) system; (Méd) diet; (de bananes, dattes) bunch; **se mettre au/suivre un ~** to go on/be on a diet

régiment [ʀeʒimɑ̃] nm regiment

région [ʀeʒjɔ̃] nf region; **régional, e, -aux** adj regional

régir [ReʒiR] /2/ vt to govern
régisseur [ReʒisœR] nm (d'un domaine) steward; (Ciné, TV) assistant director; (Théât) stage manager
registre [RaʒistR] nm register
réglage [Reglaʒ] nm adjustment
réglé, e [Regle] adj well-ordered; (arrangé) settled
règle [Regl] nf (instrument) ruler; (loi, prescription) rule; **règles** nfpl (Physiol) period sg; **en ~** (papiers d'identité) in order; **en ~ générale** as a (general) rule
règlement [Reglemã] nm (paiement) settlement; (arrêté) regulation; (règles, statuts) regulations pl, rules pl; **réglementaire** adj conforming to the regulations; (tenue, uniforme) regulation cpd; **réglementation** nf (règlements) regulations pl; **réglementer** /1/ vt to regulate
régler [Regle] /6/ vt (mécanisme, machine) to regulate, adjust; (thermostat etc) to set, adjust; (question, conflit, facture, dette) to settle; (fournisseur) to settle up with
réglisse [Reglis] nm ou f liquorice
règne [Reɲ] nm (d'un roi etc, fig) reign; **le ~ végétal/animal** the vegetable/animal kingdom; **régner** /6/ vi (roi) to rule, reign; (fig) to reign
regorger [RagɔRʒe] /3/ vi: **~ de** to overflow with, be bursting with
regret [RagRɛ] nm regret; **à ~** with regret; **sans ~** with no regrets; **regrettable** adj regrettable; **regretter** /1/ vt to regret; (personne) to miss; **non, je regrette** no, I'm sorry
regrouper [RagRupe] /1/ vt (grouper) to group together; (contenir) to include, comprise; **se regrouper** vi to gather (together)
régulier, -ière [Regylje, -jɛR] adj (gén) regular; (vitesse, qualité) steady; (répartition, pression) even; (Transports: ligne, service) scheduled, regular; (légal, réglementaire) lawful,

in order; (fam: correct) straight, on the level; **régulièrement** adv regularly; evenly
rehausser [Raose] /1/ vt (relever) to heighten, raise; (fig: souligner) to set off, enhance
rein [Rɛ̃] nm kidney; **reins** nmpl (dos) back sg
reine [Rɛn] nf queen
reine-claude [Rɛnklod] nf greengage
réinscriptible [Reɛ̃skRiptibl] adj (CD, DVD) rewritable
réinsertion [Reɛ̃sɛRsjɔ̃] nf (de délinquant) reintegration, rehabilitation
réintégrer [Reɛ̃tegRe] /6/ vt (lieu) to return to; (fonctionnaire) to reinstate
rejaillir [RaʒajiR] /2/ vi to splash up; **~ sur** (fig) (scandale) to rebound on; (gloire) to be reflected on
rejet [Raʒɛ] nm rejection; **rejeter** /4/ vt (relancer) to throw back; (vomir) to bring ou throw up; (écarter) to reject; (déverser) to throw out, discharge; **rejeter la responsabilité de qch sur qn** to lay the responsibility for sth at sb's door
rejoindre [Raʒwɛ̃dR] /49/ vt (famille, régiment) to rejoin, return to; (lieu) to get (back) to; (route etc) to meet, join; (rattraper) to catch up (with); **se rejoindre** vi to meet; **je te rejoins au café** I'll see ou meet you at the café
réjouir [ReʒwiR] /2/ vt to delight; **se ~ de qch/de faire** to be delighted about sth/to do; **réjouissances** nfpl (fête) festivities
relâche [Relɑʃ]: **sans ~** adv without respite ou a break; **relâché, e** adj loose, lax; **relâcher** /1/ vt (ressort, prisonnier) to release; (étreinte, cordes) to loosen; **se relâcher** vi (discipline) to become slack ou lax; (élève etc) to slacken off
relais [Ralɛ] nm (Sport): **(course de) ~** relay (race); **prendre le ~ (de)** to take

over (from); **~ routier** ≈ transport café (BRIT), ≈ truck stop (US)

relancer [Rəlɑ̃se] /3/ vt (balle) to throw back (again); (moteur) to restart; (fig) to boost, revive; (personne): **~ qn** to pester sb

relatif, -ive [Rəlatif, -iv] adj relative

relation [Rəlasjɔ̃] nf (rapport) relation(ship); (connaissance) acquaintance; **relations** nfpl (rapports) relations; (connaissances) connections; **être/entrer en ~(s) avec** to be in contact ou be dealing/ get in contact with

relaxer [Rəlakse] /1/: **se relaxer** vi to relax

relayer [Rəleje] /8/ vt (collaborateur, coureur etc) to relieve; **se relayer** vi (dans une activité) to take it in turns

reléguer [Rəlege] /6/ vt to relegate

relevé, e [Rəlve] adj (manches) rolled-up; (sauce) highly-seasoned ▷ nm (lecture) reading; **~ bancaire** ou **de compte** bank statement

relève [Rəlɛv] nf (personne) relief; **prendre la ~** to take over

relever [Rəlve] /5/ vt (statue, meuble) to stand up again; (personne tombée) to help up; (vitre, plafond, niveau de vie) to raise; (col) to turn up; (style, conversation) to elevate; (plat, sauce) to season; (sentinelle, équipe) to relieve; (fautes, points) to pick out; (défi) to accept, take up; (noter: adresse etc) to take down, note; (: plan) to sketch; (compteur) to read; (ramasser: cahiers, copies) to collect, take in ▷ vi: **~ de** (maladie) to be recovering from; (être du ressort de) to be a matter for; (fig) to pertain to; **se relever** vi (se remettre debout) to get up; **~ qn de** (fonctions) to relieve sb of; **~ la tête** to look up

relief [Rəljɛf] nm relief; **mettre en ~** (fig) to bring out, highlight

relier [Rəlje] /7/ vt to link up; (livre) to bind; **~ qch à** to link sth to

religieux, -euse [Rəliʒjø, -øz] adj religious ▷ nm monk

religion [Rəliʒjɔ̃] nf religion

relire [Rəlir] /43/ vt (à nouveau) to reread, read again; (vérifier) to read over

reluire [Rəlɥir] /38/ vi to gleam

remanier [Rəmanje] /7/ vt to reshape, recast; (Pol) to reshuffle

remarquable [Rəmarkabl] adj remarkable

remarque [Rəmark] nf remark; (écrite) note

remarquer [Rəmarke] /1/ vt (voir) to notice; **se remarquer** vi to be noticeable; **se faire ~** to draw attention to o.s.; **faire ~ (à qn) que** to point out (to sb) that; **faire ~ qch (à qn)** to point sth out (to sb); **remarquez, ...** mind you, ...

rembourrer [Rɑ̃bure] /1/ vt to stuff

remboursement [Rɑ̃bursəmɑ̃] nm (de dette, d'emprunt) repayment; (de frais) refund; **rembourser** /1/ vt to pay back, repay; (frais, billet etc) to refund; **se faire rembourser** to get a refund

remède [Rəmɛd] nm (médicament) medicine; (traitement, fig) remedy, cure

remémorer [Rəmemore] /1/: **se remémorer** vt to recall, recollect

remerciements [Rəmɛrsimɑ̃] nmpl thanks; **(avec) tous mes ~** (with) grateful ou many thanks

remercier [Rəmɛrsje] /7/ vt to thank; (congédier) to dismiss; **~ qn de/d'avoir fait** to thank sb for/for having done

remettre [Rəmɛtr] /56/ vt (vêtement): **~ qch** to put sth back on; (replacer): **~ qch quelque part** to put sth back somewhere; (ajouter): **~ du sel/un sucre** to add more salt/ another lump of sugar; (ajourner): **~ qch (à)** to postpone sth ou put sth off (until); **se remettre** vi to get better; **~ qch à qn** (donner) to hand over sth to sb; (prix, décoration) to present sb with sth; **se ~ de** to recover from;

s'en ~ à to leave it (up) to; **se ~ à faire/qch** to start doing/sth again
remis, e [ʀəmi, -iz] *pp de* **remettre** ▷ *nf* (*rabais*) discount; (*local*) shed; **~e en cause/question** calling into question/challenging; **~e en jeu** (*Football*) throw-in; **~e de peine** remission of sentence; **~e des prix** prize-giving
remontant [ʀəmɔ̃tɑ̃] *nm* tonic, pick-me-up
remonte-pente [ʀəmɔ̃tpɑ̃t] *nm* ski lift
remonter [ʀəmɔ̃te] /1/ *vi* to go back up; (*prix, température*) to go up again; (*en voiture*) to get back in ▷ *vt* (*pente*) to go up; (*fleuve*) to sail (*ou* swim *etc*) up; (*manches, pantalon*) to roll up; (*fam*) to turn up; (*niveau, limite*) to raise; (*fig: personne*) to buck up; (*moteur, meuble*) to put back together, reassemble; (*montre, mécanisme*) to wind up; **~ le moral à qn** to raise sb's spirits; **~ à** (*dater de*) to date *ou* go back to
remords [ʀəmɔʀ] *nm* remorse *no pl*; **avoir des ~** to feel remorse
remorque [ʀəmɔʀk] *nf* trailer; **remorquer** /1/ *vt* to tow; **remorqueur** *nm* tug(boat)
remous [ʀəmu] *nm* (*d'un navire*) (back)wash *no pl*; (*de rivière*) swirl, eddy *pl*; (*fig*) stir *sg*
remparts [ʀɑ̃paʀ] *nmpl* walls, ramparts
remplaçant, e [ʀɑ̃plasɑ̃, -ɑ̃t] *nm/f* replacement, stand-in; (*Scol*) supply (*BRIT*) *ou* substitute (*US*) teacher
remplacement [ʀɑ̃plasmɑ̃] *nm* replacement; **faire des ~s** (*professeur*) to do supply *ou* substitute teaching; (*secrétaire*) to temp
remplacer [ʀɑ̃plase] /3/ *vt* to replace; **~ qch/qn par** to replace sth/sb with
rempli, e [ʀɑ̃pli] *adj* (*emploi du temps*) full, busy; **~ de** full of, filled with

remplir [ʀɑ̃pliʀ] /2/ *vt* to fill (up); (*questionnaire*) to fill out *ou* up; (*obligations, fonction, condition*) to fulfil; **se remplir** *vi* to fill up
remporter [ʀɑ̃pɔʀte] /1/ *vt* (*marchandise*) to take away; (*fig*) to win, achieve
remuant, e [ʀəmɥɑ̃, -ɑ̃t] *adj* restless
remue-ménage [ʀəmymenaʒ] *nm inv* commotion
remuer [ʀəmɥe] /1/ *vt* to move; (*café, sauce*) to stir ▷ *vi* to move; **se remuer** *vi* to move; (*fam: s'activer*) to get a move on
rémunérer [ʀemyneʀe] /6/ *vt* to remunerate
renard [ʀənaʀ] *nm* fox
renchérir [ʀɑ̃ʃeʀiʀ] /2/ *vi* (*fig*): **~ (sur)** (*en paroles*) to add something (to)
rencontre [ʀɑ̃kɔ̃tʀ] *nf* meeting; (*imprévue*) encounter; **aller à la ~ de qn** to go and meet sb; **rencontrer** /1/ *vt* to meet; (*mot, expression*) to come across; (*difficultés*) to meet with; **se rencontrer** *vi* to meet
rendement [ʀɑ̃dmɑ̃] *nm* (*d'un travailleur, d'une machine*) output; (*d'une culture, d'un champ*) yield
rendez-vous [ʀɑ̃devu] *nm* appointment; (*d'amoureux*) date; (*lieu*) meeting place; **donner ~ à qn** to arrange to meet sb; **avoir/ prendre ~ (avec)** to have/make an appointment (with)
rendre [ʀɑ̃dʀ] /41/ *vt* (*livre, argent etc*) to give back, return; (*otages, visite, politesse, invitation*) to return; (*sang, aliments*) to bring up; (*exprimer, traduire*) to render; (*faire devenir*): **~ qn célèbre/qch possible** to make sb famous/sth possible; **se rendre** *vi* (*capituler*) to surrender, give o.s. up; (*aller*): **se ~ quelque part** to go somewhere; **se ~ compte de qch** to realize sth; **~ la monnaie** to give change
rênes [ʀɛn] *nfpl* reins

renfermé, e [ʀɑ̃fɛʀme] *adj* (*fig*) withdrawn ▷ *nm*: **sentir le ~** to smell stuffy

renfermer [ʀɑ̃fɛʀme] /1/ *vt* to contain

renforcer [ʀɑ̃fɔʀse] /3/ *vt* to reinforce; **renfort** *nm*: **renforts** *nmpl* reinforcements; **à grand renfort de** with a great deal of

renfrogné, e [ʀɑ̃fʀɔɲe] *adj* sullen, scowling

renier [ʀənje] /7/ *vt* (*parents*) to disown, repudiate; (*foi*) to renounce

renifler [ʀənifle] /1/ *vi* to sniff ▷ *vt* (*odeur*) to sniff

renne [ʀɛn] *nm* reindeer *inv*

renom [ʀənɔ̃] *nm* reputation; (*célébrité*) renown; **renommé, e** *adj* celebrated, renowned ▷ *nf* fame

renoncer [ʀənɔ̃se] /3/: **~ à** *vt* to give up; **~ à faire** to give up the idea of doing •

renouer [ʀənwe] /1/ *vt*: **~ avec** (*habitude*) to take up again

renouvelable [ʀ(ə)nuvlabl] *adj* (*contrat, bail, énergie*) renewable

renouveler [ʀənuvle] /4/ *vt* to renew; (*exploit, méfait*) to repeat; **se renouveler** *vi* (*incident*) to recur, happen again; **renouvellement** *nm* renewal

rénover [ʀenɔve] /1/ *vt* (*immeuble*) to renovate, do up; (*quartier*) to redevelop

renseignement [ʀɑ̃sɛɲmɑ̃] *nm* information *no pl*, piece of information; **(guichet des) ~s** information desk; **(service des) ~s** (*Tél*) directory inquiries (*BRIT*), information (*US*)

renseigner [ʀɑ̃seɲe] /1/ *vt*: **~ qn (sur)** to give information to sb (about); **se renseigner** *vi* to ask for information, make inquiries

rentabilité [ʀɑ̃tabilite] *nf* profitability

rentable [ʀɑ̃tabl] *adj* profitable

rente [ʀɑ̃t] *nf* income; (*pension*) pension

rentrée [ʀɑ̃tʀe] *nf*: **~ (d'argent)** cash *no pl* coming in; **la ~ (des classes ou scolaire)** the start of the new school year

rentrer [ʀɑ̃tʀe] /1/ *vi* (*entrer de nouveau*) to go (*ou* come) back in; (*entrer*) to go (*ou* come) in; (*revenir chez soi*) to go (*ou* come) (back) home; (*air, clou: pénétrer*) to go in; (*revenu, argent*) to come in ▷ *vt* to bring in; (*véhicule*) to put away; (*chemise dans pantalon etc*) to tuck in; (*griffes*) to draw in; **~ le ventre** to pull in one's stomach; **~ dans** (*heurter*) to crash into; **~ dans l'ordre** to get back to normal; **~ dans ses frais** to recover one's expenses (*ou* initial outlay)

renverse [ʀɑ̃vɛʀs]: **à la ~** *adv* backwards

renverser [ʀɑ̃vɛʀse] /1/ *vt* (*faire tomber: chaise, verre*) to knock over, overturn; (*: piéton*) to knock down; (*: liquide, contenu*) to spill, upset; (*retourner*) to turn upside down; (*: ordre des mots etc*) to reverse; (*fig: gouvernement etc*) to overthrow; (*stupéfier*) to bowl over; **se renverser** *vi* (*verre, vase*) to fall over; (*contenu*) to spill

renvoi [ʀɑ̃vwa] *nm* (*d'employé*) dismissal; (*d'élève*) expulsion; (*référence*) cross-reference; (*éructation*) belch; **renvoyer** /8/ *vt* to send back; (*congédier*) to dismiss; (*élève: définitivement*) to expel; (*lumière*) to reflect; (*ajourner*): **renvoyer qch (à)** to postpone sth (until)

repaire [ʀəpɛʀ] *nm* den

répandre [ʀepɑ̃dʀ] /41/ *vt* (*renverser*) to spill; (*étaler, diffuser*) to spread; (*chaleur, odeur*) to give off; **se répandre** *vi* to spill; to spread; **répandu, e** *adj* (*opinion, usage*) widespread

réparateur, -trice [ʀepaʀatœʀ, -tʀis] *nm/f* repairer

réparation [ʀepaʀasjɔ̃] *nf* repair

réparer [Repare] /1/ vt to repair; (fig: offense) to make up for, atone for; (: oubli, erreur) to put right

repartie [Reparti] nf retort; **avoir de la ~** to be quick at repartee

repartir [Rəpartir] /16/ vi to set off again; (voyageur) to leave again; (fig) to get going again; **~ à zéro** to start from scratch (again)

répartir [Repartir] /2/ vt (pour attribuer) to share out; (pour disperser, disposer) to divide up; (poids, chaleur) to distribute; **se répartir** vt (travail, rôles) to share out between themselves; **répartition** nf (des richesses etc) distribution

repas [Rəpa] nm meal

repassage [Rəpasaʒ] nm ironing

repasser [Rəpase] /1/ vi to come (ou go) back ▷ vt (vêtement, tissu) to iron; (examen) to retake, resit; (film) to show again; (leçon, rôle: revoir) to go over (again)

repentir [Rəpãtir] /16/ nm repentance; **se repentir** vi to repent; **se ~ d'avoir fait qch** (regretter) to regret having done sth

répercussions [Reperkysjõ] nfpl repercussions

répercuter [Reperkyte] /1/: **se répercuter** vi (bruit) to reverberate; (fig): **se ~ sur** to have repercussions on

repère [Rəper] nm mark; (monument etc) landmark

repérer [Rəpere] /6/ vt (erreur, connaissance) to spot; (abri, ennemi) to locate; **se repérer** vi to get one's bearings

répertoire [Repertwar] nm (liste) (alphabetical) list; (carnet) index notebook; (Inform) directory; (d'un théâtre, artiste) repertoire

répéter [Repete] /6/ vt to repeat; (préparer: leçon) to learn, go over; (Théât) to rehearse; **se répéter** (redire) to repeat o.s.; (se reproduire) to be repeated, recur

répétition [Repetisjõ] nf repetition; (Théât) rehearsal; **~ générale** final dress rehearsal

répit [Repi] nm respite; **sans ~** without letting up

replier [Rəplije] /7/ vt (rabattre) to fold down ou over; **se replier** vi (armée) to withdraw, fall back; **se ~ sur soi-même** to withdraw into oneself

réplique [Replik] nf (repartie, fig) reply; (Théât) line; (copie) replica; **répliquer** /1/ vi to reply; (riposter) to retaliate

répondeur [Repõdœr] nm: **~ (automatique)** (Tél) answering machine

répondre [Repõdr] /41/ vi to answer, reply; (freins, mécanisme) to respond; **~ à** to reply to, answer; (affection, salut) to return; (provocation) to respond to; (correspondre à) (besoin) to answer; (conditions) to meet; (description) to match; **~ à qn** (avec impertinence) to answer sb back; **~ de** to answer for

réponse [Repõs] nf answer, reply; **en ~ à** in reply to

reportage [Rəpɔrtaʒ] nm report

reporter¹ [Rəpɔrtɛr] nm reporter

reporter² [Rəpɔrte] vt (ajourner): **~ qch (à)** to postpone sth (until); (transférer): **~ qch sur** to transfer sth to; **se ~ à** (époque) to think back to; (document) to refer to

repos [Rəpo] nm rest; (fig) peace (and quiet); (Mil): **~!** (stand) at ease!; **ce n'est pas de tout ~!** it's no picnic!

reposant, e [R(ə)pozã, -ãt] adj restful

reposer [Rəpoze] /1/ vt (verre, livre) to put down; (délasser) to rest ▷ vi: **laisser ~** (pâte) to leave to stand

repoussant, e [Rəpusã, -ãt] adj repulsive

repousser [Rəpuse] /1/ vi to grow again ▷ vt to repel, repulse; (offre) to turn down, reject; (*tiroir, personne*) to push back; (*différer*) to put back

reprendre [ʀəpʀɑ̃dʀ] /58/ *vt* (*prisonnier, ville*) to recapture; (*firme, entreprise*) to take over; (*emprunter: argument, idée*) to take up, use; (*refaire: article etc*) to go over again; (*jupe etc*) to alter; (*réprimander*) to tell off; (*corriger*) to correct; (*travail, promenade*) to resume; (*chercher*): **je viendrai te ~ à 4 h** I'll come and fetch you *ou* I'll come back for you at 4; (*se resservir de*): **~ du pain/un œuf** to take (*ou* eat) more bread/another egg ▷ *vi* (*classes, pluie*) to start (up) again; (*activités, travaux, combats*) to resume, start (up) again; (*affaires, industrie*) to pick up; (*dire*): **reprit-il** he went on; **~ des forces** to recover one's strength; **~ courage** to take new heart; **~ la route** to resume one's journey, set off again; **~ haleine** *ou* **son souffle** to get one's breath back

représentant, e [ʀəpʀezɑ̃tɑ̃, -ɑ̃t] *nm/f* representative

représentation [ʀəpʀezɑ̃tasjɔ̃] *nf* representation; (*spectacle*) performance

représenter [ʀəpʀezɑ̃te] /1/ *vt* to represent; (*donner: pièce, opéra*) to perform; **se représenter** *vt* (*se figurer*) to imagine

répression [ʀepʀesjɔ̃] *nf* repression

réprimer [ʀepʀime] /1/ *vt* (*émotions*) to suppress; (*peuple etc*) repress

repris, e [ʀəpʀi, -iz] *pp de* **reprendre** ▷ *nm*: **~ de justice** ex-prisoner, ex-convict

reprise [ʀəpʀiz] *nf* (*recommencement*) resumption; (*économique*) recovery; (*TV*) repeat; (*Comm*) trade-in, part exchange; (*raccommodage*) mend; **à plusieurs ~s** on several occasions

repriser [ʀəpʀize] /1/ *vt* (*chaussette, lainage*) to darn; (*tissu*) to mend

reproche [ʀəpʀɔʃ] *nm* (*remontrance*) reproach; **faire des ~s à qn** to

reproach sb; **sans ~(s)** beyond *ou* above reproach; **reprocher** /1/ *vt*: **reprocher qch à qn** to reproach *ou* blame sb for sth; **reprocher qch à** (*machine, théorie*) to have sth against

reproduction [ʀəpʀɔdyksjɔ̃] *nf* reproduction

reproduire [ʀəpʀɔdɥiʀ] /38/ *vt* to reproduce; **se reproduire** *vi* (*Bio*) to reproduce; (*recommencer*) to recur, re-occur

reptile [ʀɛptil] *nm* reptile

république [ʀepyblik] *nf* republic

répugnant, e [ʀepyɲɑ̃, -ɑ̃t] *adj* repulsive

répugner [ʀepyɲe] /1/: **~ à** *vt*: **~ à qn** to repel *ou* disgust sb; **~ à faire** to be loath *ou* reluctant to do

réputation [ʀepytasjɔ̃] *nf* reputation; **réputé, e** *adj* renowned

requérir [ʀəkeʀiʀ] /21/ *vt* (*nécessiter*) to require, call for

requête [ʀəkɛt] *nf* request

requin [ʀəkɛ̃] *nm* shark

requis, e [ʀəki, -iz] *adj* required

RER *sigle m* (= *Réseau express régional*) Greater Paris high-speed train service

rescapé, e [ʀɛskape] *nm/f* survivor

rescousse [ʀɛskus] *nf*: **aller à la ~ de qn** to go to sb's aid *ou* rescue

réseau, x [ʀezo] *nm* network; **~ social** social network

réseautage [ʀezotaʒ] *nm* social networking

réservation [ʀezɛʀvasjɔ̃] *nf* reservation; booking

réserve [ʀezɛʀv] *nf* (*retenue*) reserve; (*entrepôt*) storeroom; (*restriction, aussi: d'Indiens*) reservation; (*de pêche, chasse*) preserve; **de ~** (*provisions etc*) in reserve

réservé, e [ʀezɛʀve] *adj* reserved; (*chasse, pêche*) private

réserver [ʀezɛʀve] /1/ *vt* to reserve; (*chambre, billet etc*) to book, reserve; (*mettre de côté, garder*): **~ qch pour** *ou* **à** to keep *ou* save sth for

réservoir [ʀezɛʀvwaʀ] *nm* tank

résidence [ʀezidɑ̃s] nf residence; **~ principale/secondaire** main/second home; **~ universitaire** hall of residence (BRIT), dormitory (US); **résidentiel, le** adj residential; **résider** /1/ vi: **résider à** ou **dans** ou **en** to reside in; **résider dans** (fig) to lie in

résidu [ʀezidy] nm residue no pl

résigner [ʀeziɲe] /1/: **se résigner** vi: **se ~ (à qch/à faire)** to resign o.s. (to sth/to doing)

résilier [ʀezilje] /7/ vt to terminate

résistance [ʀezistɑ̃s] nf resistance; (de réchaud, bouilloire: fil) element

résistant, e [ʀezistɑ̃, -ɑ̃t] adj (personne) robust, tough; (matériau) strong, hard-wearing

résister [ʀeziste] /1/ vi to resist; **~ à** (assaut, tentation) to resist; (matériau, plante) to withstand; (désobéir à) to stand up to, oppose

résolu, e [ʀezɔly] pp de **résoudre** ▷ adj: **être ~ à qch/faire** to be set upon sth/doing

résolution [ʀezɔlysjɔ̃] nf (fermeté, décision) resolution; (d'un problème) solution

résolvais etc [ʀezɔlve] vb voir **résoudre**

résonner [ʀezɔne] /1/ vi (cloche, pas) to reverberate, resound; (salle) to be resonant

résorber [ʀezɔʀbe] /1/: **se résorber** vi (Méd) to be resorbed; (fig) to be absorbed

résoudre [ʀezudʀ] /51/ vt to solve; **se ~ à faire** to bring o.s. to do

respect [ʀɛspɛ] nm respect; **tenir en ~** to keep at bay; **présenter ses ~s à qn** to pay one's respects to sb; **respecter** /1/ vt to respect; **respectueux, -euse** adj respectful

respiration [ʀɛspiʀasjɔ̃] nf breathing no pl

respirer [ʀɛspiʀe] /1/ vi to breathe; (fig: se reposer) to get one's breath; (: être soulagé) to breathe again ▷ vt to breathe (in), inhale; (manifester: santé, calme etc) to exude

resplendir [ʀɛsplɑ̃diʀ] /2/ vi to shine; (fig): **~ (de)** to be radiant (with)

responsabilité [ʀɛspɔ̃sabilite] nf responsibility; (légale) liability

responsable [ʀɛspɔ̃sabl] adj responsible ▷ nm/f (personne coupable) person responsible; (du ravitaillement etc) person in charge; (de parti, syndicat) official; **~ de** responsible for

ressaisir [ʀəseziʀ] /2/: **se ressaisir** vi to regain one's self-control

ressasser [ʀəsase] /1/ vt to keep turning over

ressemblance [ʀəsɑ̃blɑ̃s] nf resemblance, similarity, likeness

ressemblant, e [ʀəsɑ̃blɑ̃, -ɑ̃t] adj (portrait) lifelike, true to life

ressembler [ʀəsɑ̃ble] /1/: **~ à** vt to be like, resemble; (visuellement) to look like; **se ressembler** vi to be (ou look) alike

ressentiment [ʀəsɑ̃timɑ̃] nm resentment

ressentir [ʀəsɑ̃tiʀ] /16/ vt to feel; **se ~ de** to feel (ou show) the effects of

resserrer [ʀəseʀe] /1/ vt (nœud, boulon) to tighten (up); (fig: liens) to strengthen

resservir [ʀəseʀviʀ] /14/ vi to do ou serve again; **~ qn (d'un plat)** to give sb a second helping (of a dish); **se ~ de** (plat) to take a second helping of; (outil etc) to use again

ressort [ʀəsɔʀ] nm (pièce) spring; (force morale) spirit; **en dernier ~** as a last resort; **être du ~ de** to fall within the competence of

ressortir [ʀəsɔʀtiʀ] /16/ vi to go (ou come) out (again); (contraster) to stand out; **~ de: il ressort de ceci que** it emerges from this that; **faire ~** (fig: souligner) to bring out

ressortissant, e [ʀəsɔʀtisɑ̃, -ɑ̃t] nm/f national

ressources [ʀəsuʀs] nfpl resources

ressusciter [ʀesysite] /1/ vt (fig) to revive, bring back ▷ vi to rise (from the dead)

restant, e [ʀɛstɑ̃, -ɑ̃t] adj remaining ▷ nm: **le ~ (de)** the remainder (of); **un ~ de** (de trop) some leftover

restaurant [ʀɛstɔʀɑ̃] nm restaurant

restauration [ʀɛstɔʀasjɔ̃] nf restoration; (hôtellerie) catering; **~ rapide** fast food

restaurer [ʀɛstɔʀe] /1/ vt to restore; **se restaurer** vi to have something to eat

reste [ʀɛst] nm (restant): **le ~ (de)** the rest (of); (de trop) some leftover; **restes** nmpl leftovers; (d'une cité etc, dépouille mortelle) remains; **du ~, au ~** besides, moreover

rester [ʀɛste] /1/ vi to stay, remain; (subsister) to remain, be left; (durer) to last, live on ▷ vb impers: **il reste du pain/deux œufs** there's some bread/there are two eggs left (over); **il me reste assez de temps** I have enough time left; **il ne me reste plus qu'à ...** I've just got to ...; **restons-en là** let's leave it at that

restituer [ʀɛstitɥe] /1/ vt (objet, somme): **~ qch (à qn)** to return ou restore sth (to sb)

restreindre [ʀɛstʀɛ̃dʀ] /52/ vt to restrict, limit

restriction [ʀɛstʀiksjɔ̃] nf restriction

résultat [ʀezylta] nm result; (d'élection etc) results pl; **résultats** nmpl (d'une enquête) findings

résulter [ʀezylte] /1/: **~ de** vt to result from, be the result of

résumé [ʀezyme] nm summary, résumé; **en ~** in brief; (pour conclure) to sum up

résumer [ʀezyme] /1/ vt (texte) to summarize; (récapituler) to sum up
▮ Attention à ne pas traduire *résumer* par *to resume*.

résurrection [ʀezyʀɛksjɔ̃] nf resurrection

rétablir [ʀetabliʀ] /2/ vt to restore, re-establish; **se rétablir** vi (guérir) to recover; (silence, calme) to return, be restored; **rétablissement** nm restoring; (guérison) recovery

retaper [ʀətape] /1/ vt (maison, voiture etc) to do up; (fam: revigorer) to buck up

retard [ʀətaʀ] nm (d'une personne attendue) lateness no pl; (sur l'horaire, un programme, une échéance) delay; (fig: scolaire, mental etc) backwardness; **en ~ (de deux heures)** (two hours) late; **désolé d'être en ~** sorry I'm late; **avoir du ~** to be late; (sur un programme) to be behind (schedule); **prendre du ~** (train, avion) to be delayed; **sans ~** without delay

retardataire [ʀətaʀdatɛʀ] nm/f latecomer

retardement [ʀətaʀdəmɑ̃]: **à ~** adj delayed action cpd; **bombe à ~** time bomb

retarder [ʀətaʀde] /1/ vt to delay; (horloge) to put back; **~ qn (d'une heure)** to delay sb (an hour); (départ, date): **~ qch (de deux jours)** to put sth back (two days) ▷ vi (montre) to be slow

retenir [ʀətniʀ] /22/ vt (garder, retarder) to keep, detain; (maintenir: objet qui glisse, colère, larmes, rire) to hold back; (se rappeler) to retain; (accepter) to accept; (fig: empêcher d'agir): **~ qn (de faire)** to hold sb back (from doing); (prélever): **~ qch (sur)** to deduct sth (from); **se retenir** vi (se raccrocher): **se ~ à** to hold onto; (se contenir): **se ~ de faire** to restrain o.s. from doing; **~ son souffle** ou **haleine** to hold one's breath

retentir [ʀətɑ̃tiʀ] /2/ vi to ring out; **retentissant, e** adj resounding

retenu, e [ʀətny] adj (place) reserved ▷ nf (prélèvement) deduction; (Scol) detention; (modération) (self-) restraint

réticence [ʀetisɑ̃s] *nf* reticence *no pl*, reluctance *no pl*; **réticent, e** *adj* reticent, reluctant

rétine [ʀetin] *nf* retina

retiré, e [ʀətiʀe] *adj* (*solitaire*) secluded; (*éloigné*) remote

retirer [ʀətiʀe] /1/ *vt* (*argent, plainte*) to withdraw; (*vêtement, lunettes*) to take off, remove; (*reprendre: bagages, billets*) to collect, pick up; (*extraire*): **~ qn/qch de** to take sb away from/sth out of, remove sb/sth from

retomber [ʀətɔ̃be] /1/ *vi* (*à nouveau*) to fall again; (*atterrir: après un saut etc*) to land; (*échoir*): **~ sur qn** to fall on sb

rétorquer [ʀetɔʀke] /1/ *vt*: **~ (à qn) que** to retort (to sb) that

retouche [ʀətuʃ] *nf* (*sur vêtement*) alteration; **retoucher** /1/ *vt* (*photographie, tableau*) to touch up; (*texte, vêtement*) to alter

retour [ʀətuʀ] *nm* return; **au ~** (*en route*) on the way back; **à mon/ton ~** on my/your return; **être de ~ (de)** to be back (from); **quand serons-nous de ~?** when do we get back?; **par ~ du courrier** by return of post

retourner [ʀətuʀne] /1/ *vt* (*dans l'autre sens: matelas, crêpe*) to turn (over); (*: sac, vêtement*) to turn inside out; (*émouvoir*) to shake; (*renvoyer, restituer*): **~ qch à qn** to return sth to sb ▷ *vi* (*aller, revenir*): **~ quelque part/à** to go back *ou* return somewhere/to; **~ à** (*état, activité*) to return to, go back to; **se retourner** *vi* (*tourner la tête*) to turn round; **se ~ contre** (*fig*) to turn against

retrait [ʀətʀɛ] *nm* (*d'argent*) withdrawal; **en ~** set back; **~ du permis (de conduire)** disqualification from driving (BRIT), revocation of driver's license (US)

retraite [ʀətʀɛt] *nf* (*d'une armée, Rel.*) retreat; (*d'un employé*) retirement; (*revenu*) (retirement) pension; **prendre sa ~** to retire; **~ anticipée** early retirement; **retraité, e** *adj* retired ▷ *nm/f* (old age) pensioner

retrancher [ʀətʀɑ̃ʃe] /1/ *vt*: **~ qch de** (*nombre, somme*) to take *ou* deduct sth from; **se ~ derrière/dans** to take refuge behind/in

rétrécir [ʀetʀesiʀ] /2/ *vt* (*vêtement*) to take in ▷ *vi* to shrink; **se rétrécir** (*route, vallée*) to narrow

rétro [ʀetʀo] *adj inv*: **la mode ~** the nostalgia vogue

rétroprojecteur [ʀetʀopʀɔʒɛktœʀ] *nm* overhead projector

rétrospectif, -ive [ʀetʀɔspɛktif, -iv] *adj* retrospective ▷ *nf* (*Art*) retrospective; (*Ciné*) season, retrospective; **rétrospectivement** *adv* in retrospect

retrousser [ʀətʀuse] /1/ *vt* to roll up

retrouvailles [ʀətʀuvaj] *nfpl* reunion *sg*

retrouver [ʀətʀuve] /1/ *vt* (*fugitif, objet perdu*) to find; (*calme, santé*) to regain; (*revoir*) to see again; (*rejoindre*) to meet (again), join; **se retrouver** *vi* to meet; (*s'orienter*) to find one's way; **se ~ quelque part** to find o.s. somewhere; **s'y ~** (*y voir clair*) to make sense of it; (*rentrer dans ses frais*) to break even

rétroviseur [ʀetʀɔvizœʀ] *nm* (rear-view) mirror

réunion [ʀeynjɔ̃] *nf* (*séance*) meeting

réunir [ʀeyniʀ] /2/ *vt* (*rassembler*) to gather together; (*inviter: amis, famille*) to have round, have in; (*cumuler: qualités etc*) to combine; (*rapprocher: ennemis*) to bring together (again), reunite; (*rattacher: parties*) to join (together); **se réunir** *vi* (*se rencontrer*) to meet

réussi, e [ʀeysi] *adj* successful

réussir [ʀeysiʀ] /2/ *vi* to succeed, be successful; (*à un examen*) to pass ▷ *vt* to make a success of; **~ à faire** to succeed in doing; **~ à qn** (*être bénéfique à*) to agree with sb; **réussite** *nf* success; (*Cartes*) patience

revaloir [ʀəvalwaʀ] /29/ vt: **je vous revaudrai cela** I'll repay you some day; (en mal) I'll pay you back for this

revanche [ʀəvɑ̃ʃ] nf revenge; (sport) revenge match; **en ~** on the other hand

rêve [ʀɛv] nm dream; **de ~** dream cpd; **faire un ~** to have a dream

réveil [ʀevɛj] nm waking up no pl; (fig) awakening; (pendule) alarm (clock); **au ~** on waking up; **réveiller** /1/ vt (personne) to wake up; (fig) to awaken, revive; **se réveiller** vi to wake up

réveillon [ʀevɛjɔ̃] nm Christmas Eve; (de la Saint-Sylvestre) New Year's Eve; **réveillonner** /1/ vi to celebrate Christmas Eve (ou New Year's Eve)

révélateur, -trice [ʀevelatœʀ, -tʀis] adj: **~ (de qch)** revealing (sth)

révéler [ʀevele] /6/ vt to reveal; **se révéler** vi to be revealed, reveal itself; **se ~ facile/faux** to prove (to be) easy/false

revenant, e [ʀəvnɑ̃, -ɑ̃t] nm/f ghost

revendeur, -euse [ʀəvɑ̃dœʀ, -øz] nm/f (détaillant) retailer; (de drogue) (drug-)dealer

revendication [ʀəvɑ̃dikasjɔ̃] nf claim, demand

revendiquer [ʀəvɑ̃dike] /1/ vt to claim, demand; (responsabilité) to claim

revendre [ʀəvɑ̃dʀ] /41/ vt (d'occasion) to resell; (détailler) to sell; **à ~** (en abondance) to spare

revenir [ʀəvniʀ] /22/ vi to come back; **faire ~** (Culin) to brown; **~ cher/à 100 euros (à qn)** to cost (sb) a lot/100 euros; **~ à** (reprendre: études, projet) to return to, go back to; (équivaloir à) to amount to; **~ à qn** (part, honneur) to go to sb, be sb's; (souvenir, nom) to come back to sb; **~ sur** (question, sujet) to go back over; (engagement) to go back on; **~ à soi** to come round; **je n'en**

reviens pas I can't get over it; **~ sur ses pas** to retrace one's steps; **cela revient à dire que/au même** it amounts to saying that/to the same thing

revenu [ʀəvny] nm income; **revenus** nmpl income sg

rêver [ʀɛve] /1/ vi, vt to dream; **~ de qch/de faire** to dream of sth/of doing; **~ à** to dream of

réverbère [ʀevɛʀbɛʀ] nm street lamp ou light; **réverbérer** /6/ vt to reflect

revers [ʀəvɛʀ] nm (de feuille, main) back; (d'étoffe) wrong side; (de pièce, médaille) back, reverse; (Tennis, Ping-Pong) backhand; (de veston) lapel; (fig: échec) setback

revêtement [ʀəvɛtmɑ̃] nm (des sols) flooring; (de chaussée) surface

revêtir [ʀəvetiʀ] /20/ vt (habit) to don, put on; (prendre: importance, apparence) to take on; **~ qch de** to cover sth with

rêveur, -euse [ʀɛvœʀ, -øz] adj dreamy ▷ nm/f dreamer

revient [ʀəvjɛ̃] vb voir **revenir**

revigorer [ʀəvigɔʀe] /1/ vt (air frais) to invigorate, brace up; (repas, boisson) to revive, buck up

revirement [ʀəviʀmɑ̃] nm change of mind; (d'une situation) reversal

réviser [ʀevize] /1/ vt to revise; (machine, installation, moteur) to overhaul, service

révision [ʀevizjɔ̃] nf revision; (de voiture) servicing no pl

revivre [ʀəvivʀ] /46/ vi (reprendre des forces) to come alive again ▷ vt (épreuve, moment) to relive

revoir [ʀəvwaʀ] /30/ vt to see again ▷ nm: **au ~** goodbye

révoltant, e [ʀevɔltɑ̃, -ɑ̃t] adj revolting, appalling

révolte [ʀevɔlt] nf rebellion, revolt

révolter [ʀevɔlte] /1/ vt to revolt; **se révolter** vi: **se ~ (contre)** to rebel (against)

révolu, e [ʀevɔly] *adj* past; (*Admin*): **âgé de 18 ans ~s** over 18 years of age

révolution [ʀevɔlysjɔ̃] *nf* revolution; **révolutionnaire** *adj, nm/f* revolutionary

revolver [ʀevɔlvɛʀ] *nm* gun; (*à barillet*) revolver

révoquer [ʀevɔke] /1/ *vt* (*fonctionnaire*) to dismiss; (*arrêt, contrat*) to revoke

revu, e [ʀəvy] *pp de* **revoir** ▷ *nf* review; (*périodique*) review, magazine; (*de music-hall*) variety show; **passer en ~** (*mentalement*) to go through

rez-de-chaussée [ʀedʃose] *nm inv* ground floor

RF *sigle f* = **République française**

Rhin [ʀɛ̃] *nm*: **le ~** the Rhine

rhinocéros [ʀinɔseʀɔs] *nm* rhinoceros

Rhône [ʀon] *nm*: **le ~** the Rhone

rhubarbe [ʀybaʀb] *nf* rhubarb

rhum [ʀɔm] *nm* rum

rhumatisme [ʀymatism] *nm* rheumatism *no pl*

rhume [ʀym] *nm* cold; **~ de cerveau** head cold; **le ~ des foins** hay fever

ricaner [ʀikane] /1/ *vi* (*avec méchanceté*) to snigger; (*bêtement, avec gêne*) to giggle

riche [ʀiʃ] *adj* rich; (*personne, pays*) rich, wealthy; **~ en** rich in; **richesse** *nf* wealth; (*fig: de sol, musée etc*) richness; **richesses** *nfpl* (*ressources, argent*) wealth *sg*; (*fig: trésors*) treasures

ricochet [ʀikɔʃɛ] *nm*: **faire des ~s** to skip stones

ride [ʀid] *nf* wrinkle

rideau, x [ʀido] *nm* curtain; **~ de fer** (*lit*) metal shutter

rider [ʀide] /1/ *vt* to wrinkle; **se rider** *vi* to become wrinkled

ridicule [ʀidikyl] *adj* ridiculous ▷ *nm*: **le ~** ridicule; **ridiculiser** /1/ *vt* to ridicule; **se ridiculiser** *vi* to make a fool of o.s.

rien [ʀjɛ̃] *pron* **1**: **(ne) ... rien** nothing; (*tournure négative*) anything; **qu'est-ce que vous avez? — rien** what have you got? — nothing; **il n'a rien dit/fait** he said/did nothing, he hasn't said/done anything; **n'avoir peur de rien** to be afraid *ou* frightened of nothing, not to be afraid *ou* frightened of anything; **il n'a rien** (*n'est pas blessé*) he's all right; **ça ne fait rien** it doesn't matter
2 (*quelque chose*): **a-t-il jamais rien fait pour nous?** has he ever done anything for us?
3: **rien de**: **rien d'intéressant** nothing interesting; **rien d'autre** nothing else; **rien du tout** nothing at all
4: **rien que** just, only; nothing but; **rien que pour lui faire plaisir** only *ou* just to please him; **rien que la vérité** nothing but the truth; **rien que cela** that alone
▶ *excl*: **de rien!** not at all!
▶ *nm*: **un petit rien** (*cadeau*) a little something; **des riens** trivia *pl*; **un rien de** a hint of; **en un rien de temps** in no time at all

rieur, -euse [ʀjœʀ, -øz] *adj* cheerful

rigide [ʀiʒid] *adj* stiff; (*fig*) rigid; (*moralement*) strict

rigoler [ʀigɔle] /1/ *vi* (*rire*) to laugh; (*s'amuser*) to have (some) fun; (*plaisanter*) to be joking *ou* kidding; **rigolo, rigolote** *adj* funny ▷ *nm/f* comic; (*péj*) fraud, phoney

rigoureusement [ʀiguʀøzmɑ̃] *adv* rigorously

rigoureux, -euse [ʀiguʀø, -øz] *adj* rigorous; (*climat, châtiment*) harsh, severe

rigueur [ʀigœʀ] *nf* rigour; **"tenue de soirée de ~"** "evening dress (to be worn)"; **à la ~** at a pinch; **tenir ~ à qn de qch** to hold sth against sb

rillettes [ʀijɛt] *nfpl* ≈ potted meat *sg*
(*made from pork or goose*)

rime [ʀim] *nf* rhyme

rinçage [ʀɛ̃saʒ] *nm* rinsing (out);
(*opération*) rinse

rincer [ʀɛ̃se] /3/ *vt* to rinse; (*récipient*)
to rinse out

ringard, e [ʀɛ̃gaʀ, -aʀd] *adj* old-
fashioned

riposter [ʀiposte] /1/ *vi* to retaliate
▷ *vt*: **~ que** to retort that

rire [ʀiʀ] /36/ *vi* to laugh; (*se divertir*)
to have fun ▷ *nm* laugh; **le ~** laughter;
~ de to laugh at; **pour ~** (*pas
sérieusement*) for a joke *ou* a laugh

risible [ʀizibl] *adj* laughable

risque [ʀisk] *nm* risk; **le ~** danger;
à ses ~s et périls at his own risk;
risqué, e *adj* risky; (*plaisanterie*)
risqué, daring; **risquer** /1/ *vt* to risk;
(*allusion, question*) to venture, hazard;
se risquer *vi*: **ça ne risque rien** it's
quite safe; **il risque de se tuer** he
could get *ou* risks getting himself
killed; **ce qui risque de se produire**
what might *ou* could well happen;
il ne risque pas de recommencer
there's no chance of him doing that
again; **se risquer à faire** (*tenter*) to
dare to do

rissoler [ʀisɔle] /1/ *vi, vt*: **(faire) ~**
to brown

ristourne [ʀistuʀn] *nf* discount

rite [ʀit] *nm* rite; (*fig*) ritual

rivage [ʀivaʒ] *nm* shore

rival, e, -aux [ʀival, -o] *adj, nm/f*
rival; **rivaliser** /1/ *vi*: **rivaliser avec**
to rival, vie with; **rivalité** *nf* rivalry

rive [ʀiv] *nf* shore; (*de fleuve*) bank;
riverain, e *nm/f* riverside (*ou*
lakeside) resident; (*d'une route*) local
ou roadside resident

rivière [ʀivjɛʀ] *nf* river

riz [ʀi] *nm* rice; **rizière** *nf* paddy field

RMI *sigle m* (= *revenu minimum
d'insertion*) ≈ income support (BRIT),
≈ welfare (US)

RN *sigle f* = **route nationale**

robe [ʀɔb] *nf* dress; (*de juge,
d'ecclésiastique*) robe; (*pelage*) coat;
~ de soirée/de mariée evening/
wedding dress; **~ de chambre**
dressing gown

robinet [ʀɔbinɛ] *nm* tap (BRIT),
faucet (US)

robot [ʀɔbo] *nm* robot; **~ de cuisine**
food processor

robuste [ʀɔbyst] *adj* robust, sturdy;
robustesse *nf* robustness, sturdiness

roc [ʀɔk] *nm* rock

rocade [ʀɔkad] *nf* bypass

rocaille [ʀɔkaj] *nf* loose stones *pl*;
(*jardin*) rockery, rock garden

roche [ʀɔʃ] *nf* rock

rocher [ʀɔʃe] *nm* rock

rocheux, -euse [ʀɔʃø, -øz] *adj* rocky

rodage [ʀɔdaʒ] *nm*: **en ~** running *ou*
breaking in

rôder [ʀode] /1/ *vi* to roam *ou* wander
about; (*de façon suspecte*) to lurk
(about *ou* around); **rôdeur, -euse**
nm/f prowler

rogne [ʀɔɲ] *nf*: **être en ~** to be mad
ou in a temper

rogner [ʀɔɲe] /1/ *vt* to trim; **~ sur**
(*fig*) to cut down *ou* back on

rognons [ʀɔɲɔ̃] *nmpl* kidneys

roi [ʀwa] *nm* king; **le jour** *ou* **la fête
des R~s** Twelfth Night

rôle [ʀol] *nm* role; part

rollers [ʀɔlœʀ] *nmpl* Rollerblades®

romain, e [ʀɔmɛ̃, -ɛn] *adj* Roman
▷ *nm/f*: **R~, e** Roman

roman, e [ʀɔmɑ̃, -an] *adj* (*Archit*)
Romanesque ▷ *nm* novel; **~ policier**
detective novel

romancer [ʀɔmɑ̃se] /3/ *vt* to
romanticize; **romancier, -ière** *nm/f*
novelist; **romanesque** *adj* (*amours,
aventures*) storybook *cpd*; (*sentimental:
personne*) romantic

roman-feuilleton [ʀɔmɑ̃fœjtɔ̃] *nm*
serialized novel

romanichel, le [ʀɔmaniʃɛl] *nm/f*
gipsy

romantique [ʀɔmɑ̃tik] *adj* romantic

romarin [ʀɔmaʀɛ̃] *nm* rosemary
Rome [ʀɔm] *n* Rome
rompre [ʀɔ̃pʀ] /41/ *vt* to break;
(*entretien, fiançailles*) to break off ⊳ *vi*
(*fiancés*) to break it off; **se rompre**
vi to break; **rompu, e** *adj* (*fourbu*)
exhausted
ronce [ʀɔ̃s] *nf* bramble branch;
ronces *nfpl* brambles
ronchonner [ʀɔ̃ʃɔne] /1/ *vi* (*fam*) to
grouse, grouch
rond, e [ʀɔ̃, ʀɔ̃d] *adj* round;
(*joues, mollets*) well-rounded; (*fam:
ivre*) tight ⊳ *nm* (*cercle*) ring; (*fam:
sou*): **je n'ai plus un ~** I haven't a
penny left ⊳ *nf* (*gén: de surveillance*)
rounds *pl*, patrol; (*danse*) round
(dance); (*Mus*) semibreve (*BRIT*),
whole note (*US*); **en ~** (*s'asseoir,
danser*) in a ring; **à la ~e** (*alentour*):
à 10 km à la ~e for 10 km round;
rondelet, te *adj* plump
rondelle [ʀɔ̃dɛl] *nf* (*Tech*) washer;
(*tranche*) slice, round
rond-point [ʀɔ̃pwɛ̃] *nm*
roundabout
ronflement [ʀɔ̃fləmɑ̃] *nm* snore
ronfler [ʀɔ̃fle] /1/ *vi* to snore; (*moteur,
poêle*) to hum
ronger [ʀɔ̃ʒe] /3/ *vt* to gnaw (at);
(*vers, rouille*) to eat into; **se ~ les
sangs** to worry o.s. sick; **se ~ les
ongles** to bite one's nails; **rongeur,
-euse** [ʀɔ̃ʒœʀ, -øz] *nm/f* rodent
ronronner [ʀɔ̃ʀɔne] /1/ *vi* to purr
rosbif [ʀɔsbif] *nm*: **du ~** roasting
beef; (*cuit*) roast beef
rose [ʀoz] *nf* rose ⊳ *adj* pink;
~ bonbon *adj inv* candy pink
rosé, e [ʀoze] *adj* pinkish; (**vin**) **~**
rosé (wine)
roseau, x [ʀozo] *nm* reed
rosée [ʀoze] *nf* dew
rosier [ʀozje] *nm* rosebush, rose tree
rossignol [ʀɔsiɲɔl] *nm* (*Zool*)
nightingale
rotation [ʀɔtasjɔ̃] *nf* rotation
roter [ʀɔte] /1/ *vi* (*fam*) to burp, belch

rôti [ʀoti] *nm*: **du ~** roasting meat;
(*cuit*) roast meat; **un ~ de bœuf/porc**
a joint of beef/pork
rotin [ʀɔtɛ̃] *nm* rattan (cane);
fauteuil en ~ cane (arm)chair
rôtir [ʀotiʀ] /2/ *vt* (*aussi*: **faire ~**)
to roast ⊳ *vi* to roast; **rôtisserie** *nf*
(*restaurant*) steakhouse; (*traiteur*)
roast meat shop; **rôtissoire** *nf*
(roasting) spit
rotule [ʀɔtyl] *nf* kneecap
rouage [ʀwaʒ] *nm* cog(wheel),
gearwheel; **les ~s de l'État** the
wheels of State
roue [ʀu] *nf* wheel; **~ de secours**
spare wheel
rouer [ʀwe] /1/ *vt*: **~ qn de coups** to
give sb a thrashing
rouge [ʀuʒ] *adj, nm/f* red ⊳ *nm*
red; (**vin**) **~** red wine; **passer au ~**
(*signal*) to go red; (*automobiliste*) to
go through a red light; **sur la liste
~** ex-directory (*BRIT*), unlisted (*US*);
~ à joue blusher; **~ (à lèvres)** lipstick;
rouge-gorge *nm* robin (redbreast)
rougeole [ʀuʒɔl] *nf* measles *sg*
rougeoyer [ʀuʒwaje] /8/ *vi* to
glow red
rouget [ʀuʒɛ] *nm* mullet
rougeur [ʀuʒœʀ] *nf* redness;
rougeurs *nfpl* (*Méd*) red blotches
rougir [ʀuʒiʀ] /2/ *vi* to turn red; (*de
honte, timidité*) to blush, flush; (*de
plaisir, colère*) to blush
rouille [ʀuj] *nf* rust; **rouillé, e** *adj*
rusty; **rouiller** /1/ *vt* to rust ⊳ *vi* to
rust, go rusty
roulant, e [ʀulɑ̃, -ɑ̃t] *adj* (*meuble*)
on wheels; (*surface, trottoir, tapis*)
moving; **escalier ~** escalator
rouleau, x [ʀulo] *nm* roll; (*à mise
en plis, à peinture, vague*) roller; **~ à
pâtisserie** rolling pin
roulement [ʀulmɑ̃] *nm* (*bruit*)
rumbling *no pl*, rumble; (*rotation*)
rotation; **par ~** on a rota (*BRIT*) *ou*
rotation (*US*) basis; **~ (à billes)** ball
bearings *pl*; **~ de tambour** drum roll

r

rouler [Rule] /1/ vt to roll; (papier, tapis) to roll up; (Culin: pâte) to roll out; (fam: duper) to do, con ▷ vi (bille, boule) to roll; (voiture, train) to go, run; (automobiliste) to drive; (cycliste) to ride; (bateau) to roll; **se ~ dans** (boue) to roll in; (couverture) to roll o.s. (up) in

roulette [Rulɛt] nf (de table, fauteuil) castor; (de dentiste) drill; (jeu): **la ~** roulette; **à ~s** on castors; **ça a marché comme sur des ~s** (fam) it went off very smoothly

roulis [Ruli] nm roll(ing)

roulotte [Rulɔt] nf caravan

roumain, e [Rumɛ̃, -ɛn] adj Rumanian ▷ nm/f: **R~, e** Rumanian

Roumanie [Rumani] nf: **la ~** Rumania

rouquin, e [Rukɛ̃, -in] nm/f (péj) redhead

rouspéter [Ruspete] /6/ vi (fam) to moan

rousse [Rus] adj f voir **roux**

roussir [RusiR] /2/ vt to scorch ▷ vi (Culin): **faire ~** to brown

route [Rut] nf road; (fig: chemin) way; (itinéraire, parcours) route; (fig: voie) road, path; **il y a trois heures de ~** it's a three-hour ride ou journey; **en ~** on the way; **en ~!** let's go!; **mettre en ~** to start up; **se mettre en ~** to set off; **~ nationale** ≈ A-road (BRIT), ≈ state highway (US); **routier, -ière** adj road cpd ▷ nm (camionneur) (long-distance) lorry (BRIT) ou truck (US) driver; (restaurant) ≈ transport café (BRIT), ≈ truck stop (US)

routine [Rutin] nf routine; **routinier, -ière** [Rutinje, -jɛR] adj (péj: travail) humdrum; (: personne) addicted to routine

rouvrir [RuvRiR] /18/ vt, vi to reopen, open again; **se rouvrir** vi to open up again

roux, rousse [Ru, Rus] adj red; (personne) red-haired ▷ nm/f redhead

royal, e, -aux [Rwajal, -o] adj royal; (fig) fit for a king

royaume [Rwajom] nm kingdom; (fig) realm

Royaume-Uni [Rwajomyni] nm: **le ~** the United Kingdom

royauté [Rwajote] nf (régime) monarchy

ruban [Rybã] nm ribbon; **~ adhésif** adhesive tape

rubéole [Rybeɔl] nf German measles sg, rubella

rubis [Rybi] nm ruby

rubrique [RybRik] nf (titre, catégorie) heading; (Presse: article) column

ruche [Ryʃ] nf hive

rude [Ryd] adj (barbe, toile) rough; (métier, tâche) hard, tough; (climat) severe, harsh; (bourru) harsh, rough; (fruste: manières) rugged, tough; (fam: fameux) jolly good; **rudement** adv (très) terribly

rudimentaire [RydimãtɛR] adj rudimentary, basic

rudiments [Rydimã] nmpl: **avoir des ~ d'anglais** to have a smattering of English

rue [Ry] nf street

ruée [Rɥe] nf rush

ruelle [Rɥɛl] nf alley(way)

ruer [Rɥe] /1/ vi (cheval) to kick out; **se ruer** vi: **se ~ sur** to pounce on; **se ~ vers/dans/hors de** to rush ou dash towards/into/out of

rugby [Rygbi] nm rugby (football)

rugir [RyʒiR] /2/ vi to roar

rugueux, -euse [Rygø, -øz] adj rough

ruine [Rɥin] nf ruin; **ruiner** /1/ vt to ruin; **ruineux, -euse** adj ruinous

ruisseau, x [Rɥiso] nm stream, brook

ruisseler [Rɥisle] /4/ vi to stream

rumeur [RymœR] nf (bruit confus) rumbling; (nouvelle) rumour

ruminer [Rymine] /1/ vt (herbe) to ruminate; (fig) to ruminate on ou over, chew over

rupture [RyptyR] nf (de négociations etc) breakdown; (de contrat) breach;

(*dans continuité*) break; (*séparation, désunion*) break-up, split

rural, e, -aux [ʀyʀal, -o] *adj* rural, country *cpd*

ruse [ʀyz] *nf*: **la ~** cunning, craftiness; (*pour tromper*) trickery; **une ~** a trick, a ruse; **rusé, e** *adj* cunning, crafty

russe [ʀys] *adj* Russian ▷ *nm* (*Ling*) Russian ▷ *nm/f*: **R~** Russian

Russie [ʀysi] *nf*: **la ~** Russia

rustine [ʀystin] *nf* repair patch (for bicycle inner tube)

rustique [ʀystik] *adj* rustic

rythme [ʀitm] *nm* rhythm; (*vitesse*) rate (: *de la vie*) pace, tempo; **rythmé, e** *adj* rhythmic(al)

s' [s] *pron voir* **se**
sa [sa] *adj poss voir* **son¹**
sable [sabl] *nm* sand
sablé [sable] *nm* shortbread biscuit
sabler [sable] /1/ *vt* (*contre le verglas*) to grit; **~ le champagne** to drink champagne
sabot [sabo] *nm* clog; (*de cheval, bœuf*) hoof; **~ de frein** brake shoe
saboter [sabɔte] /1/ *vt* (*travail, morceau de musique*) to botch, make a mess of; (*machine, installation, négociation etc*) to sabotage
sac [sak] *nm* bag; (*à charbon etc*) sack; **mettre à ~** to sack; **~ à provisions/de voyage** shopping/travelling bag; **~ de couchage** sleeping bag; **~ à dos** rucksack; **~ à main** handbag
saccadé, e [sakade] *adj* jerky; (*respiration*) spasmodic
saccager [sakaʒe] /3/ *vt* (*piller*) to sack; (*dévaster*) to create havoc in
saccharine [sakaʀin] *nf* saccharin(e)

sachet [saʃɛ] nm (small) bag; (de lavande, poudre, shampooing) sachet; **~ de thé** tea bag; **du potage en ~** packet soup

sacoche [sakɔʃ] nf (gén) bag; (de bicyclette) saddlebag

sacré, e [sakre] adj sacred; (fam: satané) blasted; (: fameux): **un ~ ...** a heck of a ...

sacrement [sakrəmɑ̃] nm sacrament

sacrifice [sakrifis] nm sacrifice; **sacrifier** /7/ vt to sacrifice

sacristie [sakristi] nf sacristy; (culte protestant) vestry

sadique [sadik] adj sadistic

safran [safrɑ̃] nm saffron

sage [saʒ] adj wise; (enfant) good

sage-femme [saʒfam] nf midwife

sagesse [saʒɛs] nf wisdom

Sagittaire [saʒiter] nm: **le ~** Sagittarius

Sahara [saara] nm: **le ~** the Sahara (Desert)

saignant, e [sɛɲɑ̃, -ɑ̃t] adj (viande) rare

saigner [seɲe] /1/ vi to bleed ▷ vt to bleed; (animal) to bleed to death; **~ du nez** to have a nosebleed

saillir [sajir] /13/ vi to project, stick out; (veine, muscle) to bulge

sain, e [sɛ̃, sɛn] adj healthy; **~ et sauf** safe and sound, unharmed; **~ d'esprit** sound in mind, sane

saindoux [sɛ̃du] nm lard

saint, e [sɛ̃, sɛ̃t] adj holy ▷ nm/f saint; **la S~e Vierge** the Blessed Virgin

Saint-Esprit [sɛ̃tɛspri] nm: **le ~** the Holy Spirit ou Ghost

sainteté [sɛ̃təte] nf holiness

Saint-Sylvestre [sɛ̃silvɛstr] nf: **la ~** New Year's Eve

sais etc [sɛ] vb voir **savoir**

saisie [sezi] nf seizure; **~ (de données)** (data) capture

saisir [sezir] /2/ vt to take hold of, grab; (fig: occasion) to seize; (comprendre) to grasp; (entendre) to

get, catch; (Inform) to capture; (Culin) to fry quickly; (Jur: biens, publication) to seize; **saisissant, e** adj startling, striking

saison [sezɔ̃] nf season; **haute/ basse/morte ~** high/low/slack season; **saisonnier, -ière** adj seasonal

salade [salad] nf (Bot) lettuce etc (generic term); (Culin) (green) salad; (fam: confusion) tangle, muddle; **~ composée** mixed salad; **~ de fruits** fruit salad; **~ verte** green salad; **saladier** nm (salad) bowl

salaire [saler] nm (annuel, mensuel) salary; (hebdomadaire, journalier) pay, wages pl; **~ minimum interprofessionnel de croissance** index-linked guaranteed minimum wage

salarié, e [salarje] nm/f salaried employee; wage-earner

salaud [salo] nm (fam!) sod (!), bastard (!)

sale [sal] adj dirty, filthy; (fig: mauvais) nasty

salé, e [sale] adj (liquide, saveur, mer, goût) salty; (Culin: amandes, beurre etc) salted; (: gâteaux) savoury; (fig: grivois) spicy; (: note, facture) steep

saler [sale] /1/ vt to salt

saleté [salte] nf (état) dirtiness; (crasse) dirt, filth; (tache etc) dirt no pl; (fig: tour) filthy trick; (: chose sans valeur) rubbish no pl; (: obscénité) filth no pl

salière [saljer] nf saltcellar

salir [salir] /2/ vt to (make) dirty; (fig) to soil the reputation of; **se salir** vi to get dirty; **salissant, e** adj (tissu) which shows the dirt; (métier) dirty, messy

salle [sal] nf room; (d'hôpital) ward; (de restaurant) dining room; (d'un cinéma) auditorium (: public) audience; **~ d'attente** waiting room; **~ de bain(s)** bathroom; **~ de classe** classroom; **~ de concert** concert hall; **~ d'eau** shower-room;

~ d'embarquement (*à l'aéroport*) departure lounge; **~ de jeux** (*pour enfants*) playroom; **~ à manger** dining room; **~ des professeurs** staffroom; **~ de séjour** living room; **~ des ventes** saleroom

salon [salɔ̃] *nm* lounge, sitting room; (*mobilier*) lounge suite; (*exposition*) exhibition, show; **~ de coiffure** hairdressing salon; **~ de thé** tearoom

salope [salɔp] *nf* (*fam!*) bitch (!); **saloperie** *nf* (*fam!: action*) dirty trick; (: *chose sans valeur*) rubbish *no pl*; **salopette** [salɔpɛt] *nf* dungarees *pl*; (*d'ouvrier*) overall(s)

salsifis [salsifi] *nm* salsify

salubre [salybʀ] *adj* healthy, salubrious

saluer [salɥe] /1/ *vt* (*pour dire bonjour, fig*) to greet; (*pour dire au revoir*) to take one's leave; (*Mil*) to salute

salut [saly] *nm* (*sauvegarde*) safety; (*Rel*) salvation; (*geste*) wave; (*parole*) greeting; (*Mil*) salute ▷ *excl* (*fam: pour dire bonjour*) hi (there); (: *pour dire au revoir*) see you!, bye!

salutations [salytasjɔ̃] *nfpl* greetings; **recevez mes ~ distinguées** *ou* **respectueuses** yours faithfully

samedi [samdi] *nm* Saturday

SAMU [samy] *sigle m* (= *service d'assistance médicale d'urgence*) ≈ ambulance (service) (BRIT), ≈ paramedics (US)

sanction [sɑ̃ksjɔ̃] *nf* sanction; **sanctionner** /1/ *vt* (*loi, usage*) to sanction; (*punir*) to punish

sandale [sɑ̃dal] *nf* sandal

sandwich [sɑ̃dwitʃ] *nm* sandwich

sang [sɑ̃] *nm* blood; **en ~** covered in blood; **se faire du mauvais ~** to fret, get in a state; **sang-froid** *nm* calm, sangfroid; **de sang-froid** in cold blood; **sanglant, e** *adj* bloody

sangle [sɑ̃gl] *nf* strap

sanglier [sɑ̃glije] *nm* (wild) boar

sanglot [sɑ̃glo] *nm* sob; **sangloter** /1/ *vi* to sob

sangsue [sɑ̃sy] *nf* leech

sanguin, e [sɑ̃gɛ̃, -in] *adj* blood *cpd*

sanitaire [sanitɛʀ] *adj* health *cpd*; **sanitaires** *nmpl* (*salle de bain et w.-c.*) bathroom *sg*

sans [sɑ̃] *prép* without; **~ qu'il s'en aperçoive** without him *ou* his noticing; **un pull ~ manches** a sleeveless jumper; **~ faute** without fail; **~ arrêt** without a break; **~ ça** (*fam*) otherwise; **sans-abri** *nmpl* homeless; **sans-emploi** *nm/f inv* unemployed person; **les sans-emploi** the unemployed; **sans-gêne** *adj inv* inconsiderate

santé [sɑ̃te] *nf* health; **être en bonne ~** to be in good health; **boire à la ~ de qn** to drink (to) sb's health; **à ta** *ou* **votre ~!** cheers!

saoudien, ne [saudjɛ̃, -ɛn] *adj* Saudi (Arabian) ▷ *nm/f*: **S~, ne** Saudi (Arabian)

saoul, e [su, sul] *adj* = **soûl**

saper [sape] /1/ *vt* to undermine, sap

sapeur-pompier [sapœʀpɔ̃pje] *nm* fireman

saphir [safiʀ] *nm* sapphire

sapin [sapɛ̃] *nm* fir (tree); (*bois*) fir; **~ de Noël** Christmas tree

sarcastique [saʀkastik] *adj* sarcastic

Sardaigne [saʀdɛɲ] *nf*: **la ~** Sardinia

sardine [saʀdin] *nf* sardine

SARL [saʀl] *sigle f* (= *société à responsabilité limitée*) ≈ plc (BRIT), ≈ Inc. (US)

sarrasin [saʀazɛ̃] *nm* buckwheat

satané, e [satane] *adj* (*fam*) confounded

satellite [satelit] *nm* satellite

satin [satɛ̃] *nm* satin

satire [satiʀ] *nf* satire; **satirique** *adj* satirical

satisfaction [satisfaksjɔ̃] *nf* satisfaction

satisfaire [satisfɛʀ] /60/ *vt* to satisfy; **~ à** (*revendications, conditions*) to meet; **satisfaisant, e** adj (acceptable) satisfactory; **satisfait, e** adj satisfied; **satisfait de** happy ou satisfied with

saturer [satyʀe] /1/ vt to saturate

sauce [sos] nf sauce; (avec un rôti) gravy; **~ tomate** tomato sauce; **saucière** nf sauceboat

saucisse [sosis] nf sausage

saucisson [sosisɔ̃] nm (slicing) sausage

sauf¹ [sof] prép except; **~ si** (à moins que) unless; **~ avis contraire** unless you hear to the contrary; **~ erreur** if I'm not mistaken

sauf², sauve [sof, sov] adj unharmed, unhurt; (fig: honneur) intact, saved; **laisser la vie sauve à qn** to spare sb's life

sauge [soʒ] nf sage

saugrenu, e [sogʀəny] adj preposterous

saule [sol] nm willow (tree)

saumon [somɔ̃] nm salmon inv

saupoudrer [sopudʀe] /1/ vt: **~ qch de** to sprinkle sth with

saur [sɔʀ] adj m: **hareng ~** smoked ou red herring, kipper

saut [so] nm jump; (discipline sportive) jumping; **faire un ~ chez qn** to pop over to sb's (place); **~ en hauteur/ longueur** high/long jump; **~ à la perche** pole vaulting; **~ à l'élastique** bungee jumping; **~ périlleux** somersault

sauter [sote] /1/ vi to jump, leap; (exploser) to blow up, explode; (: fusibles) to blow; (se détacher) to pop out (ou off) ▷ vt to jump (over), leap (over); (fig: omettre) to skip, miss (out); **faire ~** to blow up; (Culin) to sauté; **~ à la corde** to skip; **~ au cou de qn** to fly into sb's arms; **~ sur une occasion** to jump at an opportunity; **~ aux yeux** to be quite obvious

sauterelle [sotʀɛl] nf grasshopper

sautiller [sotije] /1/ vi (oiseau) to hop; (enfant) to skip

sauvage [sovaʒ] adj (gén) wild; (peuplade) savage; (farouche) unsociable; (barbare) wild, savage; (non officiel) unauthorized, unofficial; **faire du camping ~** to camp in the wild ▷ nm/f savage; (timide) unsociable type

sauve [sov] adj f voir **sauf²**

sauvegarde [sovgaʀd] nf safeguard; (Inform) backup; **sauvegarder** /1/ vt to safeguard; (Inform: enregistrer) to save; (: copier) to back up

sauve-qui-peut [sovkipø] excl run for your life!

sauver [sove] /1/ vt to save; (porter secours à) to rescue; (récupérer) to salvage, rescue; **se sauver** vi (s'enfuir) to run away; (fam: partir) to be off; **sauvetage** nm rescue; **sauveteur** nm rescuer; **sauvette: à la sauvette** adv (se marier etc) hastily, hurriedly; **sauveur** nm saviour (BRIT), savior (US)

savant, e [savɑ̃, -ɑ̃t] adj scholarly, learned ▷ nm scientist

saveur [savœʀ] nf flavour ; (fig) savour

savoir [savwaʀ] /32/ vt to know; (être capable de): **il sait nager** he can swim ▷ nm knowledge; **se savoir** vi (être connu) to be known; **je n'en sais rien** I (really) don't know; **à ~ (que)** that is, namely; **faire ~ qch à qn** to let sb know sth; **pas que je sache** not as far as I know

savon [savɔ̃] nm (produit) soap; (morceau) bar ou tablet of soap; (fam): **passer un ~ à qn** to give sb a good dressing-down; **savonner** /1/ vt to soap; **savonnette** nf bar of soap

savourer [savuʀe] /1/ vt to savour; **savoureux, -euse** adj tasty; (fig: anecdote) spicy, juicy

saxo(phone) [saksɔ(fɔn)] nm sax(ophone)

scabreux, -euse [skabʀø, -øz] adj risky; (indécent) improper, shocking

scandale [skãdal] nm scandal;
faire un ~ (scène) to make a scene;
(Jur) create a disturbance; **faire ~**
to scandalize people; **scandaleux,
-euse** adj scandalous, outrageous
scandinave [skãdinav] adj
Scandinavian ▷ nm/f: **S~**
Scandinavian
Scandinavie [skãdinavi] nf: **la ~**
Scandinavia
scarabée [skaRabe] nm beetle
scarlatine [skaRlatin] nf scarlet
fever
scarole [skaRɔl] nf endive
sceau, x [so] nm seal
sceller [sele] /1/ vt to seal
scénario [senaRjo] nm scenario
scène [sɛn] nf (gén) scene; (estrade,
fig: théâtre) stage; **entrer en ~** to
come on stage; **mettre en ~** (Théât)
to stage; (Ciné) to direct; **faire une ~
(à qn)** to make a scene (with sb); **~ de
ménage** domestic fight ou scene
sceptique [sɛptik] adj sceptical
schéma [ʃema] nm (diagramme)
diagram, sketch; **schématique** adj
diagrammatic(al), schematic; (fig)
oversimplified
sciatique [sjatik] nf sciatica
scie [si] nf saw
sciemment [sjamã] adv knowingly
science [sjãs] nf science; (savoir)
knowledge; **~s humaines/sociales**
social sciences; **~s naturelles** (Scol)
natural science sg, biology sg; **~s
po** political science ou studies pl;
science-fiction nf science fiction;
scientifique adj scientific ▷ nm/f
scientist; (étudiant) science student
scier [sje] /7/ vt to saw; (retrancher) to
saw off; **scierie** nf sawmill
scintiller [sɛ̃tije] /1/ vi to sparkle;
(étoile) to twinkle
sciure [sjyR] nf: **~ (de bois)** sawdust
sclérose [skleRoz] nf: **~ en plaques
(SEP)** multiple sclerosis (MS)
scolaire [skɔlɛR] adj school cpd;
scolariser /1/ vt to provide with

schooling (ou schools); **scolarité** nf
schooling
scooter [skutœR] nm (motor) scooter
score [skɔR] nm score
scorpion [skɔRpjɔ̃] nm (signe): **le
S~** Scorpio
scotch [skɔtʃ] nm (whisky) scotch,
whisky; **Scotch®** (adhésif)
Sellotape® (BRIT), Scotch tape® (US)
scout, e [skut] adj, nm scout
script [skRipt] nm (écriture) printing;
(Ciné) (shooting) script
scrupule [skRypyl] nm scruple
scruter [skRyte] /1/ vt to scrutinize;
(l'obscurité) to peer into
scrutin [skRytɛ̃] nm (vote) ballot;
(ensemble des opérations) poll
sculpter [skylte] /1/ vt to sculpt;
(érosion) to carve; **sculpteur** nm
sculptor; **sculpture** nf sculpture
SDF sigle m (= sans domicile fixe)
homeless person; **les ~** the homeless

○ **MOT-CLÉ**

se, s' [sə, s] pron 1 (emploi réfléchi)
oneself; (: masc) himself; (: fém)
herself; (: sujet non humain) itself;
(: pl) themselves; **se savonner** to
soap o.s.
2 (réciproque) one another, each
other; **ils s'aiment** they love one
another ou each other
3 (passif): **cela se répare facilement**
it is easily repaired
4 (possessif): **se casser la jambe/se
laver les mains** to break one's leg/
wash one's hands

séance [seãs] nf (d'assemblée)
meeting, session; (de tribunal) sitting,
session; (musicale, Ciné, Théât)
performance
seau, x [so] nm bucket, pail
sec, sèche [sɛk, sɛʃ] adj dry; (raisins,
figues) dried; (insensible: cœur,
personne) hard, cold ▷ nm: **tenir au ~**
to keep in a dry place ▷ adv hard; **je le**

bois ~ I drink it straight *ou* neat; **à ~** (*puits*) dried up

sécateur [sekatœʀ] *nm* secateurs *pl* (BRIT), shears *pl*

sèche [sɛʃ] *adj f voir* **sec; sèche-cheveux** *nm inv* hair-drier; **sèche-linge** *nm inv* tumble dryer; **sèchement** *adv* (*répliquer etc*) drily

sécher [seʃe] /6/ *vt* to dry; (*dessécher: peau, blé*) to dry (out); (*: étang*) to dry up; (*fam: classe, cours*) to skip ▷ *vi* to dry; to dry out; to dry up; (*fam: candidat*) to be stumped; **se sécher** *vi* (*après le bain*) to dry o.s.; **sécheresse** *nf* dryness; (*absence de pluie*) drought; **séchoir** *nm* drier

second, e [səɡɔ̃, -ɔ̃d] *adj* second ▷ *nm* (*assistant*) second in command; (*Navig*) first mate ▷ *nf* second; (*Scol*) ≈ year in (BRIT), ≈ tenth grade (US); (*Aviat, Rail etc*) second class; **voyager en ~e** to travel second-class; **secondaire** *adj* secondary; **seconder** /1/ *vt* to assist

secouer [səkwe] /1/ *vt* to shake; (*passagers*) to rock; (*traumatiser*) to shake (up)

secourir [səkuʀiʀ] /11/ *vt* (*venir en aide à*) to assist, aid; **secourisme** *nm* first aid; **secouriste** *nm/f* first-aid worker

secours *nm* help, aid, assistance ▷ *nmpl* aid *sg*; **au ~!** help!; **appeler au ~** to shout *ou* call for help; **porter ~ à qn** to give sb assistance, help sb; **les premiers ~** first aid *sg*

○ **ÉQUIPES DE SECOURS**
○
○ Emergency phone numbers can
○ be dialled free from public phones.
○ For the police ('la police') dial 17; for
○ medical services ('le SAMU') dial 15;
○ for the fire brigade ('les sapeurs—
○ pompiers') dial 18.

secousse [səkus] *nf* jolt, bump; (*électrique*) shock; (*fig: psychologique*) jolt, shock

secret, -ète [səkʀɛ, -ɛt] *adj* secret; (*fig: renfermé*) reticent, reserved ▷ *nm* secret; (*discrétion absolue*): **le ~** secrecy; **en ~** in secret, secretly; **~ professionnel** professional secrecy

secrétaire [səkʀetɛʀ] *nm/f* secretary ▷ *nm* (*meuble*) writing desk; **~ de direction** private *ou* personal secretary; **~ d'État** ≈ junior minister; **secrétariat** *nm* (*profession*) secretarial work; (*bureau*) (secretary's) office; (*: d'organisation internationale*) secretariat

secteur [sɛktœʀ] *nm* sector; (*Admin*) district; (*Élec*): **branché sur le ~** plugged into the mains (supply)

section [sɛksjɔ̃] *nf* section; (*de parcours d'autobus*) fare stage; (*Mil: unité*) platoon; **sectionner** /1/ *vt* to sever

sécu [seky] *nf* = **sécurité sociale**

sécurité [sekyʀite] *nf* (*absence de troubles*) security; (*absence de danger*) safety; **système de ~** security (*ou* safety) system; **être en ~** to be safe; **la ~ routière** road safety; **la ~ sociale** ≈ (the) Social Security (BRIT), ≈ (the) Welfare (US)

sédentaire [sedɑ̃tɛʀ] *adj* sedentary

séduction [sedyksjɔ̃] *nf* seduction; (*charme, attrait*) appeal, charm

séduire [seduiʀ] /38/ *vt* to charm; (*femme: abuser de*) to seduce; **séduisant, e** *adj* (*femme*) seductive; (*homme, offre*) very attractive

ségrégation [segʀegasjɔ̃] *nf* segregation

seigle [sɛɡl] *nm* rye

seigneur [sɛɲœʀ] *nm* lord

sein [sɛ̃] *nm* breast; (*entrailles*) womb; **au ~ de** (*équipe, institution*) within

séisme [seism] *nm* earthquake

seize [sɛz] *num* sixteen; **seizième** *num* sixteenth

séjour [seʒuʀ] *nm* stay; (*pièce*) living room; **séjourner** /1/ *vi* to stay

sel [sɛl] *nm* salt; (*fig: piquant*) spice

sélection [seleksjɔ̃] *nf* selection; **sélectionner** /1/ *vt* to select

self [sɛlf] *nm (fam)* self-service
self-service [sɛlfsɛʀvis] *adj* self-service ▷ *nm* self-service (restaurant)
selle [sɛl] *nf* saddle; **selles** *nfpl (Méd)* stools; **seller** /1/ *vt* to saddle
selon [s(ə)lɔ̃] *prép* according to; *(en se conformant à)* in accordance with; **~ moi** as I see it; **~ que** according to
semaine [s(ə)mɛn] *nf* week; **en ~** during the week, on weekdays
semblable [sɑ̃blabl] *adj* similar; *(de ce genre)*: **de ~s mésaventures** such mishaps ▷ *nm* fellow creature *ou* man; **~ à** similar to, like
semblant [sɑ̃blɑ̃] *nm*: **un ~ de vérité** a semblance of truth; **faire ~ (de faire)** to pretend (to do)
sembler [sɑ̃ble] /1/ *vb copule* to seem ▷ *vb impers*: **il semble (bien) que/ inutile de** it (really) seems *ou* appears that/useless to; **il me semble (bien) que** it (really) seems to me that; **comme bon lui semble** as he sees fit
semelle [s(ə)mɛl] *nf* sole; *(intérieure)* insole, inner sole
semer [s(ə)me] /5/ *vt* to sow; *(fig: éparpiller)* to scatter; *(: confusion)* to spread; *(fam: poursuivants)* to lose, shake off; **semé de** *(difficultés)* riddled with
semestre [s(ə)mɛstʀ] *nm* half-year; *(Scol)* semester
séminaire [seminɛʀ] *nm* seminar
semi-remorque [s(ə)miʀəmɔʀk] *nm* articulated lorry (BRIT), semi(trailer) (US)
semoule [s(ə)mul] *nf* semolina
sénat [sena] *nm* senate; **sénateur** *nm* senator
Sénégal [senegal] *nm*: **le ~** Senegal
sens [sɑ̃s] *nm (Physiol)* sense; *(signification)* meaning, sense; *(direction)* direction; **à mon ~** to my mind; **dans le ~ des aiguilles d'une montre** clockwise; **dans le ~ contraire des aiguilles d'une montre** anticlockwise; **dans le mauvais ~** *(aller)* the wrong way;

in the wrong direction; **bon ~** good sense; **~ dessus dessous** upside down; **~ interdit, ~ unique** one-way street
sensation [sɑ̃sasjɔ̃] *nf* sensation; **faire ~** to cause a sensation, create a stir; **à ~** *(péj)* sensational; **sensationnel, le** *adj* sensational, fantastic
sensé, e [sɑ̃se] *adj* sensible
sensibiliser [sɑ̃sibilize] /1/ *vt*: **~ qn (à)** to make sb sensitive (to)
sensibilité [sɑ̃sibilite] *nf* sensitivity
sensible [sɑ̃sibl] *adj* sensitive; *(aux sens)* perceptible; *(appréciable: différence, progrès)* appreciable, noticeable; **~ à** sensitive to; **sensiblement** *adv (à peu près)*: **ils ont sensiblement le même poids** they weigh approximately the same; **sensiblerie** *nf* sentimentality

> Attention à ne pas traduire *sensible* par le mot anglais *sensible*.

sensuel, le [sɑ̃sɥɛl] *adj (personne)* sensual; *(musique)* sensuous
sentence [sɑ̃tɑ̃s] *nf (jugement)* sentence
sentier [sɑ̃tje] *nm* path
sentiment [sɑ̃timɑ̃] *nm* feeling; **recevez mes ~s respectueux** *(personne nommée)* yours sincerely; *(personne non nommée)* yours faithfully; **sentimental, e, -aux** *adj* sentimental; *(vie, aventure)* love *cpd*
sentinelle [sɑ̃tinɛl] *nf* sentry
sentir [sɑ̃tiʀ] /16/ *vt (par l'odorat)* to smell; *(par le goût)* to taste; *(au toucher, fig)* to feel; *(répandre une odeur de)* to smell of; *(: ressemblance)* to smell like ▷ *vi* to smell; **~ mauvais** to smell bad; **se ~ bien** to feel good; **se ~ mal** *(être indisposé)* to feel unwell *ou* ill; **se ~ le courage/la force de faire** to feel brave/strong enough to do; **il ne peut pas le ~** *(fam)* he can't stand him; **je ne me sens pas bien** I don't feel well

S

séparation [separasjɔ̃] nf
separation; (cloison) division,
partition

séparé, e [separe] adj (appartements,
pouvoirs) separate; (époux) separated;
séparément adv separately

séparer [separe] /1/ vt to separate;
(désunir) to drive apart; (détacher):
~ qch de to pull sth (off) from; **se
séparer** vi (époux) to separate, part;
(prendre congé: amis etc) to part; (se
diviser: route, tige etc) to divide; **se ~
de** (époux) to separate ou part from;
(employé, objet personnel) to part with

sept [sɛt] num seven; **septante** num
(BELGIQUE, SUISSE) seventy

septembre [sɛptɑ̃bʀ] nm
September

septicémie [sɛptisemi] nf blood
poisoning, septicaemia

septième [sɛtjɛm] num seventh

séquelles [sekɛl] nfpl after-effects;
(fig) aftermath sg

serbe [sɛʀb] adj Serbian

Serbie [sɛʀbi] nf: **la ~** Serbia

serein, e [səʀɛ̃, -ɛn] adj serene

sergent [sɛʀʒɑ̃] nm sergeant

série [seʀi] nf series inv; (de clés,
casseroles, outils) set; (catégorie:
Sport) rank; **en ~** in quick succession;
(Comm) mass cpd; **de ~** (voiture)
standard; **hors ~** (Comm) custom-
built; **~ noire** (crime) thriller

sérieusement [seʀjøzmɑ̃] adv
seriously

sérieux, -euse [seʀjø, -øz] adj
serious; (élève, employé) reliable,
responsible; (client, maison) reliable,
dependable ▷ nm seriousness; (d'une
entreprise etc) reliability; **garder son ~**
to keep a straight face; **prendre qch/
qn au ~** to take sth/sb seriously

serin [səʀɛ̃] nm canary

seringue [səʀɛ̃g] nf syringe

serment [sɛʀmɑ̃] nm (juré) oath;
(promesse) pledge, vow

sermon [sɛʀmɔ̃] nm sermon

séropositif, -ive [seʀopozitif, -iv]
adj HIV positive

serpent [sɛʀpɑ̃] nm snake;
serpenter /1/ vi to wind

serpillière [sɛʀpijɛʀ] nf floorcloth

serre [sɛʀ] nf (Agr) greenhouse;
serres nfpl (griffes) claws, talons

serré, e [seʀe] adj (réseau) dense;
(habits) tight; (fig: lutte, match) tight,
close-fought; (passagers etc) (tightly)
packed; **avoir le cœur ~** to have a
heavy heart

serrer [seʀe] /1/ vt (tenir) to grip
ou hold tight; (comprimer, coincer)
to squeeze; (poings, mâchoires) to
clench; (vêtement) to be too tight for;
(ceinture, nœud, frein, vis) to tighten
▷ vi: **~ à droite** to keep to the right

serrure [seʀyʀ] nf lock; **serrurier** nm
locksmith

sers, sert [sɛʀ] vb voir **servir**

servante [sɛʀvɑ̃t] nf (maid) servant

serveur, -euse [sɛʀvœʀ, -øz] nm/f
waiter (waitress)

serviable [sɛʀvjabl] adj obliging,
willing to help

service [sɛʀvis] nm service; (série
de repas): **premier ~** first sitting;
(assortiment de vaisselle) set, service;
(bureau: de la vente etc) department,
section; **faire le ~** to serve; **rendre
~ à qn** to help sb; **rendre un ~ à qn**
to do sb a favour; **être de ~** to be on
duty; **être/mettre en ~** to be in/put
into service ou operation; **~ compris/
non compris** service included/
not included; **hors ~** out of order;
~ après-vente after-sales service;
~ militaire military service; see
note **"service militaire"**; **~ d'ordre**
police (ou stewards) in charge of
maintaining order; **~s secrets** secret
service sg

● **SERVICE MILITAIRE**
●
● Until 1997, French men over
● the age of 18 who were passed
● as fit, and who were not in

full-time higher education, were required to do ten months' 'service militaire'. Conscientious objectors were required to do two years' community service.Since 1997, military service has been suspended in France. However, all sixteen-year-olds, both male and female, are required to register for a compulsory one-day training course, the 'JDC' ('journée défense et citoyenneté'), which covers basic information on the principles and organization of defence in France, and also advises on career opportunities in the military and in the voluntary sector. Young people must attend the training day before their eighteenth birthday.

serviette [sɛʀvjɛt] *nf (de table)* (table) napkin, serviette; *(de toilette)* towel; *(porte-documents)* briefcase; **~ hygiénique** sanitary towel

servir [sɛʀviʀ] /14/ *vt* to serve; *(au restaurant)* to wait on; *(au magasin)* to serve, attend to ▷ *vi (Tennis)* to serve; *(Cartes)* to deal; **se servir** *vi (prendre d'un plat)* to help o.s.; **vous êtes servi?** are you being served?; **sers-toi!** help yourself!; **se ~ de** *(plat)* to help o.s. to; *(voiture, outil, relations)* to use; **~ à qn** *(diplôme, livre)* to be of use to; **~ à qch/à faire** *(outil etc)* to be used for sth/for doing; **ça ne sert à rien** it's no use; **~ (à qn) de …** to serve as … (for sb)

serviteur [sɛʀvitœʀ] *nm* servant

ses [se] *adj poss voir* **son¹**

seuil [sœj] *nm* doorstep; *(fig)* threshold

seul, e [sœl] *adj (sans compagnie)* alone; *(unique)*: **un ~ livre** only one book, a single book; **le ~ livre** the only book ▷ *adv (vivre)* alone, on one's own; **faire qch (tout) ~** to do sth (all) on one's own *ou* (all) by oneself ▷ *nm/f*: **il en reste un(e) ~(e)** there's

only one left; **à lui (tout) ~** single-handed, on his own; **se sentir ~** to feel lonely; **parler tout ~** to talk to oneself; **seulement** *adv* only; **non seulement … mais aussi** *ou* **encore** not only … but also

sève [sɛv] *nf* sap

sévère [sevɛʀ] *adj* severe

sexe [sɛks] *nm* sex; *(organe mâle)* member; **sexuel, le** *adj* sexual

shampooing [ʃɑ̃pwɛ̃] *nm* shampoo

Shetland [ʃɛtlɑ̃d] *n*: **les îles ~** the Shetland Islands, Shetland

shopping [ʃɔpiŋ] *nm*: **faire du ~** to go shopping

short [ʃɔʀt] *nm* (pair of) shorts *pl*

MOT-CLÉ

si [si] *adv* **1** *(oui)* yes; **"Paul n'est pas venu" — "si!"** "Paul hasn't come" — "Yes he has!"; **je vous assure que si** I assure you he did/she is *etc*
2 *(tellement)* so; **si gentil/ rapidement** so kind/fast; **(tant et) si bien que** so much so that; **si rapide qu'il soit** however fast he may be
▷ *conj* if; **si tu veux** if you want; **je me demande si** I wonder if *ou* whether; **si seulement** if only
▷ *nm (Mus)* B; (: *en chantant la gamme)* ti

Sicile [sisil] *nf*: **la ~** Sicily

sida [sida] *nm* (= *syndrome immuno- déficitaire acquis)* AIDS *sg*

sidéré, e [sideʀe] *adj* staggered

sidérurgie [sideʀyʀʒi] *nf* steel industry

siècle [sjɛkl] *nm* century

siège [sjɛʒ] *nm* seat; *(d'entreprise)* head office; *(d'organisation)* headquarters *pl*; *(Mil)* siege; **~ social** registered office; **siéger** /3, 6/ *vi* to sit

sien, ne [sjɛ̃, sjɛn] *pron*: **le (la) ~(ne), les ~(ne)s** *(d'un homme)* his; *(d'une femme)* hers; *(d'une chose)* its

S

sieste [sjɛst] nf (afternoon) snooze ou nap; **faire la ~** to have a snooze ou nap

sifflement [sifləmɑ̃] nm whistle

siffler [sifle] /1/ vi (gén) to whistle; (en respirant) to wheeze; (serpent, vapeur) to hiss ▷ vt (chanson) to whistle; (chien etc) to whistle for; (fille) to whistle at; (pièce, orateur) to hiss, boo; (fin du match, départ) to blow one's whistle for; (fam: verre, bouteille) to guzzle

sifflet [siflɛ] nm whistle; **coup de ~** whistle

siffloter [siflɔte] /1/ vi, vt to whistle

sigle [sigl] nm acronym

signal, -aux [siɲal, -o] nm signal; (indice, écriteau) sign; **donner le ~ de** to give the signal for; **~ d'alarme** alarm signal; **signalement** nm description, particulars pl

signaler [siɲale] /1/ vt to indicate; (vol, perte) to report; (personne, faire un signe) to signal; **~ qch à qn/à qn que** to point out sth to sb/to sb that

signature [siɲatyʀ] nf signature; (action) signing

signe [siɲ] nm sign; (Typo) mark; **faire un ~ de la main/tête** to give a sign with one's hand/shake one's head; **faire ~ à qn** (fig: contacter) to get in touch with sb; **faire ~ à qn d'entrer** to motion (to) sb to come in; **signer** /1/ vt to sign; **se signer** vi to cross o.s.

significatif, -ive [siɲifikatif, -iv] adj significant

signification [siɲifikasjɔ̃] nf meaning

signifier [siɲifje] /7/ vt (vouloir dire) to mean; (faire connaître): **~ qch (à qn)** to make sth known (to sb)

silence [silɑ̃s] nm silence; (Mus) rest; **garder le ~ (sur qch)** to keep silent (about sth), say nothing (about sth); **silencieux, -euse** adj quiet, silent ▷ nm silencer

silhouette [silwɛt] nf outline, silhouette; (figure) figure

sillage [sijaʒ] nm wake

sillon [sijɔ̃] nm furrow; (de disque) groove; **sillonner** /1/ vt to criss-cross

simagrées [simaɡʀe] nfpl fuss sg

similaire [similɛʀ] adj similar; **similicuir** nm imitation leather; **similitude** nf similarity

simple [sɛ̃pl] adj simple; (non multiple) single; **~ messieurs/dames** nm (Tennis) men's/ladies' singles sg; **~ d'esprit** nm/f simpleton; **~ soldat** private

simplicité [sɛ̃plisite] nf simplicity; **en toute ~** quite simply

simplifier [sɛ̃plifje] /7/ vt to simplify

simuler [simyle] /1/ vt to sham, simulate

simultané, e [simyltane] adj simultaneous

sincère [sɛ̃sɛʀ] adj sincere; **sincèrement** adv sincerely; genuinely; **sincérité** nf sincerity

Singapour [sɛ̃ɡapuʀ] nm: Singapore

singe [sɛ̃ʒ] nm monkey; (de grande taille) ape; **singer** /3/ vt to ape, mimic; **singeries** nfpl antics

singulariser [sɛ̃ɡylaʀize] /1/: **se singulariser** vi to call attention to o.s.

singularité [sɛ̃ɡylaʀite] nf peculiarity

singulier, -ière [sɛ̃ɡylje, -jɛʀ] adj remarkable, singular ▷ nm singular

sinistre [sinistʀ] adj sinister ▷ nm (incendie) blaze; (catastrophe) disaster; (Assurances) damage (giving rise to a claim); **sinistré, e** adj disaster-stricken ▷ nm/f disaster victim

sinon [sinɔ̃] conj (autrement, sans quoi) otherwise, or else; (sauf) except, other than; (si ce n'est) if not

sinueux, -euse [sinɥø, -øz] adj winding

sinus [sinys] nm (Anat) sinus; (Géom) sine; **sinusite** nf sinusitis

sirène [siʀɛn] nf siren; **~ d'alarme** fire alarm; (pendant la guerre) air-raid siren

sirop [siʀo] nm (à diluer: de fruit etc) syrup; (pharmaceutique) syrup, mixture; **~ contre la toux** cough syrup ou mixture

siroter [siʀɔte] /1/ vt to sip

sismique [sismik] adj seismic

site [sit] nm (paysage, environnement) setting; (d'une ville etc: emplacement) site; **~ (pittoresque)** beauty spot; **~s touristiques** places of interest; **~ web** (Inform) website

sitôt [sito] adv: **~ parti** as soon as he etc had left; **pas de ~** not for a long time; **~ (après) que** as soon as

situation [sitɥasjɔ̃] nf situation; (d'un édifice, d'une ville) position; location; **~ de famille** marital status

situé, e [sitɥe] adj: **bien ~** well situated

situer [sitɥe] /1/ vt to site, situate; (en pensée) to set, place; **se situer** vi: **se ~ à/près de** to be situated at/near

six [sis] num six; **sixième** num sixth ▷ nf (Scol) year 7

skaï® [skaj] nm ≈ Leatherette®

skate [sket], **skate-board** [sketbɔʀd] nm (sport) skateboarding; (planche) skateboard

ski [ski] nm (objet) ski; (sport) skiing; **faire du ~** to ski; **~ de fond** cross-country skiing; **~ nautique** water-skiing; **~ de piste** downhill skiing; **~ de randonnée** cross-country skiing; **skier** /7/ vi to ski; **skieur, -euse** nm/f skier

slip [slip] nm (sous-vêtement) pants pl (BRIT), briefs pl; (de bain: d'homme) trunks pl; (: du bikini) (bikini) briefs pl

slogan [slɔgɑ̃] nm slogan

Slovaquie [slɔvaki] nf: **la ~** Slovakia

SMIC [smik] sigle m = **salaire minimum interprofessionnel de croissance**

smoking [smɔkiŋ] nm dinner ou evening suit

SMS sigle m (= short message service) (service) SMS; (message) text (message)

SNCF sigle f (= Société nationale des chemins de fer français) French railways

snob [snɔb] adj snobbish ▷ nm/f snob; **snobisme** nm snobbery, snobbishness

sobre [sɔbʀ] adj (personne) temperate, abstemious; (élégance, style) sober

sobriquet [sɔbʀike] nm nickname

social, e, -aux [sɔsjal, -o] adj social

socialisme [sɔsjalism] nm socialism; **socialiste** nm/f socialist

société [sɔsjete] nf society; (sportive) club; (Comm) company; **la ~ d'abondance/de consommation** the affluent/consumer society; **~ anonyme** ≈ limited company (BRIT), ≈ incorporated company (US)

sociologie [sɔsjɔlɔʒi] nf sociology

socle [sɔkl] nm (de colonne, statue) plinth, pedestal; (de lampe) base

socquette [sɔket] nf ankle sock

sœur [sœʀ] nf sister; (religieuse) nun, sister

soi [swa] pron oneself; **en ~** (intrinsèquement) in itself; **cela va de ~** that ou it goes without saying; **soi-disant** adj inv so-called ▷ adv supposedly

soie [swa] nf silk; **soierie** nf (tissu) silk

soif [swaf] nf thirst; **avoir ~** to be thirsty; **donner ~ à qn** to make sb thirsty

soigné, e [swaɲe] adj (tenue) well-groomed, neat; (travail) careful, meticulous

soigner [swaɲe] /1/ vt (malade, maladie: docteur) to treat; (: infirmière, mère) to nurse, look after; (travail, détails) to take care over; (jardin, chevelure, invités) to look after; **soigneux, -euse** adj tidy, neat; (méticuleux) painstaking, careful

soi-même [swamɛm] pron oneself

soin [swɛ̃] nm (application) care; (propreté, ordre) tidiness, neatness; **soins** nmpl (à un malade, blessé) treatment sg, medical attention sg; (hygiène) care sg; **avoir** ou **prendre ~**

de to take care of, look after; **avoir** *ou* **prendre ~ de faire** to take care to do; **les premiers ~s** first aid *sg*

soir [swaʀ] *nm* evening; **ce ~** this evening, tonight; **à ce ~!** see you this evening (*ou* tonight)!; **sept/dix heures du ~** seven in the evening/ ten at night; **demain ~** tomorrow evening, tomorrow night; **soirée** *nf* evening; (*réception*) party

soit [swa] *vb voir* **être** ▷ *conj* (*à savoir*) namely; (*ou*): **~ ... ~** either ... or ▷ *adv* so be it, very well; **~ que ... ~ que** *ou* **ou que** whether ... or whether

soixantaine [swasɑ̃tɛn] *nf*: **une ~ (de)** sixty or so, about sixty; **avoir la ~ (âge)** to be around sixty

soixante [swasɑ̃t] *num* sixty; **soixante-dix** *num* seventy

soja [sɔʒa] *nm* soya; (*graines*) soya beans *pl*; **germes de ~** beansprouts

sol [sɔl] *nm* ground; (*de logement*) floor; (*Agr, Géo*) soil; (*Mus*) G (: *en chantant la gamme*) so(h)

solaire [sɔlɛʀ] *adj* (*énergie etc*) solar; (*crème etc*) sun *cpd*

soldat [sɔlda] *nm* soldier

solde [sɔld] *nf* pay ▷ *nm* (*Comm*) balance; **soldes** *nmpl ou nfpl* (*Comm*) sales; **en ~** at sale price; **solder** /1/ *vt* (*marchandise*) to sell at sale price, sell off

sole [sɔl] *nf* sole *inv* (*fish*)

soleil [sɔlɛj] *nm* sun; (*lumière*) sun(light); (*temps ensoleillé*) sun(shine); **il y a** *ou* **il fait du ~** it's sunny; **au ~** in the sun

solennel, le [sɔlanɛl] *adj* solemn

solfège [sɔlfɛʒ] *nm* rudiments *pl* of music

solidaire [sɔlidɛʀ] *adj*: **être ~s** (*personnes*) to show solidarity, stand *ou* stick together; **être ~ de** (*collègues*) to stand by; **solidarité** *nf* solidarity; **par solidarité (avec)** in sympathy (with)

solide [sɔlid] *adj* solid; (*mur, maison, meuble*) solid, sturdy; (*connaissances, argument*) sound; (*personne*) robust, sturdy ▷ *nm* solid

soliste [sɔlist] *nm/f* soloist

solitaire [sɔlitɛʀ] *adj* (*sans compagnie*) solitary, lonely; (*lieu*) lonely ▷ *nm/f* (*ermite*) recluse; (*fig: ours*) loner

solitude [sɔlityd] *nf* loneliness; (*paix*) solitude

solliciter [sɔlisite] /1/ *vt* (*personne*) to appeal to; (*emploi, faveur*) to seek

sollicitude [sɔlisityd] *nf* concern

soluble [sɔlybl] *adj* soluble

solution [sɔlysjɔ̃] *nf* solution; **~ de facilité** easy way out

solvable [sɔlvabl] *adj* solvent

sombre [sɔ̃bʀ] *adj* dark; (*fig*) gloomy; **sombrer** /1/ *vi* (*bateau*) to sink; **sombrer dans** (*misère, désespoir*) to sink into

sommaire [sɔmɛʀ] *adj* (*simple*) basic; (*expéditif*) summary ▷ *nm* summary

somme [sɔm] *nf* (*Math*) sum; (*fig*) amount; (*argent*) sum, amount ▷ *nm*: **faire un ~** to have a (short) nap; **en ~**, **~ toute** all in all

sommeil [sɔmɛj] *nm* sleep; **avoir ~** to be sleepy; **sommeiller** /1/ *vi* to doze

sommet [sɔmɛ] *nm* top; (*d'une montagne*) summit, top; (*fig: de la perfection, gloire*) height

sommier [sɔmje] *nm* bed base

somnambule [sɔmnɑ̃byl] *nm/f* sleepwalker

somnifère [sɔmnifɛʀ] *nm* sleeping drug; sleeping pill *ou* tablet

somnoler [sɔmnɔle] /1/ *vi* to doze

somptueux, -euse [sɔ̃ptɥø, -øz] *adj* sumptuous

son[1], sa (*pl* **ses**) [sɔ̃, sa, se] *adj poss* (*antécédent humain: mâle*) his (: *femelle*) her; (: *valeur indéfinie*) one's, his (her); (: *non humain*) its

son[2] [sɔ̃] *nm* sound; (*de blé etc*) bran

sondage [sɔ̃daʒ] *nm*: **~ (d'opinion)** (opinion) poll

sonde [sɔ̃d] nf (Navig) lead ou sounding line; (Méd) probe; (Tech: de forage, sondage) drill

sonder [sɔ̃de] /1/ vt (Navig) to sound; (Tech) to bore, drill; (fig: personne) to sound out; **~ le terrain** (fig) to see how the land lies

songe [sɔ̃ʒ] nm dream; **songer** /3/ vi: **songer à** (rêver à) to think over; (envisager) to contemplate, think of; **songer que** to think that; **songeur, -euse** adj pensive

sonnant, e [sɔnɑ̃, -ɑ̃t] adj: **à huit heures ~es** on the stroke of eight

sonné, e [sɔne] adj (fam) cracked; **il est midi ~** it's gone twelve

sonner [sɔne] /1/ vi to ring ▷ vt (cloche) to ring; (glas, tocsin) to sound; (portier, infirmière) to ring for; **~ faux** (instrument) to sound out of tune; (rire) to ring false

sonnerie [sɔnri] nf (son) ringing; (sonnette) bell; (de portable) ringtone; **~ d'alarme** alarm bell

sonnette [sɔnɛt] nf bell; **~ d'alarme** alarm bell

sonore [sɔnɔr] adj (voix) sonorous, ringing; (salle, métal) resonant; (ondes, film, signal) sound cpd; **sonorisation** nf (équipement: de salle de conférences) public address system, P.A. system; (: de discothèque) sound system; **sonorité** nf (de piano, violon) tone; (d'une salle) acoustics pl

sophistiqué, e [sɔfistike] adj sophisticated

sorbet [sɔrbe] nm water ice, sorbet

sorcier, -ière [sɔrsje, -jɛr] nm/f sorcerer (witch ou sorceress)

sordide [sɔrdid] adj (lieu) squalid; (action) sordid

sort [sɔr] nm (fortune, destinée) fate; (condition, situation) lot; (magique): **jeter un ~** to cast a spell; **tirer au ~** to draw lots

sorte [sɔrt] nf sort, kind; **de la ~** in that way; **en quelque ~** in a way; **de (telle) ~ que** so that; **faire en ~ que** to see to it that

sortie [sɔrti] nf (issue) way out, exit; (verbale) sally; (promenade) outing; (le soir, au restaurant etc) night out; (Comm: d'un disque) release; (: d'un livre) publication; (: d'un modèle) launching; **~ de bain** (vêtement) bathrobe; **~ de secours** emergency exit

sortilège [sɔrtilɛʒ] nm (magic) spell

sortir [sɔrtir] /16/ vi (gén) to come out; (partir, se promener, aller au spectacle etc) to go out; (bourgeon, plante, numéro gagnant) to come up ▷ vt (gén) to take out; (produit, ouvrage, modèle) to bring out; (fam: dire) to come out with; **~ avec qn** to be going out with sb; **~ de** (endroit) to go (ou come) out of, leave; (cadre, compétence) to be outside; (provenir de) to come from; **s'en ~** (malade) to pull through; (d'une difficulté etc) to get through

sosie [sɔzi] nm double

sot, sotte [so, sɔt] adj silly, foolish ▷ nm/f fool; **sottise** nf silliness no pl, foolishness no pl; (propos, acte) silly ou foolish thing (to do ou say)

sou [su] nm: **près de ses ~s** tight-fisted; **sans le ~** penniless

soubresaut [subrəso] nm start; (cahot) jolt

souche [suʃ] nf (d'arbre) stump; (de carnet) counterfoil (BRIT), stub

souci [susi] nm (inquiétude) worry; (préoccupation) concern; (Bot) marigold; **se faire du ~** to worry; **soucier** /7/: **se soucier de** vt to care about; **soucieux, -euse** adj concerned, worried

soucoupe [sukup] nf saucer; **~ volante** flying saucer

soudain, e [sudɛ̃, -ɛn] adj (douleur, mort) sudden ▷ adv suddenly, all of a sudden

Soudan [sudɑ̃] nm: **le ~** Sudan

soude [sud] nf soda

s

souder [sude] /1/ vt (avec fil à souder) to solder; (par soudure autogène) to weld; (fig) to bind ou knit together

soudure [sudyʀ] nf soldering; welding; (joint) soldered joint; weld

souffle [sufl] nm (en expirant) breath; (en soufflant) puff, blow; (respiration) breathing; (d'explosion, de ventilateur) blast; (du vent) blowing; **être à bout de ~** to be out of breath; **un ~ d'air** ou **de vent** a breath of air

soufflé, e [sufle] adj (fam: ahuri, stupéfié) staggered ▷ nm (Culin) soufflé

souffler [sufle] /1/ vi (gén) to blow; (haleter) to puff (and blow) ▷ vt (feu, bougie) to blow out; (chasser: poussière etc) to blow away; (Tech: verre) to blow; (dire): **~ qch à qn** to whisper sth to sb

souffrance [sufʀɑ̃s] nf suffering; **en ~** (affaire) pending

souffrant, e [sufʀɑ̃, -ɑ̃t] adj unwell

souffre-douleur [sufʀədulœʀ] nm inv butt, underdog

souffrir [sufʀiʀ] /18/ vi to suffer; (éprouver des douleurs) to be in pain ▷ vt to suffer, endure; (supporter) to bear, stand; **~ de** (maladie, froid) to suffer from; **elle ne peut pas le ~** she can't stand ou bear him

soufre [sufʀ] nm sulphur

souhait [swɛ] nm wish; **tous nos ~s pour la nouvelle année** (our) best wishes for the New Year; **souhaitable** adj desirable

souhaiter [swete] /1/ vt to wish for; **~ la bonne année à qn** to wish sb a happy New Year; **~ que** to hope that

soûl, e [su, sul] adj drunk ▷ nm: **tout son ~** to one's heart's content

soulagement [sulaʒmɑ̃] nm relief

soulager [sulaʒe] /3/ vt to relieve

soûler [sule] /1/ vt: **~ qn** to get sb drunk; (boisson) to make sb drunk; (fig) to make sb's head spin ou reel; **se soûler** vi to get drunk

soulever [sulve] /5/ vt to lift; (vagues, poussière) to send up; (enthousiasme)

to arouse; (question, débat, protestations, difficultés) to raise; **se soulever** vi (peuple) to rise up; (personne couchée) to lift o.s. up

soulier [sulje] nm shoe

souligner [suliɲe] /1/ vt to underline; (fig) to emphasize, stress

soumettre [sumɛtʀ] /56/ vt (pays) to subject, subjugate; (rebelles) to put down, subdue; **~ qch à qn** (projet etc) to submit sth to sb; **se ~ (à)** to submit (to)

soumis, e [sumi, -iz] adj submissive; **soumission** nf submission

soupçon [supsɔ̃] nm suspicion; (petite quantité): **un ~ de** a hint ou touch of; **soupçonner** /1/ vt to suspect; **soupçonneux, -euse** adj suspicious

soupe [sup] nf soup

souper [supe] /1/ vi to have supper ▷ nm supper

soupeser [supəze] /5/ vt to weigh in one's hand(s); (fig) to weigh up

soupière [supjɛʀ] nf (soup) tureen

soupir [supiʀ] nm sigh; **pousser un ~ de soulagement** to heave a sigh of relief

soupirer [supiʀe] /1/ vi to sigh

souple [supl] adj supple; (fig: règlement, caractère) flexible; (: démarche, taille) lithe, supple; **souplesse** nf suppleness; (de caractère) flexibility

source [suʀs] nf (point d'eau) spring; (d'un cours d'eau, fig) source; **tenir qch de bonne ~/de ~ sûre** to have sth on good authority/from a reliable source

sourcil [suʀsij] nm (eye)brow; **sourciller** /1/ vi: **sans sourciller** without turning a hair ou batting an eyelid

sourd, e [suʀ, suʀd] adj deaf; (bruit, voix) muffled; (douleur) dull ▷ nm/f deaf person; **faire la ~e oreille** to turn a deaf ear; **sourdine** nf (Mus) mute; **en sourdine** softly, quietly; **sourd-muet, sourde-muette** adj with a speech and hearing impairment

souriant, e [suʀjɑ̃, -ɑ̃t] *adj* cheerful

sourire [suʀiʀ] /36/ *nm* smile ▷ *vi* to smile; **~ à qn** to smile at sb; (*fig: plaire à*) to appeal to sb; (*chance*) to smile on sb; **garder le ~** to keep smiling

souris [suʀi] *nf* mouse

sournois, e [suʀnwa, -waz] *adj* deceitful, underhand

sous [su] *prép* under; **~ la pluie/le soleil** in the rain/sunshine; **~ terre** underground; **~ peu** shortly, before long; **sous-bois** *nm inv* undergrowth

souscrire [suskʀiʀ] /39/: **~ à** *vt* to subscribe to

sous: sous-directeur, -trice *nm/f* assistant manager/manageress; **sous-entendre** /41/ *vt* to imply, infer; **sous-entendu, e** *adj* implied ▷ *nm* innuendo, insinuation; **sous-estimer** /1/ *vt* to underestimate; **sous-jacent, e** *adj* underlying; **sous-louer** /1/ *vt* to sublet; **sous-marin, e** *adj* (*flore, volcan*) submarine; (*navigation, pêche, explosif*) underwater ▷ *nm* submarine; **sous-pull** *nm* thin poloneck sweater; **soussigné, e** *adj*: **je soussigné** I the undersigned; **sous-sol** *nm* basement; **sous-titre** [sutitʀ] *nm* subtitle

soustraction [sustʀaksjɔ̃] *nf* subtraction

soustraire [sustʀɛʀ] /50/ *vt* to subtract, take away; (*dérober*): **~ qch à qn** to remove sth from sb; **se ~ à** (*autorité, obligation, devoir*) to elude, escape from

sous: sous-traitant *nm* subcontractor; **sous-traiter** /1/ *vt, vi* to subcontract; **sous-vêtement** *nm* item of underwear; **sous-vêtements** *nmpl* underwear *sg*

soutane [sutan] *nf* cassock, soutane

soute [sut] *nf* hold

soutenir [sutniʀ] /22/ *vt* to support; (*assaut, choc, regard*) to stand up to, withstand; (*intérêt, effort*) to keep up; (*assurer*): **~ que** to maintain that;

soutenu, e *adj* (*efforts*) sustained, unflagging; (*style*) elevated

souterrain, e [suteʀɛ̃, -ɛn] *adj* underground ▷ *nm* underground passage

soutien [sutjɛ̃] *nm* support; **soutien-gorge** *nm* bra

soutirer [sutiʀe] /1/ *vt*: **~ qch à qn** to squeeze *ou* get sth out of sb

souvenir [suvniʀ] /22/ *nm* (*réminiscence*) memory; (*cadeau*) souvenir ▷ *vb*: **se ~ de** to remember; **se ~ que** to remember that; **en ~ de** in memory *ou* remembrance of; **avec mes affectueux/meilleurs ~s, ...** with love from, .../regards, ...

souvent [suvɑ̃] *adv* often; **peu ~** seldom, infrequently

souverain, e [suvʀɛ̃, -ɛn] *nm/f* sovereign, monarch

soyeux, -euse [swajø, -øz] *adj* silky

spacieux, -euse [spasjø, -øz] *adj* spacious; roomy

spaghettis [spageti] *nmpl* spaghetti *sg*

sparadrap [spaʀadʀa] *nm* adhesive *ou* sticking (BRIT) plaster, bandaid® (US)

spatial, e, -aux [spasjal, -o] *adj* (*Aviat*) space *cpd*

speaker, ine [spikœʀ, -kʀin] *nm/f* announcer

spécial, e, -aux [spesjal, -o] *adj* special; (*bizarre*) peculiar; **spécialement** *adv* especially, particularly; (*tout exprès*) specially; **spécialiser** /1/: **se spécialiser** *vi* to specialize; **spécialiste** *nm/f* specialist; **spécialité** *nf* speciality; (*Scol*) special field

spécifier [spesifje] /7/ *vt* to specify, state

spécimen [spesimɛn] *nm* specimen

spectacle [spɛktakl] *nm* (*tableau, scène*) sight; (*représentation*) show; (*industrie*) show business; **spectaculaire** *adj* spectacular

spectateur, -trice [spɛktatœʀ, -tʀis] *nm/f* (*Ciné etc*) member of the audience; (*Sport*) spectator; (*d'un événement*) onlooker, witness

spéculer [spekyle] /1/ *vi* to speculate

spéléologie [speleɔlɔʒi] *nf* potholing

sperme [spɛʀm] *nm* semen, sperm

sphère [sfɛʀ] *nf* sphere

spirale [spiʀal] *nf* spiral

spirituel, le [spiʀityɛl] *adj* spiritual; (*fin, piquant*) witty

splendide [splɑ̃did] *adj* splendid

spontané, e [spɔ̃tane] *adj* spontaneous; **spontanéité** *nf* spontaneity

sport [spɔʀ] *nm* sport ▷ *adj inv* (*vêtement*) casual; **faire du ~** to do sport; **~s d'hiver** winter sports; **sportif, -ive** *adj* (*journal, association, épreuve*) sports *cpd*; (*allure, démarche*) athletic; (*attitude, esprit*) sporting

spot [spɔt] *nm* (*lampe*) spot(light); (*annonce*): **~ (publicitaire)** commercial (break)

square [skwaʀ] *nm* public garden(s)

squelette [skəlɛt] *nm* skeleton; **squelettique** *adj* scrawny

SRAS [sʀas] *sigle m* (= *syndrome respiratoire aigu sévère*) SARS

Sri Lanka [sʀilɑ̃ka] *nm*: **le ~** Sri Lanka

stabiliser [stabilize] /1/ *vt* to stabilize

stable [stabl] *adj* stable, steady

stade [stad] *nm* (*Sport*) stadium; (*phase, niveau*) stage

stage [staʒ] *nm* (*cours*) training course; **~ de formation (professionnelle)** vocational (training) course; **~ de perfectionnement** advanced training course; **stagiaire** [staʒjɛʀ] *nm/f, adj* trainee

Attention à ne pas traduire *stage* par le mot anglais *stage*.

stagner [stagne] /1/ *vi* to stagnate

stand [stɑ̃d] *nm* (*d'exposition*) stand; (*de foire*) stall; **~ de tir** (*à la foire, Sport*) shooting range

standard [stɑ̃daʀ] *adj inv* standard ▷ *nm* switchboard; **standardiste** *nm/f* switchboard operator

standing [stɑ̃diŋ] *nm* standing; **de grand ~** luxury

starter [staʀtɛʀ] *nm* (*Auto*) choke

station [stasjɔ̃] *nf* station; (*de bus*) stop; (*de villégiature*) resort; **~ de ski** ski resort; **~ de taxis** taxi rank (BRIT) *ou* stand (US); **stationnement** *nm* parking; **stationner** /1/ *vi* to park; **station-service** *nf* service station

statistique [statistik] *nf* (*science*) statistics *sg*; (*rapport, étude*) statistic ▷ *adj* statistical

statue [staty] *nf* statue

statu quo [statykwo] *nm* status quo

statut [staty] *nm* status; **statuts** *nmpl* (*Jur, Admin*) statutes; **statutaire** *adj* statutory

Sté *abr* (= *société*) soc

steak [stɛk] *nm* steak; **~ haché** hamburger

sténo [steno] *nf* (*aussi*: **~graphie**) shorthand

stérile [steʀil] *adj* sterile

stérilet [steʀilɛ] *nm* coil, loop

stériliser [steʀilize] /1/ *vt* to sterilize

stimulant, e [stimylɑ̃, -ɑ̃t] *adj* stimulating ▷ *nm* (*Méd*) stimulant; (*fig*) stimulus, incentive

stimuler [stimyle] /1/ *vt* to stimulate

stipuler [stipyle] /1/ *vt* to stipulate

stock [stɔk] *nm* stock; **stocker** /1/ *vt* to stock

stop [stɔp] *nm* (*Auto: écriteau*) stop sign; (: *signal*) brake-light; **faire du ~** (*fam*) to hitch(hike); **stopper** /1/ *vt* to stop ▷ *vi* to stop, halt

store [stɔʀ] *nm* blind; (*de magasin*) shade, awning

strabisme [strabism] *nm* squint(ing)

strapontin [strapɔ̃tɛ̃] *nm* jump *ou* foldaway seat

stratégie [strateʒi] *nf* strategy; **stratégique** *adj* strategic

stress [strɛs] nm inv stress;
stressant, e adj stressful; **stresser**
/1/ vt: **stresser qn** to make sb (feel)
tense

strict, e [strikt] adj strict; (tenue,
décor) severe, plain; **le ~ nécessaire/
minimum** the bare essentials/
minimum

strident, e [stridã, -ãt] adj shrill,
strident

strophe [strɔf] nf verse, stanza

structure [stryktyr] nf structure; **~s
d'accueil/touristiques** reception/
tourist facilities

studieux, -euse [stydjø, -øz] adj
studious

studio [stydjo] nm (logement) studio
flat (BRIT) ou apartment (US);
(d'artiste, TV etc) studio

stupéfait, e [stypefɛ, -ɛt] adj
astonished

stupéfiant, e [stypefjã, -ãt] adj
(étonnant) stunning, astonishing
▷ nm (Méd) drug, narcotic

stupéfier [stypefje] /7/ vt (étonner)
to stun, astonish

stupeur [stypœr] nf astonishment

stupide [stypid] adj stupid;
stupidité nf stupidity no pl; (parole,
acte) stupid thing (to say ou do)

style [stil] nm style

stylé, e [stile] adj well-trained

styliste [stilist] nm/f designer

stylo [stilo] nm: **~ (à encre)**
(fountain) pen; **~ (à) bille** ballpoint
pen

su, e [sy] pp de **savoir** ▷ nm: **au su de**
with the knowledge of

suave [sɥav] adj sweet

subalterne [sybaltɛrn] adj (employé,
officier, (rôle) junior; (rôle) subordinate,
subsidiary ▷ nm/f subordinate

subconscient [sypkɔ̃sjã] nm
subconscious

subir [sybir] /2/ vt (affront, dégâts,
mauvais traitements) to suffer;
(traitement, opération, châtiment) to
undergo

subit, e [sybi, -it] adj sudden;
subitement adv suddenly, all of a
sudden

subjectif, -ive [sybʒɛktif, -iv] adj
subjective

subjonctif [sybʒɔ̃ktif] nm
subjunctive

subjuguer [sybʒyge] /1/ vt to
subjugate

submerger [sybmɛrʒe] /3/ vt to
submerge; (fig) to overwhelm

subordonné, e [sybɔrdɔne] adj,
nm/f subordinate

subrepticement [sybrɛptismã]
adv surreptitiously

subside [sypsid] nm grant

subsidiaire [sypsidjɛr] adj:
question ~ deciding question

subsister [sybziste] /1/ vi (rester) to
remain, subsist; (survivre) to live on

substance [sypstãs] nf substance

substituer [sypstitɥe] /1/ vt: **~ qn/
qch à** to substitute sb/sth for; **se ~ à
qn** (évincer) to substitute o.s. for sb

substitut [sypstity] nm (succédané)
substitute

subterfuge [sybtɛrfyʒ] nm subterfuge

subtil, e [syptil] adj subtle

subvenir [sybvənir] /22/: **~ à** vt
to meet

subvention [sybvãsjɔ̃] nf subsidy,
grant; **subventionner** /1/ vt to
subsidize

suc [syk] nm (Bot) sap; (de viande,
fruit) juice

succéder [syksede] /6/: **~ à** vt to
succeed; **se succéder** vi (accidents,
années) to follow one another

succès [syksɛ] nm success; **avoir du
~** to be a success, be successful; **à ~**
successful; **~ de librairie** bestseller

successeur [syksesœr] nm
successor

successif, -ive [syksesif, -iv] adj
successive

succession [syksesjɔ̃] nf (série, Pol)
succession; (Jur: patrimoine) estate,
inheritance

succomber [sykɔ̃be] /1/ vi to die, succumb; (fig): **~ à** to succumb to

succulent, e [sykylɑ̃, -ɑ̃t] adj delicious

succursale [sykyʀsal] nf branch

sucer [syse] /3/ vt to suck; **sucette** nf (bonbon) lollipop; (de bébé) dummy (BRIT), pacifier (US)

sucre [sykʀ] nm (substance) sugar; (morceau) lump of sugar, sugar lump ou cube; **~ en morceaux/cristallisé/en poudre** lump ou cube/granulated/caster sugar; **~ glace** icing sugar (BRIT), confectioner's sugar (US); **~ d'orge** barley sugar; **sucré, e** adj (produit alimentaire) sweetened; (au goût) sweet; **sucrer** /1/ vt (thé, café) to sweeten, put sugar in; **sucrerie** nf sugar refinery; **sucreries** nfpl (bonbons) sweets, sweet things; **sucrier** nm (récipient) sugar bowl ou basin

sud [syd] nm: **le ~** the south ▷ adj inv south; (côte) south, southern; **au ~** (situation) in the south; (direction) to the south; **au ~ de** (to the) south of; **sud-africain, e** adj South African ▷ nm/f: **Sud-Africain, e** South African; **sud-américain, e** adj South American ▷ nm/f: **Sud-Américain, e** South American; **sud-est** nm, adj inv south-east; **sud-ouest** nm, adj inv south-west

Suède [syɛd] nf: **la ~** Sweden; **suédois, e** adj Swedish ▷ nm (Ling) Swedish ▷ nm/f: **Suédois, e** Swede

suer [sɥe] /1/ vi to sweat; (suinter) to ooze; **sueur** nf sweat; **en sueur** sweating, in a sweat; **avoir des sueurs froides** to be in a cold sweat

suffire [syfiʀ] /37/ vi (être assez): **~ (à qn/pour qch/pour faire)** to be enough ou sufficient (for sb/for sth/to do); **il suffit d'une négligence/qu'on oublie pour que …** it only takes one act of carelessness/one only needs to forget for …; **ça suffit!** that's enough!

suffisamment [syfizamɑ̃] adv sufficiently, enough; **~ de** sufficient, enough

suffisant, e [syfizɑ̃, -ɑ̃t] adj sufficient; (résultats) satisfactory; (vaniteux) self-important, bumptious

suffixe [syfiks] nm suffix

suffoquer [syfɔke] /1/ vt to choke, suffocate; (stupéfier) to stagger, astound ▷ vi to choke, suffocate

suffrage [syfʀaʒ] nm (Pol: voix) vote

suggérer [syɡʒeʀe] /6/ vt to suggest; **suggestion** nf suggestion

suicide [sɥisid] nm suicide; **suicider** /1/: **se suicider** vi to commit suicide

suie [sɥi] nf soot

suisse [sɥis] adj Swiss ▷ nm/f: **S~** Swiss inv ▷ nf: **la S~** Switzerland; **la S~ romande/allemande** French-speaking/German-speaking Switzerland

suite [sɥit] nf (continuation: d'énumération etc) rest, remainder; (: de feuilleton) continuation; (: second film etc sur le même thème) sequel; (série) series, succession; (conséquence) result; (ordre, liaison logique) coherence; (appartement, Mus) suite; (escorte) retinue, suite; **suites** nfpl (d'une maladie etc) effects; **une ~ de** a series ou succession of; **prendre la ~ de** (directeur etc) to succeed, take over from; **donner ~ à** (requête, projet) to follow up; **faire ~ à** to follow; **(faisant) ~ à votre lettre du** further to your letter of the; **de ~** (d'affilée) in succession; (immédiatement) at once; **par la ~** afterwards, subsequently; **à la ~** one after the other; **à la ~ de** (derrière) behind; (en conséquence de) following

suivant, e [sɥivɑ̃, -ɑ̃t] adj next, following ▷ prép (selon) according to; **au ~!** next!

suivi, e [sɥivi] adj (effort, qualité) consistent; (cohérent) coherent; **très/peu ~** (cours) well-/poorly-attended

suivre [sɥivʀ] /40/ vt (gén) to follow; (Scol: cours) to attend; (: programme) to keep up with; (Comm: article) to continue to stock ▷ vi to follow; (élève: assimiler le programme) to keep up; **se suivre** vi (accidents, personnes, voitures etc) to follow one after the other; **faire ~** (lettre) to forward; "**à ~**" "to be continued"

sujet, te [syʒɛ, -ɛt] adj: **être ~ à** (vertige etc) to be liable ou subject to ▷ nm/f (d'un souverain) subject ▷ nm subject; **au ~ de** about; **~ de conversation** topic ou subject of conversation; **~ d'examen** (Scol) examination question

super [sypɛʀ] adj inv great, fantastic

superbe [sypɛʀb] adj magnificent, superb

superficie [sypɛʀfisi] nf (surface) area

superficiel, le [sypɛʀfisjɛl] adj superficial

superflu, e [sypɛʀfly] adj superfluous

supérieur, e [sypeʀjœʀ] adj (lèvre, étages, classes) upper; **~ (à)** (plus élevé: température, niveau) higher (than); (meilleur: qualité, produit) superior (to); (excellent, hautain) superior ▷ nm/f superior; **supériorité** nf superiority

supermarché [sypɛʀmaʀʃe] nm supermarket

superposer [sypɛʀpoze] /1/ vt (faire chevaucher) to superimpose; **lits superposés** bunk beds

superpuissance [sypɛʀpɥisɑ̃s] nf superpower

superstitieux, -euse [sypɛʀstisjø, -øz] adj superstitious

superviser [sypɛʀvize] /1/ vt to supervise

supplanter [syplɑ̃te] /1/ vt to supplant

suppléant, e [sypleɑ̃, -ɑ̃t] adj (juge, fonctionnaire) deputy cpd; (professeur) supply cpd (BRIT), substitute cpd (US) ▷ nm/f (professeur) supply ou substitute teacher

suppléer [syplee] /1/ vt (ajouter: mot manquant etc) to supply, provide; (compenser: lacune) to fill in; **~ à** to make up for

supplément [syplemɑ̃] nm supplement; **un ~ de travail** extra ou additional work; **un ~ de frites** etc an extra portion of chips etc; **le vin est en ~** wine is extra; **payer un ~** to pay an additional charge; **supplémentaire** adj additional, further; (train, bus) relief cpd, extra

supplication [syplikasjɔ̃] nf supplication; **supplications** nfpl pleas, entreaties

supplice [syplis] nm torture no pl

supplier [syplije] /7/ vt to implore, beseech

support [sypɔʀ] nm support; **~ audio-visuel** audio-visual aid; **~ publicitaire** advertising medium

supportable [sypɔʀtabl] adj (douleur, température) bearable

supporter¹ [sypɔʀtɛʀ] nm supporter, fan

supporter² [sypɔʀte] vt (conséquences, épreuve) to bear, endure; (défauts, personne) to tolerate, put up with; (chose, chaleur etc) to withstand; (personne, chaleur, vin) to take

⬛ Attention à ne pas traduire supporter par to support.

supposer [sypoze] /1/ vt to suppose; (impliquer) to presuppose; **en supposant** ou **à ~ que** supposing (that)

suppositoire [sypozitwaʀ] nm suppository

suppression [sypʀesjɔ̃] nf (voir supprimer) removal; deletion; cancellation

supprimer [syprime] /1/ vt (cloison, cause, anxiété) to remove; (clause, mot) to delete; (congés, service d'autobus etc) to cancel; (emplois, privilèges, témoin gênant) to do away with

suprême [sypʀɛm] adj supreme

s

○ MOT-CLÉ

sur [syʀ] *prép* **1** (*position*) on;
(: *par-dessus*) over; (: *au-dessus*) above;
pose-le sur la table put it on the
table; **je n'ai pas d'argent sur moi** I
haven't any money on me
2 (*direction*) towards; **en allant sur
Paris** going towards Paris; **sur votre
droite** on *ou* to your right
3 (*à propos de*) on, about; **un livre/
une conférence sur Balzac** a book/
lecture on *ou* about Balzac
4 (*proportion, mesures*) out of; **un sur
10** one in 10; (*Scol*) one out of 10; **4 m
sur 2** 4 m by 2; **avoir accident sur
accident** to have one accident after
another

sûr, e [syʀ] *adj* sure, certain; (*digne de
confiance*) reliable; (*sans danger*) safe;
~ de soi self-assured, self-confident;
le plus ~ est de the safest thing is to
surcharge [syʀʃaʀʒ] *nf* (*de
passagers, marchandises*) excess load;
surcharger /3/ *vt* to overload;
(*décoration*) to overdo
surcroît [syʀkʀwa] *nm*: **~ de qch**
additional sth; **par** *ou* **de ~** moreover;
en ~ in addition
surdité [syʀdite] *nf* deafness
sûrement [syʀmã] *adv* (*sans risques*)
safely; (*certainement*) certainly
surenchère [syʀɑ̃ʃɛʀ] *nf* (*aux
enchères*) higher bid; **surenchérir** /2/
vi to bid higher; (*fig*) to try and outbid
each other
surestimer [syʀɛstime] /1/ *vt* to
overestimate
sûreté [syʀte] *nf* (*exactitude: de
renseignements etc*) reliability;
(*sécurité*) safety; (*d'un geste*)
steadiness; **mettre en ~** to put in a
safe place; **pour plus de ~** as an extra
precaution; to be on the safe side
surf [sœʀf] *nm* surfing
surface [syʀfas] *nf* surface;
(*superficie*) surface area; **une**

grande ~ a supermarket; **faire ~** to
surface; **en ~** near the surface; (*fig*)
superficially
surfait, e [syʀfɛ, -ɛt] *adj* overrated
surfer [sœʀfe] /1/ *vi* to surf; **~ sur
Internet** to surf *ou* browse the
Internet
surgelé, e [syʀʒəle] *adj* (deep-)frozen
▷ *nm*: **les ~s** (deep-)frozen food
surgir [syʀʒiʀ] /2/ *vi* to appear
suddenly; (*fig: problème, conflit*)
to arise
sur: surhumain, e *adj* superhuman;
sur-le-champ *adv* immediately;
surlendemain *nm*: **le
surlendemain (soir)** two days later
(in the evening); **le surlendemain
de** two days after; **surmenage**
nm overwork; **surmener** /5/: **se
surmener** *vi* to overwork
surmonter [syʀmɔ̃te] /1/ *vt* (*vaincre*)
to overcome; (*être au-dessus de*) to top
surnaturel, le [syʀnatyʀɛl] *adj, nm*
supernatural
surnom [syʀnɔ̃] *nm* nickname
surnombre [syʀnɔ̃bʀ] *nm*: **être en ~**
to be too many (*ou* one too many)
surpeuplé, e [syʀpœple] *adj*
overpopulated
surplace [syʀplas] *nm*: **faire du ~**
to mark time
surplomber [syʀplɔ̃be] /1/ *vi* to be
overhanging ▷ *vt* to overhang
surplus [syʀply] *nm* (*Comm*) surplus;
(*reste*): **~ de bois** wood left over
surprenant, e [syʀpʀənã, -ãt] *adj*
amazing
surprendre [syʀpʀãdʀ] /58/ *vt*
(*étonner, prendre à l'improviste*) to
amaze; (*tomber sur: intrus etc*) to
catch; (*conversation*) to overhear
surpris, e [syʀpʀi, -iz] *adj*: **~ (de/
que)** amazed *ou* surprised (at/that);
surprise *nf* surprise; **faire une
surprise à qn** to give sb a surprise;
surprise-partie *nf* party
sursaut [syʀso] *nm* start, jump; **~ de**
(*énergie, indignation*) sudden fit *ou*

burst of; **en ~** with a start; **sursauter** /1/ vi to (give a) start, jump

sursis [syRsi] nm (Jur: gén) suspended sentence; (aussi fig) reprieve

surtout [syRtu] adv (avant tout, d'abord) above all; (spécialement, particulièrement) especially; **~, ne dites rien!** whatever you do, don't say anything!; **~ pas!** certainly ou definitely not!; **~ que ...** especially as ...

surveillance [syRvejãs] nf watch; (Police, Mil) surveillance; **sous ~ médicale** under medical supervision

surveillant, e [syRvejã, -ãt] nm/f (de prison) warder; (Scol) monitor

surveiller [syRveje] /1/ vt (enfant, élèves, bagages) to watch, keep an eye on; (prisonnier, suspect) to keep (a) watch on; (territoire, bâtiment) to (keep) watch over; (travaux, cuisson) to supervise; (Scol: examen) to invigilate; **~ son langage/sa ligne** to watch one's language/figure

survenir [syRvǝniR] /22/ vi (incident, retards) to occur, arise; (événement) to take place

survêt [syRvɛt], **survêtement** [syRvɛtmã] nm tracksuit

survie [syRvi] nf survival; **survivant, e** nm/f survivor; **survivre** /46/ vi to survive; **survivre à** (accident etc) to survive

survoler [syRvole] /1/ vt to fly over; (fig: livre) to skim through

survolté, e [syRvolte] adj (fig) worked up

sus [sy(s)]: **en ~ de** prép in addition to, over and above; **en ~** in addition

susceptible [syseptibl] adj touchy, sensitive; **~ de faire** (probabilité) liable to do

susciter [sysite] /1/ vt (admiration) to arouse; (obstacles, ennuis): **~ (à qn)** to create (for sb)

suspect, e [syspɛ(kt), -ɛkt] adj suspicious; (témoignage, opinions, vin etc) suspect ▷ nm/f suspect;

suspecter /1/ vt to suspect; (honnêteté de qn) to question, have one's suspicions about

suspendre [syspãdR] /41/ vt (interrompre, démettre) to suspend; (accrocher: vêtement): **~ qch (à)** to hang sth up (on)

suspendu, e [syspãdy] adj (accroché): **~ à** hanging on (ou from); (perché): **~ au-dessus de** suspended over

suspens [syspã]: **en ~** adv (affaire) in abeyance; **tenir en ~** to keep in suspense

suspense [syspãs] nm suspense

suspension [syspãsjõ] nf suspension; (lustre) pendant light fitting

suture [sytyR] nf: **point de ~** stitch

svelte [svɛlt] adj slender, svelte

SVP abr (= s'il vous plaît) please

sweat [swit] nm (fam) sweatshirt

sweat-shirt (pl sweat-shirts) [switʃœRt] nm sweatshirt

syllabe [silab] nf syllable

symbole [sɛ̃bɔl] nm symbol; **symbolique** adj symbolic; (geste, offrande) token cpd; **symboliser** /1/ vt to symbolize

symétrique [simetRik] adj symmetrical

sympa [sɛ̃pa] adj inv (fam) nice; **sois ~, prête-le moi** be a pal and lend it to me

sympathie [sɛ̃pati] nf (inclination) liking; (affinité) fellow feeling; (condoléances) sympathy; **avoir de la ~ pour qn** to like sb; **sympathique** adj nice, friendly

Attention à ne pas traduire sympathique par sympathetic.

sympathisant, e [sɛ̃patizã, -ãt] nm/f sympathizer

sympathiser [sɛ̃patize] /1/ vi (voisins etc: s'entendre) to get on (BRIT) ou along (US) (well)

symphonie [sɛ̃fɔni] nf symphony

symptôme [sɛ̃ptom] nm symptom

synagogue [sinagɔg] *nf* synagogue
syncope [sɛ̃kɔp] *nf (Méd)* blackout;
  tomber en ~ to faint, pass out
syndic [sɛ̃dik] *nm* managing agent
syndical, e, -aux [sɛ̃dikal, -o] *adj*
  (trade-)union *cpd*; **syndicaliste** *nm/f*
  trade unionist
syndicat [sɛ̃dika] *nm (d'ouvriers,
  employés)* (trade(s)) union; **~
  d'initiative** tourist office *ou* bureau;
  syndiqué, e *adj* belonging to a
  (trade) union; **syndiquer** /1/: **se
  syndiquer** *vi* to form a trade union;
  (adhérer) to join a trade union
synonyme [sinɔnim] *adj*
  synonymous ▷ *nm* synonym; **~ de**
  synonymous with
syntaxe [sɛ̃taks] *nf* syntax
synthèse [sɛ̃tɛz] *nf* synthesis
synthétique [sɛ̃tetik] *adj* synthetic
Syrie [siri] *nf*: **la ~** Syria
systématique [sistematik] *adj*
  systematic
système [sistɛm] *nm* system; **le ~ D**
  resourcefulness

t

t' [t] *pron voir* **te**
ta [ta] *adj poss voir* **ton¹**
tabac [taba] *nm* tobacco; *(aussi:* **débit**
  ou **bureau de ~)** tobacconist's (shop)
tabagisme [tabaʒism] *nm*: **~ passif**
  passive smoking
table [tabl] *nf* table; **à ~!** dinner
  etc is ready!; **se mettre à ~** to sit
  down to eat; **mettre** *ou* **dresser/
  desservir la ~** to lay *ou* set/clear
  the table; **~ à repasser** ironing
  board; **~ de cuisson** hob; **~ des
  matières** (table of) contents *pl*; **~
  de nuit** *ou* **de chevet** bedside table;
  ~ d'orientation viewpoint indicator;
  ~ roulante (tea) trolley *(BRIT)*, tea
  wagon *(US)*
tableau, x [tablo] *nm (Art)* painting;
  (reproduction, fig) picture; *(panneau)*
  board; *(schéma)* table, chart;
  ~ d'affichage notice board; **~ de
  bord** dashboard; *(Aviat)* instrument
  panel; **~ noir** blackboard

tablette [tablɛt] nf (planche) shelf;
~ **de chocolat** bar of chocolate;
~ **tactile** (Inform) tablet
tablier [tablije] nm apron
tabou [tabu] nm taboo
tabouret [taburɛ] nm stool
tac [tak] nm: **du ~ au ~** tit for tat
tache [taʃ] nf (saleté) stain, mark;
(Art, de couleur, lumière) spot; ~ **de**
rousseur ou **de son** freckle
tâche [taʃ] nf task
tacher [taʃe] /1/ vt to stain, mark
tâcher [taʃe] /1/ vi: ~ **de faire** to try
to do, endeavour (BRIT) ou endeavor
(US) to do
tacheté, e [taʃte] adj: ~ **de** speckled
ou spotted with
tact [takt] nm tact; **avoir du ~** to
be tactful
tactique [taktik] adj tactical ▷ nf
(technique) tactics sg; (plan) tactic
taie [tɛ] nf: ~ **(d'oreiller)** pillowslip,
pillowcase
taille [taj] nf cutting; (d'arbre)
pruning; (milieu du corps) waist;
(hauteur) height; (grandeur) size;
de ~ à faire capable of doing; **de ~**
sizeable
taille-crayon(s) [tajkrɛjõ] nm inv
pencil sharpener
tailler [taje] /1/ vt (pierre, diamant) to
cut; (arbre, plante) to prune; (vêtement)
to cut out; (crayon) to sharpen
tailleur [tajœʀ] nm (couturier)
tailor; (vêtement) suit; **en ~** (assis)
cross-legged
taillis [taji] nm copse
taire [tɛʀ] /54/ vi: **faire ~ qn** to make
sb be quiet; **se taire** vi to be silent ou
quiet; **taisez-vous!** be quiet!
Taiwan [tajwan] nf Taiwan
talc [talk] nm talc, talcum powder
talent [talã] nm talent
talkie-walkie [tɔkiwɔki] nm
walkie-talkie
talon [talõ] nm heel; (de chèque, billet)
stub, counterfoil (BRIT); ~ **s plats/**
aiguilles flat/stiletto heels

talus [taly] nm embankment
tambour [tãbuʀ] nm (Mus, Tech)
drum; (musicien) drummer; (porte)
revolving door(s pl); **tambourin** nm
tambourine
Tamise [tamiz] nf: **la ~** the Thames
tamisé, e [tamize] adj (fig) subdued,
soft
tampon [tãpõ] nm (de coton, d'ouate)
pad; (aussi: ~ **hygiénique** ou
périodique) tampon; (amortisseur,
Inform: aussi: **mémoire ~**) buffer;
(bouchon) plug, stopper; (cachet,
timbre) stamp; **tamponner** /1/ vt
(timbres) to stamp; (heurter) to crash
ou ram into; **tamponneuse** adj f:
autos tamponneuses dodgems
tandem [tãdɛm] nm tandem
tandis [tãdi]: ~ **que** conj while
tanguer [tãge] /1/ vi to pitch (and
toss)
tant [tã] adv so much; ~ **de** (sable,
eau) so much; (gens, livres) so many;
~ **que** as long as; ~ **que** as much as; ~
mieux that's great; (avec une certaine
réserve) so much the better; ~ **pis** too
bad; (conciliant) never mind; ~ **bien**
que mal as well as can be expected
tante [tãt] nf aunt
tantôt [tãto] adv (parfois): **tantôt ...**
tantôt now ... now; (cet après-midi)
this afternoon
taon [tã] nm horsefly
tapage [tapaʒ] nm uproar, din
tapageur, -euse [tapaʒœʀ, -øz] adj
noisy; (voyant) loud, flashy
tape [tap] nf slap
tape-à-l'œil [tapalœj] adj inv flashy,
showy
taper [tape] /1/ vt (porte) to bang,
slam; (enfant) to slap; (dactylographier)
to type (out); (fam: emprunter): ~ **qn**
de 10 euros to touch sb for 10 euros
▷ vi (soleil) to beat down; **se taper**
vt (fam: travail) to get landed with;
(: boire, manger) to get through; ~ **sur qn** to
thump sb; (fig) to run sb down; ~ **sur**
qch (clou etc) to hit sth; (table etc) to

bang on sth; **~ à** (*porte etc*) to knock on; **~ dans** (*se servir*) to dig into; **~ des mains/pieds** to clap one's hands/ stamp one's feet; **~ (à la machine)** to type

tapi, e [tapi] *adj*: **~ dans/derrière** (*caché*) hidden away in/behind

tapis [tapi] *nm* carpet; (*petit*) rug; **~ roulant** (*pour piétons*) moving walkway; (*pour bagages*) carousel; **~ de sol** (*de tente*) groundsheet; **~ de souris** (*Inform*) mouse mat

tapisser [tapise] /1/ *vt* (*avec du papier peint*) to paper; (*recouvrir*): **~ qch (de)** to cover sth (with); **tapisserie** *nf* (*tenture, broderie*) tapestry; (*papier peint*) wallpaper

tapissier, -ière [tapisje, -jɛʀ] *nm/f*: **~-décorateur** interior decorator

tapoter [tapote] /1/ *vt* (*joue, main*) to pat; (*objet*) to tap

taquiner [takine] /1/ *vt* to tease

tard [taʀ] *adv* late ▷ *nm*: **sur le ~** late in life; **plus ~** later (on); **au plus ~** at the latest; **il est trop ~** it's too late

tarder [taʀde] /1/ *vi* (*chose*) to be a long time coming; (*personne*): **~ à faire** to delay doing; **il me tarde d'être** I am longing to be; **sans (plus) ~** without (further) delay

tardif, -ive [taʀdif, -iv] *adj* late

tarif [taʀif] *nm*: **~ des consommations** price list; **~s postaux/douaniers** postal/ customs rates; **~ des taxis** taxi fares; **~ plein/réduit** (*train*) full/reduced fare; (*téléphone*) peak/off-peak rate

tarir [taʀiʀ] /2/ *vt* to dry up, run dry

tarte [taʀt] *nf* tart; **~ aux pommes/à la crème** apple/custard tart; **~ Tatin** ≈ apple upside-down tart

tartine [taʀtin] *nf* slice of bread (and butter (*ou* jam)); **~ de miel** slice of bread and honey; **tartiner** /1/ *vt* to spread; **fromage à tartiner** cheese spread

tartre [taʀtʀ] *nm* (*des dents*) tartar; (*de chaudière*) fur, scale

tas [tɑ] *nm* heap, pile; **un ~ de** (*fig*) heaps of, lots of; **en ~** in a heap *ou* pile; **formé sur le ~** trained on the job

tasse [tɑs] *nf* cup; **~ à café/thé** coffee/teacup

tassé, e [tɑse] *adj*: **bien ~** (*café etc*) strong

tasser [tɑse] /1/ *vt* (*terre, neige*) to pack down; (*entasser*): **~ qch dans** to cram sth into; **se tasser** *vi* (*se serrer*) to squeeze up; (*s'affaisser*) to settle; (*personne: avec l'âge*) to shrink; (*fig*) to sort itself out, settle down

tâter [tɑte] /1/ *vt* to feel; (*fig*): **~ de** (*prison etc*) to have a taste of; **se tâter** (*hésiter*) to be in two minds

tatillon, ne [tatijɔ̃, -ɔn] *adj* pernickety

tâtonnement [tɑtɔnmɑ̃] *nm*: **par ~s** (*fig*) by trial and error

tâtonner [tɑtɔne] /1/ *vi* to grope one's way along

tâtons [tɑtɔ̃]: **à ~** *adv*: **chercher/ avancer à ~** to grope around for/ grope one's way forward

tatouage [tatwaʒ] *nm* tattoo

tatouer [tatwe] /1/ *vt* to tattoo

taudis [todi] *nm* hovel, slum

taule [tol] *nf* (*fam*) nick (BRIT), jail

taupe [top] *nf* mole

taureau, x [tɔʀo] *nm* bull; (*signe*): **le T~** Taurus

taux [to] *nm* rate; (*d'alcool*) level; **~ d'intérêt** interest rate

taxe [taks] *nf* tax; (*douanière*) duty; **toutes ~s comprises** inclusive of tax; **la boutique hors ~s** the duty-free shop; **~ de séjour** tourist tax; **~ à** *ou* **sur la valeur ajoutée** value added tax

taxer [takse] /1/ *vt* (*personne*) to tax; (*produit*) to put a tax on, tax

taxi [taksi] *nm* taxi; (*chauffeur: fam*) taxi driver

Tchécoslovaquie [tʃekɔslɔvaki] *nf*: **la ~** Czechoslovakia; **tchèque** *adj* Czech ▷ *nm* (*Ling*) Czech ▷ *nm/f*:

Tchèque Czech; **la République tchèque** the Czech Republic

Tchétchénie [tʃetʃeni] *nf*: **la ~** Chechnya

te, t' [tə] *pron* you; (*réfléchi*) yourself

technicien, ne [tɛknisjɛ̃, -ɛn] *nm/f* technician

technico-commercial, e, -aux [tɛknikokɔmɛʁsjal, -o] *adj*: **agent ~** sales technician

technique [tɛknik] *adj* technical ▷ *nf* technique; **techniquement** *adv* technically

techno [tɛkno] *nf*: **la (musique) ~** techno (music)

technologie [tɛknɔlɔʒi] *nf* technology; **technologique** *adj* technological

teck [tɛk] *nm* teak

tee-shirt [tiʃœʁt] *nm* T-shirt, tee-shirt

teindre [tɛ̃dʁ] /52/ *vt* to dye; **se ~ (les cheveux)** to dye one's hair; **teint, e** *adj* dyed ▷ *nm* (*du visage*) complexion; (: *momentané*) colour ▷ *nf* shade; **grand teint** colourfast

teinté, e [tɛ̃te] *adj*: **~ de** (*fig*) tinged with

teinter [tɛ̃te] /1/ *vt* (*verre*) to tint; (*bois*) to stain

teinture [tɛ̃tyʁ] *nf* dye; **~ d'iode** tincture of iodine; **teinturerie** *nf* dry cleaner's; **teinturier, -ière** *nm/f* dry cleaner

tel, telle [tɛl] *adj* (*pareil*) such; (*comme*): **~ un/des ...** like a/like ...; (*indéfini*) such-and-such a; (*intensif*): **un ~/de ~s ...** such (a)/such ...; **venez ~ jour** come on such-and-such a day; **rien de ~** nothing like it; **~ que** like, such as; **~ quel** as it is *ou* stands (*ou* was *etc*)

télé [tele] *nf* (*fam*) TV; **à la ~** on TV *ou* telly; **télécabine** *nf* (*benne*) cable car; **télécarte** *nf* phonecard; **téléchargeable** *adj* downloadable; **téléchargement** *nm* (*action*) downloading; (*fichier*) download;

télécharger /3/ *vt* (*recevoir*) to download; (*transmettre*) to upload; **télécommande** *nf* remote control; **télécopieur** *nm* fax (machine); **télédistribution** *nf* cable TV; **télégramme** *nm* telegram; **télégraphier** /7/ *vt* to telegraph, cable; **téléguider** /1/ *vt* to operate by remote control; **télématique** *nf* telematics *sg*; **téléobjectif** *nm* telephoto lens *sg*; **télépathie** *nf* telepathy; **téléphérique** *nm* cable-car

téléphone [telefɔn] *nm* telephone; **avoir le ~** to be on the (tele)phone; **au ~** on the phone; **~ sans fil** cordless (tele)phone; **téléphoner** /1/ *vi* to make a phone call; **téléphoner à** to phone, call up; **téléphonique** *adj* (tele)phone *cpd*

téléréalité [telerealite] *nf* reality TV

télescope [teleskɔp] *nm* telescope

télescoper [teleskɔpe] /1/ *vt* to smash up; **se télescoper** (*véhicules*) to concertina

télé: téléscripteur *nm* teleprinter; **télésiège** *nm* chairlift; **téléski** *nm* ski-tow; **téléspectateur, -trice** *nm/f* (television) viewer; **télétravail** *nm* telecommuting; **télévente** *nf* telesales; **téléviseur** *nm* television set; **télévision** *nf* television; **à la télévision** on television; **télévision numérique** digital TV; **télévision par câble/satellite** cable/satellite television

télex [teleks] *nm* telex

telle [tɛl] *adj f voir* **tel**; **tellement** *adv* (*tant*) so much; (*si*) so; **tellement de** (*sable, eau*) so much; (*gens, livres*) so many; **il s'est endormi tellement il était fatigué** he was so tired (that) he fell asleep; **pas tellement** not really; **pas tellement fort/lentement** not (all) that strong/slowly; **il ne mange pas tellement** he doesn't eat (all that) much

téméraire [temerɛʁ] *adj* reckless, rash

témoignage [temwaɲaʒ] nm (Jur: déclaration) testimony no pl, evidence no pl; (rapport, récit) account; (fig: d'affection etc) token, mark; (geste) expression

témoigner [temwaɲe] /1/ vt (intérêt, gratitude) to show ▷ vi (Jur) to testify, give evidence; **~ de** to bear witness to, testify to

témoin [temwɛ̃] nm witness ▷ adj: **appartement~** show flat; **être ~ de** to witness; **~ oculaire** eyewitness

tempe [tɑ̃p] nf temple

tempérament [tɑ̃peramɑ̃] nm temperament, disposition; **à ~** (vente) on deferred (payment) terms; (achat) by instalments, hire purchase cpd

température [tɑ̃peratyr] nf temperature; **avoir** ou **faire de la ~** to be running ou have a temperature

tempête [tɑ̃pɛt] nf storm; **~ de sable/neige** sand/snowstorm

temple [tɑ̃pl] nm temple; (protestant) church

temporaire [tɑ̃pɔrɛr] adj temporary

temps [tɑ̃] nm (atmosphérique) weather; (durée) time; (époque) time, times pl; (Ling) tense; (Mus) beat; (Tech) stroke; **un ~ de chien** (fam) rotten weather; **quel ~ fait-il?** what's the weather like?; **il fait beau/mauvais ~** the weather is fine/bad; **avoir le ~/tout le ~/juste le ~** to have time/plenty of time/just enough time; **en ~ de paix/guerre** in peacetime/wartime; **en ~ utile** ou **voulu** in due time ou course; **ces derniers ~** lately; **dans quelque ~** in a (little) while; **de ~ en ~, de ~ à autre** from time to time; **à ~** (partir, arriver) in time; **à ~ complet, à plein ~** adv, adj full-time; **à ~ partiel, à mi-~** adv, adj part-time; **dans le ~** at one time; **~ d'arrêt** pause, halt; **~ libre** free ou spare time; **~ mort** (Comm) slack period

tenable [tənabl] adj bearable

tenace [tənas] adj persistent

tenant, e [tənɑ̃, -ɑ̃t] nm/f (Sport): **~ du titre** title-holder

tendance [tɑ̃dɑ̃s] nf (opinions) leanings pl, sympathies pl; (inclination) tendency; (évolution) trend; **avoir ~ à** to have a tendency to, tend to

tendeur [tɑ̃dœr] nm (attache) elastic strap

tendre [tɑ̃dr] /41/ adj tender; (bois, roche, couleur) soft ▷ vt (élastique, peau) to stretch; (corde) to tighten; (muscle) to tense; (donner): **~ qch à qn** to hold sth out to sb; (offrir) to offer sb sth; (fig: piège) to set, lay; **se tendre** vi (corde) to tighten; (relations) to become strained; **~ à qch/à faire** to tend towards sth/to do; **~ l'oreille** to prick up one's ears; **~ la main/le bras** to hold out one's hand/stretch out one's arm; **tendrement** adv tenderly; **tendresse** nf tenderness

tendu, e [tɑ̃dy] pp de **tendre** ▷ adj (corde) tight; (muscles) tensed; (relations) strained

ténèbres [tenɛbr] nfpl darkness sg

teneur [tənœr] nf content; (d'une lettre) terms pl, content

tenir [tənir] /22/ vt to hold; (magasin, hôtel) to run; (promesse) to keep ▷ vi to hold; (neige, gel) to last; **se tenir** vi (avoir lieu) to be held, take place; (être: personne) to stand; **se ~ droit** to stand up (ou sit up) straight; **bien se ~** to behave well; **se ~ à qch** to hold on to sth; **s'en ~ à qch** to confine o.s. to sth; **~ à** (personne, objet) to be attached to, care about (ou for); (réputation) to care about; **~ à faire** to want to do; **~ de** (ressembler à) to take after; **ça ne tient qu'à lui** it is entirely up to him; **~ qn pour** to take sb for; **~ qch de qn** (histoire) to have heard ou learnt sth from sb; (qualité, défaut) to have inherited ou got sth from sb; **~ dans** to fit into; **~ compte de qch** to take sth into account; **~ les**

comptes to keep the books; **~ le coup** to hold out; **~ bon** to stand *ou* hold fast; **~ au chaud/à l'abri** to keep hot/under shelter *ou* cover; **un manteau qui tient chaud** a warm coat; **tiens (***ou* **tenez), voilà le stylo** there's the pen!; **tiens, voilà Alain!** look, here's Alain!; **tiens?** (*surprise*) really?

tennis [tenis] *nm* tennis; (*aussi*: **court ~**) tennis court ▷ *nmpl, nfpl* (*aussi*: **chaussures de ~**) tennis *ou* gym shoes; **~ de table** table tennis; **tennisman** *nm* tennis player

tension [tɑ̃sjɔ̃] *nf* tension; (*Méd*) blood pressure; **faire** *ou* **avoir de la ~** to have high blood pressure

tentation [tɑ̃tasjɔ̃] *nf* temptation

tentative [tɑ̃tativ] *nf* attempt

tente [tɑ̃t] *nf* tent

tenter [tɑ̃te] /1/ *vt* (*éprouver, attirer*) to tempt; (*essayer*): **~ qch/de faire** to attempt sth/to do; **~ sa chance** to try one's luck

tenture [tɑ̃tyʀ] *nf* hanging

tenu, e [təny] *pp de* **tenir** ▷ *adj*: **bien ~** (*maison, comptes*) well-kept; **~ de faire** (*obligé*) under an obligation to do ▷ *nf* (*vêtements*) clothes *pl*; (*comportement*) manners *pl*, behaviour; (*d'une maison*) upkeep; **en petite ~e** scantily dressed *ou* clad

ter [tɛʀ] *adj*: **16 ~** 16b *ou* B

terme [tɛʀm] *nm* term; (*fin*) end; **être en bons/mauvais ~s avec qn** to be on good/bad terms with sb; **à court/long ~** *adj* short-/long-term *ou* -range; *adv* in the short/long term; **avant ~** (*Méd*) prematurely; **mettre un ~ à** to put an end *ou* a stop to

terminaison [tɛʀminɛzɔ̃] *nf* (*Ling*) ending

terminal, e, -aux [tɛʀminal, -o] *nm* terminal ▷ *nf* (*Scol*) ≈ year 13 (*BRIT*), ≈ twelfth grade (*US*)

terminer [tɛʀmine] /1/ *vt* to finish; **se terminer** *vi* to end

terne [tɛʀn] *adj* dull

ternir [tɛʀniʀ] /2/ *vt* to dull; (*fig*) to sully, tarnish; **se ternir** *vi* to become dull

terrain [teʀɛ̃] *nm* (*sol, fig*) ground; (*Comm*: *étendue de terre*) land *no pl*; (: *parcelle*) plot (of land); (: *à bâtir*) site; **sur le ~** (*fig*) on the field; **~ de football/rugby** football/rugby pitch (*BRIT*) *ou* field (*US*); **~ d'aviation** airfield; **~ de camping** campsite; **~ de golf** golf course; **~ de jeu** (*pour les petits*) playground; (*Sport*) games field; **~ de sport** sports ground; **~ vague** waste ground *no pl*

terrasse [teʀas] *nf* terrace; **à la ~** (*café*) outside; **terrasser** /1/ *vt* (*adversaire*) to floor; (*maladie etc*) to lay low

terre [tɛʀ] *nf* (*gén, aussi Élec*) earth; (*substance*) soil, earth; (*opposé à mer*) land *no pl*; (*contrée*) land; **terres** *nfpl* (*terrains*) lands, land *sg*; **en ~** (*pipe, poterie*) clay *cpd*; **à** *ou* **par ~** (*mettre, être, s'asseoir*) on the ground (*ou* floor); (*jeter, tomber*) to the ground, down; **~ à ~** *adj inv* down-to-earth; **~ cuite** terracotta; **la ~ ferme** dry land; **~ glaise** clay

terreau [teʀo] *nm* compost

terre-plein [tɛʀplɛ̃] *nm* platform; (*sur chaussée*) central reservation

terrestre [teʀɛstʀ] *adj* (*surface*) earth's, of the earth; (*Bot, Zool, Mil*) land *cpd*; (*Rel*) earthly

terreur [teʀœʀ] *nf* terror *no pl*

terrible [teʀibl] *adj* terrible, dreadful; (*fam*) terrific; **pas ~** nothing special

terrien, ne [teʀjɛ̃, -ɛn] *adj*: **propriétaire ~** landowner ▷ *nm/f* (*non martien etc*) earthling

terrier [teʀje] *nm* burrow, hole; (*chien*) terrier

terrifier [teʀifje] /7/ *vt* to terrify

terrine [teʀin] *nf* (*récipient*) terrine; (*Culin*) pâté

territoire [teʀitwaʀ] *nm* territory

terroriser [teʀɔʀize] /1/ *vt* to terrorize

terrorisme [tɛrɔrism] *nm*
terrorism; **terroriste** [tɛrɔrist] *nm/f*
terrorist

tertiaire [tɛrsjɛr] *adj* tertiary ▷ *nm*
(*Écon*) service industries *pl*

tes [te] *adj poss voir* **ton¹**

test [tɛst] *nm* test

testament [tɛstamɑ̃] *nm* (*Jur*) will;
(*fig*) legacy; (*Rel*) **T~** Testament

tester [tɛste] /1/ *vt* to test

testicule [tɛstikyl] *nm* testicle

tétanos [tetanos] *nm* tetanus

têtard [tɛtar] *nm* tadpole

tête [tɛt] *nf* head; (*cheveux*) hair *no
pl*; (*visage*) face; **de ~** *adj* (*wagon etc*)
front *cpd* ▷ *adv* (*calculer*) in one's head,
mentally; **perdre la ~** (*fig*) (*s'affoler*) to
lose one's head; (*devenir fou*) to go off
one's head; **tenir ~ à qn** to stand up
to *ou* defy sb; **la ~ en bas** with one's
head down; **la ~ la première** (*tomber*)
head-first; **faire une ~** (*Football*) to
head the ball; **faire la ~** (*fig*) to sulk;
en ~ (*Sport*) in the lead; at the front
ou head; **à la ~ de** at the head of; **à ~
reposée** in a more leisurely moment;
n'en faire qu'à sa ~ to do as one
pleases; **en avoir par-dessus la ~** to
be fed up; **en ~ à ~** in private, alone
together; **de la ~ aux pieds** from
head to toe; **~ de lecture** (*playback*)
head; **~ de liste** (*Pol*) chief candidate;
~ de mort skull and crossbones; **~ de
série** (*Tennis*) seeded player, seed;
~ de Turc (*fig*) whipping boy (*BRIT*),
butt; **tête-à-queue** *nm inv*: **faire
un tête-à-queue** to spin round;
tête-à-tête *nm inv*: **en tête-à-tête**
in private, alone together

téter [tete] /6/ *vt*: **~ (sa mère)** to
suck at one's mother's breast, feed

tétine [tetin] *nf* teat; (*sucette*)
dummy (*BRIT*), pacifier (*US*)

têtu, e [tety] *adj* stubborn, pigheaded

texte [tɛkst] *nm* text; (*morceau choisi*)
passage

textile [tɛkstil] *adj* textile *cpd* ▷ *nm*
textile; (*industrie*) textile industry

Texto® [tɛksto] *nm* text (message)

texture [tɛkstyr] *nf* texture

TGV *sigle m* = **train à grande vitesse**

thaïlandais, e [tailɑ̃dɛ, -ɛz] *adj* Thai
▷ *nm/f*: **T~, e** Thai

Thaïlande [tailɑ̃d] *nf*: **la ~** Thailand

thé [te] *nm* tea; **prendre le ~** to have
tea; **~ au lait/citron** tea with milk/
lemon; **faire le ~** to make the tea

théâtral, e, -aux [teatral, -o] *adj*
theatrical

théâtre [teatr] *nm* theatre; (*péj*)
playacting; (*fig: lieu*): **le ~ de** the scene
of; **faire du ~** to act

théière [tejɛr] *nf* teapot

thème [tɛm] *nm* theme; (*Scol:
traduction*) prose (composition)

théologie [teɔlɔʒi] *nf* theology

théorie [teɔri] *nf* theory; **théorique**
adj theoretical

thérapie [terapi] *nf* therapy

thermal, e, -aux [tɛrmal, -o] *adj*:
station ~e spa; **cure ~e** water cure

thermomètre [tɛrmɔmɛtr] *nm*
thermometer

thermos [tɛrmos] *nm ou f*:
(bouteille) ~ vacuum *ou* Thermos®
flask ; *BRIT ou* bottle (*US*)

thermostat [tɛrmɔsta] *nm*
thermostat

thèse [tɛz] *nf* thesis

thon [tɔ̃] *nm* tuna (fish)

thym [tɛ̃] *nm* thyme

Tibet [tibɛ] *nm*: **le ~** Tibet

tibia [tibja] *nm* shin; shinbone, tibia

TIC *sigle fpl* (= *technologies de
l'information et de la communication*)
ICT *sg*

tic [tik] *nm* tic, (*nervous*) twitch; (*de
langage etc*) mannerism

ticket [tikɛ] *nm* ticket; **~ de caisse**
till receipt

tiède [tjɛd] *adj* lukewarm; (*vent, air*)
mild, warm; **tiédir** /2/ *vi* (*se réchauffer*)
to grow warmer; (*refroidir*) to cool

tien, tienne [tjɛ̃, tjɛn] *pron*: **le (la)
~(ne)** yours; **les ~(ne)s** yours; **à la
~ne!** cheers!

tiens [tjɛ̃] vb, excl voir **tenir**

tiercé [tjɛRse] nm system of forecast betting giving first three horses

tiers, tierce [tjɛR, tjɛRs] adj third ▷ nm (Jur) third party; (fraction) third; **le ~ monde** the third world

tige [tiʒ] nf stem; (baguette) rod

tignasse [tiɲas] nf (péj) shock ou mop of hair

tigre [tigR] nm tiger; **tigré, e** adj (rayé) striped; (tacheté) spotted; (chat) tabby; **tigresse** nf tigress

tilleul [tijœl] nm lime (tree), linden (tree); (boisson) lime(-blossom) tea

timbre [tɛ̃bR] nm (tampon) stamp; (aussi: **~-poste**) (postage) stamp; (Mus: de voix, instrument) timbre, tone

timbré, e [tɛ̃bRe] adj (fam) cracked

timide [timid] adj shy; (timoré) timid; **timidement** adv shyly; timidly; **timidité** nf shyness; timidity

tintamarre [tɛ̃tamaR] nm din, uproar

tinter [tɛ̃te] /1/ vi to ring, chime; (argent, clés) to jingle

tique [tik] nf tick (insect)

tir [tiR] nm (sport) shooting; (fait ou manière de tirer) firing no pl; (rafale) fire; (stand) shooting gallery; **~ à l'arc** archery

tirage [tiRaʒ] nm (action) printing; (Photo) print; (de journal) circulation; (de livre) (print-)run; edition; (de loterie) draw; **~ au sort** drawing lots

tire [tiR] nf: **vol à la ~** pickpocketing

tiré, e [tiRe] adj (visage, traits) drawn; **~ par les cheveux** far-fetched

tire-bouchon [tiRbuʃɔ̃] nm corkscrew

tirelire [tiRliR] nf moneybox

tirer [tiRe] /1/ vt (gén) to pull; (ligne, trait) to draw; (rideau) to draw; (carte, conclusion, chèque) to draw; (en faisant feu: balle, coup) to fire; (: animal) to shoot; (journal, livre, photo) to print; (Football: corner etc) to take ▷ vi (faire feu) to fire; (faire du tir, Football) to shoot; **se tirer** vi (fam) to push off;

(aussi: **s'en ~**) (éviter le pire) to get off; (survivre) to pull through; (se débrouiller) to manage; (extraire): **~ qch de** to take ou pull sth out of; **~ sur** (corde, poignée) to pull on ou at; (faire feu sur) to shoot ou fire at; (pipe) to draw on; (fig: avoisiner) to verge ou border on; **~ qn de** (embarras etc) to help ou get sb out of; **~ à l'arc/la carabine** to shoot with a bow and arrow/with a rifle; **~ à sa fin** to be drawing to an end; **~ qch au clair** to clear sth up; **~ au sort** to draw lots; **~ parti de** to take advantage of; **~ profit de** to profit from; **~ les cartes** to read ou tell the cards

tiret [tiRɛ] nm dash

tireur [tiRœR] nm gunman; **~ d'élite** marksman

tiroir [tiRwaR] nm drawer; **tiroir-caisse** nm till

tisane [tizan] nf herb tea

tisser [tise] /1/ vt to weave

tissu [tisy] nm fabric, material, cloth no pl; (Anat, Bio) tissue; **tissu-éponge** nm (terry) towelling no pl

titre [titR] nm (gén) title; (de journal) headline; (diplôme) qualification; (Comm) security; **en ~** (champion, responsable) official; **à juste ~** rightly; **à quel ~?** on what grounds?; **à aucun ~** on no account; **au même ~ (que)** in the same way (as); **à ~ d'information** for (your) information; **à ~ gracieux** free of charge; **à ~ d'essai** on a trial basis; **à ~ privé** in a private capacity; **~ de propriété** title deed; **~ de transport** ticket

tituber [titybe] /1/ vi to stagger ou reel (along)

titulaire [titylɛR] adj (Admin) with tenure ▷ nm/f (de permis) holder; **être ~ de** (diplôme, permis) to hold

toast [tost] nm slice ou piece of toast; (de bienvenue) (welcoming) toast; **porter un ~ à qn** to propose ou drink a toast to sb

t

toboggan [tɔbɔgɑ̃] nm slide; (Auto) flyover

toc [tɔk] nm: **en toc** imitation cpd
▷ excl: **toc, toc** knock knock

tocsin [tɔksɛ̃] nm alarm (bell)

tohu-bohu [tɔybɔy] nm commotion

toi [twa] pron you

toile [twal] nf (tableau) canvas; **de** ou **en ~** (pantalon) cotton; (sac) canvas; **~ d'araignée** cobweb; **la T~** (Internet) the Web; **~ cirée** oilcloth; **~ de fond** (fig) backdrop

toilette [twalɛt] nf (habits) outfit; **toilettes** nfpl toilet sg; **faire sa ~** to have a wash, get washed; **articles de ~** toiletries

toi-même [twamɛm] pron yourself

toit [twa] nm roof; **~ ouvrant** sun roof

toiture [twatyR] nf roof

Tokyo [tɔkjo] n Tokyo

tôle [tol] nf (plaque) steel (ou iron) sheet; **~ ondulée** corrugated iron

tolérable [tɔleRabl] adj tolerable

tolérant, e [tɔleRɑ̃, -ɑ̃t] adj tolerant

tolérer [tɔleRe] /6/ vt to tolerate; (Admin: hors taxe etc) to allow

tollé [tɔle] nm: **un ~ (de protestations)** a general outcry

tomate [tɔmat] nf tomato; **~s farcies** stuffed tomatoes

tombe [tɔ̃b] nf (sépulture) grave; (avec monument) tomb

tombeau, x [tɔ̃bo] nm tomb

tombée [tɔ̃be] nf: **à la ~ du jour** ou **de la nuit** at nightfall

tomber [tɔ̃be] /1/ vi to fall; (fièvre, vent) to drop ▷ vt: **laisser ~** (objet) to drop; (personne) to let down; (activité) to give up; **laisse ~!** forget it!; **faire ~** to knock over; **~ sur** (rencontrer) to come across; **~ de fatigue/sommeil** to drop from exhaustion/be falling asleep on one's feet; **~ à l'eau** (projet etc) to fall through; **~ en panne** to break down; **~ en ruine** to fall into ruins; **ça tombe bien/mal** (fig) that's come at the right/wrong time; **il est bien/mal tombé** (fig) he's been lucky/unlucky

tombola [tɔ̃bɔla] nf raffle

tome [tɔm] nm volume

ton¹, ta (pl **tes**) [tɔ̃, ta, te] adj poss your

ton² [tɔ̃] nm (gén) tone; (couleur) shade, tone; **de bon ~** in good taste

tonalité [tɔnalite] nf (au téléphone) dialling tone

tondeuse [tɔ̃døz] nf (à gazon) (lawn) mower; (du coiffeur) clippers pl; (pour la tonte) shears pl

tondre [tɔ̃dR] /41/ vt (pelouse, herbe) to mow; (haie) to cut, clip; (mouton, toison) to shear; (cheveux) to crop

tongs [tɔ̃g] nfpl flip-flops

tonifier [tɔnifje] /7/ vt (peau, organisme) to tone up

tonique [tɔnik] adj fortifying ▷ nm tonic

tonne [tɔn] nf metric ton, tonne

tonneau, x [tɔno] nm (à vin, cidre) barrel; **faire des ~x** (voiture, avion) to roll over

tonnelle [tɔnɛl] nf bower, arbour

tonner [tɔne] /1/ vi to thunder; **il tonne** it is thundering, there's some thunder

tonnerre [tɔnɛR] nm thunder

tonus [tɔnys] nm energy

top [tɔp] nm: **au troisième ~** at the third stroke ▷ adj: **~ secret** top secret

topinambour [tɔpinɑ̃buR] nm Jerusalem artichoke

torche [tɔRʃ] nf torch

torchon [tɔRʃɔ̃] nm cloth; (à vaisselle) tea towel ou cloth

tordre [tɔRdR] /41/ vt (chiffon) to wring; (barre, fig: visage) to twist; **se tordre** vi; **se ~ le poignet/la cheville** to twist one's wrist/ankle; **se ~ de douleur/rire** to writhe in pain/be doubled up with laughter; **tordu, e** adj (fig) twisted; (fig) crazy

tornade [tɔRnad] nf tornado

torrent [tɔRɑ̃] nm mountain stream

torsade [tɔʀsad] *nf*: **un pull à ~s** a cable sweater

torse [tɔʀs] *nm* chest; (*Anat, Sculpture*) torso; **~ nu** stripped to the waist

tort [tɔʀ] *nm* (*défaut*) fault; **torts** *nmpl* (*Jur*) fault *sg*; **avoir ~** to be wrong; **être dans son ~** to be in the wrong; **donner ~ à qn** to lay the blame on sb; **causer du ~ à** to harm; **à ~** wrongly; **à ~ et à travers** wildly

torticolis [tɔʀtikɔli] *nm* stiff neck

tortiller [tɔʀtije] /1/ *vt* to twist; (*moustache*) to twirl; **se tortiller** *vi* to wriggle; (*en dansant*) to wiggle

tortionnaire [tɔʀsjɔnɛʀ] *nm* torturer

tortue [tɔʀty] *nf* tortoise; (*d'eau douce*) terrapin; (*d'eau de mer*) turtle

tortueux, -euse [tɔʀtɥø, -øz] *adj* (*rue*) twisting; (*fig*) tortuous

torture [tɔʀtyʀ] *nf* torture; **torturer** /1/ *vt* to torture; (*fig*) to torment

tôt [to] *adv* early; **~ ou tard** sooner or later; **si ~** so early; (*déjà*) so soon; **au plus ~** at the earliest; **plus ~** earlier

total, e, -aux [tɔtal, -o] *adj, nm* total; **au ~** in total *ou* all; (*fig*) on the whole; **faire le ~** to work out the total; **totalement** *adv* totally; **totaliser** /1/ *vt* to total (up); **totalitaire** *adj* totalitarian; **totalité** *nf*: **la totalité de: la totalité des élèves** all (of) the pupils; **la totalité de la population/classe** the whole population/class; **en totalité** entirely

toubib [tubib] *nm* (*fam*) doctor

touchant, e [tuʃɑ̃, -ɑ̃t] *adj* touching

touche [tuʃ] *nf* (*de piano, de machine à écrire*) key; (*de téléphone*) button; (*Peinture etc*) stroke, touch; (*fig: de couleur, nostalgie*) touch; (*Football: aussi*: **remise en ~**) throw-in; (*aussi*: **ligne de ~**) touch-line; (*Escrime*) hit; **~ dièse** (*de téléphone, clavier*) hash key

toucher [tuʃe] /1/ *nm* touch ▷ *vt* to touch; (*palper*) to feel; (*atteindre: d'un coup de feu etc*) to hit; (*concerner*) to concern, affect; (*contacter*) to reach, contact; (*recevoir: récompense*) to receive, get; (: *salaire*) to draw, get; (*chèque*) to cash; (*aborder: problème, sujet*) to touch on; **au ~** to the touch; **~ à** to touch; (*traiter de, concerner*) to have to do with, concern; **je vais lui en ~ un mot** I'll have a word with him about it; **~ au but** (*fig*) to near one's goal; **~ à sa fin** to be drawing to a close

touffe [tuf] *nf* tuft

touffu, e [tufy] *adj* thick, dense

toujours [tuʒuʀ] *adv* always; (*encore*) still; (*constamment*) forever; **essaie ~** (you can) try anyway; **pour ~** forever; **~ est-il que** the fact remains that; **~ plus** more and more

toupie [tupi] *nf* (spinning) top

tour [tuʀ] *nf* tower; (*immeuble*) high-rise block (BRIT) *ou* building (US); (*Échecs*) castle, rook ▷ *nm* (*excursion: à pied*) stroll, walk; (: *en voiture etc*) run, ride; (: *plus long*) trip; (*Sport: aussi*: **~ de piste**) lap; (*d'être servi ou de jouer etc*) turn; (*de roue etc*) revolution; (*Pol: aussi*: **~ de scrutin**) ballot; (*ruse, de prestidigitation, de cartes*) trick; (*de potier*) wheel; (*à bois, métaux*) lathe; (*circonférence*): **de 3 m de ~** 3 m round, with a circumference *ou* girth of 3 m; **faire le ~ de** to go (a)round; (*à pied*) to walk (a)round; **faire un ~** to go for a walk; **c'est au ~ de Renée** it's Renée's turn; **à ~ de rôle, ~ à ~** in turn; **~ de taille/tête** *nm* waist/head measurement; **~ de chant** *nm* song recital; **~ de contrôle** *nf* control tower; **la ~ Eiffel** the Eiffel Tower; **le T~ de France** the Tour de France; **~ de force** *nm* tour de force; **~ de garde** *nm* spell of duty; **un 33 ~s** an LP; **un 45 ~s** a single; **~ d'horizon** *nm* (*fig*) general survey

tourbe [tuʀb] *nf* peat

tourbillon [tuʀbijɔ̃] *nm* whirlwind; (*d'eau*) whirlpool; (*fig*) whirl, swirl;

tourbillonner /1/ *vi* to whirl *ou* twirl round
tourelle [tuʀɛl] *nf* turret
tourisme [tuʀism] *nm* tourism; **agence de ~** tourist agency; **faire du ~** to go touring; (*en ville*) to go sightseeing; **touriste** *nm/f* tourist; **touristique** *adj* tourist *cpd*; (*région*) touristic (*péj*)
tourment [tuʀmɑ̃] *nm* torment; **tourmenter** /1/ *vt* to torment; **se tourmenter** to fret, worry o.s.
tournage [tuʀnaʒ] *nm* (*d'un film*) shooting
tournant, e [tuʀnɑ̃, -ɑ̃t] *adj* (*feu, scène*) revolving ▷ *nm* (*de route*) bend ; (*fig*) turning point
tournée [tuʀne] *nf* (*du facteur etc*) round; (*d'artiste, politicien*) tour; (*au café*) round (of drinks)
tourner [tuʀne] /1/ *vt* to turn; (*sauce, mélange*) to stir; (*Ciné: faire les prises de vues*) to shoot; (: *produire*) to make ▷ *vi* to turn; (*moteur*) to run; (*compteur*) to tick away; (*lait etc*) to turn (sour); **se tourner** *vi* to turn (a)round; **se ~ vers** to turn to; to turn towards; **mal ~** to go wrong; **~ autour de** to go (a)round; (*péj*) to hang (a)round; **~ à/en** to turn into; **~ en ridicule** to ridicule; **~ le dos à** (*mouvement*) to turn one's back on; (*position*) to have one's back to; **se ~ les pouces** to twiddle one's thumbs; **~ de l'œil** to pass out
tournesol [tuʀnəsɔl] *nm* sunflower
tournevis [tuʀnəvis] *nm* screwdriver
tournoi [tuʀnwa] *nm* tournament
tournure [tuʀnyʀ] *nf* (*Ling*) turn of phrase; **la ~ de qch** (*évolution*) the way sth is developing; **~ d'esprit** turn *ou* cast of mind
tourte [tuʀt] *nf* pie
tourterelle [tuʀtəʀɛl] *nf* turtledove
tous [tu, tus] *adj, pron voir* **tout**
Toussaint [tusɛ̃] *nf*: **la ~** All Saints' Day

tousser [tuse] /1/ *vi* to cough

MOT-CLÉ

tout, e (*mpl* **tous**, *fpl* **toutes**) [tu, tut, tus, tut] *adj* **1** (*avec article singulier*) all; **tout le lait** all the milk; **toute la nuit** all night, the whole night; **tout le livre** the whole book; **tout un pain** a whole loaf; **tout le temps** all the time, the whole time; **c'est tout le contraire** it's quite the opposite
2 (*avec article pluriel*) every; all; **tous les livres** all the books; **toutes les nuits** every night; **toutes les fois** every time; **toutes les trois/ deux semaines** every third/other *ou* second week, every three/two weeks; **tous les deux** both *ou* each of us (*ou* them *ou* you); **toutes les trois** all three of us (*ou* them *ou* you)
3 (*sans article*) **à tout âge** at any age; **pour toute nourriture, il avait ...** his only food was ...
▶ *pron* everything, all; **il a tout fait** he's done everything; **je les vois tous** I can see them all *ou* all of them; **nous y sommes tous allés** all of us went, we all went; **c'est tout** that's all; **en tout** in all; **tout ce qu'il sait** all he knows
▶ *nm* whole; **le tout** all of it (*ou* them); **le tout est de ...** the main thing is to ...; **pas du tout** not at all
▶ *adv* **1** (*très, complètement*) very; **tout près** *ou* **à côté** very near; **le tout premier** the very first; **tout seul** all alone; **le livre tout entier** the whole book; **tout en haut** right at the top; **tout droit** straight ahead

2: **tout en** while; **tout en travaillant** while working, as he *etc* works
3: **tout d'abord** first of all; **tout à coup** suddenly; **tout à fait** absolutely; **tout à l'heure** a short while ago; (*futur*) in a short while, shortly; **à tout à l'heure!** see you later!; **tout de même** all the same; **tout le monde** everybody; **tout simplement** quite simply; **tout de suite** immediately, straight away

toutefois [tutfwa] *adv* however
toutes [tut] *adj, pron voir* **tout**
tout-terrain [tuterɛ̃] *adj*: **vélo ~** mountain bike; **véhicule ~** four-wheel drive
toux [tu] *nf* cough
toxicomane [tɔksikɔman] *nm/f* drug addict
toxique [tɔksik] *adj* toxic
trac [tʀak] *nm* (*aux examens*) nerves *pl*; (*Théât*) stage fright; **avoir le ~** (*aux examens*) to get an attack of nerves; (*Théât*) to have stage fright
tracasser [tʀakase] /1/ *vt* to worry, bother; **se tracasser** to worry (o.s.)
trace [tʀas] *nf* (*empreintes*) tracks *pl*; (*marques, fig*) mark; (*restes, vestige*) trace; **~s de pas** footprints
tracer [tʀase] /3/ *vt* to draw; (*piste*) to open up
tract [tʀakt] *nm* tract, pamphlet
tracteur [tʀaktœʀ] *nm* tractor
traction [tʀaksjɔ̃] *nf*: **~ avant/arrière** front-wheel/rear-wheel drive
tradition [tʀadisjɔ̃] *nf* tradition; **traditionnel, le** *adj* traditional
traducteur, -trice [tʀadyktœʀ, -tʀis] *nm/f* translator
traduction [tʀadyksjɔ̃] *nf* translation
traduire [tʀadɥiʀ] /38/ *vt* to translate; (*exprimer*) to convey; **~ en français** to translate into French; **~ en justice** to bring before the courts
trafic [tʀafik] *nm* traffic; **~ d'armes** arms dealing; **trafiquant, e** *nm/f*

trafficker; (*d'armes*) dealer; **trafiquer** /1/ *vt* (*péj: vin*) to doctor; (: *moteur, document*) to tamper with
tragédie [tʀaʒedi] *nf* tragedy; **tragique** *adj* tragic
trahir [tʀaiʀ] /2/ *vt* to betray; **trahison** *nf* betrayal; (*Jur*) treason
train [tʀɛ̃] *nm* (*Rail*) train; (*allure*) pace; **être en ~ de faire qch** to be doing sth; **~ à grande vitesse** high-speed train; **~ d'atterrissage** undercarriage; **~ électrique** (*jouet*) (electric) train set; **~ de vie** style of living
traîne [tʀɛn] *nf* (*de robe*) train; **être à la ~** to lag behind
traîneau, x [tʀɛno] *nm* sleigh, sledge
traîner [tʀene] /1/ *vt* (*remorque*) to pull; (*enfant, chien*) to drag ou trail along ▷ *vi* (*robe, manteau*) to trail; (*être en désordre*) to lie around; (*marcher lentement*) to dawdle (along); (*vagabonder*) to hang about; (*durer*) to drag on; **se traîner** *vi*: **se ~ par terre** to crawl (on the ground); **~ les pieds** to drag one's feet
train-train [tʀɛ̃tʀɛ̃] *nm* humdrum routine
traire [tʀɛʀ] /50/ *vt* to milk
trait, e [tʀɛ, -ɛt] *nm* (*ligne*) line; (*de dessin*) stroke; (*caractéristique*) feature, trait; **traits** *nmpl* (*du visage*) features; **d'un ~** (*boire*) in one gulp; **de ~** (*animal*) draught ; **avoir ~ à** to concern; **~ d'union** hyphen
traitant, e [tʀɛtɑ̃, -ɑ̃t] *adj*: **votre médecin ~** your usual ou family doctor; **shampooing ~** medicated shampoo
traite [tʀɛt] *nf* (*Comm*) draft; (*Agr*) milking; **d'une (seule) ~** without stopping (once)
traité [tʀete] *nm* treaty
traitement [tʀɛtmɑ̃] *nm* treatment; (*salaire*) salary; **~ de données** ou **de l'information** data processing; **~ de texte** word processing; (*logiciel*) word processing package

traiter [tʀete] /1/ vt to treat;
(qualifier): ~ **qn d'idiot** to call sb a fool
▷ vi to deal; ~ **de** to deal with

traiteur [tʀetœʀ] nm caterer

traître, -esse [tʀetʀ, -tʀes] adj
(dangereux) treacherous ▷ nm/f
traitor (traitress)

trajectoire [tʀaʒektwaʀ] nf path

trajet [tʀaʒe] nm (parcours, voyage)
journey; (itinéraire) route; (distance à
parcourir) distance; **il y a une heure
de ~** the journey takes one hour

trampoline [tʀɑ̃pɔlin] nm
trampoline

tramway [tʀamwɛ] nm tram(way);
(voiture) tram(car) (BRIT), streetcar
(US)

tranchant, e [tʀɑ̃ʃɑ̃, -ɑ̃t] adj sharp;
(fig) peremptory ▷ nm (d'un couteau)
cutting edge; (de la main) edge; **à
double ~** double-edged

tranche [tʀɑ̃ʃ] nf (morceau) slice;
(arête) edge; ~ **d'âge/de salaires**
age/wage bracket

tranché, e [tʀɑ̃ʃe] adj (couleurs)
distinct; (opinions) clear-cut

trancher [tʀɑ̃ʃe] /1/ vt to cut, sever
▷ vi to be decisive; ~ **avec** to contrast
sharply with

tranquille [tʀɑ̃kil] adj quiet; (rassuré)
easy in one's mind, with one's mind
at rest; **se tenir ~** (enfant) to be
quiet; **avoir la conscience ~** to have
an easy conscience; **laisse-moi/
laisse-ça ~** leave me/it alone;
tranquillisant nm tranquillizer;
tranquillité nf peace (and quiet);
tranquillité d'esprit peace of mind

transférer [tʀɑ̃sfeʀe] /6/ vt to
transfer; **transfert** nm transfer

transformation [tʀɑ̃sfɔʀmasjɔ̃]
nf change, alteration; (radicale)
transformation; (Rugby) conversion;
transformations nfpl (travaux)
alterations

transformer [tʀɑ̃sfɔʀme] /1/ vt to
change; (radicalement) to transform;
(vêtement) alter; (matière première,
appartement, Rugby) to convert; ~ **en**
to turn into

transfusion [tʀɑ̃sfyzjɔ̃] nf:
~ **sanguine** blood transfusion

transgénique [tʀɑ̃sʒenik] adj
transgenic

transgresser [tʀɑ̃sgʀese] /1/ vt to
contravene

transi, e [tʀɑ̃zi] adj numb (with
cold), chilled to the bone

transiger [tʀɑ̃ziʒe] /3/ vi to
compromise

transit [tʀɑ̃zit] nm transit; **transiter**
/1/ vi to pass in transit

transition [tʀɑ̃zisjɔ̃] nf transition;
transitoire adj transitional

transmettre [tʀɑ̃smɛtʀ] /56/ vt
(passer): ~ **qch à qn** to pass sth on to
sb; (Tech, Tél, Méd) to transmit; (TV,
Radio: retransmettre) to broadcast;
transmission nf transmission

transparent, e [tʀɑ̃spaʀɑ̃, -ɑ̃t] adj
transparent

transpercer [tʀɑ̃spɛʀse] /3/ vt (froid,
pluie) to go through, pierce; (balle) to
go through

transpiration [tʀɑ̃spiʀasjɔ̃] nf
perspiration

transpirer [tʀɑ̃spiʀe] /1/ vi to
perspire

transplanter [tʀɑ̃splɑ̃te] /1/ vt
(Méd, Bot) to transplant

transport [tʀɑ̃spɔʀ] nm transport;
~**s en commun** public transport
sg; **transporter** /1/ vt to carry,
move; (Comm) to transport,
convey; **transporteur** nm haulage
contractor (BRIT), trucker (US)

transvaser [tʀɑ̃svaze] /1/ vt to
decant

transversal, e, -aux [tʀɑ̃svɛʀsal,
-o] adj (mur, chemin, rue) running at
right angles; **coupe ~e** cross section

trapèze [tʀapɛz] nm (au cirque)
trapeze

trappe [tʀap] nf trap door

trapu, e [tʀapy] adj squat, stocky

traquenard [tʀaknaʀ] nm trap

traquer [tʀake] /1/ vt to track down; (harceler) to hound

traumatiser [tʀomatize] /1/ vt to traumatize

travail, -aux [tʀavaj, -o] nm (gén) work; (tâche, métier) work no pl, job; (Écon, Méd) labour; **travaux** nmpl (de réparation, agricoles etc) work sg; (sur route) roadworks; (de construction) building (work) sg; **être sans ~** (employé) to be out of work; **~ (au) noir** moonlighting; **travaux des champs** farmwork sg; **travaux dirigés** (Scol) supervised practical work sg; **travaux forcés** hard labour sg; **travaux manuels** (Scol) handicrafts; **travaux ménagers** housework sg; **travaux pratiques** (gén) practical work sg; (en laboratoire) lab work sg

travailler [tʀavaje] /1/ vi to work; (bois) to warp ▷ vt (bois, métal) to work; (objet d'art, discipline) to work on; **cela le travaille** it is on his mind; **travailleur, -euse** adj hard-working ▷ nm/f worker; **travailleur social** social worker; **travailliste** adj ≈ Labour cpd

travaux [tʀavo] nmpl voir **travail**

travers [tʀavɛʀ] nm fault, failing; **en ~ (de)** across; **au ~ (de)** through; **de ~** (nez, bouche) crooked; (chapeau) askew; **à ~** through; **regarder de ~** (fig) to look askance at; **comprendre de ~** to misunderstand

traverse [tʀavɛʀs] nf (de voie ferrée) sleeper; **chemin de ~** shortcut

traversée [tʀavɛʀse] nf crossing

traverser [tʀavɛʀse] /1/ vt (gén) to cross; (ville, tunnel, aussi percer, fig) to go through; (ligne, trait) to run across

traversin [tʀavɛʀsɛ̃] nm bolster

travesti [tʀavɛsti] nm transvestite

trébucher [tʀebyʃe] /1/ vi: **~ (sur)** to stumble (over), trip (over)

trèfle [tʀɛfl] nm (Bot) clover; (Cartes: couleur) clubs pl; (: carte) club; **~ à quatre feuilles** four-leaf clover

treize [tʀɛz] num thirteen; **treizième** num thirteenth

tréma [tʀema] nm diaeresis

tremblement [tʀɑ̃bləmɑ̃] nm: **~ de terre** earthquake

trembler [tʀɑ̃ble] /1/ vi to tremble, shake; **~ de** (froid, fièvre) to shiver ou tremble with; (peur) to shake ou tremble with; **~ pour qn** to fear for sb

trémousser [tʀemuse] /1/: **se trémousser** vi to jig about, wriggle about

trempé, e [tʀɑ̃pe] adj soaking (wet), drenched; (Tech): **acier ~** tempered steel

tremper [tʀɑ̃pe] /1/ vt to soak, drench; (aussi: **faire ~, mettre à ~**) to soak ▷ vi to soak; (fig): **~ dans** to be involved ou have a hand in; **se tremper** vi to have a quick dip

tremplin [tʀɑ̃plɛ̃] nm springboard; (Ski) ski jump

trentaine [tʀɑ̃tɛn] nf (âge): **avoir la ~** to be around thirty; **une ~ (de)** thirty or so, about thirty

trente [tʀɑ̃t] num thirty; **être/ se mettre sur son ~ et un** to be wearing/put on one's Sunday best; **trentième** num thirtieth

trépidant, e [tʀepidɑ̃, -ɑ̃t] adj (fig: rythme) pulsating; (: vie) hectic

trépigner [tʀepiɲe] /1/ vi to stamp (one's feet)

très [tʀɛ] adv very; **~ beau/bien** very beautiful/well; **~ critiqué** much criticized; **~ industrialisé** highly industrialized

trésor [tʀezɔʀ] nm treasure; **~ (public)** public revenue; **trésorerie** nf (gestion) accounts pl; (bureaux) accounts department; **difficultés de trésorerie** cash problems, shortage of cash ou funds; **trésorier, -ière** nm/f treasurer

tressaillir [tʀesajiʀ] /13/ vi to shiver, shudder

t

tressauter [tʀesote] /1/ vi to start, jump

tresse [tʀɛs] nf braid, plait; **tresser** /1/ vt (cheveux) to braid, plait; (fil, jonc) to plait; (corbeille) to weave; (corde) to twist

tréteau, x [tʀeto] nm trestle

treuil [tʀœj] nm winch

trêve [tʀɛv] nf (Mil, Pol) truce; (fig) respite; **~ de ...** enough of this ...

tri [tʀi] nm: **faire le ~ (de)** to sort out; **le (bureau de) ~** (Postes) the sorting office

triangle [tʀijɑ̃gl] nm triangle; **triangulaire** adj triangular

tribord [tʀibɔʀ] nm: **à ~** to starboard, on the starboard side

tribu [tʀiby] nf tribe

tribunal, -aux [tʀibynal, -o] nm (Jur) court; (Mil) tribunal

tribune [tʀibyn] nf (estrade) platform, rostrum; (débat) forum; (d'église, de tribunal) gallery; (de stade) stand

tribut [tʀiby] nm tribute

tributaire [tʀibytɛʀ] adj: **être ~ de** to be dependent on

tricher [tʀiʃe] /1/ vi to cheat; **tricheur, -euse** nm/f cheat

tricolore [tʀikɔlɔʀ] adj three-coloured ; (français) red, white and blue

tricot [tʀiko] nm (technique, ouvrage) knitting no pl; (vêtement) jersey, sweater; **~ de corps, ~ de peau** vest ; **tricoter** /1/ vt to knit

tricycle [tʀisikl] nm tricycle

trier [tʀije] /7/ vt to sort (out); (Postes, Inform, fruits) to sort

trimestre [tʀimɛstʀ] nm (Scol) term; (Comm) quarter; **trimestriel, le** adj quarterly; (Scol) end-of-term

trinquer [tʀɛ̃ke] /1/ vi to clink glasses

triomphe [tʀijɔ̃f] nm triumph; **triompher** /1/ vi to triumph, win; **triompher de** to triumph over, overcome

tripes [tʀip] nfpl (Culin) tripe sg

triple [tʀipl] adj triple ▷ nm: **le ~ (de)** (comparaison) three times as much (as); **en ~ exemplaire** in triplicate; **tripler** /1/ vi, vt to triple, treble

triplés, -ées [tʀiple] nm/f pl triplets

tripoter [tʀipɔte] /1/ vt to fiddle with

triste [tʀist] adj sad; (couleur, temps, journée) dreary; (péj): **~ personnage/ affaire** sorry individual/affair; **tristesse** nf sadness

trivial, e, -aux [tʀivjal, -o] adj coarse, crude; (commun) mundane

troc [tʀɔk] nm barter

trognon [tʀɔɲɔ̃] nm (de fruit) core; (de légume) stalk

trois [tʀwa] num three; **troisième** num third ▷ nf (Scol) year 10 (BRIT), ninth grade (US); **le troisième âge** (période de vie) one's retirement years; (personnes âgées) senior citizens pl

trombe [tʀɔ̃b] nf: **des ~s d'eau** a downpour; **en ~** like a whirlwind

trombone [tʀɔ̃bɔn] nm (Mus) trombone; (de bureau) paper clip

trompe [tʀɔ̃p] nf (d'éléphant) trunk; (Mus) trumpet, horn

tromper [tʀɔ̃pe] /1/ vt to deceive; (vigilance, poursuivants) to elude; **se tromper** vi to make a mistake, be mistaken; **se ~ de voiture/jour** to take the wrong car/get the day wrong; **se ~ de 3 cm/20 euros** to be out by 3 cm/20 euros

trompette [tʀɔ̃pɛt] nf trumpet; **en ~** (nez) turned-up

trompeur, -euse [tʀɔ̃pœʀ, -øz] adj deceptive

tronc [tʀɔ̃] nm (Bot, Anat) trunk; (d'église) collection box

tronçon [tʀɔ̃sɔ̃] nm section; **tronçonner** /1/ vt to saw up; **tronçonneuse** nf chainsaw

trône [tʀon] nm throne

trop [tʀo] adv too; (avec verbe) too much; (aussi: **~ nombreux**) too many; (aussi: **~ souvent**) too often; **~ peu (nombreux)** too few; **~ longtemps** (for) too long; **~ de**

(*nombre*) too many; (*quantité*) too much; **de ~, en ~: des livres en ~** a few books too many; **du lait en ~** too much milk; **trois livres/cinq euros de ~** three books too many/five euros too much; **ça coûte ~ cher** it's too expensive

tropical, e, -aux [tʀɔpikal, -o] *adj* tropical

tropique [tʀɔpik] *nm* tropic

trop-plein [tʀɔplɛ̃] *nm* (*tuyau*) overflow *ou* outlet (pipe); (*liquide*) overflow

troquer [tʀɔke] /1/ *vt*: **~ qch contre** to barter *ou* trade sth for; (*fig*) to swap sth for

trot [tʀo] *nm* trot; **trotter**/1/ *vi* to trot

trottinette [tʀɔtinɛt] *nf* (child's) scooter

trottoir [tʀɔtwaʀ] *nm* pavement (BRIT), sidewalk (US); **faire le ~** (*péj*) to walk the streets; **~ roulant** moving walkway, travelator

trou [tʀu] *nm* hole; (*fig*) gap; (*Comm*) deficit; **~ d'air** air pocket; **~ de mémoire** blank, lapse of memory

troublant, e [tʀublɑ̃, -ɑ̃t] *adj* disturbing

trouble [tʀubl] *adj* (*liquide*) cloudy; (*image, photo*) blurred; (*affaire*) shady, murky ▷ *adv*: **voir ~** to have blurred vision ▷ *nm* agitation; **troubles** *nmpl* (*Pol*) disturbances, troubles, unrest *sg*; (*Méd*) trouble *sg*, disorders; **trouble-fête** *nm/f inv* spoilsport

troubler [tʀuble] /1/ *vt* to disturb; (*liquide*) to make cloudy; (*intriguer*) to bother; **se troubler** *vi* (*personne*) to become flustered *ou* confused

trouer [tʀue] /1/ *vt* to make a hole (*ou* holes) in

trouille [tʀuj] *nf* (*fam*): **avoir la ~** to be scared stiff

troupe [tʀup] *nf* troop; **~ (de théâtre)** (theatrical) company

troupeau, x [tʀupo] *nm* (*de moutons*) flock; (*de vaches*) herd

trousse [tʀus] *nf* case, kit; (*d'écolier*) pencil case; **aux ~s de** (*fig*) on the heels *ou* tail of; **~ à outils** toolkit; **~ de toilette** toilet bag

trousseau, x [tʀuso] *nm* (*de mariée*) trousseau; **~ de clefs** bunch of keys

trouvaille [tʀuvaj] *nf* find

trouver [tʀuve] /1/ *vt* to find; (*rendre visite*): **aller/venir ~ qn** to go/come and see sb; **se trouver** *vi* (*être*) to be; **je trouve que** I find *ou* think that; **~ à boire/critiquer** to find something to drink/criticize; **se ~ mal** to pass out

truand [tʀyɑ̃] *nm* villain; **truander** /1/ *vt*: **se faire truander** to be swindled

truc [tʀyk] *nm* (*astuce*) way; (*de cinéma, prestidigitateur*) trick effect; (*chose*) thing; thingumajig; **avoir le ~** to have the knack; **c'est pas son (*ou* mon *etc*) ~** (*fam*) it's not really his (*ou* my *etc*) thing

truffe [tʀyf] *nf* truffle; (*nez*) nose

truffé, e [tʀyfe] *adj* (*Culin*) garnished with truffles

truie [tʀɥi] *nf* sow

truite [tʀɥit] *nf* trout *inv*

truquage [tʀykaʒ] *nm* special effects *pl*

truquer [tʀyke] /1/ *vt* (*élections, serrure, dés*) to fix

TSVP *abr* (= *tournez s'il vous plaît*) PTO

TTC *abr* (= *toutes taxes comprises*) inclusive of tax

tu¹ [ty] *pron* you ▷ *nm*: **employer le tu** to use the "tu" form

tu², e [ty] *pp de* **taire**

tuba [tyba] *nm* (*Mus*) tuba; (*Sport*) snorkel

tube [tyb] *nm* tube; (*chanson, disque*) hit song *ou* record

tuberculose [tybɛʀkyloz] *nf* tuberculosis

tuer [tɥe] /1/ *vt* to kill; **se tuer** (*se suicider*) to kill o.s.; (*dans un accident*) to be killed; **se ~ au travail** (*fig*) to work o.s. to death; **tuerie** *nf* slaughter *no pl*

tue-tête [tytɛt]: **à ~** adv at the top of one's voice

tueur [tɥœʀ] nm killer; **~ à gages** hired killer

tuile [tɥil] nf tile; (fam) spot of bad luck, blow

tulipe [tylip] nf tulip

tuméfié, e [tymefje] adj puffy, swollen

tumeur [tymœʀ] nf growth, tumour

tumulte [tymylt] nm commotion; **tumultueux, -euse** adj stormy, turbulent

tunique [tynik] nf tunic

Tunis [tynis] n Tunis

Tunisie [tynizi] nf: **la ~** Tunisia; **tunisien, ne** adj Tunisian ▷ nm/f: **Tunisien, ne** Tunisian

tunnel [tynɛl] nm tunnel; **le ~ sous la Manche** the Channel Tunnel

turbulent, e [tyʀbylɑ̃, -ɑ̃t] adj boisterous, unruly

turc, turque [tyʀk] adj Turkish ▷ nm (Ling) Turkish ▷ nm/f: **Turc, Turque** Turk/Turkish woman

turf [tyʀf] nm racing; **turfiste** nm/f racegoer

Turquie [tyʀki] nf: **la ~** Turkey

turquoise [tyʀkwaz] nf, adj inv turquoise

tutelle [tytɛl] nf (Jur) guardianship; (Pol) trusteeship; **sous la ~ de** (fig) under the supervision of

tuteur, -trice [tytœʀ, -tʀis] nm/f (Jur) guardian; (de plante) stake, support

tutoyer [tytwaje] /8/ vt: **~ qn** to address sb as "tu"

tuyau, x [tɥijo] nm pipe; (flexible) tube; (fam) tip; **~ d'arrosage** hosepipe; **~ d'échappement** exhaust pipe; **tuyauterie** nf piping no pl

TVA sigle f (= taxe à ou sur la valeur ajoutée) VAT

tweet [twit] nm tweet

tympan [tɛ̃pɑ̃] nm (Anat) eardrum

type [tip] nm type; (fam) chap, guy ▷ adj typical, standard

typé, e [tipe] adj ethnic (euphémisme)

typique [tipik] adj typical

tyran [tiʀɑ̃] nm tyrant; **tyrannique** adj tyrannical

tzigane [dzigan] adj gipsy, tzigane

u

ulcère [ylsɛʀ] *nm* ulcer
ultérieur, e [ylterjœʀ] *adj*
later, subsequent; **remis à une
date ~e** postponed to a later
date; **ultérieurement** *adv* later,
subsequently
ultime [yltim] *adj* final

 MOT-CLÉ

un, une [œ̃, yn] *art indéf* a; (*devant
voyelle*) an; **un garçon/vieillard** a
boy/an old man; **une fille** a girl
▶ *pron* one; **l'un des meilleurs**
one of the best; **l'un ..., l'autre**
(the) one ..., the other; **les uns ...,
les autres** some ..., others; **l'un
et l'autre** both (of them); **l'un ou
l'autre** either (of them); **l'un l'autre,
les uns les autres** each other, one
another; **pas un seul** not a single
one; **un par un** one by one
▶ *num* one; **une pomme seulement**

one apple only, just one apple
▶ *nf*: **la une** (*Presse*) the front page

unanime [ynanim] *adj* unanimous;
unanimité *nf*: **à l'unanimité**
unanimously
uni, e [yni] *adj* (*ton, tissu*) plain;
(*surface*) smooth, even; (*famille*)
close(-knit); (*pays*) united
unifier [ynifje] /7/ *vt* to unite, unify
uniforme [ynifɔʀm] *adj* uniform;
(*surface, ton*) even ▷ *nm* uniform;
uniformiser /1/ *vt* (*systèmes*) to
standardize
union [ynjɔ̃] *nf* union; **~ de
consommateurs** consumers'
association; **~ libre: vivre en ~ libre**
(*en concubinage*) to cohabit; **l'U~
européenne** the European Union;
l'U~ soviétique the Soviet Union
unique [ynik] *adj* (*seul*) only;
(*exceptionnel*) unique; **un prix/
système ~** a single price/system;
fils/fille ~ only son/daughter,
only child; **sens ~** one-way street;
uniquement *adv* only, solely; (*juste*)
only, merely
unir [yniʀ] /2/ *vt* (*nations*) to unite;
(*en mariage*) to unite, join together;
s'unir *vi* to unite; (*en mariage*) to be
joined together
unitaire [ynitɛʀ] *adj*: **prix ~** unit price
unité [ynite] *nf* (*harmonie, cohésion*)
unity; (*Math*) unit
univers [ynivɛʀ] *nm* universe;
universel, le *adj* universal
universitaire [ynivɛʀsitɛʀ] *adj*
university *cpd*; (*diplôme, études*)
academic, university *cpd* ▷ *nm/f*
academic
université [ynivɛʀsite] *nf* university
urbain, e [yʀbɛ̃, -ɛn] *adj* urban, city
cpd, town *cpd*; **urbanisme** *nm* town
planning
urgence [yʀʒɑ̃s] *nf* urgency; (*Méd etc*)
emergency; **d'~** *adj* emergency *cpd*
▷ *adv* as a matter of urgency; **service
des ~s** emergency service

urgent, e [yRʒɑ̃, -ɑ̃t] *adj* urgent
urine [yRin] *nf* urine; **urinoir** *nm* (public) urinal
urne [yRn] *nf* (*électorale*) ballot box; (*vase*) urn
urticaire [yRtikɛR] *nf* nettle rash
us [ys] *nmpl*: **us et coutumes** (habits and) customs
usage [yzaʒ] *nm* (*emploi, utilisation*) use; (*coutume*) custom; **à l'~** with use; **à l'~ de** (*pour*) for (use of); **en ~** in use; **hors d'~** out of service; **à ~ interne** (*Méd*) to be taken (internally); **à ~ externe** (*Méd*) for external use only; **usagé, e** *adj* (*usé*) worn; **usager, -ère** *nm/f* user
usé, e [yze] *adj* worn (down *ou* out *ou* away); (*banal: argument etc*) hackneyed
user [yze] /1/ *vt* (*outil*) to wear down; (*vêtement*) to wear out; (*matière*) to wear away; (*consommer: charbon etc*) to use; **s'user** *vi* (*tissu, vêtement*) to wear out; **~ de** (*moyen, procédé*) to use, employ; (*droit*) to exercise
usine [yzin] *nf* factory
usité, e [yzite] *adj* common
ustensile [ystãsil] *nm* implement; **~ de cuisine** kitchen utensil
usuel, le [yzɥɛl] *adj* everyday, common
usure [yzyR] *nf* wear
utérus [yteRys] *nm* uterus, womb
utile [ytil] *adj* useful
utilisation [ytilizasjɔ̃] *nf* use
utiliser [ytilize] /1/ *vt* to use
utilitaire [ytilitɛR] *adj* utilitarian
utilité [ytilite] *nf* usefulness *no pl*; **de peu d'~** of little use *ou* help
utopie [ytɔpi] *nf* utopia

va [va] *vb voir* **aller**
vacance [vakãs] *nf* (*Admin*) vacancy; **vacances** *nfpl* holiday(s) *pl* (BRIT), vacation *sg* (US); **les grandes ~s** the summer holidays *ou* vacation; **prendre des/ses ~s** to take a holiday *ou* vacation/ one's holiday(s) *ou* vacation; **aller en ~s** to go on holiday *ou* vacation; **vacancier, -ière** *nm/f* holidaymaker
vacant, e [vakã, -ãt] *adj* vacant
vacarme [vakaRm] *nm* row, din
vaccin [vaksɛ̃] *nm* vaccine; (*opération*) vaccination; **vaccination** *nf* vaccination; **vacciner** /1/ *vt* to vaccinate; **être vacciné** (*fig*) to be immune
vache [vaʃ] *nf* (*Zool*) cow; (*cuir*) cowhide ▷ *adj* (*fam*) rotten, mean; **vachement** *adv* (*fam*) really; **vacherie** *nf* (*action*) dirty trick; (*propos*) nasty remark

vaciller [vasije] /1/ vi to sway, wobble; (bougie, lumière) to flicker; (fig) to be failing, falter

va-et-vient [vaevjɛ̃] nm inv (de personnes, véhicules) comings and goings pl, to-ings and fro-ings pl

vagabond, e [vagabɔ̃, -ɔ̃d] adj wandering ▷ nm (rôdeur) tramp, vagrant; (voyageur) wanderer; **vagabonder** /1/ vi to roam, wander

vagin [vaʒɛ̃] nm vagina

vague [vag] nf wave ▷ adj vague; (regard) faraway; (manteau, robe) loose(-fitting); (quelconque): **un ~ bureau/cousin** some office/cousin or other; **~ de fond** ground swell; **~ de froid** cold spell

vaillant, e [vajɑ̃, -ɑ̃t] adj (courageux) gallant; (robuste) hale and hearty

vain, e [vɛ̃, vɛn] adj vain; **en ~** in vain

vaincre [vɛ̃kʀ] /42/ vt to defeat; (fig) to conquer, overcome; **vaincu, e** nm/f defeated party; **vainqueur** nm victor; (Sport) winner

vaisseau, x [veso] nm (Anat) vessel; (Navig) ship, vessel; **~ spatial** spaceship

vaisselier [vesəlje] nm dresser

vaisselle [vesɛl] nf (service) crockery; (plats etc à laver) (dirty) dishes pl; **faire la ~** to do the washing-up (BRIT) ou the dishes

valable [valabl] adj valid; (acceptable) decent, worthwhile

valet [valɛ] nm valet; (Cartes) jack

valeur [valœʀ] nf (gén) value; (mérite) worth, merit; (Comm: titre) security; **valeurs** nfpl (morales) values; **mettre en ~** (fig) to highlight; to show off to advantage; **avoir de la ~** to be valuable; **prendre de la ~** to go up ou gain in value; **sans ~** worthless

valide [valid] adj (en bonne santé) fit; (valable) valid; **valider** /1/ vt to validate

valise [valiz] nf (suit)case; **faire sa ~** to pack one's (suit)case

vallée [vale] nf valley

vallon [valɔ̃] nm small valley

valoir [valwaʀ] /29/ vi (être valable) to hold, apply ▷ vt (prix, valeur, effort) to be worth; (causer): **~ qch à qn** to earn sb sth; **se valoir** to be of equal merit; (péj) to be two of a kind; **faire ~** (droits, prérogatives) to assert; **se faire ~** to make the most of o.s.; **à ~ sur** to be deducted from; **vaille que vaille** somehow or other; **cela ne me dit rien qui vaille** I don't like the look of it at all; **ce climat ne me vaut rien** this climate doesn't suit me; **~ la peine** to be worth the trouble, be worth it; **~ mieux: il vaut mieux se taire** it's better to say nothing; **ça ne vaut rien** it's worthless; **que vaut ce candidat?** how good is this applicant?

valse [vals] nf waltz

vandalisme [vɑ̃dalism] nm vandalism

vanille [vanij] nf vanilla

vanité [vanite] nf vanity; **vaniteux, -euse** adj vain, conceited

vanne [van] nf gate; (fam) dig

vannerie [vanʀi] nf basketwork

vantard, e [vɑ̃taʀ, -aʀd] adj boastful

vanter [vɑ̃te] /1/ vt to speak highly of, praise; **se vanter** vi to boast, brag; **se ~ de** to pride o.s. on; (péj) to boast of

vapeur [vapœʀ] nf steam; (émanation) vapour, fumes pl; **vapeurs** nfpl (bouffées) vapours; **à ~** steam-powered, steam cpd; **cuit à la ~** steamed; **vaporeux, -euse** adj (flou) hazy, misty; (léger) filmy; **vaporisateur** nm spray; **vaporiser** /1/ vt (parfum etc) to spray

varappe [vaʀap] nf rock climbing

vareuse [vaʀøz] nf (blouson) pea jacket; (d'uniforme) tunic

variable [vaʀjabl] adj variable; (temps, humeur) changeable; (divers: résultats) varied, various

varice [vaʀis] nf varicose vein

varicelle [vaʀisɛl] nf chickenpox

varié, e [vaʁje] *adj* varied; (*divers*) various; **hors-d'œuvre ~s** selection of hors d'œuvres

varier [vaʁje] /7/ *vi* to vary; (*temps, humeur*) to change ▷ *vt* to vary; **variété** *nf* variety; **spectacle de variétés** variety show

variole [vaʁjɔl] *nf* smallpox

Varsovie [vaʁsɔvi] *n* Warsaw

vas [va] *vb voir* **aller**; **~-y!** go on!

vase [vɑz] *nm* vase ▷ *nf* silt, mud; **vaseux, -euse** *adj* silty, muddy; (*fig: confus*) woolly, hazy; (: *fatigué*) peaky

vasistas [vazistɑs] *nm* fanlight

vaste [vast] *adj* vast, immense

vautour [votuʁ] *nm* vulture

vautrer [votʁe] /1/: **se vautrer** *vi*: **se ~ dans** to wallow in; **se ~ sur** to sprawl on

va-vite [vavit]: **à la ~** *adv* in a rush

VDQS *sigle m* (= *vin délimité de qualité supérieure*) *label guaranteeing quality of wine*

veau, x [vo] *nm* (*Zool*) calf; (*Culin*) veal; (*peau*) calfskin

vécu, e [veky] *pp de* **vivre**

vedette [vədɛt] *nf* (*artiste etc*) star; (*canot*) patrol boat; (*police*) launch

végétal, e, -aux [veʒetal, -o] *adj* vegetable ▷ *nm* vegetable, plant; **végétalien, ne** *adj, nm/f* vegan

végétarien, ne [veʒetaʁjɛ̃, -ɛn] *adj, nm/f* vegetarian

végétation [veʒetasjɔ̃] *nf* vegetation; **végétations** *nfpl* (*Méd*) adenoids

véhicule [veikyl] *nm* vehicle; **~ utilitaire** commercial vehicle

veille [vɛj] *nf* (*Psych*) wakefulness; (*jour*): **la ~** the day before; **la ~ au soir** the previous evening; **la ~ de** the day before; **la ~ de Noël** Christmas Eve; **la ~ du jour de l'An** New Year's Eve; **à la ~ de** on the eve of

veillée [veje] *nf* (*soirée*) evening; (*réunion*) evening gathering; **~ (funèbre)** wake

veiller [veje] /1/ *vi* to stay *ou* sit up ▷ *vt* (*malade, mort*) to watch over, sit up with; **~ à** to attend to, see to; **~ à ce que** to make sure that; **~ sur** to keep a watch *ou* an eye on; **veilleur** *nm*: **veilleur de nuit** night watchman; **veilleuse** *nf* (*lampe*) night light; (*Auto*) sidelight; (*flamme*) pilot light

veinard, e [venaʁ, -aʁd] *nm/f* lucky devil

veine [vɛn] *nf* (*Anat, du bois etc*) vein; (*filon*) vein, seam; **avoir de la ~** (*fam*) (*chance*) to be lucky

véliplanchiste [veliplɑ̃ʃist] *nm/f* windsurfer

vélo [velo] *nm* bike, cycle; **faire du ~** to go cycling; **vélomoteur** *nm* moped

velours [v(ə)luʁ] *nm* velvet; **~ côtelé** corduroy; **velouté, e** *adj* velvety ▷ *nm*: **velouté d'asperges/ de tomates** cream of asparagus/ tomato soup

velu, e [vəly] *adj* hairy

vendange [vɑ̃dɑʒ] *nf* (*aussi*: **~s**) grape harvest; **vendanger** /3/ *vi* to harvest the grapes

vendeur, -euse [vɑ̃dœʁ, -øz] *nm/f* shop *ou* sales assistant ▷ *nm* (*Jur*) vendor, seller

vendre [vɑ̃dʁ] /41/ *vt* to sell; **~ qch à qn** to sell sb sth; **"à ~"** "for sale"

vendredi [vɑ̃dʁədi] *nm* Friday; **V~ saint** Good Friday

vénéneux, -euse [venenø, -øz] *adj* poisonous

vénérien, ne [veneʁjɛ̃, -ɛn] *adj* venereal

vengeance [vɑ̃ʒɑs] *nf* vengeance *no pl*, revenge *no pl*

venger [vɑ̃ʒe] /3/ *vt* to avenge; **se venger** *vi* to avenge o.s.; **se ~ de qch** to avenge o.s. for sth; to take one's revenge for sth; **se ~ de qn** to take revenge on sb; **se ~ sur** to take revenge on

venimeux, -euse [vənimø, -øz] *adj*
poisonous, venomous; *(fig: haineux)*
venomous, vicious

venin [vənɛ̃] *nm* venom, poison

venir [v(ə)niʀ] /22/ *vi* to come; **~ de**
to come from; **~ de faire: je viens
d'y aller/de le voir** I've just been
there/seen him; **s'il vient à pleuvoir**
if it should rain; **où veux-tu en ~?**
what are you getting at?; **faire ~**
(docteur, plombier) to call (out)

vent [vɑ̃] *nm* wind; **il y a du ~** it's
windy; **c'est du ~** it's all hot air; **dans
le ~** *(fam)* trendy

vente [vɑ̃t] *nf* sale; **la ~** *(activité)*
selling; *(secteur)* sales *pl*; **mettre en
~** to put on sale; *(objets personnels)*
to put up for sale; **~ aux enchères**
auction sale; **~ de charité** jumble
(BRIT) *ou* rummage (US) sale

venteux, -euse [vɑ̃tø, -øz] *adj*
windy

ventilateur [vɑ̃tilatœʀ] *nm* fan

ventiler [vɑ̃tile] /1/ *vt* to ventilate

ventouse [vɑ̃tuz] *nf (de caoutchouc)*
suction pad

ventre [vɑ̃tʀ] *nm* (Anat) stomach;
(fig) belly; **avoir mal au ~** to have (a)
stomach ache

venu, e [v(ə)ny] *pp de* **venir**
▷ *adj*: **être mal ~ à** *ou* **de faire** to
have no grounds for doing, be in
no position to do; **mal ~** ill-timed;
bien ~ timely

ver [vɛʀ] *nm* worm; *(des fruits etc)*
maggot; *(du bois)* woodworm *no
pl*; **~ luisant** glow-worm; **~ à soie**
silkworm; **~ solitaire** tapeworm;
~ de terre earthworm

verbe [vɛʀb] *nm* verb

verdâtre [vɛʀdɑtʀ] *adj* greenish

verdict [vɛʀdik(t)] *nm* verdict

verdir [vɛʀdiʀ] /2/ *vi, vt* to turn
green; **verdure** *nf* greenery

véreux, -euse [veʀø, -øz] *adj* worm-
eaten; *(malhonnête)* shady, corrupt

verge [vɛʀʒ] *nf* (Anat) penis

verger [vɛʀʒe] *nm* orchard

verglacé, e [vɛʀglase] *adj* icy,
iced-over

verglas [vɛʀgla] *nm* (black) ice

véridique [veʀidik] *adj* truthful

vérification [veʀifikasjɔ̃] *nf*
checking *no pl*, check

vérifier [veʀifje] /7/ *vt* to check;
(corroborer) to confirm, bear out

véritable [veʀitabl] *adj* real; *(ami,
amour)* true; **un ~ désastre** an
absolute disaster

vérité [veʀite] *nf* truth; **en ~** to tell
the truth

verlan [vɛʀlɑ̃] *nm* (back) slang

vermeil, le [vɛʀmɛj] *adj* ruby red

vermine [vɛʀmin] *nf* vermin *pl*

vermoulu, e [vɛʀmuly] *adj* worm-
eaten

verni, e [vɛʀni] *adj (fam)* lucky; **cuir ~**
patent leather

vernir [vɛʀniʀ] /2/ *vt (bois, tableau,
ongles)* to varnish; *(poterie)* to glaze;
vernis *nm (enduit)* varnish; glaze; *(fig)*
veneer; **vernis à ongles** nail varnish
(BRIT) *ou* polish; **vernissage** *nm (d'une
exposition)* preview

vérole [veʀɔl] *nf (variole)* smallpox

verre [vɛʀ] *nm* glass; *(de lunettes)* lens
sg; **boire** *ou* **prendre un ~** to have a
drink; **~s de contact** contact lenses;
verrière *nf (grand vitrage)* window;
(toit vitré) glass roof

verrou [veʀu] *nm (targette)* bolt;
mettre qn sous les ~s to put sb
behind bars; **verrouillage** *nm* locking
mechanism; **verrouillage central**
ou **centralisé** central locking;
verrouiller /1/ *vt* to bolt; to lock

verrue [veʀy] *nf* wart

vers [vɛʀ] *nm* line ▷ *nmpl (poésie)* verse
sg ▷ *prép (en direction de)* toward(s);
(près de) around (about); *(temporel)*
about, around

versant [vɛʀsɑ̃] *nm* slopes *pl*, side

versatile [vɛʀsatil] *adj* fickle,
changeable

verse [vɛʀs]: **à ~** *adv*: **il pleut à ~** it's
pouring (with rain)

Verseau [vɛʀso] nm: **le ~** Aquarius

versement [vɛʀsəmɑ̃] nm
payment; **en trois ~s** in three
instalments

verser [vɛʀse] /1/ vt (liquide, grains) to
pour; (larmes, sang) to shed; (argent)
to pay; **~ sur un compte** to pay into
an account

version [vɛʀsjɔ̃] nf version; (Scol)
translation (into the mother tongue);
film en ~ originale film in the
original language

verso [vɛʀso] nm back; **voir au ~** see
over(leaf)

vert, e [vɛʀ, vɛʀt] adj green; (vin)
young; (vigoureux) sprightly ▷ nm
green; **les V~s** (Pol) the Greens

vertèbre [vɛʀtɛbʀ] nf vertebra

vertement [vɛʀtəmɑ̃] adv
(réprimander) sharply

vertical, e, -aux [vɛʀtikal, -o] adj
vertical; **verticale** nf vertical; **à la
verticale** vertically; **verticalement**
adv vertically

vertige [vɛʀtiʒ] nm (peur du vide)
vertigo; (étourdissement) dizzy spell;
(fig) fever; **vertigineux, -euse** adj
breathtaking

vertu [vɛʀty] nf virtue; **en ~ de** in
accordance with; **vertueux, -euse**
adj virtuous

verve [vɛʀv] nf witty eloquence; **être
en ~** to be in brilliant form

verveine [vɛʀvɛn] nf (Bot) verbena,
vervain; (infusion) verbena tea

vésicule [vezikyl] nf vesicle;
~ biliaire gall-bladder

vessie [vesi] nf bladder

veste [vɛst] nf jacket; **~ droite/
croisée** single-/double-breasted
jacket

vestiaire [vɛstjɛʀ] nm (au théâtre
etc) cloakroom; (de stade etc)
changing-room (BRIT), locker-room
(US)

vestibule [vɛstibyl] nm hall

vestige [vɛstiʒ] nm relic; (fig) vestige;
vestiges nmpl (d'une ville) remains

vestimentaire [vɛstimɑ̃tɛʀ] adj
(détail) of dress; (élégance) sartorial;
dépenses ~s clothing expenditure

veston [vɛstɔ̃] nm jacket

vêtement [vɛtmɑ̃] nm garment,
item of clothing; **vêtements** nmpl
clothes

vétérinaire [veteʀinɛʀ] nm/f vet,
veterinary surgeon

vêtir [vetiʀ] /20/ vt to clothe, dress

vêtu, e [vety] pp de **vêtir** ▷ adj: **~ de**
dressed in, wearing

vétuste [vetyst] adj ancient,
timeworn

veuf, veuve [vœf, vœv] adj widowed
▷ nm widower ▷ nf widow

vexant, e [vɛksɑ̃, -ɑ̃t] adj
(contrariant) annoying; (blessant)
upsetting

vexation [vɛksasjɔ̃] nf humiliation

vexer [vɛkse] /1/ vt to hurt; **se vexer**
vi to be offended

viable [vjabl] adj viable; (économie,
industrie etc) sustainable

viande [vjɑ̃d] nf meat; **je ne mange
pas de ~** I don't eat meat

vibrer [vibʀe] /1/ vi to vibrate; (son,
voix) to be vibrant; (fig) to be stirred;
faire ~ to (cause to) vibrate; to
stir, thrill

vice [vis] nm vice; (défaut) fault; **~ de
forme** legal flaw ou irregularity

vicié, e [visje] adj (air) polluted,
tainted; (Jur) invalidated

vicieux, -euse [visjø, -øz] adj
(pervers) dirty(-minded); (méchant)
nasty ▷ nm/f lecher

vicinal, e, -aux [visinal, -o] adj:
chemin ~ byroad, byway

victime [viktim] nf victim;
(d'accident) casualty

victoire [viktwaʀ] nf victory

victuailles [viktɥaj] nfpl provisions

vidange [vidɑ̃ʒ] nf (d'un fossé,
réservoir) emptying; (Auto) oil change;
(de lavabo: bonde) waste outlet;
vidanges nfpl (matières) sewage sg;
vidanger /3/ vt to empty

vide [vid] *adj* empty ▷ *nm* (*Physique*) vacuum; (*espace*) (empty) space, gap; (*futilité, néant*) void; **emballé sous ~** vacuum-packed; **avoir peur du ~** to be afraid of heights; **à ~** (*sans occupants*) empty; (*sans charge*) unladen

vidéo [video] *nf* video; **cassette ~** video cassette; **vidéoclip** *nm* music video; **vidéoconférence** *nf* videoconference

vide-ordures [vidɔʀdyʀ] *nm inv* (rubbish) chute

vider [vide] /1/ *vt* to empty; (*Culin: volaille, poisson*) to gut, clean out; **se vider** *vi* to empty; **~ les lieux** to quit *ou* vacate the premises; **videur** *nm* (*de boîte de nuit*) bouncer

vie [vi] *nf* life; **être en ~** to be alive; **sans ~** lifeless; **à ~** for life; **que faites-vous dans la ~?** what do you do?

vieil [vjɛj] *adj m voir* **vieux**; **vieillard** *nm* old man; **vieille** *adj f, nf voir* **vieux**; **vieilleries** *nfpl* old things *ou* stuff *sg*; **vieillesse** *nf* old age; **vieillir** /2/ *vi* (*prendre de l'âge*) to grow old; (*population, vin*) to age; (*doctrine, auteur*) to become dated ▷ *vt* to age; **se vieillir** to make o.s. older; **vieillissement** *nm* growing old; ageing

Vienne [vjɛn] *n* Vienna

viens [vjɛ̃] *vb voir* **venir**

vierge *adj* virgin; (*page*) clean, blank ▷ *nf* virgin; (*signe*): **la V~** Virgo

Viêtnam, Vietnam [vjɛtnam] *nm*: **le ~** Vietnam; **vietnamien, ne** *adj* Vietnamese ▷ *nm/f*: **Vietnamien, ne** Vietnamese

vieux (vieil), vieille [vjø, vjɛj] *adj* old ▷ *nm/f* old man/woman ▷ *nmpl*: **les ~** the old, old people; **un petit ~** a little old man; **mon ~/ma vieille** (*fam*) old man/girl; **prendre un coup de ~** to put years on; **~ garçon** bachelor; **~ jeu** *adj inv* old-fashioned

vif, vive [vif, viv] *adj* (*animé*) lively; (*alerte*) sharp; (*lumière, couleur*) brilliant; (*air*) crisp; (*vent, émotion*) keen; (*fort: regret, déception*) great, deep; (*vivant*): **brûlé ~** burnt alive; **de vive voix** personally; **avoir l'esprit ~** to be quick-witted; **piquer qn au ~** to cut sb to the quick; **à ~** (*plaie*) open; **avoir les nerfs à ~** to be on edge

vigne [viɲ] *nf* (*plante*) vine; (*plantation*) vineyard; **vigneron** *nm* wine grower

vignette [viɲɛt] *nf* (*pour voiture*) ≈ (road) tax disc (BRIT), ≈ license plate sticker (US); (*sur médicament*) price label (*on medicines for reimbursement by Social Security*)

vignoble [viɲɔbl] *nm* (*plantation*) vineyard; (*vignes d'une région*) vineyards *pl*

vigoureux, -euse [viguʀø, -øz] *adj* vigorous, robust

vigueur [vigœʀ] *nf* vigour; **être/ entrer en ~** to be in/come into force; **en ~** current

vilain, e [vilɛ̃, -ɛn] *adj* (*laid*) ugly; (*affaire, blessure*) nasty; (*pas sage: enfant*) naughty; **~ mot** bad word

villa [vila] *nf* (detached) house; **~ en multipropriété** time-share villa

village [vilaʒ] *nm* village; **villageois, e** *adj* village *cpd* ▷ *nm/f* villager

ville [vil] *nf* town; (*importante*) city; (*administration*): **la ~** ≈ the (town) council; **~ d'eaux** spa; **~ nouvelle** new town

vin [vɛ̃] *nm* wine; **avoir le ~ gai/ triste** to get happy/miserable after a few drinks; **~ d'honneur** reception (*with wine and snacks*); **~ ordinaire** *ou* **de table** table wine; **~ de pays** local wine

vinaigre [vinɛgʀ] *nm* vinegar; **vinaigrette** *nf* vinaigrette, French dressing

vindicatif, -ive [vɛ̃dikatif, -iv] *adj* vindictive

v

vingt [vɛ̃, vɛ̃t] (*2nd pron used when followed by a vowel*) *num* twenty; **~-quatre heures sur ~-quatre** twenty-four hours a day, round the clock; **vingtaine** *nf*: **une vingtaine (de)** around twenty, twenty or so; **vingtième** *num* twentieth

vinicole [vinikɔl] *adj* wine *cpd*; wine-growing

vinyle [vinil] *nm* vinyl

viol [vjɔl] *nm* (*d'une femme*) rape; (*d'un lieu sacré*) violation

violacé, e [vjɔlase] *adj* purplish, mauvish

violemment [vjɔlamɑ̃] *adv* violently

violence [vjɔlɑ̃s] *nf* violence

violent, e [vjɔlɑ̃, -ɑ̃t] *adj* violent; (*remède*) drastic

violer [vjɔle] /1/ *vt* (*femme*) to rape; (*sépulture*) to desecrate; (*loi, traité*) to violate

violet, te [vjɔlɛ, -ɛt] *adj, nm* purple, mauve ▷ *nf* (*fleur*) violet

violon [vjɔlɔ̃] *nm* violin; (*fam: prison*) lock-up; **~ d'Ingres** (artistic) hobby; **violoncelle** *nm* cello; **violoniste** *nm/f* violinist

vipère [vipɛʁ] *nf* viper, adder

virage [viʁaʒ] *nm* (*d'un véhicule*) turn; (*d'une route, piste*) bend

virée [viʁe] *nf* run; (*à pied*) walk; (*longue*) hike

virement [viʁmɑ̃] *nm* (*Comm*) transfer

virer [viʁe] /1/ *vt* (*Comm*) to transfer; (*fam: renvoyer*) to sack ▷ *vi* to turn; (*Chimie*) to change colour (BRIT) *ou* color (US); **~ au bleu** to turn blue; **~ de bord** to tack

virevolter [viʁvɔlte] /1/ *vi* to twirl around

virgule [viʁgyl] *nf* comma; (*Math*) point

viril, e [viʁil] *adj* (*propre à l'homme*) masculine; (*énergique, courageux*) manly, virile

virtuel, le [viʁtɥɛl] *adj* potential; (*théorique*) virtual

virtuose [viʁtɥoz] *nm/f* (*Mus*) virtuoso; (*gén*) master

virus [viʁys] *nm* virus

vis *vb* [vi] *voir* **voir, vivre** ▷ *nf* [vis] screw

visa [viza] *nm* (*sceau*) stamp; (*validation de passeport*) visa

visage [vizaʒ] *nm* face

vis-à-vis [vizavi]: **~ de** *prép* towards; **en ~** facing *ou* opposite each other

visée [vize] *nf* aiming; **visées** *nfpl* (*intentions*) designs

viser [vize] /1/ *vi* to aim ▷ *vt* to aim at; (*concerner*) to be aimed *ou* directed at; (*apposer un visa sur*) to stamp, visa; **~ à qch/faire** to aim at sth/at doing *ou* to do

visibilité [vizibilite] *nf* visibility

visible [vizibl] *adj* visible; (*disponible*): **est-il ~?** can he see me?, will he see visitors?

visière [vizjɛʁ] *nf* (*de casquette*) peak; (*qui s'attache*) eyeshade

vision [vizjɔ̃] *nf* vision; (*sens*) (eye)sight, vision; (*fait de voir*): **la ~ de** the sight of; **visionneuse** *nf* viewer

visiophone [vizjɔfɔn] *nm* videophone

visite [vizit] *nf* visit; **~ médicale** medical examination; **~ accompagnée** *ou* **guidée** guided tour; **faire une ~ à qn** to call on sb, pay sb a visit; **rendre ~ à qn** to visit sb, pay sb a visit; **être en ~ (chez qn)** to be visiting (sb); **avoir de la ~** to have visitors; **heures de ~** (*hôpital, prison*) visiting hours

visiter [vizite] /1/ *vt* to visit; **visiteur, -euse** *nm/f* visitor

vison [vizɔ̃] *nm* mink

visser [vise] /1/ *vt*: **~ qch** (*fixer, serrer*) to screw sth on

visuel, le [vizɥɛl] *adj* visual

vital, e, -aux [vital, -o] *adj* vital

vitamine [vitamin] *nf* vitamin

vite [vit] *adv* (*rapidement*) quickly, fast; (*sans délai*) quickly; soon; **~!** quick!; **faire ~** to be quick

vitesse [vitɛs] *nf* speed; (*Auto: dispositif*) gear; **prendre de la ~** to pick up *ou* gather speed; **à toute ~** at full *ou* top speed; **en ~** quickly

● **LIMITE DE VITESSE**
●
● The speed limit in France is 50
● km/h in built-up areas, 90 km/h
● on main roads, and 130 km/h on
● motorways (110 km/h when it is
● raining).

viticulteur [vitikyltœr] *nm* wine grower

vitrage [vitraʒ] *nm*: **double ~** double glazing

vitrail, -aux [vitraj, -o] *nm* stained-glass window

vitre [vitr] *nf* (window) pane; (*de portière, voiture*) window; **vitré, e** *adj* glass *cpd*

vitrine [vitrin] *nf* (shop) window; (*petite armoire*) display cabinet; **en ~** in the window

vivable [vivabl] *adj* (*personne*) livable-with; (*maison*) fit to live in

vivace [vivas] *adj* (*arbre, plante*) hardy; (*fig*) enduring

vivacité [vivasite] *nf* liveliness, vivacity

vivant, e [vivã, -ãt] *adj* (*qui vit*) living, alive; (*animé*) lively; (*preuve, exemple*) living ▷ *nm*: **du ~ de qn** in sb's lifetime; **les ~s et les morts** the living and the dead

vive [viv] *adj f voir* **vif** ▷ *vb voir* **vivre** ▷ *excl*: **~ le roi!** long live the king!; **vivement** *adv* sharply ▷ *excl*: **vivement les vacances!** roll on the holidays!

vivier [vivje] *nm* (*au restaurant etc*) fish tank; (*étang*) fishpond

vivifiant, e [vivifjã, -ãt] *adj* invigorating

vivoter [vivɔte] /1/ *vi* (*personne*) to scrape a living, get by; (*fig: affaire etc*) to struggle along

vivre [vivr] /46/ *vi, vt* to live; **vivres** *nmpl* provisions, food supplies; **il vit encore** he is still alive; **se laisser ~** to take life as it comes; **ne plus ~** (*être anxieux*) to live on one's nerves; **il a vécu** (*eu une vie aventureuse*) he has seen life; **être facile à ~** to be easy to get on with; **faire ~ qn** (*pourvoir à sa subsistance*) to provide (a living) for sb; **~ de** to live on

vlan [vlã] *excl* wham!, bang!

VO *sigle f* = **version originale**; **voir un film en VO** to see a film in its original language

vocabulaire [vɔkabylɛr] *nm* vocabulary

vocation [vɔkasjõ] *nf* vocation, calling

vœu, x [vø] *nm* wish; (*à Dieu*) vow; **faire ~ de** to take a vow of; **avec tous nos ~x** with every good wish *ou* our best wishes

vogue [vɔg] *nf* fashion, vogue; **en ~** in fashion, in vogue

voici [vwasi] *prép* (*pour introduire, désigner*) here is (+ *sg*); here are (+ *pl*); **et ~ que ...** and now it (*ou* he) ...; *voir aussi* **voilà**

voie [vwa] *nf* way; (*Rail*) track, line; (*Auto*) lane; **par ~ buccale** *ou* **orale** orally; **être en bonne ~** to be shaping *ou* going well; **mettre qn sur la ~** to put sb on the right track; **être en ~ d'achèvement/de rénovation** to be nearing completion/in the process of renovation; **à ~ unique** single-track; **route à deux/trois ~s** two-/three-lane road; **~ express** expressway; **~ ferrée** track; railway line (brit), railroad (us); **~ de garage** (*Rail*) siding; **la ~ lactée** the Milky Way; **la ~ publique** the public highway

voilà [vwala] *prép* (*en désignant*) there is (+ *sg*); there are (+ *pl*); **les ~** *ou* **voici** here *ou* there they are; **en ~** *ou* **voici un** here's one, there's one; **voici mon frère et ~ ma sœur** this is my brother and that's my sister; **~** *ou* **voici deux ans** two years ago; **~** *ou* **voici deux ans que** it's two years since; **et ~!** there we are!; **~ tout** that's all; **"~** *ou* **voici"** (*en offrant etc*) "there *ou* here you are"; **tiens! ~ Paul** look! there's Paul

voile [vwal] *nm* veil; (*tissu léger*) net ▷ *nf* sail; (*sport*) sailing; **voiler** /1/ *vt* to veil; (*fausser: roue*) to buckle; (: *bois*) to warp; **se voiler** *vi* (*lune, regard*) to mist over; (*voix*) to become husky; (*roue, disque*) to buckle; (*planche*) to warp; **voilier** *nm* sailing ship; (*de plaisance*) sailing boat; **voilure** *nf* (*de voilier*) sails *pl*

voir [vwaʀ] /30/ *vi, vt* to see; **se voir**: **cela se voit** (*c'est visible*) that's obvious, it shows; **faire ~ qch à qn** to show sb sth; **en faire ~ à qn** (*fig*) to give sb a hard time; **ne pas pouvoir ~ qn** not to be able to stand sb; **voyons!** let's see now; (*indignation etc*) come (along) now!; **ça n'a rien à ~ avec lui** that has nothing to do with him

voire [vwaʀ] *adv* or even

voisin, e [vwazɛ̃, -in] *adj* (*proche*) neighbouring; next; (*ressemblant*) connected ▷ *nm/f* neighbour; **voisinage** *nm* (*proximité*) proximity; (*environs*) vicinity; (*quartier, voisins*) neighbourhood

voiture [vwatyʀ] *nf* car; (*wagon*) coach, carriage; **~ de course** racing car; **~ de sport** sports car

voix [vwa] *nf* voice; (*Pol*) vote; **à haute ~** aloud; **à ~ basse** in a low voice; **à deux/quatre ~** (*Mus*) in two/four parts; **avoir ~ au chapitre** to have a say in the matter

vol [vɔl] *nm* (*trajet, voyage, groupe d'oiseaux*) flight; (*mode d'appropriation*) theft, stealing; (*larcin*) theft; **à ~ d'oiseau** as the crow flies; **au ~: attraper qch au ~** to catch sth as it flies past; **en ~** in flight; **~ libre** hang-gliding; **~ à main armée** armed robbery; **~ régulier** scheduled flight; **~ à voile** gliding

volage [vɔlaʒ] *adj* fickle

volaille [vɔlaj] *nf* (*oiseaux*) poultry *pl*; (*viande*) poultry *no pl*; (*oiseau*) fowl

volant, e [vɔlɑ̃, -ɑ̃t] *adj* flying ▷ *nm* (*d'automobile*) (steering) wheel; (*de commande*) wheel; (*objet lancé*) shuttlecock; (*bande de tissu*) flounce

volcan [vɔlkɑ̃] *nm* volcano

volée [vɔle] *nf* (*Tennis*) volley; **à la ~: rattraper à la ~** to catch in midair; **à toute ~** (*sonner les cloches*) vigorously; (*lancer un projectile*) with full force

voler [vɔle] /1/ *vi* (*avion, oiseau, fig*) to fly; (*voleur*) to steal ▷ *vt* (*objet*) to steal; (*personne*) to rob; **~ qch à qn** to steal sth from sb; **on m'a volé mon portefeuille** my wallet (*BRIT*) *ou* billfold (*US*) has been stolen; **il ne l'a pas volé!** he asked for it!

volet [vɔlɛ] *nm* (*de fenêtre*) shutter; (*Aviat*) flap; (*de feuillet, document*) section; (*fig: d'un plan*) facet

voleur, -euse [vɔlœʀ, -øz] *nm/f* thief ▷ *adj* thieving; **"au ~!"** "stop thief!"

volley [vɔlɛ], **volley-ball** [vɔlɛbol] *nm* volleyball

volontaire [vɔlɔ̃tɛʀ] *adj* (*acte, activité*) voluntary; (*délibéré*) deliberate; (*caractère, personne: décidé*) self-willed ▷ *nm/f* volunteer

volonté [vɔlɔ̃te] *nf* (*faculté de vouloir*) will; (*énergie, fermeté*) will(power); (*souhait, désir*) wish; **se servir/boire à ~** to take/drink as much as one likes; **bonne ~** goodwill, willingness; **mauvaise ~** lack of goodwill, unwillingness

volontiers [vɔlɔ̃tje] *adv* (*avec plaisir*) willingly, gladly; (*habituellement, souvent*) readily, willingly; **"~"** "with pleasure"

volt [vɔlt] *nm* volt

volte-face [vɔltəfas] *nf inv*: **faire ~** to do an about-turn

voltige [vɔltiʒ] *nf* (*Équitation*) trick riding; (*au cirque*) acrobatics *sg*;

voltiger [vɔltiʒe] /3/ vi to flutter (about)

volubile [vɔlybil] adj voluble

volume [vɔlym] nm volume; (Géom: solide) solid; **volumineux, -euse** adj voluminous, bulky

volupté [vɔlypte] nf sensual delight ou pleasure

vomi [vɔmi] nm vomit; **vomir** /2/ vi to vomit, be sick ▷ vt to vomit, bring up; (fig) to belch out, spew out; (exécrer) to loathe, abhor

vorace [vɔʀas] adj voracious

vos [vo] adj poss voir **votre**

vote [vɔt] nm vote; **~ par correspondance/procuration** postal/proxy vote; **voter** /1/ vi to vote ▷ vt (loi, décision) to vote for

votre [vɔtʀ] adj poss your

vôtre [votʀ] pron: **le ~, la ~, les ~s** yours; **les ~s** (fig) your family ou folks; **à la ~** (toast) your (good) health!

vouer [vwe] /1/ vt: **~ sa vie/son temps à** (étude, cause etc) to devote one's life/time to; **~ une haine/ amitié éternelle à qn** to vow undying hatred/friendship to sb

⬤ **MOT-CLÉ**

vouloir [vulwaʀ] /31/ vt **1** (exiger, désirer) to want; **vouloir faire/ que qn fasse** to want to do/sb to do; **voulez-vous du thé?** would you like ou do you want some tea?; **que me veut-il?** what does he want with me?; **sans le vouloir** (involontairement) without meaning to, unintentionally; **je voudrais ceci/faire** I would ou I'd like this/to do; **le hasard a voulu que ...** as fate would have it, ...; **la tradition veut que ...** tradition demands that ...

2 (consentir): **je veux bien** (bonne volonté) I'll be happy to; (concession) fair enough, that's fine; **oui, si on veut** (en quelque sorte) yes, if you like; **veuillez attendre** please

wait; **veuillez agréer ...** (formule épistolaire) yours faithfully

3: **en vouloir à qn** to bear sb a grudge; **s'en vouloir (de)** to be annoyed with o.s. (for); **il en veut à mon argent** he's after my money

4: **vouloir de: l'entreprise ne veut plus de lui** the firm doesn't want him any more; **elle ne veut pas de son aide** she doesn't want his help

5: **vouloir dire** to mean

▷ nm: **le bon vouloir de qn** sb's goodwill; sb's pleasure

voulu, e [vuly] pp de **vouloir** ▷ adj (requis) required, requisite; (délibéré) deliberate, intentional

vous [vu] pron you; (objet indirect) (to) you; (réfléchi: sg) yourself; (: pl) yourselves; (réciproque) each other ▷ nm: **employer le ~** (vouvoyer) to use the "vous" form; **~-même** yourself; **~-mêmes** yourselves

vouvoyer [vuvwaje] /8/ vt: **~ qn** to address sb as "vous"

voyage [vwajaʒ] nm journey, trip; (fait de voyager): **le ~** travel(ling); **partir/être en ~** to go off/be away on a journey ou trip; **faire bon ~** to have a good journey; **~ d'agrément/ d'affaires** pleasure/business trip; **~ de noces** honeymoon; **~ organisé** package tour

voyager [vwajaʒe] /3/ vi to travel; **voyageur, -euse** nm/f traveller; (passager) passenger; **voyageur (de commerce)** commercial traveller

voyant, e [vwajɑ̃, -ɑ̃t] adj (couleur) loud, gaudy ▷ nm (signal) (warning) light

voyelle [vwajɛl] nf vowel

voyou [vwaju] nm hoodlum

vrac [vʀak]: **en ~** adv loose; (Comm) in bulk

vrai, e [vʀɛ] adj (véridique: récit, faits) true; (non factice, authentique) real; **à ~ dire** to tell the truth; **vraiment** adv really;

vraisemblable *adj* likely; (*excuse*) plausible; **vraisemblablement** *adv* in all likelihood, very likely; **vraisemblance** *nf* likelihood; (*romanesque*) verisimilitude

vrombir [vʀɔ̃biʀ] /2/ *vi* to hum

VRP *sigle m* (= *voyageur, représentant, placier*) (sales) rep (*fam*)

VTT *sigle m* (= *vélo tout-terrain*) mountain bike

vu¹ [vy] *prép* (*en raison de*) in view of; **vu que** in view of the fact that

vu², e [vy] *pp de* **voir** ▷ *adj*: **bien/mal vu** (*personne*) well/poorly thought of

vue [vy] *nf* (*sens, faculté*) (eye)sight; (*panorama, image, photo*) view; **la ~ de** (*spectacle*) the sight of; **vues** *nfpl* (*idées*) views; (*dessein*) designs; **perdre la ~** to lose one's (eye)sight; **perdre de ~** to lose sight of; **hors de ~** out of sight; **à première ~** at first sight; **tirer à ~** to shoot on sight; **à ~ d'œil** visibly; **avoir ~ sur** to have a view of; **en ~** (*visible*) in sight; (*célèbre*) in the public eye; **en ~ de faire** with a view to doing; **~ d'ensemble** overall view

vulgaire [vylɡɛʀ] *adj* (*grossier*) vulgar, coarse; (*trivial*) commonplace, mundane; (*péj: quelconque*): **de ~s touristes/chaises de cuisine** common tourists/kitchen chairs; (*Bot, Zool: non latin*) common; **vulgariser** /1/ *vt* to popularize

vulnérable [vylneʀabl] *adj* vulnerable

wagon [vagɔ̃] *nm* (*de voyageurs*) carriage; (*de marchandises*) truck, wagon; **wagon-lit** *nm* sleeper, sleeping car; **wagon-restaurant** *nm* restaurant *ou* dining car

wallon, ne [walɔ̃, -ɔn] *adj* Walloon ▷ *nm* (*Ling*) Walloon ▷ *nm/f*: **W~, ne** Walloon

watt [wat] *nm* watt

WC [vese] *nmpl* toilet *sg*

Web [wɛb] *nm inv*: **le ~** the (World Wide) Web; **webcam** *nf* webcam; **webmaster, webmestre** *nm/f* webmaster

week-end [wikɛnd] *nm* weekend

western [wɛstɛʀn] *nm* western

whisky [wiski] (*pl* **whiskies**) *nm* whisky

wifi [wifi] *nm inv* wifi

WWW *sigle m* (= *World Wide Web*) WWW

xénophobe [gzenɔfɔb] *adj*
xenophobic ▷ *nm/f* xenophobe
xérès [gzerɛs] *nm* sherry
xylophone [gzilɔfɔn] *nm* xylophone

y [i] *adv* (*à cet endroit*) there; (*dessus*) on
it (*ou* them); (*dedans*) in it (*ou* them)
▷ *pron* (about *ou* on *ou* of) it (*vérifier la
syntaxe du verbe employé*); **j'y pense**
I'm thinking about it; **ça y est!** that's
it!; *voir aussi* **aller, avoir**
yacht [jɔt] *nm* yacht
yaourt [jauʀt] *nm* yogurt; **~ nature/
aux fruits** plain/fruit yogurt
yeux [jø] *nmpl de* **œil**
yoga [jɔga] *nm* yoga
yoghourt [jɔguʀt] *nm =* **yaourt**
yougoslave [jugɔslav] *adj*
Yugoslav(ian) ▷ *nm/f:* **Y~**
Yugoslav(ian)
Yougoslavie [jugɔslavi] *nf:* **la
~** Yugoslavia; **l'ex-~** the former
Yugoslavia

Z

zone [zon] *nf* zone, area;
  (*quartiers pauvres*): **la ~** the slums;
  ~ bleue ≈ restricted parking area;
  ~ industrielle (ZI) industrial estate
zoo [zoo] *nm* zoo
zoologie [zɔɔlɔʒi] *nf* zoology;
  zoologique *adj* zoological
zut [zyt] *excl* dash (it)! (*BRIT*), nuts!
  (*US*)

zapper [zape] /1/ *vi* to zap
zapping [zapiŋ] *nm*: **faire du ~** to
  flick through the channels
zèbre [zɛbʀ] *nm* (*Zool*) zebra; **zébré, e**
  adj striped, streaked
zèle [zɛl] *nm* zeal; **faire du ~** (*péj*) to
  be over-zealous; **zélé, e** *adj* zealous
zéro [zeʀo] *nm* zero, nought (*BRIT*);
  au-dessous de ~ below zero
  (Centigrade), below freezing; **partir
  de ~** to start from scratch; **trois
  (buts) à ~** three (goals to) nil
zeste [zɛst] *nm* peel, zest
zézayer [zezeje] /8/ *vi* to have a lisp
zigzag [zigzag] *nm* zigzag; **zigzaguer**
  /1/ *vi* to zigzag (along)
Zimbabwe [zimbabwe] *nm*: **le ~**
  Zimbabwe
zinc [zɛ̃g] *nm* (*Chimie*) zinc
zipper [zipe] /1/ *vt* (*Inform*) to zip
zizi [zizi] *nm* (*fam*) willy
zodiaque [zɔdjak] *nm* zodiac
zona [zona] *nm* shingles *sg*

French in focus

Introduction

French in focus gives you a fascinating introduction to the French-speaking world. The following pages look at where French is spoken throughout the world, helping you to get to know the language and the people that speak it. Practical language tips and notes on common translation difficulties will allow you to become more confident in French and a useful correspondence section gives you all the information you need to be able to communicate effectively.

We've also included a number of links to useful websites, which will give you the opportunity to read and learn more about French-speaking countries and the French language.

We hope that you will enjoy using your *French in focus* supplement. We are sure that it will help you to find out more about French-speaking countries and become more confident in writing and speaking French.

Allez-y!

France and its regions

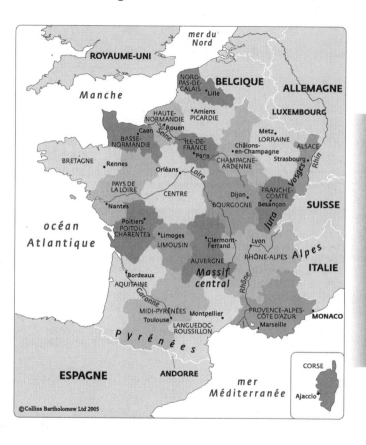

France and its regions

The six biggest French cities

City	Name of inhabitants	Population
Paris	les Parisiens	9,645,000 (Paris area)
		2,125,000 (the city proper)
Marseille–Aix-en-Provence	les Marseillais les Aixois	1,350,000
Lyon	les Lyonnais	1,349,000
Lille	les Lillois	1,001,000
Nice	les Niçois	889,000
Toulouse	les Toulousains	761,000

Note that the names of the city inhabitants start with a capital letter, but when they are used as adjectives, they begin with a small letter: *les musées parisiens* (Paris museums), *la cuisine lyonnaise* (cooking from Lyons).

French speakers often refer to mainland France as *l'Hexagone* because of its shape. The head of state is the President (*le Président de la République*), who is elected for five years. The President appoints a Prime Minister (*le Premier Ministre*), who heads the government.

France is organized into twenty-two areas called *régions*. Each *région* is made up of several smaller *départements*, four of which lie far beyond Europe's borders.

Useful links:
www.gouvernement.fr
  Office of the Prime Minister.
www.service-public.fr
  Links to most government departments.

The overseas *Départements* (*Départements d'outre-mer – DOM –* and *Régions d'outre-mer – ROM*) consist of:
• the Caribbean islands of *Martinique* and *Guadeloupe*
• *Réunion* in the Indian Ocean
• *Guyane française* in South America
They have the same legal system as mainland France.

France's overseas territories (*Collectivités d'outre-mer – COM*) include:
• *Polynésie française, Wallis-et-Futuna* and *Nouvelle-Calédonie* in the South Pacific
• *Mayotte* in the Indian Ocean
• *Saint-Pierre et Miquelon*
• polar territories in the Antarctic

A useful link:
www.outre-mer.gouv.fr
  Information on the DOM-ROM.

A snapshot of France

- France is the biggest country by area in Western Europe, covering 549 000 km² (well over twice the size of the UK).

- The Loire is the longest river in France, and is around 1010 km long. It rises in the Cévennes mountains and flows into the Atlantic Ocean at Saint-Nazaire.

- The highest mountain in the Alps, Mont Blanc (4807 m), lies just within France's border with Italy.

- 59.3 million people live in metropolitan France, and there are another 1.7 million in the overseas *départements*.

- France is the world's fifth largest economy after the US, Japan, Germany and the UK.

- The main religion in France is Roman Catholicism; Islam is the second largest religion.

- After Italy, France is the world's biggest wine-producing country.

- The Tour de France is the world's most famous cycle race. Competitors cover approximately 3500 km nationwide.

A useful link:
www.insee.fr
  The French statistical office.

The French-speaking world

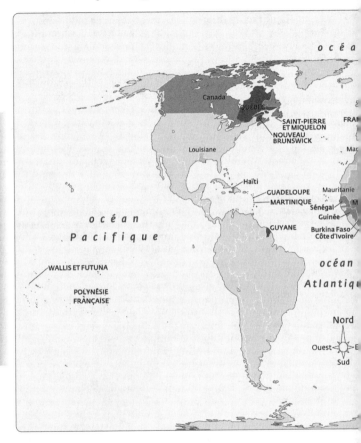

océan

Canada

QUÉBEC

SAINT-PIERRE
ET MIQUELON
NOUVEAU
BRUNSWICK

FRA

Louisiane

Mar

Haïti

GUADELOUPE
MARTINIQUE

Mauritanie

M

Sénégal
Guinée

océan
Pacifique

GUYANE

Burkina Faso
Côte d'Ivoire

océan

WALLIS ET FUTUNA

Atlantiq

POLYNÉSIE
FRANÇAISE

Nord

Ouest—E

Sud

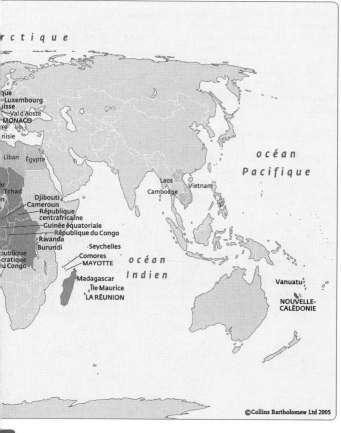

rctique

Luxembourg
uisse
Val d'Aoste
MONACO
re
nisie

Liban   Égypte

océan
Pacifique

Tchad
Djibouti
Cameroun
République
centrafricaine
Guinée équatoriale
République du Congo
Rwanda
Burundi
oublique
cratique
u Congo

Laos
Cambodge   Vietnam

Seychelles
Comores
MAYOTTE

océan
Indien

Madagascar
Île Maurice
LA RÉUNION

Vanuatu

NOUVELLE-
CALÉDONIE

©Collins Bartholomew Ltd 2005

COUNTRIES OR REGIONS WHERE FRENCH IS THE MOTHER TONGUE

Countries where French is one of the official languages

Countries or regions where French is used

7

Varieties of French

French is the first language for nearly 80 million people, which makes it the eighth most widely spoken language in the world. Around 57 million students all over the globe are currently learning French.

Outside France, French is mostly spoken in:

• Belgium and Switzerland

• Algeria, Morocco, Tunisia, Cameroon, Côte d'Ivoire and the Democratic Republic of the Congo

• Canada

A useful link :
www.academie-francaise.fr
  The Académie française web site.

Le Québec
Québec is the largest Canadian province, with an area of around 1 540 680 km². Over 80% of the province's inhabitants speak French as their first language, although it is rather different from the language of mainland France. The French spoken in Québec is called *Québécois*.

French regional languages

Other languages spoken within France:

Language	French name	Brief description	Where spoken
Alsatian	l'alsacien	Close to German	Near the border with Germany
Breton	le breton	A Celtic language	Brittany in north-west France
Basque	le basque	Not related to any other known language	Near the border with Spain
Catalan	le catalan	Close to Spanish	Near the border with Spain
Corsican	le corse	Close to Italian	The island of Corsica
Flemish	le flamand	Close to Dutch	Near the border with Belgium
Occitan	l'occitan	Close to Spanish and French	The southern part of France

Words that have crossed the Channel

When the Normans invaded England in 1066, French became the language of the ruling classes. Since then, it has played a central part in the development of English.

English has absorbed thousands of French words over time, for example, 'beef' comes from *bœuf*, 'marriage' comes from *mariage* and so on.

However, English also uses words that come directly from French and don't change at all: for example, 'au pair', 'eau de toilette' and 'rendez-vous'.

With the spread of English as a global means of communication, English terms have become more widespread in the French language.

Some of these terms mean the same in both languages:

le brunch	*un cocktail*
le hit-parade	*une interview*
un self-service	*le stress*
un tee-shirt	*les WC*
le Web	*le week-end*
un western	*un yacht*

Others have different meanings in French and English:

un agenda	diary
les baskets	trainers (BRIT), sneakers (US)
les chips	crisps (BRIT), chips (US)
la lecture	reading
un parking	a car park
un smoking	a dinner jacket
un stop	a stop sign, a brake-light

> *Be careful!*
> Some words are singular in French but plural in English and vice versa:
>
> *un jean* (a pair of) jeans
> *un short* (a pair of) shorts
> *les WC* the WC

A useful link:
www.academie-francaise.fr
The Académie française web site.

Some informal French

We all use different language styles – more relaxed, more formal – depending on the situation we find ourselves in.

When you visit a French-speaking country, you're sure to hear some informal expressions in everyday situations.

Here are some examples of French informal words:

la bagnole	car
le boulot	work
dingue	crazy
génial	fantastic
le mec	guy
moche	ugly, rotten
le prof	teacher

Informal language is marked very clearly in the dictionary to help you choose the appropriate word or phrase.

Be careful when using items marked 'informal' (*fam*) in your dictionary, and avoid ones marked 'offensive' (*fam!*) altogether.

Le verlan
Verlan is a kind of slang in which words are invented by swapping round syllables and often chopping off the end of the new word: for example, *femme* becomes *meuf*, and *Arabe* becomes *beur*.

Improving your pronunciation

There are a number of different methods you can use to improve your pronunciation and increase your confidence in speaking French:

- read out loud to yourself to improve your confidence
- listen to French radio
- watch French-language films
- chat with French-speakers

Useful links:

www.radiofrance.fr
France Info, France Inter and France Culture.

www.rfi.fr
Radio France Internationale, the equivalent of the BBC World Service.

Some points to help you with your pronunciation

- **U and ou.** For *ou*, round your lips as for English 'oo!' For *u*, round your lips but say 'ee'.

- **Silent consonant endings and *liaison*.** Consonants at the end of words are not normally pronounced but you do pronounce them when the following word starts with a vowel (*mes amis* sounds like 'may**z**amee', *c'est ici* sounds like 'se**t**eesee'). This is called *liaison*.

- **Elision.** When the words *je, le, la, me, te, se, ce* and *ne* are immediately followed by a word starting with any vowel, the *e* is dropped (and replaced by an apostrophe in writing): *j'adore l'été, elle s'habille, je t'aime.*

- **Letter *h*.** The letter *h* is never pronounced at the beginning of French words. So, *haricot* is pronounced 'areeko' and *hôtel* as 'otel'.

Words beginning with *h* can behave in one of two ways as regards pronunciation.

In some cases, the word behaves as if it began with a vowel, and preceding words like *le* and *la* are shortened: *à l'hôtel, l'huile, ils l'hébergent*. For such words liaison also takes place: *les hôtels* is pronounced as 'lay**z**otel'.

In other cases, *le, la* and similar words are not shortened: *la Hollande, le haricot*, and liaison does not happen: *les haricots* is pronounced as 'lay ariko' and not 'layzariko '. Words which behave like this are preceded by an apostrophe in the dictionary: '*hasard*.

Improving your fluency

Conversational words and phrases

In English we insert lots of words and phrases, such as *so*, *then*, *by the way*, into our conversation, to give our thoughts a structure and often to show our attitude. The French words shown below do the same thing. If you use them they will make you sound more fluent and natural.

- *alors*

  Tu as fini? **Alors** je m'en vais. (= then)

  Alors tu viens (oui ou non)? (= well, then)

- *bon*

  Bon! J'y vais. (= right!)

  Bon! Ça suffit maintenant. (= OK!)

- *ah bon*

  Je pars aux États-Unis demain. –
  Ah bon? (= really?)

- *c'est ça*

  Vous avez vingt-cinq ans, alors? – Oui,
  c'est ça. (= that's right)

- *donc*

  Voilà **donc** la solution. (= so, then)

  C'était **donc** un espion? (= then, so)

- *enfin*

  Enfin, vous voyez, c'est la catastrophe!
  (= in a word)

  Enfin, tu aurais pu le faire! (= even so)

- *de toute façon*

  De toute façon, je ne veux pas y aller.

  (= anyway)

  Tu peux m'appeler, je serai à la maison
  de toute façon. (= in any case)

- *au fait*

  Au fait, est-ce que tu as aimé le film?

  (= by the way)

  C'est quand, **au fait**, ton anniversaire?

  (= in fact)

- *en fait*

  En fait, je n'ai pas beaucoup de temps.

  (= actually)

  En fait, on devrait partir maintenant.

  (= in fact)

- *quand même*

  C'est **quand même** ennuyeux.

  (= after all)

  Merci **quand même**.

  (= all the same)

Improving your fluency

Varying the words you use to get your message across will make you sound more fluent in French. For example, you already know *J'aime* *bien les gâteaux*, but for a change you could say *J'adore les gâteaux* to mean the same thing. Here are some other suggestions:

Saying what you like or dislike

J'ai bien aimé le film.	I liked …
La visite des vignobles m'a beaucoup plu.	I really enjoyed …
Je n'aime pas (du tout) le poisson.	I don't like … (at all).
J'ai horreur du sport.	I loathe …

Expressing your opinion

Je pense que c'est trop cher.	I think …
Je trouve que c'est normal.	I think …
Je crois que c'est un peu tard.	I think …
Je suis certain/sûr que Marc va gagner.	I'm sure …
À mon avis, il n'a pas changé.	In my opinion …

Agreeing or disagreeing

Je trouve que vous avez raison.	I think you're right.
Je suis d'accord avec vous.	I agree with you.
Il a tort.	He's wrong.
Je ne suis pas d'accord.	I disagree.

Correspondence

The following section on correspondence has been designed to help you communicate confidently in written as well as spoken French. Sample letters, emails and sections on text messaging and making telephone calls will ensure that you have all the vocabulary you need to correspond successfully in French.

Text messaging

Texto	French	English
@+	à plus tard	see you later
@2m1	à demain	see you tomorrow
biîto	bientôt	soon
cpg	c'est pas grave	it's no big deal
dsl	désolé	I'm sorry
entouk	en tout cas	in any case
G la N	j'ai la haine	I'm gutted
je t'M	je t'aime	I love you
mdr	mort de rire	rolling on the floor laughing
mr6	merci	thanks
MSG	message	message
p2k	pas de quoi	you're welcome
parske	parce que	because
qqn	quelqu'un	someone
ri1	rien	nothing
svp	s'il vous plaît	please
TOK	t'es OK?	are you OK?
TOQP	t'es occupé?	are you busy?
we	week-end	weekend
Xlnt	excellent	excellent

Writing an email

| Fichier | Edition | Affichage | Outils | **Composer** | Aide | Envoyer |

	A:	michel@europost.fr		Nouveau message
	Cc:			Répondre
	Copie cachée:			Répondre à tous
				Faire suivre
	Object:	Demain soir		Fichier joint

Tu veux sortir demain soir? Le nouveau James Bond passe à l'Odéon, si ça t'intéresse.

Si tu ne peux pas demain, je suis libre samedi midi. On pourrait déjeuner ensemble.

Grosses bises

Nadia

Saying your email address
In French, when you tell someone your email address, you say:
michel arobase europost point ef-ayr

fichier (m)	file	*répondre à tous*	reply to all
édition (f)	edit	*faire suivre*	forward
affichage (m)	view	*fichier (m) joint*	attachment
outils (mpl)	tools	*à*	to
composer	compose	*cc*	cc (carbon copy)
aide (f)	help	*copie (f) cachée*	bcc (blind carbon copy)
envoyer	send	*objet (m)*	subject
nouveau message (m)	new message	*de*	from
répondre	reply	*date (f)*	date

Here is some additional useful Internet vocabulary:

barre (f) de défilement	scroll bar		*imprimer*	to print
base (f) de données	database		*l'Internet (m)*	the Internet
clavier (m)	keyboard		*liens (mpl)*	links
clic (m) droit	right click		*menu (m)*	menu
cliquer	to click		*moniteur (m)*	monitor
clore une session	to log off		*moteur (m) de recherche*	search engine
coller	to paste		*navigateur (m)*	browser
copier	to copy		*ouvrir une session*	to log on
corbeille (f)	recycle bin		*page (f) d'accueil*	home page
couper	to cut		*page (f) Web*	web page
dossier (m)	folder		*précédente*	back
double-cliquer	to double click		*rechercher*	to search
envoyé	sent		*sauvegarder*	to save
FAQ	FAQs		*site (m) Web*	website
favoris	favourites		*suivante*	forward
fenêtre (f)	window		*surfer sur Internet*	to surf the Net
feuille (f) de calcul	spreadsheet		*télécharger*	to download
fournisseur (m) d'accès à Internet	Internet Service Provider		*transmission (f) à haut débit*	broadband
historique	history		*le Web*	the (World-Wide) Web
icône (f)	icon			

Writing a personal letter

Your own name and address → Guy Leduc
18, rue des Tulipes
65004 Gervais

Town/city you are writing from, and the date → *Gervais, le 14 février 2012*

Salut Frédéric !

Merci beaucoup pour les CD que tu m'as envoyés. Tu as vraiment bien choisi puisqu'il s'agit de mes deux chanteurs préférés: je n'arrête pas de les écouter!

Sinon, rien de nouveau ici. Je passe presque tout mon temps à préparer mes examens qui commencent dans quinze jours. J'espère que je les réussirai tous, mais j'ai le trac pour mon examen de maths: c'est la matière que j'aime le moins.

Maman m'a dit que tu pars en Crète avec ta famille la semaine prochaine. Je te souhaite de très bonnes vacances, et je suis sûr que tu reviendras tout bronzé.

À bientôt!

Maxime

Writing a personal letter

Other ways of starting a personal letter	Other ways of ending a personal letter
Chers Jean et Sylvie Chère tante Laure Mon cher Laurent	Affectueusement Je t'embrasse Grosses bises (informal)

Some useful phrases

Je te remercie de ta lettre.	Thank you for your letter.
J'ai été très content d'avoir de tes nouvelles.	It was great to hear from you.
Je suis désolé de ne pas vous avoir répondu plus vite.	I'm sorry I didn't reply sooner.
Transmettez mes amitiés à Sophie.	Give my regards to Sophie.
Dis bonjour à Martin de ma part.	Say hello to Martin for me.
Maman t'embrasse.	Mum sends her love.

Writing a formal letter

Jeanne Judon ← Your own name and address
89, bd des Tertres
75008 Paris

Hôtel Renoir
→ 15, av. Jean Médecin
06000 Nice

Name and address of the person/company you are writing to

Paris, le 2 juin 2012 ← Town/city you are writing from, and the date

Madame ou Monsieur,

Suite à notre conversation téléphonique de ce matin, je vous écris afin de confirmer ma réservation pour une chambre avec salle de bains pour deux nuits du mercredi 4 au jeudi 5 juillet 2012 inclus.

Comme convenu, veuillez trouver ci-joint un chèque de 30€ correspondant au montant des arrhes.

Je vous prie de croire, Madame, Monsieur, à l'assurance de mes sentiments distingués.

Jeanne Judon

Writing a formal letter

Other ways of starting a formal letter	Other ways of ending a formal letter
Monsieur le Directeur (or *le Maire* etc) *Madame le Directeur* *Messieurs* *Madame* *Cher Monsieur* *Chère Madame*	*Veuillez accepter, [...]*, l'expression de mes sentiments distingués.* *Fill in the brackets with the words you used to start your letter: *Messieurs, chère Madame* etc.

Some useful phrases

Je vous serais reconnaissant de ...	I would be grateful if you would ...
Je vous prie de ...	Please ...
Nous vous remercions de votre lettre.	Thank you for your letter.
Dans l'attente de votre réponse ...	I look forward to hearing from you ...
Je vous remercie dès à présent de ...	Thank you in advance for ...

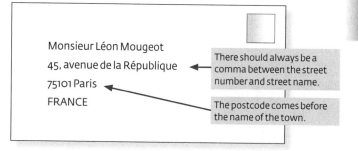

Monsieur Léon Mougeot

45, avenue de la République

75101 Paris

FRANCE

There should always be a comma between the street number and street name.

The postcode comes before the name of the town.

Making a call

Asking for information

Quel est l'indicatif de Bordeaux?	What's the code for Bordeaux?
Comment fait-on pour avoir une ligne extérieure?	How do I get an outside line?
Pouvez-vous me donner le numéro du poste de M Durand?	Could you give me the extension number for Mr Durand?

When your number answers

Bonjour! J'aimerais parler à Valérie.	Hello! Could I speak to Valérie, please?
Pourriez-vous me passer le docteur Leduc, s'il vous plaît?	Could you put me through to Dr Leduc, please?
Pourriez-vous lui demander de me rappeler, s'il vous plaît?	Would you ask him/her to call me back, please?
Je rappellerai dans une demi-heure.	I'll call back in half an hour.
Je peux laisser un message, s'il vous plaît?	Could I leave a message, please?

When you answer the telephone

Allô! C'est Marc à l'appareil.	Hello! It's Marc speaking.
C'est moi.	Speaking.
Qui est à l'appareil?	Who's speaking?

What you may hear

C'est de la part de qui?	Who shall I say is calling?
Je vous le/la passe.	I'm putting you through.
Ne quittez pas.	Please hold.
Ça ne répond pas.	There's no reply.
Voulez-vous laisser un message?	Would you like to leave a message?

Making a call

If you have a problem

Je suis désolé, j'ai dû faire un faux numéro.	I'm sorry, I must have dialled the wrong number.
La ligne est très mauvaise.	This is a very bad line.
Ça coupe.	You're breaking up.
Ma batterie est presque à plat.	My battery's low.
Je ne t'entends plus.	I can't hear you.

Saying your phone number

To tell someone your phone number in French, you divide the number up into pairs instead of saying each digit separately. For example:

01 40 32 37 12

zéro-un / quarante / trente-deux / trente-sept / douze

If there's one extra number, you say that first:

0 26 23 84 47 46

zéro / vingt-six / vingt-trois / quatre-vingt-quatre / quarante-sept / quarante-six

French phrases and sayings

In French, as in many languages, people use vivid expressions based on images from their experience of real life. We've grouped the common expressions below according to the type of image they use. For fun, we have given you the word-for-word translation as well as the true English equivalent.

Fruit and vegetables

Ce ne sont pas mes oignons!
    word for word:
→ This is none of my business!
    these aren't my onions

C'est la fin des haricots.
    word for word:
→ It's the last straw.
    it's the end of beans

être haut comme trois pommes
    word for word:
→ to be knee-high to a grasshopper
    to be high as three apples

tomber dans les pommes
    word for word:
→ to faint
    to fall into the apples

Animals and insects

donner sa langue au chat
    word for word:
→ to give in or up (*when guessing*)
    to give one's tongue to the cat

appeler un chat un chat
    word for word:
→ to call a spade a spade
    to call a cat a cat

quand les poules auront des dents
    word for word:
→ pigs might fly
    when hens have teeth

passer du coq à l'âne
    word for word:
→ to jump from one subject to another
    to go from the cockerel to the donkey

avoir un chat dans la gorge
    word for word:
→ to have a frog in one's throat
    to have a cat in one's throat

French phrases and sayings

Ce n'est pas la mer à boire.
    word for word:

→ It's not the end of the world.
    it's not like having to drink the sea

Je ne suis pas tombé de la dernière pluie.
    word for word:

→ I wasn't born yesterday.

    I didn't come down with the last shower of rain

passer entre les gouttes
    word for word:

→ to come through without a scratch
    to run between the raindrops

pleuvoir des cordes
    word for word:

→ to be bucketing down
    to be raining ropes

Ça ne me fait ni chaud ni froid.
    word for word:

→ It doesn't make any difference to me.
    it makes me neither hot nor cold

Parts of the body

avoir une dent contre quelqu'un
    word for word:

→ to have a grudge against somebody
    to have a tooth against somebody

Il n'a pas la langue dans sa poche.
    word for word:

→ He's never at a loss for words.
    he doesn't keep his tongue in his pocket

avoir un poil dans la main
    word for word:

→ to be bone idle
    to have a hair in one's hand

gagner les doigts dans le nez
    word for word:

→ to win hands down
    to win with one's fingers up one's nose

French phrases and sayings

changer d'avis comme de chemise → to be always changing one's mind
    word for word: *to change one's mind as often as one's shirt*

trouver chaussure à son pied → to find a suitable match
    word for word: *to find a shoe for one's foot*

Lâche-moi la chemise! or **Lâche-moi** → Get off my back!
les baskets!
    word for word: *let go of my shirt, let go of my trainers*

C'est bonnet blanc et blanc bonnet. → It's six of one and half a dozen of the other.
    word for word: *it's white hat and hat white*

Colours

voir tout en rose → to see life through rose-tinted spectacles
    word for word: *to see everything in pink*

avoir une peur bleue de quelque chose → to be scared stiff of something
    word for word: *to have a blue fear of something*

regarder qn dans le blanc des yeux → to look somebody straight in the eye
    word for word: *to look into the whites of somebody's eyes*

Some common translation difficulties

On the following pages we have shown some of the translation difficulties that you are most likely to come across. We hope that the tips we have given will help you to avoid these common pitfalls when writing and speaking French.

Tu or vous?

In French the word for 'you' depends on who you are talking to:

• To a person you know well, use **tu**:

Will **you** lend me this CD? → **Tu** me prêtes ce CD?

• To a person you do not know so well, use **vous**:

Have **you** met my wife? → **Vous** connaissez ma femme?

• To more than one person, whether you know them well or not, use **vous**:

Do **you** understand, children? → **Vous** comprenez, les enfants?

> ### Getting friendly
> When you get to know someone, they may ask you:
> On se tutoie? → Shall we use 'tu' to each other?
> On is the usual way of saying 'we' in conversation.
> On est allé voir la Tour Eiffel. → We went to see the Eiffel Tower.

Some common translation difficulties

Showing possession

In English -**'s** is a common way of showing who or what something belongs to. In French you have to use *de*:

my brother**'s** car	→	*la voiture **de** mon frère*
the children**'s** bedroom	→	*la chambre **des** enfants*

Singular versus plural

A word that is singular in English may be plural in French, and vice versa. Check in the dictionary if you are not sure:

Singular:
luggage

Plural:
→ ***les** bagage**s***

Plural:
my trouser**s**

Singular:
→ ***mon** pantalon*

'There is' and 'there are'

In French these are both translated by *il y a*:

There is someone at the door. → *Il y a quelqu'un à la porte.*

There are five books on the table. → *Il y a cinq livres sur la table.*

Some common translation difficulties

Using *en*

When the word *en* is used with numbers, it is often not translated in English but it can <u>never</u> be missed out in French:

I want **two (of them)**. → *J'en veux **deux**.*

Have you got a dictionary? – Yes, I've got **one**. → *Tu as un dictionnaire? – Oui, j'en ai **un**.*

Translating 'to'

'To' is generally translated by *à*, but remember:

• When you are talking about the time, use *moins*:

   five **to** ten → *dix heures **moins** cinq*

• In front of verbs, it is shown by the verb ending:

   to eat → *mang**er***
   to leave → *part**ir***
   to wait → *atten**dre***

• When you mean 'in order to', use *pour*:

   He's going into town **(in order) to** buy a present. → *Il va en ville **pour** acheter un cadeau.*

Using *ne ... pas* and other negatives

You often find the verb 'do' in English negatives, but *faire* is never used like this. You use set word pairs instead:

English negative with 'do':   French negative word pair:

I do**n't** smoke. → *Je **ne** fume **pas**.*

Do**n't** change **anything**. → ***Ne** changez **rien**.*

Some common translation difficulties

Translating 'to be'

'To be' usually corresponds to être, but remember:

- In phrases describing how you feel, use **avoir**:

to be warm/cold	→ **avoir** chaud/froid
to be hungry/thirsty	→ **avoir** faim/soif
to be afraid	→ **avoir** peur

- To describe the weather, use **faire**:

It**'s** lovely weather today.	→ Il **fait** beau aujourd'hui.

- To say your age, use **avoir**:

I**'m** fifteen.	→ J'**ai** quinze ans.

- To talk about your health, use **aller**:

I**'m** very well, thank you.	→ Je **vais** très bien, merci.

Translating verbs

Many English verbs can be followed by a preposition or adverb such as 'on' or 'back' – 'to go on', 'to give back'. These additions often give the verb a new meaning. There is no similar way of doing this in French – you just use a different word, for example:

Verb (+ preposition/adverb):	Translation:
to go	→ aller
to go on	→ continuer
to give	→ donner
to give back	→ rendre

Some common translation difficulties

Sentences that contain a verb and preposition in English might not contain a preposition in French, and vice versa. The dictionary can help you with these. For example:

- Verb + preposition:

    to pay **for** something

- Verb without preposition:

    to change something

Verb without preposition:

→ *payer quelque chose*

Verb + preposition:

→ *changer **de** quelque chose*

A [eɪ] *n* (*Mus*) la *m*

KEYWORD

a [eɪ, ə] (*before vowel and silent h* **an**)
indef art **1** un(e); **a book** un livre; **an
apple** une pomme; **she's a doctor**
elle est médecin
2 (*instead of the number "one"*) un(e);
a year ago il y a un an; **a hundred/
thousand** *etc* **pounds** cent/mille
etc livres
3 (*in expressing ratios, prices etc*): **three
a day/week** trois par jour/semaine;
10 km an hour 10 km à l'heure; **£5 a
person** 5£ par personne; **30p a kilo**
30p le kilo

A2 *n* (*BRIT Scol*) deuxième partie de
l'examen équivalent au baccalauréat
A.A. *n abbr* (*BRIT*: = *Automobile
Association*) ≈ ACF *m*; (= *Alcoholics
Anonymous*) AA

A.A.A. *n abbr* (= *American Automobile
Association*) ≈ ACF *m*
aback [ə'bæk] *adv*: **to be taken ~**
être décontenancé(e)
abandon [ə'bændən] *vt* abandonner
abattoir ['æbətwɑːᵊ] *n* (*BRIT*)
abattoir *m*
abbey ['æbɪ] *n* abbaye *f*
abbreviation [əbriːvɪ'eɪʃən] *n*
abréviation *f*
abdomen ['æbdəmən] *n* abdomen *m*
abduct [æb'dʌkt] *vt* enlever
abide [ə'baɪd] *vt* souffrir, supporter; **I
can't ~ it/him** je ne le supporte pas;
abide by *vt fus* observer, respecter
ability [ə'bɪlɪtɪ] *n* compétence *f*;
capacité *f*; (*skill*) talent *m*
able ['eɪbl] *adj* compétent(e); **to be
~ to do sth** pouvoir faire qch, être
capable de faire qch
abnormal [æb'nɔːməl] *adj*
anormal(e)
aboard [ə'bɔːd] *adv* à bord ▷ *prep* à
bord de; (*train*) dans
abolish [ə'bɔlɪʃ] *vt* abolir
abolition [æbə'lɪʃən] *n* abolition *f*
abort [ə'bɔːt] *vt* (*Med*) faire avorter;
(*Comput, fig*) abandonner; **abortion**
[ə'bɔːʃən] *n* avortement *m*; **to have
an abortion** se faire avorter

KEYWORD

about [ə'baut] *adv* **1** (*approximately*)
environ, à peu près; **about a
hundred/thousand** *etc* environ
cent/mille *etc*, une centaine (de)/
un millier (de) *etc*; **it takes about 10
hours** ça prend environ *or* à peu près
10 heures; **at about 2 o'clock** vers
2 heures; **I've just about finished** j'ai
presque fini
2 (*referring to place*) çà et là, de-ci
de-là; **to run about** courir çà et là;
to walk about se promener, aller
et venir; **they left all their things
lying about** ils ont laissé traîner
toutes leurs affaires

3: **to be about to do sth** être sur le point de faire qch
▶ *prep* **1** *(relating to)* au sujet de, à propos de; **a book about London** un livre sur Londres; **what is it about?** de quoi s'agit-il?; **we talked about it** nous en avons parlé; **what** or **how about doing this?** et si nous faisions ceci?
2 *(referring to place)* dans; **to walk about the town** se promener dans la ville

above [ə'bʌv] *adv* au-dessus ▷ *prep* au-dessus de; *(more than)* plus de; **mentioned ~** mentionné ci-dessus; **~ all** par-dessus tout, surtout

abroad [ə'brɔːd] *adv* à l'étranger

abrupt [ə'brʌpt] *adj (steep, blunt)* abrupt(e); *(sudden, gruff)* brusque

abscess ['æbsɪs] *n* abcès *m*

absence ['æbsəns] *n* absence *f*

absent ['æbsənt] *adj* absent(e); **absent-minded** *adj* distrait(e)

absolute ['æbsəluːt] *adj* absolu(e); **absolutely** [æbsə'luːtlɪ] *adv* absolument

absorb [əb'zɔːb] *vt* absorber; **to be ~ed in a book** être plongé(e) dans un livre; **absorbent cotton** *n (US)* coton *m* hydrophile; **absorbing** *adj* absorbant(e); *(book, film etc)* captivant(e)

abstain [əb'steɪn] *vi*: **to ~ (from)** s'abstenir (de)

abstract ['æbstrækt] *adj* abstrait(e)

absurd [əb'səːd] *adj* absurde

abundance [ə'bʌndəns] *n* abondance *f*

abundant [ə'bʌndənt] *adj* abondant(e)

abuse *n* [ə'bjuːs] *(insults)* insultes *fpl*, injures *fpl*; *(ill-treatment)* mauvais traitements *mpl*; *(of power etc)* abus *m* ▷ *vt* [ə'bjuːz] *(insult)* insulter; *(ill-treat)* malmener; *(power etc)* abuser de; **abusive** *adj* grossier(-ière), injurieux(-euse)

abysmal [ə'bɪzməl] *adj* exécrable; *(ignorance etc)* sans bornes

academic [ækə'dɛmɪk] *adj* universitaire; *(person: scholarly)* intellectuel(le); *(pej: issue)* oiseux(-euse), purement théorique ▷ *n* universitaire *m/f*; **academic year** *n (University)* année *f* universitaire; *(Scol)* année scolaire

academy [ə'kædəmɪ] *n (learned body)* académie *f*; *(school)* collège *m*; **~ of music** conservatoire *m*

accelerate [æk'sɛləreɪt] *vt*, *vi* accélérer; **acceleration** [æksɛlə'reɪʃən] *n* accélération *f*; **accelerator** *n (BRIT)* accélérateur *m*

accent ['æksɛnt] *n* accent *m*

accept [ək'sɛpt] *vt* accepter; **acceptable** *adj* acceptable; **acceptance** *n* acceptation *f*

access ['æksɛs] *n* accès *m*; **to have ~ to** *(information, library etc)* avoir accès à, pouvoir utiliser or consulter; *(person)* avoir accès auprès de; **accessible** [æk'sɛsəbl] *adj* accessible

accessory [æk'sɛsərɪ] *n* accessoire *m*; **~ to** *(Law)* accessoire à

accident ['æksɪdənt] *n* accident *m*; *(chance)* hasard *m*; **I've had an ~** j'ai eu un accident; **by ~** *(by chance)* par hasard; *(not deliberately)* accidentellement; **accidental** [æksɪ'dɛntl] *adj* accidentel(le); **accidentally** [æksɪ'dɛntəlɪ] *adv* accidentellement; **Accident and Emergency Department** *n (BRIT)* service *m* des urgences; **accident insurance** *n* assurance *f* accident

acclaim [ə'kleɪm] *vt* acclamer ▷ *n* acclamations *fpl*

accommodate [ə'kɔmədeɪt] *vt* loger, recevoir; *(oblige, help)* obliger; *(car etc)* contenir

accommodation, *(US)* **accommodations** [əkɔmə'deɪʃən(z)] *n, npl* logement *m*

accompaniment [ə'kʌmpənɪmənt] *n* accompagnement *m*

accompany [ə'kʌmpənɪ] vt accompagner

accomplice [ə'kʌmplɪs] n complice m/f

accomplish [ə'kʌmplɪʃ] vt accomplir; **accomplishment** n (skill: gen pl) talent m; (completion) accomplissement m; (achievement) réussite f

accord [ə'kɔːd] n accord m ▷ vt accorder; **of his own ~** de son plein gré; **accordance** n: **in accordance with** conformément à; **according: according to** prep selon; **accordingly** adv (appropriately) en conséquence; (as a result) par conséquent

account [ə'kaʊnt] n (Comm) compte m; (report) compte rendu, récit m; **accounts** npl (Comm: records) comptabilité f, comptes; **of no ~** sans importance; **on ~** en acompte; **to buy sth on ~** acheter qch à crédit; **on no ~** en aucun cas; **on ~ of** à cause de; **to take into ~**, **take ~ of** tenir compte de; **account for** vt fus (explain) expliquer, rendre compte de; (represent) représenter; **accountable** adj: **accountable (for/to)** responsable (de/devant); **accountant** n comptable m/f; **account number** n numéro m de compte

accumulate [ə'kjuːmjuleɪt] vt accumuler, amasser ▷ vi s'accumuler, s'amasser

accuracy ['ækjʊrəsɪ] n exactitude f, précision f

accurate ['ækjʊrɪt] adj exact(e), précis(e); (device) précis; **accurately** adv avec précision

accusation [ækjuːˈzeɪʃən] n accusation f

accuse [ə'kjuːz] vt: **to ~ sb (of sth)** accuser qn (de qch); **accused** n (Law) accusé(e)

accustomed [ə'kʌstəmd] adj: **~ to** habitué(e) or accoutumé(e) à

ace [eɪs] n as m

ache [eɪk] n mal m, douleur f ▷ vi (be sore) faire mal, être douloureux(-euse); **my head ~s** j'ai mal à la tête

achieve [əˈtʃiːv] vt (aim) atteindre; (victory, success) remporter, obtenir; **achievement** n exploit m, réussite f; (of aims) réalisation f

acid ['æsɪd] adj, n acide (m)

acknowledge [ək'nɒlɪdʒ] vt (also: **~ receipt of**) accuser réception de; (fact) reconnaître; **acknowledgement** n (of letter) accusé m de réception

acne ['æknɪ] n acné m

acorn ['eɪkɔːn] n gland m

acoustic [ə'kuːstɪk] adj acoustique

acquaintance [ə'kweɪntəns] n connaissance f

acquire [ə'kwaɪər] vt acquérir; **acquisition** [ækwɪ'zɪʃən] n acquisition f

acquit [ə'kwɪt] vt acquitter; **to ~ o.s. well** s'en tirer très honorablement

acre ['eɪkər] n acre f (= 4047 m²)

acronym ['ækrənɪm] n acronyme m

across [ə'krɒs] prep (on the other side) de l'autre côté de; (crosswise) en travers de ▷ adv de l'autre côté; en travers; **to run/swim ~** traverser en courant/à la nage; **~ from** en face de

acrylic [ə'krɪlɪk] adj, n acrylique (m)

act [ækt] n acte m, action f; (Theat: part of play) acte; (: of performer) numéro m; (Law) loi f ▷ vi agir; (Theat) jouer; (pretend) jouer la comédie ▷ vt (role) jouer, tenir; **to catch sb in the ~** prendre qn sur le fait or en flagrant délit; **to ~ as** servir de; **act up** (inf) vi (person) se conduire mal; (knee, back, injury) jouer des tours; (machine) être capricieux(-ieuse); **acting** adj suppléant(e), par intérim ▷ n (activity): **to do some acting** faire du théâtre (or du cinéma)

action ['ækʃən] n action f; (Mil) combat(s) m(pl); (Law) procès m, action en justice; **out of ~** hors de

combat; (*machine etc*) hors d'usage;
to take ~ agir, prendre des mesures;
action replay n (*BRIT TV*) ralenti m
activate ['æktɪveɪt] vt (*mechanism*)
actionner, faire fonctionner
active ['æktɪv] adj actif(-ive);
(*volcano*) en activité; **actively** adv
activement; (*discourage*) vivement
activist ['æktɪvɪst] n activiste m/f
activity [æk'tɪvɪtɪ] n activité f;
activity holiday n vacances actives
actor ['æktər] n acteur m
actress ['æktrɪs] n actrice f
actual ['æktjʊəl] adj réel(le),
véritable; (*emphatic use*) lui-même
(elle-même)

> Be careful not to translate *actual*
> by the French word *actuel*.

actually ['æktjʊəlɪ] adv réellement,
véritablement; (*in fact*) en fait

> Be careful not to translate
> *actually* by the French word
> *actuellement*.

acupuncture ['ækjʊpʌŋktʃər] n
acuponcture f
acute [ə'kju:t] adj aigu(ë); (*mind,
observer*) pénétrant(e)
ad [æd] n abbr = **advertisement**
A.D. adv abbr (= *Anno Domini*) ap. J.-C.
adamant ['ædəmənt] adj inflexible
adapt [ə'dæpt] vt adapter ▷ vi: **to ~
(to)** s'adapter (à); **adapter, adaptor**
n (*Elec*) adaptateur m; (*for several
plugs*) prise f multiple
add [æd] vt ajouter; (*figures: also:* **to ~
up**) additionner; **it doesn't ~ up** (*fig*)
cela ne rime à rien; **add up to** vt fus
(*Math*) s'élever à; (*fig: mean*) signifier
addict ['ædɪkt] n toxicomane
m/f; (*fig*) fanatique m/f; **addicted**
[ə'dɪktɪd] adj: **to be addicted to**
(*drink, drugs*) être adonné(e) à; (*fig:
football etc*) être un(e) fanatique
de; **addiction** [ə'dɪkʃən] n (*Med*)
dépendance f; **addictive** [ə'dɪktɪv]
adj qui crée une dépendance
addition [ə'dɪʃən] n (*adding up*)
addition f; (*thing added*) ajout m; **in ~**

de plus, de surcroît; **in ~ to** en plus de;
additional adj supplémentaire
additive ['ædɪtɪv] n additif m
address [ə'drɛs] n adresse f; (*talk*)
discours m, allocution f ▷ vt adresser;
(*speak to*) s'adresser à; **my ~ is ...** mon
adresse, c'est ...; **address book** n
carnet m d'adresses
adequate ['ædɪkwɪt] adj
(*enough*) suffisant(e); (*satisfactory*)
satisfaisant(e)
adhere [əd'hɪər] vi: **to ~ to** adhérer à;
(*fig: rule, decision*) se tenir à
adhesive [əd'hi:zɪv] n adhésif m;
adhesive tape n (*BRIT*) ruban m
adhésif; (*US Med*) sparadrap m
adjacent [ə'dʒeɪsənt] adj
adjacent(e), contigu(ë); **~ to**
adjacent à
adjective ['ædʒɛktɪv] n adjectif m
adjoining [ə'dʒɔɪnɪŋ] adj voisin(e),
adjacent(e), attenant(e)
adjourn [ə'dʒə:n] vt ajourner ▷ vi
suspendre la séance; lever la séance;
clore la session
adjust [ə'dʒʌst] vt (*machine*) ajuster,
régler; (*prices, wages*) rajuster ▷ vi:
to ~ (to) s'adapter (à); **adjustable** adj
réglable; **adjustment** n (*of machine*)
ajustage m, réglage m; (*of prices, wages*)
rajustement m; (*of person*) adaptation f
administer [əd'mɪnɪstər] vt
administrer; **administration**
[ədmɪnɪs'treɪʃən] n (*management*)
administration f; (*government*)
gouvernement m; **administrative**
[əd'mɪnɪstrətɪv] adj
administratif(-ive)
administrator [əd'mɪnɪstreɪtər] n
administrateur(-trice)
admiral ['ædmərəl] n amiral m
admiration [ædmə'reɪʃən] n
admiration f
admire [əd'maɪər] vt admirer;
admirer n (*fan*) admirateur(-trice)
admission [əd'mɪʃən] n admission
f; (*to exhibition, night club etc*) entrée f;
(*confession*) aveu m

admit [əd'mɪt] vt laisser entrer;
admettre; (agree) reconnaître,
admettre; (crime) reconnaître avoir
commis; **"children not ~ted"** "entrée
interdite aux enfants"; **admit to** vt
fus reconnaître, avouer; **admittance**
n admission f, (droit m d')entrée f;
admittedly adv il faut en convenir

adolescent [ædəʊ'lɛsnt] adj, n
adolescent(e)

adopt [ə'dɒpt] vt adopter; **adopted**
adj adoptif(-ive), adopté(e); **adoption**
[ə'dɒpʃən] n adoption f

adore [ə'dɔːʳ] vt adorer

adorn [ə'dɔːn] vt orner

Adriatic (Sea) [eɪdrɪ'ætɪk-] n: **the
Adriatic (Sea)** la mer Adriatique,
l'Adriatique f

adrift [ə'drɪft] adv à la dérive

ADSL n abbr (= asymmetric digital
subscriber line) ADSL m

adult ['ædʌlt] n adulte m/f ▷ adj
(grown-up) adulte; (for adults)
pour adultes; **adult education** n
éducation f des adultes

adultery [ə'dʌltərɪ] n adultère m

advance [əd'vɑːns] n avance f
▷ vt avancer ▷ vi s'avancer; **in ~** en
avance, d'avance; **to make ~s to
sb** (amorously) faire des avances à
qn; **~ booking** location f; **~ notice,
~ warning** préavis m; (verbal)
avertissement m; **do I need to
book in ~?** est-ce qu'il faut réserver à
l'avance?; **advanced** adj avancé(e);
(Scol: studies) supérieur(e)

advantage [əd'vɑːntɪdʒ] n (also
Tennis) avantage m; **to take ~ of**
(person) exploiter; (opportunity)
profiter de

advent ['ædvənt] n avènement m,
venue f; **A~** (Rel) avent m

adventure [əd'vɛntʃəʳ] n aventure
f; **adventurous** [əd'vɛntʃərəs] adj
aventureux(-euse)

adverb ['ædvəːb] n adverbe m

adversary ['ædvəsərɪ] n adversaire
m/f

adverse ['ædvəːs] adj adverse; (effect)
négatif(-ive); (weather, publicity)
mauvais(e); (wind) contraire

advert ['ædvəːt] n abbr (BRIT)
= **advertisement**

advertise ['ædvətaɪz] vi faire de la
publicité or de la réclame; (in classified
ads etc) mettre une annonce ▷ vt faire
de la publicité or de la réclame pour; (in
classified ads etc) mettre une annonce
pour vendre; **to ~ for** (staff) recruter
par (voie d')annonce; **advertisement**
[əd'vəːtɪsmənt] n publicité f, réclame
f; (in classified ads etc) annonce
f; **advertiser** n annonceur m;
advertising n publicité f

advice [əd'vaɪs] n conseils mpl;
(notification) avis m; **a piece of ~** un
conseil; **to take legal ~** consulter
un avocat

advisable [əd'vaɪzəbl] adj
recommandable, indiqué(e)

advise [əd'vaɪz] vt conseiller; **to
~ sb of sth** aviser or informer qn
de qch; **to ~ against sth/doing
sth** déconseiller qch/conseiller de
ne pas faire qch; **adviser, advisor**
n conseiller(-ère); **advisory** adj
consultatif(-ive)

advocate n ['ædvəkɪt] (lawyer)
avocat (plaidant); (upholder)
défenseur m, avocat(e) ▷ vt
['ædvəkeɪt] recommander, prôner;
to be an ~ of être partisan(e) de

Aegean [iː'dʒiːən] n, adj: **the ~ (Sea)**
la mer Égée, l'Égée f

aerial ['ɛərɪəl] n antenne f ▷ adj
aérien(ne)

aerobics [ɛə'rəubɪks] n aérobic m

aeroplane ['ɛərəpleɪn] n (BRIT)
avion m

aerosol ['ɛərəsɔl] n aérosol m

affair [ə'fɛəʳ] n affaire f; (also: **love ~**)
liaison f; aventure f

affect [ə'fɛkt] vt affecter; (subj:
disease) atteindre; **affected** adj
affecté(e); **affection** n affection f;
affectionate adj affectueux(-euse)

afflict [əˈflɪkt] vt affliger

affluent [ˈæfluənt] adj aisé(e), riche; **the ~ society** la société d'abondance

afford [əˈfɔːd] vt (behaviour) se permettre; (provide) fournir, procurer; **can we ~ a car?** avons-nous de quoi acheter or les moyens d'acheter une voiture?; **affordable** adj abordable

Afghanistan [æfˈgænɪstæn] n Afghanistan m

afraid [əˈfreɪd] adj effrayé(e); **to be ~ of** or **to** avoir peur de; **I am ~ that** je crains que + sub; **I'm ~ so/not** oui/non, malheureusement

Africa [ˈæfrɪkə] n Afrique f; **African** adj africain(e) ▷ n Africain(e); **African-American** adj afro-américain(e) ▷ n Afro-Américain(e)

after [ˈɑːftər] prep, adv après ▷ conj après que; **it's quarter ~ two** (us) il est deux heures et quart; **~ having done/~ he left** après avoir fait/après son départ; **to name sb ~ sb** donner à qn le nom de qn; **to ask ~ sb** demander des nouvelles de qn; **what/who are you ~?** que/qui cherchez-vous?; **~ you!** après vous!; **~ all** après tout; **after-effects** npl (of disaster, radiation, drink etc) répercussions fpl; (of illness) séquelles fpl, suites fpl; **aftermath** n conséquences fpl; **afternoon** n après-midi m/f; **after-shave (lotion)** n lotion f après-rasage; **aftersun (cream/lotion)** n après-soleil m inv; **afterwards**, (us) **afterward** [ˈɑːftəwəd(z)] adv après

again [əˈgɛn] adv de nouveau, encore (une fois); **to do sth ~** refaire qch; **~ and ~** à plusieurs reprises

against [əˈgɛnst] prep contre; (compared to) par rapport à

age [eɪdʒ] n âge m ▷ vt, vi vieillir; **he is 20 years of ~** il a 20 ans; **to come of ~** atteindre sa majorité; **it's been ~s since I saw you** ça fait une éternité que je ne t'ai pas vu

aged adj âgé(e); **~ 10** âgé de 10 ans

age: age group n tranche f d'âge; **age limit** n limite f d'âge

agency [ˈeɪdʒənsɪ] n agence f

agenda [əˈdʒɛndə] n ordre m du jour

▌ Be careful not to translate agenda by the French word agenda.

agent [ˈeɪdʒənt] n agent m; (firm) concessionnaire m

aggravate [ˈægrəveɪt] vt (situation) aggraver; (annoy) exaspérer, agacer

aggression [əˈgrɛʃən] n agression f

aggressive [əˈgrɛsɪv] adj agressif(-ive)

agile [ˈædʒaɪl] adj agile

AGM n abbr (= annual general meeting) AG f

ago [əˈgəu] adv: **two days ~** il y a deux jours; **not long ~** il n'y a pas longtemps; **how long ~?** il y a combien de temps (de cela)?

agony [ˈægənɪ] n (pain) douleur f atroce; (distress) angoisse f; **to be in ~** souffrir le martyre

agree [əˈgriː] vt (price) convenir de ▷ vi: **to ~ with** (person) être d'accord avec; (statements etc) concorder avec; (Ling) s'accorder avec; **to ~ to do** accepter de or consentir à faire; **to ~ to sth** consentir à qch; **to ~ that** (admit) convenir or reconnaître que; **garlic doesn't ~ with me** je ne supporte pas l'ail; **agreeable** adj (pleasant) agréable; (willing) consentant(e), d'accord; **agreed** adj (time, place) convenu(e); **agreement** n accord m; **in agreement** d'accord

agricultural [ægrɪˈkʌltʃərəl] adj agricole

agriculture [ˈægrɪkʌltʃər] n agriculture f

ahead [əˈhɛd] adv en avant; devant; **go right** or **straight ~** (direction) allez tout droit; **go ~!** (permission) allez-y!; **~ of** devant; (fig: schedule etc) en avance sur; **~ of time** en avance

aid [eɪd] n aide f; (device) appareil m ▷ vt aider; **in ~ of** en faveur de

aide [eɪd] n (person) assistant(e)

AIDS [eɪdz] n abbr (= acquired immune (or immuno-)deficiency syndrome) SIDA m

ailing ['eɪlɪŋ] adj (person) souffreteux(euse); (economy) malade

ailment ['eɪlmənt] n affection f

aim [eɪm] n (objective) but m; (skill): **his ~ is bad** il vise mal ▷ vt: **to take~** (with gun, camera) viser ▷ vt: **to~ sth (at)** (gun, camera) braquer or pointer qch (sur); (missile) lancer qch (à or contre or en direction de); (remark, blow) destiner or adresser qch (à); **to~ at** viser; (fig) viser (à); **to ~ to do** avoir l'intention de faire

ain't [eɪnt] (inf) = **am not**; **aren't**; **isn't**

air [ɛəʳ] n air m ▷ vt aérer; (idea, grievance, views) mettre sur le tapis ▷ cpd (currents, attack etc) aérien(ne); **to throw sth into the~** (ball etc) jeter qch en l'air; **by~** par avion; **to be on the~** (Radio, TV: programme) être diffusé(e); (: station) émettre; **airbag** n airbag m; **airbed** n (BRIT) matelas m pneumatique; **airborne** adj (plane) en vol; **as soon as the plane was airborne** dès que l'avion eut décollé; **air-conditioned** adj climatisé(e), à air conditionné; **air conditioning** n climatisation f; **aircraft** n inv avion m; **airfield** n terrain m d'aviation; **Air Force** n Armée f de l'air; **air hostess** n (BRIT) hôtesse f de l'air; **airing cupboard** n (BRIT) placard qui contient la chaudière et dans lequel on met le linge à sécher; **airlift** n pont aérien; **airline** n ligne aérienne, compagnie aérienne; **airliner** n avion m de ligne; **airmail** n: **by airmail** par avion; **airplane** n (US) avion m; **airport** n aéroport m; **air raid** n attaque aérienne; **airsick** adj: **to be airsick** avoir le mal de l'air; **airspace** n espace m aérien; **airstrip** n terrain m d'atterrissage; **air terminal** n aérogare f; **airtight** adj hermétique; **air-traffic controller** n aiguilleur m du ciel; **airy** adj bien aéré(e); (manners) dégagé(e)

aisle [aɪl] n (of church: central) allée f centrale; (: side) nef f latérale, bas-côté m; (in theatre, supermarket) allée f; (on plane) couloir m; **aisle seat** n place f côté couloir

ajar [ə'dʒɑːʳ] adj entrouvert(e)

à la carte [ælæ'kɑːt] adv à la carte

alarm [ə'lɑːm] n alarme f ▷ vt alarmer; **alarm call** n coup m de fil pour réveiller; **could I have an alarm call at 7 am, please?** pouvez-vous me réveiller à 7 heures, s'il vous plaît?; **alarm clock** n réveille-matin m inv, réveil m; **alarmed** adj (frightened) alarmé(e); (protected by an alarm) protégé(e) par un système d'alarme; **alarming** adj alarmant(e)

Albania [æl'beɪnɪə] n Albanie f

albeit [ɔːl'biːɪt] conj bien que + sub, encore que + sub

album ['ælbəm] n album m

alcohol ['ælkəhɔl] n alcool m; **alcohol-free** adj sans alcool; **alcoholic** [ælkə'hɔlɪk] adj, n alcoolique (m/f)

alcove ['ælkəuv] n alcôve f

ale [eɪl] n bière f

alert [ə'ləːt] adj alerte, vif (vive); (watchful) vigilant(e) ▷ n alerte f ▷ vt alerter; **on the~** sur le qui-vive; (Mil) en état d'alerte

algebra ['ældʒɪbrə] n algèbre m

Algeria [æl'dʒɪərɪə] n Algérie f

Algerian [æl'dʒɪərɪən] adj algérien(ne) ▷ n Algérien(ne)

Algiers [æl'dʒɪəz] n Alger

alias ['eɪlɪəs] adv alias ▷ n faux nom, nom d'emprunt

alibi ['ælɪbaɪ] n alibi m

alien ['eɪlɪən] n (from abroad) étranger(-ère); (from outer space) extraterrestre ▷ adj: **~ (to)** étranger(-ère) (à); **alienate** vt aliéner; (subj: person) s'aliéner

alight [ə'laɪt] adj en feu ▷ vi mettre pied à terre; (passenger) descendre; (bird) se poser

align [ə'laɪn] vt aligner

alike [ə'laɪk] adj semblable, pareil(le)
▷ adv de même; **to look ~** se
ressembler

alive [ə'laɪv] adj vivant(e); (active)
plein(e) de vie

○ **KEYWORD**

all [ɔːl] adj (singular) tout(e); (plural)
tous (toutes); **all day** toute la
journée; **all night** toute la nuit; **all
men** tous les hommes; **all five** tous
les cinq; **all the books** tous les livres;
all his life toute sa vie
▶ pron 1 tout; **I ate it all, I ate all
of it** j'ai tout mangé; **all of us went**
nous y sommes tous allés; **all of the
boys went** tous les garçons y sont
allés; **is that all?** c'est tout?; (in shop)
ce sera tout?
2 (in phrases): **above all** surtout,
par-dessus tout; **after all** après
tout; **at all: not at all** (in answer to
question) pas du tout; (in answer to
thanks) je vous en prie!; **I'm not at all
tired** je ne suis pas du tout fatigué(e);
anything at all will do n'importe
quoi fera l'affaire; **all in all** tout bien
considéré, en fin de compte
▶ adv: **all alone** tout(e) seul(e); **it's
not as hard as all that** ce n'est pas
si difficile que ça; **all the more/
the better** d'autant plus/mieux;
all but presque, pratiquement;
the score is 2 all le score est de 2
partout

Allah ['ælə] n Allah m
allegation [ælɪ'geɪʃən] n allégation f
alleged [ə'lɛdʒd] adj prétendu(e);
allegedly adv à ce que l'on prétend,
paraît-il
allegiance [ə'liːdʒəns] n fidélité f,
obéissance f
allergic [ə'lə:dʒɪk] adj: **~ to**
allergique à; **I'm ~ to penicillin** je
suis allergique à la pénicilline
allergy ['ælədʒɪ] n allergie f

alleviate [ə'liːvɪeɪt] vt soulager,
adoucir
alley ['ælɪ] n ruelle f
alliance [ə'laɪəns] n alliance f
allied ['ælaɪd] adj allié(e)
alligator ['ælɪgeɪtə'] n alligator m
all-in ['ɔːlɪn] adj, adv (BRIT: charge)
tout compris
allocate ['æləkeɪt] vt (share out)
répartir, distribuer; **to ~ sth to**
(duties) assigner or attribuer qch à;
(sum, time) allouer qch à
allot [ə'lɔt] vt (share out) répartir,
distribuer; **to ~ sth to** (time) allouer
qch à; (duties) assigner qch à
all-out ['ɔːlaut] adj (effort etc) total(e)
allow [ə'lau] vt (practice, behaviour)
permettre, autoriser; (sum to spend
etc) accorder, allouer; (sum, time
estimated) compter, prévoir; (claim,
goal) admettre; (concede): **to ~
that** convenir que; **to ~ sb to do**
permettre à qn de faire, autoriser qn
à faire; **he is ~ed to ...** on lui permet
de ...; **allow for** vt fus tenir compte
de; **allowance** n (money received)
allocation f (: from parent etc) subside
m; (: for expenses) indemnité f; (US:
pocket money) argent m de poche;
(Tax) somme f déductible du revenu
imposable, abattement m; **to make
allowances for** (person) essayer de
comprendre; (thing) tenir compte de
all right adv (feel, work) bien; (as
answer) d'accord
ally ['ælaɪ] n allié m ▷ vt [ə'laɪ]: **to ~
o.s. with** s'allier avec
almighty [ɔːl'maɪtɪ] adj tout(e)-
puissant(e); (tremendous) énorme
almond ['ɑːmənd] n amande f
almost ['ɔːlməust] adv presque
alone [ə'ləun] adj, adv seul(e); **to
leave sb ~** laisser qn tranquille; **to
leave sth ~** ne pas toucher à qch; **let
~ ...** sans parler de ...; encore moins ...
along [ə'lɔŋ] prep le long de ▷ adv: **is
he coming ~ with us?** vient-il avec
nous?; **he was hopping/limping ~**

il venait *or* avançait en sautillant/ boitant; **~ with** avec, en plus de; (*person*) en compagnie de; **all ~** (*all the time*) depuis le début; **alongside** *prep* (*along*) le long de; (*beside*) à côté de ▷ *adv* bord à bord; côte à côte

aloof [ə'luːf] *adj* distant(e) ▷ *adv*: **to stand ~** se tenir à l'écart *or* à distance

aloud [ə'laud] *adv* à haute voix

alphabet ['ælfəbɛt] *n* alphabet *m*

Alps [ælps] *npl*: **the ~** les Alpes *fpl*

already [ɔːl'rɛdɪ] *adv* déjà

alright ['ɔːl'raɪt] *adv* (*BRIT*) = **all right**

also ['ɔːlsəu] *adv* aussi

altar ['ɔltəʳ] *n* autel *m*

alter ['ɔltəʳ] *vt*, *vi* changer; **alteration** [ɔltə'reɪʃən] *n* changement *m*, modification *f*; **alterations** *npl* (*Sewing*) retouches *fpl*; (*Archit*) modifications *fpl*

alternate *adj* [ɔl'təːnɪt] alterné(e), alternant(e), alternatif(-ive); (*US*) = **alternative** ▷ *vi* ['ɔltəːneɪt] alterner; **to ~ with** alterner avec; **on ~ days** un jour sur deux, tous les deux jours

alternative [ɔl'təːnətɪv] *adj* (*solution, plan*) autre, de remplacement; (*lifestyle*) parallèle ▷ *n* (*choice*) alternative *f*; (*other possibility*) autre possibilité *f*; **~ medicine** médecine alternative, médecine douce; **alternatively** *adv*: **alternatively one could ...** une autre *or* l'autre solution serait de ...

although [ɔːl'ðəu] *conj* bien que + *sub*

altitude ['æltɪtjuːd] *n* altitude *f*

altogether [ɔːltə'gɛðəʳ] *adv* entièrement, tout à fait; (*on the whole*) tout compte fait; (*in all*) en tout

aluminium [ælju'mɪnɪəm], (*US*) **aluminum** [ə'luːmɪnəm] *n* aluminium *m*

always ['ɔːlweɪz] *adv* toujours

Alzheimer's (disease) ['æltshaɪməz-] *n* maladie *f* d'Alzheimer

am [æm] *vb see* **be**

a.m. *adv abbr* (= *ante meridiem*) du matin

amalgamate [ə'mælgəmeɪt] *vt*, *vi* fusionner

amass [ə'mæs] *vt* amasser

amateur ['æmətəʳ] *n* amateur *m*

amaze [ə'meɪz] *vt* stupéfier; **to be ~d (at)** être stupéfait(e) (de); **amazed** *adj* stupéfait(e); **amazement** *n* surprise *f*, étonnement *m*; **amazing** *adj* étonnant(e), incroyable; (*bargain, offer*) exceptionnel(le)

Amazon ['æməzən] *n* (*Geo*) Amazone *f*

ambassador [æm'bæsədəʳ] *n* ambassadeur *m*

amber ['æmbəʳ] *n* ambre *m*; **at ~** (*BRIT Aut*) à l'orange

ambiguous [æm'bɪgjuəs] *adj* ambigu(ë)

ambition [æm'bɪʃən] *n* ambition *f*; **ambitious** [æm'bɪʃəs] *adj* ambitieux(-euse)

ambulance ['æmbjuləns] *n* ambulance *f*; **call an ~!** appelez une ambulance!

ambush ['æmbuʃ] *n* embuscade *f* ▷ *vt* tendre une embuscade à

amen ['ɑː'mɛn] *excl* amen

amend [ə'mɛnd] *vt* (*law*) amender; (*text*) corriger; **to make ~s** réparer ses torts, faire amende honorable; **amendment** *n* (*to law*) amendement *m*; (*to text*) correction *f*

amenities [ə'miːnɪtɪz] *npl* aménagements *mpl*, équipements *mpl*

America [ə'mɛrɪkə] *n* Amérique *f*; **American** *adj* américain(e) ▷ *n* Américain(e); **American football** *n* (*BRIT*) football *m* américain

amicable ['æmɪkəbl] *adj* amical(e); (*Law*) à l'amiable

amid(st) [ə'mɪd(st)] *prep* parmi, au milieu de

ammunition [æmju'nɪʃən] *n* munitions *fpl*

amnesty ['æmnɪstɪ] *n* amnistie *f*

among(st) [ə'mʌŋ(st)] *prep* parmi, entre

amount [ə'maunt] *n* (*sum of money*) somme *f*; (*total*) montant *m*; (*quantity*) quantité *f*; nombre *m* ▷ *vi*: **to ~ to** (*total*) s'élever à; (*be same as*) équivaloir à, revenir à

amp(ère) ['æmp(ɛər)] *n* ampère *m*

ample ['æmpl] *adj* ample, spacieux(-euse); (*enough*): **this is ~** c'est largement suffisant; **to have ~ time/room** avoir bien assez de temps/place

amplifier ['æmplɪfaɪər] *n* amplificateur *m*

amputate ['æmpjuteɪt] *vt* amputer

Amtrak ['æmtræk] (*US*) *n* société mixte de transports ferroviaires interurbains pour voyageurs

amuse [ə'mju:z] *vt* amuser; **amusement** *n* amusement *m*; (*pastime*) distraction *f*; **amusement arcade** *n* salle *f* de jeu; **amusement park** *n* parc *m* d'attractions

amusing [ə'mju:zɪŋ] *adj* amusant(e), divertissant(e)

an [æn, ən, n] *indef art see* **a**

anaemic, (*US*) **anemia** [ə'ni:mɪə] *n* anémie *f*

anaemic, (*US*) **anemic** [ə'ni:mɪk] *adj* anémique

anaesthetic, (*US*) **anesthetic** [ænɪs'θɛtɪk] *n* anesthésique *m*

analog(ue) ['ænəlɒg] *adj* (*watch, computer*) analogique

analogy [ə'nælədʒɪ] *n* analogie *f*

analyse, (*US*) **analyze** ['ænəlaɪz] *vt* analyser; **analysis** (*pl* **analyses**) [ə'næləsɪs, -si:z] *n* analyse *f*; **analyst** ['ænəlɪst] *n* (*political analyst etc*) analyste *m/f*; (*US*) psychanalyste *m/f*

analyze ['ænəlaɪz] *vt* (*US*) = **analyse**

anarchy ['ænəkɪ] *n* anarchie *f*

anatomy [ə'nætəmɪ] *n* anatomie *f*

ancestor ['ænsɪstər] *n* ancêtre *m*, aïeul *m*

anchor ['æŋkər] *n* ancre *f* ▷ *vi* (*also*: **to drop ~**) jeter l'ancre, mouiller ▷ *vt*

mettre à l'ancre; (*fig*): **to ~ sth to** fixer qch à

anchovy ['æntʃəvɪ] *n* anchois *m*

ancient ['eɪnʃənt] *adj* ancien(ne), antique; (*person*) d'un âge vénérable; (*car*) antédiluvien(ne)

and [ænd] *conj* et; **~ so on** et ainsi de suite; **try ~ come** tâchez de venir; **come ~ sit here** venez vous asseoir ici; **he talked ~ talked** il a parlé pendant des heures; **better ~ better** de mieux en mieux; **more ~ more** de plus en plus

Andorra [æn'dɔ:rə] *n* (principauté *f* d')Andorre *f*

anemia *etc* [ə'ni:mɪə] *n* (*US*) = **anaemia** *etc*

anesthetic [ænɪs'θɛtɪk] *n, adj* (*US*) = **anaesthetic**

angel ['eɪndʒəl] *n* ange *m*

anger ['æŋgər] *n* colère *f*

angina [æn'dʒaɪnə] *n* angine *f* de poitrine

angle ['æŋgl] *n* angle *m*; **from their ~** de leur point de vue

angler ['æŋglər] *n* pêcheur(-euse) à la ligne

Anglican ['æŋglɪkən] *adj, n* anglican(e)

angling ['æŋglɪŋ] *n* pêche *f* à la ligne

angrily ['æŋgrɪlɪ] *adv* avec colère

angry ['æŋgrɪ] *adj* en colère, furieux(-euse); (*wound*) enflammé(e); **to be ~ with sb/at sth** être furieux contre qn/de qch; **to get ~** se fâcher, se mettre en colère

anguish ['æŋgwɪʃ] *n* angoisse *f*

animal ['ænɪməl] *n* animal *m* ▷ *adj* animal(e)

animated ['ænɪmeɪtɪd] *adj* animé(e)

animation [ænɪ'meɪʃən] *n* (*of person*) entrain *m*; (*of street, Cine*) animation *f*

aniseed ['ænɪsi:d] *n* anis *m*

ankle ['æŋkl] *n* cheville *f*

annex ['æneks] *n* (BRIT: *also*: **~e**) annexe *f* ▷ *vt* [ə'neks] annexer

anniversary [ænɪ'və:sərɪ] *n* anniversaire *m*

announce [ə'nauns] vt annoncer;
(birth, death) faire part de;
announcement n annonce f; (for
births etc: in newspaper) avis m de
faire-part; (: letter, card) faire-part
m; **announcer** n (Radio, TV: between
programmes) speaker(ine); (: in a
programme) présentateur(-trice)
annoy [ə'nɔɪ] vt agacer, ennuyer,
contrarier; **don't get ~ed!** ne
vous fâchez pas!; **annoying** adj
agaçant(e), contrariant(e)
annual ['ænjuəl] adj annuel(le) ▷ n
(Bot) plante annuelle; (book) album m;
annually adv annuellement
annum ['ænəm] n see **per**
anonymous [ə'nɔnɪməs] adj
anonyme
anorak ['ænəræk] n anorak m
anorexia [ænə'rɛksɪə] n (also: ~
nervosa) anorexie f
anorexic [ænə'rɛksɪk] adj, n
anorexique (m/f)
another [ə'nʌðər] adj: ~ **book**
(one more) un autre livre, encore un
livre, un livre de plus; (a different one)
un autre livre ▷ pron un(e) autre,
encore un(e), un(e) de plus; see
also **one**
answer ['ɑːnsər] n réponse f; (to
problem) solution f ▷ vi répondre
▷ vt (reply to) répondre à; (problem)
résoudre; (prayer) exaucer; **in ~ to
your letter** suite à or en réponse
à votre lettre; **to ~ the phone**
répondre (au téléphone); **to ~ the
bell** or **the door** aller or venir ouvrir
(la porte); **answer back** vi répondre,
répliquer; **answerphone** n (esp BRIT)
répondeur m (téléphonique)
ant [ænt] n fourmi f
Antarctic [ænt'ɑːktɪk] n: **the ~**
l'Antarctique m
antelope ['æntɪləup] n antilope f
antenatal ['æntɪ'neɪtl] adj
prénatal(e)
antenna (pl **antennae**) [æn'tɛnə,
-niː] n antenne f

anthem ['ænθəm] n: **national ~**
hymne national
anthology [æn'θɔlədʒɪ] n
anthologie f
anthropology [ænθrə'pɔlədʒɪ] n
anthropologie f
anti ['æntɪ] prefix anti-; **antibiotic**
['æntɪbaɪ'ɔtɪk] n antibiotique m;
antibody ['æntɪbɔdɪ] n anticorps m
anticipate [æn'tɪsɪpeɪt] vt
s'attendre à, prévoir; (wishes,
request) aller au devant de, devancer;
anticipation [æntɪsɪ'peɪʃən] n
attente f
anticlimax ['æntɪ'klaɪmæks] n
déception f
anticlockwise ['æntɪ'klɔkwaɪz]
(BRIT) adv dans le sens inverse des
aiguilles d'une montre
antics ['æntɪks] npl singeries fpl
anti: antidote ['æntɪdəut] n antidote
m, contrepoison m; **antifreeze**
['æntɪfriːz] n antigel m; **anti-
globalization** n antimondialisation
f; **antihistamine** [æntɪ'hɪstəmɪn] n
antihistaminique m; **antiperspirant**
[æntɪ'pəːspɪrənt] n déodorant m
antique [æn'tiːk] n (ornament) objet
m d'art ancien; (furniture) meuble
ancien ▷ adj ancien(ne); **antique
shop** n magasin m d'antiquités
antiseptic [æntɪ'sɛptɪk] adj, n
antiseptique (m)
antisocial ['æntɪ'səuʃəl] adj
(unfriendly) insociable; (against society)
antisocial(e)
antivirus [æntɪ'vaɪrəs] adj (Comput)
antivirus inv; ~ **software** (logiciel
m) antivirus
antlers ['æntləz] npl bois mpl,
ramure f
anxiety [æŋ'zaɪətɪ] n anxiété f;
(keenness): ~ **to do** grand désir or
impatience f de faire
anxious ['æŋkʃəs] adj (très)
inquiet(-ète); (always worried)
anxieux(-euse); (worrying)
angoissant(e); ~ **to do/that** (keen)

qui tient beaucoup à faire/à ce que + *sub*; impatient(e) de faire/que + *sub*

○ **KEYWORD**

any ['enɪ] *adj* **1** (*in questions etc*: *singular*) du, de l', de la; (: *plural*) des; **do you have any butter/children/ ink?** avez-vous du beurre/des enfants/de l'encre?
2 (*with negative*) de, d'; **I don't have any money/books** je n'ai pas d'argent/de livres
3 (*no matter which*) n'importe quel(le); (*each and every*) tout(e), chaque; **choose any book you like** vous pouvez choisir n'importe quel livre; **any teacher you ask will tell you** n'importe quel professeur vous le dira
4 (*in phrases*): **in any case** de toute façon; **any day now** d'un jour à l'autre; **at any moment** à tout moment, d'un instant à l'autre; **at any rate** en tout cas; **any time** n'importe quand; **he might come (at) any time** il pourrait venir n'importe quand; **come (at) any time** venez quand vous voulez
▶ *pron* **1** (*in questions etc*) en; **have you got any?** est-ce que vous en avez?; **can any of you sing?** est-ce que parmi vous il y en a qui savent chanter?
2 (*with negative*) en; **I don't have any (of them)** je n'en ai pas, je n'en ai aucun
3 (*no matter which one(s)*) n'importe lequel (or laquelle); (*anybody*) n'importe qui; **take any of those books (you like)** vous pouvez prendre n'importe lequel de ces livres
▶ *adv* **1** (*in questions etc*): **do you want any more soup/sandwiches?** voulez-vous encore de la soupe/des sandwichs?; **are you feeling any better?** est-ce que vous vous sentez mieux?
2 (*with negative*): **I can't hear him any more** je ne l'entends plus; **don't wait any longer** n'attendez pas plus longtemps; **anybody** *pron* n'importe qui; (*in interrogative sentences*) quelqu'un; (*in negative sentences*): **I don't see anybody** je ne vois personne; **if anybody should phone ...** si quelqu'un téléphone ...; **anyhow** *adv* quoi qu'il en soit; (*haphazardly*) n'importe comment; **do it anyhow you like** faites-le comme vous voulez; **she leaves things just anyhow** elle laisse tout traîner; **I shall go anyhow** j'irai de toute façon; **anyone** *pron* = **anybody**; **anything** *pron* (*no matter what*) n'importe quoi; (*in questions*) quelque chose; (*with negative*) ne ... rien; **can you see anything?** tu vois quelque chose?; **if anything happens to me ...** s'il m'arrive quoi que ce soit ...; **you can say anything you like** vous pouvez dire ce que vous voulez; **anything will do** n'importe quoi fera l'affaire; **he'll eat anything** il mange de tout; **anytime** *adv* (*at any moment*) d'un moment à l'autre; (*whenever*) n'importe quand; **anyway** *adv* de toute façon; **anyway, I couldn't come even if I wanted to** de toute façon, je ne pouvais pas venir même si je le voulais; **I shall go anyway** j'irai quand même; **why are you phoning, anyway?** au fait, pourquoi tu me téléphones?; **anywhere** *adv* n'importe où; (*in interrogative sentences*) quelque part; (*in negative sentences*): **I can't see him anywhere** je ne le vois nulle part; **can you see him anywhere?** tu le vois quelque part?; **put the books down anywhere** pose les livres n'importe où; **anywhere in the world** (*no matter where*) n'importe où dans le monde

apart [ə'pɑːt] *adv* (*to one side*) à part; de côté; à l'écart; (*separately*) séparément; **to take/pull ~** démonter; **10 miles/a long way ~** à 10 miles/très éloignés l'un de l'autre; **~ from** prep à part, excepté

apartment [ə'pɑːtmənt] n (US) appartement m, logement m; (room) chambre f; **apartment building** n (US) immeuble m; maison divisée en appartements

apathy ['æpəθɪ] n apathie f, indifférence f

ape [eɪp] n (grand) singe ▷ vt singer

aperitif [ə'perɪtɪf] n apéritif m

aperture ['æpətjuə'] n orifice m, ouverture f; (Phot) ouverture (du diaphragme)

APEX ['eɪpɛks] n abbr (Aviat: = advance purchase excursion) APEX m

apologize [ə'pɒlədʒaɪz] vi: **to ~ (for sth to sb)** s'excuser (de qch auprès de qn), présenter ses excuses (à qn pour qch)

apology [ə'pɒlədʒɪ] n excuses fpl

apostrophe [ə'pɒstrəfɪ] n apostrophe f

app n abbr (inf: Comput: = application) appli f

appal, (US) **appall** [ə'pɔːl] vt consterner, atterrer; horrifier; **appalling** adj épouvantable; (stupidity) consternant(e)

apparatus [æpə'reɪtəs] n appareil m, dispositif m; (in gymnasium) agrès mpl

apparent [ə'pærənt] adj apparent(e); **apparently** adv apparemment

appeal [ə'piːl] vi (Law) faire or interjeter appel ▷ n (Law) appel m; (request) appel; prière f; (charm) attrait m, charme m; **to ~ for** demander (instamment); implorer; **to ~ to** (beg) faire appel à; (be attractive) plaire à; **it doesn't ~ to me** cela ne m'attire pas; **appealing** adj (attractive) attrayant(e)

appear [ə'pɪə'] vi apparaître, se montrer; (Law) comparaître; (publication) paraître, sortir, être

publié(e); (seem) paraître, sembler; **it would ~ that** il semble que; **to ~ in Hamlet** jouer dans Hamlet; **to ~ on TV** passer à la télé; **appearance** n apparition f; parution f; (look, aspect) apparence f, aspect m

appendices [ə'pendɪsiːz] npl of **appendix**

appendicitis [əpendɪ'saɪtɪs] n appendicite f

appendix (pl **appendices**) [ə'pendɪks, -siːz] n appendice m

appetite ['æpɪtaɪt] n appétit m

appetizer ['æpɪtaɪzə'] n (food) amuse-gueule m; (drink) apéritif m

applaud [ə'plɔːd] vt, vi applaudir

applause [ə'plɔːz] n applaudissements mpl

apple ['æpl] n pomme f; **apple pie** n tarte f aux pommes

appliance [ə'plaɪəns] n appareil m

applicable [ə'plɪkəbl] adj applicable; **to be ~ to** (relevant) valoir pour

applicant ['æplɪkənt] n: **~ (for)** candidat(e) (à)

application [æplɪ'keɪʃən] n (also Comput) application f; (for a job, a grant etc) demande f; candidature f; **application form** n formulaire m de demande

apply [ə'plaɪ] vt: **to ~ (to)** (paint, ointment) appliquer (sur); (law, etc) appliquer (à) ▷ vi: **to ~ to** (ask) s'adresser à; (be suitable for, relevant to) s'appliquer à; **to ~ (for)** (permit, grant) faire une demande (en vue d'obtenir); (job) poser sa candidature (pour), faire une demande d'emploi (concernant); **to ~ o.s. to** s'appliquer à

appoint [ə'pɔɪnt] vt (to post) nommer, engager; (date, place) fixer, désigner; **appointment** n (to post) nomination f; (job) poste m; (arrangement to meet) rendez-vous m; **to have an appointment** avoir un rendez-vous; **to make an appointment (with)** prendre rendez-vous (avec); **I'd like to make an appointment** je voudrais prendre rendez-vous

appraisal [ə'preɪzl] n évaluation f

appreciate [ə'priːʃɪeɪt] vt (like) apprécier, faire cas de; (be grateful for) être reconnaissant(e) de; (be aware of) comprendre, se rendre compte de ▷ vi (Finance) prendre de la valeur; **appreciation** [əpriːʃɪ'eɪʃən] n appréciation f; (gratitude) reconnaissance f; (Finance) hausse f, valorisation f

apprehension [æprɪ'hɛnʃən] n appréhension f, inquiétude f

apprehensive [æprɪ'hɛnsɪv] adj inquiet(-ète), appréhensif(-ive)

apprentice [ə'prɛntɪs] n apprenti m

approach [ə'prəʊtʃ] vi approcher ▷ vt (come near) approcher de; (ask, apply to) s'adresser à; (subject, passer-by) aborder ▷ n approche f; accès m, abord m; (intellectual) démarche f

appropriate adj [ə'prəʊprɪɪt] (tool etc) qui convient, approprié(e); (moment, remark) opportun(e) ▷ vt [ə'prəʊprɪeɪt] (take) s'approprier

approval [ə'pruːvəl] n approbation f; **on ~** (Comm) à l'examen

approve [ə'pruːv] vt approuver; **approve of** vt fus (thing) approuver; (person): **they don't ~ of her** ils n'ont pas bonne opinion d'elle

approximate [ə'prɒksɪmɪt] adj approximatif(-ive); **approximately** adv approximativement

Apr. abbr = **April**

apricot ['eɪprɪkɒt] n abricot m

April ['eɪprəl] n avril m; **April Fools' Day** n le premier avril

● **APRIL FOOLS' DAY**
●
● April Fools' Day est le 1er avril, à
● l'occasion duquel on fait des farces
● de toutes sortes. Les victimes de
● ces farces sont les "April fools".

● Traditionnellement, on n'est censé
● faire des farces que jusqu'à midi.

apron ['eɪprən] n tablier m

apt [æpt] adj (suitable) approprié(e); **~ to do** (likely) susceptible de faire; ayant tendance à faire

aquarium [ə'kwɛərɪəm] n aquarium m

Aquarius [ə'kwɛərɪəs] n le Verseau

Arab ['ærəb] n Arabe m/f ▷ adj arabe

Arabia [ə'reɪbɪə] n Arabie f; **Arabian** adj arabe; **Arabic** ['ærəbɪk] adj, n arabe (m)

arbitrary ['ɑːbɪtrərɪ] adj arbitraire

arbitration [ɑːbɪ'treɪʃən] n arbitrage m

arc [ɑːk] n arc m

arcade [ɑː'keɪd] n arcade f; (passage with shops) passage m, galerie f; (with games) salle f de jeu

arch [ɑːtʃ] n arche f; (of foot) cambrure f, voûte f plantaire ▷ vt arquer, cambrer

archaeology, (US) **archeology** [ɑːkɪ'ɒlədʒɪ] n archéologie f

archbishop [ɑːtʃ'bɪʃəp] n archevêque m

archeology [ɑːkɪ'ɒlədʒɪ] (US) n = **archaeology**

architect ['ɑːkɪtɛkt] n architecte m; **architectural** [ɑːkɪ'tɛktʃərəl] adj architectural(e); **architecture** n architecture f

archive ['ɑːkaɪv] n (often pl) archives fpl

Arctic ['ɑːktɪk] adj arctique ▷ n: **the ~** l'Arctique m

are [ɑːʳ] vb see **be**

area ['ɛərɪə] n (Geom) superficie f; (zone) région f (: smaller) secteur m; (in room) coin m; (knowledge, research) domaine m; **area code** (US) n (Tel) indicatif m de zone

arena [ə'riːnə] n arène f

aren't [ɑːnt] = **are not**

Argentina [ɑːdʒən'tiːnə] n Argentine f; **Argentinian**

[ɑːdʒən'tɪnɪən] adj argentin(e) ▷ n
Argentin(e)
arguably ['ɑːgjuəblɪ] adv: **it is ~ …**
on peut soutenir que c'est …
argue ['ɑːgjuː] vi (quarrel) se disputer;
(reason) argumenter; **to ~ that**
objecter or alléguer que, donner
comme argument que
argument ['ɑːgjumənt] n (quarrel)
dispute f, discussion f; (reasons)
argument m
Aries ['ɛərɪz] n le Bélier
arise (pt **arose**, pp **arisen**) [ə'raɪz,
ə'rəuz, ə'rɪzn] vi survenir, se présenter
arithmetic [ə'rɪθmətɪk] n
arithmétique f
arm [ɑːm] n bras m ▷ vt armer; **arms**
npl (weapons, Heraldry) armes fpl; **~ in
~** bras dessus bras dessous; **armchair**
['ɑːmtʃɛəʳ] n fauteuil m
armed [ɑːmd] adj armé(e); **armed
forces** npl; **the armed forces** les
forces armées; **armed robbery** n vol
m à main armée
armour, (us) **armor** ['ɑːməʳ] n
armure f; (Mil: tanks) blindés mpl
armpit ['ɑːmpɪt] n aisselle f
armrest ['ɑːmrɛst] n accoudoir m
army ['ɑːmɪ] n armée f
A road n (BRIT) ≈ route nationale
aroma [ə'rəumə] n arôme m;
aromatherapy n aromathérapie f
arose [ə'rəuz] pt of **arise**
around [ə'raund] adv (tout) autour;
(nearby) dans les parages ▷ prep
autour de; (near) près de; (fig: about)
environ; (: date, time) vers; **is he ~?**
est-il dans les parages or là?
arouse [ə'rauz] vt (sleeper) éveiller;
(curiosity, passions) éveiller, susciter;
(anger) exciter
arrange [ə'reɪndʒ] vt arranger; **to
~ to do sth** prévoir de faire qch;
arrangement n arrangement
m; **arrangements** npl (plans etc)
arrangements mpl, dispositions fpl
array [ə'reɪ] n (of objects) déploiement
m, étalage m

arrears [ə'rɪəz] npl arriéré m; **to be in
~ with one's rent** devoir un arriéré
de loyer
arrest [ə'rɛst] vt arrêter; (sb's
attention) retenir, attirer ▷ n
arrestation f; **under ~** en état
d'arrestation
arrival [ə'raɪvl] n arrivée f; **new ~**
nouveau venu/nouvelle venue; (baby)
nouveau-né(e)
arrive [ə'raɪv] vi arriver; **arrive at** vt
fus (decision, solution) parvenir à
arrogance ['ærəgəns] n arrogance f
arrogant ['ærəgənt] adj arrogant(e)
arrow ['ærəu] n flèche f
arse [ɑːs] n (BRIT inf!) cul m (!)
arson ['ɑːsn] n incendie criminel
art [ɑːt] n art m; **Arts** npl (Scol) les
lettres fpl; **art college** n école f des
beaux-arts
artery ['ɑːtərɪ] n artère f
art gallery n musée m d'art;
(saleroom) galerie f de peinture
arthritis [ɑː'θraɪtɪs] n arthrite f
artichoke ['ɑːtɪtʃəuk] n artichaut m;
Jerusalem ~ topinambour m
article ['ɑːtɪkl] n article m
articulate adj [ɑː'tɪkjulɪt] (person)
qui s'exprime clairement et aisément;
(speech) bien articulé(e), prononcé(e)
clairement ▷ vi [ɑː'tɪkjuleɪt]
articuler, parler distinctement ▷ vt
articuler
artificial [ɑːtɪ'fɪʃəl] adj artificiel(le)
artist ['ɑːtɪst] n artiste m/f; **artistic**
[ɑː'tɪstɪk] adj artistique
art school n ≈ école f des beaux-arts

○ **KEYWORD**

as [æz] conj **1** (time: moment) comme,
alors que; à mesure que; **he came in
as I was leaving** il est arrivé comme
je partais; **as the years went by** à
mesure que les années passaient; **as
from tomorrow** à partir de demain
2 (because) comme, puisque; **he
left early as he had to be home by**

10 comme il *or* puisqu'il devait être de retour avant 10h, il est parti de bonne heure

3 (*referring to manner, way*) comme; **do as you wish** faites comme vous voudrez; **as she said** comme elle disait

▶ *adv* **1** (*in comparisons*): **as big as** aussi grand que; **twice as big as** deux fois plus grand que; **as much** *or* **many as** autant que; **as much money/many books as** autant d'argent/de livres que; **as soon as** dès que

2 (*concerning*): **as for** *or* **to that** quant à cela, pour ce qui est de cela

3: **as if** *or* **though** comme si; **he looked as if he was ill** il avait l'air d'être malade; *see also* **long; such; well**

▶ *prep* (*in the capacity of*) en tant que, en qualité de; **he works as a driver** il travaille comme chauffeur; **as chairman of the company, he ...** en tant que président de la société, il ...; **he gave me it as a present** il me l'a offert, il m'en a fait cadeau

a.s.a.p. *abbr* = **as soon as possible**

asbestos [æz'bɛstəs] *n* asbeste *m*, amiante *m*

ascent [ə'sɛnt] *n* (*climb*) ascension *f*

ash [æʃ] *n* (*dust*) cendre *f*; (*also*: **~ tree**) frêne *m*

ashamed [ə'ʃeɪmd] *adj* honteux(-euse), confus(e); **to be ~ of** avoir honte de

ashore [ə'ʃɔːʳ] *adv* à terre

ashtray ['æʃtreɪ] *n* cendrier *m*

Ash Wednesday *n* mercredi *m* des Cendres

Asia ['eɪʃə] *n* Asie *f*; **Asian** *n* (*from Asia*) Asiatique *m/f*; (BRIT: *from Indian subcontinent*) Indo-Pakistanais(e) ▶ *adj* asiatique; indo-pakistanais(e)

aside [ə'saɪd] *adv* de côté; à l'écart ▶ *n* aparté *m*

ask [ɑːsk] *vt* demander; (*invite*) inviter; **to ~ sb sth/to do sth** demander à

qn qch/de faire qch; **to ~ sb about sth** questionner qn au sujet de qch; se renseigner auprès de qn au sujet de qch; **to ~ (sb) a question** poser une question (à qn); **to ~ sb out to dinner** inviter qn au restaurant; **ask for** *vt fus* demander; **it's just ~ing for trouble** *or* **for it** ce serait chercher des ennuis

asleep [ə'sliːp] *adj* endormi(e); **to fall ~** s'endormir

AS level *n abbr* (= *Advanced Subsidiary level*) première partie de l'examen équivalent au baccalauréat

asparagus [əs'pærəgəs] *n* asperges *fpl*

aspect ['æspɛkt] *n* aspect *m*; (*direction in which a building etc faces*) orientation *f*, exposition *f*

aspire [əs'paɪəʳ] *vi*: **to ~ to** aspirer à

aspirin ['æsprɪn] *n* aspirine *f*

ass [æs] *n* âne *m*; (*inf*) imbécile *m/f*; (US *inf*!) cul *m* (!)

assassin [ə'sæsɪn] *n* assassin *m*; **assassinate** *vt* assassiner

assault [ə'sɔːlt] *n* (*Mil*) assaut *m*; (*gen*: *attack*) agression *f* ▶ *vt* attaquer; (*sexually*) violenter

assemble [ə'sɛmbl] *vt* assembler ▶ *vi* s'assembler, se rassembler

assembly [ə'sɛmblɪ] *n* (*meeting*) rassemblement *m*; (*parliament*) assemblée *f*; (*construction*) assemblage *m*

assert [ə'səːt] *vt* affirmer, déclarer; (*authority*) faire valoir; (*innocence*) protester de; **assertion** [ə'səːʃən] *n* assertion *f*, affirmation *f*

assess [ə'sɛs] *vt* évaluer, estimer; (*tax, damages*) établir *or* fixer le montant de; (*person*) juger la valeur de; **assessment** *n* évaluation *f*, estimation *f*; (*of tax*) fixation *f*

asset ['æsɛt] *n* avantage *m*, atout *m*; (*person*) atout *m*; **assets** *npl* (*Comm*) capital *m*; avoir(s) *m(pl)*; actif *m*

assign [ə'saɪn] *vt* (*date*) fixer, arrêter; **to ~ sth to** (*task*) assigner

qch à; (*resources*) affecter qch à;
assignment n (*task*) mission f;
(*homework*) devoir m
assist [ə'sɪst] vt aider, assister;
assistance n aide f, assistance f;
assistant n assistant(e), adjoint(e);
(BRIT: *also*: **shop assistant**)
vendeur(-euse)
associate adj, n [ə'səuʃɪɪt]
associé(e) ▷ vt [ə'səuʃɪeɪt] associer
▷ vi [ə'səuʃɪeɪt]: **to ~ with sb**
fréquenter qn
association [əsəusɪ'eɪʃən] n
association f
assorted [ə'sɔːtɪd] adj assorti(e)
assortment [ə'sɔːtmənt] n
assortiment m; (*of people*) mélange m
assume [ə'sjuːm] vt supposer;
(*responsibilities etc*) assumer; (*attitude,
name*) prendre, adopter
assumption [ə'sʌmpʃən] n
supposition f, hypothèse f; (*of power*)
assomption f, prise f
assurance [ə'ʃuərəns] n assurance f
assure [ə'ʃuəʳ] vt assurer
asterisk [ˈæstərɪsk] n astérisque m
asthma [ˈæsmə] n asthme m
astonish [ə'stɔnɪʃ] vt étonner,
stupéfier; **astonished** adj
étonné(e); **to be astonished at**
être étonné(e) de; **astonishing**
adj étonnant(e), stupéfiant(e);
I find it astonishing that …
je trouve incroyable que … +
sub; **astonishment** n (grand)
étonnement, stupéfaction f
astound [ə'staund] vt stupéfier,
sidérer
astray [ə'streɪ] adv: **to go ~** s'égarer;
(*fig*) quitter le droit chemin; **to lead ~**
(*morally*) détourner du droit chemin
astrology [əs'trɔlədʒɪ] n astrologie f
astronaut [ˈæstrənɔːt] n
astronaute m/f
astronomer [əs'trɔnəməʳ] n
astronome m
astronomical [æstrə'nɔmɪkl] adj
astronomique

astronomy [əs'trɔnəmɪ] n
astronomie f
astute [əs'tjuːt] adj astucieux(-euse),
malin(-igne)
asylum [ə'saɪləm] n asile m; **asylum
seeker** [-siːkəʳ] n demandeur(-euse)
d'asile

 KEYWORD

at [æt] prep **1** (*referring to position,
direction*) à; **at the top** au sommet;
at home/school à la maison or chez
soi/à l'école; **at the baker's** à la
boulangerie, chez le boulanger; **to
look at sth** regarder qch
2 (*referring to time*): **at 4 o'clock** à 4
heures; **at Christmas** à Noël; **at night**
la nuit; **at times** par moments, parfois
3 (*referring to rates, speed etc*) à; **at £1
a kilo** une livre le kilo; **two at a time**
deux à la fois; **at 50 km/h** à 50 km/h
4 (*referring to manner*): **at a stroke**
d'un seul coup; **at peace** en paix
5 (*referring to activity*): **to be at
work** (*in the office etc*) être au travail;
(*working*) travailler; **to play at
cowboys** jouer aux cowboys; **to be
good at sth** être bon en qch
6 (*referring to cause*): **shocked/
surprised/annoyed at sth** choqué
par/étonné de/agacé par qch; **I went
at his suggestion** j'y suis allé sur
son conseil
▷ n (@ *symbol*) arobase f

ate [eɪt] pt of **eat**
atheist [ˈeɪθɪɪst] n athée m/f
Athens [ˈæθɪnz] n Athènes
athlete [ˈæθliːt] n athlète m/f
athletic [æθ'lɛtɪk] adj athlétique;
athletics n athlétisme m
Atlantic [ət'læntɪk] adj atlantique
▷ n: **the ~ (Ocean)** l'(océan m)
Atlantique m
atlas [ˈætləs] n atlas m
A.T.M. n abbr (= *Automated Telling
Machine*) guichet m automatique

atmosphere ['ætməsfɪə'] n (air)
atmosphère f; (fig: of place etc)
atmosphère, ambiance f

atom ['ætəm] n atome m; **atomic**
[ə'tɔmɪk] adj atomique; **atom(ic)
bomb** n bombe f atomique

atrocity [ə'trɔsɪtɪ] n atrocité f

attach [ə'tætʃ] vt (gen) attacher;
(document, letter) joindre; **to be ~ed
to sb/sth** (to like) être attaché à qn/
qch; **to ~ a file to an email** joindre
un fichier à un e-mail; **attachment**
n (tool) accessoire m; (Comput) fichier
m joint; (love): **attachment (to)**
affection f (pour), attachement m (à)

attack [ə'tæk] vt attaquer; (task etc)
s'attaquer à ▷ n attaque f; **heart
~** crise f cardiaque; **attacker** n
attaquant m, agresseur m

attain [ə'teɪn] vt (also: **to ~ to**)
parvenir à, atteindre; (knowledge)
acquérir

attempt [ə'tɛmpt] n tentative f ▷ vt
essayer, tenter

attend [ə'tɛnd] vt (course) suivre;
(meeting, talk) assister à; (school,
church) aller à, fréquenter; (patient)
soigner, s'occuper de; **attend to**
vt fus (needs, affairs etc) s'occuper
de; (customer) s'occuper de, servir;
attendance n (being present)
présence f; (people present) assistance
f; **attendant** n employé(e);
gardien(ne) ▷ adj concomitant(e), qui
accompagne or s'ensuit

■ Be careful not to translate attend
by the French word attendre.

attention [ə'tɛnʃən] n attention f
▷ excl (Mil) garde-à-vous!; **for the ~ of**
(Admin) à l'attention de

attic ['ætɪk] n grenier m, combles mpl

attitude ['ætɪtjuːd] n attitude f

attorney [ə'təːnɪ] n (US: lawyer)
avocat m; **Attorney General** n (BRIT)
≈ procureur général; (US) ≈ garde m
des Sceaux, ministre m de la Justice

attract [ə'trækt] vt attirer;
attraction [ə'trækʃən] n (gen pl:

pleasant things) attraction f, attrait
m; (Physics) attraction; (fig: towards
sb, sth) attirance f; **attractive** adj
séduisant(e), attrayant(e)

attribute n ['ætrɪbjuːt] attribut m
▷ vt [ə'trɪbjuːt]: **to ~ sth to** attribuer
qch à

aubergine ['əubəʒiːn] n aubergine f

auburn ['ɔːbən] adj auburn inv,
châtain roux inv

auction ['ɔːkʃən] n (also: **sale by ~**)
vente f aux enchères ▷ vt (also: **to sell
by ~**) vendre aux enchères

audible ['ɔːdɪbl] adj audible

audience ['ɔːdɪəns] n (people)
assistance f, public m; (on radio)
auditeurs mpl; (at theatre) spectateurs
mpl; (interview) audience f

audit ['ɔːdɪt] vt vérifier

audition [ɔː'dɪʃən] n audition f

auditor ['ɔːdɪtə'] n vérificateur m
des comptes

auditorium [ɔːdɪ'tɔːrɪəm] n
auditorium m, salle f de concert or
de spectacle

Aug. abbr = **August**

August ['ɔːgəst] n août m

aunt [ɑːnt] n tante f; **auntie, aunty** n
diminutive of **aunt**

au pair ['əu'pɛə'] n (also: **~ girl**) jeune
fille f au pair

aura ['ɔːrə] n atmosphère f; (of person)
aura f

austerity [ɔs'tɛrɪtɪ] n austérité f

Australia [ɔs'treɪlɪə] n Australie f;
Australian adj australien(ne) ▷ n
Australien(ne)

Austria ['ɔstrɪə] n Autriche f;
Austrian adj autrichien(ne) ▷ n
Autrichien(ne)

authentic [ɔː'θɛntɪk] adj
authentique

author ['ɔːθə'] n auteur m

authority [ɔː'θɔrɪtɪ] n autorité f;
(permission) autorisation (formelle);
the authorities les autorités fpl,
l'administration f

authorize ['ɔːθəraɪz] vt autoriser

auto [ˈɔːtəʊ] *n* (*US*) auto *f*, voiture *f*; **autobiography** [ɔːtəbaɪˈɒɡrəfɪ] *n* autobiographie *f*; **autograph** [ˈɔːtəɡrɑːf] *n* autographe *m* ▷ *vt* signer, dédicacer; **automatic** [ɔːtəˈmætɪk] *adj* automatique ▷ *n* (*gun*) automatique *m*; (*car*) voiture *f* à transmission automatique; **automatically** *adv* automatiquement; **automobile** [ˈɔːtəməbiːl] *n* (*US*) automobile *f*; **autonomous** [ɔːˈtɒnəməs] *adj* autonome; **autonomy** [ɔːˈtɒnəmɪ] *n* autonomie *f*

autumn [ˈɔːtəm] *n* automne *m*

auxiliary [ɔːɡˈzɪlɪərɪ] *adj*, *n* auxiliaire (*m/f*)

avail [əˈveɪl] *vt*: **to ~ o.s. of** user de; profiter de ▷ *n*: **to no ~** sans résultat, en vain, en pure perte

availability [əveɪləˈbɪlɪtɪ] *n* disponibilité *f*

available [əˈveɪləbl] *adj* disponible

avalanche [ˈævəlɑːnʃ] *n* avalanche *f*

Ave. *abbr* = **avenue**

avenue [ˈævənjuː] *n* avenue *f*; (*fig*) moyen *m*

average [ˈævərɪdʒ] *n* moyenne *f* ▷ *adj* moyen(ne) ▷ *vt* (*a certain figure*) atteindre *or* faire *etc* en moyenne; **on ~** en moyenne

avert [əˈvəːt] *vt* (*danger*) prévenir, écarter; (*one's eyes*) détourner

avid [ˈævɪd] *adj* avide

avocado [ævəˈkɑːdəʊ] *n* (*BRIT: also*: **~ pear**) avocat *m*

avoid [əˈvɔɪd] *vt* éviter

await [əˈweɪt] *vt* attendre

awake [əˈweɪk] (*pt* **awoke**, *pp* **awoken**) *adj* éveillé(e) ▷ *vt* éveiller ▷ *vi* s'éveiller; **to be ~** être réveillé(e)

award [əˈwɔːd] *n* (*for bravery*) récompense *f*; (*prize*) prix *m*; (*Law: damages*) dommages-intérêts *mpl* ▷ *vt* (*prize*) décerner; (*Law: damages*) accorder

aware [əˈwɛər] *adj*: **~ of** (*conscious*) conscient(e) de; (*informed*) au courant de; **to become ~ of/that** prendre conscience de/que; se rendre compte de/que; **awareness** *n* conscience *f*, connaissance *f*

away [əˈweɪ] *adv* (*au*) loin; (*movement*): **she went ~** elle est partie ▷ *adj* (*not in, not here*) absent(e); **far ~** (*au*) loin; **two kilometres ~** à (une distance de) deux kilomètres, à deux kilomètres de distance; **two hours ~ by car** à deux heures de voiture *or* de route; **the holiday was two weeks ~** il restait deux semaines jusqu'aux vacances; **he's ~ for a week** il est parti (pour) une semaine; **to take sth ~ from sb** prendre qch à qn; **to take sth ~ from sth** (*subtract*) ôter qch de qch; **to work/pedal ~** travailler/pédaler à cœur joie; **to fade ~** (*colour*) s'estomper; (*sound*) s'affaiblir

awe [ɔː] *n* respect mêlé de crainte, effroi mêlé d'admiration; **awesome** [ˈɔːsəm] (*US*) *adj* (*inf: excellent*) génial(e)

awful [ˈɔːfəl] *adj* affreux(-euse); **an ~ lot of** énormément de; **awfully** *adv* (*very*) terriblement, vraiment

awkward [ˈɔːkwəd] *adj* (*clumsy*) gauche, maladroit(e); (*inconvenient*) peu pratique; (*embarrassing*) gênant

awoke [əˈwəʊk] *pt of* **awake**

awoken [əˈwəʊkən] *pp of* **awake**

axe, (*US*) **ax** [æks] *n* hache *f* ▷ *vt* (*project etc*) abandonner; (*jobs*) supprimer

axle [ˈæksl] *n* essieu *m*

ay(e) [aɪ] *excl* (*yes*) oui

azalea [əˈzeɪlɪə] *n* azalée *f*

the people at the ~ **hear me properly?** est-ce que les gens du fond m'entendent?; **~ to front** à l'envers; **~ seat/wheel** (*Aut*) siège *m*/roue *f* arrière *inv*; **~ payments/rent** arriéré *m* de paiements/loyer; **~ garden/room** jardin/pièce sur l'arrière; **he ran ~** il est revenu en courant; **throw the ball ~** renvoie la balle; **can I have it ~?** puis-je le ravoir?, peux-tu me le rendre?; **he called ~** (*again*) il a rappelé; **back down** *vi* rabattre de ses prétentions; **back out** *vi* (*of promise*) se dédire; **back up** *vt* (*person*) soutenir; (*Comput*) faire une copie de sauvegarde de; **backache** *n* mal *m* au dos; **backbencher** *n* (*BRIT*) *membre du parlement sans portefeuille*; **backbone** *n* colonne vertébrale, épine dorsale; **back door** *n* porte *f* de derrière; **backfire** *vi* (*Aut*) pétarader; (*plans*) mal tourner; **backgammon** *n* trictrac *m*; **background** *n* arrière-plan *m*; (*of events*) situation *f*, conjoncture *f*; (*basic knowledge*) éléments *mpl* de base; (*experience*) formation *f*; **family background** milieu familial; **backing** *n* (*fig*) soutien *m*, appui *m*; **backlog** *n*: **backlog of work** travail *m* en retard; **backpack** *n* sac *m* à dos; **backpacker** *n* randonneur(-euse); **backslash** *n* barre oblique inversée; **backstage** *adv* dans les coulisses; **backstroke** *n* dos crawlé; **backup** *adj* (*train, plane*) supplémentaire, de réserve; (*Comput*) de sauvegarde ▷ *n* (*support*) appui *m*, soutien *m*; (*Comput: also:* **backup file**) sauvegarde *f*; **backward** *adj* (*movement*) en arrière; (*person, country*) arriéré(e), attardé(e); **backwards** *adv* (*move, go*) en arrière; (*read a list*) à l'envers, à rebours; (*fall*) à la renverse; (*walk*) à reculons; **backyard** *n* arrière-cour *f*

B [biː] *n* (*Mus*) si *m*

B.A. *abbr* (*Scol*) = **Bachelor of Arts**

baby ['beɪbɪ] *n* bébé *m*; **baby carriage** *n* (*us*) voiture *f* d'enfant; **baby-sit** *vi* garder les enfants; **baby-sitter** *n* baby-sitter *m/f*; **baby wipe** *n* lingette *f* (*pour bébé*)

bachelor ['bætʃələʳ] *n* célibataire *m*; **B~ of Arts/Science (BA/BSc)** ≈ licencié(e) ès or en lettres/sciences

back [bæk] *n* (*of person, horse*) dos *m*; (*of hand*) dos, revers *m*; (*of house*) derrière *m*; (*of car, train*) arrière *m*; (*of chair*) dossier *m*; (*of page*) verso *m*; (*Football*) arrière *m* ▷ *vt* (*financially*) soutenir (financièrement); (*candidate: also:* **~ up**) soutenir, appuyer; (*horse: at races*) parier or miser sur; (*car*) (faire) reculer ▷ *vi* reculer; (*car etc*) faire marche arrière ▷ *adj* (*in compounds*) de derrière, à l'arrière ▷ *adv* (*not forward*) en arrière; (*returned*): **he's ~** il est rentré, il est de retour; **can**

bacon ['beɪkən] *n* bacon *m*, lard *m*

bacteria [bæk'tɪərɪə] *npl* bactéries *fpl*

bad [bæd] *adj* mauvais(e); (*child*) vilain(e); (*mistake, accident*) grave;

(*meat, food*) gâté(e), avarié(e); **his ~ leg** sa jambe malade; **to go ~** (*meat, food*) se gâter; (*milk*) tourner

bade [bæd] *pt of* **bid**

badge [bædʒ] *n* insigne *m*; (*of policeman*) plaque *f*; (*stick-on, sew-on*) badge *m*

badger ['bædʒəʳ] *n* blaireau *m*

badly ['bædlɪ] *adv* (*work, dress etc*) mal; **to reflect ~ on sb** donner une mauvaise image de qn; **~ wounded** grièvement blessé; **he needs it ~** il en a absolument besoin; **~ off** *adj, adv* dans la gêne

bad-mannered ['bæd'mænəd] *adj* mal élévé(e)

badminton ['bædmɪntən] *n* badminton *m*

bad-tempered ['bæd'tɛmpəd] *adj* (*by nature*) ayant mauvais caractère; (*on one occasion*) de mauvaise humeur

bag [bæg] *n* sac *m*; (*inf: lots of*) **~s of** des tas de; **baggage** *n* bagages *mpl*; **baggage allowance** *n* franchise *f* de bagages; **baggage reclaim** *n* (*at airport*) livraison *f* des bagages; **baggy** *adj* avachi(e), qui fait des poches; **bagpipes** *npl* cornemuse *f*

bail [beɪl] *n* caution *f* ⊳ *vt* (*prisoner: also*: **grant ~ to**) mettre en liberté sous caution; (*boat: also*: **~ out**) écoper; **to be released on ~** être libéré(e) sous caution; **bail out** *vt* (*prisoner*) payer la caution de

bait [beɪt] *n* appât *m* ⊳ *vt* appâter; (*fig: tease*) tourmenter

bake [beɪk] *vt* (faire) cuire au four ⊳ *vi* (*bread etc*) cuire (au four); (*make cakes etc*) faire de la pâtisserie; **baked beans** *npl* haricots blancs à la sauce tomate; **baked potato** *n* pomme *f* de terre en robe des champs; **baker** *n* boulanger *m*; **bakery** *n* boulangerie *f*; **baking** *n* (*process*) cuisson *f*; **baking powder** *n* levure *f* (chimique)

balance ['bæləns] *n* équilibre *m*; (*Comm: sum*) solde *m*; (*remainder*) reste

m; (*scales*) balance *f* ⊳ *vt* mettre or faire tenir en équilibre; (*pros and cons*) peser; (*budget*) équilibrer; (*account*) balancer; (*compensate*) compenser, contrebalancer; **~ of trade/ payments** balance commerciale/ des comptes *or* paiements; **balanced** *adj* (*personality, diet*) équilibré(e); (*report*) objectif(-ive); **balance sheet** *n* bilan *m*

balcony ['bælkənɪ] *n* balcon *m*; **do you have a room with a ~?** avez-vous une chambre avec balcon?

bald [bɔːld] *adj* chauve; (*tyre*) lisse

ball [bɔːl] *n* boule *f*; (*football*) ballon *m*; (*for tennis, golf*) balle *f*; (*dance*) bal *m*; **to play ~** jouer au ballon (*or* à la balle); (*fig*) coopérer

ballerina [bælə'riːnə] *n* ballerine *f*

ballet ['bæleɪ] *n* ballet *m*; (*art*) danse *f* (classique); **ballet dancer** *n* danseur(-euse) de ballet

balloon [bə'luːn] *n* ballon *m*

ballot ['bælət] *n* scrutin *m*

ballpoint (pen) ['bɔːlpɔɪnt-] *n* stylo *m* à bille

ballroom ['bɔːlrum] *n* salle *f* de bal

Baltic [bɔːltɪk] *n*: **the ~ (Sea)** la (mer) Baltique

bamboo [bæm'buː] *n* bambou *m*

ban [bæn] *n* interdiction *f* ⊳ *vt* interdire

banana [bə'nɑːnə] *n* banane *f*

band [bænd] *n* bande *f*; (*at a dance*) orchestre *m*; (*Mil*) musique *f*, fanfare *f*

bandage ['bændɪdʒ] *n* bandage *m*, pansement *m* ⊳ *vt* (*wound, leg*) mettre un pansement *or* un bandage sur

Band-Aid® ['bændeɪd] *n* (*us*) pansement adhésif

B. & B. *n abbr* = **bed and breakfast**

bandit ['bændɪt] *n* bandit *m*

bang [bæŋ] *n* détonation *f*; (*of door*) claquement *m*; (*blow*) coup (violent) ⊳ *vt* frapper (violemment); (*door*) claquer ⊳ *vi* détoner; claquer

Bangladesh [bæŋglə'dɛʃ] *n* Bangladesh *m*

Bangladeshi [bæŋglə'dɛʃɪ] adj
du Bangladesh ▷ n habitant(e) du
Bangladesh
bangle ['bæŋgl] n bracelet m
bangs [bæŋz] npl (US: fringe) frange f
banish ['bænɪʃ] vt bannir
banister(s) ['bænɪstə(z)] n(pl)
rampe f (d'escalier)
banjo ['bændʒəʊ] (pl **banjoes** or
banjos) n banjo m
bank [bæŋk] n banque f; (of river,
lake) bord m, rive f; (of earth) talus
m, remblai m ▷ vi (Aviat) virer sur
l'aile; **bank on** vt fus miser or tabler
sur; **bank account** n compte m en
banque; **bank balance** n solde m
bancaire; **bank card** (BRIT) n carte f
d'identité bancaire; **bank charges**
npl (BRIT) frais mpl de banque; **banker**
n banquier m; **bank holiday** n (BRIT)
jour férié (où les banques sont fermées);
voir article **"bank holiday"**; **banking**
n opérations fpl bancaires; profession
f de banquier; **bank manager** n
directeur m d'agence (bancaire);
banknote n billet m de banque

- **BANK HOLIDAY**
-
- Le terme bank holiday s'applique
- au Royaume-Uni aux jours fériés
- pendant lesquels banques et
- commerces sont fermés. Les
- principaux bank holidays à part Noël
- et Pâques se situent au mois de
- mai et fin août, et contrairement
- aux pays de tradition catholique,
- ne coïncident pas nécessairement
- avec une fête religieuse.

bankrupt ['bæŋkrʌpt] adj en faillite;
to go ~ faire faillite; **bankruptcy**
n faillite f
bank statement n relevé m de
compte
banner ['bænə'] n bannière f
bannister(s) ['bænɪstə(z)] n(pl)
= **banister(s)**

banquet ['bæŋkwɪt] n banquet m,
festin m
baptism ['bæptɪzəm] n baptême m
baptize [bæp'taɪz] vt baptiser
bar [bɑː'] n (pub) bar m; (counter)
comptoir m, bar; (rod: of metal etc)
barre f; (: of window etc) barreau
m; (of chocolate) tablette f, plaque
f; (fig: obstacle) obstacle m;
(prohibition) mesure f d'exclusion;
(Mus) mesure f ▷ vt (road) barrer;
(person) exclure; (activity) interdire;
~ of soap savonnette f; **behind ~s**
(prisoner) derrière les barreaux; **the
B~** (Law) le barreau; **~ none** sans
exception
barbaric [bɑː'bærɪk] adj barbare
barbecue ['bɑːbɪkjuː] n barbecue m
barbed wire ['bɑːbd-] n fil m de fer
barbelé
barber ['bɑːbə'] n coiffeur m (pour
hommes); **barber's (shop)**, (US)
barber shop n salon m de coiffure
(pour hommes)
bar code n code m à barres, code-
barre m
bare [bɛə'] adj nu(e) ▷ vt mettre à nu,
dénuder; (teeth) montrer; **barefoot**
adj, adv nu-pieds, (les) pieds nus;
barely adv à peine
bargain ['bɑːgɪn] n (transaction)
marché m; (good buy) affaire f,
occasion f ▷ vi (haggle) marchander;
(negotiate) négocier, traiter; **into
the ~** par-dessus le marché; **bargain
for** vt fus (inf): **he got more than he
~ed for!** il en a eu pour son argent!
barge [bɑːdʒ] n péniche f; **barge in** vi
(walk in) faire irruption; (interrupt talk)
intervenir mal à propos
bark [bɑːk] n (of tree) écorce f; (of dog)
aboiement m ▷ vi aboyer
barley ['bɑːlɪ] n orge f
barmaid ['bɑːmeɪd] n serveuse f (de
bar), barmaid f
barman ['bɑːmən] (irreg) n serveur m
(de bar), barman m
barn [bɑːn] n grange f

barometer [bə'rɒmɪtə'] n baromètre m

baron ['bærən] n baron m; **baroness** n baronne f

barracks ['bærəks] npl caserne f

barrage ['bærɑːʒ] n (Mil) tir m de barrage; (dam) barrage m; (of criticism) feu m

barrel ['bærəl] n tonneau m; (of gun) canon m

barren ['bærən] adj stérile

barrette [bə'rɛt] (US) n barrette f

barricade [bærɪ'keɪd] n barricade f

barrier ['bærɪə'] n barrière f

barring ['bɑːrɪŋ] prep sauf

barrister ['bærɪstə'] n (BRIT) avocat (plaidant)

barrow ['bærəu] n (cart) charrette f à bras

bartender ['bɑːtɛndə'] n (US) serveur m (de bar), barman m

base [beɪs] n base f ▷ vt (opinion, belief): **to ~ sth on** baser or fonder qch sur ▷ adj vil(e), bas(se)

baseball ['beɪsbɔːl] n base-ball m; **baseball cap** n casquette f de base-ball

Basel [bɑːl] n = **Basle**

basement ['beɪsmənt] n sous-sol m

bases ['beɪsiːz] npl of **basis**

bash [bæʃ] vt (inf) frapper, cogner

basic ['beɪsɪk] adj (precautions, rules) élémentaire; (principles, research) fondamental(e); (vocabulary, salary) de base; (minimal) réduit(e) au minimum, rudimentaire; **basically** adv (in fact) en fait; (essentially) fondamentalement; **basics** npl: **the basics** l'essentiel m

basil ['bæzl] n basilic m

basin ['beɪsn] n (vessel, also Geo) cuvette f, bassin m; (BRIT: for food) bol m; (also: **wash~**) lavabo m

basis (pl **bases**) ['beɪsɪs, -siːz] n base f; **on a part-time/trial ~** à temps partiel/à l'essai

basket ['bɑːskɪt] n corbeille f; (with handle) panier m; **basketball** n basket-ball m

Basle [bɑːl] n Bâle

Basque [bæsk] adj basque ▷ n Basque m/f; **the ~ Country** le Pays basque

bass [beɪs] n (Mus) basse f

bastard ['bɑːstəd] n enfant naturel(le), bâtard(e); (inf!) salaud m (!)

bat [bæt] n chauve-souris f; (for baseball etc) batte f; (BRIT: for table tennis) raquette f ▷ vt: **he didn't ~ an eyelid** il n'a pas sourcillé or bronché

batch [bætʃ] n (of bread) fournée f; (of papers) liasse f; (of applicants, letters) paquet m

bath (pl **baths**) [bɑːθ, bɑːðz] n bain m; (bathtub) baignoire f ▷ vt baigner, donner un bain à; **to have a ~** prendre un bain; see also **baths**

bathe [beɪð] vi se baigner ▷ vt baigner; (wound etc) laver

bathing ['beɪðɪŋ] n baignade f; **bathing costume**, (US) **bathing suit** n maillot m (de bain)

bath: bathrobe n peignoir m de bain; **bathroom** n salle f de bains; **baths** [bɑːðz] npl (BRIT: also: **swimming baths**) piscine f; **bath towel** n serviette f de bain; **bathtub** n baignoire f

baton ['bætən] n bâton m; (Mus) baguette f; (club) matraque f

batter ['bætə'] vt battre ▷ n pâte f à frire; **battered** adj (hat, pan) cabossé(e); **battered wife/child** épouse/enfant maltraité(e) or martyr(e)

battery ['bætərɪ] n (for torch, radio) pile f; (Aut, Mil) batterie f; **battery farming** n élevage m en batterie

battle ['bætl] n bataille f, combat m ▷ vi se battre, lutter; **battlefield** n champ m de bataille

bay [beɪ] n (of sea) baie f; (BRIT: for parking) place f de stationnement; (: for loading) aire f de chargement; **B~ of Biscay** golfe m de Gascogne; **to hold sb at ~** tenir qn à distance or en échec

bay leaf n laurier m

bazaar [bəˈzɑːʳ] n (shop, market) bazar m; (sale) vente f de charité

BBC n abbr (= British Broadcasting Corporation) office de la radiodiffusion et télévision britannique

B.C. adv abbr (= before Christ) av. J.-C.

KEYWORD

be [biː] (pt **was**, **were**, pp **been**) aux vb **1** (with present participle, forming continuous tenses): **what are you doing?** que faites-vous?; **they're coming tomorrow** ils viennent demain; **I've been waiting for you for 2 hours** je t'attends depuis 2 heures

2 (with pp, forming passives) être; **to be killed** être tué(e); **the box had been opened** la boîte avait été ouverte; **he was nowhere to be seen** on ne le voyait nulle part

3 (in tag questions): **it was fun, wasn't it?** c'était drôle, n'est-ce pas?; **he's good-looking, isn't he?** il est beau, n'est-ce pas?; **she's back, is she?** elle est rentrée, n'est-ce pas or alors?

4 (+to +infinitive): **the house is to be sold** (necessity) la maison doit être vendue; (future) la maison va être vendue; **he's not to open it** il ne doit pas l'ouvrir

▸ vb + complement **1** (gen) être; **I'm English** je suis anglais(e); **I'm tired** je suis fatigué(e); **I'm hot/cold** j'ai chaud/froid; **he's a doctor** il est médecin; **be careful/good/quiet!** faites attention/soyez sages/taisez-vous!; **2 and 2 are 4** 2 et 2 font 4

2 (of health) aller; **how are you?** comment allez-vous?; **I'm better now** je vais mieux maintenant; **he's very ill** il est très malade

3 (of age) avoir; **how old are you?** quel âge avez-vous?; **I'm sixteen (years old)** j'ai seize ans

4 (cost) coûter; **how much was the meal?** combien a coûté le repas?; **that'll be £5, please** ça fera 5 livres, s'il vous plaît; **this shirt is £17** cette chemise coûte 17 livres

▸ vi **1** (exist, occur etc) être, exister; **the prettiest girl that ever was** la fille la plus jolie qui ait jamais existé; **is there a God?** y a-t-il un dieu?; **be that as it may** quoi qu'il en soit; **so be it** soit

2 (referring to place) être, se trouver; **I won't be here tomorrow** je ne serai pas là demain

3 (referring to movement) aller; **where have you been?** où êtes-vous allé(s)?

▸ impers vb **1** (referring to time) être; **it's 5 o'clock** il est 5 heures; **it's the 28th of April** c'est le 28 avril

2 (referring to distance): **it's 10 km to the village** le village est à 10 km

3 (referring to the weather) faire; **it's too hot/cold** il fait trop chaud/froid; **it's windy today** il y a du vent aujourd'hui

4 (emphatic): **it's me/the postman** c'est moi/le facteur; **it was Maria who paid the bill** c'est Maria qui a payé la note

beach [biːtʃ] n plage f ▸ vt échouer

beacon [ˈbiːkən] n (lighthouse) fanal m; (marker) balise f

bead [biːd] n perle f; (of dew, sweat) goutte f; **beads** npl (necklace) collier m

beak [biːk] n bec m

beam [biːm] n (Archit) poutre f; (of light) rayon m ▸ vi rayonner

bean [biːn] n haricot m; (of coffee) grain m; **beansprouts** npl pousses fpl or germes mpl de soja

bear [bɛəʳ] n ours m ▸ vt (pt **bore**, pp **borne**) porter; (endure) supporter; (interest) rapporter ▸ vi: **to ~ right/left** obliquer à droite/gauche, se diriger vers la droite/gauche

beard [bɪəd] n barbe f

bearer [ˈbɛərəʳ] n porteur m; (of passport etc) titulaire m/f

bearing [ˈbɛərɪŋ] n maintien m, allure f; (connection) rapport m; **(ball) bearings** npl (Tech) roulement m (à billes)

beast [biːst] n bête f; (inf: person) brute f

beat [biːt] n battement m; (Mus) temps m, mesure f; (of policeman) ronde f ▷ vt, vi (pt **beat**, pp **beaten**) battre; **off the ~ en track** hors des chemins or sentiers battus; **to ~ it** (inf) ficher le camp; **beat up** vt (inf: person) tabasser; **beating** n raclée f

beautiful [ˈbjuːtɪful] adj beau (belle); **beautifully** adv admirablement

beauty [ˈbjuːtɪ] n beauté f; **beauty parlour** , (us)**beauty parlor** n institut m de beauté; **beauty salon** n institut m de beauté; **beauty spot** n (on skin) grain m de beauté; (BRIT Tourism) site naturel (d'une grande beauté)

beaver [ˈbiːvəʳ] n castor m

became [bɪˈkeɪm] pt of **become**

because [bɪˈkɔz] conj parce que; **~ of** prep à cause de

beckon [ˈbɛkən] vt (also: **~ to**) faire signe (de venir) à

become [bɪˈkʌm] vi devenir; **to ~ fat/thin** grossir/maigrir; **to ~ angry** se mettre en colère

bed [bɛd] n lit m; (of flowers) parterre m; (of coal, clay) couche f; (of sea, lake) fond m; **to go to ~** aller se coucher; **bed and breakfast** n (terms) chambre et petit déjeuner; (place) ≈ chambre f d'hôte; voir article **"bed and breakfast"**; **bedclothes** npl couvertures fpl et draps mpl; **bedding** n literie f; **bed linen** n draps mpl de lit (et taies fpl d'oreillers), literie f; **bedroom** n chambre f (à coucher); **bedside** n: **at sb's bedside** au chevet de qn; **bedside lamp** n lampe f de chevet; **bedside table** n table f de chevet; **bedsit(ter)** n (BRIT) chambre meublée, studio m; **bedspread** n couvre-lit m, dessus-de-lit m;

bedtime n: **it's bedtime** c'est l'heure de se coucher

⬤ **BED AND BREAKFAST**

⬤ Un bed and breakfast est une
⬤ petite pension dans une maison
⬤ particulière ou une ferme où l'on
⬤ peut louer une chambre avec
⬤ petit déjeuner compris pour
⬤ un prix modique par rapport
⬤ à ce que l'on paierait dans un
⬤ hôtel. Ces établissements sont
⬤ communément appelés "B & B",
⬤ et sont signalés par une pancarte
⬤ dans le jardin ou au-dessus de
⬤ la porte.

bee [biː] n abeille f

beech [biːtʃ] n hêtre m

beef [biːf] n bœuf m; **roast ~** rosbif m; **beefburger** n hamburger m

been [biːn] pp of **be**

beer [bɪəʳ] n bière f; **beer garden** n (BRIT) jardin m d'un pub (où l'on peut emmener ses consommations)

beet [biːt] n (vegetable) betterave f; (us: also: **red ~**) betterave (potagère)

beetle [ˈbiːtl] n scarabée m, coléoptère m

beetroot [ˈbiːtruːt] n (BRIT) betterave f

before [bɪˈfɔːʳ] prep (of time) avant; (of space) devant ▷ conj avant que + sub; avant de ▷ adv avant; **~ going** avant de partir; **~ she goes** avant qu'elle (ne) parte; **the week ~** la semaine précédente or d'avant; **I've never seen it ~** c'est la première fois que je le vois; **beforehand** adv au préalable, à l'avance

beg [bɛg] vi mendier ▷ vt mendier; (forgiveness, mercy etc) demander; (entreat) supplier; **to ~ sb to do sth** supplier qn de faire qch; see also **pardon**

began [bɪ'gæn] *pt of* **begin**

beggar ['bɛgəʳ] *n* mendiant(e)

begin [bɪ'gɪn] (*pt* **began**, *pp* **begun**) *vt*, *vi* commencer; **to ~ doing** *or* **to do sth** commencer à faire qch; **beginner** *n* débutant(e); **beginning** *n* commencement *m*, début *m*

begun [bɪ'gʌn] *pp of* **begin**

behalf [bɪ'hɑːf] *n* **on ~ of**, (*us*) **in ~ of** (*representing*) de la part de; (*for benefit of*) pour le compte de; **on my/his ~** de ma/sa part

behave [bɪ'heɪv] *vi* se conduire, se comporter; (*well: also: ~ o.s.*) se conduire bien *or* comme il faut; **behaviour**, (*us*) **behavior** *n* comportement *m*, conduite *f*

behind [bɪ'haɪnd] *prep* derrière; (*time*) en retard sur; (*supporting*): **to be ~ sb** soutenir qn ▷ *adv* derrière; en retard ▷ *n* derrière *m*; **~ the scenes** dans les coulisses; **to be ~ (schedule) with sth** être en retard dans qch

beige [beɪʒ] *adj* beige

Beijing ['beɪ'dʒɪŋ] *n* Pékin

being ['biːɪŋ] *n* être *m*; **to come into ~** prendre naissance

belated [bɪ'leɪtɪd] *adj* tardif(-ive)

belch [bɛltʃ] *vi* avoir un renvoi, roter ▷ *vt* (*smoke etc: also: ~ out*) vomir, cracher

Belgian ['bɛldʒən] *adj* belge, de Belgique ▷ *n* Belge *m/f*

Belgium ['bɛldʒəm] *n* Belgique *f*

belief [bɪ'liːf] *n* (*opinion*) conviction *f*; (*trust, faith*) foi *f*

believe [bɪ'liːv] *vt*, *vi* croire, estimer; **to ~ in** (*God*) croire en; (*ghosts, method*) croire à; **believer** *n* (*in idea, activity*) partisan(e); (*Rel*) croyant(e)

bell [bɛl] *n* cloche *f*; (*small*) clochette *f*, grelot *m*; (*on door*) sonnette *f*; (*electric*) sonnerie *f*

bellboy ['bɛlbɔɪ], (*us*) **bellhop** ['bɛlhɔp] *n* groom *m*, chasseur *m*

bellow ['bɛləu] *vi* (*bull*) meugler; (*person*) brailler

bell pepper *n* (*esp us*) poivron *m*

belly ['bɛlɪ] *n* ventre *m*; **belly button** (*inf*) *n* nombril *m*

belong [bɪ'lɔŋ] *vi*: **to ~ to** appartenir à; (*club etc*) faire partie de; **this book ~s here** ce livre va ici, la place de ce livre est ici; **belongings** *npl* affaires *fpl*, possessions *fpl*

beloved [bɪ'lʌvɪd] *adj* (bien-)aimé(e), chéri(e)

below [bɪ'ləu] *prep* sous, au-dessous de ▷ *adv* en dessous; en contre-bas; **see ~** voir plus bas *or* plus loin *or* ci-dessous

belt [bɛlt] *n* ceinture *f*; (*Tech*) courroie *f* ▷ *vt* (*thrash*) donner une raclée à; **beltway** *n* (*us Aut*) route *f* de ceinture; (: *motorway*) périphérique *m*

bemused [bɪ'mjuːzd] *adj* médusé(e)

bench [bɛntʃ] *n* banc *m*; (*in workshop*) établi *m*; **the B~** (*Law: judges*) la magistrature, la Cour

bend [bɛnd] (*pt*, *pp* **bent**) *vt* courber; (*leg, arm*) plier ▷ *vi* se courber ▷ *n* (*in road*) virage *m*, tournant *m*; (*in pipe, river*) coude *m*; **bend down** *vi* se baisser; **bend over** *vi* se pencher

beneath [bɪ'niːθ] *prep* sous, au-dessous de; (*unworthy of*) indigne de ▷ *adv* dessous, au-dessous, en bas

beneficial [bɛnɪ'fɪʃəl] *adj*: **~ (to)** salutaire (pour), bénéfique (à)

benefit ['bɛnɪfɪt] *n* avantage *m*, profit *m*; (*allowance of money*) allocation *f* ▷ *vt* faire du bien à, profiter à ▷ *vi*: **he'll ~ from it** cela lui fera du bien, il y gagnera *or* s'en trouvera bien

Benelux ['bɛnɪlʌks] *n* Bénélux *m*

benign [bɪ'naɪn] *adj* (*person, smile*) bienveillant(e), affable; (*Med*) bénin(-igne)

bent [bɛnt] *pt*, *pp of* **bend** ▷ *n* inclination *f*, penchant *m* ▷ *adj*: **to be ~ on** être résolu(e) à

bereaved [bɪ'riːvd] *n*: **the ~** la famille du disparu

beret ['bɛreɪ] *n* béret *m*

Berlin [bəː'lɪn] *n* Berlin

Bermuda [bə'mju:də] *n* Bermudes *fpl*

Bern [bə:n] *n* Berne

berry ['bɛrɪ] *n* baie *f*

berth [bə:θ] *n* (*bed*) couchette *f*; (*for ship*) poste *m* d'amarrage, mouillage *m* ▷ *vi* (*in harbour*) venir à quai; (*at anchor*) mouiller

beside [bɪ'saɪd] *prep* à côté de; (*compared with*) par rapport à; **that's ~ the point** ça n'a rien à voir; **to be ~ o.s. (with anger)** être hors de soi; **besides** *adv* en outre, de plus ▷ *prep* en plus de; (*except*) excepté

best [bɛst] *adj* meilleur(e) ▷ *adv* le mieux; **the ~ part of** (*quantity*) le plus clair de, la plus grande partie de; **at ~** au mieux; **to make the ~ of sth** s'accommoder de qch (du mieux que l'on peut); **to do one's ~** faire de son mieux; **to the ~ of my knowledge** pour autant que je sache; **to the ~ of my ability** du mieux que je pourrai; **best-before date** *n* date *f* de limite d'utilisation *or* de consommation; **best man** (*irreg*) *n* garçon *m* d'honneur; **bestseller** *n* best-seller *m*, succès *m* de librairie

bet [bɛt] *n* pari *m* ▷ *vt, vi* (*pt* **bet**, *pp* **betted**) parier; **to ~ sb sth** parier qch à qn

betray [bɪ'treɪ] *vt* trahir

better ['bɛtər] *adj* meilleur(e) ▷ *adv* mieux ▷ *vt* améliorer ▷ *n*: **to get the ~ of** triompher de, l'emporter sur; **you had ~ do it** vous feriez mieux de le faire; **he thought ~ of it** il s'est ravisé; **to get ~** (*Med*) aller mieux; (*improve*) s'améliorer

betting ['bɛtɪŋ] *n* paris *mpl*; **betting shop** *n* (*BRIT*) bureau *m* de paris

between [bɪ'twi:n] *prep* entre ▷ *adv* au milieu, dans l'intervalle

beverage ['bɛvərɪdʒ] *n* boisson *f* (*gén sans alcool*)

beware [bɪ'wɛər] *vi*: **to ~ (of)** prendre garde (à); **"~ of the dog"** "(attention) chien méchant"

bewildered [bɪ'wɪldəd] *adj* dérouté(e), ahuri(e)

beyond [bɪ'jɔnd] *prep* (*in space, time*) au-delà de; (*exceeding*) au-dessus de ▷ *adv* au-delà; **~ doubt** hors de doute; **~ repair** irréparable

bias ['baɪəs] *n* (*prejudice*) préjugé *m*, parti pris; (*preference*) prévention *f*; **bias(s)ed** *adj* partial(e), montrant un parti pris

bib [bɪb] *n* bavoir *m*

Bible ['baɪbl] *n* Bible *f*

bicarbonate of soda [baɪ'kɑ:bənɪt-] *n* bicarbonate *m* de soude

biceps ['baɪsɛps] *n* biceps *m*

bicycle ['baɪsɪkl] *n* bicyclette *f*; **bicycle pump** *n* pompe *f* à vélo

bid [bɪd] *n* offre *f*; (*at auction*) enchère *f*; (*attempt*) tentative *f* ▷ *vi* (*pt, pp* **bid**) faire une enchère *or* offre ▷ *vt* (*pt* **bade**, *pp* **bidden**) faire une enchère *or* offre de; **to ~ sb good day** souhaiter le bonjour à qn; **bidder** *n*: **the highest bidder** le plus offrant

bidet ['bi:deɪ] *n* bidet *m*

big [bɪg] *adj* (*in height: person, building, tree*) grand(e); (*in bulk, amount: person, parcel, book*) gros(se); **Big Apple** *n* voir article **"Big Apple"**; **bigheaded** *adj* prétentieux(-euse); **big toe** *n* gros orteil

○ **BIG APPLE**
○
○ Si l'on sait que "The Big Apple"
○ désigne la ville de New York ("apple"
○ est en réalité un terme d'argot
○ signifiant "grande ville"), on connaît
○ moins les surnoms donnés aux
○ autres grandes villes américaines.
○ Chicago est surnommée "Windy
○ City" à cause des rafales soufflant
○ du lac Michigan, La Nouvelle-
○ Orléans doit son sobriquet
○ de "Big Easy" à son style de
○ vie décontracté, et l'industrie

automobile a donné à Detroit son surnom de "Motown".

bike [baɪk] n vélo m; **bike lane** n piste f cyclable

bikini [bɪˈkiːnɪ] n bikini m

bilateral [baɪˈlætərl] adj bilatéral(e)

bilingual [baɪˈlɪŋwəl] adj bilingue

bill [bɪl] n note f, facture f; (in restaurant) addition f, note f; (Pol) projet m de loi; (us: banknote) billet m (de banque); (notice) affiche f; (of bird) bec m; **put it on my ~** mettez-le sur mon compte; **"post no ~s"** "défense d'afficher"; **to fit** or **fill the ~** (fig) faire l'affaire; **billboard** n (us) panneau m d'affichage; **billfold** [ˈbɪlfəʊld] n (us) portefeuille m

billiards [ˈbɪljədz] n (jeu m de) billard m

billion [ˈbɪljən] n (BRIT) billion m (million de millions); (us) milliard m

bin [bɪn] n boîte f; (BRIT: also: **dust~, litter ~**) poubelle f; (for coal) coffre m

bind (pt, pp **bound**) [baɪnd, baʊnd] vt attacher; (book) relier; (oblige) obliger, contraindre ▷ n (inf: nuisance) scie f

binge [bɪndʒ] n (inf): **to go on a ~** faire la bringue

bingo [ˈbɪŋgəʊ] n sorte de jeu de loto pratiqué dans des établissements publics

binoculars [bɪˈnɔkjuləz] npl jumelles fpl

bio…: biochemistry [baɪəˈkemɪstrɪ] n biochimie f; **biodegradable** [ˈbaɪəʊdɪˈgreɪdəbl] adj biodégradable; **biofuel** [ˈbaɪəufjuəl] n biocarburant; **biography** [baɪˈɔgrəfɪ] n biographie f; **biological** [baɪˈɔlədʒɪ] adj biologique; **biology** [baɪˈɔlədʒɪ] n biologie f; **biometric** [baɪəˈmetrɪk] adj biométrique

birch [bəːtʃ] n bouleau m

bird [bəːd] n oiseau m; (BRIT inf: girl) nana f; **bird flu** n grippe f aviaire; **bird of prey** n oiseau m de proie; **birdwatching** n ornithologie f (d'amateur)

Biro® [ˈbaɪərəu] n stylo m à bille

birth [bəːθ] n naissance f; **to give ~ to** donner naissance à, mettre au monde; (animal) mettre bas; **birth certificate** n acte m de naissance; **birth control** n (policy) limitation f des naissances; (methods) méthode(s) contraceptive(s); **birthday** n anniversaire m ▷ cpd (cake, card etc) d'anniversaire; **birthmark** n envie f, tache f de vin; **birthplace** n lieu m de naissance

biscuit [ˈbɪskɪt] n (BRIT) biscuit m; (us) petit pain au lait

bishop [ˈbɪʃəp] n évêque m; (Chess) fou m

bistro [ˈbiːstrəu] n petit restaurant m, bistrot m

bit [bɪt] pt of **bite** ▷ n morceau m; (Comput) bit m, élément m binaire; (of tool) mèche f; (of horse) mors m; **a ~ of** un peu de; **a ~ mad/dangerous** un peu fou/risqué; **~ by ~** petit à petit

bitch [bɪtʃ] n (dog) chienne f; (offensive) salope f (!), garce f

bite [baɪt] vt, vi (pt **bit**, pp **bitten**) mordre; (insect) piquer ▷ n morsure f; (insect bite) piqûre f; (mouthful) bouchée f; **let's have a ~ (to eat)** mangeons un morceau; **to ~ one's nails** se ronger les ongles

bitten [ˈbɪtn] pp of **bite**

bitter [ˈbɪtər] adj amer(-ère); (criticism) cinglant(e); (icy: weather, wind) glacial(e) ▷ n (BRIT: beer) bière f (à forte teneur en houblon)

bizarre [bɪˈzɑːr] adj bizarre

black [blæk] adj noir(e) ▷ n (colour) noir m; (person): **B~** noir(e) ▷ vt (BRIT Industry) boycotter; **to give sb a ~ eye** pocher l'œil à qn, faire un œil au beurre noir à qn; **to be in the ~** (in credit) avoir un compte créditeur; **~ and blue** (bruised) couvert(e) de bleus; **black out** vi (faint) s'évanouir; **blackberry** n mûre f; **blackbird** n merle m; **blackboard** n tableau noir; **black coffee** n café noir; **blackcurrant** n cassis m; **black ice** n verglas m; **blackmail** n chantage m ▷ vt faire chanter, soumettre au chantage; **black market** n marché noir; **blackout** n panne f d'électricité; (in wartime) black-out m; (TV) interruption f d'émission; (fainting) syncope f; **black pepper** n poivre noir; **black pudding** n boudin (noir); **Black Sea** n: **the Black Sea** la mer Noire

bladder ['blædə^r] n vessie f
blade [bleɪd] n lame f; (of propeller) pale f; **a ~ of grass** un brin d'herbe
blame [bleɪm] n faute f, blâme m ▷ vt: **to ~ sb/sth for sth** attribuer à qn/qch la responsabilité de qch; reprocher qch à qn/qch; **I'm not to ~** ce n'est pas ma faute
bland [blænd] adj (taste, food) doux (douce), fade
blank [blæŋk] adj blanc (blanche); (look) sans expression, dénué(e) d'expression ▷ n espace m vide, blanc m; (cartridge) cartouche f à blanc; **his mind was a ~** il avait la tête vide
blanket ['blæŋkɪt] n couverture f; (of snow, cloud) couche f
blast [blɑːst] n explosion f; (shock wave) souffle m; (of air, steam) bouffée f ▷ vt faire sauter or exploser
blatant ['bleɪtənt] adj flagrant(e), criant(e)
blaze [bleɪz] n (fire) incendie m; (fig) flamboiement m ▷ vi (fire) flamber; (fig) flamboyer, resplendir ▷ vt: **to ~ a trail** (fig) montrer la voie; **in a ~ of publicity** à grand renfort de publicité
blazer ['bleɪzə^r] n blazer m
bleach [bliːtʃ] n (also: **household ~**) eau f de Javel ▷ vt (linen) blanchir; **bleachers** npl (US Sport) gradins mpl (en plein soleil)
bleak [bliːk] adj morne, désolé(e); (weather) triste, maussade; (smile) lugubre; (prospect, future) morose
bled [blɛd] pt, pp of **bleed**

bleed (pt, pp **bled**) [bliːd, blɛd] vt saigner; (brakes, radiator) purger ▷ vi saigner; **my nose is ~ing** je saigne du nez
blemish ['blɛmɪʃ] n défaut m; (on reputation) tache f
blend [blɛnd] n mélange m ▷ vt mélanger ▷ vi (colours etc: also: **~ in**) se mélanger, se fondre, s'allier; **blender** n (Culin) mixeur m
bless (pt, pp **blessed** or **blest**) [blɛs, blɛst] vt bénir; **~ you!** (after sneeze) à tes souhaits!; **blessing** n bénédiction f; (godsend) bienfait m
blew [bluː] pt of **blow**
blight [blaɪt] vt (hopes etc) anéantir, briser
blind [blaɪnd] adj aveugle ▷ n (for window) store m ▷ vt aveugler; **the blind** npl les aveugles mpl; **blind alley** n impasse f; **blindfold** n bandeau m ▷ adj, adv les yeux bandés ▷ vt bander les yeux à
blink [blɪŋk] vi cligner des yeux; (light) clignoter
bliss [blɪs] n félicité f, bonheur m sans mélange
blister ['blɪstə^r] n (on skin) ampoule f, cloque f; (on paintwork) boursouflure f ▷ vi (paint) se boursoufler, se cloquer
blizzard ['blɪzəd] n blizzard m, tempête f de neige
bloated ['bləʊtɪd] adj (face) bouffi(e); (stomach, person) gonflé(e)
blob [blɔb] n (drop) goutte f; (stain, spot) tache f
block [blɔk] n bloc m; (in pipes) obstruction f; (toy) cube m; (of buildings) pâté m (de maisons) ▷ vt bloquer; (fig) faire obstacle à; **the sink is ~ed** l'évier est bouché; **~ of flats** (BRIT) immeuble (locatif); **mental ~** blocage m; **block up** vt boucher; **blockade** [blɔ'keɪd] n blocus m ▷ vt faire le blocus de; **blockage** n obstruction f; **blockbuster** n (film, book) grand succès; **block capitals** npl

majuscules *fpl* d'imprimerie; **block letters** *npl* majuscules *fpl*

blog [blɔg] *n* blog *m* ▷ *vi* bloguer

blogger ['blɔgə^r] *n* blogueur(-euse)

bloke [bləuk] *n* (BRIT *inf*) type *m*

blond(e) [blɔnd] *adj*, *n* blond(e)

blood [blʌd] *n* sang *m*; **blood donor** *n* donneur(-euse) de sang; **blood group** *n* groupe sanguin; **blood poisoning** *n* empoisonnement *m* du sang; **blood pressure** *n* tension (artérielle); **bloodshed** *n* effusion *f* de sang, carnage *m*; **bloodshot** *adj*: **bloodshot eyes** yeux injectés de sang; **bloodstream** *n* sang *m*, système sanguin; **blood test** *n* analyse *f* de sang; **blood transfusion** *n* transfusion *f* de sang; **blood type** *n* groupe sanguin; **blood vessel** *n* vaisseau sanguin; **bloody** *adj* sanglant(e); (BRIT *inf!*): **this bloody ...** ce foutu ..., ce putain de ... (!) ▷ *adv*: **bloody strong/good** (BRIT *inf!*) vachement *or* sacrément fort/bon

bloom [blu:m] *n* fleur *f* ▷ *vi* être en fleur

blossom ['blɔsəm] *n* fleur(s) *f(pl)* ▷ *vi* être en fleurs; (*fig*) s'épanouir

blot [blɔt] *n* tache *f* ▷ *vt* tacher; (*ink*) sécher

blouse [blauz] *n* (*feminine garment*) chemisier *m*, corsage *m*

blow [bləu] (*pt* **blew**, *pp* **blown**) *n* coup *m* ▷ *vi* souffler ▷ *vt* (*instrument*) jouer de; (*fuse*) faire sauter; **to ~ one's nose** se moucher; **blow away** *vi* s'envoler ▷ *vt* chasser, faire s'envoler; **blow out** *vi* (*fire, flame*) s'éteindre; (*tyre*) éclater; (*fuse*) sauter; **blow up** *vi* exploser, sauter ▷ *vt* faire sauter; (*tyre*) gonfler; (*Phot*) agrandir; **blow-dry** *n* (*hairstyle*) brushing *m*

blown [bləun] *pp* of **blow**

blue [blu:] *adj* bleu(e); (*depressed*) triste; **~ film/joke** film *m*/histoire *f* pornographique; **out of the ~** (*fig*) à l'improviste, sans qu'on s'y attende; **bluebell** *n* jacinthe *f* des bois;

blueberry *n* myrtille *f*, airelle *f*; **blue cheese** *n* (fromage) bleu *m*; **blues** *npl*: **the blues** (*Mus*) le blues; **to have the blues** (*inf*: *feeling*) avoir le cafard

bluff [blʌf] *vi* bluffer ▷ *n* bluff *m*; **to call sb's ~** mettre qn au défi d'exécuter ses menaces

blunder ['blʌndə^r] *n* gaffe *f*, bévue *f* ▷ *vi* faire une gaffe *or* une bévue

blunt [blʌnt] *adj* (*knife*) émoussé(e), peu tranchant(e); (*pencil*) mal taillé(e); (*person*) brusque, ne mâchant pas ses mots

blur [blə:^r] *n* (*shape*): **to become a ~** devenir flou ▷ *vt* brouiller, rendre flou(e); **blurred** *adj* flou(e)

blush [blʌʃ] *vi* rougir ▷ *n* rougeur *f*; **blusher** *n* rouge *m* à joues

board [bɔ:d] *n* (*wooden*) planche *f*; (*on wall*) panneau *m*; (*for chess etc*) plateau *m*; (*cardboard*) carton *m*; (*committee*) conseil *m*, comité *m*; (*in firm*) conseil d'administration; (*Naut, Aviat*): **on ~** à bord ▷ *vt* (*ship*) monter à bord de; (*train*) monter dans; **full ~** (BRIT) pension complète; **half ~** (BRIT) demi-pension *f*; **~ and lodging** *n* chambre *f* avec pension; **to go by the ~** (*hopes, principles*) être abandonné(e); **board game** *n* jeu *m* de société; **boarding card** *n* (*Aviat, Naut*) carte *f* d'embarquement; **boarding pass** *n* (BRIT) = **boarding card**; **boarding school** *n* internat *m*, pensionnat *m*; **board room** *n* salle *f* du conseil d'administration

boast [bəust] *vi*: **to ~ (about *or* of)** se vanter (de)

boat [bəut] *n* bateau *m*; (*small*) canot *m*; barque *f*

bob [bɔb] *vi* (*boat, cork on water*: *also*: **~ up and down**) danser, se balancer

bobby pin ['bɔbɪ-] *n* (US) pince *f* à cheveux

body ['bɔdɪ] *n* corps *m*; (*of car*) carrosserie *f*; (*fig*: *society*) organe *m*, organisme *m*; **body-building** *n* body-building *m*, culturisme *m*; **bodyguard**

n garde *m* du corps; **bodywork** *n* carrosserie *f*

bog [bɔɡ] *n* tourbière *f* ▷ *vt*: **to get ~ged down (in)** (*fig*) s'enliser (dans)

bogus ['bəʊɡəs] *adj* bidon *inv*; fantôme

boil [bɔɪl] *vt* (faire) bouillir ▷ *vi* bouillir ▷ *n* (*Med*) furoncle *m*; **to come to the** *or* (*US*) **a ~** bouillir; **boil down** *vi* (*fig*): **to ~ down to** se réduire *or* ramener à; **boil over** *vi* déborder; **boiled egg** *n* œuf *m* à la coque; **boiler** *n* chaudière *f*; **boiling** ['bɔɪlɪŋ] *adj*: **I'm boiling (hot)** (*inf*) je crève de chaud; **boiling point** *n* point *m* d'ébullition

bold [bəʊld] *adj* hardi(e), audacieux(-euse); (*pej*) effronté(e); (*outline, colour*) franc (franche), tranché(e), marqué(e)

bollard ['bɔləd] *n* (*BRIT Aut*) borne lumineuse *or* de signalisation

bolt [bəʊlt] *n* verrou *m*; (*with nut*) boulon *m* ▷ *adv*: **~ upright** droit(e) comme un piquet ▷ *vt* (*door*) verrouiller; (*food*) engloutir ▷ *vi* se sauver, filer (comme une flèche); (*horse*) s'emballer

bomb [bɔm] *n* bombe *f* ▷ *vt* bombarder; **bombard** [bɔm'baːd] *vt* bombarder; **bomber** *n* (*Aviat*) bombardier *m*; (*terrorist*) poseur *m* de bombes; **bomb scare** *n* alerte *f* à la bombe

bond [bɔnd] *n* lien *m*; (*binding promise*) engagement *m*, obligation *f*; (*Finance*) obligation; **bonds** *npl* (*chains*) chaînes *fpl*; **in ~** (*of goods*) en entrepôt

bone [bəʊn] *n* os *m*; (*of fish*) arête *f* ▷ *vt* désosser; ôter les arêtes de

bonfire ['bɔnfaɪəʳ] *n* feu *m* (de joie); (*for rubbish*) feu

bonnet ['bɔnɪt] *n* bonnet *m*; (*BRIT: of car*) capot *m*

bonus ['bəʊnəs] *n* (*money*) prime *f*; (*advantage*) avantage *m*

boo [buː] *excl* hou!, peuh! ▷ *vt* huer

book [buk] *n* livre *m*; (*of stamps, tickets etc*) carnet *m* ▷ *vt* (*ticket*) prendre;

(*seat, room*) réserver; (*football player*) prendre le nom de, donner un carton à; **books** *npl* (*Comm*) comptes *mpl*, comptabilité *f*; **I ~ed a table in the name of ...** j'ai réservé une table au nom de ...; **book in** *vi* (*BRIT: at hotel*) prendre sa chambre; **book up** *vt* réserver; **the hotel is ~ed up** l'hôtel est complet; **bookcase** *n* bibliothèque *f* (*meuble*); **booking** *n* (*BRIT*) réservation *f*; **I confirmed my booking by fax/email** j'ai confirmé ma réservation par fax/e-mail; **booking office** *n* (*BRIT*) bureau *m* de location; **book-keeping** *n* comptabilité *f*; **booklet** *n* brochure *f*; **bookmaker** *n* bookmaker *m*; **bookmark** *n* (*for book*) marque-page *m*; (*Comput*) signet *m*; **bookseller** *n* libraire *m/f*; **bookshelf** *n* (*single*) étagère *f* (à livres); (*bookcase*) bibliothèque *f*; **bookshop, bookstore** *n* librairie *f*

boom [buːm] *n* (*noise*) grondement *m*; (*in prices, population*) forte augmentation; (*busy period*) boom *m*, vague *f* de prospérité ▷ *vi* gronder; prospérer

boost [buːst] *n* stimulant *m*, remontant *m* ▷ *vt* stimuler

boot [buːt] *n* botte *f*; (*for hiking*) chaussure *f* (de marche); (*ankle boot*) bottine *f*; (*BRIT: of car*) coffre *m* ▷ *vt* (*Comput*) lancer, mettre en route; **to ~** (*in addition*) par-dessus le marché, en plus

booth [buːð] *n* (*at fair*) baraque (foraine); (*of telephone etc*) cabine *f*; (*also:* **voting ~**) isoloir *m*

booze [buːz] (*inf*) *n* boissons *fpl* alcooliques, alcool *m*

border ['bɔːdəʳ] *n* bordure *f*; bord *m*; (*of a country*) frontière *f*; **borderline** *n* (*fig*) ligne *f* de démarcation

bore [bɔːʳ] *pt of* **bear** ▷ *vt* (*person*) ennuyer, raser; (*hole*) percer; (*well, tunnel*) creuser ▷ *n* (*person*) raseur(-euse); (*boring thing*) barbe *f*;

(*of gun*) calibre m; **bored** *adj*: **to be bored** s'ennuyer; **boredom** *n* ennui m
boring ['bɔːrɪŋ] *adj* ennuyeux(-euse)
born [bɔːn] *adj*: **to be ~** naître; **I was ~ in 1960** je suis né en 1960
borne [bɔːn] *pp of* **bear**
borough ['bʌrə] *n* municipalité f
borrow ['bɔrəu] *vt*: **to ~ sth (from sb)** emprunter qch (à qn)
Bosnian ['bɔznɪən] *adj* bosniaque, bosnien(ne) ▷ *n* Bosniaque m/f, Bosnien(ne)
bosom ['buzəm] *n* poitrine f; (*fig*) sein m
boss [bɔs] *n* patron(ne) ▷ *vt* (*also*: **~ about, ~ around**) mener à la baguette; **bossy** *adj* autoritaire
both [bəuθ] *adj* les deux, l'un(e) et l'autre ▷ *pron*: **~ (of them)** les deux, tous (toutes) (les) deux, l'un(e) et l'autre; **~ of us went, we ~ went** nous y sommes allés tous les deux ▷ *adv*: **~ A and B** A et B
bother ['bɔðər] *vt* (*worry*) tracasser; (*needle, bait*) importuner, ennuyer; (*disturb*) déranger ▷ *vi* (*also*: **~ o.s.**) se tracasser, se faire du souci ▷ *n* (*trouble*) ennuis *mpl*; **to ~ doing** prendre la peine de faire; **don't ~** ce n'est pas la peine; **it's no ~** aucun problème
bottle ['bɔtl] *n* bouteille f; (*baby's*) biberon m; (*of perfume, medicine*) flacon m ▷ *vt* mettre en bouteille(s); **bottle bank** *n* conteneur m (de bouteilles); **bottle-opener** *n* ouvre-bouteille m
bottom ['bɔtəm] *n* (*of container, sea etc*) fond m; (*buttocks*) derrière m; (*of page, list*) bas m; (*of mountain, tree, hill*) pied m ▷ *adj* (*shelf, step*) du bas
bought [bɔːt] *pt, pp of* **buy**
boulder ['bəuldər] *n* gros rocher (*gén lisse, arrondi*)
bounce [bauns] *vi* (*ball*) rebondir; (*cheque*) être refusé (*étant sans provision*) ▷ *vt* faire rebondir ▷ *n* (*rebound*) rebond m; **bouncer** *n* (*inf*: *at dance, club*) videur m

bound [baund] *pt, pp of* **bind** ▷ *n* (*gen pl*) limite f; (*leap*) bond m ▷ *vi* (*leap*) bondir ▷ *vt* (*limit*) borner ▷ *adj*: **to be ~ to do sth** (*obliged*) être obligé(e) or avoir obligation de faire qch; **he's ~ to fail** (*likely*) il est sûr d'échouer, son échec est inévitable or assuré; **~ by** (*law, regulation*) engagé(e) par; **~ for** à destination de; **out of ~s** dont l'accès est interdit
boundary ['baundrɪ] *n* frontière f
bouquet ['bukeɪ] *n* bouquet m
bourbon ['buəbən] *n* (*us*: *also*: **~ whiskey**) bourbon m
bout [baut] *n* période f; (*of malaria etc*) accès m, crise f, attaque f; (*Boxing etc*) combat m, match m
boutique [buː'tiːk] *n* boutique f
bow¹ [bəu] *n* nœud m; (*weapon*) arc m; (*Mus*) archet m
bow² [bau] *n* (*with body*) révérence f, inclination f (*du buste or corps*); (*Naut*: *also*: **~s**) proue f ▷ *vi* faire une révérence, s'incliner
bowels [bauəlz] *npl* intestins *mpl*; (*fig*) entrailles *fpl*
bowl [bəul] *n* (*for eating*) bol m; (*for washing*) cuvette f; (*ball*) boule f ▷ *vi* (*Cricket*) lancer (la balle); **bowler** *n* (*Cricket*) lanceur m (de la balle); (*BRIT*: *also*: **bowler hat**) (chapeau m) melon m; **bowling** *n* (*game*) jeu m de boules, jeu de quilles; **bowling alley** *n* bowling m; **bowling green** *n* terrain m de boules (*gazonné et carré*); **bowls** *n* (*jeu m de*) boules *fpl*
bow tie [bəu-] *n* nœud m papillon
box [bɔks] *n* boîte f; (*also*: **cardboard ~**) carton m; (*Theat*) loge f ▷ *vt* mettre en boîte ▷ *vi* boxer, faire de la boxe; **boxer** ['bɔksər] *n* (*person*) boxeur m; **boxer shorts** *npl* caleçon m; **boxing** ['bɔksɪŋ] *n* (*sport*) boxe f; **Boxing Day** *n* (*BRIT*) le lendemain de Noël; *voir article* **"Boxing Day"**; **boxing gloves** *npl* gants *mpl* de boxe; **boxing ring** *n* ring m; **box office** *n* bureau m de location

b

boy [bɔɪ] *n* garçon *m*; **boy band** *n* boys band *m*

boycott ['bɔɪkɔt] *n* boycottage *m* ▷ *vt* boycotter

boyfriend ['bɔɪfrɛnd] *n* (petit) ami

bra [brɑː] *n* soutien-gorge *m*

brace [breɪs] *n* (*support*) attache *f*, agrafe *f*; (BRIT: *also*: **~s**: *on teeth*) appareil *m* (dentaire); (*tool*) vilebrequin *m* ▷ *vt* (*support*) consolider, soutenir; **braces** *npl* (BRIT: *for trousers*) bretelles *fpl*; **to ~ o.s.** (*fig*) se préparer mentalement

bracelet ['breɪslɪt] *n* bracelet *m*

bracket ['brækɪt] *n* (*Tech*) tasseau *m*, support *m*; (*group*) classe *f*, tranche *f*; (*also*: **brace ~**) accolade *f*; (*also*: **round ~**) parenthèse *f*; (*also*: **square ~**) crochet *m* ▷ *vt* mettre entre parenthèses; **in ~s** entre parenthèses *or* crochets

brag [bræg] *vi* se vanter

braid [breɪd] *n* (*trimming*) galon *m*; (*of hair*) tresse *f*, natte *f*

brain [breɪn] *n* cerveau *m*; **brains** *npl* (*intellect, food*) cervelle *f*

braise [breɪz] *vt* braiser

brake [breɪk] *n* frein *m* ▷ *vt, vi* freiner; **brake light** *n* feu *m* de stop

bran [bræn] *n* son *m*

branch [brɑːntʃ] *n* branche *f*; (*Comm*) succursale *f* (: *of bank*) agence *f*; **branch off** *vi* (*road*) bifurquer; **branch out** *vi* diversifier ses activités

brand [brænd] *n* marque (commerciale) ▷ *vt* (*cattle*) marquer (au fer rouge); **brand name** *n* nom *m* de marque; **brand-new** *adj* tout(e) neuf (neuve), flambant neuf (neuve)

brandy ['brændɪ] *n* cognac *m*

brash [bræʃ] *adj* effronté(e)

brass [brɑːs] *n* cuivre *m* (jaune), laiton *m*; **the ~** (*Mus*) les cuivres; **brass band** *n* fanfare *f*

brat [bræt] *n* (*pej*) mioche *m/f*, môme *m/f*

brave [breɪv] *adj* courageux(-euse), brave ▷ *vt* braver, affronter; **bravery** *n* bravoure *f*, courage *m*

brawl [brɔːl] *n* rixe *f*, bagarre *f*

Brazil [brəˈzɪl] *n* Brésil *m*; **Brazilian** *adj* brésilien(ne) ▷ *n* Brésilien(ne)

breach [briːtʃ] *vt* ouvrir une brèche dans ▷ *n* (*gap*) brèche *f*; (*breaking*): **~ of contract** rupture *f* de contrat; **~ of the peace** attentat *m* à l'ordre public

bread [brɛd] *n* pain *m*; **breadbin** *n* (BRIT) boîte *f* or huche *f* à pain; **breadbox** *n* (US) boîte *f* or huche *f* à pain; **breadcrumbs** *npl* miettes *fpl* de pain; (*Culin*) chapelure *f*, panure *f*

breadth [brɛtθ] *n* largeur *f*

break [breɪk] (*pt* **broke**, *pp* **broken**) *vt* casser, briser; (*promise*) rompre; (*law*) violer ▷ *vi* se casser, se briser; (*weather*) tourner; (*storm*) éclater; (*day*) se lever ▷ *n* (*gap*) brèche *f*; (*fracture*) cassure *f*; (*rest*) interruption *f*, arrêt *m* (: *short*) pause *f*; (: *at school*) récréation *f*; (*chance*) chance *f*, occasion *f* favorable; **to ~ one's leg** etc se casser la jambe etc; **to ~ a record** battre un record; **to ~ the news to sb** annoncer la nouvelle à qn; **break down** *vt* (*door etc*) enfoncer; (*figures, data*) décomposer, analyser ▷ *vi* s'effondrer; (*Med*) faire une dépression (nerveuse); (*Aut*) tomber en panne; **my car has broken down** ma voiture est en panne; **break in** *vt* (*horse etc*) dresser ▷ *vi* (*burglar*) entrer par effraction; (*interrupt*) interrompre; **break into** *vt fus* (*house*) s'introduire *or* pénétrer par effraction dans; **break off** *vi* (*speaker*) s'interrompre; (*branch*) se rompre ▷ *vt* (*talks, engagement*) rompre; **break out** vi éclater, se déclarer; (*prisoner*) s'évader; **to ~ out in spots** se couvrir de boutons; **break up** (*partnership*) cesser, prendre fin; (*marriage*) se briser; (*crowd, meeting*) se séparer; (*ship*) se disloquer; (*Scol: pupils*) être en vacances; (*line*) couper ▷ vt fracasser, casser; (*fight etc*) interrompre, faire cesser; (*marriage*) désunir; **the line's** *or* **you're ~ing up** ça coupe; **breakdown** n (*Aut*) panne f; (*in communications, marriage*) rupture f; (*Med: also:* **nervous breakdown**) dépression (nerveuse); (*of figures*) ventilation f, répartition f; **breakdown van**, (*US*) **breakdown truck** n dépanneuse f

breakfast ['brɛkfəst] n petit déjeuner m; **what time is ~?** le petit déjeuner est à quelle heure?

break: break-in n cambriolage m; **breakthrough** n percée f

breast [brɛst] n (*of woman*) sein m; (*chest*) poitrine f; (*of chicken, turkey*) blanc m; **breast-feed** vt, vi (*irreg: like* **feed**) allaiter; **breast-stroke** n brasse f

breath [brɛθ] n haleine f, souffle m; **to take a deep ~** respirer à fond; **out of ~** à bout de souffle, essoufflé(e)

Breathalyser® ['brɛθəlaɪzə'] (*BRIT*) n alcootest m

breathe [bri:ð] vt, vi respirer; **breathe in** vi inspirer ▷ vt aspirer; **breathe out** vt, vi expirer; **breathing** n respiration f

breath: breathless adj essoufflé(e), haletant(e); **breathtaking** adj stupéfiant(e), à vous couper le souffle; **breath test** n alcootest m

bred [brɛd] pt, pp of **breed**

breed [bri:d] (*pt, pp* **bred**) vt élever, faire l'élevage de ▷ vi se reproduire ▷ n race f, variété f

breeze [bri:z] n brise f

breezy ['bri:zi] adj (*day, weather*) venteux(-euse); (*manner*) désinvolte; (*person*) jovial(e)

brew [bru:] vt (*tea*) faire infuser; (*beer*) brasser ▷ vi (*fig*) se préparer, couver; **brewery** n brasserie f (*fabrique*)

bribe [braɪb] n pot-de-vin m ▷ vt acheter; soudoyer; **bribery** n corruption f

bric-a-brac ['brɪkəbræk] n bric-à-brac m

brick [brɪk] n brique f; **bricklayer** n maçon m

bride [braɪd] n mariée f, épouse f; **bridegroom** n marié m, époux m; **bridesmaid** n demoiselle f d'honneur

bridge [brɪdʒ] n pont m; (*Naut*) passerelle f (de commandement); (*of nose*) arête f; (*Cards, Dentistry*) bridge m ▷ vt (*gap*) combler

bridle ['braɪdl] n bride f

brief [bri:f] adj bref (brève) ▷ n (*Law*) dossier m, cause f; (*gen*) tâche f ▷ vt mettre au courant; **briefs** npl slip m; **briefcase** n serviette f; porte-documents m inv; **briefing** n instructions fpl; (*Press*) briefing m; **briefly** adv brièvement

brigadier [brɪgə'dɪə'] n brigadier général

bright [braɪt] adj brillant(e); (*room, weather*) clair(e); (*person: clever*) intelligent(e), doué(e); (*: cheerful*) gai(e); (*idea*) génial(e); (*colour*) vif (vive)

brilliant ['brɪljənt] adj brillant(e); (*light, sunshine*) éclatant(e); (*inf: great*) super

brim [brɪm] n bord m

brine [braɪn] n (*Culin*) saumure f

bring (*pt, pp* **brought**) [brɪŋ, brɔ:t] vt (*thing*) apporter; (*person*) amener; **bring about** vt provoquer, entraîner; **bring back** vt rapporter; (*person*) ramener; **bring down** vt (*lower*) abaisser; (*shoot down*) abattre; (*government*) faire s'effondrer; **bring in** vt (*person*) faire entrer; (*object*) rentrer; (*Pol: legislation*) introduire; (*produce: income*) rapporter; **bring on** vt (*illness, attack*) provoquer;

(player, substitute) amener; **bring out** vt sortir; (meaning) faire ressortir, mettre en relief; **bring up** vt élever; (carry up) monter; (question) soulever; (food: vomit) vomir, rendre

brink [brɪŋk] n bord m

brisk [brɪsk] adj vif (vive); (abrupt) brusque; (trade etc) actif(-ive)

bristle ['brɪsl] n poil m ▷ vi se hérisser

Brit [brɪt] n abbr (inf: = British person) Britannique m/f

Britain ['brɪtən] n (also: **Great ~**) la Grande-Bretagne

British ['brɪtɪʃ] adj britannique ▷ npl; **the ~** les Britanniques mpl; **British Isles** npl; **the British Isles** les îles fpl Britanniques

Briton ['brɪtən] n Britannique m/f

Brittany ['brɪtənɪ] n Bretagne f

brittle ['brɪtl] adj cassant(e), fragile

broad [brɔːd] adj large; (distinction) général(e); (accent) prononcé(e); **in ~ daylight** en plein jour

B road n (BRIT) ≈ route départementale

broad: **broadband** n transmission f à haut débit; **broad bean** n fève f; **broadcast** (pt, pp **broadcast**) n émission f ▷ vt (Radio) radiodiffuser; (TV) téléviser ▷ vi émettre; **broaden** vt élargir; **to broaden one's mind** élargir ses horizons ▷ vi s'élargir; **broadly** adv en gros, généralement; **broad-minded** adj large d'esprit

broccoli ['brɔkəlɪ] n brocoli m

brochure ['brəʊʃjʊəʳ] n prospectus m, dépliant m

broil [brɔɪl] vt (US) rôtir

broke [brəʊk] pt of **break** ▷ adj (inf) fauché(e)

broken ['brəʊkn] pp of **break** ▷ adj (stick, leg etc) cassé(e); (machine: also: **~ down**) fichu(e); **in ~ French/English** dans un français/anglais approximatif or hésitant

broker ['brəʊkəʳ] n courtier m

bronchitis [brɔŋ'kaɪtɪs] n bronchite f

bronze [brɔnz] n bronze m

brooch [brəʊtʃ] n broche f

brood [bruːd] n couvée f ▷ vi (person) méditer (sombrement), ruminer

broom [brum] n balai m; (Bot) genêt m

Bros. abbr (Comm: = brothers) Frères

broth [brɔθ] n bouillon m de viande et de légumes

brothel ['brɔθl] n maison close, bordel m

brother ['brʌðəʳ] n frère m; **brother-in-law** n beau-frère m

brought [brɔːt] pt, pp of **bring**

brow [brau] n front m; (eyebrow) sourcil m; (of hill) sommet m

brown [braun] adj brun(e), marron inv; (hair) châtain inv; (tanned) bronzé(e) ▷ n (colour) brun m, marron m ▷ vt brunir; (Culin) faire dorer, faire roussir; **brown bread** n pain m bis

Brownie ['braunɪ] n jeannette f éclaireuse (cadette)

brown rice n riz m complet

brown sugar n cassonade f

browse [brauz] vi (in shop) regarder (sans acheter); **to ~ through a book** feuilleter un livre; **browser** n (Comput) navigateur m

bruise [bruːz] n bleu m, ecchymose f, contusion f ▷ vt contusionner, meurtrir

brunette [bruː'nɛt] n (femme) brune

brush [brʌʃ] n brosse f; (for painting) pinceau m; (for shaving) blaireau m; (quarrel) accrochage m, prise f de bec ▷ vt brosser; (also: **~ past, ~ against**) effleurer, frôler

Brussels ['brʌslz] n Bruxelles

Brussels sprout n chou m de Bruxelles

brutal ['bruːtl] adj brutal(e)

B.Sc. n abbr = **Bachelor of Science**

BSE n abbr (= bovine spongiform encephalopathy) ESB f, BSE f

bubble ['bʌbl] n bulle f ▷ vi bouillonner, faire des bulles; (sparkle, fig) pétiller; **bubble bath** n bain moussant; **bubble gum** n chewing-gum m; **bubblejet printer** ['bʌbldʒet-] n imprimante f à bulle d'encre

buck [bʌk] n mâle m (d'un lapin, lièvre, daim etc); (US inf) dollar m ▷ vi ruer, lancer une ruade; **to pass the ~ (to sb)** se décharger de la responsabilité (sur qn)

bucket ['bʌkɪt] n seau m

buckle ['bʌkl] n boucle f ▷ vt (belt etc) boucler, attacher ▷ vi (warp) tordre, gauchir (: wheel) se voiler

bud [bʌd] n bourgeon m; (of flower) bouton m ▷ vi bourgeonner; (flower) éclore

Buddhism ['budɪzəm] n bouddhisme m

Buddhist ['budɪst] adj bouddhiste ▷ n Bouddhiste m/f

buddy ['bʌdɪ] n (US) copain m

budge [bʌdʒ] vt faire bouger ▷ vi bouger

budgerigar ['bʌdʒərɪgɑːʳ] n perruche f

budget ['bʌdʒɪt] n budget m ▷ vi: **to ~ for sth** inscrire qch au budget

budgie ['bʌdʒɪ] n = **budgerigar**

buff [bʌf] adj (couleur) chamois m ▷ n (inf: enthusiast) mordu(e)

buffalo ['bʌfələu] (pl **buffalo** or **buffaloes**) n (BRIT) buffle m; (US) bison m

buffer ['bʌfəʳ] n tampon m; (Comput) mémoire f tampon

buffet n ['bufei] (food, BRIT: bar) buffet m ▷ vt ['bʌfɪt] secouer, ébranler; **buffet car** n (BRIT Rail) voiture-bar f

bug [bʌg] n (bedbug etc) punaise f; (esp US: any insect) insecte m, bestiole f; (fig: germ) virus m, microbe m; (spy device) dispositif m d'écoute (électronique), micro clandestin; (Comput: of program) erreur f ▷ vt (room) poser des micros dans; (inf: annoy) embêter

buggy ['bʌgɪ] n poussette f

build [bɪld] n (of person) carrure f, charpente f ▷ vt (pt, pp **built**) construire, bâtir; **build up** vt accumuler, amasser; (business) développer; (reputation) bâtir; **builder** n entrepreneur m; **building** n (trade) construction f; (structure) bâtiment m, construction (: residential, offices) immeuble m; **building site** n chantier m (de construction); **building society** n (BRIT) société f de crédit immobilier

built [bɪlt] pt, pp of **build**; **built-in** adj (cupboard) encastré(e); (device) incorporé(e); intégré(e); **built-up** adj: **built-up area** zone urbanisée

bulb [bʌlb] n (Bot) bulbe m, oignon m; (Elec) ampoule f

Bulgaria [bʌl'gɛərɪə] n Bulgarie f; **Bulgarian** adj bulgare ▷ n Bulgare m/f

bulge [bʌldʒ] n renflement m, gonflement m ▷ vi faire saillie; présenter un renflement; (pocket, file): **to be bulging with** être plein(e) à craquer de

bulimia [bə'lɪmɪə] n boulimie f

bulimic [bjuː'lɪmɪk] adj, n boulimique m/f

bulk [bʌlk] n masse f, volume m; **in ~** (Comm) en gros, en vrac; **the ~ of** la plus grande or grosse partie de; **bulky** adj volumineux(-euse), encombrant(e)

bull [bul] n taureau m; (male elephant, whale) mâle m

bulldozer ['buldəuzəʳ] n bulldozer m

bullet ['bulɪt] n balle f (de fusil etc)

bulletin ['bulɪtɪn] n bulletin m, communiqué m; (also: **news ~**) (bulletin d')informations fpl; **bulletin board** n (Comput) messagerie f (électronique)

bullfight ['bulfaɪt] n corrida f, course f de taureaux; **bullfighter** n torero m; **bullfighting** n tauromachie f

bully ['bulɪ] n brute f, tyran m ▷ vt tyranniser, rudoyer

bum [bʌm] n (inf: BRIT: backside) derrière m; (esp US: tramp)

vagabond(e), traîne-savates m/f inv;
(idler) glandeur m
bumblebee ['bʌmblbiː] n bourdon m
bump [bʌmp] n (blow) coup m, choc
m; (jolt) cahot m; (on road etc, on head)
bosse f ▷ vt heurter, cogner; (car)
emboutir; **bump into** vt fus rentrer
dans, tamponner; (inf: meet) tomber
sur; **bumper** n pare-chocs m inv ▷ adj:
bumper crop/harvest récolte/
moisson exceptionnelle; **bumpy**
adj (road) cahoteux(-euse); **it was a
bumpy flight/ride** on a été secoués
dans l'avion/la voiture
bun [bʌn] n (cake) petit gâteau; (bread)
petit pain au lait; (of hair) chignon m
bunch [bʌntʃ] n (of flowers) bouquet
m; (of keys) trousseau m; (of bananas)
régime m; (of people) groupe m;
bunches npl (in hair) couettes fpl; **~ of
grapes** grappe f de raisin
bundle ['bʌndl] n paquet m ▷ vt (also:
~ up) faire un paquet de; (put): **to
~ sth/sb into** fourrer or enfourner
qch/qn dans
bungalow ['bʌŋgələu] n bungalow
m
bungee jumping
['bʌndʒiː'dʒʌmpɪŋ] n saut m à
l'élastique
bunion ['bʌnjən] n oignon m (au pied)
bunk [bʌŋk] n couchette f; **bunk
beds** npl lits superposés
bunker ['bʌŋkəʳ] n (coal store) soute f
à charbon; (Mil, Golf) bunker m
bunny ['bʌnɪ] n (also: **~ rabbit**)
lapin m
buoy [bɔɪ] n bouée f; **buoyant** adj
(ship) flottable; (carefree) gai(e),
plein(e) d'entrain; (Comm: market,
economy) actif(-ive)
burden ['bəːdn] n fardeau m, charge
f ▷ vt charger; (oppress) accabler,
surcharger
bureau (pl **bureaux**) ['bjuərəu,
-z] n (BRIT: writing desk) bureau m,
secrétaire m; (US: chest of drawers)
commode f; (office) bureau, office m

bureaucracy [bjuəˈrɔkrəsɪ] n
bureaucratie f
bureaucrat ['bjuərəkræt] n
bureaucrate m/f, rond-de-cuir m
bureau de change [-dəˈʃɑ̃ʒ] (pl
bureaux de change) n bureau m
de change
bureaux ['bjuərəuz] npl of **bureau**
burger ['bəːgəʳ] n hamburger m
burglar ['bəːgləʳ] n cambrioleur m;
burglar alarm n sonnerie f d'alarme;
burglary n cambriolage m
Burgundy ['bəːgəndɪ] n Bourgogne f
burial ['bɛrɪəl] n enterrement m
burn [bəːn] vt, vi (pt **burned**, pp
burnt) brûler ▷ n brûlure f; **burn
down** vt incendier, détruire par le feu;
burn out vt (writer etc): **to ~ o.s. out**
s'user (à force de travailler); **burning**
adj (building, forest) en flammes;
(issue, question) brûlant(e); (ambition)
dévorant(e)
Burns' Night [bəːnz-] n fête écossaise
à la mémoire du poète Robert Burns

● **BURNS' NIGHT**
●
● Burns' Night est une fête qui a lieu
● le 25 janvier, à la mémoire du poète
● écossais Robert Burns (1759–1796),
● à l'occasion de laquelle les Écossais
● partout dans le monde organisent
● un souper, en général arrosé
● de whisky. Le plat principal est
● toujours le haggis, servi avec de la
● purée de pommes de terre et de la
● purée de rutabagas. On apporte
● le haggis au son des cornemuses
● et au cours du repas on lit des
● poèmes de Burns et on chante ses
● chansons.

burnt [bəːnt] pt, pp of **burn**
burp [bəːp] (inf) n rot m ▷ vi roter
burrow ['bʌrəu] n terrier m ▷ vi (rabbit)
creuser un terrier; (rummage) fouiller
burst [bəːst] (pt, pp **burst**) vt faire
éclater; (river: banks etc) rompre ▷ vi

éclater; (*tyre*) crever ▷ *n* explosion *f*; (*also*: **~ pipe**) fuite *f* (*due à une rupture*); **a ~ of enthusiasm/energy** un accès d'enthousiasme/d'énergie; **to ~ into flames** s'enflammer soudainement; **to ~ out laughing** éclater de rire; **to ~ into tears** fondre en larmes; **to ~ open** *vi* s'ouvrir violemment *or* soudainement; **to be ~ing with** (*container*) être plein(e) (à craquer) de, regorger de; (*fig*) être débordant(e) de; **burst into** *vt fus* (*room etc*) faire irruption dans

bury ['bɛrɪ] *vt* enterrer

bus (*pl* **buses**) [bʌs, 'bʌsɪz] *n* (*auto*)bus *m*; **bus conductor** *n* receveur(-euse) *m/f* de bus

bush [buʃ] *n* buisson *m*; (*scrub land*) brousse *f*; **to beat about the ~** tourner autour du pot

business ['bɪznɪs] *n* (*matter, firm*) affaire *f*; (*trading*) affaires *fpl*; (*job, duty*) travail *m*; **to be away on ~** être en déplacement d'affaires; **it's none of my ~** cela ne me regarde pas, ce ne sont pas mes affaires; **he means ~** il ne plaisante pas, il est sérieux; **business class** *n* (*on plane*) classe *f* affaires; **businesslike** *adj* sérieux(-euse), efficace; **businessman** (*irreg*) *n* homme *m* d'affaires; **business trip** *n* voyage *m* d'affaires; **businesswoman** (*irreg*) *n* femme *f* d'affaires

busker ['bʌskəʳ] *n* (*BRIT*) artiste ambulant(e)

bus: bus pass *n* carte *f* de bus; **bus shelter** *n* abribus *m*; **bus station** *n* gare routière; **bus stop** *n* arrêt *m* d'autobus

bust [bʌst] *n* buste *m*; (*measurement*) tour *m* de poitrine ▷ *adj* (*inf: broken*) fichu(e), fini(e); **to go ~** (*inf*) faire faillite

bustling ['bʌslɪŋ] *adj* (*town*) très animé(e)

busy ['bɪzɪ] *adj* occupé(e); (*shop, street*) très fréquenté(e); (*US:*

telephone, line) occupé ▷ *vt*: **to ~ o.s.** s'occuper; **busy signal** *n* (*US*) tonalité *f* occupé *inv*

 KEYWORD

but [bʌt] *conj* mais; **I'd love to come, but I'm busy** j'aimerais venir mais je suis occupé; **he's not English but French** il n'est pas anglais mais français; **but that's far too expensive!** mais c'est bien trop cher!
▶ *prep* (*apart from, except*) sauf, excepté; **nothing but** rien d'autre que; **we've had nothing but trouble** nous n'avons eu que des ennuis; **no-one but him can do it** lui seul peut le faire; **who but a lunatic would do such a thing?** qui sinon un fou ferait une chose pareille?; **but for you/your help** sans toi/ton aide; **anything but that** tout sauf *or* excepté ça, tout mais pas ça
▶ *adv* (*just, only*) ne … que; **she's but a child** elle n'est qu'une enfant; **had I but known** si seulement j'avais su; **I can but try** je peux toujours essayer; **all but finished** pratiquement terminé

butcher ['butʃəʳ] *n* boucher *m* ▷ *vt* massacrer; (*cattle etc for meat*) tuer; **butcher's (shop)** *n* boucherie *f*

butler ['bʌtləʳ] *n* maître *m* d'hôtel

butt [bʌt] *n* (*cask*) gros tonneau *m*; (*of gun*) crosse *f*; (*of cigarette*) mégot *m*; (*BRIT fig: target*) cible *f* ▷ *vt* donner un coup de tête à

butter ['bʌtəʳ] *n* beurre *m* ▷ *vt* beurrer; **buttercup** *n* bouton *m* d'or

butterfly ['bʌtəflaɪ] *n* papillon *m*; (*Swimming: also*: **~ stroke**) brasse *f* papillon

buttocks ['bʌtəks] *npl* fesses *fpl*

button ['bʌtn] *n* bouton *m*; (*US: badge*) pin *m* ▷ *vt* (*also*: **~ up**) boutonner ▷ *vi* se boutonner

buy [baɪ] (*pt, pp* **bought**) *vt* acheter ▷ *n* achat *m*; **to ~ sb sth/sth from sb** acheter qch à qn; **to ~ sb a drink** offrir un verre *or* à boire à qn; **can I ~ you a drink?** je vous offre un verre?; **where can I ~ some postcards?** où est-ce que je peux acheter des cartes postales?; **buy out** *vt* (*partner*) désintéresser; **buy up** *vt* acheter en bloc, rafler; **buyer** *n* acheteur(-euse) *m/f*

buzz [bʌz] *n* bourdonnement *m*; (*inf*: *phone call*): **to give sb a ~** passer un coup de fil à qn ▷ *vi* bourdonner; **buzzer** *n* timbre *m* électrique

○ **KEYWORD**

by [baɪ] *prep* **1** (*referring to cause, agent*) par, de; **killed by lightning** tué par la foudre; **surrounded by a fence** entouré d'une barrière; **a painting by Picasso** un tableau de Picasso
2 (*referring to method, manner, means*): **by bus/car** en autobus/voiture; **by train** par le *or* en train; **to pay by cheque** payer par chèque; **by moonlight/candlelight** à la lueur de la lune/d'une bougie; **by saving hard, he ...** à force d'économiser, il ...
3 (*via, through*) par; **we came by Dover** nous sommes venus par Douvres
4 (*close to, past*) à côté de; **the house by the school** la maison à côté de l'école; **a holiday by the sea** des vacances au bord de la mer; **she went by me** elle est passée à côté de moi; **I go by the post office every day** je passe devant la poste tous les jours
5 (*with time: not later than*) avant; (: *during*): **by daylight** à la lumière du jour; **by night** la nuit, de nuit; **by 4 o'clock** avant 4 heures; **by this time tomorrow** d'ici demain à la même heure; **by the time I got here it was too late** lorsque je suis arrivé il était déjà trop tard
6 (*amount*) à; **by the kilo/metre** au kilo/au mètre; **paid by the hour** payé à l'heure
7 (*Math: measure*): **to divide/multiply by 3** diviser/multiplier par 3; **a room 3 metres by 4** une pièce de 3 mètres sur 4; **it's broader by a metre** c'est plus large d'un mètre
8 (*according to*) d'après, selon; **it's 3 o'clock by my watch** il est 3 heures à ma montre; **it's all right by me** je n'ai rien contre
9: **(all) by oneself** *etc* tout(e) seul(e)
▷ *adv* **1** *see* **go; pass** *etc*
2: **by and by** un peu plus tard, bientôt; **by and large** dans l'ensemble

bye(-bye) ['baɪ-] *excl* au revoir!, salut!
by-election ['baɪɪlɛkʃən] *n* (BRIT) élection (législative) partielle
bypass ['baɪpɑːs] *n* rocade *f*; (*Med*) pontage *m* ▷ *vt* éviter
byte [baɪt] *n* (*Comput*) octet *m*

C

C [siː] *n (Mus)* do *m*

cab [kæb] *n* taxi *m*; *(of train, truck)* cabine *f*

cabaret ['kæbəreɪ] *n (show)* spectacle *m* de cabaret

cabbage ['kæbɪdʒ] *n* chou *m*

cabin ['kæbɪn] *n (house)* cabane *f*, hutte *f*; *(on ship)* cabine *f*; *(on plane)* compartiment *m*; **cabin crew** *n (Aviat)* équipage *m*

cabinet ['kæbɪnɪt] *n (Pol)* cabinet *m*; *(furniture)* petit meuble à tiroirs et rayons; *(also:* **display ~**) vitrine *f*, petite armoire vitrée; **cabinet minister** *n* ministre *m (membre du cabinet)*

cable ['keɪbl] *n* câble *m* ▷ *vt* câbler, télégraphier; **cable car** *n* téléphérique *m*; **cable television** *n* télévision *f* par câble

cactus (*pl* **cacti**) ['kæktəs, -taɪ] *n* cactus *m*

café ['kæfeɪ] *n* ≈ café(-restaurant) *m* (*sans alcool*)

cafeteria [kæfɪ'tɪərɪə] *n* cafétéria *f*

caffeine ['kæfiːn] *n* caféine *f*

cage [keɪdʒ] *n* cage *f*

cagoule [kə'guːl] *n* K-way® *m*

Cairo ['kaɪərəʊ] *n* Le Caire

cake [keɪk] *n* gâteau *m*; **~ of soap** savonnette *f*

calcium ['kælsɪəm] *n* calcium *m*

calculate ['kælkjuleɪt] *vt* calculer; *(estimate: chances, effect)* évaluer; **calculation** [kælkju'leɪʃən] *n* calcul *m*; **calculator** *n* calculatrice *f*

calendar ['kæləndər] *n* calendrier *m*

calf (*pl* **calves**) [kɑːf, kɑːvz] *n (of cow)* veau *m*; *(of other animals)* petit *m*; *(also:* **~skin**) veau *m*, vachette *f*; *(Anat)* mollet *m*

calibre, *(US)* **caliber** ['kælɪbər] *n* calibre *m*

call [kɔːl] *vt* appeler; *(meeting)* convoquer ▷ *vi* appeler; *(visit: also:* **~ in, ~ round**) passer ▷ *n (shout)* appel *m*, cri *m*; *(also:* **telephone ~**) coup *m* de téléphone; **to be on ~** être de permanence; **to be ~ed** s'appeler; **can I make a ~ from here?** est-ce que je peux téléphoner d'ici?; **call back** *vi (return)* repasser; *(Tel)* rappeler ▷ *vt (Tel)* rappeler; **can you ~ back later?** pouvez-vous rappeler plus tard?; **call for** *vt fus (demand)* demander; *(fetch)* passer prendre; **call in** *vt (doctor, expert, police)* appeler, faire venir; **call off** *vt* annuler; **call on** *vt fus (visit)* rendre visite à, passer voir; *(request)* : **to ~ on sb to do** inviter qn à faire; **call out** *vi* pousser un cri ou des cris; **call up** *vt (Mil)* appeler, mobiliser; *(Tel)* appeler; **call box** *n (BRIT)* cabine *f* téléphonique; **call centre**, *(US)* **call center** *n* centre *m* d'appels; **caller** *n (Tel)* personne *f* qui appelle; *(visitor)* visiteur *m*

callous ['kæləs] *adj* dur(e), insensible

calm [kɑːm] *adj* calme ▷ *n* calme *m* ▷ *vt* calmer, apaiser; **calm down** *vi* se calmer, s'apaiser ▷ *vt* calmer, apaiser; **calmly** ['kɑːmlɪ] *adv* calmement, avec calme

Calor gas® [ˈkælə-] n (BRIT) butane m, butagaz® m

calorie [ˈkælərɪ] n calorie f

calves [kɑːvz] npl of **calf**

Cambodia [kæmˈbəʊdɪə] n Cambodge m

camcorder [ˈkæmkɔːdər] n caméscope m

came [keɪm] pt of **come**

camel [ˈkæməl] n chameau m

camera [ˈkæmərə] n appareil photo m; (Cine, TV) caméra f; **in ~** à huis clos, en privé; **cameraman** (irreg) n caméraman m; **camera phone** n téléphone m avec appareil photo

camouflage [ˈkæməflɑːʒ] n camouflage m ▷ vt camoufler

camp [kæmp] n camp m ▷ vi camper ▷ adj (man) efféminé(e)

campaign [kæmˈpeɪn] n (Mil, Pol) campagne f ▷ vi (also fig) faire campagne; **campaigner** n: **campaigner for** partisan(e) de; **campaigner against** opposant(e) à

camp: camp bed n (BRIT) lit m de camp; **camper** n campeur(-euse); (vehicle) camping-car m; **camping** camping m; **to go camping** faire du camping; **campsite** n (terrain m de) camping m

campus [ˈkæmpəs] n campus m

can¹ [kæn] n (of milk, oil, water) bidon m; (tin) boîte f (de conserve) ▷ vt mettre en conserve

KEYWORD

can² [kæn] (negative **cannot** or **can't**, conditional, pt **could**) aux vb 1 (be able to) pouvoir; **you can do it if you try** vous pouvez le faire si vous essayez; **I can't hear you** je ne t'entends pas

2 (know how to) savoir; **I can swim/play tennis/drive** je sais nager/jouer au tennis/conduire; **can you speak French?** parlez-vous français?

3 (may) pouvoir; **can I use your phone?** puis-je me servir de votre

téléphone?

4 (expressing disbelief, puzzlement etc): **it can't be true!** ce n'est pas possible!; **what can he want?** qu'est-ce qu'il peut bien vouloir?

5 (expressing possibility, suggestion etc): **he could be in the library** il est peut-être dans la bibliothèque; **she could have been delayed** il se peut qu'elle ait été retardée

Canada [ˈkænədə] n Canada m; **Canadian** [kəˈneɪdɪən] adj canadien(ne) ▷ n Canadien(ne)

canal [kəˈnæl] n canal m

canary [kəˈnɛərɪ] n canari m, serin m

cancel [ˈkænsəl] vt annuler; (train) supprimer; (party, appointment) décommander; (cross out) barrer, rayer; (cheque) faire opposition à; **I would like to ~ my booking** je voudrais annuler ma réservation; **cancellation** [kænsəˈleɪʃən] n annulation f; suppression f

Cancer [ˈkænsər] n (Astrology) le Cancer

cancer [ˈkænsər] n cancer m

candidate [ˈkændɪdeɪt] n candidat(e)

candle [ˈkændl] n bougie f; (in church) cierge m; **candlestick** n (also: **candle holder**) bougeoir m; (bigger, ornate) chandelier m

candy [ˈkændɪ] n sucre candi; (US) bonbon m; **candy bar** (US) n barre f chocolatée; **candyfloss** n (BRIT) barbe f à papa

cane [keɪn] n canne f; (for baskets, chairs etc) rotin m ▷ vt (BRIT Scol) administrer des coups de bâton à

canister [ˈkænɪstər] n boîte f (gén en métal); (of gas) bombe f

cannabis [ˈkænəbɪs] n (drug) cannabis m

canned [kænd] adj (food) en boîte, en conserve; (inf: music) enregistré(e); (BRIT inf: drunk) bourré(e); (US inf: worker) mis(e) à la porte

cannon ['kænən] (pl **cannon** or **cannons**) n (gun) canon m

cannot ['kænɔt] = **can not**

canoe [kə'nuː] n pirogue f; (Sport) canoë m; **canoeing** n (sport) canoë m

canon ['kænən] n (clergyman) chanoine m; (standard) canon m

can-opener [-'əupnəʳ] n ouvre-boîte m

can't [kɑːnt] = **can not**

canteen [kæn'tiːn] n (eating place) cantine f; (BRIT: of cutlery) ménagère f

canter ['kæntəʳ] vi aller au petit galop

canvas ['kænvəs] n toile f

canvass ['kænvəs] vi (Pol): **to ~ for** faire campagne pour ▷ vt (citizens, opinions) sonder

canyon ['kænjən] n cañon m, gorge f (profonde)

cap [kæp] n casquette f; (for swimming) bonnet m de bain; (of pen) capuchon m; (of bottle) capsule f; (BRIT: contraceptive: also: **Dutch ~**) diaphragme m ▷ vt (outdo) surpasser; (put limit on) plafonner

capability [keɪpə'bɪlɪtɪ] n aptitude f, capacité f

capable ['keɪpəbl] adj capable

capacity [kə'pæsɪtɪ] n (of container) capacité f, contenance f; (ability) aptitude f

cape [keɪp] n (garment) cape f; (Geo) cap m

caper ['keɪpəʳ] n (Culin: gen pl) câpre f; (prank) farce f

capital ['kæpɪtl] n (also: **~ city**) capitale f; (money) capital m; (also: **~ letter**) majuscule f; **capitalism** n capitalisme m; **capitalist** adj, n capitaliste m/f; **capital punishment** n peine capitale

Capitol ['kæpɪtl] n: **the ~** le Capitole

Capricorn ['kæprɪkɔːn] n le Capricorne

capsize [kæp'saɪz] vt faire chavirer ▷ vi chavirer

capsule ['kæpsjuːl] n capsule f

captain ['kæptɪn] n capitaine m

caption ['kæpʃən] n légende f

captivity [kæp'tɪvɪtɪ] n captivité f

capture ['kæptʃəʳ] vt (prisoner, animal) capturer; (town) prendre; (attention) capter; (Comput) saisir ▷ n capture f; (of data) saisie f de données

car [kɑːʳ] n voiture f, auto f; (Us Rail) wagon m, voiture

caramel ['kærəməl] n caramel m

carat ['kærət] n carat m

caravan ['kærəvæn] n caravane f; **caravan site** n (BRIT) camping m pour caravanes

carbohydrate [kɑːbəu'haɪdreɪt] n hydrate m de carbone; (food) féculent m

carbon ['kɑːbən] n carbone m; **carbon dioxide** [-daɪ'ɔksaɪd] n gaz m carbonique, dioxyde m de carbone; **carbon footprint** n empreinte f carbone; **carbon monoxide** [-mɔ'nɔksaɪd] n oxyde m de carbone

car boot sale n voir article **"car boot sale"**

⬛ **CAR BOOT SALE**
●
●
● Type de brocante très populaire, où
● chacun vide sa cave ou son grenier.
● Les articles sont présentés dans
● des coffres de voitures et la vente
● a souvent lieu sur un parking ou
● dans un champ. Les brocanteurs
● d'un jour doivent s'acquitter d'une
● petite contribution pour participer
● à la vente.

carburettor , (us)**carburetor** [kɑːbju'rɛtəʳ] n carburateur m

card [kɑːd] n carte f; (material) carton m; **cardboard** n carton m; **card game** n jeu m de cartes

cardigan ['kɑːdɪgən] n cardigan m

cardinal ['kɑːdɪnl] adj cardinal(e); (importance) capital(e) ▷ n cardinal m

cardphone ['kɑːdfəun] n téléphone m à carte (magnétique)

care [kɛəʳ] n soin m, attention f; (worry) souci m ▷ vi: **to ~ about** (feel interest for) se soucier de, s'intéresser à; (person: love) être attaché(e) à; **in sb's ~** à la garde de qn, confié à qn; **~ of** (on letter) chez; **to take ~ (to do)** faire attention (à faire); **to take ~ of** vt s'occuper de; **I don't ~** ça m'est bien égal, peu m'importe; **I couldn't ~ less** cela m'est complètement égal, je m'en fiche complètement; **care for** vt fus s'occuper de; (like) aimer
career [kəˈrɪəʳ] n carrière f ▷ vi (also: **~ along**) aller à toute allure
care: carefree adj sans souci, insouciant(e); **careful** adj soigneux(-euse); (cautious) prudent(e); **(be) careful!** (fais) attention!; **carefully** adv avec soin, soigneusement; prudemment; **caregiver** n (US) (professional) travailleur social; (unpaid) personne qui s'occupe d'un proche qui est malade; **careless** adj négligent(e); (heedless) insouciant(e); **carelessness** n manque m de soin, négligence f; insouciance f; **carer** [ˈkɛərəʳ] n (professional) travailleur social; (unpaid) personne qui s'occupe d'un proche qui est malade; **caretaker** n gardien(ne), concierge m/f
car-ferry [ˈkɑːfɛrɪ] n (on sea) ferry(-boat) m; (on river) bac m
cargo [ˈkɑːɡəu] (pl **cargoes**) n cargaison f, chargement m
car hire n (BRIT) location f de voitures
Caribbean [kærɪˈbiːən] adj, n: **the ~ (Sea)** la mer des Antilles or des Caraïbes
caring [ˈkɛərɪŋ] adj (person) bienveillant(e); (society, organization) humanitaire
carnation [kɑːˈneɪʃən] n œillet m
carnival [ˈkɑːnɪvl] n (public celebration) carnaval m; (US: funfair) fête foraine
carol [ˈkærəl] n: **(Christmas) ~** chant m de Noël

carousel [kærəˈsɛl] n (for luggage) carrousel m; (US) manège m
car park (BRIT) n parking m, parc m de stationnement
carpenter [ˈkɑːpɪntəʳ] n charpentier m; (joiner) menuisier m
carpet [ˈkɑːpɪt] n tapis m ▷ vt recouvrir (d'un tapis); **fitted ~** (BRIT) moquette f
car rental n (US) location f de voitures
carriage [ˈkærɪdʒ] n (BRIT Rail) wagon m; (horse-drawn) voiture f; (of goods) transport m (: cost) port m; **carriageway** n (BRIT: part of road) chaussée f
carrier [ˈkærɪəʳ] n transporteur m, camionneur m; (company) entreprise f de transport; (Med) porteur(-euse); **carrier bag** n (BRIT) sac m en papier or en plastique
carrot [ˈkærət] n carotte f
carry [ˈkærɪ] vt (subj: person) porter; (: vehicle) transporter; (involve: responsibilities etc) comporter, impliquer; (Med: disease) être porteur de ▷ vi (of sound) porter; **to get carried away** (fig) s'emballer, s'enthousiasmer; **carry on** vi (continue) continuer ▷ vt (conduct: business) diriger; (: conversation) entretenir; (: continue: business, conversation) continuer; **to ~ on with sth/doing** continuer qch/à faire; **carry out** vt (orders) exécuter; (investigation) effectuer
cart [kɑːt] n charrette f ▷ vt (inf) transporter
carton [ˈkɑːtən] n (box) carton m; (of yogurt) pot m (en carton)
cartoon [kɑːˈtuːn] n (Press) dessin m (humoristique); (satirical) caricature f; (comic strip) bande dessinée; (Cine) dessin animé
cartridge [ˈkɑːtrɪdʒ] n (for gun, pen) cartouche f
carve [kɑːv] vt (meat: also: **~ up**) découper; (wood, stone) tailler,

sculpter; **carving** n (in wood etc) sculpture f

car wash n station f de lavage (de voitures)

case [keɪs] n cas m; (Law) affaire f, procès m; (box) caisse f, boîte f; (for glasses) étui m; (BRIT: also: **suit~**) valise f; **in ~ of** en cas de; **in ~ he** au cas où il; **just in ~** à tout hasard; **in any ~** en tout cas, de toute façon

cash [kæʃ] n argent m; (Comm) (argent m) liquide m ▷ vt encaisser; **to pay (in) ~** payer (en argent) comptant or en espèces; **~ with order/on delivery** (Comm) payable or paiement à la commande/livraison; **I haven't got any ~** je n'ai pas de liquide; **cashback** n (discount) remise f; (at supermarket etc) retrait m (à la caisse); **cash card** n carte f de retrait; **cash desk** n (BRIT) caisse f; **cash dispenser** n distributeur m automatique de billets

cashew [kæˈʃuː] n (also: **~ nut**) noix f de cajou

cashier [kæˈʃɪəʳ] n caissier(-ère)

cashmere [ˈkæʃmɪəʳ] n cachemire m

cash point n distributeur m automatique de billets

cash register n caisse enregistreuse

casino [kəˈsiːnəu] n casino m

casket [ˈkɑːskɪt] n coffret m; (US: coffin) cercueil m

casserole [ˈkæsərəul] n (pot) cocotte f; (food) ragoût m (en cocotte)

cassette [kæˈsɛt] n cassette f; **cassette player** n lecteur m de cassettes

cast [kɑːst] (vb: pt, pp **cast**) vt (throw) jeter; (shadow: lit) projeter; (: fig) jeter; (glance) jeter ▷ n (Theat) distribution f; (also: **plaster ~**) plâtre m; **to ~ sb as Hamlet** attribuer à qn le rôle d'Hamlet; **to ~ one's vote** voter, exprimer son suffrage; **to ~ doubt on** jeter un doute sur; **cast off** vi (Naut) larguer les amarres; (Knitting) arrêter les mailles

castanets [kæstəˈnɛts] npl castagnettes fpl

caster sugar [ˈkɑːstə-] n (BRIT) sucre m semoule

cast-iron [ˈkɑːstaɪən] adj (lit) de or en fonte; (fig: will) de fer; (alibi) en béton

castle [ˈkɑːsl] n château m; (fortress) château-fort m; (Chess) tour f

casual [ˈkæʒjul] adj (by chance) de hasard, fait(e) au hasard, fortuit(e); (irregular: work etc) temporaire; (unconcerned) désinvolte; **~ wear** vêtements mpl sport inv

casualty [ˈkæʒjultı] n accidenté(e), blessé(e); (dead) victime f, mort(e); (BRIT Med: department) urgences fpl

cat [kæt] n chat m

Catalan [ˈkætəlæn] adj catalan(e)

catalogue, (US) **catalog** [ˈkætəlɔg] n catalogue m ▷ vt cataloguer

catalytic converter [kætəˈlɪtɪkkənˈvəːtəʳ] n pot m catalytique

cataract [ˈkætərækt] n (also Med) cataracte f

catarrh [kəˈtɑːʳ] n rhume m chronique, catarrhe f

catastrophe [kəˈtæstrəfı] n catastrophe f

catch [kætʃ] (pt, pp **caught**) vt attraper; (person: by surprise) prendre, surprendre; (understand) saisir; (get entangled) accrocher ▷ vi (fire) prendre; (get entangled) s'accrocher ▷ n (fish etc) prise f; (hidden problem) attrape f; (Tech) loquet m; cliquet m; **to ~ sb's attention** or **eye** attirer l'attention de qn; **to ~ fire** prendre feu; **to ~ sight of** apercevoir; **catch up** vi (with work) se rattraper, combler son retard ▷ vt (also: **~ up with**) rattraper; **catching** [ˈkætʃɪŋ] adj (Med) contagieux(-euse)

category [ˈkætɪgərı] n catégorie f

cater [ˈkeɪtəʳ] vi: **to ~ for** (BRIT: needs) satisfaire, pourvoir à; (readers, consumers) s'adresser à, pourvoir aux besoins de; (Comm: parties etc) préparer des repas pour

caterpillar ['kætəpɪlə^r] n chenille f
cathedral [kə'θi:drəl] n cathédrale f
Catholic ['kæθəlɪk] (Rel) adj catholique ▷ n catholique m/f
cattle ['kætl] npl bétail m, bestiaux mpl
catwalk ['kætwɔ:k] n passerelle f; (for models) podium m (de défilé de mode)
caught [kɔ:t] pt, pp of **catch**
cauliflower ['kɔlɪflauə^r] n chou-fleur m
cause [kɔ:z] n cause f ▷ vt causer
caution ['kɔ:ʃən] n prudence f; (warning) avertissement m ▷ vt avertir, donner un avertissement à; **cautious** adj prudent(e)
cave [keɪv] n caverne f, grotte f; **cave in** vi (roof etc) s'effondrer
caviar(e) ['kævɪɑ:^r] n caviar m
cavity ['kævɪtɪ] n cavité f; (Med) carie f
cc abbr (= cubic centimetre) cm³; (on letter etc = carbon copy) cc
CCTV n abbr = **closed-circuit television**
CD n abbr (= compact disc) CD m; **CD burner** n graveur m de CD; **CD player** n platine f laser; **CD-ROM** [si:di:'rɔm] n abbr (= compact disc read-only memory) CD-ROM m inv; **CD writer** n graveur m de CD
cease [si:s] vt, vi cesser; **ceasefire** n cessez-le-feu m
cedar ['si:də^r] n cèdre m
ceilidh ['keɪlɪ] n bal m folklorique écossais or irlandais
ceiling ['si:lɪŋ] n (also fig) plafond m
celebrate ['sɛlɪbreɪt] vt, vi célébrer; **celebration** [sɛlɪ'breɪʃən] n célébration f
celebrity [sɪ'lɛbrɪtɪ] n célébrité f
celery ['sɛlərɪ] n céleri m (en branches)
cell [sɛl] n (gen) cellule f; (Elec) élément m (de pile)
cellar ['sɛlə^r] n cave f
cello ['tʃɛləu] n violoncelle m
Cellophane® ['sɛləfeɪn] n cellophane® f

cellphone ['sɛlfəun] n (téléphone m) portable m, mobile m
Celsius ['sɛlsɪəs] adj Celsius inv
Celtic ['kɛltɪk, 'sɛltɪk] adj celte, celtique
cement [sə'mɛnt] n ciment m
cemetery ['sɛmɪtrɪ] n cimetière m
censor ['sɛnsə^r] n censeur m ▷ vt censurer; **censorship** n censure f
census ['sɛnsəs] n recensement m
cent [sɛnt] n (unit of dollar, euro) cent m (= un centième du dollar, de l'euro); see also **per cent**
centenary [sɛn'ti:nərɪ], (US) **centennial** [sɛn'tɛnɪəl] n centenaire m
center ['sɛntə^r] (US) = **centre**
centi... ['sɛntɪ]: **centigrade** adj centigrade; **centimetre**, (US) **centimeter** n centimètre m; **centipede** ['sɛntɪpi:d] n mille-pattes m inv
central ['sɛntrəl] adj central(e); **Central America** n Amérique centrale; **central heating** n chauffage central; **central reservation** n (BRIT Aut) terre-plein central
centre, (US) **center** ['sɛntə^r] n centre m ▷ vt centrer; **centre-forward** n (Sport) avant-centre m; **centre-half** n (Sport) demi-centre m
century ['sɛntjurɪ] n siècle m; **in the twentieth ~** au vingtième siècle
CEO n abbr (US) = **chief executive officer**
ceramic [sɪ'ræmɪk] adj céramique
cereal ['si:rɪəl] n céréale f
ceremony ['sɛrɪmənɪ] n cérémonie f; **to stand on ~** faire des façons
certain ['sə:tən] adj certain(e); **to make ~ of** s'assurer de; **for ~** certainement, sûrement; **certainly** adv certainement; **certainty** n certitude f
certificate [sə'tɪfɪkɪt] n certificat m
certify ['sə:tɪfaɪ] vt certifier; (award diploma to) conférer un diplôme etc

à; (*declare insane*) déclarer malade
mental(e)

cf. *abbr* (= *compare*) cf., voir

CFC *n abbr* (= *chlorofluorocarbon*) CFC *m*

chain [tʃeɪn] *n* (*gen*) chaîne *f* ▷ *vt*
(*also:* **~ up**) enchaîner, attacher (avec
une chaîne); **chain-smoke** *vi* fumer
cigarette sur cigarette

chair [tʃeəʳ] *n* chaise *f*; (*armchair*)
fauteuil *m*; (*of university*) chaire *f*; (*of
meeting*) présidence *f* ▷ *vt* (*meeting*)
présider; **chairlift** *n* télésiège *m*;
chairman (*irreg*) *n* président *m*;
chairperson (*irreg*) *n* président(e);
chairwoman (*irreg*) *n* présidente *f*

chalet [ˈʃæleɪ] *n* chalet *m*

chalk [tʃɔːk] *n* craie *f*

challenge [ˈtʃælɪndʒ] *n* défi *m* ▷ *vt*
défier; (*statement, right*) mettre
en question, contester; **to ~ sb
to do** mettre qn au défi de faire;
challenging *adj* (*task, career*) qui
représente un défi *or* une gageure;
(*tone, look*) de défi, provocateur(-trice)

chamber [ˈtʃeɪmbəʳ] *n* chambre
f; (*BRIT Law: gen pl*) cabinet *m*; **~ of
commerce** chambre de commerce;
chambermaid *n* femme *f* de
chambre

champagne [ʃæmˈpeɪn] *n*
champagne *m*

champion [ˈtʃæmpɪən] *n* (*also of
cause*) champion(ne); **championship**
n championnat *m*

chance [tʃɑːns] *n* (*luck*) hasard *m*;
(*opportunity*) occasion *f*, possibilité *f*;
(*hope, likelihood*) chance *f*; (*risk*) risque
m ▷ *vt* (*risk*) risquer ▷ *adj* fortuit(e),
de hasard; **to take a ~** prendre
un risque; **by ~** par hasard; **to ~ it**
risquer le coup, essayer

chancellor [ˈtʃɑːnsələʳ] *n* chancelier
m; **Chancellor of the Exchequer**
[-ɪksˈtʃɛkəʳ] (*BRIT*) *n* chancelier *m* de
l'Échiquier

chandelier [ʃændəˈlɪəʳ] *n* lustre *m*

change [tʃeɪndʒ] *vt* (*alter, replace:
Comm: money*) changer; (*switch,*

substitute: *hands, trains, clothes,
one's name etc*) changer de ▷ *vi*
(*gen*) changer; (*change clothes*) se
changer; (*be transformed*): **to ~ into**
se changer *or* transformer en ▷ *n*
changement *m*; (*money*) monnaie *f*;
to ~ gear (*Aut*) changer de vitesse;
to ~ one's mind changer d'avis;
a ~ of clothes des vêtements de
rechange; **for a ~** pour changer; **do
you have ~ for £10?** vous avez la
monnaie de 10 livres?; **where can
I ~ some money?** où est-ce que je
peux changer de l'argent?; **keep
the ~!** gardez la monnaie!; **change
over** *vi* (*swap*) échanger; (*change:
drivers etc*) changer; (*change sides:
players etc*) changer de côté; **to ~ over
from sth to sth** passer de qch à qch;
changeable *adj* (*weather*) variable;
change machine *n* distributeur *m* de
monnaie; **changing room** *n* (*BRIT:
in shop*) salon *m* d'essayage (*: Sport*)
vestiaire *m*

channel [ˈtʃænl] *n* (*TV*) chaîne
f; (*waveband, groove, fig: medium*)
canal *m*; (*of river, sea*) chenal *m* ▷ *vt*
canaliser; **the (English) C~** la
Manche; **Channel Islands** *npl*; **the
Channel Islands** les îles *fpl* Anglo-
Normandes; **Channel Tunnel** *n*:
the Channel Tunnel le tunnel sous
la Manche

chant [tʃɑːnt] *n* chant *m*; (*Rel*)
psalmodie *f* ▷ *vt* chanter, scander

chaos [ˈkeɪɔs] *n* chaos *m*

chaotic [keɪˈɔtɪk] *adj* chaotique

chap [tʃæp] *n* (*BRIT inf: man*) type *m*

chapel [ˈtʃæpl] *n* chapelle *f*

chapped [tʃæpt] *adj* (*skin, lips*)
gercé(e)

chapter [ˈtʃæptəʳ] *n* chapitre *m*

character [ˈkærɪktəʳ] *n* caractère *m*;
(*in novel, film*) personnage *m*; (*eccentric
person*) numéro *m*, phénomène *m*;
characteristic [ˈkærɪktəˈrɪstɪk] *adj*,
n caractéristique (*f*); **characterize**
[ˈkærɪktəraɪz] *vt* caractériser

charcoal ['tʃɑːkəul] *n* charbon *m* de bois; (*Art*) charbon

charge [tʃɑːdʒ] *n* (*accusation*) accusation *f*; (*Law*) inculpation *f*; (*cost*) prix (demandé) ▷ *vt* (*gun, battery, Mil: enemy*) charger; (*customer, sum*) faire payer ▷ *vi* foncer; **charges** *npl* (*costs*) frais *mpl*; **to reverse the ~s** (*BRIT Tel*) téléphoner en PCV; **to take ~ of** se charger de; **to be in ~ of** être responsable de, s'occuper de; **to ~ sb (with)** (*Law*) inculper qn (de); **charge card** *n* carte *f* de client (*émise par un grand magasin*); **charger** *n* (*also*: **battery charger**) chargeur *m*

charismatic [kærɪz'mætɪk] *adj* charismatique

charity ['tʃærɪtɪ] *n* charité *f*; (*organization*) institution *f* charitable or de bienfaisance, œuvre *f* (de charité); **charity shop** *n* (*BRIT*) boutique vendant des articles d'occasion au profit d'une organisation caritative

charm [tʃɑːm] *n* charme *m*; (*on bracelet*) breloque *f* ▷ *vt* charmer, enchanter; **charming** *adj* charmant(e)

chart [tʃɑːt] *n* tableau *m*, diagramme *m*; graphique *m*; (*map*) carte marine ▷ *vt* dresser or établir la carte de; (*sales, progress*) établir la courbe de; **charts** *npl* (*Mus*) hit-parade *m*; **to be in the ~s** (*record, pop group*) figurer au hit-parade

charter ['tʃɑːtə'] *vt* (*plane*) affréter ▷ *n* (*document*) charte *f*; **chartered accountant** *n* (*BRIT*) expert-comptable *m*; **charter flight** *n* charter *m*

chase [tʃeɪs] *vt* poursuivre, pourchasser; (*also*: **~ away**) chasser ▷ *n* poursuite *f*, chasse *f*

chat [tʃæt] *vi* (*also*: **have a ~**) bavarder, causer; (*on Internet*) chatter ▷ *n* conversation *f*; (*on Internet*) chat *m*; **chat up** *vt* (*BRIT inf: girl*) baratiner; **chat room** *n* (*Internet*) salon *m* de discussion; **chat show** *n* (*BRIT*) talk-show *m*

chatter ['tʃætə'] *vi* (*person*) bavarder, papoter ▷ *n* bavardage *m*, papotage *m*; **my teeth are ~ing** je claque des dents

chauffeur ['ʃəufə'] *n* chauffeur *m* (de maître)

chauvinist ['ʃəuvɪnɪst] *n* (*also*: **male ~**) phallocrate *m*, macho *m*; (*nationalist*) chauvin(e)

cheap [tʃiːp] *adj* bon marché *inv*, pas cher (chère); (*reduced: ticket*) à prix réduit; (: *fare*) réduit(e); (*joke*) facile, d'un goût douteux; (*poor quality*) à bon marché, de qualité médiocre ▷ *adv* à bon marché, pour pas cher; **can you recommend a ~ hotel/restaurant, please?** pourriez-vous m'indiquer un hôtel/restaurant bon marché?; **cheap day return** *n* billet *m* d'aller et retour réduit (*valable pour la journée*); **cheaply** *adv* à bon marché, à bon compte

cheat [tʃiːt] *vi* tricher; (*in exam*) copier ▷ *vt* tromper, duper; (*rob*): **to ~ sb out of sth** escroquer qch à qn ▷ *n* tricheur(-euse) *m/f*; escroc *m*; **cheat on** *vt fus* tromper

Chechnya [tʃɪtʃ'njɑː] *n* Tchétchénie *f*

check [tʃɛk] *vt* vérifier; (*passport, ticket*) contrôler; (*halt*) enrayer; (*restrain*) maîtriser ▷ *vi* (*official etc*) se renseigner ▷ *n* vérification *f*; contrôle *m*; (*curb*) frein *m*; (*BRIT: bill*) addition *f*; (*US*) = **cheque**; (*pattern: gen pl*) carreaux *mpl*; **to ~ with sb** demander à qn; **check in** *vi* (*in hotel*) remplir sa fiche (d'hôtel); (*at airport*) se présenter à l'enregistrement ▷ *vt* (*luggage*) (faire) enregistrer; **check off** *vt* (*tick off*) cocher; **check out** *vi* (*in hotel*) régler sa note ▷ *vt* (*investigate: story*) vérifier; **check up** *vi*: **to ~ up (on sth)** vérifier (qch); **to ~ up on sb** se renseigner sur le compte de qn; **checkbook** *n* (*US*) = **chequebook**; **checked** *adj* (*pattern, cloth*) à carreaux; **checkers** *n* (*US*) jeu *m* de dames; **check-in** *n* (*at airport: also*:

check-in desk) enregistrement m; **checking account** n (us) compte courant; **checklist** n liste f de contrôle; **checkmate** n échec et mat m; **checkout** n (in supermarket) caisse f; **checkpoint** n contrôle m; **checkroom** (us) n consigne f; **checkup** n (Med) examen médical, check-up m

cheddar ['tʃedər] n (also: ~ **cheese**) cheddar m

cheek [tʃiːk] n joue f; (impudence) toupet m, culot m; **what a ~!** quel toupet!; **cheekbone** n pommette f; **cheeky** adj effronté(e), culotté(e)

cheer [tʃɪər] vt acclamer, applaudir; (gladden) réjouir, réconforter ▷ vi applaudir ▷ n (gen pl) acclamations fpl, applaudissements mpl; bravos mpl, hourras mpl; **~s!** à la vôtre!; **cheer up** vi se dérider, reprendre courage ▷ vt remonter le moral à or de, dérider, égayer; **cheerful** adj gai(e), joyeux(-euse)

cheerio [tʃɪərɪ'əʊ] excl salut!, au revoir!

cheerleader ['tʃɪəliːdər] n membre d'un groupe de majorettes qui chantent et dansent pour soutenir leur équipe pendant les matchs de football américain

cheese [tʃiːz] n fromage m; **cheeseburger** n cheeseburger m; **cheesecake** n tarte f au fromage

chef [ʃɛf] n chef (cuisinier)

chemical ['kemɪkl] adj chimique ▷ n produit m chimique

chemist ['kemɪst] n (BRIT: pharmacist) pharmacien(ne); (scientist) chimiste m/f; **chemistry** n chimie f; **chemist's (shop)** n (BRIT) pharmacie f

cheque, (us) **check** [tʃɛk] n chèque m; **chequebook**, (us) **checkbook** n chéquier m, carnet m de chèques; **cheque card** n (BRIT) carte f (d'identité) bancaire

cherry ['tʃerɪ] n cerise f; (also: ~ **tree**) cerisier m

chess [tʃɛs] n échecs mpl

chest [tʃɛst] n poitrine f; (box) coffre m, caisse f

chestnut ['tʃesnʌt] n châtaigne f; (also: ~ **tree**) châtaignier m

chest of drawers n commode f

chew [tʃuː] vt mâcher; **chewing gum** n chewing-gum m

chic [ʃiːk] adj chic inv, élégant(e)

chick [tʃɪk] n poussin m; (inf) fille f

chicken ['tʃɪkɪn] n poulet m; (inf: coward) poule mouillée; **chicken out** vi (inf) se dégonfler; **chickenpox** n varicelle f

chickpea ['tʃɪkpiː] n pois m chiche

chief [tʃiːf] n chef m ▷ adj principal(e); **chief executive**, (us) **chief executive officer** n directeur(-trice) général(e); **chiefly** adv principalement, surtout

child (pl **children**) [tʃaɪld, 'tʃɪldrən] n enfant m/f; **child abuse** n maltraitance f d'enfants; (sexual) abus mpl sexuels sur des enfants; **child benefit** n (BRIT) ≈ allocations familiales; **childbirth** n accouchement m; **childcare** n (for working parents) garde f des enfants (pour les parents qui travaillent); **childhood** n enfance f; **childish** adj puéril(e), enfantin(e); **child minder** n (BRIT) garde f d'enfants; **children** ['tʃɪldrən] npl of **child**

Chile ['tʃɪlɪ] n Chili m

chill [tʃɪl] n (of water) froid m; (of air) fraîcheur f; (Med) refroidissement m, coup m de froid ▷ vt (person) faire frissonner; (Culin) mettre au frais, rafraîchir; **chill out** vi (inf: esp US) se relaxer

chil(l)i ['tʃɪlɪ] n piment m (rouge)

chilly ['tʃɪlɪ] adj froid(e), glacé(e); (sensitive to cold) frileux(-euse)

chimney ['tʃɪmnɪ] n cheminée f

chimpanzee [tʃɪmpæn'ziː] n chimpanzé m

chin [tʃɪn] n menton m

China ['tʃaɪnə] n Chine f

china ['tʃaɪnə] n (material) porcelaine f; (crockery) (vaisselle f en) porcelaine

Chinese [tʃaɪ'niːz] adj chinois(e) ▷ n (pl inv) Chinois(e); (Ling) chinois m

chip [tʃɪp] n (gen pl: Culin: BRIT) frite f; (: US: also: **potato ~**) chip m; (of wood) copeau m; (of glass, stone) éclat m; (also: **micro~**) puce f; (in gambling) fiche f ▷ vt (cup, plate) ébrécher; **chip shop** n (BRIT) friterie f

○ **CHIP SHOP**
○
○ Un *chip shop*, que l'on appelle
○ également un "fish-and-chip shop",
○ est un magasin où l'on vend des
○ plats à emporter. Les *chip shops* sont
○ d'ailleurs à l'origine des "takeaways".
○ On y achète en particulier du
○ poisson frit et des frites, mais
○ on y trouve également des plats
○ traditionnels britanniques ("steak
○ pies", saucisses, etc). Tous les plats
○ étaient à l'origine emballés dans du
○ papier journal. Dans certains de ces
○ magasins, on peut s'asseoir pour
○ consommer sur place.

chiropodist [kɪ'rɒpədɪst] n (BRIT) pédicure m/f

chisel ['tʃɪzl] n ciseau m

chives [tʃaɪvz] npl ciboulette f, civette f

chlorine ['klɔːriːn] n chlore m

choc-ice ['tʃɒkaɪs] n (BRIT) esquimau® m

chocolate ['tʃɒklɪt] n chocolat m

choice [tʃɔɪs] n choix m ▷ adj de choix

choir ['kwaɪə'] n chœur m, chorale f

choke [tʃəuk] vi étouffer ▷ vt étrangler; étouffer; (block) boucher, obstruer ▷ n (Aut) starter m

cholesterol [kə'lɛstərɒl] n cholestérol m

chook [tʃuk] n (AUST, NZ inf) poule f

choose (pt **chose**, pp **chosen**) [tʃuːz, tʃəuz, 'tʃəuzn] vt choisir; **to ~ to do** décider de faire, juger bon de faire

chop [tʃɒp] vt (wood) couper (à la hache); (Culin: also: **~ up**) couper (fin), émincer, hacher (en morceaux) ▷ n (Culin) côtelette f; **chop down** vt (tree) abattre; **chop off** vt trancher; **chopsticks** ['tʃɒpstɪks] npl baguettes fpl

chord [kɔːd] n (Mus) accord m

chore [tʃɔː'] n travail m de routine; **household ~s** travaux mpl du ménage

chorus ['kɔːrəs] n chœur m; (repeated part of song, also fig) refrain m

chose [tʃəuz] pt of **choose**

chosen ['tʃəuzn] pp of **choose**

Christ [kraɪst] n Christ m

christen ['krɪsn] vt baptiser; **christening** n baptême m

Christian ['krɪstɪən] adj, chrétien(ne); **Christianity** [krɪstɪ'ænɪtɪ] n christianisme m; **Christian name** n prénom m

Christmas ['krɪsməs] n Noël m or f; **happy** or **merry ~!** joyeux Noël!; **Christmas card** n carte f de Noël; **Christmas carol** n chant m de Noël; **Christmas Day** n le jour de Noël; **Christmas Eve** n la veille de Noël; la nuit de Noël; **Christmas pudding** n (esp BRIT) Christmas m pudding; **Christmas tree** n arbre m de Noël

chrome [krəum] n chrome m

chronic ['krɒnɪk] adj chronique

chrysanthemum [krɪ'sænθəməm] n chrysanthème m

chubby ['tʃʌbɪ] adj potelé(e), rondelet(te)

chuck [tʃʌk] vt (inf) lancer, jeter; (job) lâcher; **chuck out** vt (inf: person) flanquer dehors or à la porte; (: rubbish etc) jeter

chuckle ['tʃʌkl] vi glousser

chum [tʃʌm] n copain (copine)

chunk [tʃʌŋk] n gros morceau

church [tʃəːtʃ] n église f; **churchyard** n cimetière m

churn [tʃəːn] n (for butter) baratte f; (also: **milk ~**) (grand) bidon à lait

chute [ʃuːt] n goulotte f; (also: **rubbish ~**) vide-ordures m inv; (BRIT: children's slide) toboggan m

chutney ['tʃʌtnɪ] n chutney m

CIA n abbr (= Central Intelligence Agency) CIA f

CID n abbr (= Criminal Investigation Department) ≈ P.J. f

cider ['saɪdə'] n cidre m

cigar [sɪ'gɑː'] n cigare m

cigarette [sɪgə'rɛt] n cigarette f; **cigarette lighter** n briquet m

cinema ['sɪnəmə] n cinéma m

cinnamon ['sɪnəmən] n cannelle f

circle ['səːkl] n cercle m; (in cinema) balcon m ▷ vi faire or décrire des cercles ▷ vt (surround) entourer, encercler; (move round) faire le tour de, tourner autour de

circuit ['səːkɪt] n circuit m; (lap) tour m

circular ['səːkjulə'] adj circulaire ▷ n circulaire f; (as advertisement) prospectus m

circulate ['səːkjuleɪt] vi circuler ▷ vt faire circuler; **circulation** [səːkju'leɪʃən] n circulation f; (of newspaper) tirage m

circumstances ['səːkəmstənsɪz] npl circonstances fpl; (financial condition) moyens mpl, situation financière

circus ['səːkəs] n cirque m

cite [saɪt] vt citer

citizen ['sɪtɪzn] n (Pol) citoyen(ne); (resident): **the ~s of this town** les habitants de cette ville; **citizenship** n citoyenneté f; (BRIT Scol) ≈ éducation f civique

citrus fruits ['sɪtrəs-] npl agrumes mpl

city ['sɪtɪ] n (grande) ville f; **the C~** la Cité de Londres (centre des affaires); **city centre** n centre ville m; **city technology college** n (BRIT) établissement m d'enseignement technologique (situé dans un quartier défavorisé)

civic ['sɪvɪk] adj civique; (authorities) municipal(e)

civil ['sɪvɪl] adj civil(e); (polite) poli(e), civil(e); **civilian** [sɪ'vɪlɪən] adj, n civil(e)

civilization [sɪvɪlaɪ'zeɪʃən] n civilisation f

civilized ['sɪvɪlaɪzd] adj civilisé(e); (fig) où règnent les bonnes manières

civil: civil law n code civil; (study) droit civil; **civil rights** npl droits mpl civiques; **civil servant** n fonctionnaire m/f; **Civil Service** n fonction publique, administration f; **civil war** n guerre civile

CJD n abbr (= Creutzfeldt-Jakob disease) MCJ f

claim [kleɪm] vt (rights etc) revendiquer; (compensation) réclamer; (assert) déclarer, prétendre ▷ vi (for insurance) faire une déclaration de sinistre ▷ n revendication f; prétention f; (right) droit m; **(insurance) ~** demande f d'indemnisation, déclaration f de sinistre; **claim form** n (gen) formulaire m de demande

clam [klæm] n palourde f

clamp [klæmp] n crampon m; (on workbench) valet m; (on car) sabot m de Denver ▷ vt attacher; (car) mettre un sabot à; **clamp down on** vt fus sévir contre, prendre des mesures draconiennes à l'égard de

clan [klæn] n clan m

clap [klæp] vi applaudir

claret ['klærət] n (vin m de) bordeaux m (rouge)

clarify ['klærɪfaɪ] vt clarifier

clarinet [klærɪ'nɛt] n clarinette f

clarity ['klærɪtɪ] n clarté f

clash [klæʃ] n (sound) choc m, fracas m; (with police) affrontement m; (fig) conflit m ▷ vi se heurter; être or entrer en conflit; (colours) jurer; (dates, events) tomber en même temps

clasp [klɑːsp] n (of necklace, bag) fermoir m ▷ vt serrer, étreindre

class [klɑːs] n (gen) classe f; (group, category) catégorie f ▷ vt classer, classifier

classic ['klæsɪk] adj classique ▷ n (author, work) classique m; **classical** adj classique

classification [klæsɪfɪ'keɪʃən] n classification f

classify ['klæsɪfaɪ] vt classifier, classer

classmate ['klɑːsmeɪt] n camarade m/f de classe

classroom ['klɑːsrum] n (salle f de) classe f; **classroom assistant** n assistant(e) d'éducation

classy ['klɑːsɪ] (inf) adj classe (inf)

clatter ['klætər] n cliquetis m ▷ vi cliqueter

clause [klɔːz] n clause f; (Ling) proposition f

claustrophobic [klɔːstrə'fəubɪk] adj (person) claustrophobe; (place) où l'on se sent claustrophobe

claw [klɔː] n griffe f; (of bird of prey) serre f; (of lobster) pince f

clay [kleɪ] n argile f

clean [kliːn] adj propre; (clear, smooth) net(te); (record, reputation) sans tache; (joke, story) correct(e) ▷ vt nettoyer; **clean up** vt nettoyer; (fig) remettre de l'ordre dans; **cleaner** n (person) nettoyeur(-euse), femme f de ménage; (product) détachant m; **cleaner's** (also: **dry cleaner's**) teinturier m; **cleaning** n nettoyage m

cleanser ['klɛnzər] n (for face) démaquillant m

clear [klɪər] adj clair(e); (glass, plastic) transparent(e); (road, way) libre, dégagé(e); (profit, majority) net(te); (conscience) tranquille; (skin) frais (fraîche); (sky) dégagé(e) ▷ vt (road) dégager, déblayer; (table) débarrasser; (room etc: of people) faire évacuer; (cheque) compenser; (Law: suspect) innocenter; (obstacle) franchir ou sauter sans heurter ▷ vi (weather) s'éclaircir; (fog) se dissiper

▷ adv: **~ of** à distance de, à l'écart de; **to ~ the table** débarrasser la table, desservir; **clear away** vt (things, clothes etc) enlever, retirer; **to ~ away the dishes** débarrasser la table; **clear up** vt ranger, mettre en ordre; (mystery) éclaircir, résoudre; **clearance** n (removal) déblayage m; (permission) autorisation f; **clear-cut** adj précis(e), nettement défini(e); **clearing** n (in forest) clairière f; **clearly** adv clairement; (obviously) de toute évidence; **clearway** n (BRIT) route f à stationnement interdit

clench [klɛntʃ] vt serrer

clergy ['klɜːdʒɪ] n clergé m

clerk [klɑːk, US klɜːrk] n (BRIT) employé(e) de bureau; (US: salesman/woman) vendeur(-euse)

clever ['klɛvər] adj (intelligent) intelligent(e); (skilful) habile, adroit(e); (device, arrangement) ingénieux(-euse), astucieux(-euse)

cliché ['kliːʃeɪ] n cliché m

click [klɪk] vi (Comput) cliquer ▷ vt: **to ~ one's tongue** faire claquer sa langue; **to ~ one's heels** claquer des talons; **to ~ on an icon** cliquer sur une icône

client ['klaɪənt] n client(e)

cliff [klɪf] n falaise f

climate ['klaɪmɪt] n climat m; **climate change** n changement m climatique

climax ['klaɪmæks] n apogée m, point culminant; (sexual) orgasme m

climb [klaɪm] vi grimper, monter; (plane) prendre de l'altitude ▷ vt (stairs) monter; (mountain) escalader; (tree) grimper à ▷ n montée f, escalade f; **to ~ over a wall** passer par dessus un mur; **climb down** vi (re)descendre; (BRIT fig) rabattre de ses prétentions; **climber** n (also: **rock climber**) grimpeur(-euse), varappeur(-euse); (plant) plante grimpante; **climbing** n (also: **rock climbing**) escalade f, varappe f

clinch [klɪntʃ] vt (deal) conclure, sceller

cling (pt, pp **clung**) [klɪŋ, klʌŋ] vi: **to ~ (to)** se cramponner (à), s'accrocher (à); (clothes) coller (à)

Clingfilm® ['klɪŋfɪlm] n film m alimentaire

clinic ['klɪnɪk] n clinique f; centre médical

clip [klɪp] n (for hair) barrette f; (also: **paper ~**) trombone m; (TV, Cine) clip m ▷ vt (also: **~ together**: papers) attacher; (hair, nails) couper; (hedge) tailler; **clipping** n (from newspaper) coupure f de journal

cloak [kləuk] n grande cape ▷ vt (fig) masquer, cacher; **cloakroom** n (for coats etc) vestiaire m; (BRIT: W.C.) toilettes fpl

clock [klɒk] n (large) horloge f; (small) pendule f; **clock in, clock on** (BRIT) vi (with card) pointer (en arrivant); (start work) commencer à travailler; **clock off, clock out** (BRIT) vi (with card) pointer (en partant); (leave work) quitter le travail; **clockwise** adv dans le sens des aiguilles d'une montre; **clockwork** n rouages mpl, mécanisme m; (of clock) mouvement m (d'horlogerie) ▷ adj (toy, train) mécanique

clog [klɒg] n sabot m ▷ vt boucher, encrasser ▷ vi (also: **~ up**) se boucher, s'encrasser

clone [kləun] n clone m ▷ vt cloner

close¹ [kləus] adj (contact, link, watch) étroit(e); (examination) attentif(-ive), minutieux(-euse); (contest) très serré(e); (weather) lourd(e), étouffant(e); (near): **~ (to)** près (de), proche (de) ▷ adv près, à proximité; **~ to** prep près de; **~ by, ~ at hand** adj, adv tout(e) près; **a ~ friend** un ami intime; **to have a ~ shave** (fig) l'échapper belle

close² [kləuz] vt fermer ▷ vi (shop etc) fermer; (lid, door etc) se fermer; (end) se terminer, se conclure ▷ n (end)

conclusion f; **what time do you ~?** à quelle heure fermez-vous?; **close down** vi fermer (définitivement); **closed** adj (shop etc) fermé(e)

closely ['kləuslɪ] adv (examine, watch) de près

closet ['klɒzɪt] n (cupboard) placard m, réduit m

close-up ['kləusʌp] n gros plan

closing time n heure f de fermeture

closure ['kləuʒər] n fermeture f

clot [klɒt] n (of blood, milk) caillot m; (inf: person) ballot m ▷ vi (external bleeding) se coaguler

cloth [klɒθ] n (material) tissu m, étoffe f; (BRIT: also: **tea ~**) torchon m; lavette f; (also: **table~**) nappe f

clothes [kləuðz] npl vêtements mpl, habits mpl; **clothes line** n corde f (à linge); **clothes peg**, (US) **clothes pin** n pince f à linge

clothing ['kləuðɪŋ] n = **clothes**

cloud [klaud] n nuage m; **cloud over** vi se couvrir; (fig) s'assombrir; **cloudy** adj nuageux(-euse), couvert(e); (liquid) trouble

clove [kləuv] n clou m de girofle; **a ~ of garlic** une gousse d'ail

clown [klaun] n clown m ▷ vi (also: **~ about, ~ around**) faire le clown

club [klʌb] n (society) club m; (weapon) massue f, matraque f; (also: **golf ~**) club ▷ vt matraquer ▷ vi: **to ~ together** s'associer; **clubs** npl (Cards) trèfle m; **club class** n (Aviat) classe f club

clue [klu:] n indice m; (in crosswords) définition f; **I haven't a ~** je n'en ai pas la moindre idée

clump [klʌmp] n: **~ of trees** bouquet m d'arbres

clumsy ['klʌmzɪ] adj (person) gauche, maladroit(e); (object) malcommode, peu maniable

clung [klʌŋ] pt, pp of **cling**

cluster ['klʌstər] n (petit) groupe; (of flowers) grappe f ▷ vi se rassembler

clutch [klʌtʃ] n (Aut) embrayage m; (grasp): **~es** étreinte f, prise f ▷ vt (grasp) agripper; (hold tightly) serrer fort; (hold on to) se cramponner à

cm abbr (= centimetre) cm

Co. abbr = **company, county**

c/o abbr (= care of) c/o, aux bons soins de

coach [kəʊtʃ] n (bus) autocar m; (horse-drawn) diligence f; (of train) voiture f, wagon m; (Sport: trainer) entraîneur(-euse); (school: tutor) répétiteur(-trice) ▷ vt (Sport) entraîner; (student) donner des leçons particulières à; **coach station** (BRIT) n gare routière; **coach trip** n excursion f en car

coal [kəʊl] n charbon m

coalition [kəʊə'lɪʃən] n coalition f

coarse [kɔːs] adj grossier(-ère), rude; (vulgar) vulgaire

coast [kəʊst] n côte f ▷ vi (car, cycle) descendre en roue libre; **coastal** adj côtier(-ère); **coastguard** n garde-côte m; **coastline** n côte f, littoral m

coat [kəʊt] n manteau m; (of animal) pelage m, poil m; (of paint) couche f ▷ vt couvrir, enduire; **coat hanger** n cintre m; **coating** n couche f, enduit m

coax [kəʊks] vt persuader par des cajoleries

cob [kɔb] n see **corn**

cobbled ['kɔbld] adj pavé(e)

cobweb ['kɔbwɛb] n toile f d'araignée

cocaine [kə'keɪn] n cocaïne f

cock [kɔk] n (rooster) coq m; (male bird) mâle m ▷ vt (gun) armer; **cockerel** n jeune coq m

cockney ['kɔknɪ] n cockney m/f (habitant des quartiers populaires de l'East End de Londres), ≈ faubourien(ne)

cockpit ['kɔkpɪt] n (in aircraft) poste m de pilotage, cockpit m

cockroach ['kɔkrəʊtʃ] n cafard m, cancrelat m

cocktail ['kɔkteɪl] n cocktail m

cocoa ['kəʊkəʊ] n cacao m

coconut ['kəʊkənʌt] n noix f de coco

cod [kɔd] n morue fraîche, cabillaud m

C.O.D. abbr = **cash on delivery**

code [kəʊd] n code m; (Tel: area code) indicatif m

coeducational ['kəʊɛdju'keɪʃənl] adj mixte

coffee ['kɔfɪ] n café m; **coffee bar** n (BRIT) café m; **coffee bean** n grain m de café; **coffee break** n pause-café f; **coffee maker** n cafetière f; **coffeepot** n cafetière f; **coffee shop** n café m; **coffee table** n (petite) table basse

coffin ['kɔfɪn] n cercueil m

cog [kɔg] n (wheel) roue dentée; (tooth) dent f (d'engrenage)

cognac ['kɔnjæk] n cognac m

coherent [kəʊ'hɪərənt] adj cohérent(e)

coil [kɔɪl] n rouleau m, bobine f; (contraceptive) stérilet m ▷ vt enrouler

coin [kɔɪn] n pièce f (de monnaie) ▷ vt (word) inventer

coincide [kəʊɪn'saɪd] vi coïncider; **coincidence** [kəʊ'ɪnsɪdəns] n coïncidence f

Coke® [kəʊk] n coca m

coke [kəʊk] n (coal) coke m

colander ['kɔləndər] n passoire f (à légumes)

cold [kəʊld] adj froid(e) ▷ n froid m; (Med) rhume m; **it's ~** il fait froid; **to be ~** (person) avoir froid; **to catch a ~** s'enrhumer, attraper un rhume; **in ~ blood** de sang-froid; **cold sore** n bouton m de fièvre

coleslaw ['kəʊlslɔː] n sorte de salade de chou cru

colic ['kɔlɪk] n colique(s) f(pl)

collaborate [kə'læbəreɪt] vi collaborer

collapse [kə'læps] vi s'effondrer, s'écrouler; (Med) avoir un malaise ▷ n effondrement m, écroulement m; (of government) chute f

collar ['kɔlər] n (of coat, shirt) col m; (for dog) collier m; **collarbone** n clavicule f

colleague ['kɔliːg] n collègue m/f

collect [kə'lɛkt] vt rassembler; (pick up) ramasser; (as a hobby) collectionner; (BRIT: call for) (passer) prendre; (mail) faire la levée de, ramasser; (money owed) encaisser; (donations, subscriptions) recueillir ▷ vi (people) se rassembler; (dust, dirt) s'amasser; **to call ~** (US Tel) téléphoner en PCV; **collection** [kə'lɛkʃən] n collection f; (of mail) levée f; (for money) collecte f, quête f; **collective** [kə'lɛktɪv] adj collectif(-ive); **collector** n collectionneur m

college ['kɔlɪdʒ] n collège m; (of technology, agriculture etc) institut m

collide [kə'laɪd] vi: **to ~ (with)** entrer en collision (avec)

collision [kə'lɪʒən] n collision f, heurt m

cologne [kə'ləun] n (also: **eau de ~**) eau f de cologne

colon ['kəulən] n (sign) deux-points mpl; (Med) côlon m

colonel ['kə:nl] n colonel m

colonial [kə'ləunɪəl] adj colonial(e)

colony ['kɔlənɪ] n colonie f

colour, (US) **color** ['kʌləʳ] n couleur f ▷ vt colorer; (dye) teindre; (paint) peindre; (with crayons) colorier; (news) fausser, exagérer ▷ vi (blush) rougir; **I'd like a different ~** je le voudrais dans un autre coloris; **colour in** vt colorier; **colour-blind,** (US) **color-blind** adj daltonien(ne); **coloured,** (US) **colored** adj coloré(e); (photo) en couleur; **colour film,** (US) **color film** n (for camera) pellicule f (en) couleur; **colourful,** (US) **colorful** adj coloré(e), vif (vive); (personality) pittoresque, haut(e) en couleurs; **colouring,** (US) **coloring** n colorant m; (complexion) teint m; **colour television,** (US) **color television** n télévision f (en) couleur

column ['kɔləm] n colonne f; (fashion column, sports column etc) rubrique f

coma ['kəumə] n coma m

comb [kəum] n peigne m ▷ vt (hair) peigner; (area) ratisser, passer au peigne fin

combat ['kɔmbæt] n combat m ▷ vt combattre, lutter contre

combination [kɔmbɪ'neɪʃən] n (gen) combinaison f

combine [kəm'baɪn] vt combiner ▷ vi s'associer; (Chem) se combiner ▷ n ['kɔmbaɪn] (Econ) trust m; (also: **~ harvester**) moissonneuse-batteuse(-lieuse) f; **to ~ sth with sth** (one quality with another) joindre ou allier qch à qch

 KEYWORD

come (pt **came**, pp **come**) [kʌm, keɪm] vi **1** (movement towards) venir; **to come running** arriver en courant; **he's come here to work** il est venu ici pour travailler; **come with me** suivez-moi

2 (arrive) arriver; **to come home** rentrer (chez soi or à la maison); **we've just come from Paris** nous arrivons de Paris

3 (reach): **to come to** (decision etc) parvenir à, arriver à; **the bill came to £40** la note s'est élevée à 40 livres

4 (occur): **an idea came to me** il m'est venu une idée

5 (be, become): **to come loose/undone** se défaire/desserrer; **I've come to like him** j'ai fini par bien l'aimer

come across vt fus rencontrer par hasard, tomber sur

come along vi (BRIT: pupil, work) faire des progrès, avancer

come back vi revenir

come down vi descendre; (prices) baisser; (buildings) s'écrouler; (: be demolished) être démoli(e)

come from vt fus (source) venir de; (place) venir de, être originaire de

come in vi entrer; (train) arriver;

(fashion) entrer en vogue; (on deal etc) participer

come off vi (button) se détacher; (attempt) réussir

come on vi (lights, electricity) s'allumer; (central heating) se mettre en marche; (pupil, work, project) faire des progrès, avancer; **come on!** viens!, allons!, allez!

come out vi sortir; (sun) se montrer; (book) paraître; (stain) s'enlever; (strike) cesser le travail, se mettre en grève

come round vi (after faint, operation) revenir à soi, reprendre connaissance

come to vi revenir à soi

come up vi monter; (sun) se lever; (problem) se poser; (event) survenir; (in conversation) être soulevé

come up with vt fus (money) fournir; **he came up with an idea** il a eu une idée, il a proposé quelque chose

comeback ['kʌmbæk] n (Theat) rentrée f

comedian [kə'mi:dɪən] n (comic) comique m; (Theat) comédien m

comedy ['kɒmɪdɪ] n comédie f; (humour) comique m

comet ['kɒmɪt] n comète f

comfort ['kʌmfət] n confort m, bien-être m; (solace) consolation f, réconfort m ▷ vt consoler, réconforter; **comfortable** adj confortable; (person) à l'aise; (financially) aisé(e); (patient) dont l'état est stationnaire; **comfort station** n (US) toilettes fpl

comic ['kɒmɪk] adj (also: **~al**) comique ▷ n (person) comique m; (BRIT: magazine: for children) magazine m de bandes dessinées or de BD; (: for adults) illustré m; **comic book** n (US: for children) magazine m de bandes dessinées or de BD; (: for adults) illustré m; **comic strip** n bande dessinée

comma ['kɒmə] n virgule f

command [kə'mɑ:nd] n ordre m, commandement m; (Mil: authority) commandement; (mastery) maîtrise f ▷ vt (troops) commander; **to ~ sb to do** donner l'ordre or commander à qn de faire; **commander** n (Mil) commandant m

commemorate [kə'mɛməreɪt] vt commémorer

commence [kə'mɛns] vt, vi commencer

commend [kə'mɛnd] vt louer; (recommend) recommander

comment ['kɒmɛnt] n commentaire m ▷ vi: **to ~ on** faire des remarques sur; **"no ~"** je n'ai rien à déclarer"; **commentary** ['kɒməntərɪ] n commentaire m; (Sport) reportage m (en direct); **commentator** ['kɒmənteɪtə'] n commentateur m; (Sport) reporter m

commerce ['kɒmə:s] n commerce m

commercial [kə'mə:ʃəl] adj commercial(e) ▷ n (Radio, TV) annonce f publicitaire, spot m (publicitaire); **commercial break** n (Radio, TV) spot m (publicitaire)

commission [kə'mɪʃən] n (committee, fee) commission f ▷ vt (work of art) commander, charger un artiste de l'exécution de; **out of ~** (machine) hors service; **commissioner** n (Police) préfet m (de police)

commit [kə'mɪt] vt (act) commettre; (resources) consacrer; (to sb's care) confier (à); **to ~ o.s. (to do)** s'engager (à faire); **to ~ suicide** se suicider; **commitment** n engagement m; (obligation) responsabilité(s) f(pl)

committee [kə'mɪtɪ] n comité m; commission f

commodity [kə'mɒdɪtɪ] n produit m, marchandise f, article m

common ['kɒmən] adj (gen) commun(e); (usual) courant(e) ▷ n terrain communal; **commonly** adv communément, généralement; couramment; **commonplace** adj banal(e), ordinaire; **Commons**

npl (*BRIT Pol*): **the (House of) Commons** la chambre des Communes; **common sense** *n* bon sens; **Commonwealth** *n*: **the Commonwealth** le Commonwealth

communal ['kɔmjuːnl] *adj* (*life*) communautaire; (*for common use*) commun(e)

commune *n* ['kɔmjuːn] (*group*) communauté *f* ▷ *vi* [kə'mjuːn]: **to ~ with** (*nature*) communier avec

communicate [kə'mjuːnɪkeɪt] *vt* communiquer, transmettre ▷ *vi*: **to ~ (with)** communiquer (avec)

communication [kəmjuːnɪ'keɪʃən] *n* communication *f*

communion [kə'mjuːnɪən] *n* (*also*: **Holy C~**) communion *f*

communism ['kɔmjunɪzəm] *n* communisme *m*; **communist** *adj*, *n* communiste *m/f*

community [kə'mjuːnɪtɪ] *n* communauté *f*; **community centre**, (*US*) **community center** *n* foyer socio-éducatif, centre *m* de loisirs; **community service** *n* ≈ travail *m* d'intérêt général, TIG *m*

commute [kə'mjuːt] *vi* faire le trajet journalier (*de son domicile à un lieu de travail assez éloigné*) ▷ *vt* (*Law*) commuer; **commuter** *n* banlieusard(e) (*qui fait un trajet journalier pour se rendre à son travail*)

compact *adj* [kəm'pækt] compact(e) ▷ *n* ['kɔmpækt] (*also*: **powder ~**) poudrier *m*; **compact disc** *n* disque compact; **compact disc player** *n* lecteur *m* de disques compacts

companion [kəm'pænjən] *n* compagnon (compagne)

company ['kʌmpənɪ] *n* compagnie *f*; **to keep sb ~** tenir compagnie à qn; **company car** *n* voiture *f* de fonction; **company director** *n* administrateur(-trice)

comparable ['kɔmpərəbl] *adj* comparable

comparative [kəm'pærətɪv] *adj* (*study*) comparatif(-ive); (*relative*) relatif(-ive); **comparatively** *adv* (*relatively*) relativement

compare [kəm'pɛəʳ] *vt*: **to ~ sth/sb with** *or* **to** comparer qch/qn avec *or* à ▷ *vi*: **to ~ (with)** se comparer (à); être comparable (à); **comparison** [kəm'pærɪsn] *n* comparaison *f*

compartment [kəm'pɑːtmənt] *n* (*also Rail*) compartiment *m*; **a non-smoking ~** un compartiment non-fumeurs

compass ['kʌmpəs] *n* boussole *f*; **compasses** *npl* (*Math*) compas *m*

compassion [kəm'pæʃən] *n* compassion *f*, humanité *f*

compatible [kəm'pætɪbl] *adj* compatible

compel [kəm'pɛl] *vt* contraindre, obliger; **compelling** *adj* (*fig*: *argument*) irrésistible

compensate ['kɔmpənseɪt] *vt* indemniser, dédommager ▷ *vi*: **to ~ for** compenser; **compensation** [kɔmpən'seɪʃən] *n* compensation *f*; (*money*) dédommagement *m*, indemnité *f*

compete [kəm'piːt] *vi* (*take part*) concourir; (*vie*): **to ~ (with)** rivaliser (avec), faire concurrence (à)

competent ['kɔmpɪtənt] *adj* compétent(e), capable

competition [kɔmpɪ'tɪʃən] *n* (*contest*) compétition *f*, concours *m*; (*Econ*) concurrence *f*

competitive [kəm'pɛtɪtɪv] *adj* (*Econ*) concurrentiel(le); (*sports*) de compétition; (*person*) qui a l'esprit de compétition

competitor [kəm'pɛtɪtəʳ] *n* concurrent(e)

complacent [kəm'pleɪsnt] *adj* (*trop*) content(e) de soi

complain [kəm'pleɪn] *vi*: **to ~ (about)** se plaindre (de); (*in shop etc*) réclamer (au sujet de); **complaint** *n*

plainte f; (in shop etc) réclamation f;
(Med) affection f

complement ['kɔmplɪmənt] n
complément m; (esp of ship's crew
etc) effectif complet ▷ vt (enhance)
compléter; **complementary**
[kɔmplɪ'mɛntərɪ] adj complémentaire

complete [kəm'pli:t] adj
complet(-ète); (finished) achevé(e)
▷ vt achever, parachever; (set,
group) compléter; (a form) remplir;
completely adv complètement;
completion [kəm'pli:ʃən] n
achèvement m; (of contract)
exécution f

complex ['kɔmplɛks] adj complexe
▷ n (Psych, buildings etc) complexe m

complexion [kəm'plɛkʃən] n (of
face) teint m

compliance [kəm'plaɪəns] n
(submission) docilité f; (agreement):
~ with le fait de se conformer
à; **in ~ with** en conformité avec,
conformément à

complicate ['kɔmplɪkeɪt] vt
compliquer; **complicated** adj
compliqué(e); **complication**
[kɔmplɪ'keɪʃən] n complication f

compliment n ['kɔmplɪmənt]
compliment m ▷ vt ['kɔmplɪmɛnt]
complimenter; **complimentary**
[kɔmplɪ'mɛntərɪ] adj flatteur(-euse);
(free) à titre gracieux

comply [kəm'plaɪ] vi: **to ~ with** se
soumettre à, se conformer à

component [kəm'pəunənt] adj
composant(e), constituant(e) ▷ n
composant m, élément m

compose [kəm'pəuz] vt composer;
(form): **to be ~d of** se composer de;
to ~ o.s. se calmer, se maîtriser;
composer n (Mus) compositeur m;
composition [kɔmpə'zɪʃən] n
composition f

composure [kəm'pəuʒər] n calme m,
maîtrise f de soi

compound ['kɔmpaund] n (Chem,
Ling) composé m; (enclosure) enclos m,

enceinte f ▷ adj composé(e); (fracture)
compliqué(e)

comprehension [kɔmprɪ'hɛnʃən] n
compréhension f

comprehensive [kɔmprɪ'hɛnsɪv]
adj (très) complet(-ète); **~ policy**
(Insurance) assurance f tous risques;
comprehensive (school) n (BRIT)
école secondaire non sélective avec
libre circulation d'une section à l'autre,
≈ CES m

> Be careful not to translate
> comprehensive by the French word
> compréhensif.

compress vt [kəm'prɛs] comprimer;
(text, information) condenser ▷ n
['kɔmprɛs] (Med) compresse f

comprise [kəm'praɪz] vt (also: **be
~d of**) comprendre; (constitute)
constituer, représenter

compromise ['kɔmprəmaɪz] n
compromis m ▷ vt compromettre ▷ vi
transiger, accepter un compromis

compulsive [kəm'pʌlsɪv] adj
(Psych) compulsif(-ive); (book, film etc)
captivant(e)

compulsory [kəm'pʌlsərɪ] adj
obligatoire

computer [kəm'pju:tər] n ordinateur
m; **computer game** n jeu m vidéo;
computer-generated adj de
synthèse; **computerize** vt (data)
traiter par ordinateur; (system,
office) informatiser; **computer
programmer** n programmeur(-euse);
computer programming n
programmation f; **computer science**
n informatique f; **computer studies**
npl informatique f; **computing**
[kəm'pju:tɪŋ] n informatique f

con [kɔn] vt duper; (cheat) escroquer
▷ n escroquerie f

conceal [kən'si:l] vt cacher,
dissimuler

concede [kən'si:d] vt concéder
▷ vi céder

conceited [kən'si:tɪd] adj
vaniteux(-euse), suffisant(e)

conceive [kən'siːv] vt, vi concevoir

concentrate ['kɔnsəntreɪt] vi se concentrer ▷ vt concentrer

concentration [kɔnsən'treɪʃən] n concentration f

concept ['kɔnsɛpt] n concept m

concern [kən'səːn] n affaire f; (Comm) entreprise f, firme f; (anxiety) inquiétude f, souci m ▷ vt (worry) inquiéter; (involve) concerner; (relate to) se rapporter à; **to be ~ed (about)** s'inquiéter (de), être inquiet(-ète) (au sujet de); **concerning** prep en ce qui concerne, à propos de

concert ['kɔnsət] n concert m; **concert hall** n salle f de concert

concerto [kən'tʃəːtəu] n concerto m

concession [kən'sɛʃən] n (compromise) concession f; (reduced price) réduction f; **tax ~** dégrèvement fiscal; **"~s"** tarif réduit

concise [kən'saɪs] adj concis(e)

conclude [kən'kluːd] vt conclure; **conclusion** [kən'kluːʒən] n conclusion f

concrete ['kɔnkriːt] n béton m ▷ adj concret(-ète); (Constr) en béton

concussion [kən'kʌʃən] n (Med) commotion (cérébrale)

condemn [kən'dɛm] vt condamner

condensation [kɔndɛn'seɪʃən] n condensation f

condense [kən'dɛns] vi se condenser ▷ vt condenser

condition [kən'dɪʃən] n condition f; (disease) maladie f ▷ vt déterminer, conditionner; **on ~ that** à condition que + sub, à condition de; **conditional** [kən'dɪʃənl] adj conditionnel(le); **conditioner** n (for hair) baume démêlant; (for fabrics) assouplissant m

condo ['kɔndəu] n (us inf) = **condominium**

condom ['kɔndəm] n préservatif m

condominium [kɔndə'mɪnɪəm] n (us: building) immeuble m (en copropriété); (: rooms) appartement m (dans un immeuble en copropriété)

condone [kən'dəun] vt fermer les yeux sur, approuver (tacitement)

conduct n ['kɔndʌkt] conduite f ▷ vt [kən'dʌkt] conduire; (manage) mener, diriger; (Mus) diriger; **to ~ o.s.** se conduire, se comporter; **conductor** n (of orchestra) chef m d'orchestre; (on bus) receveur m; (us: on train) chef m de train; (Elec) conducteur m

cone [kəun] n cône m; (for ice-cream) cornet m; (Bot) pomme f de pin, cône

confectionery [kən'fɛkʃənrɪ] n (sweets) confiserie f

confer [kən'fəːʳ] vt: **to ~ sth on** conférer qch à ▷ vi conférer, s'entretenir

conference ['kɔnfərns] n conférence f

confess [kən'fɛs] vt confesser, avouer ▷ vi (admit sth) avouer; (Rel) se confesser; **confession** [kən'fɛʃən] n confession f

confide [kən'faɪd] vi: **to ~ in** s'ouvrir à, se confier à

confidence ['kɔnfɪdns] n confiance f; (also: **self-~**) assurance f, confiance en soi; (secret) confidence f; **in ~** (speak, write) en confidence, confidentiellement; **confident** adj (self-assured) sûr(e) de soi; (sure) sûr; **confidential** [kɔnfɪ'dɛnʃəl] adj confidentiel(le)

confine [kən'faɪn] vt limiter, borner; (shut up) confiner, enfermer; **confined** adj (space) restreint(e), réduit(e)

confirm [kən'fəːm] vt (report, Rel) confirmer; (appointment) ratifier; **confirmation** [kɔnfə'meɪʃən] n confirmation f; ratification f

confiscate ['kɔnfɪskeɪt] vt confisquer

conflict n ['kɔnflɪkt] conflit m, lutte f ▷ vi [kən'flɪkt] (opinions) s'opposer, se heurter

conform [kən'fɔːm] vi: **to ~ (to)** se conformer (à)

confront [kənˈfrʌnt] vt (two people) confronter; (enemy, danger) affronter, faire face à; (problem) faire face à; **confrontation** [kɒnfrənˈteɪʃən] n confrontation f

confuse [kənˈfjuːz] vt (person) troubler; (situation) embrouiller; (one thing with another) confondre; **confused** adj (person) dérouté(e), désorienté(e); (situation) embrouillé(e); **confusing** adj peu clair(e), déroutant(e); **confusion** [kənˈfjuːʒən] n confusion f

congestion [kənˈdʒestʃən] n (Med) congestion f; (fig: traffic) encombrement m

congratulate [kənˈɡrætjuleɪt] vt: **to ~ sb (on)** féliciter qn (de); **congratulations** [kənɡrætjuˈleɪʃənz] npl; **congratulations (on)** félicitations fpl (pour) ▷ excl: **congratulations!** (toutes mes) félicitations!

congregation [kɒnɡrɪˈɡeɪʃən] n assemblée f (des fidèles)

congress [ˈkɒnɡres] n congrès m; (Pol): **C~** Congrès m; **congressman** (irreg) n membre m du Congrès; **congresswoman** (irreg) n membre m du Congrès

conifer [ˈkɒnɪfəʳ] n conifère m

conjugate [ˈkɒndʒugeɪt] vt conjuguer

conjugation [kɒndʒəˈɡeɪʃən] n conjugaison f

conjunction [kənˈdʒʌŋkʃən] n conjonction f; **in ~ with** (conjointement) avec

conjure [ˈkʌndʒəʳ] vi faire des tours de passe-passe

connect [kəˈnekt] vt joindre, relier; (Elec) connecter; (Tel: caller) mettre en connexion; (: subscriber) brancher; (fig) établir un rapport entre, faire un rapprochement entre ▷ vi (train): **to ~ with** assurer la correspondance avec; **to be ~ed with** avoir un rapport avec; (have dealings with) avoir

des rapports avec, être en relation avec; **connecting flight** n (vol m de) correspondance f; **connection** [kəˈnekʃən] n relation f, lien m; (Elec) connexion f; (Tel) communication f; (train etc) correspondance f

conquer [ˈkɒŋkəʳ] vt conquérir; (feelings) vaincre, surmonter

conquest [ˈkɒŋkwest] n conquête f

cons [kɒnz] npl see **convenience; pro**

conscience [ˈkɒnʃəns] n conscience f

conscientious [kɒnʃɪˈenʃəs] adj consciencieux(-euse)

conscious [ˈkɒnʃəs] adj conscient(e); (deliberate: insult, error) délibéré(e); **consciousness** n conscience f; (Med) connaissance f

consecutive [kənˈsekjutɪv] adj consécutif(-ive); **on three ~ occasions** trois fois de suite

consensus [kənˈsensəs] n consensus m

consent [kənˈsent] n consentement m ▷ vi: **to ~ (to)** consentir (à)

consequence [ˈkɒnsɪkwəns] n suites fpl, conséquence f; (significance) importance f

consequently [ˈkɒnsɪkwəntlɪ] adv par conséquent, donc

conservation [kɒnsəˈveɪʃən] n préservation f, protection f; (also: **nature ~**) défense f de l'environnement

Conservative [kənˈsɜːvətɪv] adj, n (BRIT Pol) conservateur(-trice)

conservative adj conservateur(-trice); (cautious) prudent(e)

conservatory [kənˈsɜːvətrɪ] n (room) jardin m d'hiver; (Mus) conservatoire m

consider [kənˈsɪdəʳ] vt (study) considérer, réfléchir à; (take into account) penser à, prendre en considération; (regard, judge) considérer, estimer; **to ~ doing sth** envisager de faire qch; **considerable** adj considérable; **considerably** adv nettement; **considerate** adj

prévenant(e), plein(e) d'égards;
consideration [kənsɪdə'reɪʃən] n
considération f; (reward) rétribution
f, rémunération f; **considering**
prep: **considering (that)** étant
donné (que)

consignment [kən'saɪnmənt] n
arrivage m, envoi m

consist [kən'sɪst] vi: **to ~ of** consister
en, se composer de

consistency [kən'sɪstənsɪ] n
(thickness) consistance f; (fig)
cohérence f

consistent [kən'sɪstənt] adj logique,
cohérent(e)

consolation [kɒnsə'leɪʃən] n
consolation f

console¹ [kən'səul] vt consoler

console² ['kɒnsəul] n console f

consonant ['kɒnsənənt] n
consonne f

conspicuous [kən'spɪkjuəs] adj
voyant(e), qui attire l'attention

conspiracy [kən'spɪrəsɪ] n
conspiration f, complot m

constable ['kʌnstəbl] n (BRIT) ≈
agent m de police, gendarme m; **chief
~** ≈ préfet m de police

constant ['kɒnstənt] adj
constant(e); incessant(e);
constantly adv constamment,
sans cesse

constipated ['kɒnstɪpeɪtɪd]
adj constipé(e); **constipation**
[kɒnstɪ'peɪʃən] n constipation f

constituency [kən'stɪtjuənsɪ] n
(Pol: area) circonscription électorale;
(: electors) électorat m

constitute ['kɒnstɪtjuːt] vt
constituer

constitution [kɒnstɪ'tjuːʃən] n
constitution f

constraint [kən'streɪnt] n
contrainte f

construct [kən'strʌkt] vt construire;
construction [kən'strʌkʃən] n
construction f; **constructive** adj
constructif(-ive)

consul ['kɒnsl] n consul m;
consulate ['kɒnsjulɪt] n consulat m

consult [kən'sʌlt] vt consulter;
consultant n (Med) médecin
consultant; (other specialist)
consultant m, (expert-)conseil m;
consultation [kɒnsəl'teɪʃən] n
consultation f; **consulting room** n
(BRIT) cabinet m de consultation

consume [kən'sjuːm] vt
consommer; (subj: flames, hatred,
desire) consumer; **consumer** n
consommateur(-trice)

consumption [kən'sʌmpʃən] n
consommation f

cont. abbr (= continued) suite

contact ['kɒntækt] n contact m;
(person) connaissance f, relation f ▷ vt
se mettre en contact or en rapport
avec; **~ number** numéro m de
téléphone; **contact lenses** npl verres
mpl de contact

contagious [kən'teɪdʒəs] adj
contagieux(-euse)

contain [kən'teɪn] vt contenir;
to ~ o.s. se contenir, se maîtriser;
container n récipient m; (for shipping
etc) conteneur m

contaminate [kən'tæmɪneɪt] vt
contaminer

cont'd abbr (= continued) suite

contemplate ['kɒntəmpleɪt] vt
contempler; (consider) envisager

contemporary [kən'tɛmpərərɪ] adj
contemporain(e); (design, wallpaper)
moderne ▷ n contemporain(e)

contempt [kən'tɛmpt] n mépris m,
dédain m; **~ of court** (Law) outrage m
à l'autorité de la justice

contend [kən'tɛnd] vt: **to ~ that**
soutenir or prétendre que ▷ vi: **to
~ with** (compete) rivaliser avec;
(struggle) lutter avec

content [kən'tɛnt] adj content(e),
satisfait(e) ▷ vt contenter, satisfaire
▷ n ['kɒntɛnt] contenu m; (of fat,
moisture) teneur f; **contents** npl (of
container etc) contenu m; **(table of)**

~s table f des matières; **contented** adj content(e), satisfait(e)

contest n ['kɒntɛst] combat m, lutte f; (competition) concours m ▷ vt [kən'tɛst] contester, discuter; (compete for) disputer; (Law) attaquer; **contestant** [kən'tɛstənt] n concurrent(e); (in fight) adversaire m/f

context ['kɒntɛkst] n contexte m

continent ['kɒntɪnənt] n continent m; **the C~** (BRIT) l'Europe continentale; **continental** [kɒntɪ'nɛntl] adj continental(e); **continental breakfast** n café (or thé) complet; **continental quilt** n (BRIT) couette f

continual [kən'tɪnjuəl] adj continuel(le); **continually** adv continuellement, sans cesse

continue [kən'tɪnjuː] vi continuer ▷ vt continuer; (start again) reprendre

continuity [kɒntɪ'njuːɪtɪ] n continuité f; (TV) enchaînement m

continuous [kən'tɪnjuəs] adj continu(e), permanent(e); (Ling) progressif(-ive); **continuous assessment** (BRIT) n contrôle continu; **continuously** adv (repeatedly) continuellement; (uninterruptedly) sans interruption

contour ['kɒntuə'] n contour m, profil m; (also: **~ line**) courbe f de niveau

contraception [kɒntrə'sɛpʃən] n contraception f

contraceptive [kɒntrə'sɛptɪv] adj contraceptif(-ive), anticonceptionnel(le) ▷ n contraceptif m

contract n ['kɒntrækt] contrat m ▷ vi [kən'trækt] (become smaller) se contracter, se resserrer ▷ vt contracter; (Comm): **to ~ to do sth** s'engager (par contrat) à faire qch; **contractor** n entrepreneur m

contradict [kɒntrə'dɪkt] vt contredire; **contradiction** [kɒntrə'dɪkʃən] n contradiction f

contrary[1] ['kɒntrərɪ] adj contraire, opposé(e) ▷ n contraire m; **on the ~** au contraire; **unless you hear to the ~** sauf avis contraire

contrary[2] [kən'trɛərɪ] adj (perverse) contrariant(e), entêté(e)

contrast n ['kɒntrɑːst] contraste m ▷ vt [kən'trɑːst] mettre en contraste, contraster; **in ~ to** or **with** contrairement à, par opposition à

contribute [kən'trɪbjuːt] vi contribuer ▷ vt: **to ~ £10/an article to** donner 10 livres/un article à; **to ~ to** (gen) contribuer à; (newspaper) collaborer à; (discussion) prendre part à; **contribution** [kɒntrɪ'bjuːʃən] n contribution f; (BRIT: for social security) cotisation f; (to publication) article m; **contributor** n (to newspaper) collaborateur(-trice); (of money, goods) donateur(-trice)

control [kən'trəul] vt (process, machinery) commander; (temper) maîtriser; (disease) enrayer ▷ n maîtrise f; (power) autorité f; **controls** npl (of machine etc) commandes fpl; (on radio) boutons mpl de réglage; **to be in ~ of** être maître de, maîtriser; (in charge of) être responsable de; **everything is under ~** j'ai (or il a etc) la situation en main; **the car went out of ~** j'ai (or il a etc) perdu le contrôle du véhicule; **control tower** n (Aviat) tour f de contrôle

controversial [kɒntrə'vəːʃl] adj discutable, controversé(e)

controversy ['kɒntrəvəːsɪ] n controverse f, polémique f

convenience [kən'viːnɪəns] n commodité f; **at your ~** quand or comme cela vous convient; **all modern ~s, all mod cons** (BRIT) avec tout le confort moderne, tout confort

convenient [kən'viːnɪənt] adj commode

convent ['kɒnvənt] n couvent m

convention [kən'vɛnʃən] *n* convention *f*; (*custom*) usage *m*; **conventional** *adj* conventionnel(le)

conversation [kɔnvə'seɪʃən] *n* conversation *f*

conversely [kɔn'vəːslɪ] *adv* inversement, réciproquement

conversion [kən'vəːʃən] *n* conversion *f*; (*BRIT: of house*) transformation *f*, aménagement *m*; (*Rugby*) transformation *f*

convert *vt* [kən'vəːt] (*Rel, Comm*) convertir; (*alter*) transformer; (*house*) aménager ▷ *n* ['kɔnvəːt] converti(e); **convertible** *adj* convertible ▷ *n* (*voiture f*) décapotable *f*

convey [kən'veɪ] *vt* transporter; (*thanks*) transmettre; (*idea*) communiquer; **conveyor belt** *n* convoyeur *m* tapis roulant

convict *vt* [kən'vɪkt] déclarer (*or* reconnaître) coupable ▷ *n* ['kɔnvɪkt] forçat *m*, convict *m*; **conviction** [kən'vɪkʃən] *n* (*Law*) condamnation *f*; (*belief*) conviction *f*

convince [kən'vɪns] *vt* convaincre, persuader; **convinced** *adj*: **convinced of/that** convaincu(e) de/ que; **convincing** *adj* persuasif(-ive), convaincant(e)

convoy ['kɔnvɔɪ] *n* convoi *m*

cook [kuk] *vt* (faire) cuire ▷ *vi* cuire; (*person*) faire la cuisine ▷ *n* cuisinier(-ière); **cookbook** *n* livre *m* de cuisine; **cooker** *n* cuisinière *f*; **cookery** *n* cuisine *f*; **cookery book** *n* (*BRIT*) = **cookbook**; **cookie** *n* (*US*) biscuit *m*, petit gâteau sec; **cooking** *n* cuisine *f*

cool [ku:l] *adj* frais (fraîche); (*not afraid*) calme; (*unfriendly*) froid(e); (*inf: trendy*) cool *inv* (*inf*); (: *great*) super *inv* (*inf*) ▷ *vt*, *vi* rafraîchir, refroidir; **cool down** *vi* refroidir; (*fig: person, situation*) se calmer; **cool off** *vi* (*become calmer*) se calmer; (*lose enthusiasm*) perdre son enthousiasme

cop [kɔp] *n* (*inf*) flic *m*

cope [kəup] *vi* s'en sortir, tenir le coup; **to ~ with** (*problem*) faire face à

copper ['kɔpə^r] *n* cuivre *m*; (*BRIT inf: policeman*) flic *m*

copy ['kɔpɪ] *n* copie *f*; (*book etc*) exemplaire *m* ▷ *vt* copier; (*imitate*) imiter; **copyright** *n* droit *m* d'auteur, copyright *m*

coral ['kɔrəl] *n* corail *m*

cord [kɔːd] *n* corde *f*; (*fabric*) velours côtelé; (*Elec*) cordon *m* (d'alimentation), fil *m* (électrique); **cords** *npl* (*trousers*) pantalon *m* de velours côtelé; **cordless** *adj* sans fil

corduroy ['kɔːdərɔɪ] *n* velours côtelé

core [kɔː^r] *n* (*of fruit*) trognon *m*, cœur *m*; (*fig: of problem etc*) cœur ▷ *vt* enlever le trognon *or* le cœur de

coriander [kɔrɪ'ændə^r] *n* coriandre *f*

cork [kɔːk] *n* (*material*) liège *m*; (*of bottle*) bouchon *m*; **corkscrew** *n* tire-bouchon *m*

corn [kɔːn] *n* (*BRIT: wheat*) blé *m*; (*US: maize*) maïs *m*; (*on foot*) cor *m*; **~ on the cob** (*Culin*) épi *m* de maïs au naturel

corned beef ['kɔːnd-] *n* corned-beef *m*

corner ['kɔːnə^r] *n* coin *m*; (*in road*) tournant *m*, virage *m*; (*Football*) corner *m* ▷ *vt* (*trap: prey*) acculer; (*fig*) coincer; (*Comm: market*) accaparer ▷ *vi* prendre un virage; **corner shop** (*BRIT*) *n* magasin *m* du coin

cornflakes ['kɔːnfleɪks] *npl* cornflakes *mpl*

cornflour ['kɔːnflauə^r] *n* (*BRIT*) farine *f* de maïs, maïzena® *f*

cornstarch ['kɔːnstɑːtʃ] *n* (*US*) farine *f* de maïs, maïzena® *f*

Cornwall ['kɔːnwəl] *n* Cornouailles *f*

coronary ['kɔrənərɪ] *n*: **~ (thrombosis)** infarctus *m* (du myocarde), thrombose *f* coronaire

coronation [kɔrə'neɪʃən] *n* couronnement *m*

coroner ['kɔrənə^r] *n* coroner *m*, *officier de police judiciaire chargé de déterminer les causes d'un décès*

corporal ['kɔːpərl] n caporal m, brigadier m ▷ adj: **~ punishment** châtiment corporel

corporate ['kɔːpərɪt] adj (action, ownership) en commun; (Comm) de la société

corporation [kɔːpə'reɪʃən] n (of town) municipalité f, conseil municipal; (Comm) société f

corps (pl **corps**) [kɔːʳ, kɔːz] n corps m; **the diplomatic ~** le corps diplomatique; **the press ~** la presse

corpse [kɔːps] n cadavre m

correct [kə'rɛkt] adj (accurate) correct(e), exact(e); (proper) correct, convenable ▷ vt corriger; **correction** [kə'rɛkʃən] n correction f

correspond [kɔrɪs'pɔnd] vi correspondre; **to ~ to sth** (be equivalent to) correspondre à qch; **correspondence** n correspondance f; **correspondent** n correspondant(e); **corresponding** adj correspondant(e)

corridor ['kɔrɪdɔːʳ] n couloir m, corridor m

corrode [kə'rəud] vt corroder, ronger ▷ vi se corroder

corrupt [kə'rʌpt] adj corrompu(e); (Comput) altéré(e) ▷ vt corrompre; (Comput) altérer; **corruption** n corruption f; (Comput) altération f (de données)

Corsica ['kɔːsɪkə] n Corse f

cosmetic [kɔz'mɛtɪk] n produit m de beauté, cosmétique m ▷ adj (fig: reforms) symbolique, superficiel(le); **cosmetic surgery** n chirurgie f esthétique

cosmopolitan [kɔzmə'pɔlɪtn] adj cosmopolite

cost [kɔst] (pt, pp **cost**) n coût m ▷ vi coûter ▷ vt établir or calculer le prix de revient de; **costs** npl (Comm) frais mpl; (Law) dépens mpl; **how much does it ~?** combien ça coûte?; **to ~ sb time/effort** demander du temps/un effort à qn; **it ~ him his life/job** ça lui a coûté la vie/son emploi; **at all ~s** coûte que coûte, à tout prix

co-star ['kəustɑːʳ] n partenaire m/f

costly ['kɔstlɪ] adj coûteux(-euse)

cost of living n coût m de la vie

costume ['kɔstjuːm] n costume m; (BRIT: also: **swimming ~**) maillot m (de bain)

cosy, (US) **cozy** ['kəuzɪ] adj (room, bed) douillet(te); **to be ~** (person) être bien (au chaud)

cot [kɔt] n (BRIT: child's) lit m d'enfant, petit lit; (US: campbed) lit de camp

cottage ['kɔtɪdʒ] n petite maison (à la campagne), cottage m; **cottage cheese** n fromage blanc (maigre)

cotton ['kɔtn] n coton m; (thread) fil m (de coton); **cotton on** vi (inf): **to ~ on (to sth)** piger (qch); **cotton bud** (BRIT) n coton-tige® m; **cotton candy** (US) n barbe f à papa; **cotton wool** n (BRIT) ouate f, coton m hydrophile

couch [kautʃ] n canapé m; divan m

cough [kɔf] vi tousser ▷ n toux f; **I've got a ~** j'ai la toux; **cough mixture, cough syrup** n sirop m pour la toux

could [kud] pt of **can²**; **couldn't** = **could not**

council ['kaunsl] n conseil m; **city** or **town ~** conseil municipal; **council estate** n (BRIT) (quartier m or zone f de) logements loués à/par la municipalité; **council house** n (BRIT) maison f (à loyer modéré) louée par la municipalité; **councillor**, (US) **councilor** n conseiller(-ère); **council tax** n (BRIT) impôts locaux

counsel ['kaunsl] n conseil m; (lawyer) avocat(e) ▷ vt: **to ~ (sb to do sth)** conseiller (à qn de faire qch); **counselling**, (US) **counseling** n (Psych) aide psychosociale; **counsellor**, (US) **counselor** n conseiller(-ère); (US Law) avocat m

count [kaunt] vt, vi compter ▷ n compte m; (nobleman) comte m; **count in** vt (inf): **to ~ sb in on sth**

inclure qn dans qch; **count on** *vt fus* compter sur; **countdown** *n* compte *m* à rebours

counter ['kauntə^r] *n* comptoir *m*; (*in post office, bank*) guichet *m*; (*in game*) jeton *m* ▷ *vt* aller à l'encontre de, opposer ▷ *adv*: **~ to** à l'encontre de; contrairement à; **counterclockwise** (*us*) *adv* en sens inverse des aiguilles d'une montre

counterfeit ['kauntəfɪt] *n* faux *m*, contrefaçon *f* ▷ *vt* contrefaire ▷ *adj* faux(fausse)

counterpart ['kauntəpɑːt] *n* (*of person*) homologue *m/f*

countess ['kauntɪs] *n* comtesse *f*

countless ['kauntlɪs] *adj* innombrable

country ['kʌntrɪ] *n* pays *m*; (*native land*) patrie *f*; (*as opposed to town*) campagne *f*; (*region*) région *f*, pays; **country and western (music)** *n* musique *f* country; **country house** *n* manoir *m*, (petit) château; **countryside** *n* campagne *f*

county ['kauntɪ] *n* comté *m*

coup (*pl* **coups**) [kuː, kuːz] *n* (*achievement*) beau coup; (*also*: **~ d'état**) coup d'État

couple ['kʌpl] *n* couple *m*; **a ~ of** (*two*) deux; (*a few*) deux ou trois

coupon ['kuːpɔn] *n* (*voucher*) bon *m* de réduction; (*detachable form*) coupon *m* détachable, coupon-réponse *m*

courage ['kʌrɪdʒ] *n* courage *m*; **courageous** [kə'reɪdʒəs] *adj* courageux(-euse)

courgette [kuə'ʒɛt] *n* (*BRIT*) courgette *f*

courier ['kurɪə^r] *n* messager *m*, courrier *m*; (*for tourists*) accompagnateur(-trice)

course [kɔːs] *n* cours *m*; (*of ship*) route *f*; (*for golf*) terrain *m*; (*part of meal*) plat *m*; **of ~** *adv* bien sûr; **(no,) of ~ not!** bien sûr que non!, évidemment que non!; **~ of treatment** (*Med*) traitement *m*

court [kɔːt] *n* cour *f*; (*Law*) cour, tribunal *m*; (*Tennis*) court *m* ▷ *vt* (*woman*) courtiser, faire la cour à; **to take to ~** actionner *or* poursuivre en justice

courtesy ['kəːtəsɪ] *n* courtoisie *f*, politesse *f*; **(by) ~ of** avec l'aimable autorisation de; **courtesy bus, courtesy coach** *n* navette gratuite

court: court-house ['kɔːthaus] *n* (*us*) palais *m* de justice; **courtroom** ['kɔːtrum] *n* salle *f* de tribunal; **courtyard** ['kɔːtjɑːd] *n* cour *f*

cousin ['kʌzn] *n* cousin(e); **first ~** cousin(e) germain(e)

cover ['kʌvə^r] *vt* couvrir; (*Press: report on*) faire un reportage sur; (*feelings, mistake*) cacher; (*include*) englober; (*discuss*) traiter ▷ *n* (*of book, Comm*) couverture *f*; (*of pan*) couvercle *m*; (*over furniture*) housse *f*; (*shelter*) abri *m*; **covers** *npl* (*on bed*) couvertures *f*; **to take ~** se mettre à l'abri; **under ~** à l'abri; **under ~ of darkness** à la faveur de la nuit; **under separate ~** (*Comm*) sous pli séparé; **cover up** *vi*: **to ~ up for sb** (*fig*) couvrir qn; **coverage** *n* (*in media*) reportage *m*; **cover charge** *n* couvert *m* (*supplément à payer*); **cover-up** *n* tentative *f* pour étouffer une affaire

cow [kau] *n* vache *f* ▷ *vt* effrayer, intimider

coward ['kauəd] *n* lâche *m/f*; **cowardly** *adj* lâche

cowboy ['kaubɔɪ] *n* cow-boy *m*

cozy ['kəuzɪ] *adj* (*us*) = **cosy**

crab [kræb] *n* crabe *m*

crack [kræk] *n* (*split*) fente *f*, fissure *f*; (*in cup, bone*) fêlure *f*; (*in wall*) lézarde *f*; (*noise*) craquement *m*, coup (sec); (*Drugs*) crack *m* ▷ *vt* fendre, fissurer; fêler; lézarder; (*whip*) faire claquer; (*nut*) casser; (*problem*) résoudre; (*code*) déchiffrer ▷ *cpd* (*athlete*) de première classe, d'élite; **crack down on** *vt fus* (*crime*) sévir contre, réprimer; **cracked** *adj* (*cup,* *bone*) fêlé(e); (*broken*) cassé(e); (*wall*) lézardé(e); (*surface*) craquelé(e); (*inf*) toqué(e), timbré(e); **cracker** *n* (*also*: **Christmas cracker**) pétard *m*; (*biscuit*) biscuit (salé), craquelin *m*

crackle ['krækl] *vi* crépiter, grésiller

cradle ['kreɪdl] *n* berceau *m*

craft [krɑːft] *n* métier (artisanal); (*cunning*) ruse *f*, astuce *f*; (*boat: pl inv*) embarcation *f*, barque *f*; (*plane: pl inv*) appareil *m*; **craftsman** (*irreg*) *n* artisan *m* ouvrier (qualifié); **craftsmanship** *n* métier *m*, habileté *f*

cram [kræm] *vt*: **to ~ sth with** (*fill*) bourrer qch de; **to ~ sth into** (*put*) fourrer qch dans ▷ *vi* (*for exams*) bachoter

cramp [kræmp] *n* crampe *f*; **I've got ~ in my leg** j'ai une crampe à la jambe; **cramped** *adj* à l'étroit, très serré(e)

cranberry ['krænbəri] *n* canneberge *f*

crane [kreɪn] *n* grue *f*

crap [kræp] *n* (*inf!: nonsense*) conneries *fpl* (!); (!: *excrement*) merde *f* (!)

crash [kræʃ] *n* (*noise*) fracas *m*; (*of car, plane*) collision *f*; (*of business*) faillite *f* ▷ *vt* (*plane*) écraser ▷ *vi* (*plane*) s'écraser; (*two cars*) se percuter, s'emboutir; (*business*) s'effondrer; **to ~ into** se jeter *or* se fracasser contre; **crash course** *n* cours intensif; **crash helmet** *n* casque (protecteur)

crate [kreɪt] *n* cageot *m*; (*for bottles*) caisse *f*

crave [kreɪv] *vt, vi*: **to ~ (for)** avoir une envie irrésistible de

crawl [krɔːl] *vi* ramper; (*vehicle*) avancer au pas ▷ *n* (*Swimming*) crawl *m*

crayfish ['kreɪfɪʃ] *n* (*pl inv: freshwater*) écrevisse *f*; (!: *saltwater*) langoustine *f*

crayon ['kreɪən] *n* crayon *m* (de couleur)

craze [kreɪz] *n* engouement *m*

crazy ['kreɪzɪ] *adj* fou (folle); **to be ~ about sb/sth** (*inf*) être fou de qn/qch

creak [kriːk] *vi* (*hinge*) grincer; (*floor, shoes*) craquer

cream [kriːm] *n* crème *f* ▷ *adj* (*colour*) crème *inv*; **cream cheese** *n* fromage *m* à la crème, fromage blanc; **creamy** *adj* crémeux(-euse)

crease [kriːs] *n* pli *m* ▷ *vt* froisser, chiffonner ▷ *vi* se froisser, se chiffonner

create [kriː'eɪt] *vt* créer; **creation** [kriː'eɪʃən] *n* création *f*; **creative** *adj* créatif(-ive); **creator** *n* créateur(-trice)

creature ['kriːtʃər] *n* créature *f*

crèche [krɛʃ] *n* garderie *f*, crèche *f*

credentials [krɪ'dɛnʃlz] *npl* (*references*) références *fpl*; (*identity papers*) pièce *f* d'identité

credibility [krɛdɪ'bɪlɪtɪ] *n* crédibilité *f*

credible ['krɛdɪbl] *adj* digne de foi, crédible

credit ['krɛdɪt] *n* crédit *m*; (*recognition*) honneur *m*; (*Scol*) unité *f* de valeur ▷ *vt* (*Comm*) créditer; (*believe: also*: **give ~ to**) ajouter foi à, croire; **credits** *npl* (*Cine*) générique *m*; **to be in ~** (*person, bank account*) être créditeur(-trice); **to ~ sb with** (*fig*) prêter *or* attribuer à qn; **credit card** *n* carte *f* de crédit; **do you take credit cards?** acceptez-vous les cartes de crédit?; **credit crunch** *n* crise *f* du crédit

creek [kriːk] *n* (*inlet*) crique *f*, anse *f*; (*us: stream*) ruisseau *m*, petit cours d'eau

creep (*pt, pp* **crept**) [kriːp, krɛpt] *vi* ramper

cremate [krɪ'meɪt] *vt* incinérer

crematorium (*pl* **crematoria**) [krɛmə'tɔːrɪəm, -'tɔːrɪə] *n* four *m* crématoire

crept [krɛpt] *pt, pp of* **creep**

crescent ['krɛsnt] *n* croissant *m*; (*street*) rue *f* (*en arc de cercle*)

cress [krɛs] *n* cresson *m*

crest [krɛst] *n* crête *f*; (*of coat of arms*) timbre *m*

crew [kru:] *n* équipage *m*; (*Cine*) équipe *f* (de tournage); **crew-neck** *n* col ras

crib [krɪb] *n* lit *m* d'enfant; (*for baby*) berceau *m* ▷ *vt* (*inf*) copier

cricket ['krɪkɪt] *n* (*insect*) grillon *m*, cri-cri *m inv*; (*game*) cricket *m*; **cricketer** *n* joueur *m* de cricket

crime [kraɪm] *n* crime *m*; **criminal** ['krɪmɪnl] *adj*, *n* criminel(le)

crimson ['krɪmzn] *adj* cramoisi(e)

cringe [krɪndʒ] *vi* avoir un mouvement de recul

cripple ['krɪpl] *n* (*offensive*) boiteux(-euse), infirme *m/f* ▷ *vt* (*person*) estropier, paralyser; (*ship, plane*) immobiliser; (*production, exports*) paralyser

crisis (*pl* **crises**) ['kraɪsɪs, -si:z] *n* crise *f*

crisp [krɪsp] *adj* croquant(e); (*weather*) vif (vive); (*manner etc*) brusque; **crisps** (BRIT) *npl* (pommes *fpl*) chips *fpl*; **crispy** *adj* croustillant(e)

criterion (*pl* **criteria**) [kraɪ'tɪərɪən, -'tɪərɪə] *n* critère *m*

critic ['krɪtɪk] *n* critique *m/f*; **critical** *adj* critique; **criticism** ['krɪtɪsɪzəm] *n* critique *f*; **criticize** ['krɪtɪsaɪz] *vt* critiquer

Croat ['krəʊæt] *adj*, *n* = **Croatian**

Croatia [krəʊ'eɪʃə] *n* Croatie *f*; **Croatian** *adj* croate ▷ *n* Croate *m/f*; (*Ling*) croate *m*

crockery ['krɒkərɪ] *n* vaisselle *f*

crocodile ['krɒkədaɪl] *n* crocodile *m*

crocus ['krəʊkəs] *n* crocus *m*

croissant ['krwasã] *n* croissant *m*

crook [kruk] *n* (*inf*) escroc *m*; (*of shepherd*) houlette *f*; **crooked** ['krukɪd] *adj* courbé(e), tordu(e); (*action*) malhonnête

crop [krɒp] *n* (*produce*) culture *f*; (*amount produced*) récolte *f*; (*riding crop*) cravache *f* ▷ *vt* (*hair*) tondre; **crop up** *vi* surgir, se présenter, survenir

cross [krɒs] *n* croix *f*; (*Biol*) croisement *m* ▷ *vt* (*street etc*) traverser; (*arms,*

legs, *Biol*) croiser; (*cheque*) barrer ▷ *adj* en colère, fâché(e); **cross off, cross out** *vt* barrer, rayer; **cross over** *vi* traverser; **cross-Channel ferry** ['krɒs'tʃænl-] *n* ferry *m* qui fait la traversée de la Manche; **cross-country (race)** *n* cross(-country) *m*; **crossing** *n* (*sea passage*) traversée *f*; (*also:* **pedestrian crossing**) passage clouté; **how long does the crossing take?** combien de temps dure la traversée?; **crossing guard** *n* (US) *contractuel qui fait traverser la rue aux enfants*; **crossroads** *n* carrefour *m*; **crosswalk** *n* (US) passage clouté; **crossword** *n* mots *mpl* croisés

crotch [krɒtʃ] *n* (*of garment*) entrejambe *m*; (*Anat*) entrecuisse *m*

crouch [krautʃ] *vi* s'accroupir; (*hide*) se tapir; (*before springing*) se ramasser

crouton ['kru:tɒn] *n* croûton *m*

crow [krəʊ] *n* (*bird*) corneille *f*; (*of cock*) chant *m* du coq, cocorico *m* ▷ *vi* (*cock*) chanter

crowd [kraud] *n* foule *f* ▷ *vt* bourrer, remplir ▷ *vi* affluer, s'attrouper, s'entasser; **crowded** *adj* bondé(e)

crown [kraun] *n* couronne *f*; (*of head*) sommet *m* de la tête; (*of hill*) sommet *m* ▷ *vt* (*also tooth*) couronner; **crown jewels** *npl* joyaux *mpl* de la Couronne

crucial ['kru:ʃl] *adj* crucial(e), décisif(-ive)

crucifix ['kru:sɪfɪks] *n* crucifix *m*

crude [kru:d] *adj* (*materials*) brut(e); non raffiné(e); (*basic*) rudimentaire, sommaire; (*vulgar*) cru(e), grossier(-ière) ▷ *n* (*also:* **~ oil**) (pétrole *m*) brut *m*

cruel ['kruəl] *adj* cruel(le); **cruelty** *n* cruauté *f*

cruise [kru:z] *n* croisière *f* ▷ *vi* (*ship*) croiser; (*car*) rouler; (*aircraft*) voler

crumb [krʌm] *n* miette *f*

crumble ['krʌmbl] *vt* émietter ▷ *vi* (*plaster etc*) s'effriter; (*land, earth*) s'ébouler; (*building*) s'écrouler, crouler; (*fig*) s'effondrer

crumpet ['krʌmpɪt] n petite crêpe (épaisse)

crumple ['krʌmpl] vt froisser, friper

crunch [krʌntʃ] vt croquer; (underfoot) faire craquer, écraser; faire crisser ▷ n (fig) instant m or moment m critique, moment de vérité; **crunchy** adj croquant(e), croustillant(e)

crush [krʌʃ] n (crowd) foule f, cohue f; (love): **to have a ~ on sb** avoir le béguin pour qn; (drink): **lemon ~** citron pressé ▷ vt écraser; (crumple) froisser; (grind, break up: garlic, ice) piler; (: grapes) presser; (hopes) anéantir

crust [krʌst] n croûte f; **crusty** adj (bread) croustillant(e); (inf: person) revêche, bourru(e)

crutch [krʌtʃ] n béquille f; (of garment) entrejambe m; (Anat) entrecuisse m

cry [kraɪ] vi pleurer; (shout: also: **~ out**) crier ▷ n cri m; **cry out** vi (call out, shout) pousser un cri ▷ vt crier

crystal ['krɪstl] n cristal m

cub [kʌb] n petit m (d'un animal); (also: **~ scout**) louveteau m

Cuba ['kju:bə] n Cuba m

cube [kju:b] n cube m ▷ vt (Math) élever au cube

cubicle ['kju:bɪkl] n (in hospital) box m; (at pool) cabine f

cuckoo ['kuku:] n coucou m

cucumber ['kju:kʌmbə'] n concombre m

cuddle ['kʌdl] vt câliner, caresser ▷ vi se blottir l'un contre l'autre

cue [kju:] n queue f de billard; (Theat etc) signal m

cuff [kʌf] n (BRIT: of shirt, coat etc) poignet m, manchette f; (US: on trousers) revers m; (blow) gifle f; **off the ~** adv à l'improviste; **cufflinks** n boutons m de manchette

cuisine [kwɪ'zi:n] n cuisine f

cul-de-sac ['kʌldəsæk] n cul-de-sac m, impasse f

cull [kʌl] vt sélectionner ▷ n (of animals) abattage sélectif

culminate ['kʌlmɪneɪt] vi: **to ~ in** finir or se terminer par; (lead to) mener à

culprit ['kʌlprɪt] n coupable m/f

cult [kʌlt] n culte m

cultivate ['kʌltɪveɪt] vt cultiver

cultural ['kʌltʃərəl] adj culturel(le)

culture ['kʌltʃə'] n culture f

cumin ['kʌmɪn] n (spice) cumin m

cunning ['kʌnɪŋ] n ruse f, astuce f ▷ adj rusé(e), malin(-igne); (clever: device, idea) astucieux(-euse)

cup [kʌp] n tasse f; (prize, event) coupe f; (of bra) bonnet m

cupboard ['kʌbəd] n placard m

cup final n (BRIT Football) finale f de la coupe

curator [kjuə'reɪtə'] n conservateur m (d'un musée etc)

curb [kə:b] vt refréner, mettre un frein à ▷ n (fig) frein m; (us) bord m du trottoir

curdle ['kə:dl] vi (se) cailler

cure [kjuə'] vt guérir; (Culin: salt) saler; (: smoke) fumer; (: dry) sécher ▷ n remède m

curfew ['kə:fju:] n couvre-feu m

curiosity [kjuərɪ'ɔsɪtɪ] n curiosité f

curious ['kjuərɪəs] adj curieux(-euse); **I'm ~ about him** il m'intrigue

curl [kə:l] n boucle f (de cheveux) ▷ vt, vi boucler; (tightly) friser; **curl up** vi s'enrouler; (person) se pelotonner; **curler** n bigoudi m, rouleau m; **curly** adj bouclé(e); (tightly curled) frisé(e)

currant ['kʌrnt] n raisin m de Corinthe, raisin sec; (fruit) groseille f

currency ['kʌrnsɪ] n monnaie f; **to gain ~** (fig) s'accréditer

current ['kʌrnt] n courant m ▷ adj (common) courant(e); (tendency, price, event) actuel(le); **current account** n (BRIT) compte courant; **current affairs** npl (questions fpl d')actualité f; **currently** adv actuellement

curriculum (*pl* **curriculums** *or* **curricula**) [kə'rɪkjuləm, -lə] *n* programme *m* d'études; **curriculum vitae** [-'viːtaɪ] *n* curriculum vitae (CV) *m*

curry ['kʌrɪ] *n* curry *m* ▷ *vt*: **to ~ favour with** chercher à gagner la faveur *or* à s'attirer les bonnes grâces de; **curry powder** *n* poudre *f* de curry

curse [kəːs] *vi* jurer, blasphémer ▷ *vt* maudire ▷ *n* (*spell*) malédiction *f*; (*problem, scourge*) fléau *m*; (*swearword*) juron *m*

cursor ['kəːsəʳ] *n* (*Comput*) curseur *m*

curt [kəːt] *adj* brusque, sec (sèche)

curtain ['kəːtn] *n* rideau *m*

curve [kəːv] *n* courbe *f*; (*in the road*) tournant *m*, virage *m* ▷ *vi* se courber; (*road*) faire une courbe; **curved** *adj* courbe

cushion ['kuʃən] *n* coussin *m* ▷ *vt* (*fall, shock*) amortir

custard ['kʌstəd] *n* (*for pouring*) crème anglaise

custody ['kʌstədɪ] *n* (*of child*) garde *f*; (*for offenders*): **to take sb into ~** placer qn en détention préventive

custom ['kʌstəm] *n* coutume *f*, usage *m*; (*Comm*) clientèle *f*

customer ['kʌstəməʳ] *n* client(e)

customized ['kʌstəmaɪzd] *adj* personnalisé(e); (*car etc*) construit(e) sur commande

customs ['kʌstəmz] *npl* douane *f*; **customs officer** *n* douanier *m*

cut [kʌt] (*pt, pp* **cut**) *vt* couper; (*meat*) découper; (*reduce*) réduire ▷ *vi* couper ▷ *n* (*gen*) coupure *f*; (*of clothes*) coupe *f*; (*in salary etc*) réduction *f*; (*of meat*) morceau *m*; **to ~ a tooth** percer une dent; **to ~ one's finger** se couper le doigt; **to get one's hair ~** se faire couper les cheveux; **I've ~ myself** je me suis coupé; **cut back** *vt* (*plants*) tailler; (*production, expenditure*) réduire; **cut down** *vt* (*tree*) abattre; (*reduce*) réduire; **cut off** *vt* couper; (*fig*) isoler; **cut out** *vt* (*picture etc*)

découper; (*remove*) supprimer; **cut up** *vt* découper; **cutback** *n* réduction *f*

cute [kjuːt] *adj* mignon(ne), adorable

cutlery ['kʌtlərɪ] *n* couverts *mpl*

cutlet ['kʌtlɪt] *n* côtelette *f*

cut-price ['kʌt'praɪs], (*us*) **cut-rate** ['kʌt'reɪt] *adj* au rabais, à prix réduit

cutting ['kʌtɪŋ] *adj* (*fig*) cinglant(e) ▷ *n* (*BRIT: from newspaper*) coupure *f* (de journal); (*from plant*) bouture *f*

CV *n abbr* = **curriculum vitae**

cyberbullying ['saɪbəbulɪɪŋ] *n* harcèlement *m* virtuel

cyberspace ['saɪbəspeɪs] *n* cyberespace *m*

cycle ['saɪkl] *n* cycle *m*; (*bicycle*) bicyclette *f*, vélo *m* ▷ *vi* faire de la bicyclette; **cycle hire** *n* location *f* de vélos; **cycle lane, cycle path** *n* piste *f* cyclable; **cycling** *n* cyclisme *m*; **cyclist** *n* cycliste *m/f*

cyclone ['saɪkləun] *n* cyclone *m*

cylinder ['sɪlɪndəʳ] *n* cylindre *m*

cymbals ['sɪmblz] *npl* cymbales *fpl*

cynical ['sɪnɪkl] *adj* cynique

Cypriot ['sɪprɪət] *adj* cypriote, chypriote ▷ *n* Cypriote *m/f*, Chypriote *m/f*

Cyprus ['saɪprəs] *n* Chypre *f*

cyst [sɪst] *n* kyste *m*; **cystitis** [sɪs'taɪtɪs] *n* cystite *f*

czar [zɑːʳ] *n* tsar *m*

Czech [tʃɛk] *adj* tchèque ▷ *n* Tchèque *m/f*; (*Ling*) tchèque *m*; **Czech Republic** *n*: **the Czech Republic** la République tchèque

D [di:] n (Mus) ré m

dab [dæb] vt (eyes, wound) tamponner; (paint, cream) appliquer (par petites touches or rapidement)

dad, daddy [dæd, 'dædɪ] n papa m

daffodil ['dæfədɪl] n jonquille f

daft [dɑːft] adj (inf) idiot(e), stupide

dagger ['dægəʳ] n poignard m

daily ['deɪlɪ] adj quotidien(ne), journalier(-ière) ▷ adv tous les jours

dairy ['dɛərɪ] n (shop) crémerie f, laiterie f; (on farm) laiterie f; **dairy produce** n produits laitiers

daisy ['deɪzɪ] n pâquerette f

dam [dæm] n (wall) barrage m; (water) réservoir m, lac m de retenue ▷ vt endiguer

damage ['dæmɪdʒ] n dégâts mpl, dommages mpl; (fig) tort m ▷ vt endommager, abîmer; (fig) faire du tort à; **damages** npl (Law) dommages-intérêts mpl

damn [dæm] vt condamner; (curse) maudire ▷ n (inf): **I don't give a ~** je

m'en fous ▷ adj (inf: also: **~ed**): **this ~ ...** ce sacré or foutu ...; **~ (it)!** zut!

damp [dæmp] adj humide ▷ n humidité f ▷ vt (also: **~en**: cloth, rag) humecter; (: enthusiasm etc) refroidir

dance [dɑːns] n danse f; (ball) bal m ▷ vi danser; **dance floor** n piste f de danse; **dancer** n danseur(-euse); **dancing** n danse f

dandelion ['dændɪlaɪən] n pissenlit m

dandruff ['dændrəf] n pellicules fpl

D & T n abbr (BRIT Scol) = **design and technology**

Dane [deɪn] n Danois(e)

danger ['deɪndʒəʳ] n danger m; **~!** (on sign) danger!; **in ~** en danger; **he was in ~ of falling** il risquait de tomber; **dangerous** adj dangereux(-euse)

dangle ['dæŋgl] vt balancer ▷ vi pendre, se balancer

Danish ['deɪnɪʃ] adj danois(e) ▷ n (Ling) danois m

dare [dɛəʳ] vt: **to ~ sb to do** défier qn or mettre qn au défi de faire ▷ vi: **to ~ (to) do sth** oser faire qch; **I ~ say he'll turn up** il est probable qu'il viendra; **daring** adj hardi(e), audacieux(-euse) ▷ n audace f, hardiesse f

dark [dɑːk] adj (night, room) obscur(e), sombre; (colour, complexion) foncé(e), sombre ▷ n: **in the ~** dans le noir; **to be in the ~ about** (fig) ignorer tout de; **after ~** après la tombée de la nuit; **darken** vt obscurcir, assombrir ▷ vi s'obscurcir, s'assombrir; **darkness** n obscurité f; **darkroom** n chambre noire

darling ['dɑːlɪŋ] adj, n chéri(e)

dart [dɑːt] n fléchette f; (in sewing) pince f ▷ vi: **to ~ towards** se précipiter or s'élancer vers; **dartboard** n cible f (de jeu de fléchettes); **darts** n jeu m de fléchettes

dash [dæʃ] n (sign) tiret m; (small quantity) goutte f, larme f ▷ vt (throw)

jeter or lancer violemment; (*hopes*)
anéantir ▷ vi: **to ~ towards** se
précipiter or se ruer vers
dashboard ['dæʃbɔːd] n (*Aut*) tableau
m de bord
data ['deɪtə] npl données fpl;
database n base f de données; **data**
processing n traitement m des
données
date [deɪt] n date f; (*with sb*) rendez-
vous m; (*fruit*) datte f ▷ vt dater;
(*person*) sortir avec; **~ of birth** date de
naissance; **to ~** adv à ce jour; **out of ~**
périmé(e); **up to ~** à la page, mis(e) à
jour, moderne; **dated** adj démodé(e)
daughter ['dɔːtəʳ] n fille f; **daughter-**
in-law n belle-fille f, bru f
daunting ['dɔːntɪŋ] adj
décourageant(e), intimidant(e)
dawn [dɔːn] n aube f, aurore f ▷ vi
(*day*) se lever, poindre; **it ~ed on him**
that ... il lui vint à l'esprit que ...
day [deɪ] n jour m; (*as duration*)
journée f; (*period of time, age*) époque
f, temps m; **the ~ before** la veille,
le jour précédent; **the ~ after, the**
following ~ le lendemain, le jour
suivant; **the ~ before yesterday**
avant-hier; **the ~ after tomorrow**
après-demain; **by ~** de jour; **day-**
care centre ['deɪkɛə-] n (*for elderly*
etc) centre m d'accueil de jour; (*for*
children) garderie f; **daydream** vi
rêver (tout éveillé); **daylight** n
(lumière f du) jour m; **day return** n
(*BRIT*) billet m d'aller-retour (*valable*
pour la journée); **daytime** n jour m,
journée f; **day-to-day** adj (*routine,*
expenses) journalier(-ière); **day trip** n
excursion f d'une journée)
dazed [deɪzd] adj abruti(e)
dazzle ['dæzl] vt éblouir, aveugler;
dazzling adj (*light*) aveuglant(e),
éblouissant(e); (*fig*) éblouissant(e)
DC abbr (*Elec*) = **direct current**
dead [dɛd] adj mort(e); (*numb*)
engourdi(e), insensible; (*battery*) à
plat ▷ adv (*completely*) absolument,

complètement; (*exactly*) juste; **he**
was shot ~ il a été tué d'un coup
de revolver; **~ tired** éreinté(e),
complètement fourbu(e); **to stop**
~ s'arrêter pile or net; **the line is ~**
(*Tel*) la ligne est coupée; **dead end**
n impasse f; **deadline** n date for
heure f limite; **deadly** adj mortel(le);
(*weapon*) meurtrier(-ière); **Dead Sea**
n: **the Dead Sea** la mer Morte
deaf [dɛf] adj sourd(e); **deafen** vt
rendre sourd(e); **deafening** adj
assourdissant(e)
deal [diːl] n affaire f, marché m
▷ vt (*pt, pp* **dealt**) (*blow*) porter;
(*cards*) donner, distribuer; **a great**
~ of beaucoup de; **deal with** vt
fus (*handle*) s'occuper or se charger
de; (*be about*) traiter de; **dealer** n
(*Comm*) marchand m; (*Cards*) donneur
m; **dealings** npl (*in goods, shares*)
opérations fpl, transactions fpl;
(*relations*) relations fpl, rapports mpl
dealt [dɛlt] pt, pp of **deal**
dean [diːn] n (*Rel, BRIT Scol*) doyen
m; (*US Scol*) conseiller principal
(conseillère principale) d'éducation
dear [dɪəʳ] adj cher (chère); (*expensive*)
cher, coûteux(-euse) ▷ n: **my ~** mon
cher (ma chère) ▷ excl: **~ me!** mon
Dieu!; **D~ Sir/Madam** (*in letter*)
Monsieur/Madame; **D~ Mr/Mrs**
X Cher Monsieur/Chère Madame
X; **dearly** adv (*love*) tendrement;
(*pay*) cher
death [dɛθ] n mort f; (*Admin*) décès
m; **death penalty** n peine f de mort;
death sentence n condamnation
f à mort
debate [dɪ'beɪt] n discussion f, débat
m ▷ vt discuter, débattre
debit ['dɛbɪt] n débit m ▷ vt: **to ~ a**
sum to sb or **to sb's account** porter
une somme au débit de qn, débiter
qn d'une somme; **debit card** n carte
f de paiement
debris ['dɛbriː] n débris mpl,
décombres mpl

debt [dɛt] n dette f; **to be in ~** avoir des dettes, être endetté(e)

debug [diːˈbʌg] vt (Comput) déboguer

debut [ˈdeɪbjuː] n début(s) m(pl)

Dec. abbr (= December) déc

decade [ˈdɛkeɪd] n décennie f, décade f

decaffeinated [dɪˈkæfɪneɪtɪd] adj décaféiné(e)

decay [dɪˈkeɪ] n (of food, wood etc) décomposition f, pourriture f; (of building) délabrement m; (also: **tooth ~**) carie f (dentaire) ▷ vi (rot) se décomposer, pourrir; (teeth) se carier

deceased [dɪˈsiːst] n: **the ~** le (la) défunt(e)

deceit [dɪˈsiːt] n tromperie f, supercherie f; **deceive** [dɪˈsiːv] vt tromper

December [dɪˈsɛmbər] n décembre m

decency [ˈdiːsənsɪ] n décence f

decent [ˈdiːsənt] adj (proper) décent(e), convenable

deception [dɪˈsɛpʃən] n tromperie f

deceptive [dɪˈsɛptɪv] adj trompeur(-euse)

decide [dɪˈsaɪd] vt (subj: person) décider; (question, argument) trancher, régler ▷ vi se décider, décider; **to ~ to do/that** décider de faire/que; **to ~ on** décider, se décider pour

decimal [ˈdɛsɪməl] adj décimal(e) ▷ n décimale f

decision [dɪˈsɪʒən] n décision f

decisive [dɪˈsaɪsɪv] adj décisif(-ive); (manner, person) décidé(e), catégorique

deck [dɛk] n (Naut) pont m; (of cards) jeu m; (record deck) platine f; (of bus): **top ~** impériale f; **deckchair** n chaise longue

declaration [dɛkləˈreɪʃən] n déclaration f

declare [dɪˈklɛər] vt déclarer

decline [dɪˈklaɪn] n (decay) déclin m; (lessening) baisse f ▷ vt refuser, décliner ▷ vi décliner; (business) baisser

decorate [ˈdɛkəreɪt] vt (adorn, give a medal to) décorer; (paint and paper) peindre et tapisser; **decoration** [dɛkəˈreɪʃən] n (medal etc, adornment) décoration f; **decorator** n peintre m en bâtiment

decrease n [ˈdiːkriːs] diminution f ▷ vt, vi [diːˈkriːs] diminuer

decree [dɪˈkriː] n (Pol, Rel) décret m; (Law) arrêt m, jugement m

dedicate [ˈdɛdɪkeɪt] vt consacrer; (book etc) dédier; **dedicated** adj (person) dévoué(e); (Comput) spécialisé(e), dédié(e); **dedicated word processor** station f de traitement de texte; **dedication** [dɛdɪˈkeɪʃən] n (devotion) dévouement m; (in book) dédicace f

deduce [dɪˈdjuːs] vt déduire, conclure

deduct [dɪˈdʌkt] vt: **to ~ sth (from)** déduire qch (de), retrancher qch (de); **deduction** [dɪˈdʌkʃən] n (deducting, deducing) déduction f; (from wage etc) prélèvement m, retenue f

deed [diːd] n action f, acte m; (Law) acte notarié, contrat m

deem [diːm] vt (formal) juger, estimer

deep [diːp] adj profond(e); (voice) grave ▷ adv: **spectators stood 20 ~** il y avait 20 rangs de spectateurs; **4 metres ~** de 4 mètres de profondeur; **how ~ is the water?** l'eau a quelle profondeur?; **deep-fry** vt faire frire (dans une friteuse); **deeply** adv profondément; (regret, interested) vivement

deer [dɪər] n (pl inv): **(red) ~** cerf m; **(fallow) ~** daim m; **(roe) ~** chevreuil m

default [dɪˈfɔːlt] n (Comput: also: ~ **value**) valeur f par défaut; **by ~** (Law) par défaut, par contumace; (Sport) par forfait

defeat [dɪˈfiːt] n défaite f ▷ vt (team, opponents) battre

defect n [ˈdiːfɛkt] défaut m ▷ vi [dɪˈfɛkt]: **to ~ to the enemy/the West** passer à l'ennemi/l'Ouest;

defective [dɪ'fɛktɪv] *adj*
défectueux(-euse)
defence, (*US*) **defense** [dɪ'fɛns] *n*
défense *f*
defend [dɪ'fɛnd] *vt* défendre;
defendant *n* défendeur(-deresse); (*in criminal case*) accusé(e), prévenu(e);
defender *n* défenseur *m*
defense [dɪ'fɛns] *n* (*US*) = **defence**
defensive [dɪ'fɛnsɪv] *adj* défensif(-ive)
▷ *n*: **on the ~** sur la défensive
defer [dɪ'fəːʳ] *vt* (*postpone*) différer,
ajourner
defiance [dɪ'faɪəns] *n* défi *m*; **in ~ of**
au mépris de; **defiant** [dɪ'faɪənt] *adj*
provocant(e), de défi; (*person*) rebelle,
intraitable
deficiency [dɪ'fɪʃənsɪ] *n* (*lack*)
insuffisance *f* (: *Med*) carence *f*; (*flaw*)
faiblesse *f*; **deficient** [dɪ'fɪʃənt] *adj*
(*inadequate*) insuffisant(e); **to be
deficient in** manquer de
deficit ['dɛfɪsɪt] *n* déficit *m*
define [dɪ'faɪn] *vt* définir
definite ['dɛfɪnɪt] *adj* (*fixed*) défini(e),
(bien) déterminé(e); (*clear, obvious*)
net(te), manifeste; (*certain*) sûr(e); **he
was ~ about it** il a été catégorique;
definitely *adv* sans aucun doute
definition [dɛfɪ'nɪʃən] *n* définition *f*;
(*clearness*) netteté *f*
deflate [diː'fleɪt] *vt* dégonfler
deflect [dɪ'flɛkt] *vt* détourner, faire
dévier
defraud [dɪ'frɔːd] *vt*: **to ~ sb of sth**
escroquer qch à qn
defriend [diː'frɛnd] *vt* (*Internet*)
supprimer de sa liste d'amis
defrost [diː'frɔst] *vt* (*fridge*) dégivrer;
(*frozen food*) décongeler
defuse [diː'fjuːz] *vt* désamorcer
defy [dɪ'faɪ] *vt* défier; (*efforts etc*)
résister à; **it defies description** cela
défie toute description
degree [dɪ'griː] *n* degré *m*; (*Scol*)
diplôme *m* (universitaire); **a (first)
~ in maths** (BRIT) une licence en
maths; **by ~s** (*gradually*) par degrés;

to some ~ jusqu'à un certain point,
dans une certaine mesure
dehydrated [diːhaɪ'dreɪtɪd] *adj*
déshydraté(e); (*milk, eggs*) en poudre
de-icer ['diː'aɪsəʳ] *n* dégivreur *m*
delay [dɪ'leɪ] *vt* retarder; (*payment*)
différer ▷ *vi* s'attarder ▷ *n* délai *m*,
retard *m*; **to be ~ed** être en retard
delegate *n* ['dɛlɪgɪt] délégué(e) ▷ *vt*
['dɛlɪgeɪt] déléguer
delete [dɪ'liːt] *vt* rayer, supprimer;
(*Comput*) effacer
deli ['dɛlɪ] *n* épicerie fine
deliberate *adj* [dɪ'lɪbərɪt]
(*intentional*) délibéré(e); (*slow*)
mesuré(e) ▷ *vi* [dɪ'lɪbəreɪt] délibérer,
réfléchir; **deliberately** *adv* (*on
purpose*) exprès, délibérément
delicacy ['dɛlɪkəsɪ] *n* délicatesse
f; (*choice food*) mets fin *or* délicat,
friandise *f*
delicate ['dɛlɪkɪt] *adj* délicat(e)
delicatessen [dɛlɪkə'tɛsn] *n*
épicerie fine
delicious [dɪ'lɪʃəs] *adj* délicieux(-euse)
delight [dɪ'laɪt] *n* (grande) joie, grand
plaisir ▷ *vt* enchanter; **she's a ~ to
work with** c'est un plaisir de travailler
avec elle; **to take ~ in** prendre grand
plaisir à; **delighted** *adj*: **delighted
(at *or* with sth)** ravi(e) (de qch); **to
be delighted to do sth/that** être
enchanté(e) *or* ravi(e) de faire qch/
que; **delightful** *adj* (*person*) adorable;
(*meal, evening*) merveilleux(-euse)
delinquent [dɪ'lɪŋkwənt] *adj, n*
délinquant(e)
deliver [dɪ'lɪvəʳ] *vt* (*mail*) distribuer;
(*goods*) livrer; (*message*) remettre;
(*speech*) prononcer; (*Med*: *baby*)
mettre au monde; **delivery** *n* (*of
mail*) distribution *f*; (*of goods*) livraison
f; (*of speaker*) élocution *f*; (*Med*)
accouchement *m*; **to take delivery
of** prendre livraison de
delusion [dɪ'luːʒən] *n* illusion *f*
de luxe [də'lʌks] *adj* de luxe
delve [dɛlv] *vi*: **to ~ into** fouiller dans

demand [dɪ'mɑːnd] vt réclamer, exiger ▷ n exigence f; (claim) revendication f; (Econ) demande f; **in ~** demandé(e), recherché(e); **on ~** sur demande; **demanding** adj (person) exigeant(e); (work) astreignant(e)

> Be careful not to translate to demand by the French word demander.

demise [dɪ'maɪz] n décès m

demo ['dɛməu] n abbr (inf: = demonstration) (protest) manif f; (Comput) démonstration f

democracy [dɪ'mɔkrəsɪ] n démocratie f; **democrat** ['dɛməkræt] n démocrate m/f; **democratic** [dɛmə'krætɪk] adj démocratique

demolish [dɪ'mɔlɪʃ] vt démolir

demolition [dɛmə'lɪʃən] n démolition f

demon ['diːmən] n démon m

demonstrate ['dɛmənstreɪt] vt démontrer, prouver; (show) faire une démonstration de ▷ vi: **to ~ (for/against)** manifester (en faveur de/contre); **demonstration** [dɛmən'streɪʃən] n démonstration f; (Pol etc) manifestation f; **demonstrator** n (Pol etc) manifestant(e)

demote [dɪ'məut] vt rétrograder

den [dɛn] n (of lion) tanière f; (room) repaire m

denial [dɪ'naɪəl] n (of accusation) démenti m; (of rights, guilt, truth) dénégation f

denim ['dɛnɪm] n jean m; **denims** npl (blue-)jeans mpl

Denmark ['dɛnmɑːk] n Danemark m

denomination [dɪnɔmɪ'neɪʃən] n (money) valeur f; (Rel) confession f

denounce [dɪ'nauns] vt dénoncer

dense [dɛns] adj dense; (inf: stupid) obtus(e)

density ['dɛnsɪtɪ] n densité f

dent [dɛnt] n bosse f ▷ vt (also: **make a ~ in**) cabosser

dental ['dɛntl] adj dentaire; **dental floss** [-flɔs] n fil m dentaire; **dental surgery** n cabinet m de dentiste

dentist ['dɛntɪst] n dentiste m/f

dentures ['dɛntʃəz] npl dentier msg

deny [dɪ'naɪ] vt nier; (refuse) refuser

deodorant [diː'əudərənt] n déodorant m

depart [dɪ'pɑːt] vi partir; **to ~ from** (fig: differ from) s'écarter de

department [dɪ'pɑːtmənt] n (Comm) rayon m; (Scol) section f; (Pol) ministère m, département m; **department store** n grand magasin

departure [dɪ'pɑːtʃəʳ] n départ m; **a new ~** une nouvelle voie; **departure lounge** n salle f de départ

depend [dɪ'pɛnd] vi: **to ~ (up)on** dépendre de; (rely on) compter sur; **it ~s** cela dépend; **~ing on the result ...** selon le résultat ...; **dependant** n personne f à charge; **dependent** adj: **to be dependent (on)** dépendre (de) ▷ n = **dependant**

depict [dɪ'pɪkt] vt (in picture) représenter; (in words) (dé)peindre, décrire

deport [dɪ'pɔːt] vt déporter, expulser

deposit [dɪ'pɔzɪt] n (Chem, Comm, Geo) dépôt m; (of ore, oil) gisement m; (part payment) arrhes fpl, acompte m; (on bottle etc) consigne f; (for hired goods etc) cautionnement m, garantie f ▷ vt déposer; **deposit account** n compte m sur livret

depot ['dɛpəu] n dépôt m; (us Rail) gare f

depreciate [dɪ'priːʃɪeɪt] vi se déprécier, se dévaloriser

depress [dɪ'prɛs] vt déprimer; (press down) appuyer sur, abaisser; (wages etc) faire baisser; **depressed** adj (person) déprimé(e); (area) en déclin, touché(e) par le sous-emploi; **depressing** adj déprimant(e); **depression** [dɪ'prɛʃən] n dépression f

deprive [dɪ'praɪv] vt: **to ~ sb of** priver qn de; **deprived** adj déshérité(e)

dept. *abbr* (= *department*) dép, dépt

depth [dεpθ] *n* profondeur *f*; **to be in the ~s of despair** être au plus profond du désespoir; **to be out of one's ~** (BRIT: *swimmer*) ne plus avoir pied; (*fig*) être dépassé(e), nager

deputy ['dεpjutɪ] *n* (*second in command*) adjoint(e); (*Pol*) député *m*; (US: *also*: **~ sheriff**) shérif adjoint ▷ *adj*: **~ head** (*Scol*) directeur(-trice) adjoint(e), sous-directeur(-trice)

derail [dɪ'reɪl] *vt*: **to be ~ed** dérailler

derelict ['dεrɪlɪkt] *adj* abandonné(e), à l'abandon

derive [dɪ'raɪv] *vt*: **to ~ sth from** tirer qch de; trouver qch dans ▷ *vi*: **to ~ from** provenir de, dériver de

descend [dɪ'sεnd] *vt, vi* descendre; **to ~ from**, descendre de, être issu(e) de; **to ~ to** s'abaisser à; **descendant** *n* descendant(e); **descent** *n* descente *f*; (*origin*) origine *f*

describe [dɪs'kraɪb] *vt* décrire; **description** [dɪs'krɪpʃən] *n* description *f*; (*sort*) sorte *f*, espèce *f*

desert *n* ['dεzət] désert *m* ▷ *vt* [dɪ'zə:t] déserter, abandonner ▷ *vi* (*Mil*) déserter; **deserted** [dɪ'zə:tɪd] *adj* désert(e)

deserve [dɪ'zə:v] *vt* mériter

design [dɪ'zaɪn] *n* (*sketch*) plan *m*, dessin *m*; (*layout, shape*) conception *f*, ligne *f*; (*pattern*) dessin, motif(s) *m(pl)*; (*of dress, car*) modèle *m*; (*art*) design *m*, stylisme *m*; (*intention*) dessein *m* ▷ *vt* dessiner; (*plan*) concevoir; **design and technology** *n* (BRIT *Scol*) technologie *f*

designate *vt* ['dεzɪgneɪt] désigner ▷ *adj* ['dεzɪgnɪt] désigné(e)

designer [dɪ'zaɪnə'] *n* (*Archit, Art*) dessinateur(-trice); (*Industry*) concepteur *m*, designer *m*; (*Fashion*) styliste *m/f*

desirable [dɪ'zaɪərəbl] *adj* (*property, location, purchase*) attrayant(e)

desire [dɪ'zaɪə'] *n* désir *m* ▷ *vt* désirer, vouloir

desk [dεsk] *n* (*in office*) bureau *m*; (*for pupil*) pupitre *m*; (BRIT: *in shop, restaurant*) caisse *f*; (*in hotel, at airport*) réception *f*; **desk-top publishing** ['dεsktɒp-] *n* publication assistée par ordinateur, PAO *f*

despair [dɪs'pεə'] *n* désespoir *m* ▷ *vi*: **to ~ of** désespérer de

despatch [dɪs'pætʃ] *n, vt* = **dispatch**

desperate ['dεspərɪt] *adj* désespéré(e); (*fugitive*) prêt(e) à tout; **to be ~ for sth/to do sth** avoir désespérément besoin de qch/de faire qch; **desperately** *adv* désespérément; (*very*) terriblement, extrêmement; **desperation** [dεspə'reɪʃən] *n* désespoir *m*; **in (sheer) desperation** en désespoir de cause

despise [dɪs'paɪz] *vt* mépriser

despite [dɪs'paɪt] *prep* malgré, en dépit de

dessert [dɪ'zə:t] *n* dessert *m*; **dessertspoon** *n* cuiller *f* à dessert

destination [dεstɪ'neɪʃən] *n* destination *f*

destined ['dεstɪnd] *adj*: **~ for London** à destination de Londres

destiny ['dεstɪnɪ] *n* destinée *f*, destin *m*

destroy [dɪs'trɔɪ] *vt* détruire; (*injured horse*) abattre; (*dog*) faire piquer

destruction [dɪs'trʌkʃən] *n* destruction *f*

destructive [dɪs'trʌktɪv] *adj* destructeur(-trice)

detach [dɪ'tætʃ] *vt* détacher; **detached** *adj* (*attitude*) détaché(e); **detached house** *n* pavillon *m*, maison(nette) (individuelle)

detail ['di:teɪl] *n* détail *m* ▷ *vt* raconter en détail, énumérer; **in ~** en détail; **detailed** *adj* détaillé(e)

detain [dɪ'teɪn] *vt* retenir; (*in captivity*) détenir

detect [dɪ'tεkt] *vt* déceler, percevoir; (*Med, Police*) dépister; (*Mil, Radar, Tech*) détecter; **detection** [dɪ'tεkʃən] *n*

découverte f; **detective** n policier m;
private detective détective privé;
detective story n roman policier

detention [dɪˈtɛnʃən] n détention f;
(Scol) retenue f, consigne f

deter [dɪˈtəːʳ] vt dissuader

detergent [dɪˈtəːdʒənt] n détersif m,
détergent m

deteriorate [dɪˈtɪərɪəreɪt] vi se
détériorer, se dégrader

determination [dɪtəːmɪˈneɪʃən] n
détermination f

determine [dɪˈtəːmɪn] vt
déterminer; **to ~ to do** résoudre
de faire, se déterminer à faire;
determined adj (person)
déterminé(e), décidé(e);
determined to do bien décidé à faire

deterrent [dɪˈtɛrənt] n effet m de
dissuasion; force f de dissuasion

detest [dɪˈtɛst] vt détester, avoir
horreur de

detour ['diːtuəʳ] n détour m; (us Aut:
diversion) déviation f

detract [dɪˈtrækt] vt: **to ~ from**
(quality, pleasure) diminuer;
(reputation) porter atteinte à

detrimental [dɛtrɪˈmɛntl] adj: **~ to**
préjudiciable or nuisible à

devastating ['dɛvəsteɪtɪŋ]
adj dévastateur(-trice); (news)
accablant(e)

develop [dɪˈvɛləp] vt (gen)
développer; (disease) commencer
à souffrir de; (resources) mettre en
valeur, exploiter; (land) aménager
▷ vi se développer; (situation,
disease: evolve) évoluer; (facts,
symptoms: appear) se manifester,
se produire; **can you ~ this film?**
pouvez-vous développer cette
pellicule?; **developing country** n
pays m en voie de développement;
development n développement m;
(of land) exploitation f; (new fact, event)
rebondissement m, fait(s) nouveau(x)

device [dɪˈvaɪs] n (apparatus) appareil
m, dispositif m

devil ['dɛvl] n diable m; démon m

devious ['diːvɪəs] adj (person)
sournois(e), dissimulé(e)

devise [dɪˈvaɪz] vt imaginer, concevoir

devote [dɪˈvəut] vt: **to ~ sth to**
consacrer qch à; **devoted** adj
dévoué(e); **to be devoted to** être
dévoué(e) or très attaché(e) à; (book
etc) être consacré(e) à; **devotion** n
dévouement m, attachement m; (Rel)
dévotion f, piété f

devour [dɪˈvauəʳ] vt dévorer

devout [dɪˈvaut] adj pieux(-euse),
dévot(e)

dew [djuː] n rosée f

diabetes [daɪəˈbiːtiːz] n diabète m

diabetic [daɪəˈbɛtɪk] n diabétique
m/f ▷ adj (person) diabétique

diagnose [daɪəgˈnəuz] vt
diagnostiquer

diagnosis (pl **diagnoses**)
[daɪəgˈnəusɪs, -siːz] n diagnostic m

diagonal [daɪˈægənl] adj diagonal(e)
▷ n diagonale f

diagram ['daɪəgræm] n diagramme
m, schéma m

dial ['daɪəl] n cadran m ▷ vt (number)
faire, composer

dialect ['daɪəlɛkt] n dialecte m

dialling code ['daɪəlɪŋ-], (us) **dial
code** n indicatif m (téléphonique);
what's the ~ for Paris? quel est
l'indicatif de Paris?

dialling tone ['daɪəlɪŋ-], (us) **dial
tone** n tonalité f

dialogue, (us) **dialog** ['daɪəlɔg] n
dialogue m

diameter [daɪˈæmɪtəʳ] n diamètre m

diamond ['daɪəmənd] n diamant
m; (shape) losange m; **diamonds** npl
(Cards) carreau m

diaper ['daɪəpəʳ] n (us) couche f

diarrhoea, (us) **diarrhea** [daɪəˈriːə]
n diarrhée f

diary ['daɪərɪ] n (daily account) journal
m; (book) agenda m

dice [daɪs] n (pl inv) dé m ▷ vt (Culin)
couper en dés or en cubes

dictate vt [dɪk'teɪt] dicter; **dictation** [dɪk'teɪʃən] n dictée f

dictator [dɪk'teɪtəʳ] n dictateur m

dictionary ['dɪkʃənrɪ] n dictionnaire m

did [dɪd] pt of **do**

didn't [dɪdnt] = **did not**

die [daɪ] vi mourir; **to be dying for sth** avoir une envie folle de qch; **to be dying to do sth** mourir d'envie de faire qch; **die down** vi se calmer, s'apaiser; **die out** vi disparaître, s'éteindre

diesel ['diːzl] n (vehicle) diesel m; (also: ~ **oil**) carburant m diesel, gas-oil m

diet ['daɪət] n alimentation f; (restricted food) régime m ▷ vi (also: **be on a ~**) suivre un régime

differ ['dɪfəʳ] vi: **to ~ from sth** (be different) être différent(e) de qch, différer de qch; **to ~ from sb over sth** ne pas être d'accord avec qn au sujet de qch; **difference** n différence f; (quarrel) différend m, désaccord m; **different** adj différent(e); **differentiate** [dɪfə'rɛnʃɪeɪt] vi: **to differentiate between** faire une différence entre; **differently** adv différemment

difficult ['dɪfɪkəlt] adj difficile; **difficulty** n difficulté f

dig [dɪg] vt (pt, pp **dug**) (hole) creuser; (garden) bêcher ▷ n (prod) coup m de coude; (fig: remark) coup de griffe or de patte; (Archaeology) fouille f; **to ~ one's nails into** enfoncer ses ongles dans; **dig up** vt déterrer

digest vt [daɪ'dʒɛst] digérer ▷ n ['daɪdʒɛst] sommaire m, résumé m; **digestion** [dɪ'dʒɛstʃən] n digestion f

digit ['dɪdʒɪt] n (number) chiffre m (de 0 à 9); (finger) doigt m; **digital** adj (system, recording, radio) numérique, digital(e); (watch) à affichage numérique or digital; **digital camera** n appareil m photo numérique; **digital TV** n télévision f numérique

dignified ['dɪgnɪfaɪd] adj digne

dignity ['dɪgnɪtɪ] n dignité f

digs [dɪgz] npl (BRIT inf) piaule f, chambre meublée

dilemma [daɪ'lɛmə] n dilemme m

dill [dɪl] n aneth m

dilute [daɪ'luːt] vt diluer

dim [dɪm] adj (light, eyesight) faible; (memory, outline) vague, indécis(e); (room) sombre; (inf: stupid) borné(e), obtus(e) ▷ vt (light) réduire, baisser; (us Aut) mettre en code, baisser

dime [daɪm] n (us) pièce f de 10 cents

dimension [daɪ'mɛnʃən] n dimension f

diminish [dɪ'mɪnɪʃ] vt, vi diminuer

din [dɪn] n vacarme m

dine [daɪn] vi dîner; **diner** n (person) dîneur(-euse); (us: eating place) petit restaurant

dinghy ['dɪŋgɪ] n youyou m; (inflatable) canot m pneumatique; (also: **sailing ~**) voilier m, dériveur m

dingy ['dɪndʒɪ] adj miteux(-euse), minable

dining car ['daɪnɪŋ-] n (BRIT) voiture-restaurant f, wagon-restaurant m

dining room ['daɪnɪŋ-] n salle f à manger

dining table [daɪnɪŋ-] n table f de (la) salle à manger

dinkum ['dɪŋkʌm] adj (AUST, NZ inf) vrai(e); **fair ~** vrai(e)

dinner ['dɪnəʳ] n (evening meal) dîner m; (lunch) déjeuner m; (public) banquet m; **dinner jacket** n smoking m; **dinner party** n dîner m; **dinner time** n (evening) heure f du dîner; (midday) heure du déjeuner

dinosaur ['daɪnəsɔːʳ] n dinosaure m

dip [dɪp] n (slope) déclivité f; (in sea) baignade f, bain m; (Culin) ≈ sauce f ▷ vt tremper, plonger; (BRIT Aut: lights) mettre en code, baisser ▷ vi plonger

diploma [dɪ'pləumə] n diplôme m

diplomacy [dɪ'pləuməsɪ] n diplomatie f

diplomat ['dɪpləmæt] n diplomate m; **diplomatic** [dɪplə'mætɪk] adj diplomatique

dipstick ['dɪpstɪk] n (BRIT Aut) jauge f de niveau d'huile

dire [daɪəʳ] adj (poverty) extrême; (awful) affreux(-euse)

direct [daɪ'rɛkt] adj direct(e) ▷ vt (tell way) diriger, orienter; (letter, remark) adresser; (Cine, TV) réaliser; (Theat) mettre en scène; (order): **to ~ sb to do sth** ordonner à qn de faire qch ▷ adv directement; **can you ~ me to …?** pouvez-vous m'indiquer le chemin de …?; **direct debit** n (BRIT Banking) prélèvement m automatique

direction [dɪ'rɛkʃən] n direction f; **directions** npl (to a place) indications fpl; **~s for use** mode m d'emploi; **sense of ~** sens m de l'orientation

directly [dɪ'rɛktlɪ] adv (in straight line) directement, tout droit; (at once) tout de suite, immédiatement

director [dɪ'rɛktəʳ] n directeur m; (Theat) metteur m en scène; (Cine, TV) réalisateur(-trice)

directory [dɪ'rɛktərɪ] n annuaire m; (Comput) répertoire m; **directory enquiries**, (US) **directory assistance** n (Tel: service) renseignements mpl

dirt [dəːt] n saleté f; (mud) boue f; **dirty** adj sale; (joke) cochon(ne) ▷ vt salir

disability [dɪsə'bɪlɪtɪ] n invalidité f, infirmité f

disabled [dɪs'eɪbld] adj handicapé(e); (maimed) mutilé(e)

disadvantage [dɪsəd'vɑːntɪdʒ] n désavantage m, inconvénient m

disagree [dɪsə'griː] vi (differ) ne pas concorder; (be against, think otherwise): **to ~ (with)** ne pas être d'accord (avec); **disagreeable** adj désagréable; **disagreement** n désaccord m, différend m

disappear [dɪsə'pɪəʳ] vi disparaître; **disappearance** n disparition f

disappoint [dɪsə'pɔɪnt] vt décevoir; **disappointed** adj déçu(e); **disappointing** adj décevant(e); **disappointment** n déception f

disapproval [dɪsə'pruːvəl] n désapprobation f

disapprove [dɪsə'pruːv] vi: **to ~ of** désapprouver

disarm [dɪs'ɑːm] vt désarmer; **disarmament** [dɪs'ɑːməmənt] n désarmement m

disaster [dɪ'zɑːstəʳ] n catastrophe f, désastre m; **disastrous** adj désastreux(-euse)

disbelief ['dɪsbə'liːf] n incrédulité f

disc [dɪsk] n disque m; (Comput) = **disk**

discard [dɪs'kɑːd] vt (old things) se débarrasser de; (fig) écarter, renoncer à

discharge vt [dɪs'tʃɑːdʒ] (duties) s'acquitter de; (waste etc) déverser; décharger; (patient) renvoyer (chez lui); (employee, soldier) congédier, licencier ▷ n ['dɪstʃɑːdʒ] (Elec, Med) émission f; (dismissal) renvoi m licenciement m

discipline ['dɪsɪplɪn] n discipline f ▷ vt discipliner; (punish) punir

disc jockey n disque-jockey m (DJ)

disclose [dɪs'kləuz] vt révéler, divulguer

disco ['dɪskəu] n abbr discothèque f

discoloured, (US) **discolored** [dɪs'kʌləd] adj décoloré(e), jauni(e)

discomfort [dɪs'kʌmfət] n malaise m, gêne f; (lack of comfort) manque m de confort

disconnect [dɪskə'nɛkt] vt (Elec, Radio) débrancher; (gas, water) couper

discontent [dɪskən'tɛnt] n mécontentement m

discontinue [dɪskən'tɪnjuː] vt cesser, interrompre; **"~d"** (Comm) "fin de série"

discount n ['dɪskaunt] remise f, rabais m ▷ vt [dɪs'kaunt] (report etc) ne pas tenir compte de

discourage [dɪsˈkʌrɪdʒ] vt
décourager

discover [dɪsˈkʌvəʳ] vt découvrir;
discovery n découverte f

discredit [dɪsˈkrɛdɪt] vt (idea) mettre
en doute; (person) discréditer

discreet [dɪˈskriːt] adj discret(-ète)

discrepancy [dɪˈskrɛpənsɪ] n
divergence f, contradiction f

discretion [dɪˈskrɛʃən] n discrétion f;
at the ~ of à la discrétion de

discriminate [dɪˈskrɪmɪneɪt] vi: **to
~ between** établir une distinction
entre, faire la différence entre; **to ~
against** pratiquer une discrimination
contre; **discrimination**
[dɪskrɪmɪˈneɪʃən] n discrimination f;
(judgment) discernement m

discuss [dɪˈskʌs] vt discuter de;
(debate) discuter; **discussion**
[dɪˈskʌʃən] n discussion f

disease [dɪˈziːz] n maladie f

disembark [dɪsɪmˈbɑːk] vt, vi
débarquer

disgrace [dɪsˈɡreɪs] n honte f;
(disfavour) disgrâce f ▷ vt déshonorer,
couvrir de honte; **disgraceful** adj
scandaleux(-euse), honteux(-euse)

disgruntled [dɪsˈɡrʌntld] adj
mécontent(e)

disguise [dɪsˈɡaɪz] n déguisement m
▷ vt déguiser; **in ~** déguisé(e)

disgust [dɪsˈɡʌst] n dégoût m,
aversion f ▷ vt dégoûter, écœurer

disgusted [dɪsˈɡʌstɪd] adj
dégoûté(e), écœuré(e)

disgusting [dɪsˈɡʌstɪŋ] adj
dégoûtant(e)

dish [dɪʃ] n plat m; **to do** or **wash the
~es** faire la vaisselle; **dishcloth** n
(for drying) torchon m; (for washing)
lavette f

dishonest [dɪsˈɔnɪst] adj
malhonnête

dishtowel [ˈdɪʃtauəl] n (US) torchon
m (à vaisselle)

dishwasher [ˈdɪʃwɔʃəʳ] n lave-
vaisselle m

disillusion [dɪsɪˈluːʒən] vt
désabuser, désenchanter

disinfectant [dɪsɪnˈfɛktənt] n
désinfectant m

disintegrate [dɪsˈɪntɪɡreɪt] vi se
désintégrer

disk [dɪsk] n (Comput) disquette f;
single-/double-sided ~ disquette
une face/double face; **disk drive** n
lecteur m de disquette; **diskette** n
(Comput) disquette f

dislike [dɪsˈlaɪk] n aversion f,
antipathie f ▷ vt ne pas aimer

dislocate [ˈdɪsləkeɪt] vt disloquer,
déboîter

disloyal [dɪsˈlɔɪəl] adj déloyal(e)

dismal [ˈdɪzml] adj (gloomy) lugubre,
maussade; (very bad) lamentable

dismantle [dɪsˈmæntl] vt démonter

dismay [dɪsˈmeɪ] n consternation f
▷ vt consterner

dismiss [dɪsˈmɪs] vt congédier,
renvoyer; (idea) écarter; (Law) rejeter;
dismissal n renvoi m

disobedient [dɪsəˈbiːdɪənt] adj
désobéissant(e), indiscipliné(e)

disobey [dɪsəˈbeɪ] vt désobéir à

disorder [dɪsˈɔːdəʳ] n désordre
m; (rioting) désordres mpl; (Med)
troubles mpl

disorganized [dɪsˈɔːɡənaɪzd] adj
désorganisé(e)

disown [dɪsˈəun] vt renier

dispatch [dɪsˈpætʃ] vt expédier,
envoyer ▷ n envoi m, expédition f;
(Mil, Press) dépêche f

dispel [dɪsˈpɛl] vt dissiper, chasser

dispense [dɪsˈpɛns] vt (medicine)
préparer (et vendre); **dispense with**
vt fus se passer de; **dispenser** n
(device) distributeur m

disperse [dɪsˈpəːs] vt disperser ▷ vi
se disperser

display [dɪsˈpleɪ] n (of goods) étalage
m; affichage m; (Comput: information)
visualisation f; (: device) visuel m; (of
feeling) manifestation f ▷ vt montrer;
(goods) mettre à l'étalage, exposer;

(*results, departure times*) afficher; (*pej*) faire étalage de

displease [dɪs'pliːz] *vt* mécontenter, contrarier

disposable [dɪs'pəuzəbl] *adj* (*pack etc*) jetable; (*income*) disponible

disposal [dɪs'pəuzl] *n* (*of rubbish*) évacuation *f*, destruction *f*; (*of property etc*: *by selling*) vente *f*; (: *by giving away*) cession *f*; **at one's ~** à sa disposition

dispose [dɪs'pəuz] *vi*: **to ~ of** (*unwanted goods*) se débarrasser de, se défaire de; (*problem*) expédier; **disposition** [dɪspə'zɪʃən] *n* disposition *f*; (*temperament*) naturel *m*

disproportionate [dɪsprə'pɔːʃənət] *adj* disproportionné(e)

dispute [dɪs'pjuːt] *n* discussion *f*; (*also*: **industrial ~**) conflit *m* ▷ *vt* (*question*) contester; (*matter*) discuter

disqualify [dɪs'kwɔlɪfaɪ] *vt* (*Sport*) disqualifier; **to ~ sb for sth/from doing** rendre qn inapte à qch/à faire

disregard [dɪsrɪ'gɑːd] *vt* ne pas tenir compte de

disrupt [dɪs'rʌpt] *vt* (*plans, meeting, lesson*) perturber, déranger; **disruption** [dɪs'rʌpʃən] *n* perturbation *f*, dérangement *m*

dissatisfaction [dɪssætɪs'fækʃən] *n* mécontentement *m*, insatisfaction *f*

dissatisfied [dɪs'sætɪsfaɪd] *adj*: **~ (with)** insatisfait(e) (de)

dissect [dɪ'sɛkt] *vt* disséquer

dissent [dɪ'sɛnt] *n* dissentiment *m*, différence *f* d'opinion

dissertation [dɪsə'teɪʃən] *n* (*Scol*) mémoire *m*

dissolve [dɪ'zɔlv] *vt* dissoudre ▷ *vi* se dissoudre, fondre; **to ~ in(to) tears** fondre en larmes

distance ['dɪstns] *n* distance *f*; **in the ~** au loin

distant ['dɪstnt] *adj* lointain(e), éloigné(e); (*manner*) distant(e), froid(e)

distil, (*US*) **distill** [dɪs'tɪl] *vt* distiller; **distillery** *n* distillerie *f*

distinct [dɪs'tɪŋkt] *adj* distinct(e); (*clear*) marqué(e); **as ~ from** par opposition à; **distinction** [dɪs'tɪŋkʃən] *n* distinction *f*; (*in exam*) mention *f* très bien; **distinctive** *adj* distinctif(-ive)

distinguish [dɪs'tɪŋgwɪʃ] *vt* distinguer; **to ~ o.s.** se distinguer; **distinguished** *adj* (*eminent, refined*) distingué(e)

distort [dɪs'tɔːt] *vt* déformer

distract [dɪs'trækt] *vt* distraire, déranger; **distracted** *adj* (*not concentrating*) distrait(e); (*worried*) affolé(e); **distraction** [dɪs'trækʃən] *n* distraction *f*

distraught [dɪs'trɔːt] *adj* éperdu(e)

distress [dɪs'trɛs] *n* détresse *f* ▷ *vt* affliger; **distressing** *adj* douloureux(-euse), pénible

distribute [dɪs'trɪbjuːt] *vt* distribuer; **distribution** [dɪstrɪ'bjuːʃən] *n* distribution *f*; **distributor** *n* (*gen, Tech*) distributeur *m*; (*Comm*) concessionnaire *m/f*

district ['dɪstrɪkt] *n* (*of country*) région *f*; (*of town*) quartier *m*; (*Admin*) district *m*; **district attorney** *n* (*US*) ≈ procureur *m* de la République

distrust [dɪs'trʌst] *n* méfiance *f*, doute *m* ▷ *vt* se méfier de

disturb [dɪs'təːb] *vt* troubler; (*inconvenience*) déranger; **disturbance** *n* dérangement *m*; (*political etc*) troubles *mpl*; **disturbed** *adj* (*worried, upset*) agité(e), troublé(e); **to be emotionally disturbed** avoir des problèmes affectifs; **disturbing** *adj* troublant(e), inquiétant(e)

ditch [dɪtʃ] *n* fossé *m*; (*for irrigation*) rigole *f* ▷ *vt* (*inf*) abandonner; (*person*) plaquer

ditto ['dɪtəu] *adv* idem

dive [daɪv] *n* plongeon *m*; (*of submarine*) plongée *f* ▷ *vi* plonger; **to ~ into** (*bag etc*) plonger la main dans; (*place*) se précipiter dans; **diver** *n* plongeur *m*

diverse [daɪ'vəːs] *adj* divers(e)

diversion [daɪ'vəːʃən] *n* (BRIT
Aut) déviation *f*; (*distraction*, Mil)
diversion *f*

diversity [daɪ'vəːsɪtɪ] *n* diversité
f, variété *f*

divert [daɪ'vəːt] *vt* (BRIT: *traffic*)
dévier; (*plane*) dérouter; (*train, river*)
détourner

divide [dɪ'vaɪd] *vt* diviser; (*separate*)
séparer ▷ *vi* se diviser; **divided
highway** (US) *n* route *f* à quatre voies

divine [dɪ'vaɪn] *adj* divin(e)

diving ['daɪvɪŋ] *n* plongée (sous-
marine); **diving board** *n* plongeoir *m*

division [dɪ'vɪʒən] *n* division *f*;
(*separation*) séparation *f*; (Comm)
service *m*

divorce [dɪ'vɔːs] *n* divorce *m* ▷ *vt*
divorcer d'avec; **divorced** *adj*
divorcé(e); **divorcee** [dɪvɔː'siː] *n*
divorcé(e)

DIY *adj, n abbr* (BRIT) = **do-it-yourself**

dizzy ['dɪzɪ] *adj*: **I feel ~** la tête me
tourne, j'ai la tête qui tourne

DJ *n abbr* = **disc jockey**

DNA *n abbr* (= deoxyribonucleic acid)
ADN *m*

 KEYWORD

do [duː] *n* (inf: party etc) soirée *f*, fête *f*
▶ *aux vb* (pt **did**, pp **done**) **1** (in negative
constructions) non traduit; **I don't
understand** je ne comprends pas
2 (to form questions) non traduit;
didn't you know? vous ne le saviez
pas?; **what do you think?** qu'en
pensez-vous?
3 (for emphasis, in polite expressions):
**people do make mistakes
sometimes** on peut toujours se
tromper; **she does seem rather
late** je trouve qu'elle est bien en
retard; **do sit down/help yourself**
asseyez-vous/servez-vous je vous
en prie; **do take care!** faites bien
attention à vous!

4 (used to avoid repeating vb): **she
swims better than I do** elle nage
mieux que moi; **do you agree?
— yes, I do/no I don't** vous êtes
d'accord? — oui/non; **she lives
in Glasgow — so do I** elle habite
Glasgow — moi aussi; **he didn't like
it and neither did we** il n'a pas aimé
ça, et nous non plus; **who broke
it? — I did** qui l'a cassé? — c'est moi;
he asked me to help him and I did
il m'a demandé de l'aider, et c'est ce
que j'ai fait
5 (in question tags): **you like him,
don't you?** vous l'aimez bien, n'est-ce
pas?; **I don't know him, do I?** je ne
crois pas le connaître
▶ *vt* (pt **did**, pp **done**) **1** (gen: carry out,
perform etc) faire; (*visit: city, museum*)
faire, visiter; **what are you doing
tonight?** qu'est-ce que vous faites
ce soir?; **what do you do?** (job)
que faites-vous dans la vie?; **what
can I do for you?** que puis-je faire
pour vous?; **to do the cooking/
washing-up** faire la cuisine/la
vaisselle; **to do one's teeth/hair/
nails** se brosser les dents/se coiffer/
se faire les ongles
2 (Aut etc: distance) faire; (: speed) faire
du; **we've done 200 km already**
nous avons déjà fait 200 km; **the
car was doing 100** la voiture faisait
du 100 (à l'heure); **he can do 100 in
that car** il peut faire du 100 (à l'heure)
dans cette voiture-là
▶ *vi* (pt **did**, pp **done**) **1** (act, behave)
faire; **do as I do** faites comme moi
2 (get on, fare) marcher; **the firm
is doing well** l'entreprise marche
bien; **he's doing well/badly at
school** ça marche bien/mal pour lui
à l'école; **how do you do?** comment
allez-vous?; (on being introduced)
enchanté(e)!
3 (suit) aller; **will it do?** est-ce que
ça ira?
4 (be sufficient) suffire, aller; **will £10**

do? est-ce que 10 livres suffiront?; **that'll do** ça suffit, ça ira; **that'll do!** (in annoyance) ça va or suffit comme ça!; **to make do (with)** se contenter (de)

do up vt (laces, dress) attacher; (buttons) boutonner; (zip) fermer; (renovate: room) refaire; (: house) remettre à neuf

do with vt fus (need): **I could do with a drink/some help** quelque chose à boire/un peu d'aide ne serait pas de refus; **it could do with a wash** ça ne lui ferait pas de mal d'être lavé; (be connected with): **that has nothing to do with you** cela ne vous concerne pas; **I won't have anything to do with it** je ne veux pas m'en mêler

do without vi s'en passer: **if you're late for tea then you'll do without** si vous êtes en retard pour le dîner il faudra vous en passer ▷ vt fus se passer de; **I can do without a car** je peux me passer de voiture

dock [dɔk] n dock m; (wharf) quai m; (Law) banc m des accusés ▷ vi se mettre à quai; (Space) s'arrimer; **docks** npl (Naut) docks

doctor ['dɔktə'] n médecin m, docteur m; (PhD etc) docteur ▷ vt (drink) frelater; **call a ~!** appelez un docteur or un médecin!; **Doctor of Philosophy** n (degree) doctorat m; (person) titulaire m/f d'un doctorat

document ['dɔkjumənt] n document m; **documentary** [dɔkju'mɛntərɪ] adj, n documentaire (m); **documentation** [dɔkjumən'teɪʃən] n documentation f

dodge [dɔdʒ] n truc m; combine f ▷ vt esquiver, éviter

dodgy ['dɔdʒɪ] adj (BRIT inf: uncertain) douteux(-euse); (: shady) louche

does [dʌz] vb see **do**

doesn't ['dʌznt] = **does not**

dog [dɔg] n chien(ne) ▷ vt (follow closely) suivre de près; (fig: memory etc) poursuivre, harceler; **doggy bag** ['dɔgɪ-] n petit sac pour emporter les restes

do-it-yourself ['duːɪtjɔː'sɛlf] n bricolage m

dole [dəul] n (BRIT: payment) allocation f de chômage; **on the ~** au chômage

doll [dɔl] n poupée f

dollar ['dɔlə'] n dollar m

dolphin ['dɔlfɪn] n dauphin m

dome [dəum] n dôme m

domestic [də'mɛstɪk] adj (duty, happiness) familial(e); (policy, affairs, flight) intérieur(e); (animal) domestique

dominant ['dɔmɪnənt] adj dominant(e)

dominate ['dɔmɪneɪt] vt dominer

domino ['dɔmɪnəu] (pl **dominoes**) n domino m; **dominoes** n (game) dominos mpl

donate [də'neɪt] vt faire don de, donner; **donation** [də'neɪʃən] n donation f, don m

done [dʌn] pp of **do**

donkey ['dɔŋkɪ] n âne m

donor ['dəunə'] n (of blood etc) donneur(-euse); (to charity) donateur(-trice); **donor card** n carte f de don d'organes

don't [dəunt] = **do not**

donut ['dəunʌt] (US) n = **doughnut**

doodle ['duːdl] vi griffonner, gribouiller

doom [duːm] n (fate) destin m ▷ vt: **to be ~ed to failure** être voué(e) à l'échec

door [dɔː'] n porte f; (Rail, car) portière f; **doorbell** n sonnette f; **door handle** n poignée f de porte; (of car) poignée de portière; **doorknob** n poignée for bouton m de porte; **doorstep** n pas m de (la) porte, seuil m; **doorway** n (embrasure f de) porte f

dope [dəup] n (inf: drug) drogue f; (: person) andouille f ▷ vt (horse etc) doper

dormitory ['dɔ:mɪtrɪ] n (BRIT) dortoir m; (US: hall of residence) résidence f universitaire

DOS [dɒs] n abbr (= disk operating system) DOS m

dosage ['dəʊsɪdʒ] n dose f; dosage m; (on label) posologie f

dose [dəʊs] n dose f

dot [dɒt] n point m; (on material) pois m ▷ vt: **~ted with** parsemé(e) de; **on the ~** à l'heure tapante; **dotcom** n point com m, pointcom m; **dotted line** ['dɒtɪd-] n ligne pointillée; **to sign on the dotted line** signer à l'endroit indiqué or sur la ligne pointillée

double ['dʌbl] adj double ▷ adv (twice): **to cost ~ (sth)** coûter le double (de qch) or deux fois plus (que qch) ▷ n double m; (Cine) doublure f ▷ vt doubler; (fold) plier en deux ▷ vi doubler; **on the ~, at the ~** au pas de course; **double back** vi (person) revenir sur ses pas; **double bass** n contrebasse f; **double bed** n grand lit; **double-check** vt, vi revérifier; **double-click** vi (Comput) double-cliquer; **double-cross** vt doubler, trahir; **double-decker** n autobus m à impériale; **double glazing** n (BRIT) double vitrage m; **double room** n chambre f pour deux; **doubles** n (Tennis) double m; **double yellow lines** npl (BRIT Aut) double bande jaune marquant l'interdiction de stationner

doubt [daʊt] n doute m ▷ vt douter de; **no ~** sans doute; **to ~ that** douter que + sub; **doubtful** adj douteux(-euse); (person) incertain(e); **doubtless** adv sans doute, sûrement

dough [dəʊ] n pâte f; **doughnut**, (US) **donut** n beignet m

dove [dʌv] n colombe f

Dover ['dəʊvər] n Douvres

down [daʊn] n (fluff) duvet m ▷ adv en bas, vers le bas; (on the ground) par terre ▷ prep en bas de; (along) le long de ▷ vt (inf: drink) siffler; **to walk ~**

a hill descendre une colline; **to run ~ the street** descendre la rue en courant; **~ with X!** à bas X!; **down-and-out** n (tramp) clochard(e); **downfall** n chute f; ruine f; **downhill** adv: **to go downhill** descendre; (business) péricliter

Downing Street ['daʊnɪŋ-] n (BRIT): **10 ~** résidence du Premier ministre

down: download vt (Comput) télécharger; **downloadable** adj (Comput) téléchargeable; **downright** adj (lie etc) effronté(e); (refusal) catégorique

Down's syndrome [daʊnz-] n trisomie f

down: downstairs adv (on or to ground floor) au rez-de-chaussée; (on or to floor below) à l'étage inférieur; **down-to-earth** adj terre à terre inv; **downtown** adv en ville; **down under** adv en Australie or Nouvelle Zélande; **downward** ['daʊnwəd] adj, adv vers le bas; **downwards** ['daʊnwədz] adv vers le bas

doz. abbr = **dozen**

doze [dəʊz] vi sommeiller

dozen ['dʌzn] n douzaine f; **a ~ books** une douzaine de livres; **~s of** des centaines de

Dr. abbr (= doctor) Dr; (in street names); = **drive**

drab [dræb] adj terne, morne

draft [drɑːft] n (of letter, school work) brouillon m; (of literary work) ébauche f; (Comm) traite f; (US Mil: call-up) conscription f ▷ vt faire le brouillon de; (Mil: send) détacher; see also **draught**

drag [dræg] vt traîner; (river) draguer ▷ vi traîner ▷ n (inf) casse-pieds m/f; (: women's clothing): **in ~** (en) travesti; **to ~ and drop** (Comput) glisser-poser

dragonfly ['drægənflaɪ] n libellule f

drain [dreɪn] n égout m; (on resources) saignée f ▷ vt (land, marshes) assécher; (vegetables) égoutter; (reservoir etc) vider ▷ vi (water) s'écouler; **drainage** n (system) système m d'égouts; (act) drainage m; **drainpipe** n tuyau m d'écoulement

drama ['drɑːmə] n (art) théâtre m, art m dramatique; (play) pièce f; (event) drame m; **dramatic** [drə'mætɪk] adj (Theat) dramatique; (impressive) spectaculaire

drank [dræŋk] pt of **drink**

drape [dreɪp] vt draper; **drapes** npl (US) rideaux mpl

drastic ['dræstɪk] adj (measures) d'urgence, énergique; (change) radical(e)

draught, (US) **draft** [drɑːft] n courant m d'air; **on ~** (beer) à la pression; **draught beer** n bière f (à la) pression; **draughts** n (BRIT: game) (jeu m de) dames fpl

draw [drɔː] (vb: pt **drew**, pp **drawn**) vt tirer; (picture) dessiner; (attract) attirer; (line, circle) tracer; (money) retirer; (wages) toucher ▷ vi (Sport) faire match nul ▷ n match nul; (lottery) loterie f; (picking of ticket) tirage m au sort; **draw out** vi (lengthen) s'allonger ▷ vt (money) retirer; **draw up** vi (stop) s'arrêter ▷ vt (document) établir, dresser; (plan) formuler, dessiner; (chair) approcher; **drawback** n inconvénient m, désavantage m

drawer [drɔː^r] n tiroir m

drawing ['drɔːɪŋ] n dessin m; **drawing pin** n (BRIT) punaise f; **drawing room** n salon m

drawn [drɔːn] pp of **draw**

dread [drɛd] n épouvante f, effroi m ▷ vt redouter, appréhender; **dreadful** adj épouvantable, affreux(-euse)

dream [driːm] n rêve m ▷ vt, vi (pt **dreamed**, pp **dreamt**) rêver; **dreamer** n rêveur(-euse)

dreamt [drɛmt] pt, pp of **dream**

dreary ['drɪərɪ] adj triste; monotone

drench [drɛntʃ] vt tremper

dress [drɛs] n robe f; (clothing) habillement m, tenue f ▷ vt habiller; (wound) panser ▷ vi: **to get ~ed** s'habiller; **dress up** vi s'habiller; (in fancy dress) se déguiser; **dress circle** n (BRIT) premier balcon; **dresser** n (furniture) vaisselier m (: US) coiffeuse f, commode f; **dressing** n (Med) pansement m; (Culin) sauce f, assaisonnement m; **dressing gown** n (BRIT) robe f de chambre; **dressing room** n (Theat) loge f; (Sport) vestiaire m; **dressing table** n coiffeuse f; **dressmaker** n couturière f

drew [druː] pt of **draw**

dribble ['drɪbl] vi (baby) baver ▷ vt (ball) dribbler

dried [draɪd] adj (fruit, beans) sec (sèche); (eggs, milk) en poudre

drier ['draɪə^r] n = **dryer**

drift [drɪft] n (of current etc) force f; direction f; (of snow) rafale f; coulée f (on ground) congère f; (general meaning) sens général ▷ vi (boat) aller à la dérive, dériver; (sand, snow) s'amonceler, s'entasser

drill [drɪl] n perceuse f; (bit) foret m; (of dentist) roulette f, fraise f; (Mil) exercice m ▷ vt percer; (troops) entraîner ▷ vi (for oil) faire un or des forage(s)

drink [drɪŋk] n boisson f; (alcoholic) verre m ▷ vt, vi (pt **drank**, pp **drunk**) boire; **to have a ~** boire quelque chose, boire un verre; **a ~ of water** un verre d'eau; **would you like a ~?** tu veux boire quelque chose?; **drink-driving** n conduite f en état d'ivresse;

drinker n buveur(-euse); **drinking water** n eau f potable

drip [drɪp] n (drop) goutte f; (Med: device) goutte-à-goutte m inv; (: liquid) perfusion f ▷ vi tomber goutte à goutte; (tap) goutter

drive [draɪv] (pt **drove**, pp **driven**) n promenade f or trajet m en voiture; (also: **~way**) allée f; (energy) dynamisme m, énergie f; (push) effort (concerté) campagne f; (Comput: also: **disk ~**) lecteur m de disquette ▷ vt conduire; (nail) enfoncer; (push) chasser, pousser; (Tech: motor) actionner; entraîner ▷ vi (be at the wheel) conduire; (travel by car) aller en voiture; **left-/right-hand ~** (Aut) conduite f à gauche/droite; **to ~ sb mad** rendre qn fou (folle); **drive out** vt (force out) chasser; **drive-in** adj, n (esp US) drive-in m

driven ['drɪvn] pp of **drive**

driver ['draɪvəʳ] n conducteur(-trice); (of taxi, bus) chauffeur m; **driver's license** n (US) permis m de conduire

driveway ['draɪvweɪ] n allée f

driving ['draɪvɪŋ] n conduite f; **driving instructor** n moniteur m d'auto-école; **driving lesson** n leçon f de conduite; **driving licence** n (BRIT) permis m de conduire; **driving test** n examen m du permis de conduire

drizzle ['drɪzl] n bruine f, crachin m

droop [druːp] vi (flower) commencer à se faner; (shoulders, head) tomber

drop [drɔp] n (of liquid) goutte f; (fall) baisse f; (also: **parachute ~**) saut m ▷ vt laisser tomber; (voice, eyes, price) baisser; (passenger) déposer ▷ vi tomber; **drop in** vi (inf: visit): **to ~ in (on)** faire un saut (chez), passer (chez); **drop off** vi (sleep) s'assoupir ▷ vt (passenger) déposer; **drop out** vi (withdraw) se retirer; (student etc) abandonner, décrocher

drought [draut] n sécheresse f

drove [drəuv] pt of **drive**

drown [draun] vt noyer ▷ vi se noyer

drowsy ['drauzɪ] adj somnolent(e)

drug [drʌg] n médicament m; (narcotic) drogue f ▷ vt droguer; **to be on ~s** se droguer; **drug addict** n toxicomane m/f; **drug dealer** n revendeur(-euse) de drogue; **druggist** n (US) pharmacien(ne)-droguiste; **drugstore** n (US) pharmacie-droguerie f, drugstore m

drum [drʌm] n tambour m; (for oil, petrol) bidon m; **drums** npl (Mus) batterie f; **drummer** n (joueur m de) tambour m

drunk [drʌŋk] pp of **drink** ▷ adj ivre, soûl(e) ▷ n (also: **~ard**) ivrogne m/f; **to get ~** se soûler; **drunken** adj ivre, soûl(e); (rage, stupor) ivrogne, d'ivrogne

dry [draɪ] adj sec (sèche); (day) sans pluie ▷ vt sécher; (clothes) faire sécher ▷ vi sécher; **dry off** vi, vt sécher; **dry up** vi (river, supplies) se tarir; **dry-cleaner's** n teinturerie f; **dry-cleaning** n (process) nettoyage m à sec; **dryer** n (tumble-dryer) sèche-linge m inv; (for hair) sèche-cheveux m inv

DSS n abbr (BRIT) = **Department of Social Security**

DTP n abbr (= desktop publishing) PAO f

dual ['djuəl] adj double; **dual carriageway** n (BRIT) route f à quatre voies

dubious ['djuːbɪəs] adj hésitant(e), incertain(e); (reputation, company) douteux(-euse)

duck [dʌk] n canard m ▷ vi se baisser vivement, baisser subitement la tête

due [djuː] adj (money, payment) dû (due); (expected) attendu(e); (fitting) qui convient ▷ adv: **~ north** droit vers le nord; **~ to** (because of) en raison de; (caused by) dû à; **the train is ~ at 8 a.m.** le train est attendu à 8 h; **she is ~ back tomorrow** elle doit rentrer demain; **he is ~ £10** on lui doit 10 livres; **to give sb his or her ~** être juste envers qn

duel ['djuəl] n duel m

duet [dju:'et] n duo m

dug [dʌg] pt, pp of **dig**

duke [dju:k] n duc m

dull [dʌl] adj (boring) ennuyeux(-euse); (not bright) morne, terne; (sound, pain) sourd(e); (weather, day) gris(e), maussade ▷ vt (pain, grief) atténuer; (mind, senses) engourdir

dumb [dʌm] adj muet(te); (stupid) bête

dummy ['dʌmɪ] n (tailor's model) mannequin m; (mock-up) factice m, maquette f; (BRIT: for baby) tétine f ▷ adj faux (fausse), factice

dump [dʌmp] n (also: **rubbish ~**) décharge (publique); (inf: place) trou m ▷ vt (put down) déposer; déverser; (get rid of) se débarrasser de; (Comput) lister

dumpling ['dʌmplɪŋ] n boulette f (de pâte)

dune [dju:n] n dune f

dungarees [dʌŋgə'ri:z] npl bleu(s) m(pl); (for child, woman) salopette f

dungeon ['dʌndʒən] n cachot m

duplex ['dju:pleks] n (US: also: **~ apartment**) duplex m

duplicate n ['dju:plɪkət] double m ▷ vt ['dju:plɪkeɪt] faire un double de; (on machine) polycopier; **in ~** en deux exemplaires, en double

durable ['djuərəbl] adj durable; (clothes, metal) résistant(e), solide

duration [djuə'reɪʃən] n durée f

during ['djuərɪŋ] prep pendant, au cours de

dusk [dʌsk] n crépuscule m

dust [dʌst] n poussière f ▷ vt (furniture) essuyer, épousseter; (cake etc): **to ~ with** saupoudrer de; **dustbin** n (BRIT) poubelle f; **duster** n chiffon m; **dustman** (irreg) n (BRIT) boueux m, éboueur m; **dustpan** n pelle f à poussière; **dusty** adj poussiéreux(-euse)

Dutch [dʌtʃ] adj hollandais(e), néerlandais(e) ▷ n (Ling) hollandais m, néerlandais m ▷ adv: **to go ~** or **dutch** (inf) partager les frais; **the Dutch** npl les Hollandais, les Néerlandais; **Dutchman** (irreg) n Hollandais m; **Dutchwoman** (irreg) n Hollandaise f

duty ['dju:tɪ] n devoir m; (tax) droit m, taxe f; **on ~** de service; (at night etc) de garde; **off ~** libre, pas de service or de garde; **duty-free** adj exempté(e) de douane, hors-taxe

duvet ['du:veɪ] n (BRIT) couette f

DVD n abbr (= digital versatile or video disc) DVD m; **DVD burner** n graveur m de DVD; **DVD player** n lecteur m de DVD; **DVD writer** n graveur m de DVD

dwarf (pl **dwarves**) [dwɔ:f, dwɔ:vz] n (offensive) nain(e) ▷ vt écraser

dwell (pt, pp **dwelt**) [dwel, dwelt] vi demeurer; **dwell on** vt fus s'étendre sur

dwelt [dwelt] pt, pp of **dwell**

dwindle ['dwɪndl] vi diminuer, décroître

dye [daɪ] n teinture f ▷ vt teindre

dying ['daɪɪŋ] adj mourant(e), agonisant(e)

dynamic [daɪ'næmɪk] adj dynamique

dynamite ['daɪnəmaɪt] n dynamite f

dyslexia [dɪs'leksɪə] n dyslexie f

dyslexic [dɪs'leksɪk] adj, n dyslexique m/f

ancien(ne), antérieur(e) ▷ adv
plus tôt

early [ˈəːlɪ] adv tôt, de bonne heure;
(ahead of time) en avance; (near the
beginning) au début ▷ adj précoce,
qui se manifeste (or se fait) tôt or de
bonne heure; (Christians, settlers)
premier(-ière); (reply) rapide; (death)
prématuré(e); (work) de jeunesse; **to
have an ~ night/start** se coucher/
partir tôt or de bonne heure; **in the
~** or **~ in the spring/19th century**
au début or commencement du
printemps/19ème siècle; **early
retirement** n retraite anticipée

earmark [ˈɪəmɑːk] vt: **to ~ sth for**
réserver or destiner qch à

earn [əːn] vt gagner; (Comm: yield)
rapporter; **to ~ one's living** gagner
sa vie

earnest [ˈəːnɪst] adj sérieux(-euse)
▷ n: **in ~** adv sérieusement, pour
de bon

earnings [ˈəːnɪŋz] npl salaire m;
gains mpl; (of company etc) profits mpl,
bénéfices mpl

ear: earphones npl écouteurs mpl;
earplugs npl boules fpl Quiès®; (to
keep out water) protège-tympans mpl;
earring n boucle f d'oreille

earth [əːθ] n (gen, also BRIT Elec)
terre f ▷ vt (BRIT Elec) relier à la terre;
earthquake n tremblement m de
terre, séisme m

ease [iːz] n facilité f, aisance f;
(comfort) bien-être m ▷ vt (soothe:
mind) tranquilliser; (reduce: pain,
problem) atténuer; (: tension) réduire;
(loosen) relâcher, détendre; (help pass):
to ~ sth in/out faire pénétrer/sortir
qch délicatement or avec douceur,
faciliter la pénétration/la sortie de
qch; **at ~** à l'aise; (Mil) au repos

easily [ˈiːzɪlɪ] adv facilement; (by
far) de loin

east [iːst] n est m ▷ adj (wind) d'est;
(side) est inv ▷ adv à l'est, vers l'est;
the E~ l'Orient m; (Pol) les pays mpl de

E [iː] n (Mus) mi m

each [iːtʃ] adj chaque ▷ pron
chacun(e); **~ other** l'un l'autre;
they hate ~ other ils se détestent
(mutuellement); **they have 2
books ~** ils ont 2 livres chacun;
they cost £5 ~ ils coûtent 5 livres
(la) pièce

eager [ˈiːgəʳ] adj (person, buyer)
empressé(e); (keen: pupil, worker)
enthousiaste; **to be ~ to do sth**
(impatient) brûler de faire qch; (keen)
désirer vivement faire qch; **to be
~ for** (event) désirer vivement;
(vengeance, affection, information) être
avide de

eagle [ˈiːgl] n aigle m

ear [ɪəʳ] n oreille f; (of corn) épi m;
earache n mal m aux oreilles;
eardrum n tympan m

earl [əːl] n comte m

earlier [ˈəːlɪəʳ] adj (date etc) plus
rapproché(e); (edition etc) plus

l'Est; **eastbound** adj en direction de l'est; (carriageway) est inv

Easter ['iːstər] n Pâques fpl; **Easter egg** n œuf m de Pâques

eastern ['iːstən] adj de l'est, oriental(e)

Easter Sunday n le dimanche de Pâques

easy ['iːzɪ] adj facile; (manner) aisé(e) ▷ adv: **to take it** or **things ~** (rest) ne pas se fatiguer; (not worry) ne pas (trop) s'en faire; **easy-going** adj accommodant(e), facile à vivre

eat (pt **ate**, pp **eaten**) [iːt, eɪt, 'iːtn] vt, vi manger; **can we have something to ~?** est-ce qu'on peut manger quelque chose?; **eat out** vi manger au restaurant

eaten ['iːtn] pp of **eat**

eavesdrop ['iːvzdrɒp] vi: **to ~ (on)** écouter de façon indiscrète

e-book ['iːbuk] n livre m électronique

e-business ['iːbɪznɪs] n (company) entreprise f électronique; (commerce) commerce m électronique

eccentric [ɪk'sɛntrɪk] adj, n excentrique m/f

echo ['ɛkəu] (pl **echoes**) n écho m ▷ vt répéter ▷ vi résonner; faire écho

eclipse [ɪ'klɪps] n éclipse f

eco-friendly [iːkəu'frɛndlɪ] adj non nuisible à or qui ne nuit pas à l'environnement

ecological [iːkə'lɒdʒɪkəl] adj écologique

ecology [ɪ'kɒlədʒɪ] n écologie f

e-commerce [iːkɒməːs] n commerce m électronique

economic [iːkə'nɒmɪk] adj économique; (profitable) rentable; **economical** adj économique; (person) économe; **economics** n (Scol) économie f politique ▷ npl (of project etc) côté m or aspect m économique

economist [ɪ'kɒnəmɪst] n économiste m/f

economize [ɪ'kɒnəmaɪz] vi économiser, faire des économies

economy [ɪ'kɒnəmɪ] n économie f; **economy class** n (Aviat) classe f touriste; **economy class syndrome** n syndrome m de la classe économique

ecstasy ['ɛkstəsɪ] n extase f; (Drugs) ecstasy m; **ecstatic** [ɛks'tætɪk] adj extatique, en extase

eczema ['ɛksɪmə] n eczéma m

edge [ɛdʒ] n bord m; (of knife etc) tranchant m, fil m ▷ vt border; **on ~** (fig) crispé(e), tendu(e)

edgy ['ɛdʒɪ] adj crispé(e), tendu(e)

edible ['ɛdɪbl] adj comestible; (meal) mangeable

Edinburgh ['ɛdɪnbərə] n Édimbourg; voir article **"Edinburgh Festival"**

EDINBURGH FESTIVAL

Le Festival d'Édimbourg, qui se tient chaque année durant trois semaines au mois d'août, est l'un des grands festivals européens. Il est réputé pour son programme officiel mais aussi pour son festival "off" (the Fringe) qui propose des spectacles aussi bien traditionnels que résolument d'avant-garde. Pendant la durée du Festival se tient par ailleurs, sur l'esplanade du château, un grand spectacle de musique militaire, le "Military Tattoo".

---

edit ['ɛdɪt] vt (text, book) éditer; (report) préparer; (film) monter; (magazine) diriger; (newspaper) être le rédacteur or la rédactrice en chef de; **edition** [ɪ'dɪʃən] n édition f; **editor** n (of newspaper) rédacteur(-trice), rédacteur(-trice) en chef; (of sb's work) éditeur(-trice); (also): **film editor** monteur(-euse); **political/foreign editor** rédacteur politique/au service étranger; **editorial** [ɛdɪ'tɔːrɪəl] adj de la rédaction, éditorial(e) ▷ n éditorial m

educate ['ɛdjukeɪt] vt (teach) instruire; (bring up) éduquer; **educated** ['ɛdjukeɪtɪd] adj (person) cultivé(e)

education [ɛdju'keɪʃən] n éducation f; (studies) études fpl; (teaching) enseignement m, instruction f; **educational** adj pédagogique; (institution) scolaire; (game, toy) éducatif(-ive)

eel [iːl] n anguille f

eerie ['ɪərɪ] adj inquiétant(e), spectral(e), surnaturel(le)

effect [ɪ'fɛkt] n effet m ▷ vt effectuer; **effects** npl (property) effets, affaires fpl; **to take ~** (Law) entrer en vigueur, prendre effet; (drug) agir, faire son effet; **in ~** en fait; **effective** adj efficace; (actual) véritable; **effectively** adv efficacement; (in reality) effectivement, en fait

efficiency [ɪ'fɪʃənsɪ] n efficacité f; (of machine, car) rendement m

efficient [ɪ'fɪʃənt] adj efficace; (machine, car) d'un bon rendement; **efficiently** adv efficacement

effort ['ɛfət] n effort m; **effortless** adj sans effort, aisé(e); (achievement) facile

e.g. adv abbr (= exempli gratia) par exemple, p. ex.

egg [ɛg] n œuf m; **hard-boiled/soft-boiled ~** œuf dur/à la coque; **eggcup** n coquetier m; **egg plant** (US) n aubergine f; **eggshell** n coquille f d'œuf; **egg white** n blanc m d'œuf; **egg yolk** n jaune m d'œuf

ego ['iːgəu] n (self-esteem) amour-propre m; (Psych) moi m

Egypt ['iːdʒɪpt] n Égypte f; **Egyptian** [ɪ'dʒɪpʃən] adj égyptien(ne) ▷ n Égyptien(ne)

Eiffel Tower ['aɪfəl-] n tour f Eiffel

eight [eɪt] num huit; **eighteen** num dix-huit; **eighteenth** num dix-huitième; **eighth** num huitième; **eightieth** ['eɪtɪɪθ] num quatre-vingtième

eighty ['eɪtɪ] num quatre-vingt(s)

Eire ['ɛərə] n République f d'Irlande

either ['aɪðər] adj l'un ou l'autre; (both, each) chaque ▷ pron: **~ (of them)** l'un ou l'autre ▷ adv non plus ▷ conj: **~ good or bad** soit bon soit mauvais; **on ~ side** de chaque côté; **I don't like ~** je n'aime ni l'un ni l'autre; **no, I don't ~** moi non plus; **which bike do you want? — ~ will do** quel vélo voulez-vous? — n'importe lequel; **answer with ~ yes or no** répondez par oui ou par non

eject [ɪ'dʒɛkt] vt (tenant etc) expulser; (object) éjecter

elaborate adj [ɪ'læbərɪt] compliqué(e), recherché(e), minutieux(-euse) ▷ vt [ɪ'læbəreɪt] élaborer ▷ vi entrer dans les détails

elastic [ɪ'læstɪk] adj, n élastique (m); **elastic band** n (BRIT) élastique m

elbow ['ɛlbəu] n coude m

elder ['ɛldər] adj aîné(e) ▷ n (tree) sureau m; **one's ~s** ses aînés; **elderly** adj âgé(e) ▷ npl; **the elderly** les personnes âgées

eldest ['ɛldɪst] adj, n: **the ~ (child)** l'aîné(e) (des enfants)

elect [ɪ'lɛkt] vt élire; (choose): **to ~ to do** choisir de faire ▷ adj: **the president ~** le président désigné; **election** n élection f; **electoral** adj électoral(e); **electorate** n électorat m

electric [ɪ'lɛktrɪk] adj électrique; **electrical** adj électrique; **electric blanket** n couverture chauffante; **electric fire** n (BRIT) radiateur m électrique; **electrician** [ɪlɛk'trɪʃən] n électricien m; **electricity** [ɪlɛk'trɪsɪtɪ] n électricité f; **electric shock** n choc m or décharge f électrique; **electrify** [ɪ'lɛktrɪfaɪ] vt (Rail) électrifier; (audience) électriser

electronic [ɪlɛk'trɔnɪk] adj électronique; **electronic mail** n courrier m électronique; **electronics** n électronique f

elegance ['ɛlɪgəns] n élégance f

elegant ['ɛlɪgənt] *adj* élégant(e)

element ['ɛlɪmənt] *n (gen)* élément *m; (of heater, kettle etc)* résistance *f*

elementary [ɛlɪ'mɛntərɪ] *adj* élémentaire; *(school, education)* primaire; **elementary school** *n (us)* école *f* primaire

elephant ['ɛlɪfənt] *n* éléphant *m*

elevate ['ɛlɪveɪt] *vt* élever

elevator ['ɛlɪveɪtər] *n (in warehouse etc)* élévateur *m*, monte-charge *m inv; (us: lift)* ascenseur *m*

eleven [ɪ'lɛvn] *num* onze; **eleventh** *num* onzième

eligible ['ɛlɪdʒəbl] *adj* éligible; *(for membership)* admissible; **an ~ young man** un beau parti; **to be ~ for sth** remplir les conditions requises pour qch

eliminate [ɪ'lɪmɪneɪt] *vt* éliminer

elm [ɛlm] *n* orme *m*

eloquent ['ɛləkwənt] *adj* éloquent(e)

else [ɛls] *adv:* **something ~** quelque chose d'autre, autre chose; **somewhere ~** ailleurs, autre part; **everywhere ~** partout ailleurs; **everyone ~** tous les autres; **nothing ~** rien d'autre; **where ~?** à quel autre endroit?; **little ~** pas grand-chose d'autre; **elsewhere** *adv* ailleurs, autre part

elusive [ɪ'lu:sɪv] *adj* insaisissable

email ['i:meɪl] *n abbr (= electronic mail)* (e-)mail *m*, courriel *m* ▷ *vt:* **to ~ sb** envoyer un (e-)mail or un courriel à qn; **email account** *n* compte *m* (e-)mail; **email address** *n* adresse *f* (e-)mail or électronique

embankment [ɪm'bæŋkmənt] *n (of road, railway)* remblai *m*, talus *m; (of river)* berge *f*, quai *m; (dyke)* digue *f*

embargo [ɪm'bɑ:gəu] *(pl* **embargoes**) *n (Comm, Naut)* embargo *m; (prohibition)* interdiction *f*

embark [ɪm'bɑ:k] *vi* embarquer ▷ *vt* s'embarquer; **to ~ on** *(journey etc)* commencer, entreprendre; *(fig)* se lancer or s'embarquer dans

embarrass [ɪm'bærəs] *vt* embarrasser, gêner; **embarrassed** *adj* gêné(e); **embarrassing** *adj* gênant(e), embarrassant(e); **embarrassment** *n* embarras *m*, gêne *f; (embarrassing thing, person)* source *f* d'embarras

embassy ['ɛmbəsɪ] *n* ambassade *f*

embrace [ɪm'breɪs] *vt* embrasser, étreindre; *(include)* embrasser ▷ *vi* s'embrasser, s'étreindre ▷ *n* étreinte *f*

embroider [ɪm'brɔɪdər] *vt* broder; **embroidery** *n* broderie *f*

embryo ['ɛmbrɪəu] *n (also fig)* embryon *m*

emerald ['ɛmərəld] *n* émeraude *f*

emerge [ɪ'mə:dʒ] *vi* apparaître; *(from room, car)* surgir; *(from sleep, imprisonment)* sortir

emergency [ɪ'mə:dʒənsɪ] *n (crisis)* cas *m* d'urgence; *(Med)* urgence *f;* **in an ~** en cas d'urgence; **state of ~** état *m* d'urgence; **emergency brake** *(us)* *n* frein *m* à main; **emergency exit** *n* sortie *f* de secours; **emergency landing** *n* atterrissage forcé; **emergency room** *n (us Med)* urgences *fpl;* **emergency services** *npl:* **the emergency services** *(fire, police, ambulance)* les services *mpl* d'urgence

emigrate ['ɛmɪgreɪt] *vi* émigrer; **emigration** [ɛmɪ'greɪʃən] *n* émigration *f*

eminent ['ɛmɪnənt] *adj* éminent(e)

emissions [ɪ'mɪʃənz] *npl* émissions *fpl*

emit [ɪ'mɪt] *vt* émettre

emoticon [ɪ'məutɪkɔn] *n (Comput)* émoticone *m*

emotion [ɪ'məuʃən] *n* sentiment *m;* **emotional** *adj (person)* émotif(-ive), très sensible; *(needs)* affectif(-ive); *(scene)* émouvant(e); *(tone, speech)* qui fait appel aux sentiments

emperor ['ɛmpərər] *n* empereur *m*

emphasis *(pl* **emphases**) ['ɛmfəsɪs, -si:z] *n* accent *m;* **to lay** or **place**

~ on sth (*fig*) mettre l'accent sur, insister sur

emphasize ['emfəsaɪz] *vt* (*syllable, word, point*) appuyer *or* insister sur; (*feature*) souligner, accentuer

empire ['empaɪə[r]] *n* empire *m*

employ [ɪm'plɔɪ] *vt* employer; **employee** [ɪmplɔɪ'iː] *n* employé(e); **employer** *n* employeur(-euse); **employment** *n* emploi *m*; **employment agency** *n* agence for bureau *m* de placement

empower [ɪm'pauə[r]] *vt*: **to ~ sb to do** autoriser *or* habiliter qn à faire

empress ['empris] *n* impératrice *f*

emptiness ['emptɪnɪs] *n* vide *m*; (*of area*) aspect *m* désertique

empty ['emptɪ] *adj* vide; (*street, area*) désert(e); (*threat, promise*) en l'air, vain(e) ▷ *vt* vider ▷ *vi* se vider; (*liquid*) s'écouler; **empty-handed** *adj* les mains vides

EMU *n abbr* (= *European Monetary Union*) UME *f*

emulsion [ɪ'mʌlʃən] *n* émulsion *f*; (*also*: **~ paint**) peinture mate

enable [ɪ'neɪbl] *vt*: **to ~ sb to do** permettre à qn de faire

enamel [ɪ'næməl] *n* émail *m*; (*also*: **~ paint**) (peinture *f*) laque *f*

enchanting [ɪn'tʃɑːntɪŋ] *adj* ravissant(e), enchanteur(-eresse)

encl. *abbr* (*on letters etc* = *enclosed*) ci-joint(e); (: = *enclosure*) PJ *f*

enclose [ɪn'kləuz] *vt* (*land*) clôturer; (*space, object*) entourer; (*letter etc*) **to ~ (with)** joindre (à); **please find ~d** veuillez trouver ci-joint

enclosure [ɪn'kləuʒə[r]] *n* enceinte *f*

encore [ɔŋ'kɔː[r]] *excl, n* bis (*m*)

encounter [ɪn'kauntə[r]] *n* rencontre *f* ▷ *vt* rencontrer

encourage [ɪn'kʌrɪdʒ] *vt* encourager

encouraging [ɪn'kʌrɪdʒɪŋ] *adj* encourageant(e)

encyclop(a)edia [ensaɪkləu'piːdɪə] *n* encyclopédie *f*

end [end] *n* fin *f*; (*of table, street, rope etc*) bout *m*, extrémité *f* ▷ *vt* terminer; (*also*: **bring to an ~, put an ~ to**) mettre fin à ▷ *vi* se terminer, finir; **in the ~** finalement; **on ~** (*object*) debout, dressé(e); **to stand on ~** (*hair*) se dresser sur la tête; **for hours on ~** pendant des heures (et des heures); **end up** *vi*: **to ~ up in** (*condition*) finir *or* se terminer par; (*place*) finir *or* aboutir à

endanger [ɪn'deɪndʒə[r]] *vt* mettre en danger; **an ~ed species** une espèce en voie de disparition

endearing [ɪn'dɪərɪŋ] *adj* attachant(e)

endeavour (*US*) **endeavor** [ɪn'dɛvə[r]] *n* effort *m*; (*attempt*) tentative *f* ▷ *vt*: **to ~ to do** tenter *or* s'efforcer de faire

ending ['endɪŋ] *n* dénouement *m*, conclusion *f*; (*Ling*) terminaison *f*

endless ['endlɪs] *adj* sans fin, interminable

endorse [ɪn'dɔːs] *vt* (*cheque*) endosser; (*approve*) appuyer, approuver, sanctionner; **endorsement** *n* (*approval*) appui *m*, aval *m*; (BRIT: *on driving licence*) contravention *f* (*portée au permis de conduire*)

endurance [ɪn'djuərəns] *n* endurance *f*

endure [ɪn'djuə[r]] *vt* (*bear*) supporter, endurer ▷ *vi* (*last*) durer

enemy ['enəmɪ] *adj, n* ennemi(e)

energetic [enə'dʒetɪk] *adj* énergique; (*activity*) très actif(-ive), qui fait se dépenser (physiquement)

energy ['enədʒɪ] *n* énergie *f*

enforce [ɪn'fɔːs] *vt* (*law*) appliquer, faire respecter

engaged [ɪn'geɪdʒd] *adj* (BRIT: *busy, in use*) occupé(e); (*betrothed*) fiancé(e); **to get ~** se fiancer; **the line's ~** la ligne est occupée; **engaged tone** *n* (BRIT *Tel*) tonalité *f* occupé *inv*

engagement [ɪnˈgeɪdʒmənt]
n (*undertaking*) obligation *f*,
engagement *m*; (*appointment*) rendez-
vous *m inv*; (*to marry*) fiançailles *fpl*;
engagement ring *n* bague *f* de
fiançailles

engaging [ɪnˈgeɪdʒɪŋ] *adj*
engageant(e), attirant(e)

engine [ˈɛndʒɪn] *n* (*Aut*) moteur *m*;
(*Rail*) locomotive *f*

▮ Be careful not to translate *engine*
by the French word *engin*.

engineer [ɛndʒɪˈnɪər] *n* ingénieur *m*;
(*Brit: repairer*) dépanneur *m*; (*Navy,
US Rail*) mécanicien *m*; **engineering**
n engineering *m*, ingénierie *f*; (*of
bridges, ships*) génie *m*; (*of machine*)
mécanique *f*

England [ˈɪŋglənd] *n* Angleterre *f*

English [ˈɪŋglɪʃ] *adj* anglais(e) ▷ *n*
(*Ling*) anglais *m*; **the ~** *npl* les Anglais;
English Channel *n*: **the English
Channel** la Manche; **Englishman**
(*irreg*) *n* Anglais *m*; **Englishwoman**
(*irreg*) *n* Anglaise *f*

engrave [ɪnˈgreɪv] *vt* graver

engraving [ɪnˈgreɪvɪŋ] *n* gravure *f*

enhance [ɪnˈhɑːns] *vt* rehausser,
mettre en valeur

enjoy [ɪnˈdʒɔɪ] *vt* aimer, prendre
plaisir à; (*have benefit of: health,
fortune*) jouir de; (*: success*) connaître;
to ~ o.s. s'amuser; **enjoyable** *adj*
agréable; **enjoyment** *n* plaisir *m*

enlarge [ɪnˈlɑːdʒ] *vt* accroître,
(*Phot*) agrandir ▷ *vi*: **to ~ on** (*subject*)
s'étendre sur; **enlargement** *n* (*Phot*)
agrandissement *m*

enlist [ɪnˈlɪst] *vt* recruter; (*support*)
s'assurer ▷ *vi* s'engager

enormous [ɪˈnɔːməs] *adj* énorme

enough [ɪˈnʌf] *adj*: **~ time/
books** assez or suffisamment de
temps/livres ▷ *adv*: **big ~** assez or
suffisamment grand ▷ *pron*: **have
you got ~?** (en) avez-vous assez?;
~ to eat assez à manger; **that's
~, thanks** cela suffit or c'est assez,

merci; **I've had ~ of him** j'en ai
assez de lui; **he has not worked
~** il n'a pas assez or suffisamment
travaillé, il n'a pas travaillé assez or
suffisamment; **... which, funnily** or
oddly or **strangely ~ ...** qui, chose
curieuse, ...

enquire [ɪnˈkwaɪər] *vt, vi* = **inquire**

enquiry [ɪnˈkwaɪərɪ] *n* = **inquiry**

enrage [ɪnˈreɪdʒ] *vt* mettre en fureur
or en rage, rendre furieux(-euse)

enrich [ɪnˈrɪtʃ] *vt* enrichir

enrol, (*US*) **enroll** [ɪnˈrəʊl] *vt* inscrire
▷ *vi* s'inscrire; **enrolment**, (*US*)
enrollment *n* inscription *f*

en route [ɔnˈruːt] *adv* en route, en
chemin

en suite [ˈɔnswiːt] *adj*: **with ~
bathroom** avec salle de bains en
attenante

ensure [ɪnˈʃʊər] *vt* assurer, garantir

entail [ɪnˈteɪl] *vt* entraîner, nécessiter

enter [ˈɛntər] *vt* (*room*) entrer dans,
pénétrer dans; (*club, army*) entrer à;
(*competition*) s'inscrire à or pour; (*sb
for a competition*) (faire) inscrire; (*write
down*) inscrire, noter; (*Comput*) entrer,
introduire ▷ *vi* entrer

enterprise [ˈɛntəpraɪz] *n*
(*company, undertaking*) entreprise
f; (*initiative*) (esprit *m* d')initiative
f; **free ~** libre entreprise; **private
~** entreprise privée; **enterprising**
adj entreprenant(e), dynamique;
(*scheme*) audacieux(-euse)

entertain [ɛntəˈteɪn] *vt* amuser,
distraire; (*invite*) recevoir (à dîner);
(*idea, plan*) envisager; **entertainer** *n*
artiste *m/f* de variétés; **entertaining**
adj amusant(e), distrayant(e);
entertainment *n* (*amusement*)
distraction *f*, divertissement *m*,
amusement *m*; (*show*) spectacle *m*

enthusiasm [ɪnˈθuːzɪæzəm] *n*
enthousiasme *m*

enthusiast [ɪnˈθuːzɪæst] *n*
enthousiaste *m/f*; **enthusiastic**
[ɪnθuːzɪˈæstɪk] *adj* enthousiaste;

to be enthusiastic about être enthousiasmé(e) par

entire [ɪnˈtaɪəʳ] adj (tout) entier(-ère); **entirely** adv entièrement, complètement

entitle [ɪnˈtaɪtl] vt: **to ~ sb to sth** donner droit à qch à qn; **entitled** adj (book) intitulé(e); **to be entitled to do** avoir le droit de faire

entrance n [ˈɛntrns] entrée f ▷ vt [ɪnˈtrɑːns] enchanter, ravir; **where's the ~?** où est l'entrée?; **to gain ~ to** (university etc) être admis à; **entrance examination** n examen m d'entrée or d'admission; **entrance fee** n (to museum etc) prix m d'entrée; (to join club etc) droit m d'inscription; **entrance ramp** n (us Aut) bretelle f d'accès; **entrant** n (in race etc) participant(e), concurrent(e); (BRIT: in exam) candidat(e)

entrepreneur [ˈɔntrəprəˈnəːʳ] n entrepreneur m

entrust [ɪnˈtrʌst] vt: **to ~ sth to** confier qch à

entry [ˈɛntrɪ] n entrée f; (in register, diary) inscription f; **"no ~"** "défense d'entrer", "entrée interdite"; (Aut) "sens interdit"; **entry phone** n (BRIT) interphone m (à l'entrée d'un immeuble)

envelope [ˈɛnvələup] n enveloppe f

envious [ˈɛnvɪəs] adj envieux(-euse)

environment [ɪnˈvaɪərnmənt] n (social, moral) milieu m; (natural world): **the ~** l'environnement m; **environmental** [ɪnvaɪərnˈmɛntl] adj (of surroundings) du milieu; (issue, disaster) écologique; **environmentally** [ɪnvaɪərnˈmɛntlɪ] adv: **environmentally sound/ friendly** qui ne nuit pas à l'environnement

envisage [ɪnˈvɪzɪdʒ] vt (foresee) prévoir

envoy [ˈɛnvɔɪ] n envoyé(e); (diplomat) ministre m plénipotentiaire

envy [ˈɛnvɪ] n envie f ▷ vt envier; **to ~ sb sth** envier qch à qn

epic [ˈɛpɪk] n épopée f ▷ adj épique

epidemic [ɛpɪˈdɛmɪk] n épidémie f

epilepsy [ˈɛpɪlɛpsɪ] n épilepsie f; **epileptic** adj, n épileptique m/f; **epileptic fit** n crise f d'épilepsie

episode [ˈɛpɪsəud] n épisode m

equal [ˈiːkwl] adj égal(e) ▷ vt égaler; **~ to** (task) à la hauteur de; **equality** [iːˈkwɔlɪtɪ] n égalité f; **equalize** vt, vi (Sport) égaliser; **equally** adv également; (share) en parts égales; (treat) de la même façon; (pay) autant; (just as) tout aussi

equation [ɪˈkweɪʃən] n (Math) équation f

equator [ɪˈkweɪtəʳ] n équateur m

equip [ɪˈkwɪp] vt équiper; **to ~ sb/ sth with** équiper or munir qn/ qch de; **equipment** n équipement m; (electrical etc) appareillage m, installation f

equivalent [ɪˈkwɪvəlnt] adj équivalent(e) ▷ n équivalent m; **to be ~ to** équivaloir à, être équivalent(e) à

ER abbr (BRIT: = Elizabeth Regina) la reine Élisabeth; (us Med: = emergency room) urgences fpl

era [ˈɪərə] n ère f, époque f

erase [ɪˈreɪz] vt effacer; **eraser** n gomme f

erect [ɪˈrɛkt] adj droit(e) ▷ vt construire; (monument) ériger, élever; (tent etc) dresser; **erection** [ɪˈrɛkʃən] n (Physiol) érection f; (of building) construction f

ERM n abbr (= Exchange Rate Mechanism) mécanisme m des taux de change

erode [ɪˈrəud] vt éroder; (metal) ronger

erosion [ɪˈrəuʒən] n érosion f

erotic [ɪˈrɔtɪk] adj érotique

errand [ˈɛrnd] n course f, commission f

erratic [ɪˈrætɪk] adj irrégulier(-ière), inconstant(e)

error [ˈɛrəʳ] n erreur f

erupt [ɪˈrʌpt] vi entrer en éruption; (fig) éclater; **eruption** [ɪˈrʌpʃən] n éruption f; (of anger, violence) explosion f

escalate [ˈɛskəleɪt] vi s'intensifier; (costs) monter en flèche

escalator [ˈɛskəleɪtər] n escalier roulant

escape [ɪˈskeɪp] n évasion f, fuite f; (of gas etc) fuite ▷ vi s'échapper, fuir; (from jail) s'évader; (fig) s'en tirer; (leak) s'échapper ▷ vt échapper à; **to ~ from** (person) échapper à; (place) s'échapper de; (fig) fuir; **his name ~s me** son nom m'échappe

escort vt [ɪˈskɔːt] escorter ▷ n [ˈɛskɔːt] (Mil) escorte f

especially [ɪˈspɛʃlɪ] adv (particularly) particulièrement; (above all) surtout

espionage [ˈɛspɪənɑːʒ] n espionnage m

essay [ˈɛseɪ] n (Scol) dissertation f; (Literature) essai m

essence [ˈɛsns] n essence f; (Culin) extrait m

essential [ɪˈsɛnʃl] adj essentiel(le); (basic) fondamental(e); **essentials** npl éléments essentiels; **essentially** adv essentiellement

establish [ɪˈstæblɪʃ] vt établir; (business) fonder, créer; (one's power etc) asseoir, affermir; **establishment** n établissement m; (founding) création f; (institution) établissement; **the Establishment** les pouvoirs établis; l'ordre établi

estate [ɪˈsteɪt] n (land) domaine m, propriété f; (Law) biens mpl, succession f; (BRIT: also: **housing ~**) lotissement m; **estate agent** n (BRIT) agent immobilier; **estate car** n (BRIT) break m

estimate n [ˈɛstɪmət] estimation f; (Comm) devis m ▷ vt [ˈɛstɪmeɪt] estimer

etc abbr (= et cetera) etc

eternal [ɪˈtəːnl] adj éternel(le)

eternity [ɪˈtəːnɪtɪ] n éternité f

ethical [ˈɛθɪkl] adj moral(e); **ethics** [ˈɛθɪks] n éthique f ▷ npl moralité f

Ethiopia [iːθɪˈəupɪə] n Éthiopie f

ethnic [ˈɛθnɪk] adj ethnique; (clothes, food) folklorique, exotique, propre aux minorités ethniques non-occidentales; **ethnic minority** n minorité f ethnique

e-ticket [ˈiːtɪkɪt] n billet m électronique

etiquette [ˈɛtɪkɛt] n convenances fpl, étiquette f

EU n abbr (= European Union) UE f

euro [ˈjuərəu] n (currency) euro m

Europe [ˈjuərəp] n Europe f; **European** [juərəˈpiːən] adj européen(ne) ▷ n Européen(ne); **European Community** n Communauté européenne; **European Union** n Union européenne

Eurostar® [ˈjuərəustɑːr] n Eurostar® m

evacuate [ɪˈvækjueɪt] vt évacuer

evade [ɪˈveɪd] vt échapper à; (question etc) éluder; (duties) se dérober à

evaluate [ɪˈvæljueɪt] vt évaluer

evaporate [ɪˈvæpəreɪt] vi s'évaporer; (fig: hopes, fear) s'envoler; (anger) se dissiper

eve [iːv] n: **on the ~ of** à la veille de

even [ˈiːvn] adj (level, smooth) régulier(-ière); (equal) égal(e); (number) pair(e) ▷ adv même; **~ if** même si + indic; **~ though** alors même que + cond; **~ more** encore plus; **~ faster** encore plus vite; **~ so** quand même; **not ~** pas même; **~ he was there** même lui était là; **~ on Sundays** même le dimanche; **to get ~ with sb** prendre sa revanche sur qn

evening [ˈiːvnɪŋ] n soir m; (as duration, event) soirée f; **in the ~** le soir; **evening class** n cours m du soir; **evening dress** n (man's) tenue f de soirée, smoking m; (woman's) robe f de soirée

event [ɪ'vɛnt] n événement m; (Sport) épreuve f; **in the ~ of** en cas de; **eventful** adj mouvementé(e)

eventual [ɪ'vɛntʃuəl] adj final(e)

> Be careful not to translate eventual by the French word éventuel.

eventually [ɪ'vɛntʃuəlɪ] adv finalement

> Be careful not to translate eventually by the French word éventuellement.

ever ['ɛvər] adv jamais; (at all times) toujours; **why ~ not?** mais enfin, pourquoi pas?; **the best ~** le meilleur qu'on ait jamais vu; **have you ~ seen it?** l'as-tu déjà vu?, as-tu eu l'occasion or t'est-il arrivé de le voir?; **~ since** (as adv) depuis; (as conj) depuis que; **~ so pretty** si joli; **evergreen** n arbre m à feuilles persistantes

○ **KEYWORD**

every ['ɛvrɪ] adj **1** (each) chaque; **every one of them** tous (sans exception); **every shop in town was closed** tous les magasins en ville étaient fermés
2 (all possible) tous (toutes) les; **I gave you every assistance** j'ai fait tout mon possible pour vous aider; **I have every confidence in him** j'ai entièrement or pleinement confiance en lui; **we wish you every success** nous vous souhaitons beaucoup de succès
3 (showing recurrence) tous les; **every day** tous les jours, chaque jour; **every other car** une voiture sur deux; **every other/third day** tous les deux/trois jours; **every now and then** de temps en temps; **everybody** pron = **everyone**; **everyday** adj (expression) courant(e), d'usage courant; (use) courant; (clothes, life) de tous les jours; (occurrence, problem) quotidien(ne); **everyone** pron tout

le monde, tous pl; **everything** pron tout; **everywhere** adv partout; **everywhere you go you meet ...** où qu'on aille on rencontre ...

evict [ɪ'vɪkt] vt expulser

evidence ['ɛvɪdns] n (proof) preuve(s) f(pl); (of witness) témoignage m; (sign): **to show ~ of** donner des signes de; **to give ~** témoigner, déposer

evident ['ɛvɪdnt] adj évident(e); **evidently** adv de toute évidence; (apparently) apparemment

evil ['iːvl] adj mauvais(e) ▷ n mal m

evoke [ɪ'vəuk] vt évoquer

evolution [iːvə'luːʃən] n évolution f

evolve [ɪ'vɒlv] vt élaborer ▷ vi évoluer, se transformer

ewe [juː] n brebis f

ex- [ɛks] n (inf): **my ex** mon ex

ex- [ɛks] prefix ex-

exact [ɪg'zækt] adj exact(e) ▷ vt: **to ~ sth (from)** (signature, confession) extorquer qch (à); (apology) exiger qch (de); **exactly** adv exactement

exaggerate [ɪg'zædʒəreɪt] vt, vi exagérer; **exaggeration** [ɪgzædʒə'reɪʃən] n exagération f

exam [ɪg'zæm] n abbr (Scol); = **examination**

examination [ɪgzæmɪ'neɪʃən] n (Scol, Med) examen m; **to take** or **sit an ~** (BRIT) passer un examen

examine [ɪg'zæmɪn] vt (gen) examiner; (Scol, Law: person) interroger; **examiner** n examinateur(-trice)

example [ɪg'zɑːmpl] n exemple m; **for ~** par exemple

exasperated [ɪg'zɑːspəreɪtɪd] adj exaspéré(e)

excavate ['ɛkskəveɪt] vt (site) fouiller, excaver; (object) mettre au jour

exceed [ɪk'siːd] vt dépasser; (one's powers) outrepasser; **exceedingly** adv extrêmement

excel [ɪk'sɛl] vi exceller ▷ vt surpasser; **to ~ o.s.** se surpasser

excellence ['ɛksələns] n excellence f

excellent ['ɛksələnt] adj excellent(e)

except [ɪk'sɛpt] prep (also: **~ for, ~ing**) sauf, excepté, à l'exception de ▷ vt excepter; **~ if/when** sauf si/quand; **~ that** excepté que, si ce n'est que; **exception** [ɪk'sɛpʃən] n exception f; **to take exception to** s'offusquer de; **exceptional** [ɪk'sɛpʃənl] adj exceptionnel(le); **exceptionally** [ɪk'sɛpʃənəlɪ] adv exceptionnellement

excerpt ['ɛksə:pt] n extrait m

excess [ɪk'sɛs] n excès m; **excess baggage** n excédent m de bagages; **excessive** adj excessif(-ive)

exchange [ɪks'tʃeɪndʒ] n échange m; (also: **telephone ~**) central m ▷ vt: **to ~ (for)** échanger (contre); **could I ~ this, please?** est-ce que je peux échanger ceci, s'il vous plaît?; **exchange rate** n taux m de change

excite [ɪk'saɪt] vt exciter; **excited** adj (tout) excité(e); **to get excited** s'exciter; **excitement** n excitation f; **exciting** adj passionnant(e)

exclaim [ɪk'skleɪm] vi s'exclamer; **exclamation** [ɛksklə'meɪʃən] n exclamation f; **exclamation mark**, (US) **exclamation point** n point m d'exclamation

exclude [ɪk'sklu:d] vt exclure

excluding [ɪk'sklu:dɪŋ] prep: **~ VAT** la TVA non comprise

exclusion [ɪk'sklu:ʒən] n exclusion f

exclusive [ɪk'sklu:sɪv] adj exclusif(-ive); (club, district) sélect(e); (item of news) en exclusivité; **~ of VAT** TVA non comprise; **exclusively** adv exclusivement

excruciating [ɪk'skru:ʃeɪtɪŋ] adj (pain) atroce, déchirant(e); (embarrassing) pénible

excursion [ɪk'skə:ʃən] n excursion f

excuse n [ɪk'skju:s] excuse f ▷ vt [ɪk'skju:z] (forgive) excuser; **to ~ sb from** (activity) dispenser qn de; **~ me!** excusez-moi!, pardon!; **now if you will ~ me, ...** maintenant, si vous (le) permettez ...

ex-directory ['ɛksdɪ'rɛktərɪ] adj (BRIT) sur la liste rouge

execute ['ɛksɪkju:t] vt exécuter; **execution** [ɛksɪ'kju:ʃən] n exécution f

executive [ɪg'zɛkjutɪv] n (person) cadre m; (managing group) bureau m; (Pol) exécutif m ▷ adj exécutif(-ive); (position, job) de cadre

exempt [ɪg'zɛmpt] adj: **~ from** exempté(e) or dispensé(e) de ▷ vt: **to ~ sb from** exempter or dispenser qn de

exercise ['ɛksəsaɪz] n exercice m ▷ vt exercer; (patience etc) faire preuve de; (dog) promener ▷ vi (also: **to take ~**) prendre de l'exercice; **exercise book** n cahier m

exert [ɪg'zə:t] vt exercer, employer; **to ~ o.s.** se dépenser; **exertion** [ɪg'zə:ʃən] n effort m

exhale [ɛks'heɪl] vt exhaler ▷ vi expirer

exhaust [ɪg'zɔ:st] n (also: **~ fumes**) gaz mpl d'échappement; (also: **~ pipe**) tuyau m d'échappement ▷ vt épuiser; **exhausted** adj épuisé(e); **exhaustion** [ɪg'zɔ:stʃən] n épuisement m; **nervous exhaustion** fatigue nerveuse

exhibit [ɪg'zɪbɪt] n (Art) objet exposé, pièce exposée; (Law) pièce à conviction ▷ vt (Art) exposer; (courage, skill) faire preuve de; **exhibition** [ɛksɪ'bɪʃən] n exposition f

exhilarating [ɪg'zɪləreɪtɪŋ] adj grisant(e), stimulant(e)

exile ['ɛksaɪl] n exil m; (person) exilé(e) ▷ vt exiler

exist [ɪg'zɪst] vi exister; **existence** n existence f; **existing** adj actuel(le)

exit ['ɛksɪt] n sortie f ▷ vi (Comput, Theat) sortir; **where's the ~?** où est la sortie?; **exit ramp** n (US Aut) bretelle f d'accès

exotic [ɪgˈzɔtɪk] *adj* exotique
expand [ɪkˈspænd] *vt (area)* agrandir; *(quantity)* accroître ▷ *vi (trade, etc)* se développer, s'accroître; *(gas, metal)* se dilater
expansion [ɪkˈspænʃən] *n (territorial, economic)* expansion *f*; *(of trade, influence etc)* développement *m*; *(of production)* accroissement *m*; *(of population)* croissance *f*; *(of gas, metal)* expansion, dilatation *f*
expect [ɪkˈspɛkt] *vt (anticipate)* s'attendre à, s'attendre à ce que + *sub*; *(count on)* compter sur, escompter; *(require)* demander, exiger; *(suppose)* supposer; *(await: also baby)* attendre ▷ *vi*: **to be ~ing** *(pregnant woman)* être enceinte; **expectation** [ɛkspɛkˈteɪʃən] *n (hope)* attente *f*, espérance(s) *f(pl)*; *(belief)* attente
expedition [ɛkspəˈdɪʃən] *n* expédition *f*
expel [ɪkˈspɛl] *vt* chasser, expulser; *(Scol)* renvoyer, exclure
expenditure [ɪkˈspɛndɪtʃə^r] *n (act of spending)* dépense *f*; *(money spent)* dépenses *fpl*
expense [ɪkˈspɛns] *n (high cost)* coût *m*; *(spending)* dépense *f*, frais *mpl*; **expenses** *npl* frais *mpl*; dépenses; **at the ~ of** *(fig)* aux dépens de; **expense account** *n (note f de)* frais *mpl*
expensive [ɪkˈspɛnsɪv] *adj* cher (chère), coûteux(-euse); **it's too ~** ça coûte trop cher
experience [ɪkˈspɪərɪəns] *n* expérience *f* ▷ *vt* connaître; *(feeling)* éprouver; **experienced** *adj* expérimenté(e)
experiment [ɪkˈspɛrɪmənt] *n* expérience *f* ▷ *vi* faire une expérience; **experimental** [ɪkspɛrɪˈmɛntl] *adj* expérimental(e)
expert [ˈɛkspəːt] *adj* expert(e) ▷ *n* expert *m*; **expertise** [ɛkspəːˈtiːz] *n* (grande) compétence
expire [ɪkˈspaɪə^r] *vi* expirer; **expiry** *n* expiration *f*; **expiry date** *n* date

f d'expiration; *(on label)* à utiliser avant …
explain [ɪkˈspleɪn] *vt* expliquer; **explanation** [ɛkspləˈneɪʃən] *n* explication *f*
explicit [ɪkˈsplɪsɪt] *adj* explicite; *(definite)* formel(le)
explode [ɪkˈspləud] *vi* exploser
exploit *n* [ˈɛksplɔɪt] exploit *m* ▷ *vt* [ɪkˈsplɔɪt] exploiter; **exploitation** [ɛksplɔɪˈteɪʃən] *n* exploitation *f*
explore [ɪkˈsplɔː^r] *vt* explorer; *(possibilities)* étudier, examiner; **explorer** *n* explorateur(-trice)
explosion [ɪkˈspləuʒən] *n* explosion *f*; **explosive** [ɪkˈspləusɪv] *adj* explosif(-ive) ▷ *n* explosif *m*
export *vt* [ɛkˈspɔːt] exporter ▷ *n* [ˈɛkspɔːt] exportation *f* ▷ *cpd* [ˈɛkspɔːt] d'exportation; **exporter** *n* exportateur *m*
expose [ɪkˈspəuz] *vt* exposer; *(unmask)* démasquer, dévoiler; **exposed** *adj (land, house)* exposé(e); **exposure** [ɪkˈspəuʒə^r] *n* exposition *f*; *(publicity)* couverture *f*; *(Phot: speed)* (temps *m* de) pose *f*; *(: shot)* pose; **to die of exposure** *(Med)* mourir de froid
express [ɪkˈsprɛs] *adj (definite)* formel(le), exprès(-esse); *(BRIT: letter etc)* exprès *inv* ▷ *n (train)* rapide *m* ▷ *vt* exprimer; **expression** [ɪkˈsprɛʃən] *n* expression *f*; **expressway** *n (US)* voie *f* express (à plusieurs files)
exquisite [ɛkˈskwɪzɪt] *adj* exquis(e)
extend [ɪkˈstɛnd] *vt (visit, street)* prolonger; remettre; *(building)* agrandir; *(offer)* présenter, offrir; *(hand, arm)* tendre ▷ *vi (land)* s'étendre; **extension** *n (of visit, street)* prolongation *f*; *(building)* annexe *f*; *(telephone: in offices)* poste *m*; *(: in private house)* téléphone *m* supplémentaire; **extension cable, extension lead** *n (Elec)* rallonge *f*; **extensive** *adj* étendu(e), vaste; *(damage, alterations)* considérable; *(inquiries)* approfondi(e)

extent [ɪk'stɛnt] n étendue f; **to some ~** dans une certaine mesure; **to the ~ of ...** au point de ...; **to what ~?** dans quelle mesure?, jusqu'à quel point?; **to such an ~ that ...** à tel point que ...

exterior [ɛk'stɪərɪəʳ] adj extérieur(e) ▷ n extérieur m

external [ɛk'stə:nl] adj externe

extinct [ɪk'stɪŋkt] adj (volcano) éteint(e); (species) disparu(e); **extinction** n extinction f

extinguish [ɪk'stɪŋgwɪʃ] vt éteindre

extra ['ɛkstrə] adj supplémentaire, de plus ▷ adv (in addition) en plus ▷ n supplément m; (perk) à-coté m; (Cine, Theat) figurant(e)

extract vt [ɪk'strækt] extraire; (tooth) arracher; (money, promise) soutirer ▷ n ['ɛkstrækt] extrait m

extradite ['ɛkstrədaɪt] vt extrader

extraordinary [ɪk'strɔ:dnrɪ] adj extraordinaire

extravagance [ɪk'strævəgəns] n (excessive spending) prodigalités fpl; (thing bought) folie f, dépense excessive; **extravagant** adj extravagant(e); (in spending: person) prodigue, dépensier(-ière); (: tastes) dispendieux(-euse)

extreme [ɪk'stri:m] adj, n extrême (m); **extremely** adv extrêmement

extremist [ɪk'stri:mɪst] adj, n extrémiste m/f

extrovert ['ɛkstrəvə:t] n extraverti(e)

eye [aɪ] n œil m; (of needle) trou m, chas m ▷ vt examiner; **to keep an ~ on** surveiller; **eyeball** n globe m oculaire; **eyebrow** n sourcil m; **eye drops** npl gouttes fpl pour les yeux; **eyelash** n cil m; **eyelid** n paupière f; **eyeliner** n eye-liner m; **eye shadow** n ombre f à paupières; **eyesight** n vue f; **eye witness** n témoin m oculaire

F [ɛf] n (Mus) fa m

fabric ['fæbrɪk] n tissu m

fabulous ['fæbjuləs] adj fabuleux(-euse); (inf: super) formidable, sensationnel(le)

face [feɪs] n visage m, figure f; (expression) air m; (of clock) cadran m; (of cliff) paroi f; (of mountain) face f; (of building) façade f ▷ vt faire face à; (facts etc) accepter; **~ down** (person) à plat ventre; (card) face en dessous; **to lose/save ~** perdre/sauver la face; **to pull a ~** faire une grimace; **in the ~ of** (difficulties etc) face à, devant; **on the ~ of it** à première vue; **~ to ~** face à face; **face up to** vt fus faire face à, affronter; **face cloth** n (BRIT) gant m de toilette; **face pack** n (BRIT) masque m (de beauté)

facial ['feɪʃl] adj facial(e) ▷ n soin complet du visage

facilitate [fə'sɪlɪteɪt] vt faciliter

facilities [fə'sɪlɪtɪz] *npl* installations *fpl*, équipement *m*; **credit ~** facilités de paiement

fact [fækt] *n* fait *m*; **in ~** en fait

faction ['fækʃən] *n* faction *f*

factor ['fæktər] *n* facteur *m*; (*of sun cream*) indice *m* (de protection); **I'd like a ~ 15 suntan lotion** je voudrais une crème solaire d'indice 15

factory ['fæktərɪ] *n* usine *f*, fabrique *f*

factual ['fæktjuəl] *adj* basé(e) sur les faits

faculty ['fækəltɪ] *n* faculté *f*; (*US: teaching staff*) corps enseignant

fad [fæd] *n* (*personal*) manie *f*; (*craze*) engouement *m*

fade [feɪd] *vi* se décolorer, passer; (*light, sound*) s'affaiblir; (*flower*) se faner; **fade away** *vi* (*sound*) s'affaiblir

fag [fæg] (*BRIT inf*) *n* clope *f*

Fahrenheit ['fɑːrənhaɪt] *n* Fahrenheit *m inv*

fail [feɪl] *vt* (*exam*) échouer à; (*candidate*) recaler; (*subj: courage, memory*) faire défaut à ▷ *vi* échouer; (*eyesight, health, light: also: **be ~ing***) baisser, s'affaiblir; (*brakes*) lâcher; **to ~ to do sth** (*neglect*) négliger de *or* ne pas faire qch; (*be unable*) ne pas arriver *or* parvenir à faire qch; **without ~** à coup sûr; sans faute; **failing** *n* défaut *m* ▷ *prep* faute de; **failing that** à défaut, sinon; **failure** ['feɪljər] *n* échec *m*; (*person*) raté(e); (*mechanical etc*) défaillance *f*

faint [feɪnt] *adj* faible; (*recollection*) vague; (*mark*) à peine visible ▷ *n* évanouissement *m* ▷ *vi* s'évanouir; **to feel ~** défaillir; **faintest** *adj*: **I haven't the faintest idea** je n'en ai pas la moindre idée; **faintly** *adv* faiblement; (*vaguely*) vaguement

fair [fɛər] *adj* équitable, juste; (*hair*) blond(e); (*skin, complexion*) pâle, blanc (blanche); (*weather*) beau (belle); (*good enough*) assez bon(ne); (*sizeable*) considérable ▷ *adv*: **to play ~** jouer franc jeu ▷ *n* foire *f*; (*BRIT: funfair*) fête

(foraine); **fairground** *n* champ *m* de foire; **fair-haired** *adj* (*person*) aux cheveux clairs, blond(e); **fairly** *adv* (*justly*) équitablement; (*quite*) assez; **fair trade** *n* commerce *m* équitable; **fairway** *n* (*Golf*) fairway *m*

fairy ['fɛərɪ] *n* fée *f*; **fairy tale** *n* conte *m* de fées

faith [feɪθ] *n* foi *f*; (*trust*) confiance *f*; (*sect*) culte *m*, religion *f*; **faithful** *adj* fidèle; **faithfully** *adv* fidèlement; **yours faithfully** (*BRIT: in letters*) veuillez agréer l'expression de mes salutations les plus distinguées

fake [feɪk] *n* (*painting etc*) faux *m*; (*person*) imposteur *m* ▷ *adj* faux (fausse) ▷ *vt* (*emotions*) simuler; (*painting*) faire un faux de

falcon ['fɔːlkən] *n* faucon *m*

fall [fɔːl] *n* chute *f*; (*decrease*) baisse *f*; (*US: autumn*) automne *m* ▷ *vi* (*pt* **fell**, *pp* **fallen**) tomber; (*price, temperature, dollar*) baisser; **falls** *npl* (*waterfall*) chute *f* d'eau, cascade *f*; **to ~ flat** *vi* (*on one's face*) tomber de tout son long, s'étaler; (*joke*) tomber à plat; (*plan*) échouer; **fall apart** *vi* (*object*) tomber en morceaux; **fall down** *vi* (*person*) tomber; (*building*) s'effondrer, s'écrouler; **fall for** *vt fus* (*trick*) se laisser prendre à; (*person*) tomber amoureux(-euse) de; **fall off** *vi* tomber; (*diminish*) baisser, diminuer; **fall out** *vi* (*friends etc*) se brouiller; (*hair, teeth*) tomber; **fall over** *vi* tomber (par terre); **fall through** *vi* (*plan, project*) tomber à l'eau

fallen ['fɔːlən] *pp of* **fall**

fallout ['fɔːlaut] *n* retombées (radioactives)

false [fɔːls] *adj* faux (fausse); **under ~ pretences** sous un faux prétexte; **false alarm** *n* fausse alerte; **false teeth** *npl* (*BRIT*) fausses dents, dentier *m*

fame [feɪm] *n* renommée *f*, renom *m*

familiar [fə'mɪlɪər] *adj* familier(-ière); **to be ~ with sth** connaître qch;

familiarize [fə'mɪlɪəraɪz] vt: **to familiarize o.s. with** se familiariser avec

family ['fæmɪlɪ] n famille f; **family doctor** n médecin m de famille; **family planning** n planning familial

famine ['fæmɪn] n famine f

famous ['feɪməs] adj célèbre

fan [fæn] n (folding) éventail m; (Elec) ventilateur m; (person) fan m, admirateur(-trice); (Sport) supporter m/f ▷ vt éventer; (fire, quarrel) attiser

fanatic [fə'nætɪk] n fanatique m/f

fan belt n courroie f de ventilateur

fan club n fan-club m

fancy ['fænsɪ] n (whim) fantaisie f, envie f; (imagination) imagination f ▷ adj (luxury) de luxe; (elaborate: jewellery, packaging) fantaisie inv ▷ vt (feel like, want) avoir envie de; (imagine) imaginer; **to take a ~ to** se prendre d'affection pour; s'enticher de; **he fancies her** elle lui plaît; **fancy dress** n déguisement m, travesti m

fan heater n (BRIT) radiateur soufflant

fantasize ['fæntəsaɪz] vi fantasmer

fantastic [fæn'tæstɪk] adj fantastique

fantasy ['fæntəsɪ] n imagination f, fantaisie f; (unreality) fantasme m

fanzine ['fænziːn] n fanzine m

FAQ n abbr (= frequently asked question) FAQ f inv, faq f inv

far [fɑːʳ] adj (distant) lointain(e), éloigné(e) ▷ adv loin; **the ~ side/ end** l'autre côté/bout; **it's not ~ (from here)** ce n'est pas loin (d'ici); **~ away, ~ off** au loin, dans le lointain; **~ better** beaucoup mieux; **~ from** loin de; **by ~** de loin, de beaucoup; **go as ~ as the bridge** allez jusqu'au pont; **as ~ as I know** pour autant que je sache; **how ~ is it to ...?** combien y a-t-il jusqu'à ...?; **how ~ have you got with your work?** où en êtes-vous dans votre travail?

farce [fɑːs] n farce f

fare [fɛəʳ] n (on trains, buses) prix m du billet; (in taxi) prix de la course; (food) table f, chère f; **half ~** demi-tarif; **full ~** plein tarif

Far East n: **the ~** l'Extrême-Orient m

farewell [fɛə'wɛl] excl, n adieu m

farm [fɑːm] n ferme f ▷ vt cultiver; **farmer** n fermier(-ière); **farmhouse** n (maison f de) ferme f; **farming** n agriculture f; (of animals) élevage m; **farmyard** n cour f de ferme

far-reaching ['fɑː'riːtʃɪŋ] adj d'une grande portée

fart [fɑːt] (inf!) vi péter

farther ['fɑːðəʳ] adv plus loin ▷ adj plus éloigné(e), plus lointain(e)

farthest ['fɑːðɪst] superlative of **far**

fascinate ['fæsɪneɪt] vt fasciner, captiver

fascinating ['fæsɪneɪtɪŋ] adj fascinant(e)

fascination [fæsɪ'neɪʃən] n fascination f

fascist ['fæʃɪst] adj, n fasciste m/f

fashion ['fæʃən] n mode f; (manner) façon f, manière f ▷ vt façonner; **in ~** à la mode; **out of ~** démodé(e); **fashionable** adj à la mode; **fashion show** n défilé m de mannequins or de mode

fast [fɑːst] adj rapide; (clock): **to be ~** avancer; (dye, colour) grand or bon teint inv ▷ adv vite, rapidement; (stuck, held) solidement ▷ n jeûne m ▷ vi jeûner; **~ asleep** profondément endormi

fasten ['fɑːsn] vt attacher, fixer; (coat) attacher, fermer ▷ vi se fermer, s'attacher

fast food n fast food m, restauration f rapide

fat [fæt] adj gros(se) ▷ n graisse f; (on meat) gras m; (for cooking) matière grasse

fatal ['feɪtl] adj (mistake) fatal(e); (injury) mortel(le); **fatality** [fə'tælɪtɪ] n (road death etc) victime f, décès m;

fatally adv fatalement; (injured) mortellement

fate [feɪt] n destin m; (of person) sort m

father ['fɑːðəʳ] n père m; **Father Christmas** n le Père Noël; **father-in-law** n beau-père m

fatigue [fə'tiːg] n fatigue f

fattening ['fætnɪŋ] adj (food) qui fait grossir

fatty ['fætɪ] adj (food) gras(se) ▷ n (inf) gros (grosse)

faucet ['fɔːsɪt] n (US) robinet m

fault [fɔːlt] n faute f; (defect) défaut m; (Geo) faille f ▷ vt trouver des défauts à, prendre en défaut; **it's my ~** c'est de ma faute; **to find ~ with** trouver à redire or à critiquer à; **at ~** fautif(-ive), coupable; **faulty** adj défectueux(-euse)

fauna ['fɔːnə] n faune f

favour, (US) **favor** ['feɪvəʳ] n faveur f; (help) service m ▷ vt (proposition) être en faveur de; (pupil etc) favoriser; (team, horse) donner gagnant; **to do sb a ~** rendre un service à qn; **in ~ of** en faveur de; **to find ~ with sb** trouver grâce aux yeux de qn; **favourable**, (US) **favorable** adj favorable; **favourite**, (US) **favorite** ['feɪvrɪt] adj, n favori(te)

fawn [fɔːn] n (deer) faon m ▷ adj (also: **~-coloured**) fauve ▷ vi: **to ~ (up)on** flatter servilement

fax [fæks] n (document) télécopie f; (machine) télécopieur m ▷ vt envoyer par télécopie

FBI n abbr (US: = Federal Bureau of Investigation) FBI m

fear [fɪəʳ] n crainte f, peur f ▷ vt craindre; **for ~ of** de peur que + sub or de + infinitive; **fearful** adj craintif(-ive); (sight, noise) affreux(-euse), épouvantable; **fearless** adj intrépide

feasible ['fiːzəbl] adj faisable, réalisable

feast [fiːst] n festin m, banquet m; (Rel: also: **~ day**) fête f ▷ vi festoyer

feat [fiːt] n exploit m, prouesse f

feather ['feðəʳ] n plume f

feature ['fiːtʃəʳ] n caractéristique f; (article) chronique f, rubrique f ▷ vt (film) avoir pour vedette(s) ▷ vi figurer (en bonne place); **features** npl (of face) traits mpl; **a (special) ~ on sth/sb** un reportage sur qch/qn; **feature film** n long métrage

Feb. abbr (= February) fév

February ['februərɪ] n février m

fed [fɛd] pt, pp of **feed**

federal ['fɛdərəl] adj fédéral(e)

federation [fɛdə'reɪʃən] n fédération f

fed up adj: **to be ~ (with)** en avoir marre or plein le dos (de)

fee [fiː] n rémunération f; (of doctor, lawyer) honoraires mpl; (of school, college etc) frais mpl de scolarité; (for examination) droits mpl

feeble ['fiːbl] adj faible; (attempt, excuse) pauvre; (joke) piteux(-euse)

feed [fiːd] n (of animal) nourriture f, pâture f; (on printer) mécanisme m d'alimentation ▷ vt (pt, pp **fed**) (person) nourrir; (BRIT: baby: breastfeed) allaiter; (: with bottle) donner le biberon à; (horse etc) donner à manger à; (machine) alimenter; (data etc): **to ~ sth into** enregistrer qch dans; **feedback** n (Elec) effet m Larsen; (from person) réactions fpl

feel [fiːl] n (sensation) sensation f; (impression) impression f ▷ vt (pt, pp **felt**) (touch) toucher; (explore) tâter, palper; (cold, pain) sentir; (grief, anger) ressentir, éprouver; (think, believe): **to ~ (that)** trouver que; **to ~ hungry/cold** avoir faim/froid; **to ~ lonely/better** se sentir seul/mieux; **I don't ~ well** je ne me sens pas bien; **it ~s soft** c'est doux au toucher; **to ~ like** (want) avoir envie de; **feeling** n (physical) sensation f; (emotion, impression) sentiment m; **to hurt sb's feelings** froisser qn

feet [fiːt] npl of **foot**

fell [fɛl] pt of **fall** ▷ vt (tree) abattre

fellow ['fɛləʊ] n type m; (comrade) compagnon m; (of learned society) membre m ▷ cpd: **their ~ prisoners/students** leurs camarades prisonniers/étudiants; **fellow citizen** n concitoyen(ne); **fellow countryman** (irreg) n compatriote m; **fellow men** npl semblables mpl; **fellowship** n (society) association f; (comradeship) amitié f, camaraderie f; (Scol) sorte de bourse universitaire

felony ['fɛlənɪ] n crime m, forfait m

felt [fɛlt] pt, pp of **feel** ▷ n feutre m; **felt-tip** n (also: **felt-tip pen**) stylo-feutre m

female ['fiːmeɪl] n (Zool) femelle f; (pej: woman) bonne femme ▷ adj (Biol) femelle; (sex, character) féminin(e); (vote etc) des femmes

feminine ['fɛmɪnɪn] adj féminin(e)

feminist ['fɛmɪnɪst] n féministe m/f

fence [fɛns] n barrière f ▷ vi faire de l'escrime; **fencing** n (sport) escrime m

fend [fɛnd] vi: **to ~ for o.s.** se débrouiller (tout seul); **fend off** vt (attack etc) parer; (questions) éluder

fender ['fɛndər] n garde-feu m inv; (on boat) défense f; (US: of car) aile f

fennel ['fɛnl] n fenouil m

ferment vi [fə'mɛnt] fermenter ▷ n ['fəːmɛnt] (fig) agitation f, effervescence f

fern [fəːn] n fougère f

ferocious [fə'rəʊʃəs] adj féroce

ferret ['fɛrɪt] n furet m

ferry ['fɛrɪ] n (small) bac m; (large: also: **~boat**) ferry(-boat m) m ▷ vt transporter

fertile ['fəːtaɪl] adj fertile; (Biol) fécond(e); **fertilize** ['fəːtɪlaɪz] vt fertiliser; (Biol) féconder; **fertilizer** n engrais m

festival ['fɛstɪvəl] n (Rel) fête f; (Art, Mus) festival m

festive ['fɛstɪv] adj de fête; **the ~ season** (BRIT: Christmas) la période des fêtes

fetch [fɛtʃ] vt aller chercher; (BRIT: sell for) rapporter

fête [feɪt] n fête f, kermesse f

fetus ['fiːtəs] n (US) = **foetus**

feud [fjuːd] n querelle f, dispute f

fever ['fiːvər] n fièvre f; **feverish** adj fiévreux(-euse), fébrile

few [fjuː] adj (not many) peu de ▷ pron peu; **a ~** (as adj) quelques; (as pron) quelques-uns(-unes); **quite a ~ ...** adj un certain nombre de ..., pas mal de ...; **in the past ~ days** ces derniers jours; **fewer** adj moins de; **fewest** adj le moins nombreux

fiancé [fɪ'ãːŋseɪ] n fiancé m; **fiancée** n fiancée f

fiasco [fɪ'æskəʊ] n fiasco m

fib [fɪb] n bobard m

fibre, (US) **fiber** ['faɪbər] n fibre f; **fibreglass**, (US) **Fiberglass®** n fibre f de verre

fickle ['fɪkl] adj inconstant(e), volage, capricieux(-euse)

fiction ['fɪkʃən] n romans mpl, littérature f romanesque; (invention) fiction f; **fictional** adj fictif(-ive)

fiddle ['fɪdl] n (Mus) violon m; (cheating) combine f; escroquerie f ▷ vt (BRIT: accounts) falsifier, maquiller; **fiddle with** vt fus tripoter

fidelity [fɪ'dɛlɪtɪ] n fidélité f

fidget ['fɪdʒɪt] vi se trémousser, remuer

field [fiːld] n champ m; (fig) domaine m, champ; (Sport: ground) terrain m; **field marshal** n maréchal m

fierce [fɪəs] adj (look, animal) féroce, sauvage; (wind, attack, person) (très) violent(e); (fighting, enemy) acharné(e)

fifteen [fɪf'tiːn] num quinze; **fifteenth** num quinzième

fifth [fɪfθ] num cinquième

fiftieth ['fɪftɪɪθ] num cinquantième

fifty ['fɪftɪ] num cinquante; **fifty-fifty** adv moitié-moitié ▷ adj: **to have a fifty-fifty chance (of success)** avoir une chance sur deux (de réussir)

fig | 400

fig [fɪg] n figue f
fight [faɪt] (pt, pp **fought**) n (between persons) bagarre f; (argument) dispute f; (Mil) combat m; (against cancer etc) lutte f ▷ vt se battre contre; (cancer, alcoholism, emotion) combattre, lutter contre; (election) se présenter à ▷ vi se battre; (argue) se disputer; (fig): **to ~ (for/against)** lutter (pour/contre); **fight back** vi rendre les coups; (after illness) reprendre le dessus ▷ vt (tears) réprimer; **fight off** vt repousser; (disease, sleep, urge) lutter contre; **fighting** n combats mpl; (brawls) bagarres fpl

figure ['fɪgər] n (Drawing, Geom) figure f; (number) chiffre m; (body, outline) silhouette f; (person's shape) ligne f, formes fpl; (person) personnage m ▷ vt (us: think) supposer ▷ vi (appear) figurer; (us: make sense) s'expliquer; **figure out** vt (understand) arriver à comprendre; (plan) calculer

file [faɪl] n (tool) lime f; (dossier) dossier m; (folder) dossier, chemise f (: binder) classeur m; (Comput) fichier m; (row) file f ▷ vt (nails, wood) limer; (papers) classer; (Law: claim) faire enregistrer; déposer; **filing cabinet** n classeur m (meuble)

Filipino [fɪlɪ'piːnəu] adj philippin(e) ▷ n (person) Philippin(e)

fill [fɪl] vt remplir; (vacancy) pourvoir à ▷ n: **to eat one's ~** manger à sa faim; **to ~ with** remplir de; **fill in** vt (hole) boucher; (form) remplir; **fill out** vt (form, receipt) remplir; **fill up** vt remplir ▷ vi (Aut) faire le plein

fillet ['fɪlɪt] n filet m; **fillet steak** n filet m de bœuf, tournedos m

filling ['fɪlɪŋ] n (Culin) garniture f, farce f; (for tooth) plombage m; **filling station** n station-service f, station f d'essence

film [fɪlm] n film m; (Phot) pellicule f, film; (of powder, liquid) couche f, pellicule ▷ vt (scene) filmer ▷ vi tourner; **I'd like a 36-exposure ~** je

voudrais une pellicule de 36 poses; **film star** n vedette f de cinéma

filter ['fɪltər] n filtre m ▷ vt filtrer; **filter lane** n (BRIT Aut: at traffic lights) voie f de dégagement; (: on motorway) voie f de sortie

filth [fɪlθ] n saleté f; **filthy** adj sale, dégoûtant(e); (language) ordurier(-ière), grossier(-ière)

fin [fɪn] n (of fish) nageoire f; (of shark) aileron m; (of diver) palme f

final ['faɪnl] adj final(e), dernier(-ière); (decision, answer) définitif(-ive) ▷ n (BRIT Sport) finale f; **finals** npl (us) (Scol) examens mpl de dernière année; (Sport) finale f; **finale** [fɪ'nɑːlɪ] n finale m; **finalist** n (Sport) finaliste m/f; **finalize** vt mettre au point; **finally** adv (eventually) enfin, finalement; (lastly) en dernier lieu

finance [faɪ'næns] n finance f ▷ vt financer; **finances** npl finances fpl; **financial** [faɪ'nænʃəl] adj financier(-ière); **financial year** n année f budgétaire

find [faɪnd] vt (pt, pp **found**) trouver; (lost object) retrouver ▷ n trouvaille f, découverte f; **to ~ sb guilty** (Law) déclarer qn coupable; **find out** vt se renseigner sur; (truth, secret) découvrir; (person) démasquer ▷ vi: **to ~ out about** (make enquiries) se renseigner sur; (by chance) apprendre; **findings** npl (Law) conclusions fpl, verdict m; (of report) constatations fpl

fine [faɪn] adj (weather) beau (belle); (excellent) excellent(e); (thin, subtle, not coarse) fin(e); (acceptable) bien inv ▷ adv (well) très bien; (small) fin, finement ▷ n (Law) amende f; contravention f ▷ vt (Law) condamner à une amende; donner une contravention à; **he's ~** il va bien; **the weather is ~** il fait beau; **fine arts** npl beaux-arts mpl

finger ['fɪŋgər] n doigt m ▷ vt palper, toucher; **index ~** index m; **fingernail** n ongle m (de la main); **fingerprint** n empreinte digitale; **fingertip** n bout m du doigt

finish ['fɪnɪʃ] n fin f; (Sport) arrivée f; (polish etc) finition f ▷ vt finir, terminer ▷ vi finir, se terminer; **to ~ doing sth** finir de faire qch; **to ~ third** arriver or terminer troisième; **when does the show ~?** quand est-ce que le spectacle se termine?; **finish off** vt finir, terminer; (kill) achever; **finish up** vi, vt finir

Finland ['fɪnlənd] n Finlande f; **Finn** n Finnois(e), Finlandais(e); **Finnish** adj finnois(e), finlandais(e) ▷ n (Ling) finnois m

fir [fəːʳ] n sapin m

fire ['faɪəʳ] n feu m; (accidental) incendie m; (heater) radiateur m ▷ vt (discharge): **to ~ a gun** tirer un coup de feu; (fig: interest) enflammer, animer; (inf: dismiss) mettre à la porte, renvoyer ▷ vi (shoot) tirer, faire feu; **~!** au feu!; **on ~** en feu; **to set ~ to sth, set sth on ~** mettre le feu à qch; **fire alarm** n avertisseur m d'incendie; **firearm** n arme f à feu; **fire brigade** n (régiment m de sapeurs-)pompiers mpl; **fire engine** n (BRIT) pompe f à incendie; **fire escape** n escalier m de secours; **fire exit** n issue f or sortie f de secours; **fire extinguisher** n extincteur m; **fireman** (irreg) n pompier m; **fireplace** n cheminée f; **fire station** n caserne f de pompiers; **fire truck** n (US) = **fire engine**; **firewall** n (Internet) pare-feu m; **firewood** n bois m de chauffage; **fireworks** npl (display) feu(x) m(pl) d'artifice

firm [fəːm] adj ferme ▷ n compagnie f, firme f; **firmly** adv fermement

first [fəːst] adj premier(-ière) ▷ adv (before other people) le premier, la première; (before other things) en premier, d'abord; (when listing reasons etc) en premier lieu, premièrement; (in the beginning) au début ▷ n (person: in race) premier(-ière); (BRIT Scol) mention f très bien; (Aut) première f; **the ~ of January** le premier janvier; **at ~** au commencement, au début; **~ of all** tout d'abord, pour commencer; **first aid** n premiers secours or soins; **first-aid kit** n trousse f à pharmacie; **first-class** adj (ticket etc) de première classe; (excellent) excellent(e), exceptionnel(le); (post) en tarif prioritaire; **first-hand** adj de première main; **first lady** n (US) femme f du président; **firstly** adv premièrement, en premier lieu; **first name** n prénom m; **first-rate** adj excellent(e)

fiscal ['fɪskl] adj fiscal(e); **fiscal year** n exercice financier

fish [fɪʃ] n (pl inv) poisson m ▷ vt, vi pêcher; **~ and chips** poisson frit et frites; **fisherman** (irreg) n pêcheur m; **fish fingers** npl (BRIT) bâtonnets mpl de poisson (congelés); **fishing** n pêche f; **to go fishing** aller à la pêche; **fishing boat** n barque f de pêche; **fishing line** n ligne f (de pêche); **fishmonger** n (BRIT) marchand m de poisson; **fishmonger's (shop)** n (BRIT) poissonnerie f; **fish sticks** npl (US) = **fish fingers**; **fishy** adj (inf) suspect(e), louche

fist [fɪst] n poing m

fit [fɪt] adj (Med, Sport) en (bonne) forme; (proper) convenable; approprié(e) ▷ vt (subj: clothes) aller à; (put in, attach) installer, poser; (equip) équiper, garnir, munir; (suit) convenir à ▷ vi (clothes) aller; (parts) s'adapter; (in space, gap) s'adapter ▷ n (Med) accès m, crise f; (of anger) accès; (of hysterics, jealousy) crise; **~ to** (ready to) en état de; **~ for** (worthy) digne de; (capable) apte à; **to keep ~** se maintenir en forme; **this dress is a tight/good ~** cette robe est un peu juste/(me) va très bien; **a ~ of coughing** une quinte de toux; **by ~s and starts** par à-coups;

fit in vi (add up) cadrer; (integrate) s'intégrer; (to new situation) s'adapter; **fitness** n (Med) forme f physique; **fitted** adj (jacket, shirt) ajusté(e); **fitted carpet** n moquette f; **fitted kitchen** n (BRIT) cuisine équipée; **fitted sheet** n drap-housse m; **fitting** adj approprié(e) ▷ n (of dress) essayage m; (of piece of equipment) pose f, installation f; **fitting room** n (in shop) cabine f d'essayage; **fittings** npl installations fpl

five [faɪv] num cinq; **fiver** n (inf: US) billet de cinq dollars; (: BRIT) billet m de cinq livres

fix [fɪks] vt (date, amount etc) fixer; (sort out) arranger; (mend) réparer; (make ready: meal, drink) préparer ▷ n: **to be in a ~** être dans le pétrin; **fix up** vt (meeting) arranger; **to ~ sb up with sth** faire avoir qch à qn; **fixed** adj (prices etc) fixe; **fixture** n installation f (fixe); (Sport) rencontre f (au programme)

fizzy ['fɪzɪ] adj pétillant(e), gazeux(-euse)

flag [flæg] n drapeau m; (also: **~stone**) dalle f ▷ vi faiblir; fléchir; **flag down** vt héler, faire signe (de s'arrêter) à; **flagpole** n mât m

flair [fleə'] n flair m

flak [flæk] n (Mil) tir antiaérien; (inf: criticism) critiques fpl

flake [fleɪk] n (of rust, paint) écaille f; (of snow, soap powder) flocon m ▷ vi (also: **~ off**) s'écailler

flamboyant [flæm'bɔɪənt] adj flamboyant(e), éclatant(e); (person) haut(e) en couleur

flame [fleɪm] n flamme f

flamingo [flə'mɪŋɡəu] n flamant m (rose)

flammable ['flæməbl] adj inflammable

flan [flæn] n (BRIT) tarte f

flank [flæŋk] n flanc m ▷ vt flanquer

flannel ['flænl] n (BRIT: also: **face ~**) gant m de toilette; (fabric) flanelle f

flap [flæp] n (of pocket, envelope) rabat m ▷ vt (wings) battre (de) ▷ vi (sail, flag) claquer

flare [fleə'] n (signal) signal lumineux; (Mil) fusée éclairante; (in skirt etc) évasement m; **flares** npl (trousers) pantalon m à pattes d'éléphant; **flare up** vi s'embraser; (fig: person) se mettre en colère, s'emporter; (: revolt) éclater

flash [flæʃ] n éclair m; (also: **news ~**) flash m (d'information); (Phot) flash m ▷ vt (switch on) allumer (brièvement); (direct): **to ~ sth at** braquer qch sur; (send: message) câbler; (smile) lancer ▷ vi briller; jeter des éclairs; (light on ambulance etc) clignoter; **a ~ of lightning** un éclair; **in a ~** en un clin d'œil; **to ~ one's headlights** faire un appel de phares; **he ~ed by** or **past** il passa (devant nous) comme un éclair; **flashback** n flashback m, retour m en arrière; **flashbulb** n ampoule f de flash; **flashlight** n lampe f de poche

flask [flɑːsk] n flacon m, bouteille f; (also: **vacuum ~**) bouteille f thermos®

flat [flæt] adj plat(e); (tyre) dégonflé(e), à plat; (beer) éventé(e); (battery) à plat; (denial) catégorique; (Mus) bémol inv (: voice) faux (fausse) ▷ n (BRIT: apartment) appartement m; (Aut) crevaison f, pneu crevé; (Mus) bémol m; **~ out** (work) sans relâche; (race) à fond; **flatten** vt (also: **flatten out**) aplatir; (crop) coucher; (house, city) raser

flatter ['flætə'] vt flatter; **flattering** adj flatteur(-euse); (clothes etc) seyant(e)

flaunt [flɔːnt] vt faire étalage de

flavour, (US) **flavor** ['fleɪvə'] n goût m, saveur f; (of ice cream etc) parfum m ▷ vt parfumer, aromatiser; **vanilla-~ed** à l'arôme de vanille, vanillé(e); **what ~s do you have?** quels parfums avez-vous?; **flavouring**, (US) **flavoring** n arôme m (synthétique)

flaw [flɔ:] n défaut m; **flawless** adj sans défaut

flea [fli:] n puce f; **flea market** n marché m aux puces

fled [flɛd] pt, pp of **flee**

flee (pt, pp **fled**) [fli:, flɛd] vt fuir, s'enfuir de ⊳ vi fuir, s'enfuir

fleece [fli:s] n (of sheep) toison f; (top) (laine f) polaire f ⊳ vt (inf) voler, filouter

fleet [fli:t] n flotte f; (of lorries, cars etc) parc m; convoi m

fleeting ['fli:tɪŋ] adj fugace, fugitif(-ive); (visit) très bref (brève)

Flemish ['flɛmɪʃ] adj flamand(e) ⊳ n (Ling) flamand m; **the ~** npl les Flamands

flesh [flɛʃ] n chair f

flew [flu:] pt of **fly**

flex [flɛks] n fil m or câble m électrique (souple) ⊳ vt (knee) fléchir; (muscles) bander; **flexibility** n flexibilité f; **flexible** adj flexible; (person, schedule) souple; **flexitime**, (US) **flextime** n horaire m variable or à la carte

flick [flɪk] n petit coup; (with finger) chiquenaude f ⊳ vt donner un petit coup à; (switch) appuyer sur; **flick through** vt fus feuilleter

flicker ['flɪkə'] vi (light, flame) vaciller

flies [flaɪz] npl of **fly**

flight [flaɪt] n vol m; (escape) fuite f; (also: ~ of steps) escalier m; **flight attendant** n steward m, hôtesse f de l'air

flimsy ['flɪmzɪ] adj peu solide; (clothes) trop léger(-ère); (excuse) pauvre, mince

flinch [flɪntʃ] vi tressaillir; **to ~ from** se dérober à, reculer devant

fling [flɪŋ] vt (pt, pp **flung**) jeter, lancer

flint [flɪnt] n silex m; (in lighter) pierre f (à briquet)

flip [flɪp] vt (throw) donner une chiquenaude à; (switch) appuyer sur; (US: pancake) faire sauter; **to ~ sth over** retourner qch

flip-flops ['flɪpflɔps] npl (esp BRIT) tongs fpl

flipper ['flɪpə'] n (of animal) nageoire f; (for swimmer) palme f

flirt [flə:t] vi flirter ⊳ n flirteur(-euse)

float [fləut] n flotteur m; (in procession) char m; (sum of money) réserve f ⊳ vi flotter

flock [flɔk] n (of sheep) troupeau m; (of birds) vol m; (of people) foule f

flood [flʌd] n inondation f; (of letters, refugees etc) flot m ⊳ vt inonder ⊳ vi (place) être inondé; (people): **to ~ into** envahir; **flooding** n inondation f; **floodlight** n projecteur m

floor [flɔ:'] n sol m; (storey) étage m; (of sea, valley) fond m ⊳ vt (knock down) terrasser; (baffle) désorienter; **ground ~**, (US) **first ~** rez-de-chaussée m; **first ~**, (US) **second ~** premier étage; **what ~ is it on?** c'est à quel étage?; **floorboard** n planche f (du plancher); **flooring** n sol m; (wooden) plancher m; (covering) revêtement m de sol; **floor show** n spectacle m de variétés

flop [flɔp] n fiasco m ⊳ vi (fail) faire fiasco; (fall) s'affaler, s'effondrer; **floppy** adj lâche, flottant(e) ⊳ n (Comput: also: **floppy disk**) disquette f

flora ['flɔ:rə] n flore f

floral ['flɔ:rl] adj floral(e); (dress) à fleurs

florist ['flɔrɪst] n fleuriste m/f; **florist's (shop)** n magasin m or boutique f de fleuriste

flotation [fləu'teɪʃən] n (of shares) émission f; (of company) lancement m (en Bourse)

flour ['flauə'] n farine f

flourish ['flʌrɪʃ] vi prospérer ⊳ n (gesture) moulinet m

flow [fləu] n (of water, traffic etc) écoulement m; (tide, influx) flux m; (of blood, Elec) circulation f; (of river) courant m ⊳ vi couler; (traffic) s'écouler; (robes, hair) flotter

flower ['flauə^r] n fleur f ▷ vi fleurir;
flower bed n plate-bande f;
flowerpot n pot m (à fleurs)

flown [fləun] pp of **fly**

fl. oz. abbr = **fluid ounce**

flu [fluː] n grippe f

fluctuate ['flʌktjueɪt] vi varier,
fluctuer

fluent ['fluːənt] adj (speech, style)
coulant(e), aisé(e); **he speaks ~
French, he's ~ in French** il parle le
français couramment

fluff [flʌf] n duvet m; (on jacket, carpet)
peluche f; **fluffy** adj duveteux(-euse);
(toy) en peluche

fluid ['fluːɪd] n fluide m; (in diet)
liquide m ▷ adj fluide; **fluid ounce** n
(BRIT) = 0.028 l; 0.05 pints

fluke [fluːk] n coup m de veine

flung [flʌŋ] pt, pp of **fling**

fluorescent [fluə'rɛsnt] adj
fluorescent(e)

fluoride ['fluəraɪd] n fluor m

flurry ['flʌrɪ] n (of snow) rafale f,
bourrasque f; **a ~ of activity** un
affairement soudain

flush [flʌʃ] n (on face) rougeur f; (fig:
of youth etc) éclat m ▷ vt nettoyer à
grande eau ▷ vi rougir ▷ adj (level):
~ with au ras de, de niveau avec; **to ~
the toilet** tirer la chasse (d'eau)

flute [fluːt] n flûte f

flutter ['flʌtə^r] n (of panic, excitement)
agitation f; (of wings) battement m
▷ vi (bird) battre des ailes, voleter

fly [flaɪ] (pt **flew**, pp **flown**) n (insect)
mouche f; (on trousers: also: **flies**)
braguette f ▷ vt (plane) piloter;
(passengers, cargo) transporter (par
avion); (distance) parcourir ▷ vi voler;
(passengers) aller en avion; (escape)
s'enfuir, fuir; (flag) se déployer; **fly
away, fly off** vi s'envoler; **fly-drive**
n formule f avion plus voiture; **flying**
n (activity) aviation f; (action) vol
m ▷ adj: **flying visit** visite f éclair
inv; **with flying colours** haut la
main; **flying saucer** n soucoupe

volante; **flyover** n (BRIT: overpass)
pont routier

FM abbr (Radio: = frequency modulation)
FM

foal [fəul] n poulain m

foam [fəum] n écume f; (on beer)
mousse f; (also: **~ rubber**) caoutchouc
m mousse ▷ vi (liquid) écumer; (soapy
water) mousser

focus ['fəukəs] n (pl **focuses**) foyer
m; (of interest) centre m ▷ vt (field
glasses etc) mettre au point ▷ vi: **to
~ (on)** (with camera) régler la mise au
point (sur); (with eyes) fixer son regard
(sur); (fig: concentrate) se concentrer
(sur); **out of/in ~** (picture) flou(e)/
net(te); (camera) pas au point/
au point

foetus, (US) **fetus** ['fiːtəs] n fœtus m

fog [fɔg] n brouillard m; **foggy** adj:
it's foggy il y a du brouillard; **fog
lamp**, (US) **fog light** n (Aut) phare m
anti-brouillard

foil [fɔɪl] vt déjouer, contrecarrer
▷ n feuille f de métal; (kitchen foil)
papier m d'alu(minium); **to act as
a ~ to** (fig) servir de repoussoir or de
faire-valoir à

fold [fəuld] n (bend, crease) pli m; (Agr)
parc m à moutons; (fig) bercail m ▷ vt
plier; **to ~ one's arms** croiser les
bras; **fold up** vi (map etc) se plier, se
replier; (business) fermer boutique
▷ vt (map etc) plier, replier; **folder**
n (for papers) chemise f (: binder) classeur
m; (Comput) dossier m; **folding** adj
(chair, bed) pliant(e)

foliage ['fəulɪɪdʒ] n feuillage m

folk [fəuk] npl gens mpl ▷ cpd
folklorique; **folks** npl (inf: parents)
famille f, parents mpl; **folklore**
['fəuklɔː^r] n folklore m; **folk music** n
musique f folklorique; (contemporary)
musique folk, folk m; **folk song** n
chanson f folklorique; (contemporary)
chanson folk inv

follow ['fɔləu] vt suivre ▷ vi suivre;
(result) s'ensuivre; **to ~ suit** (fig) faire

de même; **follow up** vt (letter, offer) donner suite à; (case) suivre; **follower** n disciple m/f, partisan(e); **following** adj suivant(e) ▷ n partisans mpl, disciples mpl; **follow-up** n suite f; (on file, case) suivi m

fond [fɔnd] adj (memory, look) tendre, affectueux(-euse); (hopes, dreams) un peu fou (folle); **to be ~ of** aimer beaucoup

food [fuːd] n nourriture f; **food mixer** n mixeur m; **food poisoning** n intoxication f alimentaire; **food processor** n robot m de cuisine; **food stamp** n (US) bon m de nourriture (pour indigents)

fool [fuːl] n idiot(e); (Culin) mousse f de fruits ▷ vt berner, duper; **fool about, fool around** vi (pej: waste time) traînailler, glandouiller; (: behave foolishly) faire l'idiot or l'imbécile; **foolish** adj idiot(e), stupide; (rash) imprudent(e); **foolproof** adj (plan etc) infaillible

foot [pl **feet**] [fut, fiːt] n pied m; (of animal) patte f; (measure) pied (= 30.48 cm; 12 inches) ▷ vt (bill) payer; **on ~** à pied; **footage** n (Cine: length) ≈ métrage m; (: material) séquences fpl; **foot-and-mouth (disease)** [futənd'mauθ-] n fièvre aphteuse; **football** n (ball) ballon m (de football); (sport: BRIT) football m; (: US) football américain; **footballer** n (BRIT) = **football player**; **football match** n (BRIT) match m de foot(ball); **football player** n footballeur(-euse), joueur(-euse) de football; (US) joueur(-euse) de football américain; **footbridge** n passerelle f; **foothills** npl contreforts mpl; **foothold** n prise f (de pied); **footing** n (fig) position f; **to lose one's footing** perdre pied; **footnote** n note f (en bas de page); **footpath** n sentier m; **footprint** n trace f (de pied); **footstep** n pas m; **footwear** n chaussures fpl

for [fɔːʳ] prep **1** (indicating destination, intention, purpose) pour; **the train for London** le train pour (or à destination de) Londres; **he left for Rome** il est parti pour Rome; **he went for the paper** il est allé chercher le journal; **is this for me?** c'est pour moi?; **it's time for lunch** c'est l'heure du déjeuner; **what's it for?** ça sert à quoi?; **what for?** (why?) pourquoi?; (to what end?) pour quoi faire?, à quoi bon?; **for sale** à vendre; **to pray for peace** prier pour la paix

2 (on behalf of, representing) pour; **the MP for Hove** le député de Hove; **to work for sb/sth** travailler pour qn/ qch; **I'll ask him for you** je vais lui demander pour toi; **G for George** G comme Georges

3 (because of) pour; **for this reason** pour cette raison; **for fear of being criticized** de peur d'être critiqué

4 (with regard to) pour; **it's cold for July** il fait froid pour juillet; **a gift for languages** un don pour les langues

5 (in exchange for) **I sold it for £5** je l'ai vendu 5 livres; **to pay 50 pence for a ticket** payer un billet 50 pence

6 (in favour of) pour; **are you for or against us?** êtes-vous pour ou contre nous?; **I'm all for it** je suis tout à fait pour; **vote for X** votez pour X

7 (referring to distance) pour, sur; **there are roadworks for 5 km** il y a des travaux sur or pendant 5 km; **we walked for miles** nous avons marché pendant des kilomètres

8 (referring to time) pendant; depuis; pour; **he was away for 2 years** il a été absent pendant 2 ans; **she will be away for a month** elle sera absente (pendant) un mois; **it hasn't rained for 3 weeks** ça fait 3 semaines qu'il ne pleut pas, il ne pleut pas depuis 3 semaines; **I have known her for years** je la connais depuis des années; **can you do it for tomorrow?** est-ce que tu peux le faire pour demain?

9 (with infinitive clauses): **it is not for me to decide** ce n'est pas à moi de décider; **it would be best for you to leave** le mieux serait que vous partiez; **there is still time for you to do it** vous avez encore le temps de le faire; **for this to be possible ...** pour que cela soit possible ..

10 (in spite of): **for all that** malgré cela, néanmoins; **for all his work/ efforts** malgré tout son travail/tous ses efforts; **for all his complaints, he's very fond of her** il a beau se plaindre, il l'aime beaucoup
▸ conj (since, as: formal) car

forbid (pt **forbad** or **forbade**, pp **forbidden**) [fə'bɪd, -'bæd, -'bɪdn] vt défendre, interdire; **to ~ sb to do** défendre or interdire à qn de faire; **forbidden** adj défendu(e)

force [fɔːs] n force f ▸ vt forcer; (push) pousser (de force); **to ~ o.s. to do** se forcer à faire; **in ~** (rule, law, prices) en vigueur; (in large numbers) en force; **forced** adj forcé(e); **forceful** adj énergique

ford [fɔːd] n gué m

fore [fɔːʳ] n: **to the ~** en évidence; **forearm** n avant-bras m inv; **forecast** n prévision f; (also: **weather forecast**) prévisions fpl météorologiques, météo f ▸ vt (irreg: like **cast**) prévoir; **forecourt** n (of garage) devant m; **forefinger** n index m; **forefront** n: **in the forefront of** au premier rang or plan de; **foreground** n premier plan f; **forehead** ['fɔrɪd] n front m

foreign ['fɔrɪn] adj étranger(-ère); (trade) extérieur(e); (travel) à l'étranger; **foreign currency** n devises étrangères; **foreigner** n étranger(-ère); **foreign exchange** n (system) change m; (money) devises

fpl; **Foreign Office** n (BRIT) ministère m des Affaires étrangères; **Foreign Secretary** n (BRIT) ministre m des Affaires étrangères

fore: foreman (irreg) n (in construction) contremaître m; **foremost** adj le (la) plus en vue, premier(-ière) ▸ adv: **first and foremost** avant tout, tout d'abord; **forename** n prénom m

forensic [fə'rɛnsɪk] adj: **~ medicine** médecine légale

foresee (pt **foresaw**, pp **foreseen**) [fɔː'siː, -'sɔː, -'siːn] vt prévoir; **foreseeable** adj prévisible

foreseen [fɔː'siːn] pp of **foresee**

forest ['fɔrɪst] n forêt f; **forestry** n sylviculture f

forever [fə'rɛvəʳ] adv pour toujours; (fig: endlessly) continuellement

foreword ['fɔːwəːd] n avant-propos m inv

forfeit ['fɔːfɪt] vt perdre

forgave [fə'geɪv] pt of **forgive**

forge [fɔːdʒ] n forge f ▸ vt (signature) contrefaire; (wrought iron) forger; **to ~ money** (BRIT) fabriquer de la fausse monnaie; **forger** n faussaire m; **forgery** n faux m, contrefaçon f

forget (pt **forgot**, pp **forgotten**) [fə'gɛt, -'gɔt, -'gɔtn] vt, vi oublier; **I've forgotten my key/passport** j'ai oublié ma clé/mon passeport; **forgetful** adj distrait(e), étourdi(e)

forgive (pt **forgave**, pp **forgiven**) [fə'gɪv, -'geɪv, -'gɪvn] vt pardonner; **to ~ sb for sth/for doing sth** pardonner qch à qn/à qn de faire qch

forgot [fə'gɔt] pt of **forget**

forgotten [fə'gɔtn] pp of **forget**

fork [fɔːk] n (for eating) fourchette f; (for gardening) fourche f; (of roads) bifurcation f ▸ vi (road) bifurquer

forlorn [fə'lɔːn] adj (deserted) abandonné(e); (hope, attempt) désespéré(e)

form [fɔːm] n forme f; (Scol) classe f; (questionnaire) formulaire m ▸ vt former; (habit) contracter; **to ~ part**

of sth faire partie de qch; **on top ~** en pleine forme

formal ['fɔːməl] *adj* (*offer, receipt*) en bonne et due forme; (*person*) cérémonieux(-euse); (*occasion, dinner*) officiel(le); (*garden*) à la française; (*clothes*) de soirée; **formality** [fɔːˈmælɪtɪ] *n* formalité *f*

format ['fɔːmæt] *n* format *m* ⊳ *vt* (*Comput*) formater

formation [fɔːˈmeɪʃən] *n* formation *f*

former ['fɔːmə^r] *adj* ancien(ne); (*before n*) précédent(e); **the ~ ... the latter** le premier ... le second, celui-là ... celui-ci; **formerly** *adv* autrefois

formidable ['fɔːmɪdəbl] *adj* redoutable

formula ['fɔːmjulə] *n* formule *f*

fort [fɔːt] *n* fort *m*

forthcoming [fɔːˈθkʌmɪŋ] *adj* qui va paraître *or* avoir lieu prochainement; (*character*) ouvert(e), communicatif(-ive); (*available*) disponible

fortieth ['fɔːtɪɪθ] *num* quarantième

fortify ['fɔːtɪfaɪ] *vt* (*city*) fortifier; (*person*) remonter

fortnight ['fɔːtnaɪt] *n* (BRIT) quinzaine *f*, quinze jours *mpl*; **fortnightly** *adj* bimensuel(le) ⊳ *adv* tous les quinze jours

fortress ['fɔːtrɪs] *n* forteresse *f*

fortunate ['fɔːtʃənɪt] *adj* heureux(-euse); (*person*) chanceux(-euse); **it is ~ that** c'est une chance que, il est heureux que; **fortunately** *adv* heureusement, par bonheur

fortune ['fɔːtʃən] *n* chance *f*; (*wealth*) fortune *f*; **fortune-teller** *n* diseuse *f* de bonne aventure

forty ['fɔːtɪ] *num* quarante

forum ['fɔːrəm] *n* forum *m*, tribune *f*

forward ['fɔːwəd] *adj* (*movement, position*) en avant, vers l'avant; (*not shy*) effronté(e); (*in time*) en avance ⊳ *adv* (*also:* **~s**) en avant ⊳ *n* (*Sport*) avant *m* ⊳ *vt* (*letter*) faire suivre; (*parcel, goods*) expédier; (*fig*) promouvoir, favoriser; **to move ~**

avancer; **forwarding address** *n* adresse *f* de réexpédition; **forward slash** *n* barre *f* oblique

fossick ['fɔsɪk] *vi* (AUST, NZ *inf*) chercher; **to ~ around for** fouiner (*inf*) pour trouver

fossil ['fɔsl] *adj, n* fossile *m*

foster ['fɔstə^r] *vt* (*encourage*) encourager, favoriser; (*child*) élever (*sans adopter*); **foster child** *n* enfant élevé dans une famille d'accueil; **foster parent** *n* parent qui élève un enfant sans l'adopter

fought [fɔːt] *pt, pp of* **fight**

foul [faul] *adj* (*weather, smell, food*) infect(e); (*language*) ordurier(-ière) ⊳ *n* (*Football*) faute *f* ⊳ *vt* (*dirty*) salir, encrasser; **he's got a ~ temper** il a un caractère de chien; **foul play** *n* (*Law*) acte criminel

found [faund] *pt, pp of* **find** ⊳ *vt* (*establish*) fonder; **foundation** [faunˈdeɪʃən] *n* (*act*) fondation *f*; (*base*) fondement *m*; (*also:* **foundation cream**) fond *m* de teint; **foundations** *npl* (*of building*) fondations *fpl*

founder ['faundə^r] *n* fondateur *m* ⊳ *vi* couler, sombrer

fountain ['fauntɪn] *n* fontaine *f*; **fountain pen** *n* stylo *m* (à encre)

four [fɔː^r] *num* quatre; **on all ~s** à quatre pattes; **four-letter word** *n* obscénité *f*, gros mot; **four-poster** *n* (*also:* **four-poster bed**) lit *m* à baldaquin; **fourteen** *num* quatorze; **fourteenth** *num* quatorzième; **fourth** *num* quatrième ⊳ *n* (*Aut: also:* **fourth gear**) quatrième *f*; **four-wheel drive** *n* (*Aut: car*) voiture *f* à quatre roues motrices

fowl [faul] *n* volaille *f*

fox [fɔks] *n* renard *m* ⊳ *vt* mystifier

foyer ['fɔɪeɪ] *n* (*in hotel*) vestibule *m*; (*Theat*) foyer *m*

fraction ['frækʃən] *n* fraction *f*

fracture ['fræktʃə^r] *n* fracture *f* ⊳ *vt* fracturer

fragile ['frædʒaɪl] *adj* fragile
fragment ['frægmənt] *n* fragment *m*
fragrance ['freɪgrəns] *n* parfum *m*
frail [freɪl] *adj* fragile, délicat(e);
(*person*) frêle
frame [freɪm] *n* (*of building*)
charpente *f*; (*of human, animal*)
charpente, ossature *f*; (*of
picture*) cadre *m*; (*of door, window*)
encadrement *m*, chambranle *m*;
(*of spectacles: also:* **~s**) monture *f*
▷ *vt* (*picture*) encadrer; **~ of mind**
disposition *f* d'esprit; **framework** *n*
structure *f*
France [frɑːns] *n* la France
franchise ['fræntʃaɪz] *n* (*Pol*) droit *m*
de vote; (*Comm*) franchise *f*
frank [fræŋk] *adj* franc (franche)
▷ *vt* (*letter*) affranchir; **frankly** *adv*
franchement
frantic ['fræntɪk] *adj* (*hectic*)
frénétique; (*distraught*) hors de soi
fraud [frɔːd] *n* supercherie *f*, fraude *f*,
tromperie *f*; (*person*) imposteur *m*
fraught [frɔːt] *adj* (*tense: person*)
très tendu(e); (: *situation*) pénible;
~ with (*difficulties etc*) chargé(e) de,
plein(e) de
fray [freɪ] *vt* effilocher ▷ *vi* s'effilocher
freak [friːk] *n* (*eccentric person*)
phénomène *m*; (*unusual event*) hasard
m extraordinaire; (*pej: fanatic*):
health food ~ fana *m/f* or obsédé(e)
de l'alimentation saine ▷ *adj* (*storm*)
exceptionnel(le); (*accident*) bizarre
freckle ['frɛkl] *n* tache *f* de rousseur
free [friː] *adj* libre; (*gratis*) gratuit(e)
▷ *vt* (*prisoner etc*) libérer; (*jammed
object or person*) dégager; **is this seat
~?** la place est libre?; **~ (of charge)**
gratuitement; **freedom** *n* liberté *f*;
Freefone® *n* numéro vert; **free gift**
n prime *f*; **free kick** *n* (*Sport*) coup
franc; **freelance** *adj* (*journalist etc*)
indépendant(e), free-lance *inv* ▷ *adv*
en free-lance; **freely** *adv* librement;
(*liberally*) libéralement; **Freepost®** *n*
(*BRIT*) port payé; **free-range** *adj* (*egg*)

de ferme; (*chicken*) fermier; **freeway**
n (*US*) autoroute *f*; **free will** *n* libre
arbitre *m*; **of one's own free will** de
son plein gré
freeze [friːz] (*pt* **froze**, *pp* **frozen**)
vi geler ▷ *vt* geler; (*food*) congeler;
(*prices, salaries*) bloquer, geler ▷ *n*
gel *m*; (*of prices, salaries*) blocage *m*;
freezer *n* congélateur *m*; **freezing**
adj: **freezing (cold)** (*room etc*)
glacial(e); (*person, hands*) gelé(e),
glacé(e) ▷ *n*: **3 degrees below
freezing** 3 degrés au-dessous de
zéro; **it's freezing** il fait un froid
glacial; **freezing point** *n* point *m* de
congélation
freight [freɪt] *n* (*goods*) fret *m*,
cargaison *f*; (*money charged*) fret, prix
m du transport; **freight train** *n* (*US*)
train *m* de marchandises
French [frɛntʃ] *adj* français(e)
▷ *n* (*Ling*) français *m*; **the ~** *npl* les
Français; **what's the ~ (word) for
…?** comment dit-on … en français?;
French bean *n* (*BRIT*) haricot vert;
French bread *n* pain *m* français;
French dressing *n* (*Culin*) vinaigrette
f; **French fried potatoes, French
fries** (*US*) *npl* (pommes de terre
fpl) frites *fpl*; **Frenchman** (*irreg*)
n Français *m*; **French stick** *n* ≈
baguette *f*; **French window** *n* porte-
fenêtre *f*; **Frenchwoman** (*irreg*) *n*
Française *f*
frenzy ['frɛnzɪ] *n* frénésie *f*
frequency ['friːkwənsɪ] *n*
fréquence *f*
frequent *adj* ['friːkwənt] fréquent(e)
▷ *vt* [frɪ'kwɛnt] fréquenter;
frequently ['friːkwəntlɪ] *adv*
fréquemment
fresh [frɛʃ] *adj* frais (fraîche);
(*new*) nouveau (nouvelle); (*cheeky*)
familier(-ière), culotté(e); **freshen** *vi*
(*wind, air*) fraîchir; **freshen up** *vi* faire
un brin de toilette; **fresher** *n* (*BRIT
University: inf*) bizuth *m*, étudiant(e)
de première année; **freshly** *adv*

nouvellement, récemment;
freshman (*irreg*) *n* (*US*) = **fresher**;
freshwater *adj* (*fish*) d'eau douce
fret [frɛt] *vi* s'agiter, se tracasser
friction ['frɪkʃən] *n* friction *f*,
frottement *m*
Friday ['fraɪdɪ] *n* vendredi *m*
fridge [frɪdʒ] *n* (*BRIT*) frigo *m*,
frigidaire® *m*
fried [fraɪd] *adj* frit(e); **~ egg** œuf *m*
sur le plat
friend [frɛnd] *n* ami(e) ▷ *vt* (*Internet*)
ajouter comme ami(e); **friendly**
adj amical(e); (*kind*) sympathique,
gentil(le); (*place*) accueillant(e); (*Pol:
country*) ami(e) ▷ *n* (*also*: **friendly
match**) match amical; **friendship**
n amitié *f*
fries [fraɪz] (*esp US*) *npl* = **chips**
frigate ['frɪgɪt] *n* frégate *f*
fright [fraɪt] *n* peur *f*, effroi *m*; **to
give sb a ~** faire peur à qn; **to take
~** prendre peur, s'effrayer; **frighten**
vt effrayer, faire peur à; **frightened**
adj: **to be frightened (of)** avoir peur
(de); **frightening** *adj* effrayant(e);
frightful *adj* affreux(-euse)
frill [frɪl] *n* (*of dress*) volant *m*; (*of shirt*)
jabot *m*
fringe [frɪndʒ] *n* (*BRIT: of hair*) frange
f; (*edge: of forest etc*) bordure *f*
Frisbee® ['frɪzbɪ] *n* Frisbee® *m*
fritter ['frɪtər] *n* beignet *m*
frivolous ['frɪvələs] *adj* frivole
fro [frəʊ] *adv see* **to**
frock [frɒk] *n* robe *f*
frog [frɒg] *n* grenouille *f*; **frogman**
(*irreg*) *n* homme-grenouille *m*

KEYWORD

from [frɒm] *prep* **1** (*indicating starting
place, origin etc*) de; **where do you
come from?, where are you from?**
d'où venez-vous?; **where has he
come from?** d'où arrive-t-il?; **from
London to Paris** de Londres à Paris;
to escape from sb/sth échapper

à qn/qch; **a letter/telephone call
from my sister** une lettre/un appel
de ma sœur; **to drink from the
bottle** boire à (même) la bouteille;
tell him from me that … dites-lui de
ma part que …
2 (*indicating time*) (à partir) de; **from
one o'clock to** *or* **until** *or* **till two**
d'une heure à deux heures; **from
January (on)** à partir de janvier
3 (*indicating distance*) de; **the hotel
is one kilometre from the beach**
l'hôtel est à un kilomètre de la plage
4 (*indicating price, number etc*) de;
prices range from £10 to £50 les prix
varient entre 10 livres et 50 livres; **the
interest rate was increased from
9% to 10%** le taux d'intérêt est passé
de 9% à 10%
5 (*indicating difference*) de; **he can't
tell red from green** il ne peut pas
distinguer le rouge du vert; **to be
different from sb/sth** être différent
de qn/qch
6 (*because of, on the basis of*): **from
what he says** d'après ce qu'il dit;
weak from hunger affaibli par
la faim

front [frʌnt] *n* (*of house, dress*)
devant *m*; (*of coach, train*) avant *m*;
(*promenade: also*: **sea ~**) bord *m* de
mer; (*Mil, Pol, Meteorology*) front
m; (*fig: appearances*) contenance *f*,
façade *f* ▷ *adj* de devant; (*seat, wheel*)
avant *inv* ▷ *vi*: **in ~ (of)** devant;
front door *n* porte *f* d'entrée; (*of car*)
portière *f* avant; **frontier** ['frʌntɪər]
n frontière *f*; **front page** *n* première
page; **front-wheel drive** *n* traction
f avant
frost [frɒst] *n* gel *m*, gelée *f*; (*also*:
hoar~) givre *m*; **frostbite** *n* gelures
fpl; **frosting** *n* (*esp US: on cake*)
glaçage *m*; **frosty** *adj* (*window*)
couvert(e) de givre; (*weather, welcome*)
glacial(e)
froth [frɒθ] *n* mousse *f*; écume *f*

frown [fraun] n froncement m de
sourcils ▷ vi froncer les sourcils

froze [frəuz] pt of **freeze**

frozen ['frəuzn] pp of **freeze** ▷ adj
(food) congelé(e); (person, also assets)
gelé(e)

fruit [fru:t] n (pl inv) fruit m; **fruit
juice** n jus m de fruit; **fruit machine**
n (BRIT) machine f à sous; **fruit salad**
n salade f de fruits

frustrate [frʌs'treɪt] vt frustrer;
frustrated adj frustré(e)

fry (pt, pp **fried**) [fraɪ, -d] vt (faire) frire
▷ n: **small ~** le menu fretin; **frying
pan** n poêle f (à frire)

ft. abbr = **foot; feet**

fudge [fʌdʒ] n (Culin) sorte de confiserie
à base de sucre, de beurre et de lait

fuel [fjuəl] n (for heating) combustible
m; (for engine) carburant m; **fuel
tank** n (in vehicle) réservoir m de or
à carburant

fulfil, (US) **fulfill** [ful'fɪl] vt (function,
condition) remplir; (order) exécuter;
(wish, desire) satisfaire, réaliser

full [ful] adj plein(e); (details, hotel, bus)
complet(-ète); (busy: day) chargé(e);
(skirt) ample, large ▷ adv: **to know ~
well that** savoir fort bien que; **I'm ~
(up)** j'ai bien mangé; **~ employment/
fare** plein emploi/tarif; **a ~ two
hours** deux bonnes heures; **at ~
speed** à toute vitesse; **in ~** (reproduce,
quote, pay) intégralement; (write name
etc) en toutes lettres; **full-length** adj
(portrait) en pied; (coat) long(ue); **full-
length film** long métrage; **full moon**
n pleine lune; **full-scale** adj (model)
grandeur nature inv; (search, retreat)
complet(-ète), total(e); **full stop** n
point m; **full-time** adj, adv (work) à
plein temps; **fully** adv entièrement,
complètement

fumble ['fʌmbl] vi fouiller, tâtonner;
fumble with vt fus tripoter

fume [fju:m] vi (rage) rager; **fumes**
[fju:mz] npl vapeurs fpl, émanations
fpl, gaz mpl

fun [fʌn] n amusement m,
divertissement m; **to have ~**
s'amuser; **for ~** pour rire; **to make ~
of** se moquer de

function ['fʌŋkʃən] n fonction f;
(reception, dinner) cérémonie f, soirée
officielle f ▷ vi fonctionner

fund [fʌnd] n caisse f, fonds m;
(source, store) source f, mine f; **funds**
npl (money) fonds mpl

fundamental [fʌndə'mɛntl] adj
fondamental(e)

funeral ['fju:nərəl] n enterrement
m, obsèques fpl (more formal occasion);
funeral director n entrepreneur
m des pompes funèbres; **funeral
parlour** n (BRIT) dépôt m mortuaire

funfair ['fʌnfɛəʳ] n (BRIT) fête
(foraine)

fungus (pl **fungi**) ['fʌŋgəs, -gaɪ] n
champignon m; (mould) moisissure f

funnel ['fʌnl] n entonnoir m; (of ship)
cheminée f

funny ['fʌnɪ] adj amusant(e), drôle;
(strange) curieux(-euse), bizarre

fur [fə:ʳ] n fourrure f; (BRIT: in kettle
etc) (dépôt m de) tartre m; **fur coat** n
manteau m de fourrure

furious ['fjuərɪəs] adj furieux(-euse);
(effort) acharné(e)

furnish ['fə:nɪʃ] vt meubler; (supply)
fournir; **furnishings** npl mobilier m,
articles mpl d'ameublement

furniture ['fə:nɪtʃəʳ] n meubles mpl,
mobilier m; **piece of ~** meuble m

furry ['fə:rɪ] adj (animal) à fourrure;
(toy) en peluche

further ['fə:ðəʳ] adj supplémentaire,
autre; nouveau (nouvelle) ▷ adv
plus loin; (more) davantage;
(moreover) de plus ▷ vt faire avancer
or progresser, promouvoir; **further
education** n enseignement m
postscolaire (recyclage, formation
professionnelle); **furthermore** adv de
plus, en outre

furthest ['fə:ðɪst] superlative of **far**

fury ['fjuərɪ] n fureur f

fuse, (US) **fuze** [fjuːz] n fusible m;
(for bomb etc) amorce f, détonateur m
▷ vt, vi (metal) fondre; (BRIT Elec): **to**
~ the lights faire sauter les fusibles
or les plombs; **fuse box** n boîte f à
fusibles

fusion ['fjuːʒən] n fusion f

fuss [fʌs] n (anxiety, excitement) chichis
mpl, façons fpl; (commotion) tapage m;
(complaining, trouble) histoire(s) f(pl);
to make a ~ faire des façons (or des
histoires); **to make a ~ of sb** dorloter
qn; **fussy** adj (person) tatillon(ne),
difficile, chichiteux(-euse); (dress,
style) tarabiscoté(e)

future ['fjuːtʃəʳ] adj futur(e) ▷ n
avenir m; (Ling) futur m; **futures** npl
(Comm) opérations fpl à terme; **in**
(the) ~ à l'avenir

fuze [fjuːz] n, vt, vi (US) = **fuse**

fuzzy ['fʌzɪ] adj (Phot) flou(e); (hair)
crépu(e)

FYI abbr = **for your information**

g

G [dʒiː] n (Mus) sol m

g. abbr (= gram) g

gadget ['gædʒɪt] n gadget m

Gaelic ['geɪlɪk] adj, n (Ling) gaélique
(m)

gag [gæg] n (on mouth) bâillon m; (joke)
gag m ▷ vt (prisoner etc) bâillonner

gain [geɪn] n (improvement) gain m;
(profit) gain, profit m ▷ vt gagner
▷ vi (watch) avancer; **to ~ from/by**
gagner de/à; **to ~ on sb** (catch up)
rattraper qn; **to ~ 3lbs (in weight)**
prendre 3 livres; **to ~ ground** gagner
du terrain

gal. abbr = **gallon**

gala ['gɑːlə] n gala m

galaxy ['gæləksɪ] n galaxie f

gale [geɪl] n coup m de vent

gall bladder ['gɔːl-] n vésicule f
biliaire

gallery ['gælərɪ] n (also: **art ~**) musée
m; (private) galerie; (in theatre) dernier
balcon

gallon ['gæln] n gallon m (Brit = 4.543 l; US = 3.785 l)

gallop ['gæləp] n galop m ▷ vi galoper

gallstone ['gɔ:lstəun] n calcul m (biliaire)

gamble ['gæmbl] n pari m, risque calculé ▷ vt, vi jouer; **to ~ on** (fig) miser sur; **gambler** n joueur m; **gambling** n jeu m

game [geɪm] n jeu m; (event) match m; (of tennis, chess, cards) partie f; (Hunting) gibier m ▷ adj (willing): **to be ~ (for)** être prêt(e) (à or pour); **games** npl (Scol) sport m; (sport event) jeux; **big ~** gros gibier; **games console** ['geɪmz-] n console f de jeux vidéo; **game show** n jeu télévisé

gammon ['gæmən] n (bacon) quartier m de lard fumé; (ham) jambon fumé or salé

gang [gæŋ] n bande f; (of workmen) équipe f

gangster ['gæŋstər] n gangster m, bandit m

gap [gæp] n trou m; (in time) intervalle m; (difference): **~ (between)** écart m (entre)

gape [geɪp] vi (person) être or rester bouche bée; (hole, shirt) être ouvert(e)

gap year n année que certains étudiants prennent pour voyager ou pour travailler avant d'entrer à l'université

garage ['gærɑ:ʒ] n garage m; **garage sale** n vide-grenier m

garbage ['gɑ:bɪdʒ] n (us: rubbish) ordures fpl, détritus mpl; (inf: nonsense) âneries fpl; **garbage can** n (us) poubelle f, boîte f à ordures; **garbage collector** n (us) éboueur m

garden ['gɑ:dn] n jardin m; **gardens** npl (public) jardin public; (private) parc m; **garden centre** (BRIT) n pépinière f, jardinerie f; **gardener** n jardinier m; **gardening** n jardinage m

garlic ['gɑ:lɪk] n ail m

garment ['gɑ:mənt] n vêtement m

garnish ['gɑ:nɪʃ] (Culin) vt garnir ▷ n décoration f

garrison ['gærɪsn] n garnison f

gas [gæs] n gaz m; (us: gasoline) essence f ▷ vt asphyxier; **I can smell ~** ça sent le gaz; **gas cooker** n (BRIT) cuisinière f à gaz; **gas cylinder** n bouteille f de gaz; **gas fire** n (BRIT) radiateur m à gaz

gasket ['gæskɪt] n (Aut) joint m de culasse

gasoline ['gæsəli:n] n (us) essence f

gasp [gɑ:sp] n halètement m; (of shock etc): **she gave a small ~ of pain** la douleur lui coupa le souffle ▷ vi haleter; (fig) avoir le souffle coupé

gas: gas pedal n (us) accélérateur m; **gas station** n (us) station-service f; **gas tank** n (us Aut) réservoir m d'essence

gate [geɪt] n (of garden) portail m; (of field, at level crossing) barrière f; (of building, town, at airport) porte f

gateau (pl **gateaux**) ['gætəu, -z] n gros gâteau à la crème

gatecrash ['geɪtkræʃ] vt s'introduire sans invitation dans

gateway ['geɪtweɪ] n porte f

gather ['gæðər] vt (flowers, fruit) cueillir; (pick up) ramasser; (assemble: objects) rassembler; (: people) réunir; (: information) recueillir; (understand) comprendre; (Sewing) froncer ▷ vi (assemble) se rassembler; **to ~ speed** prendre de la vitesse; **gathering** n rassemblement m

gauge [geɪdʒ] n (instrument) jauge f ▷ vt jauger; (fig) juger de

gave [geɪv] pt of **give**

gay [geɪ] adj (homosexual) homosexuel(le); (colour) gai, vif (vive)

gaze [geɪz] n regard m fixe ▷ vi: **to ~ at** fixer du regard

GB abbr = **Great Britain**

GCSE n abbr (BRIT: = General Certificate of Secondary Education) examen passé à l'âge de 16 ans sanctionnant les connaissances de l'élève

gear [gɪər] n matériel m, équipement m; (Tech) engrenage m; (Aut) vitesse f ▷ vt (fig: adapt) adapter; **top** or (US) **high/low ~** quatrième (or cinquième)/première vitesse; **in ~** en prise; **gear up** vi: **to ~ up (to do)** se préparer (à faire); **gear box** n boîte f de vitesse; **gear lever** n levier m de vitesse; **gear shift** (US) n = **gear lever**; **gear stick** (BRIT) n = **gear lever**

geese [giːs] npl of **goose**

gel [dʒɛl] n gelée f

gem [dʒɛm] n pierre précieuse

Gemini ['dʒɛmɪnaɪ] n les Gémeaux mpl

gender ['dʒɛndəʳ] n genre m; (person's sex) sexe m

gene [dʒiːn] n (Biol) gène m

general ['dʒɛnərl] n général m ▷ adj général(e); **in ~** en général; **general anaesthetic**, (US) **general anesthetic** n anesthésie générale; **general election** n élection(s) législative(s); **generalize** vi généraliser; **generally** adv généralement; **general practitioner** n généraliste m/f; **general store** n épicerie f

generate ['dʒɛnəreɪt] vt engendrer; (electricity) produire

generation [dʒɛnə'reɪʃən] n génération f; (of electricity etc) production f

generator ['dʒɛnəreɪtəʳ] n générateur m

generosity [dʒɛnə'rɒsɪtɪ] n générosité f

generous ['dʒɛnərəs] adj généreux(-euse); (copious) copieux(-euse)

genetic [dʒɪ'nɛtɪk] adj génétique; **~ engineering** ingénierie m génétique; **~ fingerprinting** système m d'empreinte génétique; **genetically modified** adj (food etc) génétiquement modifié(e); **genetics** n génétique f

Geneva [dʒɪ'niːvə] n Genève f

genitals ['dʒɛnɪtlz] npl organes génitaux

genius ['dʒiːnɪəs] n génie m

gent [dʒɛnt] n abbr (BRIT inf); = **gentleman**

gentle ['dʒɛntl] adj doux (douce); (breeze, touch) léger(-ère)

gentleman ['dʒɛntlmən] (irreg) n monsieur m; (well-bred man) gentleman m

gently ['dʒɛntlɪ] adv doucement

gents [dʒɛnts] n W.-C. mpl (pour hommes)

genuine ['dʒɛnjuɪn] adj véritable, authentique; (person, emotion) sincère; **genuinely** adv sincèrement, vraiment

geographic(al) [dʒɪə'græfɪk-] adj géographique

geography [dʒɪ'ɔgrəfɪ] n géographie f

geology [dʒɪ'ɔlədʒɪ] n géologie f

geometry [dʒɪ'ɔmɪtrɪ] n géométrie f

geranium [dʒɪ'reɪnɪəm] n géranium m

geriatric [dʒɛrɪ'ætrɪk] adj gériatrique ▷ n patient(e) gériatrique

germ [dʒəːm] n (Med) microbe m

German ['dʒəːmən] adj allemand(e) ▷ n Allemand(e); (Ling) allemand m; **German measles** n rubéole f

Germany ['dʒəːmənɪ] n Allemagne f

gesture ['dʒɛstjəʳ] n geste m

KEYWORD

get [gɛt] (pt, pp **got**, (US) pp **gotten**) vi **1** (become, be) devenir; **to get old/ tired** devenir vieux/fatigué, vieillir/se fatiguer; **to get drunk** s'enivrer; **to get dirty** se salir; **to get married** se marier; **when do I get paid?** quand est-ce que je serai payé?; **it's getting late** il se fait tard

2 (go): **to get to/from** aller à/de; **to get home** rentrer chez soi; **how did you get here?** comment es-tu arrivé ici?

3 (begin) commencer or se mettre à; **to get to know sb** apprendre à

connaître qn; **I'm getting to like him** je commence à l'apprécier; **let's get going** or **started** allons-y
4 (modal aux vb): **you've got to do it** il faut que vous le fassiez; **I've got to tell the police** je dois le dire à la police

▶ vt **1**: **to get sth done** (do) faire qch; (have done) faire faire qch; **to get sth/sb ready** préparer qch/qn; **to get one's hair cut** se faire couper les cheveux; **to get the car going** or **to go** (faire) démarrer la voiture; **to get sb to do sth** faire faire qch à qn
2 (obtain: money, permission, results) obtenir, avoir; (buy) acheter; (find: job, flat) trouver; (fetch: person, doctor, object) aller chercher; **to get sth for sb** procurer qch à qn; **get me Mr Jones, please** (on phone) passez-moi Mr Jones, s'il vous plaît; **can I get you a drink?** est-ce que je peux vous servir à boire?
3 (receive: present, letter) recevoir, avoir; (acquire: reputation) avoir; (: prize) obtenir; **what did you get for your birthday?** qu'est-ce que tu as eu pour ton anniversaire?; **how much did you get for the painting?** combien avez-vous vendu le tableau?
4 (catch) prendre, saisir, attraper; (hit: target etc) atteindre; **to get sb by the arm/throat** prendre or saisir or attraper qn par le bras/à la gorge; **get him!** arrête-le!; **the bullet got him in the leg** il a pris la balle dans la jambe
5 (take, move): **to get sth to sb** faire parvenir qch à qn; **do you think we'll get it through the door?** on arrivera à le faire passer par la porte?
6 (catch, take: plane, bus etc) prendre; **where do I get the train for Birmingham?** où prend-on le train pour Birmingham?
7 (understand) comprendre, saisir; (hear) entendre; **I've got it!** j'ai compris!; **I don't get your meaning**

je ne vois or comprends pas ce que vous voulez dire; **I didn't get your name** je n'ai pas entendu votre nom
8 (have, possess): **to have got** avoir; **how many have you got?** vous en avez combien?
9 (illness) avoir; **I've got a cold** j'ai le rhume; **she got pneumonia and died** elle a fait une pneumonie et elle en est morte
get away vi partir, s'en aller; (escape) s'échapper
get away with vt fus (punishment) en être quitte pour; (crime etc) se faire pardonner
get back vi (return) rentrer ▷ vt récupérer, recouvrer; **when do we get back?** quand serons-nous de retour?
get in vi entrer; (arrive home) rentrer; (train) arriver
get into vt fus entrer dans; (car, train etc) monter dans; (clothes) mettre, enfiler, endosser; **to get into bed/a rage** se mettre au lit/en colère
get off vi (from train etc) descendre; (depart: person, car) s'en aller ▷ vt (remove: clothes, stain) enlever ▷ vt fus (train, bus) descendre de; **where do I get off?** où est-ce que je dois descendre?
get on vi (at exam etc) se débrouiller; (agree): **to get on (with)** s'entendre (avec); **how are you getting on?** comment ça va? ▷ vt fus monter dans; (horse) monter sur
get out vi sortir; (of vehicle) descendre ▷ vt sortir
get out of vt fus sortir de; (duty etc) échapper à, se soustraire à
get over vt fus (illness) se remettre de
get through vi (Tel) avoir la communication; **to get through to sb** atteindre qn
get up vi (rise) se lever ▷ vt fus monter
getaway ['gɛtəweɪ] n fuite f

Ghana ['gɑːnə] n Ghana m
ghastly ['gɑːstlɪ] adj atroce, horrible
ghetto ['gɛtəu] n ghetto m
ghost [gəust] n fantôme m, revenant m
giant ['dʒaɪənt] n géant(e) ▷ adj géant(e), énorme
gift [gɪft] n cadeau m; (donation, talent) don m; **gifted** adj doué(e); **gift shop**, (US)**gift store** n boutique f de cadeaux; **gift token, gift voucher** n chèque-cadeau m
gig [gɪg] n (inf: concert) concert m
gigabyte ['dʒɪgəbaɪt] n gigaoctet m
gigantic [dʒaɪ'gæntɪk] adj gigantesque
giggle ['gɪgl] vi pouffer, ricaner sottement
gills [gɪlz] npl (of fish) ouïes fpl, branchies fpl
gilt [gɪlt] n dorure f ▷ adj doré(e)
gimmick ['gɪmɪk] n truc m
gin [dʒɪn] n gin m
ginger ['dʒɪndʒər] n gingembre m
gipsy ['dʒɪpsɪ] n = **gypsy**
giraffe [dʒɪ'rɑːf] n girafe f
girl [gəːl] n fille f, fillette f; (young unmarried woman) jeune fille; (daughter) fille; **an English ~** une jeune Anglaise; **girl band** n girls band m; **girlfriend** n (of girl) amie f; (of boy) petite amie; **Girl Guide** n (BRIT) éclaireuse f; (Roman Catholic) guide f; **Girl Scout** n (US) = **Girl Guide**
gist [dʒɪst] n essentiel m
give [gɪv] (pt **gave**, pp **given**) vt donner ▷ vi (break) céder; (stretch: fabric) se prêter; **to ~ sb sth, ~ sth to sb** donner qch à qn; (gift) offrir qch à qn; (message) transmettre qch à qn; **to ~ sb a call/kiss** appeler/ embrasser qn; **to ~ a cry/sigh** pousser un cri/un soupir; **give away** vt donner; (give free) faire cadeau de; (betray) donner, trahir; (disclose) révéler; **give back** vt rendre; **give in** vi céder ▷ vt donner; **give out** vt (food etc) distribuer; **give up** vi

renoncer ▷ vt renoncer à; **to ~ up smoking** arrêter de fumer; **to ~ o.s. up** se rendre
given ['gɪvn] pp of **give** ▷ adj (fixed: time, amount) donné(e), déterminé(e) ▷ conj: **~ the circumstances ...** étant donné les circonstances ..., vu les circonstances ...; **~ that ...** étant donné que ...
glacier ['glæsɪər] n glacier m
glad [glæd] adj content(e); **gladly** ['glædlɪ] adv volontiers
glamorous ['glæmərəs] adj (person) séduisant(e); (job) prestigieux(-euse)
glamour, (US)**glamor** ['glæmər] n éclat m, prestige m
glance [glɑːns] n coup m d'œil ▷ vi: **to ~ at** jeter un coup d'œil à
gland [glænd] n glande f
glare [glɛər] n (of anger) regard furieux; (of light) lumière éblouissante; (of publicity) feux mpl ▷ vi briller d'un éclat aveuglant; **to ~ at** lancer un regard or des regards furieux à; **glaring** adj (mistake) criant(e), qui saute aux yeux
glass [glɑːs] n verre m; **glasses** npl (spectacles) lunettes fpl
glaze [gleɪz] vt (door) vitrer; (pottery) vernir ▷ n vernis m
gleam [gliːm] vi luire, briller
glen [glɛn] n vallée f
glide [glaɪd] vi glisser; (Aviat, bird) planer; **glider** n (Aviat) planeur m
glimmer ['glɪmər] n lueur f
glimpse [glɪmps] n vision passagère, aperçu m ▷ vt entrevoir, apercevoir
glint [glɪnt] vi étinceler
glisten ['glɪsn] vi briller, luire
glitter ['glɪtər] vi scintiller, briller
global ['gləubl] adj (world-wide) mondial(e); (overall) global(e); **globalization** n mondialisation f; **global warming** n réchauffement m de la planète
globe [gləub] n globe m
gloom [gluːm] n obscurité f; (sadness) tristesse f, mélancolie f; **gloomy**

adj (*person*) morose; (*place, outlook*) sombre

glorious ['glɔːrɪəs] *adj* glorieux(-euse); (*beautiful*) splendide

glory ['glɔːrɪ] *n* gloire *f*; splendeur *f*

gloss [glɔs] *n* (*shine*) brillant *m*, vernis *m*; (*also:* **~ paint**) peinture brillante *or* laquée

glossary ['glɔsərɪ] *n* glossaire *m*, lexique *m*

glossy ['glɔsɪ] *adj* brillant(e), luisant(e) ▷ *n* (*also:* **~ magazine**) revue *f* de luxe

glove [glʌv] *n* gant *m*; **glove compartment** *n* (*Aut*) boîte *f* à gants, vide-poches *m inv*

glow [gləu] *vi* rougeoyer; (*face*) rayonner; (*eyes*) briller

glucose ['gluːkəus] *n* glucose *m*

glue [gluː] *n* colle *f* ▷ *vt* coller

GM *abbr* (= *genetically modified*) génétiquement modifié(e)

gm *abbr* (= *gram*) g

GMO *n abbr* (= *genetically modified organism*) OGM *m*

GMT *abbr* (= *Greenwich Mean Time*) GMT

gnaw [nɔː] *vt* ronger

go [gəu] (*pt* **went**, *pp* **gone**) *vi* aller; (*depart*) partir, s'en aller; (*work*) marcher; (*break*) céder; (*time*) passer; (*be sold*): **to go for £10** se vendre 10 livres; (*become*): **to go pale/mouldy** pâlir/moisir ▷ *n* (*pl* **goes**): **to have a go (at)** essayer (de faire); **to be on the go** être en mouvement; **whose go is it?** à qui est-ce de jouer?; **he's going to do it** il va le faire, il est sur le point de le faire; **to go for a walk** aller se promener; **to go dancing/shopping** aller danser/faire les courses; **to go and see sb, go to see sb** aller voir qn; **how did it go?** comment est-ce que ça s'est passé?; **to go round the back/by the shop** passer par derrière/devant le magasin; **… to go** (*US: food*) … à emporter; **go ahead** *vi* (*take place*) avoir lieu; (*get going*) y aller; **go away**

vi partir, s'en aller; **go back** *vi* rentrer; revenir; (*go again*) retourner; **go by** *vi* (*years, time*) passer, s'écouler ▷ *vt fus* s'en tenir à; (*believe*) en croire; **go down** *vi* descendre; (*number, price, amount*) baisser; (*ship*) couler; (*sun*) se coucher ▷ *vt fus* descendre; **go for** *vt fus* (*fetch*) aller chercher; (*like*) aimer; (*attack*) s'en prendre à; attaquer; **go in** *vi* entrer; **go into** *vt fus* entrer dans; (*investigate*) étudier, examiner; (*embark on*) se lancer dans; **go off** *vi* partir, s'en aller; (*food*) se gâter; (*milk*) tourner; (*bomb*) sauter; (*alarm clock*) sonner; (*alarm*) se déclencher; (*lights etc*) s'éteindre; (*event*) se dérouler ▷ *vt fus* ne plus aimer; **the gun went off** le coup est parti; **go on** *vi* continuer; (*happen*) se passer; (*lights*) s'allumer ▷ *vt fus*: **to go on doing** continuer à faire; **go out** *vi* sortir; (*fire, light*) s'éteindre; (*tide*) descendre; **to go out with sb** sortir avec qn; **go over** *vi, vt fus* (*check*) revoir, vérifier; **go past** *vt fus*: **to go past sth** passer devant qch; **go round** *vi* (*circulate: news, rumour*) circuler; (*revolve*) tourner; (*suffice*) suffire (pour tout le monde); (*visit*): **to go round to sb's** passer chez qn; aller chez qn; (*make a detour*) se passer; (*lights*) faire un détour (par); **go through** *vt fus* (*town etc*) traverser; (*search through*) fouiller; (*suffer*) subir; **go up** *vi* monter; (*price*) augmenter ▷ *vt fus* gravir; **go with** *vt fus* aller avec; **go without** *vt fus* se passer de

go-ahead ['gəuəhɛd] *adj* dynamique, entreprenant(e) ▷ *n* feu vert

goal [gəul] *n* but *m*; **goalkeeper** *n* gardien *m* de but; **goal-post** *n* poteau *m* de but

goat [gəut] *n* chèvre *f*

gobble ['gɔbl] *vt* (*also:* **~ down, ~ up**) engloutir

god [gɔd] *n* dieu *m*; **God** Dieu; **godchild** *n* filleul(e); **goddaughter**

n filleule *f*; **goddess** *n* déesse *f*; **godfather** *n* parrain *m*; **godmother** *n* marraine *f*; **godson** *n* filleul *m*

goggles ['gɔglz] *npl* (*for skiing etc*) lunettes (protectrices); (*for swimming*) lunettes de piscine

going ['gəʊɪŋ] *n* (*conditions*) état *m* du terrain ▷ *adj*: **the ~ rate** le tarif (en vigueur)

gold [gəʊld] *n* or *m* ▷ *adj* en or; (*reserves*) d'or; **golden** *adj* (*made of gold*) en or; (*gold in colour*) doré(e); **goldfish** *n* poisson *m* rouge; **goldmine** *n* mine *f* d'or; **gold-plated** *adj* plaqué(e) or *inv*

golf [gɔlf] *n* golf *m*; **golf ball** *n* balle *f* de golf; (*on typewriter*) boule *f*; **golf club** *n* club *m* de golf; (*stick*) club *m*, crosse *f* de golf; **golf course** *n* terrain *m* de golf; **golfer** *n* joueur(-euse) de golf

gone [gɔn] *pp of* **go**

gong [gɔŋ] *n* gong *m*

good [gʊd] *adj* bon(ne); (*kind*) gentil(le); (*child*) sage; (*weather*) beau (belle) ▷ *n* bien *m*; **goods** *npl* marchandise *f*, articles *mpl*; **~!** bon!, très bien!; **to be ~ at** être bon en; **to be ~ for** être bon pour; **it's no ~ complaining** cela ne sert à rien de se plaindre; **to make ~** (*deficit*) combler; (*losses*) compenser; **for ~** (*for ever*) pour de bon, une fois pour toutes; **would you be ~ enough to …?** auriez-vous la bonté *or* l'amabilité de …?; **is this any ~?** (*will it do?*) est-ce que ceci fera l'affaire?, est-ce que cela peut vous rendre service?; (*what's it like?*) qu'est-ce que ça vaut?; **a ~ deal (of)** beaucoup (de); **a ~ many** beaucoup (de); **~ morning/ afternoon!** bonjour!; **~ evening!** bonsoir!; **~ night!** bonsoir!; (*on going to bed*) bonne nuit!; **goodbye** *excl* au revoir!; **to say goodbye to sb** dire au revoir à qn; **Good Friday** *n* Vendredi saint; **good-looking** *adj* beau (belle), bien *inv*; **good-natured** *adj* (*person*)

qui a un bon naturel; **goodness** *n* (*of person*) bonté *f*; **for goodness sake!** je vous en prie!; **goodness gracious!** mon Dieu!; **goods train** *n* (*BRIT*) train *m* de marchandises; **goodwill** *n* bonne volonté

google ['gugl] *vi* faire une recheche Google® ▷ *vt* googler

goose (*pl* **geese**) [guːs, giːs] *n* oie *f*

gooseberry ['guzbərɪ] *n* groseille *f* à maquereau; **to play ~** (*BRIT*) tenir la chandelle

goose bumps, goose pimples *npl* chair *f* de poule

gorge [gɔːdʒ] *n* gorge *f* ▷ *vt*: **to ~ o.s. (on)** se gorger (de)

gorgeous ['gɔːdʒəs] *adj* splendide, superbe

gorilla [gəˈrɪlə] *n* gorille *m*

gosh [gɔʃ] (*inf*) *excl* mince alors!

gospel ['gɔspl] *n* évangile *m*

gossip ['gɔsɪp] *n* (*chat*) bavardages *mpl*; (*malicious*) commérage *m*, cancans *mpl*; (*person*) commère *f* ▷ *vi* bavarder; cancaner, faire des commérages; **gossip column** *n* (*Press*) échos *mpl*

got [gɔt] *pt, pp of* **get**

gotten ['gɔtn] (*US*) *pp of* **get**

gourmet ['guəmeɪ] *n* gourmet *m*, gastronome *m/f*

govern ['gʌvən] *vt* gouverner; (*influence*) déterminer; **government** *n* gouvernement *m*; (*BRIT: ministers*) ministère *m*; **governor** *n* (*of colony, state, bank*) gouverneur *m*; (*of school, hospital etc*) administrateur(-trice); (*BRIT: of prison*) directeur(-trice)

gown [gaun] *n* robe *f*; (*of teacher, BRIT: of judge*) toge *f*

GP *n abbr* (*Med*) = **general practitioner**

GPS *n abbr* (= *global positioning system*) GPS *m*

grab [græb] *vt* saisir, empoigner ▷ *vi*: **to ~ at** essayer de saisir

grace [greɪs] *n* grâce *f* ▷ *vt* (*honour*) honorer; (*adorn*) orner; **5 days'**

g

~ un répit de 5 jours; **graceful** adj gracieux(-euse), élégant(e); **gracious** ['greɪʃəs] adj bienveillant(e)

grade [greɪd] n (Comm: quality) qualité f; (: size) calibre m; (: type) catégorie f; (in hierarchy) grade m, échelon m; (Scol) note f; (US: school class) classe f; (: gradient) pente f ▷ vt classer; (by size) calibrer; **grade crossing** n (US) passage m à niveau; **grade school** n (US) école f primaire

gradient ['greɪdɪənt] n inclinaison f, pente f

gradual ['grædjʊəl] adj graduel(le), progressif(-ive); **gradually** adv peu à peu, graduellement

graduate n ['grædjʊɪt] diplômé(e) d'université; (US: of high school) diplômé(e) de fin d'études ▷ vi ['grædjʊeɪt] obtenir un diplôme d'université (or de fin d'études); **graduation** [grædjʊ'eɪʃən] n cérémonie f de remise des diplômes

graffiti [grə'fiːtɪ] npl graffiti mpl

graft [grɑːft] n (Agr, Med) greffe f; (bribery) corruption f ▷ vt greffer; **hard ~** (BRIT inf) boulot acharné

grain [greɪn] n (single piece) grain m; (no pl: cereals) céréales fpl; (US: corn) blé m

gram [græm] n gramme m

grammar ['græmə'] n grammaire f; **grammar school** n (BRIT) ≈ lycée m

gramme [græm] n = **gram**

gran [græn] (inf) n (BRIT) mamie f (inf), mémé f (inf)

grand [grænd] adj magnifique, splendide; (gesture etc) noble; **grandad** n (inf) = **granddad**; **grandchild** (pl **grandchildren**) n petit-fils m, petite-fille f; **grandchildren** npl petits-enfants; **granddad** n (inf) papy m (inf), papi m (inf), pépé m (inf); **granddaughter** n petite-fille f; **grandfather** n grand-père m; **grandma** n (inf) = **gran**; **grandmother** n grand-mère f; **grandpa** n (inf) = **granddad**;

grandparents npl grands-parents mpl; **grand piano** n piano m à queue; **Grand Prix** ['grɑ̃:'priː] n (Aut) grand prix automobile; **grandson** n petit-fils m

granite ['grænɪt] n granit m

granny ['grænɪ] n (inf) = **gran**

grant [grɑːnt] vt accorder; (a request) accéder à; (admit) concéder ▷ n (Scol) bourse f; (Admin) subside m, subvention f; **to take sth for ~ed** considérer qch comme acquis; **to take sb for ~ed** considérer qn comme faisant partie du décor

grape [greɪp] n raisin m

grapefruit ['greɪpfruːt] n pamplemousse m

graph [grɑːf] n graphique m, courbe f; **graphic** ['græfɪk] adj graphique; (vivid) vivant(e); **graphics** n (art) arts mpl graphiques; (process) graphisme m ▷ npl (drawings) illustrations fpl

grasp [grɑːsp] vt saisir ▷ n (grip) prise f; (fig) compréhension f, connaissance f

grass [grɑːs] n herbe f; (lawn) gazon m; **grasshopper** n sauterelle f

grate [greɪt] n grille f de cheminée ▷ vi grincer ▷ vt (Culin) râper

grateful ['greɪtful] adj reconnaissant(e)

grater ['greɪtə'] n râpe f

gratitude ['grætɪtjuːd] n gratitude f

grave [greɪv] n tombe f ▷ adj grave, sérieux(-euse)

gravel ['grævl] n gravier m

gravestone ['greɪvstəʊn] n pierre tombale

graveyard ['greɪvjɑːd] n cimetière m

gravity ['grævɪtɪ] n (Physics) gravité f; pesanteur f; (seriousness) gravité

gravy ['greɪvɪ] n jus m (de viande), sauce f (au jus de viande)

gray [greɪ] adj (US) = **grey**

graze [greɪz] vi paître, brouter ▷ vt (touch lightly) frôler, effleurer; (scrape) écorcher ▷ n écorchure f

grease [griːs] *n* (*fat*) graisse *f*;
(*lubricant*) lubrifiant *m* ▷ *vt* graisser;
lubrifier; **greasy** *adj* gras(se),
graisseux(-euse); (*hands, clothes*)
graisseux

great [greɪt] *adj* grand(e); (*heat,
pain etc*) très fort(e), intense; (*inf*)
formidable; **Great Britain** *n* Grande-
Bretagne *f*; **great-grandfather**
n arrière-grand-père *m*; **great-
grandmother** *n* arrière-grand-mère
f; **greatly** *adv* très, grandement; (*with
verbs*) beaucoup

Greece [griːs] *n* Grèce *f*

greed [griːd] *n* (*also*: **~iness**)
avidité *f*; (*for food*) gourmandise
f; **greedy** *adj* avide; (*for food*)
gourmand(e)

Greek [griːk] *adj* grec (grecque) ▷ *n*
Grec (Grecque); (*Ling*) grec *m*

green [griːn] *adj* vert(e);
(*inexperienced*) (bien) jeune, naïf(-ïve);
(*ecological: product etc*) écologique
▷ *n* (*colour*) vert *m*; (*on golf course*)
green *m*; (*stretch of grass*) pelouse
f; **greens** *npl* (*vegetables*) légumes
verts; **green card** *n* (*Aut*) carte
verte; (*us: work permit*) permis *m* de
travail; **greengage** *n* reine-claude *f*;
greengrocer *n* (*brit*) marchand *m*
de fruits et légumes; **greengrocer's
(shop)** *n* magasin *m* de fruits et
légumes; **greenhouse** *n* serre
f; **greenhouse effect** *n*: **the
greenhouse effect** l'effet *m* de serre

Greenland ['griːnlənd] *n*
Groenland *m*

green salad *n* salade verte

greet [griːt] *vt* accueillir; **greeting** *n*
salutation *f*; **Christmas/birthday
greetings** souhaits *mpl* de Noël/de
bon anniversaire; **greeting(s) card** *n*
carte *f* de vœux

grew [gruː] *pt of* **grow**

grey, (*us*)**gray** [greɪ] *adj* gris(e);
(*dismal*) sombre; **grey-haired**, (*us*)
gray-haired *adj* aux cheveux gris;
greyhound *n* lévrier *m*

grid [grɪd] *n* grille *f*; (*Elec*) réseau *m*;
gridlock *n* (*traffic jam*) embouteillage
m

grief [griːf] *n* chagrin *m*, douleur *f*

grievance ['griːvəns] *n* doléance *f*,
grief *m*; (*cause for complaint*) grief

grieve [griːv] *vi* avoir du chagrin;
se désoler ▷ *vt* faire de la peine à,
affliger; **to ~ for sb** pleurer qn

grill [grɪl] *n* (*on cooker*) gril *m*; (*also:
mixed ~) grillade(s) *f(pl)* ▷ *vt* (*Culin*)
griller; (*inf: question*) cuisiner

grille [grɪl] *n* grillage *m*; (*Aut*)
calandre *f*

grim [grɪm] *adj* sinistre, lugubre;
(*serious, stern*) sévère

grime [graɪm] *n* crasse *f*

grin [grɪn] *n* large sourire *m* ▷ *vi*
sourire

grind [graɪnd] (*pt, pp* **ground**) *vt*
écraser; (*coffee, pepper etc*) moudre;
(*us: meat*) hacher ▷ *n* (*work*) corvée *f*

grip [grɪp] *n* (*handclasp*) poigne *f*;
(*control*) prise *f*; (*handle*) poignée
f; (*holdall*) sac *m* de voyage ▷ *vt*
saisir, empoigner; (*viewer, reader*)
captiver; **to come to ~s with** se
colleter avec, en venir aux prises
avec; **to ~ the road** (*Aut*) adhérer à
la route; **gripping** *adj* prenant(e),
palpitant(e)

grit [grɪt] *n* gravillon *m*; (*courage*) cran
m ▷ *vt* (*road*) sabler; **to ~ one's teeth**
serrer les dents

grits [grɪts] *npl* (*us*) gruau *m* de maïs

groan [grəun] *n* (*of pain*)
gémissement *m* ▷ *vi* gémir

grocer ['grəusəʳ] *n* épicier *m*;
groceries *npl* provisions *fpl*; **grocer's
(shop)**, **grocery** *n* épicerie *f*

groin [grɔɪn] *n* aine *f*

groom [gruːm] *n* (*for horses*)
palefrenier *m*; (*also:* **bride~**) marié *m*
▷ *vt* (*horse*) panser; (*fig*): **to ~ sb for**
former qn pour

groove [gruːv] *n* sillon *m*, rainure *f*

grope [grəup] *vi* tâtonner; **to ~ for**
chercher à tâtons

g

gross [grəus] *adj* grossier(-ière);
(*Comm*) brut(e); **grossly** *adv* (*greatly*)
très, grandement

grotesque [grə'tɛsk] *adj* grotesque

ground [graund] *pt, pp of* **grind** ▷ *n*
sol *m*, terre *f*; (*land*) terrain *m*, terres
fpl; (*Sport*) terrain; (*reason: gen pl*)
raison *f*; (*us: also:* **~ wire**) terre *f* ▷ *vt*
(*plane*) empêcher de décoller, retenir
au sol; (*us Elec*) équiper d'une prise
de terre; **grounds** *npl* (*gardens etc*)
parc *m*, domaine *m*; (*of coffee*) marc
m; **on the ~, to the ~** par terre;
to gain/lose ~ gagner/perdre
du terrain; **ground floor** *n* (*BRIT*)
rez-de-chaussée *m*; **groundsheet** *n*
(*BRIT*) tapis *m* de sol; **groundwork** *n*
préparation *f*

group [gru:p] *n* groupe *m* ▷ *vt* (*also:*
~ together) grouper ▷ *vi* (*also:* **~**
together) se grouper

grouse [graus] *n* (*pl inv: bird*) grouse *f*
(*sorte de coq de bruyère*) ▷ *vi* (*complain*)
rouspéter, râler

grovel ['grɔvl] *vi* (*fig*): **to ~ (before)**
ramper (devant)

grow (*pt* **grew**, *pp* **grown**) [grəu,
gru:, grəun] *vi* (*plant*) pousser,
croître; (*person*) grandir; (*increase*)
augmenter, se développer; (*become*)
devenir: **to ~ rich/weak** s'enrichir/
s'affaiblir ▷ *vt* cultiver, faire pousser;
(*hair, beard*) laisser pousser; **grow on**
vt fus: **that painting is ~ing on me**
je finirai par aimer ce tableau; **grow**
up *vi* grandir

growl [graul] *vi* grogner

grown [grəun] *pp of* **grow**; **grown-**
up *n* adulte *m/f*, grande personne

growth [grəuθ] *n* croissance *f*,
développement *m*; (*what has grown*)
pousse *f*; poussée *f*; (*Med*) grosseur
f, tumeur *f*

grub [grʌb] *n* larve *f*; (*inf: food*) bouffe *f*

grubby ['grʌbɪ] *adj* crasseux(-euse)

grudge [grʌdʒ] *n* rancune *f* ▷ *vt*: **to**
~ sb sth (*in giving*) donner qch à qn
à contre-cœur; (*resent*) reprocher

qch à qn; **to bear sb a ~ (for)** garder
rancune *or* en vouloir à qn (de)

gruelling, (*us*) **grueling** ['gruəlɪŋ]
adj exténuant(e)

gruesome ['gru:səm] *adj* horrible

grumble ['grʌmbl] *vi* rouspéter,
ronchonner

grumpy ['grʌmpɪ] *adj*
grincheux(-euse)

grunt [grʌnt] *vi* grogner

guarantee [gærən'ti:] *n* garantie *f*
▷ *vt* garantir

guard [gɑ:d] *n* garde *f*; (*one man*)
garde *m*; (*BRIT Rail*) chef *m* de train;
(*safety device: on machine*) dispositif
m de sûreté; (*also:* **fire~**) garde-feu
inv ▷ *vt* garder, surveiller; (*protect*):
to ~ sb/sth (against *or* **from)**
protéger qn/qch (contre); **to be**
on one's ~ (*fig*) être sur ses gardes;
guardian *n* gardien(ne); (*of minor*)
tuteur(-trice)

guerrilla [gə'rɪlə] *n* guérillero *m*

guess [gɛs] *vi* deviner ▷ *vt* deviner;
(*estimate*) évaluer; (*us*) croire, penser
▷ *n* supposition *f*, hypothèse *f*; **to**
take *or* **have a ~** essayer de deviner

guest [gɛst] *n* invité(e); (*in hotel*)
client(e); **guest house** *n* pension *f*;
guest room *n* chambre *f* d'amis

guidance ['gaɪdəns] *n* (*advice*)
conseils *mpl*

guide [gaɪd] *n* (*person*) guide
m/f; (*book*) guide *m*; (*also:* **Girl**
G~) éclaireuse *f*; (*Roman Catholic*)
guide *f* ▷ *vt* guider; **is there an**
English-speaking ~? est-ce que
l'un des guides parle anglais?;
guidebook *n* guide *m*; **guide dog**
n chien *m* d'aveugle; **guided tour**
n visite guidée; **what time does**
the guided tour start? la visite
guidée commence à quelle heure?;
guidelines *npl* (*advice*) instructions
générales, conseils *mpl*

guild [gɪld] *n* (*Hist*) corporation
f; (*sharing interests*) cercle *m*,
association *f*

guilt [gɪlt] n culpabilité f; **guilty** adj
coupable
guinea pig ['gɪnɪ-] n cobaye m
guitar [gɪ'tɑː'] n guitare f; **guitarist** n
guitariste m/f
gulf [gʌlf] n golfe m; (abyss) gouffre m
gull [gʌl] n mouette f
gulp [gʌlp] vi avaler sa salive; (from
emotion) avoir la gorge serrée,
s'étrangler ▷ vt (also: ~ **down**) avaler
gum [gʌm] n (Anat) gencive f; (glue)
colle f; (also: **chewing-~**) chewing-
gum m ▷ vt coller
gun [gʌn] n (small) revolver m,
pistolet m; (rifle) fusil m, carabine
f; (cannon) canon m; **gunfire** n
fusillade f; **gunman** (irreg) n bandit
armé; **gunpoint** n: **at gunpoint**
sous la menace du pistolet (or fusil);
gunpowder n poudre f à canon;
gunshot n coup m de feu
gush [gʌʃ] vi jaillir; (fig) se répandre
en effusions
gust [gʌst] n (of wind) rafale f
gut [gʌt] n intestin m, boyau m; **guts**
npl (inf: Anat) boyaux mpl; (: courage)
cran m
gutter ['gʌtə'] n (of roof) gouttière f;
(in street) caniveau m
guy [gaɪ] n (inf: man) type m; (also:
~rope) corde f; (figure) effigie de Guy
Fawkes
Guy Fawkes' Night [gaɪ'fɔːks-] n
voir article **"Guy Fawkes' Night"**

GUY FAWKES' NIGHT

Guy Fawkes' Night, que l'on appelle
également "bonfire night",
commémore l'échec du complot (le
"Gunpowder Plot") contre James
Ier et son parlement le 5 novembre
1605. L'un des conspirateurs, Guy
Fawkes, avait été surpris dans
les caves du parlement alors
qu'il s'apprêtait à y mettre le feu.
Chaque année pour le 5 novembre,
les enfants préparent à l'avance
une effigie de Guy Fawkes et ils
demandent aux passants "un
penny pour le guy" avec lequel ils
pourront s'acheter des fusées de
feu d'artifice. Beaucoup de gens
font encore un feu dans leur jardin
sur lequel ils brûlent le "guy".

gym [dʒɪm] n (also: **~nasium**)
gymnase m; (also: **~nastics**) gym f;
gymnasium n gymnase m; **gymnast**
n gymnaste m/f; **gymnastics** n,
npl gymnastique f; **gym shoes** npl
chaussures fpl de gym(nastique)
gynaecologist, (US) **gynecologist**
[gaɪnɪ'kɔlədʒɪst] n gynécologue m/f
gypsy ['dʒɪpsɪ] n gitan(e),
bohémien(ne)

h

haberdashery [hæbə'dæʃərɪ] *n* (BRIT) mercerie *f*

habit ['hæbɪt] *n* habitude *f*; (*costume: Rel*) habit *m*

habitat ['hæbɪtæt] *n* habitat *m*

hack [hæk] *vt* hacher, tailler ▷ *n* (*pej: writer*) nègre *m*; **hacker** *n* (*Comput*) pirate *m* (informatique)

had [hæd] *pt, pp of* **have**

haddock ['hædək] (*pl* **haddock** *or* **haddocks**) *n* églefin *m*; **smoked ~** haddock *m*

hadn't ['hædnt] = **had not**

haemorrhage, (US) **hemorrhage** ['hɛmərɪdʒ] *n* hémorragie *f*

haemorrhoids, (US) **hemorrhoids** ['hɛmərɔɪdz] *npl* hémorroïdes *fpl*

haggle ['hægl] *vi* marchander

Hague [heɪg] *n*: **The ~** La Haye

hail [heɪl] *n* grêle *f* ▷ *vt* (*call*) héler; (*greet*) acclamer ▷ *vi* grêler; **hailstone** *n* grêlon *m*

hair [hɛəʳ] *n* cheveux *mpl*; (*on body*) poils *mpl*; (*of animal*) pelage *m*; (*single hair: on head*) cheveu *m*; (: *on body, of animal*) poil *m*; **to do one's ~** se coiffer; **hairband** *n* (*elasticated*) bandeau *m*; (*plastic*) serre-tête *m*; **hairbrush** *n* brosse *f* à cheveux; **haircut** *n* coupe *f* (de cheveux); **hairdo** *n* coiffure *f*; **hairdresser** *n* coiffeur(-euse); **hairdresser's** *n* salon *m* de coiffure, coiffeur *m*; **hair dryer** *n* sèche-cheveux *m*, séchoir *m*; **hair gel** *n* gel *m* pour cheveux; **hair spray** *n* laque *f* (pour les cheveux); **hairstyle** *n* coiffure *f*; **hairy** *adj* poilu(e), chevelu(e); (*inf: frightening*) effrayant(e)

haka ['hɑːkə] *n* (NZ) haka *m*

hake [heɪk] (*pl* **hake** *or* **hakes**) *n* colin *m*, merlu *m*

half [hɑːf] *n* (*pl* **halves**) moitié *f*; (*of beer: also: ~ pint*) ≈ demi *m*; (*Rail, bus: also: ~ fare*) demi-tarif *m*; (*Sport: of match*) mi-temps *f* ▷ *adj* demi(e) ▷ *adv* (à) moitié, à demi; **~ an hour** une demi-heure; **~ a dozen** une demi-douzaine; **~ a pound** une demi-livre, ≈ 250 g; **two and a ~** deux et demi; **to cut sth in ~** couper qch en deux; **half board** *n* (BRIT: *in hotel*) demi-pension *f*; **half-brother** *n* demi-frère *m*; **half day** *n* demi-journée *f*; **half fare** *n* demi-tarif *m*; **half-hearted** *adj* tiède, sans enthousiasme; **half-hour** *n* demi-heure *f*; **half-price** *adj* à moitié prix ▷ *adv* (*also*: **at half-price**) à moitié prix; **half term** *n* (BRIT *Scol*) vacances *fpl* (de demi-trimestre); **half-time** *n* mi-temps *f*; **halfway** *adv* à mi-chemin; **halfway through sth** au milieu de qch

hall [hɔːl] *n* salle *f*; (*entrance way: big*) hall *m*; (: *small*) entrée *f*; (US: *corridor*) couloir *m*; (*mansion*) château *m*, manoir *m*

hallmark ['hɔːlmɑːk] *n* poinçon *m*; (*fig*) marque *f*

hallo [hə'ləu] *excl* = **hello**

hall of residence n (BRIT) pavillon m
or résidence f universitaire
Hallowe'en, Halloween
['hæləʊ'iːn] n veille f de la Toussaint

● HALLOWE'EN
●
● Selon la tradition, *Hallowe'en* est la
● nuit des fantômes et des sorcières.
● En Écosse et aux États-Unis surtout
● (et de plus en plus en Angleterre) les
● enfants, pour fêter *Hallowe'en*, se
● déguisent ce soir-là et ils vont ainsi
● de porte en porte en demandant de
● petits cadeaux (du chocolat, etc).

hallucination [həluːsɪ'neɪʃən] n
hallucination f
hallway ['hɔːlweɪ] n (entrance)
vestibule m; (corridor) couloir m
halo ['heɪləʊ] n (of saint etc) auréole f
halt [hɔːlt] n halte f, arrêt m ▷ vt faire
arrêter; (progress etc) interrompre ▷ vi
faire halte, s'arrêter
halve [hɑːv] vt (apple etc) partager or
diviser en deux; (reduce by half) réduire
de moitié
halves [hɑːvz] npl of **half**
ham [hæm] n jambon m
hamburger ['hæmbɜːgər] n
hamburger m
hamlet ['hæmlɪt] n hameau m
hammer ['hæmər] n marteau m
▷ vt (nail) enfoncer; (fig) éreinter,
démolir ▷ vi (at door) frapper à coups
redoublés; **to ~ a point home to sb**
faire rentrer qch dans la tête de qn
hammock ['hæmək] n hamac m
hamper ['hæmpər] vt gêner ▷ n
panier m (d'osier)
hamster ['hæmstər] n hamster m
hamstring ['hæmstrɪŋ] n (Anat)
tendon m du jarret
hand [hænd] n main f; (of clock)
aiguille f; (handwriting) écriture f; (at
cards) jeu m; (worker) ouvrier(-ière)
▷ vt passer, donner; **to give sb a ~**
donner un coup de main à qn; **at ~**
à portée de la main; **in ~** (situation)
en main; (work) en cours; **to be on ~**
(person) être disponible; (emergency
services) se tenir prêt(e) (à intervenir);
to ~ (information etc) sous la main,
à portée de la main; **on the one ~
..., on the other ~** d'une part ...,
d'autre part; **hand down** vt passer;
(tradition, heirloom) transmettre; (us:
sentence, verdict) prononcer; **hand in**
vt remettre; **hand out** vt distribuer;
hand over vt remettre; (powers
etc) transmettre; **handbag** n sac m
à main; **hand baggage** n = **hand
luggage**; **handbook** n manuel
m; **handbrake** n frein m à main;
handcuffs npl menottes fpl; **handful**
n poignée f
handicap ['hændɪkæp] n handicap
m ▷ vt handicaper; **mentally/
physically ~ped** handicapé(e)
mentalement/physiquement
handkerchief ['hæŋkətʃɪf] n
mouchoir m
handle ['hændl] n (of door etc)
poignée f; (of cup etc) anse f; (of knife
etc) manche m; (of saucepan) queue f;
(for winding) manivelle f ▷ vt toucher,
manier; (deal with) s'occuper de;
(treat: people) prendre; **"~ with care"**
"fragile"; **to fly off the ~** s'énerver;
handlebar(s) n(pl) guidon m
hand: hand luggage n bagages mpl
à main; **handmade** adj fait(e) à la
main; **handout** n (money) aide f, don
m; (leaflet) prospectus m; (at lecture)
polycopié m; **hands-free** adj mains
libres inv ▷ n (also: **hands-free kit**) kit
m mains libres inv
handsome ['hænsəm] adj beau
(belle); (profit) considérable
handwriting ['hændraɪtɪŋ] n
écriture f
handy ['hændɪ] adj (person)
adroit(e); (close at hand) sous la main;
(convenient) pratique
hang (pt, pp **hung**) [hæŋ, hʌŋ] vt
accrocher; (criminal) pendre ▷ vi

h

pendre; (*hair, drapery*) tomber ▷ *n*: **to get the ~ of (doing) sth** (*inf*) attraper le coup pour faire qch; **hang about, hang around** *vi* traîner; **hang down** *vi* pendre; **hang on** *vi* (*wait*) attendre; **hang out** *vt* (*washing*) étendre (dehors) ▷ *vi* (*inf: live*) habiter, percher; (: *spend time*) traîner; **hang round** *vi* = **hang about**; **hang up** *vi* (*Tel*) raccrocher ▷ *vt* (*coat, painting etc*) accrocher, suspendre

hanger ['hæŋə^r] *n* cintre *m*, portemanteau *m*

hang-gliding ['hæŋglaɪdɪŋ] *n* vol *m* libre *or* sur aile delta

hangover ['hæŋəuvə^r] *n* (*after drinking*) gueule *f* de bois

hankie, hanky ['hæŋkɪ] *n abbr* = **handkerchief**

happen ['hæpən] *vi* arriver, se passer, se produire; **what's ~ing?** que se passe-t-il?; **she ~ed to be free** il s'est trouvé (*or* se trouvait) qu'elle était libre; **as it ~s** justement

happily ['hæpɪlɪ] *adv* heureusement; (*cheerfully*) joyeusement

happiness ['hæpɪnɪs] *n* bonheur *m*

happy ['hæpɪ] *adj* heureux(-euse); **~ with** (*arrangements etc*) satisfait(e) de; **to be ~ to do** faire volontiers; **~ birthday!** bon anniversaire!

harass ['hærəs] *vt* accabler, tourmenter; **harassment** *n* tracasseries *fpl*

harbour, (*US*) **harbor** ['hɑːbə^r] *n* port *m* ▷ *vt* héberger, abriter; (*hopes, suspicions*) entretenir

hard [hɑːd] *adj* dur(e); (*question, problem*) difficile; (*facts, evidence*) concret(-ète) ▷ *adv* (*work*) dur; (*think, try*) sérieusement; **to look ~ at** regarder fixement; (*thing*) regarder de près; **no ~ feelings!** sans rancune!; **to be ~ of hearing** être dur(e) d'oreille; **to be ~ done by** être traité(e) injustement; **hardback** *n* livre relié; **hardboard** *n* Isorel® *m*; **hard disk** *n* (*Comput*) disque dur;

harden *vt* durcir; (*fig*) endurcir ▷ *vi* (*substance*) durcir

hardly ['hɑːdlɪ] *adv* (*scarcely*) à peine; (*harshly*) durement; **~ anywhere/ ever** presque nulle part/jamais

hard: hardship *n* (*difficulties*) épreuves *fpl*; (*deprivation*) privations *fpl*; **hard shoulder** *n* (*BRIT Aut*) accotement stabilisé; **hard-up** *adj* (*inf*) fauché(e); **hardware** *n* quincaillerie *f*; (*Comput, Mil*) matériel *m*; **hardware shop**, (*US*) **hardware store** *n* quincaillerie *f*; **hard-working** *adj* travailleur(-euse), consciencieux(-euse)

hardy ['hɑːdɪ] *adj* robuste; (*plant*) résistant(e) au gel

hare [hɛə^r] *n* lièvre *m*

harm [hɑːm] *n* mal *m*; (*wrong*) tort *m* ▷ *vt* (*person*) faire du mal *or* du tort à; (*thing*) endommager; **out of ~'s way** à l'abri du danger, en lieu sûr; **harmful** *adj* nuisible; **harmless** *adj* inoffensif(-ive)

harmony ['hɑːmənɪ] *n* harmonie *f*

harness ['hɑːnɪs] *n* harnais *m* ▷ *vt* (*horse*) harnacher; (*resources*) exploiter

harp [hɑːp] *n* harpe *f* ▷ *vi*: **to ~ on about** revenir toujours sur

harsh [hɑːʃ] *adj* (*hard*) dur(e); (*severe*) sévère; (*unpleasant: sound*) discordant(e); (: *light*) cru(e)

harvest ['hɑːvɪst] *n* (*of corn*) moisson *f*; (*of fruit*) récolte *f*; (*of grapes*) vendange *f* ▷ *vt* moissonner; récolter; vendanger

has [hæz] *vb see* **have**

hasn't ['hæznt] = **has not**

hassle ['hæsl] *n* (*inf: fuss*) histoire(s) *f(pl)*

haste [heɪst] *n* hâte *f*, précipitation *f*; **hasten** ['heɪsn] *vt* hâter, accélérer ▷ *vi* se hâter, s'empresser; **hastily** *adv* à la hâte; (*leave*) précipitamment; **hasty** *adj* (*decision, action*) hâtif(-ive); (*departure, escape*) précipité(e)

hat [hæt] *n* chapeau *m*

hatch [hætʃ] n (Naut: also: **~way**) écoutille f; (BRIT: also: **service ~**) passe-plats m inv ▷ vi éclore

hatchback ['hætʃbæk] n (Aut) modèle m avec hayon arrière

hate [heɪt] vt haïr, détester ▷ n haine f; **hatred** ['heɪtrɪd] n haine f

haul [hɔːl] vt traîner, tirer ▷ n (of fish) prise f; (of stolen goods etc) butin m

haunt [hɔːnt] vt (subj: ghost, fear) hanter; (: person) fréquenter ▷ n repaire m; **haunted** adj (castle etc) hanté(e); (look) égaré(e), hagard(e)

○ **KEYWORD**

have [hæv] (pt, pp **had**) aux vb
1 (gen) avoir; être; **to have eaten/ slept** avoir mangé/dormi; **to have arrived/gone** être arrivé(e)/allé(e); **having finished** or **when he had finished, he left** quand il a eu fini, il est parti; **we'd already eaten** nous avions déjà mangé
2 (in tag questions): **you've done it, haven't you?** vous l'avez fait, n'est-ce pas?
3 (in short answers and questions): **no I haven't!/yes we have!** mais non!/ mais si!; **so I have!** ah oui!, oui c'est vrai!; **I've been there before, have you?** j'y suis déjà allé, et vous?
▶ modal aux vb (be obliged): **to have (got) to do sth** devoir faire qch, être obligé(e) de faire qch; **she has (got) to do it** elle doit le faire, il faut qu'elle le fasse; **you haven't to tell her** vous n'êtes pas obligé de le lui dire; (must not) ne le lui dites surtout pas; **do you have to book?** il faut réserver?
▶ vt 1 (possess) avoir; **he has (got) blue eyes/dark hair** il a les yeux bleus/les cheveux bruns
2 (referring to meals etc): **to have breakfast** prendre le petit déjeuner; **to have dinner/lunch** dîner/ déjeuner; **to have a drink** prendre

un verre; **to have a cigarette** fumer une cigarette
3 (receive) avoir, recevoir; (obtain) avoir; **may I have your address?** puis-je avoir votre adresse?; **you can have it for £5** vous pouvez l'avoir pour 5 livres; **I must have it for tomorrow** il me le faut pour demain; **to have a baby** avoir un bébé
4 (maintain, allow): **I won't have it!** ça ne se passera pas comme ça!; **we can't have that** nous ne tolérerons pas ça
5 (by sb else): **to have sth done** faire faire qch; **to have one's hair cut** se faire couper les cheveux; **to have sb do sth** faire faire qch à qn
6 (experience, suffer) avoir; **to have a cold/flu** avoir un rhume/la grippe; **to have an operation** se faire opérer; **she had her bag stolen** elle s'est fait voler son sac
7 (+noun): **to have a swim/walk** nager/se promener; **to have a bath/shower** prendre un bain/une douche; **let's have a look** regardons; **to have a meeting** se réunir; **to have a party** organiser une fête; **let me have a try** laissez-moi essayer

haven ['heɪvn] n port m; (fig) havre m

haven't ['hævnt] = **have not**

havoc ['hævək] n ravages mpl

Hawaii [hə'waɪ:] n (îles fpl) Hawaï m

hawk [hɔːk] n faucon m

hawthorn ['hɔːθɔːn] n aubépine f

hay [heɪ] n foin m; **hay fever** n rhume m des foins; **haystack** n meule f de foin

hazard ['hæzəd] n (risk) danger m, risque m ▷ vt risquer, hasarder; **hazardous** adj hasardeux(-euse), risqué(e); **hazard warning lights** npl (Aut) feux mpl de détresse

haze [heɪz] n brume f

hazel ['heɪzl] n (tree) noisetier m ▷ adj (eyes) noisette inv; **hazelnut** n noisette f

hazy ['heɪzɪ] adj brumeux(-euse); (idea) vague

he [hiː] pron il; **it is he who ...** c'est lui qui ...; **here he is** le voici

head [hɛd] n tête f; (leader) chef m; (of school) directeur(-trice); (of secondary school) proviseur m ▷ vt (list) être en tête de; (group, company) être à la tête de; **~s or tails** pile ou face; **~ first** la tête la première; **~ over heels in love** follement or éperdument amoureux(-euse); **to ~ the ball** faire une tête; **head for** vt fus se diriger vers; (disaster) aller à; **head off** vt (threat, danger) détourner; **headache** n mal m de tête; **to have a headache** avoir mal à la tête; **heading** n titre m; (subject title) rubrique f; **headlamp** (BRIT) n = **headlight**; **headlight** n phare m; **headline** n titre m; **head office** n siège m, bureau m central; **headphones** npl casque m (à écouteurs); **headquarters** npl (of business) bureau or siège central; (Mil) quartier général; **headroom** n (in car) hauteur f de plafond; (under bridge) hauteur limite; **headscarf** n foulard m; **headset** n = **headphones**; **headteacher** n directeur(-trice); (of secondary school) proviseur m; **head waiter** n maître m d'hôtel

heal [hiːl] vt, vi guérir

health [hɛlθ] n santé f; **health care** n services médicaux; **health centre** n (BRIT) centre m de santé; **health food** n aliment(s) naturel(s); **Health Service** n: **the Health Service** (BRIT) ≈ la Sécurité Sociale; **healthy** adj (person) en bonne santé; (climate, food, attitude etc) sain(e)

heap [hiːp] n tas m ▷ vt (also: **~ up**) entasser, amonceler; **she ~ed her plate with cakes** elle a chargé son assiette de gâteaux; **~s (of)** (inf: lots) des tas (de)

hear (pt, pp **heard**) [hɪəʳ, həːd] vt entendre; (news) apprendre ▷ vi entendre; **to ~ about** entendre parler de; (have news of) avoir des nouvelles de; **to ~ from sb** recevoir des nouvelles de qn

heard [həːd] pt, pp of **hear**

hearing ['hɪərɪŋ] n (sense) ouïe f; (of witnesses) audition f; (of a case) audience f; **hearing aid** n appareil m acoustique

hearse [həːs] n corbillard m

heart [hɑːt] n cœur m; **hearts** npl (Cards) cœur m; **at ~** au fond; **by ~** (learn, know) par cœur; **to lose/take ~** perdre/prendre courage; **heart attack** n crise f cardiaque; **heartbeat** n battement m de cœur; **heartbroken** adj: **to be heartbroken** avoir beaucoup de chagrin; **heartburn** n brûlures fpl d'estomac; **heart disease** n maladie f cardiaque

hearth [hɑːθ] n foyer m, cheminée f

heartless ['hɑːtlɪs] adj (person) sans cœur, insensible; (treatment) cruel(le)

hearty ['hɑːtɪ] adj chaleureux(-euse); (appetite) solide; (dislike) cordial(e); (meal) copieux(-euse)

heat [hiːt] n chaleur f; (Sport: also: **qualifying ~**) éliminatoire f ▷ vt chauffer; **heat up** vi (liquid) chauffer; (room) se réchauffer ▷ vt réchauffer; **heated** adj chauffé(e); (fig) passionné(e), échauffé(e), excité(e); **heater** n appareil m de chauffage; radiateur m; (in car) chauffage m; (water heater) chauffe-eau m

heather ['hɛðəʳ] n bruyère f

heating ['hiːtɪŋ] n chauffage m

heatwave ['hiːtweɪv] n vague f de chaleur

heaven ['hɛvn] n ciel m, paradis m; (fig) paradis m; **heavenly** adj céleste, divin(e)

heavily ['hɛvɪlɪ] adv lourdement; (drink, smoke) beaucoup; (sleep, sigh) profondément

heavy ['hɛvɪ] adj lourd(e); (work, rain, user, eater) gros(se); (drinker, smoker) grand(e); (schedule, week) chargé(e)

Hebrew ['hi:bru:] *adj* hébraïque ▷ *n* (*Ling*) hébreu *m*

Hebrides ['hɛbrɪdi:z] *npl*; **the ~** les Hébrides *fpl*

hectare ['hɛktɑ:'] *n* (BRIT) hectare *m*

hectic ['hɛktɪk] *adj* (*schedule*) très chargé(e); (*day*) mouvementé(e); (*lifestyle*) trépidant(e)

he'd [hi:d] = **he would; he had**

hedge [hɛdʒ] *n* haie *f* ▷ *vi* se dérober ▷ *vt*: **to ~ one's bets** (*fig*) se couvrir

hedgehog ['hɛdʒhɔg] *n* hérisson *m*

heed [hi:d] *vt* (*also*: **take ~ of**) tenir compte de, prendre garde à

heel [hi:l] *n* talon *m* ▷ *vt* retalonner

hefty ['hɛftɪ] *adj* (*person*) costaud(e); (*parcel*) lourd(e); (*piece, price*) gros(se)

height [haɪt] *n* (*of person*) taille *f*, grandeur *f*; (*of object*) hauteur *f*; (*of plane, mountain*) altitude *f*; (*of ground*) hauteur, éminence *f*; (*fig: of glory, fame, power*) sommet *m*; (: *of luxury, stupidity*) comble *m*; **at the ~ of summer** au cœur de l'été; **heighten** *vt* hausser, surélever; (*fig*) augmenter

heir [ɛə'] *n* héritier *m*; **heiress** *n* héritière *f*

held [hɛld] *pt, pp of* **hold**

helicopter ['hɛlɪkɔptə'] *n* hélicoptère *m*

hell [hɛl] *n* enfer *m*; **oh ~!** (*inf*) merde!

he'll [hi:l] = **he will; he shall**

hello [hə'ləu] *excl* bonjour!; (*to attract attention*) hé!; (*surprise*) tiens!

helmet ['hɛlmɪt] *n* casque *m*

help [hɛlp] *n* aide *f*; (*cleaner etc*) femme *f* de ménage ▷ *vt, vi* aider; **~!** au secours!; **~ yourself** servez-vous; **can you ~ me?** pouvez-vous m'aider?; **can I ~ you?** (*in shop*) vous désirez?; **he can't ~ it** il n'y peut rien; **help out** *vi* aider ▷ *vt*: **to ~ sb out** aider qn; **helper** *n* aide *m/f*, assistant(e); **helpful** *adj* serviable, obligeant(e); (*useful*) utile; **helping** *n* portion *f*; **helpless** *adj* impuissant(e); (*baby*) sans défense; **helpline** *n* service *m* d'assistance téléphonique; (*free*) ≈ numéro vert

hem [hɛm] *n* ourlet *m* ▷ *vt* ourler

hemisphere ['hɛmɪsfɪə'] *n* hémisphère *m*

hemorrhage ['hɛmərɪdʒ] *n* (US) = **haemorrhage**

hemorrhoids ['hɛmərɔɪdz] *npl* (US) = **haemorrhoids**

hen [hɛn] *n* poule *f*; (*female bird*) femelle *f*

hence [hɛns] *adv* (*therefore*) d'où, de là; **2 years ~** d'ici 2 ans

hen night, hen party *n* soirée *f* entre filles (*avant le mariage de l'une d'elles*)

hepatitis [hɛpə'taɪtɪs] *n* hépatite *f*

her [hə:'] *pron* (*direct*) la, l' + *vowel or h mute*; (*indirect*) lui; (*stressed, after prep*) elle ▷ *adj* son (sa), ses *pl*; *see also* **me, my**

herb [hə:b] *n* herbe *f*; **herbal** *adj* à base de plantes; **herbal tea** *n* tisane *f*

herd [hə:d] *n* troupeau *m*

here [hɪə'] *adv* ici; (*time*) alors ▷ *excl* tiens!, tenez!; **~!** (*present*) présent!; **~ is, ~ are** voici; **~ he/she is** le (la) voici

hereditary [hɪ'rɛdɪtrɪ] *adj* héréditaire

heritage ['hɛrɪtɪdʒ] *n* héritage *m*, patrimoine *m*

hernia ['hə:nɪə] *n* hernie *f*

hero ['hɪərəu] (*pl* **heroes**) *n* héros *m*; **heroic** [hɪ'rəuɪk] *adj* héroïque

heroin ['hɛrəuɪn] *n* héroïne *f* (*drogue*)

heroine ['hɛrəuɪn] *n* héroïne *f* (*femme*)

heron ['hɛrən] *n* héron *m*

herring ['hɛrɪŋ] *n* hareng *m*

hers [hə:z] *pron* le sien(ne), les siens (siennes); *see also* **mine¹**

herself [hə:'sɛlf] *pron* (*reflexive*) se; (*emphatic*) elle-même; (*after prep*) elle; *see also* **oneself**

he's [hi:z] = **he is; he has**

hesitant ['hɛzɪtənt] *adj* hésitant(e), indécis(e)

hesitate ['hɛzɪteɪt] *vi*: **to ~ (about/to do)** hésiter (sur/à faire); **hesitation** [hɛzɪ'teɪʃən] *n* hésitation *f*

heterosexual ['hɛtərəu'sɛksjuəl] *adj, n* hétérosexuel(le)

hexagon ['hɛksəgən] *n* hexagone *m*

hey [heɪ] *excl* hé!

heyday ['heɪdeɪ] *n*: **the ~ of** l'âge *m* d'or de, les beaux jours de

HGV *n abbr* = **heavy goods vehicle**

hi [haɪ] *excl* salut!; (*to attract attention*) hé!

hibernate ['haɪbəneɪt] *vi* hiberner

hiccough, hiccup ['hɪkʌp] *vi* hoqueter ▷ *n*: **to have (the) ~s** avoir le hoquet

hid [hɪd] *pt of* **hide**

hidden ['hɪdn] *pp of* **hide** ▷ *adj*: **~ agenda** intentions non déclarées

hide [haɪd] (*pt* **hid**, *pp* **hidden**) *n* (*skin*) peau *f* ▷ *vt* cacher ▷ *vi*: **to ~ (from sb)** se cacher (de qn)

hideous ['hɪdɪəs] *adj* hideux(-euse), atroce

hiding ['haɪdɪŋ] *n* (*beating*) correction *f*, volée *f* de coups; **to be in ~** (*concealed*) se tenir caché(e)

hi-fi ['haɪfaɪ] *adj, n abbr* (= *high fidelity*) hi-fi *f inv*

high [haɪ] *adj* haut(e); (*speed, respect, number*) grand(e); (*price*) élevé(e); (*wind*) fort(e), violent(e); (*voice*) aigu(ë) ▷ *adv* haut, en haut; **20 m ~** haut(e) de 20 m; **~ in the air** haut dans le ciel; **highchair** *n* (*child's*) chaise haute; **high-class** *adj* (*neighbourhood, hotel*) chic *inv*, de grand standing; **higher education** *n* études supérieures; **high heels** *npl* talons hauts, hauts talons; **high jump** *n* (*Sport*) saut *m* en hauteur; **highlands** ['haɪləndz] *npl* région montagneuse; **the Highlands** (*in Scotland*) les Highlands *mpl*; **highlight** *n* (*fig: of event*) point culminant ▷ *vt* (*emphasize*) faire ressortir, souligner; **highlights** *npl* (*in hair*) reflets *mpl*; **highlighter** *n* (*pen*) surligneur (lumineux); **highly** *adv* extrêmement, très; (*unlikely*) fort; (*recommended, skilled, qualified*) hautement; **to speak highly of** dire beaucoup de bien de; **highness** *n*: **His/Her Highness** son Altesse *f*; **high-rise** *n* (*also*: **high-rise block, high-rise building**) tour *f* (d'habitation); **high school** *n* lycée *m*; (*us*) établissement *m* d'enseignement supérieur; **high season** *n* (*BRIT*) haute saison *f*; **high street** *n* (*BRIT*) grand-rue *f*; **high-tech** (*inf*) *adj* de pointe; **highway** *n* (*BRIT*) route *f*; (*us*) route nationale; **Highway Code** *n* (*BRIT*) code *m* de la route

hijack ['haɪdʒæk] *vt* détourner (*par la force*); **hijacker** *n* auteur *m* d'un détournement d'avion, pirate *m* de l'air

hike [haɪk] *vi* faire des excursions à pied ▷ *n* excursion *f* à pied, randonnée *f*; **hiker** *n* promeneur(-euse), excursionniste *m/f*; **hiking** *n* excursions *fpl* à pied, randonnée *f*

hilarious [hɪ'lɛərɪəs] *adj* (*behaviour, event*) désopilant(e)

hill [hɪl] *n* colline *f*; (*fairly high*) montagne *f*; (*on road*) côte *f*; **hillside** *n* (*flanc m de*) coteau *m*; **hill walking** *n* randonnée *f* de basse montagne; **hilly** *adj* vallonné(e), montagneux(-euse)

him [hɪm] *pron* (*direct*) le, l' + *vowel or h mute*; (*stressed, indirect, after prep*) lui; *see also* **me**; **himself** *pron* (*reflexive*) se; (*emphatic*) lui-même; (*after prep*) lui; *see also* **oneself**

hind [haɪnd] *adj* de derrière

hinder ['hɪndər] *vt* gêner; (*delay*) retarder

hindsight ['haɪndsaɪt] *n*: **with (the benefit of) ~** avec du recul, rétrospectivement

Hindu ['hɪndu:] *n* Hindou(e); **Hinduism** *n* (*Rel*) hindouisme *m*

hinge [hɪndʒ] n charnière f ▷ vi (fig): **to ~ on** dépendre de

hint [hɪnt] n allusion f; (advice) conseil m; (clue) indication f ▷ vt: **to ~ that** insinuer que ▷ vi: **to ~ at** faire une allusion à

hip [hɪp] n hanche f

hippie, hippy ['hɪpɪ] n hippie m/f

hippo ['hɪpəu] (pl **hippos**) n hippopotame m

hippopotamus (pl **hippopotamuses** or **hippopotami**) [hɪpə'pɔtəməs, hɪpə'pɔtəmaɪ] n hippopotame m

hippy ['hɪpɪ] n = **hippie**

hire ['haɪəʳ] vt (BRIT: car, equipment) louer; (worker) embaucher, engager ▷ n location f; **for ~** à louer; (taxi) libre; **I'd like to ~ a car** je voudrais louer une voiture; **hire(d) car** n (BRIT) voiture f de location; **hire purchase** n (BRIT) achat m (or vente f) à tempérament or crédit

his [hɪz] pron le sien(ne), les siens (siennes) ▷ adj son (sa), ses pl; **mine¹; my**

Hispanic [hɪs'pænɪk] adj (in US) hispano-américain(e) ▷ n Hispano-Américain(e)

hiss [hɪs] vi siffler

historian [hɪ'stɔːrɪən] n historien(ne)

historic(al) [hɪ'stɔrɪk(l)] adj historique

history ['hɪstərɪ] n histoire f

hit [hɪt] vt (pt, pp **hit**) frapper; (reach: target) atteindre, toucher; (collide with: car) entrer en collision avec, heurter; (fig: affect) toucher ▷ n coup m; (success) succès m; (song) tube m; (to website) visite f; (on search engine) résultat m de recherche; **to ~ it off with sb** bien s'entendre avec qn; **hit back** vi: **to ~ back at sb** prendre sa revanche sur qn

hitch [hɪtʃ] vt (fasten) accrocher, attacher; (also: **~ up**) remonter d'une saccade ▷ vi faire de l'autostop ▷ n (difficulty) anicroche f, contretemps m; **to ~ a lift** faire du stop; **hitch-hike** vi faire de l'auto-stop; **hitch-hiker** n auto-stoppeur(-euse); **hitch-hiking** n auto-stop m, stop m (inf)

hi-tech ['haɪ'tek] adj de pointe

hitman ['hɪtmæn] (irreg) n (inf) tueur m à gages

HIV n abbr (= human immunodeficiency virus) HIV m, VIH m; **~-negative** séronégatif(-ive); **~-positive** séropositif(-ive)

hive [haɪv] n ruche f

hoard [hɔːd] n (of food) provisions fpl, réserves fpl; (of money) trésor m ▷ vt amasser

hoarse [hɔːs] adj enroué(e)

hoax [həuks] n canular m

hob [hɔb] n plaque chauffante

hobble ['hɔbl] vi boitiller

hobby ['hɔbɪ] n passe-temps favori

hobo ['həubəu] n (US) vagabond m

hockey ['hɔkɪ] n hockey m; **hockey stick** n crosse f de hockey

hog [hɔg] n porc (châtré) ▷ vt (fig) accaparer; **to go the whole ~** aller jusqu'au bout

Hogmanay [hɔgmə'neɪ] n réveillon m du jour de l'An, Saint-Sylvestre f

HOGMANAY

La Saint-Sylvestre ou "New Year's Eve" se nomme *Hogmanay* en Écosse. En cette occasion, la famille et les amis se réunissent pour entendre sonner les douze coups de minuit et pour fêter le "first-footing", une coutume qui veut qu'on se rende chez ses amis et voisins en apportant quelque chose à boire (du whisky en général) et un morceau de charbon en gage de prospérité pour la nouvelle année.

hoist [hɔɪst] n palan m ▷ vt hisser

hold [həuld] (pt, pp **held**) vt tenir; (contain) contenir; (meeting)

tenir; (*keep back*) retenir; (*believe*) considérer; (*possess*) avoir ▷ vi (*withstand pressure*) tenir (bon); (*be valid*) valoir; (*on telephone*) attendre ▷ n prise f; (*find*) influence f; (*Naut*) cale f; **to catch** or **get (a) ~ of** saisir; **to get ~ of** (*find*) trouver; **~ the line!** (*Tel*) ne quittez pas!; **to ~ one's own** (*fig*) (bien) se défendre; **hold back** vt retenir; (*secret*) cacher; **hold on** vi tenir bon; (*wait*) attendre; **~ on!** (*Tel*) ne quittez pas!; **to ~ on to sth** (*grasp*) se cramponner à qch; (*keep*) conserver or garder qch; **hold out** vt offrir ▷ vi (*resist*): **to ~ out (against)** résister (devant), tenir bon (devant); **hold up** vt (*raise*) lever; (*support*) soutenir; (*delay*) retarder (: *traffic*) ralentir; (*rob*) braquer; **holdall** n (*BRIT*) fourre-tout m inv; **holder** n (*container*) support m; (*of ticket, record*) détenteur(-trice); (*of office, title, passport etc*) titulaire m/f
hole [həul] n trou m
holiday [ˈhɔlədɪ] n (*BRIT: vacation*) vacances fpl; (*day off*) jour m de congé; (*public*) jour férié; **to be on ~** être en vacances; **I'm here on ~** je suis ici en vacances; **holiday camp** n (*also*: **holiday centre**) camp m de vacances; **holiday job** n (*BRIT*) boulot m (*inf*) de vacances; **holiday-maker** n (*BRIT*) vacancier(-ière); **holiday resort** n centre m de villégiature or de vacances
Holland [ˈhɔlənd] n Hollande f
hollow [ˈhɔləu] adj creux(-euse); (*fig*) faux (fausse) ▷ n creux m; (*in land*) dépression f (de terrain), cuvette f ▷ vt: **to ~ out** creuser, évider
holly [ˈhɔlɪ] n houx m
holocaust [ˈhɔləkɔːst] n holocauste m
holy [ˈhəulɪ] adj saint(e); (*bread, water*) bénit(e); (*ground*) sacré(e)
home [həum] n foyer m, maison f; (*country*) pays natal, patrie f; (*institution*) maison ▷ adj de famille; (*Econ, Pol*) national(e), intérieur(e);

(*Sport: team*) qui reçoit; (: *match, win*) sur leur (or notre) terrain ▷ adv chez soi, à la maison; au pays natal; (*right in: nail etc*) à fond; **at ~** chez soi, à la maison; **to go** (or **come**) **~** rentrer (chez soi), rentrer à la maison (or au pays); **make yourself at ~** faites comme chez vous; **home address** n domicile permanent; **homeland** n patrie f; **homeless** adj sans foyer, sans abri; **homely** adj (*plain*) simple, sans prétention; (*welcoming*) accueillant(e); **home-made** adj fait(e) à la maison; **home match** n match m à domicile; **Home Office** n (*BRIT*) ministère m de l'Intérieur; **home owner** n propriétaire occupant; **home page** n (*Comput*) page f d'accueil; **Home Secretary** n (*BRIT*) ministre m de l'Intérieur; **homesick** adj: **to be homesick** avoir le mal du pays; (*missing one's family*) s'ennuyer de sa famille; **home town** n ville natale; **homework** n devoirs mpl
homicide [ˈhɔmɪsaɪd] n (*US*) homicide m
homoeopathic, (*US*) **homeopathic** [həumɪəuˈpæθɪk] adj (*medicine*) homéopathique; (*doctor*) homéopathe
homoeopathy, (*US*) **homeopathy** [həumɪˈɔpəθɪ] n homéopathie f
homosexual [hɔməuˈsɛksjuəl] adj, n homosexuel(le)
honest [ˈɔnɪst] adj honnête; (*sincere*) franc (franche); **honestly** adv honnêtement; franchement; **honesty** n honnêteté f
honey [ˈhʌnɪ] n miel m; **honeymoon** n lune f de miel, voyage m de noces; **we're on honeymoon** nous sommes en voyage de noces; **honeysuckle** n chèvrefeuille m
Hong Kong [ˈhɔŋˈkɔŋ] n Hong Kong
honorary [ˈɔnərərɪ] adj honoraire; (*duty, title*) honorifique; **~ degree** diplôme m honoris causa

honour, (US) **honor** ['ɔnəʳ] vt honorer ▷ n honneur m; **to graduate with ~s** obtenir sa licence avec mention; **honourable**, (US) **honorable** adj honorable; **honours degree** n (Scol) ≈ licence f avec mention

hood [hud] n capuchon m; (of cooker) hotte f; (BRIT Aut) capote f; (US Aut) capot m; **hoodie** ['hudi] n (top) sweat m à capuche

hoof (pl **hoofs** or **hooves**) [hu:f, hu:vz] n sabot m

hook [huk] n crochet m; (on dress) agrafe f; (for fishing) hameçon m ▷ vt accrocher; **off the ~** (Tel) décroché

hooligan ['hu:lɪgən] n voyou m

hoop [hu:p] n cerceau m

hoot [hu:t] vi (BRIT Aut) klaxonner; (siren) mugir; (owl) hululer

Hoover® ['hu:vəʳ] (BRIT) n aspirateur m ▷ vt: **to hoover** (room) passer l'aspirateur dans; (carpet) passer l'aspirateur sur

hooves [hu:vz] npl of **hoof**

hop [hɔp] vi sauter; (on one foot) sauter à cloche-pied; (bird) sautiller

hope [həup] vt, vi espérer ▷ n espoir m; **I ~ so** je l'espère; **I ~ not** j'espère que non; **hopeful** adj (person) plein(e) d'espoir; (situation) prometteur(-euse), encourageant(e); **hopefully** adv (expectantly) avec espoir, avec optimisme; (one hopes) avec un peu de chance; **hopeless** adj désespéré(e); (useless) nul(le)

hops [hɔps] npl houblon m

horizon [hə'raɪzn] n horizon m; **horizontal** [hɔrɪ'zɔntl] adj horizontal(e)

hormone ['hɔːməun] n hormone f

horn [hɔːn] n corne f; (Mus) cor m; (Aut) klaxon m

horoscope ['hɔrəskəup] n horoscope m

horrendous [hə'rɛndəs] adj horrible, affreux(-euse)

horrible ['hɔrɪbl] adj horrible, affreux(-euse)

horrid ['hɔrɪd] adj (person) détestable; (weather, place, smell) épouvantable

horrific [hɔ'rɪfɪk] adj horrible

horrifying ['hɔrɪfaɪɪŋ] adj horrifiant(e)

horror ['hɔrəʳ] n horreur f; **horror film** n film m d'épouvante

hors d'œuvre [ɔː'dəːvrə] n hors d'œuvre m

horse [hɔːs] n cheval m; **horseback**: **on horseback** adj, adv à cheval; **horse chestnut** n (nut) marron m (d'Inde); (tree) marronnier m (d'Inde); **horsepower** n puissance f (en chevaux); (unit) cheval-vapeur m (CV); **horse-racing** n courses fpl de chevaux; **horseradish** n raifort m; **horse riding** n (BRIT) équitation f

hose [həuz] n tuyau m; (also: **garden ~**) tuyau d'arrosage; **hosepipe** n tuyau m; (in garden) tuyau d'arrosage

hospital ['hɔspɪtl] n hôpital m; **in ~** à l'hôpital; **where's the nearest ~?** où est l'hôpital le plus proche?

hospitality [hɔspɪ'tælɪtɪ] n hospitalité f

host [həust] n hôte m; (TV, Radio) présentateur(-trice); (large number): **a ~ of** une foule de; (Rel) hostie f

hostage ['hɔstɪdʒ] n otage m

hostel ['hɔstl] n foyer m; (also: **youth ~**) auberge f de jeunesse

hostess ['həustɪs] n hôtesse f; (BRIT: also: **air ~**) hôtesse de l'air; (TV, Radio) présentatrice f

hostile ['hɔstaɪl] adj hostile

hostility [hɔ'stɪlɪtɪ] n hostilité f

hot [hɔt] adj chaud(e); (as opposed to only warm) très chaud; (spicy) fort(e); (fig: contest) acharné(e); (topic) brûlant(e); (temper) violent(e), passionné(e); **to be ~** (person) avoir chaud; (thing) être (très) chaud; **it's ~** (weather) il fait chaud; **hot dog** n hot-dog m

hotel [həu'tɛl] n hôtel m

h

hotspot ['hɔtspɔt] n (Comput: also: **wireless ~**) borne f wifi, hotspot m
hot-water bottle [hɔt'wɔːtə-] n bouillotte f
hound [haʊnd] vt poursuivre avec acharnement ▷ n chien courant
hour ['aʊəʳ] n heure f; **hourly** adj toutes les heures; (rate) horaire
house n [haʊs] maison f; (Pol) chambre f; (Theat) salle f; auditoire m ▷ vt [haʊz] (person) loger, héberger; **on the ~** (fig) aux frais de la maison; **household** n (Admin etc) ménage m; (people) famille f, maisonnée f; **householder** n propriétaire m/f; (head of house) chef m de famille; **housekeeper** n gouvernante f; **housekeeping** n (work) ménage m; **housewife** (irreg) n ménagère f; femme f au foyer; **house wine** n cuvée f maison or du patron; **housework** n (travaux mpl du) ménage m
housing ['haʊzɪŋ] n logement m; **housing development, housing estate** (BRIT) n (blocks of flats) cité f; (houses) lotissement m
hover ['hɔvəʳ] vi planer; **hovercraft** n aéroglisseur m, hovercraft m
how [haʊ] adv comment; **~ are you?** comment allez-vous?; **~ do you do?** bonjour; (on being introduced) enchanté(e); **~ long have you been here?** depuis combien de temps êtes-vous là?; **~ lovely/awful!** que or comme c'est joli/affreux!; **~ much time/many people?** combien de temps/gens?; **~ much does it cost?** ça coûte combien?; **~ old are you?** quel âge avez-vous?; **~ tall is he?** combien mesure-t-il?; **~ is school?** ça va à l'école?; **~ was the film?** comment était le film?
however [haʊ'ɛvəʳ] conj pourtant, cependant ▷ adv: **~ I do it** de quelque manière que je m'y prenne; **~ cold it is** même s'il fait très froid; **~ did you do it?** comment y êtes-vous donc arrivé?

howl [haʊl] n hurlement m ▷ vi hurler; (wind) mugir
H.P. n abbr (BRIT) = **hire purchase**
h.p. abbr (Aut) = **horsepower**
HQ n abbr (= headquarters) QG m
hr abbr (= hour) h
hrs abbr (= hours) h
HTML n abbr (= hypertext markup language) HTML m
hubcap [hʌbkæp] n (Aut) enjoliveur m
huddle ['hʌdl] vi: **to ~ together** se blottir les uns contre les autres
huff [hʌf] n: **in a ~** fâché(e)
hug [hʌg] vt serrer dans ses bras; (shore, kerb) serrer ▷ n: **to give sb a ~** serrer qn dans ses bras
huge [hjuːdʒ] adj énorme, immense
hull [hʌl] n (of ship) coque f
hum [hʌm] vt (tune) fredonner ▷ vi fredonner; (insect) bourdonner; (plane, tool) vrombir
human ['hjuːmən] adj humain(e) ▷ n (also: **~ being**) être humain
humane [hjuːˈmeɪn] adj humain(e), humanitaire
humanitarian [hjuːmænɪˈtɛərɪən] adj humanitaire
humanity [hjuːˈmænɪtɪ] n humanité f
human rights npl droits mpl de l'homme
humble ['hʌmbl] adj humble, modeste
humid ['hjuːmɪd] adj humide; **humidity** [hjuːˈmɪdɪtɪ] n humidité f
humiliate [hjuːˈmɪlɪeɪt] vt humilier
humiliating [hjuːˈmɪlɪeɪtɪŋ] adj humiliant(e)
humiliation [hjuːmɪlɪˈeɪʃən] n humiliation f
hummus ['hʊməs] n houm(m)ous m
humorous ['hjuːmərəs] adj humoristique
humour, (US) **humor** ['hjuːməʳ] n humour m; (mood) humeur f ▷ vt (person) faire plaisir à; se prêter aux caprices de

hump [hʌmp] n bosse f
hunch [hʌntʃ] n (premonition) intuition f
hundred ['hʌndrəd] num cent; **~s of** des centaines de; **hundredth** ['hʌndrədɪdθ] num centième
hung [hʌŋ] pt, pp of **hang**
Hungarian [hʌŋ'gɛərɪən] adj hongrois(e) ▷ n Hongrois(e); (Ling) hongrois m
Hungary ['hʌŋgərɪ] n Hongrie f
hunger ['hʌŋgər] n faim f ▷ vi: **to ~ for** avoir faim de, désirer ardemment
hungry ['hʌŋgrɪ] adj affamé(e); **to be ~** avoir faim; **~ for** (fig) avide de
hunt [hʌnt] vt (seek) chercher; (Sport) chasser ▷ vi (search): **to ~ for** chercher (partout); (Sport) chasser ▷ n (Sport) chasse f; **hunter** n chasseur m; **hunting** n chasse f
hurdle ['hə:dl] n (Sport) haie f; (fig) obstacle m
hurl [hə:l] vt lancer (avec violence); (abuse, insults) lancer
hurrah, hurray [hu'rɑ:, hu'reɪ] excl hourra!
hurricane ['hʌrɪkən] n ouragan m
hurry ['hʌrɪ] n hâte f, précipitation f ▷ vi se presser, se dépêcher ▷ vt (person) faire presser, faire se dépêcher; (work) presser; **to be in a ~** être pressé(e); **to do sth in a ~** faire qch en vitesse; **hurry up** vi se dépêcher
hurt [hə:t] (pt, pp **hurt**) vt (cause pain to) faire mal à; (injure, fig) blesser ▷ vi faire mal ▷ adj blessé(e); **my arm ~s** j'ai mal au bras; **to ~ o.s.** se faire mal
husband ['hʌzbənd] n mari m
hush [hʌʃ] n calme m, silence m ▷ vt faire taire; **~!** chut!
husky ['hʌskɪ] adj (voice) rauque ▷ n chien m esquimau or de traîneau
hut [hʌt] n hutte f; (shed) cabane f
hyacinth ['haɪəsɪnθ] n jacinthe f
hydrofoil ['haɪdrəfɔɪl] n hydrofoil m
hydrogen ['haɪdrədʒən] n hydrogène m

hygiene ['haɪdʒi:n] n hygiène f; **hygienic** [haɪ'dʒi:nɪk] adj hygiénique
hymn [hɪm] n hymne m; cantique m
hype [haɪp] n (inf) matraquage m publicitaire or médiatique
hyperlink ['haɪpəlɪŋk] n hyperlien m
hypermarket ['haɪpəmɑ:kɪt] (BRIT) n hypermarché m
hyphen ['haɪfn] n trait m d'union
hypnotize ['hɪpnətaɪz] vt hypnotiser
hypocrite ['hɪpəkrɪt] n hypocrite m/f
hypocritical [hɪpə'krɪtɪkl] adj hypocrite
hypothesis (pl **hypotheses**) [haɪ'pɔθɪsɪs, -si:z] n hypothèse f
hysterical [hɪ'stɛrɪkl] adj hystérique; (funny) hilarant(e)
hysterics [hɪ'stɛrɪks] npl; **to be in/ have ~** (anger, panic) avoir une crise de nerfs; (laughter) attraper un fou rire

h

I [aɪ] *pron* je; (*before vowel*) j'; (*stressed*) moi

ice [aɪs] *n* glace *f*; (*on road*) verglas *m* ▷ *vt* (*cake*) glacer ▷ *vi* (*also:* **~ over**) geler; (*also:* **~ up**) se givrer; **iceberg** *n* iceberg *m*; **ice cream** *n* glace *f*; **ice cube** *n* glaçon *m*; **ice hockey** *n* hockey *m* sur glace

Iceland [ˈaɪslənd] *n* Islande *f*; **Icelander** *n* Islandais(e); **Icelandic** [aɪsˈlændɪk] *adj* islandais(e) ▷ *n* (*Ling*) islandais *m*

ice: **ice lolly** *n* (*BRIT*) esquimau *m*; **ice rink** *n* patinoire *f*; **ice skating** *n* patinage *m* (sur glace)

icing [ˈaɪsɪŋ] *n* (*Culin*) glaçage *m*; **icing sugar** *n* (*BRIT*) sucre *m* glace

icon [ˈaɪkɔn] *n* icône *f*

ICT *n abbr* (*BRIT Scol:* = *information and communications technology*) TIC *fpl*

icy [ˈaɪsɪ] *adj* glacé(e); (*road*) verglacé(e); (*weather, temperature*) glacial(e)

I'd [aɪd] = **I would; I had**

ID card *n* carte *f* d'identité

idea [aɪˈdɪə] *n* idée *f*

ideal [aɪˈdɪəl] *n* idéal *m* ▷ *adj* idéal(e); **ideally** [aɪˈdɪəlɪ] *adv* (*preferably*) dans l'idéal; (*perfectly*): **he is ideally suited to the job** il est parfait pour ce poste

identical [aɪˈdɛntɪkl] *adj* identique

identification [aɪdɛntɪfɪˈkeɪʃən] *n* identification *f*; **means of ~** pièce *f* d'identité

identify [aɪˈdɛntɪfaɪ] *vt* identifier

identity [aɪˈdɛntɪtɪ] *n* identité *f*; **identity card** *n* carte *f* d'identité; **identity theft** *n* usurpation *f* d'identité

ideology [aɪdɪˈɔlədʒɪ] *n* idéologie *f*

idiom [ˈɪdɪəm] *n* (*phrase*) expression *f* idiomatique; (*style*) style *m*

idiot [ˈɪdɪət] *n* idiot(e), imbécile *m/f*

idle [ˈaɪdl] *adj* (*doing nothing*) sans occupation, désœuvré(e); (*lazy*) oisif(-ive), paresseux(-euse); (*unemployed*) au chômage; (*machinery*) au repos; (*question, pleasures*) vain(e), futile ▷ *vi* (*engine*) tourner au ralenti

idol [ˈaɪdl] *n* idole *f*

idyllic [ɪˈdɪlɪk] *adj* idyllique

i.e. *abbr* (= *id est: that is*) c. à d., c'est-à-dire

if [ɪf] *conj* si; **if necessary** si nécessaire, le cas échéant; **if so** si c'est le cas; **if not** sinon; **if only I could!** si seulement je pouvais!; *see also* **as; even**

ignite [ɪgˈnaɪt] *vt* mettre le feu à, enflammer ▷ *vi* s'enflammer

ignition [ɪgˈnɪʃən] *n* (*Aut*) allumage *m*; **to switch on/off the ~** mettre/couper le contact

ignorance [ˈɪgnərəns] *n* ignorance *f*

ignorant [ˈɪgnərənt] *adj* ignorant(e); **to be ~ of** (*subject*) ne rien connaître en; (*events*) ne pas être au courant de

ignore [ɪgˈnɔː] *vt* ne tenir aucun compte de; (*mistake*) ne pas relever;

(*person: pretend to not see*) faire semblant de ne pas reconnaître; (: *pay no attention to*) ignorer

ill [ɪl] *adj* (*sick*) malade; (*bad*) mauvais(e) ▷ *n* mal *m* ▷ *adv*: **to speak/think ~ of sb** dire/penser du mal de qn; **to be taken ~** tomber malade

I'll [aɪl] = **I will; I shall**

illegal [ɪˈliːgl] *adj* illégal(e)

illegible [ɪˈlɛdʒɪbl] *adj* illisible

illegitimate [ɪlɪˈdʒɪtɪmət] *adj* illégitime

ill health *n* mauvaise santé

illiterate [ɪˈlɪtərət] *adj* illettré(e)

illness [ˈɪlnɪs] *n* maladie *f*

illuminate [ɪˈluːmɪneɪt] *vt* (*room, street*) éclairer; (*for special effect*) illuminer

illusion [ɪˈluːʒən] *n* illusion *f*

illustrate [ˈɪləstreɪt] *vt* illustrer

illustration [ɪləˈstreɪʃən] *n* illustration *f*

I'm [aɪm] = **I am**

image [ˈɪmɪdʒ] *n* image *f*; (*public face*) image de marque

imaginary [ɪˈmædʒɪnərɪ] *adj* imaginaire

imagination [ɪmædʒɪˈneɪʃən] *n* imagination *f*

imaginative [ɪˈmædʒɪnətɪv] *adj* imaginatif(-ive); (*person*) plein(e) d'imagination

imagine [ɪˈmædʒɪn] *vt* s'imaginer; (*suppose*) imaginer, supposer

imbalance [ɪmˈbæləns] *n* déséquilibre *m*

imitate [ˈɪmɪteɪt] *vt* imiter; **imitation** [ɪmɪˈteɪʃən] *n* imitation *f*

immaculate [ɪˈmækjulət] *adj* impeccable; (*Rel*) immaculé(e)

immature [ɪməˈtjuəʳ] *adj* (*fruit*) qui n'est pas mûr(e); (*person*) qui manque de maturité

immediate [ɪˈmiːdɪət] *adj* immédiat(e); **immediately** *adv* (*at once*) immédiatement; **immediately next to** juste à côté de

immense [ɪˈmɛns] *adj* immense, énorme

immerse [ɪˈməːs] *vt* immerger, plonger; **to be ~d in** (*fig*) être plongé dans

immigrant [ˈɪmɪgrənt] *n* immigrant(e); (*already established*) immigré(e); **immigration** [ɪmɪˈgreɪʃən] *n* immigration *f*

imminent [ˈɪmɪnənt] *adj* imminent(e)

immoral [ɪˈmɔrl] *adj* immoral(e)

immortal [ɪˈmɔːtl] *adj, n* immortel(le)

immune [ɪˈmjuːn] *adj*: **~ (to)** immunisé(e) (contre); **immune system** *n* système *m* immunitaire

immunize [ˈɪmjunaɪz] *vt* immuniser

impact [ˈɪmpækt] *n* choc *m*, impact *m*; (*fig*) impact

impair [ɪmˈpɛəʳ] *vt* détériorer, diminuer

impartial [ɪmˈpɑːʃl] *adj* impartial(e)

impatience [ɪmˈpeɪʃəns] *n* impatience *f*

impatient [ɪmˈpeɪʃənt] *adj* impatient(e); **to get** *or* **grow ~** s'impatienter

impeccable [ɪmˈpɛkəbl] *adj* impeccable, parfait(e)

impending [ɪmˈpɛndɪŋ] *adj* imminent(e)

imperative [ɪmˈpɛrətɪv] *adj* (*need*) urgent(e), pressant(e); (*tone*) impérieux(-euse) ▷ *n* (*Ling*) impératif *m*

imperfect [ɪmˈpəːfɪkt] *adj* imparfait(e); (*goods etc*) défectueux(-euse) ▷ *n* (*Ling: also:* **~ tense**) imparfait *m*

imperial [ɪmˈpɪərɪəl] *adj* impérial(e); (*BRIT: measure*) légal(e)

impersonal [ɪmˈpəːsənl] *adj* impersonnel(le)

impersonate [ɪmˈpəːsəneɪt] *vt* se faire passer pour; (*Theat*) imiter

impetus [ˈɪmpətəs] *n* impulsion *f*; (*of runner*) élan *m*

implant [ɪm'plɑːnt] vt (Med) implanter; (fig: idea, principle) inculquer

implement n ['ɪmplɪmənt] outil m, instrument m; (for cooking) ustensile m ▷ vt ['ɪmplɪmənt] exécuter

implicate ['ɪmplɪkeɪt] vt impliquer, compromettre

implication [ɪmplɪ'keɪʃən] n implication f; **by ~** indirectement

implicit [ɪm'plɪsɪt] adj implicite; (complete) absolu(e), sans réserve

imply [ɪm'plaɪ] vt (hint) suggérer, laisser entendre; (mean) indiquer, supposer

impolite [ɪmpə'laɪt] adj impoli(e)

import vt [ɪm'pɔːt] importer ▷ n ['ɪmpɔːt] (Comm) importation f; (meaning) portée f, signification f

importance [ɪm'pɔːtns] n importance f

important [ɪm'pɔːtnt] adj important(e); **it's not ~** c'est sans importance, ce n'est pas important

importer [ɪm'pɔːtə'] n importateur(-trice)

impose [ɪm'pəuz] vt imposer ▷ vi: **to ~ on sb** abuser de la gentillesse de qn; **imposing** adj imposant(e), impressionnant(e)

impossible [ɪm'pɔsɪbl] adj impossible

impotent ['ɪmpətnt] adj impuissant(e)

impoverished [ɪm'pɔvərɪʃt] adj pauvre, appauvri(e)

impractical [ɪm'præktɪkl] adj pas pratique; (person) qui manque d'esprit pratique

impress [ɪm'prɛs] vt impressionner, faire impression sur; (mark) imprimer, marquer; **to ~ sth on sb** faire bien comprendre qch à qn

impression [ɪm'prɛʃən] n impression f; (of stamp, seal) empreinte f; (imitation) imitation f; **to be under the ~ that** avoir l'impression que

impressive [ɪm'prɛsɪv] adj impressionnant(e)

imprison [ɪm'prɪzn] vt emprisonner, mettre en prison; **imprisonment** n emprisonnement m; (period): **to sentence sb to 10 years' imprisonment** condamner qn à 10 ans de prison

improbable [ɪm'prɔbəbl] adj improbable; (excuse) peu plausible

improper [ɪm'prɔpə'] adj (unsuitable) déplacé(e), de mauvais goût; (indecent) indécent(e); (dishonest) malhonnête

improve [ɪm'pruːv] vt améliorer ▷ vi s'améliorer; (pupil etc) faire des progrès; **improvement** n amélioration f; (of pupil etc) progrès m

improvise ['ɪmprəvaɪz] vt, vi improviser

impulse ['ɪmpʌls] n impulsion f; **on ~** impulsivement, sur un coup de tête; **impulsive** [ɪm'pʌlsɪv] adj impulsif(-ive)

 KEYWORD

in [ɪn] prep **1** (indicating place, position) dans; **in the house/the fridge** dans la maison/le frigo; **in the garden** dans le or au jardin; **in town** en ville; **in the country** à la campagne; **in school** à l'école; **in here/there** ici/là **2** (with place names, of town, region, country): **in London** à Londres; **in England** en Angleterre; **in Japan** au Japon; **in the United States** aux États-Unis

3 (indicating time: during): **in spring** au printemps; **in summer** en été; **in May/2005** en mai/2005; **in the afternoon** (dans) l'après-midi; **at 4 o'clock in the afternoon** à 4 heures de l'après-midi

4 (indicating time: in the space of) en; (: future) dans; **I did it in 3 hours/ days** je l'ai fait en 3 heures/jours; **I'll**

see you in 2 weeks or **in 2 weeks'
time** je te verrai dans 2 semaines
5 (*indicating manner etc*) à; **in a loud/
soft voice** à voix haute/basse; **in
pencil** au crayon; **in writing** par
écrit; **in French** en français; **the boy
in the blue shirt** le garçon à or avec la
chemise bleue
6 (*indicating circumstances*): **in
the sun** au soleil; **in the shade** à
l'ombre; **in the rain** sous la pluie; **a
change in policy** un changement
de politique
7 (*indicating mood, state*): **in tears** en
larmes; **in anger** sous le coup de la
colère; **in despair** au désespoir; **in
good condition** en bon état; **to live
in luxury** vivre dans le luxe
8 (*with ratios, numbers*): **1 in 10
households, 1 household in 10** 1
ménage sur 10; **20 pence in the
pound** 20 pence par livre sterling;
they lined up in twos ils se mirent
en rangs (deux) par deux; **in
hundreds** par centaines
9 (*referring to people, works*) chez; **the
disease is common in children**
c'est une maladie courante chez les
enfants; **in (the works of) Dickens**
chez Dickens, dans (l'œuvre de)
Dickens
10 (*indicating profession etc*) dans; **to
be in teaching** être dans
l'enseignement
11 (*after superlative*) de; **the best
pupil in the class** le meilleur élève
de la classe
12 (*with present participle*): **in saying
this** en disant ceci
▶*adv*: **to be in** (*person: at home,
work*) être là; (*train, ship, plane*) être
arrivé(e); (*in fashion*) être à la mode;
to ask sb in inviter qn à entrer; **to
run/limp etc in** entrer en courant/
boitant *etc*
▶*n*: **the ins and outs (of)** (*of
proposal, situation etc*) les tenants et
aboutissants (de)

inability [ɪnə'bɪlɪtɪ] *n* incapacité *f*;
~ to pay incapacité de payer
inaccurate [ɪn'ækjʊrət] *adj*
inexact(e); (*person*) qui manque de
précision
inadequate [ɪn'ædɪkwət] *adj*
insuffisant(e), inadéquat(e)
inadvertently [ɪnəd'vɜːtntlɪ] *adv*
par mégarde
inappropriate [ɪnə'prəʊprɪət] *adj*
inopportun(e), mal à propos; (*word,
expression*) impropre
inaugurate [ɪ'nɔːgjʊreɪt] *vt*
inaugurer; (*president, official*) investir
de ses fonctions
Inc. *abbr* = **incorporated**
incapable [ɪn'keɪpəbl] *adj*: **~ (of)**
incapable (de)
incense *n* ['ɪnsens] encens *m* ▷*vt*
[ɪn'sens] (*anger*) mettre en colère
incentive [ɪn'sentɪv] *n*
encouragement *m*, raison *f* de se
donner de la peine
inch [ɪntʃ] *n* pouce *m* (= 25 mm; 12 *in a
foot*); **within an ~ of** à deux doigts de;
he wouldn't give an ~ (*fig*) il n'a pas
voulu céder d'un pouce
incidence ['ɪnsɪdns] *n* (*of crime,
disease*) fréquence *f*
incident ['ɪnsɪdnt] *n* incident *m*
incidentally [ɪnsɪ'dentəlɪ] *adv* (*by
the way*) à propos
inclination [ɪnklɪ'neɪʃən] *n*
inclination *f*; (*desire*) envie *f*
incline *n* ['ɪnklaɪn] pente *f*, plan
incliné ▷*vt* [ɪn'klaɪn] incliner ▷*vi*
(*surface*) s'incliner; **to be ~d to do**
(*have a tendency to do*) avoir tendance
à faire
include [ɪn'kluːd] *vt* inclure,
comprendre; **service is/is not
~d** le service est compris/n'est pas
compris; **including** *prep* y compris;
inclusion *n* inclusion *f*; **inclusive** *adj*
inclus(e), compris(e); **inclusive of
tax** taxes comprises
income ['ɪnkʌm] *n* revenu *m*; (*from
property etc*) rentes *fpl*; **income**

support n (BRIT) ≈ revenu m
minimum d'insertion, RMI m;
income tax n impôt m sur le revenu
incoming ['ɪnkʌmɪŋ] adj (passengers,
mail) à l'arrivée; (government, tenant)
nouveau (nouvelle)
incompatible [ɪnkəm'pætɪbl] adj
incompatible
incompetence [ɪn'kɒmpɪtns] n
incompétence f, incapacité f
incompetent [ɪn'kɒmpɪtnt] adj
incompétent(e), incapable
incomplete [ɪnkəm'pliːt] adj
incomplet(-ète)
inconsistent [ɪnkən'sɪstnt] adj
qui manque de constance; (work)
irrégulier(-ière); (statement) peu
cohérent(e); ~ **with** en contradiction
avec
inconvenience [ɪnkən'viːnjəns]
n inconvénient m; (trouble)
dérangement m ▷ vt déranger
inconvenient [ɪnkən'viːnjənt]
adj malcommode; (time, place) mal
choisi(e), qui ne convient pas; (visitor)
importun(e)
incorporate [ɪn'kɔːpəreɪt] vt
incorporer; (contain) contenir
incorporated [ɪn'kɔːpəreɪtɪd] adj:
~ **company** (US) ≈ société f anonyme
incorrect [ɪnkə'rɛkt] adj
incorrect(e); (opinion, statement)
inexact(e)
increase n ['ɪnkriːs] augmentation
f ▷ vi, vt [ɪn'kriːs] augmenter;
increasingly adv de plus en plus
incredible [ɪn'krɛdɪbl] adj
incroyable; **incredibly** adv
incroyablement
incur [ɪn'kəːʳ] vt (expenses) encourir;
(anger, risk) s'exposer à; (debt)
contracter; (loss) subir
indecent [ɪn'diːsnt] adj indécent(e),
inconvenant(e)
indeed [ɪn'diːd] adv (confirming,
agreeing) en effet, effectivement; (for
emphasis) vraiment; (furthermore)
d'ailleurs; **yes ~!** certainement!

indefinitely [ɪn'dɛfɪnɪtlɪ] adv (wait)
indéfiniment
independence [ɪndɪ'pɛndns] n
indépendance f; **Independence Day**
n (US) fête de l'Indépendance américaine

* **INDEPENDENCE DAY**
*
* L'Independence Day est la fête
* nationale aux États-Unis, le 4
* juillet. Il commémore l'adoption de
* la déclaration d'Indépendance, en
* 1776, écrite par Thomas Jefferson
* et proclamant la séparation des 13
* colonies américaines de la Grande-
* Bretagne.

independent [ɪndɪ'pɛndnt]
adj indépendant(e); (radio) libre;
independent school n (BRIT) école
privée
index ['ɪndɛks] n (pl **indexes**)
(in book) index m; (in library etc)
catalogue m; (pl **indices**) (ratio, sign)
indice m
India ['ɪndɪə] n Inde f; **Indian**
adj indien(ne) ▷ n Indien(ne);
(American) Indian Indien(ne)
(d'Amérique)
indicate ['ɪndɪkeɪt] vt indiquer ▷ vi
(BRIT Aut): **to ~ left/right** mettre
son clignotant à gauche/à droite;
indication [ɪndɪ'keɪʃən] n indication
f, signe m; **indicative** [ɪn'dɪkətɪv]
adj: **to be indicative of sth** être
symptomatique de qch ▷ n (Ling)
indicatif m; **indicator** n (sign)
indicateur m; (Aut) clignotant m
indices ['ɪndɪsiːz] npl of **index**
indict [ɪn'daɪt] vt accuser;
indictment n accusation f
indifference [ɪn'dɪfrəns] n
indifférence f
indifferent [ɪn'dɪfrənt] adj
indifférent(e); (poor) médiocre,
quelconque
indigenous [ɪn'dɪdʒɪnəs] adj
indigène

indigestion [ɪndɪ'dʒɛstʃən] *n* indigestion *f*, mauvaise digestion

indignant [ɪn'dɪgnənt] *adj*: **~ (at sth/with sb)** indigné(e) (de qch/contre qn)

indirect [ɪndɪ'rɛkt] *adj* indirect(e)

indispensable [ɪndɪ'spɛnsəbl] *adj* indispensable

individual [ɪndɪ'vɪdjuəl] *n* individu *m* ▷ *adj* individuel(le); *(characteristic)* particulier(-ière), original(e); **individually** *adv* individuellement

Indonesia [ɪndə'niːzɪə] *n* Indonésie *f*

indoor ['ɪndɔː'] *adj* d'intérieur; *(plant)* d'appartement; *(swimming pool)* couvert(e); *(sport, games)* pratiqué(e) en salle; **indoors** [ɪn'dɔːz] *adv* à l'intérieur

induce [ɪn'djuːs] *vt (persuade)* persuader; *(bring about)* provoquer; *(labour)* déclencher

indulge [ɪn'dʌldʒ] *vt (whim)* céder à, satisfaire; *(child)* gâter ▷ *vi*: **to ~ in sth** *(luxury)* s'offrir qch, se permettre qch; *(fantasies etc)* se livrer à qch; **indulgent** *adj* indulgent(e)

industrial [ɪn'dʌstrɪəl] *adj* industriel(le); *(injury)* du travail; *(dispute)* ouvrier(-ière); **industrial estate** *n (BRIT)* zone industrielle; **industrialist** *n* industriel *m*; **industrial park** *n (US)* zone industrielle

industry ['ɪndəstrɪ] *n* industrie *f*; *(diligence)* zèle *m*, application *f*

inefficient [ɪnɪ'fɪʃənt] *adj* inefficace

inequality [ɪnɪ'kwɔlɪtɪ] *n* inégalité *f*

inevitable [ɪn'ɛvɪtəbl] *adj* inévitable; **inevitably** *adv* inévitablement, fatalement

inexpensive [ɪnɪk'spɛnsɪv] *adj* bon marché *inv*

inexperienced [ɪnɪk'spɪərɪənst] *adj* inexpérimenté(e)

inexplicable [ɪnɪk'splɪkəbl] *adj* inexplicable

infamous ['ɪnfəməs] *adj* infâme, abominable

infant ['ɪnfənt] *n (baby)* nourrisson *m*; *(young child)* petit(e) enfant

infantry ['ɪnfəntrɪ] *n* infanterie *f*

infant school *n (BRIT)* classes *fpl* préparatoires *(entre 5 et 7 ans)*

infect [ɪn'fɛkt] *vt (wound)* infecter; *(person, blood)* contaminer; **infection** [ɪn'fɛkʃən] *n* infection *f*; *(contagion)* contagion *f*; **infectious** [ɪn'fɛkʃəs] *adj* infectieux(-euse); *(also fig)* contagieux(-euse)

infer [ɪn'fəː'] *vt*: **to ~ (from)** conclure (de), déduire (de)

inferior [ɪn'fɪərɪə'] *adj* inférieur(e); *(goods)* de qualité inférieure ▷ *n* inférieur(e); *(in rank)* subalterne *m/f*

infertile [ɪn'fəːtaɪl] *adj* stérile

infertility [ɪnfəː'tɪlɪtɪ] *n* infertilité *f*, stérilité *f*

infested [ɪn'fɛstɪd] *adj*: **~ (with)** infesté(e) (de)

infinite ['ɪnfɪnɪt] *adj* infini(e); *(time, money)* illimité(e); **infinitely** *adv* infiniment

infirmary [ɪn'fəːmərɪ] *n* hôpital *m*; *(in school, factory)* infirmerie *f*

inflamed [ɪn'fleɪmd] *adj* enflammé(e)

inflammation [ɪnflə'meɪʃən] *n* inflammation *f*

inflatable [ɪn'fleɪtəbl] *adj* gonflable

inflate [ɪn'fleɪt] *vt (tyre, balloon)* gonfler; *(fig: exaggerate)* grossir; *(: increase)* gonfler; **inflation** [ɪn'fleɪʃən] *n (Econ)* inflation *f*

inflexible [ɪn'flɛksɪbl] *adj* inflexible, rigide

inflict [ɪn'flɪkt] *vt*: **to ~ on** infliger à

influence ['ɪnfluəns] *n* influence *f* ▷ *vt* influencer; **under the ~ of alcohol** en état d'ébriété; **influential** [ɪnflu'ɛnʃl] *adj* influent(e)

influenza [ɪnflu'ɛnzə] *n* grippe *f*

influx ['ɪnflʌks] *n* afflux *m*

info ['ɪnfəu] *(inf)* *n* (= *information*) renseignements *mpl*

inform [ɪn'fɔːm] *vt*: **to ~ sb (of)** informer *or* avertir qn (de) ▷ *vi*: **to**

~ on sb dénoncer qn, informer contre qn

informal [ɪnˈfɔːml] adj (person, manner, party) simple; (visit, discussion) dénué(e) de formalités; (announcement, invitation) non officiel(le); (colloquial) familier(-ère)

information [ɪnfəˈmeɪʃən] n information(s) f(pl); renseignements mpl; (knowledge) connaissances fpl; **a piece of ~** un renseignement; **information office** n bureau m de renseignements; **information technology** n informatique f

informative [ɪnˈfɔːmətɪv] adj instructif(-ive)

infra-red [ɪnfrəˈrɛd] adj infrarouge

infrastructure [ˈɪnfrəstrʌktʃər] n infrastructure f

infrequent [ɪnˈfriːkwənt] adj peu fréquent(e), rare

infuriate [ɪnˈfjuərɪeɪt] vt mettre en fureur

infuriating [ɪnˈfjuərɪeɪtɪŋ] adj exaspérant(e)

ingenious [ɪnˈdʒiːnjəs] adj ingénieux(-euse)

ingredient [ɪnˈgriːdɪənt] n ingrédient m; (fig) élément m

inhabit [ɪnˈhæbɪt] vt habiter; **inhabitant** n habitant(e)

inhale [ɪnˈheɪl] vt inhaler; (perfume) respirer; (smoke) avaler ▷ vi (breathe in) aspirer; (in smoking) avaler la fumée; **inhaler** n inhalateur m

inherent [ɪnˈhɪərənt] adj: **~ (in** or **to)** inhérent(e) (à)

inherit [ɪnˈhɛrɪt] vt hériter (de); **inheritance** n héritage m

inhibit [ɪnˈhɪbɪt] vt (Psych) inhiber; (growth) freiner; **inhibition** [ɪnhɪˈbɪʃən] n inhibition f

initial [ɪˈnɪʃl] adj initial(e) ▷ n initiale f ▷ vt parafer; **initials** npl initiales fpl; (as signature) parafe m; **initially** adv initialement, au début

initiate [ɪˈnɪʃɪeɪt] vt (start) entreprendre; amorcer; (enterprise)

lancer; (person) initier; **to ~ proceedings against sb** (Law) intenter une action à qn, engager des poursuites contre qn

initiative [ɪˈnɪʃətɪv] n initiative f

inject [ɪnˈdʒɛkt] vt injecter; (person): **to ~ sb with sth** faire une piqûre de qch à qn; **injection** [ɪnˈdʒɛkʃən] n injection f, piqûre f

injure [ˈɪndʒər] vt blesser; (damage: reputation etc) compromettre; **to ~ o.s.** se blesser; **injured** adj (person, leg etc) blessé(e); **injury** n blessure f; (wrong) tort m

injustice [ɪnˈdʒʌstɪs] n injustice f

ink [ɪŋk] n encre f; **ink-jet printer** [ˈɪŋkdʒɛt-] n imprimante f à jet d'encre

inland adj [ˈɪnlənd] intérieur(e) ▷ adv [ɪnˈlænd] à l'intérieur, dans les terres; **Inland Revenue** n (BRIT) fisc m

in-laws [ˈɪnlɔːz] npl beaux-parents mpl; belle famille

inmate [ˈɪnmeɪt] n (in prison) détenu(e); (in asylum) interné(e)

inn [ɪn] n auberge f

inner [ˈɪnər] adj intérieur(e); **inner-city** adj (schools, problems) de quartiers déshérités

inning [ˈɪnɪŋ] n (US Baseball) tour m de batte; **innings** npl (Cricket) tour de batte

innocence [ˈɪnəsns] n innocence f

innocent [ˈɪnəsnt] adj innocent(e)

innovation [ɪnəuˈveɪʃən] n innovation f

innovative [ˈɪnəuveɪtɪv] adj novateur(-trice); (product) innovant(e)

in-patient [ˈɪnpeɪʃənt] n malade hospitalisé(e)

input [ˈɪnput] n (contribution) contribution f; (resources) ressources fpl; (Comput) entrée f (de données) (: data) données fpl ▷ vt (Comput) introduire, entrer

inquest [ˈɪnkwɛst] n enquête (criminelle); (coroner's) enquête judiciaire

inquire [ɪnˈkwaɪəʳ] *vi* demander ▷ *vt* demander; **to ~ about** s'informer de, se renseigner sur; **to ~ when/ where/whether** demander quand/ où/si; **inquiry** *n* demande *f* de renseignements; (*Law*) enquête *f*, investigation *f*; **"inquiries"** "renseignements"

ins. *abbr* = **inches**

insane [ɪnˈseɪn] *adj* fou (folle); (*Med*) aliéné(e)

insanity [ɪnˈsænɪtɪ] *n* folie *f*; (*Med*) aliénation (mentale)

insect [ˈɪnsɛkt] *n* insecte *m*; **insect repellent** *n* crème *f* anti-insectes

insecure [ɪnsɪˈkjuəʳ] *adj* (*person*) anxieux(-euse); (*job*) précaire; (*building etc*) peu sûr(e)

insecurity [ɪnsɪˈkjuərɪtɪ] *n* insécurité *f*

insensitive [ɪnˈsɛnsɪtɪv] *adj* insensible

insert *vt* [ɪnˈsəːt] insérer ▷ *n* [ˈɪnsəːt] insertion *f*

inside [ˈɪnˈsaɪd] *n* intérieur *m* ▷ *adj* intérieur(e) ▷ *adv* à l'intérieur, dedans ▷ *prep* à l'intérieur de; (*of time*): **~ 10 minutes** en moins de 10 minutes; **to go ~** rentrer; **inside lane** *n* (*Aut*: *in Britain*) voie *f* de gauche; (: *in US, Europe*) voie *f* de droite; **inside out** *adv* à l'envers; (*know*) à fond; **to turn sth inside out** retourner qch

insight [ˈɪnsaɪt] *n* perspicacité *f*; (*glimpse, idea*) aperçu *m*

insignificant [ɪnsɪɡˈnɪfɪk/nt] *adj* insignifiant(e)

insincere [ɪnsɪnˈsɪəʳ] *adj* hypocrite

insist [ɪnˈsɪst] *vi* insister; **to ~ on doing** insister pour faire; **to ~ on sth** exiger qch; **to ~ that** insister pour que + *sub*; (*claim*) maintenir or soutenir que; **insistent** *adj* insistant(e), pressant(e); (*noise, action*) ininterrompu(e)

insomnia [ɪnˈsɔmnɪə] *n* insomnie *f*

inspect [ɪnˈspɛkt] *vt* inspecter; (*BRIT*: *ticket*) contrôler; **inspection** [ɪnˈspɛkʃən] *n* inspection *f*; (*BRIT*: *of tickets*) contrôle *m*; **inspector** *n* inspecteur(-trice); (*BRIT*: *on buses, trains*) contrôleur(-euse)

inspiration [ɪnspəˈreɪʃən] *n* inspiration *f*; **inspire** [ɪnˈspaɪəʳ] *vt* inspirer; **inspiring** *adj* inspirant(e)

instability [ɪnstəˈbɪlɪtɪ] *n* instabilité *f*

install, (*US*) **instal** [ɪnˈstɔːl] *vt* installer; **installation** [ɪnstəˈleɪʃən] *n* installation *f*

instalment, (*US*) **installment** [ɪnˈstɔːlmənt] *n* (*payment*) acompte *m*, versement partiel; (*of TV serial etc*) épisode *m*; **in ~s** (*pay*) à tempérament; (*receive*) en plusieurs fois

instance [ˈɪnstəns] *n* exemple *m*; **for ~** par exemple; **in the first ~** tout d'abord, en premier lieu

instant [ˈɪnstənt] *n* instant *m* ▷ *adj* immédiat(e), urgent(e); (*coffee, food*) instantané(e), en poudre; **instantly** *adv* immédiatement, tout de suite; **instant messaging** *n* messagerie *f* instantanée

instead [ɪnˈstɛd] *adv* au lieu de cela; **~ of** au lieu de; **~ of sb** à la place de qn

instinct [ˈɪnstɪŋkt] *n* instinct *m*; **instinctive** *adj* instinctif(-ive)

institute [ˈɪnstɪtjuːt] *n* institut *m* ▷ *vt* instituer, établir; (*inquiry*) ouvrir; (*proceedings*) entamer

institution [ɪnstɪˈtjuːʃən] *n* institution *f*; (*school*) établissement *m* (scolaire); (*for care*) établissement (psychiatrique *etc*)

instruct [ɪnˈstrʌkt] *vt*: **to ~ sb in sth** enseigner qch à qn; **to ~ sb to do** charger qn or ordonner à qn de faire; **instruction** [ɪnˈstrʌkʃən] *n* instruction *f*; **instructions** *npl* (*orders*) directives *fpl*; **instructions for use** mode *m* d'emploi; **instructor** *n* professeur *m*; (*for skiing, driving*) moniteur *m*

instrument [ˈɪnstrumənt] *n* instrument *m*; **instrumental**

[ɪnstru'mɛntl] *adj* (*Mus*) instrumental(e); **to be instrumental in sth/in doing sth** contribuer à qch/à faire qch

insufficient [ɪnsə'fɪʃənt] *adj* insuffisant(e)

insulate ['ɪnsjuleɪt] *vt* isoler; (*against sound*) insonoriser; **insulation** [ɪnsju'leɪʃən] *n* isolation *f*; (*against sound*) insonorisation *f*

insulin ['ɪnsjulɪn] *n* insuline *f*

insult *n* ['ɪnsʌlt] insulte *f*, affront *m* ▷ *vt* [ɪn'sʌlt] insulter, faire un affront à; **insulting** *adj* insultant(e), injurieux(-euse)

insurance [ɪn'ʃuərəns] *n* assurance *f*; **fire/life ~** assurance-incendie/-vie; **insurance company** *n* compagnie *for* société *f* d'assurances; **insurance policy** *n* police *f* d'assurance

insure [ɪn'ʃuə'] *vt* assurer; **to ~ (o.s.) against** (*fig*) parer à

intact [ɪn'tækt] *adj* intact(e)

intake ['ɪnteɪk] *n* (*Tech*) admission *f*; (*consumption*) consommation *f*; (*BRIT Scol*): **an ~ of 200 a year** 200 admissions par an

integral ['ɪntɪɡrəl] *adj* (*whole*) intégral(e); (*part*) intégrant(e)

integrate ['ɪntɪɡreɪt] *vt* intégrer ▷ *vi* s'intégrer

integrity [ɪn'tɛɡrɪtɪ] *n* intégrité *f*

intellect ['ɪntəlɛkt] *n* intelligence *f*; **intellectual** [ɪntə'lɛktjuəl] *adj, n* intellectuel(le)

intelligence [ɪn'tɛlɪdʒəns] *n* intelligence *f*; (*Mil*) informations *fpl*, renseignements *mpl*

intelligent [ɪn'tɛlɪdʒənt] *adj* intelligent(e)

intend [ɪn'tɛnd] *vt* (*gift etc*): **to ~ sth for** destiner qch à; **to ~ to do** avoir l'intention de faire

intense [ɪn'tɛns] *adj* intense; (*person*) véhément(e)

intensify [ɪn'tɛnsɪfaɪ] *vt* intensifier

intensity [ɪn'tɛnsɪtɪ] *n* intensité *f*

intensive [ɪn'tɛnsɪv] *adj* intensif(-ive); **intensive care** *n*: **to be in intensive care** être en réanimation; **intensive care unit** *n* service *m* de réanimation

intent [ɪn'tɛnt] *n* intention *f* ▷ *adj* attentif(-ive), absorbé(e); **to all ~s and purposes** en fait, pratiquement; **to be ~ on doing sth** être (bien) décidé à faire qch

intention [ɪn'tɛnʃən] *n* intention *f*; **intentional** *adj* intentionnel(le), délibéré(e)

interact [ɪntər'ækt] *vi* avoir une action réciproque; (*people*) communiquer; **interaction** [ɪntər'ækʃən] *n* interaction *f*; **interactive** *adj* (*Comput*) interactif, conversationnel(le)

intercept [ɪntə'sɛpt] *vt* intercepter; (*person*) arrêter au passage

interchange *n* ['ɪntətʃeɪndʒ] (*exchange*) échange *m*; (*on motorway*) échangeur *m*

intercourse ['ɪntəkɔ:s] *n*: **sexual ~** rapports sexuels

interest ['ɪntrɪst] *n* intérêt *m*; (*Comm: stake, share*) participation *f*, intérêts *mpl* ▷ *vt* intéresser; **interested** *adj* intéressé(e); **to be interested in sth** s'intéresser à qch; **I'm interested in going** ça m'intéresse d'y aller; **interesting** *adj* intéressant(e); **interest rate** *n* taux *m* d'intérêt

interface ['ɪntəfeɪs] *n* (*Comput*) interface *f*

interfere [ɪntə'fɪə'] *vi*: **to ~ in** (*quarrel*) s'immiscer dans; (*other people's business*) se mêler de; **to ~ with** (*object*) tripoter, toucher à; (*plans*) contrecarrer; (*duty*) être en conflit avec; **interference** *n* (*gen*) ingérence *f*; (*Radio, TV*) parasites *mpl*

interim ['ɪntərɪm] *adj* provisoire; (*post*) intérimaire ▷ *n*: **in the ~** dans l'intérim

interior [ɪn'tɪərɪə'] *n* intérieur *m* ▷ *adj* intérieur(e); (*minister, department*)

de l'intérieur; **interior design** n
architecture f d'intérieur

intermediate [ɪntə'miːdɪət] adj
intermédiaire; (Scol: course, level)
moyen(ne)

intermission [ɪntə'mɪʃən] n pause f;
(Theat, Cine) entracte m

intern vt [ɪn'təːn] interner ▷ n
['ɪntəːn] (US) interne m/f

internal [ɪn'təːnl] adj interne; (dispute,
reform etc) intérieur(e); **Internal
Revenue Service** n (US) fisc m

international [ɪntə'næʃənl] adj
international(e) ▷ n (BRIT Sport)
international m

Internet [ɪntə'nɛt] n: **the ~** l'Internet
m; **Internet café** n cybercafé m;
Internet Service Provider n
fournisseur m d'accès à Internet;
Internet user n internaute m/f

interpret [ɪn'təːprɪt] vt
interpréter ▷ vi servir d'interprète;
interpretation [ɪntəːprɪ'teɪʃən]
n interprétation f; **interpreter** n
interprète m/f; **could you act as an
interpreter for us?** pourriez-vous
nous servir d'interprète?

interrogate [ɪn'tɛrəugeɪt] vt
interroger; (suspect etc) soumettre
à un interrogatoire; **interrogation**
[ɪntɛrəu'geɪʃən] n interrogation f; (by
police) interrogatoire m

interrogative [ɪntə'rɔgətɪv] adj
interrogateur(-trice) ▷ n (Ling)
interrogatif m

interrupt [ɪntə'rʌpt] vt, vi
interrompre; **interruption**
[ɪntə'rʌpʃən] n interruption f

intersection [ɪntə'sɛkʃən] n (of
roads) croisement m

interstate ['ɪntərsteɪt] (US) n
autoroute f (qui relie plusieurs États)

interval ['ɪntəvl] n intervalle m;
(BRIT: Theat) entracte m; (: Sport)
mi-temps f; **at ~s** par intervalles

intervene [ɪntə'viːn] vi (time)
s'écouler (entre-temps); (event)
survenir; (person) intervenir

interview ['ɪntəvjuː] n (Radio, TV)
interview f; (for job) entrevue f ▷ vt
interviewer, avoir une entrevue
avec; **interviewer** n (Radio, TV)
interviewer m

intimate adj ['ɪntɪmət] intime;
(friendship) profond(e); (knowledge)
approfondi(e) ▷ vt ['ɪntɪmeɪt]
suggérer, laisser entendre; (announce)
faire savoir

intimidate [ɪn'tɪmɪdeɪt] vt intimider

intimidating [ɪn'tɪmɪdeɪtɪŋ] adj
intimidant(e)

into ['ɪntu] prep dans; **~ pieces/
French** en morceaux/français

intolerant [ɪn'tɔlərnt] adj: **~ (of)**
intolérant(e) (de)

intranet [ɪn'trənɛt] n intranet m

intransitive [ɪn'trænsɪtɪv] adj
intransitif(-ive)

intricate ['ɪntrɪkət] adj complexe,
compliqué(e)

intrigue [ɪn'triːg] n intrigue f ▷ vt
intriguer; **intriguing** adj fascinant(e)

introduce [ɪntrə'djuːs] vt introduire;
(TV show etc) présenter; **to ~ sb
(to sb)** présenter qn (à qn); **to ~
sb to** (pastime, technique) initier qn
à; **introduction** [ɪntrə'dʌkʃən]
n introduction f; (of person)
présentation f; (to new experience)
initiation f; **introductory**
[ɪntrə'dʌktərɪ] adj préliminaire,
introductif(-ive)

intrude [ɪn'truːd] vi (person) être
importun(e); **to ~ on** or **into**
(conversation etc) s'immiscer dans;
intruder n intrus(e)

intuition [ɪntjuː'ɪʃən] n intuition f

inundate ['ɪnʌndeɪt] vt: **to ~ with**
inonder de

invade [ɪn'veɪd] vt envahir

invalid n ['ɪnvəlɪd] malade m/f;
(with disability) invalide m/f ▷ adj
[ɪn'vælɪd] (not valid) invalide, non
valide

invaluable [ɪn'væljuəbl] adj
inestimable, inappréciable

invariably [ɪnˈvɛərɪəblɪ] *adv*
invariablement; **she is ~ late** elle est
toujours en retard
invasion [ɪnˈveɪʒən] *n* invasion *f*
invent [ɪnˈvɛnt] *vt* inventer;
invention [ɪnˈvɛnʃən] *n* invention *f*;
inventor *n* inventeur(-trice)
inventory [ˈɪnvəntrɪ] *n* inventaire *m*
inverted commas [ɪnˈvəːtɪd-] *npl*
(BRIT) guillemets *mpl*
invest [ɪnˈvɛst] *vt* investir ▷ *vi*: **to ~ in**
placer de l'argent *or* investir dans; (*fig:
acquire*) s'offrir, faire l'acquisition de
investigate [ɪnˈvɛstɪgeɪt] *vt* étudier,
examiner; (*crime*) faire une enquête
sur; **investigation** [ɪnvɛstɪˈgeɪʃən] *n*
(*of crime*) enquête *f*, investigation *f*
investigator [ɪnˈvɛstɪgeɪtər] *n*
investigateur(-trice); **private ~**
détective privé
investment [ɪnˈvɛstmənt] *n*
investissement *m*, placement *m*
investor [ɪnˈvɛstər] *n* épargnant(e);
(*shareholder*) actionnaire *m/f*
invisible [ɪnˈvɪzɪbl] *adj* invisible
invitation [ɪnvɪˈteɪʃən] *n*
invitation *f*
invite [ɪnˈvaɪt] *vt* inviter; (*opinions
etc*) demander; **inviting** *adj*
engageant(e), attrayant(e)
invoice [ˈɪnvɔɪs] *n* facture *f* ▷ *vt*
facturer
involve [ɪnˈvɔlv] *vt* (*entail*) impliquer;
(*concern*) concerner; (*require*)
nécessiter; **to ~ sb in** (*theft etc*)
impliquer qn dans; (*activity, meeting*)
faire participer qn à; **involved** *adj*
(*complicated*) complexe; **to be
involved in** (*take part*) participer à;
involvement *n* (*personal role*) rôle
m; (*participation*) participation *f*;
(*enthusiasm*) enthousiasme *m*
inward [ˈɪnwəd] *adj* (*movement*)
vers l'intérieur; (*thought, feeling*)
profond(e), intime ▷ *adv* = **inwards**;
inwards *adv* vers l'intérieur
iPod® [ˈaɪpɔd] *n* iPod® *m*
IQ *n abbr* (= *intelligence quotient*) Q.I. *m*

IRA *n abbr* (= *Irish Republican Army*) IRA *f*
Iran [ɪˈrɑːn] *n* Iran *m*; **Iranian**
[ɪˈreɪnɪən] *adj* iranien(ne) ▷ *n*
Iranien(ne)
Iraq [ɪˈrɑːk] *n* Irak *m*; **Iraqi** *adj*
irakien(ne) ▷ *n* Irakien(ne)
Ireland [ˈaɪələnd] *n* Irlande *f*
iris, irises [ˈaɪrɪs, -ɪz] *n* iris *m*
Irish [ˈaɪrɪʃ] *adj* irlandais(e) ▷ *npl*:
the ~ les Irlandais; **Irishman** (*irreg*)
n Irlandais *m*; **Irishwoman** (*irreg*) *n*
Irlandaise *f*
iron [ˈaɪən] *n* fer *m*; (*for clothes*) fer *m* à
repasser ▷ *adj* de *or* en fer ▷ *vt* (*clothes*)
repasser
ironic(al) [aɪˈrɔnɪk(l)] *adj* ironique;
ironically *adv* ironiquement
ironing [ˈaɪənɪŋ] *n* (*activity*)
repassage *m*; (*clothes: ironed*) linge
repassé; (: *to be ironed*) linge à
repasser; **ironing board** *n* planche
f à repasser
irony [ˈaɪrənɪ] *n* ironie *f*
irrational [ɪˈræʃənl] *adj*
irrationnel(le); (*person*) qui n'est pas
rationnel
irregular [ɪˈrɛgjulər] *adj*
irrégulier(-ière); (*surface*) inégal(e);
(*action, event*) peu orthodoxe
irrelevant [ɪˈrɛləvənt] *adj* sans
rapport, hors de propos
irresistible [ɪrɪˈzɪstɪbl] *adj*
irrésistible
irresponsible [ɪrɪˈspɔnsɪbl] *adj* (*act*)
irréfléchi(e); (*person*) qui n'a pas le
sens des responsabilités
irrigation [ɪrɪˈgeɪʃən] *n* irrigation *f*
irritable [ˈɪrɪtəbl] *adj* irritable
irritate [ˈɪrɪteɪt] *vt* irriter; **irritating**
adj irritant(e); **irritation** [ɪrɪˈteɪʃən]
n irritation *f*
IRS *n abbr* (US) = **Internal Revenue
Service**
is [ɪz] *vb see* **be**
ISDN *n abbr* (= *Integrated Services Digital
Network*) RNIS *m*
Islam [ˈɪzlɑːm] *n* Islam *m*; **Islamic**
[ɪzˈlɑːmɪk] *adj* islamique

island ['aɪlənd] *n* île *f*; (*also:* **traffic ~**) refuge *m* (pour piétons); **islander** *n* habitant(e) d'une île, insulaire *m/f*

isle [aɪl] *n* île *f*

isn't ['ɪznt] = **is not**

isolated ['aɪsəleɪtɪd] *adj* isolé(e)

isolation [aɪsə'leɪʃən] *n* isolement *m*

ISP *n abbr* = **Internet Service Provider**

Israel ['ɪzreɪl] *n* Israël *m*; **Israeli** [ɪz'reɪlɪ] *adj* israélien(ne) ▷ *n* Israélien(ne)

issue ['ɪʃuː] *n* question *f*, problème *m*; (*of banknotes*) émission *f*; (*of newspaper*) numéro *m*; (*of book*) publication *f*, parution *f* ▷ *vt* (*rations, equipment*) distribuer; (*orders*) donner; (*statement*) publier, faire; (*certificate, passport*) délivrer; (*banknotes, cheques, stamps*) émettre, mettre en circulation; **at ~** en jeu, en cause; **to take ~ with sb (over sth)** exprimer son désaccord avec qn (sur qch)

IT *n abbr* = **information technology**

⊙ **KEYWORD**

it [ɪt] *pron* **1** (*specific: subject*) il (elle); (: *direct object*) le (la, l'); (: *indirect object*) lui; **it's on the table** c'est or il (or elle) est sur la table; **I can't find it** je n'arrive pas à le trouver; **give it to me** donne-le-moi

2 (*after prep*): **about/from/of it** en; **I spoke to him about it** je lui en ai parlé; **what did you learn from it?** qu'est-ce que vous en avez retiré?; **I'm proud of it** j'en suis fier; **in/to it** y; **put the book in it** mettez-y le livre; **he agreed to it** il y a consenti; **did you go to it?** (*party, concert etc*) est-ce que vous y êtes allé(s)?

3 (*impersonal*) il; ce, cela, ça; **it's Friday tomorrow** demain, c'est vendredi *or* nous sommes vendredi; **it's 6 o'clock** il est 6 heures; **how far is it? — it's 10 miles** c'est loin? — c'est à 10 miles; **who is it? — it's me** qui

est-ce? — c'est moi; **it's raining** il pleut

Italian [ɪ'tæljən] *adj* italien(ne) ▷ *n* Italien(ne); (*Ling*) italien *m*

italics [ɪ'tælɪks] *npl* italique *m*

Italy ['ɪtəlɪ] *n* Italie *f*

itch [ɪtʃ] *n* démangeaison *f* ▷ *vi* (*person*) éprouver des démangeaisons; (*part of body*) démanger; **I'm ~ing to do** l'envie me démange de faire; **itchy** *adj*: **my back is itchy** j'ai le dos qui démange

it'd ['ɪtd] = **it would; it had**

item ['aɪtəm] *n* (*gen*) article *m*; (*on agenda*) question *f*, point *m*; (*also:* **news ~**) nouvelle *f*

itinerary [aɪ'tɪnərərɪ] *n* itinéraire *m*

it'll ['ɪtl] = **it will; it shall**

its [ɪts] *adj* son (sa), ses *pl*

it's [ɪts] = **it is; it has**

itself [ɪt'sɛlf] *pron* (*reflexive*) se; (*emphatic*) lui-même (elle-même)

ITV *n abbr* (BRIT: = *Independent Television*) chaîne de télévision commerciale

I've [aɪv] = **I have**

ivory ['aɪvərɪ] *n* ivoire *m*

ivy ['aɪvɪ] *n* lierre *m*

jab [dʒæb] *vt*: **to ~ sth into** enfoncer or planter qch dans ▷ *n* (*Med: inf*) piqûre *f*

jack [dʒæk] *n* (*Aut*) cric *m*; (*Cards*) valet *m*

jacket ['dʒækɪt] *n* veste *f*, veston *m*; (*of book*) couverture *f*, jaquette *f*; **jacket potato** *n* pomme *f* de terre en robe des champs

jackpot ['dʒækpɔt] *n* gros lot

Jacuzzi® [dʒə'ku:zɪ] *n* jacuzzi® *m*

jagged ['dʒægɪd] *adj* dentelé(e)

jail [dʒeɪl] *n* prison *f* ▷ *vt* emprisonner, mettre en prison; **jail sentence** *n* peine *f* de prison

jam [dʒæm] *n* confiture *f*; (*also*: **traffic ~**) embouteillage *m* ▷ *vt* (*passage etc*) encombrer, obstruer; (*mechanism, drawer etc*) bloquer, coincer; (*Radio*) brouiller ▷ *vi* (*mechanism, sliding part*) se coincer, se bloquer; (*gun*) s'enrayer; **to be in a ~** (*inf*) être dans le pétrin; **to ~ sth into** (*stuff*) entasser or comprimer qch dans; (*thrust*) enfoncer qch dans

Jamaica [dʒə'meɪkə] *n* Jamaïque *f*

jammed [dʒæmd] *adj* (*window etc*) coincé(e)

janitor ['dʒænɪtə*ʳ*] *n* (*caretaker*) concierge *m*

January ['dʒænjuərɪ] *n* janvier *m*

Japan [dʒə'pæn] *n* Japon *m*; **Japanese** [dʒæpə'ni:z] *adj* japonais(e) ▷ *n* (*pl inv*) Japonais(e); (*Ling*) japonais *m*

jar [dʒɑ:ʳ] *n* (*stone, earthenware*) pot *m*; (*glass*) bocal *m* ▷ *vi* (*sound*) produire un son grinçant or discordant; (*colours etc*) détonner, jurer

jargon ['dʒɑ:gən] *n* jargon *m*

javelin ['dʒævlɪn] *n* javelot *m*

jaw [dʒɔ:] *n* mâchoire *f*

jazz [dʒæz] *n* jazz *m*

jealous ['dʒɛləs] *adj* jaloux(-ouse); **jealousy** *n* jalousie *f*

jeans [dʒi:nz] *npl* jean *m*

Jello® ['dʒɛləu] (*US*) *n* gelée *f*

jelly ['dʒɛlɪ] *n* (*dessert*) gelée *f*; (*US: jam*) confiture *f*; **jellyfish** *n* méduse *f*

jeopardize ['dʒɛpədaɪz] *vt* mettre en danger or péril

jerk [dʒə:k] *n* secousse *f*, saccade *f*; (*of muscle*) spasme *m*; (*inf*) pauvre type *m* ▷ *vt* (*shake*) donner une secousse à; (*pull*) tirer brusquement ▷ *vi* (*vehicles*) cahoter

jersey ['dʒə:zɪ] *n* tricot *m*; (*fabric*) jersey *m*

Jesus ['dʒi:zəs] *n* Jésus

jet [dʒɛt] *n* (*of gas, liquid*) jet *m*; (*Aviat*) avion *m* à réaction, jet *m*; **jet lag** *n* décalage *m* horaire; **jet-ski** *vi* faire du jet-ski or scooter des mers

jetty ['dʒɛtɪ] *n* jetée *f*, digue *f*

Jew [dʒu:] *n* Juif *m*

jewel ['dʒu:əl] *n* bijou *m*, joyau *m*; (*in watch*) rubis *m*; **jeweller**, (*US*) **jeweler** *n* bijoutier(-ière), joaillier *m*; **jeweller's (shop)** *n* (*BRIT*) bijouterie *f*, joaillerie *f*; **jewellery**, (*US*)**jewelry** *n* bijoux *mpl*

Jewish ['dʒu:ɪʃ] *adj* juif (juive)

jigsaw ['dʒɪgsɔ:] n (also: **~ puzzle**) puzzle m

job [dʒɔb] n (chore, task) travail m, tâche f; (employment) emploi m, poste m, place f; **it's a good ~ that ...** c'est heureux or c'est une chance que ... + sub; **just the ~!** (c'est) juste or exactement ce qu'il faut!; **job centre** (BRIT) n ≈ ANPE f, ≈ Agence nationale pour l'emploi; **jobless** adj sans travail, au chômage

jockey ['dʒɔkɪ] n jockey m ▷ vi: **to ~ for position** manœuvrer pour être bien placé

jog [dʒɔg] vt secouer ▷ vi (Sport) faire du jogging; **to ~ sb's memory** rafraîchir la mémoire de qn; **jogging** n jogging m

join [dʒɔɪn] vt (put together) unir, assembler; (become member of) s'inscrire à; (meet) rejoindre, retrouver; (queue) se joindre à ▷ vi (roads, rivers) se rejoindre, se rencontrer ▷ n raccord m; **join in** vi se mettre de la partie ▷ vt fus se mêler à; **join up** vi (meet) se rejoindre; (Mil) s'engager

joiner ['dʒɔɪnəʳ] (BRIT) n menuisier m

joint [dʒɔɪnt] n (Tech) jointure f; joint m; (Anat) articulation f, jointure; (BRIT Culin) rôti m; (inf: place) boîte f; (of cannabis) joint ▷ adj commun(e); (committee) mixte, paritaire; (winner) ex aequo; **joint account** n compte joint; **jointly** adv ensemble, en commun

joke [dʒəuk] n plaisanterie f; (also: **practical ~**) farce f ▷ vi plaisanter; **to play a ~ on** jouer un tour à, faire une farce à; **joker** n (Cards) joker m

jolly ['dʒɔlɪ] adj gai(e), enjoué(e); (enjoyable) amusant(e), plaisant(e) ▷ adv (BRIT inf) rudement, drôlement

jolt [dʒəult] n cahot m, secousse f; (shock) choc m ▷ vt cahoter, secouer

Jordan ['dʒɔ:dən] n (country) Jordanie f

journal ['dʒə:nl] n journal m; **journalism** n journalisme m; **journalist** n journaliste m/f

journey ['dʒə:nɪ] n voyage m; (distance covered) trajet m; **the ~ takes two hours** le trajet dure deux heures; **how was your ~?** votre voyage s'est bien passé?

joy [dʒɔɪ] n joie f; **joyrider** n voleur(-euse) de voiture (qui fait une virée dans le véhicule volé); **joy stick** n (Aviat) manche m à balai; (Comput) manche à balai, manette f (de jeu)

Jr abbr = **junior**

judge [dʒʌdʒ] n juge m ▷ vt juger; (estimate: weight, size etc) apprécier; (consider) estimer

judo ['dʒu:dəu] n judo m

jug [dʒʌg] n pot m, cruche f

juggle ['dʒʌgl] vi jongler; **juggler** n jongleur m

juice [dʒu:s] n jus m; **juicy** adj juteux(-euse)

July [dʒu:'laɪ] n juillet m

jumble ['dʒʌmbl] n fouillis m ▷ vt (also: **~ up**, **~ together**) mélanger, brouiller; **jumble sale** n (BRIT) vente f de charité

JUMBLE SALE

Les jumble sales ont lieu dans les églises, salles des fêtes ou halls d'écoles, et l'on y vend des articles de toutes sortes, en général bon marché et surtout d'occasion, pour collecter des fonds pour une œuvre de charité, une école (par exemple, pour acheter des ordinateurs), ou encore une église (pour réparer un toit etc).

jumbo ['dʒʌmbəu] adj (also: **~ jet**) (avion) gros porteur (à réaction)

jump [dʒʌmp] vi sauter, bondir; (with fear etc) sursauter; (increase) monter en flèche ▷ vt sauter, franchir ▷ n saut m, bond m; (with fear etc) sursaut m; (fence) obstacle m; **to ~ the queue** (BRIT) passer avant son tour

jumper ['dʒʌmpəʳ] n (BRIT: pullover) pull-over m; (US: pinafore dress) robe-chasuble f

jump leads, (US) **jumper cables** npl câbles mpl de démarrage

Jun. abbr = **June; junior**

junction ['dʒʌŋkʃən] n (BRIT: of roads) embranchement m; (of rails) embranchement m

June [dʒu:n] n juin m

jungle ['dʒʌŋgl] n jungle f

junior ['dʒu:nɪəʳ] adj, n: **he's ~ to me (by two years), he's my ~ (by two years)** il est mon cadet (de deux ans), il est plus jeune que moi (de deux ans); **he's ~ to me** (seniority) il est en dessous de moi (dans la hiérarchie), j'ai plus d'ancienneté que lui; **junior high school** n (US) ≈ collège m d'enseignement secondaire; see also **high school; junior school** n (BRIT) école f primaire

junk [dʒʌŋk] n (rubbish) camelote f; (cheap goods) bric-à-brac m inv; **junk food** n snacks vite prêts (sans valeur nutritive)

junkie ['dʒʌŋkɪ] n (inf) junkie m, drogué(e)

junk mail n prospectus mpl; (Comput) messages mpl publicitaires

Jupiter ['dʒu:pɪtəʳ] n (planet) Jupiter f

jurisdiction [dʒuərɪs'dɪkʃən] n juridiction f; **it falls** or **comes within/outside our ~** cela est/n'est pas de notre compétence or ressort

jury ['dʒuərɪ] n jury m

just [dʒʌst] adj juste ▷ adv: **he's ~ done it/left** il vient de le faire/partir; **~ right/two o'clock** exactement or juste ce qu'il faut/deux heures; **we were ~ going** nous partions; **I was ~ about to phone** j'allais téléphoner; **~ as he was leaving** au moment or à l'instant précis où il partait; **~ before/enough/here** juste avant/assez/là; **it's ~ me/a mistake** ce n'est que moi/(rien) qu'une erreur; **~ missed/caught** manqué/attrapé

de justesse; **~ listen to this!** écoutez un peu ça!; **she's ~ as clever as you** elle est tout aussi intelligente que vous; **it's ~ as well that you ...** heureusement que vous ...; **~ a minute!, ~ one moment!** un instant (s'il vous plaît!)

justice ['dʒʌstɪs] n justice f; (US: judge) juge m de la Cour suprême

justification [dʒʌstɪfɪ'keɪʃən] n justification f

justify ['dʒʌstɪfaɪ] vt justifier

jut [dʒʌt] vi (also: ~ out) dépasser, faire saillie

juvenile ['dʒu:vənaɪl] adj juvénile; (court, books) pour enfants ▷ n adolescent(e)

K, k [keɪ] *abbr* (= *one thousand*) K
kangaroo [kæŋgəˈru:] *n* kangourou *m*
karaoke [kɑ:rəˈəʊkɪ] *n* karaoké *m*
karate [kəˈrɑ:tɪ] *n* karaté *m*
kebab [kəˈbæb] *n* kebab *m*
keel [ki:l] *n* quille *f*; **on an even ~** (*fig*) à flot
keen [ki:n] *adj* (*eager*) plein(e) d'enthousiasme; (*interest, desire, competition*) vif (vive); (*eye, intelligence*) pénétrant(e); (*edge*) effilé(e); **to be ~ to do** *or* **on doing sth** désirer vivement faire qch, tenir beaucoup à faire qch; **to be ~ on sth/sb** aimer beaucoup qch/qn
keep [ki:p] (*pt, pp* **kept**) *vt* (*retain, preserve*) garder; (*hold back*) retenir; (*shop, accounts, promise, diary*) tenir; (*support*) entretenir; (*chickens, bees, pigs etc*) élever ▷ *vi* (*food*) se conserver; (*remain: in a certain state or place*) rester ▷ *n* (*of castle*) donjon *m*; (*food etc*): **enough for his ~** assez pour (*assurer*) sa subsistance; **to ~ doing sth** (*continue*) continuer à faire qch; (*repeatedly*) ne pas arrêter de faire qch; **to ~ sb from doing/sth from happening** empêcher qn de faire *or* que qn (ne) fasse/que qch (n')arrive; **to ~ sb happy/a place tidy** faire que qn soit content/qu'un endroit reste propre; **to ~ sth to o.s.** garder qch pour soi, tenir qch secret; **to ~ sth from sb** cacher qch à qn; **to ~ time** (*clock*) être à l'heure, ne pas retarder; **for ~s** (*inf*) pour de bon, pour toujours; **keep away** *vt*: **to ~ sth/sb away from sb** tenir qch/qn éloigné de qn ▷ *vi*: **to ~ away (from)** ne pas s'approcher (de); **keep back** *vt* (*crowds, tears, money*) retenir; (*conceal: information*): **to ~ sth back from sb** cacher qch à qn ▷ *vi* rester en arrière; **keep off** *vt* (*dog, person*) éloigner ▷ *vi*: **if the rain ~s off** s'il ne pleut pas; **~ your hands off!** pas touche! (*inf*); **"~ off the grass"** "pelouse interdite"; **keep on** *vi* continuer; **to ~ on doing** continuer à faire; **don't ~ on about it!** arrête (d'en parler)!; **keep out** *vt* empêcher d'entrer ▷ *vi* (*stay out*) rester en dehors; **"~ out"** "défense d'entrer"; **keep up** *vi* (*fig: in comprehension*) suivre ▷ *vt* continuer, maintenir; **to ~ up with sb** (*in work etc*) se maintenir au même niveau que qn; (*in race etc*) aller aussi vite que qn; **keeper** *n* gardien(ne); **keep-fit** *n* gymnastique *f* (d'entretien); **keeping** *n* (*care*) garde *f*; **in keeping with** en harmonie avec
kennel [ˈkɛnl] *n* niche *f*; **kennels** *npl* (*for boarding*) chenil *m*
Kenya [ˈkɛnjə] *n* Kenya *m*
kept [kɛpt] *pt, pp of* **keep**
kerb [kə:b] *n* (BRIT) bordure *f* du trottoir
kerosene [ˈkɛrəsi:n] *n* kérosène *m*
ketchup [ˈkɛtʃəp] *n* ketchup *m*
kettle [ˈkɛtl] *n* bouilloire *f*
key [ki:] *n* (*gen, Mus*) clé *f*; (*of piano, typewriter*) touche *f*; (*on map*) légende *f* ▷ *adj* (*factor, role, area*) clé *inv* ▷ *vt*

(*also:* **~ in**) (*text*) saisir; **can I have my ~?** je peux avoir ma clé?; **a ~ issue** un problème fondamental; **keyboard** *n* clavier *m*; **keyhole** *n* trou *m* de la serrure; **keyring** *n* porte-clés *m*

kg *abbr* (= *kilogram*) K

khaki ['kɑ:kɪ] *adj*, *n* kaki *m*

kick [kɪk] *vt* donner un coup de pied à ▷ *vi* (*horse*) ruer ▷ *n* coup *m* de pied; (*inf: thrill*): **he does it for ~s** il le fait parce que ça l'excite, il le fait pour le plaisir; **to ~ the habit** (*inf*) arrêter; **kick off** *vi* (*Sport*) donner le coup d'envoi; **kick-off** *n* (*Sport*) coup *m* d'envoi

kid [kɪd] *n* (*inf: child*) gamin(e), gosse *m/f*; (*animal*, *leather*) chevreau *m* ▷ *vi* (*inf*) plaisanter, blaguer

kidnap ['kɪdnæp] *vt* enlever, kidnapper; **kidnapping** *n* enlèvement *m*

kidney ['kɪdnɪ] *n* (*Anat*) rein *m*; (*Culin*) rognon *m*; **kidney bean** *n* haricot *m* rouge

kill [kɪl] *vt* tuer ▷ *n* mise *f* à mort; **to ~ time** tuer le temps; **killer** *n* tueur(-euse); (*murderer*) meurtrier(-ière); **killing** *n* meurtre *m*; (*of group of people*) tuerie *f*, massacre *m*; (*inf*): **to make a killing** se remplir les poches, réussir un beau coup

kiln [kɪln] *n* four *m*

kilo ['ki:ləu] *n* kilo *m*; **kilobyte** *n* (*Comput*) kilo-octet *m*; **kilogram(me)** *n* kilogramme *m*; **kilometre**, (*US*) **kilometer** ['kɪləmi:tər] *n* kilomètre *m*; **kilowatt** *n* kilowatt *m*

kilt [kɪlt] *n* kilt *m*

kin [kɪn] *n* see **next-of-kin**

kind [kaɪnd] *adj* gentil(le), aimable ▷ *n* sorte *f*, espèce *f*; (*species*) genre *m*; **to be two of a ~** se ressembler; **in ~** (*Comm*) en nature; **~ of** (*inf: rather*) plutôt; **a ~ of** une sorte de; **what ~ of ...?** quelle sorte de ...?

kindergarten ['kɪndəgɑ:tn] *n* jardin *m* d'enfants

kindly ['kaɪndlɪ] *adj* bienveillant(e), plein(e) de gentillesse ▷ *adv* avec

bonté; **will you ~ ...** auriez-vous la bonté or l'obligeance de ...

kindness ['kaɪndnɪs] *n* (*quality*) bonté *f*, gentillesse *f*

king [kɪŋ] *n* roi *m*; **kingdom** *n* royaume *m*; **kingfisher** *n* martin-pêcheur *m*; **king-size(d) bed** *n* grand lit (*de 1,95 m de large*)

kiosk ['ki:ɔsk] *n* kiosque *m*; (*BRIT: also:* **telephone ~**) cabine *f* (téléphonique)

kipper ['kɪpər] *n* hareng fumé et salé

kiss [kɪs] *n* baiser *m* ▷ *vt* embrasser; **to ~ (each other)** s'embrasser; **kiss of life** *n* (*BRIT*) bouche à bouche *m*

kit [kɪt] *n* équipement *m*, matériel *m*; (*set of tools etc*) trousse *f*; (*for assembly*) kit *m*

kitchen ['kɪtʃɪn] *n* cuisine *f*

kite [kaɪt] *n* (*toy*) cerf-volant *m*

kitten ['kɪtn] *n* petit chat, chaton *m*

kitty ['kɪtɪ] *n* (*money*) cagnotte *f*

kiwi ['ki:wi:] *n* (*also:* **~ fruit**) kiwi *m*

km *abbr* (= *kilometre*) km

km/h *abbr* (= *kilometres per hour*) km/h

knack [næk] *n*: **to have the ~ (of doing)** avoir le coup (pour faire)

knee [ni:] *n* genou *m*; **kneecap** *n* rotule *f*

kneel (*pt*, *pp* **knelt**) [ni:l, nɛlt] *vi* (*also:* **~ down**) s'agenouiller

knelt [nɛlt] *pt*, *pp of* **kneel**

knew [nju:] *pt of* **know**

knickers ['nɪkəz] *npl* (*BRIT*) culotte *f* (de femme)

knife (*pl* **knives**) [naɪf, naɪvz] *n* couteau *m* ▷ *vt* poignarder, frapper d'un coup de couteau

knight [naɪt] *n* chevalier *m*; (*Chess*) cavalier *m*

knit [nɪt] *vt* tricoter ▷ *vi* tricoter; (*broken bones*) se ressouder; **to ~ one's brows** froncer les sourcils; **knitting** *n* tricot *m*; **knitting needle** *n* aiguille *f* à tricoter; **knitwear** *n* tricots *mpl*, lainages *mpl*

knives [naɪvz] *npl of* **knife**

knob [nɔb] *n* bouton *m*; (*BRIT*): **a ~ of butter** une noix de beurre

knock [nɔk] *vt* frapper; (*bump into*) heurter; (*inf: fig*) dénigrer ▷ *vi* (*at door*

etc): **to ~ at/on** frapper à/sur ▷ *n*
coup *m*; **knock down** *vt* renverser;
(*price*) réduire; **knock off** *vi* (*inf: finish*)
s'arrêter (de travailler) ▷ *vt* (*vase,
object*) faire tomber; (*inf: steal*) piquer;
(*fig: from price etc*): **to ~ off £10** faire
une remise de 10 livres; **knock out** *vt*
assommer; (*Boxing*) mettre k.-o.; (*in
competition*) éliminer; **knock over**
vt (*object*) faire tomber; (*pedestrian*)
renverser; **knockout** *n* (*Boxing*)
knock-out *m*, K.-O. *m*; **knockout
competition** (*BRIT*) compétition *f*
avec épreuves éliminatoires
knot [nɔt] *n* (*gen*) nœud *m* ▷ *vt* nouer
know [nəu] (*pt* **knew**, *pp* **known**) *vt*
savoir; (*person, place*) connaître; **to
~ that** savoir que; **to ~ how to do**
savoir faire; **to ~ how to swim** savoir
nager; **to ~ about/of sth** (*event*) être
au courant de qch; (*subject*) connaître
qch; **I don't ~** je ne sais pas; **do you
~ where I can ...?** savez-vous où je
peux ...?; **know-all** *n* (*BRIT pej*) je-sais-
tout *m/f*; **know-how** *n* savoir-faire *m*,
technique *f*, compétence *f*; **knowing**
adj (*look etc*) entendu(e); **knowingly**
adv (*on purpose*) sciemment; (*smile,
look*) d'un air entendu; **know-it-all** *n*
(*US*) = **know-all**
knowledge ['nɔlɪdʒ] *n* connaissance
f; (*learning*) connaissances, savoir
m; **without my ~** à mon insu;
knowledgeable *adj* bien informé(e)
known [nəun] *pp of* **know** ▷ *adj* (*thief,
facts*) notoire; (*expert*) célèbre
knuckle ['nʌkl] *n* articulation *f* (des
phalanges), jointure *f*
koala [kəu'ɑːlə] *n* (*also*: **~ bear**)
koala *m*
Koran [kɔ'rɑːn] *n* Coran *m*
Korea [kə'rɪə] *n* Corée *f*; **Korean** *adj*
coréen(ne) ▷ *n* Coréen(ne)
kosher ['kəuʃər] *adj* kascher *inv*
Kosovar, Kosovan ['kɔsəvɑːr,
'kɔsəvən] *adj* kosovar(e)
Kosovo ['kɔsəvəu] *n* Kosovo *m*
Kuwait [ku'weɪt] *n* Koweït *m*

L *abbr* (*BRIT Aut*: = *learner*) signale un
conducteur débutant
l. *abbr* (= *litre*) l
lab [læb] *n abbr* (= *laboratory*) labo *m*
label ['leɪbl] *n* étiquette *f*; (*brand: of
record*) marque *f* ▷ *vt* étiqueter
labor *etc* ['leɪbər] (*US*) *n* = **labour**
laboratory [lə'bɔrətərɪ] *n*
laboratoire *m*
Labor Day *n* (*US, CANADA*) fête *f* du
travail (*le premier lundi de septembre*)

⬤ **LABOR DAY**
⬤
⬤ *Labor Day* aux États-Unis et au
⬤ Canada est fixée au premier lundi
⬤ de septembre. Instituée par le
⬤ Congrès en 1894 après avoir été
⬤ réclamée par les mouvements
⬤ ouvriers pendant douze ans, elle
⬤ a perdu une grande partie de son
⬤ caractère politique pour devenir
⬤ un jour férié assez ordinaire et

* l'occasion de partir pour un long
* week-end avant la rentrée des
* classes.

labor union *n* (*US*) syndicat *m*

Labour ['leɪbəˣ] *n* (*BRIT Pol: also:* **the ~ Party**) le parti travailliste, les travaillistes *mpl*

labour, (*US*)**labor** ['leɪbəˣ] *n* (*work*) travail *m*; (*workforce*) main-d'œuvre *f* ▷ *vi:* **to ~ (at)** travailler dur (à), peiner (sur) ▷ *vt:* **to ~ a point** insister sur un point; **in ~** (*Med*) en travail;**labourer**, (*US*)**laborer** *n* manœuvre *m*; **farm labourer** ouvrier *m* agricole

lace [leɪs] *n* dentelle *f*; (*of shoe etc*) lacet *m* ▷ *vt* (*shoe: also:* **~ up**) lacer

lack [læk] *n* manque *m* ▷ *vt* manquer de; **through** *or* **for ~ of** faute de, par manque de; **to be ~ing** manquer, faire défaut; **to be ~ing in** manquer de

lacquer ['lækəˣ] *n* laque *f*

lacy ['leɪsɪ] *adj* (*made of lace*) en dentelle; (*like lace*) comme de la dentelle

lad [læd] *n* garçon *m*, gars *m*

ladder ['lædəˣ] *n* échelle *f*; (*BRIT: in tights*) maille filée ▷ *vt, vi* (*BRIT: tights*) filer

ladle ['leɪdl] *n* louche *f*

lady ['leɪdɪ] *n* dame *f*; **"ladies and gentlemen ..."** "Mesdames (et) Messieurs ..."; **young ~** jeune fille *f*; (*married*) jeune femme *f*; **the ladies' (room)** les toilettes *fpl* des dames; **ladybird** *n*, (*US*)**ladybug** *n* coccinelle *f*

lag [læg] *n* retard *m* ▷ *vi* (*also:* **~ behind**) rester en arrière, traîner; (*fig*) rester à la traîne ▷ *vt* (*pipes*) calorifuger

lager ['lɑːgəˣ] *n* bière blonde

lagoon [lə'guːn] *n* lagune *f*

laid [leɪd] *pt, pp of* **lay**;**laid back** *adj* (*inf*) relaxe, décontracté(e)

lain [leɪn] *pp of* **lie**

lake [leɪk] *n* lac *m*

lamb [læm] *n* agneau *m*

lame [leɪm] *adj* (*also fig*) boiteux(-euse)

lament [lə'mɛnt] *n* lamentation *f* ▷ *vt* pleurer, se lamenter sur

lamp [læmp] *n* lampe *f*;**lamppost** *n* (*BRIT*) réverbère *m*;**lampshade** *n* abat-jour *m inv*

land [lænd] *n* (*as opposed to sea*) terre *f* (*ferme*); (*country*) pays *m*; (*soil*) terre; (*piece of land*) terrain *m*; (*estate*) terre(s), domaine(s) *m(pl)* ▷ *vi* (*from ship*) débarquer; (*Aviat*) atterrir; (*fig: fall*) (re)tomber ▷ *vt* (*passengers, goods*) débarquer; (*obtain*) décrocher; **to ~ sb with sth** (*inf*) coller qch à qn; **landing** *n* (*from ship*) débarquement *m*; (*Aviat*) atterrissage *m*; (*of staircase*) palier *m*;**landing card** *n* carte *f* de débarquement;**landlady** *n* propriétaire *f*, logeuse *f*; (*of pub*) patronne *f*;**landline** *n* ligne *f* fixe; **landlord** *n* propriétaire *m*, logeur *m*; (*of pub etc*) patron *m*;**landmark** *n* (*point m de*) repère *m*; **to be a landmark** (*fig*) faire date *or* époque; **landowner** *n* propriétaire foncier *or* terrien;**landscape** *n* paysage *m*;**landslide** *n* (*Geo*) glissement *m* (*de terrain*); (*fig: Pol*) raz-de-marée (*électoral*)

lane [leɪn] *n* (*in country*) chemin *m*; (*Aut: of road*) voie *f*; (: *line of traffic*) file *f*; (*in race*) couloir *m*

language ['læŋgwɪdʒ] *n* langue *f*; (*way one speaks*) langage *m*; **what ~s do you speak?** quelles langues parlez-vous?; **bad ~** grossièretés *fpl*, langage grossier;**language laboratory** *n* laboratoire *m* de langues;**language school** *n* école *f* de langue

lantern ['læntn] *n* lanterne *f*

lap [læp] *n* (*of track*) tour *m* (*de piste*); (*of body*): **in** *or* **on one's ~** sur les genoux ▷ *vt* (*also:* **~ up**) laper ▷ *vi* (*waves*) clapoter

lapel [lə'pɛl] *n* revers *m*

lapse [læps] *n* défaillance *f*; (*in behaviour*) écart *m* (*de conduite*)

▷ vi (Law) cesser d'être en vigueur; (contract) expirer; **to ~ into bad habits** prendre de mauvaises habitudes; **~ of time** laps m de temps, intervalle m
laptop (computer) ['læptɔp-] n (ordinateur m) portable m
lard [lɑːd] n saindoux m
larder ['lɑːdə'] n garde-manger m inv
large [lɑːdʒ] adj grand(e); (person, animal) gros (grosse); **at ~** (free) en liberté; (generally) en général; pour la plupart; see also **by**; **largely** adv en grande partie; (principally) surtout; **large-scale** adj (map, drawing etc) à grande échelle; (fig) important(e)
lark [lɑːk] n (bird) alouette f; (joke) blague f, farce f
larrikin ['lærɪkɪn] n (AUST, NZ inf) fripon m (inf)
laryngitis [lærɪn'dʒaɪtɪs] n laryngite f
lasagne [ləˈzænjə] n lasagne f
laser ['leɪzə'] n laser m; **laser printer** n imprimante f laser
lash [læʃ] n coup m de fouet; (also: **eye~**) cil m ▷ vt fouetter; (tie) attacher; **lash out** vi: **to ~ out (at or against sb/sth)** attaquer violemment (qn/qch)
lass [læs] (BRIT) n (jeune) fille f
last [lɑːst] adj dernier(-ière) en dernier; (most recently) la dernière fois; (finally) finalement ▷ vi durer; **~ week** la semaine dernière; **~ night** (evening) hier soir; (night) la nuit dernière; **at ~** enfin; **~ but one** avant-dernier(-ière); **lastly** adv en dernier lieu, pour finir; **last-minute** adj de dernière minute
latch [lætʃ] n loquet m; **latch onto** vt fus (cling to: person, group) s'accrocher à; (: idea) se mettre en tête
late [leɪt] adj (not on time) en retard; (far on in day etc) tardif(-ive) (: edition, delivery) dernier(-ière); (dead) défunt(e) ▷ adv tard; (behind time, schedule) en retard; **to be 10**

minutes ~ avoir 10 minutes de retard; **sorry I'm ~** désolé d'être en retard; **it's too ~** il est trop tard; **of ~** dernièrement; **in ~ May** vers la fin (du mois) de mai, fin mai; **the ~ Mr X** feu M. X; **latecomer** n retardataire m/f; **lately** adv récemment; **later** adj (date etc) ultérieur(e); (version etc) plus récent(e) ▷ adv plus tard; **latest** ['leɪtɪst] adj tout(e) dernier(-ière); **at the latest** au plus tard
lather ['lɑːðə'] n mousse f (de savon) ▷ vt savonner
Latin ['lætɪn] n latin m ▷ adj latin(e); **Latin America** n Amérique latine; **Latin American** adj latino-américain(e), d'Amérique latine ▷ n Latino-Américain(e)
latitude ['lætɪtjuːd] n (also fig) latitude f
latter ['lætə'] adj deuxième, dernier(-ière) ▷ n: **the ~** ce dernier, celui-ci
laugh [lɑːf] n rire m ▷ vi rire; **(to do sth) for a ~** (faire qch) pour rire; **laugh at** vt fus se moquer de; (joke) rire de; **laughter** n rire m; (of several people) rires mpl
launch [lɔːntʃ] n lancement m; (also: **motor ~**) vedette f ▷ vt (ship, rocket, plan) lancer; **launch into** vt fus se lancer dans
launder ['lɔːndə'] vt laver; (fig: money) blanchir
Launderette® [lɔːn'drɛt], (US) **Laundromat®** ['lɔːndrəmæt] n laverie f (automatique)
laundry ['lɔːndrɪ] n (clothes) linge m; (business) blanchisserie f; (room) buanderie f; **to do the ~** faire la lessive
lava ['lɑːvə] n lave f
lavatory ['lævətərɪ] n toilettes fpl
lavender ['lævəndə'] n lavande f
lavish ['lævɪʃ] adj (amount) copieux(-euse); (person: giving freely): **~ with** prodigue de ▷ vt: **to ~ sth on sb** prodiguer qch à qn; (money) dépenser qch sans compter pour qn

law [lɔː] n loi f; (science) droit m; **lawful**
adj légal(e), permis(e); **lawless** adj
(action) illégal(e); (place) sans loi

lawn [lɔːn] n pelouse f; **lawnmower**
n tondeuse f à gazon

lawsuit ['lɔːsuːt] n procès m

lawyer ['lɔːjəʳ] n (consultant, with
company) juriste m; (for sales, wills
etc) ≈ notaire m; (partner, in court) ≈
avocat m

lax [læks] adj relâché(e)

laxative ['læksətɪv] n laxatif m

lay [leɪ] pt of **lie** ▷ adj laïque; (not
expert) profane ▷ vt (pt, pp **laid**) poser,
mettre; (eggs) pondre; (trap) tendre;
(plans) élaborer; **to ~ the table**
mettre la table; **lay down** vt poser;
(rules etc) établir; **to ~ down the law**
(fig) faire la loi; **lay off** vt (workers)
licencier; **lay on** vt (provide: meal etc)
fournir; **lay out** vt (design) dessiner,
concevoir; (display) disposer; (spend)
dépenser; **lay-by** n (BRIT) aire f de
stationnement (sur le bas-côté)

layer ['leɪəʳ] n couche f

layman ['leɪmən] (irreg) n (Rel) laïque
m; (non-expert) profane m

layout ['leɪaut] n disposition f, plan
m, agencement m; (Press) mise f
en page

lazy ['leɪzɪ] adj paresseux(-euse)

lb. abbr (weight) = **pound**

lead[1] (pt, pp **led**) [liːd, lɛd] n (front
position) tête f; (distance, time ahead)
avance f; (clue) piste f; (Elec) fil m; (for
dog) laisse f; (Theat) rôle principal ▷ vt
(guide) mener, conduire; (be leader of)
être à la tête de ▷ vi (Sport) mener,
être en tête; **to ~ to** (road, pipe) mener
à, conduire à; (result in) conduire à;
aboutir à; **to be in the ~** (Sport) (in
race) mener, être en tête; (in match)
mener (à la marque); **to ~ sb to do
sth** amener qn à faire qch; **to ~ the
way** montrer le chemin; **lead up to** vt
conduire à; (in conversation) en venir à

lead[2] [lɛd] n (metal) plomb m; (in
pencil) mine f

leader ['liːdəʳ] n (of team) chef m;
(of party etc) dirigeant(e), leader m;
(Sport: in league) leader; (: in race)
coureur m de tête; **leadership** n
(position) direction f; **under the
leadership of ...** sous la direction de
...; **qualities of leadership** qualités
fpl de chef or de meneur

lead-free ['lɛdfriː] adj sans plomb

leading ['liːdɪŋ] adj de premier plan;
(main) principal(e); (in race) de tête

lead singer [liːd-] n (in pop group)
(chanteur m) vedette f

leaf (pl **leaves**) [liːf, liːvz] n feuille f;
(of table) rallonge f; **to turn over a
new ~** (fig) changer de conduite or
d'existence; **leaf through** vt (book)
feuilleter

leaflet ['liːflɪt] n prospectus m,
brochure f; (Pol, Rel) tract m

league [liːg] n ligue f; (Football)
championnat m; **to be in ~ with**
avoir partie liée avec, être de mèche
avec

leak [liːk] n (lit, fig) fuite f ▷ vi (pipe,
liquid etc) fuir; (shoes) prendre l'eau;
(ship) faire eau ▷ vt (liquid) répandre;
(information) divulguer

lean (pt, pp **leaned** or **leant**) [liːn,
lɛnt] adj maigre ▷ vt: **to ~ sth on**
appuyer qch sur ▷ vi (slope) pencher;
(rest): **to ~ against** s'appuyer
contre; être appuyé(e) contre; **to ~
on** s'appuyer sur; **lean forward** vi
se pencher en avant; **lean over** vi
se pencher; **leaning** n: **leaning
(towards)** penchant m (pour)

leant [lɛnt] pt, pp of **lean**

leap (pt, pp **leaped** or **leapt**) [liːp, lɛpt]
n bond m, saut m ▷ vi bondir, sauter

leapt [lɛpt] pt, pp of **leap**

leap year n année f bissextile

learn (pt, pp **learned** or **learnt**) [ləːn,
ləːnt] vt, vi apprendre; **to ~ (how)
to do sth** apprendre à faire qch;
to ~ about sth (Scol) étudier qch;
(hear, read) apprendre qch; **learner**
n débutant(e); (BRIT: also: **learner**

driver) (conducteur(-trice))
débutant(e); **learning** n savoir m
learnt [lə:nt] pp of **learn**
lease [li:s] n bail m ▷ vt louer à bail
leash [li:ʃ] n laisse f
least [li:st] adj: **the ~** (+ noun) le (la)
plus petit(e), le (la) moindre; (smallest
amount of) le moins de ▷ pron: **(the)
~** le moins ▷ adv (+ verb) le moins; (+
adj): **the ~** le (la) moins; **the ~ money**
le moins d'argent; **the ~ expensive** le
(la) moins cher (chère) **the ~ possible
effort** le moins d'effort possible; **at
~** au moins; (or rather) du moins; **you
could at ~ have written** tu aurais au
moins pu écrire; **not in the ~** pas le
moins du monde

leather ['lɛðəʳ] n cuir m
leave (pt, pp **left**) [li:v, lɛft] vt
laisser; (go away from) quitter; (forget)
oublier ▷ vi partir, s'en aller ▷ n
(time off) congé m; (Mil, also consent)
permission f; **what time does the
train/bus ~?** le train/le bus part à
quelle heure?; **to ~ sth to sb** (money
etc) laisser qch à qn; **to be left** rester;
there's some milk left over il reste
du lait; **~ it to me!** laissez-moi faire!,
je m'en occupe!; **on ~** en permission;
leave behind vt (also fig) laisser;
(forget) laisser, oublier; **leave out** vt
oublier, omettre
leaves [li:vz] npl of **leaf**
Lebanon ['lɛbənən] n Liban m
lecture ['lɛktʃəʳ] n conférence f;
(Scol) cours (magistral) ▷ vi donner
des cours; enseigner ▷ vt (scold)
sermonner, réprimander; **to give
a ~ (on)** faire une conférence (sur),
faire un cours (sur); **lecture hall**
n amphithéâtre m; **lecturer** n
(speaker) conférencier(-ière); (BRIT: at
university) professeur m (d'université),
prof m/f de fac (inf); **lecture theatre**
n = **lecture hall**

⬛ Be careful not to translate lecture
by the French word lecture.

led [lɛd] pt, pp of **lead**[1]

ledge [lɛdʒ] n (of window, on wall)
rebord m; (of mountain) saillie f,
corniche f
leek [li:k] n poireau m
left [lɛft] pt, pp of **leave** ▷ adj gauche
▷ adv à gauche ▷ n gauche f; **there
are two ~** il en reste deux; **on the
~, to the ~** à gauche; **the L~** (Pol)
la gauche; **left-hand** adj: **the left-
hand side** la gauche, le côté gauche;
left-hand drive n (vehicle) véhicule
m avec la conduite à gauche; **left-
handed** adj gaucher(-ère); (scissors
etc) pour gauchers; **left-luggage
locker** n (BRIT) (casier m à) consigne f
automatique; **left-luggage (office)**
n (BRIT) consigne f; **left-overs** npl
restes mpl; **left-wing** adj (Pol) de
gauche
leg [lɛg] n jambe f; (of animal) patte f;
(of furniture) pied m; (Culin: of chicken)
cuisse f; (of journey) étape f; **1st/2nd
~** (Sport) match m aller/retour; **~ of
lamb** (Culin) gigot m d'agneau
legacy ['lɛgəsɪ] n (also fig) héritage
m, legs m
legal ['li:gl] adj (permitted by law)
légal(e); (relating to law) juridique;
legal holiday (US) n jour férié;
legalize vt légaliser; **legally** adv
légalement
legend ['lɛdʒənd] n légende f;
legendary ['lɛdʒəndərɪ] adj
légendaire
leggings ['lɛgɪŋz] npl caleçon m
legible ['lɛdʒəbl] adj lisible
legislation [lɛdʒɪs'leɪʃən] n
législation f
legislative ['lɛdʒɪslətɪv] adj
législatif(-ive)
legitimate [lɪ'dʒɪtɪmət] adj
légitime
leisure ['lɛʒəʳ] n (free time) temps
libre, loisirs mpl; **at ~** (tout) à loisir; **at
your ~** (later) à tête reposée; **leisure
centre** n (BRIT) centre m de loisirs;
leisurely adj tranquille, fait(e) sans
se presser

lemon ['lemən] *n* citron *m*;
  lemonade *n* (*fizzy*) limonade *f*;
  lemon tea *n* thé *m* au citron

lend (*pt, pp* **lent**) [lɛnd, lɛnt] *vt*: **to ~
  sth (to sb)** prêter qch (à qn); **could
  you ~ me some money?** pourriez-
  vous me prêter de l'argent?

length [lɛŋθ] *n* longueur *f*; (*section:
  of road, pipe etc*) morceau *m*, bout *m*;
  ~ of time durée *f*; **it is 2 metres in ~**
  cela fait 2 mètres de long; **at ~** (*at last*)
  enfin, à la fin; (*lengthily*) longuement;
  lengthen *vt* allonger, prolonger ▷ *vi*
  s'allonger; **lengthways** *adv* dans le
  sens de la longueur, en long; **lengthy**
  adj (très) long (longue)

lens [lɛnz] *n* lentille *f*; (*of spectacles*)
  verre *m*; (*of camera*) objectif *m*

Lent [lɛnt] *n* carême *m*

lent [lɛnt] *pt, pp of* **lend**

lentil ['lɛntl] *n* lentille *f*

Leo ['liːəu] *n* le Lion

leopard ['lɛpəd] *n* léopard *m*

leotard ['liːətɑːd] *n* justaucorps *m*

leprosy ['lɛprəsɪ] *n* lèpre *f*

lesbian ['lɛzbɪən] *n* lesbienne *f* ▷ *adj*
  lesbien(ne)

less [lɛs] *adj* moins de ▷ *pron, adv*
  moins ▷ *prep*: **~ tax/10% discount**
  avant impôt/moins 10% de remise;
  ~ than that/you moins que cela/
  vous; **~ than half** moins de la moitié;
  ~ than ever moins que jamais; **~ and
  ~** de moins en moins; **the ~ he works
  ...** moins il travaille ...; **lessen** *vi*
  diminuer, s'amoindrir, s'atténuer ▷ *vt*
  diminuer, réduire, atténuer; **lesser**
  ['lɛsə'] *adj* moindre; **to a lesser
  extent** *or* **degree** à un degré moindre

lesson ['lɛsn] *n* leçon *f*; **to teach sb a
  ~** (*fig*) donner une bonne leçon à qn

let (*pt, pp* **let**) [lɛt] *vt* laisser; (*BRIT:
  lease*) louer; **to ~ sb do sth** laisser
  qn faire qch; **to ~ sb know sth**
  faire savoir qch à qn, prévenir qn de
  qch; **to ~ go** lâcher prise; **to ~ go of
  sth, to ~ sth go** lâcher qch; **~'s go**
  allons-y; **~ him come** qu'il vienne;

"to ~" (*BRIT*) "à louer"; **let down** *vt*
  (*lower*) baisser; (*BRIT: tyre*) dégonfler;
  (*disappoint*) décevoir; **let in** *vt* laisser
  entrer; (*visitor etc*) faire entrer; **let
  off** *vt* (*allow to leave*) laisser partir;
  (*not punish*) ne pas punir; (*firework etc*)
  faire partir; (*bomb*) faire exploser; **let
  out** *vt* laisser sortir; (*scream*) laisser
  échapper; (*BRIT: rent out*) louer

lethal ['liːθl] *adj* mortel(le), fatal(e);
  (*weapon*) meurtrier(-ère)

letter ['lɛtə'] *n* lettre *f*; **letterbox** *n*
  (*BRIT*) boîte *f* aux *or* à lettres

lettuce ['lɛtɪs] *n* laitue *f*, salade *f*

leukaemia, (*US*) **leukemia**
  [luːˈkiːmɪə] *n* leucémie *f*

level ['lɛvl] *adj* (*flat*) plat(e), plan(e),
  uni(e); (*horizontal*) horizontal(e) ▷ *n*
  niveau *m* ▷ *vt* niveler, aplanir; **A ~s**
  npl (*BRIT*) ≈ baccalauréat *m*; **to be ~
  with** être au même niveau que; **to
  draw ~ with** (*runner, car*) arriver à la
  hauteur de, rattraper; **on the ~** (*fig:
  honest*) régulier(-ière); **level crossing**
  n (*BRIT*) passage *m* à niveau

lever ['liːvə'] *n* levier *m*; **leverage** *n*
  (*influence*): **leverage (on** *or* **with)**
  prise *f* (sur)

levy ['lɛvɪ] *n* taxe *f*, impôt *m* ▷ *vt* (*tax*)
  lever; (*fine*) infliger

liability [laɪəˈbɪlətɪ] *n* responsabilité
  f; (*handicap*) handicap *m*

liable ['laɪəbl] *adj* (*subject*): **~ to**
  sujet(te) à, passible de; (*responsible*):
  ~ (for) responsable (de); (*likely*): **~ to
  do** susceptible de faire

liaise [liːˈeɪz] *vi*: **to ~ with** assurer la
  liaison avec

liar ['laɪə'] *n* menteur(-euse)

libel ['laɪbl] *n* diffamation *f*;
  (*document*) écrit *m* diffamatoire ▷ *vt*
  diffamer

liberal ['lɪbərl] *adj* libéral(e);
  (*generous*): **~ with** prodigue de,
  généreux(-euse) avec ▷ *n*: **L~** (*Pol*)
  libéral(e); **Liberal Democrat** *n* (*BRIT*)
  libéral(e)-démocrate *m/f*

liberate ['lɪbəreɪt] *vt* libérer

liberation [lɪbə'reɪʃən] n libération f
liberty ['lɪbətɪ] n liberté f; **to be at ~** (criminal) être en liberté; **at ~ to do** libre de faire; **to take the ~ of** prendre la liberté de, se permettre de
Libra ['liːbrə] n la Balance
librarian [laɪ'brɛərɪən] n bibliothécaire m/f
library ['laɪbrərɪ] n bibliothèque f
Be careful not to translate library by the French word librairie.
Libya ['lɪbɪə] n Libye f
lice [laɪs] npl of **louse**
licence, (US) **license** ['laɪsns] n autorisation f, permis m; (Comm) licence f; (Radio, TV) redevance f; **driving ~**, (US) **driver's license** permis m (de conduire)
license ['laɪsns] n (US) = **licence**; **licensed** adj (for alcohol) patenté(e) pour la vente des spiritueux, qui a une patente de débit de boissons; (car) muni(e) de la vignette; **license plate** n (US Aut) plaque f minéralogique; **licensing hours** (BRIT) npl heures fpl d'ouvertures (des pubs)
lick [lɪk] vt lécher; (inf: defeat) écraser, flanquer une piquette or raclée à; **to ~ one's lips** (fig) se frotter les mains
lid [lɪd] n couvercle m; (eyelid) paupière f
lie [laɪ] n mensonge m ▷ vi (pt, pp **lied**) (tell lies) mentir; (pt, **lay**, pp **lain**) (rest) être étendu(e) or allongé(e) or couché(e) (: object: be situated) se trouver, être; **to ~ low** (fig) se cacher, rester caché(e); **to tell ~s** mentir; **lie about**, **lie around** vi (things) traîner; (BRIT: person) traînasser, flemmarder; **lie down** vi se coucher, s'étendre
Liechtenstein ['lɪktənstaɪn] n Liechtenstein m
lie-in ['laɪɪn] n (BRIT): **to have a ~** faire la grasse matinée
lieutenant [lɛf'tɛnənt, US luː'tɛnənt] n lieutenant m
life (pl **lives**) [laɪf, laɪvz] n vie f; **to come to ~** (fig) s'animer; **life**

assurance n (BRIT) = **life insurance**; **lifeboat** n canot m or chaloupe f de sauvetage; **lifeguard** n surveillant m de baignade; **life insurance** n assurance-vie f; **life jacket** n gilet m or ceinture f de sauvetage; **lifelike** adj qui semble vrai(e) or vivant(e), ressemblant(e); (painting) réaliste; **life preserver** n (US) gilet m or ceinture f de sauvetage; **life sentence** n condamnation f à vie or à perpétuité; **lifestyle** n style m de vie; **lifetime** n: **in his lifetime** de son vivant
lift [lɪft] vt soulever, lever; (end) supprimer, lever ▷ vi (fog) se lever ▷ n (BRIT: elevator) ascenseur m; **to give sb a ~** (BRIT) emmener or prendre qn en voiture; **can you give me a ~ to the station?** pouvez-vous m'emmener à la gare?; **lift up** vt soulever; **lift-off** n décollage m
light [laɪt] n lumière f; (lamp) lampe f; (Aut: rear light) feu m; (: headlamp) phare m; (for cigarette etc): **have you got a ~?** avez-vous du feu? ▷ vt (pt, pp **lit**) (candle, cigarette, fire) allumer; (room) éclairer ▷ adj (room, colour) clair(e); (not heavy, also fig) léger(-ère); (not strenuous) peu fatigant(e); **lights** npl (traffic lights) feux mpl; **to come to ~** être dévoilé(e) or découvert(e); **in the ~ of** à la lumière de; étant donné; **light up** vi s'allumer; (face) s'éclairer; (smoke) allumer une cigarette or une pipe etc ▷ vt (illuminate) éclairer, illuminer; **light bulb** n ampoule f; **lighten** vt (light up) éclairer; (make lighter) éclaircir; (make less heavy) alléger; **lighter** n (also: **cigarette lighter**) briquet m; **light-hearted** adj gai(e), joyeux(-euse), enjoué(e); **lighthouse** n phare m; **lighting** n éclairage m; (in theatre) éclairages; **lightly** adv légèrement; **to get off lightly** s'en tirer à bon compte
lightning ['laɪtnɪŋ] n foudre f; (flash) éclair m

lightweight ['laɪtweɪt] *adj* (*suit*) léger(-ère) ▷ *n* (*Boxing*) poids léger

like [laɪk] *vt* aimer (bien) ▷ *prep* comme ▷ *adj* semblable, pareil(le) ▷ *n*: **the ~** (*pej*) (d')autres du même genre *or* acabit; **his ~s and dislikes** ses goûts *mpl or* préférences *fpl*; **I would ~, I'd ~** je voudrais, j'aimerais; **would you ~ a coffee?** voulez-vous du café?; **to be/look ~ sb/sth** ressembler à qn/qch; **what's he ~?** comment est-il?; **what does it look ~?** de quoi est-ce que ça a l'air?; **what does it taste ~?** quel goût est-ce que ça a?; **that's just ~ him** c'est bien de lui, ça lui ressemble; **do it ~ this** fais-le comme ceci; **it's nothing ~ ...** ce n'est pas du tout comme ...; **likeable** *adj* sympathique, agréable

likelihood ['laɪklɪhud] *n* probabilité *f*

likely ['laɪklɪ] *adj* (*result, outcome*) probable; (*excuse*) plausible; **he's ~ to leave** il va sûrement partir, il risque fort de partir; **not ~!** (*inf*) pas de danger!

likewise ['laɪkwaɪz] *adv* de même, pareillement

liking ['laɪkɪŋ] *n* (*for person*) affection *f*; (*for thing*) penchant *m*, goût *m*; **to be to sb's ~** être au goût de qn, plaire à qn

lilac ['laɪlək] *n* lilas *m*

Lilo® ['laɪləu] *n* matelas *m* pneumatique

lily ['lɪlɪ] *n* lis *m*; **~ of the valley** muguet *m*

limb [lɪm] *n* membre *m*

limbo ['lɪmbəu] *n*: **to be in ~** (*fig*) être tombé(e) dans l'oubli

lime [laɪm] *n* (*tree*) tilleul *m*; (*fruit*) citron vert, lime *f*; (*Geo*) chaux *f*

limelight ['laɪmlaɪt] *n*: **in the ~** (*fig*) en vedette, au premier plan

limestone ['laɪmstəun] *n* pierre *f* à chaux; (*Geo*) calcaire *m*

limit ['lɪmɪt] *n* limite *f* ▷ *vt* limiter; **limited** *adj* limité(e), restreint(e);

to be limited to se limiter à, ne concerner que

limousine ['lɪməziːn] *n* limousine *f*

limp [lɪmp] *n*: **to have a ~** boiter ▷ *vi* boiter ▷ *adj* mou (molle)

line [laɪn] *n* (*gen*) ligne *f*; (*stroke*) trait *m*; (*wrinkle*) ride *f*; (*rope*) corde *f*; (*wire*) fil *m*; (*of poem*) vers *m*; (*row, series*) rangée *f*; (*of people*) file *f*, queue *f*; (*railway track*) voie *f*; (*Comm: series of goods*) article(s) *m*(*pl*), ligne de produits; (*work*) métier *m* ▷ *vt* (*subj: trees, crowd*) border; **to ~ (with)** (*clothes*) doubler (de); (*box*) garnir *or* tapisser (de); **to stand in ~** (*us*) faire la queue; **in his ~ of business** dans sa partie, dans son rayon; **to be in ~ for sth** (*fig*) être en lice pour qch; **in ~ with** en accord avec, en conformité avec; **in a ~** aligné(e); **line up** *vi* s'aligner, se mettre en rang(s); (*in queue*) faire la queue ▷ *vt* aligner; (*event*) prévoir; (*find*) trouver; **to have sb/sth ~d up** avoir qn/qch en vue *or* de prévu(e)

linear ['lɪnɪəʳ] *adj* linéaire

linen ['lɪnɪn] *n* linge *m* (de corps *or* de maison); (*cloth*) lin *m*

liner ['laɪnəʳ] *n* (*ship*) paquebot *m* de ligne; (*for bin*) sac-poubelle *m*

line-up ['laɪnʌp] *n* (*us: queue*) file *f*; (*also*: **police ~**) parade *f* d'identification; (*Sport*) (composition *f* de l')équipe *f*

linger ['lɪŋgəʳ] *vi* s'attarder; traîner; (*smell, tradition*) persister

lingerie ['lænʒəriː] *n* lingerie *f*

linguist ['lɪŋgwɪst] *n* linguiste *m/f*; **to be a good ~** être doué(e) pour les langues; **linguistic** *adj* linguistique

lining ['laɪnɪŋ] *n* doublure *f*; (*of brakes*) garniture *f*

link [lɪŋk] *n* (*connection*) lien *m*, rapport *m*; (*Internet*) lien; (*of a chain*) maillon *m* ▷ *vt* relier, lier, unir; **links** *npl* (*Golf*) (terrain *m* de) golf *m*; **link up** *vt* relier ▷ *vi* (*people*) se rejoindre; (*companies etc*) s'associer

lion ['laɪən] n lion m; **lioness** n lionne f
lip [lɪp] n lèvre f; (of cup etc) rebord m;
lip-read vi (irreg: like **read**) lire sur les
lèvres; **lip salve** [-sælv] n pommade
f pour les lèvres, pommade rosat;
lipstick n rouge m à lèvres
liqueur [lɪ'kjuə^r] n liqueur f
liquid ['lɪkwɪd] n liquide m ⊳ adj
liquide; **liquidizer** ['lɪkwɪdaɪzə^r] n
(BRIT Culin) mixer m
liquor ['lɪkə^r] n spiritueux m, alcool m;
liquor store (US) n magasin m de vins
et spiritueux
Lisbon ['lɪzbən] n Lisbonne
lisp [lɪsp] n zézaiement m ⊳ vi
zézayer
list [lɪst] n liste f ⊳ vt (write down)
inscrire; (make list of) faire la liste de;
(enumerate) énumérer
listen ['lɪsn] vi écouter; **to ~ to**
écouter; **listener** n auditeur(-trice)
lit [lɪt] pt, pp of **light**
liter ['li:tə^r] n (US) = **litre**
literacy ['lɪtərəsɪ] n degré m
d'alphabétisation, fait m de savoir lire
et écrire; (BRIT Scol) enseignement m
de la lecture et de l'écriture
literal ['lɪtərl] adj littéral(e); **literally**
adv littéralement; (really) réellement
literary ['lɪtərərɪ] adj littéraire
literate ['lɪtərət] adj qui sait lire et
écrire; (educated) instruit(e)
literature ['lɪtrɪtʃə^r] n littérature
f; (brochures etc) copie f publicitaire,
prospectus mpl
litre, (US) **liter** ['li:tə^r] n litre m
litter ['lɪtə^r] n (rubbish) détritus mpl;
(dirtier) ordures fpl; (young animals)
portée f; **litter bin** n (BRIT) poubelle f
little ['lɪtl] adj (small) petit(e); (not
much): **~ milk** peu de lait ⊳ adv peu;
a ~ un peu (de); **a ~ milk** un peu de
lait; **a ~ bit** un peu; **as ~ as possible**
le moins possible; **~ by ~** petit à petit,
peu à peu; **little finger** n auriculaire
m, petit doigt
live¹ [laɪv] adj (animal) vivant(e), en
vie; (wire) sous tension; (broadcast)

(transmis(e)) en direct; (unexploded)
non explosé(e)
live² [lɪv] vi vivre; (reside) vivre,
habiter; **to ~ in London** habiter
(à) Londres; **where do you ~?** où
habitez-vous?; **live together** vi vivre
ensemble, cohabiter; **live up to** vt fus
se montrer à la hauteur de
livelihood ['laɪvlɪhud] n moyens mpl
d'existence
lively ['laɪvlɪ] adj vif (vive), plein(e)
d'entrain; (place, book) vivant(e)
liven up ['laɪvn-] vt (room etc) égayer;
(discussion, evening) animer ⊳ vi
s'animer
liver ['lɪvə^r] n foie m
lives [laɪvz] npl of **life**
livestock ['laɪvstɔk] n cheptel m,
bétail m
living ['lɪvɪŋ] adj vivant(e), en vie ⊳ n:
to earn or **make a ~** gagner sa vie;
living room n salle f de séjour
lizard ['lɪzəd] n lézard m
load [ləud] n (weight) poids m; (thing
carried) chargement m, charge f; (Elec,
Tech) charge ⊳ vt charger; (also: **~ up**):
to ~ (with) (lorry, ship) charger (de);
(gun, camera) charger (avec); **a ~ of**,
~s of (fig) un or des tas de, des masses
de; **to talk a ~ of rubbish** (inf) dire
des bêtises; **loaded** adj (dice) pipé(e);
(question) insidieux(-euse); (inf: rich)
bourré(e) de fric
loaf (pl **loaves**) [ləuf, ləuvz] n pain m,
miche f ⊳ vi (also: **~ about, ~ around**)
fainéanter, traîner
loan [ləun] n prêt m ⊳ vt prêter; **on ~**
prêté(e), en prêt
loathe [ləuð] vt détester, avoir en
horreur
loaves [ləuvz] npl of **loaf**
lobby ['lɔbɪ] n hall m, entrée f; (Pol)
groupe m de pression, lobby m ⊳ vt
faire pression sur
lobster ['lɔbstə^r] n homard m
local ['ləukl] adj local(e) ⊳ n (BRIT:
pub) pub m or café m du coin; **the
locals** npl les gens mpl du pays or du

coin; **local anaesthetic**, (US) **local anesthetic** n anesthésie locale; **local authority** n collectivité locale, municipalité f; **local government** n administration locale or municipale; **locally** ['ləukəlı] adv localement; dans les environs or la région

locate [ləu'keɪt] vt (find) trouver, repérer; (situate) situer; **to be ~d in** être situé à or en

location [ləu'keɪʃən] n emplacement m; **on ~** (Cine) en extérieur

> Be careful not to translate location by the French word location.

loch [lɔx] n lac m, loch m

lock [lɔk] n (of door, box) serrure f; (of canal) écluse f; (of hair) mèche f, boucle f ▷ vt (with key) fermer à clé ▷ vi (door etc) fermer à clé; (wheels) se bloquer; **lock in** vt enfermer; **lock out** vt enfermer dehors; (on purpose) mettre à la porte; **lock up** vt (person) enfermer; (house) fermer à clé ▷ vi tout fermer (à clé)

locker ['lɔkə*] n casier m; (in station) consigne f automatique; **locker-room** ['lɔkə*ru:m] (US) n (Sport) vestiaire m

locksmith ['lɔksmɪθ] n serrurier m

locomotive [ləukə'məutɪv] n locomotive f

locum ['ləukəm] n (Med) suppléant(e) de médecin etc

lodge [lɔdʒ] n pavillon m (de gardien); (also: **hunting** ~) pavillon de chasse ▷ vi (person): **to ~ with** être logé(e) chez, être en pension chez; (bullet) se loger ▷ vt (appeal etc) présenter; déposer; **to ~ a complaint** porter plainte; **lodger** n locataire m/f; (with room and meals) pensionnaire m/f

lodging ['lɔdʒɪŋ] n logement m

loft [lɔft] n grenier m; (apartment) grenier aménagé (en appartement) (gén dans ancien entrepôt ou fabrique)

log [lɔg] n (of wood) bûche f; (Naut) livre m or journal m de bord; (of car) ≈

carte grise ▷ vt enregistrer; **log in**, **log on** vi (Comput) ouvrir une session, entrer dans le système; **log off**, **log out** vi (Comput) clore une session, sortir du système

logic ['lɔdʒɪk] n logique f; **logical** adj logique

login ['lɔgɪn] n (Comput) identifiant m

Loire [lwa:] n: **the (River) ~** la Loire

lollipop ['lɔlɪpɔp] n sucette f; **lollipop man/lady** (irreg) (BRIT) n contractuel(le) qui fait traverser la rue aux enfants

lolly ['lɔlɪ] n (inf: ice) esquimau m; (: lollipop) sucette f

London ['lʌndən] n Londres; **Londoner** n Londonien(ne)

lone [ləun] adj solitaire

loneliness ['ləunlɪnɪs] n solitude f, isolement m

lonely ['ləunlɪ] adj seul(e); (childhood etc) solitaire; (place) solitaire, isolé(e)

long [lɔŋ] adj long (longue) ▷ adv longtemps ▷ vi: **to ~ for sth/to do sth** avoir très envie de qch/de faire qch, attendre qch avec impatience/ attendre avec impatience de faire qch; **how ~ is this river/course?** quelle est la longueur de ce fleuve/ la durée de ce cours?; **6 metres ~** (long) de 6 mètres; **6 months ~** qui dure 6 mois, de 6 mois; **all night ~** toute la nuit; **he no ~er comes** il ne vient plus; **I can't stand it any ~er** je ne peux plus le supporter; **~ before** longtemps avant; **before ~** (+ future) avant peu, dans peu de temps; (+ past) peu de temps après; **don't be ~!** fais vite!, dépêche-toi!; **I shan't be ~** je n'en ai pas pour longtemps; **at ~ last** enfin; **so** or **as ~ as** à condition que + sub; **long-distance** adj (race) de fond; (call) interurbain(e); **long-haul** adj (flight) long-courrier; **longing** n désir m, envie f; (nostalgia) nostalgie f ▷ adj plein(e) d'envie or de nostalgie

longitude ['lɔŋgɪtju:d] n longitude f

long: long jump n saut m en longueur; **long-life** adj (batteries etc) longue durée inv; (milk) longue conservation; **long-sighted** adj (BRIT) presbyte; (fig) prévoyant(e); **long-standing** adj de longue date; **long-term** adj à long terme

loo [luː] n (BRIT inf) w.-c. mpl, petit coin

look [lʊk] vi regarder; (seem) sembler, paraître, avoir l'air; (building etc): **to ~ south/on to the sea** donner au sud/sur la mer ▷ n regard m; (appearance) air m, allure f, aspect m; **looks** npl (good looks) physique m, beauté f; **to ~ like** ressembler à; **to have a ~** regarder; **to have a ~ at sth** jeter un coup d'œil à qch; **~ (here)!** (annoyance) écoutez!; **look after** vt fus s'occuper de; (luggage etc: watch over) garder, surveiller; **look around** vi regarder autour de soi; **look at** vt fus examiner; (problem etc) examiner; **look back** vi: **to ~ back at sth/sb** se retourner pour regarder qch/qn; **to ~ back on** (event, period) évoquer, repenser à; **look down on** vt fus (fig) regarder de haut, dédaigner; **look for** vt fus chercher; **we're ~ing for a hotel/restaurant** nous cherchons un hôtel/restaurant; **look forward to** vt fus attendre avec impatience; **~ing forward to hearing from you** (in letter) dans l'attente de vous lire; **look into** vt fus (matter, possibility) examiner, étudier; **look out** vi (beware): **to ~ out (for)** prendre garde (à), faire attention (à); **~ out!** attention!; **look out for** vt fus (seek) être à la recherche de; (try to spot) guetter; **look round** vt fus (house, shop) faire le tour de ▷ vi (turn) regarder derrière soi, se retourner; **look through** vt fus (papers, book) examiner (: briefly) parcourir; **look up** vi lever les yeux; (improve) s'améliorer ▷ vt (word) chercher; **look up to** vt fus avoir du respect pour; **lookout** n (tower etc) poste m de guet; (person)

guetteur m; **to be on the lookout (for)** guetter

loom [luːm] vi (also: **~ up**) surgir; (event) paraître imminent(e); (threaten) menacer

loony ['luːnɪ] adj, n (inf) timbré(e), cinglé(e) m/f

loop [luːp] n boucle f ▷ vt: **to ~ sth round sth** passer qch autour de qch; **loophole** n (fig) porte f de sortie; échappatoire f

loose [luːs] adj (knot, screw) desserré(e); (clothes) vague, ample, lâche; (hair) dénoué(e), épars(e); (not firmly fixed) pas solide; (morals, discipline) relâché(e); (translation) approximatif(-ive) ▷ n: **to be on the ~** être en liberté; **~ connection** (Elec) mauvais contact; **to be at a ~ end** or (US) **at ~ ends** (fig) ne pas trop savoir quoi faire; **loosely** adv sans serrer; (imprecisely) approximativement; **loosen** vt desserrer, relâcher, défaire

loot [luːt] n butin m ▷ vt piller

lop-sided ['lɔp'saɪdd] adj de travers, asymétrique

lord [lɔːd] n seigneur m; **L~ Smith** lord Smith; **the L~** (Rel) le Seigneur; **my L~** (to noble) Monsieur le comte/le baron; (to judge) Monsieur le juge; (to bishop) Monseigneur; **good L~!** mon Dieu!; **Lords** npl (BRIT Pol): **the (House of) Lords** la Chambre des Lords

lorry ['lɔrɪ] n (BRIT) camion m; **lorry driver** n (BRIT) camionneur m, routier m

lose (pt, pp **lost**) [luːz, lɔst] vt perdre ▷ vi perdre; **I've lost my wallet/passport** j'ai perdu mon portefeuille/passeport; **to ~ (time)** (clock) retarder; **lose out** vi être perdant(e); **loser** n perdant(e)

loss [lɔs] n perte f; **to make a ~** enregistrer une perte; **to be at a ~** être perplexe or embarrassé(e)

lost [lɔst] pt, pp of **lose** ▷ adj perdu(e); **to get ~** vi se perdre;

I'm ~ je me suis perdu; **~ and found property** n (US) objets trouvés; **~ and found** n (US) (bureau m des) objets trouvés; **lost property** n (BRIT) objets trouvés; **lost property office** or **department** (bureau m des) objets trouvés

lot [lɔt] n (at auctions, set) lot m; (destiny) sort m, destinée f; **the ~** (everything) le tout; (everyone) tous mpl, toutes fpl; **a ~** beaucoup; **a ~ of** beaucoup de; **~s of** des tas de; **to draw ~s (for sth)** tirer (qch) au sort

lotion ['ləʊʃən] n lotion f

lottery ['lɔtərɪ] n loterie f

loud [laʊd] adj bruyant(e), sonore; (voice) fort(e); (condemnation etc) vigoureux(-euse); (gaudy) voyant(e), tapageur(-euse) ⊳ adv (speak etc) fort; **out ~** tout haut; **loudly** adv fort, bruyamment; **loudspeaker** n haut-parleur m

lounge [laʊndʒ] n salon m; (of airport) salle f; (BRIT: also: **~ bar**) (salle de) café m or bar m ⊳ vi (also: **~ about, ~ around**) se prélasser, paresser

louse (pl **lice**) [laʊs, laɪs] n pou m

lousy ['laʊzɪ] (inf) adj (bad quality) infect(e), moche; **I feel ~** je suis mal fichu(e)

love [lʌv] n amour m ⊳ vt aimer; (caringly, kindly) aimer beaucoup; **I ~ chocolate** j'adore le chocolat; **to ~ to do** aimer beaucoup or adorer faire; **"15 ~"** (Tennis) "15 à rien or zéro"; **to be/fall in ~ with** être/ tomber amoureux(-euse) de; **to make ~** faire l'amour; **~ from Anne, ~, Anne** affectueusement, Anne; **I ~ you** je t'aime; **love affair** n liaison (amoureuse); **love life** n vie sentimentale

lovely ['lʌvlɪ] adj (pretty) ravissant(e); (friend, wife) charmant(e); (holiday, surprise) très agréable, merveilleux(-euse)

lover ['lʌvəʳ] n amant m; (person in love) amoureux(-euse); (amateur): **a ~**

of un(e) ami(e) de, un(e) amoureux(-euse) de

loving ['lʌvɪŋ] adj affectueux(-euse), tendre, aimant(e)

low [ləʊ] adj bas (basse); (quality) mauvais(e), inférieur(e) ⊳ adv bas ⊳ n (Meteorology) dépression f; **to feel ~** se sentir déprimé(e); **he's very ~** (ill) il est bien bas or très affaibli; **to turn (down) ~** vt baisser; **to be ~ on** (supplies etc) être à court de; **to reach a new** or **an all-time ~** tomber au niveau le plus bas; **low-alcohol** adj à faible teneur en alcool, peu alcoolisé(e); **low-calorie** adj hypocalorique

lower ['ləʊəʳ] adj inférieur(e) ⊳ vt baisser; (resistance) diminuer; **to ~ o.s. to** s'abaisser à

low-fat ['ləʊ'fæt] adj maigre

loyal ['lɔɪəl] adj loyal(e), fidèle; **loyalty** n loyauté f, fidélité f; **loyalty card** n carte f de fidélité

L-plates ['ɛlpleɪts] npl (BRIT) plaques fpl (obligatoires) d'apprenti conducteur

Lt abbr (= lieutenant) Lt.

Ltd abbr (Comm: = limited) ≈ SA

luck [lʌk] n chance f; **bad ~** malchance f, malheur m; **good ~!** bonne chance!; **bad** or **tough ~!** pas de chance!; **luckily** adv heureusement, par bonheur; **lucky** adj (person) qui a de la chance; (coincidence) heureux(-euse); (number etc) qui porte bonheur

lucrative ['lu:krətɪv] adj lucratif(-ive), rentable, qui rapporte

ludicrous ['lu:dɪkrəs] adj ridicule, absurde

luggage ['lʌgɪdʒ] n bagages mpl; **our ~ hasn't arrived** nos bagages ne sont pas arrivés; **could you send someone to collect our ~?** pourriez-vous envoyer quelqu'un chercher nos bagages?; **luggage rack** n (in train) porte-bagages m inv; (on car) galerie f

lukewarm ['lu:kwɔ:m] adj tiède

lull [lʌl] n accalmie f; (in conversation) pause f ▷ vt: **to ~ sb to sleep** bercer qn pour qu'il s'endorme; **to be ~ed into a false sense of security** s'endormir dans une fausse sécurité

lullaby ['lʌləbaɪ] n berceuse f

lumber ['lʌmbə'] n (wood) bois m de charpente; (junk) bric-à-brac m inv ▷ vt (BRIT inf): **to ~ sb with sth/sb** coller or refiler qch/qn à qn

luminous ['lu:mɪnəs] adj lumineux(-euse)

lump [lʌmp] n morceau m; (in sauce) grumeau m; (swelling) grosseur f ▷ vt (also: **~ together**) réunir, mettre en tas; **lump sum** n somme globale or forfaitaire; **lumpy** adj (sauce) qui a des grumeaux; (bed) défoncé(e), peu confortable

lunatic ['lu:nətɪk] n fou (folle), dément(e) ▷ adj fou (folle), dément(e)

lunch [lʌntʃ] n déjeuner m ▷ vi déjeuner; **lunch break, lunch hour** n pause f de midi, heure f du déjeuner; **lunchtime** n: **it's lunchtime** c'est l'heure du déjeuner

lung [lʌŋ] n poumon m

lure [luə'] n (attraction) attrait m, charme m; (in hunting) appât m, leurre m ▷ vt attirer or persuader par la ruse

lurk [lə:k] vi se tapir, se cacher

lush [lʌʃ] adj luxuriant(e)

lust [lʌst] n (sexual) désir (sexuel); (Rel) luxure f; (fig): **~ for** soif f de

Luxembourg ['lʌksəmbə:g] n Luxembourg m

luxurious [lʌg'zjuərɪəs] adj luxueux(-euse)

luxury ['lʌkʃəri] n luxe m ▷ cpd de luxe

Lycra® ['laɪkrə] n Lycra® m

lying ['laɪɪŋ] n mensonge(s) m(pl) ▷ adj (statement, story) mensonger(-ère), faux (fausse); (person) menteur(-euse)

Lyons ['ljɔ̃] n Lyon

lyrics ['lɪrɪks] npl (of song) paroles fpl

m. abbr (= metre) m; (= million) M; (= mile) mi

ma [mɑ:] (inf) n maman f

M.A. n abbr (Scol) = **Master of Arts**

mac [mæk] n (BRIT) imper(méable m) m

macaroni [mækə'rəunɪ] n macaronis mpl

Macedonia [mæsɪ'dəunɪə] n Macédoine f; **Macedonian** [mæsɪ'dəunɪən] adj macédonien(ne) ▷ n Macédonien(ne); (Ling) macédonien m

machine [mə'ʃi:n] n machine f ▷ vt (dress etc) coudre à la machine; (Tech) usiner; **machine gun** n mitrailleuse f; **machinery** n machinerie f, machines fpl; (fig) mécanisme(s) m(pl); **machine washable** adj (garment) lavable en machine

macho ['mætʃəu] adj macho inv

mackerel ['mækrl] n (pl inv) maquereau m

mackintosh ['mækɪntɔʃ] n (BRIT) imperméable m

mad [mæd] *adj* fou (folle); *(foolish)* insensé(e); *(angry)* furieux(-euse); **to be ~ (keen) about** *or* **on sth** *(inf)* être follement passionné de qch, être fou de qch

Madagascar [mædə'gæskər] *n* Madagascar *m*

madam ['mædəm] *n* madame *f*

mad cow disease *n* maladie *f* des vaches folles

made [meɪd] *pt, pp of* **make**; **made-to-measure** *adj* (BRIT) fait(e) sur mesure; **made-up** ['meɪdʌp] *adj* *(story)* inventé(e), fabriqué(e)

madly ['mædlɪ] *adv* follement; **~ in love** éperdument amoureux(-euse)

madman ['mædmən] *(irreg)* *n* fou *m*, aliéné *m*

madness ['mædnɪs] *n* folie *f*

Madrid [mə'drɪd] *n* Madrid

Mafia ['mæfɪə] *n* maf(f)ia *f*

mag [mæg] *n abbr* (BRIT *inf*: = *magazine*) magazine *m*

magazine [mægə'ziːn] *n* (Press) magazine *m*, revue *f*; *(Radio, TV)* magazine

maggot ['mægət] *n* ver *m*, asticot *m*

magic ['mædʒɪk] *n* magie *f* ▷ *adj* magique; **magical** *adj* magique; *(experience, evening)* merveilleux(-euse); **magician** [mə'dʒɪʃən] *n* magicien(ne)

magistrate ['mædʒɪstreɪt] *n* magistrat *m*; juge *m*

magnet ['mægnɪt] *n* aimant *m*; **magnetic** [mæg'nɛtɪk] *adj* magnétique

magnificent [mæg'nɪfɪsnt] *adj* superbe, magnifique; *(splendid: robe, building)* somptueux(-euse), magnifique

magnify ['mægnɪfaɪ] *vt* grossir; *(sound)* amplifier; **magnifying glass** *n* loupe *f*

magpie ['mægpaɪ] *n* pie *f*

mahogany [mə'hɔgənɪ] *n* acajou *m*

maid [meɪd] *n* bonne *f*; *(in hotel)* femme *f* de chambre; **old ~** *(pej)* vieille fille

maiden name *n* nom *m* de jeune fille

mail [meɪl] *n* poste *f*; *(letters)* courrier *m* ▷ *vt* envoyer (par la poste); **by ~** par la poste; **mailbox** *n* (US, *also Comput)* boîte *f* aux lettres; **mailing list** *n* liste *f* d'adresses; **mailman** *(irreg)* *n* (US) facteur *m*; **mail-order** *n* vente *f* or achat *m* par correspondance

main [meɪn] *adj* principal(e) ▷ *n* *(pipe)* conduite principale, canalisation *f*; **the ~s** *(Elec)* le secteur; **the ~ thing** l'essentiel *m*; **in the ~** dans l'ensemble; **main course** *n* (Culin) plat *m* de résistance; **mainland** *n* continent *m*; **mainly** *adv* principalement, surtout; **main road** *n* grand axe, route nationale; **mainstream** *n* *(fig)* courant principal; **main street** *n* rue *f* principale

maintain [meɪn'teɪn] *vt* entretenir; *(continue)* maintenir, préserver; *(affirm)* soutenir; **maintenance** ['meɪntənəns] *n* entretien *m*; *(Law: alimony)* pension *f* alimentaire

maisonette [meɪzə'nɛt] *n* (BRIT) appartement *m* en duplex

maize [meɪz] *n* (BRIT) maïs *m*

majesty ['mædʒɪstɪ] *n* majesté *f*; *(title)*: **Your M~** Votre Majesté

major ['meɪdʒər] *n* (Mil) commandant *m* ▷ *adj* *(important)* important(e); *(most important)* principal(e); *(Mus)* majeur(e) ▷ *vi* (US Scol): **to ~ (in)** se spécialiser (en)

Majorca [mə'jɔːkə] *n* Majorque *f*

majority [mə'dʒɔrɪtɪ] *n* majorité *f*

make [meɪk] *vt* (*pt, pp* **made**) faire; *(manufacture)* faire, fabriquer; *(earn)* gagner; *(decision)* prendre; *(friend)* se faire; *(speech)* faire, prononcer; *(cause to be)*: **to ~ sb sad** *etc* rendre qn triste *etc*; *(force)*: **to ~ sb do sth** obliger qn à faire qch, faire faire qch à qn; *(equal)*: **2 and 2 ~ 4** 2 et 2 font 4 ▷ *n* *(manufacture)* fabrication *f*; *(brand)* marque *f*; **to ~ the bed** faire le lit; **to ~ a fool of sb** *(ridicule)* ridiculiser qn; *(trick)* avoir or duper qn; **to ~ a profit** faire un or des bénéfice(s); **to ~ a loss** essuyer une perte; **to ~ it** (*in time etc*) y arriver; (*succeed*) réussir; **what time do you ~ it?** quelle heure avez-vous?; **I ~ it £249** d'après mes calculs ça fait 249 livres; **to be made of** être en; **to ~ do with** se contenter de; se débrouiller avec; **make off** *vi* filer; **make out** *vt* (*write out: cheque*) faire; (*decipher*) déchiffrer; (*understand*) comprendre; (*see*) distinguer; (*claim, imply*) prétendre, vouloir faire croire; **make up** *vt* (*invent*) imaginer, inventer; (*constitute*) constituer; (*parcel, bed*) faire ▷ *vi* se réconcilier; (*with cosmetics*) se maquiller, se farder; **to be made up of** se composer de; **make up for** *vt fus* compenser; (*lost time*) rattraper; **makeover** ['meɪkəʊvə'] *n* (*by beautician*) soins *mpl* de maquillage; (*change of image*) changement *m* d'image; **maker** *n* fabricant *m*; (*of film, programme*) réalisateur(-trice); **makeshift** *adj* provisoire, improvisé(e); **make-up** *n* maquillage *m*

making ['meɪkɪŋ] *n* (*fig*): **in the ~** en formation or gestation; **to have the ~s of** (*actor, athlete*) avoir l'étoffe de

malaria [mə'lɛərɪə] *n* malaria *f*, paludisme *m*

Malaysia [mə'leɪzɪə] *n* Malaisie *f*

male [meɪl] *n* (*Biol, Elec*) mâle *m* ▷ *adj* (*sex, attitude*) masculin(e); (*animal*) mâle; (*child etc*) du sexe masculin

malicious [mə'lɪʃəs] *adj* méchant(e), malveillant(e)

> Be careful not to translate *malicious* by the French word *malicieux*.

malignant [mə'lɪgnənt] *adj* (*Med*) malin(-igne)

mall [mɔːl] *n* (*also:* **shopping ~**) centre commercial

mallet ['mælɪt] *n* maillet *m*

malnutrition [mælnjuː'trɪʃən] *n* malnutrition *f*

malpractice [mæl'præktɪs] *n* faute professionnelle; négligence *f*

malt [mɔːlt] *n* malt *m* ▷ *cpd* (*whisky*) pur malt

Malta ['mɔːltə] *n* Malte *f*; **Maltese** [mɔːl'tiːz] *adj* maltais(e) ▷ *n* (*pl inv*) Maltais(e)

mammal ['mæml] *n* mammifère *m*

mammoth ['mæməθ] *n* mammouth *m* ▷ *adj* géant(e), monstre

man (*pl* **men**) [mæn, mɛn] *n* homme *m*; (*Sport*) joueur *m*; (*Chess*) pièce *f* ▷ *vt* (*Naut: ship*) garnir d'hommes; (*machine*) assurer le fonctionnement de; (*Mil: gun*) servir; (: *post*) être de service à; **an old ~** un vieillard; **~ and wife** mari et femme

manage ['mænɪdʒ] *vi* se débrouiller; (*succeed*) y arriver, réussir ▷ *vt* (*business*) gérer; (*team, operation*) diriger; (*control: ship*) manier, manœuvrer; (: *person*) savoir s'y prendre avec; **to ~ to do** se débrouiller pour faire; (*succeed*) réussir à faire; **manageable** *adj* maniable; (*task etc*) faisable; (*number*) raisonnable; **management** *n* (*running*) administration *f*, direction *f*; (*people in charge: of business, firm*) dirigeants *mpl*, cadres *mpl*; (: *of hotel, shop, theatre*) direction; **manager** *n* (*of business*) directeur *m*; (*of institution etc*) administrateur *m*; (*of department, unit*) responsable *m/f*, chef *m*; (*of hotel etc*) gérant *m*; (*Sport*) manager *m*; (*of artist*) impresario *m*; **manageress** *n* directrice *f*; (*of hotel etc*) gérante *f*; **managerial** [mænɪ'dʒɪərɪəl] *adj* directorial(e); (*skills*) de cadre, de gestion; **managing director** *n* directeur général

mandarin ['mændərɪn] *n* (*also:* **~ orange**) mandarine *f*

mandate ['mændeɪt] *n* mandat *m*

mandatory ['mændətərɪ] *adj* obligatoire

mane [meɪn] *n* crinière *f*

m

maneuver [mə'nu:vər] (us) n
= **manoeuvre**

mangetout ['mɔnʒ'tu:] n mangetout m inv

mango ['mæŋgəu] (pl **mangoes**) n
mangue f

man: manhole n trou m d'homme;
manhood n (age) âge m d'homme;
(manliness) virilité f

mania ['meɪnɪə] n manie f; **maniac**
['meɪnɪæk] n maniaque m/f; (fig)
fou (folle)

manic ['mænɪk] adj maniaque

manicure ['mænɪkjuər] n manucure f

manifest ['mænɪfɛst] vt manifester
▷ adj manifeste, évident(e)

manifesto [mænɪ'fɛstəu] n (Pol)
manifeste m

manipulate [mə'nɪpjuleɪt] vt
manipuler; (system, situation)
exploiter

man: mankind [mæn'kaɪnd] n
humanité f, genre humain; **manly** adj
viril(e); **man-made** adj artificiel(le);
(fibre) synthétique

manner ['mænər] n manière f,
façon f; (behaviour) attitude f,
comportement m; **manners** npl;
(good) ~s (bonnes) manières; **bad ~s**
mauvaises manières; **all ~ of** toutes
sortes de

manoeuvre, (us) **maneuver**
[mə'nu:vər] vt (move) manœuvrer;
(manipulate: person) manipuler;
(: situation) exploiter ▷ n manœuvre f

manpower ['mænpauər] n main-
d'œuvre f

mansion ['mænʃən] n château m,
manoir m

manslaughter ['mænslɔ:tər] n
homicide m involontaire

mantelpiece ['mæntlpi:s] n
cheminée f

manual ['mænjuəl] adj manuel(le)
▷ n manuel m

manufacture [mænju'fæktʃər]
vt fabriquer ▷ n fabrication f;
manufacturer n fabricant m

manure [mə'njuər] n fumier m;
(artificial) engrais m

manuscript ['mænjuskrɪpt] n
manuscrit m

many ['mɛnɪ] adj beaucoup de, de
nombreux(-euses) ▷ pron beaucoup,
un grand nombre; **a great ~** un grand
nombre (de); **~ a ...** bien des ..., plus
d'un(e) ...

map [mæp] n carte f; (of town) plan
m; **can you show it to me on the
~?** pouvez-vous me l'indiquer sur la
carte?; **map out** vt tracer; (fig: task)
planifier

maple ['meɪpl] n érable m

mar [mɑ:r] vt gâcher, gâter

marathon ['mærəθən] n
marathon m

marble ['mɑ:bl] n marbre m; (toy)
bille f

March [mɑ:tʃ] n mars m

march [mɑ:tʃ] vi marcher au pas;
(demonstrators) défiler ▷ n marche f;
(demonstration) manifestation f

mare [mɛər] n jument f

margarine [mɑ:dʒə'ri:n] n
margarine f

margin ['mɑ:dʒɪn] n marge f;
marginal adj marginal(e); **marginal
seat** (Pol) siège disputé; **marginally**
adv très légèrement, sensiblement

marigold ['mærɪgəuld] n souci m

marijuana [mærɪ'wɑ:nə] n
marijuana f

marina [mə'ri:nə] n marina f

marinade n [mærɪ'neɪd] marinade f

marinate ['mærɪneɪt] vt (faire)
mariner

marine [mə'ri:n] adj marin(e) ▷ n
fusilier marin; (us) marine m

marital ['mærɪtl] adj matrimonial(e);
marital status n situation f de
famille

maritime ['mærɪtaɪm] adj maritime

marjoram ['mɑ:dʒərəm] n
marjolaine f

mark [mɑ:k] n marque f; (of skid
etc) trace f; (brit Scol) note f; (oven

temperature): **(gas) ~ 4** thermostat m 4 ▷ vt (also Sport: player) marquer; (stain) tacher; (BRIT Scol) corriger, noter; **to ~ time** marquer le pas; **marked** adj (obvious) marqué(e), net(te); **marker** n (sign) jalon m; (bookmark) signet m

market ['mɑːkɪt] n marché m ▷ vt (Comm) commercialiser; **marketing** n marketing m; **marketplace** n place f du marché; (Comm) marché m; **market research** n étude f de marché

marmalade ['mɑːməleɪd] n confiture f d'oranges

maroon [mə'ruːn] vt: **to be ~ed** être abandonné(e); (fig) être bloqué(e) ▷ adj (colour) bordeaux inv

marquee [mɑː'kiː] n chapiteau m

marriage ['mærɪdʒ] n mariage m; **marriage certificate** n extrait m d'acte de mariage

married ['mærɪd] adj marié(e); (life, love) conjugal(e)

marrow ['mærəu] n (of bone) moelle f; (vegetable) courge f

marry ['mærɪ] vt épouser, se marier avec; (subj: father, priest etc) marier ▷ vi (also: **get married**) se marier

Mars [mɑːz] n (planet) Mars f

Marseilles [mɑː'seɪ] n Marseille

marsh [mɑːʃ] n marais m, marécage m

marshal ['mɑːʃl] n maréchal m; (us: fire, police) ≈ capitaine m; (for demonstration, meeting) membre m du service d'ordre ▷ vt rassembler

martyr ['mɑːtər] n martyr(e)

marvel ['mɑːvl] n merveille f ▷ vi: **to ~ (at)** s'émerveiller (de); **marvellous**, (us) **marvelous** adj merveilleux(-euse)

Marxism ['mɑːksɪzəm] n marxisme m

Marxist ['mɑːksɪst] adj, n marxiste (m/f)

marzipan ['mɑːzɪpæn] n pâte f d'amandes

mascara [mæs'kɑːrə] n mascara m

mascot ['mæskət] n mascotte f

masculine ['mæskjulɪn] adj masculin(e) ▷ n masculin m

mash [mæʃ] vt (Culin) faire une purée de; **mashed potato(es)** n(pl) purée f de pommes de terre

mask [mɑːsk] n masque m ▷ vt masquer

mason ['meɪsn] n (also: **stone~**) maçon m; (also: **free~**) franc-maçon m; **masonry** n maçonnerie f

mass [mæs] n multitude f, masse f; (Physics) masse; (Rel) messe f ▷ cpd (communication) de masse; (unemployment) massif(-ive) ▷ vi se masser; **masses** npl: **the ~es** les masses; **~es of** (inf) des tas de

massacre ['mæsəkər] n massacre m

massage ['mæsɑːʒ] n massage m ▷ vt masser

massive ['mæsɪv] adj énorme, massif(-ive)

mass media npl mass-media mpl

mass-produce ['mæsprə'djuːs] vt fabriquer en série

mast [mɑːst] n mât m; (Radio, TV) pylône m

master ['mɑːstər] n maître m; (in secondary school) professeur m; (in primary school) instituteur m; (title for boys): **M~ X** Monsieur X ▷ vt maîtriser; (learn) apprendre à fond; **M~ of Arts/ Science (MA/MSc)** n ≈ titulaire m/f d'une maîtrise (en lettres/science); **M~ of Arts/Science degree (MA/ MSc)** n ≈ maîtrise f; **mastermind** n esprit supérieur ▷ vt diriger, être le cerveau de; **masterpiece** n chef-d'œuvre m

masturbate ['mæstəbeɪt] vi se masturber

mat [mæt] n petit tapis; (also: **door~**) paillasson m; (also: **table~**) set m de table ▷ adj = **matt**

match [mætʃ] n allumette f; (game) match m, partie f; (fig) égal(e) ▷ vt (also: **~ up**) assortir; (go well with)

m

aller bien avec, s'assortir à; (*equal*) égaler, valoir ▷ vi être assorti(e); **to be a good ~** être assorti(e); **matchbox** n boîte f d'allumettes; **matching** adj assorti(e)

mate [meɪt] n (inf) copain (copine); (animal) partenaire m/f, mâle (femelle); (in merchant navy) second m ▷ vi s'accoupler

material [mə'tɪərɪəl] n (substance) matière f, matériau m; (cloth) tissu m, étoffe f; (information, data) données fpl ▷ adj matériel(le); (relevant: evidence) pertinent(e); **materials** npl (equipment) matériaux mpl

materialize [mə'tɪərɪəlaɪz] vi se matérialiser, se réaliser

maternal [mə'tə:nl] adj maternel(le)

maternity [mə'tə:nɪtɪ] n maternité f; **maternity hospital** n maternité f; **maternity leave** n congé m de maternité

math [mæθ] n (US: = mathematics) maths fpl

mathematical [mæθə'mætɪkl] adj mathématique

mathematician [mæθəmə'tɪʃən] n mathématicien(ne)

mathematics [mæθə'mætɪks] n mathématiques fpl

maths [mæθs] n abbr (BRIT: = mathematics) maths fpl

matinée ['mætɪneɪ] n matinée f

matron ['meɪtrən] n (in hospital) infirmière-chef f; (in school) infirmière f

matt [mæt] adj mat(e)

matter ['mætər] n question f; (Physics) matière f, substance f; (Med: pus) pus m ▷ vi importer; **matters** npl (affairs, situation) la situation; **it doesn't ~** cela n'a pas d'importance; (I don't mind) cela ne fait rien; **what's the ~?** qu'est-ce qu'il y a?, qu'est-ce qui ne va pas?; **no ~ what** quoi qu'il arrive; **as a ~ of course** tout naturellement; **as a ~ of fact** en fait; **reading ~** (BRIT) de quoi lire, de la lecture

mattress ['mætrɪs] n matelas m

mature [mə'tjuər] adj mûr(e); (cheese) fait(e); (wine) arrive(e) à maturité ▷ vi mûrir; (cheese, wine) se faire; **mature student** n étudiant(e) plus âgé(e) que la moyenne; **maturity** n maturité f

maul [mɔ:l] vt lacérer

mauve [məuv] adj mauve

max abbr = **maximum**

maximize ['mæksɪmaɪz] vt (profits etc, chances) maximiser

maximum (pl **maxima**) ['mæksɪməm, -mə] adj maximum ▷ n maximum m

May [meɪ] n mai m

may [meɪ] (conditional **might**) vi (indicating possibility): **he ~ come** il se peut qu'il vienne; (be allowed to): **~ I smoke?** puis-je fumer?; (wishes): **~ God bless you!** (que) Dieu vous bénisse!; **you ~ as well go** vous feriez aussi bien d'y aller

maybe ['meɪbi:] adv peut-être; **~ he'll ...** peut-être qu'il ...

May Day n le Premier mai

mayhem ['meɪhem] n grabuge m

mayonnaise [meɪə'neɪz] n mayonnaise f

mayor [mɛər] n maire m; **mayoress** n (female mayor) maire m; (wife of mayor) épouse f du maire

maze [meɪz] n labyrinthe m, dédale m

MD n abbr (Comm) = **managing director**

me [mi:] pron me, m' + vowel or h mute; (stressed, after prep) moi; **it's me** c'est moi; **he heard me** il m'a entendu; **give me a book** donnez-moi un livre; **it's for me** c'est pour moi

meadow ['mɛdəu] n prairie f, pré m

meagre, (US) **meager** ['mi:gər] adj maigre

meal [mi:l] n repas m; (flour) farine f; **mealtime** n heure f du repas

mean [mi:n] adj (with money) avare, radin(e); (unkind) mesquin(e), méchant(e); (shabby) misérable;

(*average*) moyen(ne) ▷ vt (pt, pp
meant) (*signify*) signifier, vouloir dire;
(*refer to*) faire allusion à, parler de;
(*intend*): **to ~ to do** avoir l'intention de
faire ▷ n moyenne f; **means** npl (*way,
money*) moyens mpl; **to be ~t for** être
destiné(e) à; **do you ~ it?** vous êtes
sérieux?; **what do you ~?** que voulez-
vous dire?; **by ~s of** (*instrument*) au
moyen de; **by all ~s** je vous en prie

meaning ['miːnɪŋ] n signification
f, sens m; **meaningful** adj
significatif(-ive); (*relationship*)
valable; **meaningless** adj dénué(e)
de sens

meant [mɛnt] pt, pp of **mean**

meantime ['miːntaɪm] adv (*also*: **in
the ~**) pendant ce temps

meanwhile ['miːnwaɪl] adv
= **meantime**

measles ['miːzlz] n rougeole f

measure ['mɛʒəʳ] vt, vi mesurer ▷ n
mesure f; (*ruler*) règle (graduée)

measurements ['mɛʒəməntz] npl
mesures fpl; **chest/hip ~** tour m de
poitrine/hanches

meat [miːt] n viande f; **I don't eat ~**
je ne mange pas de viande; **cold ~s**
(BRIT) viandes froides; **meatball** n
boulette f de viande

Mecca ['mɛkə] n la Mecque

mechanic [mɪ'kænɪk] n mécanicien
m; **can you send a ~?** pouvez-vous
nous envoyer un mécanicien?;
mechanical adj mécanique

mechanism ['mɛkənɪzəm] n
mécanisme m

medal ['mɛdl] n médaille f;
medallist, (US) **medalist** n (Sport)
médaillé(e)

meddle ['mɛdl] vi: **to ~ in** se mêler
de, s'occuper de; **to ~ with** toucher à

media ['miːdɪə] npl media mpl ▷ npl
of **medium**

mediaeval [mɛdɪ'iːvl] adj
= **medieval**

mediate ['miːdɪeɪt] vi servir
d'intermédiaire

medical ['mɛdɪkl] adj médical(e)
▷ n (*also*: **~ examination**) visite
médicale; (*private*) examen médical;
medical certificate n certificat
médical

medicated ['mɛdɪkeɪtɪd] adj
traitant(e), médicamenteux(-euse)

medication [mɛdɪ'keɪʃən] n (*drugs
etc*) médication f

medicine ['mɛdsɪn] n médecine f;
(*drug*) médicament m

medieval [mɛdɪ'iːvl] adj médiéval(e)

mediocre [miːdɪ'əukəʳ] adj médiocre

meditate ['mɛdɪteɪt] vi: **to ~ (on)**
méditer (sur)

meditation [mɛdɪ'teɪʃən] n
méditation f

Mediterranean [mɛdɪtə'reɪnɪən]
adj méditerranéen(ne); **the ~ (Sea)** la
(mer) Méditerranée

medium ['miːdɪəm] adj moyen(ne)
▷ n (pl **media**) (*means*) moyen m;
(*person*) médium m; **the happy ~**
le juste milieu; **medium-sized** adj
de taille moyenne; **medium wave**
n (Radio) ondes moyennes, petites
ondes

meek [miːk] adj doux (douce),
humble

meet (pt, pp **met**) [miːt, mɛt]
vt rencontrer; (*by arrangement*)
retrouver, rejoindre; (*for the first time*)
faire la connaissance de; (*go and
fetch*): **I'll ~ you at the station** j'irai te
chercher à la gare; (*opponent, danger,
problem*) faire face à; (*requirements*)
satisfaire à, répondre à ▷ vi (*friends*) se
rencontrer; (*again*) se retrouver; (*in session*)
se réunir; (*join: lines, roads*) se joindre;
nice ~ing you ravi d'avoir fait votre
connaissance; **meet up** vi: **to ~ up
with sb** rencontrer qn; **meet with** vt
fus (*difficulty*) rencontrer; **to ~ with
success** être couronné(e) de succès;
meeting n (*of group of people*) réunion
f; (*between individuals*) rendez-vous m;
she's at or **in a meeting** (Comm) elle
est en réunion; **meeting place** n lieu

m

m de (la) réunion; (*for appointment*) lieu de rendez-vous

megabyte ['mɛgəbaɪt] *n* (*Comput*) méga-octet *m*

megaphone ['mɛgəfəʊn] *n* porte-voix *m inv*

megapixel ['mɛgəpɪksl] *n* mégapixel *m*

melancholy ['mɛlənkəlɪ] *n* mélancolie *f* ▷ *adj* mélancolique

melody ['mɛlədɪ] *n* mélodie *f*

melon ['mɛlən] *n* melon *m*

melt [mɛlt] *vi* fondre ▷ *vt* faire fondre

member ['mɛmbər] *n* membre *m*; **M~ of the European Parliament** eurodéputé *m*; **M~ of Parliament** (*BRIT*) député *m*; **membership** *n* (*becoming a member*) adhésion *f*; admission *f*; (*members*) membres *mpl*, adhérents *mpl*; **membership card** *n* carte *f* de membre

memento [mə'mɛntəʊ] *n* souvenir *m*

memo ['mɛməʊ] *n* note *f* (de service)

memorable ['mɛmərəbl] *adj* mémorable

memorandum (*pl* **memoranda**) [mɛmə'rændəm, -də] *n* note *f* (de service)

memorial [mɪ'mɔːrɪəl] *n* mémorial *m* ▷ *adj* commémoratif(-ive)

memorize ['mɛməraɪz] *vt* apprendre *or* retenir par cœur

memory ['mɛmərɪ] *n* (*also Comput*) mémoire *f*; (*recollection*) souvenir *m*; **in ~ of** à la mémoire de; **memory card** *n* (*for digital camera*) carte *f* mémoire; **memory stick** *n* (*Comput: flash pen*) clé *f* USB; (: *card*) carte *f* mémoire

men [mɛn] *npl of* **man**

menace ['mɛnɪs] *n* menace *f*; (*inf: nuisance*) peste *f*, plaie *f* ▷ *vt* menacer

mend [mɛnd] *vt* réparer; (*darn*) raccommoder, repriser ▷ *n*: **on the ~** en voie de guérison; **to ~ one's ways** s'amender

meningitis [mɛnɪn'dʒaɪtɪs] *n* méningite *f*

menopause ['mɛnəʊpɔːz] *n* ménopause *f*

men's room (*US*) *n*: **the ~** les toilettes *fpl* pour hommes

menstruation [mɛnstru'eɪʃən] *n* menstruation *f*

menswear ['mɛnzwɛər] *n* vêtements *mpl* d'hommes

mental ['mɛntl] *adj* mental(e); **mental hospital** *n* hôpital *m* psychiatrique; **mentality** [mɛn'tælɪtɪ] *n* mentalité *f*; **mentally** *adv*: **to be mentally handicapped** être handicapé(e) mental(e); **the mentally ill** les malades mentaux

menthol ['mɛnθɔl] *n* menthol *m*

mention ['mɛnʃən] *n* mention *f* ▷ *vt* mentionner, faire mention de; **don't ~ it!** je vous en prie, il n'y a pas de quoi!

menu ['mɛnjuː] *n* (*set menu, Comput*) menu *m*; (*list of dishes*) carte *f*

MEP *n abbr* = **Member of the European Parliament**

mercenary ['məːsɪnərɪ] *adj* (*person*) intéressé(e), mercenaire ▷ *n* mercenaire *m*

merchandise ['məːtʃəndaɪz] *n* marchandises *fpl*

merchant ['məːtʃənt] *n* négociant *m*, marchand *m*; **merchant bank** *n* (*BRIT*) banque *f* d'affaires; **merchant navy**, (*US*) **merchant marine** *n* marine marchande

merciless ['məːsɪlɪs] *adj* impitoyable, sans pitié

mercury ['məːkjurɪ] *n* mercure *m*

mercy ['məːsɪ] *n* pitié *f*, merci *f*; (*Rel*) miséricorde *f*; **at the ~ of** à la merci de

mere [mɪər] *adj* simple; (*chance*) pur(e); **a ~ two hours** seulement deux heures; **merely** *adv* simplement, purement

merge [məːdʒ] *vt* unir; (*Comput*) fusionner, interclasser ▷ *vi* (*colours, shapes, sounds*) se mêler; (*roads*) se joindre; (Comm) fusionner; **merger** n (Comm) fusion f

meringue [məˈræŋ] n meringue f

merit [ˈmɛrɪt] n mérite m, valeur f ▷ vt mériter

mermaid [ˈməːmeɪd] n sirène f

merry [ˈmɛrɪ] adj gai(e); **M~ Christmas!** joyeux Noël!; **merry-go-round** n manège m

mesh [mɛʃ] n mailles fpl

mess [mɛs] n désordre m, fouillis m, pagaille f; (muddle: of life) gâchis m; (: of economy) pagaille f; (dirt) saleté f; (Mil) mess m, cantine f; **to be (in) a ~** être en désordre; **to be/get o.s. in a ~** (fig) être/se mettre dans le pétrin; **mess about, mess around** (inf) vi perdre son temps; **mess up** vt (inf: dirty) salir; (spoil) gâcher; **mess with** (inf) vt fus (challenge, confront) se frotter à; (interfere with) toucher à

message [ˈmɛsɪdʒ] n message m; **can I leave a ~?** est-ce que je peux laisser un message?; **are there any ~s for me?** est-ce que j'ai des messages?

messenger [ˈmɛsɪndʒəʳ] n messager m

Messrs, Messrs. [ˈmɛsəz] abbr (on letters: = messieurs) MM

messy [ˈmɛsɪ] adj (dirty) sale; (untidy) en désordre

met [mɛt] pt, pp of **meet**

metabolism [mɛˈtæbəlɪzəm] n métabolisme m

metal [ˈmɛtl] n métal m ▷ cpd en métal; **metallic** [mɛˈtælɪk] adj métallique

metaphor [ˈmɛtəfəʳ] n métaphore f

meteor [ˈmiːtɪəʳ] n météore m; **meteorite** [ˈmiːtɪəraɪt] n météorite m/f

meteorology [miːtɪəˈrɔlədʒɪ] n météorologie f

meter [ˈmiːtəʳ] n (instrument) compteur m; (also: **parking ~**) parc(o)mètre m; (US: unit) = **metre** ▷ vt (US Post) affranchir à la machine

method [ˈmɛθəd] n méthode f; **methodical** [mɪˈθɔdɪkl] adj méthodique

methylated spirit [ˈmɛθɪleɪtɪd-] n (BRIT) alcool m à brûler

meticulous [mɛˈtɪkjuləs] adj méticuleux(-euse)

metre, (US) **meter** [ˈmiːtəʳ] n mètre m

metric [ˈmɛtrɪk] adj métrique

metro [ˈmɛtrəu] n métro m

metropolitan [mɛtrəˈpɔlɪtən] adj métropolitain(e); **the M~ Police** (BRIT) la police londonienne

Mexican [ˈmɛksɪkən] adj mexicain(e) ▷ n Mexicain(e)

Mexico [ˈmɛksɪkəu] n Mexique m

mg abbr (= milligram) mg

mice [maɪs] npl of **mouse**

micro... [maɪkrəu] prefix micro...; **microchip** n (Elec) puce f; **microphone** n microphone m; **microscope** n microscope m

mid [mɪd] adj: **~ May** la mi-mai; **~ afternoon** le milieu de l'après-midi; **in ~ air** en plein ciel; **he's in his ~ thirties** il a dans les trente-cinq ans; **midday** n midi m

middle [ˈmɪdl] n milieu m; (waist) ceinture f, taille f ▷ adj du milieu; (average) moyen(ne); **in the ~ of the night** au milieu de la nuit; **middle-aged** adj d'un certain âge, ni vieux ni jeune; **Middle Ages** npl; **the Middle Ages** le moyen âge; **middle class(es)** n(pl): **the middle class(es)** ≈ les classes moyennes; **middle-class** adj bourgeois(e); **Middle East** n: **the Middle East** le Proche-Orient, le Moyen-Orient; **middle name** n second prénom; **middle school** n (US) école pour les enfants de 12 à 14 ans ≈ collège m; (BRIT) école pour les enfants de 8 à 14 ans

midge [mɪdʒ] n moucheron m

midget [ˈmɪdʒɪt] n (offensive) nain(e)

midnight [ˈmɪdnaɪt] n minuit m

midst [mɪdst] n: **in the ~ of** au milieu de

m

midsummer [mɪd'sʌmə^r] *n* milieu *m* de l'été

midway [mɪd'weɪ] *adj, adv*: **~ (between)** à mi-chemin (entre); **~ through ...** au milieu de ..., en plein(e) ...

midweek [mɪd'wi:k] *adv* au milieu de la semaine, en pleine semaine

midwife (*pl* **midwives**) ['mɪdwaɪf, -vz] *n* sage-femme *f*

midwinter [mɪd'wɪntə^r] *n* milieu *m* de l'hiver

might [maɪt] *vb see* **may** ▷ *n* puissance *f*, force *f*; **mighty** *adj* puissant(e)

migraine ['mi:greɪn] *n* migraine *f*

migrant ['maɪgrənt] *n* (*bird, animal*) migrateur *m*; (*person*) migrant(e) ▷ *adj* migrateur(-trice); migrant(e); (*worker*) saisonnier(-ière)

migrate [maɪ'greɪt] *vi* migrer

migration [maɪ'greɪʃən] *n* migration *f*

mike [maɪk] *n abbr* (= *microphone*) micro *m*

mild [maɪld] *adj* doux (douce); (*reproach, infection*) léger(-ère); (*illness*) bénin(-igne); (*interest*) modéré(e); (*taste*) peu relevé(e); **mildly** ['maɪldlɪ] *adv* doucement; légèrement; **to put it mildly** (*inf*) c'est le moins qu'on puisse dire

mile [maɪl] *n* mil(l)e *m* (= 1609 *m*); **mileage** *n* distance *f* en milles, ≈ kilométrage *m*; **mileometer** [maɪ'lɔmɪtə^r] *n* compteur *m* kilométrique; **milestone** *n* borne *f*; (*fig*) jalon *m*

military ['mɪlɪtərɪ] *adj* militaire

militia [mɪ'lɪʃə] *n* milice *f*

milk [mɪlk] *n* lait *m* ▷ *vt* (*cow*) traire; (*fig: person*) dépouiller, plumer; (: *situation*) exploiter à fond; **milk chocolate** *n* chocolat *m* au lait; **milkman** (*irreg*) *n* laitier *m*; **milky** *adj* (*drink*) au lait; (*colour*) laiteux(-euse)

mill [mɪl] *n* moulin *m*; (*factory*) usine *f*, fabrique *f*; (*spinning mill*) filature *f*;

(*flour mill*) minoterie *f* ▷ *vt* moudre, broyer ▷ *vi* (*also*: **~ about**) grouiller

millennium (*pl* **millenniums** or **millennia**) [mɪ'lɛnɪəm, -'lɛnɪə] *n* millénaire *m*

milli... ['mɪlɪ] *prefix* milli...; **milligram(me)** *n* milligramme *m*; **millilitre**, (*us*) **milliliter** *n* millilitre *m*; **millimetre**, (*us*) **millimeter** *n* millimètre *m*

million ['mɪljən] *n* million *m*; **a ~ pounds** un million de livres sterling; **millionaire** [mɪljə'nɛə^r] *n* millionnaire *m*; **millionth** [mɪljə'nθ] *num* millionième

milometer [maɪ'lɔmɪtə^r] *n* = **mileometer**

mime [maɪm] *n* mime *m* ▷ *vt*, *vi* mimer

mimic ['mɪmɪk] *n* imitateur(-trice) ▷ *vt*, *vi* imiter, contrefaire

min. *abbr* (= *minute(s)*) mn.; (= *minimum*) min.

mince [mɪns] *vt* hacher ▷ *n* (BRIT *Culin*) viande hachée, hachis *m*; **mincemeat** *n* hachis de fruits secs utilisés en pâtisserie; (*us*) viande hachée, hachis *m*; **mince pie** *n* sorte de tarte aux fruits secs

mind [maɪnd] *n* esprit *m* ▷ *vt* (*attend to, look after*) s'occuper de; (*be careful*) faire attention à; (*object to*): **I don't ~ the noise** je ne crains pas le bruit, le bruit ne me dérange pas; **it is on my ~** cela me préoccupe; **to change one's ~** changer d'avis; **to my ~** à mon avis, selon moi; **to bear sth in ~** tenir compte de qch; **to have sb/sth in ~** avoir qn/qch en tête; **to make up one's ~** se décider; **do you ~ if ...?** est-ce que cela vous gêne si ...?; **I don't ~** cela ne me dérange pas; (*don't care*) ça m'est égal; **~ you, ...** remarquez, ...; **never ~** peu importe, ça ne fait rien; (*don't worry*) ne vous en faites pas; **"~ the step"** "attention à la marche"; **mindless** *adj* irréfléchi(e); (*violence, crime*) insensé(e); (*boring: job*) idiot(e)

mine¹ [maɪn] *pron* le (la) mien(ne), les miens (miennes); **a friend of ~** un de mes amis, un ami à moi; **this book is ~** ce livre est à moi

mine² [maɪn] *n* mine *f* ▷ *vt* (*coal*) extraire; (*ship, beach*) miner; **minefield** *n* champ *m* de mines; **miner** *n* mineur *m*

mineral ['mɪnərəl] *adj* minéral(e) ▷ *n* minéral *m*; **mineral water** *n* eau minérale

mingle ['mɪŋgl] *vi*: **to ~ with** se mêler à

miniature ['mɪnətʃər] *adj* (en) miniature ▷ *n* miniature *f*

minibar ['mɪnɪbɑːr] *n* minibar *m*

minibus ['mɪnɪbʌs] *n* minibus *m*

minicab ['mɪnɪkæb] *n* (BRIT) taxi *m* indépendant

minimal ['mɪnɪml] *adj* minimal(e)

minimize ['mɪnɪmaɪz] *vt* (*reduce*) réduire au minimum; (*play down*) minimiser

minimum ['mɪnɪməm] *n* (*pl* **minima**) minimum *m* ▷ *adj* minimum

mining ['maɪnɪŋ] *n* exploitation minière

miniskirt ['mɪnɪskəːt] *n* mini-jupe *f*

minister ['mɪnɪstər] *n* (BRIT Pol) ministre *m*; (Rel) pasteur *m*

ministry ['mɪnɪstrɪ] *n* (BRIT Pol) ministère *m*; (Rel): **to go into the ~** devenir pasteur

minor ['maɪnər] *adj* petit(e), de peu d'importance; (Mus, poet, problem) mineur(e) ▷ *n* (Law) mineur(e)

minority [maɪ'nɔrɪtɪ] *n* minorité *f*

mint [mɪnt] *n* (plant) menthe *f*; (sweet) bonbon *m* à la menthe ▷ *vt* (coins) battre; **the (Royal) M~, the (US) M~** ≈ l'hôtel *m* de la Monnaie; **in ~ condition** à l'état de neuf

minus ['maɪnəs] *n* (also: **~ sign**) signe *m* moins ▷ *prep* moins; **12 ~ 6 equals 6** 12 moins 6 égal 6; **~ 24°C** moins 24°C

minute¹ ['mɪnɪt] *n* minute *f*; **minutes** *npl* (of meeting) procès-verbal *m*, compte rendu; **wait a ~!**

(attendez) un instant!; **at the last ~** à la dernière minute

minute² [maɪ'njuːt] *adj* minuscule; (detailed) minutieux(-euse); **in ~ detail** par le menu

miracle ['mɪrəkl] *n* miracle *m*

miraculous [mɪ'rækjuləs] *adj* miraculeux(-euse)

mirage ['mɪrɑːʒ] *n* mirage *m*

mirror ['mɪrər] *n* miroir *m*, glace *f*; (in car) rétroviseur *m*

misbehave [mɪsbɪ'heɪv] *vi* mal se conduire

misc. *abbr* = **miscellaneous**

miscarriage ['mɪskærɪdʒ] *n* (Med) fausse couche; **~ of justice** erreur *f* judiciaire

miscellaneous [mɪsɪ'leɪnɪəs] *adj* (items, expenses) divers(es); (selection) varié(e)

mischief ['mɪstʃɪf] *n* (naughtiness) sottises *fpl*; (playfulness) espièglerie *f*; (harm) mal *m*, dommage *m*; (maliciousness) méchanceté *f*; **mischievous** ['mɪstʃɪvəs] *adj* (playful, naughty) coquin(e), espiègle

misconception ['mɪskən'sɛpʃən] *n* idée fausse

misconduct [mɪs'kɔndʌkt] *n* inconduite *f*; **professional ~** faute professionnelle

miser ['maɪzər] *n* avare *m/f*

miserable ['mɪzərəbl] *adj* (person, expression) malheureux(-euse); (conditions) misérable; (weather) maussade; (offer, donation) minable; (failure) pitoyable

misery ['mɪzərɪ] *n* (unhappiness) tristesse *f*; (pain) souffrances *fpl*; (wretchedness) misère *f*

misfortune [mɪs'fɔːtʃən] *n* malchance *f*, malheur *m*

misgiving [mɪs'gɪvɪŋ] *n* (apprehension) craintes *fpl*; **to have ~s about sth** avoir des doutes quant à qch

misguided [mɪs'gaɪdɪd] *adj* malavisé(e)

m

mishap ['mɪʃæp] n mésaventure f

misinterpret [mɪsɪn'tə:prɪt] vt mal interpréter

misjudge [mɪs'dʒʌdʒ] vt méjuger, se méprendre sur le compte de

mislay [mɪs'leɪ] vt (irreg: like **lay**) égarer

mislead [mɪs'li:d] vt (irreg: like **lead¹**) induire en erreur; **misleading** adj trompeur(-euse)

misplace [mɪs'pleɪs] vt égarer; **to be ~d** (trust etc) être mal placé(e)

misprint ['mɪsprɪnt] n faute f d'impression

misrepresent [mɪsreprɪ'zent] vt présenter sous un faux jour

Miss [mɪs] n Mademoiselle

miss [mɪs] n (fail to get, attend, see) manquer, rater; (regret the absence of): **I ~ him/it** il/cela me manque ▷ vi manquer ▷ n (shot) coup manqué; **we ~ed our train** nous avons raté notre train; **you can't ~ it** vous ne pouvez pas vous tromper; **miss out** vt (BRIT) oublier; **miss out on** vt fus (fun, party) rater, manquer; (chance, bargain) laisser passer

missile ['mɪsaɪl] n (Aviat) missile m; (object thrown) projectile m

missing ['mɪsɪŋ] adj manquant(e); (after escape, disaster: person) disparu(e); **to go ~** disparaître; **~ in action** (Mil) porté(e) disparu(e)

mission ['mɪʃən] n mission f; **on a ~ to sb** en mission auprès de qn; **missionary** n missionnaire m/f

misspell ['mɪs'spel] vt (irreg: like **spell**) mal orthographier

mist [mɪst] n brume f ▷ vi (also: ~ **over**, ~ **up**) devenir brumeux(-euse); (BRIT: windows) s'embuer

mistake [mɪs'teɪk] n erreur f, faute f ▷ vt (irreg: like **take**) (meaning) mal comprendre; (intentions) se méprendre sur; **to ~ for** prendre pour; **by ~** par erreur, par inadvertance; **to make a ~** (in writing) faire une faute; (in calculating

etc) faire une erreur; **there must be some ~** il doit y avoir une erreur, se tromper; **mistaken** pp of **mistake** ▷ adj (idea etc) erroné(e); **to be mistaken** faire erreur, se tromper

mister ['mɪstər] n (inf) Monsieur m; see **Mr**

mistletoe ['mɪsltəu] n gui m

mistook [mɪs'tuk] pt of **mistake**

mistress ['mɪstrɪs] n maîtresse f; (BRIT: in primary school) institutrice f; (: in secondary school) professeur m

mistrust [mɪs'trʌst] vt se méfier de

misty ['mɪsti] adj brumeux(-euse); (glasses, window) embué(e)

misunderstand [mɪsʌndə'stænd] vt, vi (irreg: like **understand**) mal comprendre; **misunderstanding** n méprise f, malentendu m; **there's been a misunderstanding** il y a eu un malentendu

misunderstood [mɪsʌndə'stud] pt, pp of **misunderstand** ▷ adj (person) incompris(e)

misuse n [mɪs'ju:s] mauvais emploi; (of power) abus m ▷ vt [mɪs'ju:z] mal employer; abuser de

mitt(en) ['mɪt(n)] n moufle f; (fingerless) mitaine f

mix [mɪks] vt mélanger; (sauce, drink etc) préparer ▷ vi se mélanger; (socialize): **he doesn't ~ well** il est peu sociable ▷ n mélange m; **to ~ sth with sth** mélanger qch à qch; **cake ~** préparation f pour gâteau; **mix up** vt mélanger; (confuse) confondre; **to be ~ed up in sth** être mêlé(e) à qch or impliqué(e) dans qch; **mixed** adj (feelings, reactions) contradictoire; (school, marriage) mixte; **mixed grill** n (BRIT) assortiment m de grillades; **mixed salad** n salade f de crudités; **mixed-up** adj (person) désorienté(e), embrouillé(e); **mixer** n (for food) batteur m, mixeur m; (drink) boisson gazeuse (servant à couper un alcool); (person): **he is a good mixer** il est très sociable; **mixture** n assortiment

m, mélange *m*; (*Med*) préparation *f*;
mix-up *n*: **there was a mix-up** il y a
eu confusion

ml *abbr* (= millilitre(s)) ml

mm *abbr* (= millimetre) mm

moan [məun] *n* gémissement *m* ▷ *vi*
gémir; (*inf: complain*): **to ~ (about)** se
plaindre (de)

moat [məut] *n* fossé *m*, douves *fpl*

mob [mɔb] *n* foule *f*; (*disorderly*) cohue
f ▷ *vt* assaillir

mobile ['məubaɪl] *adj* mobile ▷ *n*
(*Art*) mobile *m*; (*BRIT inf: phone*)
(téléphone *m*) portable *m*, mobile *m*;
mobile home *n* caravane *f*; **mobile
phone** *n* (téléphone *m*) portable *m*,
mobile *m*

mobility [məu'bɪlɪtɪ] *n* mobilité *f*

mobilize ['məubɪlaɪz] *vt*, *vi* mobiliser

mock [mɔk] *vt* ridiculiser; (*laugh at*)
se moquer de ▷ *adj* faux (fausse);
mocks *npl* (*BRIT Scol*) examens blancs;
mockery *n* moquerie *f*, raillerie *f*

mod cons ['mɔd'kɔnz] *npl abbr*
(*BRIT*) = **modern conveniences**; *see*
convenience

mode [məud] *n* mode *m*; (*of transport*)
moyen *m*

model ['mɔdl] *n* modèle *m*; (*person:
for fashion*) mannequin *m*; (: *for artist*)
modèle ▷ *vt* (*with clay etc*) modeler
▷ *vi* travailler comme mannequin
▷ *adj* (*railway: toy*) modèle réduit *inv*;
(*child, factory*) modèle; **to ~ clothes**
présenter des vêtements; **to ~ o.s.
on** imiter

modem ['məudɛm] *n* modem *m*

moderate ['mɔdərət] *adj* modéré(e);
(*amount, change*) peu important(e)
▷ *vi* ['mɔdəreɪt] se modérer, se calmer
▷ *vt* ['mɔdəreɪt] modérer

moderation [mɔdə'reɪʃən] *n*
modération *f*, mesure *f*; **in ~** à dose
raisonnable, pris(e) *or* pratiqué(e)
modérément

modern ['mɔdən] *adj* moderne;
modernize *vt* moderniser; **modern
languages** *npl* langues vivantes

modest ['mɔdɪst] *adj* modeste;
modesty *n* modestie *f*

modification [mɔdɪfɪ'keɪʃən] *n*
modification *f*

modify ['mɔdɪfaɪ] *vt* modifier

module ['mɔdju:l] *n* module *m*

mohair ['məuhɛər] *n* mohair *m*

Mohammed [mə'hæmɛd] *n*
Mahomet *m*

moist [mɔɪst] *adj* humide, moite;
moisture ['mɔɪstʃər] *n* humidité
f; (*on glass*) buée *f*; **moisturizer**
['mɔɪstʃəraɪzər] *n* crème hydratante

mold *etc* [məuld] (*US*) = **mould**

mole [məul] *n* (*animal, spy*) taupe *f*;
(*spot*) grain *m* de beauté

molecule ['mɔlɪkju:l] *n* molécule *f*

molest [məu'lɛst] *vt* (*assault sexually*)
attenter à la pudeur de

molten ['məultən] *adj* fondu(e);
(*rock*) en fusion

mom [mɔm] *n* (*US*) = **mum**

moment ['məumənt] *n* moment *m*,
instant *m*; **at the ~** en ce moment;
momentarily *adv* momentanément;
(*US: soon*) bientôt; **momentary** *adj*
momentané(e), passager(-ère);
momentous [məu'mɛntəs] *adj*
important(e), capital(e)

momentum [məu'mɛntəm] *n* élan
m, vitesse acquise; (*fig*) dynamique *f*;
to gather ~ prendre de la vitesse; (*fig*)
gagner du terrain

mommy ['mɔmɪ] *n* (*US: mother*)
maman *f*

Monaco ['mɔnəkəu] *n* Monaco *f*

monarch ['mɔnək] *n* monarque *m*;
monarchy *n* monarchie *f*

monastery ['mɔnəstərɪ] *n*
monastère *m*

Monday ['mʌndɪ] *n* lundi *m*

monetary ['mʌnɪtərɪ] *adj* monétaire

money ['mʌnɪ] *n* argent *m*; **to
make ~** (*person*) gagner de l'argent;
(*business*) rapporter; **money belt** *n*
ceinture-portefeuille *f*; **money order**
n mandat *m*

mongrel ['mʌŋgrəl] *n* (*dog*) bâtard *m*

m

monitor ['mɒnɪtə'] n (TV, Comput)
écran m, moniteur m ▷ vt contrôler;
(foreign station) être à l'écoute de;
(progress) suivre de près
monk [mʌŋk] n moine m
monkey ['mʌŋkɪ] n singe m
monologue ['mɒnəlɒg] n monologue m
monopoly [mə'nɒpəlɪ] n monopole m
monosodium glutamate
[mɒnə'səudɪəm 'glu:təmeɪt] n
glutamate m de sodium
monotonous [mə'nɒtənəs] adj
monotone
monsoon [mɒn'su:n] n mousson f
monster ['mɒnstə'] n monstre m
month [mʌnθ] n mois m; **monthly**
adj mensuel(le) ▷ adv mensuellement
Montreal [mɒntrɪ'ɔːl] n Montréal
monument ['mɒnjumənt] n
monument m
mood [mu:d] n humeur f, disposition
f; **to be in a good/bad ~** être de
bonne/mauvaise humeur; **moody**
adj (variable) d'humeur changeante,
lunatique; (sullen) morose, maussade
moon [mu:n] n lune f; **moonlight** n
clair m de lune
moor [muə'] n lande f ▷ vt (ship)
amarrer ▷ vi mouiller
moose [mu:s] n (pl inv) élan m
mop [mɒp] n balai m à laver; (for
dishes) lavette f à vaisselle ▷ vt
éponger, essuyer; **~ of hair** tignasse
f; **mop up** vt éponger
mope [məup] vi avoir le cafard, se
morfondre
moped ['məupɛd] n cyclomoteur m
moral ['mɒrl] adj moral(e) ▷ n morale
f; **morals** npl moralité f
morale [mɒ'rɑːl] n moral m
morality [mə'rælɪtɪ] n moralité f
morbid ['mɔːbɪd] adj morbide

○ **KEYWORD**

more [mɔː'] adj 1 (greater in number
etc) plus (de), davantage (de); **more
people/work (than)** plus de gens/

de travail (que)
2 (additional) encore (de); **do you
want (some) more tea?** voulez-vous
encore du thé?; **is there any more
wine?** reste-t-il du vin?; **I have no** or **I
don't have any more money** je n'ai
plus d'argent; **it'll take a few more
weeks** ça prendra encore quelques
semaines
▷ pron plus, davantage; **more than
10** plus de 10; **it cost more than
we expected** cela a coûté plus que
prévu; **I want more** j'en veux plus or
davantage; **is there any more?** est-
ce qu'il en reste?; **there's no more**
il n'y en a plus; **a little more** un peu
plus; **many/much more** beaucoup
plus, bien davantage
▷ adv plus; **more dangerous/easily
(than)** plus dangereux/facilement
(que); **more and more expensive** de
plus en plus cher; **more or less** plus
ou moins; **more than ever** plus que
jamais; **once more** encore une fois,
une fois de plus

moreover [mɔː'rəuvə'] adv de plus
morgue [mɔːg] n morgue f
morning ['mɔːnɪŋ] n matin m; (as
duration) matinée f ▷ cpd matinal(e);
(paper) du matin; **in the ~** le matin;
7 o'clock in the ~ 7 heures du matin;
morning sickness n nausées
matinales
Moroccan [mə'rɒkən] adj
marocain(e) ▷ n Marocain(e)
Morocco [mə'rɒkəu] n Maroc m
moron ['mɔːrɒn] n (offensive) idiot(e),
minus m/f
morphine ['mɔːfiːn] n morphine f
morris dancing ['mɒrɪs-] n (BRIT)
danses folkloriques anglaises

● **MORRIS DANCING**
●
● Le morris dancing est une
● danse folklorique anglaise
● traditionnellement réservée aux

hommes. Habillés tout en blanc et portant des clochettes, ils exécutent différentes figures avec des mouchoirs et de longs bâtons. Cette danse est très populaire dans les fêtes de village.

Morse [mɔːs] n (also: **~ code**) morse m

mortal ['mɔːtl] adj, n mortel(le)

mortar ['mɔːtəʳ] n mortier m

mortgage ['mɔːɡɪdʒ] n hypothèque f; (loan) prêt m (or crédit m) hypothécaire ▷ vt hypothéquer

mortician [mɔːˈtɪʃən] n (US) entrepreneur m de pompes funèbres

mortified ['mɔːtɪfaɪd] adj mort(e) de honte

mortuary ['mɔːtjuəri] n morgue f

mosaic [məuˈzeɪɪk] n mosaïque f

Moscow ['mɔskəu] n Moscou

Moslem ['mɔzləm] adj, n = **Muslim**

mosque [mɔsk] n mosquée f

mosquito [mɔsˈkiːtəu] (pl **mosquitoes**) n moustique m

moss [mɔs] n mousse f

most [məust] adj (majority of) la plupart de; (greatest amount of) le plus de ▷ pron la plupart ▷ adv le plus; (very) très, extrêmement; **the ~** le plus; **the ~ fish** la plupart des poissons; **the ~ beautiful woman in the world** la plus belle femme du monde; **~ of** (with plural) la plupart de; (with singular) la grande partie de; **~ of them** la plupart d'entre eux; **~ of the time** la plupart du temps; **I saw ~** (a lot but not all) j'en ai vu la plupart; (more than anyone else) c'est moi qui en ai vu le plus; **at the (very) ~** au plus; **to make the ~ of** profiter au maximum de; **mostly** adv (chiefly) surtout, principalement; (usually) généralement

MOT n abbr (BRIT: = Ministry of Transport): **the ~ (test)** visite technique (annuelle) obligatoire des véhicules à moteur

motel [məuˈtɛl] n motel m

moth [mɔθ] n papillon m de nuit; (in clothes) mite f

mother ['mʌðəʳ] n mère f ▷ vt (pamper, protect) dorloter; **motherhood** n maternité f; **mother-in-law** n belle-mère f; **mother-of-pearl** n nacre f; **Mother's Day** n fête f des Mères; **mother-to-be** n future maman; **mother tongue** n langue maternelle

motif [məuˈtiːf] n motif m

motion ['məuʃən] n mouvement m; (gesture) geste m; (at meeting) motion f ▷ vt, vi: **to ~ (to) sb to do** faire signe à qn de faire; **motionless** adj immobile, sans mouvement; **motion picture** n film m

motivate ['məutɪveɪt] vt motiver

motivation [məutɪˈveɪʃən] n motivation f

motive ['məutɪv] n motif m, mobile m

motor ['məutəʳ] n moteur m; (BRIT inf: vehicle) auto f; **motorbike** n moto f; **motorboat** n bateau m à moteur; **motorcar** n (BRIT) automobile f; **motorcycle** n moto f; **motorcyclist** n motocycliste m/f; **motoring** (BRIT) n tourisme m automobile; **motorist** n automobiliste m/f; **motor racing** n (BRIT) course f automobile; **motorway** n (BRIT) autoroute f

motto ['mɔtəu] (pl **mottoes**) n devise f

mould, (US) **mold** [məuld] n moule m; (mildew) moisissure f ▷ vt mouler, modeler; (fig) façonner; **mouldy**, (US) **moldy** adj moisi(e); (smell) de moisi

mound [maund] n monticule m, tertre m

mount [maunt] n (hill) mont m, montagne f; (horse) monture f; (for picture) carton m de montage ▷ vt monter; (horse) monter à; (bike) monter sur; (picture) monter sur carton ▷ vi (inflation, tension) augmenter; **mount up** vi s'élever, monter; (bills, problems, savings) s'accumuler

mountain ['mauntɪn] n
montagne f ▷ cpd de (la) montagne;
mountain bike n VTT m, vélo
m tout terrain; **mountaineer** n
alpiniste m/f; **mountaineering** n
alpinisme m; **mountainous** adj
montagneux(-euse); **mountain
range** n chaîne f de montagnes
mourn [mɔːn] vt pleurer ▷ vi: **to
~ for sb** pleurer qn; **to ~ for sth**
se lamenter sur qch; **mourner** n
parent(e) or ami(e) du défunt;
personne f en deuil or venue rendre
hommage au défunt; **mourning** n
deuil m; **in mourning** en deuil
mouse (pl **mice**) [maus, maɪs] n
(also Comput) souris f; **mouse mat** n
(Comput) tapis m de souris
moussaka [mu'sɑːkə] n moussaka f
mousse [muːs] n mousse f
moustache, (us) **mustache**
[məs'tɑːʃ] n moustache(s) f(pl)
mouth (pl **mouths**) [mauθ, mauðz]
n bouche f; (of dog, cat) gueule f; (of
river) embouchure f; (of hole, cave)
ouverture f; **mouthful** n bouchée
f; **mouth organ** n harmonica m;
mouthpiece n (of musical instrument)
bec m, embouchure f; (spokesperson)
porte-parole m inv; **mouthwash** n
eau f dentifrice
move [muːv] n (movement)
mouvement m; (in game) coup m
(: turn to play) tour m; (change of
house) déménagement m; (change
of job) changement m d'emploi ▷ vt
déplacer, bouger; (emotionally)
émouvoir; (Pol: resolution etc)
proposer ▷ vi (gen) bouger, remuer;
(traffic) circuler; (also: **~ house**)
déménager; (in game) jouer; **can you
~ your car, please?** pouvez-vous
déplacer votre voiture, s'il vous
plaît?; **to ~ sb to do sth** pousser
or inciter qn à faire qch; **to get a ~
on** se dépêcher, se remuer; **move
back** vi revenir, retourner; **move in**
vi (to a house) emménager; (police,

soldiers) intervenir; **move off** vi
s'éloigner, s'en aller; **move on** vi
se remettre en route; **move out** vi
(of house) déménager; **move over**
vi se pousser, se déplacer; **move
up** vi avancer; (employee) avoir de
l'avancement; (pupil) passer dans
la classe supérieure; **movement** n
mouvement m
movie ['muːvɪ] n film m; **movies** npl;
the ~s le cinéma; **movie theater** (us)
n cinéma m
moving ['muːvɪŋ] adj en
mouvement; (touching)
émouvant(e)
mow (pt **mowed**, pp **mowed** or
mown) [məu, -d, -n] vt faucher;
(lawn) tondre; **mower** n (also:
lawnmower) tondeuse f à gazon
mown [məun] pp of **mow**
Mozambique [məuzəm'biːk] n
Mozambique m
MP n abbr (BRIT) = **Member of
Parliament**
MP3 n mp3 m; **MP3 player** n baladeur
m numérique, lecteur m mp3
mpg n abbr = **miles per gallon**
(30 mpg = 9,4 l. aux 100 km)
m.p.h. abbr = **miles per hour** (60 mph
= 96 km/h)
Mr, (us) **Mr.** ['mɪstər] n: **~ X** Monsieur
X, M. X
Mrs, (us) **Mrs.** ['mɪsɪz] n: **~ X**
Madame X, Mme X
Ms, (us) **Ms.** [mɪz] n (Miss or Mrs): **~ X**
Madame X, Mme X
MSP n abbr (= Member of the Scottish
Parliament) député m au Parlement
écossais
Mt abbr (Geo: = mount) Mt
much [mʌtʃ] adj beaucoup de ▷ adv,
n, pron beaucoup; **we don't have
~ time** nous n'avons pas beaucoup
de temps; **how ~ is it?** combien
est-ce que ça coûte?; **it's not ~** ce
n'est pas beaucoup; **too ~** trop (de);
so ~ tant (de); **I like it very/so ~**
j'aime beaucoup/tellement ça; **as ~**

as autant de; **that's ~ better** c'est beaucoup mieux

muck [mʌk] n (mud) boue f; (dirt) ordures fpl; **muck up** vt (inf: ruin) gâcher, esquinter; (dirty) salir; (exam, interview) se planter à; **mucky** adj (dirty) boueux(-euse), sale

mucus ['mju:kəs] n mucus m

mud [mʌd] n boue f

muddle ['mʌdl] n (mess) pagaille f, fouillis m; (mix-up) confusion f ▷ vt (also: **~ up**) brouiller, embrouiller; **to get in a ~** (while explaining etc) s'embrouiller

muddy ['mʌdɪ] adj boueux(-euse)

mudguard ['mʌdgɑ:d] n garde-boue m inv

muesli ['mju:zlɪ] n muesli m

muffin ['mʌfɪn] n (roll) petit pain rond et plat; (cake) petit gâteau au chocolat ou aux fruits

muffled ['mʌfld] adj étouffé(e), voilé(e)

muffler ['mʌflər] n (scarf) cache-nez m inv; (us Aut) silencieux m

mug [mʌg] n (cup) tasse f (sans soucoupe); (: for beer) chope f; (inf: face) bouille f; (: fool) poire f ▷ vt (assault) agresser; **mugger** ['mʌgər] n agresseur m; **mugging** n agression f

muggy ['mʌgɪ] adj lourd(e), moite

mule [mju:l] n mule f

multicoloured, (us) **multicolored** ['mʌltɪkʌləd] adj multicolore

multimedia ['mʌltɪ'mi:dɪə] adj multimédia inv

multinational [mʌltɪ'næʃənl] n multinationale f ▷ adj multinational(e)

multiple ['mʌltɪpl] adj multiple ▷ n multiple m; **multiple choice (test)** n QCM m, questionnaire m à choix multiple; **multiple sclerosis** [-sklɪ'rəusɪs] n sclérose f en plaques

multiplex (cinema) ['mʌltɪpleks-] n (cinéma m) multisalles m

multiplication [mʌltɪplɪ'keɪʃən] n multiplication f

multiply ['mʌltɪplaɪ] vt multiplier ▷ vi se multiplier

multistorey ['mʌltɪ'stɔ:rɪ] adj (BRIT: building) à étages; (: car park) à étages or niveaux multiples

mum [mʌm] n (BRIT) maman f ▷ adj: **to keep ~** ne pas souffler mot

mumble ['mʌmbl] vt, vi marmotter, marmonner

mummy ['mʌmɪ] n (BRIT: mother) maman f; (embalmed) momie f

mumps [mʌmps] n oreillons mpl

munch [mʌntʃ] vt, vi mâcher

municipal [mju:'nɪsɪpl] adj municipal(e)

mural ['mjuərl] n peinture murale

murder ['mə:dər] n meurtre m, assassinat m ▷ vt assassiner; **murderer** n meurtrier m, assassin m

murky ['mə:kɪ] adj sombre, ténébreux(-euse); (water) trouble

murmur ['mə:mər] n murmure m ▷ vt, vi murmurer

muscle ['mʌsl] n muscle m; (fig) force f; **muscular** ['mʌskjulər] adj musculaire; (person, arm) musclé(e)

museum [mju:'zɪəm] n musée m

mushroom ['mʌʃrum] n champignon m ▷ vi (fig) pousser comme un (or des) champignon(s)

music ['mju:zɪk] n musique f; **musical** adj musical(e); (person) musicien(ne) ▷ n (show) comédie musicale; **musical instrument** n instrument m de musique; **musician** [mju:'zɪʃən] n musicien(ne)

Muslim ['mʌzlɪm] adj, n musulman(e)

muslin ['mʌzlɪn] n mousseline f

mussel ['mʌsl] n moule f

must [mʌst] aux vb (obligation): **I ~ do it** je dois le faire, il faut que je le fasse; (probability): **he ~ be there by now** il doit y être maintenant, il y est probablement maintenant; (suggestion, invitation): **you ~ come and see me** il faut que vous veniez me voir ▷ n nécessité f, impératif m;

m

it's a ~ c'est indispensable; **I ~ have made a mistake** j'ai dû me tromper

mustache ['mʌstæʃ] n (US) = **moustache**

mustard ['mʌstəd] n moutarde f

mustn't ['mʌsnt] = **must not**

mute [mjuːt] adj, n muet(te)

mutilate ['mjuːtɪleɪt] vt mutiler

mutiny ['mjuːtɪnɪ] n mutinerie f ▷ vi se mutiner

mutter ['mʌtər] vt, vi marmonner, marmotter

mutton ['mʌtn] n mouton m

mutual ['mjuːtʃuəl] adj mutuel(le), réciproque; (benefit, interest) commun(e)

muzzle ['mʌzl] n museau m; (protective device) muselière f; (of gun) gueule f ▷ vt museler

my [maɪ] adj mon (ma), mes pl; **my house/car/gloves** ma maison/ma voiture/mes gants; **I've washed my hair/cut my finger** je me suis lavé les cheveux/coupé le doigt; **is this my pen or yours?** c'est mon stylo ou c'est le vôtre?

myself [maɪ'self] pron (reflexive) me; (emphatic) moi-même; (after prep) moi; see also **oneself**

mysterious [mɪs'tɪərɪəs] adj mystérieux(-euse)

mystery ['mɪstərɪ] n mystère m

mystical ['mɪstɪkl] adj mystique

mystify ['mɪstɪfaɪ] vt (deliberately) mystifier; (puzzle) ébahir

myth [mɪθ] n mythe m; **mythology** [mɪ'θɔlədʒɪ] n mythologie f

n/a abbr (= not applicable) n.a.

nag [næg] vt (scold) être toujours après, reprendre sans arrêt

nail [neɪl] n (human) ongle m; (metal) clou m ▷ vt clouer; **to ~ sth to sth** clouer qch à qch; **to ~ sb down to a date/price** contraindre qn à accepter or donner une date/un prix; **nailbrush** n brosse f à ongles; **nailfile** n lime f à ongles; **nail polish** n vernis m à ongles; **nail polish remover** n dissolvant m; **nail scissors** npl ciseaux mpl à ongles; **nail varnish** n (BRIT) = **nail polish**

naïve [naɪ'iːv] adj naïf(-ïve)

naked ['neɪkɪd] adj nu(e)

name [neɪm] n nom m; (reputation) réputation f ▷ vt nommer; (identify: accomplice etc) citer; (price, date) fixer, donner; **by ~** par son nom; de nom; **in the ~ of** au nom de; **what's your ~?** comment vous appelez-vous?, quel est votre nom?; **namely** adv à savoir

nanny ['nænɪ] n bonne f d'enfants

nap [næp] n (sleep) (petit) somme
napkin ['næpkɪn] n serviette f (de table)
nappy ['næpɪ] n (BRIT) couche f
narcotics [nɑː'kɔtɪkz] npl (illegal drugs) stupéfiants mpl
narrative ['nærətɪv] n récit m ⊳ adj narratif(-ive)
narrator [nə'reɪtəʳ] n narrateur(-trice)
narrow ['nærəu] adj étroit(e); (fig) restreint(e), limité(e) ⊳ vi (road) devenir plus étroit, se rétrécir; (gap, difference) se réduire; **to have a ~ escape** l'échapper belle; **narrow down** vt restreindre; **narrowly** adv: **he narrowly missed injury/the tree** il a failli se blesser/rentrer dans l'arbre; **he only narrowly missed the target** il a manqué la cible de peu or de justesse; **narrow-minded** adj à l'esprit étroit, borné(e); (attitude) borné(e)
nasal ['neɪzl] adj nasal(e)
nasty ['nɑːstɪ] adj (person: malicious) méchant(e); (: rude) très désagréable; (smell) dégoûtant(e); (wound, situation) mauvais(e), vilain(e)
nation ['neɪʃən] n nation f
national ['næʃənl] adj national(e) ⊳ n (abroad) ressortissant(e); (when home) national(e); **national anthem** n hymne national; **national dress** n costume national; **National Health Service** n (BRIT) service national de santé, ≈ Sécurité Sociale; **National Insurance** n (BRIT) ≈ Sécurité Sociale; **nationalist** adj, n nationaliste m/f; **nationality** [næʃə'nælɪtɪ] n nationalité f; **nationalize** vt nationaliser; **national park** n parc national; **National Trust** n (BRIT) ≈ Caisse f nationale des monuments historiques et des sites

nationwide ['neɪʃənwaɪd] adj s'étendant à l'ensemble du pays; (problem) à l'échelle du pays entier
native ['neɪtɪv] n habitant(e) du pays, autochtone m/f ⊳ adj du pays, indigène; (country) natal(e); (language) maternel(le); (ability) inné(e); **Native American** n Indien(ne) d'Amérique ⊳ adj amérindien(ne); **native speaker** n locuteur natif
NATO ['neɪtəu] n abbr (= North Atlantic Treaty Organization) OTAN f
natural ['nætʃrəl] adj naturel(le); **natural gas** n gaz naturel; **natural history** n histoire naturelle; **naturally** adv naturellement; **natural resources** npl ressources naturelles
nature ['neɪtʃəʳ] n nature f; **by ~** par tempérament, de nature; **nature reserve** n (BRIT) réserve naturelle
naughty ['nɔːtɪ] adj (child) vilain(e), pas sage
nausea ['nɔːsɪə] n nausée f
naval ['neɪvl] adj naval(e)
navel ['neɪvl] n nombril m
navigate ['nævɪgeɪt] vt (steer) diriger, piloter ⊳ vi naviguer; (Aut) indiquer la route à suivre; **navigation** [nævɪ'geɪʃən] n navigation f
navy ['neɪvɪ] n marine f
navy-blue ['neɪvɪ'bluː] adj bleu marine inv
Nazi ['nɑːtsɪ] n Nazi(e)
NB abbr (= nota bene) NB
near [nɪəʳ] adj proche ⊳ adv près ⊳ prep (also: ~ to) près de ⊳ vt approcher de; **in the ~ future** dans un proche avenir; **nearby** [nɪə'baɪ] adj proche ⊳ adv tout près, à proximité; **nearly** adv presque; **I nearly fell** j'ai failli tomber; **it's not**

nearly big enough ce n'est vraiment pas assez grand, c'est loin d'être assez grand; **near-sighted** adj myope

neat [niːt] adj (person, work) soigné(e); (room etc) bien tenu(e) or rangé(e); (solution, plan) habile; (spirits) pur(e); **neatly** adv avec soin or ordre; (skilfully) habilement

necessarily ['nɛsɪsərɪlɪ] adv nécessairement; **not ~** pas nécessairement or forcément

necessary ['nɛsɪsrɪ] adj nécessaire; **if ~** si besoin est, le cas échéant

necessity [nɪ'sɛsɪtɪ] n nécessité f; chose nécessaire or essentielle

neck [nɛk] n cou m; (of horse, garment) encolure f; (of bottle) goulot m; **~ and ~** à égalité; **necklace** ['nɛklɪs] n collier m; **necktie** ['nɛktaɪ] n (esp us) cravate f

nectarine ['nɛktərɪn] n brugnon m, nectarine f

need [niːd] n besoin m ▷ vt avoir besoin de; **to ~ to do** devoir faire; avoir besoin de faire; **you don't ~ to go** vous n'avez pas besoin or vous n'êtes pas obligé de partir; **a signature is ~ed** il faut une signature; **there's no ~ to do ....** il n'y a pas lieu de faire ..., il n'est pas nécessaire de faire …

needle ['niːdl] n aiguille f ▷ vt (inf) asticoter, tourmenter

needless ['niːdlɪs] adj inutile; **~ to say, ...** inutile de dire que …

needlework ['niːdlwəːk] n (activity) travaux mpl d'aiguille; (object) ouvrage m

needn't ['niːdnt] = need not

needy ['niːdɪ] adj nécessiteux(-euse)

negative ['nɛgətɪv] n (Phot, Elec) négatif m; (Ling) terme m de négation ▷ adj négatif(-ive)

neglect [nɪ'glɛkt] vt négliger; (garden) ne pas entretenir; (duty) manquer à ▷ n (of person, duty, garden) le fait de négliger; **(state of) ~** abandon m; **to ~ to do sth** négliger

or omettre de faire qch; **to ~ one's appearance** se négliger

negotiate [nɪ'gəʊʃɪeɪt] vi négocier ▷ vt négocier; (obstacle) franchir, négocier; **to ~ with sb for sth** négocier avec qn en vue d'obtenir qch

negotiation [nɪgəʊʃɪ'eɪʃən] n négociation f, pourparlers mpl

negotiator [nɪ'gəʊʃɪeɪtər] n négociateur(-trice)

neighbour, (us) **neighbor** ['neɪbər] n voisin(e); **neighbourhood**, (us) **neighborhood** n (place) quartier m; (people) voisinage m; **neighbouring**, (us) **neighboring** adj voisin(e), avoisinant(e)

neither ['naɪðər] adj, pron aucun(e) (des deux), ni l'un(e) ni l'autre ▷ conj: **~ do I** moi non plus ▷ adv: **~ good nor bad** ni bon ni mauvais; **~ of them** ni l'un ni l'autre

neon ['niːɔn] n néon m

Nepal [nɪ'pɔːl] n Népal m

nephew ['nɛvjuː] n neveu m

nerve [nəːv] n nerf m; (bravery) sang-froid m, courage m; (cheek) aplomb m, toupet m; **nerves** npl (nervousness) nervosité f; **he gets on my ~s** il m'énerve

nervous ['nəːvəs] adj nerveux(-euse); (anxious) inquiet(-ète), plein(e) d'appréhension; (timid) intimidé(e); **nervous breakdown** n dépression nerveuse

nest [nɛst] n nid m ▷ vi (se) nicher, faire son nid

Net [nɛt] n (Comput): **the ~** (Internet) le Net

net [nɛt] n filet m; (fabric) tulle f ▷ adj net(te) ▷ vt (fish etc) prendre au filet; **netball** n netball m

Netherlands ['nɛðələndz] npl; **the ~** les Pays-Bas mpl

nett [nɛt] adj = net

nettle ['nɛtl] n ortie f

network ['nɛtwəːk] n réseau m; **there's no ~ coverage here** (Tel) il n'y a pas de réseau ici

neurotic [njuə'rɔtɪk] *adj* névrosé(e)
neuter ['nju:tə*] *adj* neutre ▷ *vt* (*cat etc*) châtrer, coupér
neutral ['nju:trəl] *adj* neutre ▷ *n* (*Aut*) point mort
never ['nɛvə*] *adv* (ne ...) jamais; **I ~ went** je n'y suis pas allé; **I've ~ been to Spain** je ne suis jamais allé en Espagne; **~ again** plus jamais; **~ in my life** jamais de ma vie; *see also* **mind**; **never-ending** *adj* interminable; **nevertheless** [nɛvəðə'lɛs] *adv* néanmoins, malgré tout
new [nju:] *adj* nouveau (nouvelle); (*brand new*) neuf (neuve); **New Age** *n* New Age *m*; **newborn** *adj* nouveau-né(e); **newcomer** ['nju:kʌmə*] *n* nouveau venu (nouvelle venue); **newly** *adv* nouvellement, récemment
news [nju:z] *n* nouvelle(s) *f(pl)*; (*Radio, TV*) informations *fpl*, actualités *fpl*; **a piece of ~** une nouvelle; **news agency** *n* agence *f* de presse; **newsagent** *n* (*BRIT*) marchand *m* de journaux; **newscaster** *n* (*Radio, TV*) présentateur(-trice); **newsletter** *n* bulletin *m*; **newspaper** *n* journal *m*; **newsreader** *n* = **newscaster**
newt [nju:t] *n* triton *m*
New Year *n* Nouvel An; **Happy ~!** Bonne Année!; **New Year's Day** *n* le jour de l'An; **New Year's Eve** *n* la Saint-Sylvestre
New York [-'jɔ:k] *n* New York
New Zealand [-'zi:lənd] *n* Nouvelle-Zélande *f*; **New Zealander** *n* Néo-Zélandais(e)
next [nɛkst] *adj* (*in time*) prochain(e); (*seat, room*) voisin(e), d'à côté; (*meeting, bus stop*) suivant(e) ▷ *adv* la fois suivante, la prochaine fois; (*afterwards*) ensuite; **~ to** *prep* à côté de; **~ to nothing** presque rien; **~ time** *adv* la prochaine fois; **the ~ day** le lendemain, le jour suivant *or* d'après; **~ year** l'année prochaine; **~ please!** (*at doctor's etc*) au suivant!;

the week after ~ dans deux semaines; **next door** *adv* à côté ▷ *adj* (*neighbour*) d'à côté; **next-of-kin** *n* parent *m* le plus proche
NHS *n abbr* (*BRIT*) = **National Health Service**
nibble ['nɪbl] *vt* grignoter
nice [naɪs] *adj* (*holiday, trip, taste*) agréable; (*flat, picture*) joli(e); (*person*) gentil(le); (*distinction, point*) subtil(e); **nicely** *adv* agréablement; joliment; gentiment; subtilement
niche [ni:ʃ] *n* (*Archit*) niche *f*
nick [nɪk] *n* (*indentation*) encoche *f*; (*wound*) entaille *f*; (*BRIT inf*): **in good ~** en bon état ▷ *vt* (*cut*): **to ~ o.s.** se couper; (*BRIT inf: steal*) faucher, piquer; **in the ~ of time** juste à temps
nickel ['nɪkl] *n* nickel *m*; (*US*) pièce *f* de 5 cents
nickname ['nɪkneɪm] *n* surnom *m* ▷ *vt* surnommer
nicotine ['nɪkəti:n] *n* nicotine *f*
niece [ni:s] *n* nièce *f*
Nigeria [naɪ'dʒɪərɪə] *n* Nigéria *m/f*
night [naɪt] *n* nuit *f*; (*evening*) soir *m*; **at ~** la nuit; **by ~** de nuit; **last ~** (*evening*) hier soir; (*night-time*) la nuit dernière; **night club** *n* boîte *f* de nuit; **nightdress** *n* chemise *f* de nuit; **nightie** ['naɪtɪ] *n* chemise *f* de nuit; **nightlife** *n* vie *f* nocturne; **nightly** *adj* (*news*) du soir; (*by night*) nocturne ▷ *adv* (*every evening*) tous les soirs; (*every night*) toutes les nuits; **nightmare** *n* cauchemar *m*; **night school** *n* cours *mpl* du soir; **night shift** *n* équipe *f* de nuit; **night-time** *n* nuit *f*
nil [nɪl] *n* (*BRIT Sport*) zéro *m*
nine [naɪn] *num* neuf; **nineteen** *num* dix-neuf; **nineteenth** [naɪn'ti:nθ] *num* dix-neuvième; **ninetieth** ['naɪntɪɪθ] *num* quatre-vingt-dixième; **ninety** *num* quatre-vingt-dix
ninth [naɪnθ] *num* neuvième
nip [nɪp] *vt* pincer ▷ *vi* (*BRIT inf*): **to ~ out/down/up** sortir/descendre/monter en vitesse

n

nipple ['nɪpl] n (Anat) mamelon m,
bout m du sein
nitrogen ['naɪtrədʒən] n azote m

⭕ **KEYWORD**

no [nəʊ] adv (opposite of "yes") non;
are you coming? — no (I'm not)
est-ce que vous venez? — non;
**would you like some more? — no
thank you** vous en voulez encore?
— non merci
▶ adj (not any) (ne …) pas de, (ne
…) aucun(e); **I have no money/
books** je n'ai pas d'argent/de livres;
no student would have done it
aucun étudiant ne l'aurait fait; **"no
smoking"** "défense de fumer"; **"no
dogs"** "les chiens ne sont pas admis"
▶ n (pl **noes**) non m

nobility [nəʊ'bɪlɪtɪ] n noblesse f
noble ['nəʊbl] adj noble
nobody ['nəʊbədɪ] pron (ne …)
personne
nod [nɒd] vi faire un signe de (la) tête
(affirmatif ou amical); (sleep) somnoler
▶ vt: **to ~ one's head** faire un signe
de (la) tête; (in agreement) faire signe
que oui ▶ n signe m de (la) tête; **nod
off** vi s'assoupir
noise [nɔɪz] n bruit m; **I can't sleep
for the ~** je n'arrive pas à dormir à
cause du bruit; **noisy** adj bruyant(e)
nominal ['nɒmɪnl] adj (rent, fee)
symbolique; (value) nominal(e)
nominate ['nɒmɪneɪt] vt (propose)
proposer; (appoint) nommer;
nomination [nɒmɪ'neɪʃən] n
nomination f; **nominee** [nɒmɪ'niː] n
candidat agréé; personne nommée
none [nʌn] pron aucun(e); **~ of you**
aucun d'entre vous, personne parmi
vous; **I have ~ left** je n'en ai plus;
he's ~ the worse for it il ne s'en porte
pas plus mal
nonetheless ['nʌnðə'lɛs] adv
néanmoins

non-fiction [nɒn'fɪkʃən] n
littérature f non romanesque
nonsense ['nɒnsəns] n absurdités fpl,
idioties fpl; **~!** ne dites pas d'idioties!
non: **non-smoker** n non-fumeur m;
non-smoking adj non-fumeur; **non-
stick** adj qui n'attache pas
noodles ['nuːdlz] npl nouilles fpl
noon [nuːn] n midi m
no-one ['nəʊwʌn] pron = **nobody**
nor [nɔːʳ] conj = **neither** ▷ adv see
neither
norm [nɔːm] n norme f
normal ['nɔːml] adj normal(e);
normally adv normalement
Normandy ['nɔːməndɪ] n
Normandie f
north [nɔːθ] n nord m ▷ adj nord
inv; (wind) du nord ▷ adv au or vers
le nord; **North Africa** n Afrique f
du Nord; **North African** adj nord-
africain(e), d'Afrique du Nord ▷ n
Nord-Africain(e); **North America**
n Amérique f du Nord; **North
American** n Nord-Américain(e) ▷ adj
nord-américain(e), d'Amérique du
Nord; **northbound** ['nɔːθbaʊnd]
adj (traffic) en direction du nord;
(carriageway) nord inv; **north-east** n
nord-est m; **northern** ['nɔːðən] adj
du nord, septentrional(e); **Northern
Ireland** n Irlande f du Nord; **North
Korea** n Corée f du Nord; **North
Pole** n: **the North Pole** le pôle Nord;
North Sea n: **the North Sea** la mer
du Nord; **north-west** n nord-ouest m
Norway ['nɔːweɪ] n Norvège f;
Norwegian [nɔː'wiːdʒən] adj
norvégien(ne) ▷ n Norvégien(ne);
(Ling) norvégien m
nose [nəʊz] n nez m; (of dog, cat)
museau m; (fig) flair m; **nose about,
nose around** vi fouiner or fureter
(partout); **nosebleed** n saignement m
de nez; **nosey** adj (inf) curieux(-euse)
nostalgia [nɒs'tældʒɪə] n nostalgie f
nostalgic [nɒs'tældʒɪk] adj
nostalgique

nostril ['nɔstrɪl] n narine f; (of horse) naseau m

nosy ['nəʊzɪ] (inf) adj = **nosey**

not [nɔt] adv (ne ...) pas; **he is ~** or **isn't here** il n'est pas ici; **you must ~** or **mustn't do that** tu ne dois pas faire ça; **I hope ~** j'espère que non; **~ at all** pas du tout; (after thanks) de rien; **it's too late, isn't it?** c'est trop tard, n'est-ce pas?; **~ yet/now** pas encore/maintenant; see also **only**

notable ['nəʊtəbl] adj notable; **notably** adv (particularly) en particulier; (markedly) spécialement

notch [nɔtʃ] n encoche f

note [nəʊt] n note f; (letter) mot m; (banknote) billet m ▷ vt (also: **~ down**) noter; (notice) constater; **notebook** n carnet m; (for shorthand etc) bloc-notes m; **noted** ['nəʊtɪd] adj réputé(e); **notepad** n bloc-notes m; **notepaper** n papier m à lettres

nothing ['nʌθɪŋ] n rien m; **he does ~** il ne fait rien; **~ new** rien de nouveau; **for ~** (free) pour rien, gratuitement; (in vain) pour rien; **~ at all** rien du tout; **~ much** pas grand-chose

notice ['nəʊtɪs] n (announcement, warning) avis m ▷ vt remarquer, s'apercevoir de; **advance ~** préavis m; **at short ~** dans un délai très court; **until further ~** jusqu'à nouvel ordre; **to give ~, hand in one's ~** (employee) donner sa démission, démissionner; **to take ~ of** prêter attention à; **to bring sth to sb's ~** porter qch à la connaissance de qn; **noticeable** adj visible

notice board n (BRIT) panneau m d'affichage

notify ['nəʊtɪfaɪ] vt: **to ~ sb of sth** avertir qn de qch

notion ['nəʊʃən] n idée f; (concept) notion f; **notions** npl (US: haberdashery) mercerie f

notorious [nəʊ'tɔːrɪəs] adj notoire (souvent en mal)

notwithstanding [nɔtwɪθ'stændɪŋ] adv néanmoins ▷ prep en dépit de

nought [nɔːt] n zéro m

noun [naʊn] n nom m

nourish ['nʌrɪʃ] vt nourrir; **nourishment** n nourriture f

Nov. abbr (= November) nov

novel ['nɔvl] n roman m ▷ adj nouveau (nouvelle), original(e); **novelist** n romancier m; **novelty** n nouveauté f

November [nəʊ'vɛmbər] n novembre m

novice ['nɔvɪs] n novice m/f

now [naʊ] adv maintenant ▷ conj: **~ (that)** maintenant (que); **right ~** tout de suite; **by ~** à l'heure qu'il est; **that's the fashion just ~** c'est la mode en ce moment or maintenant; **~ and then, ~ and again** de temps en temps; **from ~ on** dorénavant; **nowadays** ['naʊədeɪz] adv de nos jours

nowhere ['nəʊwɛər] adv (ne ...) nulle part

nozzle ['nɔzl] n (of hose) jet m, lance f; (of vacuum cleaner) suceur m

nr abbr (BRIT) = **near**

nuclear ['njuːklɪər] adj nucléaire

nucleus (pl **nuclei**) ['njuːklɪəs, 'njuːklɪaɪ] n noyau m

nude [njuːd] adj nu(e) ▷ n (Art) nu m; **in the ~** (tout(e)) nu(e)

nudge [nʌdʒ] vt donner un (petit) coup de coude à

nudist ['njuːdɪst] n nudiste m/f

nudity ['njuːdɪtɪ] n nudité f

nuisance ['njuːsns] n: **it's a ~** c'est (très) ennuyeux or gênant; **he's a ~** il est assommant or casse-pieds; **what a ~!** quelle barbe!

numb [nʌm] adj engourdi(e); (with fear) paralysé(e)

number ['nʌmbər] n nombre m; (numeral) chiffre m; (of house, car, telephone, newspaper) numéro m ▷ vt numéroter; (amount to) compter;

n

a ~ of un certain nombre de; **they were seven in ~** ils étaient (au nombre de) sept; **to be ~ed among** compter parmi; **number plate** n (BRIT Aut) plaque f minéralogique or d'immatriculation; **Number Ten** n (BRIT: 10 Downing Street) résidence du Premier ministre

numerical [njuːˈmɛrɪkl] adj numérique

numerous [ˈnjuːmərəs] adj nombreux(-euse)

nun [nʌn] n religieuse f, sœur f

nurse [nəːs] n infirmière f; (also: **~maid**) bonne f d'enfants ▷ vt (patient, cold) soigner

nursery [ˈnəːsərɪ] n (room) nursery f; (institution) crèche f, garderie f; (for plants) pépinière f; **nursery rhyme** n comptine f, chansonnette f pour enfants; **nursery school** n école maternelle; **nursery slope** n (BRIT Ski) piste f pour débutants

nursing [ˈnəːsɪŋ] n (profession) profession f d'infirmière; (care) soins mpl; **nursing home** n clinique f; (for convalescence) maison f de convalescence or de repos; (for old people) maison de retraite

nurture [ˈnəːtʃər] vt élever

nut [nʌt] n (of metal) écrou m; (fruit: walnut) noix f; (: hazelnut) noisette f; (: peanut) cacahuète f (terme générique en anglais)

nutmeg [ˈnʌtmɛg] n (noix f) muscade f

nutrient [ˈnjuːtrɪənt] n substance nutritive

nutrition [njuːˈtrɪʃən] n nutrition f, alimentation f

nutritious [njuːˈtrɪʃəs] adj nutritif(-ive), nourrissant(e)

nuts [nʌts] (inf) adj dingue

NVQ n abbr (BRIT) = **National Vocational Qualification**

nylon [ˈnaɪlɔn] n nylon m ▷ adj de or en nylon

oak [əuk] n chêne m ▷ cpd de or en (bois de) chêne

O.A.P. n abbr (BRIT) = **old age pensioner**

oar [ɔːʳ] n aviron m, rame f

oasis (pl **oases**) [əuˈeɪsɪs, əuˈeɪsiːz] n oasis f

oath [əuθ] n serment m; (swear word) juron m; **on** (BRIT) or **under ~** sous serment; assermenté(e)

oatmeal [ˈəutmiːl] n flocons mpl d'avoine

oats [əuts] n avoine f

obedience [əˈbiːdɪəns] n obéissance f

obedient [əˈbiːdɪənt] adj obéissant(e)

obese [əuˈbiːs] adj obèse

obesity [əuˈbiːsɪtɪ] n obésité f

obey [əˈbeɪ] vt obéir à; (instructions, regulations) se conformer à ▷ vi obéir

obituary [əˈbɪtjuərɪ] n nécrologie f

object n [ˈɔbdʒɪkt] objet m; (purpose) but m, objet; (Ling) complément

m d'objet ▷ *vi* [əb'dʒɛkt]: **to ~ to**
(*attitude*) désapprouver; (*proposal*)
protester contre, élever une objection
contre; **I ~!** je proteste!; **he ~ed that
...** il a fait valoir *or* a objecté que ...;
money is no ~ l'argent n'est pas un
problème; **objection** [əb'dʒɛkʃən]
n objection *f*; **if you have no
objection** si vous n'y voyez pas
d'inconvénient; **objective** *n* objectif
m ▷ *adj* objectif(-ive)
obligation [ɔblɪ'ɡeɪʃən] *n* obligation
f, devoir *m*; (*debt*) dette *f* (de
reconnaissance)
obligatory [ə'blɪɡətərɪ] *adj*
obligatoire
oblige [ə'blaɪdʒ] *vt* (*force*): **to ~ sb to do**
obliger *or* forcer qn à faire; (*do a favour*)
rendre service à, obliger; **to be ~d to
sb for sth** être obligé(e) à qn de qch
oblique [ə'bliːk] *adj* oblique; (*allusion*)
indirect(e)
obliterate [ə'blɪtəreɪt] *vt* effacer
oblivious [ə'blɪvɪəs] *adj*: **~ of**
oublieux(-euse) de
oblong [ˈɔblɔŋ] *adj* oblong(ue) ▷ *n*
rectangle *m*
obnoxious [əb'nɔkʃəs] *adj*
odieux(-euse); (*smell*) nauséabond(e)
oboe [ˈəubəu] *n* hautbois *m*
obscene [əb'siːn] *adj* obscène
obscure [əb'skjuər] *adj* obscur(e) ▷ *vt*
obscurcir; (*hide: sun*) cacher
observant [əb'zɜːvnt] *adj*
observateur(-trice)
observation [ɔbzə'veɪʃən] *n*
observation *f*; (*by police etc*)
surveillance *f*
observatory [əb'zɜːvətrɪ] *n*
observatoire *m*
observe [əb'zɜːv] *vt* observer;
(*remark*) faire observer *or* remarquer;
observer *n* observateur(-trice)
obsess [əb'sɛs] *vt* obséder;
obsession [əb'sɛʃən] *n* obsession *f*;
obsessive *adj* obsédant(e)
obsolete [ˈɔbsəliːt] *adj* dépassé(e),
périmé(e)

obstacle [ˈɔbstəkl] *n* obstacle *m*
obstinate [ˈɔbstɪnɪt] *adj* obstiné(e);
(*pain, cold*) persistant(e)
obstruct [əb'strʌkt] *vt* (*block*)
boucher, obstruer; (*hinder*) entraver;
obstruction [əb'strʌkʃən] *n*
obstruction *f*; (*to plan, progress*)
obstacle *m*
obtain [əb'teɪn] *vt* obtenir
obvious [ˈɔbvɪəs] *adj* évident(e),
manifeste; **obviously** *adv*
manifestement; **obviously!** bien
sûr!; **obviously not!** évidemment
pas!, bien sûr que non!
occasion [ə'keɪʒən] *n* occasion *f*;
(*event*) événement *m*; **occasional**
adj pris(e) (*or* fait(e) *etc*) de temps
en temps; (*worker, spending*)
occasionnel(le); **occasionally** *adv* de
temps en temps, quelquefois
occult [ɔ'kʌlt] *adj* occulte ▷ *n*: **the ~**
le surnaturel
occupant [ˈɔkjupənt] *n* occupant *m*
occupation [ɔkju'peɪʃən] *n*
occupation *f*; (*job*) métier *m*,
profession *f*
occupy [ˈɔkjupaɪ] *vt* occuper; **to
~ o.s. with** *or* **by doing** s'occuper
à faire
occur [ə'kɜːr] *vi* se produire;
(*difficulty, opportunity*) se présenter;
(*phenomenon, error*) se rencontrer;
to ~ to sb venir à l'esprit de qn;
occurrence [ə'kʌrəns] *n* (*existence*)
présence *f*, existence *f*; (*event*) cas
m, fait *m*
ocean [ˈəuʃən] *n* océan *m*
o'clock [ə'klɔk] *adv*: **it is 5 ~** il est
5 heures
Oct. *abbr* (= *October*) oct
October [ɔk'təubər] *n* octobre *m*
octopus [ˈɔktəpəs] *n* pieuvre *f*
odd [ɔd] *adj* (*strange*) bizarre,
curieux(-euse); (*number*) impair(e);
(*not of a set*) dépareillé(e); **60-~**
60 et quelques; **at ~ times** de
temps en temps; **the ~ one out**
l'exception *f*; **oddly** *adv* bizarrement,

curieusement; **odds** npl (in betting)
cote f; **it makes no odds** cela n'a
pas d'importance; **odds and ends**
de petites choses; **at odds** en
désaccord

odometer [ɔ'dɔmitə'] n (US)
odomètre m

odour, (US)**odor** ['əudə'] n odeur f

KEYWORD

of [ɔv, əv] prep **1** (gen) de; **a friend of
ours** un de nos amis; **a boy of 10** un
garçon de 10 ans; **that was kind of
you** c'était gentil de votre part
2 (expressing quantity, amount, dates
etc) de; **a kilo of flour** un kilo de
farine; **how much of this do you
need?** combien vous en faut-il?;
there were three of them (people)
ils étaient 3; (objects) il y en avait
3; **three of us went** 3 d'entre nous
y sont allé(e)s; **the 5th of July** le 5
juillet; **a quarter of 4** (US) 4 heures
moins le quart
3 (from, out of) en, de; **a statue of
marble** une statue de or en marbre;
made of wood (fait) en bois

off [ɔf] adj, adv (engine) coupé(e);
(light, TV) éteint(e); (tap) fermé(e);
(BRIT: food) mauvais(e), avancé(e);
(: milk) tourné(e); (absent) absent(e);
(cancelled) annulé(e); (removed): **the
lid was ~** le couvercle était retiré
or n'était pas mis; (away): **to run/
drive ~** partir en courant/en voiture
▷ prep de; **to be ~** (to leave) partir, s'en
aller; **to be ~ sick** être absent pour
cause de maladie; **a day ~** un jour de
congé; **to have an ~ day** n'être pas
en forme; **he had his coat ~** il avait
enlevé son manteau; **10% ~** (Comm)
10% de rabais; **5 km ~ (the road)** à 5
km (de la route); **~ the coast** au large
de la côte; **it's a long way ~** c'est loin
(d'ici); **I'm ~ meat** je ne mange plus
de viande; je n'aime plus la viande; **on**

the ~ chance à tout hasard; **~ and
on, on and ~** de temps à autre

offence, (US)**offense** [ə'fɛns] n
(crime) délit m, infraction f; **to take ~
at** se vexer de, s'offenser de

offend [ə'fɛnd] vt (person) offenser,
blesser; **offender** n délinquant(e);
(against regulations) contrevenant(e)

offense [ə'fɛns] n (US) = **offence**

offensive [ə'fɛnsɪv] adj offensant(e),
choquant(e); (smell etc) très
déplaisant(e); (weapon) offensif(-ive)
▷ n (Mil) offensive f

offer ['ɔfə'] n offre f, proposition f ▷ vt
offrir, proposer; **"on ~"** (Comm) "en
promotion"

offhand [ɔf'hænd] adj désinvolte
▷ adv spontanément

office ['ɔfis] n (place) bureau m;
(position) charge f, fonction f;
doctor's ~ (US) cabinet (médical);
to take ~ entrer en fonctions;
office block, (US)**office building**
n immeuble m de bureaux; **office
hours** npl heures fpl de bureau; (US
Med) heures de consultation

officer ['ɔfisə'] n (Mil etc) officier m;
(also: **police ~**) agent m (de police);
(of organization) membre m du bureau
directeur

office worker n employé(e) de bureau

official [ə'fɪʃl] adj (authorized)
officiel(le) ▷ n officiel m; (civil servant)
fonctionnaire m/f; (of railways, post
office, town hall) employé(e)

off: off-licence n (BRIT: shop) débit
m de vins et de spiritueux; **off-line**
adj (Comput) (en mode) autonome
(: switched off) non connecté(e);
off-peak adj aux heures creuses;
(electricity, ticket) au tarif heures
creuses; **off-putting** adj (BRIT)
(remark) rébarbatif(-ive); (person)
rebutant(e), peu engageant(e); **off-
season** adj, adv hors-saison inv

offset ['ɔfsɛt] vt (irreg: like **set**)
(counteract) contrebalancer,
compenser

offshore [ɔfʃɔːʳ] adj (breeze) de terre; (island) proche du littoral; (fishing) côtier(-ière)

offside ['ɔf'saɪd] adj (Sport) hors jeu; (Aut: in Britain) de droite; (: in US, Europe) de gauche

offspring ['ɔfsprɪŋ] n progéniture f

often ['ɔfn] adv souvent; **how ~ do you go?** vous y allez tous les combien?; **every so ~** de temps en temps, de temps à autre

oh [əu] excl ô!, oh!, ah!

oil [ɔɪl] n huile f; (petroleum) pétrole m; (for central heating) mazout m ▷ vt (machine) graisser; **oil filter** n (Aut) filtre m à huile; **oil painting** n peinture f à l'huile; **oil refinery** n raffinerie f de pétrole; **oil rig** n derrick m; (at sea) plate-forme pétrolière; **oil slick** n nappe f de mazout; **oil tanker** n (ship) pétrolier m; (truck) camion-citerne m; **oil well** n puits m de pétrole; **oily** adj huileux(-euse); (food) gras(se)

ointment ['ɔɪntmənt] n onguent m

O.K., okay ['əu'keɪ] (inf) excl d'accord! ▷ vt approuver, donner son accord à ▷ adj (not bad) pas mal; **is it ~?, are you ~?** ça va?

old [əuld] adj vieux (vieille); (person) vieux, âgé(e); (former) ancien(ne), vieux; **how ~ are you?** quel âge avez-vous?; **he's 10 years ~** il a 10 ans, il est âgé de 10 ans; **~er brother/ sister** frère/sœur aîné(e); **old age** n vieillesse f; **old-age pensioner** n (BRIT) retraité(e); **old-fashioned** adj démodé(e); (person) vieux jeu inv; **old people's home** n (esp BRIT) maison f de retraite

olive ['ɔlɪv] n (fruit) olive f; (tree) olivier m ▷ adj (also: **~-green**) (vert) olive inv; **olive oil** n huile f d'olive

Olympic [əu'lɪmpɪk] adj olympique; **the ~ Games, the ~s** les Jeux mpl olympiques

omelet(te) ['ɔmlɪt] n omelette f

omen ['əumən] n présage m

ominous ['ɔmɪnəs] adj menaçant(e), inquiétant(e); (event) de mauvais augure

omit [əu'mɪt] vt omettre

KEYWORD

on [ɔn] prep **1** (indicating position) sur; **on the table** sur la table; **on the wall** sur le or au mur; **on the left** à gauche

2 (indicating means, method, condition etc): **on foot** à pied; **on the train/ plane** (be) dans le train/l'avion; (go) en train/avion; **on the telephone/ radio/television** au téléphone/à la radio/à la télévision; **to be on drugs** se droguer; **on holiday**, (US) **on vacation** en vacances

3 (referring to time): **on Friday** vendredi; **on Fridays** le vendredi; **on June 20th** le 20 juin; **a week on Friday** vendredi en huit; **on arrival** à l'arrivée; **on seeing this** en voyant cela

4 (about, concerning) sur, de; **a book on Balzac/physics** un livre sur Balzac/de physique

▶ adv **1** (referring to dress): **to have one's coat on** avoir (mis) son manteau; **to put one's coat on** mettre son manteau; **what's she got on?** qu'est-ce qu'elle porte?

2 (referring to covering): **screw the lid on tightly** vissez bien le couvercle

3 (further, continuously): **to walk** etc **on** continuer à marcher etc; **from that day on** depuis ce jour

▶ adj **1** (in operation: machine) en marche; (: radio, TV, light) allumé(e); (: tap, gas) ouvert(e); (: brakes) mis(e); **is the meeting still on?** (not cancelled) est-ce que la réunion a bien lieu?; **when is this film on?** quand passe ce film?

2 (inf): **that's not on!** (not acceptable) cela ne se fait pas!; (not possible) pas question!

once [wʌns] *adv* une fois; *(formerly)*
autrefois ▷ *conj* une fois que + *sub*;
~ he had left/it was done une fois
qu'il fut parti/ que ce fut terminé;
at ~ tout de suite, immédiatement;
(simultaneously) à la fois; **all at ~** *adv*
tout d'un coup; **~ a week** une fois par
semaine; **~ more** encore une fois;
~ and for all une fois pour toutes;
~ upon a time there was ... il y avait
une fois ..., il était une fois ...

oncoming ['ɔnkʌmɪŋ] *adj* (*traffic*)
venant en sens inverse

KEYWORD

one [wʌn] *num* un(e); **one hundred
and fifty** cent cinquante; **one by
one** un(e) à *or* par un(e); **one day**
un jour
▷ *adj* **1** *(sole)* seul(e), unique; **the
one book which** l'unique *or* le seul
livre qui; **the one man who** le seul
(homme) qui
2 *(same)* même; **they came in the
one car** ils sont venus dans la même
voiture
▷ *pron* **1: this one** celui-ci (celle-ci);
that one celui-là (celle-là); **I've
already got one/a red one** j'en ai
déjà un(e)/un(e) rouge; **which one
do you want?** lequel voulez-vous?
2: one another l'un(e) l'autre; **to
look at one another** se regarder
3 *(impersonal)* on; **one never knows**
on ne sait jamais; **to cut one's finger**
se couper le doigt; **one needs to eat**
il faut manger

one-off [wʌn'ɔf] *n* (*BRIT inf*)
exemplaire *m* unique
oneself [wʌn'sɛlf] *pron* se; *(after prep,
also emphatic)* soi-même; **to hurt ~**
se faire mal; **to keep sth for ~** garder
qch pour soi; **to talk to ~** se parler à
soi-même; **by ~** tout seul
one: one-shot [wʌn'ʃɔt] (*US*) *n*
= **one-off**; **one-sided** *adj* (*argument,*

decision) unilatéral(e); **one-to-one**
adj (*relationship*) univoque; **one-way**
adj (*street, traffic*) à sens unique
ongoing ['ɔngəʊɪŋ] *adj* en cours;
(relationship) suivi(e)
onion ['ʌnjən] *n* oignon *m*
on-line ['ɔnlaɪn] *adj* (*Comput*) en ligne
(*: switched on*) connecté(e)
onlooker ['ɔnlʊkəʳ] *n*
spectateur(-trice)
only ['əʊnlɪ] *adv* seulement ▷ *adj*
seul(e), unique ▷ *conj* seulement,
mais; **an ~ child** un enfant unique;
not ~ ... but also non seulement
... mais aussi; **I ~ took one** j'en ai
seulement pris un, je n'en ai pris qu'un
on-screen [ɔn'skriːn] *adj* à l'écran
onset ['ɔnsɛt] *n* début *m*; (*of winter, old
age*) approche *f*
onto ['ɔntu] *prep* sur
onward(s) ['ɔnwəd(z)] *adv* (*move*) en
avant; **from that time ~** à partir de
ce moment
oops [ups] *excl* houp!
ooze [uːz] *vi* suinter
opaque [əʊ'peɪk] *adj* opaque
open ['əʊpn] *adj* ouvert(e); *(car)*
découvert(e); *(road, view)* dégagé(e);
(meeting) public(-ique); *(admiration)*
manifeste ▷ *vt* ouvrir ▷ *vi* (*flower,
eyes, door, debate*) s'ouvrir; *(shop,
bank, museum*) ouvrir; *(book etc:
commence*) commencer, débuter;
is it ~ to public? est-ce ouvert au
public?; **what time do you ~?** à
quelle heure ouvrez-vous?; **in the ~
(air)** en plein air; **open up** *vt* ouvrir;
(blocked road) dégager ▷ *vi* s'ouvrir;
open-air *adj* en plein air; **opening** *n*
ouverture *f*; *(opportunity)* occasion
f; *(work)* débouché *m*; *(job)* poste
vacant; **opening hours** *npl* heures
fpl d'ouverture; **open learning** *n*
enseignement universitaire à la carte,
notamment par correspondance;
(distance learning) télé-enseignement
m; **openly** *adv* ouvertement;
open-minded *adj* à l'esprit ouvert;

open-necked *adj* à col ouvert;
open-plan *adj* sans cloisons; **Open University** *n* (BRIT) *cours universitaires par correspondance*

⊛ **OPEN UNIVERSITY**
⊛
⊛ L'*Open University* a été fondée en
⊛ 1969. L'enseignement comprend
⊛ des cours (certaines plages horaires
⊛ sont réservées à cet effet à la
⊛ télévision et à la radio), des devoirs
⊛ qui sont envoyés par l'étudiant
⊛ à son directeur ou sa directrice
⊛ d'études, et un séjour obligatoire en
⊛ université d'été. Il faut préparer un
⊛ certain nombre d'unités de valeur
⊛ pendant une période de temps
⊛ déterminée et obtenir la moyenne
⊛ à un certain nombre d'entre elles
⊛ pour recevoir le diplôme visé.

opera ['ɔpərə] *n* opéra *m*; **opera house** *n* opéra *m*; **opera singer** *n* chanteur(-euse) d'opéra
operate ['ɔpəreɪt] *vt* (*machine*) faire marcher, faire fonctionner ▷ *vi* fonctionner; **to ~ on sb (for)** (*Med*) opérer qn (de)
operating room *n* (US Med) salle *f* d'opération
operating theatre *n* (BRIT Med) salle *f* d'opération
operation [ɔpə'reɪʃən] *n* opération *f*; (*of machine*) fonctionnement *m*; **to have an ~ (for)** se faire opérer (de); **to be in ~** (*machine*) être en service; (*system*) être en vigueur; **operational** *adj* opérationnel(le); (*ready for use*) en état de marche
operative ['ɔpərətɪv] *adj* (*measure*) en vigueur ▷ *n* (*in factory*) ouvrier(-ière)
operator ['ɔpəreɪtə'] *n* (*of machine*) opérateur(-trice); (*Tel*) téléphoniste *m/f*
opinion [ə'pɪnjən] *n* opinion *f*, avis *m*; **in my ~** à mon avis; **opinion poll** *n* sondage *m* d'opinion

opponent [ə'pəunənt] *n* adversaire *m/f*
opportunity [ɔpə'tjuːnɪtɪ] *n* occasion *f*; **to take the ~ to do** *or* **of doing** profiter de l'occasion pour faire
oppose [ə'pəuz] *vt* s'opposer à; **to be ~d to sth** être opposé(e) à qch; **as ~d to** par opposition à
opposite ['ɔpəzɪt] *adj* opposé(e); (*house etc*) d'en face ▷ *adv* en face ▷ *prep* en face de ▷ *n* opposé *m*, contraire *m*; (*of word*) contraire
opposition [ɔpə'zɪʃən] *n* opposition *f*
oppress [ə'prɛs] *vt* opprimer
opt [ɔpt] *vi*: **to ~ for** opter pour; **to ~ to do** choisir de faire; **opt out** *vi*: **to ~ out of** choisir de ne pas participer à *or* de ne pas faire
optician [ɔp'tɪʃən] *n* opticien(ne)
optimism ['ɔptɪmɪzəm] *n* optimisme *m*
optimist ['ɔptɪmɪst] *n* optimiste *m/f*; **optimistic** [ɔptɪ'mɪstɪk] *adj* optimiste
optimum ['ɔptɪməm] *adj* optimum
option ['ɔpʃən] *n* choix *m*, option *f*; (*Scol*) matière *f* à option; **optional** *adj* facultatif(-ive)
or [ɔː'] *conj* ou; (*with negative*): **he hasn't seen or heard anything** il n'a rien vu ni entendu; **or else** sinon; ou bien
oral ['ɔːrəl] *adj* oral(e) ▷ *n* oral *m*
orange ['ɔrɪndʒ] *n* (*fruit*) orange *f* ▷ *adj* orange *inv*; **orange juice** *n* jus *m* d'orange
orbit ['ɔːbɪt] *n* orbite *f* ▷ *vt* graviter autour de
orchard ['ɔːtʃəd] *n* verger *m*
orchestra ['ɔːkɪstrə] *n* orchestre *m*; (US: *seating*) (fauteuils *mpl* d')orchestre
orchid ['ɔːkɪd] *n* orchidée *f*
ordeal [ɔː'diːl] *n* épreuve *f*
order ['ɔːdə'] *n* ordre *m*; (*Comm*) commande *f* ▷ *vt* ordonner; (*Comm*) commander; **in ~** en ordre; (*document*) en règle; **out of ~** (*not in correct order*) en désordre;

o

(*machine*) hors service; (*telephone*) en dérangement; **a machine in working ~** une machine en état de marche; **in ~ to do/that** pour faire/ que + *sub*; **could I ~ now, please?** je peux commander, s'il vous plaît?; **to be on ~** être en commande; **to ~ sb to do** ordonner à qn de faire; **order form** *n* bon *m* de commande; **orderly** *n* (*Mil*) ordonnance *f*; (*Med*) garçon *m* de salle ▷ *adj* (*room*) en ordre; (*mind*) méthodique; (*person*) qui a le l'ordre

ordinary [ˈɔːdnrɪ] *adj* ordinaire, normal(e); (*pej*) ordinaire, quelconque; **out of the ~** exceptionnel(le)

ore [ɔːr] *n* minerai *m*

oregano [ɒrɪˈgɑːnəʊ] *n* origan *m*

organ [ˈɔːgən] *n* organe *m*; (*Mus*) orgue *m*, orgues *fpl*; **organic** [ɔːˈgænɪk] *adj* organique; (*crops etc*) biologique, naturel(le); **organism** *n* organisme *m*

organization [ɔːgənaɪˈzeɪʃən] *n* organisation *f*

organize [ˈɔːgənaɪz] *vt* organiser; **organized** [ˈɔːgənaɪzd] *adj* (*planned*) organisé(e); (*efficient*) bien organisé; **organizer** *n* organisateur(-trice)

orgasm [ˈɔːgæzəm] *n* orgasme *m*

orgy [ˈɔːdʒɪ] *n* orgie *f*

oriental [ɔːrɪˈɛntl] *adj* oriental(e)

orientation [ɔːrɪɛnˈteɪʃən] *n* (*attitudes*) tendance *f*; (*in job*) orientation *f*; (*of building*) orientation, exposition *f*

origin [ˈɒrɪdʒɪn] *n* origine *f*

original [əˈrɪdʒɪnl] *adj* original(e); (*earliest*) originel(le) ▷ *n* original *m*; **originally** *adv* (*at first*) à l'origine

originate [əˈrɪdʒɪneɪt] *vi*: **to ~ from** être originaire de; (*suggestion*) provenir de; **to ~ in** (*custom*) prendre naissance dans, avoir son origine dans

Orkney [ˈɔːknɪ] *n* (*also*: **the ~s, the ~ Islands**) les Orcades *fpl*

ornament [ˈɔːnəmənt] *n* ornement *m*; (*trinket*) bibelot *m*; **ornamental** [ɔːnəˈmɛntl] *adj* décoratif(-ive); (*garden*) d'agrément

ornate [ɔːˈneɪt] *adj* très orné(e)

orphan [ˈɔːfn] *n* orphelin(e)

orthodox [ˈɔːθədɒks] *adj* orthodoxe

orthopaedic, (*us*) **orthopedic** [ɔːθəˈpiːdɪk] *adj* orthopédique

osteopath [ˈɒstɪəpæθ] *n* ostéopathe *m/f*

ostrich [ˈɒstrɪtʃ] *n* autruche *f*

other [ˈʌðər] *adj* autre ▷ *pron*: **the ~ (one)** l'autre; **~s** (*other people*) d'autres ▷ *adv*: **~ than** autrement que; à part; **the ~ day** l'autre jour; **otherwise** *adv*, *conj* autrement

Ottawa [ˈɒtəwə] *n* Ottawa

otter [ˈɒtər] *n* loutre *f*

ouch [autʃ] *excl* aïe!

ought [ɔːt] *aux vb*: **I ~ to do it** je devrais le faire, il faudrait que je le fasse; **this ~ to have been corrected** cela aurait dû être corrigé; **he ~ to win** (*probability*) il devrait gagner

ounce [auns] *n* once *f* (28.35g; 16 in a pound)

our [ˈauər] *adj* notre, nos *pl*; *see also* **my**; **ours** *pron* le (la) nôtre, les nôtres; *see also* **mine¹**; **ourselves** *pl pron* (*reflexive, after preposition*) nous; (*emphatic*) nous-mêmes; *see also* **oneself**

oust [aust] *vt* évincer

out [aut] *adv* dehors; (*published, not at home etc*) sorti(e); (*light, fire*) éteint(e); **~ there** là-bas; **he's ~** (*absent*) il est sorti; **to be ~ in one's calculations** s'être trompé dans ses calculs; **to run/back etc ~** sortir en courant/en reculant *etc*; **~ loud** *adv* à haute voix; **~ of** *prep* (*outside*) en dehors de; (*because of: anger etc*) par; (*from among*): **10 ~ of 10** 10 sur 10; (*without*): **~ of petrol** sans essence, à court d'essence; **~ of order** (*machine*) en panne; (*Tel: line*) en dérangement; **outback** n (in Australia) intérieur m; **outbound** adj: **outbound (from/for)** en partance (de/pour); **outbreak** n (of violence) éruption f, explosion f; (of disease) de nombreux cas; **the outbreak of war south of the border** la guerre qui s'est déclarée au sud de la frontière; **outburst** n explosion f, accès m; **outcast** n exilé(e); (socially) paria m; **outcome** n issue f, résultat m; **outcry** n tollé (général); **outdated** adj démodé(e); **outdoor** adj de or en plein air; **outdoors** adv dehors; au grand air

outer ['autər] adj extérieur(e); **outer space** n espace m cosmique

outfit ['autfɪt] n (clothes) tenue f

out: outgoing adj (president, tenant) sortant(e); (character) ouvert(e), extraverti(e); **outgoings** npl (BRIT: expenses) dépenses fpl; **outhouse** n appentis m, remise f

outing ['autɪŋ] n sortie f; excursion f

out: outlaw n hors-la-loi m inv ▷ vt (person) mettre hors la loi; (practice) proscrire; **outlay** n dépenses fpl; (investment) mise f de fonds; **outlet** n (for liquid etc) issue f, sortie f; (for emotion) exutoire m; (also: **retail outlet**) point m de vente; (US Elec) prise f de courant; **outline** n (shape) contour m; (summary) esquisse f, grandes lignes ▷ vt (fig: theory, plan) exposer à grands traits; **outlook** n perspective f; (point of view) attitude f; **outnumber** vt surpasser en nombre; **out-of-date** adj (passport, ticket) périmé(e); (theory, idea) dépassé(e); (custom) désuet(-ète); (clothes) démodé(e); **out-of-doors** adv = **outdoors**; **out-of-the-way** adj loin de tout; **out-of-town** adj (shopping centre etc) en périphérie; **outpatient** n malade m/f en consultation externe; **outpost** n avant-poste m; **output** n rendement m, production f; (Comput) sortie f ▷ vt (Comput) sortir

outrage ['autreɪdʒ] n (anger) indignation f; (violent act) atrocité f, acte m de violence; (scandal) scandale m ▷ vt outrager; **outrageous** [aut'reɪdʒəs] adj atroce; (scandalous) scandaleux(-euse)

outright adv [aut'raɪt] complètement; (deny, refuse) catégoriquement; (ask) carrément; (kill) sur le coup ▷ adj ['autraɪt] complet(-ète); catégorique

outset ['autset] n début m

outside [aut'saɪd] n extérieur m ▷ adj extérieur(e) ▷ adv (au) dehors, à l'extérieur ▷ prep hors de, à l'extérieur de; (in front of) devant; **at the ~** (fig) au plus or maximum; **outside lane** n (Aut: in Britain) voie f de droite; (: in US, Europe) voie de gauche; **outside line** n (Tel) ligne extérieure; **outsider** n (stranger) étranger(-ère)

out: outsize adj énorme; (clothes) grande taille inv; **outskirts** npl faubourgs mpl; **outspoken** adj très franc (franche); **outstanding** adj remarquable, exceptionnel(le); (unfinished: work, business) en suspens, en souffrance; (debt) impayé(e); (problem) non réglé(e)

outward ['autwəd] adj (sign, appearances) extérieur(e); (journey) (d')aller; **outwards** adv (esp BRIT) = **outward**

outweigh [aut'weɪ] vt l'emporter sur

oval ['əuvl] adj, n ovale m

ovary ['əuvəri] n ovaire m

oven ['ʌvn] n four m; **oven glove** n gant m de cuisine; **ovenproof** adj allant au four; **oven-ready** adj prêt(e) à cuire

over ['əuvər] adv (par-)dessus ▷ adj (finished) fini(e), terminé(e); (too much) en plus ▷ prep sur; par-dessus; (above) au-dessus de; (on the other side of) de l'autre côté de; (more than) plus de; (during) pendant; (about, concerning): **they fell out ~ money/her** ils se sont brouillés pour des

questions d'argent/à cause d'elle;
~ here ici; **~ there** là-bas; **all ~**
(everywhere) partout; **~ and ~ (again)**
à plusieurs reprises; **~ and above**
en plus de; **to ask sb ~** inviter qn (à
passer); **to fall ~** tomber; **to turn
sth ~** retourner qch

overall ['əʊvərɔːl] adj (length)
total(e); (study, impression)
d'ensemble ▷ n (BRIT) blouse f ▷ adv
[əʊvər'ɔːl] dans l'ensemble, en
général; **overalls** npl (boiler suit) bleus
mpl (de travail)

overboard ['əʊvəbɔːd] adv (Naut)
par-dessus bord

overcame [əʊvə'keɪm] pt of
overcome

overcast ['əʊvəkɑːst] adj couvert(e)

overcharge [əʊvə'tʃɑːdʒ] vt: **to ~ sb
for sth** faire payer qch trop cher à qn

overcoat ['əʊvəkəʊt] n pardessus m

overcome [əʊvə'kʌm] vt (irreg:
like **come**) (defeat) triompher
de; (difficulty) surmonter ▷ adj
(emotionally) bouleversé(e); **~ with
grief** accablé(e) de douleur

over: overcrowded adj bondé(e);
(city, country) surpeuplé(e); **overdo**
vt (irreg: like **do**) exagérer; (overcook)
trop cuire; **to overdo it, to overdo
things** (work too hard) en faire
trop, se surmener; **overdone**
[əʊvə'dʌn] adj (vegetables, steak)
trop cuit(e); **overdose** n dose
excessive; **overdraft** n découvert
m; **overdrawn** adj (account) à
découvert; **overdue** adj en retard;
(bill) impayé(e); (change) qui tarde;
overestimate vt surestimer

overflow vi [əʊvə'fləʊ] déborder
▷ n ['əʊvəfləʊ] (also: **~ pipe**) tuyau m
d'écoulement, trop-plein m

overgrown [əʊvə'grəʊn] adj (garden)
envahi(e) par la végétation

overhaul vt [əʊvə'hɔːl] réviser ▷ n
['əʊvəhɔːl] révision f

overhead adv [əʊvə'hɛd] au-dessus
▷ adj ['əʊvəhɛd] aérien(ne); (lighting)

vertical(e) ▷ n ['əʊvəhɛd] (US)
= **overheads**; **overhead projector**
n rétroprojecteur m; **overheads** npl
(BRIT) frais généraux

over: overhear vt (irreg: like **hear**)
entendre (par hasard); **overheat**
vi (engine) chauffer; **overland** adj,
adv par voie de terre; **overlap** vi se
chevaucher; **overleaf** adv au verso;
overload vt surcharger; **overlook** vt
(have view of) donner sur; (miss) oublier,
négliger; (forgive) fermer les yeux sur

overnight adv [əʊvə'naɪt] (happen)
durant la nuit; (fig) soudain ▷ adj
['əʊvənaɪt] d'une(e) nuit;
soudain(e); **to stay ~ (with sb)**
passer la nuit (chez qn); **overnight
bag** n nécessaire m de voyage

overpass ['əʊvəpɑːs] n (US: for cars)
pont autoroutier; (for pedestrians)
passerelle f, pont m

overpower [əʊvə'paʊər] vt vaincre;
(fig) accabler; **overpowering** adj
irrésistible; (heat, stench) suffocant(e)

over: overreact [əʊvəri:'ækt] vi
réagir de façon excessive; **overrule**
vt (decision) annuler; (claim) rejeter;
(person) rejeter l'avis de; **overrun**
vt (irreg: like **run**) (Mil: country etc)
occuper; (time limit etc) dépasser ▷ vi
dépasser le temps imparti

overseas [əʊvə'siːz] adv outre-mer;
(abroad) à l'étranger ▷ adj (trade)
extérieur(e); (visitor) étranger(-ère)

oversee [əʊvə'siː] vt (irreg: like **see**)
surveiller

overshadow [əʊvə'ʃædəʊ] vt (fig)
éclipser

oversight ['əʊvəsaɪt] n omission
f, oubli m

oversleep [əʊvə'sliːp] vi (irreg: like
sleep) se réveiller (trop) tard

overspend [əʊvə'spɛnd] vi (irreg: like
spend) dépenser de trop

overt [əʊ'vɜːt] adj non dissimulé(e)

overtake [əʊvə'teɪk] vt (irreg: like
take) dépasser; (BRIT Aut) dépasser,
doubler

over: overthrow vt (irreg: like **throw**)
(government) renverser; **overtime**
n heures fpl supplémentaires;
overturn vt renverser; (decision,
plan) annuler ▷ vi se retourner;
overweight adj (person) trop
gros(se); **overwhelm** vt (subj:
emotion) accabler, submerger; (enemy,
opponent) écraser; **overwhelming**
adj (victory, defeat) écrasant(e); (desire)
irrésistible

owe [əu] vt devoir; **to ~ sb sth, to ~
sth to sb** devoir qch à qn; **how much
do I ~ you?** combien est-ce que je
vous dois?; **owing to** prep à cause de,
en raison de

owl [aul] n hibou m

own [əun] vt posséder ▷ adj propre;
a room of my ~ une chambre à moi,
ma propre chambre; **to get one's
~ back** prendre sa revanche; **on
one's ~** tout(e) seul(e); **own up** vi
avouer; **owner** n propriétaire m/f;
ownership n possession f

ox (pl **oxen**) [ɔks, 'ɔksn] n bœuf m

Oxbridge ['ɔksbrɪdʒ] n (BRIT) les
universités d'Oxford et de Cambridge

oxen ['ɔksən] npl of **ox**

oxygen ['ɔksɪdʒən] n oxygène m

oyster ['ɔɪstər] n huître f

oz. abbr = **ounce; ounces**

ozone ['əuzəun] n ozone m; **ozone
friendly** adj qui n'attaque pas or qui
préserve la couche d'ozone; **ozone
layer** n couche f d'ozone

p

p abbr (BRIT) = **penny; pence**

P.A. n abbr = **personal assistant;
public address system**

p.a. abbr = **per annum**

pace [peɪs] n pas m; (speed) allure f;
vitesse f ▷ vi: **to ~ up and down** faire
les cent pas; **to keep ~ with** aller à
la même vitesse que; (events) se tenir
au courant de; **pacemaker** n (Med)
stimulateur m cardiaque; (Sport: also:
pacesetter) meneur(-euse) de train

Pacific [pə'sɪfɪk] n: **the ~ (Ocean)** le
Pacifique, l'océan m Pacifique

pacifier ['pæsɪfaɪər] n (us: dummy)
tétine f

pack [pæk] n paquet m; (of hounds)
meute f; (of thieves, wolves etc) bande
f; (of cards) jeu m; (us: of cigarettes)
paquet; (back pack) sac m à dos ▷ vt
(goods) empaqueter, emballer; (in
suitcase etc) emballer; (box) remplir;
(cram) entasser ▷ vi: **to ~ (one's
bags)** faire ses bagages; **pack in** (BRIT

inf) *vi* (*machine*) tomber en panne ▷ *vt* (*boyfriend*) plaquer; **~ it in!** laisse tomber!; **pack off** *vt*: **to ~ sb off to** expédier qn à; **pack up** *vi* (BRIT *inf*: *machine*) tomber en panne; (*person*) se tirer ▷ *vt* (*belongings*) ranger; (*goods, presents*) empaqueter, emballer

package ['pækɪdʒ] *n* paquet *m*; (*also*: **~ deal**) (*agreement*) marché global; (*purchase*) forfait *m*; (*Comput*) progiciel *m* ▷ *vt* (*goods*) conditionner; **package holiday** *n* (BRIT) vacances organisées; **package tour** *n* voyage organisé

packaging ['pækɪdʒɪŋ] *n* (*wrapping materials*) emballage *m*

packed [pækt] *adj* (*crowded*) bondé(e); **packed lunch** (BRIT) *n* repas froid

packet ['pækɪt] *n* paquet *m*

packing ['pækɪŋ] *n* emballage *m*

pact [pækt] *n* pacte *m*, traité *m*

pad [pæd] *n* bloc(-notes *m*) *m*; (*to prevent friction*) tampon *m* ▷ *vt* rembourrer; **padded** *adj* (*jacket*) matelassé(e); (*bra*) rembourré(e)

paddle ['pædl] *n* (*oar*) pagaie *f*; (US: *for table tennis*) raquette *f* de ping-pong ▷ *vi* (*with feet*) barboter, faire trempette ▷ *vt*: **to ~ a canoe** *etc* pagayer; **paddling pool** *n* petit bassin

paddock ['pædək] *n* enclos *m*; (*Racing*) paddock *m*

padlock ['pædlɔk] *n* cadenas *m*

paedophile, (US) **pedophile** ['piːdəʊfaɪl] *n* pédophile *m*

page [peɪdʒ] *n* (*of book*) page *f*; (*also*: **~ boy**) groom *m*, chasseur *m*; (*at wedding*) garçon *m* d'honneur ▷ *vt* (*in hotel etc*) (faire) appeler

pager ['peɪdʒə'] *n* bip *m* (*inf*), Alphapage® *m*

paid [peɪd] *pt, pp of* **pay** ▷ *adj* (*work, official*) rémunéré(e); (*holiday*) payé(e); **to put ~ to** (BRIT) mettre fin à, mettre par terre

pain [peɪn] *n* douleur *f*; (*inf*: *nuisance*) plaie *f*; **to be in ~** souffrir, avoir mal; **to take ~s to do** se donner du mal pour faire; **painful** *adj* douloureux(-euse); (*difficult*) difficile, pénible; **painkiller** *n* calmant *m*, analgésique *m*; **painstaking** ['peɪnzteɪkɪŋ] *adj* (*person*) soigneux(-euse); (*work*) soigné(e)

paint [peɪnt] *n* peinture *f* ▷ *vt* peindre; **to ~ the door blue** peindre la porte en bleu; **paintbrush** *n* pinceau *m*; **painter** *n* peintre *m*; **painting** *n* peinture *f*; (*picture*) tableau *m*

pair [peə'] *n* (*of shoes, gloves etc*) paire *f*; (*of people*) couple *m*; **~ of scissors** (paire de) ciseaux *mpl*; **~ of trousers** pantalon *m*

pajamas [pə'dʒɑːməz] *npl* (US) pyjama *m*

Pakistan [pɑːkɪ'stɑːn] *n* Pakistan *m*; **Pakistani** *adj* pakistanais(e) ▷ *n* Pakistanais(e)

pal [pæl] *n* (*inf*) copain (copine)

palace ['pæləs] *n* palais *m*

pale [peɪl] *adj* pâle; **~ blue** *adj* bleu pâle *inv*

Palestine ['pælɪstaɪn] *n* Palestine *f*; **Palestinian** [pælɪs'tɪnɪən] *adj* palestinien(ne) ▷ *n* Palestinien(ne)

palm [pɑːm] *n* (*Anat*) paume *f*; (*also*: **~ tree**) palmier *m* ▷ *vt*: **to ~ sth off on sb** (*inf*) refiler qch à qn

pamper ['pæmpə'] *vt* gâter, dorloter

pamphlet ['pæmflət] *n* brochure *f*

pan [pæn] *n* (*also*: **sauce~**) casserole *f*; (*also*: **frying ~**) poêle *f*

pancake ['pænkeɪk] *n* crêpe *f*

panda ['pændə] *n* panda *m*

pandemic [pæn'dɛmɪk] *n* pandémie *f*

pane [peɪn] *n* carreau *m* (de fenêtre), vitre *f*

panel ['pænl] *n* (*of wood, cloth etc*) panneau *m*; (*Radio, TV*) panel *m*, invités *mpl*; (*for interview, exams*) jury *m*

panhandler ['pænhændlə'] *n* (US *inf*) mendiant(e)

panic ['pænɪk] *n* panique *f*, affolement *m* ▷ *vi* s'affoler, paniquer

panorama [pænə'rɑ:mə] n
panorama m
pansy ['pænzɪ] n (Bot) pensée f
pant [pænt] vi haleter
panther ['pænθə^r] n panthère f
panties ['pæntɪz] npl slip m, culotte f
pantomime ['pæntəmaɪm] n (BRIT)
spectacle m de Noël

○ **PANTOMIME**
○
○ Une *pantomime* (à ne pas confondre
○ avec le mot tel qu'on l'utilise
○ en français), que l'on appelle
○ également de façon familière
○ "panto", est un genre de farce où le
○ personnage principal est souvent
○ un jeune garçon et où il y a toujours
○ une "dame", c'est-à-dire une vieille
○ femme jouée par un homme, et
○ un méchant. La plupart du temps,
○ l'histoire est basée sur un conte de
○ fées comme Cendrillon ou Le Chat
○ botté, et le public est encouragé
○ à participer en prévenant le héros
○ d'un danger imminent. Ce genre
○ de spectacle, qui s'adresse surtout
○ aux enfants, vise également un
○ public d'adultes au travers des
○ nombreuses plaisanteries faisant
○ allusion à des faits d'actualité.

pants [pænts] npl (BRIT: woman's)
culotte f, slip m; (: man's) slip, caleçon
m; (US: trousers) pantalon m
pantyhose ['pæntɪhəuz] npl (US)
collant m
paper ['peɪpə^r] n papier m; (also:
wall~) papier peint; (also: **news~**)
journal m; (academic essay) article
m; (exam) épreuve écrite ▷ adj en or
de papier ▷ vt tapisser (de papier
peint); **papers** npl (also: **identity ~s**)
papiers mpl (d'identité); **paperback**
n livre broché or non relié; (small) livre
m de poche; **paper bag** n sac m en
papier; **paper clip** n trombone m;
paper shop n (BRIT) marchand m de

journaux; **paperwork** n papiers mpl;
(pej) paperasserie f
paprika ['pæprɪkə] n paprika m
par [pɑ:^r] n pair m; (Golf) normale f du
parcours; **on a ~ with** à égalité avec,
au même niveau que
paracetamol [pærə'si:təmɒl] n
(BRIT) paracétamol m
parachute ['pærəʃu:t] n
parachute m
parade [pə'reɪd] n défilé m ▷ vt (fig)
faire étalage de ▷ vi défiler
paradise ['pærədaɪs] n paradis m
paradox ['pærədɒks] n paradoxe m
paraffin ['pærəfɪn] n (BRIT): **~ (oil)**
pétrole (lampant)
paragraph ['pærəgrɑ:f] n
paragraphe m
parallel ['pærəlɛl] adj: **~ (with** or **to)**
parallèle (à); (fig) analogue (à) ▷ n
(line) parallèle f; (fig, Geo) parallèle m
paralysed ['pærəlaɪzd] adj
paralysé(e)
paralysis (pl **paralyses**) [pə'rælɪsɪs,
-si:z] n paralysie f
paramedic [pærə'mɛdɪk] n
auxiliaire m/f médical(e)
paranoid ['pærənɔɪd] adj (Psych)
paranoïaque; (neurotic) paranoïde
parasite ['pærəsaɪt] n parasite m
parcel ['pɑ:sl] n paquet m, colis m ▷ vt
(also: **~ up**) empaqueter
pardon ['pɑ:dn] n pardon m; (Law)
grâce f ▷ vt pardonner à; (Law)
gracier; **~!** pardon!; **~ me!** (after
burping etc) excusez-moi!; **I beg your
~!** (I'm sorry) pardon!, je suis désolé!; **(I
beg your) ~?**, (US) **~ me?** (what did you
say?) pardon?
parent ['pɛərənt] n (father) père
m; (mother) mère f; **parents** npl
parents mpl; **parental** [pə'rɛntl] adj
parental(e), des parents
Paris ['pærɪs] n Paris
parish ['pærɪʃ] n paroisse f; (BRIT: civil)
≈ commune f
Parisian [pə'rɪzɪən] adj parisien(ne),
de Paris ▷ n Parisien(ne)

park [pɑːk] n parc m, jardin public
▷ vt garer ▷ vi se garer; **can I ~ here?**
est-ce que je peux me garer ici?
parking ['pɑːkɪŋ] n stationnement
m; **"no ~"** "stationnement interdit";
parking lot n (us) parking m, parc m
de stationnement; **parking meter**
n parc(o)mètre m; **parking ticket**
n P.-V. m

> Be careful not to translate parking
by the French word parking.

parkway ['pɑːkweɪ] n (us) route f
express (en site vert ou aménagé)
parliament ['pɑːləmənt] n
parlement m; **parliamentary**
[pɑːlə'mentərɪ] adj parlementaire
Parmesan [pɑːmɪ'zæn] n (also:
~ cheese) Parmesan m
parole [pə'rəʊl] n: **on ~** en liberté
conditionnelle
parrot ['pærət] n perroquet m
parsley ['pɑːslɪ] n persil m
parsnip ['pɑːsnɪp] n panais m
parson ['pɑːsn] n ecclésiastique m;
(Church of England) pasteur m
part [pɑːt] n partie f; (of machine)
pièce f; (Theat) rôle m; (of serial)
épisode m; (us: in hair) raie f ▷ adv
= **partly** ▷ vt séparer ▷ vi (people) se
séparer; (crowd) s'ouvrir; **to take ~ in**
participer à, prendre part à; **to take**
sb's ~ prendre le parti de qn, prendre
parti pour qn; **for my ~** en ce qui me
concerne; **for the most ~** en grande
partie; dans la plupart des cas; **in ~**
en partie; **to take sth in good/bad**
~ prendre qch du bon/mauvais côté;
part with vt fus (person) se séparer
de; (possessions) se défaire de
partial ['pɑːʃl] adj (incomplete)
partiel(le); **to be ~ to** aimer, avoir un
faible pour
participant [pɑː'tɪsɪpənt] n (in
competition, campaign) participant(e)
participate [pɑː'tɪsɪpeɪt] vi: **to ~**
(in) participer (à), prendre part (à)
particle ['pɑːtɪkl] n particule f; (of
dust) grain m

particular [pə'tɪkjulə^r] adj (specific)
particulier(-ière); (special) particulier,
spécial(e); (fussy) difficile, exigeant(e);
(careful) méticuleux(-euse); **in ~** en
particulier, surtout; **particularly** adv
particulièrement; (in particular) en
particulier; **particulars** npl détails
mpl; (information) renseignements mpl
parting ['pɑːtɪŋ] n séparation f; (BRIT:
in hair) raie f
partition [pɑː'tɪʃən] n (Pol) partition
f, division f; (wall) cloison f
partly ['pɑːtlɪ] adv en partie,
partiellement
partner ['pɑːtnə^r] n (Comm)
associé(e); (Sport) partenaire m/f;
(spouse) conjoint(e); (lover) ami(e); (at
dance) cavalier(-ière); **partnership** n
association f
partridge ['pɑːtrɪdʒ] n perdrix f
part-time ['pɑːt'taɪm] adj, adv à
mi-temps, à temps partiel
party ['pɑːtɪ] n (Pol) parti m;
(celebration) fête f; (: formal) réception
f; (: in evening) soirée f; (group) groupe
m; (Law) partie f
pass [pɑːs] vt (time, object) passer;
(place) passer devant; (friend)
croiser; (exam) être reçu(e) à, réussir;
(overtake) dépasser; (approve)
approuver, accepter ▷ vi passer;
(Scol) être reçu(e) or admis(e), réussir
▷ n (permit) laissez-passer m inv;
(membership card) carte f d'accès
or d'abonnement; (in mountains)
col m; (Sport) passe f; (Scol: also: **~**
mark); **to get a ~** être reçu(e) (sans
mention); **to ~ sb sth** passer qch
à qn; **could you ~ the salt/oil,**
please? pouvez-vous me passer le
sel/l'huile, s'il vous plaît?; **to make**
a ~ at sb (inf) faire des avances à qn;
pass away vi mourir; **pass by** vi
passer ▷ vt (ignore) négliger; **pass on**
vt (hand on): **to ~ on (to)** transmettre
(à); **pass out** vi s'évanouir; **pass over**
vt (ignore) passer sous silence; **pass**
up vt (opportunity) laisser passer;

passable adj (road) praticable; (work) acceptable

> Be careful not to translate to pass an exam by the French expression passer un examen.

passage ['pæsɪdʒ] n (also: **~way**) couloir m; (gen, in book) passage m; (by boat) traversée f

passenger ['pæsɪndʒəʳ] n passager(-ère)

passer-by [pɑːsə'baɪ] n passant(e)

passing place n (Aut) aire f de croisement

passion ['pæʃən] n passion f; **passionate** adj passionné(e); **passion fruit** n fruit m de la passion

passive ['pæsɪv] adj (also: Ling) passif(-ive)

passport ['pɑːspɔːt] n passeport m; **passport control** n contrôle m des passeports; **passport office** n bureau m de délivrance des passeports

password ['pɑːswəːd] n mot m de passe

past [pɑːst] prep (in front of) devant; (further than) au-delà de, plus loin que; après; (later than) après ⊳ adv: **to run ~** passer en courant ⊳ adj passé(e); (president etc) ancien(ne) ⊳ n passé m; **he's ~ forty** il a dépassé la quarantaine, il a plus de or passé quarante ans; **ten/quarter ~ eight** (BRIT) huit heures dix/un or et quart; **for the ~ few/3 days** depuis quelques jours; ces derniers/3 derniers jours

pasta ['pæstə] n pâtes fpl

paste [peɪst] n pâte f; (Culin: meat) pâté m (à tartiner); (: tomato) purée f, concentré m; (glue) colle f (de pâte) ⊳ vt coller

pastel [pæstl] adj pastel inv ⊳ n (Art: pencil) (crayon m) pastel m; (: drawing) (dessin m au) pastel; (colour) ton m pastel inv

pasteurized ['pæstəraɪzd] adj pasteurisé(e)

pastime ['pɑːstaɪm] n passe-temps m inv, distraction f

pastor ['pɑːstəʳ] n pasteur m

pastry ['peɪstrɪ] n pâte f; (cake) pâtisserie f

pasture ['pɑːstʃəʳ] n pâturage m

pasty¹ n ['pæstɪ] petit pâté (en croûte)

pasty² ['peɪstɪ] adj (complexion) terreux(-euse)

pat [pæt] vt donner une petite tape à; (dog) caresser

patch [pætʃ] n (of material) pièce f; (eye patch) cache m; (spot) tache f; (of land) parcelle f; (on tyre) rustine f ⊳ vt (clothes) rapiécer; **a bad ~** (BRIT) une période difficile; **patchy** adj inégal(e); (incomplete) fragmentaire

pâté ['pæteɪ] n pâté m, terrine f

patent ['peɪtnt, US 'pætnt] n brevet m (d'invention) ⊳ vt faire breveter ⊳ adj patent(e), manifeste

paternal [pə'təːnl] adj paternel(le)

paternity leave [pə'təːnɪtɪ-] n congé m de paternité

path [pɑːθ] n chemin m, sentier m; (in garden) allée f; (of missile) trajectoire f

pathetic [pə'θetɪk] adj (pitiful) pitoyable; (very bad) lamentable, minable

pathway ['pɑːθweɪ] n chemin m, sentier m; (in garden) allée f

patience ['peɪʃns] n patience f; (BRIT Cards) réussite f

patient ['peɪʃnt] n malade m/f; (of dentist etc) patient(e) ⊳ adj patient(e)

patio ['pætɪəu] n patio m

patriotic [pætrɪ'ɔtɪk] adj patriotique; (person) patriote

patrol [pə'trəul] n patrouille f ⊳ vt patrouiller dans; **patrol car** n voiture f de police

patron ['peɪtrən] n (in shop) client(e); (of charity) patron(ne); **~ of the arts** mécène m

patronizing ['pætrənaɪzɪŋ] adj condescendant(e)

P

pattern ['pætən] n (Sewing) patron m; (design) motif m; **patterned** adj à motifs

pause [pɔːz] n pause f, arrêt m ▷ vi faire une pause, s'arrêter

pave [peɪv] vt paver, daller; **to ~ the way for** ouvrir la voie à

pavement ['peɪvmənt] n (BRIT) trottoir m; (US) chaussée f

pavilion [pə'vɪlɪən] n pavillon m; (Sport) stand m

paving ['peɪvɪŋ] n (material) pavé m, dalle f

paw [pɔː] n patte f

pawn [pɔːn] n (Chess, also fig) pion m ▷ vt mettre en gage; **pawnbroker** n prêteur m sur gages

pay [peɪ] (pt, pp **paid**) n salaire m; (of manual worker) paie f ▷ vt payer ▷ vi payer; (be profitable) être rentable; **can I ~ by credit card?** est-ce que je peux payer par carte de crédit?; **to ~ attention (to)** prêter attention (à); **to ~ sb a visit** rendre visite à qn; **to ~ one's respects to sb** présenter ses respects à qn; **pay back** vt rembourser; **pay for** vt fus payer; **pay in** vt verser; **pay off** vt (debts) régler, acquitter; (person) rembourser ▷ vi (scheme, decision) se révéler payant(e); **pay out** vt (money) payer, sortir de sa poche; **pay up** vt (amount) payer; **payable** adj payable; **to make a cheque payable to sb** établir un chèque à l'ordre de qn; **pay-as-you-go** adj (mobile phone) à carte prépayée; **payday** n jour m de paie; **pay envelope** n (US) paie f; **payment** n paiement m; règlement m; (of deposit, cheque) versement m; **monthly payment** mensualité f; **payout** n (from insurance) dédommagement m; (in competition) prix m; **pay packet** n (BRIT) paie f; **pay phone** n cabine f téléphonique, téléphone public; **pay raise** n (US) = **pay rise**; **pay rise** n (BRIT) augmentation f (de salaire);

payroll n registre m du personnel; **pay slip** n (BRIT) bulletin m de paie, feuille f de paie; **pay television** n chaînes fpl payantes

PC n abbr = **personal computer**; (BRIT) = **police constable** ▷ adj abbr = **politically correct**

p.c. abbr = **per cent**

pcm n abbr (= per calendar month) par mois

PDA n abbr (= personal digital assistant) agenda m électronique

PE n abbr (= physical education) EPS f

pea [piː] n (petit) pois

peace [piːs] n paix f; (calm) calme m, tranquillité f; **peaceful** adj paisible, calme

peach [piːtʃ] n pêche f

peacock ['piːkɔk] n paon m

peak [piːk] n (mountain) pic m, cime f; (of cap) visière f; (fig: highest level) maximum m; (: of career, fame) apogée m; **peak hours** npl heures fpl d'affluence or de pointe

peanut ['piːnʌt] n arachide f, cacahuète f; **peanut butter** n beurre m de cacahuète

pear [pɛə^r] n poire f

pearl [pəːl] n perle f

peasant ['pɛznt] n paysan(ne)

peat [piːt] n tourbe f

pebble ['pɛbl] n galet m, caillou m

peck [pɛk] vt (also: ~ **at**) donner un coup de bec à; (food) picorer ▷ n coup m de bec; (kiss) bécot m; **peckish** adj (BRIT inf): **I feel peckish** je mangerais bien quelque chose, j'ai la dent

peculiar [pɪ'kjuːlɪə^r] adj (odd) étrange, bizarre, curieux(-euse); (particular) particulier(-ière); **~ to** particulier à

pedal ['pɛdl] n pédale f ▷ vi pédaler

pedestal ['pɛdəstl] n piédestal m

pedestrian [pɪ'dɛstrɪən] n piéton m; **pedestrian crossing** n (BRIT) passage clouté; **pedestrianized** adj: **a pedestrianized street** une rue piétonne; **pedestrian precinct**,

(US) **pedestrian zone** n (BRIT) zone piétonne

pedigree ['pɛdɪɡriː] n ascendance f; (of animal) pedigree m ▷ cpd (animal) de race

pedophile ['piːdəʊfaɪl] (US) n = **paedophile**

pee [piː] vi (inf) faire pipi, pisser

peek [piːk] vi jeter un coup d'œil (furtif)

peel [piːl] n pelure f, épluchure f; (of orange, lemon) écorce f ▷ vt peler, éplucher ▷ vi (paint etc) s'écailler; (wallpaper) se décoller; (skin) peler

peep [piːp] n (look) coup d'œil furtif; (sound) pépiement m ▷ vi jeter un coup d'œil (furtif)

peer [pɪəʳ] vi: **to ~ at** regarder attentivement, scruter ▷ n (noble) pair m; (equal) pair, égal(e)

peg [pɛɡ] n (for coat etc) patère f; (BRIT: also: **clothes ~**) pince f à linge

pelican ['pɛlɪkən] n pélican m; **pelican crossing** n (BRIT Aut) feu m à commande manuelle

pelt [pɛlt] vt: **to ~ sb (with)** bombarder qn (de) ▷ vi (rain) tomber à seaux; (inf: run) courir à toutes jambes ▷ n peau f

pelvis ['pɛlvɪs] n bassin m

pen [pɛn] n (for writing) stylo m; (for sheep) parc m

penalty ['pɛnltɪ] n pénalité f; sanction f; (fine) amende f; (Sport) pénalisation f; (Football) penalty m; (Rugby) pénalité f

pence [pɛns] npl of **penny**

pencil ['pɛnsl] n crayon m; **pencil in** vt noter provisoirement; **pencil case** n trousse f (d'écolier); **pencil sharpener** n taille-crayon(s) m inv

pendant ['pɛndnt] n pendentif m

pending ['pɛndɪŋ] prep en attendant ▷ adj en suspens

penetrate ['pɛnɪtreɪt] vt pénétrer dans; (enemy territory) entrer en

pen friend n (BRIT) correspondant(e)

penguin ['pɛŋɡwɪn] n pingouin m

penicillin [pɛnɪ'sɪlɪn] n pénicilline f

peninsula [pə'nɪnsjulə] n péninsule f

penis ['piːnɪs] n pénis m, verge f

penitentiary [pɛnɪ'tɛnʃərɪ] n (US) prison f

penknife ['pɛnnaɪf] n canif m

penniless ['pɛnɪlɪs] adj sans le sou

penny (pl **pennies** or **pence**) ['pɛnɪ, 'pɛnɪz, pɛns] n (BRIT) penny m; (US) cent m

pen pal n correspondant(e)

pension ['pɛnʃən] n (from company) retraite f; **pensioner** n (BRIT) retraité(e)

pentagon ['pɛntəɡən] n: **the P~** (US Pol) le Pentagone

penthouse ['pɛnthaus] n appartement m (de luxe) en attique

penultimate [pɪ'nʌltɪmət] adj pénultième, avant-dernier(-ière)

people ['piːpl] npl gens mpl; personnes fpl; (inhabitants) population f; (Pol) peuple m ▷ n (nation, race) peuple m; **several ~ came** plusieurs personnes sont venues; **~ say that ...** on dit or les gens disent que ...

pepper ['pɛpəʳ] n poivre m; (vegetable) poivron m ▷ vt (Culin) poivrer; **peppermint** n (sweet) pastille f de menthe

per [pəːʳ] prep par; **~ hour** (miles etc) à l'heure; (fee) (de) l'heure; **~ kilo** etc le kilo etc; **~ day/person** par jour/ personne; **~ annum** par an

perceive [pə'siːv] vt percevoir; (notice) remarquer, s'apercevoir de

per cent adv pour cent

percentage [pə'sɛntɪdʒ] n pourcentage m

perception [pə'sɛpʃən] n perception f; (insight) sensibilité f

perch [pəːtʃ] n (fish) perche f; (for bird) perchoir m ▷ vi (se) percher

percussion [pə'kʌʃən] n percussion f

perennial [pə'rɛnɪəl] n (Bot) (plante f) vivace f, plante pluriannuelle

P

perfect ['pə:fɪkt] *adj* parfait(e)
▷ *n* (*also*: **~ tense**) parfait *m* ▷ *vt*
[pə'fɛkt] (*technique, skill, work of art*)
parfaire; (*method, plan*) mettre au
point; **perfection** [pə'fɛkʃən] *n*
perfection *f*; **perfectly** ['pə:fɪktlɪ]
adv parfaitement

perform [pə'fɔ:m] *vt* (*carry out*)
exécuter; (*concert etc*) jouer,
donner ▷ *vi* (*actor, musician*) jouer;
performance *n* représentation
f, spectacle *m*; (*of an artist*)
interprétation *f*; (*Sport: of car,
engine*) performance *f*; (*of company,
economy*) résultats *mpl*; **performer** *n*
artiste *m/f*

perfume ['pə:fju:m] *n* parfum *m*

perhaps [pə'hæps] *adv* peut-être

perimeter [pə'rɪmɪtə^r] *n* périmètre
m

period ['pɪərɪəd] *n* période *f*; (*Hist*)
époque *f*; (*Scol*) cours *m*; (*full stop*)
point *m*; (*Med*) règles *fpl* ▷ *adj*
(*costume, furniture*) d'époque;
periodical [pɪərɪ'ɔdɪkl] *n* périodique
m; **periodically** *adv* périodiquement

perish ['pɛrɪʃ] *vi* périr, mourir; (*decay*)
se détériorer

perjury ['pə:dʒərɪ] *n* (*Law: in court*)
faux témoignage; (*breach of oath*)
parjure *m*

perk [pə:k] *n* (*inf*) avantage *m*,
à-côté *m*

perm [pə:m] *n* (*for hair*) permanente *f*

permanent ['pə:mənənt] *adj*
permanent(e); **permanently**
adv de façon permanente; (*move
abroad*) définitivement; (*open, closed*)
en permanence; (*tired, unhappy*)
constamment

permission [pə'mɪʃən] *n* permission
f, autorisation *f*

permit *n* ['pə:mɪt] permis *m*

perplex [pə'plɛks] *vt* (*person*) rendre
perplexe

persecute ['pə:sɪkju:t] *vt* persécuter

persecution [pə:sɪ'kju:ʃən] *n*
persécution *f*

persevere [pə:sɪ'vɪə^r] *vi* persévérer

Persian ['pə:ʃən] *adj* persan(e); **the ~
Gulf** le golfe Persique

persist [pə'sɪst] *vi*: **to ~ (in doing)**
persister (à faire), s'obstiner (à faire);
persistent *adj* persistant(e), tenace

person ['pə:sn] *n* personne *f*; **in
~** en personne; **personal** *adj*
personnel(le); **personal assistant** *n*
secrétaire personnel(le); **personal
computer** *n* ordinateur individuel,
PC *m*; **personality** [pə:sə'nælɪtɪ]
n personnalité *f*; **personally** *adv*
personnellement; **to take sth
personally** se sentir visé(e) par
qch; **personal organizer** *n* agenda
(personnel); (*electronic*) agenda
électronique; **personal stereo** *n*
Walkman® *m*, baladeur *m*

personnel [pə:sə'nɛl] *n* personnel *m*

perspective [pə'spɛktɪv] *n*
perspective *f*

perspiration [pə:spɪ'reɪʃən] *n*
transpiration *f*

persuade [pə'sweɪd] *vt*: **to ~ sb to
do sth** persuader qn de faire qch,
amener *or* décider qn à faire qch

persuasion [pə'sweɪʒən] *n*
persuasion *f*; (*creed*) conviction *f*

persuasive [pə'sweɪsɪv] *adj*
persuasif(-ive)

perverse [pə'və:s] *adj* pervers(e);
(*contrary*) entêté(e), contrariant(e)

pervert *n* ['pə:və:t] perverti(e) ▷ *vt*
[pə'və:t] pervertir; (*words*) déformer

pessimism ['pɛsɪmɪzəm] *n*
pessimisme *m*

pessimist ['pɛsɪmɪst] *n* pessimiste
m/f; **pessimistic** [pɛsɪ'mɪstɪk] *adj*
pessimiste

pest [pɛst] *n* animal *m* (*or* insecte *m*)
nuisible; (*fig*) fléau *m*

pester ['pɛstə^r] *vt* importuner,
harceler

pesticide ['pɛstɪsaɪd] *n* pesticide *m*

pet [pɛt] *n* animal familier ▷ *cpd*
(*favourite*) favori(e) ▷ *vt* (*stroke*)
caresser, câliner; **teacher's ~**

chouchou *m* du professeur; **~ hate**
bête noire
petal ['pɛtl] *n* pétale *m*
petite [pə'tiːt] *adj* menu(e)
petition [pə'tɪʃən] *n* pétition *f*
petrified ['pɛtrɪfaɪd] *adj* (*fig*) mort(e)
de peur
petrol ['pɛtrəl] *n* (BRIT) essence *f*;
I've run out of ~ je suis en panne
d'essence

▮ Be careful not to translate *petrol*
by the French word *pétrole*.

petroleum [pə'trəʊlɪəm] *n* pétrole *m*
petrol: petrol pump *n* (BRIT: *in car*,
at garage) pompe *f* à essence; **petrol
station** *n* (BRIT) station-service *f*;
petrol tank *n* (BRIT) réservoir *m*
d'essence
petticoat ['pɛtɪkəʊt] *n* jupon *m*
petty ['pɛtɪ] *adj* (*mean*) mesquin(e);
(*unimportant*) insignifiant(e), sans
importance
pew [pjuː] *n* banc *m* (d'église)
pewter ['pjuːtər] *n* étain *m*
phantom ['fæntəm] *n* fantôme *m*
pharmacist ['fɑːməsɪst] *n*
pharmacien(ne)
pharmacy ['fɑːməsɪ] *n* pharmacie *f*
phase [feɪz] *n* phase *f*, période
f; **phase in** *vt* introduire
progressivement; **phase out** *vt*
supprimer progressivement
Ph.D. *abbr* = **Doctor of Philosophy**
pheasant ['fɛznt] *n* faisan *m*
phenomena [fə'nɔmɪnə] *npl of*
phenomenon
phenomenal [fɪ'nɔmɪnl] *adj*
phénoménal(e)
phenomenon (*pl* **phenomena**)
[fə'nɔmɪnən, -nə] *n* phénomène *m*
Philippines ['fɪlɪpiːnz] *npl* (*also:*
Philippine Islands): **the ~** les
Philippines *fpl*
philosopher [fɪ'lɔsəfər] *n*
philosophe *m*
philosophical [fɪlə'sɔfɪkl] *adj*
philosophique
philosophy [fɪ'lɔsəfɪ] *n* philosophie *f*

phlegm [flɛm] *n* flegme *m*
phobia ['fəʊbjə] *n* phobie *f*
phone [fəʊn] *n* téléphone *m* ▷ *vt*
téléphoner à ▷ *vi* téléphoner; **to
be on the ~** avoir le téléphone; (*be
calling*) être au téléphone; **phone
back** *vt*, *vi* rappeler; **phone up**
vt téléphoner à ▷ *vi* téléphoner;
phone book *n* annuaire *m*; **phone
box**, (US)**phone booth** *n* cabine *f*
téléphonique; **phone call** *n* coup *m*
de fil *or* de téléphone; **phonecard** *n*
télécarte *f*; **phone number** *n* numéro
m de téléphone
phonetics [fə'nɛtɪks] *n* phonétique *f*
phoney ['fəʊnɪ] *adj* faux (fausse),
factice; (*person*) pas franc (franche)
photo ['fəʊtəʊ] *n* photo *f*; **photo
album** *n* album *m* de photos;
photocopier *n* copieur *m*;
photocopy *n* photocopie *f* ▷ *vt*
photocopier
photograph ['fəʊtəgræf] *n*
photographie *f* ▷ *vt* photographier;
photographer [fə'tɔgrəfər] *n*
photographe *m/f*; **photography**
[fə'tɔgrəfɪ] *n* photographie *f*
phrase [freɪz] *n* expression *f*; (*Ling*)
locution *f* ▷ *vt* exprimer; **phrase
book** *n* recueil *m* d'expressions (pour
touristes)
physical ['fɪzɪkl] *adj* physique;
physical education *n* éducation
f physique; **physically** *adv*
physiquement
physician [fɪ'zɪʃən] *n* médecin *m*
physicist ['fɪzɪsɪst] *n* physicien(ne)
physics ['fɪzɪks] *n* physique *f*
physiotherapist [fɪzɪəʊ'θɛrəpɪst] *n*
kinésithérapeute *m/f*
physiotherapy [fɪzɪəʊ'θɛrəpɪ] *n*
kinésithérapie *f*
physique [fɪ'ziːk] *n* (*appearance*)
physique *m*; (*health etc*) constitution *f*
pianist ['piːənɪst] *n* pianiste *m/f*
piano [pɪ'ænəʊ] *n* piano *m*
pick [pɪk] *n* (*tool: also:* **~-axe**) pic *m*,
pioche *f* ▷ *vt* choisir; (*gather*) cueillir;

P

(*remove*) prendre; (*lock*) forcer; **take your ~** faites votre choix; **the ~ of** le meilleur(e) de; **to ~ one's nose** se mettre les doigts dans le nez; **to ~ one's teeth** se curer les dents; **to ~ a quarrel with sb** chercher noise à qn; **pick on** vt fus (*person*) harceler; **pick out** vt choisir; (*distinguish*) distinguer; **pick up** vi (*improve*) remonter, s'améliorer ▷ vt ramasser; (*collect*) passer prendre; (*learn*) apprendre; (*Radio*) capter; **to ~ up speed** prendre de la vitesse; **to ~ o.s. up** se relever

pickle ['pɪkl] n (*also*: **~s**) (*as condiment*) pickles *mpl* ▷ vt conserver dans du vinaigre *or* dans de la saumure; **in a ~** (*fig*) dans le pétrin

pickpocket ['pɪkpɔkɪt] n pickpocket *m*

pick-up ['pɪkʌp] n (*also*: **~ truck**) pick-up *m inv*

picnic ['pɪknɪk] n pique-nique *m* ▷ vi pique-niquer; **picnic area** n aire *f* de pique-nique

picture ['pɪktʃər] n (*also TV*) image *f*; (*painting*) peinture *f*, tableau *m*; (*photograph*) photo(graphie) *f*; (*drawing*) dessin *m*; (*film*) film *m*; (*fig: description*) description *f* ▷ vt (*imagine*) se représenter; **pictures** *npl*: **the ~s** (*BRIT*) le cinéma; **to take a ~ of sb/sth** prendre qn/qch en photo; **would you take a ~ of us, please?** pourriez-vous nous prendre en photo, s'il vous plaît?; **picture frame** n cadre *m*; **picture messaging** n picture messaging *m*, messagerie *f* d'images

picturesque [pɪktʃəˈrɛsk] adj pittoresque

pie [paɪ] n tourte *f*; (*of fruit*) tarte *f*; (*of meat*) pâté *m* en croûte

piece [piːs] n morceau *m*; (*item*): **a ~ of furniture/advice** un meuble/conseil ▷ vt: **to ~ together** rassembler; **to take to ~s** démonter

pie chart n graphique *m* à secteurs, camembert *m*

pier [pɪər] n jetée *f*

pierce [pɪəs] vt percer, transpercer; **pierced** adj (*ears*) percé(e)

pig [pɪg] n cochon *m*, porc *m*; (*pej: unkind person*) mufle *m*; (: *greedy person*) goinfre *m*

pigeon ['pɪdʒən] n pigeon *m*

piggy bank ['pɪgɪ-] n tirelire *f*

pigsty ['pɪgstaɪ] n porcherie *f*

pigtail ['pɪgteɪl] n natte *f*, tresse *f*

pike [paɪk] n (*fish*) brochet *m*

pilchard ['pɪltʃəd] n pilchard *m* (*sorte de sardine*)

pile [paɪl] n (*pillar, of books*) pile *f*; (*heap*) tas *m*; (*of carpet*) épaisseur *f*; **pile up** vi (*accumulate*) s'entasser, s'accumuler ▷ vt (*put in heap*) empiler, entasser; (*accumulate*) accumuler; **piles** *npl* hémorroïdes *fpl*; **pile-up** n (*Aut*) télescopage *m*, collision *f* en série

pilgrim ['pɪlgrɪm] n pèlerin *m*; *voir article* **"Pilgrim Fathers"**

⬤ **PILGRIM FATHERS**
⬤
⬤ Les *Pilgrim Fathers* ("Pères pèlerins")
⬤ sont un groupe de puritains qui
⬤ quittèrent l'Angleterre en 1620 pour
⬤ fuir les persécutions religieuses.
⬤ Ayant traversé l'Atlantique à bord
⬤ du "Mayflower", ils fondèrent New
⬤ Plymouth en Nouvelle-Angleterre,
⬤ dans ce qui est aujourd'hui le
⬤ Massachusetts. Ces Pères pèlerins
⬤ sont considérés comme les
⬤ fondateurs des États-Unis, et l'on
⬤ commémore chaque année, le jour
⬤ de "Thanksgiving", la réussite de
⬤ leur première récolte.

pilgrimage ['pɪlgrɪmɪdʒ] n pèlerinage *m*

pill [pɪl] n pilule *f*; **the ~** la pilule

pillar ['pɪlər] n pilier *m*

pillow ['pɪləʊ] n oreiller *m*; **pillowcase, pillowslip** n taie *f* d'oreiller

pilot ['paɪlət] n pilote m ▷ cpd (scheme etc) pilote, expérimental(e) ▷ vt piloter; **pilot light** n veilleuse f

pimple ['pɪmpl] n bouton m

PIN n abbr (= personal identification number) code m confidentiel

pin [pɪn] n épingle f; (Tech) cheville f ▷ vt épingler; **~s and needles** fourmis fpl; **to ~ sb down** (fig) coincer qn; **to ~ sth on sb** (fig) mettre qch sur le dos de qn

pinafore ['pɪnəfɔːʳ] n tablier m

pinch [pɪntʃ] n pincement m; (of salt etc) pincée f ▷ vt pincer; (inf: steal) piquer, chiper ▷ vi (shoe) serrer; **at a ~** à la rigueur

pine [paɪn] n (also: **~ tree**) pin m ▷ vi: **to ~ for** aspirer à, désirer ardemment

pineapple ['paɪnæpl] n ananas m

ping [pɪŋ] n (noise) tintement m; **ping-pong®** n ping-pong® m

pink [pɪŋk] adj rose ▷ n (colour) rose m

pinpoint ['pɪnpɔɪnt] vt indiquer (avec précision)

pint [paɪnt] n pinte f (Brit = 0,57 l; US = 0,47 l); (BRIT inf) ≈ demi m, ≈ pot m

pioneer [paɪə'nɪəʳ] n pionnier m

pious ['paɪəs] adj pieux(-euse)

pip [pɪp] n (seed) pépin m; **pips** npl: **the ~s** (BRIT: time signal on radio) le top

pipe [paɪp] n tuyau m, conduite f; (for smoking) pipe f ▷ vt amener par tuyau; **pipeline** n (for gas) gazoduc m, pipeline m; (for oil) oléoduc m, pipeline; **piper** n (flautist) joueur(-euse) de pipeau; (of bagpipes) joueur(-euse) de cornemuse

pirate ['paɪərət] n pirate m ▷ vt (CD, video, book) pirater

Pisces ['paɪsiːz] n les Poissons mpl

piss [pɪs] vi (infl) pisser (!); **pissed** adj (infl: BRIT: drunk) bourré(e); (: US: angry) furieux(-euse)

pistol ['pɪstl] n pistolet m

piston ['pɪstən] n piston m

pit [pɪt] n trou m, fosse f; (also: **coal ~**) puits m de mine; (also: **orchestra ~**) fosse d'orchestre; (US: fruit stone)

noyau m ▷ vt: **to ~ o.s.** or **one's wits against** se mesurer à

pitch [pɪtʃ] n (BRIT Sport) terrain m; (Mus) ton m; (fig: degree) degré m; (tar) poix f ▷ vt (throw) lancer; (tent) dresser ▷ vi (fall): **to ~ into/off** tomber dans/de; **pitch-black** adj noir(e) comme poix

pitfall ['pɪtfɔːl] n piège m

pith [pɪθ] n (of orange etc) intérieur m de l'écorce

pitiful ['pɪtɪful] adj (touching) pitoyable; (contemptible) lamentable

pity ['pɪtɪ] n pitié f ▷ vt plaindre; **what a ~!** quel dommage!

pizza ['piːtsə] n pizza f

placard ['plækɑːd] n affiche f; (in march) pancarte f

place [pleɪs] n endroit m, lieu m; (proper position, job, rank, seat) place f; (home): **at/to his ~** chez lui ▷ vt (position) placer, mettre; (identify) situer; reconnaître; **to take ~** avoir lieu; **to change ~s with sb** changer de place avec qn; **out of ~** (not suitable) déplacé(e), inopportun(e); **in the first ~** d'abord, en premier; **place mat** n set m de table; (in linen etc) napperon m; **placement** n (during studies) stage m

placid ['plæsɪd] adj placide

plague [pleɪg] n (Med) peste f ▷ vt (fig) tourmenter

plaice [pleɪs] n (pl inv) carrelet m

plain [pleɪn] adj (in one colour) uni(e); (clear) clair(e), évident(e); (simple) simple; (not handsome) quelconque, ordinaire ▷ adv franchement, carrément ▷ n plaine f; **plain chocolate** n chocolat m à croquer; **plainly** adv clairement; (frankly) carrément, sans détours

plaintiff ['pleɪntɪf] n plaignant(e)

plait [plæt] n tresse f, natte f

plan [plæn] n plan m; (scheme) projet m ▷ vt (think in advance) projeter; (prepare) organiser ▷ vi faire des projets; **to ~ to do** projeter de faire

plane [pleɪn] n (Aviat) avion m; (also:
~ **tree**) platane m; (tool) rabot m; (Art,
Math etc) plan m; (fig) niveau m, plan
▷ vt (with tool) raboter
planet ['plænɪt] n planète f
plank [plæŋk] n planche f
planning ['plænɪŋ] n planification f;
family ~ planning familial
plant [plɑːnt] n plante f; (machinery)
matériel m; (factory) usine f ▷ vt
planter; (bomb) déposer, poser;
(microphone, evidence) cacher
plantation [plæn'teɪʃən] n
plantation f
plaque [plæk] n plaque f
plaster ['plɑːstər] n plâtre m; (also:
~ **of Paris**) plâtre à mouler; (BRIT: also:
sticking ~) pansement adhésif ▷ vt
plâtrer; (cover): **to ~ with** couvrir de;
plaster cast n (Med) plâtre m; (model,
statue) moule m
plastic ['plæstɪk] n plastique m ▷ adj
(made of plastic) en plastique; **plastic
bag** n sac m en plastique; **plastic
surgery** n chirurgie f esthétique
plate [pleɪt] n (dish) assiette f; (sheet of
metal, on door, Phot) plaque f; (in book)
gravure f; (dental) dentier m
plateau (pl **plateaus** or **plateaux**)
['plætəu, -z] n plateau m
platform ['plætfɔːm] n (at meeting)
tribune f; (stage) estrade f; (Rail) quai
m; (Pol) plateforme f
platinum ['plætɪnəm] n platine m
platoon [plə'tuːn] n peloton m
platter ['plætər] n plat m
plausible ['plɔːzɪbl] adj plausible;
(person) convaincant(e)
play [pleɪ] n jeu m; (Theat) pièce f (de
théâtre) ▷ vt jouer à; (team,
opponent) jouer contre; (instrument)
jouer de; (part, piece of music, note)
jouer; (CD etc) passer ▷ vi jouer; **to ~
safe** ne prendre aucun risque; **play
back** vt repasser, réécouter; **play
up** vi (cause trouble) faire des siennes;
player n joueur(-euse); (Mus)
musicien(ne); **playful** adj enjoué(e);

playground n cour f de récréation;
(in park) aire f de jeux; **playgroup** n
garderie f; **playing card** n carte f à
jouer; **playing field** n terrain m de
sport; **playschool** n = **playgroup**
playtime n (Scol) récréation f;
playwright n dramaturge m
plc abbr (BRIT: = public limited company)
≈ SARL f
plea [pliː] n (request) appel m; (Law)
défense f
plead [pliːd] vt plaider; (give as
excuse) invoquer ▷ vi (Law) plaider;
(beg): **to ~ with sb (for sth)** implorer
qn (d'accorder qch); **to ~ guilty/
not guilty** plaider coupable/non
coupable
pleasant ['plɛznt] adj agréable
please [pliːz] excl s'il te (or vous)
plaît ▷ vt plaire à ▷ vi (think fit): **do
as you ~** faites comme il vous plaira;
~ yourself! (inf) (faites) comme
vous voulez!; **pleased** adj: **pleased
(with)** content(e) (de); **pleased to
meet you** enchanté (de faire votre
connaissance)
pleasure ['plɛʒər] n plaisir m; "**it's a
~**" "je vous en prie"
pleat [pliːt] n pli m
pledge [plɛdʒ] n (promise) promesse f
▷ vt promettre
plentiful ['plɛntɪful] adj
abondant(e), copieux(-euse)
plenty ['plɛntɪ] n: **~ of** beaucoup de;
(sufficient) (bien) assez de
pliers ['plaɪəz] npl pinces fpl
plight [plaɪt] n situation f critique
plod [plɔd] vi avancer péniblement;
(fig) peiner
plonk [plɔŋk] (inf) n (BRIT: wine)
pinard m, piquette f ▷ vt: **to ~ sth
down** poser brusquement qch
plot [plɔt] n complot m, conspiration
f; (of story, play) intrigue f; (of land) lot
m de terrain, lopin m ▷ vt (mark out)
tracer point par point; (Naut) pointer;
(make graph of) faire le graphique de;
(conspire) comploter ▷ vi comploter

plough, (US) **plow** [plau] n charrue f ▷ vt (earth) labourer; **to ~ money into** investir dans

ploy [plɔɪ] n stratagème m

pls abbr (= please) SVP m

pluck [plʌk] vt (fruit) cueillir; (musical instrument) pincer; (bird) plumer; **to ~ one's eyebrows** s'épiler les sourcils; **to ~ up courage** prendre son courage à deux mains

plug [plʌg] n (stopper) bouchon m, bonde f; (Elec) prise f de courant; (Aut: also: **spark(ing) ~**) bougie f ▷ vt (hole) boucher; (inf: advertise) faire du battage pour, matraquer; **plug in** vt (Elec) brancher; **plughole** n (BRIT) trou m (d'écoulement)

plum [plʌm] n (fruit) prune f

plumber ['plʌmə'] n plombier m

plumbing ['plʌmɪŋ] n (trade) plomberie f; (piping) tuyauterie f

plummet ['plʌmɪt] vi (person, object) plonger; (sales, prices) dégringoler

plump [plʌmp] adj rondelet(te), dodu(e), bien en chair; **plump for** vt fus (inf: choose) se décider pour

plunge [plʌndʒ] n plongeon m; (fig) chute f ▷ vt plonger ▷ vi (fall) tomber, dégringoler; (dive) plonger; **to take the ~** se jeter à l'eau

pluperfect [pluː'pəːfɪkt] n (Ling) plus-que-parfait m

plural ['pluərl] adj pluriel(le) ▷ n pluriel m

plus [plʌs] n (also: **~ sign**) signe m plus; (advantage) atout m ▷ prep plus; **ten/twenty ~** plus de dix/vingt

ply [plaɪ] n (of wool) fil m ▷ vt (a trade) exercer ▷ vi (ship) faire la navette; **to ~ sb with drink** donner continuellement à boire à qn; **plywood** n contreplaqué m

P.M. n abbr (BRIT) = **prime minister**

p.m. adv abbr (= post meridiem) de l'après-midi

PMS n abbr (= premenstrual syndrome) syndrome prémenstruel

PMT n abbr (= premenstrual tension) syndrome prémenstruel

pneumatic drill [njuː'mætɪk-] n marteau-piqueur m

pneumonia [njuː'məunɪə] n pneumonie f

poach [pəutʃ] vt (cook) pocher; (steal) pêcher (or chasser) sans permis ▷ vi braconner; **poached** adj (egg) poché(e)

P.O. Box n abbr = **post office box**

pocket ['pɔkɪt] n poche f ▷ vt empocher; **to be (£5) out of ~** (BRIT) en être de sa poche (pour 5 livres); **pocketbook** n (US: wallet) portefeuille m; **pocket money** n argent m de poche

pod [pɔd] n cosse f

podcast ['pɔdkɑːst] n podcast m ▷ vi podcaster

podiatrist [pɔ'diːətrɪst] n (US) pédicure m/f

poem ['pəuɪm] n poème m

poet ['pəuɪt] n poète m; **poetic** [pəu'ɛtɪk] adj poétique; **poetry** n poésie f

poignant ['pɔɪnjənt] adj poignant(e)

point [pɔɪnt] n point m; (tip) pointe f; (in time) moment m; (in space) endroit m; (subject, idea) point, sujet m; (purpose) but m; (also: **decimal ~**): **2 ~ 3 (2.3)** 2 virgule 3 (2,3); (BRIT Elec: also: **power ~**) prise f (de courant) ▷ vt (show) indiquer; (gun etc): **to ~ sth at** braquer or diriger qch sur ▷ vi: **to ~ at** montrer du doigt; **points** npl (Rail) aiguillage m; **to make a ~ of doing sth** ne pas manquer de faire qch; **to get/miss the ~** comprendre/ne pas comprendre; **to come to the ~** en venir au fait; **there's no ~ (in doing)** cela ne sert à rien (de faire); **to be on the ~ of doing sth** être sur le point de faire qch; **point out** vt (mention) faire remarquer, souligner; **point-blank** adv (fig) catégoriquement; (also: **at point-blank range**) à bout portant; **pointed** adj (shape) pointu(e); (*remark*) plein(e) de sous-entendus; **pointer** n (*needle*) aiguille f; (*clue*) indication f; (*advice*) tuyau m; **pointless** adj inutile, vain(e); **point of view** n point m de vue

poison ['pɔɪzn] n poison m ▷ vt empoisonner; **poisonous** adj (*snake*) venimeux(-euse); (*substance, plant*) vénéneux(-euse); (*fumes*) toxique

poke [pəuk] vt (*jab with finger, stick etc*) piquer; pousser du doigt; (*put*): **to ~ sth in(to)** fourrer or enfoncer qch dans; **poke about** vi fureter; **poke out** vi (*stick out*) sortir

poker ['pəukər] n tisonnier m; (*Cards*) poker m

Poland ['pəulənd] n Pologne f

polar ['pəulər] adj polaire; **polar bear** n ours blanc

Pole [pəul] n Polonais(e)

pole [pəul] n (*of wood*) mât m, perche f; (*Elec*) poteau m; (*Geo*) pôle m; **pole bean** n (*US*) haricot m (à rames); **pole vault** n saut m à la perche

police [pə'li:s] npl police f ▷ vt maintenir l'ordre dans; **police car** n voiture f de police; **police constable** n (*BRIT*) agent m de police; **police force** n police f, forces fpl de l'ordre; **policeman** (*irreg*) n agent m de police, policier m; **police officer** n agent m de police; **police station** n commissariat m de police; **policewoman** (*irreg*) n femme-agent f

policy ['pɔlɪsɪ] n politique f; (*also*: **insurance ~**) police f (d'assurance)

polio ['pəulɪəu] n polio f

Polish ['pəulɪʃ] adj polonais(e) ▷ n (*Ling*) polonais m

polish ['pɔlɪʃ] n (*for shoes*) cirage m; (*for floor*) cire f, encaustique f; (*for nails*) vernis m; (*shine*) éclat m, poli m; (*fig: refinement*) raffinement m ▷ vt (*put polish on: shoes, wood*) cirer; (*make shiny*) astiquer, faire briller; **polish off** vt (*food*) liquider; **polished** adj (*fig*) raffiné(e)

polite [pə'laɪt] adj poli(e); **politeness** n politesse f

political [pə'lɪtɪkl] adj politique; **politically** adv politiquement; **politically correct** politiquement correct(e)

politician [pɔlɪ'tɪʃən] n homme/femme politique, politicien(ne)

politics ['pɔlɪtɪks] n politique f

poll [pəul] n scrutin m, vote m; (*also*: **opinion ~**) sondage m (d'opinion) ▷ vt (*votes*) obtenir

pollen ['pɔlən] n pollen m

polling station n (*BRIT*) bureau m de vote

pollute [pə'lu:t] vt polluer

pollution [pə'lu:ʃən] n pollution f

polo ['pəuləu] n polo m; **polo-neck** adj à col roulé ▷ n (*sweater*) pull m à col roulé; **polo shirt** n polo m

polyester [pɔlɪ'ɛstər] n polyester m

polystyrene [pɔlɪ'staɪri:n] n polystyrène m

polythene ['pɔlɪθi:n] n (*BRIT*) polyéthylène m; **polythene bag** n sac m en plastique

pomegranate ['pɔmɪgrænɪt] n grenade f

pompous ['pɔmpəs] adj pompeux(-euse)

pond [pɔnd] n étang m; (*stagnant*) mare f

ponder ['pɔndər] vt considérer, peser

pony ['pəunɪ] n poney m; **ponytail** n queue f de cheval; **pony trekking** n (*BRIT*) randonnée f équestre or à cheval

poodle ['pu:dl] n caniche m

pool [pu:l] n (*of rain*) flaque f; (*pond*) mare f; (*artificial*) bassin m; (*also*: **swimming ~**) piscine f; (*sth shared*) fonds commun; (*billiards*) poule f ▷ vt mettre en commun; **pools** npl (*football*) ≈ loto sportif

poor [puər] adj pauvre; (*mediocre*) médiocre, faible, mauvais(e) ▷ npl: **the ~** les pauvres mpl; **poorly** adv

(badly) mal, médiocrement ▷ adj
souffrant(e), malade
pop [pɒp] n (noise) bruit sec; (Mus)
musique f pop; (inf: drink) soda m; (us
inf: father) papa m ▷ vt (put) fourrer,
mettre (rapidement) ▷ vi éclater;
(cork) sauter; **pop in** vi entrer en
passant; **pop out** vi sortir; **popcorn**
n pop-corn m
pope [pəʊp] n pape m
poplar ['pɒplər] n peuplier m
popper ['pɒpər] n (BRIT) bouton-
pression m
poppy ['pɒpɪ] n (wild) coquelicot m;
(cultivated) pavot m
Popsicle® ['pɒpsɪkl] n (us) esquimau
m (glace)
pop star n pop star f
popular ['pɒpjʊlər] adj populaire;
(fashionable) à la mode; **popularity**
[pɒpjʊ'lærɪtɪ] n popularité f
population [pɒpjʊ'leɪʃən] n
population f
pop-up adj (Comput: menu, window)
pop up inv ▷ n pop up m inv, fenêtre
f pop up
porcelain ['pɔːslɪn] n porcelaine f
porch [pɔːtʃ] n porche m; (us)
véranda f
pore [pɔːr] n pore m ▷ vi: **to ~ over**
s'absorber dans, être plongé(e) dans
pork [pɔːk] n porc m; **pork chop** n
côte f de porc; **pork pie** n pâté m de
porc en croûte
porn [pɔːn] adj (inf) porno ▷ n
(inf) porno m; **pornographic**
[pɔːnə'græfɪk] adj pornographique;
pornography [pɔː'nɒgrəfɪ] n
pornographie f
porridge ['pɒrɪdʒ] n porridge m
port [pɔːt] n (harbour) port m; (Naut:
left side) bâbord m; (wine) porto m;
(Comput) port m, accès m; **~ of call**
(port d')escale f
portable ['pɔːtəbl] adj portatif(-ive)
porter ['pɔːtər] n (for luggage)
porteur m; (doorkeeper) gardien(ne);
portier m

portfolio [pɔːt'fəʊlɪəʊ] n portefeuille
m; (of artist) portfolio m
portion ['pɔːʃən] n portion f, part f
portrait ['pɔːtreɪt] n portrait m
portray [pɔː'treɪ] vt faire le
portrait de; (in writing) dépeindre,
représenter; (subj: actor) jouer
Portugal ['pɔːtjʊgl] n Portugal m
Portuguese [pɔːtjʊ'giːz] adj
portugais(e) ▷ n (pl inv) Portugais(e);
(Ling) portugais m
pose [pəʊz] n pose f ▷ vi poser;
(pretend): **to ~ as** se faire passer pour
▷ vt poser; (problem) créer
posh [pɒʃ] adj (inf) chic inv
position [pə'zɪʃən] n position f; (job,
situation) situation f ▷ vt mettre en
place or en position
positive ['pɒzɪtɪv] adj positif(-ive);
(certain) sûr(e), certain(e); (definite)
formel(le), catégorique; **positively**
adv (affirmatively, enthusiastically) de
façon positive; (inf: really) carrément
possess [pə'zɛs] vt posséder;
possession [pə'zɛʃən] n possession f;
possessions npl (belongings) affaires
fpl; **possessive** adj possessif(-ive)
possibility [pɒsɪ'bɪlɪtɪ] n possibilité f;
(event) éventualité f
possible ['pɒsɪbl] adj possible; **as big
as ~** aussi gros que possible; **possibly**
adv (perhaps) peut-être; **I cannot
possibly come** il m'est impossible
de venir
post [pəʊst] n (BRIT: mail) poste f;
(: letters, delivery) courrier m; (job,
situation) poste m; (pole) poteau m;
(Internet) post ▷ vt (Internet) poster;
(BRIT: send by post) poster; (appoint):
to ~ to affecter à; **where can I ~
these cards?** où est-ce que je peux
poster ces cartes postales?; **postage**
n tarifs mpl d'affranchissement;
postal adj postal(e); **postal order**
n mandat(-poste m) m; **postbox** n
(BRIT) boîte f aux lettres (publique);
postcard n carte postale; **postcode**
n (BRIT) code postal

poster ['pəustə^r] n affiche f
postgraduate ['pəust'grædjuət] n ≈ étudiant(e) de troisième cycle
postman ['pəustmən] (irreg) (BRIT) n facteur m
postmark ['pəustmɑːk] n cachet m (de la poste)
post-mortem [pəust'mɔːtəm] n autopsie f
post office n (building) poste f; (organization): **the Post Office** les postes fpl
postpone [pəs'pəun] vt remettre (à plus tard), reculer
posture ['pɒstʃə^r] n posture f; (fig) attitude f
postwoman ['pəust'wumən] (irreg) (BRIT) n factrice f
pot [pɒt] n (for cooking) marmite f, casserole f; (teapot) théière f; (for coffee) cafetière f; (for plants, jam) pot m; (inf: marijuana) herbe f ▷ vt (plant) mettre en pot; **to go to ~** (inf) aller à vau-l'eau
potato [pə'teɪtəu] (pl **potatoes**) n pomme f de terre; **potato peeler** n épluche-légumes m
potent ['pəutnt] adj puissant(e); (drink) fort(e), très alcoolisé(e); (man) viril
potential [pə'tɛnʃl] adj potentiel(le) ▷ n potentiel m
pothole ['pɒthəul] n (in road) nid m de poule; (BRIT: underground) gouffre m, caverne f
pot plant n plante f d'appartement
potter ['pɒtə^r] n potier m ▷ vi (BRIT): **to ~ around** or **about** bricoler; **pottery** n poterie f
potty ['pɒtɪ] n (child's) pot m
pouch [pautʃ] n (Zool) poche f; (for tobacco) blague f; (for money) bourse f
poultry ['pəultrɪ] n volaille f
pounce [pauns] vi: **to ~ (on)** bondir (sur), fondre (sur)
pound [paund] n livre f (weight = 453g, 16 ounces; money = 100 pence); (for dogs, cars) fourrière f ▷ vt (beat)

bourrer de coups, marteler; (crush) piler, pulvériser ▷ vi (heart) battre violemment, taper; **pound sterling** n livre f sterling
pour [pɔː^r] vt verser ▷ vi couler à flots; (rain) pleuvoir à verse; **to ~ sb a drink** verser or servir à boire à qn; **pour in** vi (people) affluer, se précipiter; (news, letters) arriver en masse; **pour out** vi (people) sortir en masse ▷ vt vider; (fig) déverser; (serve: a drink) verser; **pouring** adj: **pouring rain** pluie f torrentielle
pout [paut] vi faire la moue
poverty ['pɒvətɪ] n pauvreté f, misère f
powder ['paudə^r] n poudre f ▷ vt poudrer; **powdered milk** n lait m en poudre
power ['pauə^r] n (strength, nation) puissance f, force f; (ability, Pol: of party, leader) pouvoir m; (of speech, thought) faculté f; (Elec) courant m; **to be in ~** être au pouvoir; **power cut** n (BRIT) coupure f de courant; **power failure** n panne f de courant; **powerful** adj puissant(e); (performance etc) très fort(e); **powerless** adj impuissant(e); **power point** n (BRIT) prise f de courant; **power station** n centrale f électrique
p.p. abbr (= per procurationem: by proxy) p.p.
PR n abbr = **public relations**
practical ['præktɪkl] adj pratique; **practical joke** n farce f; **practically** adv (almost) pratiquement
practice ['præktɪs] n pratique f; (of profession) exercice m; (at football etc) entraînement m; (business) cabinet m ▷ vt, vi (US) = **practise**; **in ~** (in reality) en pratique; **out of ~** rouillé(e)
practise, (US) **practice** ['præktɪs] vt (work at: piano, backhand etc) s'exercer à, travailler; (train for: sport) s'entraîner à; (a sport, religion, method) pratiquer; (profession) exercer ▷ vi s'exercer, travailler; (train) s'entraîner; (lawyer, doctor) exercer; **practising**,

(US) **practicing** adj (Christian etc) pratiquant(e); (lawyer) en exercice
practitioner [præk'tɪʃənə^r] n praticien(ne)
pragmatic [præg'mætɪk] adj pragmatique
prairie ['prɛərɪ] n savane f
praise [preɪz] n éloge(s) m(pl), louange(s) f(pl) ▷ vt louer, faire l'éloge de
pram [præm] n (BRIT) landau m, voiture f d'enfant
prank [præŋk] n farce f
prawn [prɔ:n] n crevette f(rose); **prawn cocktail** n cocktail m de crevettes
pray [preɪ] vi prier; **prayer** [prɛə^r] n prière f
preach [pri:tʃ] vi prêcher; **preacher** n prédicateur m; (US: clergyman) pasteur m
precarious [prɪ'kɛərɪəs] adj précaire
precaution [prɪ'kɔ:ʃən] n précaution f
precede [prɪ'si:d] vt, vi précéder; **precedent** ['presɪdənt] n précédent m; **preceding** [prɪ'si:dɪŋ] adj qui précède (or précédait)
precinct ['pri:sɪŋkt] n (US: district) circonscription f, arrondissement m; **pedestrian ~** (BRIT) zone piétonnière; **shopping ~** (BRIT) centre commercial
precious ['prɛʃəs] adj précieux(-euse)
precise [prɪ'saɪs] adj précis(e); **precisely** adv précisément
precision [prɪ'sɪʒən] n précision f
predator ['prɛdətə^r] n prédateur m, rapace m
predecessor ['pri:dɪsɛsə^r] n prédécesseur m
predicament [prɪ'dɪkəmənt] n situation f difficile
predict [prɪ'dɪkt] vt prédire; **predictable** adj prévisible; **prediction** [prɪ'dɪkʃən] n prédiction f
predominantly [prɪ'dɔmɪnəntlɪ] adv en majeure partie; (especially) surtout

preface ['prɛfəs] n préface f
prefect ['pri:fɛkt] n (BRIT: in school) élève chargé de certaines fonctions de discipline
prefer [prɪ'fə:^r] vt préférer; **preferable** ['prɛfrəbl] adj préférable; **preferably** ['prɛfrəblɪ] adv de préférence; **preference** ['prɛfrəns] n préférence f
prefix ['pri:fɪks] n préfixe m
pregnancy ['prɛgnənsɪ] n grossesse f
pregnant ['prɛgnənt] adj enceinte; (animal) pleine
prehistoric ['pri:hɪs'tɔrɪk] adj préhistorique
prejudice ['prɛdʒudɪs] n préjugé m; **prejudiced** adj (person) plein(e) de préjugés; (in a matter) partial(e)
preliminary [prɪ'lɪmɪnərɪ] adj préliminaire
prelude ['prɛlju:d] n prélude m
premature ['prɛmətʃuə^r] adj prématuré(e)
premier ['prɛmɪə^r] adj premier(-ière), principal(e) ▷ n (Pol: Prime Minister) premier ministre; (Pol: President) chef m de l'État
premiere ['prɛmɪɛə^r] n première f
Premier League n première division
premises ['prɛmɪsɪz] npl locaux mpl; **on the ~** sur les lieux; sur place
premium ['pri:mɪəm] n prime f; **to be at a ~** (fig: housing etc) être très demandé(e), être rarissime
premonition [prɛmə'nɪʃən] n prémonition f
preoccupied [pri:'ɔkjupaɪd] adj préoccupé(e)
prepaid [pri:'peɪd] adj payé(e) d'avance
preparation [prɛpə'reɪʃən] n préparation f; **preparations** npl (for trip, war) préparatifs mpl
preparatory school n (BRIT) école primaire privée; (US) lycée privé
prepare [prɪ'pɛə^r] vt préparer ▷ vi: **to ~ for** se préparer à

prepared [prɪ'pɛəd] *adj*: **~ for** préparé(e) à; **~ to** prêt(e) à

preposition [prɛpə'zɪʃən] *n* préposition *f*

prep school *n* = **preparatory school**

prerequisite [pri:'rɛkwɪzɪt] *n* condition *f* préalable

preschool ['pri:'sku:l] *adj* préscolaire; (*child*) d'âge préscolaire

prescribe [prɪ'skraɪb] *vt* prescrire

prescription [prɪ'skrɪpʃən] *n* (*Med*) ordonnance *f* (: *medicine*) médicament *m* (obtenu sur ordonnance); **could you write me a ~?** pouvez-vous me faire une ordonnance?

presence ['prɛzns] *n* présence *f*; **in sb's ~** en présence de qn; **~ of mind** présence d'esprit

present ['prɛznt] *adj* présent(e); (*current*) présent, actuel(le) ▷ *n* cadeau *m*; (*actuality*) présent *m* ▷ *vt* [prɪ'zɛnt] présenter; (*prize, medal*) remettre; (*give*): **to ~ sb with sth** offrir qch à qn; **at ~** en ce moment; **to give sb a ~** offrir un cadeau à qn; **presentable** [prɪ'zɛntəbl] *adj* présentable; **presentation** [prɛzn'teɪʃən] *n* présentation *f*; (*ceremony*) remise *f* du cadeau (*or* de la médaille *etc*); **present-day** *adj* contemporain(e), actuel(le); **presenter** [prɪ'zɛntə'] *n* (*BRIT Radio, TV*) présentateur(-trice); **presently** *adv* (*soon*) tout à l'heure, bientôt; (*with verb in past*) peu après; (*at present*) en ce moment

preservation [prɛzə'veɪʃən] *n* préservation *f*, conservation *f*

preservative [prɪ'zə:vətɪv] *n* agent *m* de conservation

preserve [prɪ'zə:v] *vt* (*keep safe*) préserver, protéger; (*maintain*) conserver, garder; (*food*) mettre en conserve ▷ *n* (*for game, fish*) réserve *f*; (*often pl: jam*) confiture *f*

preside [prɪ'zaɪd] *vi* présider

president ['prɛzɪdənt] *n* président(e); **presidential** [prɛzɪ'dɛnʃl] *adj* présidentiel(le)

press [prɛs] *n* (*tool, machine, newspapers*) presse *f*; (*for wine*) pressoir *m* ▷ *vt* (*push*) appuyer sur; (*squeeze*) presser, serrer; (*clothes: iron*) repasser; (*insist*): **to ~ sth on sb** presser qn d'accepter qch; (*urge, entreat*): **to ~ sb to do** *or* **into doing sth** pousser qn à faire qch ▷ *vi* appuyer; **we are ~ed for time** le temps nous manque; **to ~ for sth** faire pression pour obtenir qch; **press conference** *n* conférence *f* de presse; **pressing** *adj* urgent(e), pressant(e); **press stud** *n* (*BRIT*) bouton-pression *m*; **press-up** *n* (*BRIT*) traction *f*

pressure ['prɛʃə'] *n* pression *f*; (*stress*) tension *f*; **to put ~ on sb (to do sth)** faire pression sur qn (pour qu'il fasse qch); **pressure cooker** *n* cocotte-minute® *f*; **pressure group** *n* groupe *m* de pression

prestige [prɛs'ti:ʒ] *n* prestige *m*

prestigious [prɛs'tɪdʒəs] *adj* prestigieux(-euse)

presumably [prɪ'zju:məblɪ] *adv* vraisemblablement

presume [prɪ'zju:m] *vt* présumer, supposer

pretence, (*US*) **pretense** [prɪ'tɛns] *n* (*claim*) prétention *f*; **under false ~s** sous des prétextes fallacieux

pretend [prɪ'tɛnd] *vt* (*feign*) feindre, simuler ▷ *vi* (*feign*) faire semblant

pretense [prɪ'tɛns] *n* (*US*) = **pretence**

pretentious [prɪ'tɛnʃəs] *adj* prétentieux(-euse)

pretext ['pri:tɛkst] *n* prétexte *m*

pretty ['prɪtɪ] *adj* joli(e) ▷ *adv* assez

prevail [prɪ'veɪl] *vi* (*win*) l'emporter, prévaloir; (*be usual*) avoir cours; **prevailing** *adj* (*widespread*) courant(e), répandu(e); (*wind*) dominant(e)

prevalent ['prɛvələnt] *adj* répandu(e), courant(e)

prevent [prɪ'vɛnt] *vt*: **to ~ (from doing)** empêcher (de faire); **prevention** [prɪ'vɛnʃən] *n* prévention *f*; **preventive** *adj* préventif(-ive)

preview ['pri:vju:] *n* (of film) avant-première *f*

previous ['pri:vɪəs] *adj* (last) précédent(e); (earlier) antérieur(e); **previously** *adv* précédemment, auparavant

prey [preɪ] *n* proie *f* ▷ *vi*: **to ~ on** s'attaquer à; **it was ~ing on his mind** ça le rongeait or minait

price [praɪs] *n* prix *m* ▷ *vt* (goods) fixer le prix de; **priceless** *adj* sans prix, inestimable; **price list** *n* tarif *m*

prick [prɪk] *n* (sting) piqûre *f* ▷ *vt* piquer; **to ~ up one's ears** dresser or tendre l'oreille

prickly ['prɪklɪ] *adj* piquant(e), épineux(-euse); (fig: person) irritable

pride [praɪd] *n* fierté *f*; (pej) orgueil *m* ▷ *vt*: **to ~ o.s. on** se flatter de; s'enorgueillir de

priest [pri:st] *n* prêtre *m*

primarily ['praɪmərɪlɪ] *adv* principalement, essentiellement

primary ['praɪmərɪ] *adj* primaire; (first in importance) premier(-ière), primordial(e) ▷ *n* (us: election) (élection *f*) primaire *f*; **primary school** *n* (BRIT) école *f* primaire

prime [praɪm] *adj* primordial(e), fondamental(e); (excellent) excellent(e) ▷ *vt* (fig) mettre au courant ▷ *n*: **in the ~ of life** dans la fleur de l'âge; **Prime Minister** *n* Premier ministre

primitive ['prɪmɪtɪv] *adj* primitif(-ive)

primrose ['prɪmrəuz] *n* primevère *f*

prince [prɪns] *n* prince *m*

princess [prɪn'sɛs] *n* princesse *f*

principal ['prɪnsɪpl] *adj* principal(e) ▷ *n* (head teacher) directeur *m*, principal *m*; **principally** *adv* principalement

principle ['prɪnsɪpl] *n* principe *m*; **in ~** en principe; **on ~** par principe

print [prɪnt] *n* (mark) empreinte *f*; (letters) caractères *mpl*; (fabric) imprimé *m*; (Art) gravure *f*, estampe *f*; (Phot) épreuve *f* ▷ *vt* imprimer; (publish) publier; (write in capitals) écrire en majuscules; **out of ~** épuisé(e); **print out** *vt* (Comput) imprimer; **printer** *n* (machine) imprimante *f*; (person) imprimeur *m*; **printout** *n* (Comput) sortie *f* imprimante

prior ['praɪə*] *adj* antérieur(e), précédent(e); (more important) prioritaire ▷ *adv*: **~ to doing** avant de faire

priority [praɪ'ɔrɪtɪ] *n* priorité *f*; **to have** or **take ~ over sth/sb** avoir la priorité sur qch/qn

prison ['prɪzn] *n* prison *f* ▷ *cpd* pénitentiaire; **prisoner** *n* prisonnier(-ière); **prisoner of war** *n* prisonnier(-ière) de guerre

pristine ['prɪsti:n] *adj* virginal(e)

privacy ['prɪvəsɪ] *n* intimité *f*, solitude *f*

private ['praɪvɪt] *adj* (not public) privé(e); (personal) personnel(le); (house, car, lesson) particulier(-ière); (quiet: place) tranquille ▷ *n* soldat *m* de deuxième classe; **"~"** (on envelope) "personnelle"; (on door) "privé"; **in ~** en privé; **privately** *adv* en privé; (within oneself) intérieurement; **private property** *n* propriété privée; **private school** *n* école privée

privatize ['praɪvɪtaɪz] *vt* privatiser

privilege ['prɪvɪlɪdʒ] *n* privilège *m*

prize [praɪz] *n* prix *m* ▷ *adj* (example, idiot) parfait(e); (bull, novel) primé(e) ▷ *vt* priser, faire grand cas de; **prize-giving** *n* distribution *f* des prix; **prizewinner** *n* gagnant(e)

pro [prəu] *n* (inf: Sport) professionnel(le) ▷ *prep* pro; **pros** *npl*; **the ~s and cons** le pour et le contre

probability [prɔbə'bɪlɪtɪ] *n* probabilité *f*; **in all ~** très probablement

probable ['prɔbəbl] *adj* probable

probably ['prɔbəblɪ] *adv* probablement

P

probation [prəˈbeɪʃən] n: **on ~**
(employee) à l'essai; (Law) en liberté
surveillée
probe [prəub] n (Med, Space) sonde
f; (enquiry) enquête f, investigation f
▷ vt sonder, explorer
problem [ˈprɔbləm] n problème m
procedure [prəˈsiːdʒəʳ] n (Admin,
Law) procédure f; (method) marche f à
suivre, façon f de procéder
proceed [prəˈsiːd] vi (go forward)
avancer; (act) procéder; (continue):
to ~ (with) continuer, poursuivre;
to ~ to do se mettre à faire;
proceedings npl (measures) mesures
fpl; (Law: against sb) poursuites fpl;
(meeting) réunion f, séance f; (records)
compte rendu; actes mpl; **proceeds**
[ˈprəusiːdz] npl produit m, recette f
process [ˈprəusɛs] n processus m;
(method) procédé m ▷ vt traiter
procession [prəˈsɛʃən] n défilé
m, cortège m; **funeral ~** (on foot)
cortège funèbre; (in cars) convoi m
mortuaire
proclaim [prəˈkleɪm] vt déclarer,
proclamer
prod [prɔd] vt pousser
produce n [ˈprɔdjuːs] (Agr) produits
mpl ▷ vt [prəˈdjuːs] produire; (show)
présenter; (cause) provoquer, causer;
(Theat) monter, mettre en scène;
(TV: programme) réaliser; (: play, film)
mettre en scène; (Radio: programme)
réaliser; (: play) mettre en ondes;
producer n (Theat) metteur m en
scène; (Agr, Comm, Cine) producteur
m; (TV: of programme) réalisateur
m; (: of play, film) metteur en scène;
(Radio: of programme) réalisateur; (: of
play) metteur en ondes
product [ˈprɔdʌkt] n produit
m; **production** [prəˈdʌkʃən] n
production f; (Theat) mise f en
scène; **productive** [prəˈdʌktɪv]
adj productif(-ive); **productivity**
[prɔdʌkˈtɪvɪtɪ] n productivité f
Prof. [prɔf] abbr (= professor) Prof

profession [prəˈfɛʃən] n profession
f; **professional** n professionnel(le)
▷ adj professionnel(le); (work) de
professionnel
professor [prəˈfɛsəʳ] n professeur
m (titulaire d'une chaire); (us: teacher)
professeur m
profile [ˈprəufaɪl] n profil m
profit [ˈprɔfɪt] n (from trading)
bénéfice m; (advantage) profit m
▷ vi: **to ~ (by** or **from)** profiter (de);
profitable adj lucratif(-ive), rentable
profound [prəˈfaund] adj profond(e)
programme, (us) **program**
[ˈprəugræm] n (Comput)
programme m; (Radio, TV) émission
f ▷ vt programmer; **programmer**
n programmeur(-euse);
programming, (us) **programing** n
programmation f
progress n [ˈprəugrɛs] progrès m(pl)
▷ vi [prəˈgrɛs] progresser, avancer; **in**
~ en cours; **progressive** [prəˈgrɛsɪv]
adj progressif(-ive); (person)
progressiste
prohibit [prəˈhɪbɪt] vt interdire,
défendre
project n [ˈprɔdʒɛkt] (plan) projet
m, plan m; (venture) opération f,
entreprise f; (Scol: research) étude f,
dossier m ▷ vt [prəˈdʒɛkt] projeter
▷ vi [prəˈdʒɛkt] (stick out) faire saillie,
s'avancer; **projection** [prəˈdʒɛkʃən]
n projection f; (overhang) saillie
f; **projector** [prəˈdʒɛktəʳ] n
projecteur m
prolific [prəˈlɪfɪk] adj prolifique
prolong [prəˈlɔŋ] vt prolonger
prom [prɔm] n abbr = **promenade**;
(us: ball) bal m d'étudiants; **the P~s**
série de concerts de musique classique

● **PROM**
●
●
● En Grande-Bretagne, un promenade
● concert ou prom est un concert de
● musique classique, ainsi appelé
● car, à l'origine, le public restait

debout et se promenait au lieu de rester assis. De nos jours, une partie du public reste debout, mais il y a également des places assises (plus chères). Les *Proms* les plus connus sont les Proms londoniens. La dernière séance (the "Last Night of the Proms") est un grand événement médiatique où se jouent des airs traditionnels et patriotiques. Aux États-Unis et au Canada, le *prom* ou *promenade* est un bal organisé par le lycée.

promenade [prɔməˈnɑːd] *n* (*by sea*) esplanade *f*, promenade *f*

prominent ['prɔmɪnənt] *adj* (*standing out*) proéminent(e); (*important*) important(e)

promiscuous [prəˈmɪskjuəs] *adj* (*sexually*) de mœurs légères

promise ['prɔmɪs] *n* promesse *f* ▷ *vt, vi* promettre; **promising** *adj* prometteur(-euse)

promote [prəˈməut] *vt* promouvoir; (*new product*) lancer; **promotion** [prəˈməuʃən] *n* promotion *f*

prompt [prɔmpt] *adj* rapide ▷ *n* (*Comput*) message *m* (de guidage) ▷ *vt* (*cause*) entraîner, provoquer; (*Theat*) souffler (son rôle *or* ses répliques) à; **at 8 o'clock** = à 8 heures précises; **to ~ sb to do** inciter *or* pousser qn à faire; **promptly** *adv* (*quickly*) rapidement, sans délai; (*on time*) ponctuellement

prone [prəun] *adj* (*lying*) couché(e) (face contre terre); (*liable*): **~ to** enclin(e) à

prong [prɔŋ] *n* (*of fork*) dent *f*

pronoun ['prəunaun] *n* pronom *m*

pronounce [prəˈnauns] *vt* prononcer; **how do you ~ it?** comment est-ce que ça se prononce?

pronunciation [prənʌnsɪˈeɪʃən] *n* prononciation *f*

proof [pruːf] *n* preuve *f* ▷ *adj*: **~ against** à l'épreuve de

prop [prɔp] *n* support *m*, étai *m*; (*fig*) soutien *m* ▷ *vt* (*also*: **~ up**) étayer, soutenir; **props** *npl* accessoires *mpl*

propaganda [prɔpəˈgændə] *n* propagande *f*

propeller [prəˈpɛləʳ] *n* hélice *f*

proper ['prɔpəʳ] *adj* (*suited, right*) approprié(e), bon (bonne); (*seemly*) correct(e), convenable; (*authentic*) vrai(e), véritable; (*referring to place*): **the village ~** le village proprement dit; **properly** *adv* correctement, convenablement; **proper noun** *n* nom *m* propre

property ['prɔpətɪ] *n* (*possessions*) biens *mpl*; (*house etc*) propriété *f*; (*land*) terres *fpl*, domaine *m*

prophecy ['prɔfɪsɪ] *n* prophétie *f*

prophet ['prɔfɪt] *n* prophète *m*

proportion [prəˈpɔːʃən] *n* proportion *f*; (*share*) part *f*, partie *f*; **proportions** *npl* (*size*) dimensions *fpl*; **proportional, proportionate** *adj* proportionnel(le)

proposal [prəˈpəuzl] *n* proposition *f*, offre *f*; (*plan*) projet *m*; (*of marriage*) demande *f* en mariage

propose [prəˈpəuz] *vt* proposer, suggérer ▷ *vi* faire sa demande en mariage; **to ~ to do** avoir l'intention de faire

proposition [prɔpəˈzɪʃən] *n* proposition *f*

proprietor [prəˈpraɪətəʳ] *n* propriétaire *m/f*

prose [prəuz] *n* prose *f*; (*Scol: translation*) thème *m*

prosecute ['prɔsɪkjuːt] *vt* poursuivre; **prosecution** [prɔsɪˈkjuːʃən] *n* poursuites *fpl* judiciaires; (*accusing side: in criminal case*) accusation *f*; (: *in civil case*) la partie plaignante; **prosecutor** *n* (*lawyer*) procureur *m*; (*also*: **public prosecutor**) ministère public; (*us: plaintiff*) plaignant(e)

prospect *n* ['prɔspɛkt] perspective *f*; (*hope*) espoir *m*, chances *fpl* ▷ *vt, vi*

P

[prə'spɛkt] prospecter; **prospects** npl (for work etc) possibilités fpl d'avenir, débouchés mpl; **prospective** [prə'spɛktɪv] adj (possible) éventuel(le); (future) futur(e)

prospectus [prə'spɛktəs] n prospectus m

prosper ['prɔspə'] vi prospérer; **prosperity** [prɔ'spɛrɪtɪ] n prospérité f; **prosperous** adj prospère

prostitute ['prɔstɪtjuːt] n prostituée f; **male ~** prostitué m

protect [prə'tɛkt] vt protéger; **protection** [prə'tɛkʃən] n protection f; **protective** adj protecteur(-trice); (clothing) de protection

protein ['prəutiːn] n protéine f

protest n ['prəutɛst] protestation f ▷ vi [prə'tɛst]: **to ~ against/about** protester contre/à propos de; **to ~ (that)** protester que

Protestant ['prɔtɪstənt] adj, n protestant(e)

protester, protestor [prə'tɛstə'] n (in demonstration) manifestant(e)

protractor [prə'træktə'] n (Geom) rapporteur m

proud [praud] adj fier(-ère); (pej) orgueilleux(-euse)

prove [pruːv] vt prouver, démontrer ▷ vi: **to ~ correct** etc s'avérer juste etc; **to ~ o.s.** montrer ce dont on est capable

proverb ['prɔvəːb] n proverbe m

provide [prə'vaɪd] vt fournir; **to ~ sb with sth** fournir qch à qn; **provide for** vt fus (person) subvenir aux besoins de; (future event) prévoir; **provided** conj: **provided (that)** à condition que + sub; **providing** [prə'vaɪdɪŋ] conj à condition que + sub

province ['prɔvɪns] n province f; (fig) domaine m; **provincial** [prə'vɪnʃəl] adj provincial(e)

provision [prə'vɪʒən] n (supplying) fourniture f; approvisionnement m; (stipulation) disposition f; **provisions**

npl (food) provisions fpl; **provisional** adj provisoire

provocative [prə'vɔkətɪv] adj provocateur(-trice), provocant(e)

provoke [prə'vəuk] vt provoquer

prowl [praul] vi (also: **~ about, ~ around**) rôder

proximity [prɔk'sɪmɪtɪ] n proximité f

proxy ['prɔksɪ] n: **by ~** par procuration

prudent ['pruːdnt] adj prudent(e)

prune [pruːn] n pruneau m ▷ vt élaguer

pry [praɪ] vi: **to ~ into** fourrer son nez dans

PS n abbr (= postscript) PS m

pseudonym ['sjuːdənɪm] n pseudonyme m

PSHE n abbr (BRIT Scol: = personal, social and health education) cours d'éducation personnelle, sanitaire et sociale préparant à la vie adulte

psychiatric [saɪkɪ'ætrɪk] adj psychiatrique

psychiatrist [saɪ'kaɪətrɪst] n psychiatre m/f

psychic ['saɪkɪk] adj (also: **~al**) (méta)psychique; (person) doué(e) de télépathie or d'un sixième sens

psychoanalysis (pl **psychoanalyses**) [saɪkəuə'nælɪsɪs, -siːz] n psychanalyse f

psychological [saɪkə'lɔdʒɪkl] adj psychologique

psychologist [saɪ'kɔlədʒɪst] n psychologue m/f

psychology [saɪ'kɔlədʒɪ] n psychologie f

psychotherapy [saɪkəu'θɛrəpɪ] n psychothérapie f

pt abbr = pint; pints; point; points

PTO abbr (= please turn over) TSVP

PTV abbr (US) = **pay television**

pub [pʌb] n abbr (= public house) pub m

puberty ['pjuːbətɪ] n puberté f

public ['pʌblɪk] adj public(-ique) ▷ n public m; **in ~** en public; **to make ~** rendre public

publication [pʌblɪˈkeɪʃən] n publication f

public: public company n société f anonyme; **public convenience** n (BRIT) toilettes fpl; **public holiday** n (BRIT) jour férié; **public house** n (BRIT) pub m

publicity [pʌbˈlɪsɪtɪ] n publicité f

publicize [ˈpʌblɪsaɪz] vt (make known) faire connaître, rendre public; (advertise) faire de la publicité pour

public: public limited company n ≈ société f anonyme (SA) (cotée en Bourse); **publicly** adv publiquement, en public; **public opinion** n opinion publique; **public relations** n or npl relations publiques (RP); **public school** n (BRIT) école privée; (US) école publique; **public transport**, (US) **public transportation** n transports mpl en commun

publish [ˈpʌblɪʃ] vt publier; **publisher** n éditeur m; **publishing** n (industry) édition f

pub lunch n repas m de bistrot

pudding [ˈpudɪŋ] n (BRIT: dessert) dessert m, entremets m; (sweet dish) pudding m, gâteau m

puddle [ˈpʌdl] n flaque f d'eau

puff [pʌf] n bouffée f ⊳ vt (also: ~ out: sails, cheeks) gonfler ⊳ vi (pant) haleter; **puff pastry**, (US) **puff paste** n pâte feuilletée

pull [pul] n (tug): **to give sth a ~** tirer sur qch ⊳ vt tirer; (trigger) presser; (strain: muscle, tendon) se claquer ⊳ vi tirer; **to ~ to pieces** mettre en morceaux; **to ~ one's punches** (also fig) ménager son adversaire; **to ~ one's weight** y mettre du sien; **to ~ together** se ressaisir; **to ~ sb's leg** (fig) faire marcher qn; **pull apart** vt (break) mettre en pièces, démantibuler; **pull away** vi (vehicle: move off) partir; (draw back) s'éloigner; **pull back** vt (lever etc) tirer sur; (curtains) ouvrir ⊳ vi (refrain)

s'abstenir; (Mil: withdraw) se retirer; **pull down** vt baisser, abaisser; (house) démolir; **pull in** vi (Aut) se ranger; (Rail) entrer en gare; **pull off** vt enlever, ôter; (deal etc) conclure; **pull out** vi démarrer, partir; (Aut: come out of line) déboîter ⊳ vt (from bag, pocket) sortir; (remove) arracher; **pull over** vi (Aut) se ranger; **pull up** vi (stop) s'arrêter ⊳ vt remonter; (uproot) déraciner, arracher

pulley [ˈpulɪ] n poulie f

pullover [ˈpuləuvəʳ] n pull-over m, tricot m

pulp [pʌlp] n (of fruit) pulpe f; (for paper) pâte f à papier

pulpit [ˈpulpɪt] n chaire f

pulse [pʌls] n (of blood) pouls m; (of heart) battement m; **pulses** npl (Culin) légumineuses fpl

puma [ˈpjuːmə] n puma m

pump [pʌmp] n pompe f; (shoe) escarpin m ⊳ vt pomper; **pump up** vt gonfler

pumpkin [ˈpʌmpkɪn] n potiron m, citrouille f

pun [pʌn] n jeu m de mots, calembour m

punch [pʌntʃ] n (blow) coup m de poing; (tool) poinçon m; (drink) punch m ⊳ vt (make a hole in) poinçonner, perforer; (hit): **to ~ sb/sth** donner un coup de poing à qn/sur qch; **punch-up** n (BRIT inf) bagarre f

punctual [ˈpʌŋktjuəl] adj ponctuel(le)

punctuation [pʌŋktjuˈeɪʃən] n ponctuation f

puncture [ˈpʌŋktʃəʳ] n (BRIT) crevaison f ⊳ vt crever

punish [ˈpʌnɪʃ] vt punir; **punishment** n punition f, châtiment m

punk [pʌŋk] n (person: also: ~ rocker) punk m/f; (music: also: ~ rock) le punk; (US inf: hoodlum) voyou m

pup [pʌp] n chiot m

pupil [ˈpjuːpl] n élève m/f; (of eye) pupille f

P

puppet ['pʌpɪt] n marionnette f, pantin m

puppy ['pʌpɪ] n chiot m, petit chien

purchase ['pə:tʃɪs] n achat m ▷ vt acheter

pure [pjuəʳ] adj pur(e); **purely** adv purement

purify ['pjuərɪfaɪ] vt purifier, épurer

purity ['pjuərɪtɪ] n pureté f

purple ['pə:pl] adj violet(te); (face) cramoisi(e)

purpose ['pə:pəs] n intention f, but m; **on ~** exprès

purr [pə:ʳ] vi ronronner

purse [pə:s] n (BRIT: for money) porte-monnaie m inv; (US: handbag) sac m (à main) ▷ vt serrer, pincer

pursue [pə'sju:] vt poursuivre

pursuit [pə'sju:t] n poursuite f; (occupation) occupation f, activité f

pus [pʌs] n pus m

push [puʃ] n poussée f ▷ vt pousser; (button) appuyer sur; (fig: product) mettre en avant, faire de la publicité pour ▷ vi pousser; **to ~ for** (better pay, conditions) réclamer; **push in** vi s'introduire de force; **push off** vi (inf) filer, ficher le camp; **push on** vi (continue) continuer; **push over** vt renverser; **push through** vi (in crowd) se frayer un chemin; **pushchair** n (BRIT) poussette f; **pusher** n (also: **drug pusher**) revendeur(-euse) (de drogue), ravitailleur(-euse) (en drogue); **push-up** n (US) traction f

pussy(-cat) ['pusɪ-] n (inf) minet m

put (pt, pp **put**) [put] vt mettre; (place) poser, placer; (say) dire, exprimer; (a question) poser; (case, view) exposer, présenter; (estimate) estimer; **put aside** vt mettre de côté; **put away** vt (store) ranger; **put back** vt (replace) remettre, replacer; (postpone) remettre; **put by** vt (money) mettre de côté, économiser; **put down** vt (parcel etc) poser, déposer; (in writing) mettre par écrit, inscrire; (suppress: revolt etc) réprimer, écraser; (attribute) attribuer; (animal) abattre; (cat, dog) faire piquer; **put forward** vt (ideas) avancer, proposer; **put in** vt (complaint) soumettre; (time, effort) consacrer; **put off** vt (postpone) remettre à plus tard, ajourner; (discourage) dissuader; **put on** vt (clothes, lipstick, CD) mettre; (light etc) allumer; (play etc) monter; (weight) prendre; (assume: accent, manner) prendre; (take outside) mettre dehors; (one's hand) tendre; (light etc) éteindre; (person: inconvenience) déranger, gêner; **put through** vt (Tel: caller) mettre en communication; (: call) passer; (plan) faire accepter; **put together** vt mettre ensemble; (assemble: furniture) monter, assembler; (: meal) préparer; **put up** vt (raise) lever, relever, remonter; (hang) accrocher; (build) construire, ériger; (increase) augmenter; (accommodate) loger; **put up with** vt fus supporter

putt [pʌt] n putt m; **putting green** n green m

puzzle ['pʌzl] n énigme f, mystère m; (game) jeu m, casse-tête m; (jigsaw) puzzle m; (also: **crossword ~**) mots croisés ▷ vt intriguer, rendre perplexe ▷ vi: **to ~ over** chercher à comprendre; **puzzled** adj perplexe; **puzzling** adj déconcertant(e), inexplicable

pyjamas [pɪ'dʒɑ:məz] npl (BRIT) pyjama m

pylon ['paɪlən] n pylône m

pyramid ['pɪrəmɪd] n pyramide f

Pyrenees [pɪrə'ni:z] npl Pyrénées fpl

q

quack [kwæk] n (of duck) coin-coin m inv; (pej: doctor) charlatan m
quadruple [kwɔ'dru:pl] vt, vi quadrupler
quail [kweɪl] n (Zool) caille f ▷ vi: **to ~ at** or **before** reculer devant
quaint [kweɪnt] adj bizarre; (old-fashioned) désuet(-ète); (picturesque) au charme vieillot, pittoresque
quake [kweɪk] vi trembler ▷ n abbr = **earthquake**
qualification [kwɔlɪfɪ'keɪʃən] n (often pl: degree etc) diplôme m; (training) qualification(s) f(pl); (ability) compétence(s) f(pl); (limitation) réserve f, restriction f
qualified ['kwɔlɪfaɪd] adj (trained) qualifié(e); (professionally) diplômé(e); (fit, competent) compétent(e), qualifié(e); (limited) conditionnel(le)
qualify ['kwɔlɪfaɪ] vt qualifier; (modify) atténuer, nuancer ▷ vi: **to ~ (as)** obtenir son diplôme (de); **to ~**

(for) remplir les conditions requises (pour); (Sport) se qualifier (pour)
quality ['kwɔlɪtɪ] n qualité f
qualm [kwɑ:m] n doute m; scrupule m
quantify ['kwɔntɪfaɪ] vt quantifier
quantity ['kwɔntɪtɪ] n quantité f
quarantine ['kwɔrnti:n] n quarantaine f
quarrel ['kwɔrl] n querelle f, dispute f ▷ vi se disputer, se quereller
quarry ['kwɔrɪ] n (for stone) carrière f; (animal) proie f, gibier m
quart [kwɔ:t] n ≈ litre m
quarter ['kwɔ:tər] n quart m; (of year) trimestre m; (district) quartier m; (us, CANADA: 25 cents) (pièce f de) vingt-cinq cents mpl ▷ vt partager en quartiers or en quatre; (Mil) caserner, cantonner; **quarters** npl logement m; (Mil) quartiers mpl, cantonnement m; **a ~ of an hour** un quart d'heure; **quarter final** n quart m de finale; **quarterly** adj trimestriel(le) ▷ adv tous les trois mois
quartet(te) [kwɔ:'tɛt] n quatuor m; (jazz players) quartette m
quartz [kwɔ:ts] n quartz m
quay [ki:] n (also: ~side) quai m
queasy ['kwi:zɪ] adj: **to feel ~** avoir mal au cœur
Quebec [kwɪ'bɛk] n (city) Québec; (province) Québec m
queen [kwi:n] n (gen) reine f; (Cards etc) dame f
queer [kwɪər] adj étrange, curieux(-euse); (suspicious) louche ▷ n (offensive) homosexuel m
quench [kwɛntʃ] vt: **to ~ one's thirst** se désaltérer
query ['kwɪərɪ] n question f ▷ vt (disagree with, dispute) mettre en doute, questionner
quest [kwɛst] n recherche f, quête f
question ['kwɛstʃən] n question f ▷ vt (person) interroger; (plan, idea) mettre en question or en doute; **beyond ~** sans aucun doute; **out of the ~** hors de

question; **questionable** *adj*
discutable; **question mark** *n* point
m d'interrogation; **questionnaire**
[kwɛstʃə'nɛəʳ] *n* questionnaire *m*
queue [kjuː] (BRIT) *n* queue *f*, file *f* ▷ *vi*
(*also*: **~ up**) faire la queue
quiche [kiːʃ] *n* quiche *f*
quick [kwɪk] *adj* rapide; (*mind*) vif
(vive); (*agile*) agile, vif (vive) ▷ *n*: **cut
to the ~** (*fig*) touché(e) au vif; **be
~!** dépêche-toi!; **quickly** *adv* (*fast*)
vite, rapidement; (*immediately*) tout
de suite
quid [kwɪd] *n* (*pl inv*: BRIT *inf*) livre *f*
quiet ['kwaɪət] *adj* tranquille,
calme; (*voice*) bas(se); (*ceremony,
colour*) discret(-ète) ▷ *n* tranquillité
f, calme *m*; (*silence*) silence *m*;
quietly *adv* tranquillement;
(*silently*) silencieusement; (*discreetly*)
discrètement
quilt [kwɪlt] *n* édredon *m*; (*continental
quilt*) couette *f*
quirky ['kwɜːkɪ] *adj* singulier(-ère)
quit [kwɪt] (*pt, pp* **quit** *or* **quitted**)
vt quitter ▷ *vi* (*give up*) abandonner,
renoncer; (*resign*) démissionner
quite [kwaɪt] *adv* (*rather*) assez,
plutôt; (*entirely*) complètement,
tout à fait; **~ a few of them** un assez
grand nombre d'entre eux; **that's
not ~ right** ce n'est pas tout à fait
juste; **~ (so)!** exactement!
quits [kwɪts] *adj*: **~ (with)** quitte
(envers); **let's call it ~** restons-en là
quiver ['kwɪvəʳ] *vi* trembler, frémir
quiz [kwɪz] *n* (*on TV*) jeu-concours *m*
(télévisé); (*in magazine etc*) test *m* de
connaissances ▷ *vt* interroger
quota ['kwəʊtə] *n* quota *m*
quotation [kwəʊ'teɪʃən] *n* citation *f*;
(*estimate*) devis *m*; **quotation marks**
npl guillemets *mpl*
quote [kwəʊt] *n* citation *f*; (*estimate*)
devis *m* ▷ *vt* (*sentence, author*) citer;
(*price*) donner, soumettre ▷ *vi*: **to
~ from** citer; **quotes** *npl* (*inverted
commas*) guillemets *mpl*

r

rabbi ['ræbaɪ] *n* rabbin *m*
rabbit ['ræbɪt] *n* lapin *m*
rabies ['reɪbiːz] *n* rage *f*
RAC *n abbr* (BRIT: = *Royal Automobile
Club*) ≈ ACF *m*
rac(c)oon [rə'kuːn] *n* raton *m* laveur
race [reɪs] *n* (*species*) race *f*;
(*competition, rush*) course *f* ▷ *vt*
(*person*) faire la course avec ▷ *vi*
(*compete*) faire la course, courir;
(*pulse*) battre très vite; **race car** *n* (US)
= **racing car**; **racecourse** *n* champ *m*
de courses; **racehorse** *n* cheval *m* de
course; **racetrack** *n* piste *f*
racial ['reɪʃl] *adj* racial(e)
racing ['reɪsɪŋ] *n* courses *fpl*; **racing
car** *n* (BRIT) voiture *f* de course;
racing driver *n* (BRIT) pilote *m* de
course
racism ['reɪsɪzəm] *n* racisme *m*;
racist ['reɪsɪst] *adj, n* raciste *m/f*
rack [ræk] *n* (*for guns, tools*) râtelier
m; (*for clothes*) portant *m*; (*for bottles*)

casier m; (also: **luggage ~**) filet m à bagages; (also: **roof ~**) galerie f; (also: **dish ~**) égouttoir m ▷ vt tourmenter; **to ~ one's brains** se creuser la cervelle

racket ['rækɪt] n (for tennis) raquette f; (noise) tapage m, vacarme m; (swindle) escroquerie f

racquet ['rækɪt] n raquette f

radar ['reɪdɑːʳ] n radar m

radiation [reɪdɪ'eɪʃən] n rayonnement m; (radioactive) radiation f

radiator ['reɪdɪeɪtəʳ] n radiateur m

radical ['rædɪkl] adj radical(e)

radio ['reɪdɪəu] n radio f ▷ vt (person) appeler par radio; **on the ~** à la radio; **radioactive** adj radioactif(-ive); **radio station** n station f de radio

radish ['rædɪʃ] n radis m

RAF n abbr (BRIT) = **Royal Air Force**

raffle ['ræfl] n tombola f

raft [rɑːft] n (craft: also: **life ~**) radeau m; (logs) train m de flottage

rag [ræg] n chiffon m; (pej: newspaper) feuille f, torchon m; (for charity) attractions organisées par les étudiants au profit d'œuvres de charité; **rags** npl haillons mpl

rage [reɪdʒ] n (fury) rage f, fureur f ▷ vi (person) être fou (folle) de rage; (storm) faire rage, être déchaîné(e); **it's all the ~** cela fait fureur

ragged ['rægɪd] adj (edge) inégal(e), qui accroche; (clothes) en loques; (appearance) déguenillé(e)

raid [reɪd] n (Mil) raid m; (criminal) hold-up m inv; (by police) descente f, rafle f ▷ vt faire un raid sur ou un hold-up dans ou une descente dans

rail [reɪl] n (on stair) rampe f; (on bridge, balcony) balustrade f; (of ship) bastingage m; (for train) rail m; **railcard** n (BRIT) carte f de chemin de fer; **railing(s)** n(pl) grille f; **railway**, (US) **railroad** n chemin m de fer; (track) voie f ferrée; **railway line** n (BRIT) ligne f de chemin de fer; (track)

voie ferrée; **railway station** n (BRIT) gare f

rain [reɪn] n pluie f ▷ vi pleuvoir; **in the ~** sous la pluie; **it's ~ing** il pleut; **rainbow** n arc-en-ciel m; **raincoat** n imperméable m; **raindrop** n goutte f de pluie; **rainfall** n chute f de pluie; (measurement) hauteur f des précipitations; **rainforest** n forêt tropicale; **rainy** adj pluvieux(-euse)

raise [reɪz] n augmentation f ▷ vt (lift) lever; hausser; (increase) augmenter; (morale) remonter; (standards) améliorer; (a protest, doubt) provoquer, causer; (a question) soulever; (cattle, family) élever; (crop) faire pousser; (army, funds) rassembler; (loan) obtenir; **to ~ one's voice** élever la voix

raisin ['reɪzn] n raisin sec

rake [reɪk] n (tool) râteau m; (person) débauché m ▷ vt (garden) ratisser

rally ['rælɪ] n (Pol etc) meeting m, rassemblement m; (Aut) rallye m; (Tennis) échange m ▷ vt rassembler, rallier; (support) gagner ▷ vi (sick person) aller mieux; (Stock Exchange) reprendre

RAM [ræm] n abbr (Comput: = random access memory) mémoire vive

ram [ræm] n bélier m ▷ vt (push) enfoncer; (crash into: vehicle) emboutir; (: lamppost etc) percuter

Ramadan [ræmə'dæn] n Ramadan m

ramble ['ræmbl] n randonnée f ▷ vi (walk) se promener, faire une randonnée; (pej: also: **~ on**) discourir, pérorer; **rambler** n promeneur(-euse), randonneur(-euse); **rambling** adj (speech) décousu(e); (house) plein(e) de coins et de recoins; (Bot) grimpant(e)

ramp [ræmp] n (incline) rampe f; (Aut) dénivellation f; (in garage) pont m; **on/off ~** (US Aut) bretelle f d'accès

rampage ['ræmpeɪdʒ] n: **to be on the ~** se déchaîner

r

ran [ræn] *pt of* **run**

ranch [rɑ:ntʃ] *n* ranch *m*

random ['rændəm] *adj* fait(e) or établi(e) au hasard; (*Comput, Math*) aléatoire ⊳ *n*: **at ~** au hasard

rang [ræŋ] *pt of* **ring**

range [reɪndʒ] *n* (*of mountains*) chaîne *f*; (*of missile, voice*) portée *f*; (*of products*) choix *m*, gamme *f*; (*also*: **shooting ~**) champ *m* de tir; (*also*: **kitchen ~**) fourneau *m* (de cuisine) ⊳ *vt* (*place*) mettre en rang, placer ⊳ *vi*: **to ~ over** couvrir; **to ~ from ... to** aller de ... à

ranger ['reɪndʒəʳ] *n* garde *m* forestier

rank [ræŋk] *n* rang *m*; (*Mil*) grade *m*; (*BRIT: also*: **taxi ~**) station *f* de taxis ⊳ *vi*: **to ~ among** compter or se classer parmi ⊳ *adj* (*smell*) nauséabond(e); **the ~ and file** (*fig*) la masse, la base

ransom ['rænsəm] *n* rançon *f*; **to hold sb to ~** (*fig*) exercer un chantage sur qn

rant [rænt] *vi* fulminer

rap [ræp] *n* (*music*) rap *m* ⊳ *vt* (*door*) frapper sur or à; (*table etc*) taper sur

rape [reɪp] *n* viol *m*; (*Bot*) colza *m* ⊳ *vt* violer

rapid ['ræpɪd] *adj* rapide; **rapidly** *adv* rapidement; **rapids** *npl* (*Geo*) rapides *mpl*

rapist ['reɪpɪst] *n* auteur *m* d'un viol

rapport [ræ'pɔ:ʳ] *n* entente *f*

rare [rɛəʳ] *adj* rare; (*Culin: steak*) saignant(e); **rarely** *adv* rarement

rash [ræʃ] *adj* imprudent(e), irréfléchi(e); *n* (*Med*) rougeur *f*, éruption *f*; (*of events*) série *f* (noire)

rasher ['ræʃəʳ] *n* fine tranche (de lard)

raspberry ['rɑ:zbərɪ] *n* framboise *f*

rat [ræt] *n* rat *m*

rate [reɪt] *n* (*ratio*) taux *m*, pourcentage *m*; (*speed*) vitesse *f*, rythme *m*; (*price*) tarif *m* ⊳ *vt* (*price*) évaluer, estimer; (*people*) classer; **rates** *npl* (*BRIT: property tax*) impôts

locaux; **to ~ sb/sth as** considérer qn/qch comme

rather ['rɑ:ðəʳ] *adv* (*somewhat*) assez, plutôt; (*to some extent*) un peu; **it's ~ expensive** c'est assez cher; (*too much*) c'est un peu cher; **there's ~ a lot** il y en a beaucoup; **I would** or **I'd ~ go** j'aimerais mieux or je préférerais partir; **or ~** (*more accurately*) ou plutôt

rating ['reɪtɪŋ] *n* (*assessment*) évaluation *f*; (*score*) classement *m*; (*Finance*) cote *f*; **ratings** *npl* (*Radio*) indice(s) *m(pl)* d'écoute; (*TV*) Audimat® *m*

ratio ['reɪʃɪəu] *n* proportion *f*; **in the ~ of 100 to 1** dans la proportion de 100 contre 1

ration ['ræʃən] *n* ration *f* ⊳ *vt* rationner; **rations** *npl* (*food*) vivres *mpl*

rational ['ræʃənl] *adj* raisonnable, sensé(e); (*solution, reasoning*) logique; (*Med: person*) lucide

rat race *n* foire *f* d'empoigne

rattle ['rætl] *n* (*of door, window*) battement *m*; (*of coins, chain*) cliquetis *m*; (*of train, engine*) bruit *m* de ferraille; (*for baby*) hochet *m* ⊳ *vi* cliqueter; (*car, bus*): **to ~ along** rouler en faisant un bruit de ferraille ⊳ *vt* agiter (bruyamment); (*inf: disconcert*) déconcerter

rave [reɪv] *vi* (*in anger*) s'emporter; (*with enthusiasm*) s'extasier; (*Med*) délirer ⊳ *n* (*inf: party*) rave *f*, soirée *f* techno

raven ['reɪvən] *n* grand corbeau

ravine [rə'vi:n] *n* ravin *m*

raw [rɔ:] *adj* (*uncooked*) cru(e); (*not processed*) brut(e); (*sore*) à vif, irrité(e); (*inexperienced*) inexpérimenté(e); **~ materials** matières premières

ray [reɪ] *n* rayon *m*; **~ of hope** lueur *f* d'espoir

razor ['reɪzəʳ] *n* rasoir *m*; **razor blade** *n* lame *f* de rasoir

Rd *abbr* = **road**

RE n abbr (BRIT: = religious education) instruction religieuse

re [ri:] prep concernant

reach [ri:tʃ] n portée f, atteinte f; (of river etc) étendue f ▷ vt atteindre, arriver à; (conclusion, decision) parvenir à ▷ vi s'étendre; **out of/within ~** (object) hors de/à portée; **reach out** vt tendre ▷ vi: **to ~ out (for)** allonger le bras (pour prendre)

react [ri:'ækt] vi réagir; **reaction** [ri:'ækʃən] n réaction f; **reactor** [ri:'æktər] n réacteur m

read (pt, pp **read**) [ri:d, rɛd] vi lire ▷ vt lire; (understand) comprendre, interpréter; (study) étudier; (meter) relever; (subj: instrument etc) indiquer, marquer; **read out** vt lire à haute voix; **reader** n lecteur(-trice)

readily ['rɛdɪlɪ] adv volontiers, avec empressement; (easily) facilement

reading ['ri:dɪŋ] n lecture f; (understanding) interprétation f; (on instrument) indications fpl

ready ['rɛdɪ] adj prêt(e); (willing) prêt, disposé(e); (available) disponible ▷ n: **at the ~** (Mil) prêt à faire feu; **when will my photos be ~?** quand est-ce que mes photos seront prêtes?; **to get ~** (as vi) se préparer; (as vt) préparer; **ready-cooked** adj précuit(e); **ready-made** adj tout(e) faite(e)

real [rɪəl] adj (world, life) réel(le); (genuine) véritable; (proper) vrai(e) ▷ adv (US inf: very) vraiment; **real ale** n bière traditionnelle; **real estate** n biens fonciers or immobiliers; **realistic** [rɪə'lɪstɪk] adj réaliste; **reality** [ri:'ælɪtɪ] n réalité f; **reality TV** n téléréalité f

realization [rɪəlaɪ'zeɪʃən] n (awareness) prise f de conscience; (fulfilment, also: of asset) réalisation f

realize ['rɪəlaɪz] vt (understand) se rendre compte de, prendre conscience de; (a project, Comm: asset) réaliser

really ['rɪəlɪ] adv vraiment; **~?** vraiment?, c'est vrai?

realm [rɛlm] n royaume m; (fig) domaine m

realtor ['rɪəltɔːr] n (US) agent immobilier

reappear [ri:ə'pɪər] vi réapparaître, reparaître

rear [rɪər] adj de derrière, arrière inv; (Aut: wheel etc) arrière ▷ n arrière m ▷ vt (cattle, family) élever ▷ vi (also: **~ up**: animal) se cabrer

rearrange [ri:ə'reɪndʒ] vt réarranger

rear: rear-view mirror n (Aut) rétroviseur m; **rear-wheel drive** n (Aut) traction f arrière

reason ['ri:zn] n raison f ▷ vi: **to ~ with sb** raisonner qn, faire entendre raison à qn; **it stands to ~ that** il va sans dire que; **reasonable** adj raisonnable; (not bad) acceptable; **reasonably** adv (behave) raisonnablement; (fairly) assez; **reasoning** n raisonnement m

reassurance [ri:ə'ʃuərəns] n (factual) assurance f, garantie f; (emotional) réconfort m

reassure [ri:ə'ʃuər] vt rassurer

rebate ['ri:beɪt] n (on tax etc) dégrèvement m

rebel n ['rɛbl] rebelle m/f ▷ vi [rɪ'bɛl] se rebeller, se révolter; **rebellion** [rɪ'bɛljən] n rébellion f, révolte f; **rebellious** [rɪ'bɛljəs] adj rebelle

rebuild [ri:'bɪld] vt (irreg: like **build**) reconstruire

recall vt [rɪ'kɔ:l] rappeler; (remember) se rappeler, se souvenir de ▷ n ['ri:kɔl] rappel m; (ability to remember) mémoire f

receipt [rɪ'si:t] n (document) reçu m; (for parcel etc) accusé m de réception; (act of receiving) réception f; **receipts** npl (Comm) recettes fpl; **can I have a ~, please?** je peux avoir un reçu, s'il vous plaît?

receive [rɪ'si:v] vt recevoir; (guest) recevoir, accueillir; **receiver** n (Tel)

r

récepteur m, combiné m; (*Radio*) récepteur; (*of stolen goods*) receleur m; (*for bankruptcies*) administrateur m judiciaire

recent ['ri:snt] *adj* récent(e); **recently** *adv* récemment

reception [rɪ'sɛpʃən] *n* réception f; (*welcome*) accueil m, réception; **reception desk** *n* réception f; **receptionist** *n* réceptionniste m/f

recession [rɪ'sɛʃən] *n* (*Econ*) récession f

recharge [ri:'tʃɑ:dʒ] *vt* (*battery*) recharger

recipe ['rɛsɪpɪ] *n* recette f

recipient [rɪ'sɪpɪənt] *n* (*of payment*) bénéficiaire m/f; (*of letter*) destinataire m/f

recital [rɪ'saɪtl] *n* récital m

recite [rɪ'saɪt] *vt* (*poem*) réciter

reckless ['rɛkləs] *adj* (*driver etc*) imprudent(e); (*spender etc*) insouciant(e)

reckon ['rɛkən] *vt* (*count*) calculer, compter; (*consider*) considérer, estimer; (*think*): **I ~ (that)** ... je pense (que), j'estime (que) ...

reclaim [rɪ'kleɪm] *vt* (*land: from sea*) assécher; (*demand back*) réclamer (le remboursement *or* la restitution de); (*waste materials*) récupérer

recline [rɪ'klaɪn] *vi* être allongé(e) *or* étendu(e)

recognition [rɛkəg'nɪʃən] *n* reconnaissance f; **transformed beyond ~** méconnaissable

recognize ['rɛkəgnaɪz] *vt*: **to ~ (by/ as)** reconnaître (à/comme étant)

recollection [rɛkə'lɛkʃən] *n* souvenir m

recommend [rɛkə'mɛnd] *vt* recommander; **can you ~ a good restaurant?** pouvez-vous me conseiller un bon restaurant?; **recommendation** [rɛkəmen'deɪʃən] *n* recommandation f

reconcile ['rɛkənsaɪl] *vt* (*two people*) réconcilier; (*two facts*) concilier, accorder; **to ~ o.s. to** se résigner à

reconsider [ri:kən'sɪdər] *vt* reconsidérer

reconstruct [ri:kən'strʌkt] *vt* (*building*) reconstruire; (*crime, system*) reconstituer

record *n* ['rɛkɔ:d] rapport m, récit m; (*of meeting etc*) procès-verbal m; (*register*) registre m; (*file*) dossier m; (*Comput*) article m; (*also*: **police ~**) casier m judiciaire; (*Mus: disc*) disque m; (*Sport*) record m ▷ *adj* ['rɛkɔ:d] record *inv* ▷ *vt* [rɪ'kɔ:d] (*set down*) noter; (*Mus: song etc*) enregistrer; **public ~s** archives fpl; **in ~ time** dans un temps record; **recorded delivery** *n* (*BRIT Post*): **to send sth recorded delivery** ≈ envoyer qch en recommandé; **recorder** *n* (*Mus*) flûte f à bec; **recording** *n* (*Mus*) enregistrement m; **record player** *n* tourne-disque m

recount [rɪ'kaunt] *vt* raconter

recover [rɪ'kʌvər] *vt* récupérer ▷ *vi* (*from illness*) se rétablir; (*from shock*) se remettre; **recovery** *n* récupération f; rétablissement m; (*Econ*) redressement m

recreate [ri:krɪ'eɪt] *vt* recréer

recreation [rɛkrɪ'eɪʃən] *n* (*leisure*) récréation f, détente f; **recreational drug** *n* drogue récréative; **recreational vehicle** *n* (*US*) camping-car m

recruit [rɪ'kru:t] *n* recrue f ▷ *vt* recruter; **recruitment** *n* recrutement m

rectangle ['rɛktæŋgl] *n* rectangle m; **rectangular** [rɛk'tæŋgjulər] *adj* rectangulaire

rectify ['rɛktɪfaɪ] *vt* (*error*) rectifier, corriger

rector ['rɛktər] *n* (*Rel*) pasteur m

recur [rɪ'kə:r] *vi* se reproduire; (*idea, opportunity*) se retrouver; (*symptoms*) réapparaître; **recurring** *adj* (*problem*) périodique, fréquent(e); (*Math*) périodique

recyclable [ri:'saɪkləbl] *adj* recyclable

recycle [riː'saɪkl] *vt, vi* recycler
recycling [riː'saɪklɪŋ] *n* recyclage *m*
red [rɛd] *n* rouge *m*; (*Pol: pej*) rouge *m/f* ▷ *adj* rouge; (*hair*) roux (rousse); **in the ~** (*account*) à découvert; (*business*) en déficit; **Red Cross** *n* Croix-Rouge *f*; **redcurrant** *n* groseille *f* (rouge)
redeem [rɪ'diːm] *vt* (*debt*) rembourser; (*sth in pawn*) dégager; (*fig, also Rel*) racheter
red: red-haired *adj* roux (rousse); **redhead** *n* roux (rousse); **red-hot** *adj* chauffé(e) au rouge, brûlant(e); **red light** *n*: **to go through a red light** (*Aut*) brûler un feu rouge; **red-light district** *n* quartier mal famé
red meat *n* viande *f* rouge
reduce [rɪ'djuːs] *vt* réduire; (*lower*) abaisser; **"~ speed now"** (*Aut*) "ralentir"; **to ~ sb to tears** faire pleurer qn; **reduced** *adj* réduit(e); **"greatly reduced prices"** "gros rabais"; **at a reduced price** (*goods*) au rabais; (*ticket etc*) à prix réduit; **reduction** [rɪ'dʌkʃən] *n* réduction *f*; (*of price*) baisse *f*; (*discount*) rabais *m*; réduction; **is there a reduction for children/students?** y a-t-il une réduction pour les enfants/les étudiants?
redundancy [rɪ'dʌndənsɪ] *n* (*BRIT*) licenciement *m*, mise *f* au chômage
redundant [rɪ'dʌndnt] *adj* (*BRIT: worker*) licencié(e), mis(e) au chômage; (*detail, object*) superflu(e); **to be made ~** (*worker*) être licencié, être mis au chômage
reed [riːd] *n* (*Bot*) roseau *m*
reef [riːf] *n* (*at sea*) récif *m*, écueil *m*
reel [riːl] *n* bobine *f*; (*Fishing*) moulinet *m*; (*Cine*) bande *f*; (*dance*) quadrille écossais ▷ *vi* (*sway*) chanceler
ref [rɛf] *n abbr* (*inf: = referee*) arbitre *m*
refectory [rɪ'fɛktərɪ] *n* réfectoire *m*
refer [rɪ'fəː] *vt*: **to ~ sb to** (*inquirer, patient*) adresser qn à; (*reader: to text*) renvoyer qn à ▷ *vi*: **to ~ to** (*allude to*)

parler de, faire allusion à; (*consult*) se reporter à; (*apply to*) s'appliquer à
referee [rɛfə'riː] *n* arbitre *m*; (*BRIT: for job application*) répondant(e) ▷ *vt* arbitrer
reference ['rɛfrəns] *n* référence *f*, renvoi *m*; (*mention*) allusion *f*, mention *f*; (*for job application: letter*) références; lettre *f* de recommandation; **with ~ to** en ce qui concerne; (*Comm: in letter*) me référant à; **reference number** *n* (*Comm*) numéro *m* de référence
refill *vt* [riː'fɪl] remplir à nouveau; (*pen, lighter etc*) recharger ▷ *n* ['riːfɪl] (*for pen etc*) recharge *f*
refine [rɪ'faɪn] *vt* (*sugar, oil*) raffiner; (*taste*) affiner; (*idea, theory*) peaufiner; **refined** *adj* (*person, taste*) raffiné(e); **refinery** *n* raffinerie *f*
reflect [rɪ'flɛkt] *vt* (*light, image*) réfléchir, refléter ▷ *vi* (*think*) réfléchir, méditer; **it ~s badly on him** cela le discrédite; **it ~s well on him** c'est tout à son honneur; **reflection** [rɪ'flɛkʃən] *n* réflexion *f*; (*image*) reflet *m*; **on reflection** réflexion faite
reflex ['riːflɛks] *adj, n* réflexe (*m*)
reform [rɪ'fɔːm] *n* réforme *f* ▷ *vt* réformer
refrain [rɪ'freɪn] *vi*: **to ~ from doing** s'abstenir de faire ▷ *n* refrain *m*
refresh [rɪ'frɛʃ] *vt* rafraîchir; (*subj: food, sleep etc*) redonner des forces à; **refreshing** *adj* (*drink*) rafraîchissant(e); (*sleep*) réparateur(-trice); **refreshments** *npl* rafraîchissements *mpl*
refrigerator [rɪ'frɪdʒəreɪtəʳ] *n* réfrigérateur *m*, frigidaire *m*
refuel [riː'fjuəl] *vi* se ravitailler en carburant
refuge ['rɛfjuːdʒ] *n* refuge *m*; **to take ~ in** se réfugier dans; **refugee** [rɛfju'dʒiː] *n* réfugié(e)
refund *n* ['riːfʌnd] remboursement *m* ▷ *vt* [rɪ'fʌnd] rembourser
refurbish [riː'fəːbɪʃ] *vt* remettre à neuf

r

refusal [rɪ'fjuːzəl] n refus m; **to have first ~ on sth** avoir droit de préemption sur qch

refuse¹ ['refjuːs] n ordures fpl, détritus mpl

refuse² [rɪ'fjuːz] vt, vi refuser; **to ~ to do sth** refuser de faire qch

regain [rɪ'geɪn] vt (lost ground) regagner; (strength) retrouver

regard [rɪ'gɑːd] n respect m, estime f, considération f ▷ vt considérer; **to give one's ~s to** faire ses amitiés à; **"with kindest ~s"** "bien amicalement"; **as ~s, with ~ to** en ce qui concerne; **regarding** prep en ce qui concerne; **regardless** adv quand même; **regardless of** sans se soucier de

regenerate [rɪ'dʒɛnəreɪt] vt régénérer ▷ vi se régénérer

reggae ['regeɪ] n reggae m

regiment ['redʒɪmənt] n régiment m

region ['riːdʒən] n région f; **in the ~ of** (fig) aux alentours de; **regional** adj régional(e)

register ['redʒɪstər] n registre m; (also: **electoral ~**) liste électorale ▷ vt enregistrer, inscrire; (birth) déclarer; (vehicle) immatriculer; (letter) envoyer en recommandé; (subj: instrument) marquer ▷ vi s'inscrire; (at hotel) signer le registre; (make impression) être (bien) compris(e); **registered** adj (BRIT: letter) recommandé(e); **registered trademark** n marque déposée

registrar ['redʒɪstrɑː'] n officier m de l'état civil

registration [redʒɪs'treɪʃən] n (act) enregistrement m; (of student) inscription f; (BRIT Aut: also: **~ number**) numéro m d'immatriculation

registry office ['redʒɪstrɪ-] n (BRIT) bureau m de l'état civil; **to get married in a ~** ≈ se marier à la mairie

regret [rɪ'grɛt] n regret m ▷ vt regretter; **regrettable** adj regrettable, fâcheux(-euse)

regular ['regjulər] adj régulier(-ière); (usual) habituel(le), normal(e); (soldier) de métier; (Comm: size) ordinaire ▷ n (client etc) habitué(e); **regularly** adv régulièrement

regulate ['regjuleɪt] vt régler; **regulation** [regju'leɪʃən] n (rule) règlement m; (adjustment) réglage m

rehabilitation ['riːəbɪlɪ'teɪʃən] n (of offender) réhabilitation f; (of addict) réadaptation f

rehearsal [rɪ'həːsəl] n répétition f

rehearse [rɪ'həːs] vt répéter

reign [reɪn] n règne m ▷ vi régner

reimburse [riːɪm'bəːs] vt rembourser

rein [reɪn] n (for horse) rêne f

reincarnation [riːɪnkɑː'neɪʃən] n réincarnation f

reindeer ['reɪndɪə'] n (pl inv) renne m

reinforce [riːɪn'fɔːs] vt renforcer; **reinforcements** npl (Mil) renfort(s) m(pl)

reinstate [riːɪn'steɪt] vt rétablir, réintégrer

reject n ['riːdʒɛkt] (Comm) article m de rebut ▷ vt [rɪ'dʒɛkt] refuser; (idea) rejeter; **rejection** [rɪ'dʒɛkʃən] n rejet m, refus m

rejoice [rɪ'dʒɔɪs] vi: **to ~ (at or over)** se réjouir (de)

relate [rɪ'leɪt] vt (tell) raconter; (connect) établir un rapport entre ▷ vi: **to ~ to** (connect) se rapporter à; **to ~ to sb** (interact) entretenir des rapports avec qn; **related** adj apparenté(e); **related to** (subject) lié(e) à; **relating to** prep concernant

relation [rɪ'leɪʃən] n (person) parent(e); (link) rapport m, lien m; **relations** npl (relatives) famille f; **relationship** n rapport m, lien m; (personal ties) relations fpl, rapports; (also: **family relationship**) lien de parenté; (affair) liaison f

relative ['rɛlətɪv] n parent(e) ▷ adj
relatif(-ive); (respective) respectif(-
ive); **relatively** adv relativement
relax [rɪ'læks] vi (muscle) se relâcher;
(person: unwind) se détendre ▷ vt
relâcher; (mind, person) détendre;
relaxation [riːlæk'seɪʃən] n
relâchement m; (of mind) détente f;
(recreation) détente, délassement m;
relaxed adj relâché(e); détendu(e);
relaxing adj délassant(e)
relay ['riːleɪ] n (Sport) course f de relais
▷ vt (message) retransmettre, relayer
release [rɪ'liːs] n (from prison,
obligation) libération f; (of gas etc)
émission f; (of film etc) sortie f; (new
recording) disque m ▷ vt (prisoner)
libérer; (book, film) sortir; (report,
news) rendre public, publier; (gas etc)
émettre, dégager; (free: from wreckage
etc) dégager; (Tech: catch, spring etc)
déclencher; (let go: person, animal)
relâcher; (: hand, object) lâcher; (: grip,
brake) desserrer
relegate ['rɛləgeɪt] vt reléguer; (BRIT
Sport): **to be ~d** descendre dans une
division inférieure
relent [rɪ'lɛnt] vi se laisser fléchir;
relentless adj implacable; (non-stop)
continuel(le)
relevant ['rɛləvənt] adj (question)
pertinent(e); (corresponding)
approprié(e); (fact) significatif(-ive);
(information) utile
reliable [rɪ'laɪəbl] adj (person, firm)
sérieux(-euse), fiable; (method,
machine) fiable; (news, information)
sûr(e)
relic ['rɛlɪk] n (Rel) relique f; (of the
past) vestige m
relief [rɪ'liːf] n (from pain, anxiety)
soulagement m; (help, supplies)
secours m(pl); (Art, Geo) relief m
relieve [rɪ'liːv] vt (pain, patient)
soulager; (fear, worry) dissiper; (bring
help) secourir; (take over from: gen)
relayer; (: guard) relever; **to ~ sb of
sth** débarrasser qn de qch; **to ~ o.s.**

(euphemism) se soulager, faire ses
besoins; **relieved** adj soulagé(e)
religion [rɪ'lɪdʒən] n religion f
religious [rɪ'lɪdʒəs] adj
religieux(-euse); (book) de piété;
religious education n instruction
religieuse
relish ['rɛlɪʃ] n (Culin) condiment m;
(enjoyment) délectation f ▷ vt (food
etc) savourer; **to ~ doing** se délecter
à faire
relocate [riːləu'keɪt] vt (business)
transférer ▷ vi se transférer, s'installer
or s'établir ailleurs
reluctance [rɪ'lʌktəns] n
répugnance f
reluctant [rɪ'lʌktənt] adj peu
disposé(e), qui hésite; **reluctantly**
adv à contrecœur, sans enthousiasme
rely on [rɪ'laɪ-] vt fus (be dependent on)
dépendre de; (trust) compter sur
remain [rɪ'meɪn] vi rester;
remainder n reste m; (Comm) fin f
de série; **remaining** adj qui reste;
remains npl restes mpl
remand [rɪ'mɑːnd] n: **on ~** en
détention préventive ▷ vt: **to be ~ed
in custody** être placé(e) en détention
préventive
remark [rɪ'mɑːk] n remarque f,
observation f ▷ vt (faire) remarquer,
dire; **remarkable** adj remarquable
remarry [riː'mærɪ] vi se remarier
remedy ['rɛmədɪ] n: **~ (for)** remède
m (contre or à) ▷ vt remédier à
remember [rɪ'mɛmbəʳ] vt se
rappeler, se souvenir de; (send
greetings): **~ me to him** saluez-le
de ma part; **Remembrance Day**
[rɪ'mɛmbrəns-] n (BRIT) ≈ (le jour de)
l'Armistice m, ≈ le 11 novembre

● **REMEMBRANCE DAY**
●
● Remembrance Day ou Remembrance
● Sunday est le dimanche le plus
● proche du 11 novembre, jour où
● la Première Guerre mondiale

a officiellement pris fin. Il rend
hommage aux victimes des
deux guerres mondiales. À
cette occasion, on observe deux
minutes de silence à 11h, heure de
la signature de l'armistice avec
l'Allemagne en 1918; certaines
membres de la famille royale et
du gouvernement déposent des
gerbes de coquelicots au cénotaphe
de Whitehall, et des couronnes
sont placées sur les monuments
aux morts dans toute la Grande-
Bretagne; par ailleurs, les gens
portent des coquelicots artificiels
fabriqués et vendus par des
membres de la légion britannique
blessés au combat, au profit des
blessés de guerre et de leur famille.

remind [rɪ'maɪnd] vt: **to ~ sb of sth**
rappeler qch à qn; **to ~ sb to do** faire
penser à qn à faire, rappeler à qn qu'il
doit faire; **reminder** n (Comm: letter)
rappel m; (note etc) pense-bête m;
(souvenir) souvenir m

reminiscent [remɪ'nɪsnt] adj: **~ of**
qui rappelle, qui fait penser à

remnant ['remnənt] n reste m,
restant m; (of cloth) coupon m

remorse [rɪ'mɔːs] n remords m

remote [rɪ'məut] adj éloigné(e),
lointain(e); (person) distant(e);
(possibility) vague; **remote control**
n télécommande f; **remotely** adv au
loin; (slightly) très vaguement

removal [rɪ'muːvəl] n (taking away)
enlèvement m; suppression f; (BRIT:
from house) déménagement m;
(from office: dismissal) renvoi m; (of
stain) nettoyage m; (Med) ablation
f; **removal man** (irreg) n (BRIT)
déménageur m; **removal van** n
(BRIT) camion m de déménagement

remove [rɪ'muːv] vt enlever, retirer;
(employee) renvoyer; (stain) faire
partir; (abuse) supprimer; (doubt)
chasser

Renaissance [rɪ'neɪsãns] n: **the ~** la
Renaissance

rename [riː'neɪm] vt rebaptiser

render ['rendər] vt rendre

rendezvous ['rɔndɪvuː] n rendez-
vous m inv

renew [rɪ'njuː] vt renouveler;
(negotiations) reprendre;
(acquaintance) renouer; **renewable**
adj (energy) renouvelable

renovate ['renəveɪt] vt rénover;
(work of art) restaurer

renowned [rɪ'naund] adj
renommé(e)

rent [rent] n loyer m ▷ vt louer;
rental n (for television, car) (prix m de)
location f

reorganize [riː'ɔːgənaɪz] vt
réorganiser

rep [rep] n abbr (Comm)
= **representative**

repair [rɪ'pɛər] n réparation f ▷ vt
réparer; **in good/bad ~** en bon/
mauvais état; **where can I get
this ~ed?** où est-ce que je peux faire
réparer ceci?; **repair kit** n trousse f de
réparations

repay [riː'peɪ] vt (irreg: like **pay**)
(money, creditor) rembourser; (sb's
efforts) récompenser; **repayment** n
remboursement m

repeat [rɪ'piːt] n (Radio, TV) reprise
f ▷ vt répéter; (promise, attack, also
Comm: order) renouveler; (Scol: a
class) redoubler ▷ vi répéter; **can
you ~ that, please?** pouvez-vous
répéter, s'il vous plaît?; **repeatedly**
adv souvent, à plusieurs reprises;
repeat prescription n (BRIT):
I'd like a repeat prescription
je voudrais renouveler mon
ordonnance

repellent [rɪ'pɛlənt] adj
repoussant(e) ▷ n: **insect ~**
insectifuge m

repercussions [riːpə'kʌʃənz] npl
répercussions fpl

repetition [repɪ'tɪʃən] n répétition f

repetitive [rɪ'pɛtɪtɪv] adj (movement, work) répétitif(-ive); (speech) plein(e) de redites

replace [rɪ'pleɪs] vt (put back) remettre, replacer; (take the place of) remplacer; **replacement** n (substitution) remplacement m; (person) remplaçant(e)

replay ['riːpleɪ] n (of match) match rejoué; (of tape, film) répétition f

replica ['rɛplɪkə] n réplique f, copie exacte

reply [rɪ'plaɪ] n réponse f ▷ vi répondre

report [rɪ'pɔːt] n rapport m; (Press etc) reportage m; (BRIT: also: **school ~**) bulletin m (scolaire); (of gun) détonation f ▷ vt rapporter, faire un compte rendu de; (Press etc) faire un reportage sur; (notify: accident) signaler; (: culprit) dénoncer ▷ vi (make a report) faire un rapport; **I'd like to ~ a theft** je voudrais signaler un vol; **to ~ (to sb)** (present o.s.) se présenter (chez qn); **report card** n (US, SCOTTISH) bulletin m (scolaire); **reportedly** adv: **she is reportedly living in Spain** elle habiterait en Espagne; **he reportedly told them to …** il leur aurait dit de …; **reporter** n reporter m

represent [rɛprɪ'zɛnt] vt représenter; (view, belief) présenter, expliquer; (describe): **to ~ sth as** présenter or décrire qch comme; **representation** [rɛprɪzɛn'teɪʃən] n représentation f; **representative** n représentant(e); (US Pol) député m ▷ adj représentatif(-ive), caractéristique

repress [rɪ'prɛs] vt réprimer; **repression** [rɪ'prɛʃən] n répression f

reprimand ['rɛprɪmɑːnd] n réprimande f ▷ vt réprimander

reproduce [riːprə'djuːs] vt reproduire ▷ vi se reproduire; **reproduction** [riːprə'dʌkʃən] n reproduction f

reptile ['rɛptaɪl] n reptile m

republic [rɪ'pʌblɪk] n république f; **republican** adj, n républicain(e)

reputable ['rɛpjʊtəbl] adj de bonne réputation; (occupation) honorable

reputation [rɛpjʊ'teɪʃən] n réputation f

request [rɪ'kwɛst] n demande f; (formal) requête f ▷ vt: **to ~ (of or from sb)** demander (à qn); **request stop** n (BRIT: for bus) arrêt facultatif

require [rɪ'kwaɪəʳ] vt (need: subj: person) avoir besoin de; (: thing, situation) nécessiter, demander; (want) exiger; (order): **to ~ sb to do sth/sth of sb** exiger que qn fasse qch/qch de qn; **requirement** n (need) exigence f; besoin m; (condition) condition f (requise)

resat [riː'sæt] pt, pp of **resit**

rescue ['rɛskjuː] n (from accident) sauvetage m; (help) secours mpl ▷ vt sauver

research [rɪ'səːtʃ] n recherche(s) f(pl) ▷ vt faire des recherches sur

resemblance [rɪ'zɛmbləns] n ressemblance f

resemble [rɪ'zɛmbl] vt ressembler à

resent [rɪ'zɛnt] vt être contrarié(e) par; **resentful** adj irrité(e), plein(e) de ressentiment; **resentment** n ressentiment m

reservation [rɛzə'veɪʃən] n (booking) réservation f; **to make a ~ (in an hotel/a restaurant/on a plane)** réserver or retenir une chambre/une table/une place; **reservation desk** n (US: in hotel) réception f

reserve [rɪ'zəːv] n réserve f; (Sport) remplaçant(e) ▷ vt (seats etc) réserver, retenir; **reserved** adj réservé(e)

reservoir ['rɛzəvwɑːʳ] n réservoir m

reshuffle ['riːʃʌfl] n: **Cabinet ~** (Pol) remaniement ministériel

residence ['rɛzɪdəns] n résidence f; **residence permit** n (BRIT) permis m de séjour

r

resident ['rezɪdənt] n (of country) résident(e); (of area, house) habitant(e); (in hotel) pensionnaire ▷ adj résidant(e); **residential** [rezɪ'dɛnʃəl] adj de résidence; (area) résidentiel(le); (course) avec hébergement sur place

residue ['rezɪdjuː] n reste m; (Chem, Physics) résidu m

resign [rɪ'zaɪn] vt (one's post) se démettre de ▷ vi démissionner; **to ~ o.s. to** (endure) se résigner à; **resignation** [rezɪg'neɪʃən] n (from post) démission f; (state of mind) résignation f

resin ['rezɪn] n résine f

resist [rɪ'zɪst] vt résister à; **resistance** n résistance f

resit vt [riː'sɪt] (irreg: like **sit**) (BRIT: exam) repasser ▷ n ['riːsɪt] deuxième session f (d'un examen)

resolution [rezə'luːʃən] n résolution f

resolve [rɪ'zɒlv] n résolution f ▷ vt (problem) résoudre; (decide): **to ~ to do** résoudre or décider de faire

resort [rɪ'zɔːt] n (seaside town) station f balnéaire; (for skiing) station de ski; (recourse) recours m ▷ vi: **to ~ to** avoir recours à; **in the last ~** en dernier ressort

resource [rɪ'sɔːs] n ressource f; **resourceful** adj ingénieux(-euse), débrouillard(e)

respect [rɪs'pɛkt] n respect m ▷ vt respecter; **respectable** adj respectable; (quite good: result etc) honorable; **respectful** adj respectueux(-euse); **respective** adj respectif(-ive); **respectively** adv respectivement

respite ['rɛspaɪt] n répit m

respond [rɪs'pɒnd] vi répondre; (react) réagir; **response** [rɪs'pɒns] n réponse f; (reaction) réaction f

responsibility [rɪspɒnsɪ'bɪlɪtɪ] n responsabilité f

responsible [rɪs'pɒnsɪbl] adj (liable): **~ (for)** responsable (de);

(person) digne de confiance; (job) qui comporte des responsabilités; **responsibly** adv avec sérieux

responsive [rɪs'pɒnsɪv] adj (student, audience) réceptif(-ive); (brakes, steering) sensible

rest [rɛst] n repos m; (stop) arrêt m, pause f; (Mus) silence m; (support) support m, appui m; (remainder) reste m, restant m ▷ vi se reposer; (be supported): **to ~ on** appuyer or reposer sur ▷ vt (lean): **to ~ sth on/against** appuyer qch sur/contre; **the ~ of them** les autres

restaurant ['rɛstərɒŋ] n restaurant m; **restaurant car** n (BRIT Rail) wagon-restaurant m

restless ['rɛstlɪs] adj agité(e)

restoration [rɛstə'reɪʃən] n (of building) restauration f; (of stolen goods) restitution f

restore [rɪ'stɔːʳ] vt (building) restaurer; (sth stolen) restituer; (peace, health) rétablir; **to ~ to** (former state) ramener à

restrain [rɪs'treɪn] vt (feeling) contenir; (person): **to ~ (from doing)** retenir (de faire); **restraint** n (restriction) contrainte f; (moderation) retenue f; (of style) sobriété f

restrict [rɪs'trɪkt] vt restreindre, limiter; **restriction** [rɪs'trɪkʃən] n restriction f, limitation f

rest room n (US) toilettes fpl

restructure [riː'strʌktʃəʳ] vt restructurer

result [rɪ'zʌlt] n résultat m ▷ vi: **to ~ in** aboutir à, se terminer par; **as a ~ of** à la suite de

resume [rɪ'zjuːm] vt (work, journey) reprendre ▷ vi (work etc) reprendre

résumé ['reɪzjuːmeɪ] n (summary) résumé m; (US: curriculum vitae) curriculum vitae m inv

resuscitate [rɪ'sʌsɪteɪt] vt (Med) réanimer

retail ['riːteɪl] adj de or au détail ▷ adv au détail; **retailer** n détaillant(e)

retain [rɪ'teɪn] vt (keep) garder, conserver

retaliation [rɪtælɪ'eɪʃən] n représailles fpl, vengeance f

retarded [rɪ'tɑːdɪd] adj (offensive) retardé(e)

retire [rɪ'taɪəʳ] vi (give up work) prendre sa retraite; (withdraw) se retirer, partir; (go to bed) (aller) se coucher; **retired** adj (person) retraité(e); **retirement** n retraite f

retort [rɪ'tɔːt] vi riposter

retreat [rɪ'triːt] n retraite f ▷ vi battre en retraite

retrieve [rɪ'triːv] vt (sth lost) récupérer; (situation, honour) sauver; (error, loss) réparer; (Comput) rechercher

retrospect ['rɛtrəspɛkt] n: **in ~** rétrospectivement, après coup; **retrospective** [rɛtrə'spɛktɪv] adj rétrospectif(-ive); (law) rétroactif(-ive) ▷ n (Art) rétrospective f

return [rɪ'tɜːn] n (going or coming back) retour m; (of sth stolen etc) restitution f; (Finance: from land, shares) rapport m ▷ cpd (journey) de retour; (BRIT: ticket) aller et retour; (match) retour ▷ vi (person etc: come back) revenir; (: go back) retourner ▷ vt rendre; (bring back) rapporter; (send back) renvoyer; (put back) remettre; (Pol: candidate) élire; **returns** npl (Comm) recettes fpl; (Finance) bénéfices mpl; **many happy ~s (of the day)!** bon anniversaire!; **by ~ (of post)** par retour (du courrier); **in ~ (for)** en échange (de); **a ~ (ticket) for ...** un billet aller et retour pour ...; **return ticket** n (esp BRIT) billet m aller-retour

reunion [riː'juːnɪən] n réunion f

reunite [riːjuː'naɪt] vt réunir

revamp [riː'væmp] vt (house) retaper; (firm) réorganiser

reveal [rɪ'viːl] vt (make known) révéler; (display) laisser voir; **revealing** adj révélateur(-trice); (dress) au décolleté généreux or suggestif

revel ['rɛvl] vi: **to ~ in sth/in doing** se délecter de qch/à faire

revelation [rɛvə'leɪʃən] n révélation f

revenge [rɪ'vɛndʒ] n vengeance f; (in game etc) revanche f ▷ vt venger; **to take ~ (on)** se venger (sur)

revenue ['rɛvənjuː] n revenu m

Reverend ['rɛvərənd] adj (in titles): **the ~ John Smith** (Anglican) le révérend John Smith; (Catholic) l'abbé (John) Smith; (Protestant) le pasteur (John) Smith

reversal [rɪ'vəːsl] n (of opinion) revirement m; (of order) renversement m; (of direction) changement m

reverse [rɪ'vəːs] n contraire m, opposé m; (back) dos m, envers m; (of paper) verso m; (of coin) revers m; (Aut: also: **~ gear**) marche f arrière ▷ adj (order, direction) opposé(e), inverse ▷ vt (order, position) changer, inverser; (direction, policy) changer complètement de; (decision) annuler; (roles) renverser ▷ vi (BRIT Aut) faire marche arrière; **reversing lights** npl (BRIT Aut) feux mpl de marche arrière or de recul

revert [rɪ'vəːt] vi: **to ~ to** revenir à, retourner à

review [rɪ'vjuː] n revue f; (of book, film) critique f; (of situation, policy) examen m, bilan m; (us: examination) examen ▷ vt passer en revue; faire la critique de; examiner

revise [rɪ'vaɪz] vt réviser, modifier; (manuscript) revoir, corriger ▷ vi (study) réviser; **revision** [rɪ'vɪʒən] n révision f

revival [rɪ'vaɪvəl] n reprise f; (recovery) rétablissement m; (of faith) renouveau m

revive [rɪ'vaɪv] vt (person) ranimer; (custom) rétablir; (economy) relancer; (hope, courage) raviver, faire renaître; (play, fashion) reprendre ▷ vi (person) reprendre connaissance (: from ill health) se rétablir; (hope etc) renaître; (activity) reprendre

r

revolt [rɪ'vəult] n révolte f ▷ vi
se révolter, se rebeller ▷ vt
révolter, dégoûter; **revolting** adj
dégoûtant(e)

revolution [revə'lu:ʃən] n révolution
f; (of wheel etc) tour m, révolution;
revolutionary adj, n révolutionnaire
(m/f)

revolve [rɪ'vɒlv] vi tourner

revolver [rɪ'vɒlvə'] n revolver m

reward [rɪ'wɔ:d] n récompense f
▷ vt: **to ~ (for)** récompenser (de);
rewarding adj (fig) qui (en) vaut la
peine, gratifiant(e)

rewind [ri:'waɪnd] vt (irreg: like
wind²) (tape) réembobiner

rewritable [ri:'raɪtəbl] adj (CD, DVD)
réinscriptible

rewrite [ri:'raɪt] (irreg: like **write**)
vt récrire

rheumatism ['ru:mətɪzəm] n
rhumatisme m

Rhine [raɪn] n: **the (River) ~** le Rhin

rhinoceros [raɪ'nɒsərəs] n
rhinocéros m

rhubarb ['ru:bɑ:b] n rhubarbe f

rhyme [raɪm] n rime f; (verse) vers mpl

rhythm ['rɪðm] n rythme m

rib [rɪb] n (Anat) côte f

ribbon ['rɪbən] n ruban m; **in ~s** (torn)
en lambeaux

rice [raɪs] n riz m; **rice pudding** n
riz m au lait

rich [rɪtʃ] adj riche; (gift, clothes)
somptueux(-euse); **to be ~ in sth**
être riche en qch

rid [rɪd] (pt, pp **rid**) vt: **to ~ sb of**
débarrasser qn de; **to get ~ of** se
débarrasser de

ridden ['rɪdn] pp of **ride**

riddle ['rɪdl] n (puzzle) énigme f ▷ vt:
to be ~d with être criblé(e) de; (fig)
être en proie à

ride [raɪd] (pt **rode**, pp **ridden**) n
promenade f, tour m; (distance
covered) trajet m ▷ vi (as sport)
monter (à cheval), faire du cheval;
(go somewhere: on horse, bicycle) aller

(à cheval or bicyclette etc); (travel: on
bicycle, motor cycle, bus) rouler ▷ vt (a
horse) monter; (distance) parcourir,
faire; **to ~ a horse/bicycle** monter à
cheval/à bicyclette; **to take sb for a
~** (fig) faire marcher qn; (cheat) rouler
qn; **rider** n cavalier(-ière); (in race)
jockey m; (on bicycle) cycliste m/f; (on
motorcycle) motocycliste m/f

ridge [rɪdʒ] n (of hill) faîte m; (of roof,
mountain) arête f; (on object) strie f

ridicule ['rɪdɪkju:l] n ridicule m;
dérision f ▷ vt ridiculiser, tourner en
dérision; **ridiculous** [rɪ'dɪkjuləs]
adj ridicule

riding ['raɪdɪŋ] n équitation f;
riding school n manège m, école f
d'équitation

rife [raɪf] adj répandu(e); **~ with**
abondant(e) en

rifle ['raɪfl] n fusil m (à canon rayé)
▷ vt vider, dévaliser

rift [rɪft] n fente f, fissure f; (fig:
disagreement) désaccord m

rig [rɪg] n (also: **oil ~**: on land) derrick
m; (: at sea) plate-forme pétrolière
f ▷ vt (election etc) truquer

right [raɪt] adj (true) juste, exact(e);
(correct) bon (bonne); (suitable)
approprié(e), convenable; (just)
juste, équitable; (morally good) bien
inv; (not left) droit(e) ▷ n (moral good)
bien m; (title, claim) droit m; (not left)
droite f ▷ adv (answer) correctement;
(treat) bien, comme il faut; (not on
the left) à droite ▷ vt redresser ▷ excl
bon!; **do you have the ~ time?**
avez-vous l'heure juste or exacte? **to
be ~** (person) avoir raison; (answer)
être juste or correct(e); **by ~s** en
toute justice; **on the ~** à droite; **to
be in the ~** avoir raison; **~ in the
middle** en plein milieu; **~ away**
immédiatement; **right angle** n
(Math) angle droit; **rightful** adj (heir)
légitime; **right-hand** adj: **the right-
hand side** la droite; **right-hand
drive** n conduite f à droite; (vehicle)

véhicule *m* avec la conduite à droite;
right-handed *adj* (*person*) droitier(-ière); **rightly** *adv* bien, correctement;
(*with reason*) à juste titre; **right
of way** *n* (*on path etc*) droit *m* de
passage; (*Aut*) priorité *f*; **right-wing**
adj (*Pol*) de droite

rigid ['rɪdʒɪd] *adj* rigide; (*principle,
control*) strict(e)

rigorous ['rɪgərəs] *adj*
rigoureux(-euse)

rim [rɪm] *n* bord *m*; (*of spectacles*)
monture *f*; (*of wheel*) jante *f*

rind [raɪnd] *n* (*of bacon*) couenne *f*; (*of
lemon, orange*) écorce *f*, zeste *m*; (*of cheese*)
croûte *f*

ring [rɪŋ] *n* anneau *m*; (*on finger*)
bague *f*; (*also:* **wedding ~**) alliance *f*;
(*of people, objects*) cercle *m*; (*of spies*)
réseau *m*; (*of smoke etc*) rond *m*; (*arena*)
piste *f*, arène *f*; (*for boxing*) ring *m*;
(*sound of bell*) sonnerie *f* ▷ *vi* (*pt* **rang**,
pp **rung**) (*telephone, bell*) sonner;
(*person: by telephone*) téléphoner;
(*ears*) bourdonner; (*also:* **~ out**:
voice, words) retentir ▷ *vt* (*also:* **~ up**)
téléphoner à, appeler; **to ~ the bell**
sonner; **to give sb a ~** (*Tel*) passer
un coup de téléphone *or* de fil à qn;
ring back *vt*, *vi* (*BRIT Tel*) rappeler;
ring off *vi* (*BRIT Tel*) raccrocher; **ring
up** *vt* (*BRIT Tel*) téléphoner à, appeler;
ringing tone *n* (*BRIT Tel*) tonalité *f*
d'appel; **ringleader** *n* (*of gang*) chef
m, meneur *m*; **ring road** *n* (*BRIT*)
rocade *f*; (*motorway*) périphérique *m*;
ringtone *n* (*on mobile*) sonnerie *f* (*de
téléphone portable*)

rink [rɪŋk] *n* (*also:* **ice ~**) patinoire *f*

rinse [rɪns] *n* rinçage *m* ▷ *vt* rincer

riot ['raɪət] *n* émeute *f*, bagarres
fpl ▷ *vi* (*demonstrators*) manifester
avec violence; (*population*) se
soulever, se révolter; **to run ~** se
déchaîner

rip [rɪp] *n* déchirure *f* ▷ *vt* déchirer
▷ *vi* se déchirer; **rip off** *vt* (*inf: cheat*)
arnaquer; **rip up** *vt* déchirer

ripe [raɪp] *adj* (*fruit*) mûr(e); (*cheese*)
fait(e)

rip-off ['rɪpɔf] *n* (*inf*): **it's a ~!** c'est du
vol manifeste!, c'est de l'arnaque!

ripple ['rɪpl] *n* ride *f*, ondulation *f*; (*of
applause, laughter*) cascade *f* ▷ *vi* se
rider, onduler

rise [raɪz] *n* (*slope*) côte *f*, pente *f*;
(*hill*) élévation *f*; (*increase: in wages:
BRIT*) augmentation *f*; (: *in prices,
temperature*) hausse *f*, augmentation;
(*fig: to power etc*) ascension *f* ▷ *vi*
(*pt* **rose**, *pp* **risen**) s'élever, monter;
(*prices, numbers*) augmenter, monter;
(*waters, river*) monter; (*sun, wind,
person: from chair, bed*) se lever; (*also:*
~ up: *tower, building*) s'élever; (: *rebel*)
se révolter; se rebeller; (*in rank*)
s'élever; **to give ~ to** donner lieu à;
to ~ to the occasion se montrer à
la hauteur; **risen** ['rɪzn] *pp of* **rise**;
rising *adj* (*increasing: number, prices*)
en hausse; (*tide*) montant(e); (*sun,
moon*) levant(e)

risk [rɪsk] *n* risque *m* ▷ *vt* risquer; **to
take** *or* **run the ~ of doing** courir le
risque de faire; **at ~** en danger; **at
one's own ~** à ses risques et périls;
risky *adj* risqué(e)

rite [raɪt] *n* rite *m*; **the last ~s** les
derniers sacrements

ritual ['rɪtjuəl] *adj* rituel(le) ▷ *n*
rituel *m*

rival ['raɪvl] *n* rival(e); (*in business*)
concurrent(e) ▷ *adj* rival(e); qui fait
concurrence ▷ *vt* (*match*) égaler;
rivalry *n* rivalité *f*; (*in business*)
concurrence *f*

river ['rɪvər] *n* rivière *f*; (*major: also fig*)
fleuve *m* ▷ *cpd* (*port, traffic*) fluvial(e);
up/down ~ en amont/aval;
riverbank *n* rive *f*, berge *f*

rivet ['rɪvɪt] *n* rivet *m* ▷ *vt* (*fig*) river,
fixer

Riviera [rɪvɪ'ɛərə] *n*: **the (French) ~**
la Côte d'Azur

road [rəud] *n* route *f*; (*in town*) rue *f*;
(*fig*) chemin, voie *f* ▷ *cpd* (*accident*)

r

de la route; **major/minor ~**
route principale or à priorité/voie
secondaire; **which ~ do I take for
…?** quelle route dois-je prendre pour
aller à …?; **roadblock** n barrage
routier; **road map** n carte routière;
road rage n comportement très agressif
de certains usagers de la route; **road
safety** n sécurité routière; **roadside**
n bord m de la route, bas-côté m; **road
sign** n panneau m de signalisation;
road tax n (BRIT Aut) taxe f sur les
automobiles; **roadworks** npl travaux
mpl (de réfection des routes)

roam [rəʊm] vi errer, vagabonder

roar [rɔːʳ] n rugissement m; (of crowd)
hurlements mpl; (of vehicle, thunder,
storm) grondement m ▷ vi rugir;
hurler; gronder; **to ~ with laughter**
rire à gorge déployée

roast [rəʊst] n rôti m ▷ vt (meat)
(faire) rôtir; (coffee) griller, torréfier;
roast beef n rôti m de bœuf, rosbif m

rob [rɒb] vt (person) voler; (bank)
dévaliser; **to ~ sb of sth** voler or
dérober qch à qn; (fig: deprive) priver
qn de qch; **robber** n bandit m, voleur
m; **robbery** n vol m

robe [rəʊb] n (for ceremony etc) robe
f; (also: **bath~**) peignoir m; (us: rug)
couverture f ▷ vt revêtir (d'une robe)

robin ['rɒbɪn] n rouge-gorge m

robot ['rəʊbɒt] n robot m

robust [rəʊ'bʌst] adj robuste;
(material, appetite) solide

rock [rɒk] n (substance) roche f, roc m;
(boulder) rocher m, roche; (us: small
stone) caillou m; (BRIT: sweet) ≈ sucre
m d'orge ▷ vt (swing gently: cradle)
balancer; (: child) bercer; (shake)
ébranler, secouer ▷ vi se balancer,
être ébranlé(e) or secoué(e); **on the
~s** (drink) avec des glaçons; (marriage
etc) en train de craquer; **rock and roll**
n rock (and roll) m, rock'n'roll m; **rock
climbing** n varappe f

rocket ['rɒkɪt] n fusée f; (Mil) fusée,
roquette f; (Culin) roquette

rocking chair ['rɒkɪŋ-] n fauteuil
m à bascule

rocky ['rɒkɪ] adj (hill) rocheux(-euse);
(path) rocailleux(-euse)

rod [rɒd] n (metallic) tringle f; (Tech)
tige f; (wooden) baguette f; (also:
fishing ~) canne f à pêche

rode [rəʊd] pt of **ride**

rodent ['rəʊdnt] n rongeur m

rogue [rəʊg] n coquin(e)

role [rəʊl] n rôle m; **role-model** n
modèle m à émuler

roll [rəʊl] n rouleau m; (of banknotes)
liasse f; (also: **bread ~**) petit pain;
(register) liste f; (sound: of drums etc)
roulement m ▷ vt rouler; (also: **~ up**)
(string) enrouler; (also: **~ out**: pastry)
étendre au rouleau, abaisser ▷ vi
rouler; **roll over** vi se retourner; **roll
up** vi (inf: arrive) arriver, s'amener ▷ vt
(carpet, cloth, map) rouler; (sleeves)
retrousser; **roller** n rouleau m;
(wheel) roulette f; (for road) rouleau
compresseur; (for hair) bigoudi m;
roller coaster n montagnes fpl
russes; **roller skates** npl patins mpl à
roulettes; **roller-skating** n patin m à
roulettes; **to go roller-skating** faire
du patin à roulettes; **rolling pin** n
rouleau m à pâtisserie

ROM [rɒm] n abbr (Comput: = read-only
memory) mémoire morte, ROM f

Roman ['rəʊmən] adj romain(e) ▷ n
Romain(e); **Roman Catholic** adj, n
catholique (m/f)

romance [rə'mæns] n (love affair)
idylle f; (charm) poésie f; (novel) roman
m à l'eau de rose

Romania [rəʊ'meɪnɪə] n = **Rumania**

Roman numeral n chiffre romain

romantic [rə'mæntɪk] adj
romantique; (novel, attachment)
sentimental(e)

Rome [rəʊm] n Rome

roof [ruːf] n toit m; (of tunnel, cave)
plafond m ▷ vt couvrir (d'un toit); **the
~ of the mouth** la voûte du palais;
roof rack n (Aut) galerie f

rook [ruk] *n* (*bird*) freux *m*; (*Chess*) tour *f*

room [ru:m] *n* (*in house*) pièce *f*; (*also:* **bed~**) chambre *f* (à coucher); (*in school etc*) salle *f*; (*space*) place *f*; **roommate** *n* camarade *m/f* de chambre; **room service** *n* service *m* des chambres (*dans un hôtel*); **roomy** *adj* spacieux(-euse); (*garment*) ample

rooster ['ru:stə'] *n* coq *m*

root [ru:t] *n* (*Bot, Math*) racine *f*; (*fig: of problem*) origine *f*, fond *m* ▷ *vi* (*plant*) s'enraciner

rope [rəup] *n* corde *f*; (*Naut*) cordage *m* ▷ *vt* (*tie up or together*) attacher; (*climbers: also:* **~ together**) encorder; (*area: also:* **~ off**) interdire l'accès de; (*: divide off*) séparer; **to know the ~s** (*fig*) être au courant, connaître les ficelles

rort [rɔ:t] *n* (AUST, NZ *inf*) arnaque *f* (*inf*) ▷ *vt* escroquer

rose [rəuz] *pt of* **rise** ▷ *n* rose *f*; (*also:* **~bush**) rosier *m*

rosé ['rəuzeɪ] *n* rosé *m*

rosemary ['rəuzmərɪ] *n* romarin *m*

rosy ['rəuzɪ] *adj* rose; **a ~ future** un bel avenir

rot [rɔt] *n* (*decay*) pourriture *f*; (*fig: pej: nonsense*) idioties *fpl*, balivernes *fpl* ▷ *vt, vi* pourrir

rota ['rəutə] *n* liste *f*, tableau *m* de service

rotate [rəu'teɪt] *vt* (*revolve*) faire tourner; (*change round: crops*) alterner; (*: jobs*) faire à tour de rôle ▷ *vi* (*revolve*) tourner

rotten ['rɔtn] *adj* (*decayed*) pourri(e); (*dishonest*) corrompu(e); (*inf: bad*) mauvais(e), moche; **to feel ~** (*ill*) être mal fichu(e)

rough [rʌf] *adj* (*cloth, skin*) rêche, rugueux(-euse); (*terrain*) accidenté(e); (*path*) rocailleux(-euse); (*voice*) rauque, rude; (*person, manner: coarse*) rude, fruste; (*: violent*) brutal(e); (*district, weather*) mauvais(e); (*sea*) houleux(-euse); (*plan*) ébauché(e); (*guess*) approximatif(-ive) ▷ *n* (*Golf*) rough *m* ▷ *vt*: **to ~ it** vivre à la dure; **to sleep ~** (BRIT) coucher à la dure; **roughly** *adv* (*handle*) rudement, brutalement; (*speak*) avec brusquerie; (*make*) grossièrement; (*approximately*) à peu près, en gros

roulette [ru:'lɛt] *n* roulette *f*

round [raund] *adj* rond(e) ▷ *n* rond *m*, cercle *m*; (BRIT: *of toast*) tranche *f*; (*duty: of policeman, milkman etc*) tournée *f*; (*: of doctor*) visites *fpl*; (*game: of cards, in competition*) partie *f*; (*Boxing*) round *m*; (*of talks*) série *f* ▷ *vt* (*corner*) tourner ▷ *prep* autour de ▷ *adv*: **right ~, all ~** tout autour; **~ of ammunition** cartouche *f*; **~ of applause** applaudissements *mpl*; **~ of drinks** tournée *f*; **~ of sandwiches** (BRIT) sandwich *m*; **the long way ~** (par) le chemin le plus long; **all (the) year ~** toute l'année; **it's just ~ the corner** (*fig*) c'est tout près; **to go ~ to sb's (house)** aller chez qn; **go ~ the back** passez par derrière; **enough to go ~** assez pour tout le monde; **she arrived ~ (about) noon** (BRIT) elle est arrivée vers midi; **~ the clock** 24 heures sur 24; **round off** *vt* (*speech etc*) terminer; **round up** *vt* rassembler; (*criminals*) effectuer une rafle de; (*prices*) arrondir (au chiffre supérieur); **roundabout** *n* (BRIT: *Aut*) rond-point *m* (à sens giratoire); (*: at fair*) manège *m* (de chevaux de bois) ▷ *adj* (*route, means*) détourné(e); **round trip** *n* (voyage *m*) aller et retour *m*; **roundup** *n* rassemblement *m*; (*of criminals*) rafle *f*

rouse [rauz] *vt* (*wake up*) réveiller; (*stir up*) susciter, provoquer; (*interest*) éveiller; (*suspicions*) susciter, éveiller

route [ru:t] *n* itinéraire *m*; (*of bus*) parcours *m*; (*of trade, shipping*) route *f*

routine [ru:'ti:n] *adj* (*work*) ordinaire, courant(e); (*procedure*) d'usage ▷ *n* (*habits*) habitudes *fpl*; (*pej*) train-train *m*; (*Theat*) numéro *m*

r

row¹ [rəʊ] n (line) rangée f; (of people, seats, Knitting) rang m; (behind one another: of cars, people) file f ▷ vi (in boat) ramer; (as sport) faire de l'aviron ▷ vt (boat) faire aller à la rame or à l'aviron; **in a ~** (fig) d'affilée

row² [raʊ] n (noise) vacarme m; (dispute) dispute f, querelle f; (scolding) réprimande f, savon m ▷ vi (also: **to have a ~**) se disputer, se quereller

rowboat ['rəʊbəʊt] n (US) canot m (à rames)

rowing ['rəʊɪŋ] n canotage m; (as sport) aviron m; **rowing boat** n (BRIT) canot m (à rames)

royal ['rɔɪəl] adj royal(e); **royalty** n (royal persons) (membres mpl de la) famille royale; (payment: to author) droits mpl d'auteur; (: to inventor) royalties fpl

rpm abbr (= revolutions per minute) t/mn (= tours/minute)

R.S.V.P. abbr (= répondez s'il vous plaît) RSVP

Rt. Hon. abbr (BRIT: = Right Honourable) titre donné aux députés de la Chambre des communes

rub [rʌb] n: **to give sth a ~** donner un coup de chiffon or de torchon à qch ▷ vt frotter; (person) frictionner; (hands) se frotter; **to ~ sb up** (BRIT) or **to ~ sb** (US) **the wrong way** prendre qn à rebrousse-poil; **rub in** vt (ointment) faire pénétrer; **rub off** vi partir; **rub out** vt effacer

rubber ['rʌbər] n caoutchouc m; (BRIT: eraser) gomme f (à effacer); **rubber band** n élastique m; **rubber gloves** npl gants mpl en caoutchouc

rubbish ['rʌbɪʃ] n (from household) ordures fpl; (fig: pej) choses fpl sans valeur; camelote f; (nonsense) bêtises fpl, idioties fpl; **rubbish bin** n (BRIT) boîte f à ordures, poubelle f; **rubbish dump** n (BRIT: in town) décharge publique, dépotoir m

rubble ['rʌbl] n décombres mpl; (smaller) gravats mpl; (Constr) blocage m

ruby ['ruːbɪ] n rubis m

rucksack ['rʌksæk] n sac m à dos

rudder ['rʌdər] n gouvernail m

rude [ruːd] adj (impolite: person) impoli(e); (: word, manners) grossier(-ière); (shocking) indécent(e), inconvenant(e)

ruffle ['rʌfl] vt (hair) ébouriffer; (clothes) chiffonner; (fig: person): **to get ~d** s'énerver

rug [rʌg] n petit tapis; (BRIT: blanket) couverture f

rugby ['rʌgbɪ] n (also: **~ football**) rugby m

rugged ['rʌgɪd] adj (landscape) accidenté(e); (features, character) rude

ruin ['ruːɪn] n ruine f ▷ vt ruiner; (spoil: clothes) abîmer; (: event) gâcher; **ruins** npl (of building) ruine(s)

rule [ruːl] n règle f; (regulation) règlement m; (government) autorité f, gouvernement m ▷ vt (country) gouverner; (person) dominer; (decide) décider ▷ vi commander; **as a ~** normalement, en règle générale; **rule out** vt exclure; **ruler** n (sovereign) souverain(e); (leader) chef m (d'État); (for measuring) règle f; **ruling** adj (party) au pouvoir; (class) dirigeant(e) ▷ n (Law) décision f

rum [rʌm] n rhum m

Rumania [ruːˈmeɪnɪə] n Roumanie f; **Rumanian** adj roumain(e) ▷ n Roumain(e); (Ling) roumain m

rumble ['rʌmbl] n grondement m; (of stomach, pipe) gargouillement m ▷ vi gronder; (stomach, pipe) gargouiller

rumour, (US) **rumor** ['ruːmər] n rumeur f, bruit m (qui court) ▷ vt: **it is ~ed that** le bruit court que

rump steak n romsteck m

run [rʌn] (pt **ran**, pp **run**) n (race) course f; (outing) tour m or promenade f (en voiture); (distance travelled) parcours m, trajet m; (series) suite f, série f; (*Theat*) série de représentations; (*Ski*) piste f; (*Cricket, Baseball*) point m; (*in tights, stockings*) maille filée, échelle f ▷ vt (*business*) diriger; (*competition, course*) organiser; (*hotel, house*) tenir; (*race*) participer à; (*Comput: program*) exécuter; (*to pass: hand, finger*) **to ~ sth over** promener or passer qch sur; (*water, bath*) faire couler; (*Press: feature*) publier ▷ vi courir; (*pass: road etc*) passer; (*work: machine, factory*) marcher; (*bus, train*) circuler; (*continue: play*) se jouer, être à l'affiche; (*: contract*) être valide or en vigueur; (*flow: river, bath, nose*) couler; (*colours, washing*) déteindre; (*in election*) être candidat, se présenter; **at a ~** au pas de course; **to go for a ~** aller courir or faire un peu de course à pied; (*in car*) faire un tour or une promenade (en voiture); **there was a ~ on** (*meat, tickets*) les gens se sont rués sur; **in the long ~** à la longue; **on the ~** en fuite; **I'll ~ you to the station** je vais vous emmener or conduire à la gare; **to ~ a risk** courir un risque; **run after** vt fus (*to catch up*) courir après; (*chase*) poursuivre; **run away** vi s'enfuir; **run down** vt (*Aut: knock over*) renverser; (*BRIT: reduce: production*) réduire progressivement; (*: factory/shop*) réduire progressivement la production/ l'activité de; (*criticize*) critiquer, dénigrer; **to be ~ down** (*tired*) être fatigué(e) or à plat; **run into** vt fus (*meet: person*) rencontrer par hasard; (*: trouble*) se heurter à; (*collide with*) heurter; **run off** vi s'enfuir ▷ vt (*water*) laisser s'écouler; (*copies*) tirer; **run out** vi (*person*) sortir en courant; (*liquid*) couler; (*lease*) expirer; (*money*) être épuisé(e); **run out of** vt fus se trouver à court de; **run over** vt (*Aut*) écraser ▷ vt fus (*revise*) revoir, reprendre; **run through** vt fus (*recap*) reprendre, revoir; (*play*) répéter; **run up** vi: **to ~ up against** (*difficulties*) se heurter

à; **runaway** adj (*horse*) emballé(e); (*truck*) fou (folle); (*person*) fugitif(-ive); (*child*) fugueur(-euse)

rung [rʌŋ] pp of **ring** ▷ n (*of ladder*) barreau m

runner ['rʌnəʳ] n (*in race: person*) coureur(-euse); (*: horse*) partant m; (*on sledge*) patin m; (*for drawer etc*) coulisseau m; **runner bean** n (*BRIT*) haricot m (à rames); **runner-up** n second(e)

running ['rʌnɪŋ] n (*in race etc*) course f, (*of business, organization*) direction f, gestion f ▷ adj (*water*) courant(e); (*commentary*) suivi(e); **6 days ~** 6 jours de suite; **to be in/out of the ~ for sth** être/ne pas être sur les rangs pour qch

runny ['rʌnɪ] adj qui coule

run-up ['rʌnʌp] n (*BRIT*): **~ to sth** période f précédant qch

runway ['rʌnweɪ] n (*Aviat*) piste f (d'envol or d'atterrissage)

rupture ['rʌptʃəʳ] n (*Med*) hernie f

rural ['rʊərl] adj rural(e)

rush [rʌʃ] n (*of crowd, Comm: sudden demand*) ruée f; (*hurry*) hâte f; (*of anger, joy*) accès m; (*current*) flot m; (*Bot*) jonc m ▷ vt (*hurry*) transporter or envoyer d'urgence ▷ vi se précipiter; **to ~ sth off** (*do quickly*) faire qch à la hâte; **rush hour** n heures fpl de pointe or d'affluence

Russia ['rʌʃə] n Russie f; **Russian** adj russe ▷ n Russe m/f; (*Ling*) russe m

rust [rʌst] n rouille f ▷ vi rouiller

rusty ['rʌstɪ] adj rouillé(e)

ruthless ['ruːθlɪs] adj sans pitié, impitoyable

RV n abbr (*US*) = **recreational vehicle**

rye [raɪ] n seigle m

S

Sabbath ['sæbəθ] n (*Jewish*) sabbat m; (*Christian*) dimanche m

sabotage ['sæbətɑ:ʒ] n sabotage m ▷ vt saboter

saccharin(e) ['sækərɪn] n saccharine f

sachet ['sæʃeɪ] n sachet m

sack [sæk] n (*bag*) sac m ▷ vt (*dismiss*) renvoyer, mettre à la porte; (*plunder*) piller, mettre à sac; **to get the ~** être renvoyé(e) or mis(e) à la porte

sacred ['seɪkrɪd] adj sacré(e)

sacrifice ['sækrɪfaɪs] n sacrifice m ▷ vt sacrifier

sad [sæd] adj (*unhappy*) triste; (*deplorable*) triste, fâcheux(-euse); (*inf: pathetic: thing*) triste, lamentable; (: *person*) minable

saddle ['sædl] n selle f ▷ vt (*horse*) seller; **to be ~d with sth** (*inf*) avoir qch sur les bras

sadistic [sə'dɪstɪk] adj sadique

sadly ['sædlɪ] adv tristement; (*unfortunately*) malheureusement; (*seriously*) fort

sadness ['sædnɪs] n tristesse f

s.a.e. n abbr (BRIT: = stamped addressed envelope) enveloppe affranchie pour la réponse

safari [sə'fɑ:rɪ] n safari m

safe [seɪf] adj (*out of danger*) hors de danger, en sécurité; (*not dangerous*) sans danger; (*cautious*) prudent(e); (*sure: bet*) assuré(e) ▷ n coffre-fort m; **~ and sound** sain(e) et sauf; **(just) to be on the ~ side** pour plus de sûreté, par précaution; **safely** adv (*assume, say*) sans risque d'erreur; (*drive, arrive*) sans accident; **safe sex** n rapports sexuels protégés

safety ['seɪftɪ] n sécurité f; **safety belt** n ceinture f de sécurité; **safety pin** n épingle f de sûreté or de nourrice

saffron ['sæfrən] n safran m

sag [sæg] vi s'affaisser, fléchir; (*hem, breasts*) pendre

sage [seɪdʒ] n (*herb*) sauge f; (*person*) sage m

Sagittarius [sædʒɪ'tɛərɪəs] n le Sagittaire

Sahara [sə'hɑ:rə] n: **the ~ (Desert)** le (désert du) Sahara m

said [sɛd] pt, pp of **say**

sail [seɪl] n (*on boat*) voile f; (*trip*): **to go for a ~** faire un tour en bateau ▷ vt (*boat*) manœuvrer, piloter ▷ vi (*travel: ship*) avancer, naviguer; (*set off*) partir, prendre la mer; (*Sport*) faire de la voile; **they ~ed into Le Havre** ils sont entrés dans le port du Havre; **sailboat** n (*us*) bateau m à voiles, voilier m; **sailing** n (*Sport*) voile f; **to go sailing** faire de la voile; **sailing boat** n bateau m à voiles, voilier m; **sailor** n marin m, matelot m

saint [seɪnt] n saint(e)

sake [seɪk] n: **for the ~ of** (*out of concern for*) pour (l'amour de), dans l'intérêt de; (out of consideration for) par égard pour

salad ['sæləd] n salade f; **salad cream** n (BRIT) (sorte f de) mayonnaise f; **salad dressing** n vinaigrette f

salami [sə'lɑ:mɪ] n salami m

salary ['sælərɪ] n salaire m, traitement m

sale [seɪl] n vente f; (at reduced prices) soldes mpl; **sales** npl (total amount sold) chiffre m de ventes; **"for ~"** "à vendre"; **on ~** en vente; **sales assistant** , (US) **sales clerk** n vendeur(-euse); **salesman** (irreg) n (in shop) vendeur m; **salesperson** (irreg) n (in shop) vendeur(-euse); **sales rep** n (Comm) représentant(e) m/f; **saleswoman** (irreg) n (in shop) vendeuse f

saline ['seɪlaɪn] adj salin(e)

saliva [sə'laɪvə] n salive f

salmon ['sæmən] n (pl inv) saumon m

salon ['sælɔn] n salon m

saloon [sə'lu:n] n (US) bar m; (BRIT Aut) berline f; (ship's lounge) salon m

salt [sɔ:lt] n sel m ▷ vt saler; **saltwater** adj (fish etc) (d'eau) de mer; **salty** adj salé(e)

salute [sə'lu:t] n salut m; (of guns) salve f ▷ vt saluer

salvage ['sælvɪdʒ] n (saving) sauvetage m; (things saved) biens sauvés or récupérés ▷ vt sauver, récupérer

Salvation Army [sæl'veɪʃən-] n Armée f du Salut

same [seɪm] adj même ▷ pron: **the ~** le (la) même, les mêmes; **the ~ book as** le même livre que; **at the ~ time** en même temps; (yet) néanmoins; **all** or **just the ~** tout de même, quand même; **to do the ~** faire de même, en faire autant; **to do the ~ as sb** faire comme qn; **and the ~ to you!** et à vous de même!; (after insult) toi-même!

sample ['sɑ:mpl] n échantillon m; (Med) prélèvement m ▷ vt (food, wine) goûter

sanction ['sæŋkʃən] n approbation f, sanction f ▷ vt cautionner, sanctionner; **sanctions** npl (Pol) sanctions

sanctuary ['sæŋktjuərɪ] n (holy place) sanctuaire m; (refuge) asile m; (for wildlife) réserve f

sand [sænd] n sable m ▷ vt (also: ~ **down**: wood etc) poncer

sandal ['sændl] n sandale f

sand: sandbox n (US: for children) tas m de sable; **sand castle** n château m de sable; **sand dune** n dune f de sable; **sandpaper** n papier m de verre; **sandpit** n (BRIT: for children) tas m de sable; **sands** npl plage f (de sable); **sandstone** ['sændstəun] n grès m

sandwich ['sændwɪtʃ] n sandwich m ▷ vt (also: ~ **in**) intercaler; **~ed between** pris en sandwich entre; **cheese/ham ~** sandwich au fromage/jambon

sandy ['sændɪ] adj sablonneux(-euse); (colour) sable inv, blond roux inv

sane [seɪn] adj (person) sain(e) d'esprit; (outlook) sensé(e), sain(e)

sang [sæŋ] pt of **sing**

sanitary towel , (US) **sanitary napkin** ['sænɪtərɪ-] n serviette f hygiénique

sanity ['sænɪtɪ] n santé mentale; (common sense) bon sens

sank [sæŋk] pt of **sink**

Santa Claus [sæntə'klɔ:z] n le Père Noël

sap [sæp] n (of plants) sève f ▷ vt (strength) saper, miner

sapphire ['sæfaɪər] n saphir m

sarcasm ['sɑ:kæzm] n sarcasme m, raillerie f

sarcastic [sɑ:'kæstɪk] adj sarcastique

sardine [sɑ:'di:n] n sardine f

s

SASE n abbr (US: = self-addressed stamped envelope) enveloppe affranchie pour la réponse

sat [sæt] pt, pp of **sit**

Sat. abbr (= Saturday) sa

satchel ['sætʃl] n cartable m

satellite ['sætəlaɪt] n satellite m; **satellite dish** n antenne f parabolique; **satellite navigation system** n système m de navigation par satellite; **satellite television** n télévision f par satellite

satin ['sætɪn] n satin m ⊳ adj en or de satin, satiné(e)

satire ['sætaɪər] n satire f

satisfaction [sætɪs'fækʃən] n satisfaction f

satisfactory [sætɪs'fæktərɪ] adj satisfaisant(e)

satisfied ['sætɪsfaɪd] adj satisfait(e); **to be ~ with sth** être satisfait de qch

satisfy ['sætɪsfaɪ] vt satisfaire, contenter; (convince) convaincre, persuader

Saturday ['sætədɪ] n samedi m

sauce [sɔːs] n sauce f; **saucepan** n casserole f

saucer ['sɔːsər] n soucoupe f

Saudi Arabia ['saudɪ-] n Arabie f Saoudite

sauna ['sɔːnə] n sauna m

sausage ['sɔsɪdʒ] n saucisse f; (salami etc) saucisson m; **sausage roll** n friand m

sautéed ['səuteɪd] adj sauté(e)

savage ['sævɪdʒ] adj (cruel, fierce) brutal(e), féroce; (primitive) primitif(-ive), sauvage ⊳ n sauvage m/f ⊳ vt attaquer férocement

save [seɪv] vt (person, belongings) sauver; (money) mettre de côté, économiser; (time) (faire) gagner; (keep) garder; (Comput) sauvegarder; (Sport: stop) arrêter; (avoid: trouble) éviter ⊳ vi (also: **~ up**) mettre de l'argent de côté ⊳ n (Sport) arrêt m (du ballon) ⊳ prep sauf, à l'exception de

saving ['seɪvɪŋ] n économie f; **savings** npl économies fpl

savings account n compte m d'épargne

savings and loan association (US) n ≈ société f de crédit immobilier

savoury, (US) **savory** ['seɪvərɪ] adj savoureux(-euse); (dish: not sweet) salé(e)

saw [sɔː] ⊳ pt of **see** ⊳ n (tool) scie f ⊳ vt (pt **sawed**, pp **sawed** or **sawn**) scier; **sawdust** n sciure f

sawn [sɔːn] pp of **saw**

saxophone ['sæksəfəun] n saxophone m

say [seɪ] vt (pt, pp **said**) dire ⊳ n: **to have one's ~** dire ce qu'on a à dire; **to have a ~** avoir voix au chapitre; **could you ~ that again?** pourriez-vous répéter ce que vous venez de dire?; **to ~ yes/no** dire oui/non; **my watch ~s 3 o'clock** ma montre indique 3 heures, il est 3 heures à ma montre; **that is to ~** c'est-à-dire; **that goes without ~ing** cela va sans dire, cela va de soi; **saying** n dicton m, proverbe m

scab [skæb] n croûte f; (pej) jaune m

scaffolding ['skæfəldɪŋ] n échafaudage m

scald [skɔːld] n brûlure f ⊳ vt ébouillanter

scale [skeɪl] n (of fish) écaille f; (Mus) gamme f; (of ruler, thermometer etc) graduation f, échelle (graduée); (of salaries, fees etc) barème m; (of map, also size, extent) échelle ⊳ vt (mountain) escalader; **scales** npl balance f; (larger) bascule f; (also: **bathroom ~s**) pèse-personne m inv; **~ of charges** tableau m des tarifs; **on a large ~** sur une grande échelle, en grand

scallion ['skæljən] n (US: salad onion) ciboule f

scallop ['skɔləp] n coquille f Saint-Jacques; (Sewing) feston m

scalp [skælp] n cuir chevelu ⊳ vt scalper

scalpel ['skælpl] n scalpel m

scam [skæm] n (inf) arnaque f

scampi ['skæmpɪ] npl langoustines (frites), scampi mpl

scan [skæn] vt (examine) scruter, examiner; (glance at quickly) parcourir; (TV, Radar) balayer ▷ n (Med) scanographie f

scandal ['skændl] n scandale m; (gossip) ragots mpl

Scandinavia [skændɪ'neɪvɪə] n Scandinavie f; **Scandinavian** adj scandinave ▷ n Scandinave m/f

scanner ['skænə^r] n (Radar, Med) scanner m, scanographe m; (Comput) scanner

scapegoat ['skeɪpgəut] n bouc m émissaire

scar [skɑ:^r] n cicatrice f ▷ vt laisser une cicatrice or une marque à

scarce [skɛəs] adj rare, peu abondant(e); **to make o.s. ~** (inf) se sauver; **scarcely** adv à peine, presque pas

scare [skɛə^r] n peur f, panique f ▷ vt effrayer, faire peur à; **to ~ sb stiff** faire une peur bleue à qn; **bomb ~** alerte f à la bombe; **scarecrow** n épouvantail m; **scared** adj: **to be scared** avoir peur

scarf (pl **scarves**) [skɑ:f, skɑ:vz] n (long) écharpe f; (square) foulard m

scarlet ['skɑ:lɪt] adj écarlate

scarves [skɑ:vz] npl of **scarf**

scary ['skɛərɪ] adj (inf) effrayant(e); (film) qui fait peur

scatter ['skætə^r] vt éparpiller, répandre; (crowd) disperser ▷ vi se disperser

scenario [sɪ'nɑ:rɪəu] n scénario m

scene [si:n] n (Theat, fig etc) scène f; (of crime, accident) lieu(x) m(pl), endroit m; (sight, view) spectacle m, vue f; **scenery** n (Theat) décor(s) m(pl); (landscape) paysage m; **scenic** adj offrant de beaux paysages or panoramas

scent [sɛnt] n parfum m, odeur f; (fig: track) piste f

sceptical, (US) **skeptical** ['skɛptɪkl] adj sceptique

schedule ['ʃɛdju:l, US 'skɛdju:l] n programme m, plan m; (of trains) horaire m; (of prices etc) barème m, tarif m ▷ vt prévoir; **on ~** à l'heure (prévue); à la date prévue; **to be ahead of/behind ~** avoir de l'avance/du retard; **scheduled flight** n vol régulier

scheme [ski:m] n plan m, projet m; (plot) complot m, combine f; (arrangement) arrangement m, classification f; (pension scheme etc) régime m ▷ vt, vi comploter, manigancer

schizophrenic [skɪtsə'frɛnɪk] adj schizophrène

scholar ['skɔlə^r] n érudit(e); (pupil) boursier(-ère); **scholarship** n érudition f; (grant) bourse f (d'études)

school [sku:l] n (gen) école f; (secondary school) collège m; lycée m; (in university) faculté f; (US: university) université f ▷ cpd scolaire; **schoolbook** n livre m scolaire or de classe; **schoolboy** n écolier m; (at secondary school) collégien m; lycéen m; **schoolchildren** npl écoliers mpl; (at secondary school) collégiens mpl; lycéens mpl; **schoolgirl** n écolière f; (at secondary school) collégienne f; lycéenne f; **schooling** n instruction f, études fpl; **schoolteacher** n (primary) instituteur(-trice); (secondary) professeur m

science ['saɪəns] n science f; **science fiction** n science-fiction f; **scientific** [saɪən'tɪfɪk] adj scientifique; **scientist** n scientifique m/f; (eminent) savant m

sci-fi ['saɪfaɪ] n abbr (inf: = science fiction) SF f

scissors ['sɪzəz] npl ciseaux mpl; **a pair of ~** une paire de ciseaux

scold [skəuld] vt gronder

scone [skɔn] n sorte de petit pain rond au lait

scoop [sku:p] n pelle f (à main);
(for ice cream) boule f à glace; (Press)
reportage exclusif or à sensation

scooter ['sku:təʳ] n (motor cycle)
scooter m; (toy) trottinette f

scope [skəup] n (capacity: of plan,
undertaking) portée f, envergure f; (: of
person) compétence f, capacités fpl;
(opportunity) possibilités fpl

scorching ['skɔ:tʃɪŋ] adj torride,
brûlant(e)

score [skɔ:ʳ] n score m, décompte m
des points; (Mus) partition f ▷ vt (goal,
point) marquer; (success) remporter;
(cut: leather, wood, card) entailler,
inciser ▷ vi marquer des points;
(Football) marquer un but; (keep score)
compter les points; **on that ~** sur ce
chapitre, à cet égard; **a ~ of** (twenty)
vingt; **~s of** (fig) des tas de; **to ~ 6
out of 10** obtenir 6 sur 10; **score out**
vt rayer, barrer, biffer; **scoreboard** n
tableau m; **scorer** n (Football) auteur
m du but; buteur m; (keeping score)
marqueur m

scorn [skɔ:n] n mépris m, dédain m

Scorpio ['skɔ:pɪəu] n le Scorpion

scorpion ['skɔ:pɪən] n scorpion m

Scot [skɔt] n Écossais(e)

Scotch [skɔtʃ] n whisky m, scotch m

Scotch tape® (us) n scotch® m,
ruban adhésif

Scotland ['skɔtlənd] n Écosse f

Scots [skɔts] adj écossais(e);
Scotsman (irreg) n Écossais m;
Scotswoman (irreg) n Écossaise f;
Scottish ['skɔtɪʃ] adj écossais(e); **the
Scottish Parliament** le Parlement
écossais

scout [skaut] n (Mil) éclaireur m;
(also: **boy ~**) scout m; **girl ~** (us)
guide f

scowl [skaul] vi se renfrogner, avoir
l'air maussade; **to ~ at** regarder de
travers

scramble ['skræmbl] n (rush)
bousculade f, ruée f ▷ vi grimper/
descendre tant bien que mal; **to ~
for** se bousculer or se disputer pour
(avoir); **to go scrambling** (Sport)
faire du trial; **scrambled eggs** npl
œufs brouillés

scrap [skræp] n bout m, morceau m;
(fight) bagarre f; (also: **~ iron**) ferraille
f ▷ vt jeter, mettre au rebut; (fig)
abandonner, laisser tomber ▷ vi se
bagarrer; **scraps** npl (waste) déchets
mpl; **scrapbook** n album m

scrape [skreip] vt, vi gratter, racler
▷ n: **to get into a ~** s'attirer des
ennuis; **scrape through** vi (exam etc)
réussir de justesse

scrap paper n papier m brouillon

scratch [skrætʃ] n égratignure f,
rayure f; (on paint) éraflure f; (from
claw) coup m de griffe ▷ vt (rub) (se)
gratter; (paint etc) érafler; (with claw,
nail) griffer ▷ vi (se) gratter; **to start
from ~** partir de zéro; **to be up to
~** être à la hauteur; **scratch card** n
carte f à gratter

scream [skri:m] n cri perçant,
hurlement m ▷ vi crier, hurler

screen [skri:n] n écran m; (in room)
paravent m; (fig) écran, rideau m ▷ vt
masquer, cacher; (from the wind etc)
abriter, protéger; (film) projeter;
(candidates etc) filtrer; **screening** n
(of film) projection f; (Med) test m (or
tests) de dépistage; **screenplay** n
scénario m; **screen saver** n (Comput)
économiseur m d'écran

screw [skru:] n vis f ▷ vt (also: **~ in**)
visser; **screw up** vt (paper etc) froisser;
to ~ up one's eyes se plisser les yeux;
screwdriver n tournevis m

scribble ['skrɪbl] n gribouillage m ▷ vt
gribouiller, griffonner

script [skrɪpt] n (Cine etc) scénario m,
texte m; (writing) (écriture f) script m

scroll [skrəul] n rouleau m ▷ vt
(Comput) faire défiler (sur l'écran)

scrub [skrʌb] n (land) broussailles fpl
▷ vt (floor) nettoyer à la brosse; (pan)
récurer; (washing) frotter

scruffy ['skrʌfɪ] adj débraillé(e)

scrum(mage) ['skrʌm(ɪdʒ)] n
mêlée f

scrutiny ['skru:tɪnɪ] n examen
minutieux

scuba diving ['sku:bə-] n plongée
sous-marine

sculptor ['skʌlptər] n sculpteur m

sculpture ['skʌlptʃər] n sculpture f

scum [skʌm] n écume f, mousse f;
(pej: people) rebut m, lie f

scurry ['skʌrɪ] vi filer à toute allure;
to ~ off détaler, se sauver

sea [si:] n mer f ▷ cpd marin(e), de (la)
mer, maritime; **by** or **beside the ~**
(holiday, town) au bord de la mer; **by ~**
par mer, en bateau; **out to ~** au large;
(out) at ~ en mer; **to be all at ~** (fig)
nager complètement; **seafood** n
fruits mpl de mer; **sea front** n bord m
de mer; **seagull** n mouette f

seal [si:l] n (animal) phoque m;
(stamp) sceau m, cachet m ▷ vt sceller;
(envelope) coller (: with seal) cacheter;
seal off vt (forbid entry to) interdire
l'accès de

sea level n niveau m de la mer

seam [si:m] n couture f; (of coal) veine
f, filon m

search [sə:tʃ] n (for person, thing,
Comput) recherche(s) f(pl); (of drawer,
pockets) fouille f; (Law: at sb's home)
perquisition f ▷ vt fouiller; (examine)
examiner minutieusement; scruter
▷ vi: **to ~ for** chercher; **in ~ of** à
la recherche de; **search engine** n
(Comput) moteur m de recherche;
search party n expédition f de
secours

sea: **seashore** n rivage m, plage f,
bord m de (la) mer; **seasick** adj: **to be
seasick** avoir le mal de mer; **seaside**
n bord m de mer; **seaside resort** n
station f balnéaire

season ['si:zn] n saison f ▷ vt
assaisonner, relever; **to be in/
out of ~** être/ne pas être de saison;
seasonal adj saisonnier(-ière);
seasoning n assaisonnement

m; **season ticket** n carte f
d'abonnement

seat [si:t] n siège m; (in bus, train:
place) place f; (buttocks) postérieur m;
(of trousers) fond m ▷ vt faire asseoir,
placer; (have room for) avoir des places
assises pour, pouvoir accueillir; **to be
~ed** être assis; **seat belt** n ceinture
f de sécurité; **seating** n sièges fpl,
places assises

sea: **sea water** n eau f de mer;
seaweed n algues fpl

sec. abbr (= second) sec

secluded [sɪ'klu:dɪd] adj retiré(e),
à l'écart

second ['sɛkənd] num deuxième,
second(e) ▷ adv (in race etc) en
seconde position ▷ n (unit of time)
seconde f; (Aut: also: **~ gear**)
seconde; (Comm: imperfect) article
m de second choix; (BRIT Scol) ≈
licence f avec mention ▷ vt (motion)
appuyer; **seconds** npl (inf: food) rab
m (inf); **secondary** adj secondaire;
secondary school n (age 11 to 15)
collège m; (age 15 to 18) lycée m;
second-class adj de deuxième
classe; (Rail) de seconde (classe);
(Post) au tarif réduit; (pej) de qualité
inférieure ▷ adv (Rail) en seconde;
(Post) au tarif réduit; **secondhand** adj
d'occasion; (information) de seconde
main; **secondly** adv deuxièmement;
second-rate adj de deuxième
ordre, de qualité inférieure; **second
thoughts** npl; **to have second
thoughts** changer d'avis; **on second
thoughts** or (us) **thought** à la
réflexion

secrecy ['si:krəsɪ] n secret m

secret ['si:krɪt] adj secret(-ète)
▷ n secret m; **in ~** adv en secret,
secrètement, en cachette

secretary ['sɛkrətrɪ] n secrétaire
m/f; **S~ of State (for)** (Pol) ministre
m (de)

secretive ['si:krətɪv] adj réservé(e);
(pej) cachottier(-ière), dissimulé(e)

S

secret service n services secrets

sect [sɛkt] n secte f

section ['sɛkʃən] n section f; (Comm) rayon m; (of document) section, article m, paragraphe m; (cut) coupe f

sector ['sɛktəʳ] n secteur m

secular ['sɛkjuləʳ] adj laïque

secure [sɪ'kjuəʳ] adj (free from anxiety) sans inquiétude, sécurisé(e); (firmly fixed) solide, bien attaché(e) (or fermé(e) etc); (in safe place) en lieu sûr, en sûreté ▷ vt (fix) fixer, attacher; (get) obtenir, se procurer

security [sɪ'kjuərɪtɪ] n sécurité f, mesures fpl de sécurité; (for loan) caution f, garantie f; **securities** npl (Stock Exchange) valeurs fpl, titres mpl; **security guard** n garde chargé de la sécurité; (transporting money) convoyeur m de fonds

sedan [sə'dæn] n (US Aut) berline f

sedate [sɪ'deɪt] adj calme; posé(e) ▷ vt donner des sédatifs à

sedative ['sɛdɪtɪv] n calmant m, sédatif m

seduce [sɪ'djuːs] vt séduire; **seductive** [sɪ'dʌktɪv] adj séduisant(e); (smile) séducteur(-trice); (fig: offer) alléchant(e)

see [siː] (pt **saw**, pp **seen**) vt (gen) voir; (accompany): **to ~ sb to the door** reconduire or raccompagner qn jusqu'à la porte ▷ vi voir; **to ~ that** (ensure) veiller à ce que + sub, faire en sorte que + sub, s'assurer que; **~ you soon/later/tomorrow!** à bientôt/plus tard/demain!; **see off** vt accompagner (à l'aéroport etc); **see out** vt (take to door) raccompagner à la porte; **see through** vt mener à bonne fin ▷ vt fus voir clair dans; **see to** vt fus s'occuper de, se charger de

seed [siːd] n graine f; (fig) germe m; (Tennis etc) tête f de série; **to go to ~** (plant) monter en graine; (fig) se laisser aller

seeing ['siːɪŋ] conj: **~ (that)** vu que, étant donné que

seek [siːk] (pt, pp **sought**) vt chercher, rechercher

seem [siːm] vi sembler, paraître; **there ~s to be ...** il semble qu'il y a ..., on dirait qu'il y a ...; **seemingly** adv apparemment

seen [siːn] pp of **see**

seesaw ['siːsɔː] n (jeu m de) bascule f

segment ['sɛgmənt] n segment m; (of orange) quartier m

segregate ['sɛgrɪgeɪt] vt séparer, isoler

Seine [seɪn] n: **the (River) ~** la Seine

seize [siːz] vt (grasp) saisir, attraper; (take possession of) s'emparer de; (opportunity) saisir

seizure ['siːʒəʳ] n (Med) crise f, attaque f; (of power) prise f

seldom ['sɛldəm] adv rarement

select [sɪ'lɛkt] adj choisi(e), d'élite; (hotel, restaurant, club) chic inv, sélect inv ▷ vt sélectionner, choisir; **selection** n sélection f, choix m; **selective** adj sélectif(-ive); (school) à recrutement sélectif

self (pl **selves**) [sɛlf, sɛlvz] n: **the ~** le moi inv ▷ prefix auto-; **self-assured** adj sûr(e) de soi, plein(e) d'assurance; **self-catering** adj (Brit: flat) avec cuisine, où l'on peut faire sa cuisine; (: holiday) en appartement (or chalet etc) loué; **self-centred**, (US) **self-centered** adj égocentrique; **self-confidence** n confiance f en soi; **self-confident** adj sûr(e) de soi, plein(e) d'assurance; **self-conscious** adj timide, qui manque d'assurance; **self-contained** adj (Brit: flat) avec entrée particulière, indépendant(e); **self-control** n maîtrise f de soi; **self-defence**, (US) **self-defense** n autodéfense f; (Law) légitime défense f; **self-drive** adj (Brit): **self-drive car** voiture f de location; **self-employed** adj qui travaille à son compte; **self-esteem** n amour-propre m; **self-indulgent** adj qui ne se refuse rien; **self-interest** n intérêt personnel;

selfish adj égoïste; **self-pity** n apitoiement m sur soi-même; **self-raising** [sɛlfˈreɪzɪŋ], (US) **self-rising** [sɛlfˈraɪzɪŋ] adj: **self-raising flour** farine f pour gâteaux (avec levure incorporée); **self-respect** n respect m de soi, amour-propre m; **self-service** adj, n libre-service (m), self-service (m)

sell (pt, pp **sold**) [sɛl, səʊld] vt vendre ▷ vi se vendre; **to ~ at** or **for 10 euros** se vendre 10 euros; **sell off** vt liquider; **sell out** vi: **to ~ out (of sth)** (use up stock) vendre tout son stock (de qch); **sell-by date** n date f limite de vente; **seller** n vendeur(-euse), marchand(e)

Sellotape® [ˈsɛləʊteɪp] n (BRIT) scotch® m

selves [sɛlvz] npl of **self**

semester [sɪˈmɛstər] n (esp US) semestre m

semi... [ˈsɛmɪ] prefix semi-, demi-; à demi, à moitié; **semicircle** n demi-cercle m; **semidetached (house)** n (BRIT) maison jumelée or jumelle; **semi-final** n demi-finale f

seminar [ˈsɛmɪnɑːr] n séminaire m

semi-skimmed [ˈsɛmɪˈskɪmd] adj demi-écrémé(e)

senate [ˈsɛnɪt] n sénat m; (US): **the S~** le Sénat; **senator** n sénateur m

send (pt, pp **sent**) [sɛnd, sɛnt] vt envoyer; **send back** vt renvoyer; **send for** vt fus (by post) se faire envoyer, commander par correspondance; **send in** vt (report, application, resignation) remettre; **send off** vt (goods) envoyer, expédier; (BRIT Sport: player) expulser or renvoyer du terrain; **send on** vt (BRIT: letter) faire suivre; (luggage etc: in advance) (faire) expédier à l'avance; **send out** vt (invitation) envoyer (par la poste); (emit: light, heat, signal) émettre; **send up** vt (person, price) faire monter; (BRIT: parody) mettre en boîte, parodier; **sender** n expéditeur(-trice); **send-off** n: **a good send-off** des adieux chaleureux

senile [ˈsiːnaɪl] adj sénile

senior [ˈsiːnɪər] adj (high-ranking) de haut niveau; (of higher rank): **to be ~ to sb** être le supérieur de qn; **senior citizen** n personne f du troisième âge; **senior high school** n (US) ≈ lycée m

sensation [sɛnˈseɪʃən] n sensation f; **sensational** adj qui fait sensation; (marvellous) sensationnel(le)

sense [sɛns] n sens m; (feeling) sentiment m; (meaning) sens, signification f; (wisdom) bon sens ▷ vt sentir, pressentir; **it makes ~** c'est logique; **senseless** adj insensé(e), stupide; (unconscious) sans connaissance; **sense of humour**, (US) **sense of humor** n sens m de l'humour

sensible [ˈsɛnsɪbl] adj sensé(e), raisonnable; (shoes etc) pratique

> Be careful not to translate sensible by the French word sensible.

sensitive [ˈsɛnsɪtɪv] adj: **~ (to)** sensible (à)

sensual [ˈsɛnsjuəl] adj sensuel(le)

sensuous [ˈsɛnsjuəs] adj voluptueux(-euse), sensuel(le)

sent [sɛnt] pt, pp of **send**

sentence [ˈsɛntns] n (Ling) phrase f; (Law: judgment) condamnation f, sentence f; (: punishment) peine f ▷ vt: **to ~ sb to death/to 5 years** condamner qn à mort/à 5 ans

sentiment [ˈsɛntɪmənt] n sentiment m; (opinion) opinion f, avis m; **sentimental** [sɛntɪˈmɛntl] adj sentimental(e)

separate adj [ˈsɛprɪt] séparé(e); (organization) indépendant(e); (day, occasion, issue) différent(e) ▷ vt [ˈsɛpəreɪt] séparer; (distinguish) distinguer ▷ vi [ˈsɛpəreɪt] se séparer; **separately** adv séparément; **separates** npl (clothes) coordonnés mpl; **separation** [sɛpəˈreɪʃən] n séparation f

s

September [sɛp'tɛmbə'] *n*
septembre *m*

septic ['sɛptɪk] *adj* (*wound*) infecté(e);
septic tank *n* fosse *f* septique

sequel ['si:kwl] *n* conséquence *f*;
séquelles *fpl*; (*of story*) suite *f*

sequence ['si:kwəns] *n* ordre *m*,
suite *f*; (*in film*) séquence *f*; (*dance*)
numéro *m*

sequin ['si:kwɪn] *n* paillette *f*

Serb [sə:b] *adj*, *n* = **Serbian**

Serbia ['sə:bɪə] *n* Serbie *f*

Serbian ['sə:bɪən] *adj* serbe ▷ *n* Serbe
m/f; (*Ling*) serbe *m*

sergeant ['sɑ:dʒənt] *n* sergent *m*;
(*Police*) brigadier *m*

serial ['sɪərɪəl] *n* feuilleton *m*; **serial
killer** *n* meurtrier *m* tuant en série;
serial number *n* numéro *m* de série

series ['sɪərɪz] *n* série *f*; (*Publishing*)
collection *f*

serious ['sɪərɪəs] *adj* sérieux(-euse);
(*accident etc*) grave; **seriously** *adv*
sérieusement; (*hurt*) gravement

sermon ['sə:mən] *n* sermon *m*

servant ['sə:vənt] *n* domestique *m/f*;
(*fig*) serviteur (servante)

serve [sə:v] *vt* (*employer etc*) servir,
être au service de; (*purpose*) servir
à; (*customer, food, meal*) servir; (*subj:
train*) desservir; (*apprenticeship*) faire,
accomplir; (*prison term*) faire; purger
▷ *vi* (*Tennis*) servir; (*be useful*): **to ~
as/for/to do** servir de/à/à faire ▷ *n*
(*Tennis*) service *m*; **it ~s him right**
c'est bien fait pour lui; **server** *n*
(*Comput*) serveur *m*

service ['sə:vɪs] *n* (*gen*) service *m*;
(*Aut*) révision *f*; (*Rel*) office *m* ▷ *vt*
(*car etc*) réviser; **services** *npl* (*Econ:
tertiary sector*) (secteur *m*) tertiaire
m, secteur des services; (*BRIT: on
motorway*) station-service *f*; (*Mil*): **the
S~s** *npl* les forces armées; **to be of ~
to sb, to do sb a ~** rendre service à
qn; **~ included/not included** service
compris/non compris; **service area**
n (*on motorway*) aire *f* de services;

service charge *n* (*BRIT*) service *m*;
serviceman (*irreg*) *n* militaire *m*;
service station *n* station-service *f*

serviette [sə:vi'ɛt] *n* (*BRIT*) serviette
f (de table)

session ['sɛʃən] *n* (*sitting*) séance *f*;
to be in ~ siéger, être en session ou
en séance

set [sɛt] (*pt, pp* **set**) *n* série *f*,
assortiment *m*; (*of tools etc*) jeu *m*;
(*Radio, TV*) poste *m*; (*Tennis*) set *m*;
(*group of people*) cercle *m*, milieu *m*;
(*Cine*) plateau *m*; (*Theat: stage*) scène
f; (: *scenery*) décor *m*; (*Math*) ensemble
m; (*Hairdressing*) mise *f* en plis ▷ *adj*
(*fixed*) fixe, déterminé(e); (*ready*)
prêt(e) ▷ *vt* (*place*) mettre, poser,
placer; (*fix, establish*) fixer (: *record*)
établir; (*assign: task, homework*)
donner; (*exam*) composer; (*adjust*)
régler; (*decide: rules etc*) fixer, choisir
▷ *vi* (*sun*) se coucher; (*jam, jelly,
concrete*) prendre; (*bone*) se ressouder;
to be ~ on doing être résolu(e)
à faire; **to ~ to music** mettre en
musique; **to ~ on fire** mettre le feu
à; **to ~ free** libérer; **to ~ sth going**
déclencher qch; **to ~ sail** partir,
prendre la mer; **set aside** *vt* mettre
de côté; (*time*) garder; **set down** *vt*
(*subj: bus, train*) déposer; **set in** *vi*
(*infection, bad weather*) s'installer;
(*complications*) survenir, surgir; **set
off** *vi* se mettre en route, partir ▷ *vt*
(*bomb*) faire exploser; (*cause to start*)
déclencher; (*show up well*) mettre en
valeur, faire valoir; **set out** *vi*: **to ~
out (from)** partir (de) ▷ *vt* (*arrange*)
disposer; (*state*) présenter, exposer;
to ~ out to do entreprendre de
faire; avoir pour but ou intention de
faire; **set up** *vt* (*organization*) fonder,
créer; **setback** *n* (*hitch*) revers *m*,
contretemps *m*; **set menu** *n* menu *m*

settee [sɛ'ti:] *n* canapé *m*

setting ['sɛtɪŋ] *n* cadre *m*; (*of jewel*)
monture *f*; (*position: of controls*)
réglage *m*

settle ['sɛtl] vt (argument, matter, account) régler; (problem) résoudre; (Med: calm) calmer ▷ vi (bird, dust etc) se poser; **to ~ for sth** accepter qch, se contenter de qch; **to ~ on sth** opter or se décider pour qch; **settle down** vi (get comfortable) s'installer; (become calmer) se calmer; **settle in** vi s'installer; **settle up** vi: **to ~ up with sb** régler (ce que l'on doit à) qn; **settlement** n (payment) règlement m; (agreement) accord m; (village etc) village m, hameau m

setup ['sɛtʌp] n (arrangement) manière f dont les choses sont organisées; (situation) situation f, allure f des choses

seven ['sɛvn] num sept; **seventeen** num dix-sept; **seventeenth** [sɛvn'tiːnθ] num dix-septième; **seventh** num septième; **seventieth** ['sɛvntɪɪθ] num soixante-dixième; **seventy** num soixante-dix

sever ['sɛvə'] vt couper, trancher; (relations) rompre

several ['sɛvərl] adj, pron plusieurs pl; **~ of us** plusieurs d'entre nous

severe [sɪ'vɪə'] adj (stern) sévère, strict(e); (serious) grave, sérieux(-euse); (plain) sévère, austère

sew (pt **sewed**, pp **sewn**) [səʊ, səʊd, səʊn] vt, vi coudre

sewage ['suːɪdʒ] n vidange(s) f(pl)

sewer ['suːə'] n égout m

sewing ['səʊɪŋ] n couture f; (item(s)) ouvrage m; **sewing machine** n machine f à coudre

sewn [səʊn] pp of **sew**

sex [sɛks] n sexe m; **to have ~ with** avoir des rapports (sexuels) avec; **sexism** ['sɛksɪzəm] n sexisme m; **sexist** adj sexiste; **sexual** ['sɛksjʊəl] adj sexuel(le); **sexual intercourse** n rapports sexuels; **sexuality** [sɛksju'ælɪtɪ] n sexualité f; **sexy** adj sexy inv

shabby ['ʃæbɪ] adj miteux(-euse); (behaviour) mesquin(e), méprisable

shack [ʃæk] n cabane f, hutte f

shade [ʃeɪd] n ombre f; (for lamp) abat-jour m inv; (of colour) nuance f, ton m; (us: window shade) store m; (small quantity): **a ~ of** un soupçon de ▷ vt abriter du soleil, ombrager; **shades** npl (us: sunglasses) lunettes fpl de soleil; **in the ~** à l'ombre; **a ~ smaller** un tout petit peu plus petit

shadow ['ʃædəʊ] n ombre f ▷ vt (follow) filer; **shadow cabinet** n (BRIT Pol) cabinet parallèle formé par le parti qui n'est pas au pouvoir

shady ['ʃeɪdɪ] adj ombragé(e); (fig: dishonest) louche, véreux(-euse)

shaft [ʃɑːft] n (of arrow, spear) hampe f; (Aut, Tech) arbre m; (of mine) puits m; (of lift) cage f; (of light) rayon m, trait m

shake [ʃeɪk] (pt **shook**, pp **shaken**) vt secouer; (bottle, cocktail) agiter; (house, confidence) ébranler ▷ vi trembler; **to ~ one's head** (in refusal etc) dire or faire non de la tête; (in dismay) secouer la tête; **to ~ hands with sb** serrer la main à qn; **shake off** vt secouer; (pursuer) se débarrasser de; **shake up** vt secouer; **shaky** adj (hand, voice) tremblant(e); (building) branlant(e), peu solide

shall [ʃæl] aux vb: **I ~ go** j'irai; **~ I open the door?** j'ouvre la porte?; **I'll get the coffee, ~ I?** je vais chercher le café, d'accord?

shallow ['ʃæləʊ] adj peu profond(e); (fig) superficiel(le), qui manque de profondeur

sham [ʃæm] n frime f

shambles ['ʃæmblz] n confusion f, pagaïe f, fouillis m

shame [ʃeɪm] n honte f ▷ vt faire honte à; **it is a ~ (that/to do)** c'est dommage (que + sub/de faire); **what a ~!** quel dommage!; **shameful** adj honteux(-euse), scandaleux(-euse); **shameless** adj éhonté(e), effronté(e)

shampoo [ʃæm'puː] n shampooing m ▷ vt faire un shampooing à

shandy ['ʃændɪ] n bière panachée

S

shan't [ʃɑːnt] = **shall not**

shape [ʃeɪp] n forme f ▷ vt façonner, modeler; (sb's ideas, character) former; (sb's life) déterminer ▷ vi (also: **~ up**: events) prendre tournure; (: person) faire des progrès, s'en sortir; **to take ~** prendre forme or tournure

share [ʃɛəʳ] n part f; (Comm) action f ▷ vt partager; (have in common) avoir en commun; **to ~ out (among** or **between)** partager (entre); **shareholder** n (BRIT) actionnaire m/f

shark [ʃɑːk] n requin m

sharp [ʃɑːp] adj (razor, knife) tranchant(e), bien aiguisé(e); (point, voice) aigu(ë); (nose, chin) pointu(e); (outline, increase) net(te); (cold, pain) vif (vive); (taste) piquant(e), âcre; (Mus) dièse; (person: quick-witted) vif (vive), éveillé(e); (: unscrupulous) malhonnête ▷ n (Mus) dièse m ▷ adv: **at 2 o'clock ~** à 2 heures pile or tapantes; **sharpen** vt aiguiser; (pencil) tailler; (fig) aviver; **sharpener** n (also: **pencil sharpener**) taille-crayon(s) m inv; **sharply** adv (turn, stop) brusquement; (stand out) nettement; (criticize, retort) sèchement, vertement

shatter [ˈʃætəʳ] vt briser; (fig: upset) bouleverser; (: ruin) briser, ruiner ▷ vi voler en éclats, se briser; **shattered** adj (overwhelmed, grief-stricken) bouleversé(e); (inf: exhausted) éreinté(e)

shave [ʃeɪv] vt raser ▷ vi se raser ▷ n: **to have a ~** se raser; **shaver** n (also: **electric shaver**) rasoir m électrique

shaving cream n crème f à raser

shaving foam n mousse f à raser

shavings [ˈʃeɪvɪŋz] npl (of wood etc) copeaux mpl

shawl [ʃɔːl] n châle m

she [ʃiː] pron elle

sheath [ʃiːθ] n gaine f, fourreau m, étui m; (contraceptive) préservatif m

shed [ʃɛd] n remise f, resserre f ▷ vt (pt, pp **shed**) (leaves, fur etc) perdre; (tears) verser, répandre; (workers) congédier

she'd [ʃiːd] = **she had; she would**

sheep [ʃiːp] n (pl inv) mouton m; **sheepdog** n chien m de berger; **sheepskin** n peau f de mouton

sheer [ʃɪəʳ] adj (utter) pur(e), pur et simple; (steep) à pic, abrupt(e); (almost transparent) extrêmement fin(e) ▷ adv à pic, abruptement

sheet [ʃiːt] n (on bed) drap m; (of paper) feuille f; (of glass, metal etc) feuille, plaque f

sheik(h) [ʃeɪk] n cheik m

shelf (pl **shelves**) [ʃɛlf, ʃɛlvz] n étagère f, rayon m

shell [ʃɛl] n (on beach) coquillage m; (of egg, nut etc) coquille f; (explosive) obus m; (of building) carcasse f ▷ vt (peas) écosser; (Mil) bombarder (d'obus)

she'll [ʃiːl] = **she will; she shall**

shellfish [ˈʃɛlfɪʃ] n (pl inv: crab etc) crustacé m; (: scallop etc) coquillage m ▷ npl (as food) fruits mpl de mer

shelter [ˈʃɛltəʳ] n abri m, refuge m ▷ vt abriter, protéger; (give lodging to) donner asile à ▷ vi s'abriter, se mettre à l'abri; **sheltered** adj (life) retiré(e), à l'abri des soucis; (spot) abrité(e)

shelves [ˈʃɛlvz] npl of **shelf**

shelving [ˈʃɛlvɪŋ] n (shelves) rayonnage(s) m(pl)

shepherd [ˈʃɛpəd] n berger m ▷ vt (guide) guider, escorter; **shepherd's pie** n ≈ hachis m Parmentier

sheriff [ˈʃɛrɪf] (US) n shérif m

sherry [ˈʃɛrɪ] n xérès m, sherry m

she's [ʃiːz] = **she is; she has**

Shetland [ˈʃɛtlənd] n (also: **the ~s, the ~ Isles** or **Islands**) les îles fpl Shetland

shield [ʃiːld] n bouclier m; (protection) écran m de protection f ▷ vt: **to ~ (from)** protéger (de or contre)

shift [ʃɪft] n (change) changement m; (work period) période f de travail; (of workers) équipe f, poste m ▷ vt déplacer, changer de place; (*remove*) enlever ▷ *vi* changer de place, bouger

shin [ʃɪn] *n* tibia *m*

shine [ʃaɪn] *n* éclat *m*, brillant *m* ▷ *vi* (*pt, pp* **shone**) briller ▷ *vt* (*pt, pp* **shined**) (*polish*) faire briller *or* reluire; **to ~ sth on sth** (*torch*) braquer qch sur qch

shingles ['ʃɪŋglz] *n* (*Med*) zona *m*

shiny ['ʃaɪnɪ] *adj* brillant(e)

ship [ʃɪp] *n* bateau *m*; (*large*) navire *m* ▷ *vt* transporter (par mer); (*send*) expédier (par mer); **shipment** *n* cargaison *f*; **shipping** *n* (*ships*) navires *mpl*; (*traffic*) navigation *f*; (*the industry*) industrie navale; (*transport*) transport *m*; **shipwreck** *n* épave *f*; (*event*) naufrage *m* ▷ *vt*: **to be shipwrecked** faire naufrage; **shipyard** *n* chantier naval

shirt [ʃəːt] *n* chemise *f*; (*woman's*) chemisier *m*; **in ~ sleeves** en bras de chemise

shit [ʃɪt] *excl* (*inf!*) merde (*!*)

shiver ['ʃɪvəʳ] *n* frisson *m* ▷ *vi* frissonner

shock [ʃɔk] *n* choc *m*; (*Elec*) secousse *f*, décharge *f*; (*Med*) commotion *f*, choc *m* ▷ *vt* (*scandalize*) choquer, scandaliser; (*upset*) bouleverser; **shocking** *adj* (*outrageous*) choquant(e), scandaleux(-euse); (*awful*) épouvantable

shoe [ʃuː] *n* chaussure *f*, soulier *m*; (*also*: **horse~**) fer *m* à cheval ▷ *vt* (*pt, pp* **shod**) (*horse*) ferrer; **shoelace** *n* lacet *m* (de soulier); **shoe polish** *n* cirage *m*; **shoeshop** *n* magasin *m* de chaussures

shone [ʃɔn] *pt, pp of* **shine**

shonky ['ʃɔŋkɪ] *adj* (*AUST, NZ inf*: *untrustworthy*) louche

shook [ʃuk] *pt of* **shake**

shoot [ʃuːt] (*pt, pp* **shot**) *n* (*on branch, seedling*) pousse *f* ▷ *vt* (*game: hunt*) chasser; (*: aim at*) tirer; (*: kill*) abattre; (*person*) blesser/tuer d'un coup de fusil (*or* de revolver); (*execute*) fusiller;

(*arrow*) tirer; (*gun*) tirer un coup de; (*Cine*) tourner ▷ *vi* (*with gun, bow*): **to ~ (at)** tirer (sur); (*Football*) shooter, tirer; **shoot down** *vt* (*plane*) abattre; **shoot up** *vi* (*fig: prices etc*) monter en flèche; **shooting** *n* (*shots*) coups *mpl* de feu; (*attack*) fusillade *f*; (*murder*) homicide *m* (à l'aide d'une arme à feu); (*Hunting*) chasse *f*

shop [ʃɔp] *n* magasin *m*; (*workshop*) atelier *m* ▷ *vi* (*also*: **go ~ping**) faire ses courses *or* ses achats; **shop assistant** *n* (*BRIT*) vendeur(-euse); **shopkeeper** *n* marchand(e), commerçant(e); **shoplifting** *n* vol *m* à l'étalage; **shopping** *n* (*goods*) achats *mpl*, provisions *fpl*; **shopping bag** *n* sac *m* (à provisions); **shopping centre**, (*US*)**shopping center** *n* centre commercial; **shopping mall** *n* centre commercial; **shopping trolley** *n* (*BRIT*) Caddie® *m*; **shop window** *n* vitrine *f*

shore [ʃɔːʳ] *n* (*of sea, lake*) rivage *m*, rive *f* ▷ *vt*: **to ~ (up)** étayer; **on ~** à terre

short [ʃɔːt] *adj* (*not long*) court(e); (*soon finished*) court, bref (brève); (*person, step*) petit(e); (*curt*) brusque, sec (sèche); (*insufficient*) insuffisant(e) ▷ *n* (*also*: **~ film**) court métrage; (*Elec*) court-circuit *m*; **to be ~ of sth** être à court de *or* manquer de qch; **in ~** bref; en bref; **~ of doing** à moins de faire; **everything ~ of** tout sauf; **it is ~ for** c'est l'abréviation *or* le diminutif de; **to cut ~** (*speech, visit*) abréger, écourter; **to fall ~ of** ne pas être à la hauteur de; **to run ~ of** arriver à court de, venir à manquer de; **to stop ~** s'arrêter net; **to stop ~ of** ne pas aller jusqu'à; **shortage** *n* manque *m*, pénurie *f*; **shortbread** *n* ≈ sablé *m*; **shortcoming** *n* défaut *m*; **short(crust) pastry** *n* (*BRIT*) pâte brisée; **shortcut** *n* raccourci *m*; **shorten** *vt* raccourcir; (*text, visit*) abréger; **shortfall** *n* déficit *m*; **shorthand** *n* (*BRIT*) sténo(graphie)

S

f; **shortlist** n (BRIT: for job) liste f des candidats sélectionnés; **short-lived** adj de courte durée; **shortly** adv bientôt, sous peu; **shorts** npl; **(a pair of) shorts** un short; **short-sighted** adj (BRIT) myope; (fig) qui manque de clairvoyance; **short-sleeved** adj à manches courtes; **short story** n nouvelle f; **short-tempered** adj qui s'emporte facilement; **short-term** adj (effect) à court terme

shot [ʃɔt] pt, pp of **shoot** ▷ n coup m (de feu); (try) coup, essai m; (injection) piqûre f; (Phot) photo f; **to be a good/poor ~** (person) tirer bien/mal; **like a ~** comme une flèche; (very readily) sans hésiter; **shotgun** n fusil m de chasse

should [ʃud] aux vb: **I ~ go now** je devrais partir maintenant; **he ~ be there now** il devrait être arrivé maintenant; **I ~ go if I were you** si j'étais vous j'irais; **I ~ like to** volontiers, j'aimerais bien

shoulder ['ʃəuldəʳ] n épaule f ▷ vt (fig) endosser, se charger de; **shoulder blade** n omoplate f

shouldn't ['ʃudnt] = **should not**

shout [ʃaut] n cri m ▷ vt crier ▷ vi crier, pousser des cris

shove [ʃʌv] vt pousser; (inf: put): **to ~ sth in** fourrer or ficher qch dans ▷ n poussée f

shovel ['ʃʌvl] n pelle f ▷ vt pelleter, enlever (or enfourner) à la pelle

show [ʃəu] (pt **showed**, pp **shown**) n (of emotion) manifestation f, démonstration f; (semblance) semblant m, apparence f; (exhibition) exposition f, salon m; (Theat, TV) spectacle m; (Cine) séance f ▷ vt montrer; (film) passer; (courage etc) faire preuve de, manifester; (exhibit) exposer ▷ vi se voir, être visible; **can you ~ me where it is, please?** pouvez-vous me montrer où c'est?; **to be on ~** être exposé(e); **it's just for ~** c'est juste pour l'effet; **show in**

vt faire entrer; **show off** vi (pej) crâner ▷ vt (display) faire valoir; (pej) faire étalage de; **show out** vt reconduire à la porte; **show up** vi (stand out) ressortir; (inf: turn up) se montrer ▷ vt (unmask) démasquer, dénoncer; (flaw) faire ressortir; **show business** n le monde du spectacle

shower ['ʃauəʳ] n (for washing) douche f; (rain) averse f; (of stones etc) pluie f, grêle f; (us: party) réunion organisée pour la remise de cadeaux ▷ vi prendre une douche, se doucher ▷ vt: **to ~ sb with** (gifts etc) combler qn de; **to have** or **take a ~** prendre une douche, se doucher; **shower cap** n bonnet m de douche; **shower gel** n gel m douche

showing ['ʃəuɪŋ] n (of film) projection f

show jumping [-dʒʌmpɪŋ] n concours m hippique

shown [ʃəun] pp of **show**

show-: show-off n (inf: person) crâneur(-euse), m'as-tu-vu(e); **showroom** n magasin m or salle f d'exposition

shrank [ʃræŋk] pt of **shrink**

shred [ʃrɛd] n (gen pl) lambeau m, petit morceau; (fig: of truth, evidence) parcelle f ▷ vt mettre en lambeaux, déchirer; (documents) détruire; (Culin: grate) râper; (: lettuce etc) couper en lanières

shrewd [ʃruːd] adj astucieux(-euse), perspicace; (business person) habile

shriek [ʃriːk] n cri perçant or aigu, hurlement m ▷ vt, vi hurler, crier

shrimp [ʃrɪmp] n crevette grise

shrine [ʃraɪn] n (place) lieu m de pèlerinage

shrink (pt **shrank**, pp **shrunk**) [ʃrɪŋk, ʃræŋk, ʃrʌŋk] vi rétrécir; (fig) diminuer; (also: ~ **away**) reculer ▷ vt (wool) (faire) rétrécir ▷ n (inf, pej) psychanalyste m/f; **to ~ from (doing) sth** reculer devant (la pensée de faire) qch

shrivel ['ʃrɪvl], **shrivel up** vt
ratatiner, flétrir ▷ vi se ratatiner,
se flétrir
shroud [ʃraʊd] n linceul m ▷ vt: **~ed
in mystery** enveloppé(e) de mystère
Shrove Tuesday ['ʃrəʊv-] n (le)
Mardi gras
shrub [ʃrʌb] n arbuste m
shrug [ʃrʌg] n haussement m
d'épaules ▷ vt, vi: **to ~ (one's
shoulders)** hausser les épaules;
shrug off vt faire fi de
shrunk [ʃrʌŋk] pp of **shrink**
shudder ['ʃʌdə'] n frisson m,
frémissement m ▷ vi frissonner,
frémir
shuffle ['ʃʌfl] vt (cards) battre; **to ~
(one's feet)** traîner les pieds
shun [ʃʌn] vt éviter, fuir
shut (pt, pp **shut**) [ʃʌt] vt fermer
▷ vi (se) fermer; **shut down** vt
fermer définitivement ▷ vi fermer
définitivement; **shut up** vi (inf: keep
quiet) se taire ▷ vt (close) fermer;
(silence) faire taire; **shutter** n volet m;
(Phot) obturateur m
shuttle ['ʃʌtl] n navette f; (also:
~ service) (service m de) navette
f; **shuttlecock** n volant m (de
badminton)
shy [ʃaɪ] adj timide
siblings ['sɪblɪŋz] npl (formal) frères et
sœurs mpl (de mêmes parents)
Sicily ['sɪsɪlɪ] n Sicile f
sick [sɪk] adj (ill) malade; (BRIT:
humour) noir(e), macabre; (vomiting):
to be ~ vomir; **to feel ~** avoir envie
de vomir, avoir mal au cœur; **to be ~
of** (fig) en avoir assez de; **sickening**
adj (fig) écœurant(e), révoltant(e),
répugnant(e); **sick leave** n congé m
de maladie; **sickly** adj maladif(-ive),
souffreteux(-euse); (causing nausea)
écœurant(e); **sickness** n maladie f;
(vomiting) vomissement(s) m(pl)
side [saɪd] n côté m; (of lake, road) bord
m; (of mountain) versant m; (fig: aspect)
côté, aspect m; (team: Sport) équipe

f; (TV: channel) chaîne f ▷ adj (door,
entrance) latéral(e) ▷ vi: **to ~ with sb**
prendre le parti de qn, se ranger du
côté de qn; **by the ~ of** au bord de;
~ by ~ côte à côte; **to rock from ~
to ~** se balancer; **to take ~s (with)**
prendre parti (pour); **sideboard** n
buffet m; **sideboards**, (US) **sideburns**
npl (whiskers) pattes fpl; **side effect** n
effet m secondaire; **sidelight** n (Aut)
veilleuse f; **sideline** n (Sport) (ligne f
de) touche f; (fig) activité f secondaire;
side order n garniture f; **side road** n
petite route, route transversale; **side
street** n rue transversale; **sidetrack**
vt (fig) faire dévier de son sujet;
sidewalk n (US) trottoir m; **sideways**
adv de côté
siege [siːdʒ] n siège m
sieve [sɪv] n tamis m, passoire f ▷ vt
tamiser, passer (au tamis)
sift [sɪft] vt passer au tamis or au
crible; (fig) passer au crible
sigh [saɪ] n soupir m ▷ vi soupirer,
pousser un soupir
sight [saɪt] n (faculty) vue f; (spectacle)
spectacle m ▷ vt apercevoir; **in ~**
visible; (fig) en vue; **out of ~** hors de
vue; **sightseeing** n tourisme m; **to
go sightseeing** faire du tourisme
sign [saɪn] n (gen) signe m; (with hand
etc) signe, geste m; (notice) panneau
m, écriteau m; (also: **road ~**) panneau
de signalisation ▷ vt signer; **where
do I ~?** où dois-je signer?; **sign for** vt
fus (item) signer le reçu pour; **sign in**
vi signer le registre (en arrivant); **sign
on** vi (BRIT: as unemployed) s'inscrire
au chômage; (enrol) s'inscrire ▷ vt
(employee) embaucher; **sign over**
vt: **to ~ sth over to sb** céder qch par
écrit à qn; **sign up** vi (Mil) s'engager;
(for course) s'inscrire
signal ['sɪgnl] n signal m ▷ vi (Aut)
mettre son clignotant ▷ vt (person)
faire signe à; (message) communiquer
par signaux
signature ['sɪgnətʃə'] n signature f

significance [sɪgˈnɪfɪkəns] n
signification f; importance f

significant [sɪgˈnɪfɪkənt] adj
significatif(-ive); (important)
important(e), considérable

signify [ˈsɪgnɪfaɪ] vt signifier

sign language n langage m par
signes

signpost [ˈsaɪnpəʊst] n poteau
indicateur

Sikh [siːk] adj, n Sikh m/f

silence [ˈsaɪlns] n silence m ▷ vt faire
taire, réduire au silence

silent [ˈsaɪlnt] adj silencieux(-euse);
(film) muet(te); **to keep** or **remain ~**
garder le silence, ne rien dire

silhouette [sɪluːˈɛt] n silhouette f

silicon chip [ˈsɪlɪkən-] n puce f
électronique

silk [sɪlk] n soie f ▷ cpd de or en soie

silly [ˈsɪlɪ] adj stupide, sot(te), bête

silver [ˈsɪlvər] n argent m; (money)
monnaie f (en pièces d'argent); (also:
~ware) argenterie f ▷ adj (made
of silver) d'argent, en argent; (in
colour) argenté(e); **silver-plated** adj
plaqué(e) argent

SIM card [ˈsɪm-] abbr (Tel) carte
f SIM

similar [ˈsɪmɪlər] adj: **~ (to)**
semblable (à); **similarity**
[sɪmɪˈlærɪtɪ] n ressemblance f,
similarité f; **similarly** adv de la même
façon, de même

simmer [ˈsɪmər] vi cuire à feu doux,
mijoter

simple [ˈsɪmpl] adj simple;
simplicity [sɪmˈplɪsɪtɪ] n simplicité
f; **simplify** [ˈsɪmplɪfaɪ] vt simplifier;
simply adv simplement; (without
fuss) avec simplicité; (absolutely)
absolument

simulate [ˈsɪmjuleɪt] vt simuler,
feindre

simultaneous [sɪməlˈteɪnɪəs] adj
simultané(e); **simultaneously** adv
simultanément

sin [sɪn] n péché m ▷ vi pécher

since [sɪns] adv, prep depuis ▷ conj
(time) depuis que; (because) puisque,
étant donné que, comme; **~ then,
ever ~** depuis ce moment-là

sincere [sɪnˈsɪər] adj sincère;
sincerely adv sincèrement; **yours
sincerely** (at end of letter) veuillez
agréer, Monsieur (or Madame)
l'expression de mes sentiments
distingués or les meilleurs

sing (pt **sang**, pp **sung**) [sɪŋ, sæŋ, sʌŋ]
vt, vi chanter

Singapore [sɪŋgəˈpɔːr] n
Singapour m

singer [ˈsɪŋər] n chanteur(-euse)

singing [ˈsɪŋɪŋ] n (of person, bird)
chant m

single [ˈsɪŋgl] adj seul(e), unique;
(unmarried) célibataire; (not double)
simple ▷ n (BRIT: also: **~ ticket**) aller m
(simple); (record) 45 tours m; **singles**
npl (Tennis) simple m; **every ~ day**
chaque jour sans exception; **single
out** vt choisir; (distinguish) distinguer;
single bed n lit m d'une personne or à
une place; **single file** n: **in single file**
en file indienne; **single-handed** adv
tout(e) seul(e), sans (aucune) aide;
single-minded adj résolu(e), tenace;
single parent n parent unique (or
célibataire); **single-parent family**
famille monoparentale; **single
room** n chambre f à un lit or pour une
personne

singular [ˈsɪŋgjulər] adj
singulier(-ière); (odd) singulier,
étrange; (outstanding) remarquable;
(Ling) (au) singulier, du singulier ▷ n
(Ling) singulier m

sinister [ˈsɪnɪstər] adj sinistre

sink [sɪŋk] (pt **sank**, pp **sunk**) n
évier m; (washbasin) lavabo m ▷ vt
(ship) (faire) couler, faire sombrer;
(foundations) creuser ▷ vi couler,
sombrer; (ground etc) s'affaisser; **to ~
into sth** (chair) s'enfoncer dans qch;
sink in vi (explanation) rentrer (inf),
être compris

sinus ['saɪnəs] n (Anat) sinus m inv

sip [sɪp] n petite gorgée ▷ vt boire à petites gorgées

sir [səʳ] n monsieur m; **S~ John Smith** sir John Smith; **yes ~** oui Monsieur

siren ['saɪərn] n sirène f

sirloin ['sə:lɔɪn] n (also: **~ steak**) aloyau m

sister ['sɪstəʳ] n sœur f; (nun) religieuse f, (bonne) sœur; (BRIT: nurse) infirmière f en chef; **sister-in-law** n belle-sœur f

sit (pt, pp **sat**) [sɪt, sæt] vi s'asseoir; (be sitting) être assis(e); (assembly) être en séance, siéger; (for painter) poser ▷ vt (exam) passer, se présenter à; **sit back** vi (in seat) bien s'installer, se carrer; **sit down** vi s'asseoir; **sit on** vt fus (jury, committee) faire partie de; **sit up** vi s'asseoir; (straight) se redresser; (not go to bed) rester debout, ne pas se coucher

sitcom ['sɪtkɔm] n abbr (TV: = situation comedy) sitcom f, comédie f de situation

site [saɪt] n emplacement m, site m; (also: **building ~**) chantier m; (Internet) site m web ▷ vt placer

sitting ['sɪtɪŋ] n (of assembly etc) séance f; (in canteen) service m; **sitting room** n salon m

situated ['sɪtjueɪtɪd] adj situé(e)

situation [sɪtju'eɪʃən] n situation f; **"~s vacant/wanted"** (BRIT) "offres/demandes d'emploi"

six [sɪks] num six; **sixteen** num seize; **sixteenth** [sɪks'ti:nθ] num seizième; **sixth** ['sɪksθ] num sixième; **sixth form** n (BRIT) ≈ classes fpl de première et de terminale; **sixth-form college** n lycée n'ayant que des classes de première et de terminale; **sixtieth** ['sɪkstɪɪθ] num soixantième; **sixty** num soixante

size [saɪz] n dimensions fpl; (of person) taille f; (of clothing) taille f; (of shoes) pointure f; (of problem) ampleur f; (glue) colle f; **sizeable** adj assez grand(e); (amount, problem, majority) assez important(e)

sizzle ['sɪzl] vi grésiller

skate [skeɪt] n patin m; (fish: pl inv) raie f ▷ vi patiner; **skateboard** n skateboard m, planche f à roulettes; **skateboarding** n skateboard m; **skater** n patineur(-euse); **skating** n patinage m; **skating rink** n patinoire f

skeleton ['skɛlɪtn] n squelette m; (outline) schéma m

skeptical ['skɛptɪkl] (US) adj = **sceptical**

sketch [skɛtʃ] n (drawing) croquis m, esquisse f; (outline plan) aperçu m; (Theat) sketch m, saynète f ▷ vt esquisser, faire un croquis or une esquisse de; (plan etc) esquisser

skewer ['skju:əʳ] n brochette f

ski [ski:] n ski m ▷ vi skier, faire du ski; **ski boot** n chaussure f de ski

skid [skɪd] n dérapage m ▷ vi déraper

ski: skier n skieur(-euse); **skiing** n ski m; **to go skiing** (aller) faire du ski

skilful, (US) **skillful** ['skɪlful] adj habile, adroit(e)

ski lift n remonte-pente m inv

skill [skɪl] n (ability) habileté f, adresse f, talent m; (requiring training) compétences fpl; **skilled** adj habile, adroit(e); (worker) qualifié(e)

skim [skɪm] vt (soup) écumer; (glide over) raser, effleurer ▷ vi: **to ~ through** (fig) parcourir; **skimmed milk**, (US) **skim milk** n lait écrémé

skin [skɪn] n peau f ▷ vt (fruit etc) éplucher; (animal) écorcher; **skinhead** n skinhead m; **skinny** adj maigre, maigrichon(ne)

skip [skɪp] n petit bond or saut; (BRIT: container) benne f ▷ vi gambader, sautiller; (with rope) sauter à la corde ▷ vt (pass over) sauter

ski: ski pass n forfait-skieur(s) m; **ski pole** n bâton m de ski

skipper ['skɪpəʳ] n (Naut, Sport) capitaine m; (in race) skipper m

skipping rope ['skɪpɪŋ-], (US) **skip rope** n corde f à sauter

skirt [skəːt] n jupe f ▷ vt longer, contourner

skirting board ['skəːtɪŋ-] n (BRIT) plinthe f

ski slope n piste f de ski

ski suit n combinaison f de ski

skull [skʌl] n crâne m

skunk [skʌŋk] n mouffette f

sky [skaɪ] n ciel m; **skyscraper** n gratte-ciel m inv

slab [slæb] n (of stone) dalle f; (of meat, cheese) tranche épaisse

slack [slæk] adj (loose) lâche, desserré(e); (slow) stagnant(e); (careless) négligent(e), peu sérieux(-euse) or consciencieux(-euse); **slacks** npl pantalon m

slain [sleɪn] pp of **slay**

slam [slæm] vt (door) (faire) claquer; (throw) jeter violemment, flanquer; (inf: criticize) éreinter, démolir ▷ vi claquer

slander ['slɑːndə^r] n calomnie f; (Law) diffamation f

slang [slæŋ] n argot m

slant [slɑːnt] n inclinaison f; (fig) angle m, point m de vue

slap [slæp] n claque f, gifle f; (on the back) tape f ▷ vt donner une claque or une gifle (or une tape) à ▷ adv (directly) tout droit, en plein; **to ~ on** (paint) appliquer rapidement

slash [slæʃ] vt entailler, taillader; (fig: prices) casser

slate [sleɪt] n ardoise f ▷ vt (fig: criticize) éreinter, démolir

slaughter ['slɔːtə^r] n carnage m, massacre m; (of animals) abattage m ▷ vt (animal) abattre; (people) massacrer; **slaughterhouse** n abattoir m

Slav [slɑːv] adj slave

slave [sleɪv] n esclave m/f ▷ vi (also: **~ away**) trimer, travailler comme un forçat; **slavery** n esclavage m

slay (pt **slew**, pp **slain**) [sleɪ, sluː, sleɪn] vt (literary) tuer

sleazy ['sliːzɪ] adj miteux(-euse), minable

sled [slɛd] (US) n = **sledge**

sledge [slɛdʒ] n luge f

sleek [sliːk] adj (hair, fur) brillant(e), luisant(e); (car, boat) aux lignes pures or élégantes

sleep [sliːp] n sommeil m ▷ vi (pt, pp **slept**) dormir; **to go to ~** s'endormir; **sleep in** vi (oversleep) se réveiller trop tard; (on purpose) faire la grasse matinée; **sleep together** vi (have sex) coucher ensemble; **sleeper** n (person) dormeur(-euse); (BRIT Rail: on track) traverse f; (: train) train-couchettes m; (: berth) couchette f; **sleeping bag** ['sliːpɪŋ-] n sac m de couchage; **sleeping car** n wagon-lits m, voiture-lits f; **sleeping pill** n somnifère m; **sleepover** n nuit f chez un copain or une copine; **we're having a sleepover at Jo's** nous allons passer la nuit chez Jo; **sleepwalk** vi marcher en dormant; **sleepy** adj (fig) endormi(e)

sleet [sliːt] n neige fondue

sleeve [sliːv] n manche f; (of record) pochette f; **sleeveless** adj (garment) sans manches

sleigh [sleɪ] n traîneau m

slender ['slɛndə^r] adj svelte, mince; (fig) faible, ténu(e)

slept [slɛpt] pt, pp of **sleep**

slew [sluː] pt of **slay**

slice [slaɪs] n tranche f; (round) rondelle f; (utensil) spatule f; (also: **fish ~**) pelle f à poisson ▷ vt couper en tranches (or en rondelles)

slick [slɪk] adj (skilful) bien ficelé(e); (salesperson) qui a du bagout ▷ n (also: **oil ~**) nappe f de pétrole, marée noire

slide (pt, pp **slid**) [slaɪd, slɪd] n (in playground) toboggan m; (Phot) diapositive f; (BRIT: also: **hair ~**) barrette f; (in prices) chute f, baisse f

▷ vt (faire) glisser ▷ vi glisser; **sliding** adj (door) coulissant(e)

slight [slaɪt] adj (slim) mince, menu(e); (frail) frêle; (trivial) faible, insignifiant(e); (small) petit(e), léger(-ère) before n ▷ n offense f, affront m ▷ vt (offend) blesser, offenser; **not in the ~est** pas le moins du monde, pas du tout; **slightly** adv légèrement, un peu

slim [slɪm] adj mince ▷ vi maigrir; (diet) suivre un régime amaigrissant; **slimming** n amaigrissement m ▷ adj (diet, pills) amaigrissant(e), pour maigrir; (food) qui ne fait pas grossir

slimy ['slaɪmɪ] adj visqueux(-euse), gluant(e)

sling [slɪŋ] n (Med) écharpe f; (for baby) porte-bébé m; (weapon) fronde f, lance-pierre m ▷ vt (pt, pp **slung**) lancer, jeter

slip [slɪp] n faux pas; (mistake) erreur f, bévue f; (underskirt) combinaison f; (of paper) petite feuille, fiche f ▷ vt (slide) glisser ▷ vi (slide) glisser; (decline) baisser; (move smoothly): **to ~ into/ out of** se glisser or se faufiler dans/ hors de; **to ~ sth on/off** enfiler/ enlever qch; **to give sb the ~** fausser compagnie à qn; **a ~ of the tongue** un lapsus; **slip up** vi faire une erreur, gaffer

slipped disc [slɪpt-] n déplacement m de vertèbre

slipper ['slɪpəʳ] n pantoufle f

slippery ['slɪpərɪ] adj glissant(e)

slip road n (BRIT: to motorway) bretelle f d'accès

slit [slɪt] n fente f; (cut) incision f ▷ vt (pt, pp **slit**) fendre; couper, inciser

slog [slɔg] n (BRIT: effort) gros effort; (work) tâche fastidieuse ▷ vi travailler très dur

slogan ['sləugən] n slogan m

slope [sləup] n pente f, côte f; (side of mountain) versant m; (slant) inclinaison f ▷ vi: **to ~ down** être or descendre en pente; **to ~ up** monter;

sloping adj en pente, incliné(e); (handwriting) penché(e)

sloppy ['slɔpɪ] adj (work) peu soigné(e), bâclé(e); (appearance) négligé(e), débraillé(e)

slot [slɔt] n fente f ▷ vt: **to ~ sth into** encastrer or insérer qch dans; **slot machine** n (BRIT: vending machine) distributeur m (automatique), machine f à sous; (for gambling) appareil m or machine à sous

Slovakia [sləu'vækɪə] n Slovaquie f

Slovene [sləu'vi:n] adj slovène ▷ n Slovène m/f; (Ling) slovène m

Slovenia [sləu'vi:nɪə] n Slovénie f; **Slovenian** adj, n = **Slovene**

slow [sləu] adj lent(e); (watch): **to be ~** retarder ▷ adv lentement ▷ vt, vi ralentir; **"~"** (road sign) "ralentir"; **slow down** vi ralentir; **slowly** adv lentement; **slow motion** n: **in slow motion** au ralenti

slug [slʌg] n limace f; (bullet) balle f; **sluggish** adj (person) mou (molle), lent(e); (stream, engine, trading) lent(e)

slum [slʌm] n (house) taudis m; **slums** npl (area) quartiers mpl pauvres

slump [slʌmp] n baisse soudaine, effondrement m; (Econ) crise f ▷ vi s'effondrer, s'affaisser

slung [slʌŋ] pt, pp of **sling**

slur [slə:ʳ] n (smear): **~ (on)** atteinte f (à); insinuation f (contre) ▷ vt mal articuler

slush [slʌʃ] n neige fondue

sly [slaɪ] adj (person) rusé(e); (smile, expression, remark) sournois(e)

smack [smæk] n (slap) tape f; (on face) gifle f ▷ vt donner une tape à; (on face) gifler; (on bottom) donner la fessée à ▷ vi: **to ~ of** avoir des relents de, sentir

small [smɔ:l] adj petit(e); **small ads** npl (BRIT) petites annonces; **small change** n petite or menue monnaie

smart [smɑ:t] adj élégant(e), chic inv; (clever) intelligent(e); (quick) vif (vive), prompt(e) ▷ vi faire mal, brûler;

smart card n carte f à puce; **smart phone** n smartphone m

smash [smæʃ] n (also: **~-up**) collision f, accident m; (Mus) succès foudroyant ▷ vt casser, briser, fracasser; (opponent) écraser; (Sport: record) pulvériser ▷ vi se briser, se fracasser; s'écraser; **smashing** adj (inf) formidable

smear [smɪəʳ] n (stain) tache f; (mark) trace f; (Med) frottis m ▷ vt enduire; (make dirty) salir; **smear test** n (BRIT Med) frottis m

smell [smɛl] (pt, pp smelt or smelled) n odeur f; (sense) odorat m ▷ vt sentir ▷ vi (pej) sentir mauvais; **smelly** adj qui sent mauvais, malodorant(e)

smelt [smɛlt] pt, pp of **smell**

smile [smaɪl] n sourire m ▷ vi sourire

smirk [smə:k] n petit sourire suffisant or affecté

smog [smɔg] n brouillard mêlé de fumée

smoke [sməuk] n fumée f ▷ vt, vi fumer; **do you mind if I ~?** ça ne vous dérange pas que je fume?; **smoke alarm** n détecteur m de fumée; **smoked** adj (bacon, glass) fumé(e); **smoker** n (person) fumeur(-euse); (Rail) wagon m fumeurs; **smoking** n: **"no smoking"** (sign) "défense de fumer"; **smoky** adj enfumé(e); (taste) fumé(e)

smooth [smu:ð] adj lisse; (sauce) onctueux(-euse); (flavour, whisky) moelleux(-euse); (movement) régulier(-ière), sans à-coups or heurts; (flight) sans secousses; (pej: person) doucereux(-euse), mielleux(-euse) ▷ vt (also: **~ out**) lisser, défroisser; (creases, difficulties) faire disparaître

smother ['smʌðəʳ] vt étouffer

SMS n abbr (= short message service) SMS m; **SMS message** n (message m) SMS m

smudge [smʌdʒ] n tache f, bavure f ▷ vt salir, maculer

smug [smʌg] adj suffisant(e), content(e) de soi

smuggle ['smʌgl] vt passer en contrebande or en fraude; **smuggling** n contrebande f

snack [snæk] n casse-croûte m inv; **snack bar** n snack(-bar) m

snag [snæg] n inconvénient m, difficulté f

snail [sneɪl] n escargot m

snake [sneɪk] n serpent m

snap [snæp] n (sound) claquement m, bruit sec; (photograph) photo f, instantané m ▷ adj subit(e), fait(e) sans réfléchir ▷ vt (fingers) faire claquer; (break) casser net ▷ vi se casser net or avec un bruit sec; (speak sharply) parler d'un ton brusque; **to ~ open/shut** s'ouvrir/se refermer brusquement; **snap at** vt fus (subj: dog) essayer de mordre; **snap up** vt sauter sur, saisir; **snapshot** n photo f, instantané m

snarl [snɑ:l] vi gronder

snatch [snætʃ] n ▷ vt saisir (d'un geste vif); (steal) voler; **to ~ some sleep** arriver à dormir un peu

sneak [sni:k] (US: pt, pp snuck) vi: **to ~ in/out** entrer/sortir furtivement or à la dérobée ▷ n (inf: pej: informer) faux jeton; **to ~ up on sb** s'approcher de qn sans faire de bruit; **sneakers** npl tennis mpl, baskets fpl

sneer [snɪəʳ] vi ricaner; **to ~ at sb/sth** se moquer de qn/qch avec mépris

sneeze [sni:z] vi éternuer

sniff [snɪf] vi renifler ▷ vt renifler, flairer; (glue, drug) sniffer, respirer

snigger ['snɪgəʳ] vi ricaner

snip [snɪp] n (cut) entaille f; (BRIT inf: bargain) (bonne) occasion or affaire f ▷ vt couper

sniper ['snaɪpəʳ] n tireur embusqué

snob [snɔb] n snob m/f

snooker ['snu:kəʳ] n sorte de jeu de billard

snoop [snu:p] vi: **to ~ about** fureter

snooze [snu:z] *n* petit somme ▷ *vi* faire un petit somme

snore [snɔːʳ] *vi* ronfler ▷ *n* ronflement *m*

snorkel ['snɔːkl] *n* (*of swimmer*) tuba *m*

snort [snɔːt] *n* grognement *m* ▷ *vi* grogner; (*horse*) renâcler

snow [snəu] *n* neige *f* ▷ *vi* neiger; **snowball** *n* boule *f* de neige; **snowdrift** *n* congère *f*; **snowman** (*irreg*) *n* bonhomme *m* de neige; **snowplough**, (*US*) **snowplow** *n* chasse-neige *m inv*; **snowstorm** *n* tempête *f* de neige

snub [snʌb] *vt* repousser, snober ▷ *n* rebuffade *f*

snuck [snʌk] (*US*) *pt, pp of* **sneak**

snug [snʌg] *adj* douillet(te), confortable; (*person*) bien au chaud

 KEYWORD

so [səu] *adv* **1** (*thus, likewise*) ainsi, de cette façon; **if so** si oui; **so do** or **have I** moi aussi; **it's 5 o'clock — so it is!** il est 5 heures — en effet! or c'est vrai!; **I hope/think so** je l'espère/ le crois; **so far** jusqu'ici, jusqu'à maintenant; (*in past*) jusque-là **2** (*in comparisons etc: to such a degree*) si, tellement; **so big (that)** si or tellement grand (que); **she's not so clever as her brother** elle n'est pas aussi intelligente que son frère **3**: **so much** *adj, adv* tant (de); **I've got so much work** j'ai tant de travail; **I love you so much** je vous aime tant; **so many** tant (de) **4** (*phrases*): **10 or so** à peu près or environ 10; **so long!** (*inf: goodbye*) au revoir!, à un de ces jours!; **so (what)?** (*inf*) (bon) et alors?, et après? ▷ *conj* **1** (*expressing purpose*): **so as to do** pour faire, afin de faire; **so (that)** pour que or afin que + *sub* **2** (*expressing result*) donc, par conséquent; **so that** si bien que; **so**

that's the reason! c'est donc (pour) ça!; **so you see, I could have gone** alors tu vois, j'aurais pu y aller

soak [səuk] *vt* faire or laisser tremper; (*drench*) tremper ▷ *vi* tremper; **soak up** *vt* absorber; **soaking** *adj* (*also:* **soaking wet**) trempé(e)

so-and-so ['səuənsəu] *n* (*somebody*) un(e) tel(le)

soap [səup] *n* savon *m*; **soap opera** *n* feuilleton télévisé (*quotidienneté réaliste ou embellie*); **soap powder** *n* lessive *f*, détergent *m*

soar [sɔːʳ] *vi* monter (en flèche), s'élancer; (*building*) s'élancer

sob [sɔb] *n* sanglot *m* ▷ *vi* sangloter

sober ['səubəʳ] *adj* qui n'est pas (or plus) ivre; (*serious*) sérieux(-euse), sensé(e); (*colour, style*) sobre, discret(-ète); **sober up** *vi* se dégriser

so-called ['səu'kɔːld] *adj* soi-disant *inv*

soccer ['sɔkəʳ] *n* football *m*

sociable ['səuʃəbl] *adj* sociable

social ['səuʃl] *adj* social(e); (*sociable*) sociable ▷ *n* (petite) fête; **socialism** *n* socialisme *m*; **socialist** *adj, n* socialiste (*m/f*); **socialize** *vi*: **to socialize with** (*meet often*) fréquenter; (*get to know*) lier connaissance or parler avec; **social life** *n* vie sociale; **socially** *adv* socialement, en société; **social media** *npl* médias *mpl* sociaux; **social networking** *n* réseaux *mpl* sociaux; **social networking site** *n* site *m* de réseautage; **social security** *n* aide sociale; **social services** *npl* services sociaux; **social work** *n* assistance sociale; **social worker** *n* assistant(e) sociale(e)

society [sə'saɪətɪ] *n* société *f*; (*club*) société, association *f*; (*also:* **high ~**) (haute) société, grand monde

sociology [səusɪ'ɔlədʒɪ] *n* sociologie *f*

sock [sɔk] *n* chaussette *f*

socket ['sɔkɪt] n cavité f; (Elec: also: **wall ~**) prise f de courant

soda ['səudə] n (Chem) soude f; (also: **~ water**) eau f de Seltz; (us: also: **~ pop**) soda m

sodium ['səudɪəm] n sodium m

sofa ['səufə] n sofa m, canapé m; **sofa bed** n canapé-lit m

soft [sɔft] adj (not rough) doux (douce); (not hard) doux, mou (molle); (not loud) doux, léger(-ère); (kind) doux, gentil(le); **soft drink** n boisson non alcoolisée; **soft drugs** npl drogues douces; **soften** ['sɔfn] vt (r)amollir; (fig) adoucir ▷ vi se ramollir; (fig) s'adoucir; **softly** adv doucement; (touch) légèrement; (kiss) tendrement; **software** n (Comput) logiciel m, software m

soggy ['sɔgɪ] adj (clothes) trempé(e); (ground) détrempé(e)

soil [sɔɪl] n (earth) sol m, terre f ▷ vt salir; (fig) souiller

solar ['səulə'] adj solaire; **solar power** n énergie f solaire; **solar system** n système m solaire

sold [səuld] pt, pp of **sell**

soldier ['səuldʒə'] n soldat m, militaire m

sold out adj (Comm) épuisé(e)

sole [səul] n (of foot) plante f; (of shoe) semelle f; (fish: pl inv) sole f ▷ adj seul(e), unique; **solely** adv seulement, uniquement

solemn ['sɔləm] adj solennel(le); (person) sérieux(-euse), grave

solicitor [sə'lɪsɪtə'] n (BRIT: for wills etc) ≈ notaire m; (: in court) ≈ avocat m

solid ['sɔlɪd] adj (not liquid) solide; (not hollow: mass) compact(e); (: metal, rock, wood) massif(-ive) ▷ n solide m

solitary ['sɔlɪtərɪ] adj solitaire

solitude ['sɔlɪtjuːd] n solitude f

solo ['səuləu] n solo m ▷ adv (fly) en solitaire; **soloist** n soliste m/f

soluble ['sɔljubl] adj soluble

solution [sə'luːʃən] n solution f

solve [sɔlv] vt résoudre

solvent ['sɔlvənt] adj (Comm) solvable ▷ n (Chem) (dis)solvant m

sombre, (us)**somber** ['sɔmbə'] adj sombre, morne

KEYWORD

some [sʌm] adj 1 (a certain amount or number of): **some tea/water/ice cream** du thé/de l'eau/de la glace; **some children/apples** des enfants/ pommes; **I've got some money but not much** j'ai de l'argent mais pas beaucoup

2 (certain: in contrasts): **some people say that ...** il y a des gens qui disent que ...; **some films were excellent, but most were mediocre** certains films étaient excellents, mais la plupart étaient médiocres

3 (unspecified): **some woman was asking for you** il y avait une dame qui vous demandait; **he was asking for some book (or other)** il demandait un livre quelconque; **some day** un de ces jours; **some day next week** un jour la semaine prochaine

▶ pron 1 (a certain number) quelques-un(e)s, certain(e)s; **I've got some** (books etc) j'en ai (quelques-uns); **some (of them) have been sold** certains ont été vendus

2 (a certain amount) un peu; **I've got some** (money, milk) j'en ai (un peu); **would you like some?** est-ce que vous en voulez?, en voulez-vous?; **could I have some of that cheese?** pourrais-je avoir un peu de ce fromage?; **I've read some of the book** j'ai lu une partie du livre

▶ adv: **some 10 people** quelque 10 personnes, 10 personnes environ; **somebody** ['sʌmbədɪ] pron = **someone; somehow** adv d'une façon ou d'une autre; (for some reason) pour une raison ou une autre; **someone** pron quelqu'un; **someplace** adv (us) = **somewhere**;

something pron quelque chose m;
something interesting quelque
chose d'intéressant; **something to
do** quelque chose à faire; **sometime**
adv (in future) un de ces jours, un jour
ou l'autre; (in past): **sometime last
month** au cours du mois dernier;
sometimes adv quelquefois, parfois;
somewhat adv quelque peu, un
peu; **somewhere** adv quelque part;
somewhere else ailleurs, autre part

son [sʌn] n fils m
song [sɒŋ] n chanson f; (of bird)
chant m
son-in-law ['sʌnɪnlɔ:] n gendre m,
beau-fils m
soon [su:n] adv bientôt; (early)
tôt; **~ afterwards** peu après; see
also **as**; **sooner** adv (time) plus
tôt; (preference): **I would sooner
do that** j'aimerais autant or je
préférerais faire ça; **sooner or later**
tôt ou tard
soothe [su:ð] vt calmer, apaiser
sophisticated [sə'fɪstɪkeɪtɪd] adj
raffiné(e), sophistiqué(e); (machinery)
hautement perfectionné(e), très
complexe
sophomore ['sɒfəmɔ:ʳ] n (US)
étudiant(e) de seconde année
soprano [sə'prɑ:nəu] n (singer)
soprano m/f
sorbet ['sɔ:beɪ] n sorbet m
sordid ['sɔ:dɪd] adj sordide
sore [sɔ:ʳ] adj (painful) douloureux(-
euse), sensible ▷ n plaie f
sorrow ['sɒrəu] n peine f, chagrin m
sorry ['sɒrɪ] adj désolé(e); (condition,
excuse, tale) triste, déplorable; **~!**
pardon!, excusez-moi!; **~?** pardon?;
to feel ~ for sb plaindre qn
sort [sɔ:t] n genre m, espèce f, sorte f;
(make: of coffee, car etc) marque f ▷ vt
(also: **~ out**: select which to keep) trier;
(classify) classer; (tidy) ranger; **sort
out** vt (problem) résoudre, régler
SOS n SOS m

so-so ['səusəu] adv comme ci
comme ça
sought [sɔ:t] pt, pp of **seek**
soul [səul] n âme f
sound [saund] adj (healthy) en bonne
santé, sain(e); (safe, not damaged)
solide, en bon état; (reliable, not
superficial) sérieux(-euse), solide;
(sensible) sensé(e) ▷ adv: **~ asleep**
profondément endormi(e) ▷ n (noise,
volume) son m; (louder) bruit m; (Geo)
détroit m, bras m de mer ▷ vt (alarm)
sonner ▷ vi sonner, retentir; (fig: seem)
sembler (être); **to ~ like** ressembler à;
sound bite n phrase toute faite (pour
être citée dans les médias); **soundtrack**
n (of film) bande f sonore
soup [su:p] n soupe f, potage m
sour ['sauəʳ] adj aigre; **it's ~ grapes**
c'est du dépit
source [sɔ:s] n source f
south [sauθ] n sud m ▷ adj sud inv;
(wind) du sud ▷ adv au sud, vers le
sud; **South Africa** n Afrique f du Sud;
South African adj sud-africain(e) ▷ n
Sud-Africain(e); **South America** n
Amérique f du Sud; **South American**
adj sud-américain(e) ▷ n Sud-
Américain(e); **southbound** adj en
direction du sud; (carriageway) sud inv;
south-east n sud-est m; **southern**
['sʌðən] adj (du) sud; méridional(e);
South Korea n Corée f du Sud; **South
of France** n: **the South of France**
le Sud de la France, le Midi; **South
Pole** n: **the South Pole** le Pôle Sud;
southward(s) adv vers le sud; **south-
west** n sud-ouest m
souvenir [su:və'nɪəʳ] n souvenir
m (objet)
sovereign ['sɒvrɪn] adj, n
souverain(e)
sow[1] (pt **sowed**, pp **sown**) [səu, səud,
səun] vt semer
sow[2] n [sau] truie f
soya ['sɔɪə], (US) **soy** [sɔɪ] n: **~ bean**
graine f de soja; **~ sauce** sauce f
au soja

s

spa [spɑː] n (town) station thermale; (US: also: **health ~**) établissement m de cure de rajeunissement

space [speis] n (gen) espace m; (room) place f; espace; (length of time) laps m de temps ▷ cpd spatial(e) ▷ vt (also: **~ out**) espacer; **spacecraft** n engin or vaisseau spatial; **spaceship** n = **spacecraft**

spacious ['speiʃəs] adj spacieux(-euse), grand(e)

spade [speid] n (tool) bêche f, pelle f; (child's) pelle; **spades** npl (Cards) pique m

spaghetti [spə'gɛtɪ] n spaghetti mpl

Spain [spein] n Espagne f

spam [spæm] n (Comput) pourriel m

span [spæn] n (of bird, plane) envergure f; (of arch) portée f; (in time) espace m de temps, durée f ▷ vt enjamber, franchir; (fig) couvrir, embrasser

Spaniard ['spænjəd] n Espagnol(e)

Spanish ['spænɪʃ] adj espagnol(e), d'Espagne ▷ n (Ling) espagnol m; **the Spanish** npl les Espagnols

spank [spæŋk] vt donner une fessée à

spanner ['spænə'] n (BRIT) clé f (de mécanicien)

spare [spɛə'] adj de réserve, de rechange; (surplus) de or en trop, de reste ▷ n (part) pièce f de rechange, pièce détachée ▷ vt (do without) se passer de; (afford to give) donner, accorder, passer; (not hurt) épargner; **to ~** (surplus) en surplus, de trop; **spare part** n pièce f de rechange, pièce détachée; **spare room** n chambre f d'ami; **spare time** n moments mpl de loisir; **spare tyre**, (US) **spare tire** n (Aut) pneu m de rechange; **spare wheel** n (Aut) roue f de secours

spark [spɑːk] n étincelle f

sparkle ['spɑːkl] n scintillement m, étincellement m, éclat m ▷ vi étinceler, scintiller

sparkling ['spɑːklɪŋ] adj (wine) mousseux(-euse), pétillant(e); (water) pétillant(e), gazeux(-euse)

spark plug n bougie f

sparrow ['spærəu] n moineau m

sparse [spɑːs] adj clairsemé(e)

spasm ['spæzəm] n (Med) spasme m

spat [spæt] pt, pp of **spit**

spate [speit] n (fig): **~ of** avalanche f or torrent m de

spatula ['spætjulə] n spatule f

speak (pt **spoke**, pp **spoken**) [spiːk, spəuk, 'spəukn] vt (language) parler; (truth) dire ▷ vi parler; (make a speech) prendre la parole; **to ~ to sb/of** or **about sth** parler à qn/de qch; **I don't ~ French** je ne parle pas français; **do you ~ English?** parlez-vous anglais?; **can I ~ to ...?** est-ce que je peux parler à ...?; **speaker** n (in public) orateur m; (also: **loudspeaker**) haut-parleur m; (for stereo etc) baffle m, enceinte f; (Pol): **the Speaker** (BRIT) le président de la Chambre des communes or des représentants; (US) le président de la Chambre

spear [spiə'] n lance f ▷ vt transpercer

special ['spɛʃl] adj spécial(e); **special delivery** n (Post): **by special delivery** en express; **special effects** npl (Cine) effets spéciaux; **specialist** n spécialiste m/f; **speciality** [spɛʃɪ'ælɪtɪ] n (BRIT) spécialité f; **specialize** vi: **to specialize (in)** se spécialiser (dans); **specially** adv spécialement, particulièrement; **special needs** npl (BRIT) difficultés fpl d'apprentissage scolaire; **special offer** n (Comm) réclame f; **special school** n (BRIT) établissement m d'enseignement spécialisé; **specialty** n (US) = **speciality**

species ['spiːʃiːz] n (pl inv) espèce f

specific [spə'sɪfɪk] adj (not vague) précis(e), explicite; (particular) particulier(-ière); **specifically** adv explicitement, précisément;

(intend, ask, design) expressément, spécialement

specify ['spɛsɪfaɪ] vt spécifier, préciser

specimen ['spɛsɪmən] n spécimen m, échantillon m; (Med: of blood) prélèvement m; (: of urine) échantillon m

speck [spɛk] n petite tache, petit point; (particle) grain m

spectacle ['spɛktəkl] n spectacle m; **spectacles** npl (BRIT) lunettes fpl; **spectacular** [spɛk'tækjulər] adj spectaculaire

spectator [spɛk'teɪtər] n spectateur(-trice)

spectrum (pl **spectra**) ['spɛktrəm, -rə] n spectre m; (fig) gamme f

speculate ['spɛkjuleɪt] vi spéculer; (try to guess): **to ~ about** s'interroger sur

sped [spɛd] pt, pp of **speed**

speech [spiːtʃ] n (faculty) parole f; (talk) discours m, allocution f; (manner of speaking) façon f de parler, langage m; (enunciation) élocution f; **speechless** adj muet(te)

speed [spiːd] n vitesse f; (promptness) rapidité f ▷ vi (pt, pp **sped**) (Aut: exceed speed limit) faire un excès de vitesse; **at full** or **top ~** à toute vitesse or allure; **speed up** (pt, pp **speeded up**) vi aller plus vite, accélérer ▷ vt accélérer; **speedboat** n vedette f, hors-bord m inv; **speeding** n (Aut) excès m de vitesse; **speed limit** n limitation f de vitesse, vitesse maximale permise; **speedometer** [spɪ'dɔmɪtər] n compteur m (de vitesse); **speedy** adj rapide, prompt(e)

spell [spɛl] n (also: **magic ~**) sortilège m, charme m; (period of time) (courte) période ▷ vt (pt, pp **spelled** or **spelt**) (in writing) écrire, orthographier; (aloud) épeler; (fig) signifier; **to cast a ~ on sb** jeter un sort à qn; **he can't ~** il fait

des fautes d'orthographe; **spell out** vt (explain): **to ~ sth out for sb** expliquer qch clairement à qn; **spellchecker** ['spɛltʃɛkər] n (Comput) correcteur m or vérificateur m orthographique; **spelling** n orthographe f

spelt [spɛlt] pt, pp of **spell**

spend (pt, pp **spent**) [spɛnd, spɛnt] vt (money) dépenser; (time, life) passer; (devote) consacrer; **spending** n: **government spending** les dépenses publiques

spent [spɛnt] pt, pp of **spend** ▷ adj (cartridge, bullets) vide

sperm [spəːm] n spermatozoïde m; (semen) sperme m

sphere [sfɪər] n sphère f; (fig) sphère, domaine m

spice [spaɪs] n épice f ▷ vt épicer

spicy ['spaɪsɪ] adj épicé(e), relevé(e); (fig) piquant(e)

spider ['spaɪdər] n araignée f

spike [spaɪk] n pointe f; (Bot) épi m

spill (pt, pp **spilt** or **spilled**) [spɪl, -t, -d] vt renverser; répandre ▷ vi se répandre; **spill over** vi déborder

spilt [spɪlt] pt, pp of **spill**

spin [spɪn] (pt, pp **spun**) n (revolution of wheel) tour m; (Aviat) (chute f en) vrille f; (trip in car) petit tour, balade f; (on ball) effet m ▷ vt (wool etc) filer; (wheel) faire tourner ▷ vi (turn) tourner, tournoyer

spinach ['spɪnɪtʃ] n épinards mpl

spinal ['spaɪnl] adj vertébral(e), spinal(e); **spinal cord** n moelle épinière

spin doctor n (inf) personne employée pour présenter un parti politique sous un jour favorable

spin-dryer [spɪn'draɪər] n (BRIT) essoreuse f

spine [spaɪn] n colonne vertébrale; (thorn) épine f, piquant m

spiral ['spaɪərl] n spirale f ▷ vi (fig: prices etc) monter en flèche

spire ['spaɪər] n flèche f, aiguille f

spirit ['spɪrɪt] n (soul) esprit m, âme f; (ghost) esprit, revenant m; (mood) esprit, état m d'esprit; (courage) courage m, énergie f; **spirits** npl (drink) spiritueux mpl, alcool m; **in good ~s** de bonne humeur

spiritual ['spɪrɪtjuəl] adj spirituel(le); (religious) religieux(-euse)

spit [spɪt] n (for roasting) broche f; (spittle) crachat m; (saliva) salive f ▷ vi (pt, pp **spat**) cracher; (sound) crépiter; (rain) crachiner

spite [spaɪt] n rancune f, dépit m ▷ vt contrarier, vexer; **in ~ of** en dépit de, malgré; **spiteful** adj malveillant(e), rancunier(-ière)

splash [splæʃ] n (sound) plouf m; (of colour) tache f ▷ vt éclabousser ▷ vi (also: ~ **about**) barboter, patauger; **splash out** (BRIT) faire une folie

splendid ['splendɪd] adj splendide, superbe, magnifique

splinter ['splɪntər] n (wood) écharde f; (metal) éclat m ▷ vi (wood) se fendre; (glass) se briser

split [splɪt] (pt, pp **split**) n fente f, déchirure f; (fig: Pol) scission f ▷ vt fendre, déchirer; (party) diviser; (work, profits) partager, répartir ▷ vi (break) se fendre, se briser; (divide) se diviser; **split up** vi (couple) se séparer, rompre; (meeting) se disperser

spoil (pt, pp **spoiled** or **spoilt**) [spɔɪl, -d, -t] vt (damage) abîmer; (mar) gâcher; (child) gâter

spoilt [spɔɪlt] pt, pp of **spoil** ▷ adj (child) gâté(e); (ballot paper) nul(le)

spoke [spəʊk] pt of **speak** ▷ n rayon m

spoken ['spəʊkn] pp of **speak**

spokesman ['spəʊksmən] (irreg) n porte-parole m inv

spokesperson ['spəʊkspə:sn] (irreg) n porte-parole m inv

spokeswoman ['spəʊkswʊmən] (irreg) n porte-parole m inv

sponge [spʌndʒ] n éponge f; (Culin: also: ~ **cake**) ≈ biscuit m de Savoie ▷ vt

éponger ▷ vi: **to ~ off** or **on** vivre aux crochets de; **sponge bag** n (BRIT) trousse f de toilette

sponsor ['spɒnsər] n (Radio, TV, Sport) sponsor m; (for application) parrain m, marraine f; (BRIT: for fund-raising event) donateur(-trice) ▷ vt sponsoriser; parrainer; faire un don à; **sponsorship** n sponsoring m; parrainage m; dons mpl

spontaneous [spɒn'teɪnɪəs] adj spontané(e)

spooky ['spu:kɪ] adj (inf) qui donne la chair de poule

spoon [spu:n] n cuiller f; **spoonful** n cuillerée f

sport [spɔ:t] n sport m; (person) chic type m/chic fille f ▷ vt (wear) arborer; **sport jacket** n (US) = **sports jacket**; **sports car** n voiture f de sport; **sports centre** (BRIT) n centre sportif; **sports jacket** n (BRIT) veste f de sport; **sportsman** (irreg) n sportif m; **sports utility vehicle** n véhicule m de loisirs (de type SUV); **sportswear** n vêtements mpl de sport; **sportswoman** (irreg) n sportive f; **sporty** adj sportif(-ive)

spot [spɒt] n tache f; (dot: on pattern) pois m; (pimple) bouton m; (place) endroit m, coin m ▷ vt (notice) apercevoir, repérer; **on the ~** sur place, sur les lieux; (immediately) sur le champ; **spotless** adj immaculé(e); **spotlight** n projecteur m; (Aut) phare m auxiliaire

spouse [spauz] n époux (épouse)

sprain [spreɪn] n entorse f, foulure f ▷ vt: **to ~ one's ankle** se fouler or se tordre la cheville

sprang [spræŋ] pt of **spring**

sprawl [sprɔ:l] vi s'étaler

spray [spreɪ] n jet m (en fines gouttelettes); (from sea) embruns mpl; (aerosol) vaporisateur m, bombe f; (for garden) pulvérisateur m; (of flowers) petit bouquet ▷ vt vaporiser, pulvériser; (crops) traiter

spread [sprɛd] (pt, pp **spread**) n
(distribution) répartition f; (Culin)
pâte f à tartiner; (inf: meal) festin m
▷ vt (paste, contents) étendre, étaler;
(rumour, disease) répandre, propager;
(wealth) répartir ▷ vi s'étendre; se
répandre; se propager; (stain) s'étaler;
spread out vi (people) se disperser;
spreadsheet n (Comput) tableur m
spree [spri:] n: **to go on a ~** faire
la fête
spring [sprɪŋ] (pt **sprang**, pp **sprung**)
n (season) printemps m; (leap) bond
m, saut m; (coiled metal) ressort m; (of
water) source f ▷ vi bondir, sauter;
spring up vi (problem) se présenter,
surgir; (plant, buildings) surgir de terre;
spring onion n (BRIT) ciboule f, cive f
sprinkle ['sprɪŋkl] vt: **to ~ water etc
on, ~ with water** etc asperger d'eau
etc; **to ~ sugar etc on, ~ with sugar**
etc saupoudrer de sucre etc
sprint [sprɪnt] n sprint m ▷ vi courir à
toute vitesse; (Sport) sprinter
sprung [sprʌŋ] pp of **spring**
spun [spʌn] pt, pp of **spin**
spur [spə:ʳ] n éperon m; (fig)
aiguillon m ▷ vt (also: **~ on**)
éperonner aiguillonner; **on the ~
of the moment** sous l'impulsion du
moment
spurt [spə:t] n jet m; (of blood)
jaillissement m; (of energy) regain m,
sursaut m ▷ vi jaillir, gicler
spy [spaɪ] n espion(ne) ▷ vi: **to ~ on**
espionner, épier ▷ vt (see) apercevoir
Sq. abbr (in address) = **square**
sq. abbr (Math etc) = **square**
squabble ['skwɔbl] vi se chamailler
squad [skwɔd] n (Mil, Police)
escouade f, groupe m; (Football)
contingent m
squadron ['skwɔdrn] n (Mil)
escadron m; (Aviat, Naut) escadrille f
squander ['skwɔndəʳ] vt gaspiller,
dilapider
square [skwɛəʳ] n carré m; (in town)
place f ▷ adj carré(e) ▷ vt (arrange)

régler; arranger; (Math) élever au
carré; (reconcile) concilier; **all ~**
quitte; à égalité; **a ~ meal** un repas
convenable; **2 metres ~** (de) 2 mètres
sur 2; **1 ~ metre** 1 mètre carré; **square
root** n racine carrée
squash [skwɔʃ] n (BRIT Sport) squash
m; (US: vegetable) courge f; (drink):
lemon/orange ~ citronnade f/
orangeade f ▷ vt écraser
squat [skwɔt] adj petit(e) et
épais(se), ramassé(e) ▷ vi (also:
~ down) s'accroupir; **squatter** n
squatter m
squeak [skwi:k] vi (hinge, wheel)
grincer; (mouse) pousser un petit cri
squeal [skwi:l] vi pousser un or des
cri(s) aigu(s) or perçant(s); (brakes)
grincer
squeeze [skwi:z] n pression f ▷ vt
presser; (hand, arm) serrer
squid [skwɪd] n calmar m
squint [skwɪnt] vi loucher
squirm [skwə:m] vi se tortiller
squirrel ['skwɪrəl] n écureuil m
squirt [skwə:t] vi jaillir, gicler ▷ vt
faire gicler
Sr abbr = **senior**
Sri Lanka [srɪ'læŋkə] n Sri Lanka m
St abbr = **saint**; **street**
stab [stæb] n (with knife etc) coup m
(de couteau etc); (of pain) lancée f;
(inf: try): **to have a ~ at (doing) sth**
s'essayer à (faire) qch ▷ vt poignarder
stability [stə'bɪlɪtɪ] n stabilité f
stable ['steɪbl] n écurie f ▷ adj stable
stack [stæk] n tas m, pile f ▷ vt
empiler, entasser
stadium ['steɪdɪəm] n stade m
staff [stɑ:f] n (work force) personnel
m; (BRIT Scol: also: **teaching ~**)
professeurs mpl, enseignants mpl,
personnel enseignant ▷ vt pourvoir
en personnel
stag [stæg] n cerf m
stage [steɪdʒ] n scène f; (platform)
estrade f; (point) étape f, stade m;
(profession): **the ~** le théâtre ▷ vt

(*play*) monter, mettre en scène; (*demonstration*) organiser; **in ~s** par étapes, par degrés

▮ Be careful not to translate *stage* by the French word *stage*.

stagger ['stægə'] *vi* chanceler, tituber ▷ *vt* (*person: amaze*) stupéfier; (*hours, holidays*) étaler, échelonner; **staggering** *adj* (*amazing*) stupéfiant(e), renversant(e)

stagnant ['stægnənt] *adj* stagnant(e)

stag night, stag party *n* enterrement *m* de vie de garçon

stain [steɪn] *n* tache *f*; (*colouring*) colorant *m* ▷ *vt* tacher; (*wood*) teindre; **stained glass** *n* (*decorative*) verre coloré; (*in church*) vitraux *mpl*; **stainless steel** *n* inox *m*, acier *m* inoxydable

staircase ['stɛəkeɪs] *n* = **stairway**

stairs [stɛəz] *npl* escalier *m*

stairway ['stɛəweɪ] *n* escalier *m*

stake [steɪk] *n* pieu *m*, poteau *m*; (*Comm: interest*) intérêts *mpl*; (*Betting*) enjeu *m* ▷ *vt* risquer, jouer; (*also: ~ out: area*) marquer, délimiter; **to be at ~** être en jeu

stale [steɪl] *adj* (*bread*) rassis(e); (*food*) pas frais (fraîche); (*beer*) éventé(e); (*smell*) de renfermé; (*air*) confiné(e)

stalk [stɔːk] *n* tige *f* ▷ *vt* traquer

stall [stɔːl] *n* (*in street, market etc*) éventaire *m*, étal *m*; (*in stable*) stalle *f* ▷ *vt* (*Aut*) caler; (*fig: delay*) retarder ▷ *vi* (*Aut*) caler; (*fig*) essayer de gagner du temps; **stalls** *npl* (*BRIT: in cinema, theatre*) orchestre *m*

stamina ['stæmɪnə] *n* vigueur *f*, endurance *f*

stammer ['stæmə'] *n* bégaiement *m* ▷ *vi* bégayer

stamp [stæmp] *n* timbre *m*; (*also: rubber ~*) tampon *m*; (*mark: also fig*) empreinte *f*; (*on document*) cachet *m* ▷ *vi* (*also: ~ one's foot*) taper du pied ▷ *vt* (*letter*) timbrer; (*with rubber stamp*) tamponner; **stamp out** *vt*

(*fire*) piétiner; (*crime*) éradiquer; (*opposition*) éliminer; **stamped addressed envelope** *n* (*BRIT*) enveloppe affranchie pour la réponse

stampede [stæm'piːd] *n* ruée *f*; (*of cattle*) débandade *f*

stance [stæns] *n* position *f*

stand [stænd] (*pt, pp* **stood**) *n* (*position*) position *f*; (*for taxis*) station *f* (de taxis); (*Comm*) étalage *m*, stand *m*; (*Sport: also: ~s*) tribune *f*; (*also: music ~*) pupitre *m* ▷ *vi* être *or* se tenir (debout); (*rise*) se lever, se mettre debout; (*be placed*) se trouver; (*remain: offer etc*) rester valable ▷ *vt* (*place*) mettre, poser; (*treat, invite*) offrir, payer; **to make a ~** prendre position; **to ~ for parliament** (*BRIT*) se présenter aux élections (*comme candidat à la députation*); **I can't ~ him** je ne peux pas le voir; **stand back** *vi* (*move back*) reculer, s'écarter; **stand by** *vi* (*be ready*) se tenir prêt(e) ▷ *vt fus* (*opinion*) s'en tenir à; (*person*) ne pas abandonner, soutenir; **stand down** *vi* (*withdraw*) se retirer; **stand for** *vt fus* (*signify*) représenter, signifier; (*tolerate*) supporter, tolérer; **stand in for** *vt fus* remplacer; **stand out** *vi* (*be prominent*) ressortir; **stand up** *vi* (*rise*) se lever, se mettre debout; **stand up for** *vt fus* défendre; **stand up to** *vt fus* tenir tête à, résister à

standard ['stændəd] *n* (*norm*) norme *f*, étalon *m*; (*level*) niveau *m* (voulu); (*criterion*) critère *m*; (*flag*) étendard *m* ▷ *adj* (*size etc*) ordinaire, normal(e); (*model, feature*) standard *inv*; (*practice*) courant(e); (*text*) de base; **standards** *npl* (*morals*) morale *f*, principes *mpl*; **standard of living** *n* niveau *m* de vie

stand-by ticket *n* (*Aviat*) billet *m* stand-by

standing ['stændɪŋ] *adj* debout *inv*; (*permanent*) permanent(e) ▷ *n* réputation *f*, rang *m*, standing *m*; **of many years' ~** qui dure *or* existe depuis longtemps; **standing order** n (BRIT: at bank) virement m automatique, prélèvement m bancaire

stand: standpoint n point m de vue; **standstill** n: **at a standstill** à l'arrêt; (fig) au point mort; **to come to a standstill** s'immobiliser, s'arrêter

stank [stæŋk] pt of **stink**

staple ['steɪpl] n (for papers) agrafe f ▷ adj (food, crop, industry etc) de base principal(e) ▷ vt agrafer

star [stɑːʳ] n étoile f; (celebrity) vedette f ▷ vt (Cine) avoir pour vedette; **stars** npl; **the ~s** (Astrology) l'horoscope m

starboard ['stɑːbəd] n tribord m

starch [stɑːtʃ] n amidon m; (in food) fécule f

stardom ['stɑːdəm] n célébrité f

stare [stɛəʳ] n regard m fixe ▷ vi: **to ~ at** regarder fixement

stark [stɑːk] adj (bleak) désolé(e), morne ▷ adv: **~ naked** complètement nu(e)

start [stɑːt] n commencement m, début m; (of race) départ m; (sudden movement) sursaut m; (advantage) avance f, avantage m ▷ vt commencer; (cause: fight) déclencher; (rumour) donner naissance à; (fashion) lancer; (found: business, newspaper) lancer, créer; (engine) mettre en marche ▷ vi (begin) commencer; (begin journey) partir, se mettre en route; (jump) sursauter; **when does the film ~?** à quelle heure est-ce que le film commence?; **to ~ doing** or **to do sth** se mettre à faire qch; **start off** vi commencer; (leave) partir; **start out** vi (begin) commencer; (set out) partir; **start up** vi commencer; (car) démarrer ▷ vt (fight) déclencher; (business) créer; (car) mettre en marche; **starter** n (Aut) démarreur m; (Sport: official) starter m; (BRIT Culin) entrée f; **starting point** n point m de départ

startle ['stɑːtl] vt faire sursauter; donner un choc à; **startling** adj surprenant(e), saisissante(e)

starvation [stɑːˈveɪʃən] n faim f, famine f

starve [stɑːv] vi mourir de faim ▷ vt laisser mourir de faim

state [steɪt] n état m; (Pol) État ▷ vt (declare) déclarer, affirmer; (specify) indiquer, spécifier; **States** npl; **the S~s** les États-Unis; **to be in a ~** être dans tous ses états; **stately home** ['steɪtlɪ-] n manoir m or château m (ouvert au public); **statement** n déclaration f; (Law) déposition f; **state school** n école publique; **statesman** (irreg) n homme m d'État

static ['stætɪk] n (Radio) parasites mpl; (also: **~ electricity**) électricité f statique ▷ adj statique

station ['steɪʃən] n gare f; (also: **police ~**) poste m or commissariat m (de police) ▷ vt placer, poster

stationary ['steɪʃnərɪ] adj à l'arrêt, immobile

stationer's (shop) n (BRIT) papeterie f

stationery ['steɪʃnərɪ] n papier m à lettres, petit matériel de bureau

station wagon n (US) break m

statistic [stəˈtɪstɪk] n statistique f; **statistics** n (science) statistique f

statue ['stætjuː] n statue f

stature ['stætʃəʳ] n stature f; (fig) envergure f

status ['steɪtəs] n position f, situation f; (prestige) prestige m; (Admin, official position) statut m; **status quo** [-ˈkwəʊ] n: **the status quo** le statu quo

statutory ['stætjutrɪ] adj statutaire, prévu(e) par un article de loi

staunch [stɔːntʃ] adj sûr(e), loyal(e)

stay [steɪ] n (period of time) séjour m ▷ vi rester; (reside) loger; (spend some time) séjourner; **to ~ put** ne pas bouger; **to ~ the night** passer la nuit; **stay away** vi (from person, building)

S

ne pas s'approcher; (*from event*) ne pas venir; **stay behind** *vi* rester en arrière; **stay in** *vi* (*at home*) rester à la maison; **stay on** *vi* rester; **stay out** *vi* (*of house*) ne pas rentrer; (*strikers*) rester en grève; **stay up** *vi* (*at night*) ne pas se coucher

steadily ['stɛdɪlɪ] *adv* (*regularly*) progressivement; (*firmly*) fermement; (*walk*) d'un pas ferme; (*fixedly: look*) sans détourner les yeux

steady ['stɛdɪ] *adj* stable, solide, ferme; (*regular*) constant(e), régulier(-ière); (*person*) calme, pondéré(e) ▷ *vt* assurer, stabiliser; (*nerves*) calmer; **a ~ boyfriend** un petit ami

steak [steɪk] *n* (*meat*) bifteck *m*, steak *m*; (*fish, pork*) tranche *f*

steal (*pt* **stole**, *pp* **stolen**) [stiːl, stəul, 'stəuln] *vt*, *vi* voler; (*move*) se faufiler, se déplacer furtivement; **my wallet has been stolen** on m'a volé mon portefeuille

steam [stiːm] *n* vapeur *f* ▷ *vt* (*Culin*) cuire à la vapeur ▷ *vi* fumer; **steam up** *vi* (*window*) se couvrir de buée; **to get ~ed up about sth** (*fig: inf*) s'exciter à propos de qch; **steamy** *adj* humide; (*window*) embué(e); (*sexy*) torride

steel [stiːl] *n* acier *m* ▷ *cpd* d'acier

steep [stiːp] *adj* raide, escarpé(e); (*price*) très élevé(e), excessif(-ive) ▷ *vt* (*faire*) tremper

steeple ['stiːpl] *n* clocher *m*

steer [stɪə*] *vt* diriger; (*boat*) gouverner; (*lead: person*) guider, conduire ▷ *vi* tenir le gouvernail; **steering** *n* (*Aut*) conduite *f*; **steering wheel** *n* volant *m*

stem [stɛm] *n* (*of plant*) tige *f*; (*of glass*) pied *m* ▷ *vt* contenir, endiguer; (*attack, spread of disease*) juguler

step [stɛp] *n* pas *m*; (*stair*) marche *f*; (*action*) mesure *f*, disposition *f* ▷ *vi*: **to ~ forward/back** faire un pas en avant/arrière, avancer/reculer; **steps** *npl* (*BRIT*) = **stepladder**; **to**

be in/out of ~ (with) (*fig*) aller dans le sens (de)/être déphasé(e) (par rapport à); **step down** *vi* (*fig*) se retirer, se désister; **step in** *vi* (*fig*) intervenir; **step up** *vt* (*production, sales*) augmenter; (*campaign, efforts*) intensifier; **stepbrother** *n* demi-frère *m*; **stepchild** (*pl* **stepchildren**) *n* beau-fils *m*, belle-fille *f*; **stepdaughter** *n* belle-fille *f*; **stepfather** *n* beau-père *m*; **stepladder** *n* (*BRIT*) escabeau *m*; **stepmother** *n* belle-mère *f*; **stepsister** *n* demi-sœur *f*; **stepson** *n* beau-fils *m*

stereo ['stɛrɪəu] *n* (*sound*) stéréo *f*; (*hi-fi*) chaîne *f* stéréo ▷ *adj* (*also:* **~phonic**) stéréo(phonique)

stereotype ['stɪərɪətaɪp] *n* stéréotype *m* ▷ *vt* stéréotyper

sterile ['stɛraɪl] *adj* stérile; **sterilize** ['stɛrɪlaɪz] *vt* stériliser

sterling ['stəːlɪŋ] *adj* (*silver*) de bon aloi, fin(e) ▷ *n* (*currency*) livre *f* sterling *inv*

stern [stəːn] *adj* sévère ▷ *n* (*Naut*) arrière *m*, poupe *f*

steroid ['stɪərɔɪd] *n* stéroïde *m*

stew [stjuː] *n* ragoût *m* ▷ *vt*, *vi* cuire à la casserole

steward ['stjuːəd] *n* (*Aviat, Naut, Rail*) steward *m*; **stewardess** *n* hôtesse *f*

stick [stɪk] (*pt*, *pp* **stuck**) *n* bâton *m*; (*for walking*) canne *f*; (*of chalk etc*) morceau *m* ▷ *vt* (*glue*) coller; (*thrust*): **to ~ sth into** piquer or planter or enfoncer qch dans; (*inf: put*) mettre, fourrer; (*: tolerate*) supporter ▷ *vi* (*adhere*) tenir, coller; (*remain*) rester; (*get jammed: door, lift*) se bloquer; **stick out** *vi* dépasser, sortir; **stick up** *vi* dépasser, sortir; **stick up for** *vt fus* défendre; **sticker** *n* autocollant *m*; **sticking plaster** *n* sparadrap *m*, pansement adhésif; **stick insect** *n* phasme *m*; **stick shift** *n* (*US Aut*) levier *m* de vitesses

sticky ['stɪkɪ] *adj* poisseux(-euse); (*label*) adhésif(-ive); (*fig: situation*) délicat(e)

stiff [stɪf] *adj* (*gen*) raide, rigide; (*door, brush*) dur(e); (*difficulty*) difficile, ardu(e); (*cold*) froid(e), distant(e); (*strong, high*) fort(e), élevé(e) ▷ *adv*: **to be bored/scared/frozen ~** s'ennuyer à mourir/être mort(e) de peur/froid

stifling ['staɪflɪŋ] *adj* (*heat*) suffocant(e)

stigma ['stɪgmə] *n* stigmate *m*

stiletto [stɪ'lɛtəu] *n* (BRIT: *also*: **~ heel**) talon *m* aiguille

still [stɪl] *adj* immobile ▷ *adv* (*up to this time*) encore, toujours; (*even*) encore; (*nonetheless*) quand même, tout de même

stimulate ['stɪmjuleɪt] *vt* stimuler

stimulus (*pl* **stimuli**) ['stɪmjuləs, 'stɪmjulaɪ] *n* stimulant *m*; (*Biol, Psych*) stimulus *m*

sting [stɪŋ] *n* piqûre *f*; (*organ*) dard *m* ▷ *vt, vi* (*pt, pp* **stung**) piquer

stink [stɪŋk] *n* puanteur *f* ▷ *vi* (*pt* **stank**, *pp* **stunk**) puer, empester

stir [stəː'] *n* agitation *f*, sensation *f* ▷ *vt* remuer ▷ *vi* remuer, bouger; **stir up** *vt* (*trouble*) fomenter, provoquer; **stir-fry** *vt* faire sauter ▷ *n*: **vegetable stir-fry** légumes sautés à la poêle

stitch [stɪtʃ] *n* (*Sewing*) point *m*; (*Knitting*) maille *f*; (*Med*) point de suture; (*pain*) point de côté ▷ *vt* coudre, piquer; (*Med*) suturer

stock [stɔk] *n* réserve *f*, provision *f*; (*Comm*) stock *m*; (*Agr*) cheptel *m*, bétail *m*; (*Culin*) bouillon *m*; (*Finance*) valeurs *fpl*, titres *mpl*; (*descent, origin*) souche *f* ▷ *adj* (*fig: reply etc*) classique ▷ *vt* (*have in stock*) avoir, vendre; **in ~**, en stock, en magasin; **out of ~** épuisé(e); **to take ~** (*fig*) faire le point; **~s and shares** valeurs (mobilières), titres; **stockbroker** ['stɔkbrəukə'] *n* agent *m* de change; **stock cube** *n* (BRIT Culin) bouillon-cube *m*; **stock exchange** *n* Bourse *f* (des valeurs); **stockholder** ['stɔkhəuldə'] *n* (US) actionnaire *m/f*

stocking ['stɔkɪŋ] *n* bas *m*

stock market *n* Bourse *f*, marché financier

stole [stəul] *pt of* **steal** ▷ *n* étole *f*

stolen ['stəuln] *pp of* **steal**

stomach ['stʌmək] *n* estomac *m*; (*abdomen*) ventre *m* ▷ *vt* supporter, digérer; **stomachache** *n* mal *m* à l'estomac *or* au ventre

stone [stəun] *n* pierre *f*; (*pebble*) caillou *m*, galet *m*; (*in fruit*) noyau *m*; (*Med*) calcul *m*; (BRIT: *weight*) = 6.348 kg; 14 *pounds* ▷ *cpd* de *or* en pierre ▷ *vt* (*person*) lancer des pierres sur, lapider; (*fruit*) dénoyauter

stood [stud] *pt, pp of* **stand**

stool [stuːl] *n* tabouret *m*

stoop [stuːp] *vi* (*also*: **have a ~**) être voûté(e); (*also*: **~ down**: *bend*) se baisser, se courber

stop [stɔp] *n* arrêt *m*; (*in punctuation*) point *m* ▷ *vt* arrêter; (*break off*) interrompre; (*also*: **put a ~ to**) mettre fin à; (*prevent*) empêcher ▷ *vi* s'arrêter; (*rain, noise etc*) cesser, s'arrêter; **to ~ doing sth** cesser *or* arrêter de faire qch; **to ~ sb (from) doing sth** empêcher qn de faire qch; **~ it!** arrête!; **stop by** *vi* s'arrêter (au passage); **stop off** *vi* faire une courte halte; **stopover** *n* halte *f*; (*Aviat*) escale *f*; **stoppage** *n* (*strike*) arrêt *m* de travail; (*obstruction*) obstruction *f*

storage ['stɔːrɪdʒ] *n* emmagasinage *m*

store [stɔː'] *n* (*stock*) provision *f*, réserve *f*; (*depot*) entrepôt *m*; (BRIT: *large shop*) grand magasin; (US: *shop*) magasin *m* ▷ *vt* emmagasiner; (*information*) enregistrer; **stores** *npl* (*food*) provisions; **who knows what is in ~ for us?** qui sait ce que l'avenir nous réserve *or* ce qui nous attend?; **storekeeper** *n* (US) commerçant(e)

S

storey, (US) **story** ['stɔ:rɪ] n étage m

storm [stɔ:m] n tempête f;
(thunderstorm) orage m ▷ vi (fig)
fulminer ▷ vt prendre d'assaut;
stormy adj orageux(-euse)

story ['stɔ:rɪ] n histoire f; (Press:
article) article m; (US) = **storey**

stout [staut] adj (strong) solide;
(fat) gros(se), corpulent(e) ▷ n bière
brune

stove [stəuv] n (for cooking) fourneau
m (: small) réchaud m; (for heating)
poêle m

straight [streɪt] adj droit(e);
(hair) raide; (frank) honnête, franc
(franche); (simple) simple ▷ adv (tout)
droit; (drink) sec, sans eau; **to put**
or **get ~** mettre en ordre, mettre de
l'ordre dans; (fig) mettre au clair; **~
away, ~ off** (at once) tout de suite;
straighten vt ajuster; (bed) arranger;
straighten out vt (fig) débrouiller;
straighten up vi (stand up) se
redresser; **straightforward** adj
simple; (frank) honnête, direct(e)

strain [streɪn] n (Tech) tension f;
pression f; (physical) effort m; (mental)
tension (nerveuse); (Med) entorse f;
(breed: of plants) variété f; (: of animals)
race f ▷ vt (fig: resources etc) mettre à
rude épreuve, grever; (hurt: back etc)
se faire mal à; (vegetables) égoutter;
strains npl (Mus) accords mpl, accents
mpl; **strained** adj (muscle) froissé(e);
(laugh etc) forcé(e), contraint(e);
(relations) tendu(e); **strainer** n
passoire f

strait [streɪt] n (Geo) détroit m;
straits npl; **to be in dire ~s** (fig) avoir
de sérieux ennuis

strand [strænd] n (of thread) fil m, brin
m; (of rope) toron m; (of hair) mèche f
▷ vt (boat) échouer; **stranded** adj en
rade, en plan

strange [streɪndʒ] adj (not
known) inconnu(e); (odd)
étrange, bizarre; **strangely** adv
étrangement, bizarrement; see also

enough; **stranger** n (unknown)
inconnu(e); (from somewhere else)
étranger(-ère)

strangle ['stræŋgl] vt étrangler

strap [stræp] n lanière f, courroie f,
sangle f; (of slip, dress) bretelle f

strategic [strə'ti:dʒɪk] adj
stratégique

strategy ['strætɪdʒɪ] n stratégie f

straw [strɔ:] n paille f; **that's the
last ~!** ça c'est le comble!

strawberry ['strɔ:bərɪ] n fraise f

stray [streɪ] adj (animal) perdu(e),
errant(e); (scattered) isolé(e) ▷ vi
s'égarer; **~ bullet** balle perdue

streak [stri:k] n bande f, filet m; (in
hair) raie f ▷ vt zébrer, strier

stream [stri:m] n (brook) ruisseau m;
(current) courant m, flot m; (of people)
défilé ininterrompu, flot ▷ vt (Scol)
répartir par niveau ▷ vi ruisseler; **to ~
in/out** entrer/sortir à flots

street [stri:t] n rue f; **streetcar** n (US)
tramway m; **street light** n réverbère
m; **street map, street plan** n plan
m des rues

strength [streŋθ] n force f; (of girder,
knot etc) solidité f; **strengthen** vt
renforcer; (muscle) fortifier; (building,
Econ) consolider

strenuous ['strenjuəs] adj
vigoureux(-euse), énergique; (tiring)
ardu(e), fatigant(e)

stress [stres] n (force, pressure)
pression f; (mental strain) tension
(nerveuse), stress m; (accent) accent
m; (emphasis) insistance f ▷ vt insister
sur, souligner; (syllable) accentuer;
stressed adj (tense) stressé(e);
(syllable) accentué(e); **stressful** adj
(job) stressant(e)

stretch [stretʃ] n (of sand etc) étendue
f ▷ vi s'étirer; (extend): **to ~ to** or **as
far as** s'étendre jusqu'à ▷ vt tendre,
étirer; (fig) pousser (au maximum); **at
a ~** d'affilée; **stretch out** vi s'étendre
▷ vt (arm etc) allonger, tendre; (to
spread) étendre

stretcher ['strɛtʃəʳ] n brancard m, civière f

strict [strɪkt] adj strict(e); **strictly** adv strictement

stridden ['strɪdn] pp of **stride**

stride [straɪd] n grand pas, enjambée f ▷ vi (pt **strode**, pp **stridden**) marcher à grands pas

strike [straɪk] (pt, pp **struck**) n grève f; (of oil etc) découverte f; (attack) raid m ▷ vt frapper; (oil etc) trouver, découvrir; (make: agreement, deal) conclure ▷ vi faire grève; (attack) attaquer; (clock) sonner; **to go on** or **come out on ~** se mettre en grève, faire grève; **to ~ a match** frotter une allumette; **striker** n gréviste m/f; (Sport) buteur m; **striking** adj frappant(e), saisissant(e); (attractive) éblouissant(e)

string [strɪŋ] n ficelle f, fil m; (row: of beads) rang m; (Mus) corde f ▷ vt (pt, pp **strung**): **to ~ out** échelonner; **to ~ together** enchaîner; **the strings** npl (Mus) les instruments mpl à cordes; **to pull ~s** (fig) faire jouer le piston

strip [strɪp] n bande f; (Sport) tenue f ▷ vt (undress) déshabiller; (paint) décaper; (fig) dégarnir, dépouiller; (also: **~ down**) (machine) démonter ▷ vi se déshabiller; **strip off** vt (paint etc) décaper ▷ vi (person) se déshabiller

stripe [straɪp] n raie f, rayure f; (Mil) galon m; **striped** adj rayé(e), à rayures

stripper ['strɪpəʳ] n strip-teaseuse f

strip-search ['strɪpsəːtʃ] vt: **to ~ sb** fouiller qn (en le faisant se déshabiller)

strive [straɪv] (pt **strove**, pp **striven**) [straɪv, strəuv, 'strɪvn] vi: **to ~ to do/for sth** s'efforcer de faire/d'obtenir qch

strode [strəud] pt of **stride**

stroke [strəuk] n coup m; (Med) attaque f; (Swimming: style) (sorte f de) nage f ▷ vt caresser; **at a ~** d'un (seul) coup

stroll [strəul] n petite promenade ▷ vi flâner, se promener nonchalamment; **stroller** n (us: for child) poussette f

strong [strɔŋ] adj (gen) fort(e); (healthy) vigoureux(-euse); (heart, nerves) solide; **they are 50 ~** ils sont au nombre de 50; **stronghold** n forteresse f, fort m; (fig) bastion m; **strongly** adv fortement, avec force; vigoureusement; solidement

strove [strəuv] pt of **strive**

struck [strʌk] pt, pp of **strike**

structure ['strʌktʃəʳ] n structure f; (building) construction f

struggle ['strʌgl] n lutte f ▷ vi lutter, se battre

strung [strʌŋ] pt, pp of **string**

stub [stʌb] n (of cigarette) bout m, mégot m; (of ticket etc) talon m ▷ vt: **to ~ one's toe (on sth)** se heurter le doigt de pied (contre qch); **stub out** vt écraser

stubble ['stʌbl] n chaume m; (on chin) barbe f de plusieurs jours

stubborn ['stʌbən] adj têtu(e), obstiné(e), opiniâtre

stuck [stʌk] pt, pp of **stick** ▷ adj (jammed) bloqué(e), coincé(e)

stud [stʌd] n (on boots etc) clou m; (collar stud) bouton m de col; (earring) petite boucle d'oreille; (of horses: also: **~ farm**) écurie f, haras m; (also: **~ horse**) étalon m ▷ vt (fig): **~ded with** parsemé(e) or criblé(e) de

student ['stjuːdənt] n étudiant(e) ▷ adj (life) estudiantin(e), étudiant(e), d'étudiant; (residence, restaurant) universitaire; (loan, movement) étudiant; **student driver** n (us) (conducteur(-trice)) débutant(e); **students' union** n (BRIT: association) ≈ union f des étudiants; (: building) ≈ foyer m des étudiants

studio ['stjuːdɪəu] n studio m, atelier m; (TV etc) studio; **studio flat**, (us) **studio apartment** n studio m

study ['stʌdɪ] n étude f; (room) bureau m ▷ vt étudier; (examine) examiner ▷ vi étudier, faire ses études

stuff [stʌf] n (gen) chose(s) f(pl), truc m; (belongings) affaires fpl, trucs; (substance) substance f ▷ vt rembourrer; (Culin) farcir; (inf: push) fourrer; **stuffing** n bourre f, rembourrage m; (Culin) farce f; **stuffy** adj (room) mal ventilé(e) or aéré(e); (ideas) vieux jeu inv

stumble ['stʌmbl] vi trébucher; **to ~ across** or **on** (fig) tomber sur

stump [stʌmp] n souche f; (of limb) moignon m ▷ vt: **to be ~ed** sécher, ne pas savoir que répondre

stun [stʌn] vt (blow) étourdir; (news) abasourdir, stupéfier

stung [stʌŋ] pt, pp of **sting**

stunk [stʌŋk] pp of **stink**

stunned [stʌnd] adj assommé(e); (fig) sidéré(e)

stunning ['stʌnɪŋ] adj (beautiful) étourdissant(e); (news etc) stupéfiant(e)

stunt [stʌnt] n (in film) cascade f, acrobatie f; (publicity) truc m publicitaire ▷ vt retarder, arrêter

stupid ['stjuːpɪd] adj stupide, bête; **stupidity** [stjuː'pɪdɪtɪ] n stupidité f, bêtise f

sturdy ['stɜːdɪ] adj (person, plant) robuste, vigoureux(-euse); (object) solide

stutter ['stʌtər] n bégaiement m ▷ vi bégayer

style [staɪl] n style m; (distinction) allure f, cachet m, style; (design) modèle m; **stylish** adj élégant(e), chic inv; **stylist** n (hair stylist) coiffeur(-euse)

sub... [sʌb] prefix sub..., sous-; **subconscious** adj subconscient(e)

subdued [səb'djuːd] adj (light) tamisé(e); (person) qui a perdu de son entrain

subject n ['sʌbdʒɪkt] sujet m; (Scol) matière f ▷ vt [səb'dʒɛkt]: **to ~ to** soumettre à; **to be ~ to** (law) être soumis(e) à; **subjective** [səb'dʒɛktɪv] adj subjectif(-ive); **subject matter** n (content) contenu m

subjunctive [səb'dʒʌŋktɪv] n subjonctif m

submarine [sʌbmə'riːn] n sous-marin m

submission [səb'mɪʃən] n soumission f

submit [səb'mɪt] vt soumettre ▷ vi se soumettre

subordinate [sə'bɔːdɪnət] adj (junior) subalterne; (Grammar) subordonné(e) ▷ n subordonné(e)

subscribe [səb'skraɪb] vi cotiser; **to ~ to** (opinion, fund) souscrire à; (newspaper) s'abonner à; être abonné(e) à

subscription [səb'skrɪpʃən] n (to magazine etc) abonnement m

subsequent ['sʌbsɪkwənt] adj ultérieur(e), suivant(e); **subsequently** adv par la suite

subside [səb'saɪd] vi (land) s'affaisser; (flood) baisser; (wind, feelings) tomber

subsidiary [səb'sɪdɪərɪ] adj subsidiaire; accessoire; (BRIT Scol: subject) complémentaire ▷ n filiale f

subsidize ['sʌbsɪdaɪz] vt subventionner

subsidy ['sʌbsɪdɪ] n subvention f

substance ['sʌbstəns] n substance f

substantial [səb'stænʃl] adj substantiel(le); (fig) important(e)

substitute ['sʌbstɪtjuːt] n (person) remplaçant(e); (thing) succédané m ▷ vt: **to ~ sth/sb for** substituer qch/qn à, remplacer par qch/qn; **substitution** n substitution f

subtitles ['sʌbtaɪtlz] npl (Cine) sous-titres mpl

subtle ['sʌtl] adj subtil(e)

subtract [səb'trækt] vt soustraire, retrancher

suburb ['sʌbəːb] n faubourg m; **the ~s** la banlieue; **suburban** [sə'bəːbən] adj de banlieue, suburbain(e)

subway ['sʌbweɪ] n (BRIT: *underpass*) passage souterrain; (US: *railway*) métro m

succeed [sək'si:d] vi réussir ▷ vt succéder à; **to ~ in doing** réussir à faire

success [sək'sɛs] n succès m; réussite f; **successful** adj (*business*) prospère, qui réussit; (*attempt*) couronné(e) de succès; **to be successful (in doing)** réussir (à faire); **successfully** adv avec succès

succession [sək'sɛʃən] n succession f

successive [sək'sɛsɪv] adj successif(-ive)

successor [sək'sɛsər] n successeur m

succumb [sə'kʌm] vi succomber

such [sʌtʃ] adj tel (telle); (*of that kind*): **~ a book** un livre de ce genre or pareil, un tel livre; (*so much*): **~ courage** un tel courage ▷ adv si; **~ a long trip** un si long voyage; **~ a lot of** tellement or tant de; **~ as** (*like*) tel (telle) que, comme; **as ~** adv en tant que tel (telle), à proprement parler; **such-and-such** adj tel ou tel (telle ou telle)

suck [sʌk] vt sucer; (*breast, bottle*) téter

Sudan [su'dɑːn] n Soudan m

sudden ['sʌdn] adj soudain(e), subit(e); **all of a ~** soudain, tout à coup; **suddenly** adv brusquement, tout à coup, soudain

sudoku [su'dəukuː] n sudoku m

sue [suː] vt poursuivre en justice, intenter un procès à

suede [sweɪd] n daim m, cuir suédé

suffer ['sʌfər] vt souffrir, subir; (*bear*) tolérer, supporter, subir ▷ vi souffrir; **to ~ from** (*illness*) souffrir de, avoir; **suffering** n souffrance(s) f(pl)

suffice [sə'faɪs] vi suffire

sufficient [sə'fɪʃənt] adj suffisant(e)

suffocate ['sʌfəkeɪt] vi suffoquer; étouffer

sugar ['ʃugər] n sucre m ▷ vt sucrer

suggest [sə'dʒɛst] vt suggérer, proposer; (*indicate*) sembler indiquer; **suggestion** n suggestion f

suicide ['suɪsaɪd] n suicide m; **~ bombing** attentat m suicide; *see also* **commit**; **suicide bomber** n kamikaze m/f

suit [suːt] n (*man's*) costume m, complet m; (*woman's*) tailleur m, ensemble m; (*Cards*) couleur f; (*lawsuit*) procès m ▷ vt (*subj: clothes, hairstyle*) aller à; (*be convenient for*) convenir à; (*adapt*): **to ~ sth to** adapter or approprier qch à; **well ~ed** (*couple*) faits l'un pour l'autre, très bien assortis; **suitable** adj qui convient; approprié(e), adéquat(e); **suitcase** n valise f

suite [swiːt] n (*of rooms, also Mus*) suite f; (*furniture*): **bedroom/dining room ~** (ensemble m de) chambre f à coucher/salle f à manger; **a three-piece ~** un salon (canapé et deux fauteuils)

sulfur ['sʌlfər] (US) n = **sulphur**

sulk [sʌlk] vi bouder

sulphur, (US) **sulfur** ['sʌlfər] n soufre m

sultana [sʌl'tɑːnə] n (*fruit*) raisin (sec) de Smyrne

sum [sʌm] n somme f; (*Scol etc*) calcul m; **sum up** vt résumer ▷ vi résumer

summarize ['sʌməraɪz] vt résumer

summary ['sʌmərɪ] n résumé m

summer ['sʌmər] n été m ▷ cpd d'été, estival(e); **in (the) ~** en été, pendant l'été; **summer holidays** npl grandes vacances; **summertime** n (*season*) été m

summit ['sʌmɪt] n sommet m; (*also:* **~ conference**) (conférence f au) sommet m

summon ['sʌmən] vt appeler, convoquer; **to ~ a witness** citer or assigner un témoin

sun [sʌn] n soleil m

Sun. abbr (= *Sunday*) dim

sun: sunbathe vi prendre un bain de soleil; **sunbed** n lit pliant; (*with sun lamp*) lit à ultra-violets; **sunblock** n écran m total; **sunburn** n coup m de soleil; **sunburned, sunburnt** adj bronzé(e), hâlé(e); (painfully) brûlé(e) par le soleil

Sunday ['sʌndɪ] n dimanche m

sunflower ['sʌnflauə'] n tournesol m

sung [sʌŋ] pp of **sing**

sunglasses ['sʌnglɑ:sɪz] npl lunettes fpl de soleil

sunk [sʌŋk] pp of **sink**

sun: sunlight n (lumière f du) soleil m; **sun lounger** n chaise longue; **sunny** adj ensoleillé(e); **it is sunny** il fait (du) soleil, il y a du soleil; **sunrise** n lever m du soleil; **sun roof** n (Aut) toit ouvrant; **sunscreen** n crème f solaire; **sunset** n coucher m du soleil; **sunshade** n (over table) parasol m; **sunshine** n (lumière f du) soleil m; **sunstroke** n insolation f, coup m de soleil; **suntan** n bronzage m; **suntan lotion** n lotion f or lait m solaire; **suntan oil** n huile f solaire

super ['su:pə'] adj (inf) formidable

superb [su:'pə:b] adj superbe, magnifique

superficial [su:pə'fɪʃəl] adj superficiel(le)

superintendent [su:pərɪn'tendənt] n directeur(-trice); (Police) ≈ commissaire m

superior [su'pɪərɪə'] adj supérieur(e); (smug) condescendant(e), méprisant(e) ▷ n supérieur(e)

superlative [su'pə:lətɪv] n (Ling) superlatif m

supermarket ['su:pəmɑ:kɪt] n supermarché m

supernatural [su:pə'nætʃərəl] adj surnaturel(le) ▷ n: **the ~** le surnaturel

superpower ['su:pəpauə'] n (Pol) superpuissance f

superstition [su:pə'stɪʃən] n superstition f

superstitious [su:pə'stɪʃəs] adj superstitieux(-euse)

superstore ['su:pəstɔː'] n (BRIT) hypermarché m, grande surface

supervise ['su:pəvaɪz] vt (children etc) surveiller; (organization, work) diriger; **supervision** [su:pə'vɪʒən] n surveillance f; (monitoring) contrôle m; (management) direction f; **supervisor** n surveillant(e); (in shop) chef m de rayon

supper ['sʌpə'] n dîner m; (late) souper m

supple ['sʌpl] adj souple

supplement n ['sʌplɪmənt] supplément m ▷ vt [sʌplɪ'ment] ajouter à, compléter

supplier [sə'plaɪə'] n fournisseur m

supply [sə'plaɪ] vt (provide) fournir; (equip): **to ~ (with)** approvisionner or ravitailler (en); fournir (en) ▷ n provision f, réserve f; (supplying) approvisionnement m; **supplies** npl (food) vivres mpl; (Mil) subsistances fpl

support [sə'pɔ:t] n (moral, financial etc) soutien m, appui m; (Tech) support m, soutien ▷ vt soutenir, supporter; (financially) subvenir aux besoins de; (uphold) être pour, être partisan de, appuyer; (Sport: team) être pour; **supporter** n (Pol etc) partisan(e); (Sport) supporter m

suppose [sə'pəuz] vt, vi supposer; imaginer; **to be ~d to do/be** être censé(e) faire/être; **supposedly** [sə'pəuzɪdlɪ] adv soi-disant; **supposing** conj si, à supposer que + sub

suppress [sə'pres] vt (revolt, feeling) réprimer; (information) faire disparaître; (scandal, yawn) étouffer

supreme [su'pri:m] adj suprême

surcharge ['sə:tʃɑ:dʒ] n surcharge f

sure [ʃuə'] adj (gen) sûr(e); (definite, convinced) sûr, certain(e); **~!** (of course) bien sûr!; **~ enough** effectivement; **to make ~ of sth/that** s'assurer de qch/vérifier qch/que; **surely** adv sûrement; certainement

surf [sə:f] n (waves) ressac m ▷ vt: **to ~ the Net** surfer sur Internet, surfer sur le Net

surface ['sə:fɪs] n surface f ▷ vt (road) poser un revêtement sur ▷ vi remonter à la surface; (fig) faire surface; **by ~ mail** par voie de terre; (by sea) par voie maritime

surfboard ['sə:fbɔ:d] n planche f de surf

surfer ['sə:fəʳ] n (in sea) surfeur(-euse); **web** or **Net ~** internaute m/f

surfing ['sə:fɪŋ] n (in sea) surf m

surge [sə:dʒ] n (of emotion) vague f ▷ vi déferler

surgeon ['sə:dʒən] n chirurgien m

surgery ['sə:dʒərɪ] n chirurgie f; (BRIT: room) cabinet m (de consultation); (also: **~ hours**) heures fpl de consultation

surname ['sə:neɪm] n nom m de famille

surpass [sə:'pɑ:s] vt surpasser, dépasser

surplus ['sə:pləs] n surplus m, excédent m ▷ adj en surplus, de trop; (Comm) excédentaire

surprise [sə'praɪz] n (gen) surprise f; (astonishment) étonnement m ▷ vt surprendre, étonner; **surprised** adj (look, smile) surpris(e), étonné(e); **to be surprised** être surpris; **surprising** adj surprenant(e), étonnant(e); **surprisingly** adv (easy, helpful) étonnamment, étrangement; **(somewhat) surprisingly, he agreed** curieusement, il a accepté

surrender [sə'rendəʳ] n reddition f, capitulation f ▷ vi se rendre, capituler

surround [sə'raund] vt entourer; (Mil etc) encercler; **surrounding** adj environnant(e); **surroundings** npl environs mpl, alentours mpl

surveillance [sə:'veɪləns] n surveillance f

survey n ['sə:veɪ] enquête f, étude f; (in house buying etc) inspection f, (rapport m d')expertise f; (of land) levé m ▷ vt [sə:'veɪ] (situation) passer en revue; (examine carefully) inspecter; (building) expertiser; (land) faire le levé de; (look at) embrasser du regard; **surveyor** n (of building) expert m; (of land) (arpenteur m) géomètre m

survival [sə'vaɪvl] n survie f

survive [sə'vaɪv] vi survivre; (custom etc) subsister ▷ vt (accident etc) survivre à, réchapper de; (person) survivre à; **survivor** n survivant(e)

suspect adj, n ['sʌspekt] suspect(e) ▷ vt [səs'pekt] soupçonner, suspecter

suspend [səs'pend] vt suspendre; **suspended sentence** n (Law) condamnation f avec sursis; **suspenders** npl (BRIT) jarretelles fpl; (US) bretelles fpl

suspense [səs'pens] n attente f, incertitude f; (in film etc) suspense m; **to keep sb in ~** tenir qn en suspens, laisser qn dans l'incertitude

suspension [səs'penʃən] n (gen, Aut) suspension f; (of driving licence) retrait m provisoire; **suspension bridge** n pont suspendu

suspicion [səs'pɪʃən] n soupçon(s) m(pl); **suspicious** adj (suspecting) soupçonneux(-euse), méfiant(e); (causing suspicion) suspect(e)

sustain [səs'teɪn] vt soutenir; (subj: food) nourrir, donner des forces à; (damage) subir; (injury) recevoir

SUV n abbr (esp US: = sports utility vehicle) SUV m, véhicule m de loisirs

swallow ['swɔləu] n (bird) hirondelle f ▷ vt avaler; (fig: story) gober

swam [swæm] pt of **swim**

swamp [swɔmp] n marais m, marécage m ▷ vt submerger

swan [swɔn] n cygne m

swap [swɔp] n échange m, troc m ▷ vt: **to ~ (for)** échanger (contre), troquer (contre)

swarm [swɔ:m] n essaim m ▷ vi (bees) essaimer; (people) grouiller; **to be ~ing with** grouiller de

sway [sweɪ] vi se balancer, osciller ▷ vt (influence) influencer

S

swear [swɛəʳ] (pt **swore**, pp **sworn**) vt, vi jurer; **swear in** vt assermenter; **swearword** n gros mot, juron m

sweat [swɛt] n sueur f, transpiration f ▷ vi suer

sweater ['swɛtəʳ] n tricot m, pull m

sweatshirt ['swɛtʃəːt] n sweat-shirt m

sweaty ['swɛtɪ] adj en sueur, moite or mouillé(e) de sueur

Swede [swiːd] n Suédois(e)

swede [swiːd] n (BRIT) rutabaga m

Sweden ['swiːdn] n Suède f; **Swedish** ['swiːdɪʃ] adj suédois(e) ▷ n (Ling) suédois m

sweep [swiːp] (pt, pp **swept**) n (curve) grande courbe; (also: **chimney ~**) ramoneur m ▷ vt balayer; (subj: current) emporter

sweet [swiːt] n (BRIT: pudding) dessert m; (candy) bonbon m ▷ adj doux (douce); (not savoury) sucré(e); (kind) gentil(le); (baby) mignon(ne); **sweetcorn** n maïs doux; **sweetener** ['swiːtnəʳ] n (Culin) édulcorant m; **sweetheart** n amoureux(-euse); **sweetshop** n (BRIT) confiserie f

swell [swɛl] n (of sea) houle f ▷ adj (US inf: excellent) chouette ▷ vt (increase) grossir, augmenter ▷ vi (increase) grossir, augmenter; (sound) s'enfler; (Med: also: **~ up**) enfler; **swelling** n (Med) enflure f (: lump) grosseur f

swept [swɛpt] pt, pp of **sweep**

swerve [swəːv] vi (to avoid obstacle) faire une embardée or un écart; (off the road) dévier

swift [swɪft] n (bird) martinet m ▷ adj rapide, prompt(e)

swim [swɪm] (pt **swam**, pp **swum**) n: **to go for a ~** aller nager or se baigner ▷ vi nager; (Sport) faire de la natation; (fig: head, room) tourner ▷ vt traverser (à la nage); **to ~ a length** nager une longueur; **swimmer** n nageur(-euse); **swimming** n nage f, natation f; **swimming costume** n (BRIT) maillot m (de bain); **swimming pool** n piscine f; **swimming trunks** npl maillot m de bain; **swimsuit** n maillot m (de bain)

swine flu ['swaɪn-] n grippe f A

swing [swɪŋ] (pt, pp **swung**) n (in playground) balançoire f; (movement) balancement m, oscillations fpl; (change in opinion etc) revirement m ▷ vt balancer, faire osciller; (also: **~ round**) tourner, faire virer ▷ vi se balancer, osciller; (also: **~ round**) virer, tourner; **to be in full ~** battre son plein

swipe card ['swaɪp-] n carte f magnétique

swirl [swəːl] vi tourbillonner, tournoyer

Swiss [swɪs] adj suisse ▷ n (pl inv) Suisse(-esse)

switch [swɪtʃ] n (for light, radio etc) bouton m; (change) changement m, revirement m ▷ vt (change) changer; **switch off** vt éteindre; (engine, machine) arrêter; **could you ~ off the light?** pouvez-vous éteindre la lumière?; **switch on** vt allumer; (engine, machine) mettre en marche; **switchboard** n (Tel) standard m

Switzerland ['swɪtsələnd] n Suisse f

swivel ['swɪvl] vi (also: **~ round**) pivoter, tourner

swollen ['swəulən] pp of **swell**

swoop [swuːp] n (by police etc) rafle f, descente f ▷ vi (bird: also: **~ down**) descendre en piqué, piquer

swop [swɔp] n, vt = **swap**

sword [sɔːd] n épée f; **swordfish** n espadon m

swore [swɔːʳ] pt of **swear**

sworn [swɔːn] pp of **swear** ▷ adj (statement, evidence) donné(e) sous serment; (enemy) juré(e)

swum [swʌm] pp of **swim**

swung [swʌŋ] pt, pp of **swing**

syllable ['sɪləbl] n syllabe f

syllabus ['sɪləbəs] n programme m

symbol ['sɪmbl] *n* symbole *m*;
  symbolic(al) [sɪm'bɒlɪk(l)] *adj*
  symbolique
symmetrical [sɪ'mɛtrɪkl] *adj*
  symétrique
symmetry ['sɪmɪtrɪ] *n* symétrie *f*
sympathetic [sɪmpə'θɛtɪk] *adj*
  (*showing pity*) compatissant(e);
  (*understanding*) bienveillant(e),
  compréhensif(-ive); **~ towards** bien
  disposé(e) envers

  > Be careful not to translate
  > *sympathetic* by the French word
  > *sympathique*.

sympathize ['sɪmpəθaɪz] *vi*: **to
  ~ with sb** plaindre qn; (*in grief*)
  s'associer à la douleur de qn; **to ~
  with sth** comprendre qch
sympathy ['sɪmpəθɪ] *n* (*pity*)
  compassion *f*
symphony ['sɪmfənɪ] *n* symphonie *f*
symptom ['sɪmptəm] *n* symptôme
  m; indice *m*
synagogue ['sɪnəgɒg] *n* synagogue *f*
syndicate ['sɪndɪkɪt] *n* syndicat
  m, coopérative *f*; (*Press*) agence *f*
  de presse
syndrome ['sɪndrəum] *n*
  syndrome *m*
synonym ['sɪnənɪm] *n* synonyme *m*
synthetic [sɪn'θɛtɪk] *adj* synthétique
Syria ['sɪrɪə] *n* Syrie *f*
syringe [sɪ'rɪndʒ] *n* seringue *f*
syrup ['sɪrəp] *n* sirop *m*; (*BRIT: also:*
  golden ~) mélasse raffinée
system ['sɪstəm] *n* système *m*;
  (*Anat*) organisme *m*; **systematic**
  [sɪstə'mætɪk] *adj* systématique;
  méthodique; **systems analyst** *n*
  analyste-programmeur *m/f*

ta [tɑː] *excl* (*BRIT inf*) merci!
tab [tæb] *n* (*label*) étiquette *f*; (*on
  drinks can etc*) languette *f*; **to keep ~s
  on** (*fig*) surveiller
table ['teɪbl] *n* table *f* ▷ *vt* (*BRIT:
  motion etc*) présenter; **to lay** *or*
  set the ~ mettre le couvert *or* la
  table; **tablecloth** *n* nappe *f*; **table
  d'hôte** [tɑːbl'dəut] *adj* (*meal*)
  à prix fixe; **table lamp** *n* lampe
  décorative *or* de table; **tablemat** *n*
  (*for plate*) napperon *m*, set *m*; (*for
  hot dish*) dessous-de-plat *m inv*;
  tablespoon *n* cuiller *f* de service;
  (*also*: **tablespoonful**: *as measurement*)
  cuillerée *f* à soupe
tablet ['tæblɪt] *n* (*Med*) comprimé *m*;
  (*of stone*) plaque *f*
table tennis *n* ping-pong® *m*, tennis
  m de table
tabloid ['tæblɔɪd] *n* (*newspaper*)
  quotidien *m* populaire
taboo [tə'buː] *adj, n* tabou (*m*)

t

tack [tæk] n (nail) petit clou m; (fig)
direction f ▷ vt (nail) clouer; (sew)
bâtir ▷ vi (Naut) tirer un or des bord(s);
to ~ sth on to (the end of) sth (of
letter, book) rajouter qch à la fin de qch
tackle ['tækl] n matériel m,
équipement m; (for lifting) appareil m
de levage; (Football, Rugby) plaquage
m ▷ vt (difficulty, animal, burglar)
s'attaquer à; (person: challenge)
s'expliquer avec; (Football, Rugby)
plaquer
tacky ['tækɪ] adj collant(e); (paint)
pas sec (sèche); (pej: poor-quality)
minable; (: showing bad taste)
ringard(e)
tact [tækt] n tact m; **tactful** adj
plein(e) de tact
tactics ['tæktɪks] npl tactique f
tactless ['tæktlɪs] adj qui manque
de tact
tadpole ['tædpəʊl] n têtard m
taffy ['tæfɪ] n (US) (bonbon m au)
caramel m
tag [tæg] n étiquette f
tail [teɪl] n queue f; (of shirt) pan m
▷ vt (follow) suivre, filer; **tails** npl (suit)
habit m; see also **head**
tailor ['teɪlər] n tailleur m (artisan)
Taiwan ['taɪ'wɑːn] n Taïwan (no
article); **Taiwanese** [taɪwə'niːz] adj
taïwanais(e) ▷ n inv Taïwanais(e)
take [teɪk] (pt **took**, pp **taken**) vt
prendre; (gain: prize) remporter;
(require: effort, courage) demander;
(tolerate) accepter, supporter; (hold:
passengers etc) contenir; (accompany)
emmener, accompagner; (bring,
carry) apporter, emporter; (exam)
passer, se présenter à; **to ~ sth from**
(drawer etc) prendre qch dans; (person)
prendre qch à; **I ~ it that** je suppose
que; **to be ~n ill** tomber malade;
it won't ~ long ça ne prendra pas
longtemps; **I was quite ~n with**
her/it elle/cela m'a beaucoup plu;
take after vt fus ressembler à; **take**
apart vt démonter; **take away** vt

(carry off) emporter; (remove) enlever;
(subtract) soustraire; **take back** vt
(return) rendre, rapporter; (one's
words) retirer; **take down** vt (building)
démolir; (letter etc) prendre, écrire;
take in vt (deceive) tromper, rouler;
(understand) comprendre, saisir;
(include) couvrir, englober; (lodger)
prendre; (dress, waistband) reprendre;
take off vi (Aviat) décoller ▷ vt
(remove) enlever; **take on** vt (work)
accepter, se charger de; (employee)
prendre, embaucher; (opponent)
accepter de se battre contre; **take**
out vt sortir; (remove) enlever; (invite)
sortir avec; **to ~ sth out of** (out of
drawer etc) prendre qch dans; **to ~**
sb out to a restaurant emmener
qn au restaurant; **take over** vt
(business) reprendre ▷ vi: **to ~ over**
from sb prendre la relève de qn;
take up vt (one's story) reprendre;
(dress) raccourcir; (occupy: time,
space) prendre, occuper; (engage
in: hobby etc) se mettre à; (accept:
offer, challenge) accepter; **takeaway**
(BRIT) adj (food) à emporter ▷ n (shop,
restaurant) ≈ magasin m qui vend
des plats à emporter; **taken** pp of
take; **takeoff** n (Aviat) décollage
m; **takeout** adj, n (US) = **takeaway**;
takeover n (Comm) rachat m;
takings npl (Comm) recette f
talc [tælk] n (also: **~um powder**)
talc m
tale [teɪl] n (story) conte m, histoire
f; (account) récit m; **to tell ~s** (fig)
rapporter
talent ['tælnt] n talent m, don m;
talented adj doué(e), plein(e) de
talent
talk [tɔːk] n (a speech) causerie f,
exposé m; (conversation) discussion
f; (interview) entretien m; (gossip)
racontars mpl (pej) ▷ vi parler;
(chatter) bavarder; **talks** npl (Pol etc)
entretiens mpl; **to ~ about** parler de;
to ~ sb out of/into doing persuader

qn de ne pas faire/de faire; **to ~ shop** parler métier or affaires; **talk over** vt discuter (de); **talk show** n (TV, Radio) émission-débat f

tall [tɔ:l] adj (person) grand(e); (building, tree) haut(e); **to be 6 feet ~** ≈ mesurer 1 mètre 80

tambourine [tæmbə'ri:n] n tambourin m

tame [teɪm] adj apprivoisé(e); (fig: story, style) insipide

tamper ['tæmpəʳ] vi: **to ~ with** toucher à (en cachette ou sans permission)

tampon ['tæmpən] n tampon m hygiénique or périodique

tan [tæn] n (also: **sun~**) bronzage m ▷ vt, vi bronzer, brunir ▷ adj (colour) marron clair inv

tandem ['tændəm] n tandem m

tangerine [tændʒə'ri:n] n mandarine f

tangle ['tæŋgl] n enchevêtrement m; **to get in(to) a ~** s'emmêler

tank [tæŋk] n réservoir m; (for fish) aquarium m; (Mil) char m d'assaut, tank m

tanker ['tæŋkəʳ] n (ship) pétrolier m, tanker m; (truck) camion-citerne m

tanned [tænd] adj bronzé(e)

tantrum ['tæntrəm] n accès m de colère

Tanzania [tænzə'nɪə] n Tanzanie f

tap [tæp] n (on sink etc) robinet m; (gentle blow) petite tape ▷ vt frapper or taper légèrement; (resources) exploiter, utiliser; (telephone) mettre sur écoute; **on ~** (fig: resources) disponible; **tap dancing** n claquettes fpl

tape [teɪp] n (for tying) ruban m; (also: **magnetic ~**) bande f (magnétique); (cassette) cassette f; (sticky) Scotch® m ▷ vt (record) enregistrer (au magnétoscope or sur cassette); (stick) coller avec du Scotch®; **tape measure** n mètre m à ruban; **tape recorder** n magnétophone m

tapestry ['tæpɪstrɪ] n tapisserie f

tar [tɑː] n goudron m

target ['tɑːgɪt] n cible f; (fig: objective) objectif m

tariff ['tærɪf] n (Comm) tarif m; (taxes) tarif douanier

tarmac ['tɑːmæk] n (Brit: on road) macadam m; (Aviat) aire f d'envol

tarpaulin [tɑː'pɔːlɪn] n bâche goudronnée

tarragon ['tærəgən] n estragon m

tart [tɑːt] n (Culin) tarte f; (Brit inf: pej: prostitute) poule f ▷ adj (flavour) âpre, aigrelet(te)

tartan ['tɑːtn] n tartan m ▷ adj écossais(e)

tartar(e) sauce ['tɑːtə-] n sauce f tartare

task [tɑːsk] n tâche f; **to take to ~** prendre à partie

taste [teɪst] n goût m; (fig: glimpse, idea) idée f, aperçu m ▷ vt goûter ▷ vi: **to ~ of** (fish etc) avoir le or un goût de; **you can ~ the garlic (in it)** on sent bien l'ail; **to have a ~ of sth** goûter (à) qch; **can I have a ~?** je peux goûter?; **to be in good/bad** or **poor ~** être de bon/mauvais goût; **tasteful** adj de bon goût; **tasteless** adj (food) insipide; (remark) de mauvais goût; **tasty** adj savoureux(-euse), délicieux(-euse)

tatters ['tætəz] npl: **in ~** (also: **tattered**) en lambeaux

tattoo [tə'tuː] n tatouage m; (spectacle) parade f militaire ▷ vt tatouer

taught [tɔːt] pt, pp of **teach**

taunt [tɔːnt] n raillerie f ▷ vt railler

Taurus ['tɔːrəs] n le Taureau

taut [tɔːt] adj tendu(e)

tax [tæks] n (on goods etc) taxe f; (on income) impôts mpl, contributions fpl ▷ vt taxer; imposer; (fig: patience etc) mettre à l'épreuve; **tax disc** n (Brit Aut) vignette f (automobile); **tax-free** adj exempt(e) d'impôts

taxi ['tæksɪ] n taxi m ▷ vi (Aviat) rouler (lentement) au sol; **taxi driver** n

t

chauffeur m de taxi; **taxi rank**, (US)
taxi stand n station f de taxis
tax payer [-peɪəʳ] n contribuable m/f
tax return n déclaration f d'impôts
or de revenus
TB n abbr = **tuberculosis**
tbc abbr = **to be confirmed**
tea [tiː] n thé m; (BRIT: snack: for
children) goûter m; **high ~** (BRIT)
collation combinant goûter et dîner; **tea
bag** n sachet m de thé; **tea break** n
(BRIT) pause-thé f
teach (pt, pp **taught**) [tiːtʃ, tɔːt] vt:
to ~ sb sth, to ~ sth to sb apprendre
qch à qn; (in school etc) enseigner
qch à qn ▷ vi enseigner; **teacher** n
(in secondary school) professeur m; (in
primary school) instituteur(-trice);
teaching n enseignement
m; **teaching assistant** n
aide-éducateur(-trice)
tea: teacup n tasse f à thé; **tea leaves**
npl feuilles fpl de thé
team [tiːm] n équipe f; (of animals)
attelage m; **team up** vi: **to ~ up
(with)** faire équipe (avec)
teapot ['tiːpɔt] n théière f
tear¹ ['tɪəʳ] n larme f; **in ~s** en larmes
tear² [tɛəʳ] (pt **tore**, pp **torn**) n
déchirure f ▷ vt déchirer ▷ vi se
déchirer; **tear apart** vt (also fig)
déchirer; **tear down** vt (building,
statue) démolir; (poster, flag)
arracher; **tear off** vt (sheet of paper
etc) arracher; (one's clothes) enlever
à toute vitesse; **tear up** vt (sheet
of paper etc) déchirer, mettre en
morceaux or pièces
tearful ['tɪəful] adj larmoyant(e)
tear gas ['tɪə-] n gaz m lacrymogène
tearoom ['tiːruːm] n salon m de thé
tease [tiːz] vt taquiner; (unkindly)
tourmenter
tea: teaspoon n petite cuiller; (also:
teaspoonful: as measurement) ≈
cuillerée f à café; **teatime** n l'heure f
du thé; **tea towel** n (BRIT) torchon m
(à vaisselle)

technical ['tɛknɪkl] adj technique
technician [tɛk'nɪʃən] n
technicien(ne)
technique [tɛk'niːk] n technique f
technology [tɛk'nɔlədʒɪ] n
technologie f
teddy (bear) ['tɛdɪ-] n ours m (en
peluche)
tedious ['tiːdɪəs] adj
fastidieux(-euse)
tee [tiː] n (Golf) tee m
teen [tiːn] adj = **teenage** ▷ n (US)
= **teenager**
teenage ['tiːneɪdʒ] adj (fashions etc)
pour jeunes, pour adolescents; (child)
qui est adolescent(e); **teenager** n
adolescent(e)
teens [tiːnz] npl; **to be in one's ~**
être adolescent(e)
teeth [tiːθ] npl of **tooth**
teetotal ['tiː'təutl] adj (person) qui ne
boit jamais d'alcool
telecommunications
['tɛlɪkəmjuːnɪ'keɪʃənz] n
télécommunications fpl
telegram ['tɛlɪɡræm] n
télégramme m
telegraph pole ['tɛlɪɡrɑːf-] n
poteau m télégraphique
telephone ['tɛlɪfəun] n téléphone
m ▷ vt (person) téléphoner à;
(message) téléphoner; **to be on
the ~** (be speaking) être au téléphone;
telephone book n = **telephone
directory**; **telephone box**, (US)
telephone booth n cabine f
téléphonique; **telephone call** n
appel m téléphonique; **telephone
directory** n annuaire m (du
téléphone); **telephone number** n
numéro m de téléphone
telesales ['tɛlɪseɪlz] npl télévente f
telescope ['tɛlɪskəup] n télescope m
televise ['tɛlɪvaɪz] vt téléviser
television ['tɛlɪvɪʒən] n télévision f;
on ~ à la télévision; **television
programme** n (BRIT) émission f de
télévision

tell (*pt, pp* **told**) [tɛl, təuld] *vt* dire; (*relate: story*) raconter; (*distinguish*): **to ~ sth from** distinguer qch de ▷ *vi* (*talk*): **to ~ of** parler de; (*have effect*) se faire sentir, se voir; **to ~ sb to do** dire à qn de faire; **to ~ the time** (*know how to*) savoir lire l'heure; **tell off** *vt* réprimander, gronder; **teller** *n* (*in bank*) caissier(-ière)

telly ['tɛlɪ] *n abbr* (BRIT inf: = television) télé *f*

temp [tɛmp] *n* (BRIT: = temporary worker) intérimaire *m/f* ▷ *vi* travailler comme intérimaire

temper ['tɛmpəʳ] *n* (*nature*) caractère *m*; (*mood*) humeur *f*; (*fit of anger*) colère *f* ▷ *vt* (*moderate*) tempérer, adoucir; **to be in a ~** être en colère; **to lose one's ~** se mettre en colère

temperament ['tɛmprəmənt] *n* (*nature*) tempérament *m*; **temperamental** [tɛmprə'mɛntl] *adj* capricieux(-euse)

temperature ['tɛmprətʃəʳ] *n* température *f*; **to have** *or* **run a ~** avoir de la fièvre

temple ['tɛmpl] *n* (*building*) temple *m*; (*Anat*) tempe *f*

temporary ['tɛmpərərɪ] *adj* temporaire, provisoire; (*job, worker*) temporaire

tempt [tɛmpt] *vt* tenter; **to ~ sb into doing** induire qn à faire; **temptation** *n* tentation *f*; **tempting** *adj* tentant(e); (*food*) appétissant(e)

ten [tɛn] *num* dix

tenant ['tɛnənt] *n* locataire *m/f*

tend [tɛnd] *vt* s'occuper de ▷ *vi*: **to ~ to do** avoir tendance à faire; **tendency** ['tɛndənsɪ] *n* tendance *f*

tender ['tɛndəʳ] *adj* tendre; (*delicate*) délicat(e); (*sore*) sensible ▷ *n* (*Comm: offer*) soumission *f*; (*money*): **legal ~** cours légal ▷ *vt* offrir

tendon ['tɛndən] *n* tendon *m*

tenner ['tɛnəʳ] *n* (BRIT inf) billet *m* de dix livres

tennis ['tɛnɪs] *n* tennis *m*; **tennis ball** *n* balle *f* de tennis; **tennis court** *n* (court *m* de) tennis *m*; **tennis match** *n* match *m* de tennis; **tennis player** *n* joueur(-euse) de tennis; **tennis racket** *n* raquette *f* de tennis

tenor ['tɛnəʳ] *n* (*Mus*) ténor *m*

tenpin bowling ['tɛnpɪn-] *n* (BRIT) bowling *m* (*à 10 quilles*)

tense [tɛns] *adj* tendu(e) ▷ *n* (*Ling*) temps *m*

tension ['tɛnʃən] *n* tension *f*

tent [tɛnt] *n* tente *f*

tentative ['tɛntətɪv] *adj* timide, hésitant(e); (*conclusion*) provisoire

tenth [tɛnθ] *num* dixième

tent: tent peg *n* piquet *m* de tente; **tent pole** *n* montant *m* de tente

tepid ['tɛpɪd] *adj* tiède

term [tə:m] *n* terme *m*; (*Scol*) trimestre *m* ▷ *vt* appeler; **terms** *npl* (*conditions*) conditions *fpl*; (*Comm*) tarif *m*; **in the short/long ~** à court/ long terme; **to come to ~s with** (*problem*) faire face à; **to be on good ~s with** bien s'entendre avec, être en bons termes avec

terminal ['tə:mɪnl] *adj* (*disease*) dans sa phase terminale; (*patient*) incurable ▷ *n* (*Elec*) borne *f*; (*for oil, ore etc: also Comput*) terminal *m*; (*also*: **air ~**) aérogare *f*; (BRIT: *also*: **coach ~**) gare routière

terminate ['tə:mɪneɪt] *vt* mettre fin à; (*pregnancy*) interrompre

termini ['tə:mɪnaɪ] *npl of* **terminus**

terminology [tə:mɪ'nɔlədʒɪ] *n* terminologie *f*

terminus (*pl* **termini**) ['tə:mɪnəs, 'tə:mɪnaɪ] *n* terminus *m inv*

terrace ['tɛrəs] *n* terrasse *f*; (BRIT: *row of houses*) rangée *f* de maisons (*attenantes les unes aux autres*); **the ~s** (BRIT Sport) les gradins *mpl*; **terraced** *adj* (*garden*) en terrasses; (*in a row: house*) attenant(e) aux maisons voisines

terrain [tɛ'reɪn] *n* terrain *m* (*sol*)

terrestrial [tɪˈrestrɪəl] adj terrestre

terrible [ˈterɪbl] adj terrible, atroce; (weather, work) affreux(-euse), épouvantable; **terribly** adv terriblement; (very badly) affreusement mal

terrier [ˈterɪəʳ] n terrier m (chien)

terrific [təˈrɪfɪk] adj (very great) fantastique, incroyable, terrible; (wonderful) formidable, sensationnel(le)

terrified [ˈterɪfaɪd] adj terrifié(e); **to be ~ of sth** avoir très peur de qch

terrify [ˈterɪfaɪ] vt terrifier; **terrifying** adj terrifiant(e)

territorial [terɪˈtɔːrɪəl] adj territorial(e)

territory [ˈterɪtərɪ] n territoire m

terror [ˈterəʳ] n terreur f; **terrorism** n terrorisme m; **terrorist** n terroriste m/f; **terrorist attack** n attentat m terroriste

test [tɛst] n (trial, check) essai m; (of courage etc) épreuve f; (Med) examen m; (Chem) analyse f; (Scol) interrogation f de contrôle; (also: **driving ~**) (examen du) permis m de conduire ▷ vt essayer; mettre à l'épreuve; examiner; analyser; faire subir une interrogation à

testicle [ˈtestɪkl] n testicule m

testify [ˈtestɪfaɪ] vi (Law) témoigner, déposer; **to ~ to sth** (Law) attester qch

testimony [ˈtestɪmənɪ] n (Law) témoignage m, déposition f

test: test match n (Cricket, Rugby) match international; **test tube** n éprouvette f

tetanus [ˈtetənəs] n tétanos m

text [tɛkst] n texte m; (on mobile phone) SMS m inv, texto® m ▷ vt (inf) envoyer un SMS or texto® à; **textbook** n manuel m

textile [ˈtekstaɪl] n textile m

text message n SMS m inv, texto® m

text messaging [-ˈmesɪdʒɪŋ] n messagerie textuelle

texture [ˈtekstʃəʳ] n texture f; (of skin, paper etc) grain m

Thai [taɪ] adj thaïlandais(e) ▷ n Thaïlandais(e)

Thailand [ˈtaɪlænd] n Thaïlande f

Thames [temz] n: **the (River) ~** la Tamise

than [ðæn, ðən] conj que; (with numerals): **more ~ 10/once** plus de 10/d'une fois; **I have more/less ~ you** j'en ai plus/moins que toi; **she has more apples ~ pears** elle a plus de pommes que de poires; **it is better to phone ~ to write** il vaut mieux téléphoner (plutôt) qu'écrire; **she is older ~ you think** elle est plus âgée que tu le crois

thank [θæŋk] vt remercier, dire merci à; **thanks** npl remerciements mpl; **~s!** merci!; **~ you (very much)** merci (beaucoup); **~ God** Dieu merci; **~s to** prep grâce à; **thankfully** adv (fortunately) heureusement; **Thanksgiving (Day)** n jour m d'action de grâce

● **THANKSGIVING (DAY)**

● Thanksgiving (Day) est un jour de
● congé aux États-Unis, le quatrième
● jeudi du mois de novembre,
● commémorant la bonne récolte
● que les Pèlerins venus de
● Grande-Bretagne ont eue en 1621;
● traditionnellement, c'était un jour
● où l'on remerciait Dieu et où l'on
● organisait un grand festin. Une
● fête semblable, mais qui n'a aucun
● rapport avec les Pères Pèlerins, a
● lieu au Canada le deuxième lundi
● d'octobre.

KEYWORD

that [ðæt] adj (demonstrative) ce, cet + vowel or h mute, cette f; **that man/woman/book** cet homme/ cette femme/ce livre; (not this) cet

homme-là/cette femme-là/ce livre-là; **that one** celui-là (celle-là)
▶ *pron* **1** (*demonstrative*) ce; (: *not this one*) celui; (: *that one*) celui (celle); **who's that?** qui est-ce?; **what's that?** qu'est-ce que c'est?; **is that you?** c'est toi?; **I prefer this to that** je préfère ceci à cela *or* ça; **that's what he said** c'est *or* voilà ce qu'il a dit; **will you eat all that?** tu vas manger tout ça?; **that is (to say)** c'est-à-dire, à savoir
2 (*relative: subject*) qui; (: *object*) que; (: *after prep*) lequel (laquelle), lesquels (lesquelles) *pl*; **the book that I read** le livre que j'ai lu; **the books that are in the library** les livres qui sont dans la bibliothèque; **all that I have** tout ce que j'ai; **the box that I put it in** la boîte dans laquelle je l'ai mis; **the people that I spoke to** les gens auxquels *or* à qui j'ai parlé
3 (*relative, of time*) où; **the day that he came** le jour où il est venu
▶ *conj* que; **he thought that I was ill** il pensait que j'étais malade
▶ *adv* (*demonstrative*): **I don't like it that much** ça ne me plaît pas tant que ça; **I didn't know it was that bad** je ne savais pas que c'était si *or* aussi mauvais; **it's about that high** c'est à peu près de cette hauteur

thatched [θætʃt] *adj* (*roof*) de chaume; **~ cottage** chaumière *f*
thaw [θɔː] *n* dégel *m* ▷ *vi* (*ice*) fondre; (*food*) dégeler ▷ *vt* (*food*) (faire) dégeler

 KEYWORD

the [ðiː, ðə] *def art* **1** (*gen*) le, la *f*, l' + *vowel or h mute*, les *pl* (NB: à + *le(s)* = **au(x)**; *de* + *le* = **du**; *de* + *les* = **des**); **the boy/girl/ink** le garçon/ la fille/l'encre; **the children** les enfants; **the history of the world** l'histoire du monde; **give it to the postman** donne-le au facteur; **to**

play the piano/flute jouer du piano/ de la flûte
2 (+ *adj to form n*) le, la *f*, l' + *vowel or h mute*, les *pl*; **the rich and the poor** les riches et les pauvres; **to attempt the impossible** tenter l'impossible
3 (*in titles*): **Elizabeth the First** Elisabeth première; **Peter the Great** Pierre le Grand
4 (*in comparisons*): **the more he works, the more he earns** plus il travaille, plus il gagne de l'argent

theatre, (US) **theater** ['θɪətə^r] *n* théâtre *m*; (*Med: also*: **operating ~**) salle *f* d'opération
theft [θɛft] *n* vol *m* (*larcin*)
their [ðɛə^r] *adj* leur, leurs *pl*; *see also* **my**; **theirs** *pron* le (la) leur, les leurs; *see also* **mine¹**
them [ðɛm, ðəm] *pron* (*direct*) les; (*indirect*) leur; (*stressed, after prep*) eux (elles); **give me a few of ~** donnez m'en quelques uns (*or* quelques unes); *see also* **me**
theme [θiːm] *n* thème *m*; **theme park** *n* parc *m* à thème
themselves [ðəm'sɛlvz] *pl pron* (*reflexive*) se; (*emphatic, after prep*) eux-mêmes (elles-mêmes); **between ~** entre eux (elles); *see also* **oneself**
then [ðɛn] *adv* (*at that time*) alors, à ce moment-là; (*next*) puis, ensuite; (*and also*) et puis ▷ *conj* (*therefore*) alors, dans ce cas ▷ *adj*: **the ~ president** le président d'alors *or* de l'époque; **by ~** (*past*) à ce moment-là; (*future*) d'ici là; **from ~ on** dès lors; **until ~** jusqu'à ce moment-là, jusque-là
theology [θɪ'ɔlədʒɪ] *n* théologie *f*
theory ['θɪərɪ] *n* théorie *f*
therapist ['θɛrəpɪst] *n* thérapeute *m/f*
therapy ['θɛrəpɪ] *n* thérapie *f*

 KEYWORD

there [ðɛə^r] *adv* **1**: **there is, there are** il y a; **there are 3 of them**

(*people, things*) il y en a 3; **there is no-one here/no bread left** il n'y a personne/il n'y a plus de pain; **there has been an accident** il y a eu un accident

2 (*referring to place*) là, là-bas; **it's there** c'est là(-bas); **in/on/up/down there** là-dedans/là-dessus/là-haut/en bas; **he went there on Friday** il y est allé vendredi; **I want that book there** je veux ce livre-là; **there he is!** le voilà!

3: **there, there!** (*esp to child*) allons, allons!

there: **thereabouts** *adv* (*place*) par là, près de là; (*amount*) environ, à peu près; **thereafter** *adv* par la suite; **thereby** *adv* ainsi; **therefore** *adv* donc, par conséquent

there's ['ðɛəz] = **there is**; **there has**

thermal ['θəːml] *adj* thermique; **~ underwear** sous-vêtements *mpl* en Thermolactyl®

thermometer [θəˈmɔmɪtəʳ] *n* thermomètre *m*

thermostat ['θəːməʊstæt] *n* thermostat *m*

these [ðiːz] *pl pron* ceux-ci (celles-ci) ▷ *pl adj* ces; (*not those*): **~ books** ces livres-là

thesis (*pl* **theses**) ['θiːsɪs, 'θiːsiːz] *n* thèse *f*

they [ðeɪ] *pl pron* ils (elles); (*stressed*) eux (elles); **~ say that ...** (*it is said that*) on dit que ...; **they'd** = **they had**; **they would**; **they'll** = **they shall**; **they will**; **they're** = **they are**; **they've** = **they have**

thick [θɪk] *adj* épais(se); (*stupid*) bête, borné(e) ▷ *n*: **in the ~ of** au beau milieu de, en plein cœur de; **it's 20 cm ~** ça a 20 cm d'épaisseur; **thicken** *vi* s'épaissir ▷ *vt* (*sauce etc*) épaissir; **thickness** *n* épaisseur *f*

thief (*pl* **thieves**) [θiːf, θiːvz] *n* voleur(-euse)

thigh [θaɪ] *n* cuisse *f*

thin [θɪn] *adj* mince; (*skinny*) maigre; (*soup*) peu épais(se); (*hair, crowd*) clairsemé(e) ▷ *vt* (*also:* **~ down**: *sauce, paint*) délayer

thing [θɪŋ] *n* chose *f*; (*object*) objet *m*; (*contraption*) truc *m*; **things** *npl* (*belongings*) affaires *fpl*; **the ~ is ...** c'est que ...; **the best ~ would be to** le mieux serait de; **how are ~s?** comment ça va?; **to have a ~ about** (*be obsessed by*) être obsédé(e) par; (*hate*) détester; **poor ~!** le (*or* la) pauvre!

think (*pt, pp* **thought**) [θɪŋk, θɔːt] *vi* penser, réfléchir ▷ *vt* penser, croire; (*imagine*) s'imaginer; **what did you ~ of them?** qu'avez-vous pensé d'eux?; **to ~ about sth/sb** penser à qch/qn; **I'll ~ about it** je vais y réfléchir; **to ~ of doing** avoir l'idée de faire; **I ~ so/not** je crois *or* pense que oui/non; **to ~ well of** avoir une haute opinion de; **think over** *vt* bien réfléchir à; **think up** *vt* inventer, trouver

third [θəːd] *num* troisième ▷ *n* (*fraction*) tiers *m*; (*Aut*) troisième (*vitesse*) *f*; (*BRIT Scol: degree*) ≈ licence *f* avec mention passable; **thirdly** *adv* troisièmement; **third party insurance** *n* (*BRIT*) assurance *f* au tiers; **Third World** *n*: **the Third World** le Tiers-Monde

thirst [θəːst] *n* soif *f*; **thirsty** *adj* qui a soif, assoiffé(e); (*work*) qui donne soif; **to be thirsty** avoir soif

thirteen [θəːˈtiːn] *num* treize; **thirteenth** [θəːˈtiːnθ] *num* treizième

thirtieth ['θəːtɪɪθ] *num* trentième

thirty ['θəːtɪ] *num* trente

 KEYWORD

this [ðɪs] *adj* (*demonstrative*) ce, cet + *vowel or h mute*, cette *f*; **this man/woman/book** cet homme/cette femme/ce livre; (*not that*) cet homme-ci/cette femme-ci/ce livre-ci; **this one** celui-ci (celle-ci)

▶ *pron* (*demonstrative*) ce (: *not that one*) celui-ci (celle-ci), ceci; **who's this?** qui est-ce?; **what's this?** qu'est-ce que c'est?; **I prefer this to that** je préfère ceci à cela; **this is where I live** c'est ici que j'habite; **this is what he said** voici ce qu'il a dit; **this is Mr Brown** (*in introductions*) je vous présente Mr Brown; (*in photo*) c'est Mr Brown; (*on telephone*) ici Mr Brown ▶ *adv* (*demonstrative*): **it was about this big** c'était à peu près de cette grandeur *or* grand comme ça; **I didn't know it was this bad** je ne savais pas que c'était si *or* aussi mauvais

thistle ['θɪsl] *n* chardon *m*

thorn [θɔːn] *n* épine *f*

thorough ['θʌrə] *adj* (*search*) minutieux(-euse); (*knowledge, research*) approfondi(e); (*work, person*) consciencieux(-euse); (*cleaning*) à fond; **thoroughly** *adv* (*search*) minutieusement; (*study*) en profondeur; (*clean*) à fond; (*very*) tout à fait

those [ðəuz] *pl pron* ceux-là (celles-là) ▶ *pl adj* ces; (*not these*): **~ books** ces livres-là

though [ðəu] *conj* bien que + *sub*, quoique + *sub* ▶ *adv* pourtant

thought [θɔːt] *pt, pp of* **think** ▶ *n* pensée *f*; (*idea*) idée *f*; (*opinion*) avis *m*; **thoughtful** *adj* (*deep in thought*) pensif(-ive); (*serious*) réfléchi(e); (*considerate*) prévenant(e); **thoughtless** *adj* qui manque de considération

thousand ['θauzənd] *num* mille; **one ~** mille; **two ~** deux mille; **~s of** des milliers de; **thousandth** *num* millième

thrash [θræʃ] *vt* rouer de coups; (*inf: defeat*) donner une raclée à (*inf*)

thread [θrɛd] *n* fil *m*; (*of screw*) pas *m*, filetage *m* ▶ *vt* (*needle*) enfiler

threat [θrɛt] *n* menace *f*; **threaten** *vi* (*storm*) menacer ▶ *vt*: **to threaten sb with sth/to do** menacer qn de qch/de faire; **threatening** *adj* menaçant(e)

three [θriː] *num* trois; **three-dimensional** *adj* à trois dimensions; **three-piece suite** *n* salon *m* (canapé et deux fauteuils); **three-quarters** *npl* trois-quarts *mpl*; **three-quarters full** aux trois-quarts plein

threshold ['θrɛʃhəuld] *n* seuil *m*

threw [θruː] *pt of* **throw**

thrill [θrɪl] *n* (*excitement*) émotion *f*, sensation forte; (*shudder*) frisson *m* ▷ *vt* (*audience*) électriser; **thrilled** *adj*: **thrilled (with)** ravi(e); **thriller** *n* film *m* (*or* roman *m or* pièce *f*) à suspense; **thrilling** *adj* (*book, play etc*) saisissant(e); (*news, discovery*) excitant(e)

thriving ['θraɪvɪŋ] *adj* (*business, community*) prospère

throat [θrəut] *n* gorge *f*; **to have a sore ~** avoir mal à la gorge

throb [θrɔb] *vi* (*heart*) palpiter; (*engine*) vibrer; **my head is ~bing** j'ai des élancements dans la tête

throne [θrəun] *n* trône *m*

through [θruː] *prep* à travers; (*time*) pendant, durant; (*by means of*) par, par l'intermédiaire de; (*owing to*) à cause de ▷ *adj* (*ticket, train, passage*) direct(e) ▷ *adv* à travers; **(from) Monday ~ Friday** (*us*) de lundi à vendredi; **to put sb ~ to sb** (*Tel*) passer qn à qn; **to be ~** (*BRIT Tel*) avoir la communication; (*esp us: have finished*) avoir fini; **"no ~ traffic"** (*us*) "passage interdit"; **"no ~ road"** (*BRIT*) "impasse"; **throughout** *prep* (*place*) partout dans; (*time*) durant tout(e) le ▷ *adv* partout

throw [θrəu] *n* jet *m*; (*Sport*) lancer *m* ▷ *vt* (*pt* **threw**, *pp* **thrown**) lancer, jeter; (*Sport*) lancer; (*rider*) désarçonner; (*fig*) décontenancer; **to ~ a party** donner une réception; **throw away** *vt* jeter; (*money*) gaspiller; **throw in** *vt* (*Sport: ball*) remettre en jeu; (*include*) ajouter; **throw off** *vt* se débarrasser de; **throw out** *vt* jeter; (*reject*) rejeter; (*person*) mettre à la porte; **throw up** *vi* vomir

thrown [θrəʊn] *pp of* **throw**

thru [θruː] (*US*) *prep* = **through**

thrush [θrʌʃ] *n* (*Zool*) grive *f*

thrust [θrʌst] *vt* (*pt, pp* **thrust**) pousser brusquement; (*push in*) enfoncer

thud [θʌd] *n* bruit sourd

thug [θʌg] *n* voyou *m*

thumb [θʌm] *n* (*Anat*) pouce *m* ▷ *vt*: **to ~ a lift** faire de l'auto-stop, arrêter une voiture; **thumbtack** *n* (*US*) punaise *f* (*clou*)

thump [θʌmp] *n* grand coup; (*sound*) bruit sourd ▷ *vt* cogner sur ▷ *vi* cogner, frapper

thunder ['θʌndə'] *n* tonnerre *m* ▷ *vi* tonner; (*train etc*): **to ~ past** passer dans un grondement *or* un bruit de tonnerre; **thunderstorm** *n* orage *m*

Thursday ['θəːzdɪ] *n* jeudi *m*

thus [ðʌs] *adv* ainsi

thwart [θwɔːt] *vt* contrecarrer

thyme [taɪm] *n* thym *m*

Tibet [tɪ'bɛt] *n* Tibet *m*

tick [tɪk] *n* (*sound: of clock*) tic-tac *m*; (*mark*) coche *f*; (*Zool*) tique *f* ▷ *vi* faire tic-tac ▷ *vt* (*item on list*) cocher; **in a ~** (*BRIT inf*) dans un instant; **tick off** *vt* (*item on list*) cocher; (*person*) réprimander, attraper

ticket ['tɪkɪt] *n* billet *m*; (*for bus, tube*) ticket *m*; (*in shop, on goods*) étiquette *f*; (*for library*) carte *f*; (*also*: **parking ~**) contravention *f*, p.-v. *m*; **ticket barrier** *n* (*BRIT Rail*) portillon *m* automatique; **ticket collector** *n* contrôleur(-euse); **ticket inspector** *n* contrôleur(-euse); **ticket machine** *n* billetterie *f* automatique; **ticket office** *n* guichet *m*, bureau *m* de vente des billets

tickle ['tɪkl] *vi* chatouiller ▷ *vt* chatouiller; **ticklish** *adj* (*person*)

chatouilleux(-euse); (*problem*) épineux(-euse)

tide [taɪd] *n* marée *f*; (*fig: of events*) cours *m*

tidy ['taɪdɪ] *adj* (*room*) bien rangé(e); (*dress, work*) net (nette), soigné(e); (*person*) ordonné(e), qui a de l'ordre ▷ *vt* (*also*: **~ up**) ranger

tie [taɪ] *n* (*string etc*) cordon *m*; (*BRIT: also*: **neck~**) cravate *f*; (*fig: link*) lien *m*; (*Sport: draw*) égalité *f* de points match nul ▷ *vt* (*parcel*) attacher; (*ribbon*) nouer ▷ *vi* (*Sport*) faire match nul; finir à égalité de points; **to ~ sth in a bow** faire un nœud à *or* avec qch; **to ~ a knot in sth** faire un nœud à qch; **tie down** *vt*: **to ~ sb down to** (*fig*) contraindre qn à accepter; **to feel ~d down** (*by relationship*) se sentir coincé(e); **tie up** *vt* (*parcel*) ficeler; (*dog, boat*) attacher; (*prisoner*) ligoter; (*arrangements*) conclure; **to be ~d up** (*busy*) être pris(e) *or* occupé(e)

tier [tɪə'] *n* gradin *m*; (*of cake*) étage *m*

tiger ['taɪgə'] *n* tigre *m*

tight [taɪt] *adj* (*rope*) tendu(e), raide; (*clothes*) étroit(e), très juste; (*budget, programme, bend*) serré(e); (*control*) strict(e), sévère; (*inf: drunk*) ivre, rond(e) ▷ *adv* (*squeeze*) très fort; (*shut*) à bloc, hermétiquement; **hold ~!** accrochez-vous bien!; **tighten** *vt* (*rope*) tendre; (*screw*) resserrer; (*control*) renforcer ▷ *vi* se tendre; se resserrer; **tightly** *adv* (*grasp*) bien, très fort; **tights** *npl* (*BRIT*) collant *m*

tile [taɪl] *n* (*on roof*) tuile *f*; (*on wall or floor*) carreau *m*

till [tɪl] *n* caisse (enregistreuse) ▷ *prep, conj* = **until**

tilt [tɪlt] *vt* pencher, incliner ▷ *vi* pencher, être incliné(e)

timber ['tɪmbə'] *n* (*material*) bois *m* de construction

time [taɪm] *n* temps *m*; (*epoch: often pl*) époque *f*, temps; (*by clock*) heure *f*; (*moment*) moment *m*; (*occasion, also Math*) fois *f*; (*Mus*) mesure *f* ▷ *vt* (*race*) chronométrer; (*programme*) minuter; (*visit*) fixer; (*remark etc*) choisir le moment de; **a long ~** un long moment, longtemps; **four at a ~** quatre à la fois; **for the ~ being** pour le moment; **from ~ to ~** de temps en temps; **at ~s** parfois; **in ~** (*soon enough*) à temps; (*after some time*) avec le temps, à la longue; (*Mus*) en mesure; **in a week's ~** dans une semaine; **in no ~** en un rien de temps; **any ~** n'importe quand; **on ~** à l'heure; **5 ~s 5** 5 fois 5; **what ~ is it?** quelle heure est-il?; **what ~ is the museum/shop open?** à quelle heure ouvre le musée/magasin?; **to have a good ~** bien s'amuser; **time limit** *n* limite *f* de temps, délai *m*; **timely** *adj* opportun(e); **timer** *n* (*in kitchen*) compte-minutes *m inv*; (*Tech*) minuteur *m*; **time-share** *n* maison *f*/appartement *m* en multipropriété; **timetable** *n* (*Rail*) (indicateur *m*) horaire *m*; (*Scol*) emploi *m* du temps; **time zone** *n* fuseau *m* horaire

timid ['tɪmɪd] *adj* timide; (*easily scared*) peureux(-euse)

timing ['taɪmɪŋ] *n* (*Sport*) chronométrage *m*; **the ~ of his resignation** le moment choisi pour sa démission

tin [tɪn] *n* étain *m*; (*also*: **~ plate**) fer-blanc *m*; (*BRIT*: *can*) boîte *f* (de conserve); (*for baking*) moule *m* (à gâteau); (*for storage*) boîte *f*; **tinfoil** *n* papier *m* d'étain *or* d'aluminium

tingle ['tɪŋgl] *vi* picoter; (*person*) avoir des picotements

tinker ['tɪŋkər]: **tinker with** *vt fus* bricoler, rafistoler

tinned [tɪnd] *adj* (*BRIT*: *food*) en boîte, en conserve

tin opener [-'əupnər] *n* (*BRIT*) ouvre-boîte(s) *m*

tinsel ['tɪnsl] *n* guirlandes *fpl* de Noël (argentées)

tint [tɪnt] *n* teinte *f*; (*for hair*) shampooing colorant; **tinted** *adj*

(*hair*) teint(e); (*spectacles, glass*) teinté(e)

tiny ['taɪnɪ] *adj* minuscule

tip [tɪp] *n* (*end*) bout *m*; (*gratuity*) pourboire *m*; (*BRIT*: *for rubbish*) décharge *f*; (*advice*) tuyau *m* ▷ *vt* (*waiter*) donner un pourboire à; (*tilt*) incliner; (*overturn*: *also*: **~ over**) renverser; (*empty*: *also*: **~ out**) déverser; **how much should I ~?** combien de pourboire est-ce qu'il faut laisser?; **tip off** *vt* prévenir, avertir

tiptoe ['tɪptəu] *n*: **on ~** sur la pointe des pieds

tire ['taɪər] *n* (*US*) = **tyre** ▷ *vt* fatiguer ▷ *vi* se fatiguer; **tired** *adj* fatigué(e); **to be tired of** en avoir assez de, être las (lasse) de; **tire pressure** (*US*) *n* = **tyre pressure**; **tiring** *adj* fatigant(e)

tissue ['tɪʃuː] *n* tissu *m*; (*paper handkerchief*) mouchoir *m* en papier, kleenex® *m*; **tissue paper** *n* papier *m* de soie

tit [tɪt] *n* (*bird*) mésange *f*; **to give ~ for tat** rendre coup pour coup

title ['taɪtl] *n* titre *m*

T-junction ['tiː'dʒʌŋkʃən] *n* croisement *m* en T

TM *n abbr* = **trademark**

 KEYWORD

to [tuː, tə] *prep* (*with noun/pronoun*)
1 (*direction*) à; (: *towards*) vers; envers; **to go to France/Portugal/London/school** aller en France/au Portugal/à Londres/à l'école; **to go to Claude's/the doctor's** aller chez Claude/le docteur; **the road to Edinburgh** la route d'Édimbourg
2 (*as far as*) (jusqu')à; **to count to 10** compter jusqu'à 10; **from 40 to 50 people** de 40 à 50 personnes
3 (*with expressions of time*): **a quarter to 5** 5 heures moins le quart; **it's twenty to 3** il est 3 heures moins vingt

t

4 (*for, of*) de; **the key to the front door** la clé de la porte d'entrée; **a letter to his wife** une lettre (adressée) à sa femme

5 (*expressing indirect object*) à; **to give sth to sb** donner qch à qn; **to talk to sb** parler à qn; **to be a danger to sb** être dangereux(-euse) pour qn

6 (*in relation to*) à; **3 goals to 2** 3 (buts) à 2; **30 miles to the gallon** ≈ 9,4 litres aux cent (km)

7 (*purpose, result*): **to come to sb's aid** venir au secours de qn, porter secours à qn; **to sentence sb to death** condamner qn à mort; **to my surprise** à ma grande surprise

▶ *prep* (*with vb*) **1** (*simple infinitive*): **to go/eat** aller/manger

2 (*following another vb*): **to want/ try/start to do** vouloir/essayer de/ commencer à faire

3 (*with vb omitted*): **I don't want to** je ne veux pas

4 (*purpose, result*) pour; **I did it to help you** je l'ai fait pour vous aider

5 (*equivalent to relative clause*): **I have things to do** j'ai des choses à faire; **the main thing is to try** l'important est d'essayer

6 (*after adjective etc*): **ready to go** prêt(e) à partir; **too old/young to ...** trop vieux/jeune pour ...

▶ *adv*: **push/pull the door to** tirez/ poussez la porte

toad [təud] *n* crapaud *m*; **toadstool** *n* champignon (vénéneux)

toast [təust] *n* (*Culin*) pain grillé, toast *m*; (*drink, speech*) toast *m* ▷ *vt* (*Culin*) faire griller; (*drink to*) porter un toast à; **toaster** *n* grille-pain *m inv*

tobacco [tə'bækəu] *n* tabac *m*

toboggan [tə'bɔgən] *n* toboggan *m*; (*child's*) luge *f*

today [tə'deɪ] *adv, n* (*also fig*) aujourd'hui (*m*)

toddler ['tɔdlə²] *n* enfant *m/f* qui commence à marcher, bambin *m*

toe [təu] *n* doigt *m* de pied, orteil *m*; (*of shoe*) bout *m* ▷ *vt*: **to ~ the line** (*fig*) obéir, se conformer; **toenail** *n* ongle *m* de l'orteil

toffee ['tɔfɪ] *n* caramel *m*

together [tə'gɛðə²] *adv* ensemble; (*at same time*) en même temps; **~ with** *prep* avec

toilet ['tɔɪlət] *n* (*BRIT: lavatory*) toilettes *fpl*, cabinets *mpl*; **to go to the ~** aller aux toilettes; **where's the ~?** où sont les toilettes?; **toilet bag** *n* (*BRIT*) nécessaire *m* de toilette; **toilet paper** *n* papier *m* hygiénique; **toiletries** *npl* articles *mpl* de toilette; **toilet roll** *n* rouleau *m* de papier hygiénique

token ['təukən] *n* (*sign*) marque *f*, témoignage *m*; (*metal disc*) jeton *m* ▷ *adj* (*fee, strike*) symbolique; **book/ record ~** (*BRIT*) chèque-livre/ -disque *m*

Tokyo ['təukjəu] *n* Tokyo

told [təuld] *pt, pp of* **tell**

tolerant ['tɔlərnt] *adj*: **~ (of)** tolérant(e) (à l'égard de)

tolerate ['tɔləreɪt] *vt* supporter

toll [təul] *n* (*tax, charge*) péage *m* ▷ *vi* (*bell*) sonner; **the accident ~ on the roads** le nombre des victimes de la route; **toll call** *n* (*US Tel*) appel *m* (à) longue distance; **toll-free** *adj* (*US*) gratuit(e) ▷ *adv* gratuitement

tomato [tə'mɑːtəu] (*pl* **tomatoes**) *n* tomate *f*; **tomato sauce** *n* sauce *f* tomate

tomb [tuːm] *n* tombe *f*; **tombstone** *n* pierre tombale

tomorrow [tə'mɔrəu] *adv, n* (*also fig*) demain (*m*); **the day after ~** après-demain; **a week ~** demain en huit; **~ morning** demain matin

ton [tʌn] *n* tonne *f* (*Brit: = 1016 kg; US = 907 kg; metric = 1000 kg*); **~s of** (*inf*) des tas de

tone [təun] *n* ton *m*; (*of radio, BRIT Tel*) tonalité *f* ▷ *vi* (*also*: **~ in**) s'harmoniser; **tone down** *vt* (*colour, criticism*) adoucir

tongs [tɒŋz] *npl* pinces *fpl*; (*for coal*) pincettes *fpl*; (*for hair*) fer *m* à friser

tongue [tʌŋ] *n* langue *f*; **~ in cheek** *adv* ironiquement

tonic ['tɒnɪk] *n* (*Med*) tonique *m*; (*also:* **~ water**) Schweppes® *m*

tonight [tə'naɪt] *adv, n* cette nuit; (*this evening*) ce soir

tonne [tʌn] *n* (BRIT: *metric ton*) tonne *f*

tonsil ['tɒnsl] *n* amygdale *f*; **tonsillitis** [tɒnsɪ'laɪtɪs] *n*: **to have tonsillitis** avoir une angine *or* une amygdalite

too [tuː] *adv* (*excessively*) trop; (*also*) aussi; **~ much** (*as adv*) trop; (*as adj*) trop de; **~ many** *adj* trop de

took [tʊk] *pt of* **take**

tool [tuːl] *n* outil *m*; **tool box** *n* boîte *f* à outils; **tool kit** *n* trousse *f* à outils

tooth (*pl* **teeth**) [tuːθ, tiːθ] *n* (*Anat, Tech*) dent *f*; **to brush one's teeth** se laver les dents; **toothache** *n* mal *m* de dents; **to have toothache** avoir mal aux dents; **toothbrush** *n* brosse *f* à dents; **toothpaste** *n* (*pâte f*) dentifrice *m*; **toothpick** *n* cure-dent *m*

top [tɒp] *n* (*of mountain, head*) sommet *m*; (*of page, ladder*) haut *m*; (*of box, cupboard, table*) dessus *m*; (*lid: of box, jar*) couvercle *m*; (*: of bottle*) bouchon *m*; (*toy*) toupie *f*; (*Dress: blouse etc*) haut *m*; (*: of pyjamas*) veste *f* ▷ *adj* du haut; (*in rank*) premier(-ière); (*best*) meilleur(e) ▷ *vt* (*exceed*) dépasser; (*be first in*) être en tête de; **from ~ to bottom** de fond en comble; **on ~ of** sur; (*in addition to*) en plus de; **over the ~** (*inf*) (*behaviour etc*) qui dépasse les limites; **top up**, (US) **top off** *vt* (*bottle*) remplir; (*salary*) compléter; **to ~ up one's mobile (phone)** recharger son compte; **top floor** *n* dernier étage; **top hat** *n* haut-de-forme *m*

topic ['tɒpɪk] *n* sujet *m*, thème *m*; **topical** *adj* d'actualité

topless ['tɒplɪs] *adj* (*bather etc*) aux seins nus

topping ['tɒpɪŋ] *n* (*Culin*) couche de crème, fromage etc qui recouvre un plat

topple ['tɒpl] *vt* renverser, faire tomber ▷ *vi* basculer; tomber

top-up ['tɒpʌp] *n* (*for mobile phone*) recharge *f*, minutes *fpl*; **top-up card** *n* (*for mobile phone*) recharge *f*

torch [tɔːtʃ] *n* torche *f*; (BRIT: *electric*) lampe *f* de poche

tore [tɔːʳ] *pt of* **tear²**

torment *n* ['tɔːmɛnt] tourment *m* ▷ *vt* [tɔː'mɛnt] tourmenter; (*fig: annoy*) agacer

torn [tɔːn] *pp of* **tear²**

tornado [tɔː'neɪdəʊ] (*pl* **tornadoes**) *n* tornade *f*

torpedo [tɔː'piːdəʊ] (*pl* **torpedoes**) *n* torpille *f*

torrent ['tɒrnt] *n* torrent *m*; **torrential** [tɒ'rɛnʃl] *adj* torrentiel(le)

tortoise ['tɔːtəs] *n* tortue *f*

torture ['tɔːtʃəʳ] *n* torture *f* ▷ *vt* torturer

Tory ['tɔːrɪ] *adj, n* (BRIT *Pol*) tory *m/f*, conservateur(-trice)

toss [tɒs] *vt* lancer, jeter; (BRIT: *pancake*) faire sauter; (*head*) rejeter en arrière ▷ *vi*: **to ~ up for sth** (BRIT) jouer qch à pile ou face; **to ~ a coin** jouer à pile ou face; **to ~ and turn** (*in bed*) se tourner et se retourner

total ['təʊtl] *adj* total(e) ▷ *n* total *m* ▷ *vt* (*add up*) faire le total de, additionner; (*amount to*) s'élever à

totalitarian [təʊtælɪ'tɛərɪən] *adj* totalitaire

totally ['təʊtəlɪ] *adv* totalement

touch [tʌtʃ] *n* contact *m*, toucher *m*; (*sense, skill: of pianist etc*) toucher ▷ *vt* (*gen*) toucher; (*tamper with*) toucher à; **a ~ of** (*fig*) un petit peu de; une touche de; **to get in ~ with** prendre contact avec; **to lose ~** (*friends*) se perdre de vue; **touch down** *vi* (*Aviat*) atterrir; (*on sea*) amerrir; **touchdown** *n* (*Aviat*) atterrissage *m*; (*on sea*) amerrissage *m*; (US *Football*) essai *m*; **touched** *adj* (*moved*) touché(e); **touching**

t

adj touchant(e), attendrissant(e);
touchline n (*Sport*) (ligne f de) touche
f; **touch-sensitive** *adj* (*keypad*) à
effleurement; (*screen*) tactile

tough [tʌf] *adj* dur(e); (*resistant*)
résistant(e), solide; (*meat*) dur,
coriace; (*firm*) inflexible; (*task,
problem, situation*) difficile

tour ['tuəʳ] n voyage m; (*also:*
package ~) voyage organisé; (*of
town, museum*) tour m, visite f; (*by
band*) tournée f ▷ vt visiter; **tour
guide** n (*person*) guide m/f

tourism ['tuərɪzm] n tourisme m

tourist ['tuərɪst] n touriste m/f ▷ cpd
touristique; **tourist office** n syndicat
m d'initiative

tournament ['tuənəmənt] n
tournoi m

tour operator n (*BRIT*) organisateur
m de voyages, tour-opérateur m

tow [təu] vt remorquer; (*caravan,
trailer*) tracter; **"on ~"**, (*US*) **"in ~"**
(*Aut*) "véhicule en remorque"; **tow
away** vt (*subj: police*) emmener à
la fourrière; (: *breakdown service*)
remorquer

toward(s) [tə'wɔ:d(z)] prep vers;
(*of attitude*) envers, à l'égard de; (*of
purpose*) pour

towel ['tauəl] n serviette f (de
toilette); **towelling** n (*fabric*) tissu-
éponge m

tower ['tauəʳ] n tour f; **tower block** n
(*BRIT*) tour f (d'habitation)

town [taun] n ville f; **to go to ~** aller
en ville; (*fig*) y mettre le paquet;
town centre n (*BRIT*) centre m de
la ville, centre-ville m; **town hall** n
≈ mairie f

tow truck n (*US*) dépanneuse f

toxic ['tɔksɪk] *adj* toxique

toy [tɔɪ] n jouet m; **toy with** vt fus
jouer avec; (*idea*) caresser; **toyshop** n
magasin m de jouets

trace [treɪs] n trace f ▷ vt (*draw*)
tracer, dessiner; (*follow*) suivre la
trace de; (*locate*) retrouver

tracing paper ['treɪsɪŋ-] n papier-
calque m

track [træk] n (*mark*) trace f; (*path:
gen*) chemin m, piste f; (: *of bullet etc*)
trajectoire f; (: *of suspect, animal*)
piste f; (*Rail*) voie ferrée, rails mpl;
(*Comput, Sport*) piste; (*on CD*) piste;
(*on record*) plage f ▷ vt suivre la trace or
la piste de; **to keep ~ of** suivre; **track
down** vt (*prey*) trouver et capturer;
(*sth lost*) finir par retrouver; **tracksuit**
n survêtement m

tractor ['træktəʳ] n tracteur m

trade [treɪd] n commerce m; (*skill,
job*) métier m ▷ vi faire du commerce
▷ vt (*exchange*): **to ~ sth (for sth)**
échanger qch (contre qch); **to ~
with/in** faire du commerce avec/
le commerce de; **trade in** vt (*old
car etc*) faire reprendre; **trademark**
n marque f de fabrique; **trader** n
commerçant(e), négociant(e);
tradesman (*irreg*) n (*shopkeeper*)
commerçant m; **trade union** n
syndicat m

trading ['treɪdɪŋ] n affaires fpl,
commerce m

tradition [trə'dɪʃən] n tradition f;
traditional *adj* traditionnel(le)

traffic ['træfɪk] n trafic m; (*cars*)
circulation f ▷ vi: **to ~ in** (*pej: liquor,
drugs*) faire le trafic de; **traffic circle**
n (*US*) rond-point m; **traffic island** n
refuge m (pour piétons); **traffic jam**
n embouteillage m; **traffic lights** npl
feux mpl (de signalisation); **traffic
warden** n contractuel(le)

tragedy ['trædʒədɪ] n tragédie f

tragic ['trædʒɪk] *adj* tragique

trail [treɪl] n (*tracks*) trace f, piste
f; (*path*) chemin m, piste; (*of smoke
etc*) traînée f ▷ vt (*drag*) traîner, tirer;
(*follow*) suivre ▷ vi traîner; (*in game,
contest*) être en retard; **trailer** n (*Aut*)
remorque f; (*US: caravan*) caravane f;
(*Cine*) bande-annonce f

train [treɪn] n train m; (*in underground*)
rame f; (*of dress*) traîne f; (*BRIT: series*):

~ **of events** série f d'événements
▷ vt (apprentice, doctor etc) former;
(Sport) entraîner; (dog) dresser;
(memory) exercer; (point: gun etc):
to ~ sth on braquer qch sur ▷ vi
recevoir sa formation; (Sport)
s'entraîner; **one's ~ of thought** le
fil de sa pensée; **what time does
the ~ from Paris get in?** à quelle
heure arrive le train de Paris?; **is this
the ~ for ...?** c'est bien le train pour
...?; **trainee** [treɪ'ni:] n stagiaire
m/f; (in trade) apprenti(e); **trainer** n
(Sport) entraîneur(-euse); (of dogs etc)
dresseur(-euse); **trainers** npl (shoes)
chaussures fpl de sport; **training** n
formation f; (Sport) entraînement m;
(of dog etc) dressage m; **in training**
(Sport) à l'entraînement; (fit) en
forme; **training course** n cours m de
formation professionnelle; **training
shoes** npl chaussures fpl de sport
trait [treɪt] n trait m (de caractère)
traitor ['treɪtər] n traître m
tram [træm] n (BRIT: also: **~car**)
tram(way) m
tramp [træmp] n (person)
vagabond(e), clochard(e); (inf, pej:
woman): **to be a ~** être coureuse
trample ['træmpl] vt: **to ~
(underfoot)** piétiner
trampoline ['træmpəli:n] n
trampoline m
tranquil ['træŋkwɪl] adj tranquille;
tranquillizer, (US) tranquilizer n
(Med) tranquillisant m
transaction [træn'zækʃən] n
transaction f
transatlantic ['trænzət'læntɪk] adj
transatlantique
transcript ['trænskrɪpt] n
transcription f (texte)
transfer n ['trænsfər] (gen, also Sport)
transfert m; (Pol: of power) passation
f; (of money) virement m; (picture,
design) décalcomanie f (: stick-on)
autocollant m ▷ vt [træns'fə:r]
transférer; passer; virer; **to ~ the**

charges (BRIT Tel) téléphoner en
P.C.V.
transform [træns'fɔ:m] vt
transformer; **transformation** n
transformation f
transfusion [træns'fju:ʒən] n
transfusion f
transit ['trænzɪt] n: **in ~** en transit
transition [træn'zɪʃən] n transition f
transitive ['trænzɪtɪv] adj (Ling)
transitif(-ive)
translate [trænz'leɪt] vt: **to ~
(from/into)** traduire (du/en); **can
you ~ this for me?** pouvez-vous
me traduire ceci?; **translation**
[trænz'leɪʃən] n traduction f; (Scol: as
opposed to prose) version f; **translator**
n traducteur(-trice)
transmission [trænz'mɪʃən] n
transmission f
transmit [trænz'mɪt] vt
transmettre; (Radio, TV) émettre;
transmitter n émetteur m
transparent [træns'pærnt] adj
transparent(e)
transplant ['trænspla:nt] n (Med)
transplantation f
transport n ['trænspɔ:t] transport
m ▷ vt [træns'pɔ:t] transporter;
transportation [trænspɔ:'teɪʃən] n
(moyen m de) transport m
transvestite [trænz'vestaɪt] n
travesti(e)
trap [træp] n (snare, trick) piège m;
(carriage) cabriolet m ▷ vt prendre au
piège; (confine) coincer
trash [træʃ] n (inf: pej: goods)
camelote f; (: nonsense) sottises fpl;
(US: rubbish) ordures fpl; **trash can** n
(US) poubelle f
trauma ['trɔ:mə] n traumatisme
m; **traumatic** [trɔ:'mætɪk] adj
traumatisant(e)
travel ['trævl] n voyage(s) m(pl) ▷ vi
voyager; (news, sound) se propager ▷ vt
(distance) parcourir; **travel agency** n
agence f de voyages; **travel agent** n
agent m de voyages; **travel insurance**

n assurance-voyage *f*; **traveller**, (*US*) **traveler** *n* voyageur(-euse); **traveller's cheque**, (*US*) **traveler's check** *n* chèque *m* de voyage; **travelling**, (*US*) **traveling** *n* voyage(s) *m*(*pl*); **travel-sick** *adj*: **to get travel-sick** avoir le mal de la route (*or* de mer *or* de l'air); **travel sickness** *n* mal *m* de la route (*or* de mer *or* de l'air)

tray [treɪ] *n* (*for carrying*) plateau *m*; (*on desk*) corbeille *f*

treacherous ['trɛtʃərəs] *adj* traître(sse); (*ground, tide*) dont il faut se méfier

treacle ['triːkl] *n* mélasse *f*

tread [trɛd] *n* (*step*) pas *m*; (*sound*) bruit *m* de pas; (*of tyre*) chape *f*, bande *f* de roulement ▷ *vi* (*pt* **trod**, *pp* **trodden**) marcher; **tread on** *vt fus* marcher sur

treasure ['trɛʒər] *n* trésor *m* ▷ *vt* (*value*) tenir beaucoup à; **treasurer** *n* trésorier(-ière)

treasury ['trɛʒərɪ] *n*: **the T~**, (*US*) **the T~ Department** ≈ le ministère des Finances

treat [triːt] *n* petit cadeau, petite surprise ▷ *vt* traiter; **to ~ sb to sth** offrir qch à qn; **treatment** *n* traitement *m*

treaty ['triːtɪ] *n* traité *m*

treble ['trɛbl] *adj* triple ▷ *vt*, *vi* tripler

tree [triː] *n* arbre *m*

trek [trɛk] *n* (*long walk*) randonnée *f*; (*tiring walk*) longue marche, trotte *f*

tremble ['trɛmbl] *vi* trembler

tremendous [trɪ'mɛndəs] *adj* (*enormous*) énorme; (*excellent*) formidable, fantastique

trench [trɛntʃ] *n* tranchée *f*

trend [trɛnd] *n* (*tendency*) tendance *f*; (*of events*) cours *m*; (*fashion*) mode *f*; **trendy** *adj* (*idea, person*) dans le vent; (*clothes*) dernier cri *inv*

trespass ['trɛspəs] *vi*: **to ~ on** s'introduire sans permission dans; **"no ~ing"** "propriété privée", "défense d'entrer"

trial ['traɪəl] *n* (*Law*) procès *m*, jugement *m*; (*test: of machine etc*) essai *m*; **trials** *npl* (*unpleasant experiences*) épreuves *fpl*; **trial period** *n* période *f* d'essai

triangle ['traɪæŋgl] *n* (*Math, Mus*) triangle *m*

triangular [traɪ'æŋgjʊlər] *adj* triangulaire

tribe [traɪb] *n* tribu *f*

tribunal [traɪ'bjuːnl] *n* tribunal *m*

tribute ['trɪbjuːt] *n* tribut *m*, hommage *m*; **to pay ~ to** rendre hommage à

trick [trɪk] *n* (*magic*) tour *m*; (*joke, prank*) tour, farce *f*; (*skill, knack*) astuce *f*; (*Cards*) levée *f* ▷ *vt* attraper, rouler; **to play a ~ on sb** jouer un tour à qn; **that should do the ~** (*inf*) ça devrait faire l'affaire

trickle ['trɪkl] *n* (*of water etc*) filet *m* ▷ *vi* couler en un filet *or* goutte à goutte

tricky ['trɪkɪ] *adj* difficile, délicat(e)

tricycle ['traɪsɪkl] *n* tricycle *m*

trifle ['traɪfl] *n* bagatelle *f*; (*Culin*) ≈ diplomate *m* ▷ *adv*: **a ~ long** un peu long

trigger ['trɪgər] *n* (*of gun*) gâchette *f*

trim [trɪm] *adj* (*house, garden*) bien tenu(e); (*figure*) svelte ▷ *n* (*haircut etc*) légère coupe; (*on car*) garnitures *fpl* ▷ *vt* (*cut*) couper légèrement; (*Naut: a sail*) gréer; (*decorate*): **to ~ (with)** décorer (de)

trio ['triːəu] *n* trio *m*

trip [trɪp] *n* voyage *m*; (*excursion*) excursion *f*; (*stumble*) faux pas ▷ *vi* faire un faux pas, trébucher; **trip up** *vi* trébucher ▷ *vt* faire un croc-en-jambe à

triple ['trɪpl] *adj* triple

triplets ['trɪplɪts] *npl* triplés(-ées)

tripod ['traɪpɔd] *n* trépied *m*

triumph ['traɪʌmf] *n* triomphe *m* ▷ *vi*: **to ~ (over)** triompher (de); **triumphant** [traɪ'ʌmfənt] *adj* triomphant(e)

trivial ['trɪvɪəl] *adj* insignifiant(e); (*commonplace*) banal(e)

trod [trɒd] *pt of* **tread**

trodden ['trɒdn] *pp of* **tread**

trolley ['trɒlɪ] *n* chariot *m*

trombone [trɒm'bəun] *n* trombone *m*

troop [truːp] *n* bande *f*, groupe *m*; **troops** *npl* (*Mil*) troupes *fpl* (: *men*) hommes *mpl*, soldats *mpl*

trophy ['trəufɪ] *n* trophée *m*

tropical ['trɒpɪkl] *adj* tropical(e)

trot [trɒt] *n* trot *m* ▷ *vi* trotter; **on the ~** (*BRIT fig*) d'affilée

trouble ['trʌbl] *n* difficulté(s) *f(pl)*, problème(s) *m(pl)*; (*worry*) ennuis *mpl*, soucis *mpl*; (*bother*, *effort*) peine *f*; (*Pol*) conflit(s) *m(pl)*, troubles *mpl*; (*Med*): **stomach** *etc* ~ troubles gastriques *etc* ▷ *vt* (*disturb*) déranger, gêner; (*worry*) inquiéter ▷ *vi*: **to ~ to do** prendre la peine de faire; **troubles** *npl* (*Pol etc*) troubles; (*personal*) ennuis, soucis; **to be in** ~ avoir des ennuis; (*ship*, *climber etc*) être en difficulté; **to have ~ doing sth** avoir du mal à faire qch; **it's no ~!** je vous en prie!; **the ~ is ...** le problème, c'est que ...; **what's the ~?** qu'est-ce qui ne va pas?; **troubled** *adj* (*person*) inquiet(-ète); (*times*, *life*) agité(e); **troublemaker** *n* élément perturbateur, fauteur de troubles; **troublesome** *adj* (*child*) fatigant(e), difficile; (*cough*) gênant(e)

trough [trɒf] *n* (*also*: **drinking ~**) abreuvoir *m*; (*also*: **feeding ~**) auge *f*; (*depression*) creux *m*

trousers ['trauzəz] *npl* pantalon *m*; **short ~** (*BRIT*) culottes courtes

trout [traut] *n* (*pl inv*) truite *f*

trowel ['trauəl] *n* truelle *f*; (*garden tool*) déplantoir *m*

truant ['truənt] *n*: **to play ~** (*BRIT*) faire l'école buissonnière

truce [truːs] *n* trêve *f*

truck [trʌk] *n* camion *m*; (*Rail*) wagon *m* à plate-forme; **truck driver** *n* camionneur *m*

true [truː] *adj* vrai(e); (*accurate*) exact(e); (*genuine*) vrai, véritable; (*faithful*) fidèle; **to come ~** se réaliser

truly ['truːlɪ] *adv* vraiment, réellement; (*truthfully*) sans mentir; **yours ~** (*in letter*) je vous prie d'agréer, Monsieur (*or* Madame *etc*), l'expression de mes sentiments respectueux

trumpet ['trʌmpɪt] *n* trompette *f*

trunk [trʌŋk] *n* (*of tree*, *person*) tronc *m*; (*of elephant*) trompe *f*; (*case*) malle *f*; (*US Aut*) coffre *m*; **trunks** *npl* (*also*: **swimming ~s**) maillot *m or* slip *m* de bain

trust [trʌst] *n* confiance *f*; (*responsibility*): **to place sth in sb's ~** confier la responsabilité de qch à qn; (*Law*) fidéicommis *m* ▷ *vt* (*rely on*) avoir confiance en; (*entrust*): **to ~ sth to sb** confier qch à qn; (*hope*): **to ~ (that)** espérer (que); **to take sth on ~** accepter qch les yeux fermés; **trusted** *adj* en qui l'on a confiance; **trustworthy** *adj* digne de confiance

truth [truːθ, truːðz] *n* vérité *f*; **truthful** *adj* (*person*) qui dit la vérité; (*answer*) sincère

try [traɪ] *n* essai *m*, tentative *f*; (*Rugby*) essai ▷ *vt* (*attempt*) essayer, tenter; (*test: sth new: also*: ~ **out**) essayer, tester; (*Law: person*) juger; (*strain*) éprouver ▷ *vi* essayer; **to ~ to do** essayer de faire; (*seek*) chercher à faire; **try on** *vt* (*clothes*) essayer; **trying** *adj* pénible

T-shirt ['tiːʃəːt] *n* tee-shirt *m*

tub [tʌb] *n* cuve *f*; (*for washing clothes*) baquet *m*; (*bath*) baignoire *f*

tube [tjuːb] *n* tube *m*; (*BRIT*: *underground*) métro *m*; (*for tyre*) chambre *f* à air

tuberculosis [tjubəː'kjuːləusɪs] *n* tuberculose *f*

tube station *n* (*BRIT*) station *f* de métro

tuck [tʌk] *vt* (*put*) mettre; **tuck away** *vt* cacher, ranger; (*money*) mettre de côté; (*building*): **to be ~ed away** être caché(e); **tuck in** vt rentrer; (*child*) border ▷ vi (*eat*) manger de bon appétit; attaquer le repas

tucker ['tʌkə'] n (AUST, NZ inf) bouffe f (inf)

tuck shop n (BRIT Scol) boutique f à provisions

Tuesday ['tjuːzdɪ] n mardi m

tug [tʌg] n (*ship*) remorqueur m ▷ vt tirer (sur)

tuition [tjuːˈɪʃən] n (BRIT: *lessons*) leçons fpl; (: *private*) cours particuliers; (US: *fees*) frais mpl de scolarité

tulip ['tjuːlɪp] n tulipe f

tumble ['tʌmbl] n (*fall*) chute f, culbute f ▷ vi tomber, dégringoler; **to ~ to sth** (inf) réaliser qch; **tumble dryer** n (BRIT) séchoir m (à linge) à air chaud

tumbler ['tʌmblə'] n verre (droit), gobelet m

tummy ['tʌmɪ] n (inf) ventre m

tumour, (US) **tumor** ['tjuːmə'] n tumeur f

tuna ['tjuːnə] n (pl inv: also: **~ fish**) thon m

tune [tjuːn] n (*melody*) air m ▷ vt (*Mus*) accorder; (*Radio, TV, Aut*) régler, mettre au point; **to be in/ out of ~** (*instrument*) être accordé/ désaccordé; (*singer*) chanter juste/ faux; **tune in** vi (*Radio, TV*): **to ~ in (to)** se mettre à l'écoute (de); **tune up** vi (*musician*) accorder son instrument

tunic ['tjuːnɪk] n tunique f

Tunis ['tjuːnɪs] n Tunis

Tunisia [tjuːˈnɪzɪə] n Tunisie f

Tunisian [tjuːˈnɪzɪən] adj tunisien(ne) ▷ n Tunisien(ne)

tunnel ['tʌnl] n tunnel m; (*in mine*) galerie f ▷ vi creuser un tunnel (or une galerie)

turbulence ['təːbjuləns] n (Aviat) turbulence f

turf [təːf] n gazon m; (*clod*) motte f (de gazon) ▷ vt gazonner

Turk [təːk] n Turc (Turque)

Turkey ['təːkɪ] n Turquie f

turkey ['təːkɪ] n dindon m, dinde f

Turkish ['təːkɪʃ] adj turc (turque) ▷ n (Ling) turc m

turmoil ['təːmɔɪl] n trouble m, bouleversement m

turn [təːn] n tour m; (*in road*) tournant m; (*tendency: of mind, events*) tournure f; (*performance*) numéro m; (*Med*) crise f, attaque f ▷ vt tourner; (*collar, steak*) retourner; (*age*) atteindre; (*change*): **to ~ sth into** changer qch en ▷ vi (*object, wind, milk*) tourner; (*person: look back*) se (re)tourner; (*reverse direction*) faire demi-tour; (*become*) devenir; **to ~ into** se changer en, se transformer en; **a good ~** un service; **it gave me quite a ~** ça m'a fait un coup; **"no left ~"** (*Aut*) "défense de tourner à gauche"; **~ left/right at the next junction** tournez à gauche/droite au prochain carrefour; **it's your ~** c'est (à) votre tour; **in ~** à son tour; à tour de rôle; **to take ~s** se relayer; **turn around** vi (*person*) se retourner ▷ vt (*object*) tourner; **turn away** vi se détourner, tourner la tête ▷ vt (*reject: person*) renvoyer; (: *business*) refuser; **turn back** vi revenir, faire demi-tour; **turn down** vt (*refuse*) rejeter, refuser; (*reduce*) baisser; (*fold*) rabattre; **turn in** vi (inf: *go to bed*) aller se coucher ▷ vt (*fold*) rentrer; **turn off** vi (*from road*) tourner ▷ vt (*light, radio etc*) éteindre; (*tap*) fermer; (*engine*) arrêter; **I can't ~ the heating off** je n'arrive pas à éteindre le chauffage; **turn on** vt (*light, radio etc*) allumer; (*tap*) ouvrir; (*engine*) mettre en marche; **I can't ~ the heating on** je n'arrive pas à allumer le chauffage; **turn out** vt (*light, gas*) éteindre; (*produce*) produire ▷ vi (*voters, troops*) sortir; **to ~ out to be ...** s'avérer ..., se révéler ...; **turn over** vi (*person*) se retourner ▷ vt (*object*) retourner; (*page*) tourner; **turn round** vi faire demi-tour;

(*rotate*) tourner; **turn to** *vt fus*: **to ~ to sb** s'adresser à qn; **turn up** *vi* (*person*) arriver, se pointer (*inf*); (*lost object*) être retrouvé(e) ▷ *vt* (*collar*) remonter; (*radio, heater*) mettre plus fort; **turning** *n* (*in road*) tournant *m*; **turning point** *n* (*fig*) tournant *m*, moment décisif

turnip ['tə:nɪp] *n* navet *m*

turn: turnout *n* (*of voters*) taux *m* de participation; **turnover** *n* (*Comm: amount of money*) chiffre *m* d'affaires; (*: of goods*) roulement *m*; (*of staff*) renouvellement *m*, changement *m*; **turnstile** *n* tourniquet *m* (*d'entrée*); **turn-up** *n* (*BRIT: on trousers*) revers *m*

turquoise ['tə:kwɔɪz] *n* (*stone*) turquoise *f* ▷ *adj* turquoise *inv*

turtle ['tə:tl] *n* tortue marine; **turtleneck (sweater)** *n* pullover *m* à col montant

tusk [tʌsk] *n* défense *f* (*d'éléphant*)

tutor ['tju:tə'] *n* (*BRIT Scol: in college*) directeur(-trice) d'études; (*private teacher*) précepteur(-trice); **tutorial** [tju:'tɔ:rɪəl] *n* (*Scol*) (séance *f* de) travaux *mpl* pratiques

tuxedo [tʌk'si:dəu] *n* (*US*) smoking *m*

TV [ti:'vi:] *n abbr* (= *television*) télé *f*, TV *f*

tweed [twi:d] *n* tweed *m*

tweet [twi:t] *n* (*on Twitter*) tweet *m* ▷ *vt*, *vi* tweeter

tweezers ['twi:zəz] *npl* pince *f* à épiler

twelfth [twɛlfθ] *num* douzième

twelve [twɛlv] *num* douze; **at ~ (o'clock)** à midi; (*midnight*) à minuit

twentieth ['twɛntɪɪθ] *num* vingtième

twenty ['twɛntɪ] *num* vingt; **in ~ fourteen** en deux mille quatorze

twice [twaɪs] *adv* deux fois; **~ as much** deux fois plus

twig [twɪg] *n* brindille *f* ▷ *vt*, *vi* (*inf*) piger

twilight ['twaɪlaɪt] *n* crépuscule *m*

twin [twɪn] *adj*, *n* jumeau(-elle) ▷ *vt* jumeler; **twin-bedded room** *n* = **twin room**; **twin beds** *npl* lits *mpl* jumeaux

twinkle ['twɪŋkl] *vi* scintiller; (*eyes*) pétiller

twin room *n* chambre *f* à deux lits

twist [twɪst] *n* torsion *f*, tour *m*; (*in wire, flex*) tortillon *m*; (*bend: in road*) tournant *m*; (*in story*) coup *m* de théâtre ▷ *vt* tordre; (*weave*) entortiller; (*roll around*) enrouler; (*fig*) déformer ▷ *vi* (*road, river*) serpenter; **to ~ one's ankle/wrist** (*Med*) se tordre la cheville/le poignet

twit [twɪt] *n* (*inf*) crétin(e)

twitch [twɪtʃ] *n* (*pull*) coup sec, saccade *f*; (*nervous*) tic *m* ▷ *vi* se convulser; avoir un tic

two [tu:] *num* deux; **to put ~ and ~ together** (*fig*) faire le rapprochement

type [taɪp] *n* (*category*) genre *m*, espèce *f*; (*model*) modèle *m*; (*example*) type *m*; (*Typ*) type, caractère *m* ▷ *vt* (*letter etc*) taper (à la machine); **typewriter** *n* machine *f* à écrire

typhoid ['taɪfɔɪd] *n* typhoïde *f*

typhoon [taɪ'fu:n] *n* typhon *m*

typical ['tɪpɪkl] *adj* typique, caractéristique; **typically** ['tɪpɪklɪ] *adv* (*as usual*) comme d'habitude; (*characteristically*) typiquement

typing ['taɪpɪŋ] *n* dactylo(graphie) *f*

typist ['taɪpɪst] *n* dactylo *m/f*

tyre, (*US*) **tire** ['taɪə'] *n* pneu *m*; **tyre pressure** *n* (*BRIT*) pression *f* (de gonflage)

t

U

UFO ['juːfəu] n abbr (= unidentified flying object) ovni m

Uganda [juːˈgændə] n Ouganda m

ugly ['ʌglɪ] adj laid(e), vilain(e); (fig) répugnant(e)

UHT adj abbr (= ultra-heat treated): ~ **milk** lait m UHT or longue conservation

UK n abbr = **United Kingdom**

ulcer ['ʌlsəʳ] n ulcère m; **mouth** ~ aphte f

ultimate ['ʌltɪmət] adj ultime, final(e); (authority) suprême; **ultimately** adv (at last) en fin de compte; (fundamentally) finalement; (eventually) par la suite

ultimatum (pl **ultimatums** or **ultimata**) [ʌltɪˈmeɪtəm, -tə] n ultimatum m

ultrasound ['ʌltrəsaund] n (Med) ultrason m

ultraviolet ['ʌltrəˈvaɪəlɪt] adj ultraviolet(te)

umbrella [ʌmˈbrɛlə] n parapluie m; (for sun) parasol m

umpire ['ʌmpaɪəʳ] n arbitre m; (Tennis) juge m de chaise

UN n abbr = **United Nations**

unable [ʌnˈeɪbl] adj: **to be ~ to** ne (pas) pouvoir, être dans l'impossibilité de; (not capable) être incapable de

unacceptable [ʌnəkˈsɛptəbl] adj (behaviour) inadmissible; (price, proposal) inacceptable

unanimous [juːˈnænɪməs] adj unanime

unarmed [ʌnˈɑːmd] adj (person) non armé(e); (combat) sans armes

unattended [ʌnəˈtɛndɪd] adj (car, child, luggage) sans surveillance

unattractive [ʌnəˈtræktɪv] adj peu attrayant(e); (character) peu sympathique

unavailable [ʌnəˈveɪləbl] adj (article, room, book) (qui n'est) pas disponible; (person) (qui n'est) pas libre

unavoidable [ʌnəˈvɔɪdəbl] adj inévitable

unaware [ʌnəˈwɛəʳ] adj: **to be ~ of** ignorer, ne pas savoir, être inconscient(e) de; **unawares** adv à l'improviste, au dépourvu

unbearable [ʌnˈbɛərəbl] adj insupportable

unbeatable [ʌnˈbiːtəbl] adj imbattable

unbelievable [ʌnbɪˈliːvəbl] adj incroyable

unborn [ʌnˈbɔːn] adj à naître

unbutton [ʌnˈbʌtn] vt déboutonner

uncalled-for [ʌnˈkɔːldfɔːʳ] adj déplacé(e), injustifié(e)

uncanny [ʌnˈkænɪ] adj étrange, troublant(e)

uncertain [ʌnˈsəːtn] adj incertain(e); (hesitant) hésitant(e); **uncertainty** n incertitude f, doutes mpl

unchanged [ʌnˈtʃeɪndʒd] adj inchangé(e)

uncle ['ʌŋkl] n oncle m

unclear [ʌnˈklɪə^r] *adj* (qui n'est) pas clair(e) *or* évident(e); **I'm still ~ about what I'm supposed to do** je ne sais pas encore exactement ce que je dois faire

uncomfortable [ʌnˈkʌmfətəbl] *adj* inconfortable, peu confortable; (*uneasy*) mal à l'aise, gêné(e); (*situation*) désagréable

uncommon [ʌnˈkɔmən] *adj* rare, singulier(-ière), peu commun(e)

unconditional [ʌnkənˈdɪʃənl] *adj* sans conditions

unconscious [ʌnˈkɔnʃəs] *adj* sans connaissance, évanoui(e); (*unaware*): **~ (of)** inconscient(e) (de) ⊳ *n*: **the ~** l'inconscient *m*

uncontrollable [ʌnkənˈtrəuləbl] *adj* (*child, dog*) indiscipliné(e); (*temper, laughter*) irrépressible

unconventional [ʌnkənˈvɛnʃənl] *adj* peu conventionnel(le)

uncover [ʌnˈkʌvə^r] *vt* découvrir

undecided [ʌndɪˈsaɪdɪd] *adj* indécis(e), irrésolu(e)

undeniable [ʌndɪˈnaɪəbl] *adj* indéniable, incontestable

under [ˈʌndə^r] *prep* sous; (*less than*) (de) moins de; au-dessous de; (*according to*) selon, en vertu de ⊳ *adv* au-dessous; en dessous; **~ there** là-dessous; **~ the circumstances** étant donné les circonstances; **~ repair** en (cours de) réparation; **undercover** *adj* secret(-ète), clandestin(e); **underdone** *adj* (*Culin*) saignant(e); (: *pej*) pas assez cuit(e); **underestimate** *vt* sous-estimer, mésestimer; **undergo** *vt* (*irreg: like* **go**) subir; (*treatment*) suivre; **undergraduate** *n* étudiant(e) (qui prépare la licence); **underground** *adj* souterrain(e); (*fig*) clandestin(e) ⊳ *n* (*BRIT: railway*) métro *m*; (*Pol*) clandestinité *f*; **undergrowth** *n* broussailles *fpl*, sous-bois *m*; **underline** *vt* souligner; **undermine** *vt* saper, miner; **underneath** [ʌndəˈniːθ] *adv* (en) dessous ⊳ *prep* sous, au-dessous de; **underpants** *npl* caleçon *m*, slip *m*; **underpass** *n* (*BRIT: for pedestrians*) passage souterrain; (: *for cars*) passage inférieur; **underprivileged** *adj* défavorisé(e); **underscore** *vt* souligner; **undershirt** *n* (*US*) tricot *m* de corps; **underskirt** *n* (*BRIT*) jupon *m*

understand [ʌndəˈstænd] *vt*, *vi* (*irreg: like* **stand**) comprendre; **I don't ~** je ne comprends pas; **understandable** *adj* compréhensible; **understanding** *adj* compréhensif(-ive) ⊳ *n* compréhension *f*; (*agreement*) accord *m*

understatement [ˈʌndəsteɪtmənt] *n*: **that's an ~** c'est (bien) peu dire, le terme est faible

understood [ʌndəˈstud] *pt*, *pp* *of* **understand** ⊳ *adj* entendu(e); (*implied*) sous-entendu(e)

undertake [ʌndəˈteɪk] *vt* (*irreg: like* **take**) (*job, task*) entreprendre; (*duty*) se charger de; **to ~ to do sth** s'engager à faire qch

undertaker [ˈʌndəteɪkə^r] *n* (*BRIT*) entrepreneur *m* des pompes funèbres, croque-mort *m*

undertaking [ˈʌndəteɪkɪŋ] *n* entreprise *f*; (*promise*) promesse *f*

under: underwater *adv* sous l'eau ⊳ *adj* sous-marin(e); **underway** *adj*: **to be underway** (*meeting, investigation*) être en cours; **underwear** *n* sous-vêtements *mpl*; (*women's only*) dessous *mpl*; **underwent** *pt of* **undergo**; **underworld** *n* (*of crime*) milieu *m*, pègre *f*

undesirable [ʌndɪˈzaɪərəbl] *adj* peu souhaitable; (*person, effect*) indésirable

undisputed [ˈʌndɪsˈpjuːtɪd] *adj* incontesté(e)

undo [ʌnˈduː] *vt* (*irreg: like* **do**) défaire

u

undone [ʌn'dʌn] *pp of* **undo** ▷ *adj*: **to come ~** se défaire

undoubtedly [ʌn'dautɪdlɪ] *adv* sans aucun doute

undress [ʌn'drɛs] *vi* se déshabiller

unearth [ʌn'ə:θ] *vt* déterrer; (*fig*) dénicher

uneasy [ʌn'i:zɪ] *adj* mal à l'aise, gêné(e); (*worried*) inquiet(-ète); (*feeling*) désagréable; (*peace, truce*) fragile

unemployed [ʌnɪm'plɔɪd] *adj* sans travail, au chômage ▷ *n*: **the ~** les chômeurs *mpl*

unemployment [ʌnɪm'plɔɪmənt] *n* chômage *m*; **unemployment benefit,** (*us*) **unemployment compensation** *n* allocation *f* de chômage

unequal [ʌn'i:kwəl] *adj* inégal(e)

uneven [ʌn'i:vn] *adj* inégal(e); (*quality, work*) irrégulier(-ière)

unexpected [ʌnɪk'spɛktɪd] *adj* inattendu(e), imprévu(e); **unexpectedly** *adv* (*succeed*) contre toute attente; (*arrive*) à l'improviste

unfair [ʌn'fɛəʳ] *adj*: **~ (to)** injuste (envers)

unfaithful [ʌn'feɪθful] *adj* infidèle

unfamiliar [ʌnfə'mɪlɪəʳ] *adj* étrange, inconnu(e); **to be ~ with sth** mal connaître qch

unfashionable [ʌn'fæʃnəbl] *adj* (*clothes*) démodé(e); (*place*) peu chic *inv*

unfasten [ʌn'fɑ:sn] *vt* défaire; (*belt, necklace*) détacher; (*open*) ouvrir

unfavourable, (*us*) **unfavorable** [ʌn'feɪvrəbl] *adj* défavorable

unfinished [ʌn'fɪnɪʃt] *adj* inachevé(e)

unfit [ʌn'fɪt] *adj* (*physically: ill*) en mauvaise santé; (*: out of condition*) pas en forme; (*incompetent*): **~ (for)** impropre (à); (*work, service*) inapte (à)

unfold [ʌn'fəuld] *vt* déplier ▷ *vi* se dérouler

unforgettable [ʌnfə'gɛtəbl] *adj* inoubliable

unfortunate [ʌn'fɔ:tʃnət] *adj* malheureux(-euse); (*event, remark*) malencontreux(-euse); **unfortunately** *adv* malheureusement

unfriend [ʌn'frɛnd] *vt* (*Internet*) supprimer de sa liste d'amis

unfriendly [ʌn'frɛndlɪ] *adj* peu aimable, froid(e)

unfurnished [ʌn'fə:nɪʃt] *adj* non meublé(e)

unhappiness [ʌn'hæpɪnɪs] *n* tristesse *f*, peine *f*

unhappy [ʌn'hæpɪ] *adj* triste, malheureux(-euse); (*unfortunate: remark etc*) malheureux(-euse); (*not pleased*): **~ with** mécontent(e) de, peu satisfait(e) de

unhealthy [ʌn'hɛlθɪ] *adj* (*gen*) malsain(e); (*person*) maladif(-ive)

unheard-of [ʌn'hə:dɔv] *adj* inouï(e), sans précédent

unhelpful [ʌn'hɛlpful] *adj* (*person*) peu serviable; (*advice*) peu utile

unhurt [ʌn'hə:t] *adj* indemne, sain(e) et sauf

unidentified [ʌnaɪ'dɛntɪfaɪd] *adj* non identifié(e); *see also* **UFO**

uniform ['ju:nɪfɔ:m] *n* uniforme *m* ▷ *adj* uniforme

unify ['ju:nɪfaɪ] *vt* unifier

unimportant [ʌnɪm'pɔ:tənt] *adj* sans importance

uninhabited [ʌnɪn'hæbɪtɪd] *adj* inhabité(e)

unintentional [ʌnɪn'tɛnʃənəl] *adj* involontaire

union ['ju:njən] *n* union *f*; (*also*: **trade ~**) syndicat *m* ▷ *cpd* du syndicat, syndical(e); **Union Jack** *n* drapeau du Royaume-Uni

unique [ju:'ni:k] *adj* unique

unisex ['ju:nɪsɛks] *adj* unisexe

unit ['ju:nɪt] *n* unité *f*; (*section: of furniture etc*) élément *m*, bloc *m*; (*team, squad*) groupe *m*, service *m*; **kitchen ~** élément de cuisine

unite [ju:'naɪt] *vt* unir ▷ *vi* s'unir; **united** *adj* uni(e); (*country, party*)

unifié(e); (*efforts*) conjugué(e);
United Kingdom *n* Royaume-Uni
m; **United Nations (Organization)**
n (Organisation *f* des) Nations unies;
United States (of America) *n*
États-Unis *mpl*

unity ['ju:nɪtɪ] *n* unité *f*

universal [ju:nɪ'vɜ:sl] *adj*
universel(le)

universe ['ju:nɪvɜ:s] *n* univers *m*

university [ju:nɪ'vɜ:sɪtɪ] *n*
université *f* ▷ *cpd* (*student, professor*)
d'université; (*education, year, degree*)
universitaire

unjust [ʌn'dʒʌst] *adj* injuste

unkind [ʌn'kaɪnd] *adj* peu gentil(le),
méchant(e)

unknown [ʌn'nəun] *adj* inconnu(e)

unlawful [ʌn'lɔ:ful] *adj* illégal(e)

unleaded [ʌn'lɛdɪd] *n* (*also:* ~ **petrol**)
essence *f* sans plomb

unleash [ʌn'li:ʃ] *vt* (*fig*) déchaîner,
déclencher

unless [ʌn'lɛs] *conj:* ~ **he leaves** à
moins qu'il (ne) parte; ~ **otherwise
stated** sauf indication contraire

unlike [ʌn'laɪk] *adj* dissemblable,
différent(e) ▷ *prep* à la différence de,
contrairement à

unlikely [ʌn'laɪklɪ] *adj* (*result,
event*) improbable; (*explanation*)
invraisemblable

unlimited [ʌn'lɪmɪtɪd] *adj* illimité(e)

unlisted ['ʌn'lɪstɪd] *adj* (us Tel) sur
la liste rouge

unload [ʌn'ləud] *vt* décharger

unlock [ʌn'lɔk] *vt* ouvrir

unlucky [ʌn'lʌkɪ] *adj* (*person*)
malchanceux(-euse); (*object, number*)
qui porte malheur; **to be ~** (*person*) ne
pas avoir de chance

unmarried [ʌn'mærɪd] *adj*
célibataire

unmistak(e)able [ʌnmɪs'teɪkəbl]
adj indubitable; qu'on ne peut pas ne
pas reconnaître

unnatural [ʌn'nætʃrəl] *adj* non
naturel(le); (*perversion*) contre nature

unnecessary [ʌn'nɛsəsərɪ] *adj*
inutile, superflu(e)

UNO ['ju:nəu] *n abbr* = **United
Nations Organization**

unofficial [ʌnə'fɪʃl] *adj* (*news*)
officieux(-euse), non officiel(le);
(*strike*) ≈ sauvage

unpack [ʌn'pæk] *vi* défaire sa valise
▷ *vt* (*suitcase*) défaire; (*belongings*)
déballer

unpaid [ʌn'peɪd] *adj* (*bill*) impayé(e);
(*holiday*) non-payé(e), sans salaire;
(*work*) non rétribué(e)

unpleasant [ʌn'plɛznt] *adj*
déplaisant(e), désagréable

unplug [ʌn'plʌg] *vt* débrancher

unpopular [ʌn'pɔpjulə^r] *adj*
impopulaire

unprecedented [ʌn'prɛsɪdɛntɪd]
adj sans précédent

unpredictable [ʌnprɪ'dɪktəbl] *adj*
imprévisible

unprotected ['ʌnprə'tɛktɪd] *adj*
(*sex*) non protégé(e)

unqualified [ʌn'kwɔlɪfaɪd] *adj*
(*teacher*) non diplômé(e), sans titres;
(*success*) sans réserve, total(e);
(*disaster*) total(e)

unravel [ʌn'rævl] *vt* démêler

unreal [ʌn'rɪəl] *adj* irréel(le);
(*extraordinary*) incroyable

unrealistic [ʌnrɪə'lɪstɪk] *adj* (*idea*)
irréaliste; (*estimate*) peu réaliste

unreasonable [ʌn'ri:znəbl] *adj* qui
n'est pas raisonnable

unrelated [ʌnrɪ'leɪtɪd] *adj* sans
rapport; (*people*) sans lien de parenté

unreliable [ʌnrɪ'laɪəbl] *adj* sur qui
(*or quoi*) on ne peut pas compter,
peu fiable

unrest [ʌn'rɛst] *n* agitation *f*,
troubles *mpl*

unroll [ʌn'rəul] *vt* dérouler

unruly [ʌn'ru:lɪ] *adj* indiscipliné(e)

unsafe [ʌn'seɪf] *adj* (*in danger*) en
danger; (*journey, car*) dangereux(-euse)

unsatisfactory ['ʌnsætɪs'fæktərɪ]
adj peu satisfaisant(e)

u

unscrew [ʌnˈskruː] *vt* dévisser

unsettled [ʌnˈsɛtld] *adj (restless)* perturbé(e); *(unpredictable)* instable; incertain(e); *(not finalized)* non résolu(e)

unsettling [ʌnˈsɛtlɪŋ] *adj* qui a un effet perturbateur

unsightly [ʌnˈsaɪtlɪ] *adj* disgracieux(-euse), laid(e)

unskilled [ʌnˈskɪld] *adj*: **~ worker** manœuvre *m*

unspoiled [ˈʌnˈspɔɪld], **unspoilt** [ˈʌnˈspɔɪlt] *adj (place)* non dégradé(e)

unstable [ʌnˈsteɪbl] *adj* instable

unsteady [ʌnˈstɛdɪ] *adj* mal assuré(e), chancelant(e), instable

unsuccessful [ʌnsəkˈsɛsful] *adj (attempt)* infructueux(-euse); *(writer, proposal)* qui n'a pas de succès; **to be ~** *(in attempting sth)* ne pas réussir; ne pas avoir de succès; *(application)* ne pas être retenu(e)

unsuitable [ʌnˈsuːtəbl] *adj* qui ne convient pas, peu approprié(e); *(time)* inopportun(e)

unsure [ʌnˈʃuəʳ] *adj* pas sûr(e); **to be ~ of o.s.** ne pas être sûr de soi, manquer de confiance en soi

untidy [ʌnˈtaɪdɪ] *adj (room)* en désordre; *(appearance, person)* débraillé(e); *(person: in character)* sans ordre, désordonné(e); *(work)* peu soigné(e)

untie [ʌnˈtaɪ] *vt (knot, parcel)* défaire; *(prisoner, dog)* détacher

until [ənˈtɪl] *prep* jusqu'à; *(after negative)* avant ▷ *conj* jusqu'à ce que + *sub*; *(in past, after negative)* avant que + *sub*; **~ he comes** jusqu'à ce qu'il vienne, jusqu'à son arrivée; **~ now** jusqu'à présent, jusqu'ici; **~ then** jusque-là

untrue [ʌnˈtruː] *adj (statement)* faux (fausse)

unused¹ [ʌnˈjuːzd] *adj (new)* neuf (neuve)

unused² [ʌnˈjuːst] *adj*: **to be ~ to sth/to doing sth** ne pas avoir l'habitude de qch/de faire qch

unusual [ʌnˈjuːʒuəl] *adj* insolite, exceptionnel(le), rare; **unusually** *adv* exceptionnellement, particulièrement

unveil [ʌnˈveɪl] *vt* dévoiler

unwanted [ʌnˈwɒntɪd] *adj (child, pregnancy)* non désiré(e); *(clothes etc)* à donner

unwell [ʌnˈwɛl] *adj* souffrant(e); **to feel ~** ne pas se sentir bien

unwilling [ʌnˈwɪlɪŋ] *adj*: **to be ~ to do** ne pas vouloir faire

unwind [ʌnˈwaɪnd] *vt (irreg: like* **wind²**) dérouler ▷ *vi (relax)* se détendre

unwise [ʌnˈwaɪz] *adj* imprudent(e), peu judicieux(-euse)

unwittingly [ʌnˈwɪtɪŋlɪ] *adv* involontairement

unwrap [ʌnˈræp] *vt* défaire; ouvrir

unzip [ʌnˈzɪp] *vt* ouvrir (la fermeture éclair de); *(Comput)* dézipper

 KEYWORD

up [ʌp] *prep*: **he went up the stairs/ the hill** il a monté l'escalier/la colline; **the cat was up a tree** le chat était dans un arbre; **they live further up the street** ils habitent plus haut dans la rue; **go up that road and turn left** remontez la rue et tournez à gauche

▶ *adv* **1** en haut; en l'air; *(upwards, higher)*: **up in the sky/the mountains** (là-haut) dans le ciel/les montagnes; **put it a bit higher up** mettez-le un peu plus haut; **to stand up** *(get up)* se lever, se mettre debout; *(be standing)* être debout; **up there** là-haut; **up above** au-dessus

2: **to be up** *(out of bed)* être levé(e); *(prices)* avoir augmenté *or* monté; *(finished)*: **when the year was up** à la fin de l'année

3: **up to** *(as far as)* jusqu'à; **up to now** jusqu'à présent

4: **to be up to** *(depending on)*: **it's up**

to you c'est à vous de décider; (equal to): **he's not up to it** (job, task etc) il n'en est pas capable; (inf: be doing): **what is he up to?** qu'est-ce qu'il peut bien faire?
▶ n: **ups and downs** hauts et bas mpl

up-and-coming [ʌpənd'kʌmɪŋ] adj plein(e) d'avenir or de promesses
upbringing ['ʌpbrɪŋɪŋ] n éducation f
update [ʌp'deɪt] vt mettre à jour
upfront [ʌp'frʌnt] adj (open) franc (franche) ▷ adv (pay) d'avance; **to be ~ about sth** ne rien cacher de qch
upgrade [ʌp'greɪd] vt (person) promouvoir; (job) revaloriser; (property, equipment) moderniser
upheaval [ʌp'hi:vl] n bouleversement m; (in room) branle-bas m; (event) crise f
uphill [ʌp'hɪl] adj qui monte; (fig: task) difficile, pénible ▷ adv (face, look) en amont, vers l'amont; **to go ~** monter
upholstery [ʌp'həʊlstərɪ] n rembourrage m; (cover) tissu m d'ameublement; (of car) garniture f
upload [ʌp'ləʊd] vt (Comput) télécharger
upmarket [ʌp'mɑ:kɪt] adj (product) haut de gamme inv; (area) chic inv
upon [ə'pɒn] prep sur
upper ['ʌpə'] adj supérieur(e); du dessus ▷ n (of shoe) empeigne f; **upper-class** adj de la haute société, aristocratique; (district) élégant(e), huppé(e); (accent, attitude) caractéristique des classes supérieures
upright ['ʌpraɪt] adj droit(e); (fig) droit, honnête
uprising ['ʌpraɪzɪŋ] n soulèvement m, insurrection f
uproar ['ʌprɔ:'] n tumulte m, vacarme m; (protests) protestations fpl
upset n ['ʌpsɛt] dérangement m ▷ vt [ʌp'sɛt] (irreg: like **set**) (glass etc) renverser; (plan) déranger;

(person: offend) contrarier; (: grieve) faire de la peine à; bouleverser ▷ adj [ʌp'sɛt] contrarié(e); peiné(e); **to have a stomach ~** (BRIT) avoir une indigestion
upside down ['ʌpsaɪd-] adv à l'envers; **to turn sth ~** (fig: place) mettre sens dessus dessous
upstairs [ʌp'stɛəz] adv en haut ▷ adj (room) du dessus, d'en haut ▷ n: **the ~** l'étage m
up-to-date ['ʌptə'deɪt] adj moderne; (information) très récent(e)
upward ['ʌpwəd] adj ascendant(e); vers le haut ▷ adv = **upwards**
upwards adv vers le haut; (more than): **~ of** plus de
uranium [juə'reɪnɪəm] n uranium m
Uranus [juə'reɪnəs] n Uranus f
urban ['ə:bən] adj urbain(e)
urge [ə:dʒ] n besoin (impératif), envie (pressante) ▷ vt (person): **to ~ sb to do** exhorter qn à faire, pousser qn à faire, recommander vivement à qn de faire
urgency ['ə:dʒənsɪ] n urgence f; (of tone) insistance f
urgent ['ə:dʒənt] adj urgent(e); (plea, tone) pressant(e)
urinal ['juərɪnl] n (BRIT: place) urinoir m
urinate ['juərɪneɪt] vi uriner
urine ['juərɪn] n urine f
URL abbr (= uniform resource locator) URL f
US n abbr = **United States**
us [ʌs] pron nous; see also **me**
USA n abbr = **United States of America**
USB stick n clé f USB
use n [ju:s] emploi m, utilisation f; (usefulness) utilité f ▷ vt [ju:z] se servir de, utiliser, employer; **in ~** en usage; **out of ~** hors d'usage; **to be of ~** servir, être utile; **it's no ~** ça ne sert à rien; **to have the ~ of** avoir l'usage de; **she ~d to do it** elle le faisait (autrefois), elle avait coutume de le

u

faire; **to be ~d to** avoir l'habitude de, être habitué(e) à; **use up** vt finir, épuiser; (*food*) consommer; **used** [juːzd] *adj* (*car*) d'occasion; **useful** *adj* utile; **useless** *adj* inutile; (*inf: person*) nul(le); **user** *n* utilisateur(-trice), usager *m*; **user-friendly** *adj* convivial(e), facile d'emploi

usual ['juːʒuəl] *adj* habituel(le); **as ~** comme d'habitude; **usually** *adv* d'habitude, d'ordinaire

ute [juːt] *n* (AUST, NZ) pick-up *m inv*

utensil [juː'tɛnsl] *n* ustensile *m*; **kitchen ~s** batterie *f* de cuisine

utility [juː'tɪlɪtɪ] *n* utilité *f*; (*also:* **public ~**) service public

utilize ['juːtɪlaɪz] *vt* utiliser; (*make good use of*) exploiter

utmost ['ʌtməʊst] *adj* extrême, le plus grand(e) ▷ *n*: **to do one's ~** faire tout son possible

utter ['ʌtəʳ] *adj* total(e), complet(-ète) ▷ *vt* prononcer, proférer; (*sounds*) émettre; **utterly** *adv* complètement, totalement

U-turn ['juː'təːn] *n* demi-tour *m*; (*fig*) volte-face *f inv*

v. *abbr* = **verse**; (= *vide*) v.; (= *versus*) vs; (= *volt*) V

vacancy ['veɪkənsɪ] *n* (*job*) poste vacant; (*room*) chambre *f* disponible; **"no vacancies"** "complet"

vacant ['veɪkənt] *adj* (*post*) vacant(e); (*seat etc*) libre, disponible; (*expression*) distrait(e)

vacate [və'keɪt] *vt* quitter

vacation [və'keɪʃən] *n* (*esp US*) vacances *fpl*; **on ~** en vacances; **vacationer, vacationist** (*US*) *n* vacancier(-ière)

vaccination [væksɪ'neɪʃən] *n* vaccination *f*

vaccine ['væksiːn] *n* vaccin *m*

vacuum ['vækjum] *n* vide *m*; **vacuum cleaner** *n* aspirateur *m*

vagina [və'dʒaɪnə] *n* vagin *m*

vague [veɪg] *adj* vague, imprécis(e); (*blurred: photo, memory*) flou(e)

vain [veɪn] *adj* (*useless*) vain(e); (*conceited*) vaniteux(-euse); **in ~** en vain

Valentine's Day ['væləntaɪnz-] n
Saint-Valentin f
valid ['vælɪd] adj (document) valide,
valable; (excuse) valable
valley ['vælɪ] n vallée f
valuable ['væljuəbl] adj (jewel)
de grande valeur; (time, help)
précieux(-euse); **valuables** npl objets
mpl de valeur
value ['vælju:] n valeur f ▷ vt (fix
price) évaluer, expertiser; (appreciate)
apprécier; **values** npl (principles)
valeurs fpl
valve [vælv] n (in machine) soupape f;
(on tyre) valve f; (Med) valve, valvule f
vampire ['væmpaɪə'] n vampire m
van [væn] n (Aut) camionnette f
vandal ['vændl] n vandale m/f;
vandalism n vandalisme m;
vandalize vt saccager
vanilla [və'nɪlə] n vanille f
vanish ['vænɪʃ] vi disparaître
vanity ['vænɪtɪ] n vanité f
vapour, (us) **vapor** ['veɪpə'] n
vapeur f; (on window) buée f
variable ['vɛərɪəbl] adj variable;
(mood) changeant(e)
variant ['vɛərɪənt] n variante f
variation [vɛərɪ'eɪʃən] n variation f;
(in opinion) changement m
varied ['vɛərɪd] adj varié(e), divers(e)
variety [və'raɪətɪ] n variété f;
(quantity) nombre m, quantité f
various ['vɛərɪəs] adj divers(e),
différent(e); (several) divers, plusieurs
varnish ['vɑːnɪʃ] n vernis m ▷ vt vernir
vary ['vɛərɪ] vt, vi varier, changer
vase [vɑːz] n vase m
Vaseline® ['væsɪliːn] n vaseline f
vast [vɑːst] adj vaste, immense;
(amount, success) énorme
VAT [væt] n abbr (BRIT: = value added
tax) TVA f
vault [vɔːlt] n (of roof) voûte f; (tomb)
caveau m; (in bank) salle f des coffres;
chambre forte ▷ vt (also: **~ over**)
sauter (d'un bond)
VCR n abbr = **video cassette recorder**

VDU n abbr = **visual display unit**
veal [viːl] n veau m
veer [vɪə'] vi tourner; (car, ship) virer
vegan ['viːgən] n végétalien(ne)
vegetable ['vɛdʒtəbl] n légume m
▷ adj végétal(e)
vegetarian [vɛdʒɪ'tɛərɪən] adj,
n végétarien(ne); **do you have
any ~ dishes?** avez-vous des plats
végétariens?
vegetation [vɛdʒɪ'teɪʃən] n
végétation f
vehicle ['viːɪkl] n véhicule m
veil [veɪl] n voile m
vein [veɪn] n veine f; (on leaf) nervure f
Velcro® ['vɛlkrəu] n velcro® m
velvet ['vɛlvɪt] n velours m
vending machine ['vɛndɪŋ-] n
distributeur m automatique
vendor ['vɛndə'] n vendeur(-euse);
street ~ marchand ambulant
Venetian blind [vɪ'niːʃən-] n store
vénitien
vengeance ['vɛndʒəns] n
vengeance f; **with a ~** (fig) vraiment,
pour de bon
venison ['vɛnɪsn] n venaison f
venom ['vɛnəm] n venin m
vent [vɛnt] n conduit m d'aération;
(in dress, jacket) fente f ▷ vt (fig: one's
feelings) donner libre cours à
ventilation [vɛntɪ'leɪʃən] n
ventilation f, aération f
venture ['vɛntʃə'] n entreprise f ▷ vt
risquer, hasarder ▷ vi s'aventurer, se
risquer; **a business ~** une entreprise
commerciale
venue ['vɛnjuː] n lieu m
Venus ['viːnəs] n (planet) Vénus f
verb [vəːb] n verbe m; **verbal** adj
verbal(e)
verdict ['vəːdɪkt] n verdict m
verge [vəːdʒ] n bord m; **"soft ~s"**
(BRIT) "accotements non stabilisés";
on the ~ of doing sur le point de faire
verify ['vɛrɪfaɪ] vt vérifier
versatile ['vəːsətaɪl] adj
polyvalent(e)

V

verse [vəːs] n vers mpl; (stanza) strophe f; (in Bible) verset m

version ['vəːʃən] n version f

versus ['vəːsəs] prep contre

vertical ['vəːtɪkl] adj vertical(e)

very ['vɛrɪ] adv très ▷ adj: **the ~ book which** le livre même que; **the ~ last** le tout dernier; **at the ~ least** au moins; **~ much** beaucoup

vessel ['vɛsl] n (Anat, Naut) vaisseau m; (container) récipient m; see also **blood vessel**

vest [vɛst] n (BRIT: underwear) tricot m de corps; (US: waistcoat) gilet m

vet [vɛt] n abbr (BRIT: = veterinary surgeon) vétérinaire m/f; (US: = veteran) ancien(ne) combattant(e) ▷ vt examiner minutieusement

veteran ['vɛtərn] n vétéran m; (also: **war ~**) ancien combattant

veterinary surgeon ['vɛtrɪnərɪ-] (BRIT) n vétérinaire m/f

veto ['viːtəu] n (pl **vetoes**) veto m ▷ vt opposer son veto à

via ['vaɪə] prep par, via

viable ['vaɪəbl] adj viable

vibrate [vaɪ'breɪt] vi: **to ~ (with)** vibrer (de)

vibration [vaɪ'breɪʃən] n vibration f

vicar ['vɪkər] n pasteur m (de l'Église anglicane)

vice [vaɪs] n (evil) vice m; (Tech) étau m; **vice-chairman** (irreg) n vice-président(e)

vice versa ['vaɪsɪ'vəːsə] adv vice versa

vicinity [vɪ'sɪnɪtɪ] n environs mpl, alentours mpl

vicious ['vɪʃəs] adj (remark) cruel(le), méchant(e); (blow) brutal(e); (dog) méchant(e), dangereux(-euse); **a ~ circle** un cercle vicieux

victim ['vɪktɪm] n victime f

victor ['vɪktər] n vainqueur m

Victorian [vɪk'tɔːrɪən] adj victorien(ne)

victorious [vɪk'tɔːrɪəs] adj victorieux(-euse)

victory ['vɪktərɪ] n victoire f

video ['vɪdɪəu] n (video film) vidéo f; (also: **~ cassette**) vidéocassette f; (also: **~ cassette recorder**) magnétoscope m ▷ vt (with recorder) enregistrer; (with camera) filmer; **video camera** n caméra f vidéo inv; **video game** n jeu m vidéo inv; **videophone** n vidéophone m; **video recorder** n magnétoscope m; **video shop** n vidéoclub m; **video tape** n bande f vidéo inv; (cassette) vidéocassette f

vie [vaɪ] vi: **to ~ with** lutter avec, rivaliser avec

Vienna [vɪ'ɛnə] n Vienne

Vietnam, Viet Nam ['vjɛt'næm] n Viêt-nam or Vietnam m; **Vietnamese** [vjɛtnə'miːz] adj vietnamien(ne) ▷ n (pl inv) Vietnamien(ne)

view [vjuː] n vue f; (opinion) avis m, vue ▷ vt voir, regarder; (situation) considérer; (house) visiter; **on ~** (in museum etc) exposé(e); **in full ~ of sb** sous les yeux de qn; **in my ~** à mon avis; **in ~ of the fact that** étant donné que; **viewer** n (TV) téléspectateur(-trice); **viewpoint** n point m de vue

vigilant ['vɪdʒɪlənt] adj vigilant(e)

vigorous ['vɪgərəs] adj vigoureux(-euse)

vile [vaɪl] adj (action) vil(e); (smell, food) abominable; (temper) massacrant(e)

villa ['vɪlə] n villa f

village ['vɪlɪdʒ] n village m; **villager** n villageois(e)

villain ['vɪlən] n (scoundrel) scélérat m; (BRIT: criminal) bandit m; (in novel etc) traître m

vinaigrette [vɪneɪ'grɛt] n vinaigrette f

vine [vaɪn] n vigne f

vinegar ['vɪnɪgər] n vinaigre m

vineyard ['vɪnjɑːd] n vignoble m

vintage ['vɪntɪdʒ] n (year) année f, millésime m ▷ cpd (car) d'époque; (wine) de grand cru

vinyl ['vaɪnl] n vinyle m
viola [vɪ'əʊlə] n alto m
violate ['vaɪəleɪt] vt violer
violation [vaɪə'leɪʃən] n violation f; **in ~ of** (rule, law) en infraction à, en violation de
violence ['vaɪələns] n violence f
violent ['vaɪələnt] adj violent(e)
violet ['vaɪələt] adj (colour) violet(te) ▷ n (plant) violette f
violin [vaɪə'lɪn] n violon m
VIP n abbr (= very important person) VIP m
virgin ['vɜːdʒɪn] n vierge f
Virgo ['vɜːgəʊ] n la Vierge
virtual ['vɜːtjʊəl] adj (Comput, Physics) virtuel(le); (in effect): **it's a ~ impossibility** c'est quasiment impossible; **virtually** adv (almost) pratiquement; **virtual reality** n (Comput) réalité virtuelle
virtue ['vɜːtjuː] n vertu f; (advantage) mérite m, avantage m; **by ~ of** en vertu or raison de
virus ['vaɪərəs] n (Med, Comput) virus m
visa ['viːzə] n visa m
vise [vaɪs] n (us Tech) = **vice**
visibility [vɪzɪ'bɪlɪtɪ] n visibilité f
visible ['vɪzəbl] adj visible
vision ['vɪʒən] n (sight) vue f, vision f; (foresight, in dream) vision
visit ['vɪzɪt] n visite f; (stay) séjour m ▷ vt (person: us: also: **~ with**) rendre visite à; (place) visiter; **visiting hours** npl heures fpl de visite; **visitor** n visiteur(-euse); (to one's house) invité(e); **visitor centre**, (us) **visitor center** n hall m or centre m d'accueil
visual ['vɪzjʊəl] adj visuel(le); **visualize** vt se représenter
vital ['vaɪtl] adj vital(e); **of ~ importance (to sb/sth)** d'une importance capitale (pour qn/qch)
vitality [vaɪ'tælɪtɪ] n vitalité f
vitamin ['vɪtəmɪn] n vitamine f
vivid ['vɪvɪd] adj (account) frappant(e), vivant(e); (light, imagination) vif (vive)

V-neck ['viːnɛk] n décolleté m en V
vocabulary [vəʊ'kæbjʊlərɪ] n vocabulaire m
vocal ['vəʊkl] adj vocal(e); (articulate) qui n'hésite pas à s'exprimer, qui sait faire entendre ses opinions
vocational [vəʊ'keɪʃənl] adj professionnel(le)
vodka ['vɒdkə] n vodka f
vogue [vəʊg] n: **to be in ~** être en vogue or à la mode
voice [vɔɪs] n voix f ▷ vt (opinion) exprimer, formuler; **voice mail** n (system) messagerie f vocale, boîte f vocale; (device) répondeur m
void [vɔɪd] n vide m ▷ adj (invalid) nul(le); (empty): **~ of** vide de, dépourvu(e) de
volatile ['vɒlətaɪl] adj volatil(e); (fig: person) versatile; (: situation) explosif(-ive)
volcano [vɒl'keɪnəʊ] (pl **volcanoes**) n volcan m
volleyball ['vɒlɪbɔːl] n volley(-ball) m
volt [vəʊlt] n volt m; **voltage** n tension f, voltage m
volume ['vɒljuːm] n volume m; (of tank) capacité f
voluntarily ['vɒləntrɪlɪ] adv volontairement
voluntary ['vɒləntərɪ] adj volontaire; (unpaid) bénévole
volunteer [vɒlən'tɪəʳ] n volontaire m/f ▷ vt (information) donner spontanément ▷ vi (Mil) s'engager comme volontaire; **to ~ to do** se proposer pour faire
vomit ['vɒmɪt] n vomissure f ▷ vt, vi vomir
vote [vəʊt] n vote m, suffrage m; (votes cast) voix f, vote; (franchise) droit m de vote ▷ vt (chairman) élire; (propose): **to ~ that** proposer que + sub ▷ vi voter; **~ of thanks** discours m de remerciement; **voter** n électeur(-trice); **voting** n scrutin m, vote m
voucher ['vaʊtʃəʳ] n (for meal, petrol, gift) bon m

vow [vau] n vœu m, serment m
  ▷ vi jurer
vowel ['vauəl] n voyelle f
voyage ['vɔɪɪdʒ] n voyage m par mer,
  traversée f
vulgar ['vʌlgəʳ] adj vulgaire
vulnerable ['vʌlnərəbl] adj
  vulnérable
vulture ['vʌltʃəʳ] n vautour m

waddle ['wɔdl] vi se dandiner
wade [weɪd] vi: **to ~ through**
  marcher dans, patauger dans; (fig:
  book) venir à bout de
wafer ['weɪfəʳ] n (Culin) gaufrette f
waffle ['wɔfl] n (Culin) gaufre f ▷ vi
  parler pour ne rien dire; faire du
  remplissage
wag [wæg] vt agiter, remuer ▷ vi
  remuer
wage [weɪdʒ] n (also: **~s**) salaire m,
  paye f ▷ vt: **to ~ war** faire la guerre
wag(g)on ['wægən] n (horse-drawn)
  chariot m; (BRIT Rail) wagon m (de
  marchandises)
wail [weɪl] n gémissement m; (of siren)
  hurlement m ▷ vi gémir; (siren) hurler
waist [weɪst] n taille f, ceinture f;
  waistcoat n (BRIT) gilet m
wait [weɪt] n attente f ▷ vi attendre;
  to ~ for sb/sth attendre qn/qch; **to
  keep sb ~ing** faire attendre qn; **~ for
  me, please** attendez-moi, s'il vous

plaît; **I can't ~ to ...** (fig) je meurs d'envie de ...; **to lie in ~ for** guetter; **wait on** vt fus servir; **waiter** n garçon m (de café), serveur m; **waiting list** n liste f d'attente; **waiting room** n salle f d'attente; **waitress** ['weɪtrɪs] n serveuse f

waive [weɪv] vt renoncer à, abandonner

wake [weɪk] (pt **woke** or **waked**, pp **woken** or **waked**) vt (also: ~ **up**) réveiller ▷ vi (also: ~ **up**) se réveiller ▷ n (for dead person) veillée f mortuaire; (Naut) sillage m

Wales [weɪlz] n pays m de Galles; **the Prince of Wales** le prince de Galles

walk [wɔːk] n promenade f; (short) petit tour; (gait) démarche f; (path) chemin m; (in park etc) allée f ▷ vi marcher; (for pleasure, exercise) se promener ▷ vt (distance) faire à pied; (dog) promener; **10 minutes' ~ from** à 10 minutes de marche de; **to go for a ~** se promener; faire un tour; **from all ~s of life** de toutes conditions sociales; **walk out** vi (go out) sortir; (as protest) partir (en signe de protestation); (strike) se mettre en grève; **to ~ out on sb** quitter qn; **walker** n (person) marcheur(-euse); **walkie-talkie** ['wɔːkɪ'tɔːkɪ] n talkie-walkie m; **walking** n marche f à pied; **walking shoes** npl chaussures fpl de marche; **walking stick** n canne f; **Walkman®** n Walkman® m; **walkway** n promenade f, cheminement piéton

wall [wɔːl] n mur m; (of tunnel, cave) paroi f

wallet ['wɔlɪt] n portefeuille m; **I can't find my ~** je ne retrouve plus mon portefeuille

wallpaper ['wɔːlpeɪpəʳ] n papier peint ▷ vt tapisser

walnut ['wɔːlnʌt] n noix f; (tree, wood) noyer m

walrus ['wɔːlrəs] (pl **walrus** or **walruses**) n morse m

waltz [wɔːlts] n valse f ▷ vi valser

wand [wɔnd] n (also: **magic ~**) baguette f (magique)

wander ['wɔndəʳ] vi (person) errer, aller sans but; (thoughts) vagabonder ▷ vt errer dans

want [wɔnt] vt vouloir; (need) avoir besoin de ▷ n: **for ~ of** par manque de, faute de; **to ~ to do** vouloir faire; **to ~ sb to do** vouloir que qn fasse; **wanted** adj (criminal) recherché(e) par la police

war [wɔːʳ] n guerre f; **to make ~ (on)** faire la guerre (à)

ward [wɔːd] n (in hospital) salle f; (Pol) section électorale; (Law: child: also: ~ **of court**) pupille m/f

warden ['wɔːdn] n (BRIT: of institution) directeur(-trice); (of park, game reserve) gardien(ne); (BRIT: also: **traffic ~**) contractuel(le)

wardrobe ['wɔːdrəub] n (cupboard) armoire f; (clothes) garde-robe f

warehouse ['wɛəhaus] n entrepôt m

warfare ['wɔːfɛəʳ] n guerre f

warhead ['wɔːhɛd] n (Mil) ogive f

warm [wɔːm] adj chaud(e); (person, thanks, welcome, applause) chaleureux(-euse); **it's ~** il fait chaud; **I'm ~** j'ai chaud; **warm up** vi (person, room) se réchauffer; (athlete, discussion) s'échauffer ▷ vt (food) (faire) réchauffer; (water) (faire) chauffer; (engine) faire chauffer; **warmly** adv (dress) chaudement; (thank, welcome) chaleureusement; **warmth** n chaleur f

warn [wɔːn] vt avertir, prévenir; **to ~ sb (not) to do** conseiller à qn de (ne pas) faire; **warning** n avertissement m; (notice) avis m; **warning light** n avertisseur lumineux

warrant ['wɔrnt] n (guarantee) garantie f; (Law: to arrest) mandat m d'arrêt; (: to search) mandat de perquisition ▷ vt (justify, merit) justifier

warranty ['wɔrəntɪ] n garantie f

w

warrior ['wɔrɪəʳ] n guerrier(-ière)

Warsaw ['wɔːsɔː] n Varsovie

warship ['wɔːʃɪp] n navire m de guerre

wart [wɔːt] n verrue f

wartime ['wɔːtaɪm] n: **in ~** en temps de guerre

wary ['wɛərɪ] adj prudent(e)

was [wɔz] pt of **be**

wash [wɔʃ] vt laver ▷ vi se laver; (sea): **to ~ over/against sth** inonder/ baigner qch ▷ n (clothes) lessive f; (washing programme) lavage m; (of ship) sillage m; **to have a ~** se laver, faire sa toilette; **wash up** vi (BRIT) faire la vaisselle; (US: have a wash) se débarbouiller; **washbasin** n lavabo m; **washer** n (Tech) rondelle f, joint m; **washing** n (BRIT: linen etc: dirty) linge m; (: clean) lessive f; **washing line** n (BRIT) corde f à linge; **washing machine** n machine f à laver; **washing powder** n (BRIT) lessive f (en poudre)

Washington ['wɔʃɪŋtən] n Washington m

wash: washing-up n (BRIT) vaisselle f; **washing-up liquid** n (BRIT) produit m pour la vaisselle; **washroom** n (US) toilettes fpl

wasn't ['wɔznt] = **was not**

wasp [wɔsp] n guêpe f

waste [weɪst] n gaspillage m; (of time) perte f; (rubbish) déchets mpl; (also: **household ~**) ordures fpl ▷ adj (land, ground: in city) à l'abandon; (leftover): **~ material** déchets ▷ vt gaspiller; (time, opportunity) perdre; **waste ground** n (BRIT) terrain m vague; **wastepaper basket** n corbeille f à papier

watch [wɔtʃ] n montre f; (act of watching) surveillance f; (guard: Mil) sentinelle f; (: Naut) homme m de quart; (Naut: spell of duty) quart m ▷ vt (look at) observer (: match, programme) regarder; (spy on, guard) surveiller; (be careful of) faire attention à ▷ vi regarder; (keep guard) monter la

garde; **to keep ~** faire le guet; **watch out** vi faire attention; **watchdog** n chien m de garde; (fig) gardien(ne); **watch strap** n bracelet m de montre

water ['wɔːtəʳ] n eau f ▷ vt (plant, garden) arroser ▷ vi (eyes) larmoyer; **in British ~s** dans les eaux territoriales Britanniques; **to make sb's mouth ~** mettre l'eau à la bouche de qn; **water down** vt (milk etc) couper avec de l'eau; (fig: story) édulcorer; **watercolour**, (US) **watercolor** n aquarelle f; **watercress** n cresson m (de fontaine); **waterfall** n chute f d'eau; **watering can** n arrosoir m; **watermelon** n pastèque f; **waterproof** adj imperméable; **water-skiing** n ski m nautique

watt [wɔt] n watt m

wave [weɪv] n vague f; (of hand) geste m, signe m; (Radio) onde f; (in hair) ondulation f; (fig) vague ▷ vi faire signe de la main; (flag) flotter au vent; (grass) ondoyer ▷ vt (handkerchief) agiter; (stick) brandir; **wavelength** n longueur f d'ondes

waver ['weɪvəʳ] vi vaciller; (voice) trembler; (person) hésiter

wavy ['weɪvɪ] adj (hair, surface) ondulé(e); (line) onduleux(-euse)

wax [wæks] n cire f; (for skis) fart m ▷ vt cirer; (car) lustrer; (skis) farter ▷ vi (moon) croître

way [weɪ] n chemin m, voie f; (distance) distance f; (direction) chemin, direction f; (manner) façon f, manière f; (habit) habitude f, façon; **which ~? — this ~/that ~** par où or de quel côté? — par ici/par là; **to lose one's ~** perdre son chemin; **on the ~ (to)** en route (pour); **to be on one's ~** être en route; **to be in the ~** bloquer le passage; (fig) gêner; **it's a long ~ away** c'est loin d'ici; **to go out of one's ~ to do** (fig) se donner beaucoup de mal pour faire; **to be under ~** (work, project) être en cours; **in a ~** dans un sens; **by the ~** à propos; **"~ in"** (BRIT) "entrée"; **"~ out"** (BRIT) "sortie"; **the ~ back** le chemin du retour; **"give ~"** (BRIT Aut) "cédez la priorité"; **no ~!** (inf) pas question!

W.C. n abbr (BRIT: = water closet) w.-c. mpl, waters mpl

we [wiː] pl pron nous

weak [wiːk] adj faible; (health) fragile; (beam etc) peu solide; (tea, coffee) léger(-ère); **weaken** vi faiblir ▷ vt affaiblir; **weakness** n faiblesse f; (fault) point m faible

wealth [wɛlθ] n (money, resources) richesse(s) f(pl); (of details) profusion f; **wealthy** adj riche

weapon ['wɛpən] n arme f; **~s of mass destruction** armes fpl de destruction massive

wear [wɛəʳ] (pt **wore**, pp **worn**) n (use) usage m; (deterioration through use) usure f ▷ vt (clothes) porter; (put on) mettre; (damage: through use) user ▷ vi (last) faire de l'usage; (rub etc through) s'user; **sports/baby~** vêtements mpl de sport/pour bébés; **evening ~** tenue f de soirée; **wear off** vi disparaître; **wear out** vt user; (person, strength) épuiser

weary ['wɪərɪ] adj (tired) épuisé(e); (dispirited) las (lasse); abattu(e) ▷ vi: **to ~ of** se lasser de

weasel ['wiːzl] n (Zool) belette f

weather ['wɛðəʳ] n temps m ▷ vt (storm: lit, fig) essuyer; (crisis) survivre à; **under the ~** (fig: ill) mal fichu(e); **weather forecast** n prévisions fpl météorologiques, météo f

weave (pt **wove**, pp **woven**) [wiːv, wəuv, 'wəuvn] vt (cloth) tisser; (basket) tresser

web [wɛb] n (of spider) toile f; (on duck's foot) palmure f; (fig) tissu m; (Comput): **the (World-Wide) W~** le Web; **web address** n adresse f Web; **webcam** n webcam f; **web page** n (Comput) page f Web; **website** n (Comput) site m Web

wed [wɛd] (pt, pp **wedded**) vt épouser ▷ vi se marier

we'd [wiːd] = **we had**; **we would**

wedding ['wɛdɪŋ] n mariage m; **wedding anniversary** n anniversaire m de mariage; **silver/ golden wedding anniversary** noces fpl d'argent/d'or; **wedding day** n jour m du mariage; **wedding dress** n robe f de mariée; **wedding ring** n alliance f

wedge [wɛdʒ] n (of wood etc) coin m; (under door etc) cale f; (of cake) part f ▷ vt (fix) caler; (push) enfoncer, coincer

Wednesday ['wɛdnzdɪ] n mercredi m

wee [wiː] adj (SCOTTISH) petit(e); tout(e) petit(e)

weed [wiːd] n mauvaise herbe ▷ vt désherber; **weedkiller** n désherbant m

week [wiːk] n semaine f; **a ~ today/ on Tuesday** aujourd'hui/mardi en huit; **weekday** n jour m de semaine; (Comm) jour ouvrable; **weekend** n week-end m; **weekly** adv une fois par semaine, chaque semaine ▷ adj, n hebdomadaire (m)

weep [wiːp] (pt, pp **wept**) vi (person) pleurer

weigh [weɪ] vt, vi peser; **to ~ anchor** lever l'ancre; **weigh up** vt examiner

weight [weɪt] n poids m; **to put on/ lose ~** grossir/maigrir; **weightlifting** n haltérophilie f

weir [wɪəʳ] n barrage m

weird [wɪəd] adj bizarre; (eerie) surnaturel(le)

welcome ['wɛlkəm] adj bienvenu(e) ▷ n accueil m ▷ vt accueillir; (also: **bid ~**) souhaiter la bienvenue à; (be glad of) se réjouir de; **you're ~!** (after thanks) de rien, il n'y a pas de quoi

weld [wɛld] vt souder

welfare ['wɛlfɛəʳ] n (wellbeing) bien-être m; (social aid) assistance sociale; **welfare state** n État-providence m

well [wɛl] n puits m ▷ adv bien ▷ adj: **to be ~** aller bien ▷ excl eh bien!; (relief also) bon!; (resignation) enfin!; **~ done!** bravo!; **get ~ soon!** remets-toi

W

vite!; **to do ~** bien réussir; (*business*) prospérer; **as ~** (*in addition*) aussi, également; **as ~ as** aussi bien que *or* de; en plus de

we'll [wi:l] = **we will**; **we shall**

well: well-behaved *adj* sage, obéissant(e); **well-built** *adj* (*person*) bien bâti(e); **well-dressed** *adj* bien habillé(e), bien vêtu(e); **well-groomed** [-'gru:md] *adj* très soigné(e)

wellies ['wɛlɪz] *npl* (BRIT *inf*) = **wellingtons**

wellingtons ['wɛlɪŋtənz] *npl* (*also:* **wellington boots**) bottes *fpl* en caoutchouc

well: well-known *adj* (*person*) bien connu(e); **well-off** *adj* aisé(e), assez riche; **well-paid** [wel'peɪd] *adj* bien payé(e)

Welsh [wɛlʃ] *adj* gallois(e) ▷ *n* (*Ling*) gallois *m*; **the Welsh** *npl* (*people*) les Gallois; **Welshman** (*irreg*) *n* Gallois *m*; **Welshwoman** (*irreg*) *n* Galloise *f*

went [wɛnt] *pt of* **go**

wept [wɛpt] *pt*, *pp of* **weep**

were [wəːʳ] *pt of* **be**

we're [wɪəʳ] = **we are**

weren't [wəːnt] = **were not**

west [wɛst] *n* ouest *m* ▷ *adj* (*wind*) d'ouest; (*side*) ouest *inv* ▷ *adv* à *or* vers l'ouest; **the W~** l'Occident *m*, l'Ouest; **westbound** ['wɛstbaund] *adj* en direction de l'ouest; (*carriageway*) ouest *inv*; **western** *adj* occidental(e), de *or* à l'ouest ▷ *n* (*Cine*) western *m*; **West Indian** *adj* antillais(e) ▷ *n* Antillais(e); **West Indies** [-'ɪndɪz] *npl* Antilles *fpl*

wet [wɛt] *adj* mouillé(e); (*damp*) humide; (*soaked: also:* **~ through**) trempé(e); (*rainy*) pluvieux(-euse); **to get ~** se mouiller; **"~ paint"** "attention peinture fraîche"; **wetsuit** *n* combinaison *f* de plongée

we've [wi:v] = **we have**

whack [wæk] *vt* donner un grand coup à

whale [weɪl] *n* (*Zool*) baleine *f*

wharf (*pl* **wharves**) [wɔːf, wɔːvz] *n* quai *m*

 KEYWORD

what [wɔt] *adj* **1** (*in questions*) quel(le); **what size is he?** quelle taille fait-il?; **what colour is it?** de quelle couleur est-ce?; **what books do you need?** quels livres vous faut-il?

2 (*in exclamations*): **what a mess!** quel désordre!; **what a fool I am!** que je suis bête!

▷ *pron* **1** (*interrogative*) que; de/à/ en *etc* quoi; **what are you doing?** que faites-vous?, qu'est-ce que vous faites?; **what is happening?** qu'est-ce qui se passe?, que se passe-t-il?; **what are you talking about?** de quoi parlez-vous?; **what are you thinking about?** à quoi pensez-vous?; **what is it called?** comment est-ce que ça s'appelle?; **what about me?** et moi?; **what about doing …?** et si on faisait …?

2 (*relative: subject*) ce qui; (*: direct object*) ce que; (*: indirect object*) ce à quoi, ce dont; **I saw what you did/was on the table** j'ai vu ce que vous avez fait/ce qui était sur la table; **tell me what you remember** dites-moi ce dont vous vous souvenez; **what I want is a cup of tea** ce que je veux, c'est une tasse de thé

▷ *excl* (*disbelieving*) quoi!, comment!

whatever [wɔt'ɛvəʳ] *adj*: **take ~ book you prefer** prenez le livre que vous préférez, peu importe lequel; **~ book you take** quel que soit le livre que vous preniez ▷ *pron*: **do ~ is necessary** faites (tout) ce qui est nécessaire; **~ happens** quoi qu'il arrive; **no reason ~** *or* **whatsoever** pas la moindre raison; **nothing ~** *or* **whatsoever** rien du tout

whatsoever [wɔtsəu'ɛvəʳ] *adj see*
whatever
wheat [wiːt] *n* blé *m*, froment *m*
wheel [wiːl] *n* roue *f*; (*Aut: also:*
steering ~) volant *m*; (*Naut*)
gouvernail *m* ▷ *vt* (*pram etc*) pousser,
rouler ▷ *vi* (*birds*) tournoyer; (*also:*
~ round: *person*) se retourner, faire
volte-face; **wheelbarrow** *n* brouette *f*;
wheelchair *n* fauteuil roulant; **wheel
clamp** *n* (*Aut*) sabot *m* (de Denver)
wheeze [wiːz] *vi* respirer
bruyamment

KEYWORD

when [wɛn] *adv* quand; **when did he
go?** quand est-ce qu'il est parti?
▷ *conj* **1** (*at, during, after the time that*)
quand, lorsque; **she was reading
when I came in** elle lisait quand *or*
lorsque je suis entré
2 (*on, at which*): **on the day when I
met him** le jour où je l'ai rencontré
3 (*whereas*) alors que; **I thought I
was wrong when in fact I was right**
j'ai cru que j'avais tort alors qu'en fait
j'avais raison

whenever [wɛn'ɛvəʳ] *adv* quand
donc ▷ *conj* quand; (*every time that*)
chaque fois que
where [wɛəʳ] *adv, conj* où; **this is
~** c'est là que; **whereabouts** *adv*
où donc ▷ *n*: **nobody knows his
whereabouts** personne ne sait où
il se trouve; **whereas** *conj* alors que;
whereby *adv* (*formal*) par lequel (*or*
laquelle *etc*); **wherever** *adv* où donc
▷ *conj* où que + *sub*; **sit wherever
you like** asseyez-vous (là) où vous
voulez
whether ['wɛðəʳ] *conj* si; **I don't
know ~ to accept or not** je ne sais
pas si je dois accepter ou non; **it's
doubtful ~** il est peu probable que
+ *sub*; **~ you go or not** que vous y
alliez ou non

KEYWORD

which [wɪtʃ] *adj* **1** (*interrogative, direct,
indirect*) quel(le); **which picture
do you want?** quel tableau voulez-
vous?; **which one?** lequel (laquelle)?
2: **in which case** auquel cas; **we
got there at 8pm, by which time
the cinema was full** quand nous
sommes arrivés à 20h, le cinéma
était complet
▷ *pron* **1** (*interrogative*) lequel
(laquelle), lesquels (lesquelles) *pl*;
I don't mind which peu importe
lequel; **which (of these) are yours?**
lesquels sont à vous?; **tell me which
you want** dites-moi lesquels *or* ceux
que vous voulez
2 (*relative: subject*) qui; (*: object*) que;
sur/vers *etc* lequel (laquelle) (*NB: à +
lequel = **auquel**; de + lequel = **duquel**);
**the apple which you ate/which
is on the table** la pomme que vous
avez mangée/qui est sur la table; **the
chair on which you are sitting** la
chaise sur laquelle vous êtes assis;
the book of which you spoke le
livre dont vous avez parlé; **he said he
knew, which is true/I was afraid
of** il a dit qu'il le savait, ce qui est vrai/
ce que je craignais; **after which**
après quoi

whichever [wɪtʃ'ɛvəʳ] *adj*: **take ~
book you prefer** prenez le livre que
vous préférez, peu importe lequel; **~
book you take** quel que soit le livre
que vous preniez
while [waɪl] *n* moment *m* ▷ *conj*
pendant que; (*as long as*) tant que;
(*as, whereas*) alors que; (*though*) bien
que + *sub*, quoique + *sub*; **for a ~**
pendant quelque temps; **in a ~** dans
un moment
whilst [waɪlst] *conj* = **while**
whim [wɪm] *n* caprice *m*
whine [waɪn] *n* gémissement *m*; (*of
engine, siren*) plainte stridente ▷ *vi*

W

gémir, geindre, pleurnicher; (dog, engine, siren) gémir

whip [wɪp] n fouet m; (for riding) cravache f; (Pol: person) chef m de file (assurant la discipline dans son groupe parlementaire) ▷ vt fouetter; (snatch) enlever (or sortir) brusquement; **whipped cream** n crème fouettée

whirl [wə:l] vi tourbillonner; (dancers) tournoyer ▷ vt faire tourbillonner; faire tournoyer

whisk [wɪsk] n (Culin) fouet m ▷ vt (eggs) fouetter, battre; **to ~ sb away** or **off** emmener qn rapidement

whiskers ['wɪskəz] npl (of animal) moustaches fpl; (of man) favoris mpl

whisky, (IRISH, US) **whiskey** ['wɪskɪ] n whisky m

whisper ['wɪspər] n chuchotement m ▷ vt, vi chuchoter

whistle ['wɪsl] n (sound) sifflement m; (object) sifflet m ▷ vi siffler ▷ vt siffler, siffloter

white [waɪt] adj blanc (blanche); (with fear) blême ▷ n blanc m; (person) blanc (blanche); **White House** n (US): **the White House** la Maison-Blanche; **whitewash** n (paint) lait m de chaux ▷ vt blanchir à la chaux; (fig) blanchir

whiting ['waɪtɪŋ] n (pl inv: fish) merlan m

Whitsun ['wɪtsn] n la Pentecôte

whittle ['wɪtl] vt: **to ~ away, to ~ down** (costs) réduire, rogner

whizz [wɪz] vi aller (or passer) à toute vitesse

who [hu:] pron qui

whoever [hu:'ɛvər] pron: **~ finds it** celui (celle) qui le trouve (, qui que ce soit), quiconque le trouve; **ask ~ you like** demandez à qui vous voulez; **~ he marries** qui que ce soit or quelle que soit la personne qu'il épouse; **~ told you that?** qui a bien pu vous dire ça?, qui donc vous a dit ça?

whole [həul] adj (complete) entier(-ière), tout(e); (not broken) intact(e), complet(-ète) ▷ n (entire unit) tout

m; (all): **the ~ of** la totalité de, tout(e) le; **the ~ of the town** la ville tout entière; **on the ~, as a ~** dans l'ensemble; **wholefood(s)** n(pl) aliments complets; **wholeheartedly** [həul'hɑ:tɪdlɪ] adv sans réserve; **to agree wholeheartedly** être entièrement d'accord; **wholemeal** adj (BRIT: flour, bread) complet(-ète); **wholesale** n (vente f en) gros m ▷ adj (price) de gros; (destruction) systématique; **wholewheat** adj = **wholemeal**; **wholly** adv entièrement, tout à fait

KEYWORD

whom [hu:m] pron 1 (interrogative) qui; **whom did you see?** qui avez-vous vu?; **to whom did you give it?** à qui l'avez-vous donné?
2 (relative) que à/de etc qui; **the man whom I saw/to whom I spoke** l'homme que j'ai vu/à qui j'ai parlé

whore [hɔ:r] n (inf: pej) putain f

KEYWORD

whose [hu:z] adj 1 (possessive, interrogative): **whose book is this?, whose is this book?** à qui est ce livre?; **whose pencil have you taken?** à qui est le crayon que vous avez pris?, c'est le crayon de qui que vous avez pris?; **whose daughter are you?** de qui êtes-vous la fille?
2 (possessive, relative): **the man whose son you rescued** l'homme dont or de qui vous avez sauvé le fils; **the girl whose sister you were speaking to** la fille à la sœur de qui or de laquelle vous parliez; **the woman whose car was stolen** la femme dont la voiture a été volée
▷ pron à qui; **whose is this?** à qui est ceci?; **I know whose it is** je sais à qui c'est

why [waɪ] *adv* pourquoi; **why not?** pourquoi pas?
▸ *conj*: **I wonder why he said that** je me demande pourquoi il a dit ça; **that's not why I'm here** ce n'est pas pour ça que je suis là; **the reason why** la raison pour laquelle
▸ *excl* eh bien!, tiens!; **why, it's you!** tiens, c'est vous!; **why, that's impossible!** voyons, c'est impossible!

wicked ['wɪkɪd] *adj* méchant(e); (*mischievous: grin, look*) espiègle, malicieux(-euse); (*crime*) pervers(e); (*inf: very good*) génial(e) (*inf*)
wicket ['wɪkɪt] *n* (*Cricket: stumps*) guichet *m*; (: *grass area*) espace compris entre les deux guichets
wide [waɪd] *adj* large; (*area, knowledge*) vaste, très étendu(e); (*choice*) grand(e) ▷ *adv*: **to open ~** ouvrir tout grand; **to shoot ~** tirer à côté; **it is 3 metres ~** cela fait 3 mètres de large; **widely** *adv* (*different*) radicalement; (*spaced*) sur une grande étendue; (*believed*) généralement; (*travel*) beaucoup; **widen** *vt* élargir ▷ *vi* s'élargir; **wide open** *adj* grand(e) ouvert(e); **widespread** *adj* (*belief etc*) très répandu(e)
widow ['wɪdəu] *n* veuve *f*; **widower** *n* veuf *m*
width [wɪdθ] *n* largeur *f*
wield [wi:ld] *vt* (*sword*) manier; (*power*) exercer
wife (*pl* **wives**) [waɪf, waɪvz] *n* femme *f*, épouse *f*
Wi-Fi ['waɪfaɪ] *n* wifi *m*
wig [wɪg] *n* perruque *f*
wild [waɪld] *adj* sauvage; (*sea*) déchaîné(e); (*idea, life*) fou (folle); (*behaviour*) déchaîné(e), extravagant(e); (*inf: angry*) hors de soi, furieux(-euse) ▷ *n*: **the ~** la nature; **wilderness** ['wɪldənɪs] *n*

désert *m*, région *f* sauvage; **wildlife** *n* faune *f* (et flore *f*); **wildly** *adv* (*behave*) de manière déchaînée; (*applaud*) frénétiquement; (*hit, guess*) au hasard; (*happy*) follement

will [wɪl] *aux vb* **1** (*forming future tense*): **I will finish it tomorrow** je le finirai demain; **I will have finished it by tomorrow** je l'aurai fini d'ici demain; **will you do it? — yes I will/ no I won't** le ferez-vous? — oui/non
2 (*in conjectures, predictions*): **he will** or **he'll be there by now** il doit être arrivé à l'heure qu'il est; **that will be the postman** ça doit être le facteur
3 (*in commands, requests, offers*): **will you be quiet!** voulez-vous bien vous taire!; **will you help me?** est-ce que vous pouvez m'aider?; **will you have a cup of tea?** voulez-vous une tasse de thé?; **I won't put up with it!** je ne le tolérerai pas!
▸ *vt* (*pt, pp* **willed**): **to will sb to do** souhaiter ardemment que qn fasse; **he willed himself to go on** par un suprême effort de volonté, il continua
▸ *n* **1** volonté *f*; **against one's will** à contre-cœur
2 (*document*) testament *m*

willing ['wɪlɪŋ] *adj* de bonne volonté, serviable; **he's ~ to do it** il est disposé à le faire, il veut bien le faire; **willingly** *adv* volontiers
willow ['wɪləu] *n* saule *m*
willpower ['wɪl'pauə'] *n* volonté *f*
wilt [wɪlt] *vi* dépérir
win [wɪn] (*pt, pp* **won**) *n* (*in sports etc*) victoire *f* ▷ *vt* (*battle, money*) gagner; (*prize, contract*) remporter; (*popularity*) acquérir ▷ *vi* gagner; **win over** *vt* convaincre
wince [wɪns] *vi* tressaillir
wind[1] [wɪnd] *n* (*also Med*) vent *m*; (*breath*) souffle *m* ▷ *vt* (*take breath*

away) couper le souffle à; **the ~(s)**
(*Mus*) les instruments *mpl* à vent
wind² (*pt, pp* **wound**) [waɪnd,
waʊnd] *vt* enrouler; (*wrap*)
envelopper; (*clock, toy*) remonter ▷ *vi*
(*road, river*) serpenter; **wind down** *vt*
(*car window*) baisser; (*fig: production,
business*) réduire progressivement;
wind up *vt* (*clock*) remonter; (*debate*)
terminer, clôturer
windfall ['wɪndfɔ:l] *n* coup *m* de
chance
wind farm *n* ferme *f* éolienne
winding ['waɪndɪŋ] *adj* (*road*)
sinueux(-euse); (*staircase*)
tournant(e)
windmill ['wɪndmɪl] *n* moulin *m*
à vent
window ['wɪndəu] *n* fenêtre *f*; (*in car,
train: also:* **~pane**) vitre *f*; (*in shop etc*)
vitrine *f*; **window box** *n* jardinière *f*;
window cleaner *n* (*person*) laveur(-
euse) de vitres; **window pane** *n*
vitre *f*, carreau *m*; **window seat** *n* (*on
plane*) place *f* côté hublot; **windowsill**
n (*inside*) appui *m* de la fenêtre;
(*outside*) rebord *m* de la fenêtre
windscreen ['wɪndskri:n] *n* pare-
brise *m inv*; **windscreen wiper** *n*
essuie-glace *m inv*
windshield ['wɪndʃi:ld] (*US*) *n*
= **windscreen**
windsurfing ['wɪndsə:fɪŋ] *n*
planche *f* à voile
wind turbine [-tə:baɪn] *n* éolienne *f*
windy ['wɪndɪ] *adj* (*day*) de vent,
venteux(-euse); (*place, weather*)
venteux; **it's ~** il y a du vent
wine [waɪn] *n* vin *m*; **wine bar** *n* bar
m à vin; **wine glass** *n* verre *m* à vin;
wine list *n* carte *f* des vins; **wine
tasting** *n* dégustation *f* (de vins)
wing [wɪŋ] *n* aile *f*; **wings** *npl* (*Theat*)
coulisses *fpl*; **wing mirror** *n* (*BRIT*)
rétroviseur latéral
wink [wɪŋk] *n* clin *m* d'œil ▷ *vi* faire un
clin d'œil; (*blink*) cligner des yeux
winner ['wɪnər] *n* gagnant(e)

winning ['wɪnɪŋ] *adj* (*team*)
gagnant(e); (*goal*) décisif(-ive);
(*charming*) charmeur(-euse)
winter ['wɪntər] *n* hiver *m* ▷ *vi*
hiverner; **in ~** en hiver; **winter
sports** *npl* sports *mpl* d'hiver;
wintertime *n* hiver *m*
wipe [waɪp] *n*: **to give sth a ~**
donner un coup de torchon/de
chiffon/d'éponge à qch ▷ *vt* essuyer;
(*erase: tape*) effacer; **to ~ one's
nose** se moucher; **wipe out** *vt*
(*debt*) éteindre, amortir; (*memory*)
effacer; (*destroy*) anéantir; **wipe up**
vt essuyer
wire ['waɪər] *n* fil *m* (de fer); (*Elec*)
fil électrique; (*Tel*) télégramme
m ▷ *vt* (*house*) faire l'installation
électrique de; (*also:* **~ up**)
brancher; (*person: send telegram to*)
télégraphier à
wireless ['waɪəlɪs] *adj* sans fil;
wireless technology *n* technologie
f sans fil
wiring ['waɪərɪŋ] *n* (*Elec*) installation
f électrique
wisdom ['wɪzdəm] *n* sagesse *f*; (*of
action*) prudence *f*; **wisdom tooth** *n*
dent *f* de sagesse
wise [waɪz] *adj* sage, prudent(e);
(*remark*) judicieux(-euse)
wish [wɪʃ] *n* (*desire*) désir *m*; (*specific
desire*) souhait *m*, vœu *m* ▷ *vt*
souhaiter, désirer, vouloir; **best ~es**
(*on birthday etc*) meilleurs vœux; **with
best ~es** (*in letter*) bien amicalement;
to ~ sb goodbye dire au revoir à qn;
he ~ed me well il m'a souhaité bonne
chance; **to ~ to do/sb to do** désirer
or vouloir faire/que qn fasse; **to ~ for**
souhaiter
wistful ['wɪstful] *adj* mélancolique
wit [wɪt] *n* (*also:* **~s**: *intelligence*)
intelligence *f*, esprit *m*; (*presence of
mind*) présence *f* d'esprit; (*wittiness*)
esprit; (*person*) homme/femme
d'esprit
witch [wɪtʃ] *n* sorcière *f*

with [wɪð, wɪθ] *prep* **1** (*in the company of*) avec; (: *at the home of*) chez; **we stayed with friends** nous avons logé chez des amis; **I'll be with you in a minute** je suis à vous dans un instant **2** (*descriptive*): **a room with a view** une chambre avec vue; **the man with the grey hat/blue eyes** l'homme au chapeau gris/aux yeux bleus **3** (*indicating manner, means, cause*): **with tears in her eyes** les larmes aux yeux; **to walk with a stick** marcher avec une canne; **red with anger** rouge de colère; **to shake with fear** trembler de peur; **to fill sth with water** remplir qch d'eau **4** (*in phrases*): **I'm with you** (*I understand*) je vous suis; **to be with it** (*inf: up-to-date*) être dans le vent

withdraw [wɪθ'drɔː] *vt* (*irreg: like* **draw**) retirer ▷ *vi* se retirer; **withdrawal** *n* retrait *m*; (*Med*) état *m* de manque; **withdrawn** *pp of* **withdraw** ▷ *adj* (*person*) renfermé(e) **withdrew** [wɪθ'druː] *pt of* **withdraw**
wither ['wɪðəʳ] *vi* se faner
withhold [wɪθ'həuld] *vt* (*irreg: like* **hold**) (*money*) retenir; (*decision*) remettre; **to ~ (from)** (*permission*) refuser (à); (*information*) cacher (à)
within [wɪð'ɪn] *prep* à l'intérieur de ▷ *adv* à l'intérieur; **~ his reach** à sa portée; **~ sight of** en vue de; **~ a mile of** à moins d'un mille de; **~ the week** avant la fin de la semaine
without [wɪð'aut] *prep* sans; **~ a coat** sans manteau; **~ speaking** sans parler; **to go** *or* **do ~ sth** se passer de qch
withstand [wɪθ'stænd] *vt* (*irreg: like* **stand**) résister à
witness ['wɪtnɪs] *n* (*person*) témoin *m* ▷ *vt* (*event*) être témoin de; (*document*)

attester l'authenticité de; **to bear ~ to sth** témoigner de qch
witty ['wɪtɪ] *adj* spirituel(le), plein(e) d'esprit
wives [waɪvz] *npl of* **wife**
wizard ['wɪzəd] *n* magicien *m*
wk *abbr* = **week**
wobble ['wɔbl] *vi* trembler; (*chair*) branler
woe [wəu] *n* malheur *m*
woke [wəuk] *pt of* **wake**
woken ['wəukn] *pp of* **wake**
wolf (*pl* **wolves**) [wulf, wulvz] *n* loup *m*
woman (*pl* **women**) ['wumən, 'wɪmɪn] *n* femme *f* ▷ *cpd*: **~ doctor** femme *f* médecin; **~ teacher** professeur *m* femme
womb [wuːm] *n* (*Anat*) utérus *m*
women ['wɪmɪn] *npl of* **woman**
won [wʌn] *pt, pp of* **win**
wonder ['wʌndəʳ] *n* merveille *f*, miracle *m*; (*feeling*) émerveillement *m* ▷ *vi*: **to ~ whether/why** se demander si/pourquoi; **to ~ at** (*surprise*) s'étonner de; (*admiration*) s'émerveiller de; **to ~ about** songer à; **it's no ~ that** il n'est pas étonnant que + *sub*; **wonderful** *adj* merveilleux(-euse)
won't [wəunt] = **will not**
wood [wud] *n* (*timber, forest*) bois *m*; **wooden** *adj* en bois; (*fig: actor*) raide; (: *performance*) qui manque de naturel; **woodwind** *n*: **the woodwind** les bois *mpl*; **woodwork** *n* menuiserie *f*
wool [wul] *n* laine *f*; **to pull the ~ over sb's eyes** (*fig*) en faire accroire à qn; **woollen**, (*us*) **woolen** *adj* de or en laine; **woolly**, (*us*) **wooly** *adj* laineux(-euse); (*fig: ideas*) confus(e)
word [wəːd] *n* mot *m*; (*spoken*) mot, parole *f*; (*promise*) parole; (*news*) nouvelles *fpl* ▷ *vt* rédiger, formuler; **in other ~s** en d'autres termes; **to have a ~ with sb** toucher un mot à qn; **to break/keep one's ~** manquer à sa parole/tenir (sa) parole;

wording n termes mpl, langage m; (of document) libellé m; **word processing** n traitement m de texte; **word processor** n machine f de traitement de texte

wore [wɔːʳ] pt of **wear**

work [wəːk] n travail m; (Art, Literature) œuvre f ▷ vi travailler; (mechanism) marcher, fonctionner; (plan etc) marcher; (medicine) agir ▷ vt (clay, wood etc) travailler; (mine etc) exploiter; (machine) faire marcher or fonctionner; (miracles etc) faire; **works** n (BRIT: factory) usine f; **how does this ~?** comment est-ce que ça marche?; **the TV isn't ~ing** la télévision est en panne or ne marche pas; **to be out of ~** être au chômage or sans emploi; **to ~ loose** se défaire, se desserrer; **work out** vi (plans etc) marcher; (Sport) s'entraîner ▷ vt (problem) résoudre; (plan) élaborer; **it ~s out at £100** ça fait 100 livres; **worker** n travailleur(-euse), ouvrier(-ière); **work experience** n stage m; **workforce** n main-d'œuvre f; **working class** n classe ouvrière ▷ adj: **working-class** ouvrier(-ière), de la classe ouvrière; **working week** n semaine f de travail; **workman** (irreg) n ouvrier m; **work of art** n œuvre f d'art; **workout** n (Sport) séance f d'entraînement; **work permit** n permis m de travail; **workplace** n lieu m de travail; **worksheet** n (Scol) feuille f d'exercices; **workshop** n atelier m; **work station** n poste m de travail; **work surface** n plan m de travail; **worktop** n plan m de travail

world [wəːld] n monde m ▷ cpd (champion) du monde; (power, war) mondial(e); **to think the ~ of sb** (fig) ne jurer que par qn; **World Cup** n: **the World Cup** (Football) la Coupe du monde; **world-wide** adj universel(le); **World-Wide Web** n: **the World-Wide Web** le Web

worm [wəːm] n (also: **earth~**) ver m

worn [wɔːn] pp of **wear** ▷ adj usé(e); **worn-out** adj (object) complètement usé(e); (person) épuisé(e)

worried ['wʌrɪd] adj inquiet(-ète); **to be ~ about sth** être inquiet au sujet de qch

worry ['wʌrɪ] n souci m ▷ vt inquiéter ▷ vi s'inquiéter, se faire du souci; **worrying** adj inquiétant(e)

worse [wəːs] adj pire, plus mauvais(e) ▷ adv plus mal ▷ n pire m; **to get ~** (condition, situation) empirer, se dégrader; **a change for the ~** une détérioration; **worsen** vt, vi empirer; **worse off** adj moins à l'aise financièrement; (fig): **you'll be worse off this way** ça ira moins bien de cette façon

worship ['wəːʃɪp] n culte m ▷ vt (God) rendre un culte à; (person) adorer

worst [wəːst] adj le (la) pire, le (la) plus mauvais(e) ▷ adv le plus mal ▷ n pire m; **at ~** au pis aller

worth [wəːθ] n valeur f ▷ adj: **to be ~** valoir; **it's ~ it** cela en vaut la peine, ça vaut la peine; **it is ~ one's while (to do)** ça vaut le coup (inf) (de faire); **worthless** adj qui ne vaut rien; **worthwhile** adj (activity) qui en vaut la peine; (cause) louable

worthy ['wəːðɪ] adj (person) digne; (motive) louable; **~ of** digne de

KEYWORD

would [wʊd] aux vb **1** (conditional tense): **if you asked him he would do it** si vous le lui demandiez, il le ferait; **if you had asked him he would have done it** si vous le lui aviez demandé, il l'aurait fait
2 (in offers, invitations, requests): **would you like a biscuit?** voulez-vous un biscuit?; **would you close the door please?** voulez-vous fermer la porte, s'il vous plaît?
3 (in indirect speech): **I said I would do**

it j'ai dit que je le ferais
4 (*emphatic*): **it would** have to
snow today! naturellement il neige
aujourd'hui!, il fallait qu'il neige
aujourd'hui!
5 (*insistence*): **she wouldn't do it** elle
n'a pas voulu *or* elle a refusé de le faire
6 (*conjecture*): **it would have been
midnight** il devait être minuit; **it
would seem so** on dirait bien
7 (*indicating habit*): **he would go
there on Mondays** il y allait le lundi

wouldn't ['wʊdnt] = **would not**
wound¹ [wuːnd] *n* blessure *f* ▷ *vt*
blesser
wound² [waʊnd] *pt, pp of* **wind²**
wove [wəʊv] *pt of* **weave**
woven ['wəʊvn] *pp of* **weave**
wrap [ræp] *vt* (*also:* **~ up**) envelopper;
(*parcel*) emballer; (*wind*) enrouler;
wrapper *n* (*on chocolate etc*) papier *m*;
(BRIT: *of book*) couverture *f*; **wrapping**
n (*of sweet, chocolate*) papier *m*; (*of
parcel*) emballage *m*; **wrapping
paper** *n* papier *m* d'emballage; (*for
gift*) papier cadeau
wreath [riːθ] *n* couronne *f*
wreck [rɛk] *n* (*sea disaster*) naufrage
m; (*ship*) épave *f*; (*vehicle*) véhicule
accidentée; (*pej: person*) loque
(humaine) ▷ *vt* démolir; (*fig*) briser,
ruiner; **wreckage** *n* débris *mpl*; (*of
building*) décombres *mpl*; (*of ship*)
naufrage *m*
wren [rɛn] *n* (*Zool*) troglodyte *m*
wrench [rɛntʃ] *n* (*Tech*) clé *f* (à
écrous); (*tug*) violent mouvement de
torsion; (*fig*) déchirement *m* ▷ *vt* tirer
violemment sur, tordre; **to ~ sth from**
arracher qch (violemment) à *or* de
wrestle ['rɛsl] *vi*: **to ~ (with
sb)** lutter (avec qn); **wrestler** *n*
lutteur(-euse); **wrestling** *n* lutte *f*;
(BRIT: *also:* **all-in wrestling**) catch *m*
wretched ['rɛtʃɪd] *adj* misérable
wriggle ['rɪgl] *vi* (*also:* **~ about**) se
tortiller

wring (*pt, pp* **wrung**) [rɪŋ, rʌŋ] *vt*
tordre; (*wet clothes*) essorer; (*fig*): **to ~
sth out of** arracher qch à
wrinkle ['rɪŋkl] *n* (*on skin*) ride *f*; (*on
paper etc*) pli *m* ▷ *vt* rider, plisser ▷ *vi*
se plisser
wrist [rɪst] *n* poignet *m*
write (*pt* **wrote**, *pp* **written**) [raɪt,
rəʊt, 'rɪtn] *vt, vi* écrire; (*prescription*)
rédiger; **write down** *vt* noter; (*put
in writing*) mettre par écrit; **write off**
vt (*debt*) passer aux profits et pertes;
(*project*) mettre une croix sur; (*smash
up: car etc*) démolir complètement;
write out *vt* écrire; (*copy*) recopier;
write-off *n* perte totale; **the car is a
write-off** la voiture est bonne pour la
casse; **writer** *n* auteur *m*, écrivain *m*
writing ['raɪtɪŋ] *n* écriture *f*; (*of
author*) œuvres *fpl*; **in ~** par écrit;
writing paper *n* papier *m* à lettres
written ['rɪtn] *pp of* **write**
wrong [rɒŋ] *adj* (*incorrect*) faux
(fausse); (*incorrectly chosen: number,
road etc*) mauvais(e); (*not suitable*)
qui ne convient pas; (*wicked*) mal;
(*unfair*) injuste ▷ *adv* mal ▷ *n* tort *m*
▷ *vt* faire du tort à, léser; **you are ~
to do it** tu as tort de le faire; **you are
~ about that, you've got it ~** tu te
trompes; **what's ~?** qu'est-ce qui
ne va pas?; **what's ~ with the car?**
qu'est-ce qu'elle a, la voiture?; **to
go ~** (*person*) se tromper; (*plan*) mal
tourner; (*machine*) se détraquer; **I
took a ~ turning** je me suis trompé
de route; **wrongly** *adv* à tort; (*answer,
do, count*) mal, incorrectement;
wrong number *n* (*Tel*): **you have
the wrong number** vous vous êtes
trompé de numéro
wrote [rəʊt] *pt of* **write**
wrung [rʌŋ] *pt, pp of* **wring**
WWW *n abbr* = **World-Wide Web**

w

XL *abbr* (= *extra large*) XL
Xmas [ˈɛksməs] *n abbr* = **Christmas**
X-ray [ˈɛksreɪ] *n* (*ray*) rayon *m* X;
(*photograph*) radio(graphie) *f* ▷ *vt*
radiographier
xylophone [ˈzaɪləfəun] *n*
xylophone *m*

yacht [jɔt] *n* voilier *m*; (*motor, luxury
yacht*) yacht *m*; **yachting** *n* yachting
m, navigation *f* de plaisance
yard [jɑːd] *n* (*of house etc*) cour *f*; (*us:
garden*) jardin *m*; (*measure*) yard *m*
(= 914 *mm*; 3 *feet*); **yard sale** *n* (*us*)
brocante *f* (dans son propre jardin)
yarn [jɑːn] *n* fil *m*; (*tale*) longue
histoire
yawn [jɔːn] *n* bâillement *m* ▷ *vi* bâiller
yd. *abbr* = **yard; yards**
yeah [jɛə] *adv* (*inf*) ouais
year [jɪəʳ] *n* an *m*, année *f*; (*Scol etc*)
année; **to be 8 ~s old** avoir 8 ans;
an eight-~-old child un enfant de
huit ans; **yearly** *adj* annuel(le) ▷ *adv*
annuellement; **twice yearly** deux
fois par an
yearn [jəːn] *vi*: **to ~ for sth/to do**
aspirer à qch/à faire
yeast [jiːst] *n* levure *f*
yell [jɛl] *n* hurlement *m*, cri *m* ▷ *vi*
hurler

yellow ['jɛləu] *adj, n* jaune (*m*);
  Yellow Pages® *npl* (*Tel*) pages *fpl*
  jaunes
yes [jɛs] *adv* oui; (*answering negative
  question*) si ▷ *n* oui *m*; **to say ~ (to)**
  dire oui (à)
yesterday ['jɛstədɪ] *adv, n* hier (*m*);
  ~ morning/evening hier matin/soir;
  all day ~ toute la journée d'hier
yet [jɛt] *adv* encore; (*in questions*) déjà
  ▷ *conj* pourtant, néanmoins; **it is not
  finished ~** ce n'est pas encore fini *or*
  toujours pas fini; **have you eaten ~?**
  vous avez déjà mangé?; **the best ~**
  le meilleur jusqu'ici *or* jusque-là; **as ~**
  jusqu'ici, encore
yew [ju:] *n* if *m*
Yiddish ['jɪdɪʃ] *n* yiddish *m*
yield [ji:ld] *n* production *f*, rendement
  m; (*Finance*) rapport *m* ▷ *vt* produire,
  rendre, rapporter; (*surrender*) céder
  ▷ *vi* céder; (*us Aut*) céder la priorité
yob(bo) ['jɔb(əu)] *n* (BRIT *inf*)
  loubar(d)*n*
yoga ['jəugə] *n* yoga *m*
yog(h)urt ['jɔgət] *n* yaourt *m*
yolk [jəuk] *n* jaune *m* (d'œuf)

 KEYWORD

you [ju:] *pron* **1** (*subject*) tu; (: *polite
  form*) vous; (: *plural*) vous; **you are
  very kind** vous êtes très gentil; **you
  French enjoy your food** vous autres
  Français, vous aimez bien manger;
  you and I will go toi et moi *or* vous
  et moi, nous irons; **there you are!**
  vous voilà!
  2 (*object: direct, indirect*) te, t' + *vowel*;
  vous; **I know you** je te *or* vous
  connais; **I gave it to you** je te l'ai
  donné, je vous l'ai donné
  3 (*stressed*) toi; vous; **I told you to do
  it** c'est à toi *or* vous que j'ai dit de le faire
  4 (*after prep, in comparisons*) toi; vous;
  it's for you c'est pour toi *or* vous;
  she's younger than you elle est plus
  jeune que toi *or* vous

  5 (*impersonal: one*) on; **fresh air does
  you good** l'air frais fait du bien; **you
  never know** on ne sait jamais; **you
  can't do that!** ça ne se fait pas!

you'd [ju:d] = **you had; you would**
you'll [ju:l] = **you will; you shall**
young [jʌŋ] *adj* jeune ▷ *npl* (*of animal*)
  petits *mpl*; **the ~** (*people*) les jeunes, la
  jeunesse; **my ~er brother** mon frère
  cadet; **youngster** *n* jeune *m/f*; (*child*)
  enfant *m/f*
your [jɔ:ʳ] *adj* ton (ta), tes *pl*; (*polite
  form, pl*) votre, vos *pl*; *see also* **my**
you're [juəʳ] = **you are**
yours [jɔ:z] *pron* le (la) tien(ne), les
  tiens (tiennes); (*polite form, pl*) le (la)
  vôtre, les vôtres; **is it ~?** c'est à toi (*or*
  à vous)?; **a friend of ~** un(e) de tes
  (*or* de vos) amis; *see also* **faithfully;
  mine¹; sincerely**
yourself [jɔ:'sɛlf] *pron* (*reflexive*) te;
  (: *polite form*) vous; (*after prep*) toi;
  vous; (*emphatic*) toi-même; vous-
  même; *see also* **oneself; yourselves**
  pl pron vous; (*emphatic*) vous-mêmes;
  see also **oneself**
youth [ju:θ] *n* jeunesse *f*; (*young man*)
  jeune homme *m*; **youth club** *n* centre
  m de jeunes; **youthful** *adj* jeune;
  (*enthusiasm etc*) juvénile; **youth
  hostel** *n* auberge *f* de jeunesse
you've [ju:v] = **you have**
Yugoslav ['ju:gəuslɑ:v] *adj* (*Hist*)
  yougoslave ▷ *n* Yougoslave *m/f*
Yugoslavia [ju:gəu'slɑ:vɪə] *n* (*Hist*)
  Yougoslavie *f*

y

zoology [zuːˈɒlədʒɪ] n zoologie f
zoom [zuːm] vi: **to ~ past** passer en
trombe; **zoom lens** n zoom m
zucchini [zuːˈkiːnɪ] n (US) courgette f

Z

zeal [ziːl] n (revolutionary etc) ferveur f;
(keenness) ardeur f, zèle m
zebra [ˈziːbrə] n zèbre m; **zebra
crossing** n (BRIT) passage clouté or
pour piétons
zero [ˈzɪərəu] n zéro m
zest [zɛst] n entrain m, élan m; (of
lemon etc) zeste m
zigzag [ˈzɪgzæg] n zigzag m ▷ vi
zigzaguer, faire des zigzags
Zimbabwe [zɪmˈbɑːbwɪ] n
Zimbabwe m
zinc [zɪŋk] n zinc m
zip [zɪp] n (also: **~ fastener**) fermeture
f éclair® or à glissière ▷ vt (file)
zipper; (also: **~ up**) fermer (avec une
fermeture éclair®); **zip code** n (US)
code postal; **zip file** n (Comput) fichier
m zip inv; **zipper** n (US) = **zip**
zit [zɪt] (inf) n bouton m
zodiac [ˈzəudɪæk] n zodiaque m
zone [zəun] n zone f
zoo [zuː] n zoo m

VERB TABLES

Introduction

The **Verb Tables** in the following section contain 29 tables of French verbs (some regular and some irregular) in alphabetical order. Each table shows you the following forms: **Present**, **Perfect**, **Future**, **Subjunctive**, **Imperfect**, **Conditional**, **Imperative** and the **Present** and **Past Participles**.

In order to help you use the verbs shown in Verb Tables correctly, there are also a number of example phrases at the bottom of each page to show the verb as it is used in context.

In French there are both **regular** verbs (their forms follow the normal rules) and **irregular** verbs (their forms do not follow the normal rules). The regular verbs in these tables are:

donner (regular-**er** verb, Verb Table 11)
finir (regular-**ir** verb, Verb Table 16)
attendre (regular-**re** verb, Verb Table 3)

The irregular verbs are shown in full.

For a further list of French irregular verb forms see pages xv–xvi.

▶ **aller** (to go)

PRESENT

je	vais
tu	vas
il/elle/on	va
nous	allons
vous	allez
ils/elles	vont

PRESENT SUBJUNCTIVE

j'	aille
tu	ailles
il/elle/on	aille
nous	allions
vous	alliez
ils/elles	aillent

PERFECT

je	suis allé(e)
tu	es allé(e)
il/elle/on	est allé(e)
nous	sommes allé(e)s
vous	êtes allé(e)(s)
ils/elles	sont allé(e)s

IMPERFECT

j'	allais
tu	allais
il/elle/on	allait
nous	allions
vous	alliez
ils/elles	allaient

FUTURE

j'	irai
tu	iras
il/elle/on	ira
nous	irons
vous	irez
ils/elles	iront

CONDITIONAL

j'	irais
tu	irais
il/elle/on	irait
nous	irions
vous	iriez
ils/elles	iraient

IMPERATIVE

va / allons / allez

PAST PARTICIPLE

allé

PRESENT PARTICIPLE

allant

EXAMPLE PHRASES

Vous **allez** au cinéma? Are you going to the cinema?
Je **suis allé** à Londres. I went to London.
Est-ce que tu **es** déjà **allé** en Allemagne? Have you ever been to Germany?

je/j' = I **tu** = you **il** = he/it **elle** = she/it **on** = we/one **nous** = we **vous** = you **ils/elles** = they

▶ **attendre** (to wait)

PRESENT

j'	attends
tu	attends
il/elle/on	attend
nous	attendons
vous	attendez
ils/elles	attendent

PRESENT SUBJUNCTIVE

j'	attende
tu	attendes
il/elle/on	attende
nous	attendions
vous	attendiez
ils/elles	attendent

PERFECT

j'	ai attendu
tu	as attendu
il/elle/on	a attendu
nous	avons attendu
vous	avez attendu
ils/elles	ont attendu

IMPERFECT

j'	attendais
tu	attendais
il/elle/on	attendait
nous	attendions
vous	attendiez
ils/elles	attendaient

FUTURE

j'	attendrai
tu	attendras
il/elle/on	attendra
nous	attendrons
vous	attendrez
ils/elles	attendront

CONDITIONAL

j'	attendrais
tu	attendrais
il/elle/on	attendrait
nous	attendrions
vous	attendriez
ils/elles	attendraient

IMPERATIVE

attends / attendons / attendez

PAST PARTICIPLE

attendu

PRESENT PARTICIPLE

attendant

EXAMPLE PHRASES

Attends-moi! Wait for me!
Tu **attends** depuis longtemps? Have you been waiting long?
Je l'**ai attendu** à la poste. I waited for him at the post office.
Je m'**attends** à ce qu'il soit en retard. I expect he'll be late.

je/j' = I **tu** = you **il** = he/it **elle** = she/it **on** = we/one **nous** = we **vous** = you **ils/elles** = they

▶ **avoir** (to have)

PRESENT		PRESENT SUBJUNCTIVE	
j'	ai	j'	aie
tu	as	tu	aies
il/elle/on	a	il/elle/on	ait
nous	avons	nous	ayons
vous	avez	vous	ayez
ils/elles	ont	ils/elles	aient

PERFECT		IMPERFECT	
j'	ai eu	j'	avais
tu	as eu	tu	avais
il/elle/on	a eu	il/elle/on	avait
nous	avons eu	nous	avions
vous	avez eu	vous	aviez
ils/elles	ont eu	ils/elles	avaient

FUTURE		CONDITIONAL	
j'	aurai	j'	aurais
tu	auras	tu	aurais
il/elle/on	aura	il/elle/on	aurait
nous	aurons	nous	aurions
vous	aurez	vous	auriez
ils/elles	auront	ils/elles	auraient

IMPERATIVE

aie / ayons / ayez

PAST PARTICIPLE

eu

PRESENT PARTICIPLE

ayant

EXAMPLE PHRASES

Il **a** les yeux bleus. He's got blue eyes.
Quel âge **as**-tu? How old are you?
Il **a eu** un accident. He's had an accident.
J'**avais** faim. I was hungry.
Il y **a** beaucoup de monde. There are lots of people.

je/j' = I **tu** = you **il** = he/it **elle** = she/it **on** = we/one **nous** = we **vous** = you **ils/elles** = they

▶ **boire** (to drink)

PRESENT

je	bois
tu	bois
il/elle/on	boit
nous	buvons
vous	buvez
ils/elles	boivent

PRESENT SUBJUNCTIVE

je	boive
tu	boives
il/elle/on	boive
nous	buvions
vous	buviez
ils/elles	boivent

PERFECT

j'	ai bu
tu	as bu
il/elle/on	a bu
nous	avons bu
vous	avez bu
ils/elles	ont bu

IMPERFECT

je	buvais
tu	buvais
il/elle/on	buvait
nous	buvions
vous	buviez
ils/elles	buvaient

FUTURE

je	boirai
tu	boiras
il/elle/on	boira
nous	boirons
vous	boirez
ils/elles	boiront

CONDITIONAL

je	boirais
tu	boirais
il/elle/on	boirait
nous	boirions
vous	boiriez
ils/elles	boiraient

IMPERATIVE

bois / buvons / buvez

PAST PARTICIPLE

bu

PRESENT PARTICIPLE

buvant

EXAMPLE PHRASES

*Qu'est-ce que tu veux **boire**?* What would you like to drink?
*Il ne **boit** jamais d'alcool.* He never drinks alcohol.
*J'**ai bu** un litre d'eau.* I drank a litre of water.

je/j' = I **tu** = you **il** = he/it **elle** = she/it **on** = we/one **nous** = we **vous** = you **ils/elles** = they

▶ connaître (to know)

PRESENT

je	connais
tu	connais
il/elle/on	connaît
nous	connaissons
vous	connaissez
ils/elles	connaissent

PRESENT SUBJUNCTIVE

je	connaisse
tu	connaisses
il/elle/on	connaisse
nous	connaissions
vous	connaissiez
ils/elles	connaissent

PERFECT

j'	ai connu
tu	as connu
il/elle/on	a connu
nous	avons connu
vous	avez connu
ils/elles	ont connu

IMPERFECT

je	connaissais
tu	connaissais
il/elle/on	connaissait
nous	connaissions
vous	connaissiez
ils/elles	connaissaient

FUTURE

je	connaîtrai
tu	connaîtras
il/elle/on	connaîtra
nous	connaîtrons
vous	connaîtrez
ils/elles	connaîtront

CONDITIONAL

je	connaîtrais
tu	connaîtrais
il/elle/on	connaîtrait
nous	connaîtrions
vous	connaîtriez
ils/elles	connaîtraient

IMPERATIVE

connais / connaissons / connaissez

PAST PARTICIPLE

connu

PRESENT PARTICIPLE

connaissant

EXAMPLE PHRASES

Je ne **connais** pas du tout cette région. I don't know the area at all.
Vous **connaissez** M Amiot? Do you know Mr Amiot?
Il n'**a** pas **connu** son grand-père. He never knew his granddad.
Ils **se sont connus** à Rouen. They first met in Rouen.

je/j' = I **tu** = you **il** = he/it **elle** = she/it **on** = we/one **nous** = we **vous** = you **ils/elles** = they

▶ **courir** (to run)

PRESENT

je	cours
tu	cours
il/elle/on	court
nous	courons
vous	courez
ils/elles	courent

PRESENT SUBJUNCTIVE

je	coure
tu	coures
il/elle/on	coure
nous	courions
vous	couriez
ils/elles	courent

PERFECT

j'	ai couru
tu	as couru
il/elle/on	a couru
nous	avons couru
vous	avez couru
ils/elles	ont couru

IMPERFECT

je	courais
tu	courais
il/elle/on	courait
nous	courions
vous	couriez
ils/elles	couraient

FUTURE

je	courrai
tu	courras
il/elle/on	courra
nous	courrons
vous	courrez
ils/elles	courront

CONDITIONAL

je	courrais
tu	courrais
il/elle/on	courrait
nous	courrions
vous	courriez
ils/elles	courraient

IMPERATIVE

cours / courons / courez

PAST PARTICIPLE

couru

PRESENT PARTICIPLE

courant

EXAMPLE PHRASES

*Je ne **cours** pas très vite.* I can't run very fast.
*Elle est sortie en **courant**.* She ran out.
*Ne **courez** pas dans le couloir.* Don't run in the corridor.
*J'**ai couru** jusqu'à l'école.* I ran all the way to school.

je/j' = I **tu** = you **il** = he/it **elle** = she/it **on** = we/one **nous** = we **vous** = you **ils/elles** = they

▶ **croire** (to believe)

PRESENT

je	crois
tu	crois
il/elle/on	croit
nous	croyons
vous	croyez
ils/elles	croient

PRESENT SUBJUNCTIVE

je	croie
tu	croies
il/elle/on	croie
nous	croyions
vous	croyiez
ils/elles	croient

PERFECT

j'	ai cru
tu	as cru
il/elle/on	a cru
nous	avons cru
vous	avez cru
ils/elles	ont cru

IMPERFECT

je	croyais
tu	croyais
il/elle/on	croyait
nous	croyions
vous	croyiez
ils/elles	croyaient

FUTURE

je	croirai
tu	croiras
il/elle/on	croira
nous	croirons
vous	croirez
ils/elles	croiront

CONDITIONAL

je	croirais
tu	croirais
il/elle/on	croirait
nous	croirions
vous	croiriez
ils/elles	croiraient

IMPERATIVE

crois / croyons / croyez

PAST PARTICIPLE

cru

PRESENT PARTICIPLE

croyant

EXAMPLE PHRASES

*Je ne te **crois** pas.* I don't believe you.
*J'**ai cru** que tu n'allais pas venir.* I thought you weren't going to come.
*Elle **croyait** encore au père Noël.* She still believed in Santa.

▶ **devoir** (to have to; to owe)

PRESENT

je	dois
tu	dois
il/elle/on	doit
nous	devons
vous	devez
ils/elles	doivent

PRESENT SUBJUNCTIVE

je	doive
tu	doives
il/elle/on	doive
nous	devions
vous	deviez
ils/elles	doivent

PERFECT

j'	ai dû
tu	as dû
il/elle/on	a dû
nous	avons dû
vous	avez dû
ils/elles	ont dû

IMPERFECT

je	devais
tu	devais
il/elle/on	devait
nous	devions
vous	deviez
ils/elles	devaient

FUTURE

je	devrai
tu	devras
il/elle/on	devra
nous	devrons
vous	devrez
ils/elles	devront

CONDITIONAL

je	devrais
tu	devrais
il/elle/on	devrait
nous	devrions
vous	devriez
ils/elles	devraient

IMPERATIVE

dois / devons / devez

PAST PARTICIPLE

dû (**NB**: due, dus, dues)

PRESENT PARTICIPLE

devant

EXAMPLE PHRASES

*Je **dois** aller faire les courses ce matin.* I have to do the shopping this morning.
*À quelle heure est-ce que tu **dois** partir?* What time do you have to leave?
*Il **a dû** faire ses devoirs hier soir.* He had to do his homework last night.
*Il **devait** prendre le train pour aller travailler.* He had to go to work by train.

---

je/j' = I **tu** = you **il** = he/it **elle** = she/it **on** = we/one **nous** = we **vous** = you **ils/elles** = they

▶ **dire** (to say)

PRESENT		PRESENT SUBJUNCTIVE	
je	dis	je	dise
tu	dis	tu	dises
il/elle/on	dit	il/elle/on	dise
nous	disons	nous	disions
vous	dites	vous	disiez
ils/elles	disent	ils/elles	disent

PERFECT		IMPERFECT	
j'	ai dit	je	disais
tu	as dit	tu	disais
il/elle/on	a dit	il/elle/on	disait
nous	avons dit	nous	disions
vous	avez dit	vous	disiez
ils/elles	ont dit	ils/elles	disaient

FUTURE		CONDITIONAL	
je	dirai	je	dirais
tu	diras	tu	dirais
il/elle/on	dira	il/elle/on	dirait
nous	dirons	nous	dirions
vous	direz	vous	diriez
ils/elles	diront	ils/elles	diraient

IMPERATIVE

dis / disons / dites

PAST PARTICIPLE

dit

PRESENT PARTICIPLE

disant

EXAMPLE PHRASES

*Qu'est-ce qu'elle **dit**?* What is she saying?
*"Bonjour!", **a-t-il dit**.* "Hello!" he said.
*Ils m'**ont dit** que le film était nul.* They told me that the film was rubbish.
*Comment ça **se dit** en anglais?* How do you say that in English?

---

je/j' = I **tu** = you **il** = he/it **elle** = she/it **on** = we/one **nous** = we **vous** = you **ils/elles** = they

▶ **donner** (to give)

PRESENT

je	donne
tu	donnes
il/elle/on	donne
nous	donnons
vous	donnez
ils/elles	donnent

PRESENT SUBJUNCTIVE

je	donne
tu	donnes
il/elle/on	donne
nous	donnions
vous	donniez
ils/elles	donnent

PERFECT

j'	ai donné
tu	as donné
il/elle/on	a donné
nous	avons donné
vous	avez donné
ils/elles	ont donné

IMPERFECT

je	donnais
tu	donnais
il/elle/on	donnait
nous	donnions
vous	donniez
ils/elles	donnaient

FUTURE

je	donnerai
tu	donneras
il/elle/on	donnera
nous	donnerons
vous	donnerez
ils/elles	donneront

CONDITIONAL

je	donnerais
tu	donnerais
il/elle/on	donnerait
nous	donnerions
vous	donneriez
ils/elles	donneraient

IMPERATIVE

donne / donnons / donnez

PAST PARTICIPLE

donné

PRESENT PARTICIPLE

donnant

EXAMPLE PHRASES

Donne-moi la main. Give me your hand.
Est-ce que je t'**ai donné** mon adresse? Did I give you my address?
L'appartement **donne** sur la place. The flat overlooks the square.

---

je/j' = I **tu** = you **il** = he/it **elle** = she/it **on** = we/one **nous** = we **vous** = you **ils/elles** = they

▶ **écrire** (to write)

PRESENT		PRESENT SUBJUNCTIVE	
j'	écris	j'	écrive
tu	écris	tu	écrives
il/elle/on	écrit	il/elle/on	écrive
nous	écrivons	nous	écrivions
vous	écrivez	vous	écriviez
ils/elles	écrivent	ils/elles	écrivent

PERFECT		IMPERFECT	
j'	ai écrit	j'	écrivais
tu	as écrit	tu	écrivais
il/elle/on	a écrit	il/elle/on	écrivait
nous	avons écrit	nous	écrivions
vous	avez écrit	vous	écriviez
ils/elles	ont écrit	ils/elles	écrivaient

FUTURE		CONDITIONAL	
j'	écrirai	j'	écrirais
tu	écriras	tu	écrirais
il/elle/on	écrira	il/elle/on	écrirait
nous	écrirons	nous	écririons
vous	écrirez	vous	écririez
ils/elles	écriront	ils/elles	écriraient

IMPERATIVE

écris / écrivons / écrivez

PAST PARTICIPLE

écrit

PRESENT PARTICIPLE

écrivant

EXAMPLE PHRASES

Tu **as écrit** à ta correspondante récemment? Have you written to your penfriend lately?
Elle **écrit** des romans. She writes novels.
Comment ça **s'écrit**, "brouillard"? How do you spell "brouillard"?

▶ **être** (to be)

PRESENT

je	suis
tu	es
il/elle/on	est
nous	sommes
vous	êtes
ils/elles	sont

PRESENT SUBJUNCTIVE

je	sois
tu	sois
il/elle/on	soit
nous	soyons
vous	soyez
ils/elles	soient

PERFECT

j'	ai été
tu	as été
il/elle/on	a été
nous	avons été
vous	avez été
ils/elles	ont été

IMPERFECT

j'	étais
tu	étais
il/elle/on	était
nous	étions
vous	étiez
ils/elles	étaient

FUTURE

je	serai
tu	seras
il/elle/on	sera
nous	serons
vous	serez
ils/elles	seront

CONDITIONAL

je	serais
tu	serais
il/elle/on	serait
nous	serions
vous	seriez
ils/elles	seraient

IMPERATIVE

sois / soyons / soyez

PAST PARTICIPLE

été

PRESENT PARTICIPLE

étant

EXAMPLE PHRASES

*Mon père **est** professeur.* My father's a teacher.
*Quelle heure **est**-il? – Il **est** dix heures.* What time is it? – It's 10 o'clock.
*Ils ne **sont** pas encore arrivés.* They haven't arrived yet.

je/j' = I **tu** = you **il** = he/it **elle** = she/it **on** = we/one **nous** = we **vous** = you **ils/elles** = they

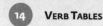

▶ **faire** (to do; to make)

PRESENT

je	fais
tu	fais
il/elle/on	fait
nous	faisons
vous	faites
ils/elles	font

PRESENT SUBJUNCTIVE

je	fasse
tu	fasses
il/elle/on	fasse
nous	fassions
vous	fassiez
ils/elles	fassent

PERFECT

j'	ai fait
tu	as fait
il/elle/on	a fait
nous	avons fait
vous	avez fait
ils/elles	ont fait

IMPERFECT

je	faisais
tu	faisais
il/elle/on	faisait
nous	faisions
vous	faisiez
ils/elles	faisaient

FUTURE

je	ferai
tu	feras
il/elle/on	fera
nous	ferons
vous	ferez
ils/elles	feront

CONDITIONAL

je	ferais
tu	ferais
il/elle/on	ferait
nous	ferions
vous	feriez
ils/elles	feraient

IMPERATIVE

fais / faisons / faites

PAST PARTICIPLE

fait

PRESENT PARTICIPLE

faisant

EXAMPLE PHRASES

*Qu'est-ce que tu **fais**?* What are you doing?
*Qu'est-ce qu'il **a fait**?* What has he done? *or* What did he do?
*J'**ai fait** un gâteau.* I've made a cake *or* I made a cake.
*Il **s'est fait** couper les cheveux.* He's had his hair cut.

je/j' = I **tu** = you **il** = he/it **elle** = she/it **on** = we/one **nous** = we **vous** = you **ils/elles** = they

▶ **falloir** (to be necessary)

PRESENT

il faut

PRESENT SUBJUNCTIVE

il faille

PERFECT

il a fallu

IMPERFECT

il fallait

FUTURE

il faudra

CONDITIONAL

il faudrait

IMPERATIVE

not used

PAST PARTICIPLE

fallu

PRESENT PARTICIPLE

not used

EXAMPLE PHRASES

Il **faut** se dépêcher! We have to hurry up!
Il me **fallait** de l'argent. I needed money.
Il **faudra** que tu sois là à 8 heures. You'll have to be there at 8.

je/j' = I **tu** = you **il** = he/it **elle** = she/it **on** = we/one **nous** = we **vous** = you **ils/elles** = they

▶ **finir** (to finish)

PRESENT

je	finis
tu	finis
il/elle/on	finit
nous	finissons
vous	finissez
ils/elles	finissent

PRESENT SUBJUNCTIVE

je	finisse
tu	finisses
il/elle/on	finisse
nous	finissions
vous	finissiez
ils/elles	finissent

PERFECT

j'	ai fini
tu	as fini
il/elle/on	a fini
nous	avons fini
vous	avez fini
ils/elles	ont fini

IMPERFECT

je	finissais
tu	finissais
il/elle/on	finissait
nous	finissions
vous	finissiez
ils/elles	finissaient

FUTURE

je	finirai
tu	finiras
il/elle/on	finira
nous	finirons
vous	finirez
ils/elles	finiront

CONDITIONAL

je	finirais
tu	finirais
il/elle/on	finirait
nous	finirions
vous	finiriez
ils/elles	finiraient

IMPERATIVE

finis / finissons / finissez

PAST PARTICIPLE

fini

PRESENT PARTICIPLE

finissant

EXAMPLE PHRASES

Finis *ta soupe!* Finish your soup!
J'ai **fini**! I've finished!
Je **finirai** *mes devoirs demain.* I'll finish my homework tomorrow.

---

je/j' = I **tu** = you **il** = he/it **elle** = she/it **on** = we/one **nous** = we **vous** = you **ils/elles** = they